22nd Annual Conference of the European Association for Machine Translation (EAMT2020)

Online
3 – 5 November 2020

Editors:

Andre Martins
Helena Moniz
Sara Fumega
Bruno Martins
Fernando Batista
Luisa Coheur
Carla Parra
Isabel Trancoso

Marco Turchi
Arianna Bisazza
Joss Moorkens
Ana Guerberof
Mary Nurminen
Lena Marg
Mikel L. Forcada

ISBN: 978-1-7138-1995-0

EAMT2020

Proceedings of the

22nd Annual Conference of the European Association for Machine Translation

3 – 5 November 2020
Online Conference

in place of
Instituto Superior Técnico, Lisbon, Portugal

Edited by

André Martins, Helena Moniz, Sara Fumega, Bruno Martins, Fernando Batista, Luisa Coheur,
Carla Parra, Isabel Trancoso, Marco Turchi, Arianna Bisazza, Joss Moorkens, Ana Guerberof,
Mary Nurminen, Lena Marg, Mikel L. Forcada

Organised by

Contents

Sponsors

Foreword from the General Chair

Bem-vindas e bem-vindos!

As president of the European Association for Machine Translation (EAMT) and General Chair of the 22nd Annual Conference of the EAMT, it's a pleasure for me to write these opening words to the Proceedings of EAMT 2020.

But on the other hand, I have some mixed feeling when I write these lines. Due to the COVID-19 crisis, we have not been able to meet in Lisbon, in person, in May. And that's so sad.

The organizers have reacted swiftly to make EAMT 2020 possible. First, we postponed it in hopes that we would be able to meet in November. But then reality struck and it was clear that not even that would be possible. Finally, it was decided that EAMT 2020 will be an on-line conference, from November 3 to November 5, 2020. We'll still have a single-room conference (including boaster sessions for papers accepted as posters), and we will do our best to make it as interactive and lively as possible. Details will be published in the EAMT 2020 website. Of course, registration fees have been reduced accordingly.

Reviewing had finished and acceptance decisions had been made, so it didn't make much sense to hold the publication of these Proceedings; here they are! Authors can now freely disseminate the papers in this volume. You can see them as a snapshot of active research and development by the best groups in Europe and around the world — I am sure authors will add new and interesting results when we *meet*.

You'll soon see an attractive three-day, four-track programme put together by our programme chairs: Arianna Bisazza and Marco Turchi, research track co-chairs, Mary Nurminen and Lena Marg, user track co-chairs, and Ana Guerberof and Joss Moorkens, translator track co-chairs; I thank them for the hard work. Finally, as General Chair, I took care of the fourth track, the projects/products track. The technical coordination of the reviewing was done by Carolina Scarton (thanks, Carol!). I also feel honored to have Lucia Specia (Imperial College London) as our invited speaker.

To give you a historical note, the EAMT started organizing annual workshops in 1996; later, these workshops became annual conferences, and were hosted all around Europe. Years ago, the venue steadily moved from west to east: from Barcelona (2009) to Saint-Raphaël (2010) to Leuven (2011) to Trento (2012) to Dubrovnik (2014) —after skipping one year to host the successful world-wide MT Summit 2013 in Nice—; then it turned around to go west again at

Antalya (2015), to go to Riga (2016), then Prague (2017), then Alacant (2018) and now —after skipping another year to host another successful MT Summit in Dublin— well, virtually, Lisbon. It's hard to go further westwards, so the next venue will take place east from Lisbon, as we will announce in November.

By the way, if you have not done so yet, and live in Europe, North Africa, or the Middle East, please consider joining the EAMT. Our membership rates are low, particularly for students and people not based in Europe. You will benefit from discounts when attending not only our conferences, but also the conferences held by our partner associations the Asia-Pacific Association for Machine Translation (AAMT) and the Association for Machine Translation in the Americas (AMTA). You will also have an exclusive chance to benefit from funding for your activities related to machine translation. And perhaps you can get even more involved and participate in serving the European machine translation community by becoming a member of the Executive Committee of the EAMT.

EAMT 2020 would have never been possible without the generous offer to host and the hard work subsequently done by the local organizing committee at Unbabel, but also at the *Instituto Superior Técnico*, the *Instituto de Engenharia de Sistemas e Computadores, Investigação e Desenvolvimento* and the *Instituto Universitário de Lisboa*, particularly André Martins, Helena Moniz, Sara Fumega, Bruno Martins, Fernando Batista, Luisa Coheur, Carla Parra Escartín, and Isabel Trancoso.

It is also with great pleasure that I thank our sponsors Banco Português de Investimento (gold sponsor), STAR Group and Microsoft (silver sponsors), Unbabel, text&form, TAUS, Pangeanic, and Crosslang (bronze sponsors), and Apertium and Prompsit (supporting sponsors), particularly for the flexibility shown when adapting to the changes in how the conference is run. EAMT 2020 would not be possible without the amazing engagement of these companies. I am also thankful for the ample support received from the local institutions in Lisbon.

Finally, I would like to thank future EAMT 2020 attendees for participating but also for their understanding. I hope the conference leads to new friendships —first virtual, and soon, I hope, face to face— and all sorts of fruitful collaboration in the field of translation technologies.

Oh, and please be sure to visit Lisbon when they let us travel freely. It was there waiting for us, and it will be when this nightmare is over. I'm looking forward to it.

(I wish we were in) Lisboa, 2020

Mikel L. Forcada
President of the EAMT
General Chair of EAMT 2020
Professor of Computer Languages and Systems Universitat d'Alacant
Alacant, Valencian Country, Spain.
Email: `mlf@ua.es`

Message from the Organising Committee Chairs

On behalf of the organising committee, we want to take this opportunity to give you a big thank you for joining us in the 22nd Annual Conference of the European Association for Machine Translation, EAMT 2020.

Sadly, this year, the COVID-19 crisis forced us to a last minute change, and we won't be able to welcome you to Lisbon, as we wished so much. However, Unbabel and INESC-ID are extremely proud and honored to host the EAMT conference in fully virtual mode for the first time, from the 3rd to the 5th of November of 2020.

This was of course a very hard decision. In the hope that we could still host a presencial conference, we started by postponing the dates to the first week of November and securing a venue at Instituto Superior Técnico. However, it later became clear that a physical meeting would be impossible under the current circumstances, and together with the board of the European Association for Machine Translation we decided to make EAMT 2020 an on-line conference, with reduced registration fees. We would like to thank all the support from the European Association for Machine Translation in this process, in particular from its president Mikel Forcada and its secretary Carol Scarton for all their help in making this change happen smoothly. We also thank the sponsors and supporting organizations for their flexibility in adapting to a virtual conference.

We are sure EAMT 2020 will be a success with the contribution of everyone! According to our predictions, we expect this edition of the EAMT conference to have one of the highest number of attendees ever. We will have a single-room conference with live talks and booster sessions for papers accepted as posters. We will do our best to make it as interactive and lively as possible. We will plan for virtual social events keeping the best spirit of Lisbon. Stay tuned!

We look forward to your active participation during the three days of the conference. Do not hesitate to ask questions when the session chairs invite you to do so. Please, contribute to make this edition of the conference a fruitful forum where a multidisciplinary group of researchers, developers, practitioners, leaders, vendors, users, and translators all share experiences and motivating ideas.

Finally, we would like to express our sincere appreciation to the people and organisations that have made this conference possible: the European Association for Machine Translation, in particular Mikel Forcada and Carol Scarton for all their support in changing the conference to virtual mode, our gold sponsor (Banco Português de Investimento), Silver sponsors (STAR Group and Microsoft), Bronze sponsors (Unbabel, Text&Form, TAUS, Pangeanic, and Crosslang), supporters (Apertium and Prompsit), institutional partners Unbabel, *Instituto Superior Técnico*, the *Instituto de Engenharia de Sistemas e Computadores, Investigação e Desenvolvimento* and the *Instituto Universitário de Lisboa*, programme chairs (Marco Turchi, Arianna Bisazza, Joss Moorkens, Ana Guerberof, Mary Nurminen, and Lena Marg), keynote speaker (Lucia Specia), and, finally but so importantly, our colleagues Sara Fumega, Bruno Martins, Fernando Batista, Luisa Coheur, Carla Parra Escartín, and Isabel Trancoso, who have worked extraordinarily hard to make this conference as pleasant and inspiring as possible.

André Martins
IST and Unbabel

Helena Moniz
INESC-ID and Unbabel

Preface by the Programme Chairs

It is our pleasure to welcome you to the 22nd annual conference of the European Association for Machine Translation (EAMT) to be held remotely from November 3 to 5, 2020. Organizing this edition in the time of a pandemic that brought about traveling and many other restrictions has been a sort of roller coaster. The whole organizing committee has worked hard to maintain the usual standards of quality and confirm the EAMT conference as the most important event in Europe in the area of machine translation for researchers, users and professional translators.

Following the success of the previous edition, this year once again there are four tracks: research, user, translators, and project/product. The research track concerns novel and significant research results in any aspect of MT and related areas while the user track reports users' experiences with MT in industry, government, NGOs, as well as innovative uses of MT. The translator track focuses on translators' interaction with MT, including MT evaluation using professional translators, post-editing practices and tools, usability, and pricing. The project/product track offers projects and products the opportunity to be presented to the wide audience of the conference.

This year we have received 47 submissions to the research track, 15 submissions to the user track, 13 submissions to the translators' track, and 22 descriptions of projects and products. Each submission to the research, user and translator tracks was peer reviewed by two or three independent members of the Programme Committee depending on the specific track. In the research track, 25 papers (53%) were accepted for publication, whereas 12 papers (80%) were accepted for the user track, and 9 papers (69%) for the translators track. Aside from regular papers from the four tracks, the programme includes an invited talk by Lucia Specia, from the University of Sheffield and Imperial College London, on "Exploring NMT's bag of tricks for translation quality estimation and evaluation". We will also have a presentation by the winner of the EAMT Best Thesis Award, Felix Stahlberg, with his thesis "The Roles of Language Models and Hierarchical Models in Neural Sequence-to-Sequence Prediction" (University of Cambridge).

We would like to thank everyone who, by offering their flexibility and extra efforts, made it possible to deal with continuously moving deadlines. In particular, we thank the Programme Committee members whose names are listed below for their high-quality reviews and recommendation which have been very useful for the Programme Chairs to make decisions. We would also like to thank all the authors for trying their best to incorporate the reviewers' suggestions when preparing the final versions of their papers. For the papers which were not accepted, we

hope that the reviewers' comments will be useful for improving them. Finally, thanks to Mikel
Forcada and Carol Scarton for all of their help and advice!

Arianna Bisazza
University of Groningen

Ana Guerberof-Arenas
University of Surrey

Joss Moorkens
Dublin City University

Marco Turchi
Fondazione Bruno Kessler

EAMT 2020 Committees

General Chair

Mikel L. Forcada, Universitat d'Alacant

Programme Chairs

Research track

Marco Turchi, FBK
Arianna Bisazza, Groningen Univ.

User track

Mary Nurminen, Tampere University
Lena Marg, Welocalize

Translators' track

Joss Moorkens, DCU
Ana Guerberof, Univ. of Surrey

Organising committee

André Martins, IST and Unbabel (co-chair)
Helena Moniz, INESC-ID and Unbabel (co-chair)
Sara Fumega, Unbabel
Bruno Martins, IST and INESC-ID
Fernando Batista, INESC-ID and ISCTE-UL
Luisa Coheur, IST and INESC-ID
Isabel Trancoso, IST and INESC-ID

Programme Committee

Research track

Tamer Alkhouli, RWTH Aachen University
Mihael Arcan, National University of Ireland Galway
Duygu Ataman, University of Zürich
Anabela Barreiro, INESC-ID
Rachel Bawden, The University of Edinburgh
Núria Bel, Universitat Pompeu Fabra
Luisa Bentivogli, Fondazione Bruno Kessler
José G. C. de Souza, eBay Inc.
Iacer Calixto, University of Amsterdam
Michael Carl, Kent State University
Helena Caseli, Federal University of São Carlos (UFSCar)
Sheila Castilho, Dublin City University
Mauro Cettolo, Fondazione Bruno Kessler
Boxing Chen, Alibaba Group
Colin Cherry, National Research Council Canada
Vishal Chowdhary, Microsoft
Chenhui Chu, Osaka University
Joke Daems, Ghent University
Mattia Antonino Di Gangi, Fondazione Bruno Kessler, University of Trento
Christian Dugast, tech2biz
Cristina España-Bonet, UdS and DFKI
Miquel Esplà, Universitat d'Alacant
Mireia Farrús, Universitat Pompeu Fabra
Marcello Federico, Amazon AI
Orhan Firat, Google
Mark Fishel, University of Tartu
George Foster, Google
Markus Freitag, Google AI
Roman Grundkiewicz, The University of Edinburgh
Nizar Habash, Columbia University
Barry Haddow, The University of Edinburgh
Gholamreza Haffari, Simon Fraser University
Teresa Herrmann, Fujitsu
Vu Hoang, The University of Melbourne
Christopher Hokamp, CNGL - Dublin City University
Matthias Huck, Ludwig Maximilian University of Munich
Julia Ive, King's College London
Shahram Khadivi, eBay
Philipp Koehn, Johns Hopkins University
Julia Kreutzer, Google AI
Roland Kuhn, National Research Council of Canada
Anoop Kunchukuttan, Microsoft
Surafel Melaku Lakew, University of Trento
Alon Lavie, Carnegie Mellon University
Gregor Leusch, eBay
Samuel Läubli, University of Zurich

Lieve Macken, Ghent University
Andreas Maletti, Universität Leipzig
Daniel Marcu, ISI/USC
Antonio Valerio Miceli Barone, University of Edinburgh
Joss Moorkens, Dublin City University
Mathias Müller, University of Zurich
Maria Nadejde, The University of Edinburgh
Matteo Negri, Fondazione Bruno Kessler
Jan Niehues, Maastricht University
Sharon O'Brien, Dublin City University
Constantin Orasan, University of Surrey
Daniel Ortiz-Martínez, Universitat Politecnica de Valencia
Myle Ott, Facebook
Carla Parra Escartín, Unbabel, Lda.
Pavel Pecina, Charles University In Prague
Stephan Peitz, Apple
Sergio Penkale, Lingo24
Martin Popel, UFAL, Charles University
Andrei Popescu-Belis, HEIG-VD / HES-SO
Maja Popovic, ADAPT Centre @ DCU
Marta R. Costa-Jussà, Institute For Infocomm Research
Matīss Rikters, Tilde
Rudolf Rosa, Charles University
Germán Sanchis-Trilles, Sciling S.L.
Yves Scherrer, University of Helsinki
Rico Sennrich, University of Zurich
Dimitar Shterionov, Dublin City University
Patrick Simianer, Lilt, Inc.
Felix Stahlberg, Google Research
Dario Stojanovski, Ludwig Maximilian University of Munich
Víctor M. Sánchez-Cartagena, Universitat d'Alacant
Felipe Sánchez-Martínez, Universitat d'Alacant
Aleš Tamchyna, Memsource a. s.
Jörg Tiedemann, University of Helsinki
Antonio Toral, University of Groningen
Ke Tran, Amazon
Francis M. Tyers, Indiana University Bloomington
Vincent Vandeghinste, Instituut voor de Nederlandse Taal // Centre for Computational Linguistics, KU Leuven
David Vilar, Amazon
Martin Volk, University of Zurich
Marion Weller-Di Marco, CIS - University of Munich
François Yvon, LIMSI/CNRS et Université Paris-Sud
Jiajun Zhang, Institute of Automation Chinese Academy of Sciences

User track

Nora Aranberri, University of the Basque Country
Adam Bittlingmayer, ModelFront
Bianka Buschbeck, Systran
Dave Clarke, Welocalize
Michael Denkowski, Amazon
Félix Do Carmo, University of Surrey
Thierry Etchegoyhen, Vicomtech-IK4
Valeria Filippello, SDL
Federico Gaspari, Università per Stranieri "Dante Alighieri" di Reggio Calabria
Kim Harris
Georg Kirchner, Dell
Maarit Koponen, University of Helsinki
László Laki, Globalese
Jay Marciano, Lionbridge
Marianna Martindale, University of Maryland
Morgan O'Brien, McAfee
Niko Papula, Multilizer
Daniel Prou, European Commission
Gema Ramírez-Sánchez, Prompsit Language Engineering
Steve Richardson, The Church of Jesus Christ of Latter-day Saints
Jon Ritzdorf, Moravia
Laura Rossi, LexisNexis
Yury Sharshov, LexisNexis Univentio
Dimitar Shterionov, Dublin City University
Charlotte Tesselaar, LexisNexis Univentio
Joachim Vandenbogaert, Crosslang
Andy Way, ADAPT Centre, Dublin City University
Chris Wendt, Microsoft
Masaru Yamada, Kansai University
Anna Zaretskaya, TransPerfect

Subreviewers

Natasha Latysheva, Welocalize

Translators' track

Khetam Alsharou, Imperial College London
Frank Austermuhl, Aston University
Sarah Bawa Mason, University of Portsmouth
Sarah Berthaud, Galway-Mayo Institute of Technology
Pat Cadwell, Dublin City University
Sheila Castilho, Dublin City University
Joke Daems, Ghent University
Christophe Declercq, KU Leuven
Félix do Carmo, University of Surrey
Gökhan Dogru, Universitat Autònoma de Barcelona
Joanna Drugan, University of East Anglia
Maria Fernandez Parra, Swansea University
Joanna Gough, University of Surrey
Dorothy Kenny, Dublin City University
Maarit Koponen, University of Helsinki
Ralph Krüger, TH Köln
Carlos la Orden Tovar, InsideLoc
Claire Larsonneur, Université Paris 8
Krzysztof Loboda, Jagiellonian University
Rudy Loock, Université de Lille
Lieve Macken, Ghent University
Javier Mallo, Freelance Spanish Language Consultant
Giulia Mattoni, Vistatec
Lucas Nunes Vieira, University of Bristol
Sharon O'Brien, Dublin City University
Antoni Oliver, Universitat Oberta de Catalunya
Maeve Olohan, University of Manchester
Constantin Orasan, University of Surrey
David Orrego Carmona, Aston University
Carla Parra Escartín, Unbabel
Mary Phelan, Dublin City University
Rubén Rodríguez de la Fuente, PayPal
Alessandra Rossetti, Dublin City University
Caroline Rossi, Université Grenoble Alpes
Andrew Rothwell, Swansea University
Akiko Sakamoto, University of Portsmouth
Vilelmini Sosoni, Ionian University
Carlos Teixeira, IOTA Localization Services and Trinity College Dublin

Invited Speech

Exploring NMT's bag of tricks for translation quality estimation and evaluation

Lucia Specia, Imperial College and Sheffield University, UK

Neural machine translation (NMT) has become the de facto automated translation technology for language pairs where enough parallel data is available. Nevertheless, translation models are not bulletproof. Given the generally very fluent translations produced by these models, automatically assessing their general quality is arguably more challenging, yet paramount. In this talk I will argue that the solution to this problem can to a large extent be provided by NMT models themselves. I will discuss experiments demonstrating that such models provide valuable information for both translation evaluation and quality estimation. Namely, they allow for better supervised as well as fully unsupervised quality estimation models, as well as more for reliable multi-reference evaluation approaches.

EAMT 2019 Best Thesis Award — Anthony C Clarke Award

Ten PhD theses defended in 2019 were received as candidates for the 2019 edition of the Anthony C Clarke Award - EAMT Best Thesis Award, and all ten were eligible. 36 reviewers and six EAMT Executive Committee members were recruited to examine and score the theses, considering how challenging the problem tackled in each thesis was, how relevant the results were for machine translation as a field, and what the strength of its impact in terms of scientific publications was. Two EAMT Executive Committee members also analysed all theses.

The year of 2019 was again a very good year for PhD theses in machine translation. The scores of the best theses were very close, which made it very hard to select a winner. A panel of five EAMT Executive Committee members (André Martins, Lucia Specia, Khalil Sima'an, Carolina Scarton, and Mikel L. Forcada) was assembled to process the reviews and select a winner.

The panel has decided to grant the 2019 edition of the EAMT Best Thesis Award, Anthony C Clarke Award, to **Felix Stahlberg** for his thesis "The Roles of Language Models and Hierarchical Models in Neural Sequence-to-Sequence Prediction", University of Cambridge, supervised by Bill Byrne.

The Roles of Language Models and Hierarchical Models in Neural Sequence-to-Sequence Prediction

Felix Stahlberg[1]
Department of Engineering
University of Cambridge
Trumpington St, Cambridge CB2 1PZ, UK
`fs439@cantab.ac.uk`

With the advent of deep learning, research in many areas of machine learning is converging towards the same set of methods and models. For example, long short-term memory networks (Hochreiter and Schmidhuber, 1997) are not only popular for various tasks in natural language processing (NLP) such as speech recognition, machine translation, handwriting recognition, syntactic parsing, etc., but they are also applicable to seemingly unrelated fields such as bioinformatics (Min et al., 2016). Recent advances in contextual word embeddings like BERT (Devlin et al., 2019) boast with achieving state-of-the-art results on 11 NLP tasks with the same model. Before deep learning, a speech recognizer and a syntactic parser used to have little in common as systems were much more tailored towards the task at hand.

At the core of this development is the tendency to view each task as yet another data mapping problem, neglecting the particular characteristics and (soft) requirements that tasks often have in practice. This often goes along with a sharp break of deep learning methods with previous research in the specific area. This thesis can be understood as an antithesis to the prevailing paradigm. We show how traditional symbolic statistical machine translation (Koehn, 2009) models can still improve neural machine translation (Kalchbrenner and Blunsom, 2013; Sutskever et al., 2014; Bahdanau et al., 2015, NMT) while reducing the risk of common pathologies of NMT such as hallucinations and neologisms. Other external symbolic models such as spell checkers and morphology databases help neural models to correct grammatical errors in text.

We also focus on language models that often do not play a role in vanilla end-to-end approaches and apply them in different ways to word reordering, grammatical error correction, low-resource NMT, and document-level NMT. Finally, we demonstrate the benefit of hierarchical models in sequence-to-sequence prediction. Hand-engineered covering grammars are effective in preventing catastrophic errors in neural text normalization systems. Our operation sequence model for interpretable NMT represents translation as a series of actions that modify the translation state, and can also be seen as derivation in a formal grammar.

This thesis also focuses on the decoding aspect of neural sequence models. We argue that NMT decoding is very similar to navigating through a weighted graph structure or finite state machine, with the only difference that the state space may not be finite. This view enables us to use a wide range of search algorithms, and provides a strong formal framework for pairing NMT with other kinds of models. In particular, we apply exact shortest path search algorithms for graphs, such as depth-first search, to NMT, and show that beam decoding fails to find the global best model score in most cases. However, these search errors, paradoxically, often prevent the decoder from suffering from a frequent but very serious model error in NMT, namely that the empty hypothesis often has the global best model score.

The main contributions of this thesis are implemented in a novel open-source NMT decoding framework called SGNMT[2] which allows paring neural translation models with different kinds of constraints and symbolic models. SGNMT is compatible to a range of popular toolkits such as Ten-

[1]Now at Google Research.

[2]`https://ucam-smt.github.io/sgnmt/html/`

Martins, Moniz, Fumega, Martins, Batista, Coheur, Parra, Trancoso, Turchi, Bisazza, Moorkens, Guerberof, Nurminen, Marg, Forcada (eds.)
Proceedings of the 22nd Annual Conference of the European Association for Machine Translation, p. 5–6
Lisboa, Portugal, November 2020.

sor2Tensor (Vaswani et al., 2018) and fairseq (Ott et al., 2019) for neural models, KenLM (Heafield, 2011) for language modelling, and OpenFST (Allauzen et al., 2007) for finite state transducers. SGNMT has been used for: (1) teaching as SGNMT has been used for course work and student theses in the MPhil in Machine Learning and Machine Intelligence at the University of Cambridge, (2) research as most of the research work of the Cambridge MT group, including four successful WMT submissions, is based on SGNMT, and (3) technology transfer as SGNMT has helped to transfer research findings from the laboratory to the industry, eg. into a product of SDL plc.

The Apollo repository of the University of Cambridge provides open access to the full thesis (https://doi.org/10.17863/CAM.49422).

Acknowledgements

The author would like to thank his Ph.D. supervisor, Bill Byrne, and his thesis examiners, Paula Buttery and Adam Lopez. The author was financially supported by the U.K. Engineering and Physical Sciences Research Council (EPSRC grant EP/L027623/1). Some of the work has been performed using resources provided by the Cambridge Tier-2 system operated by the University of Cambridge Research Computing Service[3] funded by EPSRC Tier-2 capital grant EP/P020259/1.

References

Allauzen, Cyril, Michael Riley, Johan Schalkwyk, Wojciech Skut, and Mehryar Mohri. 2007. Openfst: A general and efficient weighted finite-state transducer library. In Holub, Jan and Jan Žďárek, editors, *Implementation and Application of Automata*, pages 11–23, Berlin, Heidelberg. Springer Berlin Heidelberg.

Bahdanau, Dzmitry, Kyung Hyun Cho, and Yoshua Bengio. 2015. Neural machine translation by jointly learning to align and translate. In *3rd International Conference on Learning Representations, ICLR 2015*, January.

Devlin, Jacob, Ming-Wei Chang, Kenton Lee, and Kristina Toutanova. 2019. BERT: Pre-training of deep bidirectional transformers for language understanding. In *Proceedings of the 2019 Conference of the North American Chapter of the Association for Computational Linguistics: Human Language Technologies, Volume 1 (Long and Short Papers)*, pages 4171–4186, Minneapolis, Minnesota, June. Association for Computational Linguistics.

Heafield, Kenneth. 2011. KenLM: Faster and smaller language model queries. In *Proceedings of the Sixth Workshop on Statistical Machine Translation*, pages 187–197, Edinburgh, Scotland, July. Association for Computational Linguistics.

Hochreiter, Sepp and Jürgen Schmidhuber. 1997. Long short-term memory. *Neural computation*, 9(8):1735–1780.

Kalchbrenner, Nal and Phil Blunsom. 2013. Recurrent continuous translation models. In *Proceedings of the 2013 Conference on Empirical Methods in Natural Language Processing*, pages 1700–1709, Seattle, Washington, USA, October. Association for Computational Linguistics.

Koehn, Philipp. 2009. *Statistical machine translation*. Cambridge University Press.

Min, Seonwoo, Byunghan Lee, and Sungroh Yoon. 2016. Deep learning in bioinformatics. *Briefings in Bioinformatics*, 18(5):851–869, 07.

Ott, Myle, Sergey Edunov, Alexei Baevski, Angela Fan, Sam Gross, Nathan Ng, David Grangier, and Michael Auli. 2019. fairseq: A fast, extensible toolkit for sequence modeling. In *Proceedings of the 2019 Conference of the North American Chapter of the Association for Computational Linguistics (Demonstrations)*, pages 48–53, Minneapolis, Minnesota, June. Association for Computational Linguistics.

Sutskever, Ilya, Oriol Vinyals, and Quoc V Le. 2014. Sequence to sequence learning with neural networks. In Ghahramani, Z., M. Welling, C. Cortes, N. D. Lawrence, and K. Q. Weinberger, editors, *Advances in Neural Information Processing Systems 27*, pages 3104–3112. Curran Associates, Inc.

Vaswani, Ashish, Samy Bengio, Eugene Brevdo, Francois Chollet, Aidan Gomez, Stephan Gouws, Llion Jones, Łukasz Kaiser, Nal Kalchbrenner, Niki Parmar, Ryan Sepassi, Noam Shazeer, and Jakob Uszkoreit. 2018. Tensor2Tensor for neural machine translation. In *Proceedings of the 13th Conference of the Association for Machine Translation in the Americas (Volume 1: Research Papers)*, pages 193–199, Boston, MA, March. Association for Machine Translation in the Americas.

---

[3]http://www.hpc.cam.ac.uk

Research papers

Comprehension and Trust in Crises:
Investigating the Impact of Machine Translation and Post-Editing

Alessandra Rossetti[1,2], **Sharon O'Brien**[1,2], **Patrick Cadwell**[2]
[1] ADAPT Centre
[2] School of Applied Language and Intercultural Studies
Dublin City University, Dublin
Ireland
{alessandra.rossetti, sharon.obrien, patrick.cadwell}
@dcu.ie

Abstract

We conducted a survey to understand the impact of machine translation and post-editing awareness on comprehension of and trust in messages disseminated to prepare the public for a weather-related crisis, i.e. flooding. The translation direction was English–Italian. Sixty-one participants—all native Italian speakers with different English proficiency levels—answered our survey. Each participant read and evaluated between three and six crisis messages using ratings and open-ended questions on comprehensibility and trust. The messages were in English and Italian. All the Italian messages had been machine translated and post-edited. Nevertheless, participants were told that only half had been post-edited, so that we could test the impact of post-editing awareness. We could not draw firm conclusions when comparing the scores for trust and comprehensibility assigned to the three types of messages—English, post-edits, and purported raw outputs. However, when scores were triangulated with open-ended answers, stronger patterns were observed, such as the impact of fluency of the translations on their comprehensibility and trustworthiness. We found correlations between comprehensibility and trustworthiness, and identified other factors influencing these aspects, such as the clarity and soundness of the messages. We conclude by outlin-

ing implications for crisis preparedness, limitations, and areas for future research.

1 Introduction

Societies are becoming increasingly multicultural and multilingual, mainly as a result of economic migration and displacement (O'Brien and Federici, 2019). In Ireland, for example, there are more than 500 thousand non-Irish nationals, the majority of whom come from a country where English is not the official language, e.g. Poland, Lithuania, Brazil, and Italy (Central Statistics Office, 2016). Non-native speakers of a language—and especially those with limited proficiency—need to overcome considerable communication challenges in the contexts of crises (Santos-Hernández and Morrow, 2013; Sherly et al., 2015).

Taking again Ireland as an example, flooding is the most common hazard that the country needs to manage (Jeffers, 2011). When substantial, flooding poses a threat to infrastructure, business, and also people's health (Major Emergency Management, 2016). In order to be safe and act upon the messages sent by emergency responders, linguistically diverse communities need to be able to comprehend and trust those messages (Alexander and Pescaroli, 2019). Machine translation (MT) and post-editing (PE) can play a role in crisis communication but their application needs careful consideration.

This paper describes the results of a survey whose goal was to address two important gaps in relation to the role of MT and PE as enablers of multilingual communication in crises. Specifically, we set out to gather empirical evidence on the impact of MT and of PE awareness on comprehension of and trust in messages disseminated by emergency responders to prepare the public for a

Martins, Moniz, Fumega, Martins, Batista, Coheur, Parra, Trancoso, Turchi, Bisazza, Moorkens, Guerberof, Nurminen, Marg, Forcada (eds.)
Proceedings of the 22nd Annual Conference of the European Association for Machine Translation, p. 9–18
Lisboa, Portugal, November 2020.

specific weather-related crisis: flooding. The translation direction under analysis was English to Italian (see Section 3 for our research questions). The choice of this translation direction was motivated by the substantial number of native speakers of Italian living in English-speaking countries where flooding is common, such as the United Kingdom and Ireland (Central Statistics Office, 2016).

It is worth underlining the lack of clear distinctions between the concepts of *crisis, emergency, disaster,* or *hazard.* For the purpose of this study, we adopted a broad definition of *crisis,* understood as a non-routine and disruptive event, that poses a threat, and that usually involves the phases of preparation, response, and recovery (Alexander, 2002; Cadwell et al., 2019).

The remainder of this paper is organized as follows: Section 2 reviews and summarizes related work on MT, PE, comprehension, and trust, with a special focus on crisis contexts. Section 3 presents our research questions and the methodology that we adopted in order to answer them. Section 4 reports on the results of our survey, which are then discussed in Section 5, along with implications, limitations, and avenues for future research.

2   Related Work

Translation of crisis information into the first language of the target audience facilitates comprehension, as has been shown, for example, in the case of the 2014 Ebola outbreak (O'Brien and Cadwell, 2017). However, the importance of translation in crises is still either not acknowledged or discussed only superficially in policy documents and institutional checklists (O'Brien et al., 2018; O'Brien and Federici, 2019). This is surprising when considering that misunderstandings due to lack of translation have often resulted in increased vulnerability and loss of lives (Santos-Hernández and Morrow, 2013; Alexander and Pescaroli, 2019).

In addition to comprehension, the language in which information is conveyed can influence trust in the message, particularly in crisis situations (Translators without Borders, 2019). Previous research on trust, translation, and crises has mainly focused on how translation influences reasoning about trust among people affected by a crisis (Cadwell, 2015), with trust emerging as one of the challenges in the communication efforts of humanitarian organisations, along with low literacy levels and cultural sensitivity (Federici et al., 2019).

In crisis situations, MT has been a component of some communications, as shown, for instance, during the Haiti earthquake (Lewis, 2010) and, more recently, in refugee settings (Translators without Borders, 2016). MT is particularly helpful when large quantities of texts need quick translations into multiple languages (Cadwell et al., 2019). The utility of MT in crisis settings involving low-resource languages has also been empirically tested (Cadwell et al., 2019).

The relationship between MT and trust has received some attention since machine-translated outputs are far from flawless and fully accurate, even after the quality improvements introduced by the neural paradigm (Toral et al., 2018), thus often requiring PE. Research has revolved around approaches to identify machine-translated words, sentences or documents that pass a predetermined quality threshold and are therefore more trustworthy (Soricut and Echihabi, 2010).

The availability of these confidence, or trust, scores seems to be welcomed by translators (Moorkens and O'Brien, 2013), but the scores should be accompanied by an explanation of how they were obtained (Cadwell et al., 2017). Attention has also been given to the level of trust that professional translators attribute to machine-translated outputs and specific MT engines (Guerberof, 2013; Teixeira, 2014; Cadwell et al., 2017). Furthermore, lack of trust in MT has emerged as one of the reasons for its non-adoption among language service providers (Porro Rodríguez et al., 2017). Previous works have also focused on students, with mixed results—from a general lack of trust (Koponen, 2015; Briggs, 2018), to a tendency to almost uncritically trust the output (Depraetere, 2010).

More relevant to our research, a limited number of studies have focused on end users of MT—who often read translations for gist understanding (Specia and Shah, 2018)—and on their reliance on MT to locate information on websites (Gaspari, 2007), as well as on their tendency to use MT to translate from languages or documents of which they already have some knowledge, which might indicate a lack of complete trust in the output (Nurminen and Papula, 2018).

Research has also focused on the broader areas of acceptability, usability, readability, and comprehensibility of machine-translated texts among end users, and on how these aspects are influenced by different PE levels (Castilho and O'Brien, 2016; Screen, 2019). However, most of the research so far has focused on technical documents.

Accordingly, there is a lack of empirical evidence on: (i) the potential benefits of MT (as opposed to lack of translation) for end users' comprehension of and trust in crisis communication; and (ii) the potential impact on comprehension and trust of being aware that crisis messages have been post-edited. We set out to fill these research gaps.

3   Methodology

3.1 Research Questions

Having in mind the research gaps outlined in Section 2.2, we conducted a survey to address the following research questions (RQ):

RQ1. What is the impact of machine translation on comprehension of and trust in messages disseminated to prepare the public for a weather-related crisis?

RQ2. What is the impact of post-editing awareness on comprehension of and trust in messages disseminated to prepare the public for a weather-related crisis?

As specified in Section 1, the translation direction under analysis was English to Italian.

3.2 Survey Setup and Circulation

All of the survey questions and instructions were in Italian. The survey received approval from Dublin City University Research Ethics Committee (DCUREC/2019/209). It was preceded by a plain language statement and an informed consent form (also in Italian) describing the research in lay terms for the participants.

Initially, the survey targeted native speakers of Italian living in English-speaking countries, as they would represent a realistic audience for crisis messages delivered by emergency responders in English. However, an initial analysis of the responses from this pool of Italian participants showed that their self-reported level of English was very high (Section 4.1). Accordingly, to gather data from Italian speakers with lower levels of English proficiency—thus gaining a broader range of perspectives—we also circulated a slightly modified version of the survey among native speakers of Italian living in Italy (see Section 3.3 for details on the slightly modified version). These participants were also a realistic audience considering the high number of Italians who travel from Italy to English-speaking countries for tourism, school- or business-related purposes (Tourism Ireland, 2018).

The survey in both its versions was circulated online through word-of-mouth; social media; and newsletters from universities, Italian embassies, and organisations promoting Italian culture in English-speaking countries (from the United States, to Ireland, to New Zealand).

3.3 Survey Structure and Experimental Design

The survey began with two questions to check participants' eligibility, namely: (i) that their native language was Italian; and (ii) that they lived in an English-speaking country. In the version of the survey targeting Italians in Italy, the second eligibility question was not present.

The survey then continued with a series of questions on the participants' demographic characteristics and background, namely their age, gender, self-reported level of English proficiency, frequency of use of English, familiarity with MT systems, and reasons for their use. With regard to the questions on self-reported English proficiency and on the frequency of use of the English language, these questions were taken from Anderson et al. (2018), and they involved asking participants: (i) to rate their English conversation, writing, reading, and listening skills on a scale from 1 (low) to 5 (high); and (ii) to indicate how often they spoke, wrote, listened, and read in English. Native speakers of Italian in English-speaking countries were also asked about how much time they had lived abroad, and the frequency of flooding in their country of residence (Section 4.1).

The participants were subsequently presented with information and instructions regarding the experimental tasks. Specifically, they would first be shown three messages dealing with preparation for a flooding crisis: one message would be in English, while the other two would be Italian translations of two different messages. They were also told that, of the two translations, one had been produced by Google Translate and had not been corrected by anyone, while the other had also been produced by Google Translate but then corrected by a native speaker of Italian. We used *corrected* (rather than *post-edited*) because our participants might not have been familiar with the concept of PE. We also specified that we would let them know which MT output had been post-edited/corrected beforehand.

At this stage, we used deception since both machine-translated messages had actually been post-edited by the first author (see Section 3.4 for details on PE level). We used deception for two reasons. First, if we had not post-edited one of the two machine-translated messages, we would have introduced MT quality as a confounding variable—in other words, the different quality of the two machine-translated messages would have been likely to influence comprehensibility and trust scores. By post-editing both outputs, we ensured quality was comparable, and this allowed us to determine whether awareness of PE in itself influenced scores of comprehensibility and trust given by end users. Secondly, due to the critical nature of the messages, we deemed it risky to circulate unedited content with potential errors.

We adopted a within-subjects design whereby, for each of the three messages (one in English and two Italian translations), each participant was instructed to answer the following questions:

(i) How much do you trust this message on a scale from 1 (don't trust it at all) to 4 (trust it completely)?

(ii) How likely are you to comply with these instructions on a scale from 1 (very unlikely) to 4 (very likely)?

(iii) How comprehensible do you find this message on a scale from 1 (totally incomprehensible) to 4 (easily comprehensible)?

All participants read and evaluated the same messages, and each message was always seen in the same condition. We added a question on compliance as an additional measure of trust (Liu et al., 2018). We used four-point scales to avoid mid-point bias. For each of the three questions, participants were also given the option to explain the reasons behind their scores as answers to open-ended questions. Finally, after reading and scoring the first set of three messages, participants could either conclude the survey, or read and evaluate a set of three more messages. To counterbalance a potential fatigue effect, the order in which the English message and the two Italian translations were presented to participants varied between the first and the second set of messages, but not within set.

3.4 Experimental Materials

We took the crisis preparedness messages from the Irish website *Be Winter Ready*.[1] The PE applied to the machine-translated messages can be classified as full PE since we aimed to produce outputs that were both fluent and accurate (TAUS, 2010). Average BLEU score based on comparisons between raw and post-edited messages was 55.76. However, as the extracts in Section 4.2 show, a few participants believed that the fluency could have been improved further.

Since the readability level of the English source messages—both the one that we kept in English and the ones that we machine translated into Italian—might have represented a confounding variable influencing comprehensibility scores, we selected messages with a similar or almost similar readability level. Specifically, according to the Flesch-Kincaid Grade Level formula, all English messages could be understood by readers between 11 and 16 years of age.

To further ensure comparability, the three messages in each of the two sets (Section 3.3) began with the same introductory sentence. The three messages in the first set all began with "If you find that you are in a flood prone area, there are a number of steps that you can take to make your property more resilient to flooding. For example…", as they dealt with property protection. On the other hand, the three messages in the second set revolved around people protection and began with the introductory sentence "If you find that you are in a flood prone area, there are a number of steps that you can take. For example…". These introductory sentences were then followed by specific instructions, such as "Assess if your property is at risk from flooding" in the first set, or "Have medication to hand (if needed)" in the second set. To avoid a learning effect, the three instructions in each set were different.

4 Results

4.1 Participants' Background

A total of 61 participants took part in the survey. All the participants were native speakers of Italian, with 48 of them living in an English-

---

12

speaking country and 13 living in Italy. Most participants were aged between 29-39 (46%), followed by participants aged 40-50 (29%). We achieved good balance between male (52%) and female (46%) participants—2% of the participants did not specify their gender.

Among the 48 participants based outside Italy, most of them reported having lived in an English-speaking country either between five and ten years (N=13), or between ten and 20 years (N=13), with seven also stating that they had lived in an English-speaking country for more than 20 years. Unsurprisingly, when asked to self-report their level of English proficiency in terms of conversation, reading, writing, and listening, most participants within this cohort reported five out of five. Furthermore, the vast majority of them stated that they spoke, wrote, read, and listened in English either always or most of the time.

In contrast, most participants based in Italy reported having a lower level of English proficiency—most of them selected one (out of five) to rate their English conversation skills, and three (out of five) to rate their listening, writing, and reading skills. In line with these scores, most of the participants based in Italy stated that they spoke, listened, and wrote in English only rarely. However, most of them reported reading in English sometimes. In other words, our two cohorts of participants—namely, Italians living in English-speaking countries and Italians living in Italy—were different enough in terms of English proficiency, which allowed us to gather data from a broad range of potential users of crisis communications (Section 4.2).

42% of the 48 participants living in an English-speaking country stated that flooding—namely, the weather-related crisis that is the focus of our study—was common where they lived, with 14% not knowing, as shown in Figure 1.

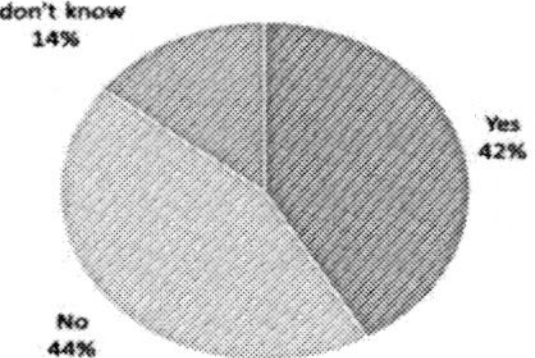

Figure 1. Percentage of participants (not) familiar with flooding

With regard to the use of MT systems, of all the 61 participants, 48 reported using MT systems. The reasons for their use of MT are reported in Figure 2, where the number of selections is higher than the number of participants because participants could select more than one option. Assimilation was the most common reason, followed by dissemination. This result was relevant as it showed that these end users could potentially use MT to translate crisis messages delivered in a language with which they were not familiar.

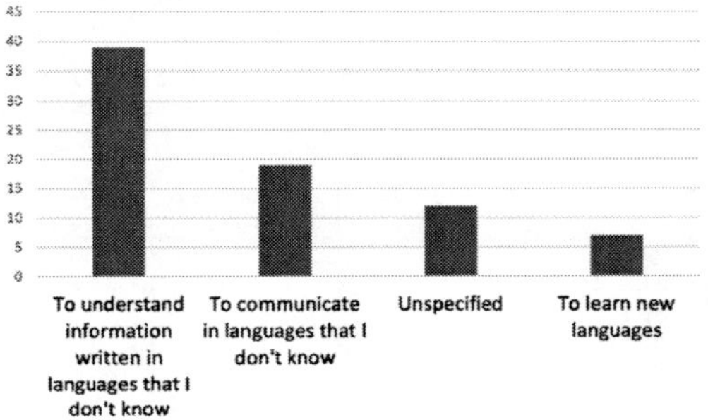

Figure 2. Participants' reasons for use of MT

4.2 Comprehensibility and Trust

The tables below contain descriptive statistics—mean and standard deviation (SD). Table 1 reports the comprehensibility scores. Table 2 contains the trust scores, and Table 3 shows the trust as compliance scores. In each table, we first reported the scores provided by all 61 survey participants combined, and then by Italians living in English-speaking countries and by Italians living in Italy separately, as these two groups differed substantially in terms of English proficiency (Section 4.1). We combined scores assigned by participants to both sets of messages (Section 3.4). In the interests of clarity, in the tables and elsewhere in this paper we used *raw messages* for those MT outputs that had also been post-edited even though participants thought that they had not been—our deception condition (Section 3.3). The highest scores are highlighted in bold.

With regard to comprehensibility (Table 1), it can be observed that: (i) the messages labelled as post-edited received the highest average scores by all three cohorts of participants; (ii) participants living in Italy—and having a lower level of English proficiency—seemed to benefit more from the translations labelled as raw, compared with the English messages, than participants living in English-speaking countries. As far as trust is concerned (Table 2), results were more varied: (i) the messages labelled as post-edited were not associated with highest average scores; but again (ii) differently from participants in English-speaking countries, participants living in Italy showed higher trust in the messages labelled as raw, compared with the English messages. With regard to trust measured in terms of compliance (Table 3), we observed that, regardless of their level of English proficiency, participants showed higher compliance with the message in English, compared with the Italian translations. It should be noted, however, that the differences in scores reported in Tables 1-3 are slight, and a series of repeated measures ANOVAs run in SPSS found these differences to be not significant (p>.05).

	Comprehensibility		
	English messages	**Raw messages**	**Post-edited messages**
Total participants (N=61)	3.45 (.83)	3.54 (.75)	**3.64 (.64)**
Italians abroad (N=48)	3.66 (.62)	3.64 (.63)	**3.74 (.51)**
Italians in Italy (N=13)	2.71 (1.04)	3.18 (1.01)	**3.29 (.92)**

Table 1. Comprehensibility scores

	Trust		
	English messages	**Raw messages**	**Post-edited messages**
Total participants (N=61)	**3.36 (.80)**	3.29 (.82)	3.35 (.90)
Italians abroad (N=48)	**3.49 (.74)**	3.34 (.77)	3.46 (.78)
Italians in Italy (N=13)	2.88 (.85)	**3.12 (.99)**	2.94 (1.19)

Table 2. Trust scores

	Trust (compliance)		
	English messages	**Raw Messages**	**Post-edited messages**
Total participants (N=61)	**3.53 (.75)**	3.35 (.90)	3.38 (.95)
Italians abroad (N=48)	**3.67 (.59)**	3.46 (.80)	3.56 (.78)
Italians in Italy (N=13)	**3.00 (1.0)**	2.94 (1.14)	2.76 (1.25)

Table 3. Compliance (trust) scores

Using SPSS software, we also examined potential correlations between comprehensibility scores and trust scores. The results, reported in Table 4, showed that comprehensibility scores and trust scores had a statistically significant linear relationship for all three types of messages (p<.01). The direction of the relationship was positive, and the strength of this association went from moderate to fairly strong (.5 < r_s < .7). In other words, regardless of how the messages were labelled (i.e. raw MT vs. PE) and regardless of translation, greater comprehensibility was often associated with greater trust.

	Trust	**Trust (compliance)**
Comprehensibility	*English messages* .69*	*English messages* .66*
	Raw messages .53*	*Raw messages* .66*
	Post-edited messages .55*	*Post-edited messages* .62*

Table 4. Results of the Spearman Correlation[2]

The qualitative data collected through the open-ended questions in the survey (Section 3.3), and coded with the NVivo software, complemented these scores and guided their interpretation. We used thematic analysis (Braun and Clarke, 2012) to identify the main reasons behind the comprehensibility and trust scores that the participants assigned. Our analysis identified seven themes in the participants' responses, namely: clarity; soundness; helpfulness; fluency; style; source; and individual differences.

Figure 3 shows how many times each reason was mentioned per message and per each object of investigation among native Italian speakers living in English-speaking countries. Figure 4 reports the same data for the cohort living in Italy. Again, we counted and analysed the answers given by the participants when evaluating both sets of crisis messages (Section 3.3). Participants could indicate more than one reason for each of their scores.

In line with the moderate to fairly strong correlations in Table 4, Figures 3 and 4 show that clarity (defined as simplicity and comprehensibility of language) was regarded by numerous participants as a reason to trust the messages. For participants living in Italy and having lower English proficiency, clarity was needed to trust the messages particularly when the messages were in English, which might explain the slightly lower average score that they assigned to the trustworthiness of English messages (Table 2).

---

[2] Statistical significance (*) is at the .01 level.

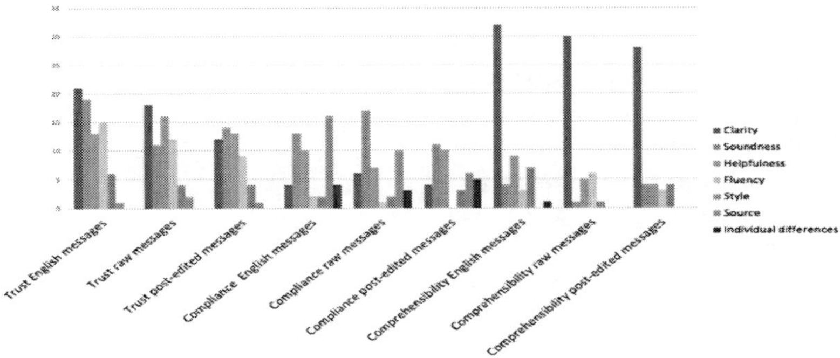

Figure 3. Mentions of themes by participants in English-speaking countries, cross-referenced with experimental conditions

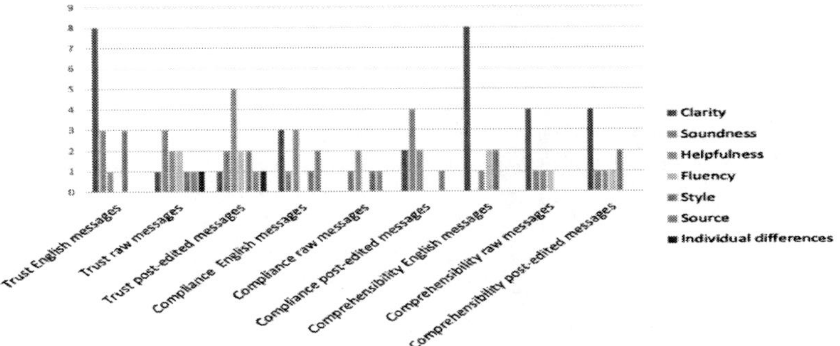

Figure 4. Mentions of themes by participants in Italy, cross-referenced with experimental conditions

As would be expected, clarity also emerged as a common reason influencing comprehensibility scores. A few participants mentioned the features that rendered a message clear, such as the absence of technical terms, simple noun and verb phrases, or the use of common words. It should be remembered that our experimental materials could be understood by readers between 11 and 16 years of age (Section 3.4).

When evaluating their level of compliance, clarity seemed to be less relevant to participants. In contrast, the soundness, the helpfulness, and the source of the messages seemed to be determining factors. Often, the soundness and helpfulness of the messages also determined the participants' level of trust in the messages. See, for examples, extracts below[3] in which participants explain why they would trust and comply with a specific crisis message:

P10: Logical and reasonable explanation.

P20: It's reasonable, and the task can be carried out easily, and it's for my benefit.

P09: In general, if it [the message] comes from emergency managers, it means that the information provided is accurate.

Another aspect occasionally influencing trust seemed to be style—this theme included the tone and register of the message. Specifically, several participants mentioned the authoritative tone, the directness of the message, and the sense of competence emerging from the messages—especially those in English—as reasons to trust them.

Individual differences, and especially previous experience of a weather-related crisis, also emerged as a reason for compliance among Italians living in English-speaking countries. This is not surprising considering that almost half of them reported living in a country where flooding is common (Figure 1).

Considering the specific focus of this paper on the impact of MT and PE (Section 3.1), as well as on how messages were labelled, it is interesting to notice that the theme of fluency—capturing participants' mentions of how (un)natural the language of the translated messages was—emerged as one of the reasons behind participants' trust and comprehensibility

---

[3] The answers in Italian were translated into English by the first author.

scores. See, for instance, the following explanations for assigning a specific score:

P14: The translation is correct, but it could be improved.

P22: Even though the message is clear, it's obvious that it's a raw translation.

P26: Message clear and simple, with no errors.

P05: Because it contains no errors, and you can't tell that it's an automatic translation.

P07: The message has been translated clearly and correctly, with no obvious grammar or syntactical errors.

P27: Convoluted, not fluid.

Despite these mentions of translation, Figure 3 and Figure 4 show that the other themes—and especially clarity, soundness, helpfulness, and source—had a stronger impact on participants' reported comprehensibility and trust. Interestingly, this observation on the somewhat lower impact of translation, and of how translation was labelled, is in line with the slight differences reported in Tables 1-3 between the scores assigned to English messages, to messages labelled as raw MT, and to those labelled as post-edited. Furthermore, participants' responses to the open-ended questions seemed to cluster around the same themes depending on whether the question was on trust, compliance, or comprehensibility, and regardless of whether they were reading the English message, the purported raw translation, or the post-edited translation. For instance, the importance of the source (i.e. emergency managers) was mentioned by several participants when indicating the reasons behind compliance, but was absent when they discussed their comprehensibility scores (Figures 3-4).

5 Discussion and Conclusions

With this survey, we set out to investigate the impact of MT and PE awareness, in the English to Italian direction, on comprehension of and trust in messages disseminated to the public in the context of preparation for a specific weather-related crisis, i.e. flooding (Section 3.1).

Overall, we found slight and non-significant differences in terms of scores between English, purported raw, and post-edited messages. However, some interesting trends emerged, namely: (i) some beneficial effect of MT on comprehension and trust among end users with low English proficiency; (ii) a tendency to comply more with messages in English, possibly as a result of their authoritative tone/style (Section 4.2); and (iii) labelling of messages as *post-edited* resulting in some improvement in comprehension, but not in trust. The absence of a beneficial effect of PE awareness on trust might be due to: (i) the purported MT outputs having also been post-edited and, therefore, appearing equally trustworthy; (ii) the fact that the fluency of the declared post-edits could have been improved further (Section 4.2). In line with these points, the fluency of the translations had some impact on how comprehensible and trustworthy the messages appeared to be to our participants. Interestingly, after comparing the influence of different PE levels among end users, Van Egdom and Pluymaekers (2019) found that full PE led to positive judgements in terms of language use and style, but did not result in a significant improvement of the perceptions (including trustworthiness) of the sender of a product.

Regardless of how the messages were labelled, several aspects of crisis messages were recognized as particularly important by participants, especially the clarity, the soundness, the helpfulness, and the source of the messages. The importance of clarity for comprehension could be expected. On the other hand, results regarding trust are particularly interesting as they align with models of trust (Mayer et al., 1995) according to which the decision to trust is determined by, among others: the competence of the trustee (e.g. their ability to provide accurate and sensible information), corresponding to soundness in our study; their intentions (e.g. to help the public affected by a crisis), corresponding to our helpfulness theme; and their adherence to a set of accepted principles, e.g. as imposed by the profession on emergency managers, who were the source of our messages. Furthermore, trust models discuss the trustor's propensity to trust (Mayer et al., 1995), which, in our study, seemed to be mainly determined by previous experience of flooding.

A final interesting finding from this study was the demonstration that greater comprehension is associated with greater trust. This finding provides empirical evidence of the role that clear crisis communications—through plain language and/or translation—can play in establishing a relationship of trust between emergency managers and the public, thus leading to higher compliance with instructions for crisis preparedness. A similar result, although related to advertisement disclaimers, is reported in Herbst et al. (2013).

This study has several limitations, particularly the high level of English proficiency of most participants, and the limited number of messages that were evaluated. Larger-scale experimental studies with different setups are warranted. Additional research should focus on: the impact of different PE levels; the impact of labelling human translations as post-edits; different language pairs; and end users less familiar with MT (Figure 2). It might also be interesting to observe end users' interactions with MT and to explain them using a trust and credibility lens (see e.g. Gao et al. 2014). Finally, future qualitative research could help determine the directionality of the relationship between comprehension and trust.

Acknowledgement This research has been funded by Science Foundation Ireland through the SFI Research Centres Programme and is co-funded under the European Regional Development Fund through Grant n. 13/RC/2106. Data from this study are available upon request.

References

Alexander, David. 2002. *Principles of Emergency Planning and Management*. Dunedin Academic Press Ltd, Edinburgh, United Kingdom.

Alexander, David, and Gianluca Pescaroli. 2019. The Role of Translators and Interpreters in Cascading Crises and Disasters: Towards a Framework for Confronting the Challenges. *Disaster Prevention and Management*, 29(1). doi:10.1108/DPM-12-2018-0382.

Anderson, John, Lorinda Mak, Aram Keyvani Chahi, and Ellen Bialystok. 2018. The Language and Social Background Questionnaire: Assessing Degree of Bilingualism in a Diverse Population. *Behavior Research Methods*, 50(1):250–263.

Braun, Virginia, and Victoria Clarke. 2012. Thematic Analysis. *APA Handbook of Research Methods in Psychology: Vol. 2: Research Designs*. American Psychological Association, Washington, 57–71.

Briggs, Neil. 2018. Neural Machine Translation Tools in the Language Learning Classroom: Students' Use, Perceptions, and Analyses. *JALT CALL Journal*, 14(1):2–24.

Cadwell, Patrick. 2015. *Translation and Trust: A Case Study of how Translation Was Experienced by Foreign Nationals Resident in Japan for the 2011 Great East Japan Earthquake*. PhD thesis, Dublin City University.

Cadwell, Patrick, Sharon O'Brien, and Carlos Teixeira. 2017. Resistance and Accommodation: Factors for the (Non-) Adoption of Machine Translation among Professional Translators. *Perspectives*, 26(3):301–321.

Cadwell, Patrick, Sharon O'Brien, and Eric DeLuca. 2019. More than Tweets: A Critical Reflection on Developing and Testing Crisis Machine Translation Technology. *Translation Spaces*, 8(2):300–333.

Castilho, Sheila, and Sharon O'Brien. 2016. Evaluating the Impact of Light Post-Editing on Usability. *10th International Conference on Language Resources and Evaluation*, Portorož, Slovenia, 310–316.

Central Statistics Office. 2016. *Census 2016 – Non-Irish Nationalities Living in Ireland*. https://bit.ly/2vNMCsv (Accessed 3 February 2020).

Depraetere, Ilse. 2010. What Counts as Useful Advice in a University Post-Editing Training Context? Report on a Case Study. *14th Annual Meeting of the European Association for Machine Translation*, Saint-Raphaël, France.

Federici, Federico, Brian Gerber, Sharon O'Brien, and Patrick Cadwell. 2019. *The International Humanitarian Sector and Language Translation in Crisis Situations. Assessment of Current Practices and Future Needs*. INTERACT The International Network on Crisis Translation, London, Dublin, Phoenix.

Gao, Ge, Bin Xu, Dan Cosley, and Susan Fussell. 2014. How Beliefs about the Presence of Machine Translation Impact Multilingual Collaborations. *17th ACM Conference on Computer Supported Cooperative Work & Social Computing*, Baltimore, USA, 1549–1560.

Gaspari, Federico. 2007. *The Role of Online MT in Webpage Translation*. PhD thesis, The University of Manchester.

Guerberof, Ana. 2013. What do Professional Translators Think about Post-Editing? *The Journal of Specialised Translation*, 19:75–95.

Herbst, Kenneth, Sean Hannah, and David Allan. 2013. Advertisement Disclaimer Speed and Corporate Social Responsibility: "Costs" to Consumer Comprehension and Effects on Brand Trust and Purchase Intention. *Journal of Business Ethics*, 117: 297–311.

Jeffers, James. 2011. The Cork City Flood of November 2009: Lessons for Flood Risk Management and Climate Change Adaptation at the Urban Scale. *Irish Geography*, 44(1):61–80.

Koponen, Maarit. 2015. How to Teach Machine Translation Post-Editing? Experiences from a Post-Editing Course. *4th Workshop on Post-Editing*

Technology and Practice, Miami, United States, 2–15.

Lewis, William. 2010. Haitian Creole: How to Build and Ship an MT Engine from Scratch in 4 days, 17 hours, & 30 minutes. *14th Annual Meeting of the European Association for Machine Translation*, Saint-Raphaël, France.

Liu, Rui, Runtong Zhang, and Xinyi Lu. 2018. An Empirical Study on the Relationship between the Satisfaction of Internet Health Information and Patient Compliance Based on Trust Perspective. *8th International Conference on Information Communication and Management*, Edinburgh, United Kingdom.

Major Emergency Management. 2016. *A Framework for Major Emergency Management.* https://bit.ly/2Vxqb3G (Accessed 3 February 2020).

Mayer, Roger, James Davis, and David Schoorman. 1995. An Integrative Model of Organizational Trust. *Academy of Management Review*, 20(3): 709–734.

Moorkens, Joss, and Sharon O'Brien. 2013. User Attitudes to Post-Editing Interface. *MT Summit XIV Workshop on Post-editing Technology and Practice*, Nice, France, 19–25.

Nurminen, Mary, and Niko Papula. 2018. Gist MT Users: A Snapshot of the Use and Users of One Online MT Tool. *21st Annual Conference of the European Association for Machine Translation*, Alacant, Spain, 199–208.

O'Brien, Sharon, and Federico Federici. 2019. Crisis Translation: Considering Language Needs in Multilingual Disaster Settings. *Disaster Prevention and Management,* 29(1). doi:10.1108/DPM-11-2018-0373.

O'Brien, Sharon, Federico Federici, Patrick Cadwell, Jay Marlowe, and Brian Gerber. 2018. Language Translation during Disaster: A Comparative Analysis of Five National Approaches. *International Journal of Disaster Risk Reduction*, 31:627–636.

O'Brien, Sharon, and Patrick Cadwell. 2017. Translation Facilitates Comprehension of Health-Related Crisis Information: Kenya as an Example. *Journal of Specialised Translation*, 28:23–51.

Porro Rodríguez, Victoria, Lucia Morado Vázquez, and Pierrette Bouillon. Study on the Use of Machine Translation and Post-Editing in Swiss-Based Language Service Providers. *Parallèles*, 29(2):19–35.

Santos-Hernández, Jenniffer, and Betty Hearn Morrow. 2013. Language and Literacy. Deborah S. K. Thomas, Brenda D. Phillips, William E. Lovekamp, and Alice Fothergill (eds). *Social Vulnerability to Disasters*, 2nd ed. CRC Press, Florida, 265–280.

Screen, Benjamin. 2019. What Effect does Post-Editing Have on the Translation Product from an End-User's Perspective? *The Journal of Specialised Translation,* 31:133–157.

Sherly, Mazhuvanchery, Subhankar Karmakarm, Devanathan Parthasarathy, Terence Chan, and Christian Rau. 2015. Disaster Vulnerability Mapping for a Densely Populated Coastal Urban Area: An Application to Mumbai, India. *Annals of the American Association of Geographers*, 105(6). doi:10.1080/00045608.2015.1072792.

Soricut, Radu, and Abdessamad Echihabi. 2010. TrustRank: Inducing Trust in Automatic Translations via Ranking. *48th Annual Meeting of the Association for Computational Linguistics*, Uppsala, Sweden, 612–621.

Specia, Lucia, and Kashif Shah. 2018. Machine Translation Quality Estimation: Applications and Future Perspectives. *Translation Quality Assessment: From Principles to Practice.* Springer, Cham, Switzerland.

TAUS 2010. *MT Post-Editing Guidelines.* https://bit.ly/2S15RH6 (Accessed 23 April 2020).

Teixeira, Carlos. 2014. Perceived vs. Measured Performance in the Post-Editing of Suggestions from Machine Translation and Translation Memories. *Third Workshop on Post-Editing Technology and Practice*, Vancouver, Canada, 45–59.

Toral, Antonio, Sheila Castilho, Ke Hu, and Andy Way. 2018. Attaining the Unattainable? Reassessing Claims of Human Parity in Neural Machine Translation. *Third Conference on Machine Translation*, Brussels, Belgium, 113–123.

Tourism Ireland 2018. *Visitor Facts and Figures.* https://bit.ly/36X51Qf (Accessed 3 February 2020).

Translators without Borders 2016. *Translators without Borders Develops the World's First Crisis-Specific Machine Translation System for Kurdish Languages.* https://bit.ly/3bjSfiq (Accessed 3 February 2020).

Translators without Borders 2019. *Misunderstanding + Misinformation = Mistrust.* https://bit.ly/37PRtHH (Accessed 3 February 2020).

Van Egdom, Gys-Walt, and Mark Pluymaekers. 2019. Why Go the Extra Mile? How Different Degrees of Post-Editing Affect Perceptions of Texts, Senders and Products among End Users. *Journal of Specialised Translation*, 31:158–176.

Efficiently Reusing Old Models Across Languages via Transfer Learning

Tom Kocmi   **Ondřej Bojar**

Charles University, Faculty of Mathematics and Physics
Institute of Formal and Applied Linguistics
Malostranské náměstí 25, 118 00 Prague, Czech Republic
`{kocmi,bojar}@ufal.mff.cuni.cz`

Abstract

Recent progress in neural machine translation is directed towards larger neural networks trained on an increasing amount of hardware resources. As a result, NMT models are costly to train, both financially, due to the electricity and hardware cost, and environmentally, due to the carbon footprint. It is especially true in transfer learning for its additional cost of training the "parent" model before transferring knowledge and training the desired "child" model. In this paper, we propose a simple method of reusing an already trained model for different language pairs where there is no need for modifications in model architecture. Our approach does not need a separate parent model for each investigated language pair, as it is typical in NMT transfer learning. To show the applicability of our method, we recycle a Transformer model trained by different researchers and use it to seed models for different language pairs. We achieve better translation quality and shorter convergence times than when training from random initialization.

1   Introduction

Neural machine translation (NMT), the current prevalent approach to automatic translation, is known to require large amounts of parallel training sentences and an extensive amount of training time on dedicated hardware. The total training time significantly increases, especially when training strong baselines, searching for best hyperparameters or training multiple models for various language pairs.

Schwartz et al. (2019) analyzed 60 papers from top AI conferences and found out that 80% of them target accuracy over efficiency, and only a small portion of papers argue for a new efficiency result. They also noted that the increasing financial cost of the computations could make it difficult for researchers to engage in deep learning research or limit training strong baselines. Furthermore, increased computational requirements have also an environmental cost. Strubell et al. (2019) estimated that training a single Transformer "big" model produces 87 kg of CO_2 and that the massive Transformer architecture parameter search produced 298 tonnes of CO_2.[1]

However, a lot of research has been already invested into cutting down the long training time by the design of NMT model architectures, promoting self-attentive (Vaswani et al., 2017) or convolutional (Gehring et al., 2017) over recurrent ones (Bahdanau et al., 2014) or the implementation of heavily optimized toolkits (Junczys-Dowmunt et al., 2018).

In this paper, we propose a novel view on reusing already trained "parent" models without the need to prepare a parent model in advance or modify its training hyper-parameters. Furthermore, we propose a second method based on a vocabulary transformation technique that makes even larger improvements, especially for languages using an alphabet different from the re-used parent model. Our transfer learning approach leads to better performance as well as faster convergence speed of the "child" model compared to training the model from scratch. We document that our methods are

---

[1]The paper reports numbers based on the U.S. energy mix.

Martins, Moniz, Fumega, Martins, Batista, Coheur, Parra, Trancoso, Turchi, Bisazza, Moorkens, Guerberof, Nurminen, Marg, Forcada (eds.)
Proceedings of the 22nd Annual Conference of the European Association for Machine Translation, p. 19–28
Lisboa, Portugal, November 2020.

not restricted only to low-resource languages, but they can be used even for high-resource ones.

Previous transfer learning techniques (Neubig and Hu, 2018; Kocmi and Bojar, 2018) rely on a shared vocabulary between the parent and child models. As a result, these techniques separately train parent model for each different child language pair. In contrast, our approach can re-use one parent model for multiple various language pairs, thus further lowering the total training time needed.

In order to document that our approach is not restricted to parent models trained by us, we re-use parent model trained by different researchers: we use the winning model of WMT 2019 for Czech-English language pair (Popel et al., 2019).

The paper is organized as follows: Section 2 describes the method of Direct Transfer learning, including our improvement of vocabulary transformation. Section 3 presents the model, training data, and our experimental setup. Section 4 describes the results of our methods followed by the analysis in Section 5. Related work is summarized in Section 6 and we conclude the discussion in Section 7.

2 Transfer Learning

In this work, we present the use of transfer learning to reduce the training time and improve the performance in comparison to training from random initialization even for high-resource language pairs.

Transfer learning is an approach of using training data from a related task to improve the accuracy of the main task in question (Tan et al., 2018). One of the first transfer learning techniques in NMT was proposed by Zoph et al. (2016). They used word-level NMT and froze several model parts, especially embeddings of words that are shared between parent and child model.

We build upon the work of Kocmi and Bojar (2018), who simplified the transfer learning technique thanks to the use of subword units (Wu et al., 2016) in contrast to word-level NMT transfer learning (Zoph et al., 2016) and extended the applicability to unrelated languages.

Their only requirement, and also the main disadvantage of the method, is that the vocabulary has to be shared and constructed for the given parent and child languages jointly, which makes the parent model usable only for the particular child language pair. This substantially increases the overall training time needed to obtain the desired NMT system for the child language pair.

The method of Kocmi and Bojar (2018) consists of three steps: (1) construct the vocabulary from both the parent and child corpora, (2) train the parent model with the shared vocabulary until convergence, and (3) continue training on the child training data.

Neubig and Hu (2018) call such approaches warm-start, where we use the child language pair to influence the parent model. In our work, we focus on the so-called cold-start scenario, where the parent model is trained without a need to know the language pair in advance. Therefore we cannot make any modifications of the parent training to better handle the child language pair. The cold-start transfer learning is expected to have slightly worse performance than the warm-start approach. However, it allows reusing one parent model for multiple child language pairs, which reduces the total training time in comparison to the use of warm-start transfer learning.

We present two approaches: Direct Transfer that ignores child-specific vocabulary altogether; and Transformed Vocabulary, which modifies vocabulary of the already trained parent. Thus, one parent model can be used for multiple child language pairs.

2.1 Direct Transfer

Direct Transfer can be seen as a simplification of Kocmi and Bojar (2018). We ignore the specifics of the child vocabulary and train the child model using the parent vocabulary. We suppose that the subword vocabulary can handle the child language pair, although it is not optimized for it.

We take an already trained model and use it as initialization for a child model using a different language pair. We continue the training process without any change to the vocabulary or hyper-parameters. This applies even to the training parameters, such as the learning rate or moments.

This method of continued training on different data while preserving hyper-parameters is used under the name "continued training" or "fine-tuning" (Hinton and Salakhutdinov, 2006; Miceli Barone et al., 2017), but it is mostly used as a domain adaptation within a given language pair.

Direct Transfer relies on the fact that the current NMT uses subword units instead of words. The subwords are designed to handle unseen words or even characters, breaking the input into shorter units, possibly down to individual bytes as implemented, for example, by Tensor2Tensor (Vaswani et al., 2018).

Avg. # per:	Child-specific		EN-CS vocab.	
	Sent.	Word	Sent.	Word
Odia	95.8	3.7	496.8	19.1
Estonian	26.0	1.1	56.2	2.3
Finnish	22.9	1.1	55.9	2.6
German	27.4	1.3	55.4	2.5
Russian	33.3	1.3	134.9	5.3
French	42.0	1.6	65.7	2.5

Table 1: Average number of tokens per sentence (column "Sent.") and average number of tokens per word (column "Word") when the training corpus is segmented by child-specific or parent-specific vocabulary. "Child-specific" represents the effect of using vocabulary customized for examined language. "EN-CS" corresponds to the use of English-Czech vocabulary.

	Segmented sentence
Original	Сьерра-Леоне
EN-RU	Сьерра_ ▮- ▮Леоне_
EN-CS	С▮ь▮ер▮ра▮_ ▮- ▮_▮\▮10▮51▮;▮ле▮о▮не_

Figure 1: Illustration of segmentation of Russian phrase (gloss: Sierra Leone) with English-Czech and English-Russian vocabulary from our experiments. The character ▮ represents splits.

This property ensures that the parent vocabulary can, in principle, serve for any child language pair, but it can be highly suboptimal, segmenting child words into too many subwords.

We present an example of a Russian phrase and its segmentation based on English-Czech or English-Russian vocabulary in Figure 1. When using child-specific vocabulary, the segmentation works as expected, splitting the phrase into three tokens. However, when we use a vocabulary that contains only the Cyrillic alphabet[2] and not many longer sequences of characters, the sentence is split into 13 tokens. We can notice that English-Czech wordpiece vocabulary is missing a character "Л", thus it breaks it into the byte representation "\1051;".

We examine the influence of parent-specific vocabulary on the training dataset of the child. Table 1 documents the segmenting effect of different vocabularies. If we compare the child-specific and parent-specific ("EN-CS") vocabulary, the average number of tokens per sentence or per word increases more than twice. For example, German has twice as many tokens per word compared to its child-specific vocabulary, and Russian has four times more tokens

[2]This happened solely due to noise in the Czech-English parent training data.

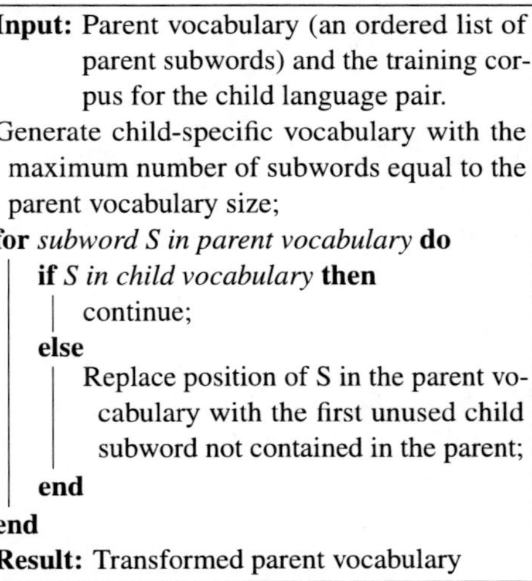

Input: Parent vocabulary (an ordered list of parent subwords) and the training corpus for the child language pair.
Generate child-specific vocabulary with the maximum number of subwords equal to the parent vocabulary size;
for *subword S in parent vocabulary* **do**
    if *S in child vocabulary* **then**
        continue;
    else
        Replace position of S in the parent vocabulary with the first unused child subword not contained in the parent;
    end
end
Result: Transformed parent vocabulary

Algorithm 1: Transforming parent vocabulary to contain child subwords and match positions for subwords common for both of language pairs.

due to Cyrillic. Odia is affected even more.

Thus, we see that ignoring the vocabulary mismatch introduces a problem for NMT models in the form of an increasing split ratio of tokens. As expected, this is most noticeable for languages using different scripts.

2.2 Vocabulary Transformation

Using parent vocabulary roughly doubles the number of subword tokens per word, as we showed in the previous section. This problem would not happen with child-specific vocabulary. However, we are using an already trained parent with its vocabulary. Therefore, we propose a vocabulary transformation method that replaces subwords in the parent wordpiece (Wu et al., 2016) vocabulary with subwords from the child-specific vocabulary.

NMT models associate each vocabulary item with its vector representation (embedding). When transferring the model from the parent to the child, we decide which subwords should preserve their embedding as trained in the parent model and which embeddings should be remapped to new subwords from the child vocabulary. The goal is to preserve embeddings of subwords that are contained in both parent and child vocabulary. In other words, we reuse embeddings of subwords common to both parent and child vocabularies and reuse the vocabulary entries of subwords not occurring in the child data for other, unrelated, subwords that the child data need. Obviously, the embeddings for these subwords will need to be retrained.

Our Transformed Vocabulary method starts by constructing the child-specific vocabulary with the size equal to the parent vocabulary size (the parent model is trained, thus it has a fixed number of embeddings). Then, as presented in Algorithm 1, we generate an ordered list of child subwords, where subwords known to the parent vocabulary are on the same positions as in the parent vocabulary, and other subwords are assigned arbitrarily to places where parent-only subwords were stored.

We experimented with several possible mappings between the parent and child vocabulary. We tried to assign subwords based on frequency, by random assignment, or based on Levenshtein distance of parent and child subwords. However, all the approaches reached comparable performance; neither of them significantly outperformed the others. One exception is when assigning all subwords randomly, even those that are shared between parent and child. This method leads to worse performance, having several BLEU points lower than other approaches. Another approach would be to use pretrained subword embeddings similarly as proposed Kim et al. (2019). However, in this paper, we focus on showing, that transfer learning can be as simple as not using any modifications at all.

3 Experiments

In this section, we first provide the details of the NMT model used in our experiments and the examined set of language pairs. We then discuss the convergence and a stopping criterion and finally present the results of our method for recycling the NMT model as well as improvements thanks to the vocabulary transformation.

3.1 Parent Model and its Training Data

In order to document that our method functions in general and is not restricted to our laboratory setting, we do not train the parent model ourselves. Instead, we recycle two systems trained by Popel et al. (2019), namely the English-to-Czech and Czech-to-English winning models of WMT 2019 News Translation Task. It is important to note, that we use two parent models and for experiments we always use the parent model with English on the same side, e.g. English-to-Russian child has English-to-Czech as a parent. We leave experimenting with different parents or various combinations for future works, because the goal of this work is to make approach most simple.

We decided to use this model for several reasons. It is trained to translate into Czech, a high-resource language that is dissimilar from any of the languages used in this work.[3] At the same time, it is trained using the state-of-the-art Transformer architecture as implemented in the Tensor2Tensor framework.[4] (Vaswani et al., 2018). We use Tensor2Tensor in version 1.8.0.

The model is described in Popel (2018). It is based on the "Big GPU Transformer" setup as defined by Vaswani et al. (2017) with a few modifications. The model uses reverse square root learning rate decay with 8000 warm-up steps and a learning rate of 1. It uses the Adafactor optimizer, the batch size of 2900 subword units, disabled layer dropout.

Due to the memory constraints, we drop training sentences longer than 100 subwords. We use child hyper-parameter setting equal to the parent model. However, some hyper-parameters like learning rate, dropouts, optimizer, and others could be modified for the training of the child model. We leave these experiments for future work.

We train models on single GPU GeForce 1080Ti with 11GB memory. In this setup, 10000 training steps take on average approximately one and a half hours. Popel et al. (2019) trained the model on 8 GPUs for 928k steps, which means that on the single GPU, the parent model would need at least 7424k steps, i.e. more than 45 days of training.

In our experiments, we train all child models up to 1M steps and then take the model with the best performance on the development set. Because some of the language pairs, especially the low-resource ones, converge within first 100k steps, we use a weak early stopping criterion that stops the training whenever there was no improvement larger than 0.5% of maximal reached BLEU over the past 50% of training evaluations (minimum of training steps is 100k). This stopping criterion makes sure that no model is stopped prematurely.

---

[3] The linguistically most similar language of our language selection is Russian, but we do not transliterate Cyrillic into Latin script. Therefore, the system cannot associate similar Russian and Czech words based on appearance.
[4] `https://github.com/tensorflow/tensor2tensor`

Language pair	Pairs	Training set	Development set	Test set
EN - Odia	27k	Parida et al. (2018)	Parida et al. (2018)	Parida et al. (2018)
EN - Estonian	0.8M	Europarl, Rapid	WMT dev 2018	WMT 2018
EN - Finnish	2.8M	Europarl, Paracrawl, Rapid	WMT 2015	WMT 2018
EN - German	3.5M	Europarl, News commentary, Rapid	WMT 2017	WMT 2018
EN - Russian	12.6M	News Commentary, Yandex, and UN Corpus	WMT 2012	WMT 2018
EN - French	34.3M	Commoncrawl, Europarl, Giga FREN, News commentary, UN corpus	WMT 2013	WMT dis. 2015

Table 2: Corpora used for each language pair. The names specify the corpora from WMT 2018 News Translation Task data. Column "Pairs" specify the total number of sentence pairs in training data.

Language pair	Baseline		Direct Transfer		Transformed Vocab			
	BLEU	Steps	BLEU	Steps	BLEU	Steps	Δ BLEU	Speed-up
English-to-Odia	3.54	45k	0.26	47k	**6.38** ‡*	**38k**	2.84	16 %
English-to-Estonian	16.03	95k	**20.75** ‡	**75k**	20.27 ‡	**75k**	4.24	21 %
English-to-Finnish	14.42	420k	16.12 ‡	**255k**	**16.73** ‡*	270k	2.31	36 %
English-to-German	36.72	270k	38.58 ‡	190k	**39.28** ‡*	**110k**	2.56	59 %
English-to-Russian	27.81	1090k	27.04	630k	**28.65** ‡*	**450k**	0.84	59 %
English-to-French	33.72	820k	34.41 ‡	**660k**	**34.46** ‡	720k	0.74	12 %
Estonian-to-English	21.07	70k	24.36 ‡	**30k**	**24.64** ‡*	60k	3.57	14 %
Russian-to-English	30.31	980k	23.41	**420k**	**31.38** ‡*	700k	1.07	29 %

Table 3: Translation quality and training time. "Baseline" is trained from scratch with its own vocabulary and child corpus only. "Direct Transfer" is initialized with parent model using the parent vocabulary and continues training. "Transformed Vocab" has the same initialization but merges the parent and child vocabulary as described in Section 2.2. Best score and lowest training time in each row in bold. The statistical significance is computed against the baseline (‡) or against "Direct Transfer" (*). Last two columns show improvements of Transformed Vocabulary in comparison to the baseline.

3.2 Studied Language Pairs

We use several child language pairs to show that our approach is useful for various sizes of corpora, language pairs, and scripts. To cover this range of situations, we select languages in Table 2. Future works could focus also on languages outside from Indo-European family, such as Chinese.

Another decision behind selecting these language pairs is to include language pairs reaching various levels of translation quality. This is indicated by automatic scores of the baseline setups ranging from 3.54 BLEU (English-to-Odia) to 36 BLEU (English-to-German)[5], see Table 3.

The sizes of corpora are in Table 2. The smallest language pair is English-Odia, which uses the Brahmic writing script and contains only 27 thousand training pairs. The largest is the high-resource English-French language pair.

For most of the language pairs, we use training data from WMT (Bojar et al., 2018).[6] We use the training data without any preprocessing, not even

tokenization.[7] See Table 2 for the list of used corpora for each language pair. For some languages, we have opted out from using all available corpora in order to experiment on languages containing various magnitudes of parallel sentences.

For high-resource English-French language pair, we perform a corpora cleaning using language detection Langid.py (Lui and Baldwin, 2012). We drop all sentences that are not recognized as the correct language. It removes 6.5M (15.9 %) sentence pairs from the English-French training corpora.

4 Results

All reported results are calculated on the test data and evaluated with SacreBLEU (Post, 2018). The results are in Table 3. We discuss separately the training time, automatically assessed translation quality using the parent and the Transformed Vocabulary, and comparison to Kocmi and Bojar (2018) in the following sections.

Baselines use the same architecture, and they are trained solely on the child training data with the use of child-specific vocabulary. We compute

---

[5]The systems submitted to WMT 2018 for English-to-German translation have better performance than our baseline due to the fact, that we decided not to use Commoncrawl, which artificially made English-German parallel data less resourceful.

[6]http://www.statmt.org/wmt18/

[7]While the recommended best practice in past WMT evaluations was to use Moses tokenizer. It is not recommended for Tensor2Tensor with its build-in tokenizer any more.

statistical significance with a paired bootstrap resampling (Koehn, 2004). We use 1000 samples and a confidence level of 0.05. Statistically significant improvements are marked by ‡.

4.1 Direct Transfer Learning

First, we compare the Direct Transfer learning in contrast to the baseline. We see that Direct Transfer learning is significantly better than the baseline in both translation directions in all cases except for Odia and Russian, which we will discuss later. We get improvements for various language types, as discussed in Section 3.2. The largest improvement is of 4.72 BLEU for the low-resource language pair of Estonian-English, but we also get an improvement of 0.69 BLEU for the high-resource pair French-English.

The results are even more surprising when we take into account the fact that the model uses the parent vocabulary, and it is thus segmenting words into considerably more subwords. This suggests that the Transformer architecture generalizes very well to short subwords. However, the worse performance of English-Odia and English-Russian can be attributed to the different writing script. The Odia script is not contained in the parent vocabulary at all, leading to segmenting of each word into individual bytes, the only common units with the parent vocabulary. Therefore, to avoid problems with filtering, we increase the filtering limit of long sentences during training from 100 to 500 subwords for these two language pairs (see Section 3.1).

4.2 Results with Transformed Vocabulary

As the results in Table 3 confirm, Transformed Vocabulary successfully tackles the problem of the child language using a different writing script. We see "Transformed Vocab" delivering the best performance for all language pairs except for English-to-Estonian, significantly improving over baseline and even over "Direct Transfer" in most cases.

4.3 Training Time

In the introduction, we discussed that recent development in NMT focuses mainly on the performance over efficiency (Schwartz et al., 2019). Therefore, in this section, we discuss the amount of training time required for our method to converge. We are reporting the number of updates (i.e. steps) needed to get the model used for evaluation.[8]

---

[8]Another possibility would be to report wall-clock time. However, that is influenced by server load and other factors. The

	Language pair	Baseline	Transf. vocab	Warm Start
BLEU	To Estonian	16.03	20.27	**20.75**
BLEU	To Russian	27.81	28.65	**29.03** ‡
BLEU	From Estonian	21.07	24.64	**26.00** ‡
BLEU	From Russian	30.31	**31.38**	31.15
Steps	To Estonian	95k	**75k**	735k
Steps	To Russian	1090k	**450k**	1510k
Steps	From Estonian	70k	**60k**	700k
Steps	From Russian	980k	**700k**	1465k

Table 4: Comparison of our Transformed Vocabulary method with Kocmi and Bojar (2018) (abridged as "Warm Start"). The top half of table compares results in BLEU, the bottom half the number of steps needed to convergence. Steps of Kocmi and Bojar (2018) method are reported as the sum of parent and child training, due to the nature of the method.

We see in Table 3 that both our methods converged in a lower number of steps than the baseline. For the Transformed Vocabulary method, we get a speed-up of 12–59 %. The reduction in the number of steps is most visible in English-to-German and English-to-Russian. It is important to note that the number of steps to the convergence is not precisely comparable, and some tolerance must be taken into account. It is due to the fluctuation in the training process. However, in neither of our experiments, Transformed Vocabulary is slower than baseline. Thus we conclude that our Transformed Vocabulary method takes fewer training steps to finish training than training a model from scratch.

4.4 Comparison to Kocmi and Bojar (2018)

We replicated the experiments of Kocmi and Bojar (2018) with the identical framework and hyperparameter setting in order to compare their method to ours. We experiment with Estonian-English and Russian-English language pair in both translation directions. Their approach needs an individual parent for every child model, so we train four models: two English-to-Czech and two Czech-to-English on the same parent training data as Kocmi and Bojar (2018). All vocabularies contain 32k subwords. We compare their method with our Transformed Vocabulary. Furthermore, the results of Direct Transfer in Table 3 are also comparable with this experiment.

In Table 4, we see that their method reaches a slightly better performance in three translation models, where English-to-Russian and Estonian-to-English are significantly (‡) better than Transformed Vocabulary technique; the other two are on par with our method, which is understandable. The Transformed Vocabulary cannot outperform

---

number of steps is better for the comparison as long as the batch size stays the same across experiments.

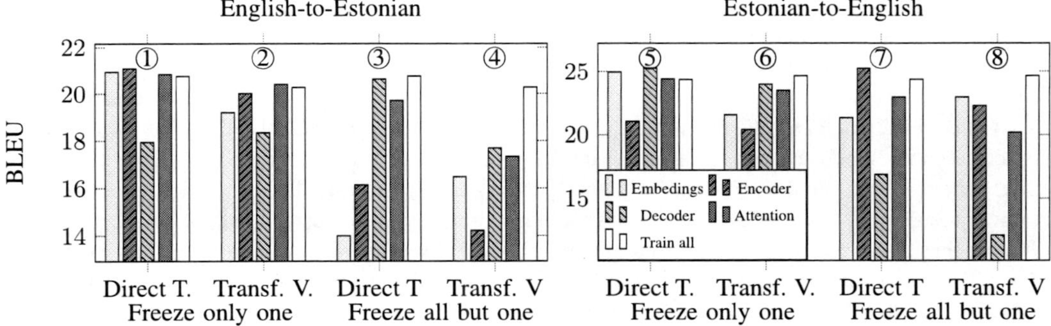

Figure 2: Child BLEU scores when trained with some parameters frozen. The left plot shows English-to-Estonian and the right is Estonian-to-English. In both plots, the first two groups are experiments where one component is frozen and the second two are when all components but one are frozen.

the warm-start technique since the warm-start parent model has the advantage of being trained with the vocabulary prepared for the investigated child.

However, when we compare the total number of steps needed to reach the performance, both our approaches are significantly faster than Kocmi and Bojar (2018). The most substantial improvements are roughly ten times faster for Estonian-to-English, and the smallest difference for English-to-Russian is two times faster. This is mostly because their method first needs to train the parent model that is specialized for the child, while our method can directly re-use any already trained model. Moreover, we can see that their method is even slower than the baseline model.

5 Analysis by Freezing Parameters

To discover which transferred parameters are the most helpful for the child model and which need to be changed the most, we follow the analysis used by Thompson et al. (2018): When training the child, we freeze some of the parameters.

Based on the internal layout of the Transformer model in Tensor2Tensor, we divide the model into four components. (i) Word embeddings (shared between encoder and decoder) map each subword unit to a dense vector representation. (ii) The encoder component includes all the six feed-forward layers converting the input sequence to the deeper representation. (iii) The decoder component consists again of six feed-forward layers preparing the choice of the next output subword unit. (iv) The multi-head attention is used throughout encoder and decoder, as self-attention layers interweaved with the feed-forward layers.

We run two sets of experiments: either freeze only one out of the four components and leave the rest of the model updating or freeze everything but the examined component. We also test it on two translation directions: English-to-Estonian in the left hand part of Figure 2 and Estonian-to-English in the right hand part. In both cases, English-Czech (in the corresponding direction, i.e. with English on the correct side) serves as the parent. We discuss individual components separately, indexing the experiments ① to ⑧.

Similarly to Thompson et al. (2018) in domain adaptation, we observe that parent embeddings serve well in Direct Transfer, freezing them has a minimal impact compared to the baseline in ① and ⑤. The frozen embeddings in Transformed Vocabulary (②, ⑥) results in significant performance drops which can be attributed to the arbitrary assignment of embeddings to new subwords.

The comparison of all but embeddings frozen in ④ and ⑧ (Transformed Vocabulary) is interesting. In ⑧, the performance of the network can be recovered close to the baseline by retraining either parent source embeddings or the encoder. These two components can compensate for each other. This differs from the case with English reused in the source (④) where updating embeddings to the child language is insufficient: the decoder must be updated to produce fluent output in the new target language and even with the decoder updated, the loss compared to the baseline is quite substantial.

The most important component for transfer learning is generally the component handling the new language: decoder in English-to-Estonian and encoder in the reverse. With this component fixed, the performance drops the most with this component fixed (①, ②, ⑤, ⑥) and among the least with this component free to update (③, ④, ⑦, ⑧). This confirms that at least for examined language pair, the Transformer model lends itself very well to encoder or decoder re-use.

Other results in Figure 2 reveal that the architecture can compensate for some of the training deficiencies. Freezing the encoder ①, ② (resp. decoder for Estonian-to-English ⑤, ⑥) or attention is not that critical as the frozen decoder (resp. encoder). The bad result of the encoder ③, ④ (resp. decoder ⑦, ⑧) being the only non-frozen component shows that model is not capable of providing all the needed capacity for the new language, unlike the self-attention where the loss is not that large. This behaviour correlates with our intuition that the model needs to update the most the component that handles the differing language with the parent model (in our case Czech).

All in all, these experiments illustrate the robustness of the Transformer model that it is able to train and reasonably well utilize pre-trained weights even if they are severely crippled.

6   Related Work

This paper focuses on re-using an existing NMT model in order to improve the performance in terms of training time and translation quality without any need to modify the model or pre-trained weights.

Lakew et al. (2018) presented two model modifications for multilingual MT and showed that transfer learning could be extended to transferring from the parent to the first child, followed by the second child and then the third one. They achieved improvements with dynamically updating embeddings for the vocabulary of a target language.

The use of other language pairs for improving results for the target language pair has been approached from various angles. One option is to build multilingual models (Liu et al., 2020), ideally so that they are capable of zero-shot, i.e. translating in a translation direction that was never part of the training data. Johnson et al. (2017) and Lu et al. (2018) achieve this with a unique language tag that specifies the desired target language. The training data includes sentence pairs from multiple language pairs, and the model implicitly learns translation among many languages. In some cases, it achieves zero-shot and can translate between languages never seen together. Gu et al. (2018) tackled the problem by creating universal embedding space across multiple languages and training many-to-one

MT system. Firat et al. (2016) propose multi-way multi-lingual systems. Their goal is to reduce the total number of parameters needed to train multiple source and target models. In all cases, the methods are dependent on a special training schedule.

The lack of parallel data in low-resource language pairs can also be tackled by unsupervised translation (Artetxe et al., 2018; Lample et al., 2018). The general idea is to train monolingual autoencoders for both source and target languages separately, followed by mapping both embeddings to the same space and training simultaneously two models, each translating in a different direction. In an iterative training, this pair of NMT systems is further refined, each system providing training data for the other one by back-translating monolingual data (Sennrich et al., 2016).

For very closely related language pairs, transliteration can be used to generate training data from a high-resourced pair to support the low-resourced one as described in Karakanta et al. (2018).

7   Conclusion

In this paper, we focus on a setting where existing models are re-used without any preparation for knowledge transfer of original model ahead of its training. This is a relevant and prevailing situation in academia due to computing restrictions, and industry, where updating existing models and scaling to more language pairs is essential. We evaluate and propose methods of re-using Transformer NMT models for any "child" language pair regardless of the original "parent" training languages and especially showing, that no modification is better than training from scratch.

The techniques are simple, effective, and applicable to models trained by others which makes it more likely that our experimental results will be replicated in practice. We showed that despite the random assignment of subwords, the Transformed Vocabulary improves the performance and shortens the training time of the child model compared to training from random initialization.

Furthermore, we showed that this approach is not restricted to low-resource languages, and we documented that the highest improvements are (expectably) due to the shared English knowledge. Moreover, we confirmed the robustness of the Transformer and its ability to achieve good results in adverse conditions like very fragmented subword units or parts of the network frozen.

The warm-start approach by Kocmi and Bojar (2018) performs slightly better than our Transformed Vocabulary, but it needs to be trained for a significantly longer time. This leaves room for approaches that also focus on the efficiency of the training process. We perceive our approach as a technique for increasing the performance of a model without an increase in training time. Thus, re-using older models in cold-start scenario of transfer learning can be used in standard NMT training pipelines without any performance or speed losses instead of random initialization as is the common practice currently.

Acknowledgements

This study was supported in parts by the grants 18-24210S of the Czech Science Foundation and 825303 (Bergamot) of the European Union. This work has been using language resources and tools stored and distributed by the LINDAT/CLARIN project of the Ministry of Education, Youth and Sports of the Czech Republic (LM2015071).

References

Artetxe, Mikel, Gorka Labaka, Eneko Agirre, and Kyunghyun Cho. 2018. Unsupervised neural machine translation. In *Proceedings of the Sixth International Conference on Learning Representations*.

Bahdanau, Dzmitry, Kyunghyun Cho, and Yoshua Bengio. 2014. Neural machine translation by jointly learning to align and translate. In *ICLR 2015*.

Bojar, Ondřej, Christian Federmann, Mark Fishel, Yvette Graham, Barry Haddow, Matthias Huck, Philipp Koehn, and Christof Monz. 2018. Findings of the 2018 conference on machine translation (wmt18). In *Proceedings of the Third Conference on Machine Translation, Volume 2: Shared Task Papers*, pages 272–307, Belgium, Brussels, October. Association for Computational Linguistics.

Firat, Orhan, Kyunghyun Cho, and Yoshua Bengio. 2016. Multi-Way, Multilingual Neural Machine Translation with a Shared Attention Mechanism. In *Proceedings of the 2016 Conference of the North American Chapter of the Association for Computational Linguistics: Human Language Technologies*, pages 866–875, San Diego, California, June. Association for Computational Linguistics.

Gehring, Jonas, Michael Auli, David Grangier, Denis Yarats, and Yann N Dauphin. 2017. Convolutional sequence to sequence learning. *arXiv preprint arXiv:1705.03122*.

Gu, Jiatao, Hany Hassan, Jacob Devlin, and Victor O.K. Li. 2018. Universal neural machine translation for extremely low resource languages. In *Proceedings of the 2018 Conference of the North American Chapter of the Association for Computational Linguistics: Human Language Technologies, Volume 1 (Long Papers)*, pages 344–354, New Orleans, Louisiana, June. Association for Computational Linguistics.

Hinton, Geoffrey E. and Ruslan R. Salakhutdinov. 2006. Reducing the dimensionality of data with neural networks. *science*, 313(5786):504–507.

Johnson, Melvin, Mike Schuster, Quoc Le, Maxim Krikun, Yonghui Wu, Zhifeng Chen, Nikhil Thorat, Fernand a Vigas, Martin Wattenberg, Greg Corrado, Macduff Hughes, and Jeffrey Dean. 2017. Google's multilingual neural machine translation system: Enabling zero-shot translation. *Transactions of the Association for Computational Linguistics*, 5:339–351.

Junczys-Dowmunt, Marcin, Roman Grundkiewicz, Tomasz Dwojak, Hieu Hoang, Kenneth Heafield, Tom Neckermann, Frank Seide, Ulrich Germann, Alham Fikri Aji, Nikolay Bogoychev, André F. T. Martins, and Alexandra Birch. 2018. Marian: Fast neural machine translation in C++. In *Proceedings of ACL 2018, System Demonstrations*, pages 116–121, Melbourne, Australia, July. Association for Computational Linguistics.

Karakanta, Alina, Jon Dehdari, and Josef van Genabith. 2018. Neural machine translation for low-resource languages without parallel corpora. *Machine Translation*, 32(1):167–189, Jun.

Kim, Yunsu, Yingbo Gao, and Hermann Ney. 2019. Effective cross-lingual transfer of neural machine translation models without shared vocabularies. In Korhonen, Anna, David R. Traum, and Lluís Màrquez, editors, *Proceedings of the 57th Conference of the Association for Computational Linguistics, ACL 2019, Florence, Italy, July 28- August 2, 2019, Volume 1: Long Papers*, pages 1246–1257. Association for Computational Linguistics.

Kocmi, Tom and Ondřej Bojar. 2018. Trivial Transfer Learning for Low-Resource Neural Machine Translation. In *Proceedings of the 3rd Conference on Machine Translation (WMT)*, Brussels, Belgium, November.

Koehn, Philipp. 2004. Statistical significance tests for machine translation evaluation. In *Proceedings of EMNLP*, volume 4, pages 388–395.

Lakew, Surafel M, Aliia Erofeeva, Matteo Negri, Marcello Federico, and Marco Turchi. 2018. Transfer learning in multilingual neural machine translation with dynamic vocabulary. *IWSLT*.

Lample, Guillaume, Myle Ott, Alexis Conneau, Ludovic Denoyer, and Marc'Aurelio Ranzato. 2018. Phrase-based & neural unsupervised machine translation. In *Proceedings of the 2018 Conference on Empirical Methods in Natural Language Processing*.

Liu, Yinhan, Jiatao Gu, Naman Goyal, Xian Li, Sergey Edunov, Marjan Ghazvininejad, Mike Lewis, and Luke Zettlemoyer. 2020. Multilingual denoising pre-training for neural machine translation. *arXiv preprint arXiv:2001.08210.*

Lu, Yichao, Phillip Keung, Faisal Ladhak, Vikas Bhardwaj, Shaonan Zhang, and Jason Sun. 2018. A neural interlingua for multilingual machine translation. In *Proceedings of the Third Conference on Machine Translation: Research Papers*, pages 84–92, Belgium, Brussels, October. Association for Computational Linguistics.

Lui, Marco and Timothy Baldwin. 2012. langid.py: An off-the-shelf language identification tool. In *Proceedings of the ACL 2012 System Demonstrations*, pages 25–30, Jeju Island, Korea, July. Association for Computational Linguistics.

Miceli Barone, Antonio Valerio, Barry Haddow, Ulrich Germann, and Rico Sennrich. 2017. Regularization techniques for fine-tuning in neural machine translation. In *Proceedings of the 2017 Conference on Empirical Methods in Natural Language Processing*, pages 1489–1494, Copenhagen, Denmark, September. Association for Computational Linguistics.

Neubig, Graham and Junjie Hu. 2018. Rapid adaptation of neural machine translation to new languages. In *Proceedings of the 2018 Conference on Empirical Methods in Natural Language Processing*, pages 875–880, Brussels, Belgium, October. Association for Computational Linguistics.

Parida, Shantipriya, Ondrej Bojar, and Satya Ranjan Dash. 2018. Odiencorp: Odia-english and odia-only corpus for machine translation. In *Smart Computing and Informatics*. Springer.

Popel, Martin, Dominik Machaček, Michal Auersperger, Ondřej Bojar, and Pavel Pecina. 2019. English-czech systems in wmt19: Document-level transformer. In *Proceedings of the Fourth Conference on Machine Translation (Volume 2: Shared Task Papers, Day 1)*, pages 342–348, Florence, Italy, August. Association for Computational Linguistics.

Popel, Martin. 2018. CUNI Transformer Neural MT System for WMT18. In *Proceedings of the Third Conference on Machine Translation*, pages 486–491, Belgium, Brussels, October. Association for Computational Linguistics.

Post, Matt. 2018. A call for clarity in reporting bleu scores. In *Proceedings of the Third Conference on Machine Translation, Volume 1: Research Papers*, pages 186–191, Belgium, Brussels, October. Association for Computational Linguistics.

Schwartz, Roy, Jesse Dodge, Noah A Smith, and Oren Etzioni. 2019. Green ai. *arXiv preprint arXiv:1907.10597.*

Sennrich, Rico, Barry Haddow, and Alexandra Birch. 2016. Improving Neural Machine Translation Models with Monolingual Data. In *Proceedings of the 54th Annual Meeting of the Association for Computational Linguistics (Volume 1: Long Papers)*, pages 86–96, Berlin, Germany, August. Association for Computational Linguistics.

Strubell, Emma, Ananya Ganesh, and Andrew McCallum. 2019. Energy and policy considerations for deep learning in NLP. In *Proceedings of the 57th Annual Meeting of the Association for Computational Linguistics*, pages 3645–3650, Florence, Italy, July. Association for Computational Linguistics.

Tan, Chuanqi, Fuchun Sun, Tao Kong, Wenchang Zhang, Chao Yang, and Chunfang Liu. 2018. A survey on deep transfer learning. In *International Conference on Artificial Neural Networks*, pages 270–279. Springer.

Thompson, Brian, Huda Khayrallah, Antonios Anastasopoulos, Arya D. McCarthy, Kevin Duh, Rebecca Marvin, Paul McNamee, Jeremy Gwinnup, Tim Anderson, and Philipp Koehn. 2018. Freezing subnetworks to analyze domain adaptation in neural machine translation. In *Proceedings of the Third Conference on Machine Translation: Research Papers*, pages 124–132, Belgium, Brussels, October. Association for Computational Linguistics.

Vaswani, Ashish, Noam Shazeer, Niki Parmar, Jakob Uszkoreit, Llion Jones, Aidan N Gomez, Łukasz Kaiser, and Illia Polosukhin. 2017. Attention is all you need. In Guyon, I., U. V. Luxburg, S. Bengio, H. Wallach, R. Fergus, S. Vishwanathan, and R. Garnett, editors, *Advances in Neural Information Processing Systems 30*, pages 6000–6010. Curran Associates, Inc.

Vaswani, Ashish, Samy Bengio, Eugene Brevdo, Francois Chollet, Aidan Gomez, Stephan Gouws, Llion Jones, Lukasz Kaiser, Nal Kalchbrenner, Niki Parmar, Ryan Sepassi, Noam Shazeer, and Jakob Uszkoreit. 2018. Tensor2Tensor for Neural Machine Translation. In *Proceedings of the 13th Conference of the Association for Machine Translation in the Americas (Volume 1: Research Papers)*, pages 193–199, Boston, MA, March. Association for Machine Translation in the Americas.

Wu, Yonghui, Mike Schuster, Zhifeng Chen, Quoc V Le, Mohammad Norouzi, Wolfgang Macherey, Maxim Krikun, Yuan Cao, Qin Gao, Klaus Macherey, et al. 2016. Google's neural machine translation system: Bridging the gap between human and machine translation. *arXiv preprint arXiv:1609.08144.*

Zoph, Barret, Deniz Yuret, Jonathan May, and Kevin Knight. 2016. Transfer learning for low-resource neural machine translation. In *Proceedings of the 2016 Conference on Empirical Methods in Natural Language Processing*, pages 1568–1575, Austin, Texas, November. Association for Computational Linguistics.

Efficient Transfer Learning for Quality Estimation with Bottleneck Adapter Layer

Hao Yang, Minghan Wang, Ning Xie, Ying Qin, Yao Deng
Huawei Translation Service Center, Beijing, China
{yanghao30,wangminghan,nicolas.xie,qinying,dengyao3}@huawei.com

Abstract

The Predictor-Estimator framework for quality estimation (QE) is commonly used for its strong performance, where the predictor and estimator works on feature extraction and quality evaluation, respectively. However, training the predictor from scratch is computationally expensive. In this paper, we propose an efficient transfer learning framework to transfer knowledge from NMT dataset into QE models. A Predictor-Estimator alike model named BAL-QE is also proposed, aiming to extract high quality features with pretrained NMT model, and make classification with a fine-tuned Bottleneck Adapter Layer (BAL). The experiment shows that BAL-QE achieves 97% of the SOTA performance in WMT19 En-De and En-Ru QE tasks by only training 3% of parameters within 4 hours on 4 Titan XP GPUs. Compared with the commonly used NuQE baseline, BAL-QE achieves 47% (En-Ru) and 75% (En-De) of performance promotions.

1 Introduction & Related work

Translation quality estimation (QE) has become one of the important research topics in the discipline of machine translation (MT). QE aims to solve the problem of how to evaluate the quality of the translation results and predict the types of errors and locations (Specia et al., 2013), with only source sentences and machine translation re-

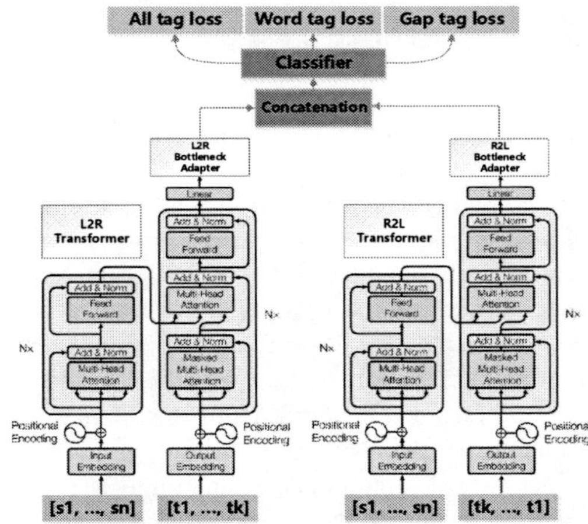

Figure 1: The architecture of BAL-QE, where two Transformers are used to produce features in both direction, then, being processed by dual Bottleneck Adapters and fed into classifiers.

sults, without the post edited reference. (Junczys-Dowmunt, 2019; Yang et al., 2019b; Yang et al., 2019a). QE tasks can be divided into word level, phrase level and sentence level. In this paper, we only focus on word-level QE tasks.

There are two main categories of neural network machine translation quality estimation systems, end-to-end neural network framework and two-stage neural network architecture. A representative architecture of the first one is named Neural QE (NuQE) (Kreutzer et al., 2015; Martins et al., 2016), which directly predicts sequence labels by passing source and MT results into a unified model composed with several bi-LSTM layers. The other one is Predictor-Estimator architecture (Kim and Lee, 2016; Kim et al., 2017; Wang et al., 2018; Li et al., 2018), which is composed of two subsequent neural models: 1) a word prediction model that

Martins, Moniz, Fumega, Martins, Batista, Coheur, Parra, Trancoso, Turchi, Bisazza, Moorkens, Guerberof, Nurminen, Marg, Forcada (eds.)
Proceedings of the 22nd Annual Conference of the European Association for Machine Translation, p. 29–34
Lisboa, Portugal, November 2020.

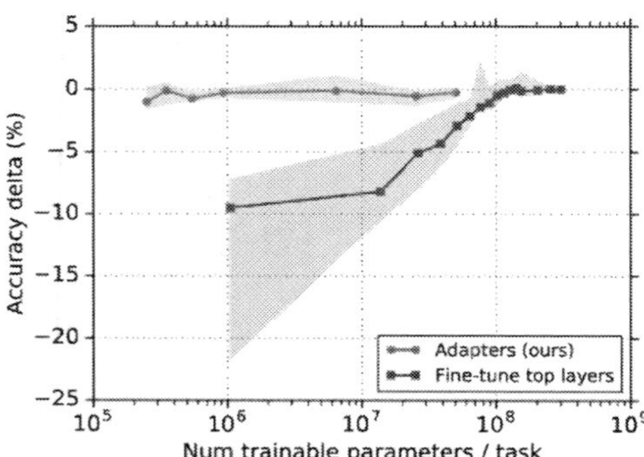

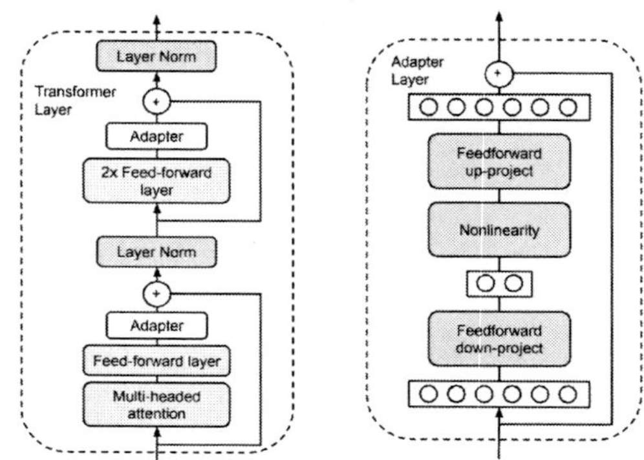

Figure 2: (Houlsby et al., 2019) The performance gain of the transfer learning on 18 GLUE corpus, which is based on adapters, which achieves 99.6% of SOTA performance by only adding 3% of training parameters

Figure 3: (Houlsby et al., 2019) Bottleneck Adapter Layer for Transformer fine-tuning. Only three green parts in the right, including Feedforward down-project, Nonlinearity and Feedforward up-project, are need to be trained, the parameters of the left transformer are fixed, total training parameters ratio is 3%.

predicts each word given the left and right context of the source and target corpus, and 2) a quality estimation model, which estimates word-level labels based on the features generated by the predictor. Because the predictor itself can be regarded as a neural machine translation (NMT) system, which can be trained based on a large volume of external parallel corpora and provides high quality semantic features, Predictor-Estimator framework is much better than NuQE.

Transfer learning (TL) or fine-tuning large pre-trained language models (PLMs) is an effective method in NLP, which can produce strong performance on many NLP tasks (Dai and Le, 2015; Howard and Ruder, 2018; Radford et al., 2018). There are two types of transfer learning. The first one is full-parameter fine-tuning with in-domain data, which aims to fit the distribution of in-domain data without damaging out-domain performance. The other one is to add additional layers to the original architecture as adapters and only update those newly added layers, resulting in a significant speed-up for fine-tuning. The Bottleneck Adapter Layer (BAL) (Houlsby et al., 2019; Rebuffi et al., 2017) proposed by Google in 2019, shows that BAL-based transfer learning could obtain 99.6% of the SOTA performance by only training 3% of the parameters.

The contribution of our paper is as follows:

- We propose an efficient transfer learning framework which transfers knowledge learned from NMT tasks to QE tasks by fine-tuning the pre-trained NMT model with QE data.

- We propose the BAL-QE which achieves 97% of the SOTA performance by only training the Bottleneck layer which is equivalent to 3% of parameters of the entire model, and converges within 4 hours. The model is open-sourced.

2 Modelling of BAL-QE

2.1 Modelling of QE

For a word-level QE task, tokens correctly translated should be tagged as OK, while mistranslated or ignored tagged as BAD. Besides, there should be tags for gaps. We consider gaps as the position between each two words. Words correctly aligned with the source are tagged as OK, otherwise as BAD. If one or more words are missing in the translation, their positions (gap) are tagged as BAD, and OK otherwise. (Wang et al., 2019).

More formally, QE can be considered as taking two sequences as inputs (i.e. source text and the translated text (MT) required for evaluation) and outputs a single sequence (i.e. tags), as shown in Figure 4. When there are K tokens in MT, the word tag should have same length, and the gap tag should have a length of $K + 1$ which is the number of positions between two words as well as the beginning and the end. The length of all tags is $2K + 1$, representing the combination of word and gap tags. Here, we define the QE system as a function f:

$$[e_1, ..., e_{2K+1}] = f([x_1, ..., x_m], [\hat{y}_1, ..., \hat{y}_k]) \quad (1)$$

Source   *the part of the regular expression within the forward slashes defines the pattern .*

MT   *der Teil des regul?ren Ausdrucks innerhalb der umgekehrten Schr?gstrich definiert Muster .*

PE(ref)   *der Teil des regul?ren Ausdrucks innerhalb des umgekehrten Schr?gstrichs definiert das Muster .*

Word Tag   **OK OK OK OK OK OK BAD OK BAD OK OK OK**

Gap Tag   **OK OK OK OK OK OK OK OK OK OK OK BAD OK OK**

All Tag (merge two)   **OK OK OK OK OK OK OK OK OK OK OK OK OK BAD OK OK OK BAD OK OK BAD OK OK OK OK**

Figure 4: An example of QE, where the word tag represents for whether the predicted token is correct, the gap tag means whether there are missing words between two predicted words. All tag is the staggered arrangements of the word and the gap tag.

where e represents tags, x is source text and $\hat{y}$ is the translation. We stagger the word tags and gap tags one by one to create the all tag sequence, where even indices are word tags and odd indices are gap tags (counting from 1). For a word tag, if the tag is BAD, it means the translated word is incorrect or has to be deleted. For a gap tag, if the tag is BAD, it means there are missing words in the gap.

2.2 Optimized Loss Function

With the improvement of the performance of NMT systems, the proportion of BAD tags becomes much fewer than OK tags in QE corpus. Therefore the loss function has to be optimized to handle such imbalance. We optimize the imbalance from three aspects: 1) Improving the effect of BAD tags on the model. 2) Optimizing three losses with appropriate weights. 3) Applying MCC as evaluation metrics to obtain reasonable results.

To improve the effect of BAD tags, we use a hyper-parameter α in the loss function to control the punishments of incorrect prediction of BAD tags. The newly introduced loss is denoted as follows:

$$\mathcal{L}^* = \begin{cases} -[y \log p + (1-y) \log(1-p)], & \text{if } y = 1 \\ -\alpha[y \log p + (1-y) \log(1-p)], & \text{if } y = 0 \end{cases} \tag{2}$$

where $y = 1$ represents for OK tag and $y = 0$ represents for BAD tag. The α is set as 9 in the experiment due to the ratio of OK and BAD is 0.88:0.12 and 0.93:0.07 for word and gap tag respectively (Wang et al., 2018; Wang et al., 2019).

Apart from the imbalance optimized loss, we also use multi-task learning to optimize the model by simultaneously optimizing the loss of words, gaps and all tags. The merged loss is represented as:

$$\mathcal{L} = \sum_{t \in \mathcal{T}} \lambda_t \mathcal{L}_t^* \tag{3}$$

where $\mathcal{T} = \{\text{all-tag}, \text{word-tag}, \text{gap-tag}\}$, and $\sum_{t \in \mathcal{T}} \lambda_t = 1$.

2.3 Evaluation Metrics

QE can be considered as a sequential labelling problem with two classes. A fine-grained F1-score and MCC are used to evaluate the results because of the imbalance. The fine-grained F1-score is composed of F1_{all}, F1_{word} and F1_{gap}. For each F1, it can be computed as $\text{F1}_t = \text{F1}_{t\text{-OK}} \times \text{F1}_{t\text{-BAD}}$, $t \in \mathcal{T}$. The F1 is calculated as standard form: F1=(2 $\times$ precision $\times$ recall) / (precision + recall)

Additionally, we use Matthews correlation coefficient (MCC) for producing unbiased evaluations over the unbalanced predictions. MCC is computed as follows:

$$S = \frac{TP + FN}{N} \tag{4}$$

$$P = \frac{TP + FP}{N} \tag{5}$$

$$MCC = \frac{\frac{TP}{N} - SP}{\sqrt{SP(1-S)(1-P)}} \tag{6}$$

2.4 Model Architecture of BAL-QE

When applying transfer learning on QE, we need a pre-trained NMT model and an adapter layer for

		MT(ALL)				MT(Word)				MT(Gap)			
		$F1_{all}$	F1-BAD	F1-OK	MCC	$F1_{word}$	F1-BAD	F1-OK	MCC	$F1_{gap}$	F1-BAD	F1-OK	MCC
EN_RU	UNBABEL	**0.45961**	**0.478018**	**0.960251**	**0.401625**	**0.48894**	**0.529076**	**0.924197**	**0.418838**	**0.18664**	**0.189196**	**0.984127**	**0.1836**
	ETRI	0.3895	0.4051	0.9617	0.3325	0.4215	0.4561	0.924	0.34675	0.1609	0.1631	0.9803	0.152
	baseline	0.2412	0.250005	0.9325	0.2145	0.222286	0.284211	0.914	0.21913	0.101053	0.102	0.932	0.096
	Uni BAL-QE	0.35055	0.36459	0.942	0.29925	0.37935	0.41049	0.922	0.312075	0.1358	0.14679	0.972	0.1368
	Bi BAL-QE	**0.424555**	**0.441559**	**0.96098**	**0.367063**	**0.45522**	**0.492588**	**0.924098**	**0.382794**	**0.1876**	**0.176148**	**0.982213**	**0.1678**
EN_DE	UNBABEL	**0.4523324**	**0.47**	**0.962**	**0.380471**	**0.495305**	**0.5336**	**0.933962**	**0.367166**	**0.313835**	**0.317975**	**0.987382**	**0.2737**
	ETRI	0.4028	0.4198	0.9595	0.342088	0.4307	0.464	0.9283	0.319275	0.2729	0.2765	0.9871	0.238
	baseline	0.2974	0.311702	0.954984	0.254	0.319795	0.34452	0.927326	0.237062	0.202628	0.205301	0.985366	0.175172
	Uni BAL-QE	0.346408	0.361028	0.955679	0.294195	0.370402	0.39904	0.948718	0.274577	0.234694	0.23779	0.987342	0.20468
	Bi BAL-QE	**0.4275662**	**0.4449**	**0.96075**	**0.361279**	**0.463003**	**0.4988**	**0.931131**	**0.343221**	**0.293368**	**0.297238**	**0.987241**	**0.25585**

Table 1: The experimental result, note that top-2 results are bold. $F1_{all}$, $F1_{word}$, $F1_{tag}$ are the multiplication of F1-OK and F1-BAD in specific level.

Split	Pair	Sentences	Words	BAD source	BAD target	HTER
Train	EN-DE	13,442	234,725	28,549(12.16%)	37.040(7.06%)	0.15($\pm$0.19)
	EN-RU	15,089	148,551	15,599 (10.50%)	18,380 (6.15%)	0.13 ($\pm$0.24)
Dev	EN-DE	1,000	17,669	2,113 (11.96%)	2,654 (6.73%)	0.15 ($\pm$0.19)
	EN-RU	1,000	9,710	1,055 (10.87%)	1,209 (6.17%)	0.13 ($\pm$0.23)
Test	EN-DE	1,023	17,649	2,415 (13.68%)	3,136 (8.04%)	0.17 ($\pm$0.19)
	EN-RU	1,023	7,778	1,049 (13.49%)	1,165 (7.46%)	0.17 ($\pm$0.28)

Table 2: The detail of WMT19 QE dataset

downstream tasks. However, different from original MT tasks which generate tokens depending on previous history, the input of QE is a known sequence which means that when evaluating the token in the current step, we can use future contexts. Therefore, we propose the BAL-QE model which contains three parts: 1) Two pre-trained NMT models, M_{L2R} and M_{R2L}. 2) Two Bottleneck Adapters for decoders of M_{L2R} and M_{R2L}. 3) A classifier layer.

The two pre-trained NMT models are Transformer-big (Ng et al., 2019; Junczys-Dowmunt, 2019), including 6 encoders and 6 decoders composed of multi-head self-attentions and cross-attentions. The only difference of the two Transformers used in BAL-QE is the generating direction.

As shown in Figure 3, the Bottleneck Adapter is like an auto-encoder (Houlsby et al., 2019; Artetxe and Schwenk, 2019; Howard and Ruder, 2018; Rebuffi et al., 2017), which is composed of three parts: 1) The feed-forward down-project, which maps the input vector into low-dimensional space. 2) The nonlinear layer, which is actually is an activation function. 3) The feed-forward up-project, which recovers the vector back to high-dimensional space. 4) A residual connection between the inputs and outputs.

The last classifier layer is a linear layer, which takes the concatenated output vectors from two adapters as input, and makes binary classification of each tag. Not surprisingly, we find that bidirectional predictor (dual Transformer) could improve 8% of the performance compared with unidirectional predictor (single Transformer).

3 Experiment

3.1 Dataset

The Dataset used in the experiment is from WMT19 Quality Evaluation Task1, including two languages (En-De, En-Ru). There are 13,000 sentence pairs for En-De, with approximately 234,000 tokens. The proportion of BAD tag in German MT sentences is 7.06%. En-Ru contains totally 15,000 sentence pairs with 148,000 tokens and 6.15% of BAD tags. More details are shown in Table 2.

3.2 Setup of Pre-training Two Transformers

The pre-training of the Transformer is similar with the setup of FAIR SOTA model in WMT19 (Ng et al., 2019), which is implemented with fairseq[1]. BPE is used for tokenizing, where 32000 tokens are reserved. We use UN corpus and Common Crawl parallel corpus with the size of

---

[1] https://github.com/pytorch/fairseq

	Total Params	Training Params	Training Ratio
Uni BAL-QE	216,235,012	6,323,204	2.92%
Bi BAL-QE	432,470,002	12,646,406	2.92%

Table 3: The comparison of parameters of BAL-QE

27,000,000. We also use back-translation to produce 20,000,000 augmented corpus. The BLEU of M_{L2R} and M_{R2L} are 42.3 and 41.8 for EN-DE, 36.2 and 35.9 for EN-RU respectively, with less than 2% of difference compared with the SOTA result of published fairseq implementation.

3.3 Setup of Fine-tuning BAL-QE

In the fine-tuning of BAL-QE, the parameter of two Transformers are fixed, and we only update the two adapters as well as the classifier, which means that only 2.92% of parameters are trained in the fine-tuning, as shown in Table 3. Adam is used as the optimizer with a triangular learning rate schedule with peak learning rate as 5e-5. We use a maximum of 1,024 tokens per batch and save checkpoints every 1,000 steps, on the exponential moving averaged parameters (Junczys-Dowmunt, 2019) with a decay rate of 1e-4. BPE is applied with subword-nmt, and 32,000 tokens are reserved. It takes 2 hours and 38 minutes and 4 hours and 02 minutes to train the unidirectional and bidirectional BAL-QE on 4 Titan XP GPUs, respectively.

3.4 Analysis

As shown in Table 1, MT (ALL), MT (Word) and MT (Gap) represents evaluation results of All Tag, Word Tag and Gap Tag, respectively. The baseline is a model of NuQE. On En-De and Ee-Ru datasets, the unidirectional BAL-QE improves performance by 17% and 45%, and the bidirectional BAL-QE improves by 44% and 75%, compared with the baseline. All metrics of bidirectional BAL-QE achieves top-2 rank, and the F1-OK of En-Ru achieves the SOTA result.

4   Conclusion

This paper proposes a Predictor-Estimator QE model based on the Bottleneck Adapter Layer and the Transformer. An efficient transfer learning framework is also proposed, which could transfer knowledge learned from NMT parallel corpora into the QE task to improve the training efficiency of the proposed BAL-QE model. Experiments shows that partially training the model (estimator) could effectively speed up the training and achieves 97% of the SOTA performance.

References

Artetxe, Mikel and Holger Schwenk. 2019. Massively multilingual sentence embeddings for zero-shot cross-lingual transfer and beyond. *Transactions of the Association for Computational Linguistics*, 7:597–610.

Dai, Andrew M and Quoc V Le. 2015. Semi-supervised sequence learning. In *Advances in neural information processing systems*, pages 3079–3087.

Houlsby, Neil, Andrei Giurgiu, Stanislaw Jastrzebski, Bruna Morrone, Quentin De Laroussilhe, Andrea Gesmundo, Mona Attariyan, and Sylvain Gelly. 2019. Parameter-efficient transfer learning for NLP. *arXiv preprint arXiv:1902.00751*.

Howard, Jeremy and Sebastian Ruder. 2018. Universal language model fine-tuning for text classification. *arXiv preprint arXiv:1801.06146*.

Junczys-Dowmunt, Marcin. 2019. Microsoft translator at wmt 2019: Towards large-scale document-level neural machine translation. *arXiv preprint arXiv:1907.06170*.

Kim, Hyun and Jong-Hyeok Lee. 2016. Recurrent neural network based translation quality estimation. In *Proceedings of the First Conference on Machine Translation: Volume 2, Shared Task Papers*, pages 787–792.

Kim, Hyun, Jong-Hyeok Lee, and Seung-Hoon Na. 2017. Predictor-estimator using multilevel task learning with stack propagation for neural quality estimation. In *Proceedings of the Second Conference on Machine Translation*, pages 562–568.

Kreutzer, Julia, Shigehiko Schamoni, and Stefan Riezler. 2015. Quality estimation from scratch (quetch): Deep learning for word-level translation quality estimation. In *Proceedings of the Tenth Workshop on Statistical Machine Translation*, pages 316–322.

Li, Maoxi, Qingyu Xiang, Zhiming Chen, and Mingwen Wang. 2018. A unified neural network for quality estimation of machine translation. *IEICE TRANSACTIONS on Information and Systems*, 101(9):2417–2421.

Martins, André FT, Ramón Astudillo, Chris Hokamp, and Fabio Kepler. 2016. Unbabel's participation in the WMT16 word-level translation quality estimation shared task. In *Proceedings of the First Conference on Machine Translation: Volume 2, Shared Task Papers*, pages 806–811.

Ng, Nathan, Kyra Yee, Alexei Baevski, Myle Ott, Michael Auli, and Sergey Edunov. 2019. Facebook FAIR's WMT19 News Translation Task Submission. *arXiv preprint arXiv:1907.06616*.

Radford, Alec, Karthik Narasimhan, Tim Salimans, and Ilya Sutskever. 2018. Improving language understanding by generative pre-training. *URL https://s3-us-west-2. amazonaws. com/openai-assets/researchcovers/languageunsupervised/language understanding paper. pdf.*

Rebuffi, Sylvestre-Alvise, Hakan Bilen, and Andrea Vedaldi. 2017. Learning multiple visual domains with residual adapters. In *Advances in Neural Information Processing Systems*, pages 506–516.

Specia, Lucia, Kashif Shah, José GC De Souza, and Trevor Cohn. 2013. QuEst-A translation quality estimation framework. In *Proceedings of the 51st Annual Meeting of the Association for Computational Linguistics: System Demonstrations*, pages 79–84.

Wang, Jiayi, Kai Fan, Bo Li, Fengming Zhou, Boxing Chen, Yangbin Shi, and Luo Si. 2018. Alibaba submission for WMT18 quality estimation task. In *Proceedings of the Third Conference on Machine Translation: Shared Task Papers*, pages 809–815.

Wang, Ziyang, Hui Liu, Hexuan Chen, Kai Feng, Zeyang Wang, Bei Li, Chen Xu, Tong Xiao, and Jingbo Zhu. 2019. NiuTrans Submission for CCMT19 Quality Estimation Task. In *China Conference on Machine Translation*, pages 82–92. Springer.

Yang, Hao, Gengui Xie, Ying Qin, and Song Peng. 2019a. Domain Specific NMT based on Knowledge Graph Embedding and Attention. In *2019 21st International Conference on Advanced Communication Technology (ICACT)*, pages 516–521. IEEE.

Yang, Muyun, Xixin Hu, Hao Xiong, Jiayi Wang, Yiliyaer Jiaermuhamaiti, Zhongjun He, Weihua Luo, and Shujian Huang. 2019b. CCMT 2019 Machine Translation Evaluation Report. In *China Conference on Machine Translation*, pages 105–128. Springer.

When and Why is Unsupervised Neural Machine Translation Useless?

Yunsu Kim　**Miguel Graça**[†]　**Hermann Ney**
Human Language Technology and Pattern Recognition Group
RWTH Aachen University, Aachen, Germany
`{surname}@cs.rwth-aachen.de`

Abstract

This paper studies the practicality of the current state-of-the-art unsupervised methods in neural machine translation (NMT). In ten translation tasks with various data settings, we analyze the conditions under which the unsupervised methods fail to produce reasonable translations. We show that their performance is severely affected by linguistic dissimilarity and domain mismatch between source and target monolingual data. Such conditions are common for low-resource language pairs, where unsupervised learning works poorly. In all of our experiments, supervised and semi-supervised baselines with 50k-sentence bilingual data outperform the best unsupervised results. Our analyses pinpoint the limits of the current unsupervised NMT and also suggest immediate research directions.

1　Introduction

Statistical methods for machine translation (MT) require a large set of sentence pairs in two languages to build a decent translation system (Resnik and Smith, 2003; Koehn, 2005). Such bilingual data is scarce for most language pairs and its quality varies largely over different domains (Al-Onaizan et al., 2002; Chu and Wang, 2018). Neural machine translation (NMT) (Bahdanau et al., 2015; Vaswani et al., 2017), the standard paradigm of MT these days, has been claimed to suffer from the data scarcity more severely than phrase-based MT (Koehn and Knowles, 2017).

Unsupervised NMT, which trains a neural translation model only with monolingual corpora, was

proposed for those scenarios which lack bilingual data (Artetxe et al., 2018b; Lample et al., 2018a). Despite its progress in research, the performance of the unsupervised methods has been evaluated mostly on high-resource language pairs, e.g. German↔English or French↔English (Artetxe et al., 2018b; Lample et al., 2018a; Yang et al., 2018; Artetxe et al., 2018a; Lample et al., 2018b; Ren et al., 2019b; Artetxe et al., 2019; Sun et al., 2019; Sen et al., 2019). For these language pairs, huge bilingual corpora are already available, so there is no need for unsupervised learning in practice. Empirical results in these tasks do not carry over to low-resource language pairs; they simply fail to produce any meaningful translations (Neubig and Hu, 2018; Guzmán et al., 2019).

This paper aims for a more comprehensive and pragmatic study on the performance of unsupervised NMT. Our experiments span ten translation tasks in the following five language pairs:

- German↔English: similar languages, abundant bilingual/monolingual data

- Russian↔English: distant languages, abundant bilingual/monolingual data, similar sizes of the alphabet

- Chinese↔English: distant languages, abundant bilingual/monolingual data, very different sizes of the alphabet

- Kazakh↔English: distant languages, scarce bilingual data, abundant monolingual data

- Gujarati↔English: distant languages, scarce bilingual/monolingual data

For each task, we compare the unsupervised performance with its supervised and semi-supervised counterparts. In addition, we make the monolingual training data vary in size and domain to cover many more scenarios, showing under which conditions unsupervised NMT works poorly.

Here is a summary of our contributions:

[†] The author is now at DeepL GmbH.

Martins, Moniz, Fumega, Martins, Batista, Coheur, Parra, Trancoso, Turchi, Bisazza, Moorkens, Guerberof, Nurminen, Marg, Forcada (eds.)
Proceedings of the 22nd Annual Conference of the European Association for Machine Translation, p. 35–44
Lisboa, Portugal, November 2020.

- We thoroughly evaluate the performance of state-of-the-art unsupervised NMT in numerous real and artificial translation tasks.

- We provide guidelines on whether to employ unsupervised NMT in practice, by showing how much bilingual data is sufficient to outperform the unsupervised results.

- We clarify which factors make unsupervised NMT weak and which points must be improved, by analyzing the results both quantitatively and qualitatively.

2 Related Work

The idea of unsupervised MT dates back to word-based decipherment methods (Knight et al., 2006; Ravi and Knight, 2011). They learn only lexicon models at first, but add alignment models (Dou et al., 2014; Nuhn, 2019) or heuristic features (Naim et al., 2018) later. Finally, Artetxe et al. (2018a) and Lample et al. (2018b) train a fully-fledged phrase-based MT system in an unsupervised way.

With neural networks, unsupervised learning of a sequence-to-sequence NMT model has been proposed by Lample et al. (2018a) and Artetxe et al. (2018b). Though having slight variations (Yang et al., 2018; Sun et al., 2019; Sen et al., 2019), unsupervised NMT approaches commonly 1) learn a shared model for both source→target and target→source 2) using iterative back-translation, along with 3) a denoising autoencoder objective. They are initialized with either cross-lingual word embeddings or a cross-lingual language model (LM). To further improve the performance at the cost of efficiency, Lample et al. (2018b), Ren et al. (2019b) and Artetxe et al. (2019) combine unsupervised NMT with unsupervised phrase-based MT. On the other hand, one can also avoid the long iterative training by applying a separate denoiser directly to the word-by-word translations from cross-lingual word embeddings (Kim et al., 2018; Pourdamghani et al., 2019).

Unsupervised NMT approaches have been so far evaluated mostly on high-resource language pairs, e.g. French→English, for academic purposes. In terms of practicality, they tend to underperform in low-resource language pairs, e.g. Azerbaijani→English (Neubig and Hu, 2018) or Nepali→English (Guzmán et al., 2019). To the best of our knowledge, this work is the first to systematically evaluate and analyze unsupervised learning for NMT in various data settings.

3 Unsupervised NMT

This section reviews the core concepts of the recent unsupervised NMT framework and describes to which points they are potentially vulnerable.

3.1 Bidirectional Modeling

Most of the unsupervised NMT methods share the model parameters between source→target and target→source directions. They also often share a joint subword vocabulary across the two languages (Sennrich et al., 2016b).

Sharing a model among different translation tasks has been shown to be effective in multilingual NMT (Firat et al., 2016; Johnson et al., 2017; Aharoni et al., 2019), especially in improving performance on low-resource language pairs. This is due to the commonality of natural languages; learning to represent a language is helpful to represent other languages, e.g. by transferring knowledge of general sentence structures. It also provides good regularization for the model.

Unsupervised learning is an extreme scenario of MT, where bilingual information is very weak. To supplement the weak and noisy training signal, knowledge transfer and regularization are crucial, which can be achieved by the bidirectional sharing. It is based on the fact that a translation problem is dual in nature; source→target and target→source tasks are conceptually related to each other.

Previous works on unsupervised NMT vary in the degree of sharing: the whole encoder (Artetxe et al., 2018b; Sen et al., 2019), the middle layers (Yang et al., 2018; Sun et al., 2019), or the whole model (Lample et al., 2018a; Lample et al., 2018b; Ren et al., 2019a; Conneau and Lample, 2019).

Note that the network sharing is less effective among linguistically distinct languages in NMT (Kocmi and Bojar, 2018; Kim et al., 2019a). It still works as a regularizer, but transferring knowledge is harder if the morphology or word order is quite different. We show how well unsupervised NMT performs on such language pairs in Section 4.1.

3.2 Iterative Back-Translation

Unsupervised learning for MT assumes no bilingual data for training. A traditional remedy for the data scarcity is generating synthetic bilingual data from monolingual text (Koehn, 2005; Schwenk, 2008; Sennrich et al., 2016a). To train a bidirectional model of Section 3.1, we need bilingual data of both translation directions. Therefore, most unsupervised NMT methods back-translate in both directions, i.e. source and target monolingual data to target and source language, respectively.

In unsupervised learning, the synthetic data should be created not only once at the beginning but also repeatedly throughout the training. At the early stages of training, the model might be too weak to generate good translations. Hence, most methods update the training data as the model gets improved during training. The improved model for source→target direction back-translates source monolingual data, which improves the model for target→source direction, and vice versa. This cycle is called dual learning (He et al., 2016) or iterative back-translation (Hoang et al., 2018). Figure 1 shows the case when it is applied to a fully shared bidirectional model.

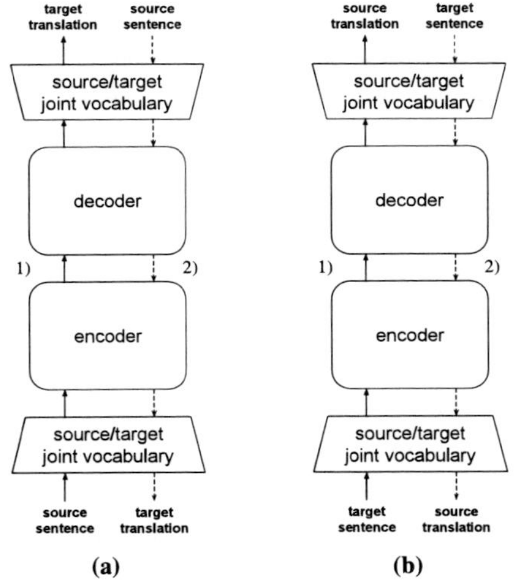

Figure 1: Iterative back-translation for training a bidirectional sequence-to-sequence model. The model first translates monolingual sentences (solid arrows), and then gets trained with the translation as the input and the original as the output (dashed arrows). This procedure alternates between **(a)** source→target and **(b)** target→source translations.

One can tune the amount of back-translations per iteration: a mini-batch (Artetxe et al., 2018b; Yang et al., 2018; Conneau and Lample, 2019; Ren et al., 2019a), the whole monolingual data (Lample et al., 2018a; Lample et al., 2018b; Sun et al., 2019), or some size in between (Artetxe et al., 2019; Ren et al., 2019b).

However, even if carefully scheduled, the iterative training cannot recover from a bad optimum if the initial model is too poor. Experiments in Section 4.5 highlight such cases.

3.3 Initialization

To kickstart the iterative training, the model should be able to generate meaningful translations already in the first iteration. We cannot expect the training to progress from a randomly initialized network and the synthetic data generated by it.

Cross-lingual embeddings give a good starting point for the model by defining a joint continuous space shared by multiple languages. Ideally, in such a space, close embedding vectors are semantically related to each other regardless of their languages; they can be possible candidates for translation pairs (Mikolov et al., 2013). It can be learned either in word level (Artetxe et al., 2017; Conneau et al., 2018) or in sentence level (Conneau and Lample, 2019) using only monolingual corpora.

In the word level, we can initialize the embedding layers with cross-lingual word embedding vectors (Artetxe et al., 2018b; Lample et al., 2018a; Yang et al., 2018; Lample et al., 2018b; Artetxe et al., 2019; Sun et al., 2019). On the other hand, the whole encoder/decoder parameters can be initialized with cross-lingual sequence training (Conneau and Lample, 2019; Ren et al., 2019a; Song et al., 2019).

Cross-lingual word embedding has limited performance among distant languages (Søgaard et al., 2018; Nakashole and Flauger, 2018) and so does cross-lingual LM (Pires et al., 2019). Section 4.5 shows the impact of a poor initialization.

3.4 Denoising Autoencoder

Initializing the word embedding layers furnishes the model with cross-lingual matching in the lexical embedding space, but does not provide any information on word orders or generation of text. Cross-lingual LMs encode word sequences in different languages, but they are not explicitly trained to reorder source words to the target language syntax. Both ways do not initialize the crucial parameters for reordering: the encoder-decoder attention and the recurrence on decoder states.

As a result, an initial model for unsupervised NMT tends to generate word-by-word translations with little reordering, which are very non-fluent when source and target languages have distinct word orders. Training on such data discourages the model from reordering words, which might cause a vicious cycle by generating even less-reordered synthetic sentence pairs in the next iterations.

Accordingly, unsupervised NMT employs an

		de-en		ru-en		zh-en		kk-en		gu-en	
		German	English	Russian	English	Chinese	English	Kazakh	English	Gujarati	English
Language family		Germanic	Germanic	Slavic	Germanic	Sinitic	Germanic	Turkic	Germanic	Indic	Germanic
Alphabet Size		60	52	66	52	8,105	52	42	52	91	52
Monolingual	Sentences	100M		71.6M		30.8M		18.5M		4.1M	
	Words	1.8B	2.3B	1.1B	2.0B	1.4B	699M	278.5M	421.5M	121.5M	93.8M
Bilingual	Sentences	5.9M		25.4M		18.9M		222k		156k	
	Words	137.4M	144.9M	618.6M	790M	440.3M	482.9M	1.6M	1.9M	2.3M	1.5M

Table 1: Training data statistics.

additional training objective of denoising autoencoding (Hill et al., 2016). Given a clean sentence, artificial noises are injected, e.g. deletion or permutation of words, to make a corrupted input. The denoising objective trains the model to reorder the noisy input to the correct syntax, which is essential for generating fluent outputs. This is done for each language individually with monolingual data, as shown in Figure 2.

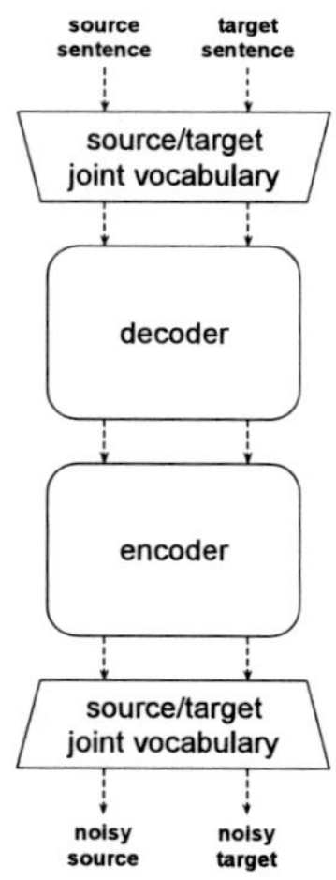

Figure 2: Denoising autoencoder training for source or target language.

Once the model is sufficiently trained for denoising, it is helpful to remove the objective or reduce its weight (Graça et al., 2018). At the later stages of training, the model gets improved in reordering and translates better; learning to denoise might hurt the performance in clean test sets.

4 Experiments and Analysis

Data   Our experiments were conducted on WMT 2018 German↔English and Russian↔ English, WMT 2019 Chinese↔English, Kazakh↔ English, and Gujarati↔English (Table 1). We pre-

processed the data using the MOSES[1] tokenizer and a frequent caser. For Chinese, we used the JIEBA segmenter[2]. Lastly, byte pair encoding (BPE) (Sennrich et al., 2016b) was learned jointly over source and target languages with 32k merges and applied without vocabulary threshold.

Model   We used 6-layer Transformer base architecture (Vaswani et al., 2017) by default: 512-dimension embedding/hidden layers, 2048-dimension feedforward sublayers, and 8 heads.

Decoding and Evaluation   Decoding was done with beam size 5. We evaluated the test performance with SACREBLEU (Post, 2018).

Unsupervised Learning   We ran XLM[3] by Conneau and Lample (2019) for the unsupervised experiments. The back-translations were done with beam search for each mini-batch of 16k tokens. The weight of the denoising objective started with 1 and linearly decreased to 0.1 until 100k updates, and then decreased to 0 until 300k updates.

The model's encoder and decoder were both initialized with the same pre-trained cross-lingual LM. We removed the language embeddings from the encoder for better cross-linguality (see Section 4.6). Unless otherwise specified, we used the same monolingual training data for both pre-training and translation training. For the pre-training, we set the batch size to 256 sentences (around 66k tokens).

Training was done with Adam (Kingma and Ba, 2014) with an initial learning rate of 0.0001, where dropout (Srivastava et al., 2014) of probability 0.1 was applied to each layer output and attention components. With a checkpoint frequency of 200k sentences, we stopped the training when the validation perplexity (pre-training) or BLEU (translation training) was not improved for ten check-

---

[1] http://www.statmt.org/moses
[2] https://github.com/fxsjy/jieba
[3] https://github.com/facebookresearch/XLM

Approach	BLEU [%]									
	de-en	en-de	ru-en	en-ru	zh-en	en-zh	kk-en	en-kk	gu-en	en-gu
Supervised	39.5	39.1	29.1	24.7	26.2	39.6	10.3	2.4	9.9	3.5
Semi-supervised	43.6	41.0	30.8	28.8	25.9	42.7	12.5	3.1	14.2	4.0
Unsupervised	23.8	20.2	12.0	9.4	1.5	2.5	2.0	0.8	0.6	0.6

Table 2: Comparison among supervised, semi-supervised, and unsupervised learning. All bilingual data was used for the (semi-)supervised results and all monolingual data was used for the unsupervised results (see Table 1). All results are computed on newstest2019 of each task, except for de-en/en-de and ru-en/en-ru on newstest2018.

points. We extensively tuned the hyperparameters for a single GPU with 12GB memory, which is widely applicable to moderate industrial/academic environments. All other hyperparameter values follow the recommended settings of XLM.

Supervised Learning   Supervised experiments used the same hyperparameters as the unsupervised learning, except 12k tokens for the batch size, 0.0002 for the initial learning rate, and 10k batches for each checkpoint.

If the bilingual training data contains less than 500k sentence pairs, we reduced the BPE merges to 8k, the batch size to 2k, and the checkpoint frequency to 4k batches; we also increased the dropout rate to 0.3 (Sennrich and Zhang, 2019).

Semi-supervised Learning   Semi-supervised experiments continued the training from the supervised baseline with back-translations added to the training data. We used 4M back-translated sentences for the low-resource cases, i.e. if the original bilingual data has less than 500k lines, and 10M back-translated sentences otherwise.

4.1   Unsupervised vs. (Semi-)Supervised

We first address the most general question of this paper: For NMT, can unsupervised learning replace semi-supervised or supervised learning? Table 2 compares the unsupervised performance to simple supervised and semi-supervised baselines.

In all tasks, unsupervised learning shows much worse performance than (semi-)supervised learning. It produces readable translations in two high-resource language pairs (German↔English and Russian↔English), but their scores are only around half of the semi-supervised systems. In other three language pairs, unsupervised NMT fails to converge at any meaningful optimum, reaching less than 3% BLEU scores. Note that, in these three tasks, source and target languages are very different in the alphabet, morphology, and

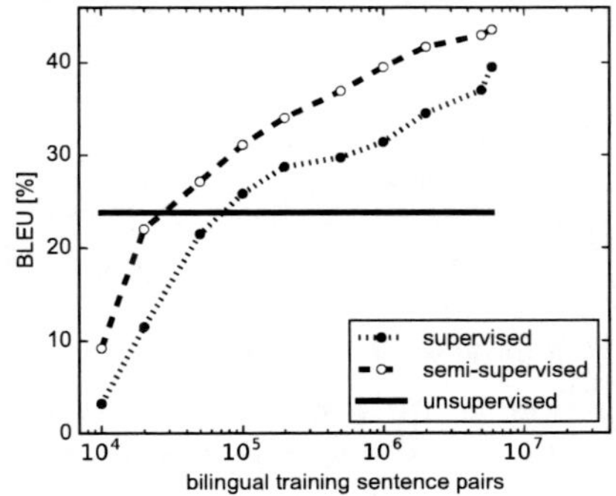

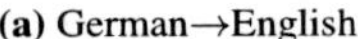

(a) German→English

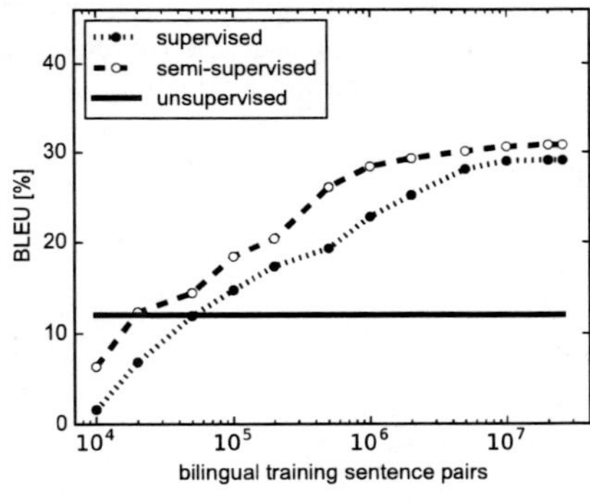

(b) Russian→English

Figure 3: Supervised and semi-supervised learning over bilingual training data size. Unsupervised learning (horizontal line) uses all monolingual data of Table 1.

word order, etc. The results in Kazakh↔English and Gujarati↔English show that the current unsupervised NMT cannot be an alternative to (semi-)supervised NMT in low-resource conditions.

To discover the precise condition where the unsupervised learning is useful in practice, we vary the size of the given bilingual training data for (semi-)supervised learning and plot the results in Figure 3. Once we have 50k bilingual sentence pairs in German↔English, simple semi-supervised learning already outperforms unsupervised learning with 100M monolingual sentences in each language. Even without back-translations (supervised), 100k-sentence bilingual data is sufficient to surpass unsupervised NMT.

In the Russian↔English task, the unsupervised learning performance can be more easily achieved with only 20k bilingual sentence pairs using semi-supervised learning. This might be due to that Russian and English are more distant to each other than German and English, thus bilingual training signal is more crucial for Russian↔English.

Note that for these two language pairs, the bilingual data for supervised learning are from many different text domains, whereas the monolingual data are from exactly the same domain of the test sets. Even with such an advantage, the large-scale unsupervised NMT cannot compete with supervised NMT with tiny out-of-domain bilingual data.

4.2 Monolingual Data Size

In this section, we analyze how much monolingual data is necessary to make unsupervised NMT produce reasonable performance. Figure 4 shows the unsupervised results with different amounts of monolingual training data. We keep the equal size for source and target data, and the domain is also the same for both (web-crawled news).

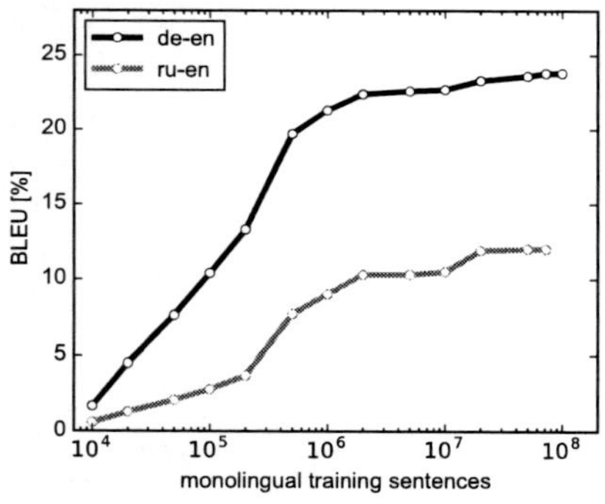

Figure 4: Unsupervised NMT performance over the size of monolingual training data, where source and target sides have the same size.

For German→English, training with only 1M sentences already gives a reasonable performance, which is only around 2% BLEU behind the 100M-sentence case. The performance starts to saturate already after 5M sentences, with only marginal improvements by using more than 20M sentences. We observe a similar trend in Russian→English.

This shows that, for the performance of unsupervised NMT, using a massive amount of monolingual data is not as important as the similarity of source and target languages. Comparing to supervised learning (see Figure 3), the performance saturates faster when increasing the training data, given the same model size.

4.3 Unbalanced Data Size

What if the size of available monolingual data is largely different for source and target languages? This is often the case for low-resource language pairs involving English, where there is plenty of data for English but not for the other side.

Our experiments so far intentionally use the same number of sentences for both sides. In Figure 5, we reduced the source data gradually while keeping the large target data fixed. To counteract the data imbalance, we oversampled the smaller side to make the ratio of source-target 1:1 for BPE learning and mini-batch construction (Conneau and Lample, 2019). We compare such unbalanced data settings to the previous equal-sized source/target settings.

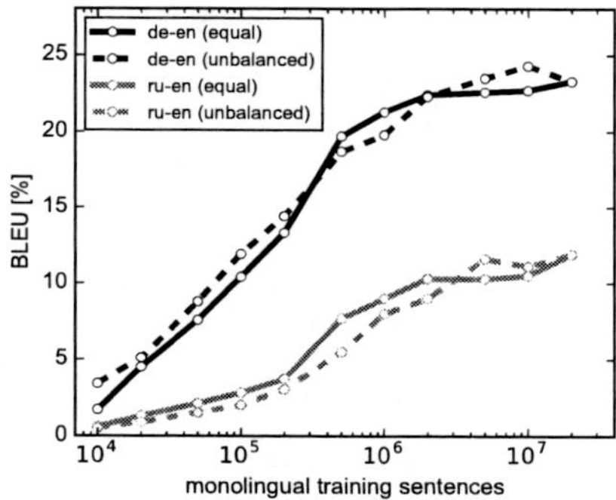

Figure 5: Unsupervised NMT performance over source training data size, where the target training data is fixed to 20M sentences (dashed line). Solid line is the case where the target data has the same number of sentences as the source side.

Interestingly, when we decrease the target data accordingly (balanced, solid line), the performance is similar or sometimes better than using the full target data (unbalanced, dashed line). This means that it is not beneficial to use oversized data on one side in unsupervised NMT training.

If the data is severely unbalanced, the distribution of the smaller side should be much sparser than that of the larger side. The network tries to generalize more on the smaller data, reserving the model capacity for smoothing (Olson et al., 2018). Thus it learns to represent a very different distribution of each side, which is challenging in a shared model (Section 3.1). This could be the reason for no merit in using larger data on one side.

4.4 Domain Similarity

In high-resource language pairs, it is feasible to collect monolingual data of the same domain on both source and target languages. However, for low-resource language pairs, it is difficult to match the data domain of both sides on a large scale. For example, our monolingual data for Kazakh is mostly from Wikipedia and Common Crawl, while the English data is solely from News Crawl. In this section, we study how the domain similarity of monolingual data on the two sides affects the performance of unsupervised NMT.

In Table 3, we artificially change the domain of the source side to politics (UN Corpus[4]) or random (Common Crawl), while keeping the target domain fixed to newswire (News Crawl). The results show that the domain matching is critical for unsupervised NMT. For instance, although German and English are very similar languages, we see the performance of German↔English deteriorate down to -11.8% BLEU by the domain mismatch.

Domain (en)	Domain (de/ru)	BLEU [%]			
		de-en	en-de	ru-en	en-ru
	Newswire	23.3	19.9	11.9	9.3
Newswire	Politics	11.5	12.2	2.3	2.5
	Random	18.4	16.4	6.9	6.1

Table 3: Unsupervised NMT performance where source and target training data are from different domains. The data size on both sides is the same (20M sentences).

Table 4 shows a more delicate case where we keep the same domain for both sides (newswire) but change the providers and years of the news articles. Our monolingual data for Chinese (Table 1) consist mainly of News Crawl (from years 2008-2018) and Gigaword 4th edition (from years 1995-2008). We split out the News Crawl part (1.7M sentences) and trained an unsupervised NMT model with the same amount of English monolingual data (from News Crawl 2014-2017). Surprisingly, this experiment yields much better results than using all available data. Even if the size is small, the source and target data are collected in the same way (web-crawling) from similar years (2010s), which seems to be crucial for unsupervised NMT to work.

On the other hand, when using the Gigaword part (28.6M sentences) on Chinese, unsupervised

[4]https://conferences.unite.un.org/uncorpus

Years (en)	Years (zh)	#sents (en/zh)	BLEU [%]	
			zh-en	en-zh
2014-2017	2008-2018	1.7M	5.4	15.1
	1995-2008	28.6M	1.5	1.9

Table 4: Unsupervised NMT performance where source and target training data are from the same domain (newswire) but different years.

learning again does not function properly. Now the source and target text are from different decades; the distribution of topics might be different. Also, the Gigaword corpus is from traditional newspaper agencies which can have a different tone from the online text of News Crawl. Despite the large scale, unsupervised NMT proves to be sensitive to a subtle discrepancy of topic, style, period, etc. between source and target data.

These results agree with Søgaard et al. (2018) who show that modern cross-lingual word embedding methods fail in domain mismatch scenarios.

4.5 Initialization vs. Translation Training

Thus far, we have seen a number of cases where unsupervised NMT breaks down. But which part of the learning algorithm is more responsible for the performance: initialization (Section 3.3) or translation training (Section 3.2 and 3.4)?

In Figure 6, we control the level of each of the two training stages and analyze its impact on the final performance. We pre-trained two cross-lingual LMs as initializations of different quality: bad (using 10k sentences) and good (using 20M sentences). For each initial point, we continued the translation training with different amounts of data from 10k to 20M sentences.

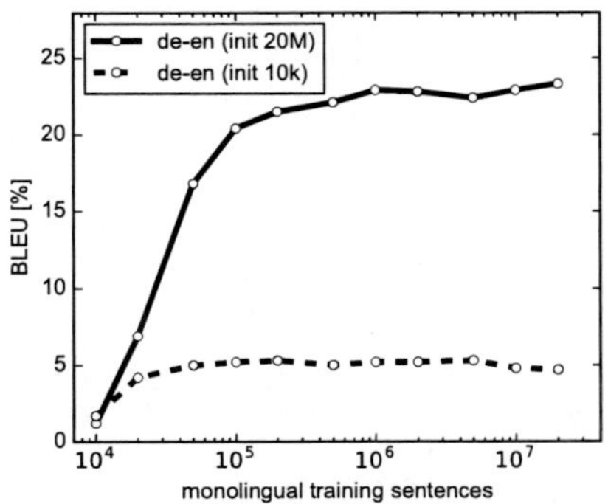

Figure 6: Unsupervised NMT performance over the training data size for translation training, where the pre-training data for initialization is fixed (10k or 20M sentences).

From the bad initialization, unsupervised learning cannot build a reasonable NMT model, no mat-

Task	BLEU [%]	Source input	System output	Reference output
de-en	23.8	Seit der ersten <u>Besichtigung</u> wurde die *1.000 Quadratfuß* große ...	Since the first <u>Besichtigung</u>, the *3,000 square* fueled ...	Since the first viewing, the 1,000sq ft flat has ...
	10.4	*München* 1856: *Vier* Karten, die Ihren Blick auf die *Stadt* verändern	*Austrailia* 1856: *Eight* things that can keep your way to the *UK*	Munich 1856: Four maps that will change your view of the city
ru-en	12.0	В ходе <u>первоочередных оператив-но-следственных мероприятий</u> установлена личность роженицы	The <u>первоочередных оператив-но-следственных мероприятий</u> have been established by the dolphin	The identity of the mother was determined during preliminary investigative and operational measures
zh-en	1.5	... <u>调整要兼顾生产需要</u>和<u>消费需求</u>。	... <u>调整要兼顾生产需要</u> and <u>消费需求</u>。	... adjustment must balance production needs with consumer demands.

Table 5: Problematic translation outputs from unsupervised NMT systems (<u>input copying</u>, *ambiguity in the same context*).

ter how much data is used in translation training. When the initial model is strong, it is possible to reach 20% BLEU by translation training with only 100k sentences. Using 1M sentences in translation training, the performance is already comparable to its best. Once the model is pre-trained well for cross-lingual representations, fine-tuning the translation-specific components seems manageable with relatively small data.

This demonstrates the importance of initialization over translation training in the current unsupervised NMT. Translation training relies solely on model-generated inputs, i.e. back-translations, which do not reflect the true distribution of the input language when generated with a poor initial model. On Figure 7, we plot all German→English unsupervised results we conducted up to the previous section. It shows that the final performance generally correlates with the initialization quality.

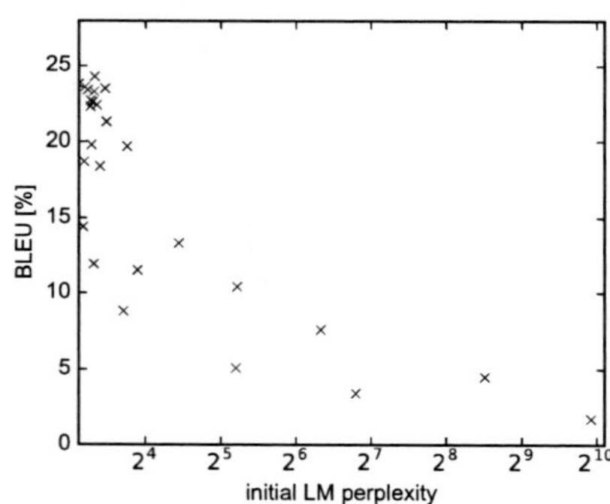

Figure 7: Unsupervised NMT performance over the validation perplexity of the initial cross-lingual LM (**de-en**).

4.6 Qualitative Examples

In this section, we analyze translation outputs of unsupervised systems to find out why they record such low BLEU scores. Do unsupervised systems have particular problems in the outputs other than limited adequacy/fluency?

Table 5 shows translation examples from the unsupervised systems. The first notable problem is copying input words to the output. This happens when the encoder has poor cross-linguality, i.e. does not concurrently model two languages well in a shared space. The decoder then can easily detect the input language by reading the encoder and may emit output words in the same language.

A good cross-lingual encoder should not give away information on the input language to the decoder. The decoder must instead rely on the ouptut language embeddings or an indicator token (e.g. `<2en>`) to determine the language of output tokens. As a simple remedy, we removed the language embeddings from the encoder and obtained consistent improvements, e.g. from 4.3% to 11.9% BLEU in Russian→English. However, the problem still remains partly even in our best-performing unsupervised system (the first example).

The copying occurs more often in inferior systems (the last example), where the poor initial cross-lingual LM is the main reason for the worse performance (Section 4.5). Note that the auto-encoding (Section 3.4) also encourages the model to generate outputs in the input language.

Another problem is that the model cannot distinguish words that appear in the same context. In the second example, the model knows that *Vier* in German (*Four* in English) is a number, but it generates a wrong number in English (*Eight*). The initial LM is trained to predict either *Four* or *Eight* given the same surrounding words (e.g. 1856, things) and has no clue to map *Four* to *Vier*.

The model cannot learn these mappings by itself with back-translations. This problem can be partly solved by subword modeling (Bojanowski et al., 2017) or orthographic features (Riley and Gildea, 2018; Artetxe et al., 2019), which are however not effective for language pairs with disjoint alphabets.

5 Conclusion and Outlook

In this paper, we examine the state-of-the-art unsupervised NMT in a wide range of tasks and data settings. We find that the performance of unsupervised NMT is seriously affected by these factors:

- Linguistic similarity of source and target languages
- Domain similarity of training data between source and target languages

It is very hard to fulfill these in low-/zero-resource language pairs, which makes the current unsupervised NMT useless in practice. We also find that the performance is not improved by using massive monolingual data on one or both sides.

In practice, a simple, non-tuned semi-supervised baseline with only less than 50k bilingual sentence pairs is sufficient to outperform our best large-scale unsupervised system. At this moment, we cannot recommend unsupervised learning for building MT products if there are at least small bilingual data.

For the cases where there is no bilingual data available at all, we plan to systematically compare the unsupervised NMT to pivot-based methods (Kim et al., 2019b; Currey and Heafield, 2019) or multilingual zero-shot translation (Johnson et al., 2017; Aharoni et al., 2019).

To make unsupervised NMT useful in the future, we suggest the following research directions:

Language-/Domain-agnostic LM   We show in Section 4.5 that the initial cross-lingual LM actually determines the performance of unsupervised NMT. In Section 4.6, we argue that the poor performance is due to input copying, for which we blame a poor cross-lingual LM. The LM pre-training must therefore handle dissimilar languages and domains equally well. This might be done by careful data selection or better regularization methods.

Robust Translation Training   On the other hand, the current unsupervised NMT lacks a mechanism to bootstrap out of a poor initialization. Inspired by classical decipherment methods (Section 2), we might devalue noisy training examples or artificially simplify the problem first.

References

Aharoni, Roee, Melvin Johnson, and Orhan Firat. 2019. Massively multilingual neural machine translation. In *NAACL-HLT*, pages 3874–3884.

Al-Onaizan, Yaser, Ulrich Germann, Ulf Hermjakob, Kevin Knight, Philipp Koehn, Daniel Marcu, and Kenji Yamada. 2002. Translation with scarce bilingual resources. *Machine Translation*, 17(1):1–17.

Artetxe, Mikel, Gorka Labaka, and Eneko Agirre. 2017. Learning bilingual word embeddings with (almost) no bilingual data. In *ACL*, pages 451–462.

Artetxe, Mikel, Gorka Labaka, and Eneko Agirre. 2018a. Unsupervised statistical machine translation. In *EMNLP*, page 3632–3642.

Artetxe, Mikel, Gorka Labaka, Eneko Agirre, and Kyunghyun Cho. 2018b. Unsupervised neural machine translation. In *ICLR*.

Artetxe, Mikel, Gorka Labaka, and Eneko Agirre. 2019. An effective approach to unsupervised machine translation. In *ACL*, pages 194–203.

Bahdanau, Dzmitry, Kyunghyun Cho, and Yoshua Bengio. 2015. Neural machine translation by jointly learning to align and translate. In *ICLR*.

Bojanowski, Piotr, Edouard Grave, Armand Joulin, and Tomas Mikolov. 2017. Enriching word vectors with subword information. *TACL*, 5:135–146.

Chu, Chenhui and Rui Wang. 2018. A survey of domain adaptation for neural machine translation. In *COLING*, pages 1304–1319.

Conneau, Alexis and Guillaume Lample. 2019. Cross-lingual language model pretraining. In *NeurIPS*, pages 7057–7067.

Conneau, Alexis, Guillaume Lample, Marc'Aurelio Ranzato, Ludovic Denoyer, and Hervé Jégou. 2018. Word translation without parallel data. In *ICLR*.

Currey, Anna and Kenneth Heafield. 2019. Zero-resource neural machine translation with monolingual pivot data. In *WNGT*, pages 99–107.

Dou, Qing, Ashish Vaswani, and Kevin Knight. 2014. Beyond parallel data: Joint word alignment and decipherment improves machine translation. In *EMNLP*, pages 557–565.

Firat, Orhan, Kyunghyun Cho, and Yoshua Bengio. 2016. Multi-way, multilingual neural machine translation with a shared attention mechanism. In *NAACL-HLT*, pages 866–875.

Graça, Miguel, Yunsu Kim, Julian Schamper, Jiahui Geng, and Hermann Ney. 2018. The RWTH aachen university English-German and German-English unsupervised neural machine translation systems for WMT 2018. In *WMT*.

Guzmán, Francisco, Peng-Jen Chen, Myle Ott, Juan Pino, Guillaume Lample, Philipp Koehn, Vishrav Chaudhary, and Marc'Aurelio Ranzato. 2019. The FLORES evaluation datasets for low-resource machine translation: Nepali–English and Sinhala–English. In *EMNLP-IJCNLP*, pages 6097–6110.

He, Di, Yingce Xia, Tao Qin, Liwei Wang, Nenghai Yu, Tie-Yan Liu, and Wei-Ying Ma. 2016. Dual learning for machine translation. In *NIPS*, pages 820–828.

Hill, Felix, Kyunghyun Cho, and Anna Korhonen. 2016. Learning distributed representations of sentences from unlabelled data. In *NAACL-HLT*, pages 1367–1377.

Hoang, Vu Cong Duy, Philipp Koehn, Gholamreza Haffari, and Trevor Cohn. 2018. Iterative back-translation for neural machine translation. In *WNGT*, pages 18–24.

Johnson, Melvin, Mike Schuster, Quoc V Le, Maxim Krikun, Yonghui Wu, Zhifeng Chen, Nikhil Thorat, Fernanda Viégas, Martin Wattenberg, Greg Corrado, et al. 2017. Google's multilingual neural machine translation system: Enabling zero-shot translation. *TACL*, 5(1):339–351.

Kim, Yunsu, Jiahui Geng, and Hermann Ney. 2018. Improving unsupervised word-by-word translation with language model and denoising autoencoder. In *EMNLP*, pages 862–868.

Kim, Yunsu, Yingbo Gao, and Hermann Ney. 2019a. Effective cross-lingual transfer of neural machine translation models without shared vocabularies. In *ACL*, pages 1246–1257.

Kim, Yunsu, Petre Petrov, Pavel Petrushkov, Shahram Khadivi, and Hermann Ney. 2019b. Pivot-based transfer learning for neural machine translation between non-English languages. In *EMNLP-IJCNLP*, pages 866–876.

Kingma, Diederik P and Jimmy Ba. 2014. Adam: A method for stochastic optimization.

Knight, Kevin, Anish Nair, Nishit Rathod, and Kenji Yamada. 2006. Unsupervised analysis for decipherment problems. In *COLING/ACL*, pages 499–506.

Kocmi, Tom and Ondřej Bojar. 2018. Trivial transfer learning for low-resource neural machine translation. In *WMT*, pages 244–252.

Koehn, Philipp and Rebecca Knowles. 2017. Six challenges for neural machine translation. In *WNMT*, pages 28–39.

Koehn, Philipp. 2005. Europarl: A parallel corpus for statistical machine translation. In *MT Summit*, pages 79–86.

Lample, Guillaume, Ludovic Denoyer, and Marc'Aurelio Ranzato. 2018a. Unsupervised machine translation using monolingual corpora only. In *ICLR*.

Lample, Guillaume, Myle Ott, Alexis Conneau, Ludovic Denoyer, and Marc'Aurelio Ranzato. 2018b. Phrase-based & neural unsupervised machine translation. In *EMNLP*, pages 5039–5049.

Mikolov, Tomas, Kai Chen, Greg Corrado, and Jeffrey Dean. 2013. Efficient estimation of word representations in vector space.

Naim, Iftekhar, Parker Riley, and Daniel Gildea. 2018. Feature-based decipherment for machine translation. *Computational Linguistics*, 44(3):525–546.

Nakashole, Ndapandula and Raphael Flauger. 2018. Characterizing departures from linearity in word translation. In *ACL*, pages 221–227.

Neubig, Graham and Junjie Hu. 2018. Rapid adaptation of neural machine translation to new languages. In *EMNLP*, pages 875–880.

Nuhn, Malte. 2019. *Unsupervised Training with Applications in Natural Language Processing*. Ph.D. thesis, Computer Science Department, RWTH Aachen University.

Olson, Matthew, Abraham Wyner, and Richard Berk. 2018. Modern neural networks generalize on small data sets. In *NIPS*, pages 3619–3628.

Pires, Telmo, Eva Schlinger, and Dan Garrette. 2019. How multilingual is multilingual bert? In *ACL*, pages 4996–5001.

Post, Matt. 2018. A call for clarity in reporting bleu scores. In *WMT*, pages 186–191.

Pourdamghani, Nima, Nada Aldarrab, Marjan Ghazvininejad, Kevin Knight, and Jonathan May. 2019. Translating translationese: A two-step approach to unsupervised machine translation. In *ACL*, pages 3057–3062.

Ravi, Sujith and Kevin Knight. 2011. Deciphering foreign language. In *ACL*, pages 12–21.

Ren, Shuo, Yu Wu, Shujie Liu, Ming Zhou, and Shuai Ma. 2019a. Explicit cross-lingual pre-training for unsupervised machine translation. In *EMNLP-IJCNLP*, pages 770–779.

Ren, Shuo, Zhirui Zhang, Shujie Liu, Ming Zhou, and Shuai Ma. 2019b. Unsupervised neural machine translation with smt as posterior regularization.

Resnik, Philip and Noah A. Smith. 2003. The web as a parallel corpus. *Computational Linguistics*, 29(3):349–380.

Riley, Parker and Daniel Gildea. 2018. Orthographic features for bilingual lexicon induction. In *ACL*, pages 390–394.

Schwenk, Holger. 2008. Investigations on large-scale lightly-supervised training for statistical machine translation. In *IWSLT*.

Sen, Sukanta, Kamal Kumar Gupta, Asif Ekbal, and Pushpak Bhattacharyya. 2019. Multilingual unsupervised NMT using shared encoder and language-specific decoders. In *ACL*, pages 3083–3089.

Sennrich, Rico and Biao Zhang. 2019. Revisiting low-resource neural machine translation: A case study. In *ACL*, pages 211–221.

Sennrich, Rico, Barry Haddow, and Alexandra Birch. 2016a. Improving neural machine translation models with monolingual data. In *ACL*, pages 86–96.

Sennrich, Rico, Barry Haddow, and Alexandra Birch. 2016b. Neural machine translation of rare words with subword units. In *ACL*, pages 1715–1725.

Søgaard, Anders, Sebastian Ruder, and Ivan Vulić. 2018. On the limitations of unsupervised bilingual dictionary induction. In *ACL*, pages 778–788.

Song, Kaitao, Xu Tan, Tao Qin, Jianfeng Lu, and Tie-Yan Liu. 2019. Mass: Masked sequence to sequence pre-training for language generation. In *ICML*, pages 5926–5936.

Srivastava, Nitish, Geoffrey Hinton, Alex Krizhevsky, Ilya Sutskever, and Ruslan Salakhutdinov. 2014. Dropout: a simple way to prevent neural networks from overfitting. *The journal of machine learning research*, 15(1):1929–1958.

Sun, Haipeng, Rui Wang, Kehai Chen, Masao Utiyama, Eiichiro Sumita, and Tiejun Zhao. 2019. Unsupervised bilingual word embedding agreement for unsupervised neural machine translation. In *ACL*, pages 1235–1245.

Vaswani, Ashish, Noam Shazeer, Niki Parmar, Jakob Uszkoreit, Llion Jones, Aidan N Gomez, Łukasz Kaiser, and Illia Polosukhin. 2017. Attention is all you need. In *NIPS*, pages 5998–6008.

Yang, Zhen, Wei Chen, Feng Wang, and Bo Xu. 2018. Unsupervised neural machine translation with weight sharing. In *ACL*, pages 46–55.

Incorporating External Annotation to improve Named Entity Translation in NMT

Maciej Modrzejewski **Thanh-Le Ha** **Alexander Waibel**
Institute for Anthropomatics and Robotics
KIT - Karlsruhe Institute of Technology, Germany
`maciej.modrzejewski@student.kit.edu`
`firstname.lastname@kit.edu`

Miriam Exel **Bianka Buschbeck**
SAP SE, Walldorf, Germany
`firstname.lastname@sap.com`

Abstract

The correct translation of named entities (NEs) still poses a challenge for conventional neural machine translation (NMT) systems. This study explores methods incorporating named entity recognition (NER) into NMT with the aim to improve named entity translation. It proposes an annotation method that integrates named entities and inside–outside–beginning (IOB) tagging into the neural network input with the use of source factors. Our experiments on English→German and English→ Chinese show that just by including different NE classes and IOB tagging, we can increase the BLEU score by around 1 point using the standard test set from WMT2019 and achieve up to 12% increase in NE translation rates over a strong baseline.

1 Introduction

The translation of named entities (NE) is challenging because new phrases appear on a daily basis and many named entities are domain specific, not to be found in bilingual dictionaries. Improving named entity translation is important to translation systems and cross-language information retrieval applications (Jiang et al., 2007). Conventional neural machine translation (NMT) systems are expected to translate NEs by learning complex linguistic aspects and ambiguous terms from the training corpus only. When faced with named entities, they are found to be occasionally distorting location, organization or person names and even sometimes ignoring low-frequency proper names altogether (Koehn and Knowles, 2017).

This paper explores methods incorporating named entity recognition (NER) into NMT with the aim to improve NE translation. NER systems are often adopted as an early annotation step in many Natural Language Processing (NLP) pipelines for applications such as question answering and information retrieval. This work explores an annotation method that integrates named entities and inside–outside–beginning (IOB) (Ramshaw and Marcus, 1999) tagging into the neural network input with the use of source factors. In our experiments, we focus on three NE classes: organization, location and person, and use the state-of-the-art encoder-decoder Transformer network. We also investigate how the granularity of NE class labels influences NE translation quality and conclude that specific labels contribute to the NE translation improvement. Further, we execute an extensive evaluation of the MT output assessing the influence of our annotation method on NE translation. Our experiments on English→German and English→Chinese show that by just including different NE classes and IOB tagging, we can increase the BLEU score by around 1 point using the standard test set from WMT2019 and achieve up to 12% increase in NE translation rates over a strong baseline.

2 Related Work

Several research groups propose translating named entities prior to the translation of the whole sentence by an external named entity translation model. Li et al., (2018a); Yan et al., (2018); Wang et al., (2017) follow the "tag-replace" training method using an external character-level

Martins, Moniz, Fumega, Martins, Batista, Cohéur, Parra, Trancoso, Turchi, Bisazza, Moorkens, Guerberof, Nurminen, Marg, Forcada (eds.)
Proceedings of the 22nd Annual Conference of the European Association for Machine Translation, p. 45–51
Lisboa, Portugal, November 2020.

En	BPE only	Belfast - Gi@@ ants won thanks to Patri@@ ck D@@ w@@ yer
En	fine-grained	Belfast$_2$ -$_0$ Gi@@$_3$ ants$_3$ won$_0$ thanks$_0$ to$_0$ Patri@@$_1$ ck$_1$ D@@$_1$ w@@$_1$ yer$_1$
En	coarse-grained	Belfast$_1$ -$_0$ Gi@@$_1$ ants$_1$ won$_0$ thanks$_0$ to$_0$ Patri@@$_1$ ck$_1$ D@@$_1$ w@@$_1$ yer$_1$
En	IOB tagging	Belfast$_B$ -$_O$ Gi@@$_B$ ants$_I$ won$_O$ thanks$_O$ to$_O$ Patri@@$_B$ ck$_I$ D@@$_I$ w@@$_I$ yer$_I$
En	Inline Ann.	<LOC> Belfast </LOC> - <ORG> Gi@@ ants </ORG> won thanks to <PER>
	(fine-grained)	Patri@@ ck D@@ w@@ yer </PER>

Table 1: Different annotation configurations; i. fine-grained: (0) for a regular *sub-word* (default), (1) for NE class *Person*, (2) for NE class *Location*, (3) for NE class *Organization* ii. coarse-grained: (0) default, (1) to denote a NE

sequence-to-sequence model to translate named entities. Li et al. (2018b) explore inserting inline annotations into the data providing information about named entity features. Such annotations are inserted into the source sentence in form of XML tags, consisting of XML boundary tags and NE class labels.

Recently, researchers have shown the benefit of explicitly encoding linguistic features, in form of source factors, into NMT (Sennrich and Haddow, 2016; García-Martínez et al., 2016). Dinu et al. (2019) use source factors successfully to enforce terminology. The work of Ugawa et al. (2018) is similar to ours, in the way that they also incorporate NE tags with the use of source factors into the NMT model to improve named entity translation. They, however, introduce a chunk-level long short-term memory (LSTM) (Hochreiter and Schmidhuber, 1997) layer over a word-level LSTM layer into the encoder to better handle compound named entities. Furthermore, they use a different network architecture (LSTM), and apply a different annotation technique (IO tagging) than we explore (IOB tagging). Finally, the work at hand provides an extensive evaluation of NE quality translation (Section 5.2), including a human assessment (Section 5.3).

3 NMT with NE tagging

We explore incorporating NE information as additional parallel streams (source factors) to signal NE occurrence in the fashion described in Sennrich and Haddow (2016). Source factors provide additional word-level information, are applied to the source language only, and take form of supplementary embeddings that are either added or concatenated to the word embeddings. This is illustrated with the following formula:

$$E \cdot x = \bigoplus_{f \in F} E_f \cdot x_{if} \qquad (1)$$

where $\bigoplus \in \{\sum, \|\}$, $(\cdot)$ denotes a matrix-vector multiplication, E_f is a feature embedding matrix,

x_i is the i-th word from the source sentence, and F is a finite, arbitrary set of word features. While we use a state-of-the-art encoder-decoder Transformer network, our approach does not modify the standard NMT model architecture, thus can be applied to any sequence-to-sequence NMT model.

Further, we also explore whether the NE class granularity may influence translation quality and help decrease word ambiguity. For this purpose, we define a "fine-grained" case, where we use specific NE class labels (e.g. person, location, organization) and also a "coarse-grained" case, where we use two different source factor values only: (0) as default and (1) to denote a named entity in a generic manner. Additionally, we investigate whether inside–outside–beginning (IOB) tagging (Ramshaw and Marcus, 1999) used to signalize where a NE begins and ends as a second input feature may guide models to translate compound named entities better. In IOB tagging, (B) indicates the beginning, (I) the inside and (O) the outside of a NE (a regular word or a sequence of words).

We annotate source sentences with an external NER system. Examples for the different annotation strategies (that we experiment with) are presented in Table 1. Each sub-word is assigned an index denoting its corresponding source factor value.

As our goal resembles that of Li et al. (2018b), we compare our approach against their inline annotation method with XML boundary tags. Li et al. (2018b) use specific NE class labels, which correspond to the "fine-grained" case in our work. We refer to their approach as "Inline Ann. (fine-grained)" and present this annotation method in Table 1.

4 Experiments

4.1 Parallel data & pre-processing

We train NMT systems for English→German and English→Chinese on data of the WMT2019 news

	En→De	En→Zh
No. of sentences	2,146,644	2,128,234
No. of sentences with NE	1,082,873	1,153,545
Percentage	≈ 50.44%	≈ 53.95%
ORG labels	983,558 (53%)	1,325,462 (57%)
PER labels	223,309 (12%)	211,892 (9%)
LOC labels	639,304 (35%)	796,269 (34%)

Table 2: Occurrences of NE annotations in the training datasets

Label type	Variant	IOB	En→De	En→Zh
fine-grained	sum	no	**33.61**	26.29
fine-grained	concat 8	yes	33.11	**26.45**
fine-grained	sum	yes	33.07	26.26
coarse-grained	concat 8	yes	32.90	26.08
coarse-grained	sum	yes	32.70	26.34
Baseline		no	32.60	26.29
Inline Ann. (fine-grained)		no	32.50	26.05

Table 3: BLEU scores on *newstest2019* (WMT2019)

translation task.[1] For English→German we use the data from Europarl v9 and news commentary data v14. For English→Chinese the models are trained on news commentary v14 and UN Parallel Corpus v1.0. The latter dataset is shortened to match the size of the training dataset for English→German by using the newest data from the end of the corpus for training, see also Table 2.

As NE Recognition is an active research field and the search for best recognition methods continues, the quality of NER systems may vary under different research scenarios and domains (Goyal et al., 2018). Incorrect NE annotation in the data may influence the results of this work negatively. Therefore, we focus on three well-researched NE classes: *Person*, *Location* and *Organization*, limiting, thus, the possibility of incorrect annotation.

We use spaCy Named Entity Recognition (NER) system[2] to recognize named entities in the source sentences. The ratio of sentences in the training data with at least one named entity occurrence (based on three NE classes) in the source sentence amounts to 50.44% for En–De and 53.95% for En–Zh. Table 2 presents the details.

We tokenize the English and German corpora using the spaCy Tokenizer[3], and use the OpenNMT Tokenizer[4] (mode aggressive) on the Chinese side. Further, we perform a joint source and target Byte-Pair encoding (BPE) (Sennrich et al., 2016) for English→German and disjoint for English→Chinese, both with 32,000 merge operations. For every source sentence in the training data (after applying BPE), we generate two files with source factors: i. marking named entities (either the coarse-grained or the fine-grained case), ii. marking IOB tagging. The baseline model is trained with no external annotation.

4.2 NMT architecture

We use the Sockeye machine translation framework (Hieber et al., 2017) for our experiments and train our models with a Transformer network (Base) (Vaswani et al., 2017) with 6 encoding and 6 decoding layers all with 2048 hidden units. We use word embeddings of size 512, dropout probability for multi-head attention of size 0.1, batch size of 4096 tokens, a maximum sequence length of 100 and source factor embedding of size 8 for the concatenation case. Each model is trained on 1 GPU Tesla T4. Training finishes if there is no improvement for 32 consecutive checkpoints on the validation data *newstest2018* (validation data from the WMT2019 news translation task).

5 Results

5.1 General translation quality

We perform the evaluation on the standard test dataset *newstest2019* from the WMT2019 news translation task. It has identical content for En–De and En–Zh and contains 1997 sentences, in which 63.95% of the sentences on the English side contain at least one named entity. There are 2681 named entity occurrences; 908 belong to the label *Location* (34% of all NEs), 870 to the label *Person* (32%) and 903 to the label *Organization* (34%); annotated with spaCy NER. Each sentence with named entity occurrence contains, on average, approx. 2 NEs. To assess the general translation quality, we calculate the BLEU score using the evaluation script *multi-bleu-detok.perl* from Moses (Koehn et al., 2007). We detokenize the MT output with *detokenizer.perl* (Koehn et al., 2007) for En–De and use OpenNMT *detokenize* function to do the same for En–Zh.

Table 3 displays the results. Column "Label type" denotes whether specific ("fine-grained") or generic ("coarse-grained") NE labels are used; column "Variant" describes whether source factors are added ("sum") or concatenated ("concat") to

---

[1]http://www.statmt.org/wmt19/translation-task.html
[2]https://spacy.io/usage/linguistic-features\#named-entities
[3]https://spaCy.io/api/tokenizer
[4]https://github.com/OpenNMT/Tokenizer

En→De						
Label type	Variant	IOB	LOC	PER	ORG	Total
fine-grained	sum	no	73.68	70.11	61.79	69.89
fine-grained	concat 8	yes	72.87	**71.96**	63.41	70.67
fine-grained	sum	yes	**75.71**	70.85	**69.11**	**72.39**
coarse-grained	concat 8	yes	74.09	71.22	62.60	70.67
coarse-grained	sum	yes	75.30	71.22	65.04	71.61
Baseline		no	74.09	71.59	60.16	70.36
Inline Ann. (fine-grained)		no	70.45	67.16	61.79	67.39

Table 4: Results of the automatic in-depth analysis on *random300* dataset for En–De with spaCy NER, *NE match rate* in %

En→Zh						
Label type	Variant	IOB	LOC	PER	ORG	Total
fine-grained	sum	no	**41.67**	20.07	31.62	24.41
fine-grained	concat 8	yes	33.33	**23.36**	36.76	**27.96**
fine-grained	sum	yes	**41.67**	20.44	33.09	25.12
coarse-grained	concat 8	yes	33.33	22.63	33.09	26.30
coarse-grained	sum	yes	33.33	21.90	**38.97**	27.73
Baseline		no	33.33	18.98	35.29	24.64
Inline Ann. (fine-grained)		no	33.33	19.71	34.56	24.88

Table 5: Results of the automatic in-depth analysis on *random300* dataset for for En–Zh with Stanford NER, *NE match rate* in %

the word embeddings; column "IOB" describes whether IOB tagging is used as a second source factor stream.

Almost all models annotated with source factors show improvements w.r.t BLEU in comparison to the baseline; with one En–Zh model being insignificantly worse. Overall, the fine-grained model with source factors added and no use of IOB tagging seems to perform best and achieves around one BLEU point more than the baseline (for En–De). As the BLEU score only assesses the quality of NE translation indirectly, we do not deem it to be a reliable evaluation metric to assess the NE translation quality. As named entities affect only a small part of a sentence, we do not expect high BLEU variations and continue with the in-depth named entity analysis in the next section.

5.2 Automatic hit/miss NE evaluation

In this section we execute an automatic in-depth analysis of NE translation quality with spaCy (German models) and Stanford NER (Finkel et al., 2005) (Chinese models). For this purpose, we randomly select 100 sentences from *newstest2019* containing at least one named entity for each of the three classes (PER, LOC, ORG) on the English side of the corpus, in total 300 sentences. We refer to this dataset in later part of this work as *random300*. We annotate the reference sentence with an external NER system (spaCy or Stanford NER) to find named entities and compare if they appear in the hypothesis in the same form (string-based). If yes, we define this case as a "hit", otherwise as a "miss" and calculate the result according to the *NE match rate* formula: $\frac{hit}{hit+miss}$. Table 4 and Table 5 display the results. Column "Total" calculates the accumulated *NE match rate* for three named entity classes.

At first glance, we see that the result values for En–De are significantly higher than for En–

Zh. We attribute this to the transliteration issues which emerge while translating from English to Chinese and, thus, occurring mismatch between the reference and hypothesis translation. In general, the baseline models show high performance as a certain amount of NEs has already been seen by the network in the training data. Furthermore, we observe improvements in named entity translation for En–De and En–Zh among almost all classes, showing that augmenting source sentences with NE information leads to their improved translation. There is, however, no consistent improvement in the models not using IOB tagging annotation. Their total *NE match rate* values are lower than that one of the baseline models. As such, IOB tagging, indicating compound named entities, proves to be an important piece of information for the NMT systems. Further, augmenting the model with exact NE class labels (fine-grained case) seems to achieve higher *NE match rates* in comparison to the coarse-grained case. Additionally, coarse-grained models perform better than the baseline. This finding indicates that the mere information that a word is a NE proves to be useful to the NMT system even if the class is not clearly specified. Inline Annotation does not deliver promising results, contrary to the findings of Li et al. (2018b), with the total *NE match rate* below that one of the baseline system (En–De) or insignificantly above (En–Zh).

Validation of the *NE match rates* After having executed the automatic in-depth analysis with spaCy NER, we wish to validate the results of the En–De models with a second state-of-the-art NER system: Stanford NER. The analysis is conducted in an identical way as earlier and only the En–De models are analyzed. At the point of writing this paper, spaCy does not provide a Chinese model. Table 6 presents the results. Column "Total" cal-

En→De						
Label type	Variant	IOB	LOC	PER	ORG	Total
fine-grained	sum	no	76.25	76.14	60.00	73.70
fine-grained	concat 8	yes	75.62	77.16	64.62	74.88
fine-grained	sum	yes	**80.00**	**78.68**	**69.23**	**76.78**
coarse-grained	concat 8	yes	75.62	77.66	67.69	75.36
coarse-grained	sum	yes	77.50	76.65	**69.23**	76.48
Baseline		no	78.75	76.65	60.00	74.64
Inline Ann. (fine-grained)		no	73.75	74.11	60.00	71.80

Table 6: Results of the automatic in-depth analysis on *random300* dataset for En–De with Stanford NER, *NE match rate* in %

En→De						
Label type	Variant	IOB	LOC	PER	ORG	Total
fine-grained	sum	yes	93.02	83.52	78.01	85.17
Baseline		no	89.77	82.05	70.92	82.14
En→Zh						
fine-grained	concat 8	yes	73.85	67.04	64.27	68.05
Baseline		no	71.43	61.90	57.35	63.24

Table 7: Results of the human in-depth evaluation on *random300* dataset, *NE match rate* in %

culates the accumulated *NE match rate* for three named entity classes.

First, we observe that the overall *NE match rates* are higher than in Table 4. We attribute this phenomenon to the fact that Stanford NER recognizes a different set of NEs in the reference sentences than spaCy does. This, however, is not problematic as we are interested in the variations in *NE match rates* between the models. In general, there are no differences in the results of the automatic in-depth analysis, regardless whether spaCy or Stanford is used to conduct it. All models trained with IOB tags translate NEs more accurately than the baseline model does. Again, fine-grained model trained with IOB tags and source factors added to the word embeddings achieves the highest *NE match rate*. The model trained without IOB tags has a lower *NE match rate* than the baseline re-confirming thus the usefulness of the IOB tags.

5.3 Human hit/miss NE evaluation

As NER systems are prone to delivering inaccurate results,[5] we also perform a human evaluation. It consists in recognizing NEs in the reference translation, comparing them to the corresponding NE translation in the MT output and calculating the *NE match rate* on the *random300* dataset. We compare the baseline and the best model (highest total *NE match rate* in Tables 4 and 5) for En–De and En–Zh and refer to them as *annotated* models. If a NE is in a different form in the hypothesis than the reference proposes or a NE is transliterated into or from Chinese, but its form is still grammatically and semantically correct, its occurrence is counted as correct. Human evaluation is executed by one native speaker for each language pair. Table 7

presents the results of the human hit/miss evaluation. Column "Total" calculates the accumulated *NE match rate* for three named entity classes.

The *NE match rate* for human hit/miss evaluation is higher than for its automatic counterpart. This is due to the fact that all false positives in the reference and false negatives in the hypothesis are eliminated. Most importantly, we can state that the *annotated* models perform consistently better than the baseline and, in fact, the incorporation of external annotation in form of source factors into the source sentence leads to an improvement in NE translation. There is an increase of 3.67% in the total *NE match rate* value for En–De and 7.61% for En–Zh. Furthermore, we observe the greatest *NE match rate* improvement when translating organizations' names (+9.99% for En–De, and +12.07% for En–Zh).

5.4 Accuracy of spaCy NER

While executing the human hit/miss NE evaluation, we also annotated false positives and false negatives in the reference, executing, thus, a quality check of spaCy NER on data from the news domain (on *random300* dataset, German model only). Precision value is 84.43% and recall amounts to 85.93%. The above observation leads to the conclusion that incorrect NE annotation may occur relatively frequently in the training data. We hypothesize that NE annotation with source factors may lead to better results if the training data is fully correctly annotated.

5.5 Discussion

In this section we discuss our observations based on the human evaluation and provide translation examples. The use of source factors seems to alleviate the problem of ignoring low-frequency proper names as the *annotated* models appear to consistently react to NE occurrence by producing a translation. The baseline, however, may ignore more complex NEs, producing, thus, under-

<hr>

[5]spaCy's German model has 83% F1-Score (https://spaCy.io/models/de) with a warning that it may "perform inconsistently on many genres", the same holds for Stanford NER: https://nlp.stanford.edu/projects/project-ner.shtml.

Source	Palin, 29, of Wasilla, Alaska, was arrested (...) according to a report released Saturday by **Alaska State Troopers**.
Reference	Palin, 29, aus Wasilla, Alaska, wurde (...) verhaftet. Gegen ihn liegt bereits ein Bericht (...), so eine Meldung, die am Samstag von den **Alaska State Troopers** veröffentlicht wurde.
Annotated	Palin, 29 von Wasilla, Alaska, wurde (...) verhaftet (...), wie ein am Samstag von **Alaska State Troopers** veröffentlichter Bericht besagt.
Baseline	Laut einem Bericht von **Alaska**, der Samstag veröffentlicht wurde, wurde Palin, 29 von Wasilla, Alaska, (...) verhaftet (...).
Source	Saipov, 30, allegedly used a **Home Depot** rental truck (...).
Reference	Saipov, 30, hat (...) angeblich einen Leihwagen von **Home Depot** (...) benutzt (...).
Annotated	Saipov, 30, soll einen Mietwagen aus dem **Home Depot** benutzt haben (...).
Baseline	Saipov, 30, soll einen **Home Department Depot** Rental benutzt haben (...).
Source	The pair's business had been likened to **Gwyneth Paltrow's Goop** brand.
Reference	Das Geschäft der beiden war mit der Marke **Goop** von **Gwyneth Paltrow** verglichen worden.
Annotated	Das Geschäft des Paares wurde mit der Marke **Gop** von **Gwyneth Paltrow** verglichen.
Baseline	Das Geschäft des Paares wurde mit der Marke von **Gwyneth Palop** verglichen.
Source	The **Giants** got an early two-goal lead through strikes from Patrick Dwyer and **Francis** Beauvillier.
Reference	Die **Giants** hatten durch Treffer von Patrick Dwyer und **Francis** Beauvillier eine frühe Zwei-Tore-Führung.
Annotated	Die **Giganten** bekamen durch die Streiks von Patrick Dwyer und **Franziskus** Beauvillier ein frühes Ziel.
Baseline	Die **Giganten** erhielten durch die Streiks von Patrick Dwyer und **Francis** Beauvillier ein frühes Ziel.

Table 8: Translation examples: Comparison of the *annotated* model and baseline for En–De

translation as in the *Alaska State Troopers* example in Table 8. Furthermore, source factors seem to guide the *annotated* models better (in comparison to the baseline) to prevent over-translation, as shown in the *Home Depot* example or miss-translation (*Gwyneth Paltrow's Goop*), both examples are in Table 8.

On the other hand, a frequent cause of errors in the *annotated* models stems from the fact that organizations' or persons' names are translated verbatim instead of being kept in their original forms, as in the *Francis/Franziskus* and *Giants/Giganten* example in Table 8. This problem concerns both the *annotated* model and the baseline. This behavior may not be desirable for persons' names, yet for organizations' names the desired output is dependent on the context and translation language pairs.

6 Conclusion

Our work focused on establishing if annotating named entities with the use of source factors leads to their more accurate translation. We can state that the general translation quality with the *annotated* models improves (improvements in BLEU score). Additionally, in-depth automatic and human named entity evaluation prove that the same holds true for NE translation.

The accuracy of named entity annotation plays a crucial role during the annotation of named entities in the training data as well as during evaluation (automatic hit/miss analysis). By establishing spaCy's F1-Score on *random300* during the human hit/miss analysis to amount to approx. 85%, we conclude that the accuracy of any NER system greatly influences the practicability of our approach. Therefore, the improvement of named entity translation is closely related to the improvement of NER systems.

Acknowledgements

We would like to thank Zihan Chen for her help with the human evaluation of the En–Zh translation.

References

Dinu, Georgiana, Prashant Mathur, Marcello Federico, and Yaser Al-Onaizan. 2019. Training neural machine translation to apply terminology constraints. In *Proceedings of the 57th Annual Meeting of the Association for Computational Linguistics*, pages 3063–3068.

Finkel, Jenny Rose, Trond Grenager, and Christopher Manning. 2005. Incorporating non-local information into information extraction systems by gibbs sampling. In *Proceedings of the 43rd annual meeting on Association for Computational Linguistics*, pages 363–370. Association for Computational Linguistics.

García-Martínez, Mercedes, Loïc Barrault, and Fethi Bougares. 2016. Factored neural machine translation. *arXiv preprint arXiv:1609.04621*.

Goyal, Archana, Vishal Gupta, and Manish Kumar. 2018. Recent named entity recognition and classification techniques: a systematic review. *Computer Science Review*, 29:21–43.

Hieber, Felix, Tobias Domhan, Michael Denkowski, David Vilar, Artem Sokolov, Ann Clifton, and Matt Post. 2017. Sockeye: A toolkit for neural machine translation. *arXiv preprint arXiv:1712.05690*.

Hochreiter, Sepp and Jürgen Schmidhuber. 1997. LSTM can solve hard long time lag problems. In *Advances in neural information processing systems*, pages 473–479.

Jiang, Long, Ming Zhou, Lee-Feng Chien, and Cheng Niu. 2007. Named entity translation with web mining and transliteration. In *Proceedings of the 20th international joint conference on Artifical Intelligence*, pages 1629–1634.

Koehn, Philipp and Rebecca Knowles. 2017. Six challenges for neural machine translation. In *Proceedings of the First Workshop on Neural Machine Translation*, pages 28–39.

Koehn, Philipp, Hieu Hoang, Alexandra Birch, Chris Callison-Burch, Marcello Federico, Nicola Bertoldi, Brooke Cowan, Wade Shen, Christine Moran, Richard Zens, et al. 2007. Moses: Open source toolkit for statistical machine translation. In *Proceedings of the 45th annual meeting of the Association for Computational Linguistics companion volume proceedings of the demo and poster sessions*, pages 177–180.

Li, Xiaoqing, Jinghui Yan, Jiajun Zhang, and Chengqing Zong. 2018a. Neural name translation improves neural machine translation. In *China Workshop on Machine Translation*, pages 93–100. Springer.

Li, Zhongwei, Xuancong Wang, Aiti Aw, Eng Siong Chng, and Haizhou Li. 2018b. Named-entity tagging and domain adaptation for better customized translation. In *Proceedings of the Seventh Named Entities Workshop*, pages 41–46.

Ramshaw, Lance A and Mitchell P Marcus. 1999. Text chunking using transformation-based learning. In *Natural language processing using very large corpora*, pages 157–176. Springer.

Sennrich, Rico and Barry Haddow. 2016. Linguistic input features improve neural machine translation. In *Proceedings of the First Conference on Machine Translation: Volume 1, Research Papers*, pages 83–91.

Sennrich, Rico, Barry Haddow, and Alexandra Birch. 2016. Neural machine translation of rare words with subword units. In *Proceedings of the 54th Annual Meeting of the Association for Computational Linguistics (Volume 1: Long Papers)*, pages 1715–1725.

Ugawa, Arata, Akihiro Tamura, Takashi Ninomiya, Hiroya Takamura, and Manabu Okumura. 2018. Neural machine translation incorporating named entity. In *Proceedings of the 27th International Conference on Computational Linguistics*, pages 3240–3250.

Vaswani, Ashish, Noam Shazeer, Niki Parmar, Jakob Uszkoreit, Llion Jones, Aidan N Gomez, Łukasz Kaiser, and Illia Polosukhin. 2017. Attention is all you need. In *Advances in neural information processing systems*, pages 5998–6008.

Wang, Yuguang, Shanbo Cheng, Liyang Jiang, Jiajun Yang, Wei Chen, Muze Li, Lin Shi, Yanfeng Wang, and Hongtao Yang. 2017. Sogou neural machine translation systems for wmt17. In *Proceedings of the Second Conference on Machine Translation*, pages 410–415.

Yan, Jinghui, Jiajun Zhang, JinAn Xu, and Chengqing Zong. 2018. The impact of named entity translation for neural machine translation. In *China Workshop on Machine Translation*, pages 63–73. Springer.

Unified Humor Detection Based on Sentence-pair Augmentation and Transfer Learning

Minghan Wang[1], Hao Yang[1], Ying Qin[1], Shiliang Sun[2], Yao Deng[1]
Huawei Translation Service Center, Beijing, China
East China Normal University, Shanghai, China
{wangminghan, yanghao30, qinying, dengyao3}@huawei.com
slsun@cs.ecnu.edu.cn

Abstract

We propose a unified multilingual model for humor detection which can be trained under a transfer learning framework. 1) The model is built based on pre-trained multilingual BERT, thereby is able to make predictions on Chinese, Russian and Spanish corpora. 2) We step out from single sentence classification and propose sequence-pair prediction which considers the inter-sentence relationship. 3) We propose the Sentence Discrepancy Prediction (SDP) loss, aiming to measure the semantic discrepancy of the sequence-pair, which often appears in the setup and punchline of a joke. Our method achieves two SoTA and a second-place on three humor detection corpora in three languages (Russian, Spanish and Chinese), and also improves F1-score by 4%-6%, which demonstrates its effectiveness in multilingual humor detection tasks.

1 Introduction

Machine learning has been adopted in computational linguistic for understanding natural languages for several decades. With the development of representation learning, rich semantics can be encoded into the dense vectors named as embedding, which significantly improves the ability of algorithms in understanding fine-grained emotions, for example, judging whether a sentence is humorous, often formulated as a binary classification problem. There can be many applications of humor detection such as language understanding in

Figure 1: An example from HAHA corpus shows that the semantic discrepancy exists in a joke, where the **urinated stones** is a disease in the left picture and is an action in the right image, originated from the second and the third sentence in the joke:
"-Doctor, my kidney hurts a lot
*-Have you **urinated stones**?*
*-Yes doctor, I **urinated stones**, cars, trees, posts ..."*

dialogue system and sentiment classification in social network platforms. In this paper, we focus on humor detection based on deep learning methods.

Many algorithms has been used to solve these problems such as conventional machine learning algorithms like TF-IDF representation with SVM classifier, or deep learning based like BERT (Devlin et al., 2019). However, most of these algorithms are typically designed for universal tasks but ignoring the difference (e.g. the paragraph structure and semantic features) between humor detection and other document classification tasks.

From a linguistic perspective, there are two critical features that often appear in jokes, which inspire us to model them explicitly and make specific optimization for the task:

- Good setup and a punchline is the core of many jokes. The setup can be considered as the background of a story, and the punchline is the surprise or the exception that is commonly contradict to intuition, which is the trigger to make the reader laugh. The punchline often appears at the ends of the joke, should be short enough, and often has signif-

Martins, Moniz, Fumega, Martins, Batista, Coheur, Parra, Trancoso, Turchi, Bisazza, Moorkens, Guerberof, Nurminen, Marg, Forcada (eds.)
Proceedings of the 22nd Annual Conference of the European Association for Machine Translation, p. 53–59
Lisboa, Portugal, November 2020.

icant semantic discrepancy to the setup. The discrepancy could be a turning or a reinforcement. For example, *"One of the most wonderful things in life is to wake up and enjoy a cuddle with somebody; unless you are in prison."* or *"A wife is like a hand grenade. Take off the ring and say good bye to your house."*, another example is shown in Figure. 1. Therefore, we may try to decompose the joke to model the setup and the punchline separately.

- The topic of the joke determines whether it is funny for most of the people. Social events, politics and daily life are mostly used as materials to write a joke, which means there are usually commonsense in the joke and requires prior knowledge to understand the conflict in the punchline. Because jokes are often very short, where items, roles and activities must be widely understood by readers. Therefore, a pre-trained language model is fairly appropriate for this task as it could provide better language representation learned from large corpus.

By reviewing features of jokes, we can start our study by making two assumptions. 1) Most of jokes have punchline, and can be appropriately modeled. 2) Most of punchlines have semantic discrepancies with setup, and can be considered as a factor in the determination of humorous.

Therefore, we propose a method for humor detection which can be described as three stages. **1)** Data augmentation with paragraph decomposition. **2)** Fine-tuning BERT on the task specific labels with the help of Sentence Discrepancy Prediction (SDP). **3)** Making predictions based on decomposed paragraphs. The contribution of our work can be summarized as following:

- We propose a data augmentation method named paragraph decomposition which is specifically appropriate for humor detection tasks.

- We propose a method to explicitly detect the semantic discrepancy in sentence pairs, named SDP.

- The proposed method is evaluated on three languages, which demonstrate its effectiveness in multilingual scenarios.

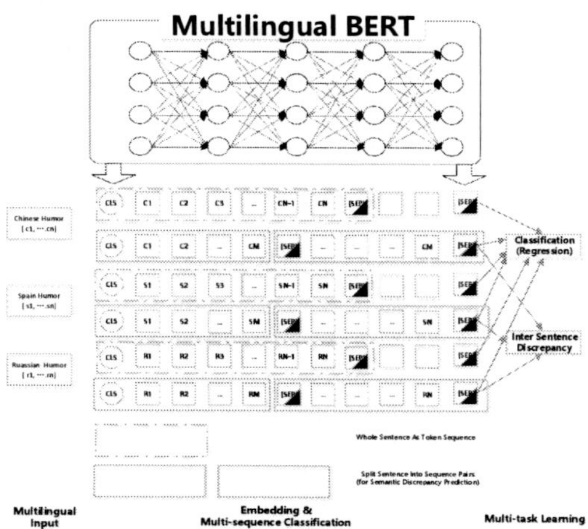

Figure 2: The architecture of our model, where two types of inputs are from three languages. The first type is normal sequence without being decomposed, and is only optimized by a classification/regression loss. The second type is decomposed sequence with additional inter sentence discrepancy loss as well as the classification/regression loss. All forms of inputs are encoded with a unified model based on the multilingual BERT.

2 Related Work

In recent years, many studies on humor detection have been published. Some researchers focuses on employing state-of-the-art studies like BERT (Devlin et al., 2019) to make better predictions, others attempts to improve simple networks like LSTM (Hochreiter and Schmidhuber, 1996) and CNN (Krizhevsky et al., 2012) or even conventional machine learning algorithms to compete with deep neural networks. At the same time, researchers have made available several high-quality datasets in different languages which significant help investigations on this area.

(Weller and Seppi, 2019) propose a BERT based humor detection model, fine-tuned on corpus collected from Reddit, Short Jokes and Pun of the Day (Yang et al., 2015), which achieves significant improvement on the performance comparing with many CNN based models.

(Chiruzzo et al., 2019) summaries a series of works from teams who build models and conduct experiments on HAHA dataset in the IberLEF 2019. (Ismailov, 2019) propose the method based on a pre-trained multilingual BERT, and further pre-train it on the domain dataset. Finally, the model is fine-tuned with task specific labels. Apart from that, they combine the prediction of Naive Bayes with TF-IDF and NN outputs with logistic regression to produce the final prediction, which achieves the best result in the HAHA 2019 challenge. Other teams also follows the framework by combining deep pre-trained models with conventional algorithms to acquire competitive predictions.

(Blinov et al., 2019; Chiruzzo et al., 2019; Yang et al., 2015) release large corpus in different languages like Russian and Spanish, which give chances for researchers to build and evaluate their models on more diverse datasets. At the same time, they evaluate their datasets with proposed models and make detailed analysis which successfully demonstrates the good quality of the corpus.

By reviewing previous works and analyzing their results, we choose to follow a similar pipeline to start our work based on the pre-trained multilingual BERT and evaluate our method on three datasets in different languages aiming to investigate whether the feature of punchline exists in jokes from different cultures and can be detected with the model.

3 Approach

In this section, we introduce details of our method in the three stages which is shown in Figure 2, and we also discuss the advantages of our method comparing with others.

3.1 Paragraph Decomposition

We have briefly introduced the feature of a joke in the introduction section and pointed out the importance of the punchline. However, there is no publicly available large dataset with exact labeled location of the punchline sentence, which stops us from decomposing the joke into the setup and the punchline directly. Therefore, we apply two ways to decompose a joke into a sentence pair.

- **Decomposing from the middle.** The first method is the simplest way, which inserts a [SEP] token in the middle of the paragraph without considering real punctuations of the paragraph. We use **PD$_M$** to represent such method.

- **Decomposing from the last sentence.** The second way is to insert the [SEP] before the last sentence of the paragraph. We use **PD$_L$** to represent such method.

The major purpose of decomposing paragraphs into segment pairs is to convert the problem of a single document classification problem to paragraph pair classification. Two benefits can be achieved. 1) Tasks which heavily depend on understanding the semantic relationship between consecutive segments can be benefit from PD, such as natural language inference and humor detection. 2) From the experiment, we find that treating a long sequence (e.g. more than 300 tokens) as a single paragraph (without [SEP] in the middle) will dramatically drop the performance of BERT in a humor classification task; however, by adding [SEP] at the appropriate position, the performance can be optimized. We assume that in the pre-training of Next Sentence Prediction (NSP) in BERT, the [SEP] could affect the self-attention to attend tokens in the pre-/post-segment separately, which somewhat decreases the context length.

3.2 Sentence Discrepancy Prediction

As already stated, the punchline of a joke often has semantic discrepancy to the setup. Therefore, we explicitly model it by using original classification label as the SDP label, which means paragraphs labeled as humours (positive sample marked as 1) are considered to have a setup and a punchline with large semantic discrepancy. On the other hand, a negative sample (marked as -1) is considered to have no setup and punchline thus has no discrepancy between any sentences or sub-sentences inside the paragraph.

Specifically, we define $v_{i,\text{cls}}$ and $v_{i,\text{sep}}$ as the representation of the sentence pair from joke i, which can be obtained with the representation of [CLS] at the beginning and the [SEP] of the decomposed position, respectively.

Then, we choose to use the **cosine** as the scoring function to measure the semantic similarity of v_{cls} and v_{sep}. denoted as:

$$s_i = \cos(g(v_{i,\text{cls}}), g(v_{i,\text{sep}})), \qquad (1)$$

where g is a linear transformation.

Finally, we define the SDP loss as L_{SDP}:

$$\mathcal{L}_{\text{SDP}} = \frac{1}{N} \sum_i^N (y_i + s_i)^2, \qquad (2)$$

where $y \in \{-1, 1\}$ is the label comes from the binary classification task but scaled into -1 to 1. The purpose of this loss is to leverage the vector of two segments in the semantic space to the opposite direction if the paragraph is a joke (i.e. the paragraph has a punchline thus the angle of the pre and the post segment should be large), and to the same direction (i.e. small angle for a non-humorous paragraph) if there is no discrepancy.

3.3 Fine-Tuning

Instead of simply fine-tuning the model with a single loss computed from the predicted logits and ground-truth, we fine-tune the model with two tasks sharing same labels but providing different contributions. The first loss comes from the conventional classification task, and the second one is from the sentence discrepancy prediction.

We define a task specific prediction heads implemented by a linear transformation, denoted as f; the input of the prediction head is the representation of the [CLS] token, represented as v_{cls}; $\hat{y}$ denotes the predicted logits. More formally:

$$\hat{y} = f(v_{\text{cls}}; \theta_f), \tag{3}$$

Weighted cross-entropy is used as the loss function to deal with the imbalance of the datasets; the label weights are calculated as follows:

$$w_c = \frac{N}{N_c \times C}, \tag{4}$$

where N is the number of samples in the training set; C is the number of classes (e.g. 2 for binary classification) and N_c is the number of samples classified as c. Therefore, the loss function can be rewritten as:

$$\mathcal{L}_{\text{CLS}} = -\frac{1}{N} \sum_i^N \sum_c^C w_c y_{i,c} \log P(y_{i,c}|x_i) \tag{5}$$

To train the model with two tasks, we define $\mathcal{L}(\theta)$ as:

$$\mathcal{L}(\theta) = \mathcal{L}_{\text{CLS}} + \lambda \mathcal{L}_{\text{SDP}} \tag{6}$$

where λ is the factor to scale the SDP loss. Note that the parameters of BERT aren't frozen and can be updated during the fine-tuning.

3.4 Segment Ensemble

Although the paragraph decomposition could change the view of the model to encode the paragraph, it might also introduce noise and cause the damage on the semantic representation. Therefore, we use another BERT, fine-tuned on the **undecomposed** corpus to produce vanilla prediction, and ensemble it with the decomposed prediction. An average pooling is performed on the logits of

		Train	Dev	Test
FUN	samples	246,415	5,000	61,794
	tokens	17.69	17.59	18.17
(RU)	positive	50.00%	50.48%	50.0%
HAHA	samples	22,000	2,000	6,000
	tokens	15.48	15.56	16.35
(ES)	positive	38.59%	38.20%	39.03%
CCL	samples	11,494	1,642	3,284
	tokens	38.33	39.15	38.71
(ZH)	positive	70.34%	69.49%	70.34%

Table 1: Details about three datasets. ZH, RU and ES are the abbreviation of Chinese, Russian and Spanish respectively. Tokens are the average tokens per line in specific subset. Positives are the proportion of the positive samples in specific subset, which indicates that HAHA and CCL is relatively imbalanced comparing with FUN.

two models. Note that the vanilla fine-tuned BERT is also considered as the **baseline** model; we use **SE** to represent segment ensemble for simplicity.

4 Experiments

In this section, we introduce the details of the datasets, as well as the experimental setup.

4.1 Data

We perform experiments on three following datasets organized in three languages respectively. The detail can be found in Table 1

4.1.1 CCL

This dataset is published in the CCL2019 Chinese Humor Detection Competition[1], which has two subsets where the first one is composed of 21,552 samples for binary classification. 21,885 jokes in the second subsets are labeled in three levels and can be formulated as a tri-class classification problem. However, we only perform experiments on the first subsets for compatibility with other two datasets. Note that the golden labels of development set and test set are not released, and can only be assessed by the competition organizer, therefore, we randomly split a dev and test set from the original train set for convenient. The experimental results reported later is from the test set on our own splitting, and we also present the score on the leaderboard of our model. Overlength jokes are removed from the training set and are trimmed to 512 tokens during validation. Macro F1-score is used as the evaluation metric.

---

[1] https://github.com/DUTIR-Emotion-Group/CCL2019-Chinese-Humor-Computation

Method	CCL	FUN	HAHA
Random (baseline)	0.5844	0.4991	0.4314
Fasttext (baseline)	0.8267	0.7982	0.7302
[2019]QingBoAI (ensemble)	0.9488	-	-
[2019]**ours (ensemble)**	0.8968	-	-
[2019]SanQunWuDui (ensemble)	0.8683	-	-
SVM	-	0.798	-
[2019]ULMFun	-	0.9070	-
[2019]adilism (ensemble)	-	-	0.821
[2019]Kevin & Hiromi (ensemble)	-	-	0.816
[2019]bfarzin (ensemble)	-	-	0.810
BERT (baseline)	0.8468	0.9022	0.7896
BERT-SDP (PD_L)	0.8635	0.9115	0.7975
BERT-SDP (PD_M)	0.8692	0.9126	0.8120
BERT-SDP (PD_M+SE)	**0.9017**[2nd]	**0.9138**[1st]	**0.8217**[1st]

Table 2: Our method achieves top 2 result in all three datasets comparing with both ensemble and single models published in 2019, which demonstrates the effectiveness of our approach in scenarios like multilingual and imbalanced data. Note that the second group are from the leaderboard of CCL competition which we participated in and achieved the second place. The third group is the result published in original FUN (Blinov et al., 2019). The fourth group is from the report of HAHA at IberLEF 2019 (Chiruzzo et al., 2019), which we didn't participate in and is shown for comparison purposes.

4.1.2 FUN

FUN is proposed in (Blinov et al., 2019), mainly collected from several Russian social network websites; it only contains binary labels (i.e. classifying whether a paragraph is humorous). Note that FUN is the largest dataset in our experiment, consisting of more than 313,210 samples, where 1877 are manually labeled and considered as golden truth which is not used for evaluation due to its limited size. 5000 samples are further split as a dev set from the train set. Macro F1-score is the evaluation metric.

4.1.3 HAHA

HAHA (Chiruzzo et al., 2019) is a Spanish corpus collected from twitter for the competition of IberLEF 2019. There are 30,000 samples where 11,595 tweets are labeled as humorous (38.7%). The humorous tweets are further annotated with real number scores in the range of 1 to 5. We only do the first task (i.e. binary classification) aiming to make comparable settings among three datasets with macro F1-score. In addition, we further split the train set into train and dev for tuning hyperparameters.

4.2 Experimental Setup

The BERT model we used is implemented with transformers (Wolf et al., 2019). All three datasets are encoded with BERT-base-multilingual-cased.

We use pytorch[2] to implement the classification head f and the SDP head g after the BERT encoder. The model is trained on 4 Titan Xp GPUs where each has 12 GB memory, the batch size is set to 96. We use the AdamW (Loshchilov and Hutter, 2019) as the optimizer with the peak learning rate of 1e-4.

We perform experiment on the BERT baseline as well as 3 variants of our approaches, including two decomposition strategies and the segment ensemble. Besides the baseline BERT, all 3 variants use the SDP loss with $\lambda = 0.1$.

5 Analysis

The experimental results is shown in Table 2, which is separated into three groups. The first group contains baseline methods including a random predictor and a fasttext (Bojanowski et al., 2016) model. The second group are SOTA methods in CCL 2019 competition, where the second place is obtained by our ensemble model. The third group is published in original FUN (Blinov et al., 2019), where SVM is their baseline and ULMFun is a fine-tuned ULMFiT (Howard and Ruder, 2018). The fourth group are results published in the report of IberLEF 2019 (Chiruzzo et al., 2019), which we didn't participate in, and is shown for comparison purposes. The last group are the ab-

---

[2]https://pytorch.org/

ZH	猫似乎只是在削尖他们的爪子。 [SEP] 实际上， 他们正在锻炼腿部肌肉。	0.61
	猫似乎只是在削尖他们的爪子。 实际上， 他们正在锻炼腿部肌肉。[SEP]	0.55
EN	Cats seem to be just sharpening their claws. [SEP] In fact, they are exercising leg muscles.	0.61
	Cats seem to be just sharpening their claws. In fact, they are exercising leg muscles. [SEP]	0.55

Table 3: An example shows that correctly decomposing the joke could encourage the model to produce higher probability for the correct class.

lation study evaluated on a BERT baseline and 3 variants of our approach. Note that the score gap on the CCL column in the second and last group is caused by the different test set. We can see all of them have the improvements of performance comparing with baselines.

We find a representative case from CCL dataset, which is shown in Table.3. We can see that decomposing the joke from the start of the second sentence achieves higher probability and the second sentence is actually the punchline of this joke.

Although the score of HAHA is acceptable, we find some cases showing that the tweets published in HAHA is relatively unclean, with noisy characters like hashtags or being barely readable even by human, which also happens in FUN. As shown in Table. 4, repeatedly appeared "JA" and hashtags may corrupt the paragraph decomposition algorithm and produce unreasonable paragraph pairs. At the same time, BERT is not pretrained on tweets or corpus from social networks which means the token representations of FUN and HAHA is insufficient to encode correct semantics.

6 Conclusion

We propose the SDP and paragraph decomposition to for humor detection, by linking the classification label to the inter-sentence discrepancy prediction. Our proposed method achieves competitive performance on three dataset with different languages. Although our SDP algorithm has achieved great performance on humor detection tasks, how to generalize it to other NLP tasks remains as our future work.

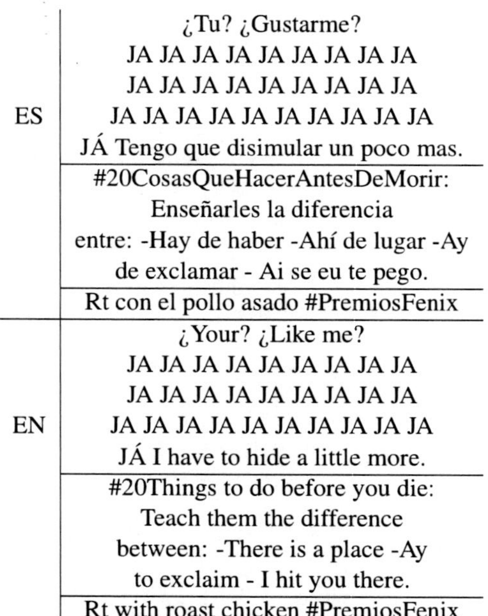

ES	¿Tu? ¿Gustarme? JA JA JA JA JA JA JA JA JA JA JA JA JA JA JA JA JA JA JA JA JA JA JA JA JA JA JA JÁ Tengo que disimular un poco mas.
	#20CosasQueHacerAntesDeMorir: Enseñarles la diferencia entre: -Hay de haber -Ahí de lugar -Ay de exclamar - Ai se eu te pego.
	Rt con el pollo asado #PremiosFenix
EN	¿Your? ¿Like me? JA JA JA JA JA JA JA JA JA JA JA JA JA JA JA JA JA JA JA JA JA JA JA JA JA JA JA JÁ I have to hide a little more.
	#20Things to do before you die: Teach them the difference between: -There is a place -Ay to exclaim - I hit you there.
	Rt with roast chicken #PremiosFenix

Table 4: An example shows that uncleaned tweets from HAHA could dramatically corrupt the performance of paragraph decomposition and BERT encoder

References

Blinov, Vladislav, Valeria Bolotova-Baranova, and Pavel Braslavski. 2019. Large dataset and language model fun-tuning for humor recognition. In *Proceedings of the 57th Conference of the Association for Computational Linguistics, ACL 2019, Florence, Italy, July 28- August 2, 2019, Volume 1: Long Papers*, pages 4027–4032.

Bojanowski, Piotr, Edouard Grave, Armand Joulin, and Tomas Mikolov. 2016. Enriching word vectors with subword information. *CoRR*, abs/1607.04606.

Chiruzzo, Luis, Santiago Castro, Mathías Etcheverry, Diego Garat, Juan José Prada, and Aiala Rosá. 2019. Overview of HAHA at iberlef 2019: Humor analysis based on human annotation. In *Proceedings of the Iberian Languages Evaluation Forum co-located with 35th Conference of the Spanish Society for Natural Language Processing, IberLEF@SEPLN 2019, Bilbao, Spain, September 24th, 2019.*, pages 132–144.

Devlin, Jacob, Ming-Wei Chang, Kenton Lee, and Kristina Toutanova. 2019. BERT: pre-training of deep bidirectional transformers for language understanding. In *Proceedings of the 2019 Conference of the North American Chapter of the Association for Computational Linguistics: Human Language Technologies, NAACL-HLT 2019, Minneapolis, MN, USA, June 2-7, 2019, Volume 1 (Long and Short Papers)*, pages 4171–4186.

Hochreiter, Sepp and Jürgen Schmidhuber. 1996. LSTM can solve hard long time lag problems. In *Advances in Neural Information Processing Systems 9, NIPS, Denver, CO, USA*, pages 473–479.

Howard, Jeremy and Sebastian Ruder. 2018. Universal language model fine-tuning for text classification. In *Proceedings of the 56th Annual Meeting of the Association for Computational Linguistics, ACL 2018, Melbourne, Australia, July 15-20, 2018, Volume 1: Long Papers*, pages 328–339.

Ismailov, Adilzhan. 2019. Humor analysis based on human annotation challenge at iberlef 2019: First-place solution. In *Proceedings of the Iberian Languages Evaluation Forum co-located with 35th Conference of the Spanish Society for Natural Language Processing, IberLEF@SEPLN 2019, Bilbao, Spain, September 24th, 2019.*, pages 160–164.

Krizhevsky, Alex, Ilya Sutskever, and Geoffrey E. Hinton. 2012. Imagenet classification with deep convolutional neural networks. In *Advances in Neural Information Processing Systems 25: 26th Annual Conference on Neural Information Processing Systems 2012. Proceedings of a meeting held December 3-6, 2012, Lake Tahoe, Nevada, United States.*, pages 1106–1114.

Loshchilov, Ilya and Frank Hutter. 2019. Decoupled weight decay regularization. In *7th International Conference on Learning Representations, ICLR 2019, New Orleans, LA, USA, May 6-9, 2019*.

Weller, Orion and Kevin D. Seppi. 2019. Humor detection: A transformer gets the last laugh. *CoRR*, abs/1909.00252.

Wolf, Thomas, Lysandre Debut, Victor Sanh, Julien Chaumond, Clement Delangue, Anthony Moi, Pierric Cistac, Tim Rault, R'emi Louf, Morgan Funtowicz, and Jamie Brew. 2019. Huggingface's transformers: State-of-the-art natural language processing. *ArXiv*, abs/1910.03771.

Yang, Diyi, Alon Lavie, Chris Dyer, and Eduard H. Hovy. 2015. Humor recognition and humor anchor extraction. In *Proceedings of the 2015 Conference on Empirical Methods in Natural Language Processing, EMNLP 2015, Lisbon, Portugal, September 17-21, 2015*, pages 2367–2376.

A multi-source approach for Breton–French hybrid machine translation

Víctor M. Sánchez-Cartagena, Mikel L. Forcada, Felipe Sánchez-Martínez

Dep. de Llenguatges i Sistemes Informàtics, Universitat d'Alacant
E-03690 Sant Vicent del Raspeig (Spain)
{vmsanchez,mlf,fsanchez}@dlsi.ua.es

Abstract

Corpus-based approaches to machine translation (MT) have difficulties when the amount of parallel corpora to use for training is scarce, especially if the languages involved in the translation are highly inflected. This problem can be addressed from different perspectives, including data augmentation, transfer learning, and the use of additional resources, such as those used in rule-based MT (RBMT). This paper focuses on the hybridisation of RBMT and neural MT (NMT) for the Breton–French under-resourced language pair in an attempt to study to what extent the RBMT resources help improve the translation quality of the NMT system. We combine both translation approaches in a multi-source NMT architecture and find out that, even though the RBMT system has a low performance according to automatic evaluation metrics, using it leads to improved translation quality.

1 Introduction

Corpus-based approaches to machine translation (MT), such as neural MT (NMT), struggle when the size of the available parallel corpora for a given language pair is scarce (Koehn and Knowles, 2017). Even though the problem can be partially mitigated with accurate hyper-parameter tuning (Sennrich and Zhang, 2019), taking advantage of additional resources can help to further improve the quality of the system.

Monolingual texts in both languages can be leveraged with the help of back-translation (Sennrich et al., 2016a; Hoang et al., 2018) to generate synthetic parallel corpora. It is also possible to use only monolingual corpora and follow an unsupervised NMT approach (Artetxe et al., 2018). Parallel corpora from related language pairs can also be leveraged thanks to multilingual NMT (Johnson et al., 2017) and other forms of transfer learning (Kocmi and Bojar, 2018).

In addition to the use of corpora, linguistic resources can also be used to improve NMT. If morphological analysers or syntactic parsers are available, they can be used to build a richer representation of the words being translated (Sennrich and Haddow, 2016; Nadejde et al., 2017). Even full rule-based MT (RBMT) systems can be combined with NMT in order to build hybrid systems (Huang et al., 2020).

In this work, we focus on an under-resourced language pair: Breton–French, and study mechanisms to build a hybrid system by combining NMT with the Breton–French system built with the Apertium RBMT platform (Forcada et al., 2011).

We aim at producing sentences that combine knowledge extracted from the parallel corpus and from the RBMT system. Hence, we go beyond approaches that simply choose the best system (either RBMT or NMT) for each input sentence (see below). We use multi-source NMT and formalise the problem of combining both sources of knowledge as an automatic post-editing (Chatterjee et al., 2018) problem. In this way, we are able to explore different ways of generating the RBMT output, using different resources, to study which resources are more useful for the hybrid approach.

The rest of the paper is organised as follows. The remainder of this section lists previous works related to the hybridisation of RBMT and corpus-based systems, including approaches for integrating external bilingual segments into NMT. Section 2 then explains the resources available for Breton–

Martins, Moniz, Fumega, Martins, Batista, Coheur, Parra, Trancoso, Turchi, Bisazza, Moorkens, Guerberof, Nurminen, Marg, Forcada (eds.)
Proceedings of the 22nd Annual Conference of the European Association for Machine Translation, p. 61–70
Lisboa, Portugal, November 2020.

French and the challenges of translating between Breton and French. Section 3 describes the hybrid architecture chosen. Section 4 presents the experiments carried out and discusses the results obtained. The paper ends with some concluding remarks.

Hybrid systems combining rule-based and corpus-based approaches. The creation of hybrid systems combining RBMT and statistical MT (SMT) has been explored by many authors. The most relevant approach for this work (Tyers, 2009) enlarged the training corpus of an SMT system with 116,500 *sentence pairs* made up of all possible inflected Breton forms and their inflected French translations as present in an earlier version of the Apertium Breton–French system we are using. Schwenk et al. (2009) followed a similar approach for other language pairs. More sophisticated approaches (Eisele et al., 2008; Enache et al., 2012; Sánchez-Cartagena et al., 2016) involve modifying the SMT architecture.

Concerning the combination of RBMT and NMT, a relevant line of research involves choosing the best output (either RBMT or NMT) for each source sentence. For instance, Huang et al. (2020) propose training an automatic classifier for this task and use some features to help predict how difficult is the source sentence for each system: for instance, the degree of morphological and syntactic ambiguity is useful to estimate how difficult is the sentence for the RBMT system, while the token frequency on the training corpus can help to assess how difficult it is for the NMT system. Similarly, Singh et al. (2019) use confidence scores computed for each system to choose the best alternative for each source sentence. Torregrosa et al. (2019) experimented with the integration of RBMT bilingual dictionaries and syntactic parsers into NMT without success.

Finally, the multi-source architecture studied in this paper has been preliminary explored by Sánchez-Cartagena et al. (2019). The main differences with this work are: i) they did not study the impact of the different components of the RBMT system; and ii) they did not perform a hyper-parameter search, which could explain the poor performance of their transformer systems. In addition, we conduct an automatic analysis of the errors produced by our hybrid approach.

Integration of bilingual segments into NMT. The integration of bilingual segments, which could be produced by an RBMT system, into an NMT system has received some attention recently. One of the first approaches (Arthur et al., 2016), which can only be applied to single-token bilingual segments, used the attention weights of a recurrent attentional encoder–decoder (Bahdanau et al., 2015) model to decide the target language (TL) word translation probabilities that needed to be boosted in the final softmax layer. Tang et al. (2016) and Wang et al. (2017) relied on a phrase memory for NMT that could contain multiple-token bilingual segments. They modelled decoding as a mixture of two processes: generating a word with the standard NMT model, or introducing a phrase from the phrase memory. Zhang et al. (2017) formalised the strategy of Tang et al. (2016) as a *posterior regularization* approach (Ganchev et al., 2010). Feng et al. (2018) designed a phrase attention mechanism that could be used either without additional supervision or with an external bilingual lexicon. Another related line of research modifies the beam search algorithm to meet some terminological constraints (Chatterjee et al., 2017; Post and Vilar, 2018).

2 Breton–French machine translation

The Breton language (*Brezhoneg* in Breton) is a Celtic language of the Brittonic group that is spoken in the west of Brittany (*Breizh Izel* or "Lower Brittany") in France, and the main language with which it has contact is French, the only official language; in fact, Breton, spoken by about 200,000 people, has virtually no legal recognition in France.

Resources for Breton: Programs like Firefox, Google applications and some Microsoft programs have been localized and there is a 70,000-page Breton Wikipedia. There is little software dedicated to Breton; most of it free/open-source, such as the Apertium MT system and the LanguageTool spelling and grammar checker. This software and services such as the Freelang online dictionary[1] are based on linguistic resources such as morphological analyzers, monolingual and bilingual dictionaries. As for bilingual text corpora, today OPUS[2] contains about 400,000 sentence pairs, most of them very specialized, in the field of computer science.

The Apertium Breton–French system: The Apertium platform[3] contains an MT system designed to allow French-speaking readers to access written Breton content (*gisting*).[4] This MT system

---

[1] https://www.freelang.com/enligne/breton.php
[2] http://opus.nlpl.eu
[3] http://www.apertium.org
[4] Developers deliberately chose not develop French–Breton MT, deeming it too risky in terms of the socio-linguistic situation, as users would assume the machine-translated Breton to be

(Tyers, 2010), the only one in the world for Breton, was released in May 2009 as the result of the joint efforts of the *Ofis ar Brezhoneg*,[5] the Spanish company Prompsit Language Engineering, and the Universitat d'Alacant and is based on the Apertium platform (Forcada et al., 2011). Dictionary development started with the free dictionaries for Breton in Lexilogos.[6] Development of the Apertium Breton–French MT system slowly continues. The quality of the French generated is not suitable for publishing, but may be used to get a rough idea of the meaning of a Breton text.

Automatic inference of translation rules for Breton–French: There have been attempts to improve the Apertium Breton–French system in an unsupervised way. In particular, Sánchez-Cartagena et al. (2015) proposed an algorithm for the automatic inference of shallow-transfer rules from small parallel corpora and existing RBMT dictionaries. The result of applying the algorithm to the Apertium Breton–French system using just the parallel data prepared by Tyers (2009) was a set of rules whose quality, as measured by automatic MT evaluation metrics, was close to the existing hand-crafted ones.

3 System architecture

We propose combining the explicit linguistic knowledge encoded in the Breton–French Apertium system with the implicit knowledge encoded in a parallel corpus by means of multi-source NMT (Zoph and Knight, 2016). Given a source-language (SL) sentence to be translated, our proposed architecture proceeds as follows (see Figure 1): First, the SL sentence is translated with the RBMT system; then the original SL sentence and its RBMT translation are passed as inputs to the multi-source NMT system, which produces the final translation. At training time, the SL side of the parallel sentences in the training corpus is translated with Apertium to obtain a "trilingual" parallel corpus. As it is common practice, the multi-source system works on byte-pair-encoding (BPE) sub-word units (Sennrich et al., 2016b) obtained from both inputs and the output together.

With this architecture, we expect the NMT system to learn to translate from the SL text with help from the RBMT output. It could also be seen the other way round: the NMT system postedits the

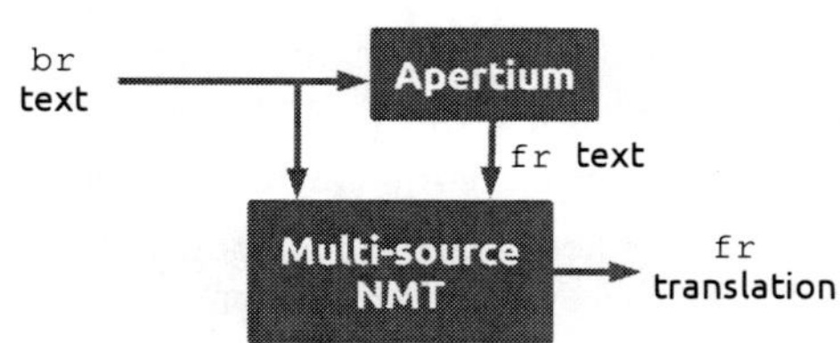

Figure 1: Multi-source NMT approach followed to integrate the linguistic knowledge encoded in the Apertium Breton–French RBMT system.

RBMT output with the help of the SL sentence. In fact, this architecture has been successfully applied for automatic post-editing (Junczys-Dowmunt and Grundkiewicz, 2018).

The Apertium architecture as well as the multi-source NMT architecture used in our experiments are described in the remainder of this section.

3.1 Apertium rule-based machine translation

Apertium is a free/open-source RBMT system that follows a shallow-transfer architecture. What follows is brief description of its modules; for a complete description of the system we refer the reader to the work by Forcada et al. (2011).

- A *morphological analyser* segments the text in surface forms (*words*, or, where detected, multi-word lexical units) and delivers, for each one, one or more *lexical forms* consisting of lemma, lexical category and morphological inflection information.

- A *part-of-speech tagger*, which combines a constraint grammar (Karlsson et al., 1995) with a first-order hidden Markov model (Cutting et al., 1992), selects the most likely lexical form corresponding to an ambiguous surface form.

- A *lexical transfer* module which reads each SL lexical form and delivers the corresponding TL lexical form by looking it up in a bilingual dictionary.

- A shallow *structural transfer* module that performs syntactic operations on the sequence of lexical forms to improve the grammaticality of the output.[7]

- A *morphological generator* which delivers a TL surface form for each TL lexical form, by suitably inflecting it.

---

good and use it improperly as if it were correct (Jakez, 2009 personal communication).

[5] Now *Ofis Publik ar Brezhoneg*

[6] https://www.lexilogos.com/breton_dictionnaire.htm

---

[7] This shallow model does not rely on a full parse tree of the whole sentence and, therefore, RBMT systems that perform full syntactic analysis are more effective than Apertium when dealing, for instance, with long-range reorderings.

- A *post-generator* which performs inter-word orthographic operations: contractions, elisions marked by apostrophes, etc.[8]

3.2 Multi-source neural machine translation

We experimented with the transformer (Vaswani et al., 2017) and the recurrent attentional encoder–decoder (Bahdanau et al., 2015, hereinafter recurrent) NMT architectures. In both cases, we followed the multi-source architectures implemented in the Marian toolkit (Junczys-Dowmunt et al., 2018), which are described next.

Our recurrent NMT systems follow the same architecture as Nematus (Sennrich et al., 2017b), namely a bidirectional gated recurrent unit (GRU) encoder, a conditional GRU decoder with attention (Miceli Barone et al., 2017, Sec. 4.2) and a deep output that combines the context vector, the recurrent hidden state and the embedding of the previous symbol. The multi-source recurrent NMT system contains two encoders (one for each input) which do not share parameters. The modifications in the decoder that allow it to accommodate the two encoders are the following:

- The initial state of the decoder is obtained after concatenating the averaged encoder states of the two input sequences.
- The conditional GRU (cGRU) unit with attention in the decoder is replaced by a doubly-attentive cGRU cell (Calixto et al., 2017) featuring two independent attention mechanisms.
- The context vector used in the deep output is replaced by the concatenation of the context vectors of the two inputs.

For further details, the reader is referred to Junczys-Dowmunt and Grundkiewicz (2017).

Our transformer models follow the architecture proposed by Vaswani et al. (2017). A transformer model contains an encoder and a decoder. The encoder is made of stacked layers, each containing a self-attention unit and a feed-forward unit. The decoder is also made of stacked layers, each containing a self-attention unit, an encoder–decoder attention unit and feed-forward unit. The multi-source transformer systems contain two encoders and two encoder–decoder attention units in each decoder layer. This transformer multi-source architecture was also used in the winning submission to the 2018 WMT automatic post-editing shared task (Chatterjee et al., 2018). For further details, the reader is referred to Junczys-Dowmunt and Grundkiewicz (2018).

Corpus	# sent.	# br tokens	# fr tokens
train	139,489	1,096,311	1,116,100
dev	2,000	25,291	24,835
test	3,000	37,054	36,346

Table 1: Number of parallel sentences and tokens in Breton and French for the corpora used for train/dev/test corpora.

4 Experiments and results

For the experiments we used the following corpora available at OPUS:[9] Tatoeba, GNOME, OfisPublik, KDE4, wikimedia, Ubuntu and OpenSubtitles. For development and testing we used the same portions of the OfisPublik corpus used by Sánchez-Cartagena et al. (2015), the rest of corpora, after de-duplication, were used for training. Table 1 reports the amount of parallel sentences and tokens in each language for the training, development, and test corpora.

Concerning Apertium, we used the Breton–French data available at `https://github.com/apertium/apertium-br-fr`. In addition to the shallow-transfer rules included in these linguistic data, we also experimented with shallow-transfer rules automatically inferred from the portion of the OfisPublik corpus included in the training corpus using the algorithm by Sánchez-Cartagena et al. (2015).

In order to determine the appropriate amount of BPE operations and hyper-parameter values to be used for the two models we proceed as follows: First we tried with 5,000, 10,000, 20,000, and 30,000 BPE operations with a baseline system not using any Apertium data. When doing so the rest of hyper-parameters were set to the values recommended by Sennrich et al. (2017a) for the recurrent model and by Vaswani et al. (2017) for the base transformer model, respectively, except for the model size which was set to 512. Training stopped after 5 validations without any perplexity improvement on the development corpus; validations were performed every 1,000 mini-batches; each minibatch contained 8,000 tokens. The best results were obtained with 20,000 BPE operations for the recurrent model and 5,000 for the transformer. We then performed a grid search to find the appropriate hyper-parameters for each model. The hyper-parameters tried for the recurrent model are:

- Embedding sizes in $\{512, 256, 128\}$. For each embedding size the hidden size was set to twice the size of the embeddings.

---

[8]In French: *à + lequel → auquel*; *de + hôtels → d'hôtels*, etc.

[9]`http://opus.nlpl.eu`

- Encoder and decoder cell depths in $\{1, 2, 4, 8\}$. We used the same value for both so as not to explore the Cartesian product. Cell depth is defined as the number of GRU transitions in the deep transition architecture proposed by Miceli Barone et al. (2017, Sec. 4.2).

The hyper-parameters tried for the transformer model are:

- Attention heads in $\{2, 4, 8\}$.
- Model size in $\{512, 256, 128\}$.
- Encoder and decoder layers in $\{2, 4, 6\}$. As before, we used the same value for both to avoid exploring the Cartesian product.

The best results for the recurrent model were obtained with an embedding size of 512 and encoder and decoder cell depths of 2. For the transformer, the best results were obtained with 4 attention heads, model size of 512 and 4 encoder and decoder layers. These hyper-parameters are the ones used for the rest of experiments reported.

Table 2 provides the BLEU and chrF2++ scores for the reference systems and for the different ways of exploiting the linguistic resources in Apertium, as explained next. For the reference NMT systems and the different multi-source NMT configurations we have tried, the table reports the mean and standard deviation of the scores obtained after three different training executions.

An explanation of the different reference systems follows:

- Baseline NMT system (*base NMT*) trained solely on the training corpus (see Table 1).
- Baseline NMT system trained on a concatenation of the training corpus and the entries in the Breton–French bilingual dictionary of Apertium (*base+dic NMT*). Tyers (2009) explains how all the inflected bilingual entries can be obtained from the Apertium dictionaries; some of them may have more than one translation equivalent while others may be multiword entries. The amount of bilingual entries obtained from the current version is 125,829, of which 57 have more than one translation equivalent and 2,228 are multiword entries.
- Apertium with hand-crafted rules (*RBMT man. rules*): the full RBMT system. The linguistic resources used by this system are: morphological analyser for Breton, morphological generator for French, part-of-speech tagger of Breton, Breton–French bilingual dictionary of lemmas and shallow structural transfer rules.

- Apertium with automatically-inferred rules (*RBMT auto rules*). Same as above but using the shallow structural transfer rules automatically inferred by Sánchez-Cartagena et al. (2015), instead of using hand-crafted rules.
- Apertium with no structural transfer rules (*RBMT no rules*). Same as above but using no structural transfer rules. After morphological analysis and part-of-speech tagging the lexical forms in Breton are translated into lexical forms in French one by one, without applying any structural transfer to make the output more grammatical, except for very simple one-word rules that ensure that the morphological features sent to the French generator for each separate word are valid.

As regards the different ways of exploiting the linguistic resources in Apertium, we generated the additional input translation provided to the multi-source NMT system with the same RBMT configurations used as reference systems (see above) as well as a word-for-word translation obtained using exactly the same bilingual dictionary we used for the *base+dic NMT* reference system. As this dictionary contains multi-word lexical units, we translated word for word in a left-to-right, longest-match fashion so that the bilingual entry covering the longest sequence of tokens is selected when there is more than one possibility. When the bilingual dictionary contained more than one translation per source word, they were all included in the output separated by a special token. This happened to 495 source words in the training corpus.

The results in Table 2 show that the use of Apertium resources improves translation quality according to both BLEU and chrF2++. The best improvement, about 1.3 BLEU points, is obtained when the additional input to the multi-source NMT system is obtained without structural transfer rules (*RBMT no rules*). However, if we pay closer attention to the performance of the reference system *RBMT no rules* on its own, the scores it obtains are worse than those obtained with hand-crafted rules (*RBMT man. rules*) and automatically inferred rules (*RBMT auto rules*). This results suggest that Apertium may be helping the NMT system to perform a better lexical selection, since the improvement in the grammaticality of the Apertium output provided by the shallow-transfer rules has no effect on the quality of the final translation. In any case, the use of a morphological analyser and part-of-speech tagger for Breton has a positive effect on the translation quality of the multi-source NMT system; compare the

BLEU	Recurrent	Transformer
reference systems		
base NMT	21.25 ± 0.12	18.45 ± 0.08
base+dic NMT	21.26 ± 0.24	18.50 ± 0.15
RBMT man. rules	12.45	
RBMT auto rules	12.16	
RBMT no rules	8.78	
multi-source		
RBMT man. rules	21.36 ± 0.46	19.16 ± 0.02
RBMT auto rules	22.24 ± 0.46	19.48 ± 0.18
RBMT no rules	$\mathbf{22.59 \pm 0.06}$	19.70 ± 0.15
word-for-word	21.73 ± 0.22	18.24 ± 0.13

chrF2++	Recurrent	Transformer
reference systems		
base NMT	38.38 ± 0.13	36.94 ± 0.03
base+dic NMT	38.68 ± 0.13	37.25 ± 0.09
RBMT man. rules	35.16	
RBMT auto rules	33.86	
RBMT no rules	30.91	
multi-source		
RBMT man. rules	39.58 ± 0.27	38.80 ± 0.08
RBMT auto rules	40.12 ± 0.34	39.03 ± 0.15
RBMT no rules	$\mathbf{40.49 \pm 0.10}$	39.19 ± 0.17
word-for-word	39.20 ± 0.10	37.17 ± 0.17

Table 2: BLEU and chrF2++ evaluation scores for different reference systems and for the different multi-source NMT configurations we have tried. RBMT stands for the Apertium rule-based MT used.

performance of *RBMT no rules* with the *word-for-word* translation which uses a bilingual dictionary of surface forms. Finally, the addition of the bilingual dictionary to the training corpus seems to have no effect on translation quality.

In order to get a deeper insight about the effect of the different hybridisation strategies, we carried out an automatic error analysis following the strategy of Toral and Sánchez-Cartagena (2017). We used Hjerson (Popović, 2011), [10] which classifies errors into five word-level categories: inflection errors, reordering errors, missing words, extra words and incorrect lexical choices. As it is difficult to automatically distinguish between the latter three categories (Popović and Ney, 2011), we grouped them into a unique category named *lexical errors*. Hjerson works on the surface form and lemma of the words in the reference translations and MT outputs. The lemmas used were obtained with the StandfordNLP lemmatiser (Qi et al., 2018).

We computed the relative difference in the num-

ber of Hjerson errors in the test set between the multi-source NMT systems and the *base NMT* system; [11] a positive value means that the multi-source system made more errors than the *base NMT* system. Table 3 shows, for the recurrent and transformer architectures, the relative difference computed for each error category and for the total number of errors. As each training was repeated 3 times, the table reports the average and standard deviation of the relative difference for the 9 possible combinations between training runs. In order to contextualise the relative differences, Table 4 reports the average and standard deviation of the total number of errors of each type in the baseline system.

For the recurrent architecture, the addition of expanded dictionaries to the bilingual training corpus does not significantly alter the number of errors. One possible explanation could be that the potential gains of introducing more lexical knowledge in the system are neutralised by the presence of single-word sentences in the training corpus, that could harm the fluency of the generated sentences.

Multi-source NMT systems, on the contrary, tend to make fewer lexical errors than the *base NMT* system. This happens for three out the four multi-source systems, where the system with hand-crafted rules is the only one in which the reduction in lexical errors is not statistically significant. Neither automatically inferred nor hand-crafted transfer rules cause a statistically significant impact in the amount of inflection errors, and both of them make reordering errors increase. The multi-source system without transfer rules is the best performing system according to automatic evaluation metrics because it is the one that brings the largest reduction in lexical errors, which constitute the most frequent error category (see Table 4). It is worth noting that the bilingual dictionary in Apertium contains a single translation for each SL lexical form, hence its lexical selection capabilities are poor. Overall, it seems that the multi-source system is able to make a better use of the translations from the bilingual dictionary when they are sequentially placed in the additional input rather than when they have been processed by transfer rules.

Concerning the transformer architecture, some differences in the way the different error categories change can be observed. The transformer seems to be more robust to the addition of dictionaries to the training corpus: adding them leads to a statistically significant reduction in lexical errors. Moreover, the transformer multi-source systems make more

---

[10] https://github.com/cidermole/hjerson

[11] Computed as $\dfrac{\#errors\_multi\_source - \#errors\_base}{\#errors\_base}$.

Recurrent	inflection	reordering	lexical	total
reference systems				
base+dic NMT	-0.019 ± 0.024	-0.022 ± 0.022	0.012 ± 0.024	0.007 ± 0.020
multi-source				
RBMT man. rules	0.006 ± 0.020	0.031 ± 0.017	-0.017 ± 0.032	-0.011 ± 0.028
RBMT auto rules	-0.015 ± 0.028	0.039 ± 0.025	-0.049 ± 0.024	-0.040 ± 0.021
RBMT no rules	0.008 ± 0.016	0.045 ± 0.018	**-0.066 ± 0.031**	**-0.052 ± 0.026**
word-for-ford	-0.005 ± 0.021	0.005 ± 0.022	-0.030 ± 0.027	-0.025 ± 0.023

Transformer	inflection	reordering	lexical	total
reference systems				
base+dic NMT	-0.010 ± 0.015	-0.012 ± 0.017	-0.009 ± 0.004	-0.010 ± 0.003
multi-source				
RBMT man. rules	0.048 ± 0.018	**0.112 ± 0.017**	-0.014 ± 0.006	0.001 ± 0.005
RBMT auto rules	0.048 ± 0.018	0.093 ± 0.019	-0.024 ± 0.004	-0.010 ± 0.003
RBMT no rules	**0.060 ± 0.016**	0.092 ± 0.032	-0.023 ± 0.003	-0.008 ± 0.004
word-for-ford	0.007 ± 0.021	-0.003 ± 0.018	-0.005 ± 0.004	-0.004 ± 0.003

Table 3: For each NMT architecture, average and standard deviation of the relative changes in the amount of errors for each error category (inflection, reordering, lexical and total). Increases in the amount of error whose confidence interval does not intersect with zero are shown in red, decreases whose confidence interval does not intersect with zero are shown in green. For each error type, the largest relative change is shown in **bold**.

	Recurrent	Transformer
inflection	1971 ± 27	1869 ± 27
reordering	2969 ± 44	2910 ± 42
lexical	30641 ± 726	27599 ± 84

Table 4: For each architecture, absolute number of errors for each type detected by the Hjerson tool on the translation of the test set with the baseline NMT system.

inflection and reordering errors than the recurrent ones. Nevertheless, the lexical errors behave in a similar way in both multi-source architectures: the configuration that leads to the largest reduction in the number of lexical errors is the RBMT system with no transfer rules.

Table 5 shows how the different systems evaluated translate a few sentences from the test set. In the first example, the baseline system is not able to correctly translate the Breton words *e-barzh* and *e-maez*, whose meaning is correctly captured by the Apertium dictionaries. The multi-source systems are able to produce the right translations (*entrées* and *sorties*, respectively *entrances* and *exits* in English) or at least related words, while the *base+dic NMT* repeats *entrées*. In the second example, whose sentence structure is more complex, the baseline system fails to produce a translation that conveys the meaning of the fragment of the reference *On leur a donné le nom de satellites galiléens, en hommage à Galilée*, which roughly means *They were given the name of Galilean satel-*

lites, in homage to Galileo. Only two hybrid systems were able to generate a translation that captures that meaning of the fragment: the multi-source systems without transfer rules and with automatically inferred rules.

5 Concluding remarks

This paper focused on the hybridisation of RBMT and NMT for the Breton–French under-resourced language pair. The aim of the paper is to study to what extent the resources from the Apertium RBMT system help the NMT system to improve its output. We combined both translation approaches in a multi-source NMT architecture and explore the use of different resources in the Apertium Breton–French system to generate the RBMT translation to be used as an additional input.

Despite the low performance of the RBMT system, the hybrid system is able to outperform a pure NMT baseline. The best translation performance is achieved with a hybrid system whose RBMT subsystem contains no transfer rules at all but takes advantage of the Breton morphological analyser and part-of-speech tagger, the French generator and post-generator and the bilingual dictionary.

The fact that the use of no transfer rules provides the best results while the RBMT system using no transfer rules, when evaluated in isolation, performs worse than the rest of RBMT configurations may seem contradictory. However, the automatic error analysis revealed that the hybrid systems using

#	system	sentence
1	source	Staliañ panelloù divyezhek evit **mont e-barzh ha mont e-maez** ar gumun.
	baseline	mise en place d'une signalétique bilingue sur **le site internet** de la commune.
	RBMT no rules	Installer panneaux bilingues pour **aller à l'intérieur et aller hors** de le commune.
	RBMT auto rules	Installer panneaux bilingues pour **aller à l'intérieur et aller hors** de la commune.
	RBMT man. rules	Installer des panneaux bilingues pour **aller à l'intérieur et aller hors** de la commune.
	base+dic NMT	Installation de panneaux bilingues **à l'entrée et de l'entrée** de la commune.
	ms. word-for-word	Mise en place des panneaux bilingues aux **entrées et sorties** de la commune.
	ms. RBMT no rules	Mise en place de panneaux bilingues pour **entrer et sortie** de la commune.
	ms. RBMT auto rules	Il s'agit pour l'installation de panneaux bilingues aux **entrées et sorties** de la commune.
	ms. RBMT man. rules	Installation de panneaux bilingues **d'entrée et de sortie** d'agglomération.
	reference	Mise en place de panneaux bilingues aux **entrées et sorties** de la commune.
2	source	Adplanedennoù galilean a vez graet anezho e koun Galileo Galilei, ar steredoniour italian a zizoloas anezho e 1610 gant ul lunedenn hepken.
	baseline	Les satellites galiléens Galilei, l'astronome italien redécouvre en 1610 avec un œil nu.
	RBMT no rules	Satellites galilean a être faire d'eux dans mémoire Galileo Galilei, le astronome italienne a découvrir d'eux dans 1610 avec un lunette seulement.
	RBMT auto rules	Satellites galilean qui les faire des en mémoire Galileo Galilei, le astronome italien qui découvrir des à 1610 par une lunette seulement.
	RBMT man. rules	Satellites galilean Il est fait d'eux dans mémoire Galileo Galilei, l'astronome italien découvrit d'eux dans 1610 avec une lunette seulement.
	base+dic NMT	Les satellites galiléens sont des satellites galiléens, dont l'astronome italien découvre en 1610 à un œil nu.
	ms. word-for-word	Les satellites galiléens de Galilée, l'astronome italienne traversent en 1610 par une lunette uniquement.
	ms. RBMT no rules	**Satellites galiléens sont évoqués dans la mémoire Galileo Galilei, l'astronome italienne** vous découvrira en 1610 avec une lunette unique.
	ms. RBMT auto rules	**De plus, les satellites galiléens forment la mémoire Galileo** qui les découvre en 1610 par une lunette unique.
	ms. RBMT man. rules	Les satellites galiléens, l'astronome italien découvrit en 1610 par une lunette seulement.
	reference	**On leur a donné le nom de satellites galiléens, en hommage à Galilée (astronome Italien)** qui les découvrit en 1610 avec une simple lunette.

Table 5: Translations into French of different Breton sentences extracted from the test set and produced by the different hybrid strategies evaluated (recurrent architecture; *ms.* stands for *multi-source*). The most remarkable differences are highlighted.

no transfer rules make fewer lexical errors, which account for most of the errors produced by the systems, but more reordering and inflection errors.

Since transfer rules seem not to be needed in our multi-source approach to succeed and morphological analysers, morphological generators and small bilingual dictionaries are available for many under-resourced language pairs, we hope that the hybrid approach presented in this paper opens the door to the development of more accurate hybrid systems in under-resource scenarios.

Acknowledgments: Work funded by the European Union's Horizon 2020 research and innovation programme under grant agreement number 825299, project Global Under-Resourced Media Translation (GoURMET). We thank NVIDIA Corporation the donation of one of the GPUs used for training.

References

Artetxe, M., G. Labaka, E. Agirre, and K. Cho. 2018. Unsupervised neural machine translation. In *Proceedings of the Sixth International Conference on Learning Representations*, Vancouver, Canada, May.

Arthur, P., G. Neubig, and S. Nakamura. 2016. Incorporating discrete translation lexicons into neural machine translation. In *Proceedings of the 2016 Conference on Empirical Methods in Natural Language Processing*, pages 1557–1567, Austin, Texas, November.

Bahdanau, D., K. Cho, and Y. Bengio. 2015. Neural machine translation by jointly learning to align and translate. In *Proceedings of the 3rd International Conference on Learning Representations*, San Diego, CA, USA, May.

Calixto, I., Q. Liu, and N. Campbell. 2017. Doubly-attentive decoder for multi-modal neural machine translation. In *Proceedings of the 55th Annual Meeting of the Association for Computational Linguistics (Volume 1: Long Papers)*, pages 1913–1924, Vancouver, Canada, July.

Chatterjee, R., M. Negri, M. Turchi, M. Federico, L. Specia, and F. Blain. 2017. Guiding neural machine translation decoding with external knowledge. In *Proceedings of the Second Conference on Machine Translation*, pages 157–168, Copenhagen, Denmark, September.

Chatterjee, R., M. Negri, R. Rubino, and M. Turchi. 2018. Findings of the WMT 2018 shared task on automatic post-editing. In *Proceedings of the Third Conference on Machine Translation, Volume 2: Shared Task Papers*, pages 723–738, Belgium, Brussels, October.

Cutting, D., J. Kupiec, J. Pedersen, and P. Sibun. 1992. A practical part-of-speech tagger. In *Proceedings of the Third Conference on Applied Natural Language Processing*, pages 133–140, Trento, Italy.

Eisele, A., C. Federmann, H. Saint-Amand, M. Jellinghaus, T. Herrmann, and Y. Chen. 2008. Using Moses to integrate multiple rule-based machine translation engines into a hybrid system. In *Proceedings of the Third Workshop on Statistical Machine Translation*, pages 179–182, Columbus, Ohio, USA, June.

Enache, R., C. España Bonet, A. Ranta, and L. Màrquez Villodre. 2012. A hybrid system for patent translation. In *Proceedings of the 16th Annual Conference of the European Association for Machine Translation*, pages 269–276, Trento, Italy, May.

Feng, J., L. Kong, P.-S. Huang, C. Wang, D.Huang, J. Mao, K. Qiao, and D. Zhou. 2018. Neural phrase-to-phrase machine translation. *CoRR*, abs/1811.02172.

Forcada, M.L., M. Ginestí-Rosell, J. Nordfalk, J. O'Regan, S. Ortiz-Rojas, J.A. Pérez-Ortiz, F. Sánchez-Martínez, G. Ramírez-Sánchez, and F.M. Tyers. 2011. Apertium: a free/open-source platform for rule-based machine translation. *Machine translation*, 25(2):127–144.

Ganchev, K., J. Graça, J. Gillenwater, and B. Taskar. 2010. Posterior regularization for structured latent variable models. *Journal of Machine Learning Research*, 11:2001–2049.

Hoang, V.C.D., P. Koehn, G. Haffari, and T. Cohn. 2018. Iterative back-translation for neural machine translation. In *Proceedings of the 2nd Workshop on Neural Machine Translation and Generation*, pages 18–24, Melbourne, Australia, July.

Huang, J.-X., K.-S. Lee, and Y.-K. Kim. 2020. Hybrid translation with classification: Revisiting rule-based and neural machine translation. *Electronics*, 9(2).

Johnson, M., M. Schuster, Q.V. Le, M. Krikun, Y. Wu, Z. Chen, N. Thorat, F. Viégas, M. Wattenberg, G. Corrado, M. Hughes, and J. Dean. 2017. Google's multilingual neural machine translation system: Enabling zero-shot translation. *Transactions of the Association for Computational Linguistics*, 5:339–351.

Junczys-Dowmunt, M. and R. Grundkiewicz. 2017. An exploration of neural sequence-to-sequence architectures for automatic post-editing. In *Proceedings of the Eighth International Joint Conference on Natural Language Processing (Volume 1: Long Papers)*, pages 120–129, Taipei, Taiwan, November.

Junczys-Dowmunt, M. and R. Grundkiewicz. 2018. MS-UEdin submission to the WMT2018 APE shared task: Dual-source transformer for automatic post-editing. In *Proceedings of the Third Conference on Machine Translation: Shared Task Papers*, pages 822–826, Belgium, Brussels, October.

Junczys-Dowmunt, M., R. Grundkiewicz, T. Dwojak, H. Hoang, K. Heafield, T. Neckermann, F. Seide, U. Germann, A. Fikri Aji, N. Bogoychev, A.F.T. Martins, and A. Birch. 2018. Marian: Fast neural machine translation in C++. In *Proceedings of ACL 2018, System Demonstrations*, pages 116–121, Melbourne, Australia, July.

Karlsson, F., A. Voutilainen, J. Heikkilä, and A. Anttila. 1995. Constraint grammar: A language-independent system for parsing unrestricted text. mouton de gruyter.

Kocmi, T. and O. Bojar. 2018. Trivial transfer learning for low-resource neural machine translation. In *Proceedings of the Third Conference on Machine Translation: Research Papers*, pages 244–252, Brussels, Belgium, October.

Koehn, P. and R. Knowles. 2017. Six challenges for neural machine translation. In *Proceedings of the First Workshop on Neural Machine Translation*, pages 28–39, Vancouver, Canada, August.

Miceli Barone, A.V., J. Helcl, R. Sennrich, B. Haddow, and A. Birch. 2017. Deep architectures for neural machine translation. In *Proceedings of the Second Conference on Machine Translation*, pages 99–107, Copenhagen, Denmark, September.

Nadejde, M., S. Reddy, R. Sennrich, T. Dwojak, M. Junczys-Dowmunt, P. Koehn, and A. Birch. 2017. Predicting target language CCG supertags improves neural machine translation. In *Proceedings of the Second Conference on Machine Translation, Volume 1: Research Papers*, pages 68–79, Copenhagen, Denmark, September.

Popović, M. and H. Ney. 2011. Towards automatic error analysis of machine translation output. *Computational Linguistics*, 37(4):657–688.

Popović, M. 2011. Hjerson: An open source tool for automatic error classification of machine translation output. *The Prague Bulletin of Mathematical Linguistics*, 96:59–67.

Post, M. and D. Vilar. 2018. Fast lexically constrained decoding with dynamic beam allocation for neural machine translation. In *Proceedings of the 2018 Conference of the North American Chapter of the Association for Computational Linguistics: Human Language Technologies, Volume 1 (Long Papers)*, pages 1314–1324, New Orleans, USA, June.

Qi, P., T. Dozat, Y. Zhang, and C.D. Manning. 2018. Universal dependency parsing from scratch. In *Proceedings of the CoNLL 2018 Shared Task: Multilingual Parsing from Raw Text to Universal Dependencies*, pages 160–170, Brussels, Belgium, October.

Sánchez-Cartagena, V. M., J. A. Pérez-Ortiz, and F. Sánchez-Martínez. 2015. A generalised alignment template formalism and its application to the inference of shallow-transfer machine translation rules from scarce bilingual corpora. *Computer Speech & Language*, 32(1):46 – 90.

Sánchez-Cartagena, V. M., J. A. Pérez-Ortiz, and F. Sánchez-Martínez. 2016. Integrating rules and dictionaries from shallow-transfer machine translation into phrase-based statistical machine translation. *Journal of Artificial Intelligence Research*, 55(1):17–61.

Sánchez-Cartagena, V. M., J. A. Pérez-Ortiz, and F. Sánchez-Martínez. 2019. The Universitat d'alacant submissions to the English-to-Kazakh news translation task at WMT 2019. In *Proceedings of the Fourth Conference on Machine Translation (Volume 2: Shared Task Papers, Day 1)*, pages 356–363, Florence, Italy, August.

Schwenk, H., S. Abdul-Rauf, L. Barrault, and J. Senellart. 2009. SMT and SPE machine translation systems for WMT'09. In *Proceedings of the Fourth Workshop on Statistical Machine Translation*, pages 130–134, Athens, Greece, March.

Sennrich, R. and B. Haddow. 2016. Linguistic input features improve neural machine translation. In *Proceedings of the First Conference on Machine Translation: Volume 1, Research Papers*, pages 83–91, Berlin, Germany, August.

Sennrich, R. and B. Zhang. 2019. Revisiting low-resource neural machine translation: A case study. In *Proceedings of the 57th Annual Meeting of the Association for Computational Linguistics*, pages 211–221, Florence, Italy, July.

Sennrich, R., B. Haddow, and A. Birch. 2016a. Improving neural machine translation models with monolingual data. In *Proceedings of the 54th Annual Meeting of the Association for Computational Linguistics (Volume 1: Long Papers)*, pages 86–96, Berlin, Germany, August.

Sennrich, R., B. Haddow, and A. Birch. 2016b. Neural machine translation of rare words with subword units. In *Proceedings of the 54th Annual Meeting of the Association for Computational Linguistics (Volume 1: Long Papers)*, pages 1715–1725, Berlin, Germany, August.

Sennrich, R., A. Birch, A. Currey, U. Germann, B. Haddow, K. Heafield, A.V. Miceli Barone, and P. Williams. 2017a. The University of Edinburgh's Neural MT Systems for WMT17. In *Proceedings of the Second Conference on Machine Translation, Volume 2: Shared Task Papers*, pages 389–399, Copenhagen, Denmark, September.

Sennrich, R., O. Firat, K. Cho, A. Birch, B. Haddow, J. Hitschler, M. Junczys-Dowmunt, S. Läubli, A.V. Miceli Barone, J. Mokry, and M. Nadejde. 2017b. Nematus: a toolkit for neural machine translation. In *Proceedings of the Software Demonstrations of the 15th Conference of the European Chapter of the Association for Computational Linguistics*, pages 65–68, Valencia, Spain, April.

Singh, M., R. Kumar, and I. Chana. 2019. Improving neural machine translation using rule-based machine translation. In *Proceedings of the 7th International Conference on Smart Computing Communications*, pages 1–5, Miri, Malaysia, June.

Tang, Y., F. Meng, Z. Lu, H. Li, and P.L.H. Yu. 2016. Neural machine translation with external phrase memory. *CoRR*, abs/1606.01792.

Toral, A. and V. M. Sánchez-Cartagena. 2017. A multi-faceted evaluation of neural versus phrase-based machine translation for 9 language directions. In *Proceedings of the 15th Conference of the European Chapter of the Association for Computational Linguistics: Volume 1, Long Papers*, pages 1063–1073, Valencia, Spain, April.

Torregrosa, D., N. Pasricha, M. Masoud, B. R. Chakravarthi, J. Alonso, N. Casas, and M. Arcan. 2019. Leveraging rule-based machine translation knowledge for under-resourced neural machine translation models. In *Proceedings of Machine Translation Summit XVII Volume 2: Translator, Project and User Tracks*, pages 125–133, Dublin, Ireland, August.

Tyers, F.M. 2009. Rule-based augmentation of training data in Breton–French statistical machine translation. In *Proceedings of the 13th Annual Conference of the European Association of Machine Translation*, pages 213–218, Barcelona, Spain, May.

Tyers, F.M. 2010. Rule-based Breton to French machine translation. In *Proceedings of the 14th Annual Conference of the European Association of Machine Translation*, pages 174–181, Saint-Raphaël, France, May.

Vaswani, A., N. Shazeer, N. Parmar, J. Uszkoreit, L. Jones, A.N. Gomez, Ł. Kaiser, and I. Polosukhin. 2017. Attention is all you need. In *Advances in Neural Information Processing Systems 30*, pages 5998–6008. Curran Associates, Inc.

Wang, X., Z. Tu, D. Xiong, and M. Zhang. 2017. Translating phrases in neural machine translation. In *Proceedings of the 2017 Conference on Empirical Methods in Natural Language Processing*, pages 1421–1431, Copenhagen, Denmark, September.

Zhang, J., Y. Liu, H. Luan, J. Xu, and M. Sun. 2017. Prior knowledge integration for neural machine translation using posterior regularization. In *Proceedings of the 55th Annual Meeting of the Association for Computational Linguistics (Volume 1: Long Papers)*, pages 1514–1523, Vancouver, Canada, July.

Zoph, B. and K. Knight. 2016. Multi-source neural translation. In *Proceedings of the 2016 Conference of the North American Chapter of the Association for Computational Linguistics: Human Language Technologies*, pages 30–34, San Diego, CA, USA, June.

Leveraging Multilingual Resources for Language Invariant Sentiment Analysis

Allen J. Antony   **Arghya Bhattacharya**   **Jaipal Singh Goud**   **Radhika Mamidi**

Language Technologies Research Centre
International Institute of Information Technology - Hyderabad
Gachibowli, Hyderabad, Telangana-500032
{allen.antony@research., arghya.b@research.,
jaipal.singh@research.,radhika.mamidi@}iiit.ac.in

Abstract

Sentiment analysis is a widely researched NLP problem with state-of-the-art solutions capable of attaining human-like accuracies for various languages. However, these methods rely heavily on large amounts of labelled data or sentiment weighted language specific lexical resources that are unavailable for low-resource languages. Our work attempts to tackle this data scarcity issue by introducing a neural architecture for language invariant sentiment analysis capable of leveraging various monolingual datasets for training without any kind of cross-lingual supervision. The proposed architecture attempts to learn language agnostic sentiment features via adversarial training on multiple resource-rich languages which can then be leveraged for inferring sentiment information at a sentence level on a low resource language. Our model outperforms the current state-of-the-art methods on the Multilingual Amazon Review Text Classification dataset (Prettenhofer and Stein, 2010) and achieves significant performance gains over prior work on the low resource Sentiraama corpus (Gangula and Mamidi, 2018). A detailed analysis of our research highlights the ability of our architecture to perform significantly well in the presence of minimal amounts of training data for low resource languages.

1 Introduction

Sentiment analysis refers to a series of methods, techniques, and tools aimed at extracting the intended sentiment from a written opinion. Traditional sentiment analysis techniques have relied on using supervised term weighting methods including terms' distribution of classes, word-level polarity scoring and using SVMs (Durant and Smith, 2006) and Naive Bayes classifiers (Prasad, 2010) for pattern extraction using hand-crafted features. The advent of deep learning techniques for sentiment analysis has now enabled the extraction of high quality sentiment data from written texts. One majorly overlooked factor in the performance of these neoteric approaches is their dependency on large annotated datasets compiled from multiple data sources related to or sourced from newspapers, tweets, photos and product reviews. (Socher et al., 2013; Kim, 2014; Tai et al., 2015; Iyyer et al., 2015; Wang et al., 2016).

Given global nature of the current information sharing infrastructure, most data generated belongs to one of the three languages : English, Mandarin or Spanish. This abundance of raw data aids and motivates the creation of annotated resources in these languages. Conversely, the paucity of annotated data in most languages makes it a challenging task to develop deep learning based solutions for them. Hence there is a pressing need to pay special attention to developing solutions capable of sentiment analysis in a low resource setting.

Some of the initial methods that attempt to tackle this problem of data scarcity using transfer learning (training a neural model on one language and applying the trained model on another language via weight sharing) do not perform well due to the limited overlap between the vocabularies of

Martins, Moniz, Fumega, Martins, Batista, Coheur, Parra, Trancoso, Turchi, Bisazza, Moorkens, Guerberof, Nurminen, Marg, Forcada (eds.)
Proceedings of the 22nd Annual Conference of the European Association for Machine Translation, p. 71–79
Lisboa, Portugal, November 2020.

the different languages and difference in their syntactic structure (Chen et al., 2018b).

Cross-lingual sentiment classification (CLSC) methods try to alleviate this problem by leveraging labeled data from one language to improve the performance on another language (Bel et al., 2003). However, these methods typically rely on auxiliary cross-lingual resources such as a parallel corpora (Yarowsky et al., 2001; Xu and Yang, 2017), bilingual lexicons (Mihalcea et al., 2007) or the use of machine translation systems (Kanayama et al., 2004; Wan, 2009; Prettenhofer and Stein, 2010; Can et al., 2018). Unfortunately, the curation of such cross-lingual resources is both a time and a labour intensive task. Hence, there is a need for architectures that can perform well in the absence of such cross-lingual resources.

In this paper, we address this problem by presenting a neural *Language Invariant Sentiment Analyzer* (LISA) architecture that is capable of training on multiple monolingual sentiment labelled datasets to learn language agnostic sentiment features that can be transferred to perform sentiment analysis in low-resource languages **without leveraging any form of cross-lingual supervision**.

Approach : We formulate this problem as a *multi-lingual transfer learning* (MLTL) language adaptation task where we attempt to learn language agnostic sentiment features via adversarial training on labelled documents $(s_1, s_2...s_n)$ from multiple (source) languages to improve the performance on documents $(t_1, t_2...t_m)$ from a low resource (target) language. The key components of our approach include learning monolingual word embeddings from $s_1, s_2...s_n, t_1, t_2...t_m$ and projecting them to a shared multilingual semantic space. We employ an LSTM network to learn latent features (z) from this multilingual space which is then used by a sentiment classifier $(\mathcal{S}_C)$ to predict the sentiment polarity of a document $d \in \{s_1...s_n, t_1...t_m\}$. Concurrently, a language classifier $(\mathcal{C}_L)$ is trained to predict the language of document d based on z. During the adversarial training we try to minimize the binary cross-entropy loss of $\mathcal{C}_S$, while at the same time we maximize the cross-entropy loss of $\mathcal{C}_L$. This results in a setting where the LSTM learns to produce latent features z that predicts the sentiment of document d correctly independent of the language of document d. We hy-

pothesize that in this setting, the latent features (z) trained would contain sentiment features that are language agnostic.

In summary, the main contributions of this paper are :

- We introduce a language independent neural architecture for sentiment analysis without the use of language specific features or cross-lingual supervision.

- We provide extensive evaluations of the LISA architecture in two settings :
  (i) **Low-resource Setting** : Where labeled data in the target language is available in limited amounts.
  (ii) **No-resource Setting** : Where the is no labeled data available in the target language.

- Our experiments on the Multilingual Amazon Review Text Classification dataset and the Sentiraama dataset show that the proposed LISA architecture achieves better performance compared to prior work in the low-resource setting.

The paper is structured as follows : Section 2 highlights the related prior work in the field of CLSC. Section 3 introduces the datasets that are used in our experiments. Section 4 presents the methodology used to align multiple monolingual semantic spaces to a common multilingual semantic space. Section 5 describes in detail the various components of the LISA architecture. Section 6 explains the adversarial training methodology employed. Section 7 describes our experimental setup and provides a detailed comparison of our approach with prior work in both the low-resource and no-resource setting. Section 8 addresses the advantages and shortcomings of the proposed approach and state our concluding remarks.

2   Background and Related Work

CLSC using Machine Translation Systems : The most straightforward approach in CLSC involves using machine translation systems to translate sentences, words, phrases or documents in the target language to the source language and then learning a classifier in the source language to predict the sentiment (Kanayama et al., 2004; Wan, 2008; Wan, 2009; Banea et al., 2010; Lu et al., 2011; Can et al., 2018). The baseline CL-MT (Prettenhofer and Stein, 2010) method uses this technique by using Google Translate[1] to translate documents in the target language to the source language and learns a classifier in the source language using the bag-of-words features. Similarly, the **BiDRL** model (Zhou et al., 2016) used Google Translate and employed a joint learning approach to simultaneously learn both word and document representations in both source and target language which are then used for sentiment classification. However, these methods are overly reliant on the performance of the machine translation system utilized, which in many cases, are less than satisfactory.

CLSC using cross-lingual resources : Most popular methods in CLSC makes use of cross-lingual resources to bridge the language barrier and induce inter-language correspondence. Bel et al. (2003) used a bilingual dictionary to translate documents in the target language to the source language and trained a classifier in the source language for text classification. Mihalcea et al. (2007) used a bilingual lexicon to translate subjective words and phrases in the source language into the target language. Shi et al. (2010) utilizes a bilingual dictionary to translate the classification model from a source language to a target language rather than the documents themselves. Balamurali et al. (2012) used WordNet senses as features for CLSA in Indian languages (Hindi and Marathi). The **CLMM** model (Meng et al., 2012) treated the source language and the target language words in an unlabeled bilingual parallel dataset as generated simultaneously by a set of mixture components. The **CR-RL** approach (Xiao and Guo, 2013) learned word embeddings by using a set of bilingual word pairs where one part of the word vector contains language specific features and the other part contains language independent features. **CL-SCL** model (Prettenhofer and Stein, 2010) leveraged structural correspondence learning with the help of a bilingual dictionary to learn a source-target feature space. Pham et al. (2015) used a parallel corpus between the source language and the target language to learn bilingual paragraph vectors (**Bi-PV**). UMM (Xu and Wan, 2017) learned multilingual sentiment-aware word representations based on unlabeled parallel data and used pivot languages to transfer sentiment information in the absence of parallel data . The **CLDFA** approach (Xu and Yang, 2017) adopted cross-lingual distillation and adversarial techniques on parallel corpora for CLSC. Our work draws inspiration from the **ADAN-GRL** model (Chen et al., 2018b) which employed language adversarial training to learn language invariant features from bilingual word embeddings (BWE) which were created using a parallel corpus. In fact, our proposed model can be considered as a cross-lingually unsupervised variant of the **ADAN-GRL** model as we do not rely on parallel corpora to learn word representations. Furthermore, the **ADAN-GRL** model is limited by the BWE to only incorporate two language pairs (source and target) during training, whereas our LISA system is capable of leveraging multiple source languages and the target language for adversarial training.

CLSC without cross-lingual supervision Neoteric advances by Chen et al. (2018a) alleviates the need for cross-lingual resources by introducing a shared-private Mixture-of-Experts model (**MoE**) that learns both language specific features and language invariant features without cross-lingual supervision. Our work, although related to **MoE** in objective with respect to the lack of cross-lingual supervision, differs in the methodology. Direct comparison of our architecture against **MoE** (Table 4) proves that the (language invariant) features extracted by our architecture contains more sentiment related information than the (language specific + language invariant) features extracted by **MoE**.

3 Dataset Description

We conduct our experiments on two publicly available sentiment classification datasets :

The Multilingual Amazon Review Text Classification dataset (Prettenhofer and Stein, 2010) consists of sentiment labelled data in multiple languages. The vast amount of prior work on this dataset helps us to directly compare our results with the pre-existing state-of-the-art CLSC methods.

The Sentiraama Corpus (Gangula and Mamidi, 2018) is a real-world low resource sentiment corpus in Telugu (an agglutinating Indian language). We use this dataset to test the robustness of our system and evaluate our results in a truly low resource setting.

In the following subsections we describe both the corpora in detail.

---

[1] https://translate.google.com/

3.1 Multilingual Amazon Review Text Classification dataset

The Multilingual Amazon Review Dataset contains sentiment labeled product reviews in four languages (English, German, French and Japanese) across three domains (Books, Dvd and Music). The German, French and Japanese reviews were crawled from Amazon and the corpus was enhanced with English reviews from Blitzer et al. (2007). Each review contains a domain label, a review summary, a review text, and a rating from the set $\{1, 2, 4, 5\}$ where $\{1, 2\}$ denotes negative sentiment and $\{4, 5\}$ denotes positive sentiment. The reviews in each domain for each language are split into three disjoint balanced sets, namely, Train set, Test set and Unlabeled set. The dataset statistics are presented in Table 1.

		Train	Test	Unlabelled
English	Books	2000	2000	50000
	DVD	2000	2000	30000
	Music	2000	2000	25220
German	Books	2000	2000	165470
	DVD	2000	2000	91516
	Music	2000	2000	60392
French	Books	2000	2000	32870
	DVD	2000	2000	9358
	Music	2000	2000	15940
Japanese	Books	2000	2000	169780
	DVD	2000	2000	68326
	Music	2000	2000	55892

Table 1: Multilingual Amazon Review Text Classification dataset statistics.

3.2 Sentiraama Dataset

The Sentiraama dataset consists of sentiment labelled documents in four domains : Books, Movies, Products and Song Lyrics. Each document is given a positive or a negative label. The corpus statistics are presented in Table 2.

	Books	Movies	Products	Lyrics
Positive	100	136	100	230
Negative	100	131	100	109
Total	200	267	200	339

Table 2: Sentiraama corpus statistics.

To avoid cross-domain discrepancies we restrict our experiments to the Books and Movies domain as it has similar counterparts in the Multilingual Amazon Review Dataset, i.e, Books and Dvd respectively. We divide the Books and Movie domains of the Sentiraama dataset to create a Train set and a Test set using an 80-20 train-test split. The statistics of the subset of the corpus that are used in our experiments are listed in Table 3.

	Books		Movies	
	+ve	-ve	+ve	-ve
Train	80	80	108	105
Test	20	20	28	26

Table 3: Subset of the Sentiraama corpus used in our experiments.

4 Multilingual Word Representation

For our experiments, we train fastText embeddings (Bojanowski et al., 2017) to project each word to a monolingual semantic space for each language in the datasets described in Section 3. We then employ the unsupervised MUSE approach (Conneau et al., 2017) to align the monolingual spaces of each language in an adversarial manner to a common multilingual semantic space. While training MUSE we use English as the target semantic space and align all the other monolingual semantic spaces to this space. Let $\mathcal{X} = \{x_1, x_2, \ldots x_a\}$ and $\mathcal{Y} = \{y_1, y_2, \ldots y_b\}$ be the source and target fastText word embeddings respectively. Let W be a linear mapping from $\mathcal{X}$ to $\mathcal{Y}$. A discriminator is trained to discriminate between elements randomly sampled from $W\mathcal{X}$ and $\mathcal{Y}$ while W (which acts as the generator) is jointly trained to fool the discriminator. The discriminator loss function $\mathcal{L}_D(\theta_D|W)$ is formulated as:

$$\mathcal{L}_D(\theta_D|W) = -\frac{1}{a}\sum_{i=1}^{a} log P_{\theta_D}(source = 1|Wx_i)$$

$$-\frac{1}{b}\sum_{i=1}^{b} log P_{\theta_D}(source = 0|y_i)$$

The Mapping objective function used to train W is given by:

$$\mathcal{L}_W(W|\theta_D) = -\frac{1}{a}\sum_{i=1}^{a} log P_{\theta_D}(source = 0|Wx_i)$$

$$-\frac{1}{b}\sum_{i=1}^{b} log P_{\theta_D}(source = 1|y_i)$$

Where θ_D denotes the discriminator parameters and $P_{\theta_D}(source = 1|z)$ is the probability that a

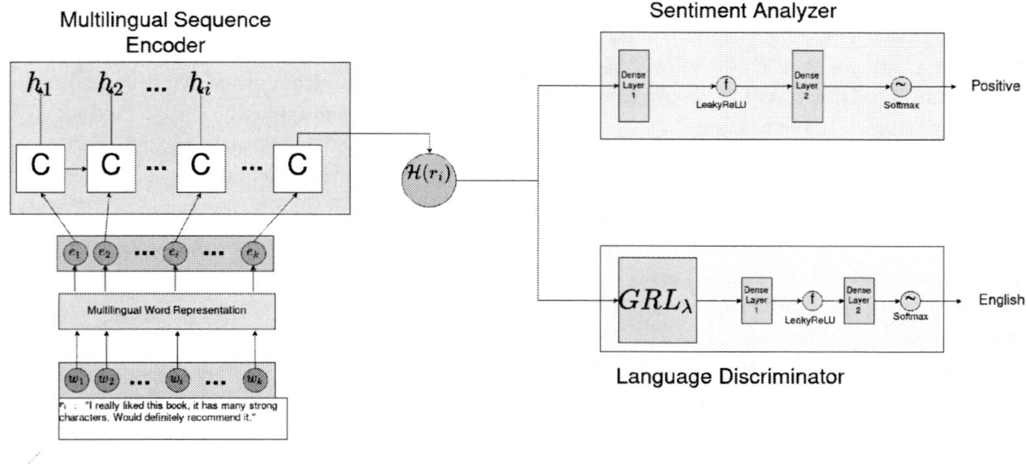

Figure 1: The LISA architecture.

vector z is the mapping of a source embedding according to the discriminator.

Next, a synthetic parallel vocabulary consisting of the most frequent words and their mutual nearest neighbors are extracted from the resulting shared embedding space W to fine-tune the mapping using the closed-form Procrustes solution (Schönemann, 1966) given by:

$$W^* = \underset{W \in O_d(\mathbb{R})}{argmin} \|WX - Y\|_F = UV^T$$

$$\text{with } U\Sigma V^T = \text{SVD}(YX^T)$$

Where X and Y are two aligned matrices containing the embeddings of the words in the trained space W, d represents the dimension of the embeddings, $O_d(\mathbb{R})$ is the space of d x d matrices of real numbers with the orthogonality constraint and $\text{SVD}(YX^T)$ represents the singular value decomposition of YX^T.

5 LISA Architecture

The input to the LISA model is a review r_i that is made up of a sequence of words $w_1, w_2, \ldots w_k$. Each review r_i is associated with a language label $l_i \in L$ where $L = \{l_1, l_2, \ldots l_p\}$ is the set of all language labels used in training. Additionally, each review r_i is also associated with a sentiment label $t_i \in \{positive, negative\}$ which denotes the sentiment polarity of the review. We project each word w_i to the multilingual semantic space (from section 4) to obtain a sequence of n-dimensional word embeddings $e_1, e_2, \ldots e_k$ where $e_i \in \mathbb{R}^n$.

The following subsections describe in detail the individual components of the LISA architecture. Figure 1 shows the overall architecture of the proposed model.

5.1 Multilingual Sequence Encoder ($\mathcal{H}$)

The Multilingual Sequence Encoder ($\mathcal{H}$) processes the sequence of word embeddings $(e_1, e_2, \ldots e_k)$ and transforms it into an m-dimensional (hidden) vector $\mathcal{H}(r_i)$. To this end, the embeddings for all the words in review r_i are passed sequentially through a Long Short-Term Memory (LSTM) network (Hochreiter and Schmidhuber, 1997). LSTMs are a variant of RNNs that learns features that model the long-term dependencies between the words. The LSTM network, at each time step outputs a hidden state h_i for every input word embedding e_i, such that :

$$h_i = \text{LSTM}(e_i, h_{i-1}) \in \mathbb{R}^m$$

The final hidden state $\mathcal{H}(r_i) = h_k$ is then passed through a Language Discriminator ($\mathcal{C}_L$) and a Sentiment Analyzer ($\mathcal{C}_S$).

5.2 Language Discriminator ($\mathcal{C}_L$)

The goal of the Language Discriminator ($\mathcal{C}_L$) is to predict the language label l_i based on $\mathcal{H}(r_i)$. In other words, $\mathcal{C}_L$ tries to predict the language from which the sequence of words $w_1, w_2, \ldots w_k$ come from. The $\mathcal{C}_L$ comprises of a Gradient Reversal Layer (GRL_λ), followed by two Dense Layers and an output Softmax Layer that applies the softmax function over all the languages used in training. During backpropagation, GRL_λ multiplies the gradients by a factor of $-\lambda$ and during the forward pass it acts as the identity function. λ is hyperparameter in the network.

5.3 Sentiment Analyzer ($\mathcal{C}_\mathcal{S}$)

The Sentiment Analyzer ($\mathcal{C}_\mathcal{S}$), as the name suggests, tries to predict the sentiment label t_i of the input review r_i based on $\mathcal{H}(r_i)$. The $\mathcal{C}_\mathcal{S}$ is made up of two Dense Layers followed by an output Softmax Layer that applies the the softmax function over the two sentiment polarities (positive and negative).

6 Adversarial Training

Inspired by recent works (Goodfellow et al., 2014; Ganin et al., 2016; Beutel et al., 2017), we train the LISA model using adversarial training on a set of labeled reviews $R = \{r_1, r_2, \ldots r_n\}$. The aim of the LISA model is to predict the sentiment label t_i for a given review r_i independent of the language label l_i.

We formulate the learning objective in a way that minimizes the sentiment classification loss from $\mathcal{C}_\mathcal{S}$ and maximizes the language classification loss from $\mathcal{C}_\mathcal{L}$. As a result, the LISA model tries to jointly optimize the below functions:

$$\arg \min_{\mathcal{H}, \mathcal{C}_\mathcal{S}} f(\mathcal{C}_\mathcal{S}(\mathcal{H}(r_i)), t_i) - f(\mathcal{C}_\mathcal{L}(\mathcal{H}(r_i)), l_i) \tag{1}$$

$$\arg \max_{\mathcal{C}_\mathcal{L}} f(\mathcal{C}_\mathcal{L}(\mathcal{H}(r_i)), l_i) \tag{2}$$

Where f denotes the loss function used. This results in a setting where the $\mathcal{C}_\mathcal{L}$ tries to predict l_i based on a given $\mathcal{H}(r_i)$ and the encoder $\mathcal{H}$ tries to 'fool' the $\mathcal{C}_\mathcal{L}$ by learning to create $\mathcal{H}(r_i)$ that is minimally influenced by the language label l_i while at the same time, is maximally influenced by the $\mathcal{C}_\mathcal{S}$ to predict he sentiment label t_i correctly.

The M-LiST model (Goud et al., 2019) presents a similar setting for the task of open domain event detection that was trained using a Gradient Reversal Layer GRL_λ (Ganin et al., 2016) between $\mathcal{H}$ and C_L. By using GRL_λ, the optimization functions (equations 1 and 2) can be simplified as :

$$\arg \min_{\mathcal{H}, \mathcal{C}_\mathcal{S}, \mathcal{C}_\mathcal{L}} f(\mathcal{C}_\mathcal{S}(\mathcal{H}(r_i)), t_i) +$$
$$f(\mathcal{C}_\mathcal{L}(GRL_\lambda(\mathcal{H}(r_i))), l_i) \tag{3}$$

7 Experiments and Results

In this section we present an extensive set of experiments conducted on the Multilingual Amazon Review Text Classification dataset and the Telugu Sentiraama sentiment classification corpus. We evaluate our approach in the two settings described below :

Low-resource setting : We evaluate the performance of the LISA architecture in the low-resource setting (termed **LISA-LR**) by training it on the Train sets from multiple source languages and the limited Train set in the target language and then testing on the Test set of the target language.

No-resource setting : In the no-resource setting, we assume that the training data is not available for the target language. We train the LISA model (termed **LISA-NR**) on the Train sets of the source languages and evaluate the model on the target language Test set.

LISA - No Language Discriminator : To show the effectiveness of the Language Discriminator ($\mathcal{C}_\mathcal{L}$), we conduct ablation experiments in the low-resource setting where we remove $\mathcal{C}_\mathcal{L}$ from the LISA architecture. In this variant of the LISA model (termed **LISA-NoLD**), the Sentiment Analyzer only depends on the MUSE embeddings to learn $\mathcal{H}(r_i)$ to learn sentiment features. Our experiments show that **LISA-LR** performs significantly better in most cases than **LISA-NoLD**.

For the Multilingual Amazon Review Text Classification dataset in the low-resource setting, we train **LISA-LR** on the Train sets of all the four languages. We then test it on the Test set of the target language. In the no-resource setting, we train **LISA-NR** on the Train sets of three languages and test it on the Test set of the fourth language. We do this for each domain in the corpus independently. We compare our results against prior state-of-the-art methods that uses Machine Translation Systems (**CL-MT** and **BiDRL**), methods that leverage cross-lingual supervision (**UMM, Bi-PV, CR-RL** and **CL-SCL**) and the cross-lingually unsupervised **MAN-MoE** method of Chen et al. (2018a). The results are presented in Table 4.

For the Sentiraama Corpus in the low-resource setting, we train **LISA-LR** by leveraging the Train sets of all the languages in the Multilingual Amazon dataset along with the Sentiraama Train Set. We then test the system on the Sentiraama Test set.

	German			French			Japanese		
	Books	DVD	Music	Books	DVD	Music	Books	DVD	Music
CL-MT	79.68	77.92	77.22	80.76	78.83	75.78	70.22	71.30	72.02
BiDRL	84.14	84.05	84.67	84.39	83.60	82.52	73.15	76.78	78.77
UMM	81.65	81.27	81.32	80.27	80.27	79.41	71.23	72.55	75.38
Bi-PV	79.51	78.60	82.45	84.25	79.60	80.09	71.75	75.40	75.45
CR-RL	79.89	77.14	77.27	78.25	74.83	78.71	71.11	73.12	74.38
CL-SCL	79.50	76.92	77.79	78.49	78.80	77.92	73.09	71.07	75.11
MAN-MoE	82.40	78.80	77.15	81.10	84.25	80.90	62.78	69.10	72.60
LISA-LR	**85.45**	**84.90**	**86.55**	**86.25**	**85.35**	**85.60**	**79.20**	**83.30**	80.892
LISA-NR	55.60	55.50	58.90	68.95	70.65	64.30	62.20	56.50	59.80
LISA-NoLD	81.20	77.70	80.75	82.80	80.10	80.50	79.05	83.15	**82.542**

Table 4: Results on the Multilingual Amazon Review Text Classification dataset. The numbers denote binary classification accuracies.

In the no-resource setting, **LISA-NR** only utilizes the Train set of all the languages in the Multilingual Amazon dataset and test the system on the Sentiraama Test set. We do this for the Books and Movies domain separately. We evaluate the results of **LISA-LR**, **LISA-NR** and **LISA-NoLD** against the Bernoulli Naive Bayes (Rish and others, 2001) and SVM (Joachims, 1998) baselines that use TF-IDF features which were set by Gangula and Mamidi (2018). The experimental results are given in Table 5

	Books	Movies
SVM	55	51.851
Naive Bayes	65	75.9
LISA-LR	**72.5**	**85.185**
LISA-NR	57.5	57.407
LISA-NoLD	67.5	68.51

Table 5: Results on the Sentiraama Dataset. The numbers denote binary classification accuracies. Note that the Naive Bayes and SVM accuracies presented in the table differ from the ones presented by Gangula and Mamidi (2018). We attribute this to the difference in the train/test splits and the the lack preprocessing guidelines which makes it hard to adequately replicate their results.

8 Analysis and Conclusion

Analysis : The results on the Multilingual Amazon Review Text Classification dataset proves our hypothesis that our model learns language invariant features that can be generalized across languages. The empirical results in Table 4 show that our model outperforms pre-existing state-of-the-art methods on this dataset. While our experiments on the Sentiraama dataset proves that our model can be applied in a real-world setting to enhance sentiment retrieval in a truly low resource language. The ablation experiments (LISA-NoLD vs LISA-LR) show that between language pairs that have similar syntactic structure (example : English, French and German), LISA-LR performs much better than LISA-NoLD. This shows the the performance gains over prior work are not just due to the use of MUSE embeddings. Rather, they are attributed to the adversarial training of the Language Discriminator and the Sentiment classifier that extracts language agnostic sentiment features from the MUSE semantic space. But for Japanese (which is dissimilar with respect to other languages in the corpus), the results show that LISA-LR does not have a significant boots over LISA-NoLD. This is because our language adversarial training will retain only features that are invariant across all four languages, which is restrictive such that the information learnt will be too sparse to be useful. Finally, the poor performance of LISA-NR shows that our approach cannot be used for Zero-Shot learning but will achieve state-of-the-art performance in the presence of limited amounts of data.

Conclusions : In this paper, we present the LISA model which focuses on exploiting language invariant features for multilingual sentiment analysis without any form of cross-lingual supervision. We back our claims by conducting a wide range of experiments over the Multilingual Amazon Review Text Classification dataset and the Sentiraama dataset which is a real-world low resource dataset. We show that our model outperforms not only the existing cross-lingually unsupervised methods but also methods that rely on strong cross-lingual supervision. Additionally, our model sets the new state-of-the-art accuracies for the Sentiraama corpus.

References

Balamurali, AR, Aditya Joshi, and Pushpak Bhattacharyya. 2012. Cross-lingual sentiment analysis for indian languages using linked wordnets. *Proceedings of COLING 2012: Posters*, pages 73–82.

Banea, Carmen, Rada Mihalcea, and Janyce Wiebe. 2010. Multilingual subjectivity: Are more languages better? In *Proceedings of the 23rd international conference on computational linguistics*, pages 28–36. Association for Computational Linguistics.

Bel, Nuria, Cornelis HA Koster, and Marta Villegas. 2003. Cross-lingual text categorization. In *International Conference on Theory and Practice of Digital Libraries*, pages 126–139. Springer.

Beutel, Alex, Jilin Chen, Zhe Zhao, and Ed H Chi. 2017. Data decisions and theoretical implications when adversarially learning fair representations. *arXiv preprint arXiv:1707.00075*.

Blitzer, John, Mark Dredze, and Fernando Pereira. 2007. Domain adaptation for sentiment classification. In *45th Annv. Meeting of the Assoc. Computational Linguistics (ACL'07)*.

Bojanowski, Piotr, Edouard Grave, Armand Joulin, and Tomas Mikolov. 2017. Enriching word vectors with subword information. *Transactions of the Association for Computational Linguistics*, 5:135–146.

Can, Ethem F, Aysu Ezen-Can, and Fazli Can. 2018. Multilingual sentiment analysis: An rnn-based framework for limited data. *arXiv preprint arXiv:1806.04511*.

Chen, Xilun, Ahmed Hassan Awadallah, Hany Hassan, Wei Wang, and Claire Cardie. 2018a. Zero-resource multilingual model transfer: Learning what to share. *arXiv preprint arXiv:1810.03552*.

Chen, Xilun, Yu Sun, Ben Athiwaratkun, Claire Cardie, and Kilian Weinberger. 2018b. Adversarial deep averaging networks for cross-lingual sentiment classification. *Transactions of the Association for Computational Linguistics*, 6:557–570.

Conneau, Alexis, Guillaume Lample, Marc'Aurelio Ranzato, Ludovic Denoyer, and Hervé Jégou. 2017. Word translation without parallel data. *arXiv preprint arXiv:1710.04087*.

Durant, Kathleen T and Michael D Smith. 2006. Mining sentiment classification from political web logs.

Gangula, Rama Rohit Reddy and Radhika Mamidi. 2018. Resource creation towards automated sentiment analysis in telugu (a low resource language) and integrating multiple domain sources to enhance sentiment prediction. In *Proceedings of the Eleventh International Conference on Language Resources and Evaluation (LREC-2018)*.

Ganin, Yaroslav, Evgeniya Ustinova, Hana Ajakan, Pascal Germain, Hugo Larochelle, François Laviolette, Mario Marchand, and Victor Lempitsky. 2016. Domain-adversarial training of neural networks. *The Journal of Machine Learning Research*, 17(1):2096–2030.

Goodfellow, Ian, Jean Pouget-Abadie, Mehdi Mirza, Bing Xu, David Warde-Farley, Sherjil Ozair, Aaron Courville, and Yoshua Bengio. 2014. Generative adversarial nets. In *Advances in neural information processing systems*, pages 2672–2680.

Goud, Jaipal Singh, Pranav Goel, Allen J Antony, and Manish Shrivastava. 2019. Leveraging multilingual resources for open-domain event detection. In *Workshop on Interoperable Semantic Annotation (ISA-15)*, page 76.

Hochreiter, Sepp and Jürgen Schmidhuber. 1997. Long short-term memory. *Neural computation*, 9(8):1735–1780.

Iyyer, Mohit, Varun Manjunatha, Jordan Boyd-Graber, and Hal Daumé III. 2015. Deep unordered composition rivals syntactic methods for text classification. In *Proceedings of the 53rd Annual Meeting of the Association for Computational Linguistics and the 7th International Joint Conference on Natural Language Processing (Volume 1: Long Papers)*, volume 1, pages 1681–1691.

Joachims, Thorsten. 1998. Text categorization with support vector machines: Learning with many relevant features. In *European conference on machine learning*, pages 137–142. Springer.

Kanayama, Hiroshi, Tetsuya Nasukawa, and Hideo Watanabe. 2004. Deeper sentiment analysis using machine translation technology. In *COLING 2004: Proceedings of the 20th International Conference on Computational Linguistics*.

Kim, Yoon. 2014. Convolutional neural networks for sentence classification. *arXiv preprint arXiv:1408.5882*.

Lu, Bin, Chenhao Tan, Claire Cardie, and Benjamin K Tsou. 2011. Joint bilingual sentiment classification with unlabeled parallel corpora. In *Proceedings of the 49th Annual Meeting of the Association for Computational Linguistics: Human Language Technologies-Volume 1*, pages 320–330. Association for Computational Linguistics.

Meng, Xinfan, Furu Wei, Xiaohua Liu, Ming Zhou, Ge Xu, and Houfeng Wang. 2012. Cross-lingual mixture model for sentiment classification. In *Proceedings of the 50th Annual Meeting of the Association for Computational Linguistics: Long Papers-Volume 1*, pages 572–581. Association for Computational Linguistics.

Mihalcea, Rada, Carmen Banea, and Janyce Wiebe. 2007. Learning multilingual subjective language via cross-lingual projections. In *Proceedings of the 45th annual meeting of the association of computational linguistics*, pages 976–983.

Pham, Hieu, Thang Luong, and Christopher Manning. 2015. Learning distributed representations for multilingual text sequences. In *Proceedings of the 1st Workshop on Vector Space Modeling for Natural Language Processing*, pages 88–94.

Prasad, Suhaas. 2010. Micro-blogging sentiment analysis using bayesian classification methods. In *Technical Report*. Stanford University.

Prettenhofer, Peter and Benno Stein. 2010. Cross-language text classification using structural correspondence learning. In *Proceedings of the 48th annual meeting of the association for computational linguistics*, pages 1118–1127.

Rish, Irina et al. 2001. An empirical study of the naive bayes classifier. In *IJCAI 2001 workshop on empirical methods in artificial intelligence*, volume 3, pages 41–46.

Schönemann, Peter H. 1966. A generalized solution of the orthogonal procrustes problem. *Psychometrika*, 31(1):1–10.

Shi, Lei, Rada Mihalcea, and Mingjun Tian. 2010. Cross language text classification by model translation and semi-supervised learning. In *Proceedings of the 2010 Conference on Empirical Methods in Natural Language Processing*, pages 1057–1067. Association for Computational Linguistics.

Socher, Richard, Alex Perelygin, Jean Wu, Jason Chuang, Christopher D Manning, Andrew Ng, and Christopher Potts. 2013. Recursive deep models for semantic compositionality over a sentiment treebank. In *Proceedings of the 2013 conference on empirical methods in natural language processing*, pages 1631–1642.

Tai, Kai Sheng, Richard Socher, and Christopher D Manning. 2015. Improved semantic representations from tree-structured long short-term memory networks. *arXiv preprint arXiv:1503.00075*.

Wan, Xiaojun. 2008. Using bilingual knowledge and ensemble techniques for unsupervised chinese sentiment analysis. In *Proceedings of the conference on empirical methods in natural language processing*, pages 553–561. Association for Computational Linguistics.

Wan, Xiaojun. 2009. Co-training for cross-lingual sentiment classification. In *Proceedings of the Joint Conference of the 47th Annual Meeting of the ACL and the 4th International Joint Conference on Natural Language Processing of the AFNLP: Volume 1-volume 1*, pages 235–243. Association for Computational Linguistics.

Wang, Yequan, Minlie Huang, Li Zhao, et al. 2016. Attention-based lstm for aspect-level sentiment classification. In *Proceedings of the 2016 conference on empirical methods in natural language processing*, pages 606–615.

Xiao, Min and Yuhong Guo. 2013. Semi-supervised representation learning for cross-lingual text classification. In *Proceedings of the 2013 Conference on Empirical Methods in Natural Language Processing*, pages 1465–1475.

Xu, Kui and Xiaojun Wan. 2017. Towards a universal sentiment classifier in multiple languages. In *Proceedings of the 2017 Conference on Empirical Methods in Natural Language Processing*, pages 511–520.

Xu, Ruochen and Yiming Yang. 2017. Cross-lingual distillation for text classification. *arXiv preprint arXiv:1705.02073*.

Yarowsky, David, Grace Ngai, and Richard Wicentowski. 2001. Inducing multilingual text analysis tools via robust projection across aligned corpora. In *Proceedings of the first international conference on Human language technology research*, pages 1–8. Association for Computational Linguistics.

Zhou, Xinjie, Xiaojun Wan, and Jianguo Xiao. 2016. Cross-lingual sentiment classification with bilingual document representation learning. In *Proceedings of the 54th Annual Meeting of the Association for Computational Linguistics (Volume 1: Long Papers)*, volume 1, pages 1403–1412.

Low-Resource Unsupervised NMT: Diagnosing the Problem and Providing a Linguistically Motivated Solution

Lukas Edman, Antonio Toral, Gertjan van Noord
Center for Language and Cognition
University of Groningen
`{j.l.edman, a.toral.ruiz, g.j.m.van.noord}@rug.nl`

Abstract

Unsupervised Machine Translation has been advancing our ability to translate without parallel data, but state-of-the-art methods assume an abundance of monolingual data. This paper investigates the scenario where monolingual data is limited as well, finding that current unsupervised methods suffer in performance under this stricter setting. We find that the performance loss originates from the poor quality of the pretrained monolingual embeddings, and we propose using linguistic information in the embedding training scheme. To support this, we look at two linguistic features that may help improve alignment quality: dependency information and sub-word information. Using dependency-based embeddings results in a complementary word representation which offers a boost in performance of around 1.5 BLEU points compared to standard WORD2VEC when monolingual data is limited to 1 million sentences per language. We also find that the inclusion of sub-word information is crucial to improving the quality of the embeddings.

1 Introduction

Machine Translation (MT) is a rapidly advancing field of Natural Language Processing, where there is an ever-increasing number of claims of MT systems reaching human parity (Hassan et al., 2018; Barrault et al., 2019). However, most of the focus has been on MT systems under the assumption that there is a large amount of parallel data available, which is only the case for a select number of language pairs.

Recently, there have been approaches that do away with this assumption, requiring only monolingual data, with the first methods based solely around neural MT (NMT), using aligned pretrained embeddings to bootstrap the translation process, and refining the translation with a neural model via denoising and back-translation (Artetxe et al., 2017b; Lample et al., 2017). More recently, statistical MT (SMT) approaches as well as hybrid approaches, combining SMT and NMT, have proven more successful (Lample et al., 2018; Artetxe et al., 2019).

While the unsupervised approaches so far have done away with the assumption of parallel data, they still assume an abundance of monolingual data for the two languages, typically assuming at least 10 million sentences per language. This amount of data is not available for every language, notably languages without much of a digital presence. For example, Fulah is a language spoken in West and Central Africa by over 20 million people, however there is a scarce amount of data freely available online. This motivates a new paradigm in unsupervised MT: Low-Resource Unsupervised MT (LRUMT).

In this paper, we investigate the reasons why current unsupervised NMT methods fail in the low-resource setting, addressing the source of the issue, and we propose a potential solution to make unsupervised NMT more robust to the lack of availability of monolingual data.

We start by giving a brief overview of the work so far in unsupervised MT in Section 2, establishing the general pipeline used to train an unsupervised system. We then identify the source of

Martins, Moniz, Fumega, Martins, Batista, Coheur, Parra, Trancoso, Turchi, Bisazza, Moorkens, Guerberof, Nurminen, Marg, Forcada (eds.)
Proceedings of the 22nd Annual Conference of the European Association for Machine Translation, p. 81–90
Lisboa, Portugal, November 2020.

the performance problem in LRUMT in Section 3, and propose potential improvements in Section 4. Lastly, in Section 5, we present our conclusions and lines for future work.

2 An Unsupervised MT Overview

The typical unsupervised NMT pipeline can be broken down into 3 sequential steps:

1. Train monolingual embeddings for each language

2. Align embeddings with a mapping algorithm

3. Train NMT system, initialized with aligned embeddings

In the first step, monolingual embeddings (which we will also refer to as pretrained embeddings) are most often trained in the style of WORD2VEC's skip-gram algorithm (Mikolov et al., 2013). To incorporate sub-word information, Lample et al. (2018) use FASTTEXT (Bojanowski et al., 2017), which formulates a word's embedding as the sum of its character n-gram embeddings. Artetxe (2019) uses a WORD2VEC extension PHRASE2VEC (Artetxe et al., 2018b), which learns embeddings of word n-grams up to trigrams, effectively creating embeddings for phrases.

The second step involves the alignment of the two monolingual embeddings such that the embeddings of words with identical or similar meaning across language appear close in the shared embedding space. Artetxe et al. achieve this using VECMAP (Artetxe et al., 2018a), which learns a linear transformation between the two embeddings into a shared space. If there is a large shared vocabulary between the two languages, it is also possible to concatenate the monolingual corpora and train a single embedding for both languages, effectively completing steps 1 and 2 simultaneously (Lample et al., 2018).

The third and final step is to train the NMT model. The architecture can be any encoder-decoder model, with the condition that it can translate in both directions. Models typically share an encoder and decoder for both languages, with a language token provided only to the decoder. Two objectives are used to train the model: denoising and on-the-fly back-translation. Denoising is monolingual; the model is given an altered sentence (e.g. with word order shuffling or word removal) and trained to reconstruct the original, un-

altered sentence. On-the-fly back-translation involves first translating a sentence from the source language (s_{src}) to the target language (s'_{tgt}). This creates a pseudo-parallel sentence pair (s'_{tgt}, s_{src}), so the output s'_{tgt} is translated back to the source language (creating s''_{src}), and the model is trained to reconstruct the original source sentence, minimizing the difference between s''_{src} and s_{src}. Denoising and back-translation are carried out alternately during training.

The unsupervised SMT approach is fairly similar, with a replacement of step 3 (or in the hybrid approach, a step added between steps 2 and 3). In Artetxe et al. (2019) for example, a phrase-based SMT model is built by constructing a phrase table that is initialized using the aligned cross-lingual phrase embeddings, and tuning it using an unsupervised variant of the Minimum Error Rate Training (Och, 2003) method. For the hybrid model, the SMT system can then create pseudo-parallel data used to train the NMT model, alongside denoising and back-translation. In the remainder of this paper, we focus on the purely NMT approach to unsupervised MT.

3 The Role of Pretrained Embeddings in Unsupervised MT

With the pipeline established, we now turn to the LRUMT setting. In LRUMT, the existing unsupervised approaches fail somewhere along the pipeline, but simply measuring MT performance does not make it clear where this failure occurs. We speculate that the failure is relative to the quality of the pretrained word embeddings, and subsequent quality of the cross-lingual alignment. We test this hypothesis in this section.

The aligned pretrained embeddings of an unsupervised NMT system are what jump-starts the process of translation. From aligned pretrained embeddings alone, we can effectively do word-for-word translation, which is commonly measured using Bilingual Lexicon Induction (BLI). Without well-aligned pretrained embeddings, denoising and back-translation alone are not enough to produce meaningful translations.

For our following experiments[1], we train on English and German sentences from the WMT Monolingual News Crawl from years 2007 to 2017, use *newstest* 2015 for development and *newstest*

---

[1]Our code for running our experiments can be found at: https://github.com/Leukas/LRUMT

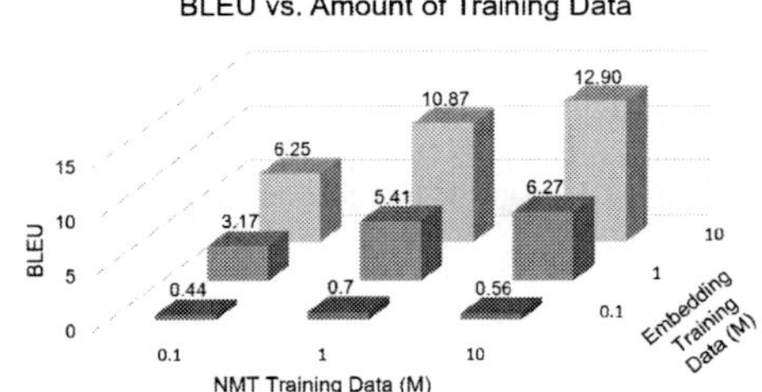

Figure 1: English→German BLEU scores of unsupervised NMT systems where the amount of training data used for the pre-trained embedding training and the amount used for the NMT model training is varied.

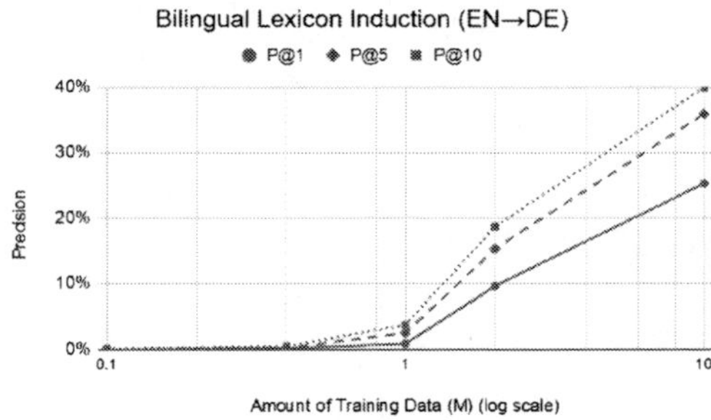

Figure 2: BLI of standard WORD2VEC using various amounts of training data, measured with precision at 1, 5, and 10.

2016 for testing, following Lample et al. (2018). The training data is filtered such that sentences that contain between 3-80 words are kept. We then truncate the corpora to sizes ranging from 0.1 to 10 million sentences per language, specified as necessary. We used UDPIPE (Straka and Straková, 2017) for tokenization[2], MOSES (Koehn et al., 2007) for truecasing, and we apply 60 thousand BPE joins (following Lample et al. (2018)) across both corpora using fastBPE.[3,4] We train the word embeddings using the WORD2VEC skipgram model, with the same hyperparameters as used in Artetxe et al. (2017b), except using an embedding dimension size of 512.[5] For embedding alignment, we use the completely unsupervised version of VECMAP with default parameters. We then train our unsupervised NMT models using Lample et al. (2018)'s implementation, using the default parameters, with the exception of 10 back-translation processors rather than 30 due to hardware limitations. We use the early stopping criterion from Lample et al. (2018).[6]

To demonstrate the importance of a large amount of training data, we vary the amount of monolingual data used for training the embeddings as well as the amount used for training the NMT

system in Figure 1.[7] Even if we then use 10 million sentences per language to train the NMT system, using only 100 thousand sentences per language to train the embeddings results in a BLEU score below 1. Conversely, the NMT system can achieve a BLEU score of around 6 using embeddings trained on 10 million sentences, even when the NMT system is only trained on 100 thousand sentences per language.

We also provide Figure 2, showing the BLI scores of the aligned embeddings (using the English→German test set from Artetxe et al. (2017a)[8]) as we vary the amount of training data used for the embeddings. We can see that the BLI scores decrease dramatically as the amount of sentences decreases, matching the trend of the results from Figure 1. Although BLI has been criticized for not always correlating with downstream tasks (Glavas et al., 2019), in this case, poor alignment corresponds to poor MT performance.

In these experiments, we use VECMAP for aligning embeddings. VECMAP's algorithm begins by initializing a bilingual dictionary, which uses a word's relations to the other words in the same language, with the idea being that "apple" would be close to "pear" but far from "motorcycle" in every language, for example. However, if the quality of embeddings is poor, the random initialization of embeddings has a greater dampening effect. Using embedding similarity tasks (shown in Table 1), we find this to be the case.

We measure the quality of the monolingual embeddings using 3 similarity datasets for English:

---

[2]We use UDPIPE's tokenizer over the commonly used MOSES as UDPIPE learns tokenization from gold-standard labels based on the UD tokenizing standard, allowing for higher-quality dependency parsing (which will be used in Section 4).

[3]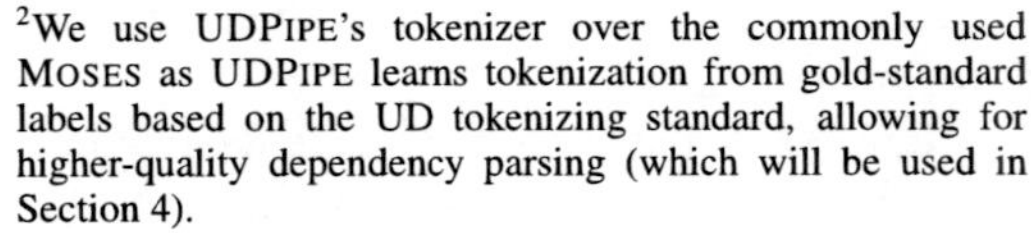https://github.com/glample/fastBPE

[4]BPE is not applied when measuring BLI or word similarity.

[5]We use a dimension size of 512 to match the embedding size used in Lample et al. (2018)'s Transformer model.

[6]We also limit training to 24 hours. On the GPU we used to train our experiments, an Nvidia V100, limiting the training time only affected systems which used 10 million sentences per language.

[7]Although we only show results for an unsupervised NMT system, the state-of-the-art SMT systems also require initialization from pretrained embeddings. Therefore, we expect the same trend would appear.

[8]We modify the test set by truecasing it in order to match our models.

Word Similarity	Amount of Data (M)		
	0.1	1	10
EN - MEN	0.138	0.421	0.705
EN - WS353	0.018	0.461	0.628
EN - SIMLEX	0.011	0.232	0.300
DE - SIMLEX_DE	0.017	0.051	0.293

Table 1: The Spearman correlation of the similarity of word pairs (measured by cosine similarity) and human evaluation. Evaluation done using: `https://github.com/kudkudak/word-embeddings-benchmarks`

MEN (Bruni et al., 2014), WS353 (Agirre et al., 2009), and SIMLEX999 (Hill et al., 2015). We also use Multilingual SIMLEX999 (Leviant and Reichart, 2015) for German and denote this as `SIMLEX_DE`.

As we can see in Table 1, the correlation to human judgment on similarity tasks decreases dramatically as the amount of data used to train the models decreases. The poor correlation when data is limited explains VECMAP's poor alignment, as it relies on word similarity being relatively equivalent across languages for its initialization step.

4 Getting More out of Scarce Data

With the source of the problem established as the drop in quality of embeddings, we ask ourselves: how can we prevent this drop in a low-resource scenario, where considerably less monolingual data is available? We argue that the conventional word embedding methods (i.e. WORD2VEC) do not use all of the information present within sentences during the training process.

Word embedding algorithms typically define a context-target pair as a word and its neighboring words in a sentence, respectively. While this method works with a large amount of data available, it relies on the fact that a word is seen in several different contexts in order to be represented in the embedding space with respect to its meaning. When data is limited, the contexts contain too much variability to allow for a meaningful representation to be learned.

To test this, we use an embedding strategy that has a different definition of the context: dependency-based word embeddings (Levy and Goldberg, 2014). These embeddings model the syntactic similarity between words rather than semantic similarity, providing an embedding representation complementary to standard embeddings.

This section presents our findings using

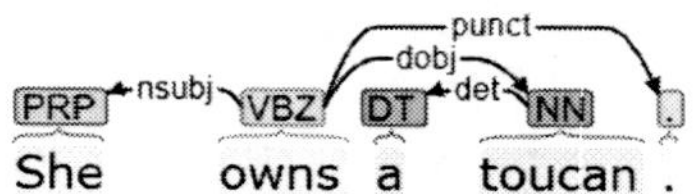

Figure 3: Example of a dependency-parsed sentence.

dependency-based embeddings (4.1). We also consider the effect of using sub-word information via FASTTEXT (4.2). With the previous two approaches, we find that ensembling models can be useful, and investigate this further (4.3). Finally, we vary context window size and report on its effect (4.4).

4.1 Dependency-Based Embeddings

Dependency parsing offers a formalization of the grammatical relationship between the words in a sentence. For each sentence, a dependency parser will create a tree in which words are connected if they have a dependency relation between them. As shown in Figure 3, the `nsubj` relation denotes the subject-to-verb relation between `she` and `owns`, for example.

Levy and Goldberg (2014) use dependency information to train word embeddings, defining the context as the parent and child relation(s) of the target word. This has two effects that distinguish dependency-based embeddings from standard embeddings. Firstly, the context is limited to syntactically-related words. For example, determiners are always limited to a context of a noun. Therefore, words of the same part-of-speech tend to be closer in the embedding space, since they have similar contexts. Secondly, the context is not limited by the distance between words in a sentence. For example, Figure 4 shows a long-range dependency between `item` and `rack`. This relation would only be captured by a standard word embedding algorithm with a large context window of length 14 or greater, whereas in the dependency-based version `rack` is one of 4 tokens in `item`'s context, and `item` is one of 6 tokens in `rack`'s context.

Levy and Goldberg (2014) also require the embedding model to predict the relation between the target word and a context word, and whether it is a parent or child relation. This explicitly trains the model to understand the syntactic relationship between two words, which provides information on the function of a word in a sentence. For example, referring back to Figure 3, the fact that `owns` has

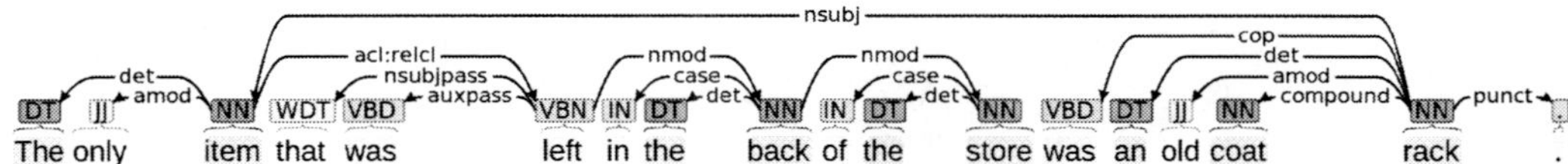

Figure 4: Example of a sentence with a long-range dependency, in this case, an `nsubj` relation between `item` and `rack`.

a `dobj` relation means that `owns` is a transitive verb. Although this information could be learned implicitly by regular WORD2VEC, as the amount of training data decreases, it becomes much harder to learn without explicit labels.

Due to their reduced context variability and their explicit learning of linguistic information, we expect dependency-based embeddings to achieve a better alignment in the low-resource setting.

In the following experiments, we use the same settings as mentioned in Section 3, apart from those explicitly mentioned. With the addition of dependency parsing into the pipeline, we apply a parser on the tokenized sentences, while truecasing is learned prior to but applied after parsing. We use the StanfordNLP parser (Qi et al., 2019), using the pretrained English and German models provided to parse our data.

Although the dependency parser that we use is supervised, therefore requiring dependency data, it is possible to train a dependency parser in an unsupervised fashion (He et al., 2018). Regardless, a dependency parser extracts linguistic information that is present in a sentence, thus our dependency-based method can still show whether using such linguistic information for training embeddings is useful for their alignment.

For training dependency-based word embeddings, we apply Levy and Goldberg (2014)'s dependency-based WORD2VEC, and compare this against the standard WORD2VEC. For the dependency-based embeddings, we use the same hyperparameters as we use for WORD2VEC.

To achieve considerable results in unsupervised NMT, it is necessary that we apply Byte-Pair Encoding (BPE) (Gage, 1994). In the dependency-based pipeline, this is learned after truecasing and applied after dependency parsing. In order to apply BPE to dependency-parsed sentences, any words that are split into multiple sub-word units will have a `bpe` relation or relations connecting them. We connected sub-word units from left-to-right, where the leftmost unit was the parent of all other units.[9]

Amount (M)	Reg	DP	Reg+DP
0.1	0.00%	0.00%	0.00%
0.4	0.27%	0.18%	**0.62%**
1	2.49%	5.05%	**9.64%**
2	15.28%	11.32%	**18.66%**
10	35.86%	25.03%	**36.06%**

Table 2: BLI P@5 scores for aligned standard (Reg), dependency-based (DP), and hybrid (Reg+DP) WORD2VEC embeddings. The best scores are shown in bold.

In addition to the standard and dependency-based word embeddings, we also combine the two approaches, forming a hybrid embedding. This is done by training word embeddings using both methods separately with half the embedding dimension size (i.e. 256), concatenating them, and aligning them with VECMAP. We use the + symbol to denote a combined model.

Table 2 shows the BLI accuracies for the standard WORD2VEC (Reg), dependency-based WORD2VEC (DP), and hybrid (Reg+DP) embeddings as we vary the amount of monolingual sentences available to the embedding algorithms. We can see that the hybrid model outperforms the other two models at each threshold for data, apart from 100 thousand, where all three models fail entirely. Although the dependency-based model performs relatively poorly in cases where more than 1 million sentences are available, we see that the hybrid model still outperforms the regular model, which would indicate that the dependency-based model is providing complementary information to the regular model.

We also include Table 3, which shows the English→German BLEU scores[10] of our NMT systems using the pretrained standard, dependency-based, and hybrid embeddings. Here, we see that the standard embeddings outperform the other two models when they are given 2 million or more sentences to train on. We suspect

---

[9]We experimented with several methods of connecting the relations, considering token length and frequency, but we found that the connection method had little impact on the resulting BLEU scores.

[10]We report the German→English BLEU scores in Table 8 in Appendix A.

Amount (M)	Reg	DP	Reg+DP
0.1	0.44	**0.97**	0.4
0.4	1.58	2.56	**3.26**
1	5.41	5.9	**6.99**
2	**9.31**	7.82	8.82
10	**12.9**	10.28	11.41

Table 3: English→German BLEU scores for NMT models using pretrained standard (Reg), dependency-based (DP), and hybrid (Reg+DP) embeddings. The best scores are shown in bold.

Amount (M)	Fast	Fast+Reg	Fast+DP
0.1	0.24%	0.36%	**1.45%**
0.4	0.18%	1.06%	**19.98%**
1	0.78%	**29.86%**	25.66%
2	34.09%	**35.64%**	29.98%
10	47.36%	**50.61%**	50.34%

Table 4: BLI P@5 scores for aligned FASTTEXT (Fast), and two hybrid models consisting of FASTTEXT with regular (Fast+Reg) and FASTTEXT with dependency-based (Fast+DP) WORD2VEC embeddings. The best scores are shown in bold.

Amount (M)	Fast	Fast+Reg	Fast+DP
0.1	0.77	**1.94**	1.16
0.4	**7.47**	7.28	5.32
1	**10.37**	9.37	7.48
2	**11.49**	11.48	10.12
10	**13.98**	13.89	11.77

Table 5: English→German BLEU scores for aligned FASTTEXT (Fast), and two hybrid models consisting of FASTTEXT with regular (Fast+Reg) and FASTTEXT with dependency-based (Fast+DP) WORD2VEC embeddings. The best scores are shown in bold.

this difference in performance is due to the inclusion of BPE, as that is the only difference in preprocessing. When adding the bpe relation to our dependency-parsed sentences, we may inadvertently isolate some sub-word units from their natural contexts. As we treat the leftmost unit as the parent, the other units will only have a relation to the leftmost unit, limiting their context and potentially adversely affecting their embedded representation.

Despite the potentially adverse effects of BPE, we see that dependency-based embeddings and hybrid embeddings outperform standard embeddings when monolingual data is limited to 1 million sentences per language or fewer.

4.2 Considering Sub-word Information

As Lample et al. (2018) and Artetxe et al. (2019) established, considering sub-word information proves very effective in increasing the performance of unsupervised MT systems. We follow Lample et al. (2018) and achieve this by using FASTTEXT. As FASTTEXT represents words as a summation of character n-grams, rarer words can have a meaningful representation if they are composed of common character n-grams. So as data becomes more scarce, FASTTEXT effectively relies on morphemes to represent words.

For FASTTEXT, we use the same hyperparameters as used for the regular WORD2VEC, apart from the context size, in which we follow Lample et al. (2018) and use a size of 5. Additionally, we create hybrid models of FASTTEXT and regular WORD2VEC concatenated (Fast+Reg), as well as FASTTEXT and dependency-based WORD2VEC concatenated (Fast+DP). The resulting BLI scores are shown in Table 4.

We can see that the inclusion of sub-word information via FASTTEXT has a very large impact on the alignment quality in general: for FAST-TEXT alone, the alignment scores improve over the regular and dependency-based models, provided there are 2 million or more sentences. Unlike with regular embeddings, the Fast+DP model does not provide improvements when there are at least 1 million sentences available. With all three FAST-TEXT-based models, we see a drastic improvement from 0-2% up to 20-35% when the amount of data is increased, however the Fast+DP model has this increase with less data, which may indicate that dependency information is useful in the lower resource setting.

For 100 thousand sentences, we do see some improvement, but with a P@5 of less than 2%, it is clear that none of the embedding methods tested are capable of providing embeddings of a high enough quality to allow for a decent unsupervised alignment.

While the inclusion of sub-word information via FASTTEXT outperforms the dependency-based embeddings alone, the two are not mutually exclusive: it is feasible to train a variant of FASTTEXT that uses contexts based on dependency relations to get the best of both worlds. From simple concatenation, the Fast+DP hybrid embeddings proved useful for cases where only 100-400 thousand sentences per language were available.

Table 5 shows the resulting BLEU scores for

FASTTEXT and the two previously described hybrid models.[11][12] With at least 400 thousand sentences available, we see that the non-hybrid model and the Fast+Reg hybrid perform similarly, but the Fast+DP hybrid performs worse than the other two. With only 100 thousand sentences available, both hybrid models perform better than the non-hybrid model, with Fast+Reg giving the best performance.

The BLEU scores from Table 5 as well as Table 3 seem to indicate that hybridization does not necessarily lead to better translation quality, despite often giving a higher BLI score. The BLEU score of the Fast+DP model trained on 400 thousand sentences per language stands out in particular, as the corresponding BLI score appears to indicate that the quality of the alignment should be much better than the other two models. We speculate that this could be due to one of two things: either it is due to the inclusion of BPE (as we previously discussed), or it is an artifact of VECMAP's training. Concerning the latter, VECMAP may be aligning the embeddings to the point where they are close enough for the NMT system to understand which words correspond to which, but not to the point where a large number of words will have their corresponding words in the other language close enough to be counted for the BLI precision at 5 score. Therefore, the large jump in BLI scores can be misleading in terms of alignment quality for unsupervised NMT.

Overall, the performance of FASTTEXT indicates that the use of sub-word information is very important to the performance of the NMT system, as we see both BLI and BLEU score improvements when comparing FASTTEXT to standard WORD2VEC. Along with the performance of the dependency-based embeddings, this supports the idea that linguistic information as a whole can be useful in improving translation quality in unsupervised NMT.

4.3 Ensembling of Embeddings

As our hybrid embeddings have shown to have an increase in performance, we note that this could be due to the effect of ensembling two embeddings with different random weight initializations rather than due to the differences between the embedding algorithms. To test this, we train two embeddings using the same algorithm (but different weight initializations) and concatenate them in the same manner as the hybrid models. Using this method, we produce Reg+Reg, DP+DP, and Fast+Fast, and we compare them to our hybrid models in Table 6.

The scores show that the improvement found in Reg+DP is greater than the improvement found by ensembling either of its two constituent models. This indicates that there is a complementary relationship between regular and dependency-based WORD2VEC. As for Fast+Fast, the model performs better than the two hybrid models using FASTTEXT when the number of sentences ranges from 400 thousand to 2 million, with the greatest improvement found at 400 thousand sentences per language. While there is a greater improvement from Fast+Fast compared to Fast+Reg and Fast+DP, this may be more due to the poor quality of the Reg and DP components of the hybrid models, whose contribution may be hindering the alignment rather than helping. Overall, ensembling 2 embeddings from the same embedding algorithm yields marginal improvements in alignment quality, whereas ensembling 2 embeddings from different algorithms can potentially yield greater benefits.

4.4 Context Size

Seeing as the context plays a role in the alignment quality of embeddings, we vary the context window size of WORD2VEC and FASTTEXT embeddings to see its effect. Additionally, using a context size of 1 with WORD2VEC produces embeddings which are better suited for inducing part-of-speech tags (Lin et al., 2015), which could also aid with alignment. As such we test on context sizes of 1, 3, 5, and 10.

The results overwhelmingly indicate that a larger context size is better for alignment when there are at least 1 million sentences per language available. This may explain why the dependency-based embeddings do not perform well relative to the standard WORD2VEC and FASTTEXT embeddings. In the sentence in Figure 4, for example, the

---

[11] We report the German→English BLEU scores in Table 9 in Appendix A.

[12] The BLEU scores are not directly comparable to the results of Lample et al. (2018) for a couple of reasons (apart from the hardware limitation previously mentioned): 1. We use VECMAP to align embeddings, whereas they concatenate corpora and train a singular embedding. 2. We use a maximum of 10 million sentences per language, they use the entire WMT News Crawl dataset, which is well over 100 million sentences per language.

Amount (M)	Reg+Reg	DP+DP	Reg+DP	Fast+Fast	Fast+Reg	Fast+DP
0.1	0.00%	0.00%	0.00%	0.84%	0.36%	**1.45%**
0.4	0.09%	0.44%	**0.62%**	**24.14%**	1.06%	19.98%
1	6.07%	4.67%	**9.64%**	**31.26%**	29.86%	25.66%
2	15.50%	11.46%	**18.66%**	**35.86%**	35.64%	29.98%
10	35.93%	25.30%	**36.06%**	47.16%	**50.61%**	50.34%

Table 6: BLI comparison of ensemble models (Reg+Reg, DP+DP, and Fast+Fast), to the aforementioned hybrid models (Reg+DP, Fast+Reg, and Fast+DP).

Amount (M)	WORD2VEC				FASTTEXT			
	1	3	5	10	1	3	5	10
0.1	0.00%	**0.12%**	0.00%	0.00%	0.12%	**0.60%**	0.24%	0.00%
0.4	0.00%	0.00%	0.00%	**0.27%**	0.18%	0.27%	0.18%	**0.35%**
1	0.00%	0.08%	1.48%	**2.49%**	0.00%	0.23%	0.78%	**28.07%**
2	3.16%	5.66%	13.15%	**15.28%**	23.14%	32.33%	34.09%	**35.05%**
10	27.06%	32.27%	33.90%	**35.86%**	39.92%	45.20%	47.36%	**48.58%**

Table 7: BLI P@5 scores for aligned FASTTEXT, and WORD2VEC, with varying window sizes of 1, 3, 5, and 10.

largest context is 6 for the word `rack`, and the average context size is 1.83. Given the increases we see from WORD2VEC and FASTTEXT with a larger context size, it is likely we will see a large increase in alignment quality for dependency-based embeddings as well if they can be trained with a larger context.

5 Conclusion and Future Work

Unsupervised NMT has made great strides in making MT more accessible for language pairs that lack parallel corpora. We attempt to further this accessibility by introducing LRUMT, where monolingual data is also limited. Our results show that, in the current state-of-the-art pipeline, the quality of the pretrained word embeddings is the main issue, and that using syntactically-motivated dependency-based embeddings has the potential to improve performance when monolingual data is limited.

We also see that the inclusion of sub-word information for training word embeddings provides a crucial performance increase, which provides further evidence that using the latent linguistic information in a sentence can improve embedding alignment quality.

Finally, on the topic of context size, we find that a larger context size is almost always better, most noticeably when more data is available. This helps explain the poorer performance of the dependency-based embeddings on larger amounts of data.

To improve upon dependency-based embeddings for unsupervised NMT, we consider two avenues to explore: including sub-word information and increasing the context size. To include sub-word information, it should be possible to combine the training methods of FASTTEXT and dependency-based WORD2VEC. To increase the context size, one might consider including a word's grandparent, grandchildren, and siblings (its parent's other children) as part of the context.

We also note that we currently use a pretrained dependency parser, trained on labelled dependency data, which is often harder to come by than parallel data. We plan to switch to using unsupervised dependency parsing techniques to ensure this method is accessible for all languages.

Furthermore, there are several potential methods for incorporating more linguistic information into embeddings. One such possibility would be to use a morphological segmenter such as MORFESSOR (Virpioja et al., 2013) rather than BPE, which would likely provide better results for more morphologically-rich languages. As we only test on English–German, our future work will test this new paradigm on other language pairs, particularly those in which unsupervised NMT fails to perform such as English into morphologically-rich languages.

References

Agirre, Eneko, Enrique Alfonseca, Keith Hall, Jana Kravalova, Marius Pasca, and Aitor Soroa. 2009.

A study on similarity and relatedness using distributional and wordnet-based approaches.

Artetxe, Mikel, Gorka Labaka, and Eneko Agirre. 2017a. Learning bilingual word embeddings with (almost) no bilingual data. In *Proceedings of the 55th Annual Meeting of the Association for Computational Linguistics (Volume 1: Long Papers)*, pages 451–462.

Artetxe, Mikel, Gorka Labaka, Eneko Agirre, and Kyunghyun Cho. 2017b. Unsupervised neural machine translation. *arXiv preprint arXiv:1710.11041*.

Artetxe, Mikel, Gorka Labaka, and Eneko Agirre. 2018a. A robust self-learning method for fully unsupervised cross-lingual mappings of word embeddings. In *Proceedings of the 56th Annual Meeting of the Association for Computational Linguistics (Volume 1: Long Papers)*, pages 789–798.

Artetxe, Mikel, Gorka Labaka, and Eneko Agirre. 2018b. Unsupervised statistical machine translation. In *Proceedings of the 2018 Conference on Empirical Methods in Natural Language Processing*, Brussels, Belgium, November. Association for Computational Linguistics.

Artetxe, Mikel, Gorka Labaka, and Eneko Agirre. 2019. An effective approach to unsupervised machine translation. *arXiv preprint arXiv:1902.01313*.

Barrault, Loïc, Ondřej Bojar, Marta R Costa-jussà, Christian Federmann, Mark Fishel, Yvette Graham, Barry Haddow, Matthias Huck, Philipp Koehn, Shervin Malmasi, et al. 2019. Findings of the 2019 conference on machine translation (wmt19). In *Proceedings of the Fourth Conference on Machine Translation (Volume 2: Shared Task Papers, Day 1)*, pages 1–61.

Bojanowski, Piotr, Edouard Grave, Armand Joulin, and Tomas Mikolov. 2017. Enriching word vectors with subword information. *Transactions of the Association for Computational Linguistics*, 5:135–146.

Bruni, Elia, Nam-Khanh Tran, and Marco Baroni. 2014. Multimodal distributional semantics. *Journal of Artificial Intelligence Research*, 49:1–47.

Gage, Philip. 1994. A new algorithm for data compression. *The C Users Journal*, 12(2):23–38.

Glavas, Goran, Robert Litschko, Sebastian Ruder, and Ivan Vulic. 2019. How to (properly) evaluate cross-lingual word embeddings: On strong baselines, comparative analyses, and some misconceptions. *arXiv preprint arXiv:1902.00508*.

Hassan, Hany, Anthony Aue, Chang Chen, Vishal Chowdhary, Jonathan Clark, Christian Federmann, Xuedong Huang, Marcin Junczys-Dowmunt, William Lewis, Mu Li, et al. 2018. Achieving human parity on automatic chinese to english news translation. *arXiv preprint arXiv:1803.05567*.

He, Junxian, Graham Neubig, and Taylor Berg-Kirkpatrick. 2018. Unsupervised learning of syntactic structure with invertible neural projections. *arXiv preprint arXiv:1808.09111*.

Hill, Felix, Roi Reichart, and Anna Korhonen. 2015. Simlex-999: Evaluating semantic models with (genuine) similarity estimation. *Computational Linguistics*, 41(4):665–695.

Koehn, Philipp, Hieu Hoang, Alexandra Birch, Chris Callison-Burch, Marcello Federico, Nicola Bertoldi, Brooke Cowan, Wade Shen, Christine Moran, Richard Zens, et al. 2007. Moses: Open source toolkit for statistical machine translation. In *Proceedings of the 45th annual meeting of the association for computational linguistics companion volume proceedings of the demo and poster sessions*, pages 177–180.

Lample, Guillaume, Alexis Conneau, Ludovic Denoyer, and Marc'Aurelio Ranzato. 2017. Unsupervised machine translation using monolingual corpora only. *arXiv preprint arXiv:1711.00043*.

Lample, Guillaume, Myle Ott, Alexis Conneau, Ludovic Denoyer, and Marc'Aurelio Ranzato. 2018. Phrase-based & neural unsupervised machine translation. *arXiv preprint arXiv:1804.07755*.

Leviant, Ira and Roi Reichart. 2015. Separated by an un-common language: Towards judgment language informed vector space modeling. *arXiv preprint arXiv:1508.00106*.

Levy, Omer and Yoav Goldberg. 2014. Dependency-based word embeddings. In *Proceedings of the 52nd Annual Meeting of the Association for Computational Linguistics (Volume 2: Short Papers)*, volume 2, pages 302–308.

Lin, Chu-Cheng, Waleed Ammar, Chris Dyer, and Lori Levin. 2015. Unsupervised pos induction with word embeddings. *arXiv preprint arXiv:1503.06760*.

Mikolov, Tomas, Ilya Sutskever, Kai Chen, Greg S Corrado, and Jeff Dean. 2013. Distributed representations of words and phrases and their compositionality. In *Advances in neural information processing systems*, pages 3111–3119.

Och, Franz Josef. 2003. Minimum error rate training in statistical machine translation. In *Proceedings of the 41st Annual Meeting on Association for Computational Linguistics-Volume 1*, pages 160–167. Association for Computational Linguistics.

Qi, Peng, Timothy Dozat, Yuhao Zhang, and Christopher D Manning. 2019. Universal dependency parsing from scratch. *arXiv preprint arXiv:1901.10457*.

Straka, Milan and Jana Straková. 2017. Tokenizing, pos tagging, lemmatizing and parsing ud 2.0 with udpipe. In *Proceedings of the CoNLL 2017 Shared Task: Multilingual Parsing from Raw Text to Universal Dependencies*, pages 88–99, Vancouver, Canada, August. Association for Computational Linguistics.

Virpioja, Sami, Peter Smit, Stig-Arne Grönroos, Mikko Kurimo, et al. 2013. Morfessor 2.0: Python implementation and extensions for morfessor baseline.

A German→English Results

We report the BLEU scores for German→English in Tables 8 and 9. Comparing these BLEU scores to the respective English→German BLEU scores in Tables 3 and 5, we see that the best performing models are the same for both translation directions. This suggests that the translation direction is not important for evaluating the relative differences unsupervised NMT systems. However, since English and German are related languages, this could also simply be a feature of this language pair.

Amount (M)	Reg	DP	Reg+DP
0.1	0.54	**1.20**	0.57
0.4	1.95	2.91	**3.71**
1	6.99	7.14	**8.74**
2	**11.90**	10.03	11.44
10	**16.97**	12.95	15.07

Table 8: German→English BLEU scores for NMT models using pretrained standard (Reg), dependency-based (DP), and hybrid (Reg+DP) embeddings. The best scores are shown in bold.

Amount (M)	Fast	Fast+Reg	Fast+DP
0.1	1.11	**2.39**	1.35
0.4	**10.01**	9.98	7.10
1	**13.68**	12.38	9.99
2	**15.27**	14.82	13.15
10	**18.40**	18.31	15.16

Table 9: German→English BLEU scores for aligned FASTTEXT (Fast), and two hybrid models consisting of FASTTEXT with regular (Fast+Reg) and FASTTEXT with dependency-based (Fast+DP) WORD2VEC embeddings. The best scores are shown in bold.

Revisiting Round-Trip Translation for Quality Estimation

Jihyung Moon
Naver Papago

Hyunchang Cho
Naver Papago

Eunjeong L. Park
Naver Papago

`{jihyung.moon, hyunchang.cho, lucypark}@navercorp.com`

Abstract

Quality estimation (QE) is the task of automatically evaluating the quality of translations without human-translated references. Calculating BLEU between the input sentence and round-trip translation (RTT) was once considered as a metric for QE, however, it was found to be a poor predictor of translation quality. Recently, various pre-trained language models have made breakthroughs in NLP tasks by providing semantically meaningful word and sentence embeddings. In this paper, we employ semantic embeddings to RTT-based QE. Our method achieves the highest correlations with human judgments, compared to previous WMT 2019 quality estimation metric task submissions. While backward translation models can be a drawback when using RTT, we observe that with semantic-level metrics, RTT-based QE is robust to the choice of the backward translation system. Additionally, the proposed method shows consistent performance for both SMT and NMT forward translation systems, implying the method does not penalize a certain type of model.

1   Introduction

A good machine translation (MT) system converts one language to another while preserving the meaning of a sentence. Given a pair of well-performing translation systems between two languages, the meaning of a sentence should remain

Input (en)	'We know it won't change students' behaviour instantly.
Reference (de)	Wir wissen, dass es das Verhalten der Studenten nicht sofort ändern wird.
Output (de)	„Wir wissen, dass es das Verhalten der Schüler nicht sofort ändern wird.
Round-trip (en)	"We know that it will not change student behavior immediately.

RTT-SENTBLEU: 14.99 (rank: 1947/1997)
RTT-SBERT(*): 98.07 (rank: 1001/1997)
RTT-BERTSCORE(*): 97.04 (rank: 1033/1997)

Table 1: A sample of RTT-based evaluation methods with an example from the WMT19 English–German evaluation set. * denotes our proposed semantic-level methods (Detailed definitions are described in Section 3). Note that SENTBLEU could not capture the similarity of the input and RTT.

intact even after a round-trip translation (RTT) – the process of translating text from the source to target language (forward translation, FT) and translating the result back into the source language (backward translation, BT). If the MT systems work reasonably well and no human-produced reference translations are provided, using RTT for translation evaluation seems like a natural choice.

However, in the early 2000s, this practice was not recommended to be used as a translation evaluation method (Huang, 1990; Somers, 2005; van Zaanen and Zwarts, 2006). This argument was largely supported by the poor correlation between BLEU (Papineni et al., 2002) for reference and translated output and BLEU for input and RTT (We address this method again in Section 3 as RTT-BLEU). However, BLEU only measures surface-level lexical similarity, thus penalizing paraphrased sentences resulting from the round-trip translation as shown in Table 1.

On the other hand, human evaluations con-

Martins, Moniz, Fumega, Martins, Batista, Coheur, Parra, Trancoso, Turchi, Bisazza, Moorkens, Guerberof, Nurminen, Marg, Forcada (eds.)
Proceedings of the 22nd Annual Conference of the European Association for Machine Translation, p. 91–104
Lisboa, Portugal, November 2020.

ducted on input sentences and translated outputs show a significant positive correlation with human evaluations on input sentences and round-trip sentences (Aiken and Park, 2010). The result implies if a suitable semantic-level metric is provided, RTT-based method can be used for MT evaluation. Meanwhile, recently introduced pre-trained language models e.g., BERT (Devlin et al., 2019) and SBERT (Reimers and Gurevych, 2019), are effective for many natural language processing tasks including semantic similarity detection (Cer et al., 2017). BERTSCORE (Zhang et al., 2019a) and YISI (Lo, 2019) leveraged such models for MT evaluation and confirmed the efficacy.

In this paper, we revisit RTT with recently proposed semantic-level metrics for MT quality estimation. Quality estimation (QE) aims to measure how good a translation is without any human-translated references (Fonseca et al., 2019) as opposed to reference-based metrics such as BLEU or CHRF. Therefore, with these metrics, it is easy to evaluate translations beyond reference-ready domains, e.g., user logs in commercial services.

We start by investigating RTT-based QE metrics on different BT systems to choose a proper BT system to examine RTT-based methods across different language pairs. Then we compare the methods on NMT with statistical machine translation (SMT) systems and demonstrate the compatibility of our methods. Across the experiments, RTT-based QE metrics with semantic-level similarities outperform lexical-based similarity metrics. We find the results are related to the metric's ability of detecting paraphrases.

The main contributions of this work are as follows:

- We reconsider RTT with suitable semantic-level metrics, specifically SBERT and BERTSCORE in our settings, and show it can be used to measure translation quality.

- We observe RTT methods using SBERT and BERTSCORE are robust to the choice of BT systems.

- We present RTT with semantic similarity measurements consistently exhibit high-performance across different FT systems: SMT and NMT.

- We find the paraphrase detection ability of metrics is related to the performance of RTT-based QE.

2　Related Work

2.1　Quality Estimation

One goal of QE is to estimate the quality for machine translated sentences without reference translations, but the definition of quality has gradually changed. Traditional QE aimed to estimate the required amount of post-editing efforts for a given translation in the word, sentence or document level. In the sentence level, this can be understood as estimating the Human Translation Error Rate (HTER) (Snover et al., 2006), or the rate of edit operations which include the insertions of words, deletions or replacements. The recently proposed view of "QE-as-a-metric" (Fonseca et al., 2019)[1] differs from traditional quality estimation in that it directly aims to estimate the absolute score of a translation, and can be directly compared with previous reference-based metrics. While reference-based metrics easily achieve above 0.9 Pearson correlation with direct human assessments in the system-level and up to 0.4 correlation in the sentence-level, QE-based metrics typically score less (Ma et al., 2019).

YISI (Lo, 2019) is the best performing QE metric from the recent QE-as-a-metrics subtask submitted to the quality estimation shared task of WMT19 (Ma et al., 2019)[2]. It takes contextual embeddings extracted from BERT and computes F-scores of semantic phrases using the cosine similarity of words weighting by their inverse document frequency (idf). YISI has variants for both situations where the references exist (YISI-1) or does not exist (YISI-2).

2.2　Round-trip Translation

RTT had frequently been used for a means of evaluating MT systems until Somers (2005) and van Zaanen and Zwarts (2006) claimed that RTT is inappropriate as a QE metric for translations. The idea was supported by the low correlations between a BLEU score for the input and RTT (RTT-BLEU) and a BLEU score for the reference and output. However, BLEU is not an adequate metric to validate RTT for QE. When Aiken and Park (2010) re-assessed RTT with human judgments, there was a significant positive correlation

---

[1] Since WMT20, this was modified to the "sentence-level direct assessment task".

[2] We excluded UNI and its variants from consideration, since they do not have any open publications to refer to. See Table 2 in (Ma et al., 2019).

between the human scores of round-trip translations and one-way translations.

Recently, RTT has been employed for other purposes: generating paraphrased sentences and modeling purposes. Yu et al. (2010) exploit RTT-based
features to estimate the quality of spoken language
translation and improve the accuracy of QE model.
Mallinson et al. (2017) reassess using RTT for
generating paraphrases in the context of NMT.
Junczys-Dowmunt and Grundkiewicz (2017) and
Lichtarge et al. (2019) generate large amounts of
artificial data to train an automatic post editing
model and grammatical error correction, respectively. Vaibhav et al. (2019) also uses RTT to augment bilingual data for NMT. Lample et al. (2018)
measures RTT-BLEU for model selection purposes
and Hassan et al. (2018) uses RTT as a feature to
re-rank translation hypotheses.

2.3 Sentence Similarity Methods

Lexical metrics, such as BLEU (Papineni et al.,
2002) and CHRF (Popović, 2015), have long and
widely been used for translation evaluation. Both
metrics compute strict matching between translation output and reference at the surface level.
BLEU counts the n-gram matches of the output and
reference over the number of tokens of output as
well as the length similarity of the output and reference. CHRF computes F-score based on character-
level n-grams. However, they cannot capture the
semantic similarity of output and reference sentences beyond lexical relatedness or overlap. In
this sense, lexical-based metrics may not be the
best way to measure the similarity of paraphrases.

BERT (Devlin et al., 2019), a pre-trained language representation model, made breakthroughs
on many natural language processing tasks, including the sentence similarity prediction task (Cer
et al., 2017). The methods using BERT's embedding vectors were also introduced to MT evaluation, the task that needs semantic-level similarity measurement, and show the best performance (Ma et al., 2019; Lo, 2019; Zhang et al.,
2019a). BERTSCORE (Zhang et al., 2019a) leverages BERT wordpiece embeddings to compute sentence similarity of two monolingual sentences.
When BERTSCORE is applied to the output and
reference, it outperforms BLEU and CHRF. Meanwhile, SENTENCE-BERT (SBERT) (Reimers and
Gurevych, 2019), a fine-tuned BERT, is introduced
to derive more semantically meaningful sentence-

level representation than BERT. From the encouraging results of the embedding-based methods, we
would expect the embeddings to catch the semantic similarity of input and round-trip sentences.

3 RTT-based QE Metrics

Given an input sentence $x = (x_1, x_2, x_3, ..., x_n)$
and a round-trip sentence $\hat{x} = (\hat{x}_1, \hat{x}_2, \hat{x}_3, ..., \hat{x}_m)$,
an RTT-based QE metric f is a scalar function
computing the similarity of x and $\hat{x}$. We consider
the scalar output as a quality for the translation of
x. The validity of f is assessed primarily by Pearson correlation against the human judgments.

Previously, only surface-level similarity metrics
were used for f. In this paper, we propose to use
semantic-level metrics which can capture higher-
level concepts of the similarity. Detailed implementations are described in the Appendix A.

3.1 Surface-level Metrics

RTT-BLEU / RTT-SENTBLEU BLEU (Papineni et al., 2002) has originally designed to measure system-level translation performance. To evaluate a sentence-level translation, SENTBLEU, the
smoothed version of BLEU, has been used (Ma
et al., 2019; Ma et al., 2018). Since system-level
BLEU and sentence-level BLEU exploit different computation method, we also separate BLEU-
based RTT QE metric for the system-level and
sentence-level. Specifically, RTT-BLEU is either
BLEU or SACREBLEU-BLEU (Post, 2018) on
system-level input sentences and round-trip sentences while RTT-SENTBLEU is SENTBLEU on
a single input sentence and round-trip sentence.

RTT-CHRF Sentence-level score is produced
by CHRF and system-level score is the average
of the segment score obtained by SACREBLEU-
CHRF[3] (Post, 2018).

3.2 Semantic-level Metrics

In our settings, the semantic-level metrics are represented by the cosine similarity of SBERT embeddings and BERTSCORE. For all metrics, system-
level score is an averaged sentence-level scores.

RTT-SBERT RTT-SBERT calculates the cosine
similarity of x and $\hat{x}$ embedding vectors extracted
from SBERT (Reimers and Gurevych, 2019). We

---

[3]It is widely known that their scores are slightly different from
the average of CHRF even with the same parameters. Since
SACREBLEU is standard, we take SACREBLEU-CHRF for the
system-level score.

use a publicly available pre-trained SBERT[4]. Note that released models support Arabic, Chinese, Dutch, English, French, German, Italian, Korean, Polish, Portuguese, Russian, Spanish, and Turkish.

RTT-BERTSCORE RTT-BERTSCORE computes F-score based on wordpiece-level embedding similarities of x and $\hat{x}$ weighted by inverse document frequency (idf), where each embedding is taken from BERT. The idf weights penalize common wordpiece similarities, such as end of sentence symbols. Given L input sentences $\{x^k\}_{k=1}^{L}$, the idf score of x_i is defined as:

$$\text{idf}(x_i) = -\log \frac{1}{L} \sum_{i=1}^{L} \mathbb{1}[x_i \in x^k]$$

4 Experimental Settings

We compare RTT-based semantic-level QE metrics to lexical-level QE metrics in various conditions. Initially, we prepare different BT systems to see the impact of the BT system to the performance change in RTT-based metrics. Then, with a suitable BT system, we observe the proposed metrics on WMT 2019 metrics task evaluation dataset. We also examine whether our methods are biased to the certain type of FT system. Furthermore, we investigate relations of the performance of RTT-based QE metrics and their paraphrase detection ability.

4.1 Data

WMT metrics task evaluation set The WMT19 dataset includes translations from English to Czech, German, Finnish, Gujarati, Kazakh, Lithuanian, Russian, and Chinese, and from the same set except Czech to English. Translation outputs were provided by the WMT19 submitted systems where all were NMT. Each system was not necessarily present in all language pairs, therefore, English–German received 22 submissions whereas German–English received 16 (see n in Table 3). The human scores were gathered by using Direct Assessment (DA) for the translations of all systems on a scale of 0-100 points then standardized for each annotator. System's performance is an average over all assessed sentences produced by the given system and sentence-level golden truth is a relative ranking of DA judgments (DARR). In WMT19,

QE-as-a-metrics were also assessed by the same standard as the reference-based metrics, namely Pearson correlation coefficient and Kendall's τ-like formulation against DARR, therefore, performance could be compared directly with BLEU (Papineni et al., 2002) and CHRF (Popović, 2015).

We also use WMT12 metrics task evaluation set to assess RTT-based metrics on SMT. It includes translations from English to Czech, French, German, and Spanish and vice versa. We select English–German, German–English, and English–Czech which also appeared in WMT 2019. The annotators were asked to evaluate sentences by ranking translated outputs from randomly selected 5 systems. A ratio of wins is used for the system's performance (Callison-Burch et al., 2012).

PAWS PAWS (Paraphrase Adversaries from Word Scrambling) (Zhang et al., 2019b) is a paraphrase identification dataset constructed from sentences in Wikipedia (Wiki) and Quora Question Pairs (QQP) corpus. We denote dataset as PAWS$_{\text{Wiki}}$ and PAWS$_{\text{QQP}}$ respectively.

Paraphrased sentences are generated by controlled word swapping and back translation, followed by fluency and paraphrase judgments by human raters. Paraphrase and non-paraphrase pairs are mixed and to make dataset more challenging, both pairs have high lexical overlap.

4.2 Backward Translation (BT)

To estimate the quality of MT systems with RTT, a BT system is required. The choice of the BT system seemingly has the potential to largely affect the performance of RTT-based QE metrics, so we run experiments to verify the effect of BT system qualities. We compare two types of models–the system trained solely on WMT19 news translation task training corpus and online system–with different performance in terms of BLEU. The BT systems trained on the WMT19 news dataset could be considered adequate to evaluate the WMT19 submitted FT systems since both systems are trained on the same domain. On the other hand, online systems could also be desirable, because the online systems are trained on a huge amount of corpus mixed with various domains and would outperform the trained models on WMT19 dataset. If the online systems show more favorable results, then RTT-based QE metrics can be more practical in terms of the easy access to a BT system on any

---

[4]`https://github.com/UKPLab/`
`sentence-transformers`

Backward translations		Pearson correlations				Variance ($\times 10^{-4}$)	
Systems	BLEU	RTT-BLEU	RTT-CHRF	RTT-SBERT	RTT-BERTSCORE	RTT-SBERT	RTT-BERTSCORE
Google	**46.96**	0.797	0.853	0.941	0.951	5.08	1.96
Microsoft	42.68	**0.845**	**0.877**	**0.948**	0.955	5.12	2.07
Amazon	40.89	0.776	0.804	0.941	**0.956**	4.86	1.88
Facebook-FAIR	42.17	0.788	0.865	0.940	0.934	4.84	1.27
Transformer Big (100k)	38.96	0.739	0.818	0.939	0.937	4.58	1.57
Transformer Big (40k)	36.38	0.707	0.795	0.938	0.935	4.22	1.36
Transformer Big (20k)	34.75	0.617	0.759	0.931	0.860	3.97	1.15
Transformer Big (10k)	31.30	0.509	0.749	0.908	0.789	3.17	0.91

Table 2: Performance of RTT-based QE metrics on 22 English–German FT systems with various German–English BT systems. The variance of the best metrics, RTT-SBERT and RTT-BERTSCORE, are described, additionally.

language pair.

To examine the impact of the BT systems, we choose English–German, which is the most submitted language pair. For trained BT systems, we use Facebook-FAIR[5], the best system in WMT19 on German–English, and the Transformer Big model (Vaswani et al., 2017) saved at 10k, 20k, 40k, and 100k iterations during training on the WMT19 corpus. Details of the Transformers are described in Appendix B. We also try three online systems, namely Google, Microsoft, and Amazon, showing different BLEU on WMT19 German–English evaluation set. Each system was requested on Oct 2019, Nov 2019, and Dec 2019.

4.3 Forward Translation (FT)

The metric might penalize or favor a certain type of models. For instance, BLEU has been argued to penalize rule-based systems against statistical systems (Hovy, 2007).

To investigate whether RTT-based QE metrics penalize FT systems based on their architecture, we assess RTT-based QE metrics on both NMT and SMT. As the all models submitted to WMT19 are NMT (Ma et al., 2019), and the models submitted to WMT12 are SMT or rule-based model (Callison-Burch et al., 2012), we denote the former as NMT and the latter as SMT. We compare RTT-based QE metrics' performance with Pearson correlation coefficient for the language pairs both appeared on WMT19 and WMT12, English–Czech, English–German, and German–English.

5 Results

5.1 Sensitivity to Backward Translation

Due to the nature of RTT-based QE metrics, a BT system is needed. We use a variety of BT sys-

tems in terms of the training recipe and BLEU on WMT19 German–English testset and observe the performance of RTT-based QE metrics evaluated by Pearson correlation (r) with human scores (Ma et al., 2019; Ma et al., 2018). Note that well-performing metrics achieve high correlation coefficient.

According to Table 2, RTT-BERTSCORE and RTT-SBERT not only outperform the other metrics but are also robust to the type and performance of the BT systems. On the other hand, RTT-BLEU and RTT-CHRF are sensitive to the performance of the BT systems, and the correlations fall behind RTT-BERTSCORE and RTT-SBERT. Since BT systems scoring low BLEU have less chance of having same word orders in RTT as with input sentences, the performance of surface-form metrics, RTT-BLEU and RTT-CHRF, decrease more sharply than RTT-SBERT and RTT-BERTSCORE.

The best correlation of each metric is accomplished when the online system is used for the BT system. Even though Microsoft and Facebook-FAIR exhibit a similar BLEU score, metrics are more successful when using the Microsoft system. This can be explained by a variance of RTT-based QE metrics score. In average, the variance of RTT-SBERT and RTT-BERTSCORE using the online BT systems is higher than that of trained ones. The trained BT systems might over-translate a fault translation output similar to the original input, e.g., Kim Jong Un – Kim – Kim Jong Un, that make QE metrics hard to distinguish good systems to the bad ones.

Surprisingly, the best BT system in terms of BLEU does not always guarantee the best RTT-based QE metrics. Despite Google's highest BLEU score, the performance of RTT-based QE metrics is lower than or similar to that of Microsoft. This assures that BLEU is not the only feature that affect

[5]Submitted model is publicly available via PyTorch (https://pytorch.org/hub/pytorch_fairseq_translation).

| src lang | de | fi | gu | kk | lt | ru | zh | | en | en | en | en | en | en | en | en | |
tgt lang	en	en	en	en	en	en	en	avg. (std.)	cs	de	fi	gu	kk	lt	ru	zh	avg. (std.)
n	16	12	11	11	11	14	15		11	22	12	11	11	12	12	12	
BLEU[*]	.849	.982	.834	.946	.961	.879	.899	.907 (.057)	.897	.921	.969	.737	.852	.989	.986	.901	.907 (.084)
CHRF[*]	.917	.992	.955	.978	.940	.945	.956	.955 (.025)	.990	.979	.986	.841	.972	.981	.943	.880	.947 (.056)
SACREBLEU-BLEU[*]	.813	.985	.834	.946	.955	.873	.903	.901 (.065)	.994	.969	.966	.736	.852	.986	.977	.801	.910 (.100)
SACREBLEU-CHRF[*]	.910	.990	.952	.969	.935	.919	.955	.947 (.028)	.983	.976	.980	.841	.967	.966	.985	.796	.937 (.074)
QE as a Metric																	
Individual Best[*]	.850	.930	.566	.324	.487	.808	.947	- (-)	.871	.936	.907	.314	.339	.810	.919	.118	- (-)
YiSi-2[*]	**.796**	.642	.566	.324	.442	.339	**.940**	.578 (.232)	.324	.924	.696	.314	.339	.055	.766	.097	.439 (.319)
RTT-BLEU	.130	**.827**	.641	.859	.596	.295	.825	.596 (.284)	-.625	.797	.417	.608	.930	-.334	.572	-.599	.221 (.637)
RTT-CHRF	.495	.810	**.778**	.776	.692	.524	.875	.707 (.146)	-.408	.842	.487	.586	.423	-.153	.750	-.310	.277 (.493)
RTT-SBERT	.761	-	-	-	-	**.867**	.889	.839 (.005)	.470	.941	.804	.710	.950	**.410**	.833	**.256**	**.672** (.261)
RTT-BERTSCORE	.654	.819	.729	**.889**	**.712**	.816	.912	**.790** (.095)	**.473**	**.951**	**.819**	**.737**	**.966**	.342	**.869**	.071	.654 (.324)

Table 3: Pearson correlations of system-level metrics with human judgments on WMT19. The best correlations of QE-as-a-metric within the same language pair are highlighted in bold. * denotes that reported correlations are from WMT19 metrics task (Ma et al., 2019).

| src lang | de | fi | gu | kk | lt | ru | zh | | en | en | en | en | en | en | en | en | |
tgt lang	en	en	en	en	en	en	en	avg. (std.)	cs	de	fi	gu	kk	lt	ru	zh	avg. (std.)
n	85k	38k	31k	27k	22k	46k	31k		27k	100k	32k	11k	18k	17k	24k	19k	
SENTBLEU[*]	.056	.233	.188	.377	.262	.125	.323	.223 (.111)	.367	.248	.396	.465	.392	.334	.469	.270	.368 (.081)
CHRF[*]	.122	.286	.256	.389	.301	.180	.371	.272 (.096)	.455	.326	.514	.534	.479	.446	.539	.301	.449 (.091)
QE as a Metric																	
Individual Best[*]	.022	.211	-.001	.096	.075	.089	.253	- (-)	.069	.236	.351	.147	.187	.003	.226	.044	- (-)
YiSi-2[*]	**.068**	.126	-.001	.096	.075	**.053**	.253	.096 (.080)	**.069**	**.212**	.239	.147	.187	.003	-.155	.044	.093 (.131)
RTT-SENTBLEU	-.169	.095	.111	.140	.086	-.104	.168	.047 (.130)	-.122	-.001	.088	.374	.399	-.110	.157	-.106	.085 (.211)
RTT-CHRF	-.114	.141	**.184**	.130	.099	-.050	.195	.083 (.119)	-.093	.055	.119	.395	.310	-.069	.195	-.075	.105 (.185)
RTT-SBERT	-.066	-	-	-	-	-.013	.225	.049 (.024)	.025	.169	.268	.444	.503	**.070**	.371	**.064**	.239 (.185)
RTT-BERTSCORE	-.085	**.185**	.167	**.204**	**.118**	-.020	**.255**	**.118** (.125)	.065	.194	**.292**	**.494**	**.579**	.069	**.391**	.056	**.268** (.205)

Table 4: Kendall's τ formulation of segment-level metric scores with human judgments on WMT19. The best correlations of QE-as-a-metric within the same language pair are highlighted in bold. For some language pairs, QE metrics obtain negative correlations. * denotes that reported correlations are from WMT19 metrics task (Ma et al., 2019).

the performance of the RTT-based QE metrics.

5.2 Performance across Language Pairs

Provided from the results in Section 5.1, we use one of the online systems to get RTT for all language pairs in WMT19. Specifically, we use Google Translate, because of its coverage of supported language pairs and its overall performance across all language pairs.

We conduct the same experiments as in the WMT19 metrics shared task to directly compare with the previous QE-as-a-metrics. Individual best results of previous methods and YISI-2 are provided to compare RTT-based QE metrics within the same reference-free metrics. Note that YISI was the only QE-as-a-metric scoring on all language pairs, at the same time, achieving the best performance in total (Ma et al., 2019). We also include commonly used reference requiring metrics, namely BLEU, CHRF, SACREBLEU-BLEU, and SACREBLEU-CHRF, to see how far QE metrics can get without reference translation. The metrics are evaluated in system-level and sentence-

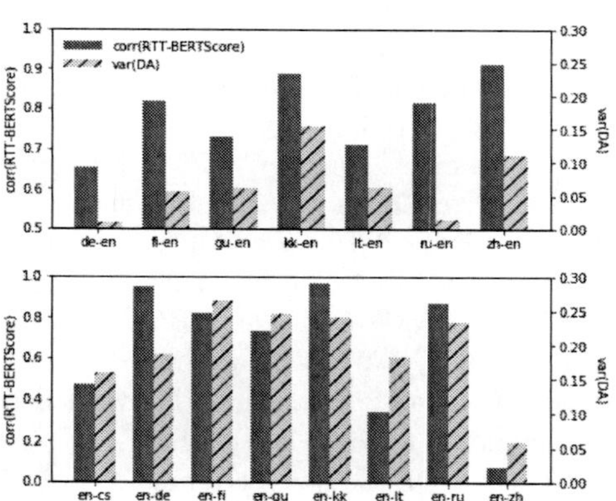

Figure 1: System-level correlations of RTT-BERTSCORE and variance of DA scores.

level for all language pairs. Specifically, Pearson correlation is applied to assess system-level metrics and Kendall's τ-like formulation against the DARR to measure sentence-level metrics.

Table 3 illustrates the system-level correlations with human judgments on both to-English and out-of-English language pairs. Across all language

Language Pairs	Systems (n)	Pearson correlations				
		BLEU	RTT-BLEU	RTT-CHRF	RTT-SBERT	RTT-BERTSCORE
English–Czech	SMT (12)	0.615	0.261	0.342	0.482	**0.620**
	NMT (11)	0.897	-0.625	-0.408	0.470	**0.473**
English–German	SMT (12)	0.582	0.523	0.553	0.742	**0.765**
	NMT (22)	0.921	0.797	0.842	0.941	**0.951**
German–English	SMT (13)	0.841	0.530	0.374	**0.712**	0.682
	NMT (16)	0.849	0.130	0.495	**0.761**	0.654

Table 5: Pearson correlations of BLEU and RTT-based QE metrics where FT systems are SMT and NMT. We reveal the number of systems in parenthesis.

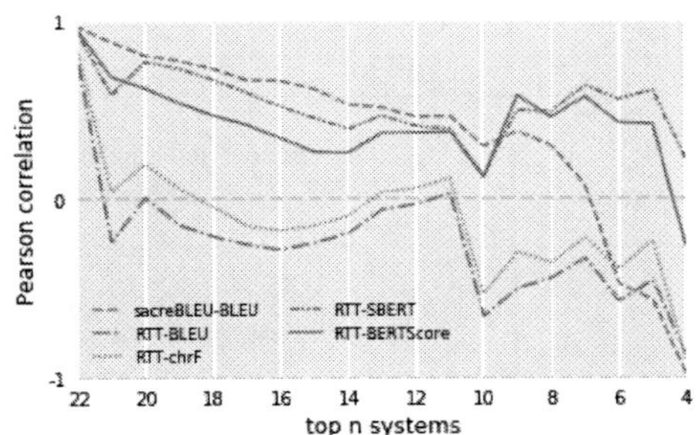

Figure 2: Pearson correlations of RTT-based QE metrics and SACREBLEU-BLEU for English–German system-level evaluation for all systems (left) down to top 4 systems (right).

Metrics	PAWS$_{\text{WiKi}}$	PAWS$_{\text{QQP}}$
SENTBLEU	0.639	0.354
CHRF	0.584	0.405
SBERT	0.656	**0.545**
BERTSCORE	**0.718**	0.509

Table 6: AUC scores of precision-recall curves of BERT-based metrics on PAWS$_{\text{WiKi}}$ and PAWS$_{\text{QQP}}$ testing set.

pairs except German–English, BERT-based RTT QE metrics outperform RTT-BLEU and RTT-CHRF. For some language pairs, Gujarati–English, Kazakh–English, Russian–English, English–German, English–Gujarati, and English–Kazakh, RTT-BERT-based metrics show comparable result to BLEU, however, QE metrics still fall behind the reference-based metrics on average. Surprisingly enough, the high Pearson correlation coefficients are mostly achieved on low-resource language pairs. Results in Figure 1 suggest that this might due to the high variance of the system's DA scores which implies distinguishing good systems to the bad ones is relatively easy.

To present a more reliable view, we draw plots of Pearson correlation while reducing MT systems to top n ones as in Ma et al. (2019). Figure 2 depicts English–German, and all language pairs are in Appendix C. In general, correlations of SACREBLEU-BLEU and RTT-based QE metrics tend towards 0 or negative, whereas the reference-based metric shows a rather continuous degradation than RTT-based metrics. RTT-SBERT and RTT-BERTSCORE are better at retaining positive correlations compared to RTT-BLEU and

RTT-CHRF, however, their consistency is weaker than SACREBLEU-BLEU except for some language pairs (English–German, English–Gujarati, English–Kazakh, and Finnish–English).

Metrics performance on sentence-level is described in Table 4[6]. Sentence-level quality estimation is considered as a more difficult task than that of system-level. This is supported by the poor correlation coefficients of even SENTBLEU and CHRF. Similar to the system-level results, QE metrics fall short of the reference-based metrics. For language pairs with high DA score variance, again, RTT-BERT-based metrics provide comparable performance with reference-based metrics.

5.3 Sensitivity to Forward Translation

A certain type of FT system could be penalized by one metric according to its computation method. For this reason, we observe the performance of RTT-based QE metrics on different FT systems: SMT and NMT. SMT denotes the systems submitted to WMT12 and NMT represents the systems submitted to WMT19. Same as the Section 5.2, we use Google Translate for the BT system and evaluate the metrics with Pearson correlation coefficient. Results are shown in Table 5.

RTT-SBERT and RTT-BERTSCORE demonstrate the most promising performance regardless of the FT systems. In contrast, RTT-BLEU and RTT-CHRF seem to favor SMT. The correlation

---

[6]Instead of BLEU, we report SENTBLEU.

Case	Sentences	Label	Ranks (out of 677)	
(a)	**sentence 1**: What are some example of *deep web and dark web* ? **sentence 2**: What are some example of *dark web and deep web* ?	1	SENTBLEU: 534 CHRF: 416	SBERT: 242 BERTSCORE: 101
(b)	**sentence 1**: What was the CD that Deanna and family *were* listening to at the beginning of Try (S5E15) of Season 5 of the Walking Dead and why was they listening to it ? **sentence 2**: What was the CD that Deanna and family *was* listening to at the beginning of Try (S5E15) of Season 5 of the Walking Dead and why were they listening to it ?	1	SENTBLEU: 100 CHRF: 142	SBERT: 14 BERTSCORE: 2
(c)	**sentence 1**: How is dark/vacuum energy created with the universe conserved if it is not *created* ? Can infinite of these be *conserved* ? **sentence 2**: How is dark/vacuum energy created with the universe conserved if it is not *conserved* ? Can infinite of these be *created* ?	0	SENTBLEU: 119 CHRF: 90	SBERT: 353 BERTSCORE: 501

Table 7: Example sentences on PAWS$_{QQP}$ dataset. Label 1 indicates paraphrased, and 0 represents dissimilarity. The higher the metric rank, the more similar the two sentences are.

Case	Sentences	Label	Ranks (out of 8000)	
(d)	**sentence 1**: Other famous spa towns include Sandanski , Hisarya , *Kyustendil , Devin , Bankya ,* Varshets , and Velingard . **sentence 2**: Other famous spa towns include Sandanski , Hisarya , *Bankya , Devin , Kyustendil ,* Varshets and Velingard .	1	SENTBLEU: 2510 CHRF: 1521	SBERT: 884 BERTSCORE: 533
(e)	**sentence 1**: *Southport Tower* is the first new tower to be built at the *southern* end of *the Macleod Trail* in almost 20 years . **sentence 2**: *Macleod Trail* is the first new tower to be built at the *south* end of *Southport Tower* in almost 20 years .	0	SENTBLEU: 2942 CHRF: 1446	SBERT: 4374 BERTSCORE: 7505

Table 8: Example sentences on PAWS$_{Wiki}$ dataset. Label 1 indicates paraphrased, and 0 represents dissimilarity. The higher the metric ranks, the more similar the two sentences are.

coefficient gap between BLEU and both RTT-BLEU and RTT-CHRF is smaller when FT system is SMT.

5.4 Paraphrase Detection

The results from all the previous sections consistently show the outstanding performance of RTT-SBERT and RTT-BERTSCORE. We see this in a view of paraphrase detection ability of SBERT and BERTSCORE. To confirm our assumption, we compare the area-under-curve (AUC) scores of precision-recall curves of the four metrics used to measure input and RTT on PAWS dataset. The higher the score is, the better the metric at paraphrase detection. Table 6 depicts the results. Note that SBERT indicates the cosine similarity of the embedding vectors of two sentence pairs extracted from the model.

As expected, BERTSCORE and SBERT outperform SENTBLEU and CHRF. In case (a) of Table 7 and case (d) of Table 8, we can find SENTBLEU and CHRF are sensitive to the change of word order. Additionally, they are hard to distinguish paraphrases on long sentences. From case (b), (c), (d), and (e), lexical-based metrics constantly view the sentences are not paraphrased.

The results imply that metrics capability to measure the semantic similarity is highly correlated to the performance of RTT-based QE metrics.

6 Conclusions

We have presented round-trip translation for translation quality estimation. It can be used for QE with suitable semantic-level similarity metrics like SBERT (Reimers and Gurevych, 2019) and BERTSCORE (Zhang et al., 2019a). RTT-SBERT and RTT-BERTSCORE are robust to the choice of a BT system, which alleviates the disadvantages of RTT being dependent on the BT system. Moreover, both QE metrics significantly outperform the state-of-the-art QE metric, YISI-2. When the performance gap between the FT systems is large, RTT-SBERT and RTT-BERTSCORE provide comparable performance to BLEU. They also perform well irrespective of the modeling architecture of FT systems. In future work, it would be interesting to investigate when RTT-based metrics become more reliable or unreliable.

We find the high performance of RTT-SBERT and RTT-BERTSCORE is owing to SBERT and BERTSCORE's ability to detect paraphrased sentences. If better sentence similarity measurements appear, the performance of RTT-based metrics would increase as well. With the growing amount of the data and the advance of computing power, there certainly be a better measurement, thus RTT-based QE metric is also promising.

References

Aiken, Milam and Park, Mina. 2010. The efficacy of round-trip translation for MT evaluation. *Translation Journal* Volume 14 1–10.

Cer, Daniel and Diab, Mona and Agirre, Eneko and Lopez-Gazpio, Inigo and Specia, Lucia. 2017. SemEval-2017 Task 1: Semantic Textual Similarity Multilingual and Crosslingual Focused Evaluation. *Proceedings of the 11th International Workshop on Semantic Evaluation* (SemEval-2017) 1–14.

Callison-Burch, Chris and Koehn, Philipp and Monz, Christof and Post, Matt and Soricut, Radu and Specia, Lucia. 2012. Findings of the 2012 Workshop on Statistical Machine Translation. *Proceedings of the Seventh Workshop on Statistical Machine Translation* 10–51.

Devlin, Jacob and Chang, Ming-Wei and Lee, Kenton and Toutanova, Kristina. 2019. BERT: Pre-training of Deep Bidirectional Transformers for Language Understanding. *Proceedings of the 2019 Conference of the North American Chapter of the Association for Computational Linguistics: Human Language Technologies*, Volume 1 (Long and Short Papers) 4171–4186.

Federmann, Christian and Elachqar, Oussama and Quirk, Chris. 2019. Multilingual Whispers: Generating Paraphrases with Translation. *Proceedings of the 5th Workshop on Noisy User-generated Text* (W-NUT 2019) 17–26.

Fonseca, Erick and Yankovskaya, Lisa and Martins, André FT and Fishel, Mark and Federmann, Christian. 2019. Findings of the WMT 2019 Shared Tasks on Quality Estimation. *Proceedings of the Fourth Conference on Machine Translation* (Volume 3: Shared Task Papers, Day 2) 1–10.

Hassan, Hany and Aue, Anthony and Chen, Chang and Chowdhary, Vishal and Clark, Jonathan and Federmann, Christian and Huang, Xuedong and Junczys-Dowmunt, Marcin and Lewis, William and Li, Mu and others 2018. Achieving human parity on automatic chinese to english news translation. *arXiv preprint arXiv:1803.05567*

Hovy, Edward. 2007. Investigating why BLEU penalizes non-statistical systems. *Proceedings of the eleventh MT Summit*

Huang, Xiuming. 1990. A machine translation system for the target language inexpert. In *COLING 1990 Volume 3: Papers presented to the 13th International Conference on Computational Linguistics*

Junczys-Dowmunt, Marcin and Grundkiewicz, Roman. 2017. An Exploration of Neural Sequence-to-Sequence Architectures for Automatic Post-Editing. *Proceedings of the Eighth International Joint Conference on Natural Language Processing* (Volume 1: Long Papers) 120–129.

Lample, Guillaume and Ott, Myle and Conneau, Alexis and Denoyer, Ludovic and Ranzato, Marc'Aurelio 2018. Phrase-based & neural unsupervised machine translation. *Proceedings of the 2018 Conference on Empirical Methods in Natural Language Processing* 5039–5049.

Lichtarge, Jared and Alberti, Chris and Kumar, Shankar and Shazeer, Noam and Parmar, Niki and Tong, Simon. 2019. Corpora Generation for Grammatical Error Correction. *Proceedings of the 2019 Conference of the North American Chapter of the Association for Computational Linguistics: Human Language Technologies,* Volume 1 (Long and Short Papers) 3291–3301.

Liu, Yinhan and Ott, Myle and Goyal, Naman and Du, Jingfei and Joshi, Mandar and Chen, Danqi and Levy, Omer and Lewis, Mike and Zettlemoyer, Luke and Stoyanov, Veselin. 2019. Roberta: A robustly optimized bert pre-training approach. *arXiv preprint arXiv:1907.11692*

Lo, Chi-kiu. 2019. YiSi-A unified semantic MT quality evaluation and estimation metric for languages with different levels of available resources. *Proceedings of the Fourth Conference on Machine Translation* (Volume 2: Shared Task Papers, Day 1) 507–513.

Ma, Qingsong and Wei, Johnny and Bojar, Ondřej and Graham, Yvette. 2019. Results of the WMT19 Metrics Shared Task: Segment-Level and Strong MT Systems Pose Big Challenges. *Proceedings of the Fourth Conference on Machine Translation* (Volume 2: Shared Task Papers, Day 1) 62–90

Ma, Qingsong and Bojar, Ondřej and Graham, Yvette. 2018. Results of the WMT18 Metrics Shared Task: Both characters and embeddings achieve good performance. *Proceedings of the third conference on machine translation: shared task papers* 671–688.

Mallinson, Jonathan and Sennrich, Rico and Lapata, Mirella. 2017. Paraphrasing revisited with neural machine translation. *Proceedings of the 15th Conference of the European Chapter of the Association for Computational Linguistics* (Volume 1, Long Papers) 881–893.

Papineni, Kishore and Roukos, Salim and Ward, Todd and Zhu, Wei-Jing. 2002. BLEU: a method for automatic evaluation of machine translation. *Proceedings of the 40th annual meeting on association for computational linguistics* 311–318

Popović, Maja. 2015. chrF: character n-gram F-score for automatic MT evaluation. *Proceedings of the*

Tenth Workshop on Statistical Machine Translation 392–395

Post, Matt. 2018. A Call for Clarity in Reporting BLEU Scores. *WMT 2018* 186

Reimers, Nils and Gurevych, Iryna. 2019. Sentence-BERT: Sentence Embeddings using Siamese BERT-Networks. *Proceedings of the 2019 Conference on Empirical Methods in Natural Language Processing and the 9th International Joint Conference on Natural Language Processing* (EMNLP-IJCNLP) 3973–3983.

Somers, Harold. 2005. Round-trip translation: What is it good for? *Proceedings of the Australasian Language Technology Workshop* 127–133.

Snover, Matthew and Dorr, Bonnie and Schwartz, Richard and Micciulla, Linnea and Makhoul, John 2006. A study of translation edit rate with targeted human annotation. *Proceedings of association for machine translation in the Americas* Volume 200 6.

Vaibhav, Vaibhav and Singh, Sumeet and Stewart, Craig and Neubig, Graham 2019. Improving robustness of machine translation with synthetic noise. *Proceedings of the 2019 Conference of the North American Chapter of the Association for Computational Linguistics: Human Language Technologies*, Volume 1 (Long and Short Papers) 1916–1920.

van Zaanen, Menno and Zwarts, Simon. 2006. Unsupervised measurement of translation quality using multi-engine, bi-directional translation. In *Proceedings of the 19th Australian joint conference on Artificial Intelligence: advances in Artificial Intelligence* 1208–1214.

Vaswani, Ashish and Shazeer, Noam and Parmar Niki and Uszkoreit, Jakob and Jones, Llion and N. Gomez, Aidan and Kaiser, Łukasz and Polosukhin, Illia. 2017. Attention is all you need. *Advances in neural information processing systems* 5998–6008.

Yu, Dong and Wei, Wei and Jia, Lei and Xu, Bo. 2010. Confidence estimation for spoken language translation based on Round Trip Translation. In *7th International Symposium on Chinese Spoken Language Processing* 426–429.

Zhang, Tianyi and Kishore, Varsha and Wu, Felix and Weinberger, Kilian Q and Artzi, Yoav. 2019a. Bertscore: Evaluating text generation with bert. *arXiv preprint arXiv:1904.09675*

Zhang, Yuan and Baldridge, Jason and He, Luheng. 2019b. PAWS: Paraphrase Adversaries from Word Scrambling. *Proc. of NAACL*

Appendix A   Metrics Implementation

RTT-BLEU / RTT-SENTBLEU SACREBLEU-BLEU (Post, 2018) is used for system-level score and SENTBLEU for sentence-level which is a smoothed version of BLEU. Following WMT19 metrics task (Ma et al., 2019), we ran SACREBLEU-BLEU[7] with `BLEU+case.lc+lang.de-en+numrefs.1+smooth.exp+tok.intl+version.1.3.6` and SENTBLEU with `sentence-Bleu` in the Moses toolkit[8]. Since Chinese tokenization is not supported by the `tok.intl` included in the package, we preprocess Chinese sentences with `tokenizeChinese.py`[9].

RTT-CHRF We also take the same computation procedure with WMT19 SACREBLEU-CHRF[7] and CHRF[10]. We ran `chrF3+case.mixed+lang.de-en+numchars.6+numrefs.1+space.False+tok.13a+version.1.3.6.` and python script `chrF++.py` with the parameters `-nw 0 -b 3` respectively.

RTT-SBERT We use `bert-large-nli-mean-tokens` for English and `distiluse-base-multilingual-cased` for the others.

RTT-BERTSCORE BERTSCORE is publicly available[11] and it uses the same model and layer applied in RTT-BERT.

Appendix B   German–English Transformer big model configurations

Hyperparameters of German–English transformer model used in Section 4.2 generally followed transformer big configuration of Vaswani et al. (2017), except for three shared embedding matrices of encoder input, decoder input, and decoder output. In other words, we set the matrices' variables independently.

For training data, we used all downloadable parallel corpus on WMT19 news translation task for German–English: Europarl, ParaCrawl, CommonCrawl corpus, News Commentary, Wiki titles, and Rapid corpus of EU press releases. Then, we cleaned corpora by filtering sentence pairs whose token length ratio is bigger than 1.5 or less than 0.66 and left 37,066,883 parallel lines.

We normalized corpora with `normalize-punctuation.perl` in the Moses toolkit[12] and tokenized them using bype-pair encoding implemented in Google's SentencePiece[13]. Encoding models for German and English are separately trained with vocabulary size 32K.

Finally, we trained model with mini batch containing approximately 35K tokens of English and 35K of German for each iteration.

---

[7] https://github.com/mjpost/sacreBLEU
[8] https://github.com/moses-smt/mosesdecoder/tree/master/mert/sentence-bleu.cpp
[9] http://hdl.handle.net/11346/WMT17-TVXH
[10] https://github.com/m-popovic/chrF/chrF++.py
[11] https://github.com/Tiiiger/bert_score
[12] https://github.com/moses-smt/mosesdecoder/blob/master/scripts/tokenizer/normalize-punctuation.perl
[13] https://github.com/google/sentencepiece

Appendix C   Correlations for Top-N Systems

C.1   de-en

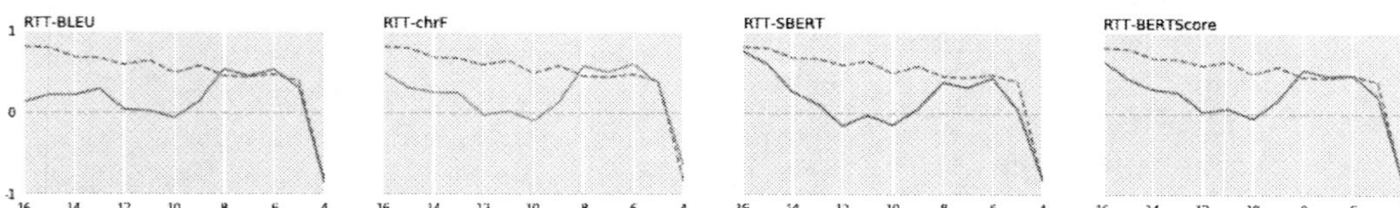

C.2   en-cs

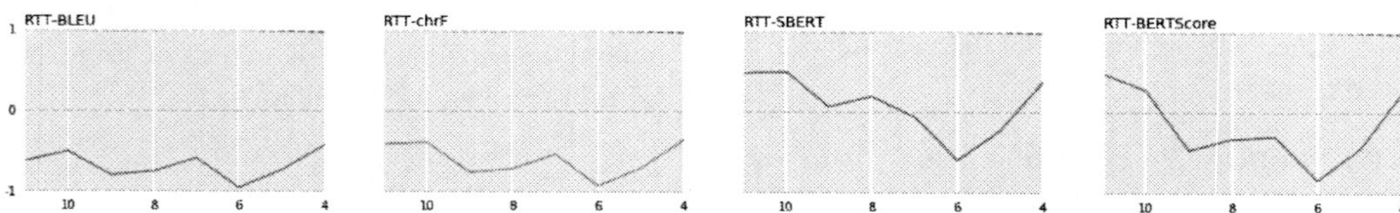

C.3   en-de

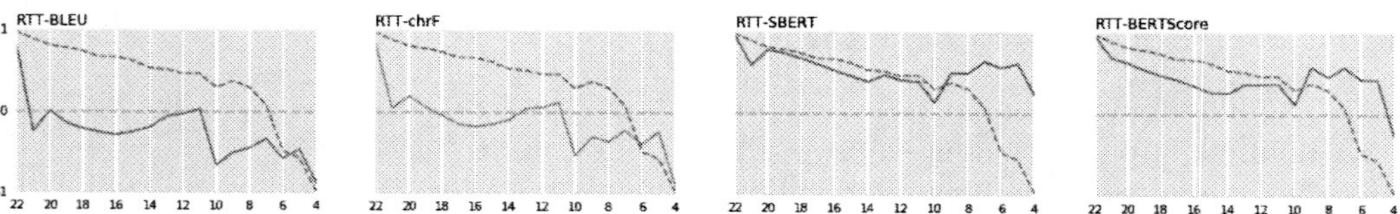

C.4   en-fi

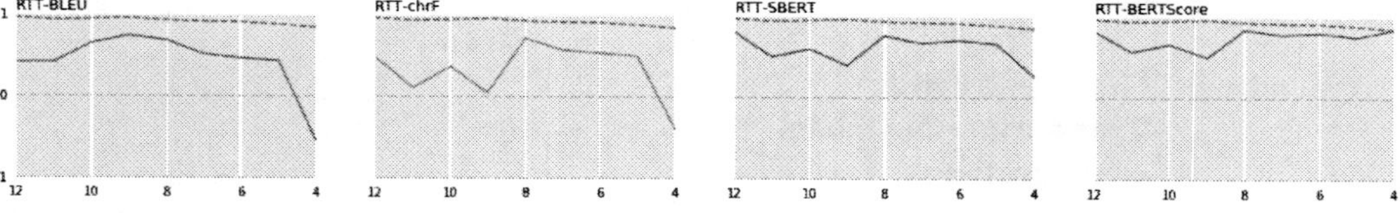

C.5   en-gu

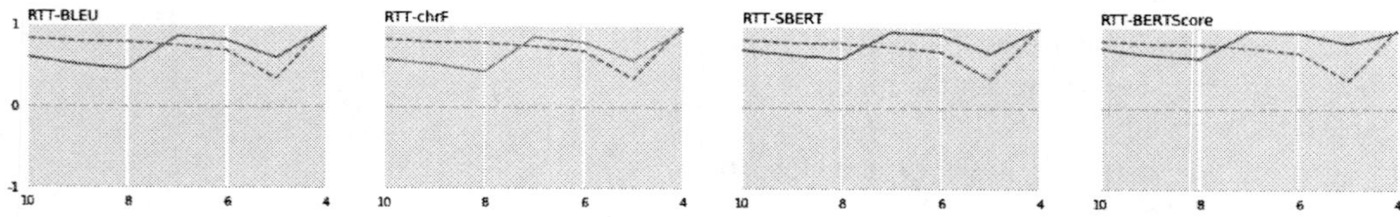

C.6 en-kk

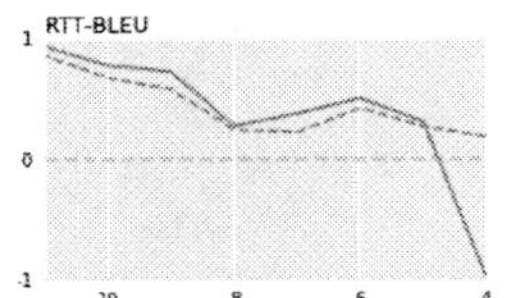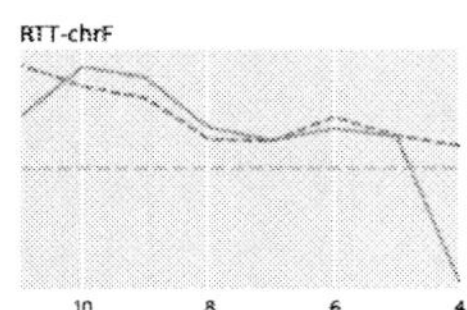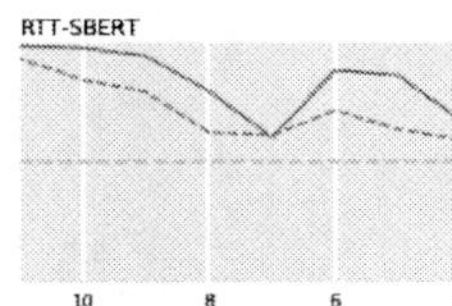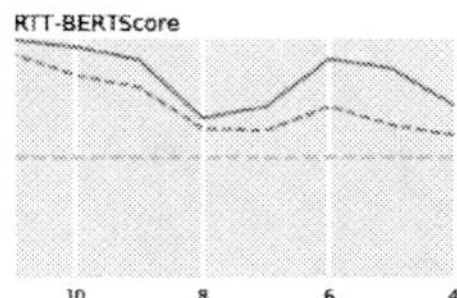

C.7 en-lt

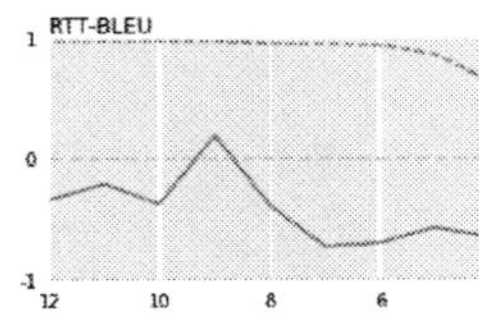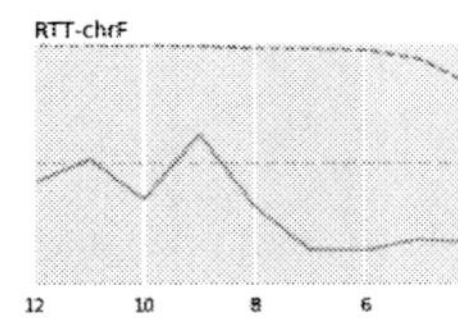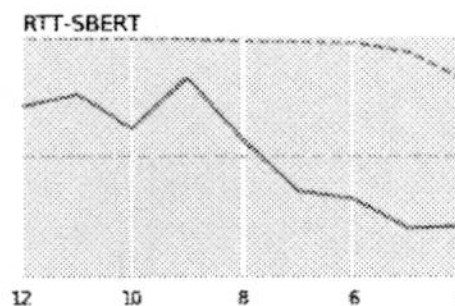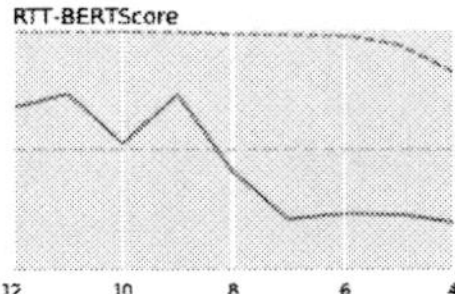

C.8 en-ru

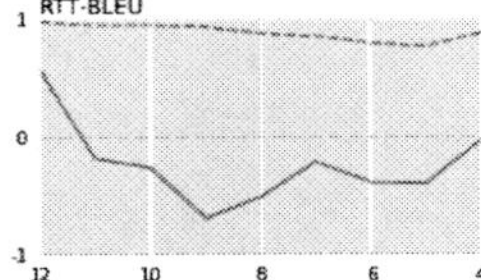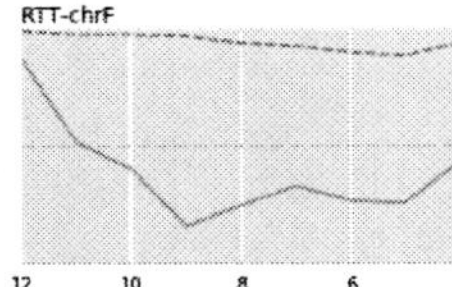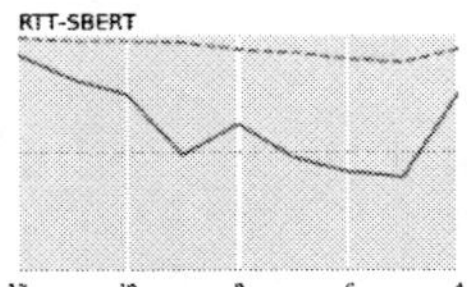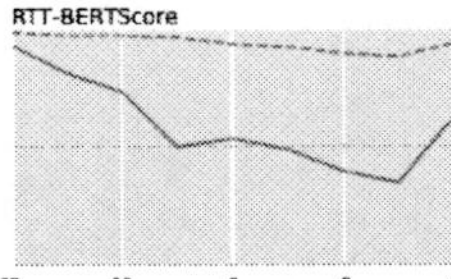

C.9 en-zh

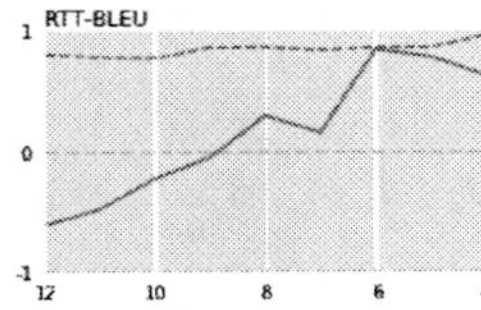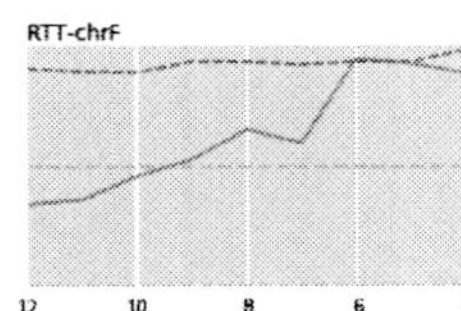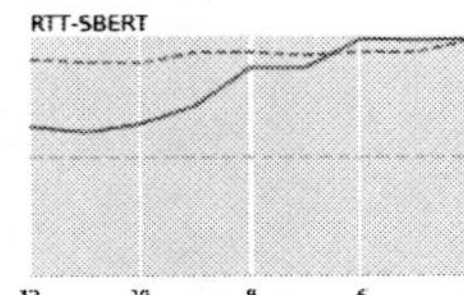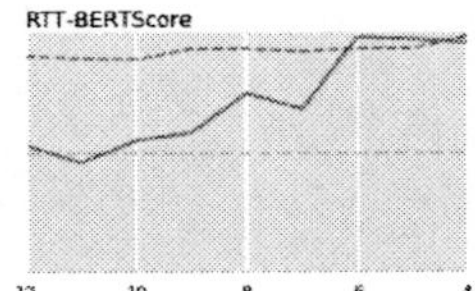

C.10 fi-en

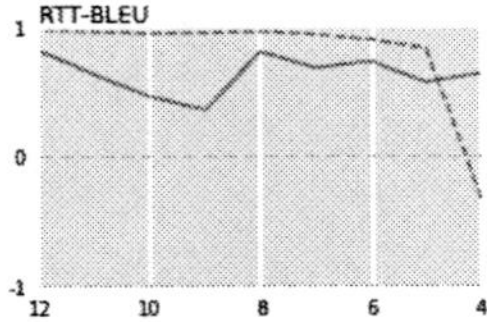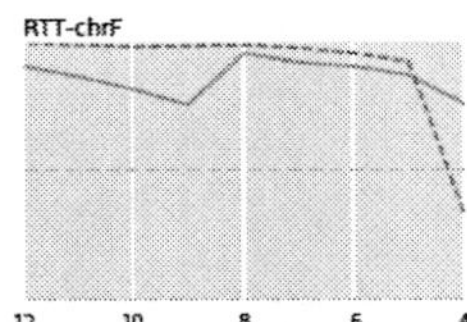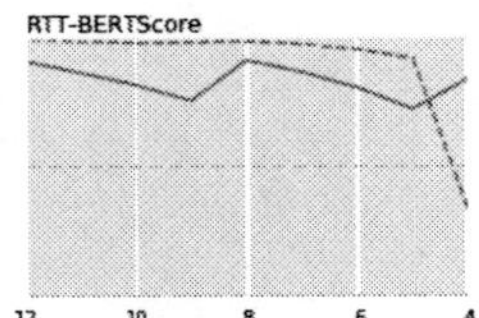

C.11 gu-en

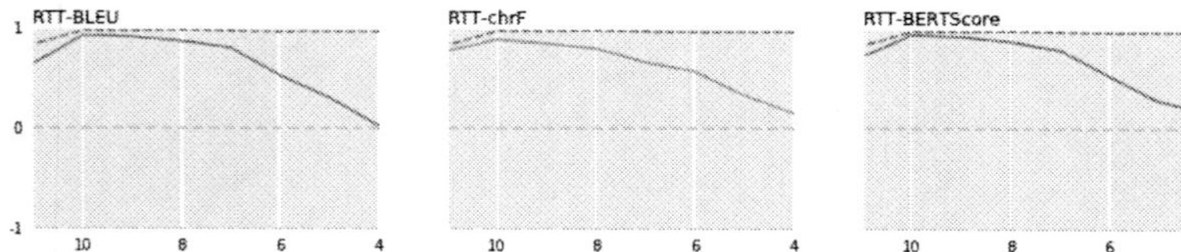

C.12 kk-en

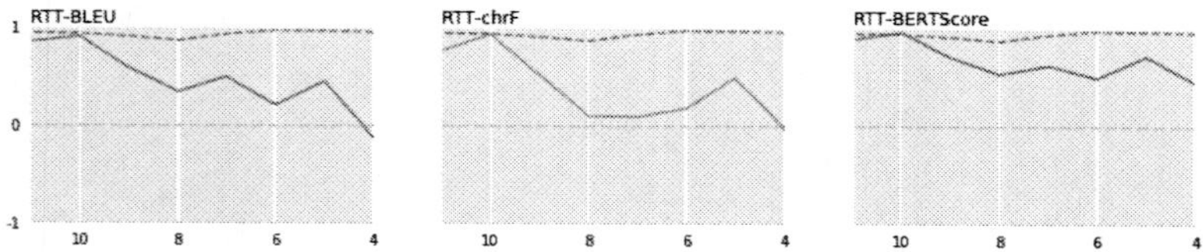

C.13 lt-en

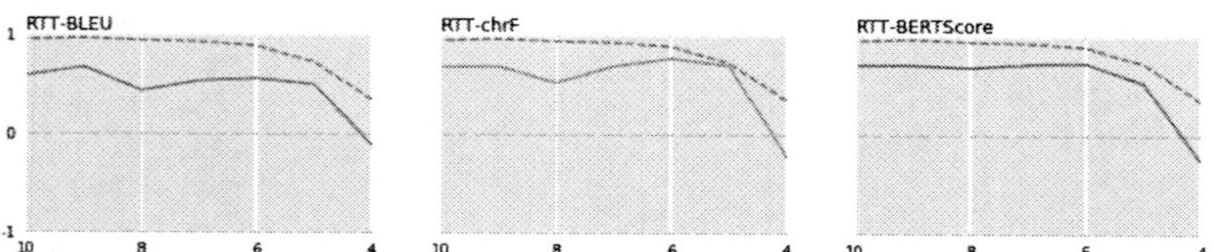

C.14 ru-en

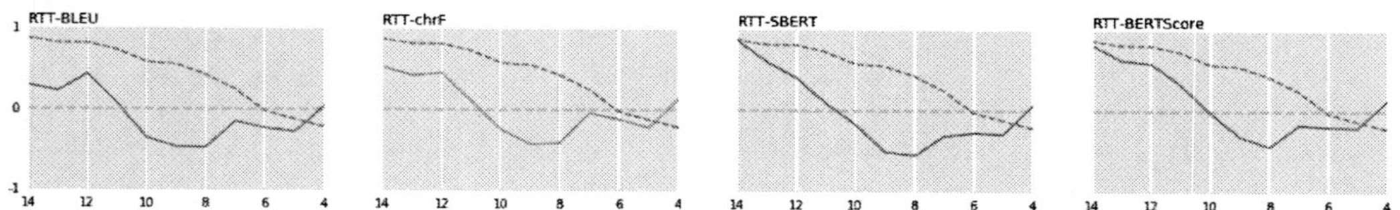

C.15 zh-en

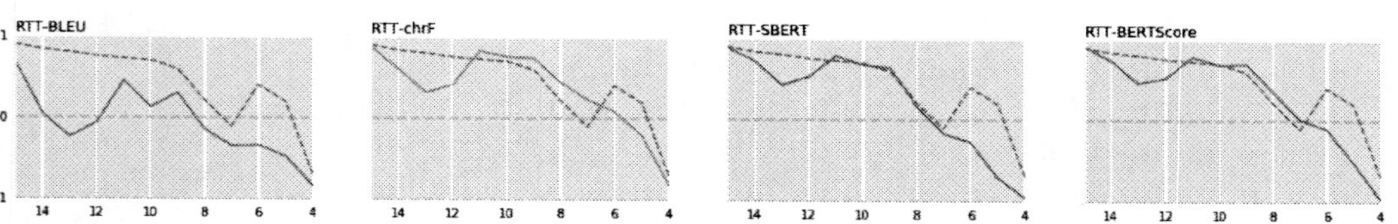

Double Attention-based Multimodal Neural Machine Translation with Semantic Image Regions

Yuting Zhao[1], Mamoru Komachi[1], Tomoyuki Kajiwara[2], Chenhui Chu[2]
[1]Tokyo Metropolitan University, 6-6 Asahigaoka, Hino, Tokyo 191-0065, Japan
[2]Osaka University, 2-8 Yamadaoka, Suita, Osaka 565-0871, Japan
`zhao-yuting@ed.tmu.ac.jp`
`komachi@tmu.ac.jp`
`{kajiwara,chu}@ids.osaka-u.ac.jp`

Abstract

Existing studies on multimodal neural machine translation (MNMT) have mainly focused on the effect of combining visual and textual modalities to improve translations. However, it has been suggested that the visual modality is only marginally beneficial. Conventional visual attention mechanisms have been used to select the visual features from equally-sized grids generated by convolutional neural networks (CNNs), and may have had modest effects on aligning the visual concepts associated with textual objects, because the grid visual features do not capture semantic information. In contrast, we propose the application of semantic image regions for MNMT by integrating visual and textual features using two individual attention mechanisms (double attention). We conducted experiments on the Multi30k dataset and achieved an improvement of 0.5 and 0.9 BLEU points for English→German and English→French translation tasks, compared with the MNMT with grid visual features. We also demonstrated concrete improvements on translation performance benefited from semantic image regions.

1 Introduction

Neural machine translation (NMT) (Sutskever et al., 2014; Bahdanau et al., 2015) has achieved state-of-the-art translation performance. Recently,

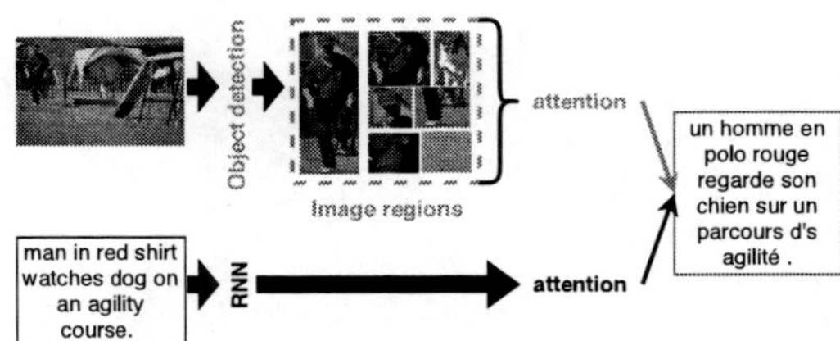

Figure 1: Overview of our MNMT model.

many studies (Specia et al., 2016; Elliott et al., 2017; Barrault et al., 2018) have been increasingly focusing on incorporating multimodal contents, particularly images, to improve translations. Hence, researchers in this field have established a shared task called multimodal machine translation (MMT), which consists of translating a target sentence from a source language description into another language using information from the image described by the source sentence.

The first MMT study by (Elliott et al., 2015) demonstrated the potential of improving the translation quality by using image. To effectively use an image, several subsequent studies (Gao et al., 2015; Huang et al., 2016; Calixto and Liu, 2017) incorporated global visual features extracted from the entire image by convolutional neural networks (CNNs) into a source word sequence or hidden states of a recurrent neural network (RNN). Furthermore, other studies started using local visual features in the context of an attention-based NMT. These features were extracted from equally-sized grids in an image by a CNN. For instance, multimodal attention (Caglayan et al., 2016b) has been designed for a mix of text and local visual features. Additionally, double attention mechanisms (Calixto et al., 2017) have been proposed for text

Martins, Moniz, Fumega, Martins, Batista, Coheur, Parra, Trancoso, Turchi, Bisazza, Moorkens, Guerberof, Nurminen, Marg, Forcada (eds.)
Proceedings of the 22nd Annual Conference of the European Association for Machine Translation, p. 105–114
Lisboa, Portugal, November 2020.

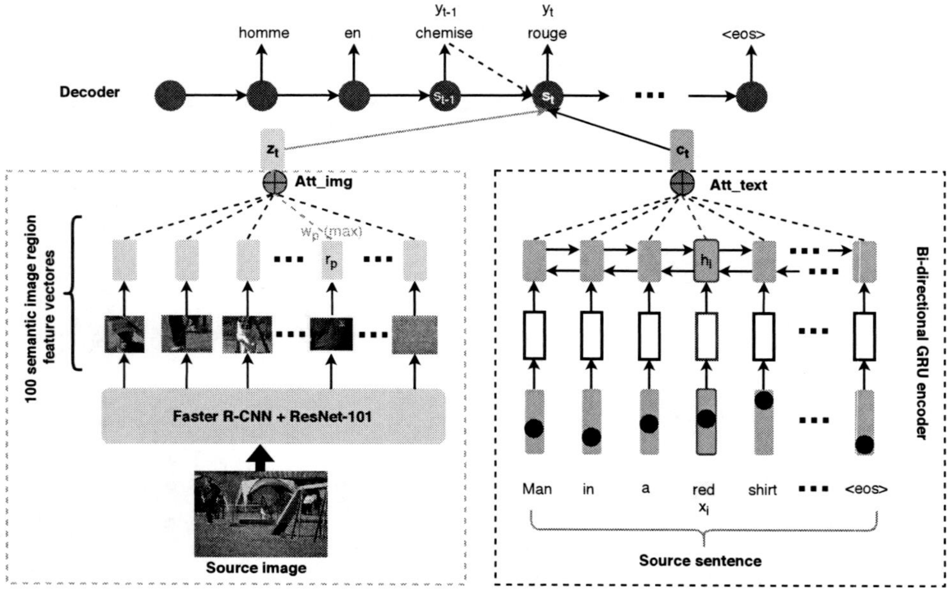

Figure 2: Our model of double attention-based MNMT with semantic image regions.

and local visual features, respectively. Although previous studies improved the use of local visual features and the text modality, these improvements were minor. As discussed in (Delbrouck and Dupont, 2017), these local visual features may not be suitable to attention-based NMT, because the attention mechanism cannot understand complex relationships between textual objects and visual concepts.

Other studies utilized richer local visual features to MNMT such as dense captioning features (Delbrouck et al., 2017). However, their efforts have not convincingly demonstrated that visual features can improve the translation quality. Caglayan et al. (2019) demonstrated that, when the textual context is limited, visual features can assist in generating better translations. MMT models disregard visual features because the quality of the image features or the way in which they are integrated into the model are not satisfactory. Therefore, which types of visual features are suitable to MNMT, and how these features should be integrated into MNMT, still remain open questions.

This paper proposes the integration of semantic image region features into a double attention-based NMT architecture. In particular, we combine object detection with a double attention mechanism to fully exploit visual features for MNMT. As shown in Figure 1, we use the semantic im-

age region features extracted by an object detection model, namely, Faster R-CNN (Ren et al., 2015). Compared with the local visual features extracted from equally-sized grids, we believe that our semantic image region features contain object attributes and relationships that are important to the source description. Moreover, we expect that the model would be capable of making selective use of the extracted semantic image regions when generating a target word. To this end, we integrate semantic image region features using two attention mechanisms: one for the semantic image regions and the other one for text. Code and pre-trained models are publicly available at: https://github.com/Zhao-Yuting/MNMT-with-semantic-regions.

The main contributions of this study are as follows:

- We verified that the translation quality can significantly improve by leveraging semantic image regions.

- We integrated semantic image regions into a double attention-based MNMT, which resulted in the improvement of translation performance above the baselines.

- We carried out a detailed analysis to identify the advantages and shortcomings of the proposed model.

2 MNMT with Semantic Image Regions

In Figure 2, our model comprises three parts: the source-sentence side, source-image side, and decoder. Inspired by (Calixto et al., 2017), we integrated the visual features using an independent attention mechanism. From the source sentence $X = (x_1, x_2, x_3, \cdots, x_n)$ to the target sentence $Y = (y_1, y_2, y_3, \cdots, y_m)$, the image-attention mechanism focuses on all semantic image regions to calculate the image context vector z_t, while the text-attention mechanism computes the text context vector c_t. The decoder uses a conditional gated recurrent unit (cGRU)[1] with attention mechanisms to generate the current hidden state s_t and target word y_t.

At time step t, first, a hidden state proposal $\hat{s}_t$ is computed in cGRU, as presented below, and then used to calculate the image context vector z_t and text context vector c_t.

$$
\begin{aligned}
\hat{\xi}_t &= \sigma(W_\xi E_Y[y_{t-1}] + U_\xi s_{t-1}) \\
\hat{\gamma}_t &= \sigma(W_\gamma E_Y[y_{t-1}] + U_\gamma s_{t-1}) \\
\ddot{s}_t &= \tanh\left(W E_Y[y_{t-1}] + \hat{\gamma}_t \odot (U s_{t-1})\right) \\
\hat{s}_t &= (1 - \hat{\xi}_t) \odot \ddot{s}_t + \hat{\xi}_t \odot s_{t-1}
\end{aligned}
\tag{1}
$$

where W_ξ, U_ξ, W_γ, U_γ, W, and U are training parameters; E_Y is the target word vector.

2.1 Source-sentence side

The source sentence side comprises a bi-directional GRU encoder and "soft" attention mechanism (Xu et al., 2015). Given a source sentence $X = (x_1, x_2, x_3, \cdots, x_n)$, the encoder updates the forward GRU hidden states by reading x from left to right, generates the forward annotation vectors $(\overrightarrow{h_1}, \overrightarrow{h_2}, \overrightarrow{h_3}, \cdots, \overrightarrow{h_n})$, and finally updates the backward GRU with the annotation vectors $(\overleftarrow{h_1}, \overleftarrow{h_2}, \overleftarrow{h_3}, \cdots, \overleftarrow{h_n})$. By concatenating the forward and backward vectors $h_i = [\overrightarrow{h_i}; \overleftarrow{h_i}]$, every h_i encodes the entire sentence while focusing on the x_i word, and all words in a sentence are denoted as $C = (h_1, h_2, \cdots, h_n)$. At each time step t, the text context vector c_t is generated as follows:

$$
\begin{aligned}
e_{t,i}^{\text{text}} &= (V^{\text{text}})^{\mathrm{T}} \tanh(U^{\text{text}} \hat{s}_t + W^{\text{text}} h_i) \\
\alpha_{t,i}^{\text{text}} &= \mathrm{softmax}(e_{t,i}^{\text{text}}) \\
c_t &= \sum_{i=1}^{n} \alpha_{t,i}^{\text{text}} h_i
\end{aligned}
\tag{2}
$$

(a) Grids.	(b) Image regions.

Figure 3: Comparing between (a) coarse grids and (b) semantic image regions.

where V^{text}, U^{text}, and W^{text} are training parameters; $e_{t,i}^{\text{text}}$ is the attention energy; $\alpha_{t,i}^{\text{text}}$ is the attention weight matrix of the source sentence.

2.2 Source-image side

In this part, we discuss the integration of semantic image regions into MNMT using an image attention mechanism.

Semantic image region feature extraction. As shown in Figure 3, instead of extracting equally-sized grid features using CNNs, we extract semantic image region features using object detection. This study applied the Faster R-CNN in conjunction with the ResNet-101 (He et al., 2016) CNN pre-trained on Visual Genome (Krishna et al., 2017) to extract 100 semantic image region features from each image. Each semantic image region feature is a vector r with a dimension of 2048, and all of these features in an image are denoted as $R = (r_1, r_2, r_3, \cdots, r_{100})$.

Image-attention mechanism. The image-attention mechanism is also a type of "soft" attention. This mechanism focuses on 100 semantic image region feature vectors at every time step and computes the image context vector z_t.

First, we calculate the attention energy $e_{t,p}^{\text{img}}$, which is an attention model that scores the degree of output matching between the inputs around position p and the output at position t, as follows:

$$
e_{t,p}^{\text{img}} = (V^{\text{img}})^{\mathrm{T}} \tanh(U^{\text{img}} \hat{s}_t + W^{\text{img}} r_p)
\tag{3}
$$

where V^{img}, U^{img}, and W^{img} are training parameters. Then the weight matrix $\alpha_{t,p}^{\text{img}}$ of each r_p is computed as follows:

$$
\alpha_{t,p}^{\text{img}} = \mathrm{softmax}(e_{t,p}^{\text{img}})
\tag{4}
$$

At each time step, the image-attention mechanism dynamically focuses on the semantic image region features and computes the image context vector z_t,

---

[1] https://github.com/nyu-dl/dl4mt-tutorial/blob/master/docs/cgru.pdf

as follows:

$$z_t = \beta_t \sum_{p=1}^{100} \alpha_{t,p}^{\text{img}} r_p \tag{5}$$

For z_t, at each decoding time step t, a gating scalar $\beta_t \in [0,1]$ (Xu et al., 2015) is used to adjust the proportion of the image context vector according to the previous hidden state of the decoder s_{t-1}.

$$\beta_t = \sigma(W_\beta s_{t-1} + b_\beta) \tag{6}$$

where W_β and b_β are training parameters.

2.3 Decoder

At each time step t of the decoder, the new hidden state s_t is computed in cGRU, as follows:

$$
\begin{aligned}
\xi_t &= \sigma(W_\xi^{\text{text}} c_t + W_\xi^{\text{img}} z_t + \bar{U}_\xi \hat{s}_t) \\
\gamma_t &= \sigma(W_\gamma^{\text{text}} c_t + W_\gamma^{\text{img}} z_t + \bar{U}_\gamma \hat{s}_t) \\
\bar{s}_t &= \tanh\left(W^{\text{text}} c_t + W^{\text{img}} z_t + \gamma_t \odot (\bar{U}\hat{s}_t)\right) \\
s_t &= (1 - \xi_t) \odot \bar{s}_t + \xi_t \odot \hat{s}_t
\end{aligned}
\tag{7}
$$

where $W_\xi^{\text{text}}, W_\xi^{\text{img}}, \bar{U}_\xi, W_\gamma^{\text{text}}, W_\gamma^{\text{img}}, \bar{U}_\gamma, W^{\text{text}}$, W^{img}, and $\bar{U}$ are model parameters; ξ_t and γ_t are the output of the update/reset gates; $\bar{s}_t$ is the proposed updated hidden state.

Finally, the conditional probability of generating a target word $p(y_t|y_{t-1}, s_t, C, R)$ is computed by a nonlinear, potentially multi-layered function, as follows:

$$\text{softmax}(L_o \tanh(L_s s_t + L_c c_t + L_z z_t + L_w E_Y[y_{t-1}])) \tag{8}$$

where L_o, L_s, L_c, L_z, and L_w are training parameters.

3 Experiments

3.1 Dataset

We conducted experiments for the English→German (En→De) and English→French (En→Fr) tasks using the Multi30k dataset (Elliott et al., 2016). The dataset contains 29k training and 1,014 validation images. For testing, we used the 2016 testset, which contains 1,000 images. Each image was paired with image descriptions expressed by both the original English sentences and the sentences translated into multiple languages.

For preprocessing, we lowercased and tokenized the English, German, and French descriptions with the scripts in the Moses SMT Toolkit.[2] Subsequently, we converted the space-separated tokens into subword units using the byte pair encoding (BPE) model.[3] Finally, the number of subwords in a description was limited to a maximum of 80.

3.2 Settings

Ours. We integrated the semantic image regions by modifying the double attention model of (Calixto et al., 2017). In the source-sentence, we reused the original implementation. In the source-image, we modified the image attention mechanism to focus on 100 semantic image region features with a dimension of 2048 at each time step. The parameter settings were consistent with the baseline doubly-attentive MNMT model, wherein we set the hidden state dimension of the 2-layer GRU encoder and 2-layer cGRU decoder to 500, source word embedding dimension to 500, batch size to 40, beam size to 5, text dropout to 0.3, and image region dropout to 0.5. We trained the model using stochastic gradient descent with ADADELTA (Zeiler, 2012) and a learning rate of 0.002, for 25 epochs. Finally, after both the validation perplexity and accuracy converged, we selected the converged model for testing.

Baseline Doubly-attentive MNMT. We trained a doubly-attentive MNMT model[4] as a baseline. For the text side, the implementation was based on OpenNMT model.[5] For the image side, attention was applied to the visual features extracted from 7×7 image grids by CNNs. For the image feature extraction, we compared three pre-trained CNN methods: VGG-19, ResNet-50, and ResNet-101.

Baseline OpenNMT. We trained a text-only attentive NMT model using OpenNMT as the other baseline. The model was trained on En→De and En→Fr, wherein only the textual part of Multi30k was used. The model comprised a 2-layer bidirectional GRU encoder and 2-layer cGRU decoder with attention.

For baselines, we used the original implementations and ensured the parameters were consistent with our model.

---

[2] https://github.com/moses-smt/mosesdecoder
[3] https://github.com/rsennrich/subword-nmt
[4] https://github.com/iacercalixto/MultimodalNMT
[5] https://github.com/OpenNMT/OpenNMT-py

	En→De		En→Fr	
Model	BLEU	METEOR	BLEU	METEOR
OpenNMT (text-only)	34.7±0.3	53.2±0.4	56.6±0.1	72.1±0.1
Doubly-attentive MNMT (VGG-19)	36.4±0.2	55.0±0.1	57.4±0.4	72.4±0.4
Doubly-attentive MNMT (ResNet-50)	36.5±0.2	54.9±0.4	57.5±0.4	72.6±0.4
Doubly-attentive MNMT (ResNet-101)	36.5±0.3	54.9±0.3	57.3±0.2	72.4±0.2
Ours (Faster R-CNN + ResNet-101)	**37.0±0.1**[†]	**55.3±0.2**	**58.2±0.5**[†‡]	**73.2±0.2**
vs. OpenNMT (text-only)	(↑ 2.3)	(↑ 2.1)	(↑ 1.6)	(↑ 1.1)
vs. Doubly-attentive MNMT (ResNet-101)	(↑ 0.5)	(↑ 0.4)	(↑ 0.8)	(↑ 0.9)
Caglayan et al. (2017) (text-only)	38.1±0.8	57.3±0.5	52.5±0.3	69.6±0.1
Caglayan et al. (2017) (grid)	37.0±0.8	57.0±0.3	53.5±0.8	70.4±0.6
Caglayan et al. (2017) (global)	38.8±0.5	57.5±0.2	54.5±0.8	71.2±0.4

Table 1: BLEU and METEOR scores for different models on the En→De and En→Fr 2016 testset of Multi30k. All scores are averages of three runs. We present the results using the mean and the standard deviation. † and ‡ indicate that the result is significantly better than OpenNMT and double-attentive MNMT at p-value < 0.01, respectively. Additionally, we report the best results of using grid and global visual features on Multi30k dataset according to (Caglayan et al., 2017), which is the state-of-the-art system for En→De translation on this dataset.

3.3 Evaluation

We evaluated the quality of the translation according to the token level BLEU (Papineni et al., 2002) and METEOR (Denkowski and Lavie, 2014) metrics. We trained all models (baselines and proposed model) three times and calculated the BLEU and METEOR scores, respectively. Based on the calculation results, we report the mean and standard deviation over three runs.

Moreover, we report the statistical significance with bootstrap resampling (Koehn, 2004) using the merger of three test translation results. We defined the threshold for the statistical significance test as 0.01, and report only if the p-value was less than the threshold.

4 Results

In Table 1, we present the results for the Open-NMT, doubly-attentive MNMT and our model on Multi30k dataset. Additionally, we also compared with Caglayan et al. (2017), which achieved the best performance under the same condition with our experiments.

Comparing the baselines, the doubly-attentive MNMT outperformed OpenNMT. Because there did not exist a big difference amongst the three image feature extraction methods for the doubly-attentive MNMT model, we only used ResNet-101 in our model.

Compared with the OpenNMT baseline, the pro-posed model improved both BLEU scores and ME-TEOR scores for En→De and En→Fr tasks. Additionally, the results of our proposed model are significantly better than the results obtained by the baseline with a p-value < 0.01 for both tasks.

Compared with the doubly-attentive MNMT (ResNet-101) baseline, the proposed model also improved the BLEU scores and METEOR scores for both tasks. Moreover, the results are significantly better than the baseline results with a p-value < 0.01 for En→Fr task.

For comparison with Caglayan et al. (2017), we report their results for the text-only NMT base-line, grid and global visual features for MNMT method. With the grid visual features, their results surpassed the text-only NMT baseline for En→Fr, but failed to surpass the text-only NMT baseline for En→De with regard to both metrics. With the global visual features, their results surpassed the text-only NMT baseline.

For En→De, though Caglayan et al. (2017) (global) achieved higher scores than our model, the improvements were minor. In terms of relative improvement compared with the text-only NMT baseline, their results improved the BLEU score by 1.8% and METEOR score by 0.3%. In contrast, our model improved the BLEU score by 6.6% and METEOR score by 3.9%.

For En→Fr, our results outperform Caglayan et al. (2017) (global) with regard to both metrics.

In terms of relative improvement compared with the text-only NMT baseline, their results improved the BLEU score by 1.9% and METEOR score by 1.1% with the grid visual features and improved the BLEU score by 3.8% and METEOR score by 2.3% with the global visual features. Our model improved the BLEU score by 2.8% and METEOR score by 1.5%.

5 Analysis

5.1 Pairwise evaluation of translations

We randomly investigated 50 examples from the En→Fr task to evaluate our model in detail. We compared the translations of our model with the baselines to identify improvement or deterioration in the translation. Then we categorized all examples into five types: 1) those whose translation performance were better than both baselines; 2) those whose translation performance were better than the doubly-attentive MNMT (ResNet-101) baseline; 3) those whose translation performance were better than the OpenNMT baseline; 4) those whose translation performance did not change; 5) those whose translation performance deteriorated. We counted the number and proportion of all types.

In Table 2, we can see that in nearly half of the examples, the translation performance is better than at least one baseline. Moreover, amongst a total of 50 examples, 14 examples are better than the doubly-attentive MNMT (ResNet-101) baseline and just two examples of local deterioration were found compared with the baselines.

5.2 Qualitative analysis

In Figure 4, we chose four examples to analyze our model in detail. The first two rows explain the advantages of our model, while the last two rows explain the shortcomings.

At each time step, the semantic image region is shown with deep or shallow transparency in the image, according to its assigned attention weight. As the weight increases, the image region becomes more transparent. Considering the number of 100 bounding boxes in one image and the overlapping areas, we visualized the top five weighted semantic image regions. The most weighted image region is indicated by the blue lines, and the target word generated at that time step is indicated by the red text along with the bounding box. Then, we analyzed whether the semantic image regions had a positive or negative effect at the time step when

Better than both baselines	8	(16%)
Better than MNMT baseline	6	(12%)
Better than NMT baseline	10	(20%)
No change	24	(48%)
Deteriorated	2	(4%)

Table 2: The amount and proportion of each type of examples in all investigated examples.

the target word was generated.

Advantages. In the first row, we can see that our model is better at translating the verb "grabbing" compared with both baselines. For the text-only OpenNMT, the translation of the word "grabbing" is incorrect. In English it is translated as "strolling with." The doubly-attentive MNMT (ResNet-101) translated "grab" into "agrippe," which failed to transform the verb into the present participle form. In contrast, although the reference is "saisissant" and our model generated "agrippant," the two words are synonyms. Our approach improved the translation performance both in terms of meaning and verb deformation, owing to the semantic image regions. We visualized the consecutive time steps of generating the word "agrippant" in context. Along with the generation of "agrippant," the attention focused on the image region where the action was being performed, and thus captured the state of the action at that moment.

In the second row, the noun "terrier" could not be translated by the baselines. This word means "a lively little dog" in English. As we can see, when the target word "terrier" was generated in our model, the attented semantic image region at that time step provided the exact object-level visual feature to the translation.

Shortcomings. The example in the third row reflects improvement and deficiency. Both baselines lack the sentence components of the adverbial "happily." In contrast, our model translated "happily" into "joyeusement," which is a better translation than both baselines. However, according to the image, the semantic image region with the largest attention weight did not carry the facial expression of a boy.

Although the maximum weight of the semantic image region was not accurately assigned, other heavily weighted semantic image regions, which contain the object attributes, may assist the translation. There may be two reasons for this: the func-

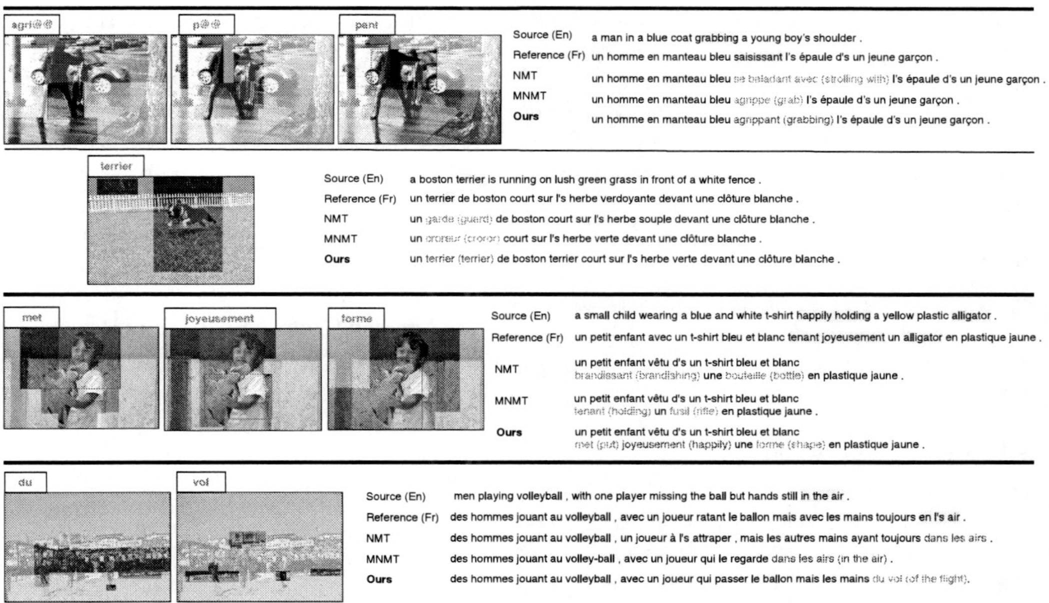

Figure 4: Translations from the baselines and our model for comparison. We highlight the words that distinguish the results. Blue words are marked for better translation and red words are marked for worse translation. We also visualize the semantic image regions that the words attend to.

tion of the attention mechanism is not sufficiently effective, or there exists an excessive amount of semantic image regions.

On the other hand, for the generation of the word "holding" and "alligator," the most weighted semantic image regions were not closely attended to. There was a slight deviation between the image regions and semantics. Owing to the inaccuracy of the image region that was drawn upon the object, the semantic feature was not adequately extracted. This indicates that the lack of specificity in the visual feature quality can diminish the detail of the information being conveyed.

In the last row, we presented one of the two examples with local deterioration. The "air" is correctly translated by baselines. However, our model translated "in the air" into "du vol (of the flight)." We observed that the transparent semantic image regions with the five top weights in the image were very scattered and unconnected. Amongst them, none of the semantic image regions matched the feature of "air." We speculate that the word "air" is difficult to interpret depending on visual features. On the other hand, our model translated it into "vol (flight)," which is close to another meaning of the polysemous "air," not something else.

Summary. In our model, the improvement of translation performance benefits from semantic image regions. The semantic image region visual features include the object, object attributes, and scene understanding, may assist the model in performing a better translation on the verb, noun, adverb and so on.

On the other hand, there are some problems:

- In some cases, although the translation performance improved, the image attention mechanism did not assign the maximum weight to the most appropriate semantic image region.

- When the object attributes cannot be specifically represented by image regions, incorrect visual features conveyed by the semantic image regions may interfere with the translation performance.

- If the image attention mechanism leads to the wrong focused semantic image region, it will bring negative effects on translation performance.

In our investigation, we did not identify any clear examples of successful disambiguation. In contrast, there is one example of detrimental results upon disambiguation. If the semantic image regions did not have good coverage of the semantic features or the image attention mechanism worked poorly, the disambiguation of polysemous words would not only fail, but ambiguous translation would also take place.

6 Related Work

From the first shared task at WMT 2016,[6] many MMT studies have been conducted. Existing studies have fused either global or local visual image features into MMT.

6.1 Global visual feature

Calixto and Liu (2017) incorporated global visual features into source sentence vectors and encoder/decoder hidden states. Elliott and Kádár (2017) utilized global visual features to learn both machine translation and visually grounding task simultaneously. As for the best system in WMT 2017,[7] Caglayan et al. (2017) proposed different methods to incorporate global visual features based on attention-based NMT model such as initial encoder/decoder hidden states using element-wise multiplication. Delbrouck and Dupont (2018) proposed a variation of the conditional gated recurrent unit decoder, which receives the global visual features as input. Calixto et al. (2019) incorporated global visual features through latent variables. Although their results surpassed the performance of the NMT baseline, the visual features of an entire image are complex and non-specific, so that the effect of the image is not fully exerted.

6.2 Local visual features

Grid visual features. Fukui et al. (2016) applied multimodal compact bilinear pooling to combine the grid visual features and text vectors, but their model does not convincingly surpass an attention-based NMT baseline. Caglayan et al. (2016a) integrated local visual features extracted by ResNet-50 and source text vectors into an NMT decoder using shared transformation. They reported that the results obtained by their method did not surpass the results obtained by NMT systems. Caglayan, Barrault, and Bougares (2016b) proposed a multimodal attention mechanism based on (Caglayan et al., 2016a). They integrated two modalities by computing the multimodal context vector, wherein the local visual features were extracted by the ResNet-50 CNN. Similarly, Calixto et al. (2016) incorporated multiple multimodal attention mechanisms into decoder using grid visual features by VGG-19 CNN. Because the grid regions do not contain semantic visual features, the multimodal attention mechanism can not capture useful information with grid visual features.

Therefore, instead of multimodal attention, Calixto, Liu, and Campbell (2017) proposed two individual attention mechanisms focusing on two modalities. Similarly, Libovický and Helcl (2017) proposed two attention strategies that can be applied to all hidden layers or context vectors of each modality. But they still used grid visual features extracted by a CNN pre-trained on ImageNet. Caglayan et al. (2017) integrated a text context vector and visual context vectors by grid visual features to generate a multimodal context vector. Their results did not surpass those of the baseline NMT for the English–German task.

Helcl, Libovický, and Variš (2018) set an additional attention sub-layer after the self-attention based on the Transformer architecture, and integrated grid visual features extracted by a pretrained CNN. Caglayan et al. (2018) enhanced the multimodal attention into the filtered attention, which filters out grid regions irrelevant to translation and focuses on the most important part of the grid visual features. They made efforts to integrate a stronger attention function, but the considered regions were still grid visual features.

Image region visual features. Huang et al. (2016) extracted global visual features from entire images using a CNN and four regional bounding boxes from an image by a R-CNN.[8] They integrated the features into the beginning or end of the encoder hidden states. Because the global visual features were unable to provide extra supplementary information, they achieved slight improvement above the attention-based NMT. Notably, detailed regional visual features lead to better NMT translation performance.

Toyama et al. (2017) proposed a transformation to mix global visual feature vectors and object-level visual feature vectors extracted by a Fast R-CNN.[9] They incorporated multiple image features into the encoder and the head of the source se-

---

[6]http://www.statmt.org/wmt16/multimodal-task.html
[7]http://www.statmt.org/wmt17/multimodal-task.html
[8]https://github.com/rbgirshick/rcnn
[9]https://github.com/rbgirshick/fast-rcnn

quence and target sequence. Their model does not benefit from the object-level regions because the integration method cannot adequately handle visual feature sequences. Delbrouck, Dupont, and Seddati (2017) used two types of visual features, which had been extracted by ResNet-50 pretrained on ImageNet, and DenseCap[10] pretrained on Visual Genome, respectively. They integrated the features into their multimodal embeddings and found that the regional visual features (extracted by DenseCap) resulted in improved translations. However, they did not clarify whether the improvement in the regional visual features was brought by the multimodal embeddings or the attention model.

For the best system in WMT 2018,[11] Grönroos et al. (2018) used different types of visual features, such as the scene type, action type, and object type. They integrated these features into the transformer architecture using multimodal settings. However, they found that the visual features only exerted a minor effect in their system. Anderson et al. (2018) proposed a bottom-up and top-down model, which calculates attention at the level of objects. This model was used in visual question answering and image captioning tasks.

7 Conclusion

This paper proposed a model that integrates semantic image regions with two individual attention mechanisms. We achieved significantly improved translation performance above two baselines, and verified that this improvement mainly benefited from the semantic image regions. Additionally, we analyzed the advantages and shortcomings of our model by comparing examples and visualization of semantic image regions. In the future, we plan to use much finer visual information such as instance semantic segmentation to improve the quality of visual features. In addition, as English entity and image region alignment has been manually annotated to the Multi30k dataset, we plan to use it as supervision to improve accuracy of the attention mechanism.

Acknowledgments

This work was supported by Microsoft Research Asia Collaborative Research Grant, Grant-in-Aid for Young Scientists #19K20343 and Grant-in-Aid for Research Activity Start-up #18H06465, JSPS.

---

[10]https://github.com/jcjohnson/densecap
[11]http://www.statmt.org/wmt18/multimodal-task.html

References

Anderson, Peter, Xiaodong He, Chris Buehler, Damien Teney, Mark Johnson, Stephen Gould, and Lei Zhang. 2018. Bottom-up and top-down attention for image captioning and visual question answering. In *CVPR*, pages 6077–6086.

Bahdanau, Dzmitry, Kyunghyun Cho, and Yoshua Bengio. 2015. Neural machine translation by jointly learning to align and translate. *ICLR*, abs/1409.0473.

Barrault, Loïc, Fethi Bougares, Lucia Specia, Chiraag Lala, Desmond Elliott, and Stella Frank. 2018. Findings of the third shared task on multimodal machine translation. In *WMT*, pages 304–323.

Caglayan, Ozan, Walid Aransa, Yaxing Wang, Marc Masana, Mercedes García-Martínez, Fethi Bougares, Loïc Barrault, and Joost van de Weijer. 2016a. Does multimodality help human and machine for translation and image captioning? In *WMT*, pages 627–633.

Caglayan, Ozan, Loïc Barrault, and Fethi Bougares. 2016b. Multimodal attention for neural machine translation. *CoRR*.

Caglayan, Ozan, Walid Aransa, Adrien Bardet, Mercedes García-Martínez, Fethi Bougares, Loïc Barrault, Marc Masana, Luis Herranz, and Joost van de Weijer. 2017. LIUM-CVC submissions for WMT17 multimodal translation task. In *WMT*, pages 432–439.

Caglayan, Ozan, Adrien Bardet, Fethi Bougares, Loïc Barrault, Kai Wang, Marc Masana, Luis Herranz, and Joost van de Weijer. 2018. LIUM-CVC submissions for WMT18 multimodal translation task. In *WMT*, pages 597–602.

Calixto, Iacer and Qun Liu. 2017. Incorporating global visual features into attention-based neural machine translation. In *EMNLP*, pages 992–1003.

Calixto, Iacer, Desmond Elliott, and Stella Frank. 2016. DCU-UvA multimodal MT system report. In *WMT*, pages 634–638.

Calixto, Iacer, Qun Liu, and Nick Campbell. 2017. Doubly-attentive decoder for multi-modal neural machine translation. In *ACL*, pages 1913–1924.

Calixto, Iacer, Miguel Rios, and Wilker Aziz. 2019. Latent variable model for multi-modal translation. In *ACL*, pages 6392–6405.

Delbrouck, Jean-Benoit and Stéphane Dupont. 2017. An empirical study on the effectiveness of images in multimodal neural machine translation. In *EMNLP*, pages 910–919.

Delbrouck, Jean-Benoit and Stéphane Dupont. 2018. UMONS submission for WMT18 multimodal translation task. In *WMT*, pages 643–647.

Delbrouck, Jean-Benoit, Stéphane Dupont, and Omar Seddati. 2017. Visually grounded word embeddings and richer visual features for improving multimodal neural machine translation. In *GLU*, pages 62–67.

Denkowski, Michael and Alon Lavie. 2014. Meteor universal: Language specific translation evaluation for any target language. In *WMT*, pages 376–380.

Elliott, Desmond and Ákos Kádár. 2017. Imagination improves multimodal translation. In *IJCNLP*, pages 130–141.

Elliott, Desmond, Stella Frank, and Eva Hasler. 2015. Multi-language image description with neural sequence models. *CoRR*.

Elliott, Desmond, Stella Frank, Khalil Sima'an, and Lucia Specia. 2016. Multi30k: Multilingual English-German image descriptions. In *VL*, pages 70–74.

Elliott, Desmond, Stella Frank, Loïc Barrault, Fethi Bougares, and Lucia Specia. 2017. Findings of the second shared task on multimodal machine translation and multilingual image description. In *WMT*, pages 215–233.

Fukui, Akira, Dong Huk Park, Daylen Yang, Anna Rohrbach, Trevor Darrell, and Marcus Rohrbach. 2016. Multimodal compact bilinear pooling for visual question answering and visual grounding. In *WMT*, pages 457–468.

Gao, Haoyuan, Junhua Mao, Jie Zhou, Zhiheng Huang, Lei Wang, and Wei Xu. 2015. Are you talking to a machine? dataset and methods for multilingual image question answering. In *NIPS*, pages 2296–2304.

Grönroos, Stig-Arne, Benoit Huet, Mikko Kurimo, Jorma Laaksonen, Bernard Merialdo, Phu Pham, Mats Sjöberg, Umut Sulubacak, Jörg Tiedemann, Raphael Troncy, and Raúl Vázquez. 2018. The MeMAD submission to the WMT18 multimodal translation task. In *WMT*, pages 603–611.

He, Kaiming, Xiangyu Zhang, Shaoqing Ren, and Jian Sun. 2016. Deep residual learning for image recognition. In *CVPR*, pages 770–778.

Helcl, Jindřich, Jindřich Libovický, and Dušan Variš. 2018. CUNI system for the WMT18 multimodal translation task. In *WMT*, pages 616–623.

Huang, Po-Yao, Frederick Liu, Sz-Rung Shiang, Jean Oh, and Chris Dyer. 2016. Attention-based multimodal neural machine translation. In *WMT*, pages 639–645.

Koehn, Philipp. 2004. Statistical significance tests for machine translation evaluation. In *EMNLP*, pages 388–395.

Krishna, Ranjay, Yuke Zhu, Oliver Groth, Justin Johnson, Kenji Hata, Joshua Kravitz, Stephanie Chen, Yannis Kalantidis, Li-Jia Li, David A. Shamma, Michael S. Bernstein, and F. Li. 2017. Visual genome: Connecting language and vision using crowdsourced dense image annotations. *IJCV*, 123(1):32–73.

Libovický, Jindřich and Jindřich Helcl. 2017. Attention strategies for multi-source sequence-to-sequence learning. In *ACL*, pages 196–202.

Papineni, Kishore, Salim Roukos, Todd Ward, and Wei-Jing Zhu. 2002. BLEU: a method for automatic evaluation of machine translation. In *ACL*, pages 311–318.

Ren, Shaoqing, Kaiming He, Ross Girshick, and Jian Sun. 2015. Faster R-CNN: Towards real-time object detection with region proposal networks. In *ICCV*, pages 91–99.

Specia, Lucia, Stella Frank, Khalil Sima'an, and Desmond Elliott. 2016. A shared task on multimodal machine translation and crosslingual image description. In *WMT*, pages 543–553.

Sutskever, Ilya, Oriol Vinyals, and Quoc V Le. 2014. Sequence to sequence learning with neural networks. In *NIPS*, pages 3104–3112.

Toyama, Joji, Masanori Misono, Masahiro Suzuki, Kotaro Nakayama, and Yutaka Matsuo. 2017. Neural machine translation with latent semantic of image and text. *ArXiv*, abs/1611.08459.

Xu, Kelvin, Jimmy Ba, Ryan Kiros, Kyunghyun Cho, Aaron Courville, Ruslan Salakhudinov, Rich Zemel, and Yoshua Bengio. 2015. Show, attend and tell: Neural image caption generation with visual attention. In *ICML*, pages 2048–2057.

Zeiler, Matthew D. 2012. ADADELTA: an adaptive learning rate method. *CoRR*.

MT for subtitling: User evaluation of post-editing productivity

Maarit Koponen *   **Umut Sulubacak** *   **Kaisa Vitikainen** [†*]   **Jörg Tiedemann** *

* University of Helsinki
{name.surname}@helsinki.fi

[†] Yle
{name.surname}@yle.fi

Abstract

This paper presents a user evaluation of machine translation and post-editing for TV subtitles. Based on a process study where 12 professional subtitlers translated and post-edited subtitles, we compare effort in terms of task time and number of keystrokes. We also discuss examples of specific subtitling features like condensation, and how these features may have affected the post-editing results. In addition to overall MT quality, segmentation and timing of the subtitles are found to be important issues to be addressed in future work.

1 Introduction

Developments in machine translation (MT) in the last two decades have led to significant improvements in translation quality. The success and popularity of statistical machine translation (SMT) systems were matched and eventually surpassed by neural machine translation (NMT). As quality has improved, the use of MT and post-editing (PE) has also increased in professional translation workflows. Broadly, PE refers to the practice of using MT output as a raw version checked and corrected by the translator. The use of MT and PE has been found to increase productivity in various translation scenarios (e.g. Plitt and Masselot, 2010). However, this workflow appears less common in the field of audiovisual translation (AVT). For example, Bywood et al. (2017) note that while specialised subtitling software with various functionalities are used, technologies like translation memory (TM) or MT have not been widely adopted in AVT. Matusov et al. (2019) suggest that a reason for the lower rate of MT adoption in the AVT field may be that current NMT systems are not suited for the particular features of subtitle translation.

This paper presents a pilot study carried out in November 2019 examining how the use of MT and PE in the subtitling workflow affects the work and productivity of subtitlers. In the study, 12 professional subtitle translators worked on a series of tasks in four language pairs (Finnish→English, Finnish→Swedish, English→Finnish, and Swedish→Finnish). They created interlingual (translated) subtitles for short video clips both with and without MT output. To assess productivity and effort, keylogging data were recorded during these tasks. Task time and technical effort represented by keystrokes were compared between post-editing and translation from scratch.

We first discuss related work on MT for subtitling and approaches to user evaluation of MTPE in Section 2. The MT models and subtitle alignment are presented in Section 3. Section 4 outlines the user data collection, and Section 5 presents the analysis of productivity measures. Section 6 discusses observations on PE changes, followed by future work and conclusions.

2 Related work

2.1 Machine translation for subtitling

Interlingual translated subtitles are a solution (along with dubbing and voice-overs) for bringing movies, television series, documentaries and other video material to audiences who do not understand the original language of the video. Whether dub-

Martins, Moniz, Fumega, Martins, Batista, Coheur, Parra, Trancoso, Turchi, Bisazza, Moorkens, Guerberof, Nurminen, Marg, Forcada (eds.)
Proceedings of the 22nd Annual Conference of the European Association for Machine Translation, p. 115–124
Lisboa, Portugal, November 2020.

bing or subtitling is used varies in different countries and also contexts. Finland, where this study was carried out, is one of the countries where subtitling is predominant for most content types (only children's programming tends to be dubbed).

Subtitling has some features which differentiate it from text translation. Firstly, the source text in subtitling is spoken language, or written representation of spoken language when intralingual subtitles in the language of the original video are used as the source in so-called template translation (e.g. Bywood et al., 2017). The translated subtitles represent source language speech in written target language. Secondly, subtitles have certain technical restrictions related to the number of characters and lines in one subtitle frame, and the length of time the frame is shown on the screen. For example, at the broadcasting company where this study was carried out, subtitle frames contain a maximum of two lines consisting of a maximum of 37 characters, and each frame is on screen from 2 seconds up to 6 seconds. Therefore, subtitle translation commonly involves condensation through solutions like omissions and paraphrases (Pedersen, 2017). Burchardt et al. (2016) also note that issues such as wide variation in subject matter, disfluencies and lack of context in the spoken language as well as the effect of the visual context may present additional challenges for MT.

On the other hand, some authors have suggested that the generally short and relatively simple sentences typical of subtitles would be well-suited for MT. For example, Volk et al. (2010) discuss an SMT system for Swedish→Danish MT of subtitles. In a PE experiment with 6 translators, they report relatively little was edited (average BLEU score between MT and PE for three different TV genres 65.8), with 22% of segments not changed at all. However, no process-based effort measures are reported in that study.

The eTITLE project (Melero et al., 2006) developed a web-based subtitling platform (for English, Spanish, Catalan and Czech) which offered translation memories and MT output from third-party MT engines as a tool for subtitlers. Their tool contains modules for condensation of the machine-translated subtitles and for subtitle placement. Melero et al. (2006) present a user evaluation where one translator translated parts of a movie (English→Czech) either based on the English source text or using MTPE, and report that subtitling the parts with MT was approximately 17% faster than the parts without.

In another study, de Sousa et al. (2011) experimented with MT and TM for DVD subtitling (English→Portuguese). Based on an experiment where 11 volunteers (described as "native speakers of Brazilian Portuguese and fluent speakers of English" with "some experience with translation tasks") alternately translated and post-edited 250 source sentences, de Sousa et al. (2011) report that MTPE was on average 40% faster than translation from scratch.

The SUMAT project (Bywood et al., 2017) developed a cloud-based platform for subtitle translation using MT and post-editing in multiple language pairs, and involved a large-scale user evaluation of productivity and usability of MTPE for subtitling. They collected time data and subjective feedback from 19 professional subtitle translators who translated two files using a source language template, and post-edited MT with and without quality estimation filtering. Bywood et al. (2017) found that MTPE improved productivity (in terms of task time) on average by nearly 40%, although considerable variation was observed in different language pairs and content types. They report the highest increase in English→Dutch (86%) whereas in Spanish→English, a 3.4% decrease of productivity was observed. On average, productivity increased by approximately 14% for scripted vs 50% for unscripted content (Bywood et al., 2017).

Matusov et al. (2019) customised an English→Spanish NMT system for subtitle translation using OpenSubtitles parallel data and other "conversational corpora" like GlobalVoices and TED talks. They report a user experiment where two professional translators subtitled a documentary and a sitcom episode partly from scratch and partly using a source language template and by post-editing two different MT outputs. Based on the experiments, Matusov et al. (2019) estimate average time savings by the translators to be approximately 25% with the customised MT and 5% with the baseline system.

2.2 User evaluation of MT and PE effort

Common approaches to evaluating MT quality include automatic MT metrics such as BLEU (Papineni et al., 2002) or (H)TER (Snover et al., 2006), which calculate similarity scores or edit rates based on the overlap of words or n-grams between an MT hypothesis and one or more reference translations. These metrics are sometimes used to compare MT output and post-edited versions of the MT as representation of PE effort in terms of the number of words changed during PE (e.g. Volk et al., 2010). However, this product-based approach cannot fully capture the actual effort involved in the PE process. For a more accurate picture of the feasibility of using MTPE, evaluations need to address PE effort in terms of time, technical effort required carrying out for corrections, as well as cognitive effort required for identifying errors and deciding what actions are needed (see Krings, 2001).

Temporal effort can be measured by recording task times (e.g. to the nearest minute) and comparing different types of tasks, such as MTPE versus translation "from scratch" (without MT output), or PE of different MT outputs. More fine-grained time data can be collected using keystroke logging tools like Inputlog (Leijten and Van Waes, 2013), which also provide information about the technical effort involved. Cognitive effort is the most difficult of the three to capture. Approaches to measuring cognitive effort include examining pauses in keylogging, introspective methods, and eyetracking. For an overview of process methodologies, see e.g. Saldanha and O'Brien (2013).

Like the previous studies on MT for subtitling in Section 2.1, the user evaluation reported in this paper addresses productivity in MTPE compared to translation from scratch. However, where prior work has mainly focused on task time or throughput (words or subtitles translated per time unit), we also examine technical effort through keylogging. Effort measures (task time, number of keystrokes) were analysed comparing subtitling from scratch and MT post-editing (see Section 4).

3 Automatic subtitle translation

3.1 Datasets and MT models

For the assessment of MT in subtitle translation, we created sentence-level and document-level translation models from all the parallel data available in OPUS.[1] For Finnish↔Swedish, this includes a bit over 30 million training examples,[2] and for Finnish↔English, roughly 44 mil-

lion.[3] The training data comes from diverse backgrounds, with sources ranging from Bible translations to software localisation data, official EU publications, and data mined from unrestricted web crawls.

The largest portion of training data is a collection of movie and TV show subtitles derived from the OpenSubtitles (v2018) dataset. For Finnish↔Swedish, this collection contains over 15 million translation units, and for Finnish↔English, it contains almost 30 million translation units. Even though this sub-corpus is quite noisy as well, it fits the task rather well, and we can therefore expect that our models should have a decent performance in the subtitle translation task even without further fine-tuning.

The models we trained rely on the Transformer architecture (Vaswani et al., 2017), the current state of the art in NMT. We apply the implementation from the MarianNMT toolkit (Junczys-Dowmunt et al., 2018), which offers fast training and decoding with the latest features of production-ready NMT. We use the common settings of a multi-layer transformer, with 6 layers on both the encoder and the decoder, and 8 attention heads in each layer. We enable label smoothing and dropout, and use tied embeddings with a shared vocabulary, basically following the recommendations for training transformer models in the MarianNMT documentation. For text segmentation, we apply SentencePiece (Kudo and Richardson, 2018) with models that are trained independently for source and target languages for a vocabulary size of 32,000 in each language. We do not apply any further pre-processing to keep the setup as general as possible, apart from some basic normalisation of Unicode punctuation characters, and parallel corpus filtering using standard scripts from the Moses SMT package (Koehn et al., 2007).

For the document-level models, we apply the concatenative models proposed by Tiedemann and Scherrer (2017) and Junczys-Dowmunt (2019) using units of a maximum length of 100 tokens. Note that sentences and sentence fragments in subtitles are typically very short, and 100 tokens typically cover substantial amounts of context beyond sentence boundaries. We mark sentence bound-

---

[1] http://opus.nlpl.eu
[2] OPUS corpora used: bible-uedin, DGT, EMEA, EUbookshop, EUconst, Europarl, Finlex, fiskmo, GNOME, infopankki, JRC-Acquis, KDE4, MultiParaCrawl, OpenSubtitles, PHP, QED, Tatoeba, TildeMODEL, Ubuntu, wikimedia
[3] OPUS corpora used: bible-uedin, Books, DGT, ECB, EMEA, EUbookshop, EUconst, Europarl, GNOME, infopankki, JRC-Acquis, KDE4, OpenSubtitles, ParaCrawl, PHP, QED, Tatoeba, TildeMODEL, Ubuntu

aries with special tokens, chunking the training and test data sequentially from the beginning to the end without any overlaps. This procedure creates roughly 3.3 million pseudo-documents for Finnish↔Swedish and 4.7 million documents for Finnish↔English. This means that we have on average about 9 sentences per document, which are concatenated into one long string with boundary markers between sentences.

During test time, we proceed in the same way, creating pseudo-documents from the original input by concatenating subsequent sentences and splitting when a segment exceeds 100 tokens. Sentence-level models are translated in the usual way. In order to examine the translation quality, we applied our models to a dedicated test set taken from a larger set of subtitles from public broadcasts with audio in Finnish, Swedish or English. Intralingual subtitles in the language of the original audio were aligned with interlingual subtitles of the same programme in one of the other two languages. However, it should be noted that the interlingual subtitles are not direct translations of the intralingual subtitles as such. The alignment of subtitle segments in the test set was manually checked and non-corresponding segments were removed. The Finnish and Swedish parts of the dataset also contain intralingual subtitles for the deaf or hard-of-hearing, which were separated in the test set as their own subsets.

The translation results are shown in Table 1, where scores are listed separately for different subsets. Note that the document-level results need to be treated in a special way as they do not automatically match the sentence-level reference translations even when splitting on generated sentence boundary markers. To ensure that the reference and the system output correspond to each other, we apply a standard sentence alignment algorithm implemented in the hunalign package (Varga et al., 2005). We use the re-alignment flag to enable lexical matching as well, which is very beneficial in this monolingual alignment task. BLEU scores may have been negatively affected by this procedure as this alignment is not perfect.

Overall, the results indicate that document-level models seem to be beneficial in the subtitle translation case. The automatic evaluation scores consistently show an improvement over the corresponding sentence-level models for both language pairs and in all directions. However, this encouraging

benchmark	sentence-level		document-level	
	BLEU	**chrF$_2$**	**BLEU**	**chrF$_2$**
fi→sv	18.8	0.443	19.3	0.451
sv→fi	15.7	0.449	16.8	0.462
fi→en	21.5	0.458	23.6	0.472
en→fi	16.0	0.444	17.1	0.454

Table 1: Comparison of BLEU and chrF$_2$ scores on the benchmark test set for the sentence-level and document-level systems in the language pairs Finnish→Swedish, Swedish→Finnish, Finnish→English, and English→Finnish.

result unfortunately does not carry over to the manual assessment (see Section 5). A reason for this may be at least partially related to the problem of segmentation and time frame alignment, which we introduce below.

3.2 Subtitle frame alignment

In both sentence-level and document-level translation, we have to treat the results in a way that maps the translations back into the time slots allocated for the original subtitles. Those time slots may include more than one sentence, and sentences may stretch over multiple time slots. Because our translation models are trained on sentence-aligned data, we need to extract sentences first from subtitles, too. We do this using the techniques proposed by Tiedemann (2008), which were also applied to the OpenSubtitles corpus in our training data.

Subtitles converted to sentence-level segments in XML:

```
<s id="13">
    <time id="T16S" value="00:01:05,960" />
We have to make readmission agreements with other countries, -
    <time id="T16E" value="00:01:12,360" />
    <time id="T17S" value="00:01:12,440" />
so that they would be willing.
</s>
<s id="14">
We have to cooperate closely.
    <time id="T17E" value="00:01:17,440" />
</s>
```

Mapped back to subtitle frames after translation:

```
16
00:01:05,960 --> 00:01:12,360
Meidän on tehtävä
takaisinottosopimuksia muiden maiden kanssa,

17
00:01:12,440 --> 00:01:17,440
jotta ne olisivat halukkaita.
Meidän on tehtävä tiivistä yhteistyötä.
```

Figure 1: Pre- and post-processing of subtitle data before and after translation. Sentences may run over several subtitle frames and multiple sentences and sentence fragments can also appear in the same time frame. The translation comes from a document-level model.

Mapping back to subtitle frames and their time allocations is implemented as another alignment algorithm. We apply a simple length-based algorithm for this, assuming that there is a strong length correlation between the source- and target-language subtitles. The difference to traditional sentence alignment is that we are now only interested in 1-to-n alignments, meaning that each existing subtitle frame in the original input should be filled with one or more segments from the translation. The segments on the target side that we consider are clauses from the generated sentences. For simplicity, we split on any punctuation in the output that is followed by space to approximate the structural segmentation. We then apply the traditional Gale & Church algorithm (Gale and Church, 1993) to optimise the global alignment between source segments (original subtitle frame data) and target segments. For this, we adjust the parameters of the algorithm in two ways: (i) we remove priors and apply a uniform distribution over possible alignment types, and (ii) we change the set of alignment types to include all possible mappings from one source segment to a maximum of four target segments. The mapping between source and target is then created using the original algorithm that ensures a globally optimal mapping according to the model (see Figure 1 for an example). Furthermore, we apply simple heuristics to insert line breaks in order to make subtitles conform to length and formatting constraints. The implementation of the entire procedure is available as an open source package[4].

4   User PE data collection

The subtitling tasks for productivity data collection were carried out in November 2019 at the premises of the Finnish Broadcasting Company Yle. In total 12 translators (3 per language pair) participated in the tasks: 8 in-house translators and 4 freelancers with experience of working for Yle. The participants have between 4 and 30 years of professional subtitling experience in their language pair. Only 2 stated they had previously used MT for subtitling, and 7 others had used MT for other purposes.

The subtitling tasks were carried out using the subtitlers' preferred software (Wincaps Q4 or Spot). To replicate their normal working environment, an external monitor and keyboard were provided, and they had access to the internet as well as terminology and other resources normally used in their work. Process data were logged using Inputlog (Leijten and Van Waes, 2013), which

records all keyboard and mouse activity. Windows 10 screen recording software was used to capture video to support the analysis. Pre- and post-task questionnaires were used to collect background information and participants' subjective assessment of the MT output and PE experience. After the tasks, a brief semi-structured interview was also carried out to collect more detailed feedback regarding problems in the workflow and the participants' views on potential improvements. In this paper, we focus on an analysis of the process data.

Subtitling tasks were carried out in 4 language pairs: Finnish→English, Finnish→Swedish, English→Finnish, and Swedish→Finnish. For each source language, six clips were selected from a dataset provided by Yle. Three clips were selected from unscripted European election debates, and three clips from semi-scripted lifestyle or cultural programmes. The individual clips were selected so that each clip (i) forms a coherent, self-contained section of the programme, (ii) is approximately 3 minutes long, and (iii) contains 30–35 subtitle segments.

Each participant completed a total of six tasks where they subtitled two clips "from scratch" without MT output, two clips using output from a sentence-level MT system, and two clips using output from a document-level MT system. The clips and MT outputs were rotated in a round-robin format so that each clip was subtitled once in each condition (no MT output, sentence-level MT output, document-level MT output) by a different participant. Task order was also varied to minimise facilitation effect. The participants were instructed to produce subtitles that would be acceptable for broadcasting, and to use the resources they normally would for their work, but to not spend excessive time in "polishing" any given wording or researching information. No explicit time limit was given for each task, rather, the participants were instructed to work at their own pace.

In the from scratch condition, the participants also created the segmentation and timing of the subtitles following their normal work process. Subtitling templates are not used by Yle for these content types. In the MTPE condition, the participants worked with output that was pre-segmented and timed based on the intralingual subtitles used as source text for the MT (see Section 3.2).

To assess productivity, the process logs were analysed using Inputlog's analysis functions. The

---

[4]https://github.com/Helsinki-NLP/subalign

task time and the number of keystrokes logged were used as productivity measures. Using Inputlog filters, we focused only on task time and keystrokes in the subtitling software, excluding other activity such as internet searches for terminology or other information. Based on the final subtitles produced, edit rate between the MT output and the final versions were calculated using HTER (Snover et al., 2006) and characTER (Wang et al., 2016). As PE of the subtitles involved also changes to the segmentation, e.g. adding or deleting frames and moving words between frames, subtitle segmentation was ignored and edit rates were calculated as document-level scores to focus on edits affecting the textual content. These measures were then compared between the tasks of creating interlingual subtitles from scratch and MTPE, as well as between PE of the sentence-level and document-level MT outputs described in Section 3.1.

5 Comparison of subtitling productivity

Figure 2 shows a comparison of the average subtitling task time for subtitling from scratch and subtitling with MTPE. The topmost three bars show averages for post-editing the sentence- and document-level MT output and for translation from scratch across all language pairs, while the bottom pairs of bars show averages for PE (either MT output) compared to from scratch. On average, post-editing machine-translated subtitles (regardless of MT output) was slightly faster than creating subtitles from scratch. Some differences can be seen between the language pairs: the largest difference in task times is seen in Swedish→Finnish, while the task times for Finnish→English and Finnish→Swedish are nearly equal. No clear difference could be observed between the two different MT outputs, although on average post-editing the sentence-level MT output appeared to be slightly faster.

Figure 3 shows a comparison of technical effort in terms of the average number of keystrokes used when producing subtitles. The topmost three bars show averages for post-editing the sentence- and document-level MT output and for translation from scratch across all language pairs, while the bottom pairs of bars show averages for PE (either MT output) compared to from scratch. On average, post-editing machine-translated subtitles (regardless of MT output) involved fewer keystrokes than

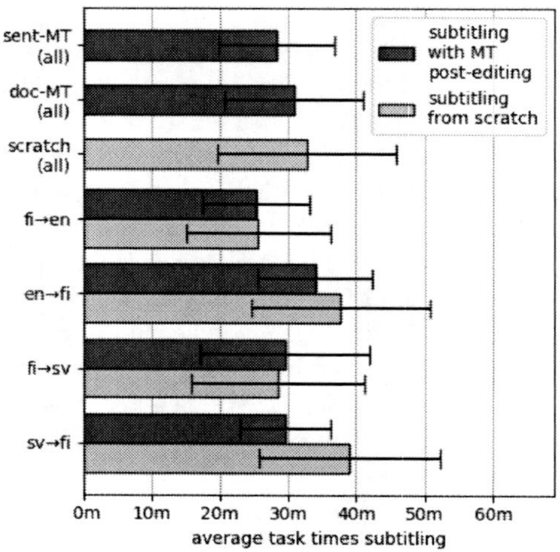

Figure 2: Average task times subtitling through post-editing and from scratch. The top three bars show averages for post-editing sentence- and document-level MT, and subtitling from scratch. The bottom pairs of bars are averages for each language pair. Error bars indicate standard deviation.

creating subtitles from scratch. The reduction in the number of keystrokes is more pronounced than in the case of task times, and seen in all language pairs. Again, no clear difference could be observed between the two different MT outputs, although on average post-editing the sentence-level MT output appeared to involve slightly less technical effort.

Although a detailed analysis of the types of keystrokes is not within the scope of this paper, some observations can be made regarding the distribution of keystroke types. Intuitively, PE reduced the need for text producing keystrokes on average by 54% compared to from scratch, as the MT output provides some of the text needed. However, the number of text deleting keystrokes was 24% higher in PE, as correcting the output also involves removing words or characters. In the from scratch case, the participants needed to create and set the timing for each subtitle frame themselves, which requires keystrokes and/or mouse clicks. In MTPE, the MT output was already segmented and timed based on the intralingual subtitles used as source text, which reduced the associated keystrokes by approximately 32%, but the number of keystrokes shows that the participants found it necessary to change both the segmentation and timing. Changes to subtitle segmentation are discussed in more detail below.

To examine the number of changes between

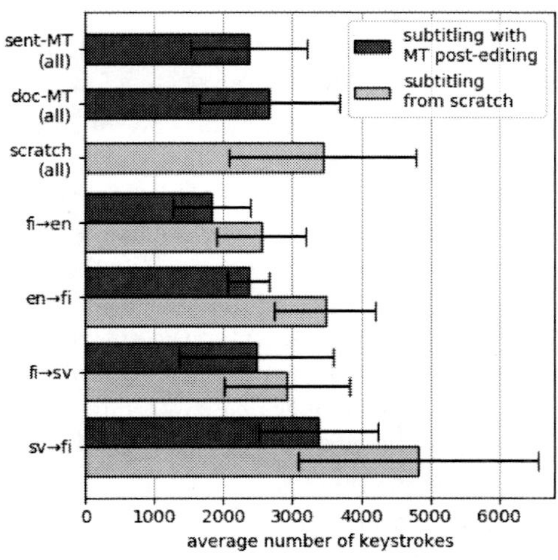

Figure 3: Average numbers of keystrokes subtitling through post-editing and from scratch. The top three bars show averages for post-editing sentence- and document-level MT, and subtitling from scratch. The bottom pairs of bars are averages for each language pair. Error bars indicate standard deviation.

the MT outputs and final PE versions, edit rates were calculated using word-based HTER and character-level characTER. Table 2 shows the HTER and characTER scores for the sentence-level and document-level MT across all four language pairs and for each language pair. The high edit rates (overall average HTER 57.7 and characTER 46.8) indicate considerable rewriting during PE, particularly in the case of English→Finnish. The high HTER score in this language pair may be due to the fact that word-based metrics do not distinguish changed words and changed word forms, which are common in morphologically-rich target languages like Finnish. The considerable difference in the characTER and HTER scores in English→Finnish suggests word form edits are indeed more common in this language pair. However, a similar effect is not seen in Swedish→Finnish. A preliminary analysis of the edits indicates that the participants working on this language pair have added words more frequently than participants in other language pairs. Corresponding to the process metrics, average edit rate for the sentence-level MT output is slightly lower than for the document-level MT. At least partly, this may be explained by the observation that repetition of words or phrases was more common in the document-level MT output.

In addition to the textual content of the MT sub-

	HTER	characTER
sent-level	55.1 ± 17.7	45.0 ± 12.3
doc-level	60.3 ± 16.1	48.7 ± 11.1
fi→en	45.6 ± 17.7	39.3 ± 13.5
en→fi	74.1 ± 12.7	48.9 ± 6.4
fi→sv	52.7 ± 13.2	44.1 ± 11.4
sv→fi	58.4 ± 9.5	55.1 ± 9.2
overall	**57.7 ± 16.9**	**46.8 ± 11.8**

Table 2: Comparison of word-level (HTER) and character-level (characTER) edit rates divided by MT system (sentence-level vs document-level) and language pair (Finnish→English, English→Finnish, Finnish→Swedish, Swedish→Finnish).

titles, the participants edited both the segmentation of that content into subtitle frames and timing of the frames. On average, the participants increased the number of subtitle frames in the clips by 7% by splitting or adding frames. This tendency was particularly noticeable in Swedish→Finnish (+19%). English→Finnish was the only language pair where the participants reduced the number of subtitle frames (–4%) for example by joining and condensing the textual content of the frames. Comparing the timestamps of the original subtitle frames used for the MT output and the frames in the post-edited files, we observed that only 24% of the original timed frames had been retained in PE. For 27% of frames, either the in or out time had been changed, and for 49% both in and out time were changed.

The intralingual subtitles used as source text were not translated as isolated subtitle frames but rather as sentences or longer passages and then aligned back to the frames (see Section 3.2). However, the heuristics used for alignment were not always successful. In some cases, splitting a segment due to punctuation caused the next segment to become too long and started to push content into the following frames, causing the subtitles to fall out of sync with the audio. Similar issues were also observed due to repetition in the MT output. It is also possible that the sync issues arising from incorrect segmentation may have lead the participants to also change the timing of subtitle frames.

6 Discussion of PE changes

Considerable variation in task times and numbers of keystrokes was observed between different participants. Productivity gains were most evident for participants with the longest average task times overall. However, 5 out of the 12 participants were in fact slower in PE. Two of them also used slightly more keystrokes, but three were slower despite using fewer keystrokes in PE. These findings are similar to other process studies both on subtitling and other text types (e.g. Plitt and Masselot, 2010; Bywood et al., 2017) showing that potential productivity gains from MTPE vary, and that participants who are already fast benefit less. Fewer keystrokes not necessarily leading to time saving has also been observed in other studies. While the number of keystrokes reflects the technical effort needed, it does not capture the amount of cognitive effort involved in recognising potential errors and deciding on necessary changes.

The edit rates of different participants also vary. At the level of individual subtitlers, average HTER scores range from 31.9 (Finnish→English, participant C) to 84.8 (English→Finnish, participant C). These edit rates are comparable to the HTER scores reported by Matusov et al. (2019) for different MT system outputs, genres and post-editors, which range from 27.8 to 82.7. In our study, the two participants with the highest average edit rates both worked on English→Finnish, and the two with the lowest average edit rates on Finnish→English, but differences are also evident within the same language pair. Since the participants post-edited different MT versions, some variation may be explained by different output quality, but to some extent these differences may also reflect individual preferences. Qualitative observations suggest that while some edits relate to clear MT errors, many are also caused by what appear to be preferential edits; for example, in the Finnish→English clips, one participant accepts the translation "financial discipline" for the Finnish *talouskuri* while another replaces it with "austerity".

A possible factor affecting both productivity and number of changes is PE experience. The participants in this study had little prior experience with MT specifically for subtitling. The subtitlers' productivity and approach to the task may therefore have been affected by the fact that PE was unfamiliar and different from their normal work processes. As Bywood et al. (2017) also note, psychological factors such as unfamiliarity and irritation with MT errors influence productivity. These factors may have also led to preferential and possibly unnecessary changes. More practice working with MT output and pre-segmented subtitles may affect their approaches, e.g. by reducing preferential changes, and increase productivity in this task.

As noted in Section 2.1, the spoken content of the videos and subtitles as a written representation of spoken language differ from each other. Due to technical restrictions, condensation is common in subtitle translation, and may affect the edit rate to some extent. On the other hand, because the source text for the subtitlers consists of not only the written subtitles, but also the audiovisual context, they may make changes based on information in the audio or video of the clip being subtitled.

An example of condensation through omission and paraphrasing can be seen in Table 3, where the participant has combined two subtitle frames (0001 and 0002) in the intralingual subtitles and the MT. This type of condensation was observed particularly in English→Finnish, where the participants reduced the number of subtitle frames.

In contrast to condensation, the participants sometimes added content to subtitles. While some additions correspond to missing words in the MT output, others in fact involve content not present in the intralingual subtitles used as source text for MT. The intralingual subtitles themselves already involve some condensation and paraphrasing, and therefore do not match exactly the spoken audio. Particularly in the Swedish "lifestyle" clips, the intralingual subtitles appear to have been very condensed, and the participants post-editing Swedish→Finnish added both textual content and new subtitle frames. These additions show one effect of the multimodal context: having the omitted information present in the audio led the participants to make additions that would have been unlikely or impossible if only the written subtitles had been available.

Subtitle translators are also affected by the visual context of the video. Changes related to the visual context occur, for example, when the subtitler chooses to replace a pronoun with the referent seen in the video. An example of this appears in one of the Swedish→Finnish clips involving cooking. The expression *de ska kokas mjuka* 'they should be cooked soft' in the dialogue is correctly translated in both MT outputs using the Finnish pronoun *ne* 'they'. However, both participants post-editing MT output for this clip replaced the pronoun with *hedelmät* 'fruit', referring to the fruit being cooked.

Source	MT output (doc)	Post-edited
0001 00:00:00:00 00:00:02:24 Viikonloppuna on vaalitarkkailijoita -	0001 00:00:00:00 00:00:02:24 There will be election observers this weekend -	0001 00:00:00:00 00:00:04:17 There are more election observers there than ever before.
0002 00:00:00:00 00:00:02:24 enemmän kuin ehkä missään muissa vaaleissa	0002 00:00:00:00 00:00:02:24 more than there may be in any other election.	

Table 3: An example of condensation of subtitle content by a post-editor.

These observations suggest that not all changes during PE correspond to MT errors. However, a detailed analysis of the MT outputs and changes carried out during PE would be needed to establish to what extent changes relate to MT errors, subtitling features like condensation, or preferential edits.

7 Future work

Based on the experiment and user feedback, segmentation of the interlingual subtitle content into appropriate chunks is an important issue to be addressed, although using subtitle timing from pre-existing intralingual subtitles was to some extent useful. Potential directions for improving segmentation and timing could involve the use of time information to split the data into coherent blocks separated by significant breaks, and the integration of speaker information into the translation engines to segment subtitles into dialogue turns by leveraging speaker labels or diarisation output. Multimodality can also play a crucial role in segmentation as visual and auditory cues may help in improving the division of verbal content into discourse units. We plan to implement an end-to-end system for subtitle translation and segmentation after Matusov et al. (2019), and investigate how well such a system could generate organic subtitles.

Multimodality may also be useful in optimising translation quality. Augmenting subtitles with information from the visual and auditory modalities could help improve translation accuracy in general. For example, visual information could be helpful in resolving ambiguity. In future work, we will explore incorporating multimodal features in translation in connection with non-linguistic context for language grounding and disambiguation.

A more detailed manual analysis of the types of PE changes made by the participants and their potential explanations (MT errors, subtitling conventions, or preferential changes) is currently underway. Feedback collected from the participants is also being analysed for information regarding the user experience. A second round of user evaluations is also planned for 2020 to collect further data and assess the effect of the new developments of our MT approaches, and to give the participants more experience with post-editing subtitles.

8 Conclusion

This paper presented a user evaluation pilot study of MT and post-editing for subtitles. Based on an analysis of process data collected from 12 professional subtitlers in four language pairs, we presented a comparison of productivity in terms of task time and number of keystrokes when post-editing MT subtitles vs translating from scratch. On average, our results indicate MTPE to be slightly faster and to involve fewer keystrokes than subtitling from scratch. However, considerable variation was observed between different language pairs and participants. We also discussed examples of specific subtitling features like condensation, and how these features may have affected the post-editing results. In addition to overall MT quality, the segmentation and the timing of the subtitles were found to be important issues to be addressed in future work.

Acknowledgments

This work is part of the MeMAD project, funded by the European Union's Horizon 2020 Research and Innovation Programme (Grant Agreement No 780069).

References

Burchardt, A., Lommel, A., Bywood, L., Harris, K., and Popović, M. (2016). Machine translation quality in an audiovisual context. *Target*, 28(2):206–221.

Bywood, L., Georgakopoulou, P., and Etchegoyhen, T. (2017). Embracing the threat: machine translation as a solution for subtitling. *Perspectives: Studies in Translatology*, 25(3):492–508.

de Sousa, S. C., Aziz, W., and Specia, L. (2011). Assessing the post-editing effort for automatic and semi-automatic translations of DVD subtitles. In *Proceedings of RANLP 2011*, pages 97–103.

Gale, W. A. and Church, K. W. (1993). A program for aligning sentences in bilingual corpora. *Computational Linguistics*, 19(1):75–102.

Junczys-Dowmunt, M. (2019). Microsoft Translator at WMT 2019: Towards large-scale document-level neural machine translation. In *Proceedings of the Fourth Conference on Machine Translation*, pages 225–233.

Junczys-Dowmunt, M., Grundkiewicz, R., Dwojak, T., Hoang, H., Heafield, K., Neckermann, T., Seide, F., Germann, U., Aji, A. F., Bogoychev, N., Martins, A. F. T., and Birch, A. (2018). Marian: Fast neural machine translation in C++. In *Proceedings of ACL 2018, System Demonstrations*, pages 116–121.

Koehn, P., Zens, R., Dyer, C., Bojar, O., Constantin, A., Herbst, E., Hoang, H., Birch, A., Callison-Burch, C., Federico, M., Bertoldi, N., Cowan, B., Shen, W., and Moran, C. (2007). Moses: Open source toolkit for statistical machine translation. In *Proceedings of the 45th ACL*.

Krings, H. P. (2001). *Repairing texts: Empirical investigations of machine translation post-editing process*. The Kent State University Press, Kent, OH.

Kudo, T. and Richardson, J. (2018). SentencePiece: A simple and language independent subword tokenizer and detokenizer for neural text processing. In *Proceedings of the 2018 EMNLP*, pages 66–71.

Leijten, M. and Van Waes, L. (2013). Keystroke logging in writing research: Using Inputlog to analyze and visualize writing processes. *Written Communication*, 30(3):358–392.

Matusov, E., Wilken, P., and Georgakopoulou, Y. (2019). Customizing neural machine translation for subtitling. In *Proceedings of the Fourth Conference on Machine Translation*, pages 82–93.

Melero, M., Oliver, A., and Badia, T. (2006). Automatic multilingual subtitling in the eTITLE project. In *Proceedings of Translating and the Computer 28*, pages 1–18.

Papineni, K., Roukos, S., Ward, T., and Zhu, W.-J. (2002). BLEU: a method for automatic evaluation of machine translation. In *Proceedings of the 40th ACL*, pages 311–318.

Pedersen, J. (2017). The FAR model: assessing quality in interlingual subtitling. *The Journal of Specialised Translation*, 28:210–229.

Plitt, M. and Masselot, F. (2010). A productivity test of statistical machine translation post-editing in a typical localisation context. *The Prague Bulletin of Mathematical Linguistics*, 93:7–16.

Saldanha, G. and O'Brien, S. (2013). *Research Methodologies in Translation Studies*. Routledge, London and New York.

Snover, M., Dorr, B., Schwartz, R., Micciulla, L., and Makhoul, J. (2006). A study of translation edit rate with targeted human annotation. In *Proceedings of AMTA 2006*.

Tiedemann, J. (2008). Synchronizing translated movie subtitles. In *Proceedings of LREC'08*.

Tiedemann, J. and Scherrer, Y. (2017). Neural machine translation with extended context. In *Proceedings of the Third DiscoMT*, pages 82–92.

Varga, D., Németh, L., Halácsy, P., Kornai, A., Trón, V., and Nagy, V. (2005). Parallel corpora for medium density languages. In *Proceedings of RANLP 2005*, pages 590–596.

Vaswani, A., Shazeer, N., Parmar, N., Uszkoreit, J., Jones, L., Gomez, A. N., Kaiser, Ł., and Polosukhin, I. (2017). Attention is all you need. In *Advances in Neural Information Processing Systems 30*, pages 5998–6008.

Volk, M., Sennrich, R., Hardmeier, C., and Tidström, F. (2010). Machine translation of TV subtitles for large scale production. In *Proceedings of the Second Joint EM+/CNGL Workshop*, pages 53–62.

Wang, W., Peter, J.-T., Rosendahl, H., and Ney, H. (2016). CharacTer: Translation edit rate on character level. In *Proceedings of the First Conference on Machine Translation*, pages 505–510.

Fine-grained Human Evaluation of Transformer and Recurrent Approaches to Neural Machine Translation for English-to-Chinese

Yuying Ye
Digital Humanities Programme
University of Groningen
The Netherlands
y.ye.yuying@gmail.com

Antonio Toral
Center for Language and Cognition
University of Groningen
The Netherlands
a.toral.ruiz@rug.nl

Abstract

This research presents a fine-grained human evaluation to compare the Transformer and recurrent approaches to neural machine translation (MT), on the translation direction English-to-Chinese. To this end, we develop an error taxonomy compliant with the Multidimensional Quality Metrics (MQM) framework that is customised to the relevant phenomena of this translation direction. We then conduct an error annotation using this customised error taxonomy on the output of state-of-the-art recurrent- and Transformer-based MT systems on a subset of WMT2019's news test set. The resulting annotation shows that, compared to the best recurrent system, the best Transformer system results in a 31% reduction of the total number of errors and it produced significantly less errors in 10 out of 22 error categories. We also note that two of the systems evaluated do not produce any error for a category that was relevant for this translation direction prior to the advent of NMT systems: Chinese classifiers.

1 Introduction

The field of machine translation (MT) has been revolutionised in the past few years by the emergence of a new approach: neural MT (NMT). NMT is a dynamic research area and we have witnessed two mainstream architectures already, the first of which is based on recurrent neural networks (RNN) with attention (Bahdanau et al., 2014) while the second, referred to as Transformer, makes use of the self-attention mechanism in non-recurrent networks (Vaswani et al., 2017).

Several studies have analysed in depth, using both automatic and human evaluation methods, the resulting translations of NMT systems under the recurrent architecture and compared them to the translations of the previous mainstream approach to MT: statistical MT (Koehn et al., 2003), e.g. (Bentivogli et al., 2016; Castilho et al., 2017; Klubička et al., 2018; Popović, 2017; Shterionov et al., 2018). However, while the Transformer architecture has brought, at least when trained with sufficient data, considerable gains over the recurrent architecture (Vaswani et al., 2017), the research conducted to date that analyses the resulting translations of these two neural approaches is, to the best of our knowledge, limited to automatic approaches (Burlot et al., 2018; Lakew et al., 2018; Tang et al., 2018a; Tang et al., 2018b; Tran et al., 2018; Yang et al., 2019).

In this paper we conduct a detailed human analysis of the outputs produced by state-of-the-art recurrent and Transformer NMT systems. Namely, we manually annotate the errors found according to a detailed error taxonomy which is compliant with the hierarchical listing of issue types defined as part of the Multidimensional Quality Metrics (MQM) framework (Lommel et al., 2014). We carry out this analysis for the news domain in the English-to-Chinese translation direction. To this end, we define an error taxonomy that is relevant to the problematic linguistic phenomena of this translation direction. This taxonomy is then used to annotate errors produced by NMT systems that fall under the recurrent and Transformer architectures.

The main contributions of this paper can then be

Martins, Moniz, Fumega, Martins, Batista, Coheur, Parra, Trancoso, Turchi, Bisazza, Moorkens, Guerberof, Nurminen, Marg, Forcada (eds.)
Proceedings of the 22nd Annual Conference of the European Association for Machine Translation, p. 125–134
Lisboa, Portugal, November 2020.

summarised as follows:

1. We develop an MQM-compliant error taxonomy tailored to the English-to-Chinese translation direction.

2. We conduct, to the best of our knowledge, the first human fine-grained error analysis of Transformer-based versus recurrent NMT.

The rest of the paper is arranged in the following way. Section 2 presents a brief review of related work. Next, Section 3 outlines the recurrent- and Transformer-based NMT systems and the dataset used in our experiments. Subsequently, Section 4 presents the methodology for error annotation and the definition of the error taxonomy, followed by results and statistical analysis of the annotation. Finally, Section 5 gives a conclusion and suggestions for future work.

2 Related Work

This section provides an overview of related research on the two topics that correspond to our main contributions: human error analysis of MT outputs for the language pair English–Chinese (Section 2.1) and analyses of MT systems based on the recurrent and Transformer architectures (Section 2.2).

2.1 Human Error Analyses of MT for Chinese

One of the first taxonomies of MT errors, by Vilar et al. (2006), had a specific error typology for the Chinese-to-English translation direction, in accordance with the specific relevant phenomena of this language pair. Compared to their base taxonomy, a refined categorisation of word order was added to mark syntactic mistakes that appear in translations of questions, infinitives, declarative and subordinate sentences. In addition, the error type *Unknown words* was refined into four sub-types: *Person, Location, Organisation* and *Other proper names*.

Li et al. (2009) carried out an error analysis for the Chinese-to-Korean translation direction with only three categories from the taxonomy of Vilar et al. (2006) (*Missing words, Wrong word order* and *Incorrect words*), and they replaced *Incorrect words* with two more specific categories: one for both wrong lexical choices and extra words and

another for wrong modality. The simplified taxonomy was used to check if their method of reordering verb phrases, prepositional phrases and modality-bearing words in the Chinese data resulted in an improved MT system.

Hsu (2014) adapted the classification scheme of Farrús et al. (2010) to conduct an error analysis for the Chinese-to-English translation direction. The error taxonomy of Farrús et al. (2010) was originally defined for Catalan→Spanish. Its first level corresponded to five types of errors, related to different linguistic levels: orthographic, morphological, lexical, semantic and syntactic.

Castilho et al. (2017) assessed the output of two MT systems (statistical and recurrent) on patents, also for the Chinese-to-English translation direction. For this, they used a custom error taxonomy consisting of the error types *Punctuation, Part of speech, Omission, Addition, Wrong terminology, Literal translation*, and *Word form*.

Hassan et al. (2018) analysed the output of a Transformer-based MT system, again for the Chinese-to-English translation direction, using a two-level taxonomy based on that by Vilar et al. (2006). The first level contains nine error types: *Missing words, Word repetition, Named entity, Word order, Incorrect words, Unknown words, Collocation, Factoid,* and *Ungrammatical*. Only the error type *Named entity* has a second level, with five subcategories: *Person, Location, Organisation, Event,* and *Other*.

As we can observe in these related works, fine-grained human evaluation for the English–Chinese language pair has been hitherto conducted, to the best of our knowledge, (i) only for the Chinese-to-English direction and (ii) with error taxonomies that were either developed prior to the advent of the MQM framework or that were designed ad-hoc and were not thoroughly motivated. The position of our paper in these regards is thus clearly novel: (i) our analysis is for the English-to-Chinese translation direction and (ii) we devise and use an error taxonomy that is compliant with the MQM framework.

2.2 Analyses of Recurrent versus Transformer MT Systems

Tang et al. (2018a) compared recurrent- and Transformer-based MT systems on a syntactic task that involves long-range dependencies (subject-verb agreement) and on a semantic task (word sense disambiguation) The recurrent system outperformed Transformer on the syntactic task while Transformer was better than the recurrent system on the semantic task. The latter finding was corroborated by Tang et al. (2018b).

Tran et al. (2018) compared the recurrent and Transformer architectures with respect to their ability to model hierarchical structure in a monolingual setting, by means of two tasks: subject-verb agreement and logical inference. On both tasks, the recurrent system outperformed Transformer, slightly but consistently.

Burlot et al. (2018) confronted English→Czech Transformer- and recurrent-based MT systems submitted to WMT2018[1] on a test suite that addresses morphological competence, based on the error typology by Burlot and Yvon (2017). The recurrent system outperformed Transformer on cases that involve number, gender and tense, while both architectures performed similarly on agreement. It is worth noting that agreement here regards local agreement (e.g. an adjective immediately followed by a noun), while the aforementioned cases of agreement in which a recurrent system outperforms Transformer (Tang et al., 2018a; Tran et al., 2018) regard long-distance agreement.

Yang et al. (2019) assessed the ability of both architectures to learn word order. When trained on a specific task related to word order, word reordering detection, a recurrent system outperformed Transformer. However, when trained on a downstream task, MT, Transformer was able to learn better positional information.

Lakew et al. (2018) evaluated multilingual NMT systems under the Transformer and recurrent architectures in terms of their morphological, lexical, and word order errors. In both architectures lexical errors were found to be the most prominent ones, followed by morphological, and lastly come reordering errors. The authors compared the number of errors in bilingual, multilingual and zero-shot systems, both for recurrent and Transformer, and found multilingual and zero-shot systems to be more competitive with respect to bilingual models for Transformer than for recurrent.

3 Machine Translation Systems

This section reports on the MT systems and the dataset used in our experiments.

We have used output from systems that fall under the recurrent and Transformer architectures and were top-ranked at the news translation shared task at the Conference on Machine Translation (WMT). We chose the University of Edinburgh's MT system (Sennrich et al., 2017) as our recurrent NMT system due to the fact that this system had the highest BLEU score (36.3) for the translation direction English→Chinese at WMT2017[2] and it was ranked first (tied with other two systems) in the human evaluation.

As for the Transformer-based MT system used in our research, we have taken the PATECH submission to WMT2019.[3] We conducted our experiments before the human evaluation of WMT2019 was available, and therefore we chose the PATECH's system based on the automatic evaluation of WMT2019, in which this system was the best performing one.[4] However, PATECH's system was not included in the human evaluation of WMT2019. Therefore we carried out an additional annotation on the top-performing system from that human evaluation: the Transformer system developed by Kingsoft AI Lab (Guo et al., 2019), hereafter referred to as KSAI.

Before our human error analysis, we would like to compare the recurrent and Transformer MT systems in terms of an automatic evaluation metric. This is not possible from their outputs since they correspond to two different test sets (`newstest2017` and `newstest2019`). In order to be able to compare them, we asked the developer of the recurrent system to provide us with the output from their system for `newstest2019`. As shown in Table 1, the use of the Transformer architecture leads to a considerable improvement compared to the recurrent system (on average 31.4% relative in terms of BLEU). While the gap between the two architectures is large based on BLEU, this is an overall metric and therefore does not provide any insight into which aspects of the translation have improved with Transformer with respect to the recurrent system. To gain further insight we conduct a fine-grained human error analysis in the following section.

---

[1] `http://www.statmt.org/wmt18/`

[2] `http://www.statmt.org/wmt17/`

[3] `http://matrix.statmt.org/systems/show/4243`

[4] `http://matrix.statmt.org/matrix/systems_list/1908`

RNN	Transformer (PATECH)	Transformer (KSAI)
33.1	44.6	42.4

Table 1: Automatic evaluation (BLEU scores) of the 3 MT systems on the WMT 2019 news test set.

4 Error Annotation

This section details the annotation setup (Section 4.1), explains how we defined our MQM-compliant error taxonomy adapted to the relevant characteristics of translating from English into Chinese and the challenges faced by NMT systems in this translation direction (Section 4.2) and presents the results of the annotation, as well as analysis and discussion thereof (Section 4.3).

4.1 Annotation Setup

We use `translate5`,[5] an open-source web-based tool, as the annotation environment. `translate5` was installed on a cloud server, so that it could be accessed remotely by annotators. The source text and reference translation are provided next to the NMT translations.

The annotation was performed by two annotators who are native Chinese speakers with fluent English. They both had an academic background and experience in translation. Prior to annotation, they were fully informed on the annotation environment and were provided with annotation instructions, comprising MQM's usage guidelines and decision tree (Burchardt and Lommel, 2014).

The dataset used in our experiments is the test set from WMT2019 (`newstest2019`) for English→Chinese. This test set is chosen due to the fact that we have outputs for the RNN- and Transformer-based MT systems (see Section 3), and also because it is a commonly-used benchmark in the MT community. In our error annotation we use two subsets of this test set.

- A calibration set, made of the first 40 sentences from the testset. This refers to a small sample of annotation data that annotators work on before the actual annotation task takes place. Its purpose is twofold: (i) we use it to find out which error types occur in the translations and therefore use it to guide the refinement of the error taxonomy in a data-driven way; (ii) we also use it to identify disagreements between the annotators.

- An evaluation set, made up of 100 sentences from the test set. In order to have intersentential context, these sentences are taken from six documents (five full documents and the first sentences of the sixth document up to 100 sentences are reached). Using this evaluation set led then to the annotation of 500 sentences (100 distinct sentences times two MT systems (RNN and PATECH) times two annotators, plus the annotation of the 100 sentences for a third system (KSAI) by one annotator).

The annotators annotated the calibration set with our custom error taxonomy (see Figure 2), after which they discussed difficult cases and reached agreement on how to annotate them. Then they annotated the translations of the evaluation set. Once annotators started working on the evaluation set, they were not allowed to discuss problems in annotation any more.

4.2 Error Taxonomy

We decided to develop our error taxonomy based on the MQM framework developed at the QT-LaunchPad project (Lommel et al., 2014), after reviewing different translation quality evaluation frameworks. MQM stands out with its extensive standardised issue types[6] which are provided with clear definitions and explanations. In addition, a thorough guideline and decision tree[7] are available to assist annotators. Furthermore, this framework allows the building of customised error taxonomies.

Following the method of Klubička et al. (2018), our customisation process started with the sample MQM-compliant hierarchy for diagnostic MT evaluation (Figure 1) as the initial stage of our error taxonomy. The sample MQM tagset went through the preliminary selection of issue types to be used for fine-grained MT evaluation.

We annotated the calibration set with the sample MQM-compliant hierarchy to find out what types of errors occur in the outputs of our MT systems. Based on the results of the calibration set, we defined the complete tagset (shown in Figure 2). In the following subsections we provide detailed information concerning each of the modifications made to the error taxonomy.

---

[5] `http://www.translate5.net`

[6] `http://www.qt21.eu/mqm-definition/issues-list-2015-12-30.html`
[7] `http://www.qt21.eu/downloads/MQM-usage-guidelines.pdf`

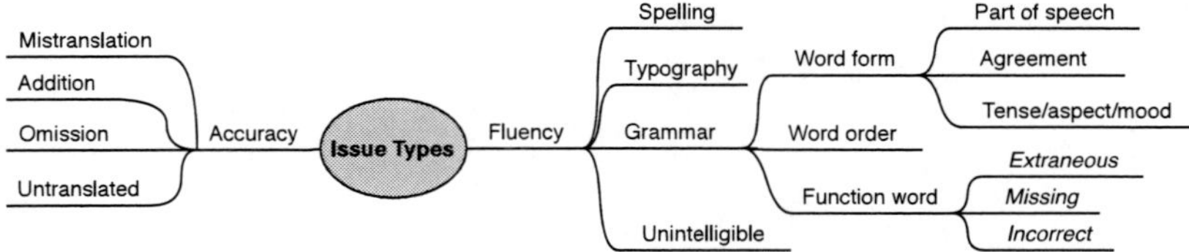

Figure 1: The sample MQM-compliant error hierarchy for diagnostic MT evaluation. The italicised issue types are not included in the standard MQM issue types.

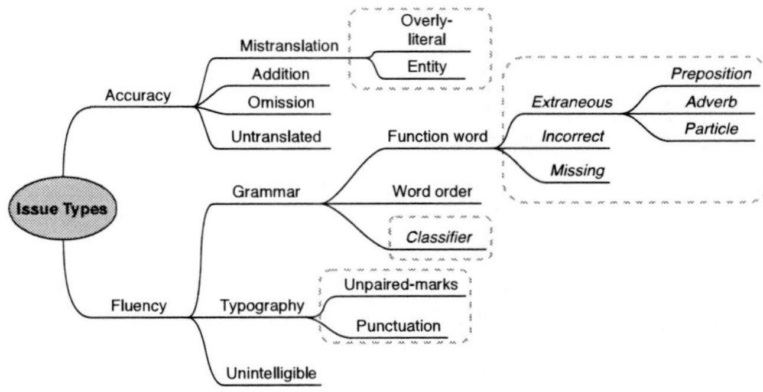

Figure 2: The MQM-compliant error taxonomy for the translation direction English→Chinese. All the changes are marked by boxes with grey dotted lines and the issue types that are not included in the MQM issue types are italicised.

4.2.1 Word Form & Spelling

Given that Chinese is an analytic language without inflection and its writing system is logographic, the issue types *Word form* and *Spelling* are of no interest to our research agenda.

4.2.2 Classifier

We add one of the distinctive features of Chinese part-of-speech, the usage of classifiers, which have been researched thoroughly in Chinese linguistics (Jin, 2018) and Chinese language processing (Huang et al., 2017). In short, classifiers are special linguistic units located behind a number, demonstrative or certain quantifiers. These classifiers do not have a counterpart in English, which might give rise to translation problems. Examples of classifiers are shown in Table 2. How MT systems handle such a specific linguistic phenomenon is of interest to us.

Pronoun	Classifier	Noun
每(*mei*) Every	个(*ge*)	角落(*jiaoluo*) corner
一(*yi*) One	架(*jia*)	飞机(*feiji*) plane

Table 2: Examples of classifiers in Chinese. The classifiers are underscored.

4.2.3 Typography

We extend the issue type *Typography* into two specific subtypes, based on the result of the calibration set. Though an unpaired quote or a misuse of punctuation is less likely to damage the comprehension of the content critically than other errors, as stated in Vilar et al. (2006), the Chinese→English error annotation conducted by Hsu (2014) shows that punctuation accounts for 10% of the errors. Such a high amount of punctuation mistakes could be a nuisance in the MT output. Incorrect usage of *Typography* could negatively influence the reception of a translation, since the reader might consider such an error as a sign of lack of professionalism, and therefore react by distrusting the content.

4.2.4 Mistranslation

Preliminarily, we observe that *Mistranslation* is a major issue in the calibration set and that related translation errors *Overly-literal* and *Entity* appear frequently. We have thus decided to specify them as sub-types of *Mistranslation*. Vilar et al. (2006) also included entity errors in their error typology for the Chinese→English language pair and further divided them into specific sub-types. As their result showed, this issue type only amounted to a small percentage of the errors. Therefore, the issue type *Entity* is not further specified in our taxonomy.

4.2.5 Function word

Function word is extended to one extra layer under *Extraneous* with the intention of covering westernised Chinese expressions that were observed in the calibration set. Westernised Chinese refers to a cross-lingual phenomenon of imposing English grammar on Chinese, which is manifested in many problematic forms, abuse of function words especially (Tse, 2001). The relations between sentence parts, tenses and aspects are often shown through word order, particles or context in Chinese, due to its lack of inflection. Specifying the types of extraneous function words into three common types, *Preposition*, *Adverb* and *Particle* could be useful to discuss whether there is difference among these word classes.

The two other sub-types of *Function word* (*Incorrect* and *Missing*) are not specified in conformity with the initial examination of the data. Not only might adding the extra layer for both sub-error types not prove practical, but it is also not advised by the MQM guidelines to have the error taxonomy so big that it could challenge annotators' memory limit (Burchardt and Lommel, 2014).

4.3 Results and Discussion

4.3.1 Inter-annotator Agreement

Inter-annotator agreement (IAA) was calculated with Cohen's Kappa (κ) (Cohen, 1960) on the annotations of the calibration and evaluation sets for the RNN and PATECH's Transformer systems (Table 3). It is worth noting that the IAA values of the evaluation set improve considerably upon those of the calibration set ($\kappa = 0.44$ versus 0.27). It shows that the discussion of annotation disagreements can contribute to improving the level of agreement notably.

IAA	RNN	Transformer (PATECH)	Both
Calibration set	0.31	0.22	0.27
Evaluation set	0.45	0.43	0.44

Table 3: Total and average inter-annotator agreement (Cohen's κ values) for the MQM calibration set and evaluation set.

As shown in Table 3, the difference of IAA scores between Transformer and RNN is slight in our evaluation set. The average IAA value

(0.44), corresponds to moderate agreement, according to Cohen (1960). When interpreting these results, it should be taken into account that IAA scores are known to be low in human evaluation of MT. For example, Callison-Burch et al. (2007) observed fair agreements for fluency and accuracy for eight language pairs, and, though the MQM framework is rigorously defined and supported by clear guidelines, in the experiments by Lommel and Burchardt (2014) MQM led to relatively low IAA, due to span-level difference, ambiguous categorisation and differences of opinion. Klubička et al. (2018) reported a moderate agreement on English–Croatian, higher than that by Lommel and Burchardt (2014), probably because the agreement was calculated on errors annotated for each sentence, thus not taking the spans of the annotations into account. Our own IAA results do not differ greatly with aforementioned research.

	RNN	Transformer (PATECH)	Both
Accuracy	0.60	**0.61**	**0.61**
Mistranslation	0.50	0.52	0.51
Entity	-0.03	0.39	0.18
Overly-literal	0.24	0.21	0.23
Omission	0.52	**0.67**	0.60
Addition	0.37	0.00	0.19
Untranslated	**0.73**	**0.71**	**0.72**
Fluency	0.01	0.07	0.04
Grammar	0.36	0.24	0.30
Function word	0.17	-0.01	0.08
Extraneous	0.32	-0.01	0.16
Preposition	**0.65**	-0.01	0.32
Adverb	0.00	N/A	N/A
Particle	-0.02	-0.03	-0.03
Incorrect	-0.02	-0.01	-0.02
Missing	0.32	0.00	0.16
Word order	0.45	0.29	0.37
Classifier	N/A	N/A	N/A
Unintelligible	0.20	-0.02	0.09
Typography	0.22	0.28	0.25
Punctuation	0.21	0.29	0.25
Unpaired-mark	N/A	N/A	N/A

Table 4: Inter-annotator agreement (Cohen's κ values) on the evaluation set for the RNN and PATECH's Transformer systems and their average. Substantial scores (0.61–0.80) are shown in bold. N/A is given to the error categories that were never used, since no data points could be used to calculate the IAA score.

In addition to overall IAA, Cohen's (κ) was also calculated for each issue type in the evaluation set individually (Table 4). For both systems, the IAA scores for *Accuracy* and its sub-types are considerably higher than those under *Fluency*. It is an expected result taken into account that accuracy errors are more straightforward and less open to interpretation. The κ values are relatively consistent between Transformer and RNN, except a striking plunge in agreement scores for Transformer in some categories (*Function word* and its subtypes, *Word order* and *Unintelligible*) and the opposite, a considerably lower agreement for RNN, for *Entity*.

The source of these disagreements can be traced back to the annotation output. For example, in the case of *Unintelligible*, the evaluators annotated different sentences with this error category. As for *Entity*, it is worth mentioning that disagreement arose over this category in the annotation of the calibration set. It seems that, despite the discussion, the understanding of entity was still not shared by the two annotators. It is also possible that due to the improved translation quality of Transformer, mistakes such as *Function word* are more subtle and harder to detect.

4.3.2 Annotated Errors

Table 5 presents the overall number of annotated error tags in the output of each system by each annotator. One can clearly observe that both annotators have annotated relatively less errors in Transformer's output (PATECH) than in RNN's; the error reduction is of 35% in the case of annotator 1 and of 27% in the case of the second annotator. The Transformer system from KSAI only reduces the number of errors by 12.5%, compared to the RNN system.

System	RNN	Transformer (PATECH)	Transformer (KSAI)
Annotator 1	168	109	147
Annotator 2	193	141	

Table 5: Total amounts of error per annotator and system, as annotated in MQM.

To delve deeper into the error distribution, we plot a histogram to show how many errors appear in each sentence and how many of these sentences are there in the output from each system. The mean of both annotators' annotations for the first two systems are used, amounting to 100 sentences per system. The histogram is shown in Figure 3. It can be observed that more than 35 sentences in the Transformer (PATECH) output are not annotated with any error while only slightly over 20 sentences in the RNN are marked as errorless. The two systems have similar amount of sentences with one mistake, while PATECH's output contains considerably less sentences than RNN with more than one error.

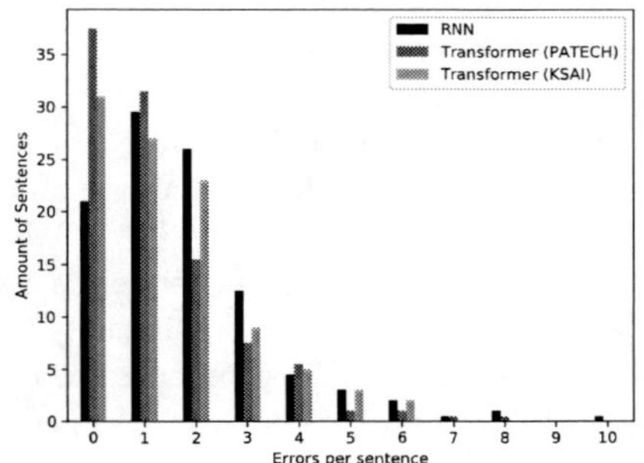

Figure 3: Error distribution per system. For RNN and Transformer (PATECH), the average of annotation data from both annotators has been used.

We can also see notable differences between the two Transformer systems in Figure 3. Fewer sentences in the KSAI's output are annotated without error, while considerably more sentences are tagged with two errors in this output than in PATECH's system.

While comparing the systems in terms of their total number of errors gives us a clear indication of their relative performance, we note that a fairer comparison should take into account their outputs' lengths. To that end, we make use of the normalisation approach proposed by Klubička et al. (2018): tokens annotated with errors are counted for each system's output and they are then used to compute each system's error ratio, which equals to the total number of erroneous tokens (Chinese characters) divided by the total number of tokens in the system's output. This error ratio can serve then as a general score for each system. We also apply the same normalisation procedure to each issue type. Statistical significance for the total amount of errors and each issue type is computed with a pairwise chi-squared (χ^2) test (Plackett, 1983), following its application to normalised MQM errors introduced by Klubička et al. (2018).

Table 6 shows the error ratios (both overall and for each issue type) for each system, together with an indication of whether there are significant differences between each pair of systems. In terms of total error ratio, compared to RNN, the error reduction by PATECH amounts to 34% relative (11.85% versus 17.93%) and is significant ($p < 0.001$). No significant difference is observed between the two Transformer-based systems.

For nearly half of the error types, the decrease in error ratio for Transformer (PATECH), compared to RNN, is statistically significant. For example, the number of tokens with *Fluency* errors decreased by 45% (6.45% verse 3.56%, $p < 0.001$). The reduction is particularly notable for its child category *Unintelligible*, for which the number of erroneous tokens decreased by 55% (2.1% verse 0.93%, $p < 0.001$). This Transformer-based system also managed to generate significantly less extraneous *Function words*, gaining a decrease of 47% (0.51% verse 0.27%, $p < 0.05$). In addition, Transformer manages to produce significantly less extraneous *Prepositions*, (0.2% verse 0.04%, $p < 0.05$). Though it also produces less *Overly-literal* translations (1.20% verse 0.86%) and no extraneous *Adverb* (0.06% verse 0%), these differences are not significant.

Conversely, this Transformer-based system underperforms on *Punctuation* (0.2% verse 0.37%), although the difference is not significant. By tracing this back to the annotation, we can observe that Transformer (PATECH) produces several cases of missing, wrong or redundant punctuation marks. For example, in one instance an English period (.) was used instead of a Chinese full stop (。). This Transformer system also had issues with adding guillemets (《》) around newspaper names and putting commas after adverbials, which are required in Chinese grammar.

Between the two Transformer systems, we can see that except for the category *Entity* and *Untranslated*, the two Transformer systems do not produce statistically significant different amount of errors. It proves that there are few significant discrepancies between these two systems.

Finally, we note that the error category *Unpaired-mark*, has not been used by any of the annotators for any of the three MT systems and the category *Classifier* has only been used to annotate 6 tokens (0.16%) in the third system's output. While these categories were relevant in MT in the past (see Section 2), our results seem to indicate that they can be considered to have been solved by NMT.

	RNN	Transformer (PATECH)	Transformer (KSAI)
Accuracy	**11.48**	8.29**	7.41
Mistranslation	**7.49**	4.50**	4.39
Entity	0.24	0.23	**0.59***
Overly-literal	1.20	0.86	0.51
Omission	**0.61**	0.33**	0.35
Addition	0.23	0.19	0.22
Untranslated	3.16	**3.27**	2.45*
Fluency	**6.45**	3.56**	3.02
Grammar	**3.08**	1.83**	2.24
Function word	**0.51**	0.27**	0.40
Extraneous	**0.35**	0.12**	0.30
Preposition	**0.20**	0.04**	0.13
Adverb	0.06	0	0.05
Particle	0.07	0.08	0.08
Incorrect	0.06	0.08	0
Missing	0.10	0.07	0.11
Word order	**2.32**	1.41**	1.46
Classifier	0	0	0.16
Unintelligible	**2.10**	0.93**	0
Typography	0.20	0.37	0.59
Punctuation	0.20	0.37	0.59
Unpaired-mark	0	0	0
Total error ratio	**17.93**	11.85**	10.40

Table 6: Error ratio (%) for each error type and overall. The annotations on RNN and Transformer (PATECH) from both annotators are concatenated. * indicates p-value < 0.05 and ** p-value < 0.001, when a system is compared to the system adjacent to its left side. Numbers shown in bold indicate that the system has significantly more erroneous tokens in the pair comparison.

5 Conclusion

This paper presented a fine-grained manual evaluation for English→Chinese on the two mainstream architectures of NMT: RNN and Transformer. The evaluation was approached in the form of a human error annotation based on a customised MQM error taxonomy.

The error taxonomy was developed from the MQM core taxonomy for MT evaluation. Chinese linguistic features and issues emerged in the calibration set were taken into account by including customised error types, such as *Extraneous function word*, *Classifier* and *Typography*. The error type *Extraneous function word* underpins investigating westernised Chinese phenomena of extraneous function words by specifying it into three word classes: *Preposition*, *Adverb* and *Particle*.

From our analysis, it is clear that Transformer-based systems generate significantly more accurate, fluent and comprehensible translation with less westernised Chinese expressions. However, Transformer systems do not handle typography as well as RNN. We also note that none of the MT systems did produce any errors related to unpaired-marks and only one system produced errors related to classifiers, which were very unfrequent (0.16% of the tokens). We can conclude that Transformer systems produce an overall better translation compared to RNN when translating from English to Chinese, which corroborates findings of prior studies on other language pairs. A limitation worth mentioning is that our annotation was conducted by only two annotators on a limited amount of data.

Our taxonomy could be of use for further error analysis on Chinese MT quality. Future research could include a larger annotation sample to investigate if punctuation is a a common issue in NMT systems based on Transformer and to verify that NMT is able to produce correct classifiers. Also, as Transformer still shows a major problem in mistranslation, the error taxonomy can be extended with more specific categories to explore this issue in more detail.

The annotations for the three MT systems and the code used for the analysis thereof are publicly available.[8]

Acknowledgements

We would like to thank Rico Sennrich, for translating the test set used in this paper with a system he had co-developed for a previous edition of the WMT news translation shared task, and Filip Klubička, for providing us with the code to perform the statistical analysis of MQM output.

References

Bahdanau, Dzmitry, Kyunghyun Cho, and Yoshua Bengio. 2014. Neural Machine Translation by Jointly Learning to Align and Translate. In *Proceedings of International Conference on Learning Representations 2015*, pages 1–15, San Diego, CA, USA, September.

Bentivogli, Luisa, Arianna Bisazza, Mauro Cettolo, and Marcello Federico. 2016. Neural versus Phrase-Based Machine Translation Quality: a Case Study. In *Proceedings of the 2016 Conference on Empirical Methods in Natural Language Processing*, pages 257–267, Austin, Texas. Association for Computational Linguistics.

Burchardt, Aljoscha and Arle Lommel, 2014. *Practical Guidelines for the Use of MQM in Scientific Research on Translation Quality*.

Burlot, Franck and François Yvon. 2017. Evaluating the morphological competence of machine translation systems. In *Proceedings of the Second Conference on Machine Translation*, pages 43–55, Copenhagen, Denmark, September. Association for Computational Linguistics.

Burlot, Franck, Yves Scherrer, Vinit Ravishankar, Ondřej Bojar, Stig-Arne Grönroos, Maarit Koponen, Tommi Nieminen, and François Yvon. 2018. The WMT'18 morpheval test suites for English-Czech, English-German, English-Finnish and Turkish-English. In *Proceedings of the Third Conference on Machine Translation: Shared Task Papers*, pages 546–560, Belgium, Brussels, October. Association for Computational Linguistics.

Callison-Burch, Chris, Cameron Fordyce, Philipp Koehn, Christof Monz, and Josh Schroeder. 2007. (Meta-) evaluation of machine translation. In *Proceedings of the Second Workshop on Statistical Machine Translation - StatMT '07*, pages 136–158, Prague, Czech Republic. Association for Computational Linguistics.

Castilho, Sheila, Joss Moorkens, Federico Gaspari, Iacer Calixto, John Tinsley, and Andy Way. 2017. Is Neural Machine Translation the New State of the Art? *The Prague Bulletin of Mathematical Linguistics*, 108(1):109–120.

Cohen, Jacob. 1960. A coefficient of agreement for nominal scales. *Educational and Psychological Measurement*, 20(1):37–46.

Farrús, Mireia, Marta Costa-jussa, Jose Bernardo Mariño Acebal, and José Fonollosa. 2010. Linguistic-based evaluation criteria to identify statistical machine translation errors. In *Proceedings of the 13th Annual Conference of the EAMT*, pages 52–57, Barcelona, Spain, 01.

Guo, Xinze, Chang Liu, Xiaolong Li, Yiran Wang, Guoliang Li, Feng Wang, Zhitao Xu, Liuyi Yang, Li Ma, and Changliang Li. 2019. Kingsoft's neural machine translation system for WMT19. In *Proceedings of the Fourth Conference on Machine Translation (Volume 2: Shared Task Papers, Day 1)*, pages 196–202, Florence, Italy, August. Association for Computational Linguistics.

Hassan, Hany, Anthony Aue, Chang Chen, Vishal Chowdhary, Jonathan Clark, Christian Federmann, Xuedong Huang, Marcin Junczys-Dowmunt, William Lewis, Mu Li, Shujie Liu, Tie-Yan Liu, Renqian Luo, Arul Menezes, Tao Qin, Frank Seide,

---

[8] https://github.com/yy-ye/mqm-analysis

Xu Tan, Fei Tian, Lijun Wu, and Ming Zhou. 2018. Achieving human parity on automatic chinese to english news translation. *arXiv:1803.05567 [cs]*, pages 1–25, 03.

Hsu, John D. 2014. Error Classification of Machine Translation A Corpus-based Study on Chinese-English Patent Translation. *Translation Studies Quarterly*, 18:121–136.

Huang, Chu-Ren, Shu-Kai Hsieh, Keh-Jiann Chen, Shu-Kai Hsieh, and Keh-Jiann Chen. 2017. *Mandarin Chinese Words and Parts of Speech : A Corpus-based Study*. Routledge, 7.

Jin, Jing. 2018. *Partition and Quantity : Numeral Classifiers, Measurement, and Partitive Constructions in Mandarin Chinese*. Routledge, 06.

Klubička, Filip, Antonio Toral, and Víctor M. Sánchez-Cartagena. 2018. Quantitative Fine-Grained Human Evaluation of Machine Translation Systems: a Case Study on English to Croatian. *arXiv e-prints*, 32(3):195–215.

Koehn, Philipp, Franz Josef Och, and Daniel Marcu. 2003. Statistical phrase-based translation. In *Proceedings of the 2003 Conference of the North American Chapter of the Association for Computational Linguistics on Human Language Technology - Volume 1*, NAACL '03, pages 48–54, Stroudsburg, PA, USA. Association for Computational Linguistics.

Lakew, Surafel Melaku, Mauro Cettolo, and Marcello Federico. 2018. A comparison of transformer and recurrent neural networks on multilingual neural machine translation. In *Proceedings of the 27th International Conference on Computational Linguistics*, pages 641–652, Santa Fe, New Mexico, USA, August. Association for Computational Linguistics.

Li, Jin-Ji, Jungi Kim, Dong-Il Kim, and Jong-Hyeok Lee. 2009. Chinese Syntactic Reordering for Adequate Generation of Korean Verbal Phrases in Chinese-to-Korean SMT. In *Proceedings of the Fourth Workshop on Statistical Machine Translation*, pages 190–196. Association for Computational Linguistics.

Lommel, Arle and Aljoscha Burchardt. 2014. Assessing inter-annotator agreement for translation error annotation. In *MTE: Workshop on Automatic and Manual Metrics for Operational Translation Evaluation*, Reykjavik, Iceland.

Lommel, Arle, Hans Uszkoreit, and Aljoscha Burchardt. 2014. Multidimensional quality metrics (mqm): A framework for declaring and describing translation quality metrics. *Tradumàtica: tecnologies de la traducció*.

Plackett, R. L. 1983. Karl pearson and the chi-squared test. *International Statistical Review / Revue Internationale de Statistique*, 51(1):59–72.

Popović, Maja. 2017. Comparing language related issues for nmt and pbmt between german and english. *The Prague Bulletin of Mathematical Linguistics*, 108(1):209–220.

Sennrich, Rico, Alexandra Birch, Anna Currey, Ulrich Germann, Barry Haddow, Kenneth Heafield, Antonio Valerio Miceli Barone, and Philip Williams. 2017. The University of Edinburgh's Neural MT Systems for WMT17. In *Proceedings of the Second Conference on Machine Translation*, pages 389–399, Copenhagen, Denmark, 09. Association for Computational Linguistics.

Shterionov, Dimitar, Riccardo Superbo, Pat Nagle, Laura Casanellas, Tony O'dowd, and Andy Way. 2018. Human versus automatic quality evaluation of nmt and pbsmt. *Machine Translation*, 32(3):217–235.

Tang, Gongbo, Mathias Müller, Annette Rios, and Rico Sennrich. 2018a. Why self-attention? a targeted evaluation of neural machine translation architectures. *arXiv preprint arXiv:1808.08946*.

Tang, Gongbo, Rico Sennrich, and Joakim Nivre. 2018b. An analysis of attention mechanisms: The case of word sense disambiguation in neural machine translation. In *Proceedings of the Third Conference on Machine Translation: Research Papers*, pages 26–35, Brussels, Belgium, October. Association for Computational Linguistics.

Tran, Ke, Arianna Bisazza, and Christof Monz. 2018. The importance of being recurrent for modeling hierarchical structure. In *Proceedings of the 2018 Conference on Empirical Methods in Natural Language Processing*, pages 4731–4736, Brussels, Belgium. Association for Computational Linguistics.

Tse, Yiu Kay 谢耀基. 2001. "hanyu yufan ouhua zongshu"汉语语法欧化综述[a review on the westernised chineses grammar]. 语文研究, 1:17–22.

Vaswani, Ashish, Noam Shazeer, Niki Parmar, Jakob Uszkoreit, Llion Jones, Aidan N. Gomez, Lukasz Kaiser, and Illia Polosukhin. 2017. Attention is all you need. abs/1706.03762.

Vilar, David, Jia Xu, Luis Fernando D'Haro, and Hermann Ney. 2006. Error Analysis of Statistical Machine Translation Output. In *Proceedings of the Fifth International Conference on Language Resources and Evaluation (LREC'06)*, pages 697–702.

Yang, Baosong, Longyue Wang, Derek F. Wong, Lidia S. Chao, and Zhaopeng Tu. 2019. Assessing the ability of self-attention networks to learn word order. In *Proceedings of the 57th Annual Meeting of the Association for Computational Linguistics*, pages 3635–3644, Florence, Italy, July. Association for Computational Linguistics.

Correct Me If You Can: Learning from Error Corrections and Markings

Julia Kreutzer* and **Nathaniel Berger*** and **Stefan Riezler**[†,*]
*Computational Linguistics & [†]IWR
Heidelberg University, Germany
{kreutzer, berger, riezler}@cl.uni-heidelberg.de

Abstract

Sequence-to-sequence learning involves a trade-off between signal strength and annotation cost of training data. For example, machine translation data range from costly expert-generated translations that enable supervised learning, to weak quality-judgment feedback that facilitate reinforcement learning. We present the first user study on annotation cost and machine learnability for the less popular annotation mode of error markings. We show that error markings for translations of TED talks from English to German allow precise credit assignment while requiring significantly less human effort than correcting/post-editing, and that error-marked data can be used successfully to fine-tune neural machine translation models.

1 Introduction

Successful machine learning for structured output prediction requires the effort of annotating sufficient amounts of gold-standard outputs—a task that can be costly if structures are complex and expert knowledge is required, as for example in neural machine translation (NMT) (Bahdanau et al., 2015). Approaches that propose to train sequence-to-sequence prediction models by reinforcement learning from task-specific scores, for example BLEU in machine translation (MT), shift the problem by simulating such scores by evaluating machine translation output against expert-generated reference structures (Ranzato et al., 2016; Bahdanau et al., 2017; Kreutzer et al., 2017; Sokolov et al., 2017). An alternative approach that proposes to considerably reduce human annotation effort by allowing to mark errors in machine outputs, for example erroneous words or phrases in a machine translation, has recently been proposed and been investigated in simulation studies by Marie and Max (2015); Domingo et al. (2017); Petrushkov et al. (2018). This approach takes the middle ground between supervised learning from error corrections as in machine translation post-editing[1] (or from translations created from scratch) and reinforcement learning from sequence-level bandit feedback (this includes self-supervised learning where all outputs are rewarded uniformly). Error markings are highly promising since they suggest an interaction mode with low annotation cost, yet they can enable precise token-level credit/blame assignment, and thus can lead to an effective fine-grained discriminative signal for machine learning and data filtering.

Our work is the first to investigate learning from error markings in a user study. Error corrections and error markings are collected from junior professional translators, analyzed, and used as training data for fine-tuning neural machine translation systems. The focus of our work is on the learnability from error corrections and error markings, and on the behavior of annotators as teachers to a machine translation system. We find that error markings require significantly less effort (in terms of key-stroke-mouse-ratio (KSMR) and time) and result in a lower correction rate (ratio of words marked as incorrect or corrected in a post-edit). Furthermore, they are less prone to over-editing

---

[1]In the following we will use the more general term error corrections and MT specific term post-edits interchangeably.

Martins, Moniz, Fumega, Martins, Batista, Coheur, Parra, Trancoso, Turchi, Bisazza, Moorkens, Guerberof, Nurminen, Marg, Forcada (eds.)
Proceedings of the 22nd Annual Conference of the European Association for Machine Translation, p. 135–144
Lisboa, Portugal, November 2020.

than error corrections. Perhaps surprisingly, agreement between annotators of which words to mark or to correct was lower for markings than for post-edits. However, despite of the low inter-annotator agreement, fine-tuning of neural machine translation could be conducted successfully from data annotated in either mode. Our data set of error corrections and markings is publicly available.[2]

2 Related Work

Prior work closest to ours is that of Marie and Max (2015); Domingo et al. (2017); Petrushkov et al. (2018), however, these works were conducted by simulating error markings by heuristic matching of machine translations against independently created human reference translations. Thus the question of the practical feasibility of machine learning from noisy human error markings is left open.

User studies on machine learnability from human post-edits, together with thorough performance analyses with mixed effects models, have been presented by Green et al. (2014); Bentivogli et al. (2016); Karimova et al. (2018). Albeit showcasing the potential of improving NMT through human corrections of machine-generated outputs, these works do not consider "weaker" annotation modes like error markings. User studies on the process and effort of machine translation post-editing are too numerous to list—a comprehensive overview is given in Koponen (2016). In contrast to works on interactive-predictive translation (Foster et al., 1997; Knowles and Koehn, 2016; Peris et al., 2017; Domingo et al., 2017; Lam et al., 2018), our approach does not require an online interaction with the human and allows to investigate, filter, pre-process, or augment the human feedback signal before making a machine learning update.

Machine learning from human feedback beyond the scope of translations, has considered learning from human pairwise preferences (Christiano et al., 2017), from human corrective feedback (Celemin et al., 2018), or from sentence-level reward signals on a Likert scale (Kreutzer et al., 2018). However, none of these studies has considered error markings on tokens of output sequences, despite its general applicability to a wide range of learning tasks.

------

[2]https://www.cl.uni-heidelberg.de/
statnlpgroup/humanmt/

3 User Study on Human Error Markings and Corrections

The goal of the annotation study is to compare the novel error marking mode to the widely adopted machine translation post-editing mode. We are interested in finding an interaction scenario that costs little time and effort, but still allows to teach the machine how to improve its translations. In this section we present the setup, measure and compare the observed amount of effort and time that went into these annotations, and discuss the reliability and adoption of the new marking mode. Machine learnability, i.e. training of an NMT system on human-annotated data is discussed in Section 4.

3.1 Participants

We recruited 10 participants that described themselves as native German speakers and having either a C1 or C2 level in English, as measured by the Common European Framework of Reference levels. 8 participants were students studying translation or interpretation and 2 participants were students studying computational linguistics. All participants were paid 100€ for their participation in the study, which was done online, and limited to a maximum of 6 hours, and it took them between 2 and 4.5 hours excluding breaks. They agreed to the usage of the recorded data for research purposes.

3.2 Interface

The annotation interface has three modes: (1) markings, (2) corrections, and (3) the user-choice mode, where annotators first choose between (1) and (2) before submitting their annotation. While the first two modes are used for collecting training data for the MT model, the third mode is used for evaluative purposes to investigate which mode is preferable when given the choice. In any case, annotators are presented the source sentence, the target sentence and an instruction to either mark or correct (aka post-edit) the translation or choose an editing mode. They also had the option to pause and resume the session. No document-level context was presented, i.e., translated sentences were judged in isolation, but in consecutive order like they appeared in the original documents to provide a reasonable amount of context. They received detailed instructions (see Appendix A) on how to proceed with the annotation. Each annotator worked on 300 sentences, 100 for each mode, and an extra 15 sentences for intra-annotator agree-

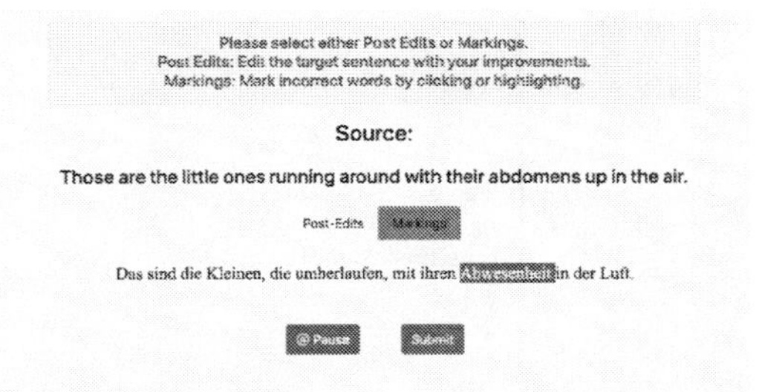

Figure 1: Interface for marking of translation outputs following user choice between markings and post-edits.

ment measures that were repeated after each mode. After the completion of the annotation task they answered a survey about the preferred mode, the perceived editing/marking speed, user-choice policies, and suggestions for improvement. A sreenshot of the interface showing a marking operation is shown in Figure 1. The code for the interface is publicly available[3].

3.3 Data

We selected a subset of 30 TED talks to create the three data sets from the IWSLT17 machine translation corpus[4]. The talks were filtered by the following criteria: single speakers, no music/singing, low intra-line final-sentence punctuation (indicating bad segmentation), length between 80 and 149 sentences. One additional short talk was selected for testing the inter- and intra-annotator reliability. We filtered out those sentences where model hypothesis and references were equal, in order to save annotation effort where it is clearly not needed, and also removed the last line from every talk (usually "thank you"). For each talk, one topic of a set of keywords provided by TED was selected. See Appendix B for a description of how data was split across annotators.

3.4 Effort and Time

Correcting one translated sentence took on average approximately 5 times longer than marking errors, and required 42 more actions, i.e., clicks and keystrokes. That is 0.6 actions per character for post-edits, while only 0.03 actions per character for markings. This measurement aligns with the unanimous subjective impression of the participants that they were faster in marking mode.

To investigate the sources of variance affecting time and effort, we use Linear Mixed Effect Models (LMEM) (Barr et al., 2013) and build one with KSMR as response variable, and another one for the total edit duration (excluding breaks) as response variable, and with the editing `mode` (correcting vs. marking) as fixed effect. For both response variables, we model users[5], talks and target lengths[6] as random effects, e.g., the one for KSMR:

$$\text{KSMR} \sim \texttt{mode} + (1 \mid \texttt{user\_id}) + (1 \mid \texttt{talk\_id})$$
$$+ (1 \mid \texttt{trg\_length}) \qquad (1)$$

We use the implementation in the R package `lmer4` (Bates et al., 2015) and fit the models with restricted maximum likelihood. Inspecting the intercepts of the fitted models, we confirm that KSMR is significantly ($p = 0.01$) higher for post edits than for markings (+3.76 on average). The variance due to the user (0.69) is larger than due to the talk (0.54) and the length $(0.05)^7$. Longer sentences have a slightly higher KSMR than shorter ones. When modeling the topics as random effects (rather than the talks), the highest KSMR (judging by individual intercepts) was obtained for physics and biodiversity and the lowest for language and diseases. This might be explained by e.g. the MT training data or the raters expertise.

Analyzing the LMEM for editing duration, we find that post-editing takes on average 42s longer than marking, which is significant at $p = 0.01$. The variance due to the target length is the largest, followed by the one due to the talk and the one due to the user is smallest. Long sentences have a six time higher editing duration on average than shorter ones. With respect to topics, the longest editing was done for topics like physics and evolution, shortest for diseases and health.

3.4.1 Annotation Quality

The corrections increased the quality, measured by comparison to reference translations, by 2.1 points in BLEU and decreased TER by 1 point. While this indicates a general improvement, it has to be taken with a grain of salt, since the post-edits

---

[3]`https://github.com/StatNLP/`
`mt-correct-mark-interface`
[4]`https://sites.google.com/site/`
`iwsltevaluation2017/`

[5]Random effects are denoted, e.g., by `(1|user_id)`.
[6]Target lengths measured by number of characters were binned into two groups at the limit of 176 characters.
[7]Note that KSMR is already normalized by reference length, hence the small effect of target length. In a LMER for the raw action count (clicks+key strokes), this effect had a larger impact.

src	I am a nomadic artist.
hyp	Ich bin ein nomadischer Künstler.
pe	Ich bin ein nomadischer Künstler.
ref	Ich <u>wurde</u> zu einer nomadischen Künstler<u>in</u>.
src	I look at the chemistry of the ocean today.
hyp	Ich betrachte <u>heute</u> die Chemie des Ozeans.
pe	Ich erforsche <u>täglich</u> die Chemie der Meere.
ref	Ich untersuche die Chemie der Meere <u>der Gegenwart</u>.
src	There's even a software called <u>cadnano</u> that allow …
hyp	Es gibt sogar eine Software namens <u>Caboano</u>, die …
pe	Es gibt sogar eine Software namens <u>Caboano</u>, die …
ref	Es gibt sogar eine Software namens "<u>cadnano</u>", …
src	It was a thick forest.
hyp	Es <u>war</u> ein dicker Wald.
pe	Es <u>handelte sich um</u> einen dichten Wald.
ref	<u>Auf der Insel war</u> dichter Wald.

Table 1: Examples of post-editing to illustrate differences between reference translations (*ref*) and post-edits (*pe*). Example 1: The gender in the German translation could not be inferred from the context, since speaker information is unavailable to post-editor. Example 2: "today" is interpreted as adverb by the NMT, this interpretation is kept in the post-edit ("telephone game" effect). Example 3: Another case of the "telephone game" effect: the name of the software is changed by the NMT, and not corrected by post-editors. Example 4: Over-editing by post-editor, and more information in the reference translation than in the source.

src	Each year, it sends up a new generation of shoots.
ann	Jedes Jahr <u>sendet</u> es eine neue Generation von <u>Shoots.</u>
sim	Jedes Jahr <u>sendet es eine</u> neue <u>Generation von Shoots.</u>
ref	Jedes Jahr wachsen neue Triebe.
src	He killed 63 percent of the Hazara population.
ann	Er <u>starb</u> 63 Prozent der Bevölkerung <u>Hazara.</u>
sim	Er <u>starb</u> 63 <u>Prozent</u> der Bevölkerung <u>Hazara.</u>
ref	Er tötete 63% der Hazara-Bevölkerung.
src	They would ordinarily support fish and other wildlife.
ann	Sie <u>würden</u> Fisch und andere wild lebende Tiere unterstützen.
sim	<u>Sie</u> würden Fisch und andere <u>wild</u> <u>lebende</u> <u>Tiere</u> <u>unterstützen.</u>
ref	Normalerweise würden sie Fisch und andere Wildtiere ernähren.

Table 2: Examples of markings to illustrate differences between human markings (*ann*) and simulated markings (*sim*). Marked parts are underlined. Example 1: "es" not clear from context, less literal reference translation. Example 2: Word omission (preposition after "Bevölkerung") or incorrect word order is not possible to mark. Example 3: Word order differs between MT and references, word omission ("ordinarily") not marked.

are heavily biased by the structure, word choice etc. by the machine translation, which might not necessarily agree with the reference translations, while still being accurate.

How good are the corrections? We therefore manually inspect the post-edits to get insights into the differences between post-edits and references. Table 1 provides a set of examples[8] with their analysis in the caption. Besides the effect of "literalness" (Koponen, 2016), we observe three major problems:

1. *Over-editing*: Editors edited translations even though they are adequate and fluent.

2. *"Telephone game" effect*: Semantic mistakes (that do not influence fluency) introduced by the MT system flow into the post-edit and remain uncorrected, when more obvious corrections are needed elsewhere in the sentence.

3. *Missing information*: Since editors only observe a portion of the complete context, i.e., they do not see the video recording of the speaker or the full transcript of the talk, they are not able to convey as much information as the reference translations.

---

[8]Selected because of their differences to references.

How good are the markings? Markings, in contrast, are less prone to over-editing, since they have fewer degrees of freedom. They are equally exposed to problem (3) of missing context, and another limitation is added: Word omissions and word order problems cannot be annotated. Table 2 gives a set of examples that illustrate these problems. While annotators were most likely not aware of problems (1) and (2), they might have sensed that information was missing, as well as the additional limitations of markings. The simulation of markings from references as used in previous work (Petrushkov et al., 2018; Marie and Max, 2015) seems overly harsh for the generated target translations, e.g., marking "Hazara-Bevölkerung" as incorrect, even though it is a valid translation of "Hazara population".

Mode	Intra-Rater (Mean / Std.) α	Inter-Rater α
Marking	0.522 / 0.284	0.201
Correction	0.820 / 0.171	0.542
User-Chosen	0.775 / 0.179	0.473

Table 3: Intra- and Inter-rater agreement calculated by Krippendorff's α.

How reliable are corrections and markings? In addition to the absolute quality of the annotations, we are interested in measuring their reliability: Do annotators agree on which parts of a translation to mark or edit? While there are many possible valid translations, and hence many ways to annotate one given translation, it has been shown that learnability profits from annotations with less conflicting information (Kreutzer et al.,

2018). In order to quantify agreement for both modes on the same scale, we reduce both annotations to sentence-level quality judgments, which for markings is the ratio of words that were marked as incorrect in a sentence, and for corrections the ratio of words that was actually edited. If the hypothesis was perfect, no markings nor edits would be required, and if it was completely wrong, all of it had to be marked or edited. After this reduction, we measure agreement with Krippendorff's α (Krippendorff, 2013), see Table 3.

Which mode do annotators prefer? In the user-choice mode, where annotators can choose for each sentence whether they would like to mark or correct it, markings were chosen much more frequently than post-edits (61.9%). Annotators did not agree on the preferred choice of mode for the repeated sentences ($\alpha = -0.008$), which indicates that there is no obvious policy when one of the modes would be advantageous over the other. In the post-annotation questionnaire, however, 60% of the participants said they generally preferred post-edits over markings, despite markings being faster, and hence resulting in a higher hourly pay.

To better understand the differences in modes, we asked them about their policies in the user-choice mode where for each sentence they would have to decide individually if they want to mark or post-edit it. The most commonly described policy is decide based on error types and frequency: choose post-edits when insertions or re-ordering is needed, and markings preferably for translations with word errors (less effort than doing a lookup or replacement). One person preferred post-edits for short translations, markings for longer ones, another three generally preferred markings generally, and one person preferred post-edits. Where annotators found the interface to need improvements was (1) in the presentation of inter-sentential context, (2) in the display of overall progress and (3) an option to edit previously edited sentences. For the marking mode they requested an option to mark missing parts or areas for re-ordering.

Do markings and corrections express the same translation quality judgment? We observe that annotators find more than twice as many token corrections in post-edit mode than in marking mode[9]

<hr>

[9]The automatically assessed translation quality for the baseline model does not differ drastically between the portions selected per mode.

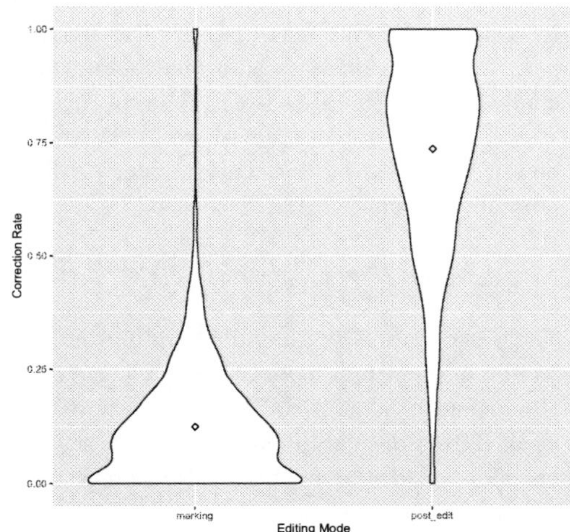

Figure 2: Correction rate by annotation mode. The correction rate describes the ratio of words in the translation that were marked as incorrect (in marking mode) or edited (in post-editing mode). Means are indicated with diamonds.

This is partially caused by the reduced degrees of freedom in marking mode, but also underlines the general trend towards over-editing when in post-edit mode. If markings and post-edits were used to compute a quality metric based on the correction rate, translations are judged as much worse in post-editing mode than in marking mode (Figure 2). This also holds for whole sentences, where 273 (26.20%) were left un-edited in marking mode, and only 3 (0.29%) in post-editing mode.

4 Machine Learnability of NMT from Human Markings and Corrections

The hypotheses presented to the annotators were generated by an NMT model. The goal is to use the supervision signal provided by the human annotation to improve the underlying model by machine learning. Learnability is concerned with the question of how strong a signal is necessary in order to see improvements in NMT fine-tuning on the respective data.

Definition. Let $x = x_1 \ldots x_S$ be a sequence of indices over a source vocabulary $\mathcal{V}_{\text{SRC}}$, and $y = y_1 \ldots y_T$ a sequence of indices over a target vocabulary $\mathcal{V}_{\text{TRG}}$. The goal of sequence-to-sequence learning is to learn a function for mapping a input sequence x into an output sequences y. For the example of machine translation, y

is a translation of x, and a model parameterized by a set of weights θ is optimized to maximize $p_\theta(y \mid x)$. This quantity is further factorized into conditional probabilities over single tokens $p_\theta(y \mid x) = \prod_{t=1}^{T} p_\theta(y_t \mid x; y_{<t})$, where the latter distribution is defined by the neural model's softmax-normalized output vector:

$$p_\theta(y_t \mid x; y_{<t}) = \texttt{softmax}(\mathrm{NN}_\theta(x; y_{<t})). \quad (2)$$

There are various options for building the architecture of the neural model NN_θ, such as recurrent (Bahdanau et al., 2015), convolutional (Gehring et al., 2017) or attentional (Vaswani et al., 2017) encoder-decoder architectures (or a mix thereof (Chen et al., 2018)).

Learning from Error Corrections. The standard supervised learning mode in human-in-the-loop machine translation assumes a fully corrected output y^* for an input x that is treated similar to a gold standard reference translation (Turchi et al., 2017). Model adaptation can be performed by maximizing the likelihood of the user-provided corrections where

$$L(\theta) = \sum_{x,y^*} \sum_{t=1}^{T} \log p_\theta(y_t^* \mid x; y_{<t}^*), \quad (3)$$

using stochastic gradient descent techniques (Bottou et al., 2018).

Learning from Error Markings. A weaker feedback mode is to let a human teacher mark the correct parts of the machine-generated output $\hat{y}$ (Marie and Max, 2015; Petrushkov et al., 2018; Domingo et al., 2017). As a consequence every token in the output receives a reward δ_t^m, either δ_t^+ if marked as correct, or δ_t^- otherwise. Petrushkov et al. (2018) proposed a model with $\delta_t^+ = 1$ and $\delta_t^- = 0$, but this weighting schemes leads to the ignorance of incorrect outputs in the gradient and the rewarding of correct tokens. Instead, we find it beneficial to penalize incorrect tokens, with e.g. $\delta_t^- = -0.5$, and reward correct tokens $\delta_t^+ = 0.5$, which aligns with the findings from Lam et al. (2019). The objective of the learning system is to maximize the likelihood of the correct parts of the output where

$$L(\theta) = \sum_{x,\hat{y}} \sum_{t=1}^{T} \delta_t^m \log p_\theta(\hat{y}_t \mid x; \hat{y}_{<t}). \quad (4)$$

Domain	train	dev	test
WMT17	5,919,142	2,169	3,004
IWSLT17	206,112	2,385	1,138
Selection	1035 corr / 1042 mark		1,043

Table 4: Data sizes (en-de), official splits from WMT17 and IWSLT17. Our target-domain data is a subset of selected talks from IWSLT2017 training data totalling 3,120 sentences.

4.1 NMT Fine-Tuning

NMT Model and Data. The goal is to adapt a general-domain NMT model to a new domain with either post-edits or markings. For the general-domain NMT system, we use the pre-trained 4-layer LSTM encoder-decoder Joey NMT WMT17 model (Kreutzer et al., 2019) for translations from English to German[10]. The model is trained on a joint vocabulary with 30k subwords (Sennrich et al., 2016). Model outputs are de-tokenized and un-BPEd before being presented to the annotators. With the help of human annotations we then adapt this model to the domain of TED talk transcripts by continuing learning on the annotated data. Hyperparameters including learning rate schedule, dropout and batch size for this fine-tuning step are tuned on the IWSLT17 dev set. For the marking mode, the weights δ^+ and δ^- are tuned in addition. As test data, we use the split of the selected talks that was annotated in the user-mode, since the purpose of this split was the evaluation of user preference. There is no overlap in the three data splits, but they have the same distribution over topics, so that we can both measure local adaptation and draw comparisons between modes. Data sizes are given in Table 4.

Evaluation. The models are evaluated with TER (Snover et al., 2006), BLEU (Papineni et al., 2002) and METEOR (Lavie and Denkowski, 2009)[11] against references translations. Significance is tested with approximate randomization for three runs for each system (Clark et al., 2011).

4.2 Results

Corrections, Markings and Quality Judgments. Table 5 compares the models after fine-tuning with

---

[10]Pre-trained model: `https://github.com/joeynmt/joeynmt/blob/master/README.md#wmt17`; modified fork of Joey NMT: `https://github.com/StatNLP/joeynmt/tree/mark`

[11]Computed with MultEval v0.5.1 (Clark et al., 2011) on tokenized outputs.

	System	TER ↓	BLEU ↑	METEOR ↑
1	WMT baseline	58.6	23.9	42.7
Error Corrections				
2	Full	57.4*	24.6*	44.7*
3	Small	57.9*	24.1	44.2*
Error Markings				
4	0/1	57.5*	24.4*	44.0*
5	-0.5/0.5	57.4*	24.6*	44.2*
6	random	58.1*	24.1	43.5*
Quality Judgments				
7	from corrections	57.4*	24.6*	44.7*
8	from markings	57.6*	24.5*	43.8*

Table 5: Results on the test set with feedback collected from humans. Decoding with beam search of width 5 and length penalty of 1. Significant ($p <= 0.05$) improvements over the baseline are marked with *. Full error corrections and error markings only significantly differ in terms of METEOR.

corrections and markings with the original WMT out-of-domain model.

The "small" model trained with error corrections is trained on one fifth of the data, which is comparable to the effort it takes to collect the error markings. Both error corrections and markings can be reduced to sentence-level quality judgments, where all tokens receive the same weight in Eq. $\delta = \frac{\#marked}{hyptokens}$ or $\delta = \frac{\#corrected}{hyptokens}$. In addition, we compare the markings against a random choice of marked tokens per sentence.[12] We see that both models trained on corrections and markings improve significantly over the baseline (rows 2 and 3). Tuning the weights for (in)correct tokens makes a small but significant difference for learning from markings (rows 4 and 5). These human markings lead to significantly better models than random markings (row 6). When reducing both types of human feedback to sentence-level quality judgments, no loss in comparison to error corrections and a small loss for markings (rows 7 and 8) is observed. We suspect that the small margin between results for learning from corrections and markings is due to evaluating against references. Effects like over-editing (see Section 3.4.1) produce training data that lead the model to generate outputs that diverge more from independent references and therefore score lower than deserved under all metrics except for METEOR.

Human Evaluation. It is infeasible to collect markings or corrections for all our systems for a

<hr>

[12]Each token is marked with probability $p_{mark} = 0.5$.

more appropriate comparison than to references, but for that purpose we conduct a small human evaluation study. Three bilingual raters receive 120 translations of the test set ($\sim$10%) and the corresponding source sentences for each mode and judge whether the translation is better, as good as, or worse than the baseline: 64% of the translations obtained from learning from error markings are judged at least as good as the baseline, compared to 65.2% for the translations obtained from learning from error corrections. Table 6 shows the detailed proportions excluding identical translations.

System	$>$ BL	$=$ BL	$<$ BL
Error Markings	**43.0%**	21.0%	36.4%
Error Corrections	**49.1%**	16.1%	34.7%

Table 6: Human preferences for comparisons between baseline (BL) translations and the NMT system fine-tuned on error markings and corrections. $>$: better than the baseline, $<$ worse than the baseline.

Effort vs. Translation Quality. Figure 3 illustrates the relation between the total time spent on annotations and the resulting translation quality for corrections and markings trained on a selection of subsets of the full annotated data: The overall trend shows that both modes benefit from more training data, with more variance for the marking mode, but also a steeper descent. From a total annotation amount of approximately 20,000s on ($\approx$ 5.5h), markings are the more efficient choice.

4.2.1 LMEM Analysis

We fit a LMEM for sentence-level quality scores of the baseline, and three runs each for the NMT systems fine-tuned on markings and post-edits respectively, and inspect the influence of the system as a fixed effect, and sentence id, topic and source length as random effects.

```
TER ~ system + (1 | talk_id/sent_id)
       + (1 | topic) + (1 | src_length)
```

The fixed effect is significant at $p = 0.05$, i.e., the quality scores of the three systems differ significantly under this model. The global intercept lies at 64.73, the one for marking 1.23 below, and the one for post-editing 0.96 below. The variance in TER is for the largest part explained by the sentence, then the talk, the source length, and the least by the topic.

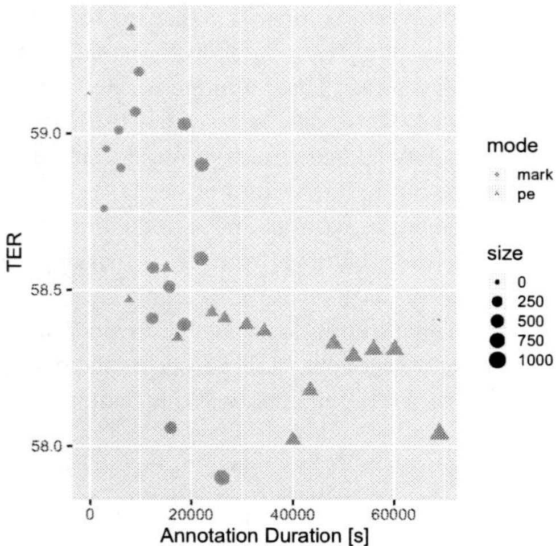

Figure 3: Improvement in TER for training data of varying size: lower is better. Scores are collected across two runs with a random selection of $k \in [125, 250, 375, 500, 625, 750, 875]$ training data points.

5   Conclusion

We presented the first user study on the annotation process and the machine learnability of human error markings of translation outputs. This annotation mode has so far been given less attention than error corrections or quality judgments, and has until now only been investigated in simulation studies. We found that both according to automatic evaluation metrics and by human evaluation, fine-tuning of NMT models achieved comparable gains by learning from error corrections and markings. However, error markings required several orders of magnitude less human annotation effort.

In future work we will investigate the integration of automatic markings into the learning process, and we will explore online adaptation possibilities.

Acknowledgments

We would like to thank the anonymous reviewers for their feedback, Michael Staniek and Michael Hagmann for the help with data processing and analysis, and Sariya Karimova and Tsz Kin Lam for their contribution to a preliminary study. The research reported in this paper was supported in part by the German research foundation (DFG) under grant RI-2221/4-1.

References

Bahdanau, D., Brakel, P., Xu, K., Goyal, A., Lowe, R., Pineau, J., Courville, A., and Bengio, Y. (2017). An actor-critic algorithm for sequence prediction. In *Proceedings of the International Conference on Learning Representations (ICLR)*, Toulon, France.

Bahdanau, D., Cho, K., and Bengio, Y. (2015). Neural machine translation by jointly learning to align and translate. In *Proceedings of the International Conference on Learning Representations (ICLR)*, San Diego, CA.

Barr, D. J., Roger, L., Scheepers, C., and Tily, H. J. (2013). Random effects structure for confirmatory hypothesis testing: Keep it maximal. *J. Mem. Lang*, 68(3):255–278.

Bates, D., Mächler, M., Bolker, B., and Walker, S. (2015). Fitting linear mixed-effects models using lme4. *Journal of Statistical Software*, 67(1):1–48.

Bentivogli, L., Bisazza, A., Cettolo, M., and Federico, M. (2016). Neural versus phrase-based machine translation quality: a case study. In *Proceedings of the 2016 Conference on Empirical Methods in Natural Language Processing (EMNLP)*, Austin, TX.

Bottou, L., Curtis, F. E., and Nocedal, J. (2018). Optimization methods for large-scale machine learning. *SIAM Review*, 60(2):223–311.

Celemin, C., del Solar, J. R., and Kober, J. (2018). A fast hybrid reinforcement learning framework with human corrective feedback. *Autonomous Robots*.

Chen, M. X., Firat, O., Bapna, A., Johnson, M., Macherey, W., Foster, G., Jones, L., Schuster, M., Shazeer, N., Parmar, N., Vaswani, A., Uszkoreit, J., Kaiser, L., Chen, Z., Wu, Y., and Hughes, M. (2018). The best of both worlds: Combining recent advances in neural machine translation. In *Proceedings of the 56th Annual Meeting of the Association for Computational Linguistics (ACL)*, Melbourne, Australia.

Christiano, P. F., Leike, J., Brown, T., Martic, M., Legg, S., and Amodei, D. (2017). Deep reinforcement learning from human preferences. In *Advances in Neural Information Processing Systems (NIPS)*, Long Beach, CA.

Clark, J. H., Dyer, C., Lavie, A., and Smith, N. A. (2011). Better hypothesis testing for statistical machine translation: Controlling for optimizer instability. In *Proceedings of the 49th Annual Meeting of the Association for Computational Linguistics: Human Language Technologies (ACL-HLT)*, Portland, OR.

Domingo, M., Peris, Á., and Casacuberta, F. (2017). Segment-based interactive-predictive machine translation. *Machine Translation*, 31(4):163–185.

Foster, G., Isabelle, P., and Plamondon, P. (1997). Target-text mediated interactive machine translation. *Machine Translation*, 12(1-2):175–194.

Gehring, J., Auli, M., Grangier, D., Yarats, D., and Dauphin, Y. (2017). Convolutional sequence to sequence learning. In *Proceedings of the 55th Annual Meeting of the Association for Computational Linguistics (ACL)*, Vancouver, Canada.

Green, S., Wang, S. I., Chuang, J., Heer, J., Schuster, S., and Manning, C. D. (2014). Human effort and machine learnability in computer aided translation. In *Proceedings the onference on Empirical Methods in Natural Language Processing (EMNLP)*, Doha, Qatar.

Karimova, S., Simianer, P., and Riezler, S. (2018). A user-study on online adaptation of neural machine translation to human post-edits. *Machine Translation*, 32(4):309–324.

Knowles, R. and Koehn, P. (2016). Neural interactive translation prediction. In *Proceedings of the Conference of the Association for Machine Translation in the Americas (AMTA)*, Austin, TX.

Koponen, M. (2016). *Machine Translation Post-Editing and Effort. Empirical Studies on the Post-Editing Process*. PhD thesis, University of Helsinki.

Kreutzer, J., Bastings, J., and Riezler, S. (2019). Joey NMT: A minimalist NMT toolkit for novices. In *Proceedings of the 2019 Conference on Empirical Methods in Natural Language Processing and the 9th International Joint Conference on Natural Language Processing (EMNLP-IJCNLP)*, Hong Kong, China.

Kreutzer, J., Sokolov, A., and Riezler, S. (2017). Bandit structured prediction for neural sequence-to-sequence learning. In *Proceedings of the 55th Annual Meeting of the Association for Computational Linguistics (ACL)*, Vancouver, Canada.

Kreutzer, J., Uyheng, J., and Riezler, S. (2018). Reliability and learnability of human bandit feedback for sequence-to-sequence reinforcement learning. In *Proceedings of the 56th Annual Meeting of the Association for Computational Linguistics (ACL)*, Melbourne, Australia.

Krippendorff, K. (2013). *Content Analysis. An Introduction to Its Methodology*. Sage, third edition.

Lam, T. K., Kreutzer, J., and Riezler, S. (2018). A reinforcement learning approach to interactive-predictive neural machine translation. In *Proceedings of the 21st Annual Conference of the European Association for Machine Translation (EAMT)*, Alicante, Spain.

Lam, T. K., Schamoni, S., and Riezler, S. (2019). Interactive-predictive neural machine translation through reinforcement and imitation. In *Proceedings of Machine Translation Summit XVII (MTSUMMIT)*, Dublin, Ireland.

Lavie, A. and Denkowski, M. J. (2009). The meteor metric for automatic evaluation of machine translation. *Machine Translation*, 23(2-3):105–115.

Marie, B. and Max, A. (2015). Touch-based pre-post-editing of machine translation output. In *Proceedings of the Conference on Empirical Methods in Natural Language Processing (EMNLP)*, Lisbon, Portugal.

Papineni, K., Roukos, S., Ward, T., and Zhu, W.-J. (2002). Bleu: a method for automatic evaluation of machine translation. In *Proceedings of the 40th Annual Meeting of the Association for Computational Linguistics (ACL)*, Philadelphia, PA.

Peris, Á., Domingo, M., and Casacuberta, F. (2017). Interactive neural machine translation. *Computer Speech & Language*, 45:201–220.

Petrushkov, P., Khadivi, S., and Matusov, E. (2018). Learning from chunk-based feedback in neural machine translation. In *Proceedings of the 56th Annual Meeting of the Association for Computational Linguistics (ACL)*, Melbourne, Australia.

Ranzato, M., Chopra, S., Auli, M., and Zaremba, W. (2016). Sequence level training with recurrent neural networks. In *Proceedings of the International Conference on Learning Representation (ICLR)*, San Juan, Puerto Rico.

Sennrich, R., Haddow, B., and Birch, A. (2016). Neural machine translation of rare words with subword units. In *Proceedings of the 54th Annual Meeting of the Association for Computational Linguistics (ACL)*, Berlin, Germany.

Snover, M., Dorr, B., Schwartz, R., Micciulla, L., and Makhoul, J. (2006). A study of translation edit rate with targeted human annotation. In *Proceedings of the Conference of the Association for Machine Translation in the Americas (AMTA)*, Cambridge, MA.

Sokolov, A., Kreutzer, J., Sunderland, K., Danchenko, P., Szymaniak, W., Fürstenau, H., and Riezler, S. (2017). A shared task on bandit learning for machine translation. In *Proceedings of the Second Conference on Machine Translation*, Copenhagen, Denmark.

Turchi, M., Negri, M., Farajian, M. A., and Federico, M. (2017). Continuous learning from human post-edits for neural machine translation. *The Prague Bulletin of Mathematical Linguistics (PBML)*, 1(108):233–244.

Vaswani, A., Shazeer, N., Parmar, N., Uszkoreit, J., Jones, L., Gomez, A. N., Kaiser, L., and Polosukhin, I. (2017). Attention is all you need. In *Advances in Neural Information Processing Systems (NIPS)*, Long Beach, CA.

Appendix

A Annotator Instructions

The annotators received the following instructions:
- You will be shown a source sentence, its translation and an instruction.
- Read the source sentence and the translation.
- Follow the instruction by either marking the incorrect words of the translation by clicking on them or highlighting them, correcting the translation by deleting, inserting and replacing words or parts of words, or choosing between modes (i) and (ii), and then click "submit".
  - In (ii), if you make a mistake and want to start over, you can click on the button "reset".
  - In (i), to highlight, click on the word you would like to start highlighting from, keep the mouse button pushed down, drag the pointer to the word you would like to stop highlighting on, and release the mouse button while over that word.
- If you want to take a short break (get a coffee, etc.), click on "pause" to pause the session. We're measuring time it takes to work on each sentence, so please do not overuse this button (e.g. do not press pause while you're making your decisions), but also do not feel rushed if you feel uncertain about a sentence.
- Instead, if you want to take a longer break, just log out. The website will return you return you to the latest unannotated sentence when you log back in. If you log out in the middle of an annotation, your markings or post-edits will not be saved.
- After completing all sentences (ca. 300), you'll be asked to fill a survey about your experience.
- Important:
  - Please do not use any external dictionaries or translation tools.
  - You might notice that some sentences reappear, which is desired. Please try to be consistent with repeated sentences.
  - There is no way to return and re-edit previous sentences, so please make sure you're confident with the edits/markings you provided before you click "submit".

B Creating Data Splits

In order to have users see a wider range of talks, each talk was split into three parts (beginning, middle, and end). Each talk part was assigned an annotation mode. Parts were then assigned to users using the following constraints:
- Each user should see nine document parts.
- No user should see the same document twice.
- Each user should see three sections in post-editing, marking, and user-choice mode.
- Each user should see three beginning, three middle, and three ending sections.
- Each document should be assigned each of the three annotation modes.

To avoid assigning post-editing to every beginning section, marking to every middle section, and user-choice to every ending section, assignment was done with an integer linear program with the above constraints. Data was presented to users in the order [Post-edit, Marking, User Chosen, Agreement].

Quality In, Quality Out: Learning from Actual Mistakes

Frédéric Blain[1]   **Nikolaos Aletras**[1]   **Lucia Specia**[1,2]
[1]Department of Computer Science, University of Sheffield
[2]Department of Computing, Imperial College London
United Kingdom
{f.blain,n.aletras,l.specia}@sheffield.ac.uk

Abstract

Approaches to Quality Estimation (QE) of machine translation have shown promising results at predicting quality scores for translated sentences. However, QE models are often trained on noisy approximations of quality annotations derived from the proportion of post-edited words in translated sentences instead of direct human annotations of translation errors. The latter is a more reliable ground-truth but more expensive to obtain. In this paper, we present the first attempt to model the task of predicting the proportion of *actual* translation errors in a sentence while minimising the need for direct human annotation. For that purpose, we use transfer-learning to leverage large scale noisy annotations and small sets of high-quality human annotated translation errors to train QE models. Experiments on four language pairs and translations obtained by statistical and neural models show consistent gains over strong baselines.

1 Introduction

Quality Estimation (QE) for Machine Translation (MT) is the task of predicting the overall quality of an automatically generated translation *e.g.*, on either word, sentence or document level (Blatz et al., 2004; Ueffing and Ney, 2007). In opposition to automatic metrics and manual evaluation which rely on gold standard reference translations, QE models can produce quality estimates on unseen data,

and at runtime. QE has already proven its usefulness in many applications such as improving productivity in post-editing of MT, and recent neural-based approaches to QE have been shown to provide promising performance in predicting quality of neural MT output (Fonseca et al., 2019).

QE models are trained under full supervision, which requires to have quality-labelled training data at hand. Obtaining annotated data for all the domains and languages of interest is costly and often impractical. As a result, QE models can suffer from the same limitations as neural MT models themselves, such as drastic degradation of their performance on out-of-domain data. As an alternative, QE models are often trained under weak supervision, using training instances labelled from noisy or limited sources (e.g. data labelled with automatic metrics for MT).

Here, we focus on sentence-level QE, where given a pair of sentences (the source and its translation), the aim is to train supervised Machine Learning (ML) models that can predict a quality label as a numerical value. The most widely used label for sentence-level QE is the Human-mediated Translation Edit Rate (HTER) (Snover et al., 2006), which represents the *post-editing effort*. HTER consists of the minimum number of edits a human language expert is required to make in order to fix the translation errors in a sentence, taking values between 0 and 1. The main limitation of HTER is that it does not represent an actual translation error rate, but its noisy approximation. The noise stems mostly from errors in the heuristics used to automatically align the machine translation and its post-edited version, but also from the fact that some edits represent preferential choices of humans, rather than errors. To overcome such limitations, QE models can be improved by using data that has been

Martins, Moniz, Fumega, Martins, Batista, Coheur, Parra, Trancoso, Turchi, Bisazza, Moorkens, Guerberof, Nurminen, Marg, Forcada (eds.)
Proceedings of the 22nd Annual Conference of the European Association for Machine Translation, p. 145–153
Lisboa, Portugal, November 2020.

Es ist wichtig, dass Sie, bevor Sie IVEMEND bekommen, Ihren Arzt informieren, wenn Sie stillen oder stillen möchten.

It is important that you before you start receiving IVEMEND, tell your doctor if you are breast-feeding or plan to breast-feed.

Ann-1   It is important that you tell your doctor if you are breast-feeding or plan to breast-feed before you start receiving IVEMEND.

Ann-2   It is important that you [[1] before you start receiving IVEMEND][[2] ,] tell your doctor if you are breast-feeding or plan to breast-feed. | 1. Word order   2. Typography

Figure 1: Example of a German sentence (top) and its automatic translation into English. The HTER between the translation and its post-edited version (ANN-1) is 0.091, while the proportion of fine-grained expert-annotated MT errors (ANN-2), is $6/23 = 0.261$.

directly annotated for translation errors by human experts. Figure 1 shows an example of the discrepancy between the HTER score and the proportion of *actual* errors from expert annotation, for a raw translation and its post-edited version.

Annotations of MT errors usually follow fine-grained error taxonomies such as the Multidimensional Quality Metrics (MQM) framework (Lommel et al., 2014). While such annotations provide highly reliable labelled data, they are more expensive to produce than HTER. This often results in datasets that are orders of magnitude smaller than HTER-based ones. This makes it hard to only use such high-quality resources for training neural-based QE models, which typically require large amounts of training data.

In this paper, we use transfer-learning to develop QE models by exploiting the advantages of both noisy and high-quality labelled data. We leverage information from large amounts of HTER data and small amounts of MQM annotations to train more reliable sentence-level QE models. Our aim is to predict the proportion of *actual* errors in MT outputs. More fine-grained error prediction is left for future work.

Main contributions: (1) We introduce a new task of predicting the proportion of actual translation errors using transfer-learning for QE[1], by leveraging large scale noisy HTER annotations and smaller but of higher quality expert MQM annotations; (2) we show that our simple yet effective approach using transfer-learning yields better performance at predicting the proportion of actual errors in MT, compared to models trained directly on expert-annotated MQM or HTER-only data; (3) we report experiments on four language pairs and both statistical and neural MT systems.

2 Related Work

Quality labels for sentence-level QE Quirk (2004) introduced the use of manually created

quality labels for evaluating MT systems. With a rather small dataset (approximately 350 sentences), they reported better results than those obtained with a much larger set of instances annotated automatically. Similarly, Specia et al. (2009) proposed the use of a (1-4) *Likert* scale representing a translator's perception on quality with regard to the degree of difficulty to fix a translation. However, sentence-level quality annotations appear to be subjective while agreement between annotators is generally low (Specia, 2011). More recently, sentence-level QE models are most typically trained on HTER scores (Bojar et al., 2013; Bojar et al., 2014; Bojar et al., 2015; Bojar et al., 2016; Bojar et al., 2017; Specia et al., 2018; Fonseca et al., 2019).

Transfer-learning for QE Transfer-learning (TL) is a machine learning approach where models trained on a *source* task are adapted to a related *target* task (Pan et al., 2010; Yosinski et al., 2014). Transfer-learning methods have been widely used in NLP, *e.g.*, machine translation (Zoph et al., 2016) and text classification (Howard and Ruder, 2018). Previous work on TL for QE focused on adapting models for labels produced by different annotators (Cohn and Specia, 2013; Shah and Specia, 2016) which is different to this work.

More recent work on TL techniques for QE explore pre-trained word representations. This was first done by POSTECH (Kim et al., 2017), best performing neural-based architecture in the QE shared task at WMT'17 (Bojar et al., 2017). POSTECH re-purposes a recurrent neural network encoder pre-trained on large parallel corpora, to predict HTER scores using multi-task learning at different levels of granularity (*e.g.*, word, phrase, or sentence). Then, Kepler et al. (2019) used a predictor-estimator architecture similar to POSTECH alongside very large scale pre-trained representations from BERT (Devlin et al., 2018) and XLM (Lample and Conneau, 2019), and ensembling techniques, to win the QE tasks at WMT'19 (Fonseca

[1]https://github.com/sheffieldnlp/tlqe

et al., 2019). These models are pre-trained on un-labelled data, as opposed to noisier labelled data, and aim to predict HTER scores, which is different to the focus of this paper.

To the best of our knowledge, this paper is the first attempt to repurpose a QE model pre-trained on one quality label to a model that predicts another quality label; we first train a model on noisy HTER data to predict post-editing effort, and leverage its knowledge to train a model capable of predicting the *actual* proportion of translation errors using expert-annotated MQM data.

3 Transfer-Learning Approach

We use inductive transfer-learning (Pan et al., 2010), where given a source learning task $\mathcal{T}_S$ and a target task $\mathcal{T}_T$, the aim is to improve performance in the latter by re-using knowledge from $\mathcal{T}_S$, where $\mathcal{T}_S \neq \mathcal{T}_T$. Here, $\mathcal{T}_S$ corresponds to predicting *post-editing effort* based on noisy HTER annotations, and $\mathcal{T}_T$ to predicting the proportion of *actual* proportion of errors based on MQM annotations.

3.1 Source task QE model

BiRNN-HTER   We use the BiRNN model proposed by Ive et al. (2018) as our base model to predict HTER scores. Figure 2 illustrates the high-level architecture of the model. Words in source and translated sentences are first mapped into embedding vectors. Then, the word embeddings are passed through bidirectional Gated Recurrent Unit encoders (Cho et al., 2014) to learn context-aware word representations in both the source and target sentences. The two sentence representations are learned independently from each other before being concatenated as a weighted sum of their word vectors, generated by an attention mechanism. The concatenated representation is finally passed through a dense layer with sigmoid activation to generate the quality estimate. BiRNN performed competitively in the WMT'18 shared task on QE (Specia et al., 2018) without relying on any parallel data nor expensive pre-training regimes such as the POSTECH approach (Section 2). Overall, it is easier and faster to train with a smaller number of parameters compared to POSTECH, which makes it more suitable for this task.

3.2 Adaptation to the target task

Our target task is to predict the proportion (between 0 and 1) of actual MQM errors in a translated sentence. Therefore, we adapt our BiRNN-HTER model to the target task.

BiRNN-MQM$_{TL}$ We first replace the BiRNN-HTER output layer with two new layers: (1) a fully-connected layer followed by a rectified linear unit (Nair and Hinton, 2010) as the activation function; and (2) a fully-connected output layer with a sigmoid activation to produce the predictions. We train these two layers on target task data by freezing the rest of the model.

BiRNN-MQM$_{TL}$+FT   We further *fine-tune* our BiRNN-MQM$_{TL}$ model on the target task data using a small learning rate following (Howard and Ruder, 2018).

Hybrid   Finally, we hypothesise that linguistic information (*e.g.*, number of tokens in the source/target sentence, language model probability of source/target sentence, etc.) might be complementary to the source-target representations obtained by our BiRNN-MQM$_{TL}$+FT model. For that purpose, we first extract a representation of the source and translated sentence by removing the BiRNN-MQM$_{TL}$+FT output layer and then we concatenate it with the widely used 17 black-box sentence-level QE features extracted with the open-source QuEst++ toolkit (Specia et al., 2015). The joint neural and linguistic information of the source and target sentences is fed into a linear regression[2] model using a L2 regularisation penalty.

4 Experimental Setup

4.1 Data

For our experiments, we use the freely available QT21 dataset[3] (Specia et al., 2017) used in the QE shared task (Bojar et al., 2017; Specia et al., 2018). This dataset contains both post-edited (HTER) and error-annotated (MQM) data in four language pairs: English into German, Latvian and Czech, and German into English; and phrase-based statistical (PBMT) and neural (NMT) translation models. The annotation for errors was produced by professional translators using the MQM taxonomy

---

[2]We also tried to jointly feed the features during fine-tuning but did not yield better performance.
[3]http://www.qt21.eu/resources/data/

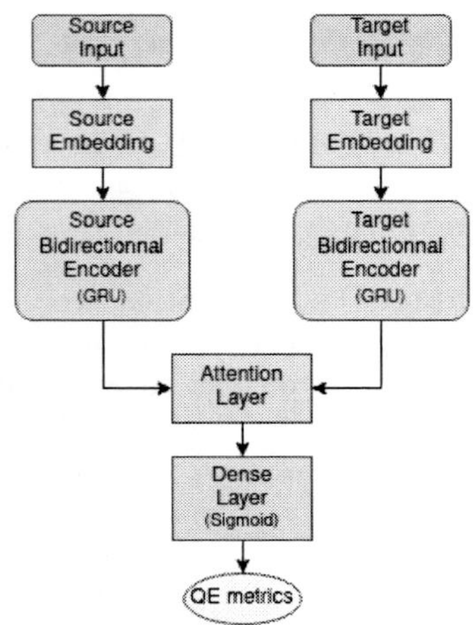

Figure 2: High-level architecture of the BiRNN sentence-level QE model.

	HTER data (Source)		MQM data (Target)	
	# sentences		# sentences	
	PBMT	NMT	PBMT	NMT
EN-DE	25,305	12,564	2,655	3,386
EN-LV	10,561	11,116	3,284	3,244
DE-EN	25,922	–	3,374	–
EN-CS	37,725	–	3,460	–

Table 1: Statistics for HTER and MQM data for statistical (PBMT) and neural (NMT) translation systems across language pairs.

with 21 error categories (*e.g.*, mistranslation, morphology, etc.). To obtain a score for the entire sentence, we divide the number of words annotated with any error category by the length of the sentence. Predicting the actual type of MQM errors is left for future work. Note that the MQM-annotated sentences are a subset of the HTER data (*i.e.* some of them have both annotations), so we removed these from the HTER data.

By design, all sentences selected for MQM annotation have at least one error. In order to increase the size and variety of the MQM dataset, we doubled the number of MQM-annotated sentences by taking sentences for which no edit was made during PE (*i.e.* perfect translations with zero MQM errors). Table 1 summarises the statistics of the labelled data used for our experiments.

4.2 Baseline and comparison models

To assess our models, we compare them against the following baselines.

BiRNN-HTER A BiRNN-HTER model trained on the HTER data and used as is, to predict the pro-

portion of MQM errors. That is using the source task base model to predict the scores in the target task.

BiRNN-MQM This is the same BiRNN architecture as our source task model (BiRNN-HTER) but trained from-scratch on the MQM data without transfer-learning.

LR-QEfeat A feature-based approach used in the WMT shared tasks as an official baseline. We use the 17 black-box sentence-level QE features introduced above (see Section 3.2) to train a linear regression[4] model with a L2 regularization penalty.

4.3 Model hyper-parameters

For the BiRNN-HTER model, we use default parameters as in (Ive et al., 2018). For the BiRNN-MQM_{TL}, we use a 5-fold Cross Validation approach. We use a dense layer[5] of 50 and choose the number of epochs in $\{1, .., 40\}$, training learning rate in $\{1e^{-2}, 1e^{-3}\}$ and fine-tuning learning rate in $\{1e^{-3}, 1e^{-4}\}$ on a validation set, by minimising the Mean Absolute Error (MAE) between the predicted score and gold standard labels. We also experimented with two approaches for fine-tuning: (1) unfreezing all the layers at the same time; and (2) a gradual unfreezing approach proposed by (Howard and Ruder, 2018). We use Adam (Kingma and Ba, 2014) with default parameters, and a batch size of 100. For the Hybrid model, we optimise the L2 regularisation penalty.

Table 2 reports on the optimal values determined by hyper-parameters optimisation.

5 Results

Tables 3 and 4 show respectively the average absolute Pearson's r correlation co-efficient and the Root Mean Square Error (the official metrics for this task (Graham, 2015)) between actual and predicted MQM error proportions in six combinations of MT models (PBMT, NMT) and language pairs (EN-DE, EN-LV, DE-EN and EN-CS).

First, we observe that the baseline model (LR-QEfeat) performs fairly well on predicting the proportion of errors, especially for the EN-DE and EN-CS PBMT. However, it is not robust across language pairs and types of translation systems.

---

[4]We have also tested a Support Vector Regression with a radial basis function kernel, but it yielded lower performance.
[5]We did not observe noticeable differences in performance using smaller or larger size in early experimentation.

	Training		Fine-tuning	
	Epochs	Learning rate	Epochs/Method	Learning rate
EN-DE$_{NMT}$	22	0.01	gradual unfreezing	0.001
EN-LV$_{NMT}$	16	0.001	gradual unfreezing	0.001
EN-DE$_{PBMT}$	15	0.001	1	0.001
EN-LV$_{PBMT}$	18	0.01	gradual unfreezing	0.001
DE-EN$_{PBMT}$	19	0.01	1	0.001
EN-CS$_{PBMT}$	18	0.001	gradual unfreezing	0.001

Table 2: Optimal values selected for the adaptation of the source task sentence-level BiRNN QE model (BiRNN-HTER) to the target task (*i.e.* proportion of *actual* MT error in MT). For each language pair: number of epochs and learning rates for the training, and number of epochs or method used for the fine-tuning of the model.

	EN-DE$_{NMT}$	EN-LV$_{NMT}$	EN-DE$_{PBMT}$	EN-LV$_{PBMT}$	DE-EN$_{PBMT}$	EN-CS$_{PBMT}$
(1) LR-QEfeat	0.152 ±0.06	0.404 ±0.19	0.585 ±0.02	0.471 ±0.06	0.329 ±0.02	0.635 ±0.02
(2) BiRNN-HTER	0.297 ±0.04	0.003 ±0.09	0.146 ±0.06	0.110 ±0.05	0.113 ±0.07	0.426 ±0.05
(3) BiRNN-MQM	<u>0.584</u> ±0.04	0.542 ±0.05	<u>0.619</u> ±0.05	0.583 ±0.03	0.606 ±0.08	<u>0.757</u> ±0.01
(4) BiRNN-MQM$_{TL}$	<u>0.575</u> ±0.04	0.596 ±0.06	<u>0.644</u> ±0.02	0.612 ±0.03	0.594 ±0.02	<u>0.787</u> ±0.03
(5) BiRNN-MQM$_{TL}$+FT	**0.649** ±**0.05**	**0.612** ±**0.06**	<u>0.648</u> ±0.04	<u>0.649</u> ±0.04	<u>0.601</u> ±0.05	<u>0.793</u> ±0.02
(6) Hybrid	<u>0.644</u> ±0.05	0.522 ±0.28	**<u>0.658</u>** ±**0.04**	**<u>0.655</u>** ±**0.03**	**<u>0.610</u>** ±**0.05**	**<u>0.795</u>** ±**0.02**

Table 3: Average absolute **Pearson's** r correlation between actual and **predicted MQM error proportions** across all folds in six combinations of MT models and language pairs: **(1)** feature-based baseline (LR-QEfeat) – **(2)** BiRNN model trained on HTER data, and used as is – **(3)** BiRNN model trained from scratch on MQM annotated data – **(4)** BiRNN MQM trained with transfer-learning, *i.e.* trained on HTER data and adapted using MQM data – **(5)** BiRNN-MQM$_{TL}$ model fine-tuned with additional training epochs – **(6)** fine-tuned BiRNN-MQM$_{TL}$+FT model used as feature extractor along with the 17 sentence-level QE features and a linear regression algorithm (Hybrid). Measurements not significantly outperformed by any other overall, are underlined. Significance is computed with Hotelling-Williams test (Williams, 1959).

	EN-DE$_{NMT}$	EN-LV$_{NMT}$	EN-DE$_{PBMT}$	EN-LV$_{PBMT}$	DE-EN$_{PBMT}$	EN-CS$_{PBMT}$
(1) LR-QEfeat	0.112 ±0.01	0.157 ±0.10	0.161 ±0.01	0.114 ±0.01	0.115 ±0.00	0.175 ±0.01
(2) BiRNN-HTER	0.117 ±0.01	0.523 ±0.01	0.250 ±0.01	0.460 ±0.01	0.605 ±0.03	0.333 ±0.01
(3) BiRNN-MQM	0.093 ±0.01	0.108 ±0.01	0.157 ±0.01	0.110 ±0.01	**0.097** ±0.00	0.152 ±0.01
(4) BiRNN-MQM$_{TL}$	0.094 ±0.01	**0.102** ±0.01	0.158 ±0.01	0.108 ±0.01	0.110 ±0.00	0.145 ±0.01
(5) BiRNN-MQM$_{TL}$+FT	0.091 ±0.01	0.105 ±0.01	0.152 ±0.01	0.100 ±0.01	0.100 ±0.00	0.139 ±0.01
(6) Hybrid	**0.087** ±0.01	0.212 ±0.26	**0.149** ±0.01	**0.098** ±0.01	**0.097** ±0.00	**0.138** ±0.01

Table 4: Average absolute **RMSE** between actual and **predicted MQM error proportions** across all folds in six combinations of MT models and language pairs: **(1)** feature-based baseline (LR-QEfeat) – **(2)** BiRNN model trained on HTER data, and used as is – **(3)** BiRNN model trained from scratch on MQM annotated data – **(4)** BiRNN MQM trained with transfer-learning, *i.e.* trained on HTER data and adapted using MQM data – **(5)** BiRNN-MQM$_{TL}$ model fine-tuned with additional training epochs – **(6)** fine-tuned BiRNN-MQM$_{TL}$+FT model used as feature extractor along with the 17 sentence-level QE features and a linear regression algorithm (Hybrid). Measurements not significantly outperformed by any other overall, are underlined. Significance is computed with Hotelling-Williams test (Williams, 1959).

Second, the BiRNN-HTER model, trained on HTER data and used as is, is not able to predict the proportion of actual MQM errors. Surprisingly, the BiRNN-MQM model trained on MQM data directly achieves relatively good performance for all language pairs. This seems to confirm that (i) the BiRNN architecture, as simple as it may be, allows to train models that perform well while keeping low the computational resources required; and (ii) that HTER is a noisy approximation of the quality of a translation and post-edits are not actually well-aligned to actual translation errors.

Overall, the best performing model is BiRNN-MQM$_{TL}$ with transfer-learning and fine-tuning, while our Hybrid model seems to further improve performance in predicting quality on statistical MT output. This is in line with recent findings demonstrating the benefits of feature-based approaches for predicting the quality of statistical MT, but not for predicting the quality of neural MT, which is better modelled with learned representations using neural networks (Specia et al., 2018). This also confirms our main hypothesis that noisy data, but from a closely related task, encapsulates useful information that our TL model is able to leverage.

6 Leveraging Pre-trained Token-level Representations

As reported in (Fonseca et al., 2019), state-of-the-art models for supervised QE follow current trend in the NLP community in 2019: leveraging large-scale pre-trained language models to compute word- or sentence-level representations. Following (Kepler et al., 2019) and their Transformer-based Predictor-Estimator model, we considered two variants of our BiRNN-HTER model introduced in Section 3:

LM-BiRNN By default, the weights of both the source and target bidirectional GRU encoders of the BiRNN model are first randomly initiated and then learned, simultaneously, during training of the task at hand. In this variant, we first learn the weights of each encoder independently in a language modelling fashion with a Cross-Entropy loss, using the additional resources provided by the organisers of the WMT'18 QE shared task[6]. We then reuse the learned weights to initiate each encoder of the BiRNN model.

BERT-BiRNN In this variant of the BiRNN model, the token-level representations are extracted from a pre-trained multilingual base cased BERT (Devlin et al., 2018) model. Concretely, we replace both the source and the target embedding layers in Figure 2 by a single custom *BERT embedding* layer. During training, we fine-tune the weights of the word embeddings layer, as well as the weights of the last 4 encoding layers of the BERT model.

In the rest of the paper, and similarly to the naming of our models in Sections 3.1 and 3.2, we will refer to as "BERT-BiRNN-HTER", "BERT-BiRNN-MQM" and "BERT-BiRNN-MQM$_{TL}$", the three variants of this model trained from scratch on the source task (-HTER), on the target task (-MQM) and adapted to the target task using TL (-MQM$_{TL}$), respectively.

6.1 Experimental Results

We evaluate the benefit of using pre-trained token-level representations, by comparing the performance of our previously introduced BERT variants, against our base BiRNN model.

Predicting HTER

Table 5 summarises the performance of each model at predicting HTER scores on the HTER data described in Table 1. We include the BiRNN-HTER models from Tables 3 and 4 (row (2)) for direct comparison when trained at predicting HTER.

<hr>

[6]http://statmt.org/wmt18/quality-estimation-task.html

First, we observe that, overall, relying on pre-trained token representation helps to improve the performance of our BiRNN model, confirming the findings in (Fonseca et al., 2019). Second, while relying on advanced token representations such as those extracted from BERT significantly help improving across language pairs and types of translation, relying on simpler representations seems to mainly help on neural-based MT output, and with limited gains.

However, pre-trained representations usually require to be fine-tuned for the task at hand. In our scenario of application, where only a few datapoints of the target task is available, this may be a challenging task when using complex and deep architectures such as the BERT model, which contains millions of parameters trained on large scale training data (BERT models are trained on the Wikipedia dataset).

Predicting MQM with Transfer-Learning

We replicated the experimental settings for inductive transfer-learning described in Section 4, by considering this time the BERT variant of our base BiRNN model. Our experimental results are summarised in Tables 6 and 7, which report on Pearson's r correlation and RMSE, respectively. We include LR-QEfeat, the feature-based approach, as well as the default BiRNN-HTER and BiRNN-MQM models from Tables 3 and 4 (rows (1)-(4)) for direct comparison when trained at predicting MQM error proportions.

First, we observe that when our BiRNN model is trained at predicting the source task (HTER) and used as is to predict on the target task (MQM), more advanced representations can help improve its performance (rows (2) *vs.* (b)). However, both variants are usually outperformed by the baseline model (LR-QEfeat) on predicting the proportion of errors, apart from EN-DE NMT.

Second, when trained from scratch on MQM annotated data, the BERT-BiRNN model is significantly outperformed by our base BiRNN model across all language pairs and types of translation (rows (3) *vs.* (c)). While we previously observed the benefit of using advanced representations from BERT when at least 10,000 training datapoints are available (see Table 5), we now observe degraded performances when the number of training set is lower than 4,000 datapoints.

Third, when trained on HTER data and adapted

	EN-DE$_{NMT}$	EN-LV$_{NMT}$	EN-DE$_{PBMT}$	EN-LV$_{PBMT}$	DE-EN$_{PBMT}$	EN-CS$_{PBMT}$
(2) BiRNN-HTER	0.290	0.436	0.347	0.416	0.505	0.480
(a) LM-BiRNN-HTER	0.372	0.443	0.395	0.384	0.495	0.476
(b) BERT-BiRNN-HTER	**0.390**	**0.561**	**0.612**	**0.520**	**0.641**	**0.537**

Table 5: Absolute **Pearson's** r correlation between actual and **predicted HTER scores**, for the HTER data introduced in Table 1: **(2)** default BiRNN model trained on HTER data – **(a)** BiRNN model with the weights of each source and target encoders pre-trained in a language modelling fashion using the additional resources of the QE shared task at WMT'18 – **(b)** BiRNN model with token-level representations extracted from a pre-trained multilingual base cased BERT model. Measurements not significantly outperformed by any other overall, are underlined. Significance is computed with Hotelling-Williams test (Williams, 1959).

	EN-DE$_{NMT}$	EN-LV$_{NMT}$	EN-DE$_{PBMT}$	EN-LV$_{PBMT}$	DE-EN$_{PBMT}$	EN-CS$_{PBMT}$
(1) LR-QEfeat	0.152 ±0.06	0.404 ±0.19	0.585 ±0.02	0.471 ±0.06	0.329 ±0.02	0.635 ±0.02
(2) BiRNN-HTER	0.297 ±0.04	0.003 ±0.09	0.146 ±0.06	0.110 ±0.05	0.113 ±0.07	0.426 ±0.05
(b) BERT-BiRNN-HTER	0.211 ±0.03	0.220 ±0.04	0.467 ±0.04	0.302 ±0.05	0.311 ±0.09	0.175 ±0.03
(3) BiRNN-MQM	**0.584** ±0.04	**0.542** ±0.05	**0.619** ±0.05	**0.583** ±0.03	**0.606** ±0.08	**0.757** ±0.01
(c) BERT-BiRNN-MQM	0.227 ±0.05	0.343 ±0.07	0.445 ±0.02	0.451 ±0.05	0.276 ±0.06	0.461 ±0.05
(4) BiRNN-MQM$_{TL}$	**0.575** ±0.04	**0.596** ±0.06	**0.644** ±0.02	**0.612** ±0.03	**0.594** ±0.02	**0.787** ±0.03
(d) BERT-BiRNN-MQM$_{TL}$	0.189 ±0.06	0.349 ±0.06	0.510 ±0.03	0.491 ±0.07	0.083 ±0.03	0.477 ±0.06

Table 6: Average absolute **Pearson's** r correlation between actual and **predicted MQM error proportions** across all folds in six combinations of MT models and language pairs: **(1)** feature-based baseline (LR-QEfeat) – **(2)** default BiRNN model trained on HTER data, and used as is – **(b)** BERT-BiRNN model trained on HTER data, and used as is – **(3)** BiRNN model trained from scratch on MQM annotated data – **(c)** BERT-BiRNN model trained from scratch on MQM annotated data – **(4)** BiRNN-MQM model trained with transfer-learning, *i.e.* trained on HTER data and adapted using MQM data. **(d)** BERT-BiRNN-MQM model trained with transfer-learning, *i.e.* trained on HTER data and adapted using MQM data. Measurements not significantly outperformed by any other overall, are underlined. Significance is computed with Hotelling-Williams test (Williams, 1959).

	EN-DE$_{NMT}$	EN-LV$_{NMT}$	EN-DE$_{PBMT}$	EN-LV$_{PBMT}$	DE-EN$_{PBMT}$	EN-CS$_{PBMT}$
(1) LR-QEfeat	0.112 ±0.01	0.157 ±0.10	0.161 ±0.01	0.114 ±0.01	0.115 ±0.00	0.175 ±0.01
(2a) BiRNN-HTER	0.117 ±0.01	0.523 ±0.01	0.250 ±0.01	0.460 ±0.01	0.605 ±0.03	0.333 ±0.01
(b) BERT-BiRNN-HTER	0.117 ±0.01	0.249 ±0.01	0.184 ±0.01	0.146 ±0.00	0.206 ±0.01	0.294 ±0.01
(3) BiRNN-MQM	**0.093** ±0.01	**0.108** ±0.01	**0.157** ±0.01	**0.110** ±0.01	**0.097** ±0.00	**0.152** ±0.01
(c) BERT-BiRNN-MQM	0.113 ±0.01	0.121 ±0.01	0.189 ±0.01	0.128 ±0.02	0.120 ±0.01	0.204 ±0.01
(4) BiRNN-MQM$_{TL}$	**0.094** ±0.01	**0.102** ±0.01	**0.158** ±0.01	**0.108** ±0.01	**0.110** ±0.00	**0.145** ±0.01
(d) BERT-BiRNN-MQM$_{TL}$	0.116 ±0.01	0.123 ±0.01	0.178 ±0.01	0.116 ±0.01	0.137 ±0.01	0.207 ±0.02

Table 7: Average absolute **RMSE** between actual and **predicted MQM error proportions** across all folds in six combinations of MT models and language pairs: **(1)** feature-based baseline (LR-QEfeat) – **(2)** default BiRNN model trained on HTER data, and used as is – **(b)** BERT-BiRNN model trained on HTER data, and used as is – **(3)** BiRNN model trained from scratch on MQM annotated data – **(c)** BERT-BiRNN model trained from scratch on MQM annotated data – **(4)** BiRNN-MQM model trained with transfer-learning, *i.e.* trained on HTER data and adapted using MQM data. **(d)** BERT-BiRNN-MQM model trained with transfer-learning, *i.e.* trained on HTER data and adapted using MQM data. Measurements not significantly outperformed by any other overall, are underlined. Significance is computed with Hotelling-Williams test (Williams, 1959).

using MQM data (rows (4) *vs.* (d)), we observe that the performance of the BERT-BiRNN model slightly improve compared to training from scratch on MQM data (row (c)) across all language pairs but EN-DE$_{NMT}$ and DE-EN$_{PBMT}$. For the latter, we even observe a significant drop in the performance of the model. There is no obvious explanations for that, so we hope that further experiments would help us to understand the reasons behind it. On the one hand, this confirms that fine-tuning deep architectures such as BERT to extract advanced token level representation is a challenging task when only a few training instances is available. On the other hand, we saw the benefit of using advanced representation from pre-trained models such as BERT, and plan to continue working towards that research direction.

7 Conclusions

We introduced a new task of predicting the proportion of actual errors in a translated sentence as an alternative to the commonly used noisy estimate HTER. The reported results from using inductive transfer-learning are particularly encouraging considering the simplicity of our BiRNN model. Our transfer-learning method helps to train models which are better at predicting the proportion of actual errors for different language pairs and translation systems, compared to models trained on the target task only.

However, whereas we were expecting to observe significant gains with the use of more advanced token-level pre-trained representations (here from BERT), we report drastic degradation in performances for this configuration when re-purposing the QE models via transfer-learning. These somewhat counter-intuitive results are an indication that further work can be done in this area to refine our transfer-learning approach, as the use of large scale pre-trained representations has become a common practice in NLP applications, including QE.

In addition to this, we plan in furture to estimate the quality of machine translation using more fine-grained MQM annotations for subsentence-level QE.

Acknowledgements

This work was supported by the Bergamot project (EU H2020 Grant No. 825303).

References

Blatz, John, Erin Fitzgerald, George Foster, Simona Gandrabur, Cyril Goutte, Alex Kulesza, Alberto Sanchis, and Nicola Ueffing. 2004. Confidence estimation for machine translation. In *COLING*.

Bojar, Ondrej, Christian Buck, Chris Callison-Burch, Christian Federmann, Barry Haddow, Philipp Koehn, Christof Monz, Matt Post, Radu Soricut, and Lucia Specia. 2013. Findings of the 2013 Workshop on Statistical Machine Translation. In *Eighth Workshop on Statistical Machine Translation*, WMT, pages 1–44, Sofia, Bulgaria.

Bojar, Ondrej, Christian Buck, Christian Federmann, Barry Haddow, Philipp Koehn, Johannes Leveling, Christof Monz, Pavel Pecina, Matt Post, Herve Saint-Amand, Radu Soricut, Lucia Specia, and Aleš Tamchyna. 2014. Findings of the 2014 workshop on statistical machine translation. In *Ninth Workshop on Statistical Machine Translation*, WMT, pages 12–58, Baltimore, Maryland.

Bojar, Ondřej, Rajen Chatterjee, Christian Federmann, Barry Haddow, Matthias Huck, Chris Hokamp, Philipp Koehn, Varvara Logacheva, Christof Monz, Matteo Negri, Matt Post, Carolina Scarton, Lucia Specia, and Marco Turchi. 2015. Findings of the 2015 Workshop on Statistical Machine Translation. In *Proceedings of the Tenth Workshop on Statistical Machine Translation*, pages 1–46, Lisbon, Portugal, September.

Bojar, Ondřej, Rajen Chatterjee, Christian Federmann, Yvette Graham, Barry Haddow, Matthias Huck, Antonio Jimeno Yepes, Philipp Koehn, Varvara Logacheva, Christof Monz, Matteo Negri, Aurelie Neveol, Mariana Neves, Martin Popel, Matt Post, Raphael Rubino, Carolina Scarton, Lucia Specia, Marco Turchi, Karin Verspoor, and Marcos Zampieri. 2016. Findings of the 2016 conference on machine translation. In *Proceedings of the First Conference on Machine Translation*, pages 131–198, Berlin, Germany, August.

Bojar, Ondřej, Rajen Chatterjee, Christian Federmann, Yvette Graham, Barry Haddow, Shujian Huang, Matthias Huck, Philipp Koehn, Qun Liu, Varvara Logacheva, Christof Monz, Matteo Negri, Matt Post, Raphael Rubino, Lucia Specia, and Marco Turchi. 2017. Findings of the 2017 conference on machine translation (wmt17). In *Proceedings of the Second Conference on Machine Translation, Volume 2: Shared Task Papers*, pages 169–214, Copenhagen, Denmark, September.

Cho, Kyunghyun, Bart Van Merriënboer, Caglar Gulcehre, Dzmitry Bahdanau, Fethi Bougares, Holger Schwenk, and Yoshua Bengio. 2014. Learning phrase representations using rnn encoder-decoder for statistical machine translation. *arXiv preprint arXiv:1406.1078*.

Cohn, Trevor and Lucia Specia. 2013. Modelling annotator bias with multi-task gaussian processes: An application to machine translation quality estimation. In *51st Annual Meeting of the Association for Computational Linguistics*, ACL, pages 32–42, Sofia, Bulgaria.

Devlin, Jacob, Ming-Wei Chang, Kenton Lee, and Kristina Toutanova. 2018. Bert: Pre-training of deep bidirectional transformers for language understanding. *arXiv preprint arXiv:1810.04805*.

Fonseca, Erick, Lisa Yankovskaya, André FT Martins, Mark Fishel, and Christian Federmann. 2019. Findings of the WMT 2019 Shared Tasks on Quality Estimation. In *Proceedings of the Fourth Conference on Machine Translation (Volume 3: Shared Task Papers, Day 2)*, pages 1–10.

Graham, Yvette. 2015. Improving evaluation of machine translation quality estimation. In *Proceedings of the 53rd Annual Meeting of the Association for Computational Linguistics and the 7th International Joint Conference on Natural Language Processing (Volume 1: Long Papers)*, pages 1804–1813, Beijing, China, July. Association for Computational Linguistics.

Howard, Jeremy and Sebastian Ruder. 2018. Universal language model fine-tuning for text classification. *arXiv preprint arXiv:1801.06146*.

Ive, Julia, Frédéric Blain, and Lucia Specia. 2018. DeepQuest: a framework for neural-based quality estimation. In *Proceedings of COLING 2018, the 27th International Conference on Computational Linguistics: Technical Papers*, Santa Fe, new Mexico.

Kepler, Fábio, Jonay Trénous, Marcos Treviso, Miguel Vera, António Góis, M Amin Farajian, António V Lopes, and André FT Martins. 2019. Unbabel's participation in the wmt19 translation quality estimation shared task. *arXiv preprint arXiv:1907.10352*.

Kim, Hyun, Jong-Hyeok Lee, and Seung-Hoon Na. 2017. Predictor-estimator using multilevel task learning with stack propagation for neural quality estimation. In *Proceedings of the Second Conference on Machine Translation*, pages 562–568.

Kingma, Diederik P and Jimmy Ba. 2014. Adam: A method for stochastic optimization. *arXiv preprint arXiv:1412.6980*.

Lample, Guillaume and Alexis Conneau. 2019. Cross-lingual language model pretraining. *arXiv preprint arXiv:1901.07291*.

Lommel, Arle Richard, Aljoscha Burchardt, and Hans Uszkoreit. 2014. Multidimensional quality metrics (MQM): A framework for declaring and describing translation quality metrics. *Tradumàtica: tecnologies de la traducció*, 0(12):455–463, 12.

Nair, Vinod and Geoffrey E Hinton. 2010. Rectified linear units improve restricted boltzmann machines. In *Proceedings of the 27th international conference on machine learning (ICML-10)*, pages 807–814.

Pan, Sinno Jialin, Qiang Yang, et al. 2010. A survey on transfer learning. *IEEE Transactions on knowledge and data engineering*, 22(10):1345–1359.

Quirk, Christopher. 2004. Training a sentence-level machine translation confidence measure. In *LREC*. Citeseer.

Shah, Kashif and Lucia Specia. 2016. Large-scale multitask learning for machine translation quality estimation. In *Conference of the North American Chapter of the Association for Computational Linguistics: Human Language Technologies*, pages 558–567, San Diego, California.

Snover, Matthew, Bonnie Dorr, Richard Schwartz, Linnea Micciulla, and John Makhoul. 2006. A study of translation edit rate with targeted human annotation. In *Proceedings of association for machine translation in the Americas*, volume 200.

Specia, Lucia, Marco Turchi, Nicola Cancedda, Marc Dymetman, and Nello Cristianini. 2009. Estimating the Sentence-Level Quality of Machine Translation Systems. In *13th Annual Conference of the European Association for Machine Translation*, EAMT, pages 28–37, Barcelona, Spain.

Specia, Lucia, Gustavo Paetzold, and Carolina Scarton. 2015. Multi-level translation quality prediction with quest++. *Proceedings of ACL-IJCNLP 2015 System Demonstrations*, pages 115–120.

Specia, Lucia, Kim Harris, Frédéric Blain, Aljoscha Burchardt, Viviven Macketanz, Inguna Skadina, Matteo Negri, , and Marco Turchi. 2017. Translation quality and productivity: A study on rich morphology languages. In *Machine Translation Summit XVI*, pages 55–71, Nagoya, Japan.

Specia, Lucia, Frédéric Blain, Varvara Logacheva, Ramón Astudillo, and André F. T. Martins. 2018. findings of the wmt 2018 shared task on quality estimation. In *Proceedings of the Third Conference on Machine Translation, Volume 2: Shared Task Papers*, pages 702–722, Belgium, Brussels, October.

Specia, Lucia. 2011. Exploiting objective annotations for measuring translation post-editing effort. In *Proceedings of the 15th Conference of the European Association for Machine Translation*, pages 73–80.

Ueffing, Nicola and Hermann Ney. 2007. Word-level confidence estimation for machine translation. *Computational Linguistics*, 33(1):9–40.

Williams, Evan James. 1959. *Regression Analysis*, volume 14. Wiley, New York, USA.

Yosinski, Jason, Jeff Clune, Yoshua Bengio, and Hod Lipson. 2014. How transferable are features in deep neural networks? In *Advances in neural information processing systems*, pages 3320–3328.

Zoph, Barret, Deniz Yuret, Jonathan May, and Kevin Knight. 2016. Transfer learning for low-resource neural machine translation. In *Proceedings of the 2016 Conference on Empirical Methods in Natural Language Processing*, pages 1568–1575.

Fine-Grained Error Analysis on English-to-Japanese Machine Translation in the Medical Domain

Takeshi Hayakawa
Graduate School of Information
Science and Technology,
Osaka University, Osaka, Japan
ASCA Corporation, Osaka, Japan
hayakawa.takeshi@ist.osaka-u.ac.jp

Yuki Arase
Graduate School of Information
Science and Technology,
Osaka Un iversity, Osaka, Japan
arase@ist.osaka-u.ac.jp

Abstract

We performed a detailed error analysis in domain-specific neural machine translation (NMT) for the English and Japanese language pair with fine-grained manual annotation. Despite its importance for advancing NMT technologies, research on the performance of domain-specific NMT and non-European languages has been limited. In this study, we designed an error typology based on the error types that were typically generated by NMT systems and might cause significant impact in technical translations: "Addition," "Omission," "Mistranslation," "Grammar," and "Terminology." The error annotation was targeted to the medical domain and was performed by experienced professional translators specialized in medicine under careful quality control. The annotation detected $4,912$ errors on $2,480$ sentences, and the frequency and distribution of errors were analyzed. We found that the major errors in NMT were "Mistranslation" and "Terminology" rather than "Addition" and "Omission," which have been reported as typical problems of NMT. Interestingly, more errors occurred in documents for professionals compared with those for the general public. The results of our annotation work will be published as a parallel corpus with error labels, which are expected to contribute to developing better NMT models, automatic evaluation metrics, and quality estimation models.

1 Introduction

We performed a manual annotation of translation errors using fine-grained error typology in domain-specific neural machine translation (NMT) of Japanese and English language pairs. Although several approaches have been proposed to evaluate the performance of NMT, it has been commonly presented as scores of automatic evaluation, and detailed analysis of problems in NMT is limited. Previous studies (Specia et al., 2017; Kepler et al., 2019) annotated errors in MT outputs; however, they targeted only on a general domain and European languages. Detailed error detection is essential, especially in the domain-specific settings, where tiny mistakes, such as incorrect translation of a technical term, leads to significant misunderstanding.

To tackle this problem, we performed an annotation-based analysis of errors that occurred in NMT for a specific technical domain. Professional translators annotated types and positions of errors that occurred in translation from English to Japanese. The error typology was designed based on an existing framework, Multidimensional Quality Metrics (MQM) (Lommel et al., 2014), which was customized to our study. We selected medicine as the domain field because medical translation is in growing demand in the society to enrich healthcare information, which requires highly specific domain expertise. Recent issues regarding public health, such as the pandemic

Martins, Moniz, Fumega, Martins, Batista, Coheur, Parra, Trancoso, Turchi, Bisazza, Moorkens, Guerberof, Nurminen, Marg, Forcada (eds.)
Proceedings of the 22nd Annual Conference of the European Association for Machine Translation, p. 155–164
Lisboa, Portugal, November 2020.

of coronavirus disease 2019, highlight demands on sharing correct and understandable information throughout the world including Asian countries. We prepared five medical contents with English-to-Japanese translation data using state-of-the-art NMT systems. As a result, $4,912$ errors in five types were annotated on $2,480$ sentences. We also analyzed the annotation results in detail to reveal distributions and characteristics of errors produced by current NMT systems.

The results of annotation will be published as a parallel corpus with error labels. This is the first corpus of error annotation (1) on domain-specific and (2) on English-to-Japanese NMT outputs. Such corpora annotating errors in machine translation (MT) are valuable resources to understand problems in NMT models, develop automatic evaluation metrics, and estimate the quality of machine translation (Blatz et al., 2004).

2   Related Work

Our annotation corpus is based on the error typology that conforms to structured categories of quality metrics for translation quality. Previous studies employed a few different typologies, such as MQM and SCATE (Smart Computer-aided Translation Environment) (Tezcan et al., 2017). Among them, MQM is one of the most common frameworks for quality assessment of human translation. The framework of the typology in our study also refers to the MQM.

QT21 Consortium has published post edited and error annotated data for machine translations in four languages: Czech, English, German, and Latvian (Specia et al., 2017) based on MQM. This data just included languages in Europe, and prior studies that used the MQM have evaluated translation of European languages (Klubička et al., 2018; Van Brussel et al., 2018). Our corpus in English to Japanese will add a useful resource of annotation. The shared task of quality estimation in the Conference on Machine Translation (WMT) has also employed the MQM for document-level quality estimation since 2018. Approaches of quality estimation tasks with MQM include word-level annotation (Specia et al., 2018) and the estimation of MQM score

with prediction models (Kepler et al., 2019). Nonetheless, there has been a limited resource for domain-specific translation (Rigouts Terryn et al., 2019), which is indispensable to develop an evaluation strategy for appropriateness of word choice in the technical context.

3   Error Typology & Development of Annotation Guidelines

In this study, we developed customized error-typology criteria for the evaluation of domain-specific NMT. Our typology was based on MQM. The major error categories in MQM are "Accuracy," "Fluency," "Design," "Locale convention," "Style," "Terminology," and "Verity," of which subcategories are defined for a specific type of incorrectness.

We selected and customized several error subtypes in the original MQM for annotation that were applicable to translations by NMT systems. In this paper, we focused on subtypes that annotation results confirmed as the major problems of the current NMT systems, namely, "Addition," "Omission," and "Mistranslation" from "Accuracy;" "Terminology;" and "Grammar" from "Fluency;" as summarized in Table 1.

We customized these error subtypes to handle domain specificity and the Japanese language due to different systems of grammar and sociolinguistic register from Western languages. The following sections describe these error types and guidelines given to annotators to identify each error.[1]

3.1   Addition and Omission

Over- and under-generations are typical errors in NMT because of the lack of a mechanism to explicitly track source-sentence coverage (Tu et al., 2016). These were categorized as "Addition" and "Omission," respectively.

"Addition" and "Omission" errors occur only in target and source sentences, respectively. Our guidelines instructed annotators to assign a label of "Addition" on the word(s) of target sentence that does not semantically correspond to any word in the source sentence. On the contrary, the guidelines required to attach a label of "Omission" to the word(s) of

---

[1] The guidelines are attached to our corpus to be released.

Error type	Description of error	Annotation span	Annotation side
Addition	The target text includes text not present in the source.*	Word/Phrase	Target
Omission	Content is missing from the translation that is present in the source.*	Word/Phrase	Source
Mistranslation	The target content does not accurately represent the source content.*	Word/Phrase	Source
Terminology	The target text is not suitable in terms of the domain of document.	Word/Phrase	Source
Grammar	Syntax or function words are presented incorrectly.	Word/Phrase	Target

Table 1: Error typology (Descriptions with asterisks are cited from MQM Issue Types.)

the source sentence of which translation did not appear in the target sentence. In cases that grammatical words specific to the target language were not translated, this kind of errors was not considered as "Omission" but as "Grammar."

Relevant error subtypes to "Addition" and "Omission" defined in MQM are "Over-translation" and "Under-translation." These apply to a translation output that is more or less specific than the source sentence, respectively. Different from human translation, our annotation results revealed that Over- and Under-translations were far infrequent in current NMT systems.

3.2 Mistranslation

This type of error refers to the semantic difference between words or phrases in source and target sentences. The wrong choice of meaning in polysemous words was included in the "Mistranslation," as well as incorrect translation.

The guidelines instructed annotators to assign a label of "Mistranslation" on the word(s) of a source sentence that was incorrectly translated. We distinguished mistranslation and terminological errors to identify domain-specific errors. Hence, inappropriate use of words with the same or similar meaning in translation was categorized to "Mistranslation," as discussed below.

3.3 Terminology

We incorporated the appropriateness of word choice to our typology as the category of "Terminology," to ensure applicability to measure the domain specificity of translation outputs. We defined terminology errors as a translated word that was unsuitable to the description in the medical field, even though the meaning of the word was acceptable in the translation of the general domain.

The "Mistranslation" and "Terminology" errors were distinguished whether a translation output correctly reflected the meaning of the source sentence.

Our guidelines instructed annotators that the errors in the choice of technical terms with similar meaning should be labeled as "Terminology," instead of "Mistranslation." On the contrary, if a translated word(s) was semantically incorrect, the word was assigned the "Mistranslation" label, irrespective of the presence of "Terminology" error. The labels of "Terminology" were placed on the source sentence.

For example, the word "primary" means "most important" or "coming earliest" in general, but when used as "primary tumor" in the context of medicine, it means "the originally developed cancer cells in the body." Hence, translating "primary tumor" as "most important tumor" is regarded as "Terminology" error, while translating into "new tumor" is regarded as a "Mistranslation" error.

3.4 Grammar

Grammatical errors in English-to-Japanese translation affect the quality of translation more significantly. This is because grammatical errors in English-to-Japanese translation are characterized by incorrect understanding of syntax, which often changes the meaning of source sentence. For example, incorrect translation output of Japanese particles may be presented as the conversion between subjective and objective cases.

The guidelines instructed annotators to assign a label of "Grammar" on the target sentence for the errors of incorrect syntax representation, grammatically inappropriate output, and wrong order of words.

3.5 Sides of Annotation

The right-most column of Table 1 shows whether annotations were conducted on source sentences or translation outputs for each error type. Since MQM has not determined which side of the sentence the error should be labeled, in this study, we defined the annotation side specific to each error type. "Addition" and "Omission" were marked on target and source sides, respectively, because their occurrences are one-sided. As for "Mistranslation" and "Terminology," we attached the labels on only source sentences for simplicity of the annotation process. The alignment of these source words and phrases to the target-side is subject to our future work. The "Grammar" error was marked in the target-side because annotators can identify ungrammatical parts in a sentence, but it was hard to determine what caused these grammatical errors.

4 Annotation Setup

In this section, we describe the annotation procedure and resources used to perform the annotation.

4.1 Annotation Procedure

First of all, annotators were instructed to read through the annotation guidelines before starting the annotation and to be familiar with the standards. The annotators were provided triples of a source sentence, reference translation, and MT output, and worked for annotation through October to December 2018. The annotators identified spans of word/phrase/sentence presenting errors and assigned the corresponding error types as labels on the sentence level. Annotation could be overlapped on the same spans for different types of errors.

4.2 NMT Systems

Distribution of the occurrence of errors might depend on a certain translation system; therefore, we used multiple systems to reduce the effect of such dependency. We used state-of-the-art NMT systems for English-to-Japanese translation available in October 2018 at the time of annotation, as described below.

- Google's neural machine translation system (GNMT) (Wu et al., 2016)

- NICT's neural machine translation system (Wang et al., 2018) (NICT NMT)

The preliminary investigation confirmed that there was no substantial difference between both systems. The corpus-level BLEU scores of GNMT and NICT NMT were 36.20 and 35.70, respectively. The mean normalized Levenshtein distance[2] of each sentence between references and translation outputs of GNMT and NICT NMT were 0.64 ($\pm$0.23) and 0.64 ($\pm$0.22), respectively. Paired bootstrap resampling test (Koehn, 2004) showed no significant difference in the two NMT systems for corpus BLEU ($p = 0.17$) as well as Student's t-test for normalized Levenshtein distance ($p = 0.63$); hence, we did not distinguish their outputs in the later processes.

4.3 Corpora for Annotation

Our annotation corpus consisted of $2,480$ sentences from the medical/pharmaceutical domain in English. We collected the sentences from five sources of documents with different types: MSD Manual Consumer Version (Merck and Co., Inc., 2015a), MSD Manual Professional Version (Merck and Co., Inc., 2015c), New England Journal of Medicine (Massachusetts Medical Society, 2019), Journal of Clinical Oncology (American Society of Clinical Oncology, 2019), and ICH guidelines (Singh, 2015). Two versions of MSD manual are for the same topics of medical information but differentiated by expertise levels of contents: Professional Version includes highly technical terms for health professionals, and Consumer Version is written for the general population without domain knowledge.[3] New England Journal of Medicine and Journal of Clinical Oncology are standard academic journals of medicine. ICH guidelines consist of international regulations for pharmaceutical manufacturing processes. The source sentences were randomly extracted from each document.

We obtained the Japanese translation of the corpora from the two NMT systems. The set of target sentence was produced by randomly

---

[2] Levenshtein distance divided by the length of reference and target sentences.

[3] Therefore, the Consumer and Professional versions consist of comparable sentences with different expertise levels but are not exactly parallel.

Source	Expertise Level	Number of sentences	Mean number of words per sentence	BLEU	normalized Levenshtein distance
MSD Manual Consumer Version	General	580	17.88 ($\pm$7.89)	31.58	0.66 ($\pm$0.23)
MSD Manual Professional Version	Professional	560	19.50 ($\pm$9.48)	38.93	0.59 ($\pm$0.24)
New England Journal of Medicine	Professional	420	29.96 ($\pm$17.12)	37.65	0.62 ($\pm$0.21)
Journal of Clinical Oncology	Professional	420	22.99 ($\pm$12.09)	36.29	0.69 ($\pm$0.24)
ICH guidelines	Professional	500	18.08 ($\pm$5.77)	33.67	0.66 ($\pm$0.21)
Total		2,480	21.20 ($\pm$11.61)	35.95	0.64 ($\pm$0.23)

Table 2: Statistics of language resource for annotation

selecting each translated sentence from the two NMT outputs (50% for each), to prepare bilingual pairs of the 2,480 sentences. Table 2 shows the statistics of our annotation corpus.

These source sentences have corresponding Japanese versions, which were prepared by human translation with the professional review (Merck and Co., Inc., 2015d; Merck and Co., Inc., 2015b; Nankodo Co.,Ltd., 2019; American Society of Clinical Oncology, 2018; Pharmaceuticals and Medical Devices Agency, 2018). These Japanese versions were used as the reference translations.[4]

4.4 Annotators

To ensure the quality of annotation, we recruited three professional translators in the medical/pharmaceutical field. All the annotators were native Japanese translators with an academic background in biology or pharmacology. Year of translation experience ranged from three to eight years. The annotators identified errors and their types in an NMT output referring to corresponding source and reference translations.

5 Quality Control of Annotation

This kind of error annotation is inevitably subjective, because the ability to detect errors in translation depends on the level of expertise. In addition, determination of the type and span of errors should be contingent on the preference of each annotator, which may cause the variation of the annotation work.[5]

In this study, to collect reliable annotations alleviating such subjectivity, we conducted a pilot study and reconciliation of annotated labels.

5.1 Pilot Study

We performed a pilot study with the annotators using an independent data, consisted of 100 pairs of sentences.

Annotations on the pilot study were thoroughly reviewed by the authors and feedbacked to the annotators when there were misunderstandings of the guidelines. Also, questions raised by any annotator and the answers were shared to ensure that annotators have the same understanding of the task.

5.2 Reconciliation of Annotation

Once the annotators completed the annotation, they reviewed all the annotation results from the other annotators. They judged whether to accept or reject each annotation label. When two or more annotators voted to accept an annotation label, the corresponding annotation is retained, otherwise discarded.

The first annotation process identified 7,424 errors. The three annotators assigned 3,115 labels on average, with a standard deviation of 37.82. After the reconciliation process, the total number of errors with types was reduced to 4,912. Among these, 4,572 annotations were agreed by all the three annotators, and the rest 340 were agreed by two, which shows that our final annotation results are highly reliable. Note that 2,352 errors with the same labels and spans were consolidated as one error. Errors with overlapping span but with different labels were kept as independent annotations. Annotations on partially overlapping span with same error type were combined to one annotation that had larger span (e.g. Two annotations on "a condition" and "condition"

---

[4] Some of the Japanese articles in the MSD manual are comparable but not parallel translations because of difference in edition and local regulation. Therefore, we manually selected sentences ensuring the equivalence of the translation pairs.

[5] Due to this variation, a common metric to measure the agreement of annotations, i.e., Fleiss' Kappa, is not applicable.

were combined to that on "a condition.").

We confirmed that "Terminology," "Addition," and "Omission" errors were highly agreed (96.8%, 71.4%, and 64.1% of errors were accepted by at least two annotators). On the other hand, "Mistranslation" and "Grammar" errors had an opposite tendency (46.0% and 47.4% were accepted by at least two annotators). The disagreement of annotation separating "Mistranslation" and "Terminology" was effectively combined through the reconciliation work. The judgment of "Mistranslation" and "Terminology" errors tended to be more subjective, which caused disagreement. These results imply that the many cases of disagreement were reconciled as "Terminology" error, rejecting the annotation of "Mistranslation." In addition, annotators commented that "Addition" and "Omission" errors were harder to detect and large part of disagreement in these errors were due to oversight. Therefore, the reconciliation resulted in the high acceptance ratios.

5.3 Annotation Examples

Table 3 shows examples of annotation results after reconciliation, in which underlined phrases in the text indicate errors. The first case is an example of "Addition," in which the same words of "長期的な (long-term)" appear twice in the target sentence. The second appearance was annotated as "Addition." In the second case, the translation corresponding to the words "both of" in the source sentence is not included in the target sentence. This type of error was annotated as "Omission." The third and fourth cases represented "Terminology" errors. In the third case, the word "at 90 days" was used to mean a time point; however, the MT output referred to duration, and thus annotated as "Mistranslation." In the fourth case, "may" was used to express a possibility, which was not reflected in the target output. The fifth case is an example of "Grammar." In this case, the coordination in the source sentence means "low vitamin D intake or low calcium intake;" however, the translation in the target text means "low vitamin D, and calcium intake." This type of syntax error was annotated as "Grammar." The sixth and seventh cases represented "Terminology" errors. In the sixth case, "fluid" specifically had the mean-

ing of water, which was translated into a word suggesting general liquid. In the seventh case, the word "response" corresponded to several words in Japanese, and the selection of words was not correct to represent the reduction of cancer cells.

Both "Mistranslation" and "Terminology" are the issue of word choice; however, there is a substantial difference in the two error types, as presented in these examples. Our typology design allowed distinguishing these two error types in a specific domain by fine-grained annotation.

6 Analysis of Annotation Results

We conducted an in-depth analysis of annotation results from four perspectives:

- Frequency and distribution of errors in current NMT systems (Section 6.1),
- Possible factors affecting error occurrence (Section 6.2),
- Co-occurrence of errors to reveal dependence among error types (Section 6.3), and
- Correlation with conventional automatic metrics for machine translation evaluation to investigate their powers of the test (Section 6.4).

6.1 Error Distribution

The rate of error occurrence was 1.98 per sentence, with a standard deviation of 2.07. The rate of error occurrence per source word was 0.09. This means that, on average, NMT outputs included approximately two errors within one sentence, although the high standard deviation suggested that the distribution of the presence of errors was somewhat dispersed. As shown in Figure 1, most of the sentences had errors of five or less (94.60%), and 572 sentences (23.06%) had no error.

Table 4 shows the distribution of errors by error types. Errors in terms of "Terminology" accounted for more than one-third. The second-largest proportion was "Mistranslation" (22.78%) followed by "Grammar" errors (20.38%).

6.2 Factors affecting to Error Occurrence

We investigated possible factors that may affect the occurrence of errors in NMT outputs. Namely, we investigated the effects of

Error type	Source	Target	Reference
Addition	Even former athletes who stop exercising do not retain measurable <u>long-term</u> benefits.	運動をやめた元スポーツ選手でさえ、<u>長期的な</u> (long-term) 長期的な (long-term) 利益を維持することはできない。	元運動選手であっても、運動をやめてしまえば、その効果を長期間維持することはできません。
Omission	Regular exercise can improve <u>both of</u> these qualities.	通常の運動は、これらの性質を改善することができる。	定期的な運動によってその<u>両方</u> (both of) を向上させることができます。
Mistranslation	The primary end point was a composite of death, the need for dialysis, or a persistent increase of at least 50% from baseline in the serum creatinine level <u>at 90 days</u>.	主要なエンドポイントは、死亡、透析の必要性、または<u>90日間</u> (for 90 days) の血清クレアチニンレベルのベースラインからの少なくとも 50%の持続的な増加の複合物であった。	<u>90日の時点</u> (at 90 days) における死亡、透析の必要性、血清クレアチニン値のベースラインから 50% 以上の上昇の持続の複合を主要評価項目とした。
Mistranslation	When men with BPH urinate, the bladder <u>may not empty completely</u>.	BPH の男性が排尿すると、膀胱が完全に空になることはありません (will not empty)。	前立腺肥大症の男性が排尿する場合、膀胱が完全に空にならないことがあります (may not empty)。
Grammar	Aging, estrogen deficiency, low vitamin D or calcium intake, and certain disorders can decrease the amounts of the components that maintain bone density and strength.	老化、エストロゲン欠乏、<u>低ビタミンDまたはカルシウム摂取</u> (low vitamin D, and calcium intake)、およびある種の障害は、骨密度および強度を維持する成分の量を減少させる可能性がある。	加齢、エストロゲンの不足、<u>ビタミンDやカルシウムの摂取不足</u> (low vitamin D or calcium intake)、およびある種の病気によって、骨密度や骨の強度を維持する成分の量が減少することがあります。
Terminology	Maintaining adequate levels of <u>fluid</u> and sodium helps prevent heat illnesses.	十分な量の<u>液体</u> (liquid) とナトリウムを維持することは、熱病予防に役立ちます。	十分な<u>水分</u> (water) およびナトリウム値を維持することが、熱中症の予防に役立つ。
Terminology	The rate of any complete or partial <u>response</u> to cabozantinib, vandetanib, and sunitinib was 37%, 18%, and 22%, respectively.	カボザンチブ、バンデタニブ、およびスニチニブに対する完全または部分<u>応答</u> (answer) の割合は、それぞれ 37%、18%および 22%であった。	完全/部分<u>奏効</u> (response) 率は Cabozantinib 37%、Vandetanib 18%、および Sunitinib 22%であった。

Table 3: Examples of annotation results (Underlines indicate the errors with corresponding English translations in parentheses. Underlines and parentheses are for explanation and do not included in the actual annotation corpus.)

Subtype	Occurrence (%)	Mean per sentence (SD)
Addition	230 (4.68%)	0.09 (±0.40)
Omission	794 (16.16%)	0.32 (±0.73)
Mistranslation	1,119 (22.78%)	0.45 (±0.75)
Grammar	1,001 (20.38%)	0.40 (±0.74)
Terminology	1,768 (35.99%)	0.71 (±0.95)
Total	4,912 (100.00%)	1.98 (±2.07)

Table 4: Error occurrence based on the typology

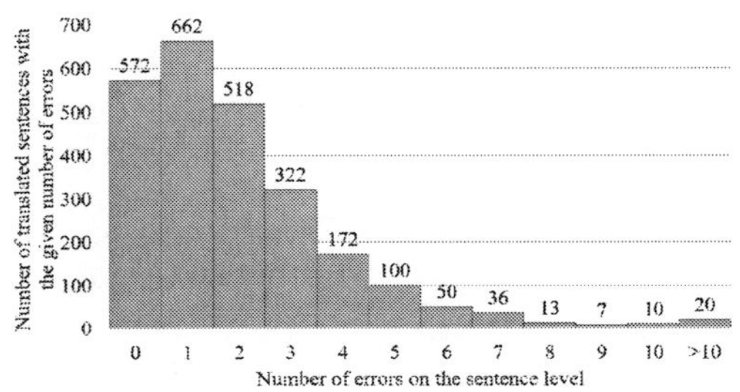

Figure 1: Distribution of errors in sentence ()

of source documents, and terminology.[6]

6.2.1 Length of Source Sentence

One of the most intuitive factors that affect the quality of NMT outputs is the length of the source sentence, i.e., longer sentences are more difficult to translate. As expected, source length was confirmed to have a high correlation with error occurrence. The correlation coefficients were $\rho = 0.65$ for the number of words in a sentence ($p < 0.0001$).

the length of source sentences, expertise level

---

[6] These are dependent factors for each other, but we independently investigated their effects for simplicity.

6.2.2 Effect of Expertise Levels of Documents

We assumed that sentences from documents for experts were more challenging for NMT systems due to discrepancies in terminologies from those of the general domain. Among the sources of our corpora, two versions of MSD Manuals were about the same topics of medical information but distinguished by the levels of expertise: the Consumer Version was targeted at the general population, and the Professional Version was at health professionals. Source sentences of the Professional Version and the Consumer Version had $2,819$ and $2,123$ unique words, respectively, of which overlapped presence was limited to 984 words.

The difference in error occurrence was summarized in Table 5. Overall, translations of the Professional Version had a larger number of errors $(1,108)$ than those of Consumer Version (770). Specifically, the errors of "Mistranslation," "Grammar," and "Terminology" were significantly more frequent on translations of Professional Version than on those of Consumer Version.[7] These results confirm our assumption that expertise levels of source documents negatively affect to the translation quality of current NMT systems.

6.2.3 Error Occurrence Dependent on Terms

Table 4 shows that the most common error types in NMT outputs are incorrect translations of terms, i.e., "Mistranslation" and "Terminology," which took up in total of 58.77% of errors. In this section, we further investigated what kind of words tend to cause these errors.

Table 6 ranks the most frequent words that were annotated as "Mistranslation" and "Terminology," respectively.[8] Frequent "Mistranslation" words included numbers and units ("days," and "months"), comparative words ("more," "less," and "versus"), and auxiliaries ("may"). In our analysis, these types of words more frequently produced incorrect translation than proper nouns, verbs, or other specific words in medicine. These words look simple

but require different translations depending on co-occurring words and the context.

"Terminology" errors list different types of words from "Mistranslation." The high-ranked words such as "primary" and "response" are polysemous in the domain of medicine, which was failed to translate correctly by NMT systems.

6.3 Co-occurrence of Error Types

In this section, we investigated the interaction between error types to examine if some errors tend to lead to other types of errors. To determine the tendency of co-occurrence of the errors, we computed correlation coefficients of combinations of error types.

Table 7 shows combinations of error types whose correlation coefficients were larger than 0.3. The highest co-occurrence was observed in the combination of "Addition" and "Omission." Notably, in the total of 176 occurrences of "Addition" errors, 100 (56.82%) were accompanied by "Omission" errors. The errors of "Addition" and "Omission" were typically caused by over-generation and under-generation in NMT, respectively. This result revealed that over and under generations affect each other; over-generation of unnecessary phrases may lead to under generation of necessary phrases, and vice versa.

It is reasonable that "Addition" and "Omission" co-occur with "Grammar" errors, because the insertion of unnecessary words or deletion of necessary words may corrupt grammatical structures. The other way around is also possible, i.e., source sentences that an NMT system fails to capture correct grammatical structures are difficult to translate, which results in "Addition" and "Omission" errors.

The high co-occurrence of these errors suggests that the common problems of machine translation may mutually have causal correlations.

6.4 Correlation with Automatic Metrics

Finally, we investigated the correlation between annotated errors and BLEU scores as the most commonly used automatic evaluation metric. Specifically, we calculated a correlation coefficient between the number of errors in a sentence and sentence BLEU score. In addition, we also calculated the correlation with

---

[7] Although a significant difference was also confirmed on "Addition," we omit it due to their small numbers of occurrences.

[8] Stop words, such as short function words and punctuation marks, were filtered out from the ranking for brevity.

Subtype	Occurrence		p-value
	Consumer	Professional	
	(Merck and Co., Inc., 2015a)	(Merck and Co., Inc., 2015c)	
Addition	26	46	0.0300
Omission	142	168	0.1071
Mistranslation	225	265	0.0489
Grammar	102	224	< 0.0001
Terminology	275	405	0.0001
Total	770	1, 108	

Table 5: Error occurrence by expertise levels of documents (Student t-test was used to calculate p-values)

Mistranslation		Terminology	
count	word	count	word
27	may	61	primary
15	more	33	response
14	days	33	common
12	less	28	survival
11	pneumonitis	28	outcome
10	rate	26	end
10	versus	22	point
9	common	19	fluid
9	therapy	18	active
9	months	17	benefit
9	active	17	therapy
8	falls	16	rate
7	medical	16	analysis
7	benefit	15	Secondary
7	drug	14	drug
7	ratio	14	overall
7	arms	14	ovarian
6	illness	14	studies
6	disease	13	outcomes
6	number	12	cancer

Table 6: Ranking of words with "Mistranslation" and "Terminology" errors

Error Combination	ρ	p value
Addition & Omission	0.43	< 0.0001
Omission & Grammar	0.35	< 0.0001
Addition & Grammar	0.31	< 0.0001

Table 7: Highly correlate error types ($\rho > 0.3$)

fairly simple metric, normalized Levenshtein distance between the translation outputs and reference translations as a baseline.

The correlation coefficient of error occurrence and sentence BLEU was $\rho = -0.18$ ($p < 0.0001$) while that of normalized Levenshtein distance was $\rho = 0.27$ ($p < 0.0001$). The sentence BLEU showed an even lower correlation than the normalized Levenshtein distance. This result indicates that sentence BLEU is not only ignorant of errors in translation output but also fails to evaluate the overall translation quality. Our annotation corpus contributes to design new automatic evaluation metrics that have the power to discriminate errors.

7 Discussion and Future Work

We performed the error analysis of NMT for the English and Japanese language pair in the medical domain, based on fine-grained and quality-controlled manual annotation.

In the analysis of detected 4, 912 errors on 2, 480 sentences, we found that the major errors in NMT were "Mistranslation" and "Terminology," rather than "Addition" and "Omission." The errors of "Addition" and "Omission" have been deemed typical in NMT as over-generation and under-generation, respectively; however, our results revealed that the semantic and terminology errors were more common in domain-specific technical documents. Interestingly, these errors were often observed in quantitative and polysemous words. This finding suggests future challenges in machine translation research targeting in the representation of numeric and multi-sense words.

We found more errors in documents for health-care professionals compared with those for the general public, specifically in terms of errors in "Grammar" and "Terminology." This finding encourages further research to improve the performance of NMT in documents that include sentences with complex syntax and highly-specialized technical terms.

The results of annotation will be published as a parallel corpus with detailed error labels, which is expected to be a valuable resource to improve NMT models, develop automatic evaluation metrics, and estimate qualities of machine translation. The limitations in current automatic evaluation metrics are partly attributable to insufficient understanding of the real performance of NMT systems. Furthermore, the dependence on the reference translation is problematic. The similarity to the reference does not necessarily represent the semantic accordance of the translation to the source sentence. Natural language is characterized by its ambiguity, such as multiple meanings and contextual implications, and thus translation should not have the unique correct answer. While verbatim similarly to the reference enforces a strict constraint, it does not ensure the actual quality of translation. Better estimation of translation quality should incorporate features reflecting the actual quality of translation, such as semantic accuracy and linguistic fluency.

We believe our corpus contributes to research on evaluation or estimation models of NMT performance to overcome these limitations. Essentially, it is a valuable resource for assessing the domain-specificity of translation outputs. As future works, we will develop quality estimation models using the corpus to allow fine-grained and domain-specific evaluation. Also, we will extend the annotation corpus in other domains and language pairs.

Acknkowlegement

This work was supported by NTT communication science laboratories.

References

American Society of Clinical Oncology. 2018. Journal of Clinical Oncology (Japanese Version). http://usaco.jcoabstracts.jp/contents/.

American Society of Clinical Oncology. 2019. Journal of Clinical Oncology. http://ascopubs. org/journal/jco/.

J. Blatz et al. 2004. Confidence estimation for machine translation. In COLING 2004: Proceedings of the 20th International Conference on Computational Linguistics, pages 315–321.

F. Kepler et al. 2019. Unbabel's participation in the WMT19 translation quality estimation shared task. In Proceedings of the Fourth Conference on Machine Translation, pages 78–84.

F. Klubička, A. Toral, V. M. Sánchez-Cartagena. 2018. Quantitative fine-grained human evaluation of machine translation systems: a case study on english to croatian. Machine Translation, 32(3):195–215.

P. Koehn. 2004. Statistical significance tests for machine translation evaluation. In Proceedings of the 2004 Conference on Empirical Methods in Natural Language Processing, pages 388–395.

A. Lommel, H. Uszkoreit, A. Burchardt. 2014. Multidimensional quality metrics (mqm): A framework for declaring and describing translation quality metrics. Tradumàtica, (12):0455–463.

Massachusetts Medical Society. 2019. The New England Journal of Medicine. https://www. nejm.org/.

Merck and Co., Inc. 2015a. MSD MANUAL Consumer Version. https://www.msdmanuals.com/ home/.

Merck and Co., Inc. 2015b. MSD MANUAL Consumer Version (Japanese Version). https://www.msdmanuals.com/ja-jp/.

Merck and Co., Inc. 2015c. MSD MANUAL Professional Version. https://www.msdmanuals. com/professional/.

Merck and Co., Inc. 2015d. MSD MANUAL Professional Version (Japanese Version). https://www.msdmanuals.com/ja-jp/.

Nankodo Co.,Ltd. 2019. The New England Journal of Medicine (Japanese Version). https://www. nejm.jp/.

Pharmaceuticals and Medical Devices Agency. 2018. ICH guidelines (Japanese Version). https://www.pmda.go.jp/int-activities/ int-harmony/ich/0070.html.

A. Rigouts Terryn et al. 2019. Pilot study on medical translations in lay language: Post-editing by language specialists, domain specialists or both? In Translating and the Computer 41. Editions Tradulex.

J. Singh. 2015. International conference on harmonization of technical requirements for registration of pharmaceuticals for human use. Journal of pharmacology & pharmacotherapeutics, 6(3):185.

L. Specia et al. 2017. Translation quality and productivity: A study on rich morphology languages. In Proceedings of Machine Translation Summit XVI, pages 55–71.

L. Specia et al. 2018. Findings of the wmt 2018 shared task on quality estimation. In Proceedings of the Third Conference on Machine Translation: Shared Task Papers, pages 689–709.

A. Tezcan, V. Hoste, L. Macken. 2017. Scate taxonomy and corpus of machine translation errors. In Trends in e-tools and resources for translators and interpreters, pages 219–244.

Z. Tu et al. 2016. Modeling coverage for neural machine translation. arXiv preprint arXiv:1601.04811.

L. Van Brussel, A. Tezcan, L. Macken. 2018. A fine-grained error analysis of nmt, smt and rbmt output for english-to-dutch. In Proceedings of the Eleventh International Conference on Language Resources and Evaluation (LREC 2018).

R. Wang et al. 2018. Sentence selection and weighting for neural machine translation domain adaptation. IEEE/ACM Transactions on Audio, Speech, and Language Processing, 26(10):1727–1741.

Y. Wu et al. 2016. Google's neural machine translation system: Bridging the gap between human and machine translation. arXiv preprint arXiv:1609.08144.

With or without you? Effects of using machine translation to write flash fiction in the foreign language

Nora Aranberri
IXA research group
University of the Basque Country UPV/EHU
`nora.aranberri@ehu.eus`

Abstract

The improvement in the quality of machine translation (MT) for both majority and minority languages in recent years is resulting in its steady adoption. This is not only happening among professional translators but also among users who occasionally find themselves in situations where translation is required or MT presents itself as a easier means to producing a text. This work sets to explore the effect using MT has in flash fiction produced in the foreign language. Specifically, we study the impact in surface closeness, syntactic and lexical complexity, and edits. Results show that texts produced with MT seem to fit closer to certain traits of the foreign language and that differences in the use of part-of-speech categories and structures emerge. Moreover, the analysis of the post-edited texts reveals that participants approach the editing of the MT output differently, displaying a wide range in the number of edits.

1 Introduction

In recent years, the quality of machine translation (MT) has greatly improved, and as a consequence, increasingly more users are adopting the technology. These users can have varying profiles. On the one hand, we find professional translators, and on the other hand, we have users who do not belong directly in the translation industry but still, occasionally, need translations. Among the latter, we can distinguish scenarios where MT is used in professional settings and scenarios where MT is used to reduce the translation effort in the private sphere.

A good few studies have been conducted on the impact of MT for professional translators but still numerous questions remain unanswered. Among others, this research has focused on analysing how translating using MT differs from translating from scratch and on ways to optimally provide the automated translation to these professionals. However, little research has been carried out on non-professional translators, even when freely available online systems have been providing automated translations for a long time, since 2006 in the case of Google Translate. This situation leaves us with little insight into what happens when non-specialists avail of MT.

The scarce research carried out on regular users has mainly focused on measuring the usefulness of MT for assimilation, that is, to facilitate comprehension. Nurminen (2018) reported that people are using MT increasingly more for gisting purposes and that they are prepared to accept different quality levels for comprehension and for publication.

Bowker (2009) and Bowker and Ciro (2015) focused their efforts on the Canadian context. In the former study, the author examined the potential acceptance of MT output by minority communities. She reported a positive attitude towards output that had undergone rapid post-editing for assimilation purposes but the need for at least full post-editing for texts intended for cultural preservation. The latter study analysed the usefulness of machine translation to make the Ottawa Public Library website more accessible to Spanish speakers. Authors reported that users would be willing to ac-

Martins, Moniz, Fumega, Martins, Batista, Coheur, Parra, Trancoso, Turchi, Bisazza, Moorkens, Guerberof, Nurminen, Marg, Forcada (eds.)
Proceedings of the 22nd Annual Conference of the European Association for Machine Translation, p. 165–174
Lisboa, Portugal, November 2020.

cept MT output, post-edited at different levels, for certain services.

Focusing on romance languages, another group of researchers studied MT in reference to the concept of intercomprehension, that is, the ability of speakers of different languages to understand one another (Martín, 2005; Martín Peris, 2011). Jordan-Nuñez, Forcada and Clua (2017) studied if users perceive MT output, non-native and native texts differently, and examined the usefulness of MT to improve comprehension in cases where native language texts would not be available. They highlighted that the efficiency seems to vary according to the level of specialisation of the texts, their domain and the MT system used.

Almost no research has been carried out on the effects of using MT to produce texts by regular users. The few efforts made in this area have mostly focused on the use of MT by non-native English speakers for academic publishing. Parra Escartín et al. (2017) studied five medical practitioners' papers and O'Brien, Simard and Goulet (2018) examined abstracts of ten scholars. Both studies found that whereas these professionals were able to correct and improve the MT output, their final versions still required further editing to be adequate for publication. Bowker and Ciro (2019) provide an overview of this user group and make a first attempt at establishing a framework for MT literacy for scholar communication. Further research in this line will prove essential to train different user groups in the optimal use of this technology, as non-language-specialists seem to be willing to accept low quality MT output when translating familiar topics (2014).

Within this context, the current work focuses on non-specialist users. We concentrate on using a series of metrics to compare texts produced by those users in the foreign language with and without MT. In particular, we aim to examine the effects of using MT in terms of accuracy, fluency and complexity. In the future this should be complemented with further qualitative analyses to account for word and word-sequence choices and editing.

2 Experimental set-up

2.1 Participants

A total of 40 participants from the Basque Country voluntarily got involved in the experiment, granting the permission to use their contributions for research purposes. All participants were students in the 19-25 age-range. As per the two official languages of the region, as can be seen in Figure 1, 85% report having Spanish as their mother tongue and Basque as a second language. The reported level of competence in both languages is similar, around 60% for Basque and 68% for Spanish, indicating a C1 level according to the CEFR[1]. The main difference is that while for Basque the remaining 40% report a B2 level, for Spanish, this is divided into B2 (25%) and C2 (7%). A clear difference between the languages is their reported use, which shows that while 75% report using Spanish more than 75% of the time, this range is only reported by 12% for Basque. Even so, it must be noted that the language of instruction of all participants is Basque.

Regarding the foreign language, English in this case, the reported level of competence is more widespread even when almost half classify themselves within the B2 level, and almost 40% within the B1 level. As expected, over 75% of the participants report using English less than 25% of the time. All in all, given their reported level of competence in their main and foreign languages, this group of participants proved adequate to study the impact of using MT to produce texts in a foreign language where their competence is low, starting from their language of instruction. Therefore, the foreign language is at the independent user level according to the CEFR, whereas their main language of instruction is at the proficient user level.

2.2 Tasks

This experiment aims to recreate a real scenario where a user avails of MT due to his/her lack of full competence in the foreign language. Considering that each user has a different language competence and style (even in their main languages), we decided to ask each of them to produce their own *source* texts. Also, as they would in a real context, we allowed them to use any language resource except MT to complete the tasks. This mainly involved online bilingual dictionaries and grammar-related sites.

Letting participants completely freely choose the text to write would have biased the results. Therefore, in order to make it possible to compare the results and draw conclusions from the work

[1]Common European Framework of Reference for Languages – Self-assessment Grid available at https://europass.cedefop.europa.eu/sites/default/files/cefr-en.pdf

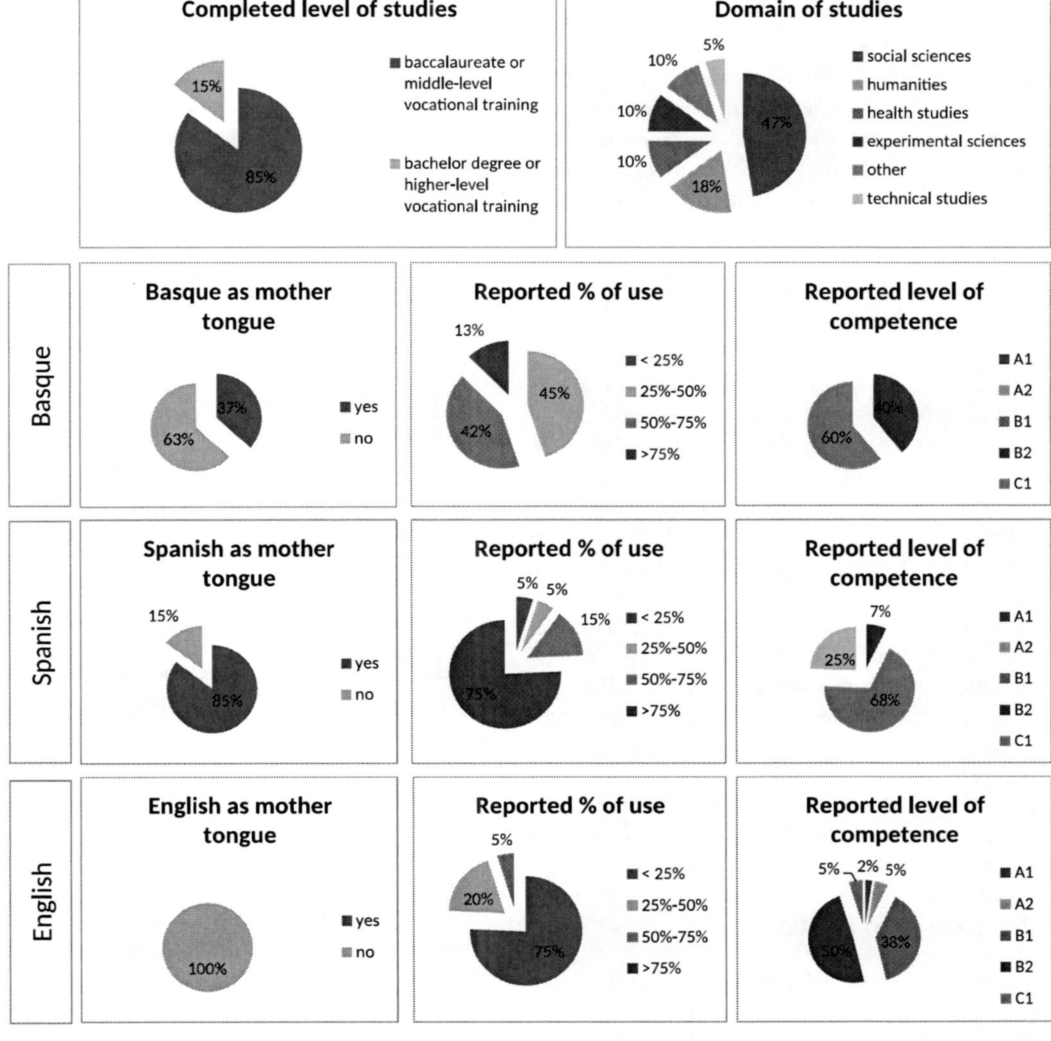

Figure 1: Studies- and language-related information of participants. Notice that legends for all possible answers have been displayed for the individual diagrams for easy comparison.

they performed, we set a guided task that aimed to somewhat define the genre, the domain and the length of the text to be produced, while still providing ample room for free contribution. Specifically, participants were asked to write a piece of flash fiction, that is, a short narrative with a full plot, a tool used successfully to promote writing within young adults (Batchelor and King, 2014). Aware of the effort of dealing with long texts in a foreign language, we asked participants to write texts of around 150 words. Also, the stories should be based on a storyboard.

The use of storyboards in linguistic research is widely accepted (Bochnak and Matthewson, 2015). Contrary to targeted storyboards which aim to elicit specific language, we opted for non-targeted storyboards, which aim to elicit language in general, and mainly, narratives (Burton and Matthewson, 2015). Storyboards would also help participants avoid the *blank page effect* when we asked them to come up with creative stories on the spot. We opted for persona-based scenarios (Cooper et al., 2003), which, according to Grudin and Pruitt (2002), are more effective, as the user may feel more represented in the storyline. We provided participants with hints about the setting, the actors and the goal or ending, and asked them to invent the actions and write a complete story (Kantola and Jokela, 2007; Rosson et al., 2002). The storyboards created for this experiment consisted of three vignettes: (1) the initial situation where the setting and the characters were presented, one of the characters being the participant, (2) a blank vignette representing the events and actions the participants would have to create, and (3) the final situation showing the setting and characters at the end of the story.

Given that the goal of the experiment was to compare the difference between writing texts in the foreign language from scratch and using MT, participants were asked to write two stories based on two storyboards. First, they wrote a piece of flash fiction in English. Secondly, they wrote another piece in Basque and edited its English MT output until they were satisfied with the final result. The participants worked on a customised web site where the different tasks were presented to them, with their respective storyboards and the MT version for their second text, which was obtained through the Google Translator API for the Basque–English pair. They were also asked to fill in an initial questionnaire about their studies and language competence and use, and to answer a final question to assess the level of help provided by the MT system. We also collected the users' permission to use their contribution through this site.

3 Analysis of results

The analysis presented here focuses on using a series of metrics to compare texts produced in both set-ups, (1) when participants write directly in the foreign language, English, and (2) when they start with their main working language, Basque, and edit the English MT output provided by Google's Translator. Many researchers in the area of language acquisition have long considered complexity, accuracy and fluency as the three main aspects that capture the foreign language competence (see Housen and Kuiken (2009) for a discussion). In reference to the experiment that concerns us, this means that texts can be classified as better or worse depending on how natural and native-like they sound, the grammatical and lexical inaccuracies they contain, and the complexity of the structures included. Therefore, for this study, we concentrate on the surface closeness, syntactic and lexical complexity, and edit types, while also considering participants' view on usefulness. We report count averages together with the standard deviations, and when possible, calculate statistical significance of the differences (with a 95% confidence interval) using the unpaired Student's t-test to compare the two set-ups (significance is marked with a †).

3.1 Does the text produced using MT look more like English?

Let us focus on accuracy and fluency first. Not fully competent speakers tend to make grammatical mistakes and awkward lexical choices to a higher or lower degree. However, if the source text presented to a machine translation system is written by a fully competent speaker, that is, it includes no errors and it is natural, given the features of current neural MT systems, the system is expected to produce a fluent output with no (or few) grammatical mistakes and a (relatively) sound lexical choice. Whereas meaning issues might be present, that is, the output does not express exactly what the user intended to, the machine translated texts tend to comply with the target language features to a considerable degree.

To observe whether participants produced a text that reads more like English with or without using MT, we measured textual closeness through perplexity. In machine translation research, perplexity is used to measure how much a translation fits a language model. In other words, a low perplexity indicates that a text is similar to the language model used as reference. For that reason, we compared the perplexities of the texts produced by the participants in both set-ups in order to find out which of the two displayed sequences that were closer to the language model. We calculated the perplexity at word- and POS-level to account for the surface form but also for a structure-level form, albeit shallow.

To train the language models, we first compiled the corpus for English. Whereas languages tend to comply with overall linguistic features that are intrinsic to them, it is also true that each textual genre brings its own linguistic features and distributions with it. Therefore, if we are to measure surface closeness, it is only fair that the language model is trained using texts that belong to the same genre as the one produced by the participants. As, to our best knowledge, no purposely-build corpus of flash fiction is readily available for NLP testing, we

Level	Original English		Post-edited English		
	Average	Std. dev.	Average	Std. dev.	t-test
token-based	177.480	135.268	**111.380**	35.002	t(78) = 2.992, p = 0.0037[†]
POS-based	10.582	5.813	**7.765**	1.080	t(78) = 3.013, p = 0.0035[†]

Table 1: Results for the perplexity metric

opted for a main news corpus and complemented it with a number of popular classic literature works that recount stories, tales and adventures. Specifically, we used the first 3 million lines (74.7 million words) of the News Crawl corpus 2019, shuffled and deduplicated,[2] and a 0.5-million-word corpus of stories obtained through the Gutenberg Project.[3]

We built the language models with Modified Kneser-Ney smoothing and no pruning. For the word-level model, we considered n-grams up to n = 5. For the POS-level model, we used *ixa-pipes* (Agerri et al., 2014) to annotate the English corpus at POS level first. The tool uses the Penn Treebank POS tagset, which consist of 36 classes. For the language model, we considered n-grams up to n = 6 and had to assign default parameters to singletons, even when they are not present in the PoS-annotated corpus.

The results show that, on average, perplexities are lower for the post-edited texts both at word-level and at POS-level, the difference being statistically very significant (see Table 1). This indicates that participants obtain surface sequences that are more similar to English when using MT than when they produce the texts directly in that language. Even when MT systems have been reported to produce output that has interference from the source language (Toral, 2019), it seems that participants' competence in the foreign language (independent users according to the CEFR) is not sufficient to outperform the MT system. Participants might be producing either word sequences that are closer to their main languages or word sequences that are incorrect in the foreign language and therefore, using MT seems to help them produce texts that read more like English.

Let us now turn to the complexity aspect. Leaving aside the correctness and appropriateness of the language, a feature that displays the language competence of a person is his or her ability to exploit the linguistic resources available in a language. In line with this, we would expect that texts written directly in the main language of a person display more diversity, precision and information density as the person has the ability and resources necessary for it. Machine translation could prove beneficial in overcoming the more limited access to resources in the foreign language by allowing users to produce the text in their main language, for which their linguistic ability is high, and obtain a foreign language text that mirrors that complexity. Whereas MT is not designed to help with other discourse or textual factors such as adequacy, coherence or cohesion, which are properties linked to cross-linguistic communicative strategies, it does provide the opportunity to assist with the selection and sentence-level arrangement of linguistic elements.

To observe whether differences emerged in the texts produced by the participants in terms of complexity, we looked at a number of lexical and syntactic features. We considered that lexical complexity could be accounted for in terms of frequency, diversity and density. To obtain those measures, we used the information provided by the *ixa-pipes* through the *Analhitza* application (Otegi et al., 2017) to obtain the relevant counts for types, tokens and POS.

We first considered POS frequency. This analysis was intended to observe whether certain grammatical categories were more or less present when writing in one of the two set-ups. For example, we can argue that nouns and verbs are more basic and central categories than adjectives and adverbs, which are used to modify the former. Similarly, pronouns, prepositions and conjunctions are considered to be more complex categories and a higher level of competence is required to use them.

By considering the POS proportions in both set-ups (see Table 2), we observe that some differences emerge. Whereas not significant differences were noticed for the more basic categories, it was interesting to see that the use of prepositions or subordinate conjunctions and pronouns was significantly higher when using MT.

We next considered lexical diversity, that is, the

---

[2]http://data.statmt.org/news-crawl/en/
[3]https://www.gutenberg.org/ - We used 9 books covering some of the works by Arthur Conan Doyle, Agatha Christie, the Grimm brothers, Mark Twain, and H.G. Wells.

POS	Original English		Post-edited English		
	Average	Std. dev.	Average	Std. dev.	t-test
nouns	18.809	3.630	20.010	2.247	$t(78) = 1.7792$, p = 0.0791
adjectives	4.408	1.986	4.341	1.666	$t(78) = 0.1635$, p = 0.8705
verbs	**22.896**	2.450	21.143	2.019	$t(78) = 3.4758$, p = 0.0008[†]
adverbs	5.222	1.898	5.726	1.713	$t(78) = 1.2451$, p = 0.2168
determiners	10.444	1.867	11.243	2.921	$t(78) = 1.4583$, p = 0.1488
prep. or sub. conj.	3.682	1.287	**4.949**	1.299	$t(78) = 4.3803$, p = 0.0001[†]
pronouns	12.209	2.422	**15.061**	2.192	$t(78) = 5.5214$, p = 0.0001[†]

Table 2: Results for the lexical proportion metric

POS	Original English		Post-edited English		
	Average	Std. dev.	Average	Std. dev.	t-test
nouns	0.722	0.088	0.697	0.091	$t(78) = 1.2825$, p = 0.2035
adjectives	0.910	0.137	0.942	0.0821	$t(78) = 1.2592$, p = 0.2117
verbs	0.580	0.068	0.601	0.0694	$t(78) = 1.3732$, p = 0.1736
adverbs	**0.752**	0.164	0.601	0.069	$t(78) = 5.3829$, p = 0.0001[†]
determiners	0.235	0.086	0.295	0.394	$t(78)= 0.9399$, p = 0.3502
prep. or sub. conj.	**0.300**	0.109	0.213	0.077	$t(78) = 4.0763$, p = 0.0001[†]
pronouns	0.470	0.098	0.444	0.099	$t(78) = 1.1933$, p = 0.2364
overall	0.530	0.039	0.553	0.054	$t(78) = 2.1830$, p = 0.0320[†]

Table 3: Results for the lexical variety metric

Original English		Post-edited English		
Average	Std. dev.	Average	Std. dev.	t-test
0.499	0.029	0.512	0.023	$t(78) = 2.2566$, p = 0.0268

Table 4: Results for the lexical density metric

variation in the words used to produce the text. We would expect that a lower competence would result in lower diversity, as the lexical resources available would be more limited. This should result in the use of more generic words and absence of synonyms and hyponyms.

However, lexical diversity as measured by the type/token ratio does not exhibit differences between the set-ups (see Table 3). In fact, it seems that the diversity for adverbs and prepositions or subordinate conjunctions is very significantly higher in the text written directly in English. There may be several reasons why this is the case. Firstly, we must remember that research has shown that MT output results in a lower lexical variety as compared with manual translation (Toral, 2019), which indicates a tendency to reduce the vocabulary produced. Secondly, we must also bear in mind that the task carried out by the participants involved writing a short piece of fiction. It is possible that, given the limited size of the text, lexi-cal diversity is not the optimum metric to account for complexity. A more qualitative analysis that considers the exact words used and their respective difficulty could shed light into these questions. It might be the case that the diversity is similar in both set-ups, but that the precision and difficulty of the words produced is greater in one over the other.

Finally, we considered the lexical density of the texts. It is possible that a higher competence in a language allows for condensing more details within the texts. In this case, the MT system would allow this condensation to be transferred to the final English text. A comparison between the average lexical density, measured as the ratio of the number of content words and the total number of words, displayed no significant differences (see Table 4). Again, a qualitative analysis would be necessary to pinpoint the reasons for this trend, which could be related to MT weakness or to the limited communicative competence of the partici-pants.

Semantic functions	Original English		Post-edited English		
	Average	Std. dev.	Average	Std. dev.	t-test
coordinating conjuctions	6.78	2.87	**10.03**	3.69	t(78) = 4.3978, p = 0.0001[†]
subordinating conjuctions	4.50	1.93	4.43	2.79	t(78) = 0.1397, p = 0.8893
manner	0.83	0.90	0.75	1.01	t(78) = 0.3509, p = 0.7266
purpose or reason	2.10	1.24	1.55	1.36	t(78) = 1.8944, p = 0.0619
temporal	8.13	3.34	8.73	3.30	t(78) = 0.8089, p = 0.4210
object	**21.30**	6.43	16.35	6.36	t(78) = 3.4607, p = 0.0009[†]
object complement	4.03	2.73	4.75	2.58	t(78) = 1.2205, p = 0.2260
predicative complement	**7.48**	2.79	5.63	2.74	t(78) = 2.9896, p = 0.0037[†]
noun modifier	38.38	10.57	**43.43**	10.72	t(78) = 2.1222, p = 0.0370[†]
adjectival or adverbial modifier	3.38	2.00	4.10	2.35	t(78) = 1.4867, p = 0.1411
prepositional modifier	14.15	5.45	**20.48**	6.48	t(78) = 4.7236, p = 0.0001[†]
apposition	1.48	1.57	1.10	1.06	t(78) = 1.2537, p = 0.2137
n. of sentences	14.13	5.09	14.13	4.88	t(78) = 0.0000, p = 1.0000
sentence length	14.08	2.70	14.95	2.43	t(78) = 1.5234, p = 0.1317

Table 5: Results for the syntactic complexity metric

The study of the syntactic complexity was carried out focusing on the presence of certain structures in the text produced by the participants. As the language competence of a learner increases, the basic subject and predicate sentence structure gains intricacy, and additional elements, constituents and semantic roles start to be present.

In order to check whether differences existed in the texts produced in the set-ups, we examined the occurrence of a number of syntactic-semantic characteristics of the texts. Specifically, we focused on semantic dependency relations, which represent the grammatical function in terms of the role that each dependent element plays with respect to its head.

We automatically analysed the texts produced by participants using *ixa-pipes*, which provides a wrapper for the English dependency parser and semantic role labeller based on mate-tools (Björkelund et al., 2009; Vossen and others, 2016) and it is trained on the dependency structures as defined for the CoNLL-2008 Shared Task (Johansson, 2008). We selected 12 dependency relations (see Table 5) that signal complexity, such as the presence of coordinating and subordinating conjunctions, elements that indicate manner, purpose, reason or temporal modifiers, prepositional modifier or adjectival and adverbial modifiers. It is expected that the number of these complex relations will be higher in the texts written using MT because participants were able to express themselves more competently in the language of instruction.

The results in Table 5 show the average occurrence of each type of relation in both set-ups.

Whereas the rates for most relations do not seem to vary, several differences surface. The post-edited texts display a significantly higher presence of coordinating conjunctions, nouns modifiers and prepositional modifiers. Also, the presence of objects and predicative complements is higher when writing directly in the foreign language. However, we must concede that the latter are often compulsory elements required by transitive verbs, whereas modifiers and conjunction can be freely used to produce more elaborate text. As a result, we could argue that writing in their language of instruction and using MT to translate it into the foreign language is allowing participants to produce more complex structures to a certain degree.

3.2 How do users approach the MT version?

The fact that MT might prove useful in obtaining a more fluent and complex text in the foreign language does not guarantee that the produced text will be error-free and absolutely natural-sounding, or that it will express exactly what the user intended. MT is still imperfect and users still have to perform an additional step before they can consider the text finished: post-editing. In order to fully identify the effects MT has in foreign language text production, it is necessary to analyse what users do with the MT output. Are they able to identify errors and awkward sequences introduced by the system? Can they measure to what extent the system is expressing what they originally intended? Are they aware of the impact the nuances introduced by the system may produce on readers?

As a first step toward identifying user editing

Metric	Average	Std. dev.
TER	9.69	8.43
number of edits	24.02	23.59
insertions	4.88	7.19
deletions	6.25	6.82
substitutions	11.40	11.60
shifts	1.53	1.92

Table 6: Edit information calculated by the TER metric

behaviour, we used edit distance measurements as calculated by TER. Given the shared foreign language competence of the participants, and the characteristics imposed on the text by the task description (text genre, initial and final settings and characters, length considerations), we assumed that the quality of the source texts was rather similar, which should, in turn, result in MT output of rather similar quality, allowing some room for comparison.

As we can observe in Table 6, the average TER value is close to 10, which is a rather good score for the metric, indicating that participants did not consider that a high number of changes were necessary to improve the MT output. The reasons for this can vary. On the one hand, it is possible that the MT quality was very good, and therefore, no changes were necessary. However, it is also possible that the MT output was imperfect but the participants were not sufficiently competent to improve the output, or even identify mistakes.

Nevertheless, it is interesting to consider the standard deviation, which indicates a rather dissimilar behaviour among participants. A closer inspection showed that 12.5% did not introduce any change in the MT output, whereas 20% modified more than one in every five words. Therefore, we can argue that the approach followed to edit the MT output was diverse. The total edits performed and its standard deviation also reflect this trend. Whereas we see the average at 24.02 edits, the standard deviation is extremely high at 23.59.

It is worth noting that changes introduced by the users may originate from diverse needs and also lead to different outcomes. Just to mention a few, we identified cases where editing was performed to adjust the meaning expressed by the MT output to the originally intended (see Example 1), to make stylistic changes – with various results (see Example 2), or even with the intention of improving the MT output but introducing errors (see Example 3).

Example 1: Required meaning adjustments.
Basque source: *Plater bat jan eta beste bat ateratzen zuen.*
MT output: He ate one dish and took another.
Post-editing: When one dish was finished she served another.

Example 2: Stylistic changes.
Basque source: *Udako oporrak ziren.*
MT output: It was a summer vacation.
Post-editing: This story happened in a summer holiday.

Example 3: Introduction of errors.
Basque source: *Zer esango diot?*
MT output: What will I say?
Post-editing: What will I told her?

Even when we must remember that the optimisation logic used by the TER metric does not always match the linguistic intuition used by users when editing text, it is worth considering the edit types calculated by the metric. We see that shifts were, by far, the less frequent, which indicates that the MT system output the information in an acceptable order for the participants. Insertions and deletions remained at around 5-6 on average, and substitutions were twice as frequent at 11.40 on average.

The observed results reveal the complexity of the editing behaviour in this type of set-up and, albeit out of the scope of the present analysis, call for a comprehensive manual analysis of the edits to shed light into behavioural patterns.

3.3 How do participants view machine translation?

Let us finally address participants' perception of MT usefulness. After performing both tasks, participants were asked to assess how much the MT system made the task easier for them. In a scale of 1-5, where 1 is not at all and 5 is completely, participants rated the usefulness of the MT system to produce short fiction narratives at 3.95 on average, with a standard deviation of 0.95. This clearly shows the positive attitude towards the technology.

Participants reporting a very positive attitude towards machine translation emphasised that they greatly valued that the MT output provided them with the translation of words that were unknown to them and that the system dealt with verb tenses and forms properly for them. They also claimed that the MT system showed them translations they would have never considered, as they differed considerably from the original structure or use of words, allowing them to learn alternative ways to express their ideas. While they acknowledged the difference between Basque and English in terms of *how things are said*, they conceded that they produce foreign language texts that follow their main language's patterns. These participants noted that they had to make few changes, which involved either correcting errors or adjusting the meaning.

Participants who were more critical towards MT tended to acknowledged its value and then added the negative aspects encountered during the task. Among their complains, worries and regrets were the fact that the MT service was not interactive, that they could keep parts of the output but had to modify others, that the meaning was sometimes distorted, and that the system was unable to handle irony or identify specific intents. It was interesting to read a comment conceding the lack of competence in the foreign language to properly assess the quality of the MT output.

4 Conclusions

Given the increase in the translation quality provided by automatic systems, the option of using online freely available systems to produce text in a language in which we are not fully competent by exploiting our main language is more and more appealing. With this in mind, this work analyses the effects of using MT when writing flash fiction in the foreign language.

To examine this, we asked participants, who were advanced users of Basque (language of instruction) and independent users of English (foreign language), to write two pieces of flash fiction of around 150 words each, with and without using MT. We compared features of the stories produced in each set-up with the aim to examine the effect of starting the writing process in a language in which the participants were competent and having an MT system provide them with a preliminary translation. Specifically, we aimed to observe whether MT can help to produce a text that sounds more English, and whether it can increase the complexity of the text. To that end, we compared word- and POS-level perplexities, lexical proportions, diversity and density, and the frequency of semantic relations that involve complex structures.

Results suggest that using MT participants produced final foreign language texts that followed English word- and POS-sequences more closely, indicating a higher fluency. We also observed that the proportion of pronouns and prepositions or subordinate conjunctions was higher in this set-up, even when no significant difference was observed in lexical variety and density. Dependency relations, in turn, revealed that the frequency of noun and prepositional modifiers, as well as coordinating conjunctions was also significantly higher. Overall, we can conclude that the texts produced using MT display certain traits that are typical of better quality texts.

We also considered the post-editing work of the participants. By examining TER scores and edits counts, we discovered that the participants approach the MT output differently. While it is true that the edit-distance is rather low in general, some make no changes to the output, whereas others change over 20% of the words, with most staying somewhere in between. Finally, it was encouraging to learn that participants perceived that the MT system was useful for the task (it obtained a score of 3.9 on average in a 1–5 scale), which shows the advance of MT quality for Basque and the positive attitude towards the technology.

While this research has revealed a number of interesting features from a quantitative perspective, further research into the actual lexical choice in each of the set-ups is now necessary to highlight differences in terms of lexical precision and difficulty between set-ups. Also, what remains to properly account for is the level of proficiency participants show in addressing MT output. Interesting results would be provided by research reporting on the elements that prompt users to introduce changes and on the impact these have at a linguistic level but also from the reader's perspective. Complementary research on the linguistic characteristics of the texts and user performance could also shed light into second language acquisition processes and teaching opportunities, as well as guide MT development.

Acknowledgements

The research leading to this work was partially funded by the Spanish MEIC and MCIU (UnsupNMT TIN2017-91692-EXP and DOMINO PGC2018-102041-B-I00, co-funded by EU FEDER), and the BigKnowledge project (BBVA foundation grant 2018).

References

Agerri, Rodrigo, Josu Bermudez, and German Rigau. 2014. Ixa pipeline: Efficient and ready to use multilingual nlp tools. In *Ninth International Conference on Language Resources and Evaluation, May 26-31, Reykjavik, Iceland*, pages 3823–3828.

Aranberri, Nora, Gorka Labaka, A Diaz de Ilarraza, and Kepa Sarasola. 2014. Comparison of post-editing productivity between professional translators and lay users. In *Proceeding of AMTA Third Workshop on Post-editing Technology and Practice, October 22-26, Vancouver, Canada*, pages 20–33.

Batchelor, Katherine E. and April King. 2014. Freshmen and five hundred words. *Journal of Adolescent & Adult Literacy*, 58(2):111–121.

Björkelund, Anders, Love Hafdell, and Pierre Nugues. 2009. Multilingual semantic role labeling. In *Proceedings of the Thirteenth Conference on Computational Natural Language Learning: Shared Task, June 4-5, Boulder, Colorado*, pages 43–48.

Bochnak, M Ryan and Lisa Matthewson. 2015. *Methodologies in semantic fieldwork*. Oxford University Press, USA.

Bowker, Lynne and Jairo Buitrago Ciro. 2015. Investigating the usefulness of machine translation for newcomers at the public library. *Translation and Interpreting Studies. The Journal of the American Translation and Interpreting Studies Association*, 10(2):165–186.

Bowker, Lynne and Jairo Buitrago Ciro. 2019. *Machine translation and global research: Towards improved machine translation literacy in the scholarly community*. Emerald Group Publishing.

Bowker, Lynne. 2009. Can machine translation meet the needs of official language minority communities in Canada? A recipient evaluation. *Linguistica Antverpiensia, New Series–Themes in Translation Studies*, (8):123–155.

Burton, Strang and Lisa Matthewson. 2015. Targeted construction storyboards in semantic fieldwork. In M. Ryan Bochnak, Lisa Matthewson, editor, *Methodologies in semantic fieldwork*, chapter 5, pages 135–156. Oxford University Press, USA.

Cooper, Alan, Robert Reimann, and Hugh Dubberly. 2003. *About face 2.0: The essentials of interaction design*. John Wiley & Sons, Inc.

Grudin, Jonathan and John Pruitt. 2002. Personas, participatory design and product development: An infrastructure for engagement. In *Proceedings of the Participatory Design Conference, June 23-25, Malmo, Sweden*, pages 144–161.

Housen, Alex and Folkert Kuiken. 2009. Complexity, accuracy, and fluency in second language acquisition. *Applied linguistics*, 30(4):461–473.

Johansson, Richard. 2008. Dependency syntax in the conll shared task 2008.

Jordan-Nuñez, Kenneth, Mikel L. Forcada and Steve Clua. 2017. Usefulness of MT output for comprehension – analysis from the point of view of linguistic intercomprehension. In *Proceedings of MT Summit XVI, Sep. 18-22, Nagoya, Japan*, pages 241–253.

Kantola, Niina and Timo Jokela. 2007. SVSb: simple and visual storyboards: developing a visualisation method for depicting user scenarios. In *Proceedings of the 19th Australasian conference on Computer-Human Interaction: Entertaining User Interfaces, November 28-30, Adelaide, Australia*, pages 49–56.

Martín Peris, Ernesto. 2011. La intercomprensión: concepto y procedimientos para su desarrollo en las lenguas románicas. *Y. Ruiz de Zarobe y L. Ruiz de Zarobe, La lectura en lengua extranjera, London: Portal Editions*, pages 246–270.

Martín, Ernesto. 2005. *EuroComRom-los siete tamices: un fácil aprendizaje de la lectura en todas las lenguas románicas;[con CD-ROM; español-català-français-italiano-português-româna-galego-occitan]*. Shaker.

Nurminen, Mary and Niko Papula. 2018. Gist MT users: A snapshot of the use and users of one online MT tool. In *Proceedings of the 21st Annual Conference of the European Association for Machine Translation, May 28-30, Alacant*, pages 199–208.

Otegi, Arantxa, Oier Imaz, Arantza Díaz de Ilarraza, Mikel Iruskieta, and Larraitz Uria. 2017. Analhitza: a tool to extract linguistic information from large corpora in humanities research. *Procesamiento del lenguaje natural*, 58:77–84.

O'Brien, Sharon, Michel Simard, and Marie-Josée Goulet. 2018. Machine translation and self-post-editing for academic writing support: Quality explorations. In Moorkens, J. et al., editor, *Translation Quality Assessment*, pages 237–262. Springer.

Parra Escartín, Carla, Sharon O'Brien, Marie-Josée Goulet, and Michel Simard. 2017. Machine translation as an academic writing aid for medical practitioners. In *MT Summit XV, Sep. 18-22, Nagoya, Japan*, pages 254–267.

Rosson, Mary Beth, John M Carroll, and Natalie Hill. 2002. *Usability engineering: scenario-based development of human-computer interaction*. Morgan Kaufmann.

Toral, Antonio. 2019. Post-editese: an exacerbated translationese. In *Proceedings of MT Summit XVII, August 19-23, Dublin, Ireland*, pages 273–281.

Vossen, Piek et al. 2016. Newsreader: Using knowledge resources in a cross-lingual reading machine to generate more knowledge from massive streams of news. *Knowledge-Based Systems*, 110:60–85.

Intelligent Translation Memory Matching and Retrieval
with Sentence Encoders

Tharindu Ranasinghe◇, Constantin Orăsan♡ and Ruslan Mitkov◇
◇Research Group in Computational Linguistics, University of Wolverhampton, UK
♡Centre for Translation Studies, University of Surrey, UK
{t.d.ranasinghehehettiarachchige, r.mitkov}@wlv.ac.uk
c.orasan@surrey.ac.uk

Abstract

Matching and retrieving previously translated segments from a Translation Memory is the key functionality in Translation Memories systems. However this matching and retrieving process is still limited to algorithms based on edit distance which we have identified as a major drawback in Translation Memories systems. In this paper we introduce sentence encoders to improve the matching and retrieving process in Translation Memories systems - an effective and efficient solution to replace edit distance based algorithms.

1 Introduction

Translation Memories (TMs) are "structured archives of past translations" which store pairs of corresponding text segments[1] in source and target languages known as "translation units" (Simard, 2020). TMs are used during the translation process in order to reuse previously translated segments. The original idea of TMs was proposed more than forty years ago when (Arthern, 1979) noticed that the translators working for the European Commission were wasting valuable time by re-translating (parts of) texts that had already been translated before. He proposed the creation of a computerised storage of source and target texts which could easily improve the performance of translators and that could be part of a computer-based terminology system. Based on this idea,

many commercial TM systems appeared on the market in the early 1990s. Since then the use of this particular technology has kept growing and recent studies show that it is used on regular basis by a large proportion of translators (Zaretskaya et al., 2018).

Translation Memories systems help translators by continuously trying to provide them with so-called matches, which are translation proposals retrieved from its database. These matches are identified by comparing automatically the segment that has to be translated with all the segments stored in the database. There are three kinds of matches: exact, fuzzy and no matches. Exact matches are found if the segment to be translated is identical to one stored in the TM. Fuzzy matches are used in cases where it is possible to identify a segment which is similar enough to the one to be translated, and therefore, it is assumed that the translator will spend less time editing the translation retrieved from the database than translating the segment from scratch. No matches occur in cases where it is not possible to identify a fuzzy match (i.e. there is no segment similar enough to the one to be translated to be worth using its translation).

TMs distinguish between fuzzy matches and no matches by calculating the similarity between segments using a similarity measure and comparing it to a threshold. Most of the existing TM systems rely on a variant of the edit distance as the similarity measure and consider a fuzzy match when the edit distance score is between 70% and 95%.[2] The main justification for using

---

[1]Segments are typically sentences, but there are implementations which consider longer or shorter units.

[2]It is unclear the origin for these value, but they are widely used by translators. Most of the tools allow translators to customise the value of this threshold according to their needs. Translators use their experience to decide which value for the

Martins, Moniz, Fumega, Martins, Batista, Coheur, Parra, Trancoso, Turchi, Bisazza, Moorkens, Guerberof, Nurminen, Marg, Forcada (eds.)
Proceedings of the 22nd Annual Conference of the European Association for Machine Translation, p. 175–184
Lisboa, Portugal, November 2020.

this measure is the fact that edit distance can be easily calculated, is fast, and is largely language independent. However, edit distance is unable to capture correctly the similarity between segments when different wording and syntactic structures are used to express the same idea. As a result, even if the TM contains a semantically similar segment, the retrieval algorithm will not be able to identify it in most of the cases.

Researchers tried to address this shortcoming of the edit distance metric by employing similarity metrics that can identify semantically similar segments even when they are different at token level. Section 2 discusses some of the approaches proposed so far. Recent research on the topic of text similarity employed methods that rely on deep learning and various vector based representations used in this field (Ranasinghe et al., 2019b; Tai et al., 2015; Mueller and Thyagarajan, 2016). One of the reasons for this is that calculating the similarity between vectors is more straightforward than calculating the similarity between texts. It is easy to calculate how close or distant two vectors are by using well understood mathematical distance metrics. In addition, deep learning based methods proved more robust in numerous NLP applications.

In this paper we propose a novel TM matching and retrieval method based on the Universal Sentence Encoder (Cer et al., 2018) which has the capability to capture semantically similar segments in TMs better than methods based on edit distance. We selected the Universal Sentence Encoder as our sentence encoder since it outperforms other sentence encoders like Infersent (Conneau et al., 2017) in many Natural Language Processing tasks including Semantic Retrieval (Cer et al., 2018). Also the recently release of Multilingual Universal Sentence Encoder [3] is available on 16 different languages (Yang et al., 2019). Since we are planning to expand our research to other language pairs than the English - Spanish pair investigated in this paper, the multilingual aspect of the Universal Sentence Encoder can prove very useful.

The rest of the paper is organised as follows. Section 2 briefly describes several approaches used to improve the matching and retrieval in TMs. Section 3 contains information about the

settings of the experiments carried out in this paper. It includes the experiments that were done for semantic textual similarity tasks comparing the Universal Sentence Encoder and edit distance. The same section also presents the results of the experiments on real world TMs. Section 4 discusses the results and describes future research directions. The implementation of the methods presented in this paper is available on Github.[4]

2   Related Work

Despite being the most used tools by professional translators, Translation Memories have rarely been criticised because of the quality of the segments they retrieve. Instead, quite often the requests from translators focus on the quality of the user interface, the need to handle different file formats, their speed and possibility of working in the cloud (Zaretskaya et al., 2018). Most of the current work on TMs is focused on the development of addons like terminology managers and plugins which integrate machine translation engines, as well as project management features (Gupta et al., 2016). Even though retrieval of previously translated segments is a key feature in a TM system, this process is still very much limited to edit-distance based measures.

Researchers working on natural language processing have proposed a number of methods which try to improve the existing matching and retrieval approaches used by translation memories. However, the majority of these approaches are not suitable for large TMs, like the ones normally employed by professional translators or were evaluated on very small number of segments. Planas and Furuse (1999) extend the edit distance metric to incorporate lemmas and part-of-speech information when calculating the similarity between two segments, but they test their approach on less than 150 segments from two domains using two translation memories with less than 40,000 segments in total. Lemmas and part-of-speech information is also used in (Hodász and Pohl, 2005) in order to improve matching, especially for morphologically rich languages like Hungarian. They also experiment with sentence skeletons in which NPs are automatically aligned between source and target. Unfortunately, the paper presents only preliminary results. Pekar and Mitkov (2007) show how it is possible to improve the quality of matching by taking into consideration the syntactic structure of sentences. Unfortunately, the evaluation is carried out on only a handful of carefully selected segments. Another method which performs matching at level of syntactic trees is proposed in (Vanallemeersch and Vandeghinste, 2014). The results presented in their paper are preliminary and the authors notice that tree matching method is "prohibitively slow".

More recent work has focused on incorporating paraphrases into the matching and retrieving algorithm (Utiyama et al., 2011; Gupta and Orasan, 2014; Chatzitheodorou, 2015). Utiyama et al. (2011) proposed a finite transducer which considers paraphrases during the matching. The evaluation shows that the method improves both precision and recall of matching, but it was carried out with only one translator and focused only on segments with exactly the same meaning. Gupta and Orasan (2014) proposed a variant of the edit distance metric which incorporates paraphrases from PPDB[5] using greedy approximation and dynamic programming. Both automatic evaluation and evaluation with translators show the advantages of using this approach (Gupta et al., 2016). Chatzitheodorou (2015) follows a similar approach. They use NooJ[6] to create paraphrases for the verb constructions in all source translation units to expand the fuzzy matching capabilities when searching in the TM. Evaluation with professional translators showed that the proposed method helps and speeds up the translation process.

To best of our knowledge, deep learning methods have not been used successfully in translation memories. Gupta (2016) presents an attempt to use ReVal, an evaluation metric that was successfully applied in the WMT15 metrics task (Gupta et al., 2015). Unfortunately, none of the neural based methods used are able to lead to better results than the standard edit distance.

3 Experiments and Results

As mentioned above, the purpose of this research is to find out whether it is possible to improve the quality of the retrieved segments by using the Universal Sentence Encoder (Cer et al., 2018) released by Google as the sentence encoder for this experiment. It comes with two versions: one trained with a Transformer encoder and the other trained with a Deep Averaging Network (DAN) (Cer et al., 2018). The transformer encoder architecture uses an attention mechanism (Vaswani et al., 2017) to compute context aware representations of words in a sentence and average those representations to calculate the embedding for the sentence. The DAN encoder begins by averaging together word and bi-gram level embeddings. Sentence embeddings are then obtained by passing the averaged representation through a feedforward deep neural network (DNN). The architecture of the DAN encoder is similar to the one proposed in (Iyyer et al., 2015).

The two architectures have a trade-off of accuracy and computational resource requirement. The one that relies on a Transformer encoder has higher accuracy, but is computationally more expensive. In contrast the one with DAN encoding is computationally less expensive, but has a slightly lower accuracy. For the experiments presented in this paper we used both architectures. The trained Universal Sentence Encoder model for English is available on TensorFlow Hub[7].

3.1 Experiments on STS

In order to assess the performance of the two architectures described in the previous section, we applied them on several Semantic Textual Similarity (STS) datasets and compared their results with those obtained when only edit distance is employed. This was done only to find out how well our unsupervised methods capture semantic textual similarity in comparison to a simple edit distance.

In this section we present the datasets that we used, the method and the results.

3.1.1 Dataset

We carried out these experiments using two datasets: the SICK dataset (Bentivogli et al., 2016) and SemEval 2017 Task 1 dataset (Cer et al., 2017) which we will refer to as STS2017 dataset.

The SICK data contains 9,927 sentence pairs with a 5,000/4,927 training/test split. Each pair is annotated with a relatedness score between 1 and 5, corresponding to the average relatedness judged by 10 different individuals. Table 1 shows a few examples from the SICK training dataset.

---

[5]http://paraphrase.org/
[6]https://nooj4nlp.net.cutestat.com/

[7]https://tfhub.dev/google/universal-sentence-encoder/4

Sentence Pair	Similarity
1. A little girl is looking at a woman in costume. 2. A young girl is looking at a woman in costume.	4.7
1. A person is performing tricks on a motorcycle. 2. The performer is tricking a person on a motorcycle.	2.6
1. Someone is pouring ingredients into a pot. 2. A man is removing vegetables from a pot.	2.8
1. Nobody is pouring ingredients into a pot. 2. Someone is pouring ingredients into a pot.	3.5

Table 1: Example sentence pairs from the SICK training data

The STS2017 test datset has 250 sentence pairs annotated with a relatedness score between [1,5]. As the training data for the competition, participants were encouraged to make use of all existing data sets from prior STS evaluations including all previously released trial, training and evaluation data [8]. Once we combined them all STS2017 had 8527 sentence pairs with a 8227/250 training/test split. Table 2 shows a few examples from the STS2017 dataset.

Sentence Pair	Similarity
1. Two people in snowsuits are lying in the snow and making snow angels. 2. Two angels are making snow on the lying children	2.5
1. A group of men play soccer on the beach. 2. A group of boys are playing soccer on the beach.	3.6
1. One woman is measuring another woman's ankle. 2. A woman measures another woman's ankle.	5.0
1. A man is cutting up a cucumber. 2. A man is slicing a cucumber.	4.2

Table 2: Example sentence pairs from the STS2017 data

3.1.2 Method

We followed a simple approach to calculate the similarity between two sentences. Each sentence was passed through the Universal Sentence Encoder to acquire the corresponding sentence vector for each sentence. The Universal Sentence Encoder uses a 512 dimension vector to represent a sentence. If the two vectors for two sentences X and Y are a and b correspondingly, we calculate the cosine similarity between a and b as of equation 1 and use that value to represent the similarity between the two sentences.

$$\cos(\mathbf{a}, \mathbf{b}) = \frac{\mathbf{ab}}{\|\mathbf{a}\|\|\mathbf{b}\|}$$
$$= \frac{\sum_{i=1}^{n} \mathbf{a}_i \mathbf{b}_i}{\sqrt{\sum_{i=1}^{n} (\mathbf{a}_i)^2} \sqrt{\sum_{i=1}^{n} (\mathbf{b}_i)^2}} \quad (1)$$

Simple edit distance between two sentences was used as a baseline. In order to convert

[8]http://alt.qcri.org/semeval2017/task1/

it to a similarity metric, we converted the edit distance between two sentences to the negative value and performed a min-max normalisation over the whole dataset to bring it to a value between 0 and 1.

3.1.3 Results

All the results were evaluated using the three evaluation metrics normally employed in STS tasks: Pearson correlation (τ), Spearman correlation (ρ) and Mean Squared Error (MSE). Table 3 contains results for SICK dataset and Table 4 for STS2017 dataset.

Algorithm	τ	ρ	MSE
DAN Encoder	0.761	0.708	0.514
Transformer	0.780	0.721	0.426
Edit Distance	0.321	0.422	3.112

Table 3: Results for SICK dataset

Algorithm	τ	ρ	MSE
DAN Encoder	0.744	0.708	0.612
Transformer	0.723	0.721	0.451
Edit Distance	0.360	0.481	2.331

Table 4: Results for STS2017 dataset

As shown in Tables 3 and 4 both architectures of Universal Sentence Encoder outperform edit distance significantly in all three evaluation metrics for both datasets. This is not surprising given how simple edit distance is, but reinforces our motivation to use better methods to capture semantic similarity in translation memories. Table 5 shows some of the example sentences where Universal Sentence Encoder architectures showed promising results against the baseline - edit distance.

As can be seen in table 5 both architectures of Universal Sentence Encoder handle semantic textual similarity better than edit distance in many cases where the word order is changed in two sentences, but the meaning remains same. This detection of similarity even when the word order is changed will be important in segment matching and retrieval in TMs.

3.2 Experiments on Translation Memories

In this section we present the experiments we conducted on TMs using the Universal Sentence Encoder. First we introduce the dataset that

Sentence 1	Sentence 2	GOLD	ED	Transf.	DAN
Israel expands subsidies to settlements	Israel widens settlement subsidies	1.0000	0.0214	0.8524	0.8231
A man plays the guitar and sings.	A man is singing and playing a guitar.	1.0000	0.0124	0.7143	0.7006
A man with no shirt is holding a football	A football is being held by a man with no shirt	1.0000	0.0037	0.9002	0.8358
EU ministers were invited to the conference but canceled because the union is closing talks on agricultural reform, said Gerry Kiely, a EU agriculture representative in Washington.	Gerry Kiely, a EU agriculture representative in Washington, said EU ministers were invited but canceled because the union is closing talks on agricultural reform.	1.0000	0.1513	0.7589	0.7142

Table 5: Examples of sentence pairs where Universal Sentence Encoder performed significantly better than edit Distance in the STS task. GOLD column shows the score assigned by humans, normalised between 0 and 1. The ED column shows the similarity obtained regarding the edit distance. Transf and DAN columns show the similarity obtained by Transformer and DAN architecture in Universal Sentence Encoder respectively.

we used and then we present the methodology employed and the evaluation results.

3.2.1 Dataset

In order to conduct the experiments, we used DGT-Translation Memory, a translation memory made publicly available by The European Commission's (EC) Directorate General for Translation, together with the EC's Joint Research Centre. It consists of segments and their professionally produced translations covering twenty-two official European Union (EU) languages and their 23 language-pair combinations (Steinberger et al., 2012). It is typically used by researches who work on TMs (Gupta et al., 2016; Baisa et al., 2015).

We used the English - Spanish segment pairs for the experiments, but our approach is easily adoptable to any language pair as long as there are embeddings available for the source language. We used data from the year 2018: *2018 Volume 1* was used as the translation memory and *2018 Volume 3* was used as the input segments. The translation memory we built from *2018 volume 1* had 230,000 segment pairs, whilst the *2018 volume 3* had 66,500 segment pairs which we used as input segments.

3.2.2 Method

We conducted the following steps for both architectures in Universal Sentence Encoder.

1. Calculated the sentence embeddings for each segment in the translation memory (230,000 segments) and stored the vectors in a AquilaDB[9] database. AquilaDB is a Decentralized vector database to store Feature Vectors and perform K Nearest Neighbour retrieval. It is build on top of popular Apache CouchDB[10]. A record of the database has 3 fields: source segment, target segment and source segment vector.

2. Calculated the sentence embedding for one incoming segment.

3. Calculated the cosine similarity of that embedding with each of the embedding in the database using equation 1. We retrieve the embedding that had the highest cosine similarity with the input segment embedding and retrieve the corresponding target segment for the embedding as the translation memory match. We used *'getNearest'* functionality provided by AquilaDB for this step.

The efficiency of the TM matching and retrieval is a key-factor for translators who are using them. Therefore, we first analysed the efficiency of each architecture in Universal Sentence Encoder. The results are shown in table 6. The experiments were carried out on an Intel(R) Core(TM) i7-8700 CPU @ 3.20GHz desktop computer. The performance of the Universal Sentence Encoder will be more

[9]https://github.com/a-mma/AquilaDB
[10]https://github.com/apache/couchdb

efficient in a GPU (Graphics Processing Unit). Nonetheless we carried our experiments without using a GPU since the translators using translation memory tools would probably not have access to a GPU on daily basis.

Architecture	Step 1	Step 2	Step 3
DAN Encoder	78s	0.77s	0.40s
Transformer	108s	1.23s	0.40s

Table 6: Time efficiency of each architecture in Universal Sentence Encoder

When we calculated the sentence embeddings for the segments in the translation memory in Step 1, we processed the segments in batches of 256 segments. As can be seen in the table 6, DAN Architecture had the maximum efficiency providing sentence embeddings within 78 seconds for 230,000 segments. The Transformer architecture was not too far behind, being able to calculate the embeddings of the 230,000 segments in 108 seconds.

The next column in table 6 reports the time taken from each sentence encoder to embed a single segment. We did not consider input segments as batches as we did earlier for the segments in the translation memory. We assumed that since the translators translate the segments one by one it would not be fair to encode the input segments in batches. In that step too, the DAN Architecture was more efficient than the Transformer Architecture.

The next column is the time taken to retrieve the best match from the translation memory. It includes the time taken to calculate the cosine similarity of the segment embeddings of the segments of the translation memory with the segment embedding of the input segment. Also, it includes the time taken to sort the similarities and get the index of the highest similarity and retrieve the corresponding segment which we considered as the best match for the input segment from the translation memory. As shown in the table 6 both architectures took approximately similar time for this step since the size of the embedding is same for both architectures.

As a whole, time taken to acquire the best match from the translation memory is the combined time taken to step 2 and step 3. Therefore, the time taken by the Transformer Encoder to retrieve a match from the translation memory

for one incoming sentence is just 1.6s, which is reasonable. In light of this, we decided to use the Transformer Architecture for future experiments since it is efficient enough and since it was reported that it provides better accuracy in semantic retrieval tasks than the DAN Architecture (Cer et al., 2018).

3.2.3 Results

In order to compare the results obtained by our method with those of an existing translation memory tool we used Okapi which uses simple edit distance to retrieve matches from the translation memory. We calculated the METEOR score (Denkowski and Lavie, 2014) between the actual translation of the incoming segment and the match we retrieved from the translation memory with the transformer architecture of the Universal Sentence Encoder. We repeated the same process with the match we retrieved from Okapi. We used METEOR score since we believed it can capture the semantic similarity between two segments better than the BLEU score (Denkowski and Lavie, 2014).

To understand the performance of our method, we first removed the segments where the match provided by Okapi and the Universal Sentence Encoder was same. Then, to have a better analysis of the results, we divided the results in to 5 partitions. The first partition contained the matches derived from Okapi that had a fuzzy match score between 0.8 and 1. We calculated the average METEOR score for the segments retrieved from Okapi and for the segments retrieved from Universal Sentence Encoder in the particular partition. We performed the same process for all the partitions: fuzzy match score ranges 0.6-0.8, 0.4-0.6, 0.2-0.4 and 0-0.2.

As shown in table 7 Universal Sentence Encoder performs better than Okapi for the fuzzy match scores below 0.8, which means that the Universal Sentence Encoder performs better when Okapi fails to find a significantly similar match in TM. However, this is not a surprise given that METEOR score is largely based on overlapping ngrams, and therefore will reward segments that have a high fuzzy match score.

However, we noticed that in most cases, the difference between the actual translation and the suggested match from either Okapi or Universal Sentence Encoder is just a number, a location, an organisation or a name of a person. We

Fuzzy score	Okapi	USE	Amount
0.8-1.0	**0.931**	0.854	1624
0.6-0.8	0.693	**0.702**	4521
0.4-0.6	0.488	**0.594**	6712
0.2-0.4	0.225	**0.318**	13136
0-0.2	0.011	**0.134**	24612

Table 7: Result comparison between Okapi and the Universal Sentence Encoder for each partition. Fuzzy score column represents the each partition. Okapi column shows the average METEOR score between the matches provided by the Okapi and the actual translations in that partition. USE column shows the average METEOR score between the matches provided by the Universal Sentence Encoder and the actual translations in that partition. Amount column shows the number of sentences in each partition. Bold shows the best result for that partition

Fuzzy score	Okapi	USE	Amount
0.8-1.0	**0.942**	0.889	1512
0.6-0.8	0.705	**0.726**	3864
0.4-0.6	0.496	**0.602**	6538
0.2-0.4	0.228	**0.320**	13128
0-0.2	0.011	**0.134**	24612

Table 8: Result comparison between Okapi and the Universal Sentence Encoder for each partition after performing NER. The Fuzzy score column represents each partition. The Okapi column shows the average METEOR score between the matches provided by the Okapi and the actual translations in that partition. The USE column shows the average METEOR score between the matches provided by the Universal Sentence Encoder and the actual translations in that partition. The Amount column shows the number of sentences in each partition. Bold shows the best result for that partition

thought this might affect the results since we are depending on the Universal Sentence Encoder's ability to retrieve semantically similar segments from the TM. For this reason, we applied a Named Entity Recognition (NER) pipeline on the actual translations, segments retrieved from Okapi and the segments retrieved from Universal Sentence Encoder. Since the target language is Spanish, we used the Spanish NER pipeline provided by Spacy that was trained on the AnCora and WikiNER corpus[11]. We detected locations, organisations and person names with the NER pipeline and replaced them with a placeholder. We also used Añotador [12] to detect dates in the segments and replaced them too with a placeholder. Last, we used a regular expression to detect number sequences in the segments and replaced them too with a place holder. After that we removed the cases where the match provided by Okapi and the Universal Sentence Encoder is same and recalculated the results in table 7 following the same process.

As shown in table 8 for the cases where the fuzzy match score is above 0.8, the segments retrieved by Okapi are still better than the segments retrieved from the Universal Sentence Encoder. However for the cases where the fuzzy match score is below 0.8 the Universal Sentence Encoder seems to be better than Okapi. After performing NER, the results of the Universal Sentence Encoder improved significantly in most of the partitions: specially in 0.6-0.8 partition.

Given the fact that METEOR relies largely on string overlap we assumed that it is unable to capture the fact that the segments retrieved using the Universal Sentence Encoder are semantically equivalent. Therefore, we asked three native Spanish speakers to compare the segments from Okapi and report the sentences where Universal Encoder performed significantly better than Okapi. Due to the time restrictions they did not have time to go through all the segments. But their opinion was generally that the Universal Sentence Encoder was better at identifying semantically similar segments in the TM. Table 9 presents sample segments they provided.

4 Conclusion and Future Work

In this paper we have proposed a new TM matching and retrieval method based on the Universal Sentence Encoder. Our assumption was that by using this representation we will be able to retrieve better segments from a TM than when using a standard edit distance. As shown in 3.2.3 section, the Universal Sentence Encoder performs better than Okapi for fuzzy match scores ranged below 0.8. Therefore, we believe that the sentence encoders can improve the matching and retrieval in TMs and should be explored more. Usually TM matches with lower fuzzy match scores (¡ 0.8) are not used by professional translators, or when used, they lead to a decrease in translation productivity. But our method can provide better matches to sentences below fuzzy match score 0.8, hence will be able to improve the translation productivity. According to the annotation guidelines of (Cer et al., 2017) a semantic textual similarity score of 0.8 means *"The two sentences are mostly*

[11]https://spacy.io/models/es
[12]http://annotador.oeg-upm.net/

Source segment	Human Translated segment	Universal Sentence Encoder Suggestion	Okapi Suggestion
If applicable	En su caso	si procede	No procede
Date of granting	Fecha de concesión de la subvención	Fecha de autorización	Fecha de la garantía otorgada
This Decision shall be kept under constant review and shall be renewed or amended, as appropriate, if the Council deems that its objectives have not been met.'	La presente Decisión estará sujeta a revisión continua y se prorrogará o modificará, según proceda, si el Consejo estima que no se han cumplido sus objetivos.	Será prorrogada o modificada, según proceda, si el Consejo considera que no se han cumplido sus objetivos.	Se prorrogará o modificará, si procede, en caso de que el Consejo estime que no se han cumplido los objetivos de la misma.
The information shall include:	Esta información incluirá:	Esa información podrá versar sobre lo siguiente:	Los indicadores clave de rendimiento incluirán:
General characteristics of the finished product	Características generales del producto terminado	descripción del producto final,	Características generales del componente de servicios de copernicus
Such reports shall be made publicly available.	Dichos informes se harán públicos.	Sus informes se harán públicos.	Se pondrá a disposición del público un resumen de las evaluaciones.
The Commission decision to initiate the procedure ('the Opening Decision') was published in the Official Journal of the European Union.	La Decisión de la Comisión de incoar el procedimiento (en lo sucesivo, Decisión de incoación) se publicó en el Diario Oficial de la Unión Europea.	La Decisión de la Comisión de incoar el procedimiento (en lo sucesivo, Decisión de incoación) fue publicada en el Diario Oficial de la Unión Europea.	La decisión de la Comisión de incoar el procedimiento se publicó en el Diario Oficial de la Unión Europea.
Chapter 2 is amended as follows:	El capítulo 2 se modifica como sigue:	la parte 2 se modifica como sigue:	la sección 2 queda modificada como sigue:

Table 9: Example segments where Universal Sentence Encoder suggestion was better than the Okapi suggestion

equivalent, but some unimportant details differ" and semantic textual similarity score of 0.6 means *"The two sentences are roughly equivalent, but some important information differs/missing"*. If we further analyse the fuzzy match score range 0.6-0.8, as shown in table 10, the mean semantic textual similarity for the sentences provided by Universal Sentence Encoder is 0.768. Therefore, we assume that the matches retrieved from the Universal Sentence Encoder in the fuzzy match score range 0.6-0.8 will help to improve the translation productivity. However, this is something that we plan to analyse further by carrying out evaluations with professional translators.

In the future, we also plan to experiment with other sentence encoders such as Infersent (Conneau et al., 2017) and SBERT (Reimers and Gurevych, 2019) and with alternative algorithms which are capable to capture semantic textual similarity between two sentences. We will try unsupervised methods like word vector averaging

Fuzzy score	Mean STS score
0.8 - 1.0	0.952
0.6 - 0.8	0.768
0.4 - 0.6	0.642
0.2 - 0.4	0.315
0 - 0.2	0.121

Table 10: Mean STS score for the sentences retrieved by Universal Sentence Encoder for each fuzzy match score. Fuzzy score column shows the fuzzy match score ranges and Mean STS score column shows that mean STS score for the sentence retrieved by Universal Sentence Encoder for that fuzzy match score range.

and word moving distance (Ranasinghe et al., 2019a) as well as supervised algorithms such as Siamese neural networks (Ranasinghe et al., 2019b) and transformers (Devlin et al., 2018).

5 Acknowledgment

We would like to acknowledge Rocío Caro Quintana from University of Wolverhampton, Encarnación Núñez Ignacio from University of Wolverhampton and Bellés-Calvera, Lucía from Jaume I University: the team of volunteer annotators that provided their free time and efforts to manually evaluate the results between Universal Sentence Encoder and edit Distance.

Also we would like to acknowledge María Navas-Loro and Pablo Calleja from Polytechnic University of Madrid for providing Añotador for free to detect dates in the Spanish segments.

References

Arthern, Peter J. 1979. Machine translation and computerized terminology systems: A translator's viewpoint. *Translating and the Computer, Proceedings of a Seminar, London 14th November 1978. Amsterdam: North-Holland Publishing Company*, pages 77–108.

Baisa, Vít, Aleš Horák, and Marek Medveď. 2015. Increasing coverage of translation memories with linguistically motivated segment combination methods. In *Proceedings of the Workshop Natural Language Processing for Translation Memories*, pages 31–35, Hissar, Bulgaria, September. Association for Computational Linguistics.

Bentivogli, Luisa, Raffaella Bernardi, Marco Marelli, Stefano Menini, Marco Baroni, and Roberto Zamparelli. 2016. Sick through the semeval glasses. lesson learned from the evaluation of compositional distributional semantic models on full sentences through semantic relatedness and textual entailment. *Language Resources and Evaluation*, 50:95–124.

Cer, Daniel M., Mona T. Diab, Eneko Agirre, Iñigo Lopez-Gazpio, and Lucia Specia. 2017. Semeval-2017 task 1: Semantic textual similarity multilingual and crosslingual focused evaluation. In *SemEval@ACL*.

Cer, Daniel, Yinfei Yang, Sheng-yi Kong, Nan Hua, Nicole Limtiaco, Rhomni St. John, Noah Constant, Mario Guajardo-Cespedes, Steve Yuan, Chris Tar, Brian Strope, and Ray Kurzweil. 2018. Universal sentence encoder for English. In *Proceedings of the 2018 Conference on Empirical Methods in Natural Language Processing: System Demonstrations*, pages 169–174, Brussels, Belgium, November. Association for Computational Linguistics.

Chatzitheodorou, Konstantinos. 2015. Improving translation memory fuzzy matching by paraphrasing. In *Proceedings of the Workshop Natural Language Processing for Translation Memories*, pages 24–30, Hissar, Bulgaria, September. Association for Computational Linguistics.

Conneau, Alexis, Douwe Kiela, Holger Schwenk, Loïc Barrault, and Antoine Bordes. 2017. Supervised learning of universal sentence representations from natural language inference data. In *Proceedings of the 2017 Conference on Empirical Methods in Natural Language Processing*, pages 670–680, Copenhagen, Denmark, September. Association for Computational Linguistics.

Denkowski, Michael and Alon Lavie. 2014. Meteor universal: Language specific translation evaluation for any target language. In *Proceedings of the EACL 2014 Workshop on Statistical Machine Translation*.

Devlin, Jacob, Ming-Wei Chang, Kenton Lee, and Kristina Toutanova. 2018. BERT: pre-training of deep bidirectional transformers for language understanding. *CoRR*, abs/1810.04805.

Gupta, Rohit and Constantin Orasan. 2014. Incorporating paraphrasing in translation memory matching and retrieval. In *Proceedings of the Seventeenth Annual Conference of the European Association for Machine Translation (EAMT2014)*, pages 3–10.

Gupta, Rohit, Constantin Orăsan, and Josef van Genabith. 2015. ReVal: A Simple and Effective Machine Translation Evaluation Metric Based on Recurrent Neural Networks. In *Proceedings of the 2015 Conference on Empirical Methods in Natural Language Processing*, pages 1066–1072, Lisbon, Portugal, September.

Gupta, Rohit, Constantin Orăsan, Marcos Zampieri, Mihaela Vela, Josef van Genabith, and Ruslan Mitkov. 2016. Improving translation memory matching and retrieval using paraphrases. *Machine Translation*, 30(1-2):19–40.

Gupta, Rohit. 2016. *USE OF LANGUAGE TECHNOLOGY TO IMPROVE MATCHING AND*

RETRIEVAL IN TRANSLATION MEMORY. Ph.D. thesis, University of Wolverhampton.

Hodász, Gábor and Gábor Pohl. 2005. MetaMorpho TM: a linguistically enriched translation memory. In *In International Workshop, Modern Approaches in Translation Technologies*.

Iyyer, Mohit, Varun Manjunatha, Jordan Boyd-Graber, and Hal Daumé III. 2015. Deep unordered composition rivals syntactic methods for text classification. In *Proceedings of the 53rd Annual Meeting of the Association for Computational Linguistics and the 7th International Joint Conference on Natural Language Processing (Volume 1: Long Papers)*, pages 1681–1691, Beijing, China, July. Association for Computational Linguistics.

Mueller, Jonas and Aditya Thyagarajan. 2016. Siamese recurrent architectures for learning sentence similarity. In *Proceedings of the Thirtieth AAAI Conference on Artificial Intelligence*, AAAI'16, page 2786–2792. AAAI Press.

Pekar, Viktor and Ruslan Mitkov. 2007. New Generation Translation Memory: Content-Sensitive Matching. In *Proceedings of the 40th Anniversary Congress of the Swiss Association of Translators, Terminologists and Interpreters*.

Planas, Emmanuel and Osamu Furuse. 1999. Formalizing Translation Memories. In *Proceedings of the 7th Machine Translation Summit*, pages 331–339.

Ranasinghe, Tharindu, Constantin Orasan, and Ruslan Mitkov. 2019a. Enhancing unsupervised sentence similarity methods with deep contextualised word representations. In *Proceedings of the International Conference on Recent Advances in Natural Language Processing (RANLP 2019)*, pages 994–1003, Varna, Bulgaria, September. INCOMA Ltd.

Ranasinghe, Tharindu, Constantin Orasan, and Ruslan Mitkov. 2019b. Semantic textual similarity with Siamese neural networks. In *Proceedings of the International Conference on Recent Advances in Natural Language Processing (RANLP 2019)*, pages 1004–1011, Varna, Bulgaria, September. INCOMA Ltd.

Reimers, Nils and Iryna Gurevych. 2019. Sentence-bert: Sentence embeddings using siamese bert-networks. In *Proceedings of the 2019 Conference on Empirical Methods in Natural Language Processing*. Association for Computational Linguistics, 11.

Simard, Michel. 2020. Building and using parallel text for translation. In O'Hagan, Minako, editor, *The Routledge Handbook of Translation and Technology*, chapter 5, pages 78 —— 90. Routledge.

Steinberger, Ralf, Andreas Eisele, Szymon Klocek, Spyridon Pilos, and Patrick Schlüter. 2012. DGT-TM: A freely available translation memory in 22 languages. In *Proceedings of the Eighth International Conference on Language Resources and Evaluation (LREC'12)*, pages 454–459, Istanbul, Turkey, May. European Language Resources Association (ELRA).

Tai, Kai Sheng, Richard Socher, and Christopher D. Manning. 2015. Improved semantic representations from tree-structured long short-term memory networks. In *Proceedings of the 53rd Annual Meeting of the Association for Computational Linguistics and the 7th International Joint Conference on Natural Language Processing (Volume 1: Long Papers)*, pages 1556–1566, Beijing, China, July. Association for Computational Linguistics.

Utiyama, Masao, Graham Neubig, Takashi Onishi, and Eiichiro Sumita. 2011. Searching Translation Memories for Paraphrases. In *Proceedings of the 13th Machine Translation Summit*, pages 325–331, Xiamen, China, September.

Vanallemeersch, Tom and Vincent Vandeghinste. 2014. Improving fuzzy matching through syntactic knowledge. In *Translating and the Computer 36*, volume 36, pages 90 – 99, London, UK.

Vaswani, Ashish, Noam Shazeer, Niki Parmar, Jakob Uszkoreit, Llion Jones, Aidan N. Gomez, undefinedukasz Kaiser, and Illia Polosukhin. 2017. Attention is all you need. In *Proceedings of the 31st International Conference on Neural Information Processing Systems*, NIPS'17, page 6000–6010, Red Hook, NY, USA. Curran Associates Inc.

Yang, Yinfei, Daniel Matthew Cer, Amin Ahmad, Mandy Guo, Jax Law, Noah Constant, Gustavo Hernández Ábrego, Steve Yuan, Chris Tar, Yun-Hsuan Sung, Brian Strope, and Ray Kurzweil. 2019. Multilingual universal sentence encoder for semantic retrieval. *ArXiv*, abs/1907.04307.

Zaretskaya, Anna, Gloria Corpas Pastor, and Miriam Seghiri. 2018. User Perspective on Translation Tools: Findings of a User Survey. In Corpas Pastor, Gloria and Isabel Duran, editors, *Trends in E-tools and Resources for Translators and Interpreters*, pages 37 – 56. Brill.

Reassessing Claims of Human Parity and Super-Human Performance in Machine Translation at WMT 2019

Antonio Toral

Center for Language and Cognition
University of Groningen
The Netherlands
`a.toral.ruiz@rug.nl`

Abstract

We reassess the claims of human parity and super-human performance made at the news shared task of WMT 2019 for three translation directions: English→German, English→Russian and German→English. First we identify three potential issues in the human evaluation of that shared task: (i) the limited amount of intersentential context available, (ii) the limited translation proficiency of the evaluators and (iii) the use of a reference translation. We then conduct a modified evaluation taking these issues into account. Our results indicate that all the claims of human parity and super-human performance made at WMT 2019 should be refuted, except the claim of human parity for English→German. Based on our findings, we put forward a set of recommendations and open questions for future assessments of human parity in machine translation.

1 Introduction

The quality of the translations produced by machine translation (MT) systems has improved considerably since the adoption of architectures based on neural networks (Bentivogli et al., 2016). To the extent that, in the last two years, there have been claims of MT systems reaching human parity and even super-human performance (Hassan et al., 2018; Bojar et al., 2018; Barrault et al., 2019). Following Hassan et al. (2018), we consider that human parity is achieved for a given task t if the performance attained by a computer on t is equivalent to that of a human, i.e. there is no significant difference between the performance obtained by human and by machine. Super-human performance is achieved for t if the performance achieved by a computer is significantly better than that of a human.

Two claims of human parity in MT were reported in 2018. One by Microsoft, on news translation for Chinese→English (Hassan et al., 2018), and another at the news translation task of WMT for English→Czech (Bojar et al., 2018), in which MT systems Uedin (Haddow et al., 2018) and Cuni-Transformer (Kocmi et al., 2018) reached human parity and super-human performance, respectively. In 2019 there were additional claims at the news translation task of WMT (Barrault et al., 2019): human parity for German→English, by several of the submitted systems, and for English→Russian, by system Facebook-FAIR (Ng et al., 2019), as well as super-human performance for English→German, again by Facebook-FAIR.

The claims of human parity and super-human performance in MT made in 2018 (Hassan et al., 2018; Bojar et al., 2018) have been since refuted given three issues in their evaluation setups (Läubli et al., 2018; Toral et al., 2018): (i) part of the source text of the test set was not original text but translationese, (ii) the sentences were evaluated in isolation, and (iii) the evaluation was not conducted by translators. However, the evaluation setup of WMT 2019 was modified to address some of these issues: the first issue (translationese) was fully addressed, while the second (sentences evaluated in isolation) was partially addressed, as we will motivate in Section 2.1, whereas the third (human evaluation conducted by non-translators) was not acted upon. Given that some of the issues that led to refute the claims of human parity in MT

Martins, Moniz, Fumega, Martins, Batista, Coheur, Parra, Trancoso, Turchi, Bisazza, Moorkens, Guerberof, Nurminen, Marg, Forcada (eds.)
Proceedings of the 22nd Annual Conference of the European Association for Machine Translation, p. 185–194
Lisboa, Portugal, November 2020.

made in 2018 have been addressed in the set-up of the experiments leading to the claims made in 2019, but that some of the issues still remain, we reassess these later claims.

The remainder of this paper is organised as follows. Section 2 discusses the potential issues in the setup of the human evaluation at WMT 2019. Next, in Section 3 we conduct a modified evaluation of the MT systems that reached human parity or super-human performance at WMT 2019. Finally, Section 4 presents our conclusions and recommendations.

2 Potential Issues in the Human Evaluation of WMT 2019

This section discusses the potential issues that we have identified in the human evaluation of the news translation task at WMT 2019, and motivates why they might have had contributed to the fact that some of the systems evaluated therein reached human parity or super-human performance. These issues concern the limited amount of intersentential context provided to the evaluators (Section 2.1), the fact that the evaluations were not conducted by translators (Section 2.2) and the fact that the evaluation was reference-based for one of the translation directions (Section 2.3).

2.1 Limited Intersentential Context

In the human evaluation at previous editions of WMT evaluators had no access to intersentential context since the sentences were shown to evaluators in random order. That changed in WMT 2019 (Barrault et al., 2019), which had two evaluation settings that contained intersentential context:

- Document-level (DR+DC), inspired by Läubli et al. (2018), in which the whole document is available and it is evaluated globally (see top of Figure 1). While the evaluator has access to the whole document, this set-up has the drawback of resulting in very few ratings (one per document) and hence suffers from low statistical power (Graham et al., 2019).

- Sentence-by-sentence with document context (SR+DC), in which segments are provided in the "natural order as they appear in the document" and they are assessed individually (see bottom of Figure 1). Such a set-up results in a much higher number of ratings compared to the previous evaluation setting (DR+DC):

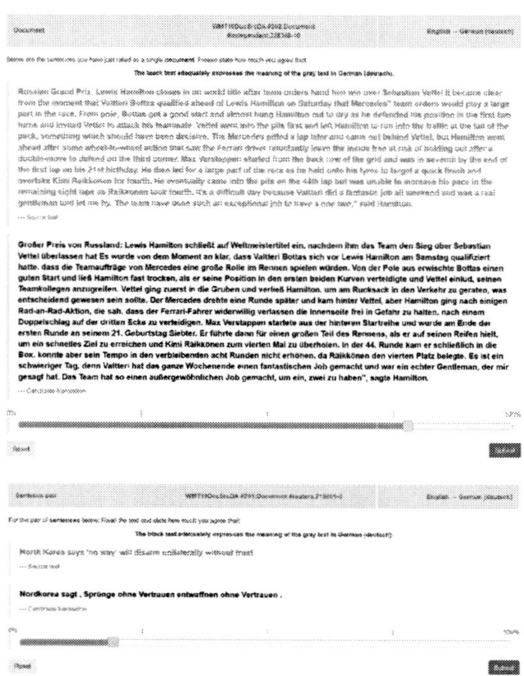

Figure 1: A snapshot of an assessment using setting DR+DC (top) and SR+DC (bottom) at WMT 2019, taken from Barrault et al. (2019)

one per sentence rather than one per document. The problem with the current setting is that the evaluator can access limited intersentential context since only the current sentence is shown. This poses two issues, with respect to previous and following sentences in the document being evaluated. With respect to previous sentences, while the evaluator has seen them recently, he/she might have forgotten some details of a previous sentence that are relevant for the evaluation of the current sentence, e.g. in long documents. As for following sentences, the evaluator does not have access to them while evaluating the current sentence, which may be useful in some cases, e.g. when evaluating the first sentence of a document, i.e. the title of the newstory, since in some cases this may present an ambiguity for which having access to subsequent sentences could be useful.

SR+DC was the set-up used for the official rankings of WMT 2019, from which the claims of human parity and super-human performance were derived. The requirement of information from both previous and following sentences in human evaluation of MT has been empirically proven in contemporary research (Castilho et al., in press 2020).

In our evaluation setup, evaluators are shown local context (the source sentences immediately preceding and following the current one) and are provided with global context: the whole source document as a separate text file. Evaluators are told to use the global context if the local context does not provide enough information to evaluate a sentence. In addition, evaluators are asked to evaluate all the sentences of a document in a single session.

2.2 Proficiency of the Evaluators

The human evaluation of WMT 2019 was conducted by crowd workers and by MT researchers. The first type of evaluators provided roughly two thirds of the judgments (487,674) while the second type contributed the remaining one third (242,424). Of the judgments provided by crowd workers, around half of them (224,046) were by "workers who passed quality control".

The fact that the evaluation was not conducted by translators might be problematic since it has been found that crowd workers lack knowledge of translation and, compared to professional translators, tend to be more accepting of (subtle) translation errors (Castilho et al., 2017).

Taking this into account, we will reassess the translations of the systems that achieved human parity or super-human performance at WMT 2019 with translators and non-translators. The latter are native speakers of the target language who are not translators but who have an advanced level of the source language (at least C1 in the Common European Framework of Reference for Languages).

2.3 Reference-based Evaluation

While for two of the translation directions for which there were claims of human parity at WMT 2019 the human evaluation was reference-free (from English to both German and Russian), for the remaining translation direction for which there was a claim of parity (German to English), the human evaluation was reference-based. In a reference-free evaluation, the evaluator assesses the quality of a translation with respect to the source sentence. Hence evaluators need to be proficient in both the source and target languages. Differently, in a reference-based evaluation, the evaluator assesses a translation with respect, not (only) to the source sentence, but (also) to a reference translation.

The advantage of a reference-based evaluation is that it can be carried out by monolingual speakers, since only proficiency in the target language is required. However, the dependence on reference translations in this type of evaluation can lead to reference bias. Such a bias is hypothesised to result in (i) inflated scores for candidate translations that happen to be similar to the reference translation (e.g. in terms of syntactic structure and lexical choice) and to (ii) penalise correct translations that diverge from the reference translation. Recent research has found both evicence that this is the case (Fomicheva and Specia, 2016; Bentivogli et al., 2018) and that it is not (Ma et al., 2017).

In the context of WMT 2019, in the translation directions that followed a reference-free human evaluation, the human translation (used as reference for the automatic evaluation) could be compared to MT systems in the human evaluation, just by being part of the pool of translations to be evaluated. However, in the translation directions that followed a reference-based human evaluation, such as German→English, the reference translation could not be evaluated against the MT systems, since it was itself the gold standard. A second human translation was used to this end. In a nutshell, for English→German and English→Russian there is one human translation, referred to as HUMAN, while for German→English there are two human translations, one was used as reference and the other was evaluated against the MT systems, to which we refer to as REF and HUMAN, respectively.

The claim of parity for German→English results therefore from the fact that HUMAN and the output of an MT system (Facebook-FAIR) were compared separately to a gold standard translation, REF, and the overall ratings that they obtained were not significantly different from each other. If there was reference bias in this case, it could be that HUMAN was penalised for being different than REF. To check whether this could be the case we use BLEU (Papineni et al., 2002) as a proxy to measure the similarity between all the pairs of the three relevant translations: REF, HUMAN and the best MT system. Table 1 shows the three pairwise scores.[1] HUMAN appears to be markedly differ-

---

[1] We use the `multi-bleu.perl` implementation of BLEU, giving as parameters one of the translations as the reference and the other as the hypothesis. Changing the order of the parameters results in very minor variations in the score.

ent than MT and REF, which are more similar to each other.

MT, REF	MT, HUMAN	REF, HUMAN
35.9	26.5	21.9

Table 1: BLEU scores between pairs of three translations (REF, HUMAN and the best MT system) for German→English at the news translation task of WMT 2019.

These results indicate thus that HUMAN could have been penalised for diverging from the reference translation REF, which could have contributed to the best MT system reaching parity. In our experiments, we will conduct a reference-free evaluation for this translation direction comparing this MT system to both human translations.

3 Evaluation

3.1 Experimental Setup

We conduct a human evaluation[2] for the three translation directions of WMT 2019 for which there were claims of human parity or super-human performance: German→English, English→German and English→Russian. We evaluate the first twenty documents of the test set for each of these language pairs. These amount to 317 sentences for German→English and 302 for both English→German and English→Russian (the English side of the test set in all from-English translation directions is common).

We conduct our evaluation with the Appraise toolkit (Federmann, 2012), by means of relative rankings, rather than direct assessment (DA) (Graham et al., 2017) as in Barrault et al. (2019). While DA has some advantages over ranking, their outcomes correlate strongly ($R > 0.9$ in Bojar et al. (2016)) and the latter is more appropriate for our evaluation for two reasons: (i) it allows us to show the evaluator all the translations that we evaluate at once, so that they are directly compared (DA only shows one translation at a time, entailing that the translations evaluated are indirectly compared to each other) and (ii) it allows us to show local context to the evaluator (DA only shows the sentence that is being currently evaluated).

Evaluators are shown two translations for both English→German and English→Russian: one by a human (referred to as HUMAN) and one by the best MT system[3] submitted to that translation direction (referred to as MT). For German→English there are three translations (see Section 2.3): two by humans (HUMAN and REF) and one by an MT system. The MT system is Facebook-FAIR for all three translation directions. The order in which the translations are shown is randomised.

For each source sentence, evaluators rank the translations thereof, with ties being allowed. Evaluators could also avoid ranking the translations of a sentence, if they detected an issue that prevented them from being able to rank them, by using the button flag error; they were instructed to do so only when strictly necessary. Figure 2 shows a snapshot of our evaluation.

From the relative rankings, we extract the number of times one of the translations is better than the other and the number of times they are tied. Statistical significance is conducted with two-tailed sign tests, the null hypothesis being that evaluators do not prefer the human translation over MT or viceversa (Läubli et al., 2018). We report the number of successes x, i.e. number of ratings in favour of the human translation, and the number of trials n, i.e. number of all ratings except for ties.

Five evaluators took part in the evaluation for English→German (two translators and three non-translators), six took part for English→Russian (four translators and two non-translators) and three took part for German→English (two translators and one non-translator).

Immediately after completing the evaluation, the evaluators completed a questionnaire (see Appendix A). It contained questions about their linguistic proficiency in the source and target languages, their amount of translation experience, the frequency with which they used the local and global contextual information, whether they thought that one of the translations was normally better than the other(s) and whether they thought that the translations were produced by human translators or MT systems.

In the remaining of this section we present the results of our evaluation for the three language pairs, followed by the inter-annotator agreement and the responses to the questionnaire.

[2]Code and data available at `https://github.com/antot/human_parity_eamt2020`

[3]The MT system with the highest normalised average DA score in the human evaluation of WMT 2019.

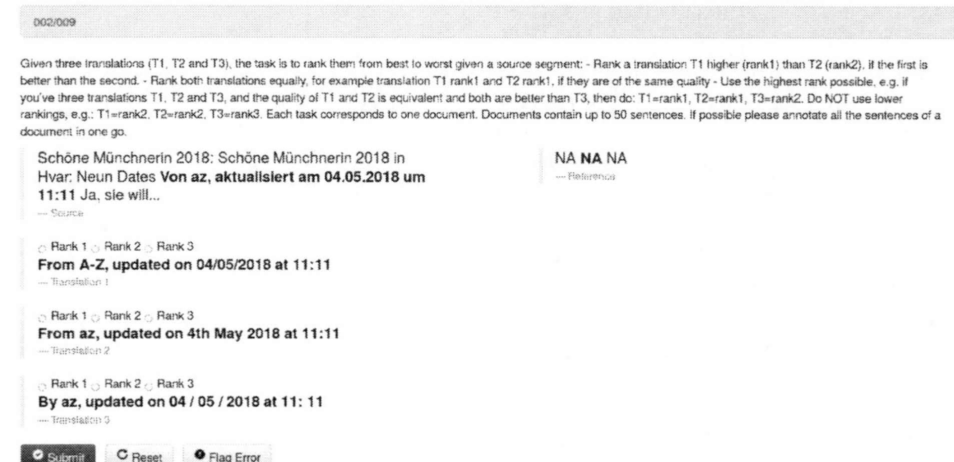

Figure 2: A snapshot of our human evaluation, for the German→English translation direction, for the second segment of a document that contains nine segments. The evaluator ranks three translations, two of which are produced by human translators (REF and HUMAN) while the remaining one comes from an MT system (Facebook-FAIR), by comparing them to the source, since no reference translation is provided. Local context (immediately preceeding and following source sentences) is provided inside the evaluation tool and global context (the whole source document) is provided as a separate file.

3.2 Results for English→German

Figure 3 shows the percentages of rankings[4] for which translators and non-translators preferred the translation by the MT system, that by the human translator or both were considered equivalent (tie). Non-translators preferred the translation by the MT engine slightly more frequently than the human translation (42.3% vs 36.7%) while the opposite is observed for translators (36.9% for HU-MAN vs 34.9% for MT). However, these differences are not significant for either translators ($x = 222$, $n = 432$, $p = 0.6$) nor for non-translators ($x = 332$, $n = 715$, $p = 0.06$). In other words, according to our results there is no super-human performance, since MT is not found to be significantly better than HUMAN (which was the case at WMT 2019) but HUMAN is not significantly better than MT either. Therefore our evaluation results in human parity, since the performance of the MT system and HUMAN are not significantly different in the eyes of the translators and the non-translators that conducted the evaluation.

Figure 4 shows the results for each evaluator separately, with ties omitted to ease the visualisation. We observe a similar trend across all the non-translators: a slight preference for MT over

Figure 3: Results for English→German for translators ($n = 602$) and non-translators ($n = 905$)

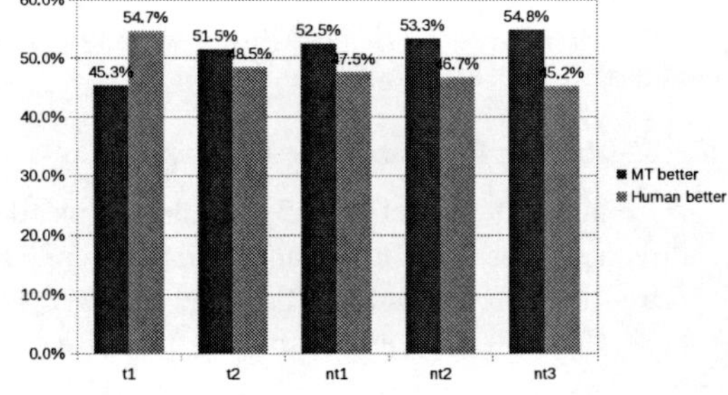

Figure 4: Results for English→German for each evaluator separately: translators t1 and t2 and non-translators nt1, nt2 and nt3.

---

[4]We show percentages instead of absolute numbers in order to be able to compare the rankings by translators and non-translators, as the number of translators and non-translators is not the same.

HUMAN, where the first is preferred in 52.5% to 54.8% of the times whereas the second is preferred in 45.2% to 47.5% of the cases. However, the two translators do not share the same trend; translator t1 prefers HUMAN more often than MT (54.7% vs 45.3%) while the trend is the opposite for translator t2, albeit more slightly (51.5% MT vs 48.5% HUMAN).

3.3 Results for English→Russian

Figure 5 shows the results for English→Russian. In this translation direction both translators and non-translators prefer HUMAN more frequently than MT: 42.3% vs 34.4% ($x = 499$, $n = 905$, $p < 0.01$) and 45.5% vs 35.8% ($x = 275$, $n = 491$, $p < 0.01$), respectively. Since the differences are significant in both cases, our evaluation refutes the claim of human parity made at WMT 2019 for this translation direction.

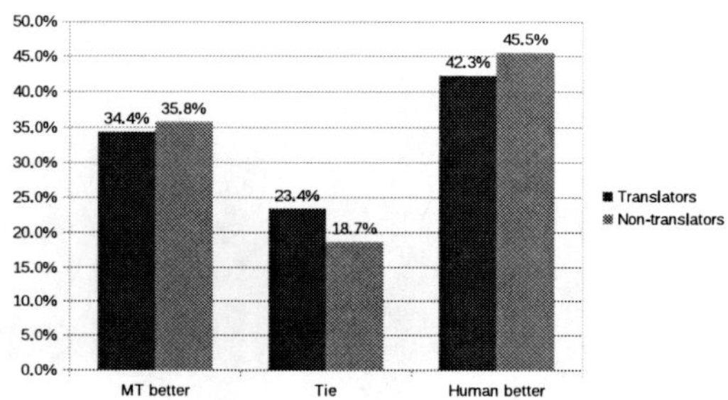

Figure 5: Results for English→Russian for translators ($n = 1181$) and non-translators ($n = 604$)

Again we zoom in on the results by the individual evaluators, as depicted in Figure 6. It can be seen that all but one of the evaluators, translator t1, prefer HUMAN considerably more often than MT. However, the differences are only significant for t3 ($x = 114$, $n = 178$, $p < 0.001$) and nt2 ($x = 119$, $n = 202$, $p < 0.05$), probably due to the small number of observations.

3.4 Results for German→English

As explained in section 2.3, for this translation direction there are two human translations, referred to as HUMAN and REF, and one MT system. Hence we can establish three pairwise comparisons: REF–MT, HUMAN–MT and HUMAN–REF. The results for them are shown in Figure 7, Figure 8 and Figure 9, respectively.

Both translators preferred the translation by the MT system slightly more often than the human

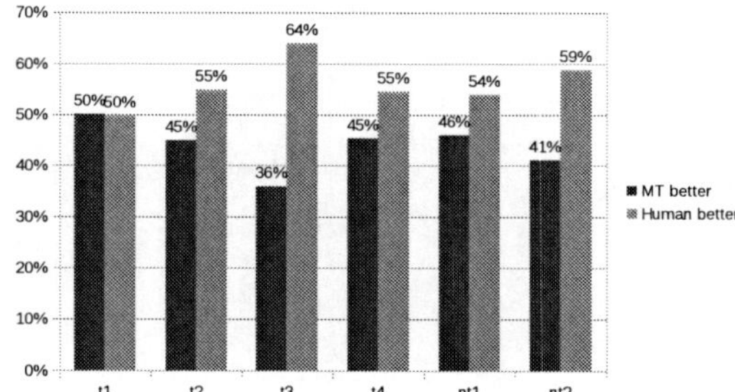

Figure 6: Results for English→Russian for each evaluator separately: translators t1, t2, t3 and t4 and non-translators nt1 and nt2.

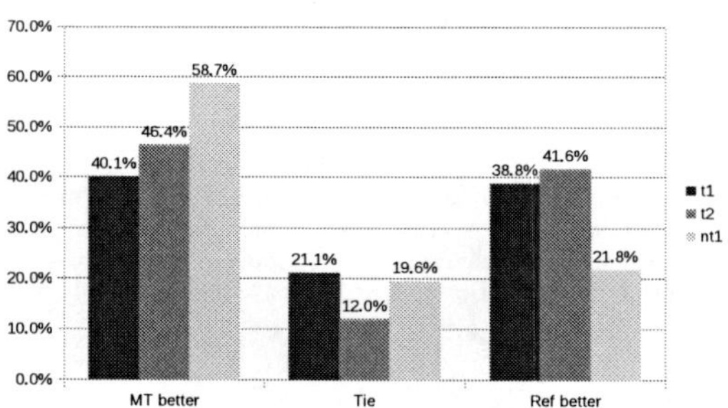

Figure 7: Results for German→English for REF and MT, with translators t1 and t2 and non-translator nt1.

translation REF, 40% vs 39% and 46% vs 42%, but the difference is not significant ($x = 255$, $n = 529$, $p = 0.4$). The non-translator preferred the translation by MT considerably more often than REF: 59% vs 22%, with the diffence being significant ($x = 69$, $n = 255$, $p < 0.001$). In other words, compared to REF, the human translation used as gold standard at WMT 2019, the MT system achieves human parity according to the two translators and super-human performance according to the non-translator.

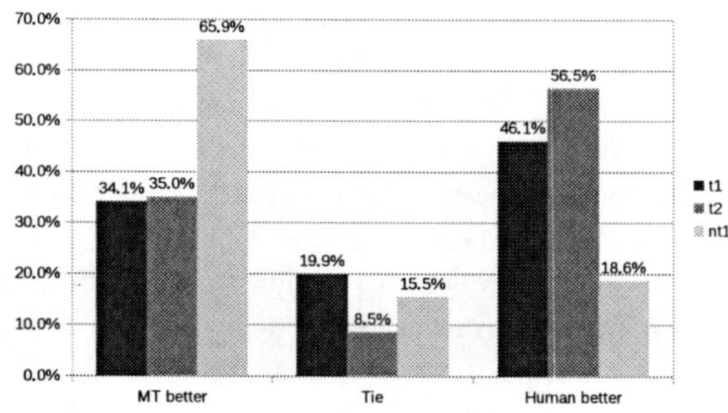

Figure 8: Results for German→English for HUMAN and MT, with translators t1 and t2 and non-translator nt1.

Now we discuss the results of comparing the

MT system to the other human translation, HU-MAN (see Figure 8). The outcome according to the non-translator is, as in the previous comparison between REF and MT, super-human performance ($x = 59$, $n = 268$, $p < 0.001$), which can be expected since this evaluator prefers MT much more often than HUMAN: 66% vs 19% of the times. We expected that the results for the translators would also follow a similar trend to their outcome when they compared MT to the other human translation (REF), i.e. human parity. However, we observe a clear preference for HUMAN over MT: 46% vs 34% and 57% vs 35%, resulting in a significant difference ($x = 325$, $n = 544$, $p < 0.001$).

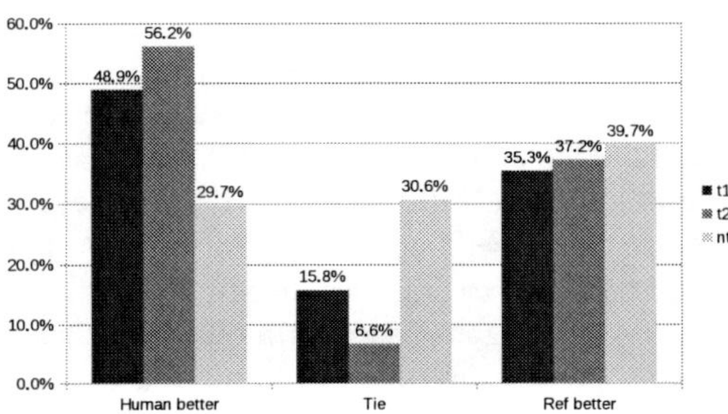

Figure 9: Results for German→English for REF and HU-MAN, with translators t1 and t2 and non-translator nt1.

The last comparison is shown in Figure 9 and concerns the two human translations: REF and HUMAN. The two translators exhibit a clear preference for HUMAN over REF: 49% vs 35% and 56% vs 37%, ($x = 230$, $n = 563$, $p < 0.001$). Conversely, the non-translator preferred REF significantly more often than HUMAN ($x = 126$, $n = 220$, $p < 0.05$): 40% vs 30%.

Given that (i) parity was found between MT and HUMAN in the reference-based evaluation of WMT, where REF was the reference translation, that (ii) HUMAN is considerably different than REF and MT (see Section 2.3) and that (iii) HUMAN is found to be significantly better than REF by translators in our evaluation, it seems that reference bias played a role in the claim of parity at WMT.

3.5 Results of the Inter-annotator Agreement

We now report the inter-annotator agreement (IAA) between the evaluators. Since we have two types of evaluators, translators and non-translators, we report the IAA for both of them. IAA is calculated in terms of Cohen's kappa coefficient (κ) as it was done at WMT 2016 (Bojar et al., 2016, Sec-

tion 3.3).

	Evaluators	
Direction	**ts**	**nts**
English→German	0.326	0.266
English→Russian	0.239	0.238
German→English	0.320	NA

Table 2: Inter-annotator agreement with Cohen's κ among translators (ts) and non-translators (nts) for the three translation directions.

Table 2 shows the IAA coefficients. For English→German, the IAA among translators ($\kappa = 0.326$) is considerably higher, 23% relative, than among non-translators ($\kappa = 0.266$). For English→Russian, both types of evaluators agree at a very similar level ($\kappa = 0.239$ and $\kappa = 0.238$). Finally, for German→English, we cannot establish a direct comparison between the IAA of translators and non-translators, since there was only one non-translator. However, we can compare the IAA of the two translators ($\kappa = 0.32$) to that of each of the translators and the non-translator: $\kappa = 0.107$ between the first translator and the non-translator and $\kappa = 0.125$ between the second translator and the non-translator. The agreement between translators is therefore 176% higher than between one translator and the non-translator.

In a nutshell, for the three translation directions the IAA of translators is higher than, or equivalent to, that of non-translators, which corroborates previous findings by Toral et al. (2018), where the IAA was 0.254 for translators and 0.13 for non-translators.

3.6 Results of the Questionnaire

The questionnaire (see Appendix A) contained two 5-point Likert questions about how often additional context, local and global, was used. In both cases, translators made slightly less use of context than non-translators: $M = 2.9$, $SD = 2.0$ versus $M = 3.5$, $SD = 1.0$ for local context and $M = 1.4$, $SD = 0.7$ versus $M = 2$, $SD = 0.9$ for global context. Our interpretation is that translators felt more confident to rank the translations and thus used additional contextual information to a lesser extent. If an evaluator used global context, they were asked to specify whether they used it mostly for some sentences in particular (those at the beginning, middle or at the end of the documents) or not. Out of 8 respondents, 5 reported to have used global context mostly for sentences regardless of their position in the document and the remaining 3 mostly for sentences at the beginning.

In terms of the perceived quality of the translations evaluated, all non-translators found one of the translations to be clearly better in general. Five out of the eight translators gave that reply too while the other three translators found all translations to be of similar quality (not so good).

Asked whether they thought the translations had been produced by MT systems or by humans, all evaluators replied that some were by humans and some by MT systems, except one translator, who thought that all the translations were by MT systems, and one non-translator who answered that he/she did not know.

4 Conclusions and Future Work

We have conducted a modified evaluation on the MT systems that reached human parity or super-human performance at the news shared task of WMT 2019. According to our results: (i) for English→German, the claim of super-human performance is refuted, but there is human parity; (ii) for English→Russian, the claim of human parity is refuted; (iii) for German→English, for which there were two human translations, the claim of human parity is refuted with respect to the best of the human translations, but not with respect to the worst.

Based on our findings, we put forward a set of recommendations for human evaluation of MT in general and for the assessment of human parity in MT in particular:

1. Global context (i.e. the whole document) should be available to the evaluator. Some of the evaluators have reported that they needed that information to conduct some of the rankings and contemporary research (Castilho et al., in press 2020) has demonstrated that such knowledge is indeed required for the evaluation of some sentences.

2. If the evaluation is to be as accurate as possible then it should be conducted by professional translators. Our evaluation has corroborated that evaluators that do not have translation proficiency evaluate MT systems more leniently than translators and that inter-annotator agreement is higher among the latter (Toral et al., 2018).

3. Reference-based human evaluation should be in principle avoided, given the reference bias issue (Bentivogli et al., 2018), which according to our results seems to have played a role in the claim of human parity for German→English at WMT 2019. That said, we note that there is also research that concludes that there is no evidence of reference bias (Ma et al., 2017).

The first two recommendations were put forward recently (Läubli et al., 2020) and are corroborated by our findings. We acknowledge that our conclusions and recommendations are somewhat limited since they are based on a small number of sentences (just over 300 for each translation direction) and evaluators (14 in total).

Claims of human parity are of course not specific to translation. Super-human performance has been reported to have been achieved in many other tasks, including board games, e.g. chess (Hsu, 2002) and Go (Silver et al., 2017). However, we argue that assessing human parity in translation, and probably in other language-related tasks too, is not as straightforward as in other tasks such as board games, and that the former task poses, at least, two open questions, which we explore briefly in the following to close the paper.

1. Against whom should the machine be evaluated? In other words, should one claim human parity if the output of an MT system is perceived to be indistiguishable from that by an *average* professional translator or should we only compare to a *champion* professional translator? In other tasks it is the latter case, e.g. chess in which DEEP BLUE outperformed world champion Gary Kasparov. Related, we note that in tasks such as chess it is straightforward to define the concept of a player being better than another: whoever wins more games, the rules of which are deterministic. But in the case of translation, it is not so straightforward to define whether a translator is better than another. This question is pertinent since, as we have seen for German→English (Section 3.4), where we had translations by two professional translators, the choice of which one is used to evaluate an MT system against can lead to a claim of human parity or not. In addition, the reason why one claim remains after our evaluation (human parity for English→German) might be that the human translation therein is not *as*

good as it could be. Therefore, once the three potential issues that we have put forward (see Section 2) are solved, we think that an important potential issue that should be studied, and which we have not considered, has to do with the quality of the human translation used.

2. Who should assess claims of human parity and super-human performance? Taking again the example of chess, this is straightforward since one can just count how many games each contestant (machine and human) wins. In translation, however, we need a person with knowledge of both languages to assess the translations. We have seen that the outcome is dependent to some extent on the level of translation proficiency of the evaluator: it is more difficult to find human parity if the translations are evaluated by professional translators than if the evaluation is carried out by bilingual speakers without any translation proficiency. Taking into account that most of the users of MT systems are not translators, should we in practice consider human parity if those users do not perceive a significant difference between human and machine translations, even if an experienced professional translator does?

Acknowledgments

This research has received funding from CLCG's 2019 budget for research participants. I am grateful for valuable comments from Barry Haddow, co-organiser of WMT 2019. I would also like to thank the reviewers; their comments have definitely led to improve this paper.

References

Barrault, Loïc, Ondřej Bojar, Marta R. Costa-jussà, Christian Federmann, Mark Fishel, Yvette Graham, Barry Haddow, Matthias Huck, Philipp Koehn, Shervin Malmasi, Christof Monz, Mathias Müller, Santanu Pal, Matt Post, and Marcos Zampieri. 2019. Findings of the 2019 conference on machine translation (WMT19). In *Proceedings of the Fourth Conference on Machine Translation (Volume 2: Shared Task Papers, Day 1)*, pages 1–61, Florence, Italy, August. Association for Computational Linguistics.

Bentivogli, Luisa, Arianna Bisazza, Mauro Cettolo, and Marcello Federico. 2016. Neural versus phrase-based machine translation quality: a case study. In *Proceedings of the 2016 Conference on Empirical Methods in Natural Language Processing*, pages 257–267, Austin, Texas.

Bentivogli, Luisa, Mauro Cettolo, Marcello Federico, and Federmann Christian. 2018. Machine translation human evaluation: an investigation of evaluation based on post-editing and its relation with direct assessment. In *15th International Workshop on Spoken Language Translation 2018*, pages 62–69.

Bojar, Ondřej, Rajen Chatterjee, Christian Federmann, Yvette Graham, Barry Haddow, Matthias Huck, Antonio Jimeno Yepes, Philipp Koehn, Varvara Logacheva, Christof Monz, Matteo Negri, Aurelie Neveol, Mariana Neves, Martin Popel, Matt Post, Raphael Rubino, Carolina Scarton, Lucia Specia, Marco Turchi, Karin Verspoor, and Marcos Zampieri. 2016. Findings of the 2016 conference on machine translation. In *Proceedings of the First Conference on Machine Translation*, pages 131–198, Berlin, Germany, August.

Bojar, Ondej, Christian Federmann, Mark Fishel, Yvette Graham, Barry Haddow, Matthias Huck, Philipp Koehn, and Christof Monz. 2018. Findings of the 2018 conference on machine translation (wmt18). In *Proceedings of the Third Conference on Machine Translation, Volume 2: Shared Task Papers*, pages 272–307, Belgium, Brussels, October. Association for Computational Linguistics.

Castilho, Sheila, Joss Moorkens, Federico Gaspari, Rico Sennrich, Vilelmini Sosoni, Panayota Georgakopoulou, Pintu Lohar, Andy Way, Antonio Valerio Miceli Barone, and Maria Gialama. 2017. A Comparative Quality Evaluation of PBSMT and NMT using Professional Translators. In *MT Summit 2017*, pages 116–131, Nagoya, Japan.

Castilho, Sheila, Maja Popovic, and Andy Way. in press 2020. On Context Span Needed for Machine Translation Evaluation. In *Proceedings of the Twelvfth International Conference on Language Resources and Evaluation (LREC 2020)*. European Language Resources Association (ELRA).

Federmann, Christian. 2012. Appraise: An open-source toolkit for manual evaluation of machine translation output. *The Prague Bulletin of Mathematical Linguistics*, 98:25–35, September.

Fomicheva, Marina and Lucia Specia. 2016. Reference bias in monolingual machine translation evaluation. In *Proceedings of the 54th Annual Meeting of the Association for Computational Linguistics (Volume 2: Short Papers)*, pages 77–82, Berlin, Germany, August. Association for Computational Linguistics.

Graham, Yvette, Timothy Baldwin, Alistair Moffat, and Justin Zobel. 2017. Can machine translation systems be evaluated by the crowd alone. *Natural Language Engineering*, 23(1):3–30.

Graham, Yvette, Barry Haddow, and Philipp Koehn. 2019. Translationese in machine translation evaluation. *arXiv preprint arXiv:1906.09833*.

Haddow, Barry, Nikolay Bogoychev, Denis Emelin, Ulrich Germann, Roman Grundkiewicz, Kenneth Heafield, Antonio Valerio Miceli Barone, and Rico Sennrich. 2018. The university of edinburgh's submissions to the wmt18 news translation task. In *Proceedings of the Third Conference on Machine Translation, Volume 2: Shared Task Papers*, pages 403–413, Belgium, Brussels, October. Association for Computational Linguistics.

Hassan, Hany, Anthony Aue, Chang Chen, Vishal Chowdhary, Jonathan Clark, Christian Federmann, Xuedong Huang, Marcin Junczys-Dowmunt, Will Lewis, Mu Li, Shujie Liu, Tie-Yan Liu, Renqian Luo, Arul Menezes, Tao Qin, Frank Seide, Xu Tan, Fei Tian, Lijun Wu, Shuangzhi Wu, Yingce Xia, Dongdong Zhang, Zhirui Zhang, and Ming Zhou. 2018. Achieving Human Parity on Automatic Chinese to English News Translation.

Hsu, Feng-Hsiung. 2002. *Behind Deep Blue: Building the Computer That Defeated the World Chess Champion*. Princeton University Press, Princeton, NJ, USA.

Kocmi, Tom, Roman Sudarikov, and Ondej Bojar. 2018. Cuni submissions in wmt18. In *Proceedings of the Third Conference on Machine Translation, Volume 2: Shared Task Papers*, pages 435–441, Belgium, Brussels, October. Association for Computational Linguistics.

Läubli, Samuel, Rico Sennrich, and Martin Volk. 2018. Has Machine Translation Achieved Human Parity? A Case for Document-level Evaluation. In *Proceedings of the 2018 Conference on Empirical Methods in Natural Language Processing*, Brussels, Belgium.

Läubli, Samuel, Sheila Castilho, Graham Neubig, Rico Sennrich, Qinlan Shen, and Antonio Toral. 2020. A set of recommendations for assessing human–machine parity in language translation. *Journal of Artificial Intelligence Research*, 67:653–672.

Ma, Qingsong, Yvette Graham, Timothy Baldwin, and Qun Liu. 2017. Further investigation into reference bias in monolingual evaluation of machine translation. In *Proceedings of the 2017 Conference on Empirical Methods in Natural Language Processing*, pages 2476–2485, Copenhagen, Denmark, September. Association for Computational Linguistics.

Ng, Nathan, Kyra Yee, Alexei Baevski, Myle Ott, Michael Auli, and Sergey Edunov. 2019. Facebook fairs wmt19 news translation task submission. In *Proceedings of the Fourth Conference on Machine Translation (Volume 2: Shared Task Papers, Day 1)*, pages 314–319, Florence, Italy, August. Association for Computational Linguistics.

Papineni, Kishore, Salim Roukos, Todd Ward, and Wei-Jing Zhu. 2002. Bleu: a method for automatic evaluation of machine translation. In *Proceedings of the 40th Annual Meeting of the Association for Computational Linguistics*, pages 311–318, Philadelphia,

Pennsylvania, USA, July. Association for Computational Linguistics.

Silver, David, Thomas Hubert, Julian Schrittwieser, Ioannis Antonoglou, Matthew Lai, Arthur Guez, Marc Lanctot, Laurent Sifre, Dharshan Kumaran, Thore Graepel, Timothy P. Lillicrap, Karen Simonyan, and Demis Hassabis. 2017. Mastering chess and shogi by self-play with a general reinforcement learning algorithm. *CoRR*, abs/1712.01815.

Toral, Antonio, Sheila Castilho, Ke Hu, and Andy Way. 2018. Attaining the unattainable? reassessing claims of human parity in neural machine translation. In *Proceedings of the Third Conference on Machine Translation, Volume 1: Research Papers*, pages 113–123, Belgium, Brussels, October. Association for Computational Linguistics.

A Post-experiment Questionnaire

1. Rate your knowledge of the source language

   - None; A1; A2; B1; B2; C1; C2; native

2. Rate your knowledge of the target language

   - None; A1; A2; B1; B2; C1; C2; native

3. How much experience do you have translating from the source to the target language?

   - None, and I am not a translator; None, but I am a translator; Less than 1 year; between 1 and 2 years; between 2 and 5 years; more than 5 years

4. During the experiment, how often did you use the local context shown in the web application (i.e. source sentences immediately preceding and immediately following the current sentence)?

   - Never; rarely; sometimes; often; always

5. During the experiment, how often did you use the global context provided (i.e. the whole source document provided as a text file)?

   - Never; rarely; sometimes; often; always

6. If you used the global context, was that the case for ranking some sentences in particular?

   - Yes, mainly those at the beginning of documents, e.g. headlines
   - Yes, mainly those in the middle of documents
   - Yes, mainly those at the end of documents
   - No, I used the global context regardless of the position of the sentences to be ranked

7. About the translations you ranked

   - Normally one was clearly better
   - All were of similar quality, and they were not so good
   - All were of similar quality, and they were very good

8. The translations that you evaluated were in your opinion:

   - All produced by human translators
   - All produced by machine translation systems
   - Some produced by humans and some by machine translation systems
   - I don't know

Modelling Source- and Target-Language Syntactic Information as Conditional Context in Interactive Neural Machine Translation

Kamal Kumar Gupta, Rejwanul Haque,[†] Asif Ekbal, Pushpak Bhattacharyya and Andy Way[†]
Department of Computer Science and Engineering, Indian Institute of Technology Patna, Patna, India
[†]ADAPT Centre, School of Computing, Dublin City University, Dublin, Ireland
`kamal.pcs17,asif,pb@iitp.ac.in`
[†]`firstname.lastname@adaptcentre.ie`

Abstract

In interactive machine translation (MT), human translators correct errors in automatic translations in collaboration with the MT systems, which is seen as an effective way to improve the productivity gain in translation. In this study, we model source-language syntactic constituency parse and target-language syntactic descriptions in the form of supertags as conditional context for interactive prediction in neural MT (NMT). We found that the supertags significantly improve productivity gain in translation in interactive-predictive NMT (INMT), while syntactic parsing somewhat found to be effective in reducing human efforts in translation. Furthermore, when we model this source- and target-language syntactic information together as the conditional context, both types complement each other and our fully syntax-informed INMT model shows statistically significant reduction in human efforts for a French–to–English translation task in a reference-simulated setting, achieving 4.30 points absolute (corresponding to 9.18% relative) improvement in terms of word prediction accuracy (WPA) and 4.84 points absolute (corresponding to 9.01% relative) reduction in terms of word stroke ratio (WSR) over the baseline.

1 Introduction

Interactive MT (IMT) is viewed as an effective mean to increase productivity in the translation industry. In principle, IMT aims to reduce human

effort in automatic translation workflows by employing an iterative collaborative strategy with its two most important components, the human agent and the MT engine. Figure 1 represents the interactive protocol.

Figure 1: Interactive protocol in collaboration with an MT system and a user. The user wants to translate the French sentence 'Nous décidons donc, citoyens, de prendre les choses en main.' to English. The reference translation is 'we decide therefore, citizens, to take control of things' which is used here to simulate the user. The user corrects the first wrong word (*things*) from the hypothesis. The validated prefix (magenta phrase) and the last modified word (*control*) are fed back to the NMT system which generates a correct suffix (*of things*).

As of today, NMT (Bahdanau et al., 2015; Vaswani et al., 2017) represents the state-of-the-art in MT research. This has led researchers to test interactive-predictive protocol on NMT too, and papers (Knowles and Koehn, 2016; Peris et al., 2017) that pursued this line of research suggest that NMT is superior than phrase-based statistical MT (Koehn et al., 2003) as far as interactive-predictive translation is concerned.

In a different MT research context, Nădejde et al. (2017) have successfully integrated CCG (combinatory categorical grammar) syntactic categories (Steedman, 2000) into the target-side of the then state-of-the-art recurrent neural network (RNN) MT models (Bahdanau et al., 2015). In this work, we investigate the possibility of modelling the target-language syntax in the form of supertags (Bangalore and Joshi, 1999; Steedman, 2000) as a conditional context in an interactive-predictive protocol on Transformer (Vaswani et al.,

Martins, Moniz, Fumega, Martins, Batista, Coheur, Parra, Trancoso, Turchi, Bisazza, Moorkens, Guerberof, Nurminen, Marg, Forcada (eds.)
Proceedings of the 22nd Annual Conference of the European Association for Machine Translation, p. 195–204
Lisboa, Portugal, November 2020.

2017), the current state-of-the-art NMT model. In a reference-simulated setting, we found that our target-language syntax-informed interactive setup can significantly reduce human effort in a French-to-English translation task.

We also extract syntactic features from constituency-based parse trees of the source French sentences following Akoury et al. (2019), and use them as the conditional context in the interactive-predictive Transformer framework. Experiments show that this contextual information can reduce human efforts in translation to some extent.

In addition, we apply the above strategies together, and model supertags and constituency parse tree-based features collectively as the conditional context for interactive prediction in NMT. Our experimental results indicate that these syntactic feature types are complementary. As a result, this collaborative strategy turns out to be the best-performing in the French-to-English task while significantly outperforming those setups that include either feature type on WPA and WSR. To the best of our knowledge, this is the very first study that investigates the possibility of integrating syntactic knowledge into an interactive MT model.

2   Related Work

Foster et al. (1997) were the first to introduce the idea of interactive-predictive MT as an alternative to pure post-editing MT. There have been a number of papers that explored this strategy in order to minimise human effort in translation and cover many use-cases involving SMT: e.g. applying online (Ortiz-Martínez, 2016) and active (González-Rubio et al., 2012) learning techniques, use of translation memories (Barrachina et al., 2009; Green et al., 2014), predicting the partially typed words and prefix matching (Koehn et al., 2014), word-graphs for reducing response time (Sanchis-Trilles et al., 2014), alignment based post-editing (Simianer et al., 2016), segment-based approaches (Peris et al., 2017), suggesting more than one suffix (Koehn, 2009), and exploring multimodal interaction (Alabau et al., 2014). This use-case has also been moderately tested on NMT, e.g. (Knowles and Koehn, 2016; Wuebker et al., 2016; Peris and Casacuberta, 2018; Lam et al., 2019). To the best of our knowledge, no one has investigated the interactive-predictive protocol on the state-of-the-art Transformer.

The strategy of exploiting syntactic knowledge from the source and/or target languages for im-proving the translation quality is not new in MT research. It was successfully applied in the era of classical MT (Hassan et al., 2007; Haque et al., 2011), and is continually being applied to improve the current state-of-the-art NMT models, e.g. (Luong et al., 2016; Nădejde et al., 2017).

3   Fully Syntactified Interactive NMT

This section presents our fully syntactified interactive NMT model. In NMT, at time step i, the conditional probability of predicting output token y_i given a source sentence x_1^J and the previously generated output token $y_1, ..., y_{i-1}$ is modelled as $\mathrm{p}(y_i|\{y_1, ..., y_{i-1}\}, x_1^J)$.

In the interactive protocol, the user corrects the wrongly translated word (by the MT system) which appears at the left-most side. The feedback is returned back to the MT system in the form of $\hat{y}_1^{i-1}$ which is the validated prefix together with the corrected word $\hat{y}_{i-1}$. Thus, in interactive NMT, the conditional context becomes $\hat{y}_1^{i-1}$, and the conditional probability of predicting output token y_i is modelled as $\mathrm{p}(y_i|\{\hat{y}_1, ..., \hat{y}_{i-1}\}, x_1^J)$. This model serves as our baseline in this work.

In our supertag-based interactive-predictive scenario, we first predict the CCG supertag ($\hat{s}_i$) of the word (y_i) to be predicted next. As a result, the length of the conditional context becomes twice the number of words in context plus one. As far as the target-syntactified interactive NMT is concerned, the conditional probability of predicting the output token y_i is modelled as $\mathrm{p}(y_i|\{\hat{s}_1, \hat{y}_1, ..., \hat{s}_{i-1}, \hat{y}_{i-1}, \hat{s}_i\}, x_1^J)$, where $\hat{s}_1^{i-1}$ is the CCG sequence of the validated prefix $\hat{y}_1^{i-1}$ and $\hat{s}_i$ is the supertag of the word (y_i) to be predicted next.

As for the modelling of source-side syntax, we extract a chunk sequence from the constituency parse tree of a source sentence by setting random a maximum chunk size ($\{1...6\}$) for every sentence (cf. Section 4.2).

Let us define a chunk sequence c_1^M extracted from the input source sentence x_1^J, where M is the number of chunk identifiers (a concatenation of the constituent type and subtree size) of the chunk sequence. This results in an input sequence l_1^{J+M}, where J is the total number of words arbitrarily separated by M number of chunk identifiers. In this model, at time step i, the conditional probability of predicting output token y_i given a source sequence (words and chunk identifiers) l_1^{J+M}, and the validated prefix together with the corrected token $\hat{y}_1, ..., \hat{y}_{i-1}$ is modelled as $p(y_i | \{\hat{y}_1, ..., \hat{y}_{i-1}\}, l_1^{J+M})$.

In our fully syntactified interactive NMT model, the conditional probability of predicting the output token y_i is modelled as $p(y_i | \{\hat{s}_1, \hat{y}_1, ..., \hat{s}_{i-1}, \hat{y}_{i-1}, \hat{s}_i\}, l_1^{J+M})$, where $\hat{s}_1^{i-1}$ is the CCG sequence of the validated prefix $\hat{y}_1^{i-1}$, $\hat{s}_i$ is the supertag of the word (y_i) to be predicted next, and l_1^{J+M} is the input sequence constituting J and M numbers of words and chunk identifiers, respectively.

4 Syntactic Context Features

4.1 Modelling CCG Supertags as Target Language Context

This section explains why we consider a rich and complex syntactic feature, supertags, as context in our experiments. Supertags (Bangalore and Joshi, 1999; Steedman, 2000) are known to be context-sensitive tags that preserve the global syntactic information at local lexical level. Having this property, supertags resolve ambiguity in short- and long-distance dependencies by capturing the preceding and succeeding syntactic dependencies of a lexical term. For example, they signify whether a particular lexical term is expecting a preposition as an argument in order to complete the sentence.

The interactive neural MT models predict a new hypothesis primarily based on the validated context (prefix) including the left-most modified word by the user. In the case of our syntax-informed model, prediction of the next word is also conditioned on CCG supertags (Steedman, 2000) of the validated prefix and the word to be predicted next. Our intuition underpinning this is that such kinds of rich syntactic knowledge sources, which inherently capture long-distance word-to-word dependencies in a sentence, may be useful to improve the prediction quality of interactive NMT, especially for the longer sentences.

4.2 Modelling Syntactic Parse as Source Language Context

Following Akoury et al. (2019) we extract a chunk sequence from the constituency parse tree of a source sentence. Akoury et al. (2019) conducted a series of experiments for getting optimal value (k) for the maximum size of a chunk (subtree). In particular, they tested random and fixed value for (k). The random k ($\{1...6\}$) was found to be best-performing when chunk identifiers were autoregressively predicted in the target using Transformer (Akoury et al., 2019). In our experiments, we adopted their best-up and set the maximum size of a chunk (subtree) random ($\{1...6\}$) for every sentence. Note that a chunk identifier represents a concatenation of the constituent type and subtree size (e.g. VP2). In our case, the chunk identifiers encode additional contextual knowledge on the source side. We adopt the procedure described in Akoury et al. (2019) in order to extract chunk sequences for the source French sentences using the Berkeley Neural Parser.[1] As an example, Table 1 shows a chunk sequence extracted from a French sentence 'si le cliquable doit être à l'état pressé' in row B. The third row of the table (cf. row C) shows the resulting input sequence which is a combination of words and chunk identifiers. As for the chunk identifier, we see from Table 1 that NP3 is a combination of the constituency label NP and the number of terminals of the subtree ('l' état pressé'), i.e. 3. Note that for this example sentence the maximum size of a subtree was 3.

5 Experimental Setups

5.1 Methods of forming conditional syntactic context

In theory, prediction of an output token in the interactive-predictive scenario is conditioned on a user-validated prefix and the input sentence. As discussed above, we model rich syntactic features from the constituency-based parse trees as source context with an expectation to improve the prediction quality in INMT. Hence, in our case, the source-side context is an input sequence of words and chunk identifiers. In interactive mode, if the user makes a correction, the conditional context is modified, i.e. the validated prefix including the last modified word is provided to the MT model for the prediction of the remaining hypothesis. Nonetheless, the source-side context including our syntactic parse features remains unchanged over the course of generation of the target translation.

We model target-side syntactic contexts (CCG supertags) as conditional context in two different ways as follows. In our first setup, we directly use the supertags that are predicted by Transformer as a part of the conditional context for the prediction of the remaining hypothesis. It implies that the setup follows the interleaving technique of Nǎdejde et al. (2017) in which the CCG tag of a token is kept before its token as shown in Table 1. For example, $word_i$ is produced by the decoder in a hypothesis having ccg_i as its CCG supertag that was predicted in the previous time step. If the

[1]https://github.com/nikitakit/
self-attentive-parser

A	à la 4e séance , M Oberthür a rendu compte des résultats des consultations
B	P1 NP3 PONCT1 NC1 PONCT1 VN3 P+D1 NP3
C	P1 à NP3 la 4e séance PONCT1 , NC1 M PONCT1 Oberthür VN3 a rendu compte P+D1 des NP3 résultats des consultations
D	P1 à NP3 la 4e séance PONCT1 , NC1 M PONCT1 Ober@@ PONCT1 th@@ PONCT1 ü@@ PONCT1 r VN3 a rendu compte P+D1 des NP3 résultats des consultations
E	at the 4th meeting , Mr. Oberthür reported on the results of the consultations
F	(S/S)/NP at NP[nb]/N the N/N 4th N meeting N/N , N/N Mr. N Oberthür (S[dcl]\NP)/NP reported PP/NP on NP[nb]/N the N results (NP\NP)/NP of NP[nb]/N the N consultations
G	(S/S)/NP at NP[nb]/N the N/N 4th N meeting N/N , N/N Mr. N Ober@@ N th@@ N ü@@ N r (S[dcl]\NP)/NP reported PP/NP on NP[nb]/N the N results (NP\NP)/NP of NP[nb]/N the N consultations

Table 1: A: a French sentence, B: chunk identifiers, C: input sequence: a combination of the French words and chunk identifiers, D: the segmented version of the French sentence, E: an English sentence, F: the English sentence with CCG supertags, G: the segmented version of the English sentence.

Input sentence	il y a des voitures neuve et chère à tout les coins de rue, exactement comme avant la crise de 2008.
Input sequence with parsing info	VN3 il y a DET1 des NC1 voitures AP3 neuve et chère P1 à ADJ1 tout DET1 les NC1 coins P1 de NC1 rue PONCT1 , ADV1 exactement P1 comme P1 avant DET1 la NC1 crise PP2 de 2008 PONCT1 .
Reference	there are new and expensive cars on every street corner , exactly like before the 2008 crisis .
Initial hypothesis	there (S[dcl]\NP[thr])/NP are N/N new conj and N/N sh@@ N/N ere N cars ((S\NP)\(S\NP))/NP across NP[nb]/N the N/N streets N , ((S\NP)\(S\NP))/((S\NP)\(S\NP)) just ((S\NP)\(S\NP))/((S\NP)\(S\NP)) as ((S\NP)\(S\NP))/PP prior PP/NP to NP[nb]/N the N/N 2008 N/N crisis N .
Hypothesis after several iterations	NP[thr] there (S[dcl]\NP[thr])/NP are N/N new conj and N/N expensive N cars ((S\NP)\(S\NP))/NP on NP[nb]/N every N/N street N corner **((S\NP)\(S\NP))/((S\NP)\(S\NP))** **just** ((S\NP)\(S\NP))/((S\NP)\(S\NP)) as ((S\NP)\(S\NP))/PP prior PP/NP to NP[nb]/N the N/N 2008 N/N crisis N .
INMT interface	there are new and expensive cars on every street corner **just** as prior to the 2008 crisis .
Correction by user	there are new and expensive cars on every street corner , as prior to the 2008 crisis .
Applying on the fly CCG supertagger	NP[thr] there (S[dcl]\NP[thr])/NP are N/N new conj and N/N expensive N cars ((S\NP)\(S\NP))/NP on NP[nb]/N every N/N street N/N corner **N** , ((S\NP)\(S\NP))/((S\NP)\(S\NP)) as ((S\NP)\(S\NP))/PP prior PP/NP to NP[nb]/N the N/N 2008 N/N crisis N .
New hypothesis	there are new and expensive cars on every street corner , exactly like before the 2008 crisis .

Table 2: An example showing applying *On the fly CCG supertagger* on hypothesis.

user sees that $word_i$ is not appropriate in the context (i.e. it is incorrectly predicted by the system), the user edits/removes $word_i$ and replaces it with a new token $word_{new}$. Now, when the modified context (i.e. validated prefix) is fed back to the NMT model, $word_{new}$ will have the tag of $word_i$, i.e. ccg_i. In other words, the final two tokens of the conditional context would be ccg_i $word_{new}$. We carried out an analysis to see how closely these supertags are related to the new words added by the user (cf. Section 6.4). In this regard, we applied BPE segmentation on the training sentences. The sub-word units of a word inherit the CCG category of the word. As an example, we show an English sentence with supertags in Table 1. We see from row E of Table 1 that CCG 'N' of a word 'Oberthür' is distributed over its sub-words (i.e. Ober@@ th@@ ü@@ and r). Our first experimental setup is referred to as PredCCG.

Akoury et al. (2019) showed that integrating target-side ground-truth syntactic information into Transformer at decoding time significantly improved translation quality, and their syntax-based model outperformed the baseline Transformer model by a large margin in terms of BLEU (Papineni et al., 2002). In reality, there is no way of obtaining the target-side ground-truth syntactic information at decoding time. However, in interactive-predictive mode, we found a way to obtain a slightly better CCG sequence for the partial translation (i.e. validated prefix) and inject them into the model at run-time, which we believe can positively impact the model's subsequent predictions. In other words, in our second setup, we integrate a CCG supertagger into our INMT framework, and apply that on the validated prefix and unchecked suffix on the fly. The tagger is invoked when the user makes a correction. As an example, when the user inserts a new token $word_{new}$ in place of an incorrectly predicted token ($word_i$), the CCG supertagger is invoked and applied to the validated prefix and unchecked suffix on the fly. In Table 2, we show how *On the fly CCG supertagger* is applied in our interactive interface. We see from rows 6 and 7 of Table 2 that the user replaces the wrongly predicted token *just* with a correct token ','. The CCG supertag ((S\NP)\(S\NP))/((S\NP)\(S\NP)) of the incorrect token 'just' is assigned to the new token ',' which is incorrect in this context. When the user commits this change, *On the fly CCG supertagger* is invoked and applied to the corrected hypothesis (a combination of validated prefix and unchecked suffix). As can be seen from row 8 of Table 2, a new CCG tag sequence is generated for the hypothesis, and we see that CCG (N) of the newly added token ',' is correct. Finally, INMT predicts another suggestion (row 9 of Table 2) where we see the remaining predictions are correct in the context. We call this experimental setup OnflyCCG. Note that the model is trained at sub-word level and generates sub-words at output; however, word level tokens are presented to the user. Naturally, *On the fly CCG supertagger* is applied to a hypothesis of word level.

5.2 MT systems

We carry out experiments with French-to-English with the UN corpus[2] (Ziemski et al., 2016). The training and development sets contain 12,238,995 and 1,500 sentences, respectively. We use 1,500 sentences from the WMT15 news test set *newstest2015* as our test set. In order to build our MT systems, we use the Sockeye[3] (Hieber et al., 2018) toolkit. Our training setups are as follows. The tokens of the training, evaluation and validation sets are segmented into sub-word units using BPE. We performed 30,000 join operations. We use 6 layers in the encoder and decoder sides, an 8-head attention, hidden layer of size 512, embedding vector of size 512, learning rate 0.0002, and minimum batch size of 1,800 tokens. EasyCCG[4] (Lewis and Steedman, 2014), a CCG supertagger, is used for generating the CCG sequence for the English sentences.

Transformer (Baseline)	26.90
Source Syntactified (SS)	26.96
Target Syntactified (TS)	27.10
Fully Syntactified (FS)	27.36 (p-value: 0.059)

Table 3: The BLEU scores of baseline and syntactified NMT systems.

Table 3 shows the performance of our baseline and syntax-sensitive NMT systems in terms of BLEU. The second and third rows represent the NMT models that incorporate source- and target-language syntactic contexts, respectively, which we call source- (SS) and target-syntactified (TS) NMT systems, respectively. We see from Table 3 that the BLEU scores of these two MT systems and Transformer are very similar. Additionally, we performed statistical significance test using bootstrap resampling methods (Koehn, 2004).

We found that the differences of the BLEU scores of these MT systems are not statistically significant.

The fourth row shows the BLEU score of the NMT system that integrates both the source- and target-language syntactic contexts (i.e. supertags and syntactic parse, respectively) together. We call this model our fully syntactified (FS) NMT system. The FS NMT system produces a 0.46 BLEU point (corresponding to 1.7% relative) gain on the test set over the baseline. The differences of the BLEU scores of the FS and baseline Transformer models are not statistically significant either. When we integrate the source- and target-language syntactic contexts individually into Transformer, they do not positively impact the system's performance. However, when we integrate them collectively into the model, we see that they bring a moderate gain in terms of BLEU over the baseline, and the gain is very close to the significance level (p-value: 0.059) too. It seems that both contextual features complement each other and bring about an (moderate) improvement. Although the primary objective of this work is to observe the prediction of Transformer in an interactive-predictive platform while modelling different syntactic constraints as conditional context, this can also be seen as an important finding to MT research.

6 Results and Discussion

In this section, first we explain the strategy that we adopted for evaluating the interactive-predictive MT systems. Then, we present our evaluation results along with some discussions and analysis.

6.1 Evaluation Plan for INMT

We evaluate the performance of the INMT systems using two evaluation metrics, WSR and WPA. WSR denotes the total number of token replacements required to obtain the desired hypothesis (Peris et al., 2017). WPA is the percentage of words that the INMT system predicts correctly, given a prefix of all the previous translator-produced words (Knowles and Koehn, 2016). WSR and WPA are calculated on word level. The process of evaluating translations in interactive scenarios is expensive as it requires human evaluators. As an alternative, we adopted a reference-simulated evaluation strategy as in Peris et al. (2017), where instead of taking feedback from the real user, the reference sentence is used as the feedback. In other words, each time an interactive MT model generates a hypothesis it is com-

[2]https://www.statmt.org/wmt13/training-parallel-un.tgz
[3]https://github.com/awslabs/sockeye
[4]https://github.com/mikelewis0/easyccg

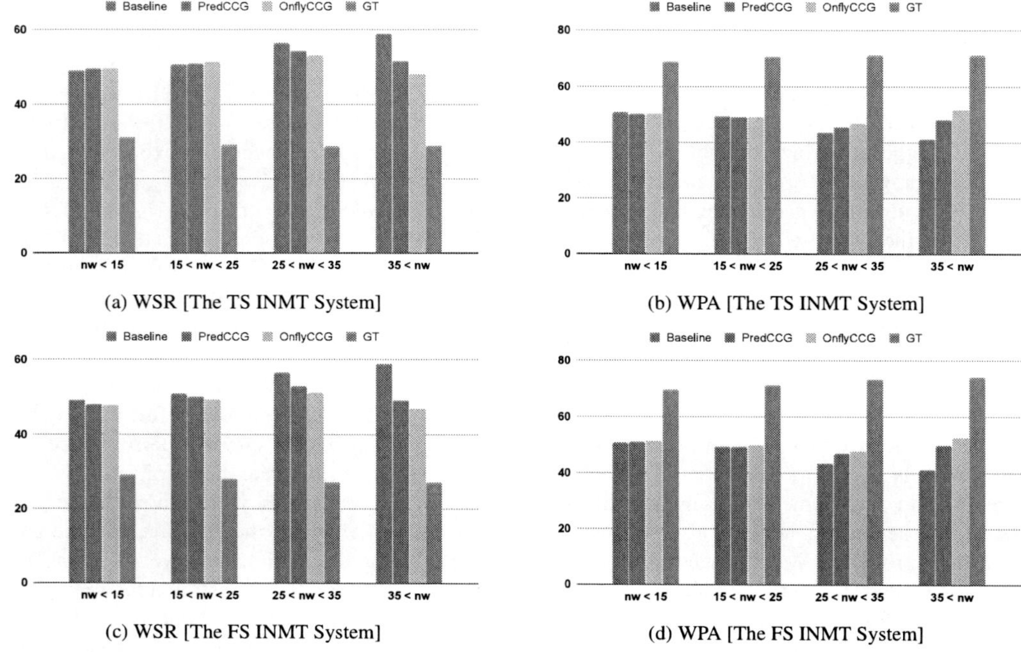

(a) WSR [The TS INMT System] (b) WPA [The TS INMT System]

(c) WSR [The FS INMT System] (d) WPA [The FS INMT System]

Figure 2: WSR and WPA scores of the syntax-informed and baseline INMT systems with respect to sentence lengths.

pared with the reference sentence from left to right.

6.2 Evaluation Results

6.2.1 The SS INMT System

In this section, we present the evaluation results that we obtain using the source-language syntactic constituency parse as conditional context in the interactive-predictive Transformer model. The WSR and WPA scores of the baseline and SS Transformer models are shown in Table 4. Note that WSR is an error metric, which means that lower scores are better. We see from the table that integrating this context into the model brought about a 0.56 point absolute (corresponding to 1.04% relative) reduction and a 0.31 point absolute (corresponding to 0.66% relative) gain in terms of WSR and WPA, respectively, over the baseline. We use approximate randomization (Yeh, 2000) to test the statistical significance of the difference between the two systems. We found that these differences are not statistically significant. These results indicate that using the syntactic

	Baseline	SS INMT
WSR	53.77	53.21
WPA	46.82	47.13

Table 4: Performance of the SS INMT System.

constituency parse as context in interactive neural MT models has only a minor impact on reducing human effort in translation.

6.2.2 The TS INMT System

In this section, we obtain experimental results to evaluate the interactive-predictive Transformer model that uses target-language supertags as conditional context on the test set. We report the results in Table 5. The third and fourth columns of Table 5 represent two setups (PredCCG and OnflyCCG) that we describe in Section 5.1. The first column of the table represents the baseline Transformer system. The gains in WSR and WPA over the baseline are found to be the highest when *On the fly CCG supertagger* is applied on the user modified hypothesis (cf. Section 5.1). With this, we achieve a 3.16 point absolute (corresponding to 5.87% relative) reduction and a 2.65 point absolute (corresponding to 5.65% relative) improvement in terms of WSR and WPA, respectively, on the test set over the baseline. These differences are statistically significant. When we compare PredCCG and OnflyCCG setups, we see that OnflyCCG brings a 1.09 WSR point absolute (corresponding to 2.10% relative) reduction and a 1.18 WPA point absolute (corresponding to 2.44% relative) improvement over the PredCCG setup, which

200

	Baseline	PredCCG	OnflyCCG	GT
WSR	53.77	**51.70**	**50.61**	**29.44**
WPA	46.82	**48.29**	**49.47**	**70.53**

Table 5: Performance of the TS INMT System

are statistically significant too. This indicates that especially with the OnflyCCG setup supertags as target-language context can have significant impact on reducing human effort in translation.

For comparison we also report the WPA and WSR scores of our TS INMT system on an ideal setup, i.e. when we feed Transformer with ground-truth CCG supertags instead of those predicted by the Transformer or generated by *On the fly CCG supertagger*. As expected, this setup surpasses the baseline and context-based setups by a large margins in terms of WSR and WPA.

6.2.3   The FS INMT System

As discussed above, we use both source and target syntax as the conditional context in interactive prediction in NMT. The first two rows of Table 6 represent the evaluation results obtained by integrating both as a collective feature into the INMT model. This feature brings about a statistically significant improvements in terms of WPA and WSR, respectively, over the baseline across two setups: PredCCG and OnflyCCG. We see from Table 6 that OnflyCCG is the best-performing setup that produces a 4.84 point absolute (corresponding to 9.01% relative) reduction and a 4.30 point absolute (corresponding to 9.18% relative) improvement in terms of WSR and WPA, respectively over the baseline.

	Baseline	PredCCG	OnflyCCG	GT
WSR	53.77	**50.03**	**48.93**	**28.24**
WPA	46.82	**49.67**	**51.12**	**71.69**
WSR		-1.67	-1.68	-1.20
WPA		+1.38	+1.65	+1.16

Table 6: Performance of the FS INMT System.

As for PredCCG and OnflyCCG, the FS INMT model with OnflyCCG statistically significantly surpassed the one with PredCCG as far as reduction of human effort is concerned. As above, we see that the ideal setup (GT) again surpasses the baseline and context-based setups by large margins. We make a comparison of Table 5 and 6 for the three setups (PredCCG, OnflyCCG, and GT), and differences in WSR and WPA scores are presented in the last rows of Table 6. We see consistent reductions in WSR and improvements in WPA

across the three setups with the combined contextual features, which are statistically significant.

CCG as target context and, to a certain extent, syntactic parse as source context were found to be effective in reducing human effort when applied individually. Nevertheless, CCG (target) and syntactic parse (source) together as a context turn out to be the best-performing setup with statistically significant gains over either feature type. In this sense, we can say that source and target-side syntactic contextual features complement each other as far as neural interactive prediction is concerned. We conjecture that since the conditional context includes source-language syntactic constituency parse and target-language syntactic constructs in the form of CCG supertags together, it provides the NMT model with better syntactic agreement between the source and target sentences, which, in turn, helps the model generate better predictions.

6.3   Impact on Sentence Lengths

For further analysis, we place the sentences of our test set into four sets (c.f. Figure 2) as per the sentence length measures, i.e. number of words $nw<15$, $15<nw\leq25$, $25<nw\leq35$ and $35<nw$. This division was made based on the lengths of reference sentences. In Figure 2, we plot the distributions of WPA and WSR scores over the sentence length-based sets. As can be seen from the figure, both the TS and FS INMT systems produce increasingly better WSR and WPA scores as the length of the reference sentences increases. As discussed above, supertags encode wider context of a sentence, which could help the decoder to capture long-range word-to-word dependencies at generation time. In other words, as the length of the validated prefix increases, the corresponding CCG supertag sequences help better predict the subsequent tokens correctly.

6.4   CCG supertags of the Words of User Choice

	Fr–>En (TS)		Fr–>En (FS)	
	PredCCG	OnflyCCG	PredCCG	OnflyCCG
Whole testset	41.07	23.95	39.58	22.52
nw <15	40.64	23.88	40.25	22.02
$15<nw<25$	40.84	23.04	39.44	21.92
$25<nw<35$	42.80	25.28	40.19	23.35
$35<nw$	39.32	24.33	38.06	22.89

Table 7: % of CCG supertags that becomes incorrect when the user replace the incorrectly predicted token in hypothesis with the token of his choice.

As mentioned in Section 5.1, we came up with two different ways to use the target-language supertags as conditional context for the predictions in INMT. First, in the PredCCG setup, if the user makes a correction, the user's choice of word inherits the CCG supertag of the word that the user has just corrected, which, in fact, is predicted by the INMT system. The new word and the incorrect word that the user has just corrected could be syntactically or semantically different. As a result, the supertag that the new word inherits could be incorrect. We calculate the percentage of CCG supertags that are incorrect for the new words when the predicted words were wrong and edited by the user. We also produce such statistics for the second experimental setup, OnflyCCG. In Table 7, we show the percentage of CCG supertags those were incorrectly assigned to new words on both the experimental setups. We clearly see from the table that the second setup (OnflyCCG) is far better than the first setup (PredCCG) in terms of assigning correct CCG tags to the new words that the user has just corrected, i.e. better by 17.06% to 17.12%. This is seen consistently across the sentence length-based sets too. When we compare this across the TS and FS INMT systems, we see that the percentage of correctly assigned CCG tags to the words of the user's choice in the FS INMT system is higher (by 1.43%) than the TS INMT system on the test set.

6.5 Latency for the CCG supertagger

We calculate the average delay for a correction (i.e. processing time) by the user for baseline, PredCCG, OnflyCCG and GT (ground-truth) setups using the TS INMT system, which are shown in Table 8. We see from the table that the delays are comparable across the systems. As for Onfly-

Baseline	PredCCG	OnflyCCG	GT
0.28	0.35	0.47	0.28

Table 8: Average Latency (in seconds) for generating modified hypothesis

CCG, we exclusively calculate the average latency for applying the CCG supertagger, which is found to be 0.12 seconds only. Hence, the supertagger does not bring much computational overhead and impact latency as far as translation time in the interactive-predictive platform is concerned.

6.6 Average Number of Partial Hypothesis Processed

In the interactive protocol, when the user makes a correction, the MT system re-translates the source

sentence given the validated partial hypothesis. Finally, the new translation is shown to the user. In

	PredCCG	OnflyCCG	GT
Baseline	8.91		
SS	8.84		
TS		8.56	8.38	5.72
FS		8.24	8.11	5.36

Table 9: Average number of partial hypothesis processed.

Table 9, we show the average number of partial hypotheses processed (i.e. how many the MT system has to re-translate) for each sentence in the test set. For this analysis, we consider all the experimental setups (PredCCG, OnflyCCG and GT) and MT system types (SS, TS and FS INMT). We see from Table 9 that the OnflyCCG on FS INMT setup wins out if we omit the ideal setup (GT). In other words, source- and target-language syntactic contexts in combination have more impact in INMT than either type individually.

7 Conclusion

In this paper, we have integrated a rich and complex syntactic knowledge in the form of supertags and/or syntactic constituency parse into the current state-of-the-art neural MT model, Transformer. Furthermore, we tested whether integration of such knowledge sources into Transformer could indeed reduce human efforts in translation in an interactive-predictive scenario. We carried out our experiments on French-to-English, a high resource widely-used translation-pair in industry. We compared our syntax-informed and baseline Transformer models on an interactive-predictive platform. The use of syntactic constituency parse as conditional context has minor impact on reducing human effort in translation. We modelled target-language supertags as conditional context in interactive NMT in two different ways, and both of these significantly positively impact productivity in translation.

Interestingly, supertags (target) and constituency parse (source) together as a context turns out to be the best-performing setup with significant gains over either feature type. In this sense, we can say that source and target-side syntactic contextual features complement as far as neural interactive prediction is concerned. In fact, the conditional context in this setup includes both source-language constituency parse and target-language CCG, which essentially provides the INMT model with better syntactic agreement between the source and target sentences.

We conjecture that this could be the reason why this collaborative strategy turned out to be best-performing.

Our analysis shows that the OnflyCCG setup (where CCG assigned by *On the fly CCG supertagger*) significantly outperformed PredCCG (where CCG predicted by Transformer) in terms of assigning correct CCG to the words of user's choice by large margins (17.06% to 17.12%). In fact, our proposed setup (OnflyCCG), to a certain extent, provides a way to inject correct context into the interactive model. This could be the reason why OnflyCCG turned out to be best-performing.

Our analysis unraveled many sides of our syntax-aware models in an interactive-predictive environment. For an example, we particularly found that our syntax-informed interactive-predictive models have positively impacted more for the translation of longer sentences. Given the importance of interactive MT in translation industry, the findings of this work can be crucial for their production as our methods can positively impact their productivity gain in translation.

Given the fact that linguistic tools such as supertaggers and constituency parsers are only readily available for a handful of languages, in future, we will continue to pursue this line of investigation with exploring integration of language-independent contextual knowledge in interactive-predictive NMT. In future, we plan to evaluate our interactive MT systems with human agents.

8   Acknowledgement

Authors gratefully acknowledge the generous grant of TDIL, MeiTY, Govt. of India for the project "Hindi to English Machine Translation for Judicial Domain [11(3)/2015-HCC(TDIL]" to carry out this research. Asif Ekbal acknowledges Young Faculty Research Fellowship (YFRF), supported by Visvesvaraya PhD scheme for Electronics and IT, Ministry of Electronics and Information Technology (MeitY), Government of India, being implemented by Digital India Corporation (formerly MediaLab Asia). Rejwanul Haque and Andy Way acknowledge the ADAPT Centre for Digital Content Technology, funded under the Science Foundation Ireland (SFI) Research Centres Programme (Grant No. 13/RC/2106) and is co-funded under the European Regional Development Fund.

References

Akoury, N., Krishna, K., and Iyyer, M. (2019). Syntactically supervised transformers for faster neural machine translation. In *Proceedings of the 57th Conference of the Association for Computational Linguistics, ACL 2019, Volume 1: Long Papers*, pages 1269–1281, Florence, Italy.

Alabau, V., Sanchis, A., and Casacuberta, F. (2014). Improving on-line handwritten recognition in interactive machine translation. *Pattern Recognition*, 47(3):1217–1228.

Bahdanau, D., Cho, K., and Bengio, Y. (2015). Neural machine translation by jointly learning to align and translate. In *3rd International Conference on Learning Representations (ICLR 2015)*, San Diego, CA.

Bangalore, S. and Joshi, A. K. (1999). Supertagging: An approach to almost parsing. *Computational Linguistics*, 25(2):237–265.

Barrachina, S., Bender, O., Casacuberta, F., Civera, J., Cubel, E., Khadivi, S., Lagarda, A., Ney, H., Tomás, J., Vidal, E., et al. (2009). Statistical approaches to computer-assisted translation. *Computational Linguistics*, 35(1):3–28.

Foster, G., Isabelle, P., and Plamondon, P. (1997). Target-text mediated interactive machine translation. *Machine Translation*, 12:175–194.

González-Rubio, J., Ortiz-Martínez, D., and Casacuberta, F. (2012). Active learning for interactive machine translation. In *Proceedings of the 13th Conference of the European Chapter of the Association for Computational Linguistics*, pages 245–254, Avignon, France.

Green, S., Chuang, J., Heer, J., and Manning, C. D. (2014). Predictive translation memory: A mixed-initiative system for human language translation. In *Proceedings of the 27th annual ACM symposium on User interface software and technology*, pages 177–187.

Haque, R., Naskar, S. K., van den Bosch, A., and Way, A. (2011). Integrating source-language context into phrase-based statistical machine translation. *Machine Translation*, 25(3):239–285.

Hassan, H., Sima'an, K., and Way, A. (2007). Supertagged phrase-based statistical machine translation. In *Proceedings of the 45th Annual Meeting of the Association of Computational Linguistics*, pages 288–295, Prague, Czech Republic.

Hieber, F., Domhan, T., Denkowski, M., Vilar, D., Sokolov, A., Clifton, A., and Post, M. (2018). The sockeye neural machine translation toolkit at AMTA 2018. In *Proceedings of the 13th Conference of the Association for Machine Translation in the Americas (Volume 1: Research Papers)*, pages 200–207, Boston, MA.

Knowles, R. and Koehn, P. (2016). Neural interactive translation prediction. In *Proceedings of the Association for Machine Translation in the Americas*, pages 107–120, Austin, TX.

Koehn, P. (2004). Statistical significance tests for machine translation evaluation. In *Proceedings of the 2004 Conference on Empirical Methods in Natural Language Processing (EMNLP)*, pages 388–395, Barcelona, Spain.

Koehn, P. (2009). A process study of computer-aided translation. *Machine Translation*, 23(4):241–263.

Koehn, P., Och, F. J., and Marcu, D. (2003). Statistical phrase-based translation. In *HLT-NAACL 2003: conference combining Human Language Technology conference series and the North American Chapter of the Association for Computational Linguistics conference series*, pages 48–54, Edmonton, AB.

Koehn, P., Tsoukala, C., and Saint-Amand, H. (2014). Refinements to interactive translation prediction based on search graphs. In *Proceedings of the 52nd Annual Meeting of the Association for Computational Linguistics (Volume 2: Short Papers)*, pages 574–578, Baltimore, MD.

Lam, T. K., Schamoni, S., and Riezler, S. (2019). Interactive-predictive neural machine translation through reinforcement and imitation. In *Proceedings of Machine Translation Summit XVII Volume 1: Research Track*, pages 96–106, Dublin, Ireland.

Lewis, M. and Steedman, M. (2014). A* CCG parsing with a supertag-factored model. In *Proceedings of the 2014 Conference on Empirical Methods in Natural Language Processing (EMNLP)*, pages 990–1000, Doha, Qatar.

Luong, M.-T., Le, Q. V., Sutskever, I., Vinyals, O., and Kaiser, L. (2016). Multi-task sequence to sequence learning. In *International Conference on Learning Representations (ICLR)*, San Juan, Puerto Rico.

Nădejde, M., Reddy, S., Sennrich, R., Dwojak, T., Junczys-Dowmunt, M., Koehn, P., and Birch, A. (2017). Predicting target language CCG supertags improves neural machine translation. In *Proceedings of the Second Conference on Machine Translation*, pages 68–79, Copenhagen, Denmark.

Ortiz-Martínez, D. (2016). Online learning for statistical machine translation. *Computational Linguistics*, 42(1):121–161.

Papineni, K., Roukos, S., Ward, T., and Zhu, W.-J. (2002). BLEU: a method for automatic evaluation of machine translation. In *ACL-2002: 40th Annual Meeting of the Association for Computational Linguistics*, pages 311–318, Philadelphia, PA.

Peris, Á. and Casacuberta, F. (2018). Active learning for interactive neural machine translation of data streams. In *Proceedings of the 22nd Conference on Computational Natural Language Learning*, pages 151–160, Brussels, Belgium.

Peris, Á., Domingo, M., and Casacuberta, F. (2017). Interactive neural machine translation. *Computer Speech & Language*, 45:201–220.

Sanchis-Trilles, G., Ortiz-Martínez, D., and Casacuberta, F. (2014). Efficient wordgraph pruning for interactive translation prediction. In *Proceedings of the 17th Annual Conference of the European Association for Machine Translation (EAMT)*, pages 27–34, Prague, Czech Republic.

Simianer, P., Karimova, S., and Riezler, S. (2016). A post-editing interface for immediate adaptation in statistical machine translation. In *Proceedings of COLING 2016, the 26th International Conference on Computational Linguistics: System Demonstrations*, pages 16–20, Osaka, Japan.

Steedman, M. (2000). The syntactic process. *MIT Press*, 24.

Vaswani, A., Shazeer, N., Parmar, N., Uszkoreit, J., Jones, L., Gomez, A. N., Kaiser, Ł., and Polosukhin, I. (2017). Attention is all you need. In *Advances in neural information processing systems*, pages 5998–6008.

Wuebker, J., Green, S., DeNero, J., Hasan, S., and Luong, M.-T. (2016). Models and inference for prefix-constrained machine translation. In *Proceedings of the 54th Annual Meeting of the Association for Computational Linguistics (Volume 1: Long Papers)*, pages 66–75, Berlin, Germany.

Yeh, A. (2000). More accurate tests for the statistical significance of result differences. In *Proceedings of the 18th conference on Computational linguistics - Volume 2, COLING 2000*, pages 947–953, Saarbrücken, Germany.

Ziemski, M., Junczys-Dowmunt, M., and Pouliquen, B. (2016). The united nations parallel corpus v1.0. In *Proceedings of the Tenth International Conference on Language Resources and Evaluation (LREC'16)*, pages 3530–3534, Portorož, Slovenia.

Learning Non-Monotonic Automatic Post-Editing of Translations from Human Orderings

António Góis[*]
Unbabel
Lisbon, Portugal
antoniogois@gmail.com

Kyunghyun Cho
New York University
Facebook AI
New York, USA
kyunghyun.cho@nyu.edu

André Martins
Unbabel
Instituto de Telecomunicações
Lisbon, Portugal
andre.martins@unbabel.com

Abstract

Recent research in neural machine translation has explored flexible generation orders, as an alternative to left-to-right generation. However, training non-monotonic models brings a new complication: how to search for a good ordering when there is a combinatorial explosion of orderings arriving at the same final result? Also, how do these automatic orderings compare with the actual behaviour of human translators? Current models rely on manually built biases or are left to explore all possibilities on their own. In this paper, we analyze the orderings produced by human post-editors and use them to train an automatic post-editing system. We compare the resulting system with those trained with left-to-right and random post-editing orderings. We observe that humans tend to follow a nearly left-to-right order, but with interesting deviations, such as preferring to start by correcting punctuation or verbs.

1 Introduction

Neural sequence generation models have been widely adopted for tasks such as machine translation (MT) (Bahdanau et al., 2015; Vaswani et al., 2017) and automatic post-editing of translations (Junczys-Dowmunt and Grundkiewicz, 2016; Chatterjee et al., 2016; Correia and Martins, 2019; Lopes et al., 2019). These models typically generate one word at a time, and rely on a factoriza-

0 : Die LMS geöffnet *ist* .	[I:2:**ist**]
1 : Die LMS **ist** geöffnet *ist* .	[D:4:*ist*]
2 : Die LMS **ist** geöffnet .	

Table 1: Example of a small post-edit from the training set. Each action is represented by three features: its type (I for insert and D for delete), its position in the sentence and the token to insert/delete. In this example, the token marked *in red* needs to be removed since it is incorrectly placed. The **blue** token is inserted to obtain the correct pe.

tion that imposes a left-to-right generation ordering. Recent alternatives allow for different generation orderings (Welleck et al., 2019; Stern et al., 2019; Gu et al., 2019a), or even for parallel generation of multiple tokens (Gu et al., 2018; Stern et al., 2019; Gu et al., 2019b; Zhou et al., 2020), which allows exploiting dependencies among non-consecutive tokens. One potential difficulty when training non-monotonic models is how to learn a good generation ordering. There are exponentially many valid orderings to generate a given sequence, and a model should prefer those that lead to accurate translations and can be efficiently learned. In previous work, to guide the search for a good ordering, oracle policies have been provided (Welleck et al., 2019), or another kind of inductive bias such as a loss function tailored to promote certain orderings (Stern et al., 2019). However, no supervision has been used with orderings that go beyond simple patterns, such as left-to-right, random ordering with a uniform distribution, or a balanced binary tree.

While prior work has focused on learning generation orderings in an unsupervised manner, in this paper we ask the question of whether human generation orderings can be a useful source of supervision. One such possible source lies in the keystrokes of humans typing. It is known that

[*]Work partly done during a research visit at New York University.

Martins, Moniz, Fumega, Martins, Batista, Coheur, Parra, Trancoso, Turchi, Bisazza, Moorkens, Guerberof, Nurminen, Marg, Forcada (eds.)
Proceedings of the 22nd Annual Conference of the European Association for Machine Translation, p. 205–214
Lisboa, Portugal, November 2020.

edit operations performed by human translators are not arbitrary (Góis and Martins, 2019). But it is not known how the orderings preferred by humans look like, or how they compare to orders learned by models.

To investigate this question, we propose a model that learns generation orderings in a supervised manner from human keystrokes. Since a human is free to move back and forth arbitrarily while editing text, the chosen order of operations can be used as an additional learning signal. More specifically, we do this in the context of **automatic post-editing (APE)** (Simard et al., 2007). APE consists in improving the output of a blackbox MT system by automatically fixing its mistakes. The act of post-editing text can be fully specified as a sequence of delete (DEL) and insert (INS) **actions** in given positions. Furthermore, if we do not include redundant actions in a sequence, that sequence can be arbitrarily reordered while still producing the same output. For instance, in Table 1, we can switch the order of the two actions, as long as we rectify to delete position 3 instead of position 4.

We compare a model trained with human orderings to others trained with left-to-right and random orderings. We show that the resulting non-monotonic APE system learned from human orderings outperforms systems learned on random orderings and performs comparably or slightly better than a system learned with left-to-right orderings.

2 Dataset

2.1 WMT data and keystrokes

The dataset used in this paper is the keystrokes dataset introduced by Specia et al. (2017) in the scope of the QT21 project. This dataset consists of triplets required to train an APE system: *source* sentences (src), *machine-translation* outputs (mt) and *human post-edits* (pe). Features about the post-editing process are also provided, including the keystroke logging. In particular, we focus on the language pair English to German (En-De) in the Information Technology (IT) domain, translated with a Phrase-Based Statistical MT system (PBSMT) – this dataset has a large intersection with the data used in the WMT 2016-18 APE shared tasks (Chatterjee et al., 2018). This allows for comparison with systems previously submitted to the shared task by using the exact same development and test sets, while augmenting the

	size	mt=pe	min-edit	human-edit
train with keystrokes	16,068	18.2%	6.6	14.48
full train	23,000	14.6%	11.8	—
dev '16	1,000	6.0%	11.3	—

Table 2: WMT-APE datasets: Original training set and development set from the WMT-APE shared task, and subset of the training set also found in the dataset from Specia et al. (2017). mt=pe is the percentage of samples where the mt output is already correct. min-edit is the average count of actions (DEL ans INS) required to change mt into pe, computed from Levenshtein distance. human-edit is the average count of actions computed from human keystrokes. Both average action counts exclude samples with zero actions.

training set with keystroke logging information.

Out of 23,000 training samples provided by the WMT 2016-17 shared tasks, 16,068 are also present in the dataset from Specia et al. (2017). This intersection is obtained by requiring the same triplet (src, mt, pe) to be present in both datasets. Since the WMT dataset comes already pre-processed, the following pre-processing is applied to the dataset containing keystrokes, to increase their intersection: using tools from Moses (Koehn et al., 2007), we apply En punctuation-normalization to the whole triplet, followed by tokenization of the corresponding language (either En or De). Additionally, we preprocess the raw keystrokes to obtain word-level DEL and INS actions (detailed in §2.2).

Table 2 shows statistics from WMT's original data and training set after intersecting with the keystrokes dataset from Specia et al. (2017). We denote by min-edit the average count of DEL and INS obtained from the Levenshtein distance. Average count of human actions (human-edit) is only available for the subset of the training data found in the keystrokes dataset. Also note that keystrokes will not be required during inference, only for training. Once a model is already trained, the only input required is a (src, mt) pair in order to predict a full sequence of actions and produce the final pe. This allows to use the exact same development and test sets as in the shared task, without losing any samples.

2.2 Preprocessing raw keystrokes

The original keystrokes logging provides character-level changes made by the human editor. Since this information is too fine-grained for our model, we preprocess the raw keystokes to obtain word-level DEL and INS. Our starting

src	When you decrease opacity , the underlying artwork becomes visible through the surface of the object , stroke , fill , or text .
mt	Wenn Sie die Deckkraft verringern , wird das zugrunde liegende Bildmaterial durch die Oberfläche des Objekts , Kontur , Fläche oder Text angezeigt .
pe	Wenn Sie die Deckkraft verringern , wird das darunterliegende Bildmaterial durch die Oberfläche des Objekts , der Kontur , der Fläche bzw. des Textes sichtbar .
l2r	D:8:zugrunde D:8:liegende I:8:darunterliegende I:16:der I:19:der D:21:oder D:21:Text D:21:angezeigt I:21:bzw. I:22:des I:23:Textes I:24:sichtbar STOP
shuff	D:20:oder I:22:bzw. D:20:Text I:22:des I:10:darunterliegende D:8:zugrunde I:23:sichtbar I:19:der I:24:Textes I:17:der D:22:angezeigt D:8:liegende STOP
h-ord	I:17:der I:20:der D:22:oder I:24:bzw. I:25:des D:22:Text I:25:Textes D:8:zugrunde D:8:liegende I:8:darunterliegende D:21:angezeigt I:24:sichtbar STOP
human	I:17:der I:20:der D:22:oder I:22:bzw. I:23:des D:24:Text I:24:Textes D:8:zugrunde D:8:liegende I:8:darunterliegende D:25:. D:24:angezeigt I:24:sichtbar I:25:. STOP

Table 3: Example of a sentence and its minimum-edit actions ordered in three different ways: left-to-right (*l2r*), randomly shuffled (*shuff*) and following human order (*h-ord*). The unfiltered human actions are also presented (*human*). We can see that the human chose to first insert the two words marked in blue, later moving back in the sentence to edit the leftmost mistakes.

point is the sequence of strings containing the mt state after each keystroke. We track which word is currently being edited and store an action to summarize the change. Replacements are represented as a DEL followed by INS. Multiple words may be changed simultaneous, either by selecting and deleting a block of words or by pasting text. Block changes assume a left-to-right sequence of actions.

Table 3 contains an example of a preprocessed sequence of keystrokes in the last line (*human*). When applied to the mt, the sentence is converted to pe. Note that this kind of action sequences may be impossible to re-order due to redundant actions — for a token t not present in mt nor pe, the actions INS:0:t DEL:0:t cannot be switched.

We perform an additional step to eliminate redundant actions performed by human post-editors. Editors may take paths significantly longer than the minimum edit distance. During experiments these longer paths proved harmful for the model, so we designed a way to filter all actions which are not relevant. First, an optimal action sequence that minimizes edit (Levenshtein) distance is obtained with dynamic programming. Since by definition this sequence does not contain redundant actions, these actions can be reordered to produce the same output. This provides a chance to experiment with different orders, such as left-to-right or human order. To align the unfiltered human actions with the minimum-edit actions, we first match human actions to machine actions that insert/delete the same token. Then, we break ties by aligning each machine action to the human action applied

to the closest position in the sentence. Note that in some cases this alignment is not possible – for instance in Table 1, if the editor had moved the word *geöffnet* instead of *ist*, the alignment would have failed. However, in practice this only happens in around 1% of the samples. In such cases, we simply keep the unfiltered human order.

For reproducibility purposes, we provide the dataset containing the (src, mt, pe) triplets, together with the four kinds of action sequences seen in Table 3, in `https://github.com/ antoniogois/keystrokes_ape`.

2.3 Analysis of action sequences

Given the actions provided by the minimum-edit distance between mt and pe it is possible to reorder them arbitrarily, as explained in the previous section. In Figure 1 we visualize three different kinds of orderings: the one produced by human post-editors, a random ordering, and the ordering obtained by processing the sentence left-to-right.

We show, in the vertical axis of Figure 1, in which position of the sentence an action is applied, relatively to the other actions of the same sample. On the left-hand plot we display two samples. Sample A contains 3 actions, applying the leftmost action followed by the rightmost and finally an action applied in a sentence position somewhere in between the first two. This could be generated from random shuffling or human-order, but never from the artificial left-to-right order. On the other hand, Sample B contains 5 actions which could have been ordered by any of the three methods. In practice, 2.0% of the human-ordered samples fol-

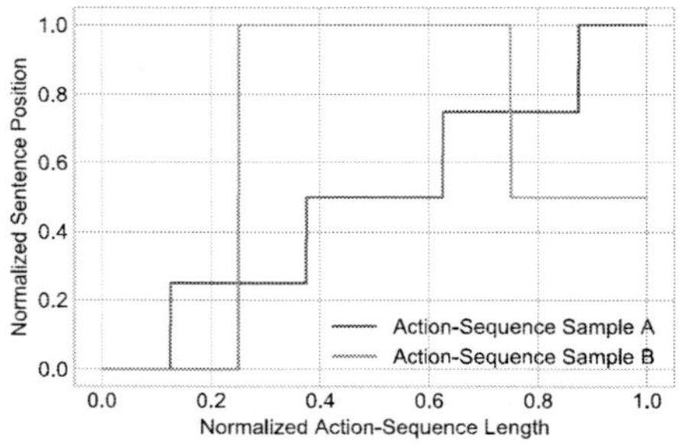 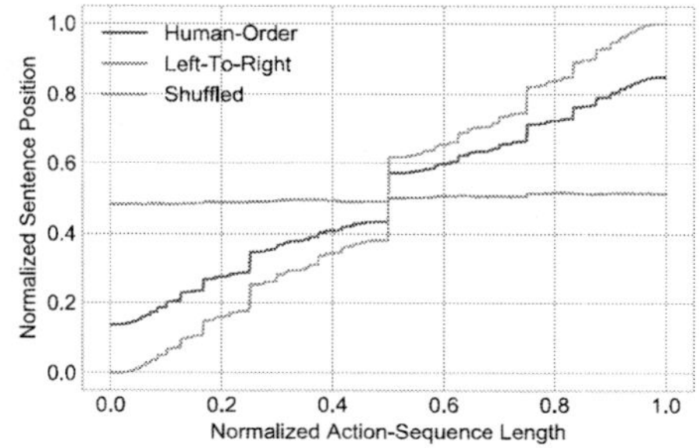

Figure 1: Relative positions of actions in a sequence. Each action-sequence length is normalized to 1, and we show the order by which actions were applied. For instance, sample A in the left-hand plot contains 3 actions, applied in a non-monotonic order — first the leftmost action, then the rightmost and finally the middle-action (e.g. corresponding to actions in positions 3, 8 and 5 of a sentence). Samples A and B represent respectively 2.0% and 4.2% of the human action-sequences. The right-hand plot shows the average of all sequences, in human order, left-to-right and shuffled. Human-order tends to follow a left-to-right order, but not as strict as the artificial left-to-right. The shuffled sequences do not follow any pattern, as expected.

low sample A, and 4.2% follow sample B.

On the right-hand plot we visualize the average line for each of the three orders. We can see that human actions tend to follow a left-to-right order, but not as strictly as the artificial left-to-right. Shuffled sequences are equally likely to start on the far left or far right of the sentence.

Relative orderings displayed in Figure 1 can be represented as a permutation of the sequence $(0, 1, ..., \#actions)$, i.e. Sample A would be $(0, 2, 1)$ and Sample B $(0, 1, 2, 3, 4)$. This way it is possible to use Kendall's τ distance (Kendall, 1938) to measure how far we are from a pure left-to-right order. We show this in Table 4, together with the percentage of actions which are a jump-back (applied to a position in the sentence to the left of the previous action) requiring a jump of at least 1 or 4 tokens. We confirm that the human-order is nearly left-to-right, but with some deviations.

	Jump-Back	JB$\geq$4	Kendall's τ
l2r	0.00%	0.00%	0.00
shuff	39.43%	21.34%	0.48
h-ord	14.87%	4.26%	0.16

Table 4: Statistics of action orders following left-to-right, random shuffle and human-order. Jump-Back counts actions applied to any position before the previous action, whereas JB$\geq$4 requires a jump of at least 4 tokens. Kendall's τ distance is measured between the sequence $(0, 1, ..., \#actions)$ and its permutation matching the order of the actions in the sentence.

In Figure 2 we visualize the words preferred by human editors as first action. We count how many times each word is picked as the first action (with-

out discriminating `DEL` and `INS`), both for human order and left-to-right order. We subtract human occurrences by left-to-right occurrences, keeping only words with a difference of at least 5, and group them by part-of-speech tags. We can see that humans prefer to begin with punctuation, whereas a left-to-right order favours determinants, which tend to appear in the beginning of the sentence.

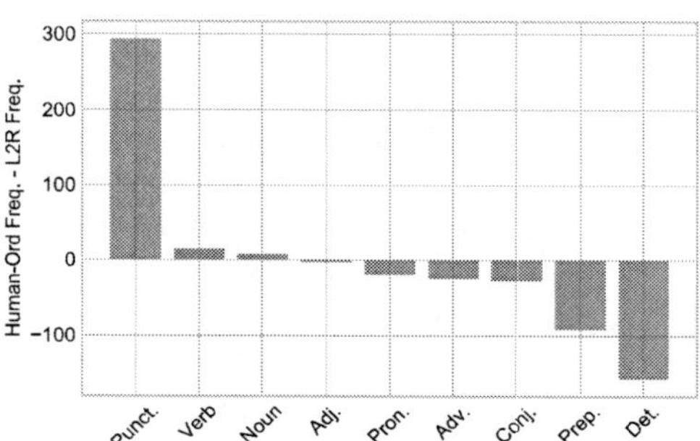

Figure 2: Part-of-speech tags preferred by humans as a first action — positive values indicate tags preferred by humans, negative values indicate tags preferred by left-to-right order. We count occurrences of each word as first action in both human action sequences and left-to-right sequences. We subtract humans counts by left-to-right counts, discard words with a difference lower than 5, and group results by part-of-speech tag.

3 Model

Inspired by recent work in non-monotonic generation (Stern et al., 2019; Gu et al., 2019a; Emelianenko et al., 2019), we propose a model that receives a `src`, `mt` pair and outputs one action at a time. When a new action is predicted, there is no explicit memory of previous time-steps. The model can only observe the current state of the `mt`, which may have been changed by previous actions of the model.

This model is based on a Transformer-Encoder pre-trained with BERT (Devlin et al., 2019). After producing one hidden state for each token, a linear transformation outputs two values per token: the logit of deleting that token and of inserting a word to its right. Out of all possible `DEL` or `INS` positions, the most likely operation is selected. A special operation is reserved to represent End-of-Decoding. If an `INS` operation is chosen, we still need to choose which token to insert. Another linear transformation is applied to the hidden state of the chosen position. We obtain a distribution over the vocabulary and select the most likely token. Figure 3 illustrates this procedure.

After a `DEL` or `INS` is applied, we repeat this procedure using the updated `mt`. Decoding can end in three different ways:

- When the `STOP` action is predicted;

- When the model enters a loop;

- When a limit of 50 actions is reached.

Once decoding ends, the model outputs the final post-edited `mt`.

Model details. We use BERT's implementation from Wolf et al. (2019) together with OpenNMT (Klein et al., 2017), both based on PyTorch (Paszke et al., 2019). The pretrained BERT-Encoder contains 12 layers, embedding size and hidden size of 768.

We begin with an input sequence x. This sequence is the concatenation of:

```
src + [SEP] + <S> + mt + <T>
```
where `<S>` and `<T>` are auxiliary tokens used to allow `INS` in position 0 and to represent End-of-Decoding. Tokens before and after `[SEP]` have a different segment embedding, to help differentiate between `src` and `mt` tokens. Let N be the length of x after applying a BERT pre-trained tokenizer (Wolf et al., 2019). This sequence is the input of the BERT-Encoder with hidden dimension $h = 768$. The output is a matrix $H \in \mathbb{R}^{N \times h}$. We call each possible `DEL` position and each `INS` position an **edit-operation**. Note that this does not yet include the choice of a token from the vocabulary. For each token in the partially generated

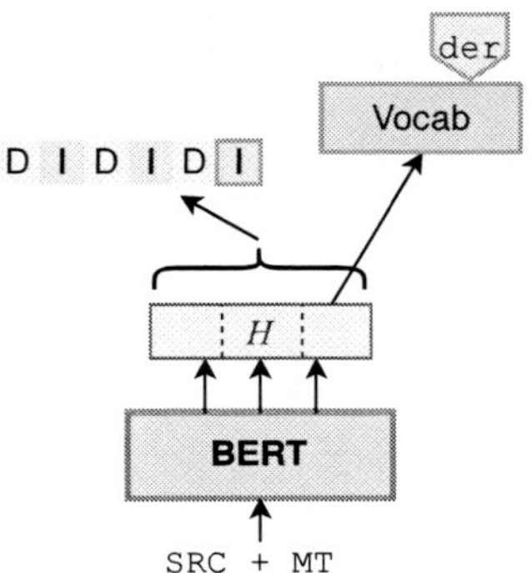

Figure 3: Our proposed model for automatic post-editing. A BERT-Encoder receives as input `src` and `mt` to produce a hidden representation H. We apply a linear transformation to the full H, obtaining a probability distribution over all possible actions. If the chosen action is an `INS`, we obtain a distribution over the vocabulary by applying another linear transformation to H's row of the chosen action position.

sentence, we obtain the logit of `INS` (on the position to its right) and `DEL` (of the token itself) using a learnable matrix $W \in \mathbb{R}^{h \times 2}$. The distribution probability over all possible edit-operations is defined as:

$$p(\text{edit\_op}) = \text{softmax}(\text{flatten}(HW)) \quad (1)$$

To represent the End-of-Decoding operation, we use the action `DEL<T>`. All unavailable actions are masked: `DEL<S>`, `INS-after<T>`, and edit-operations on `src`. When the model predicts an `INS`, a token is then predicted for that position. Let i be the chosen position, $h_i \in \mathbb{R}^h$ the ith row in H, and $V \in \mathbb{R}^{|v| \times h}$ the matrix mapping to all tokens in a vocabulary of size v:

$$p(\text{token} \mid \text{edit\_op}) = \text{softmax}(V h_i) \quad (2)$$

The predicted action is applied and we repeat this procedure using the updated x. Since no history of previous actions is kept, this opens the possibility of entering a loop. To handle loops, when we re-visit a state x we stop decoding. Alternatively, we tried applying the Nth most likely action on the Nth visit to a given x, but this degraded performance slightly.

4 Training

During training, the model may have several correct actions to choose from, even if we only consider actions following a minimum edit distance

	dev 2016		test 2016		test 2017		test 2018	
	TER ↓	BLEU ↑	TER ↓	BLEU ↑	TER ↓	BLEU ↑	TER ↓	BLEU ↑
MT baseline (uncorrected)	24.81	62.92	24.76	62.11	24.48	62.49	24.24	62.99
l2r	22.33 (±0.13)	67.04 (±0.11)	**22.53** (**±0.26**)	**66.23** (**±0.26**)	**22.63** (**±0.3**)	**65.84** (**±0.29**)	22.97 (±0.20)	65.49 (±0.26)
shuff	22.47 (±0.15)	66.74 (±0.22)	22.87 (±0.23)	65.89 (±0.28)	23.24 (±0.25)	65.14 (±0.24)	22.94 (±0.12)	65.39 (±0.18)
h-ord	**22.15** (**±0.23**)	**67.19** (**±0.15**)	22.65 (±0.16)	66.15 (±0.19)	22.75 (±0.08)	65.63 (±0.04)	**22.70** (**±0.15**)	**65.72** (**±0.22**)
Correia and Martins (2019) (seq2seq BERT)	—	—	18.05	72.39	18.07	71.90	18.91	70.94
Bérard et al. (2017) (actions)	23.07	—	22.89	—	23.08	65.57	—	—

Table 5: Results on development set and test sets used in WMT 2018 APE shared task. We show our system's performance trained by each of the three proposed orderings, and two other models for comparison. Correia and Martins (2019) is a monotonic model following the sequence-to-sequence architecture and pre-trained on BERT (seq2seq BERT). Bérard et al. (2017) predict a sequence of actions in a left-to-right order.

path. We compare different ground-truth action sequences based on minimum edit actions, all arriving at the same `pe`:

- Left-to-right (*l2r*);

- Randomly shuffled (*shuff*);

- Human-ordered (*h-ord*).

Minimum edit actions are generated using the dynamic programming algorithm to compute Levenshtein distance. The algorithm is set to output left-to-right actions, but since its output contains no redundant actions, they can be arbitrarily re-ordered. One simple way to re-order the actions is by randomly shuffling them. A more sophisticated alternative consists in matching each minimum-edit action to a human action, as described in §2.2.

We also experimented with unfiltered human actions. However this resulted in significantly inferior performance, possibly due to the hesitations made by humans typing, who may add and delete words unnecessary for the final `pe`.

Training details. We train the model by maximizing the likelihood of the action sequences provided as ground truth. Following Correia and Martins (2019) we use Adam (Kingma and Ba, 2015) with a triangular schedule, increasing linearly for the first 5,000 steps until 5×10^{-5}, applying a linear decay afterwards. BERT components have ℓ_2 weight decay of 10^{-4}. We apply dropout (Srivastava et al., 2014) with $p_{drop} = 0.1$ and, for the loss of vocabulary distribution, label-smoothing with

$\epsilon = 0.1$ (Pereyra et al., 2017). We use batch size of 512 tokens and save checkpoints every 10,000 steps.

5 Experiments

We compare the effect of using different action orders on the development set and test sets of WMT 2018 APE shared task (Chatterjee et al., 2018).

By using only training data overlapping with WMT's training sets (as described in §2.1), we are able to use WMT's development and test sets for evaluation. This allows to compare the performance of our model with that of previous submissions. Note however that our systems are in disadvantage, due to being trained on fewer data: out of the original 23,000 training samples we only found 16,068 in Specia et al. (2017).

5.1 Performance of models

We explore three different ways to order the actions provided by minimum edit distance: *l2r*, *shuff* and *h-ord*. For each run, we pick the best checkpoint measured by TER in the development set, and evaluate on 3 test sets. Table 5 shows the average and standard deviation of 5 runs. Depending on the dataset chosen, the best performance is achieved by either *l2r* or *h-ord*, with small variations between the two. Random shuffling is consistently worse than the alternatives, by a margin of around 0.3 TER. All three alternatives significantly improve the uncorrected MT baseline.

To compare with existing results, we choose two models. Correia and Martins (2019) use an archi-

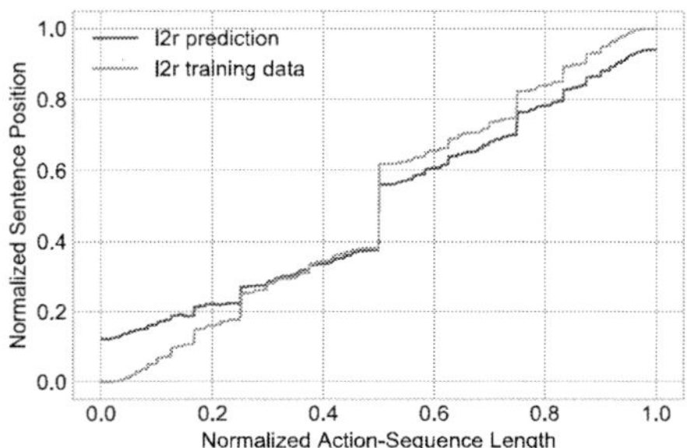

Figure 4: Relative positions of actions in a sequence, as explained in Figure 1. Comparing the original full left-to-right training data curve (orange) with the model predictions (blue), we see that the model became slightly non-monotonic.

tecture based on a monotonic autoregressive decoder (factorized in a left-to-right order). They propose a strategy that leverages on the pretrained BERT transformer (Devlin et al., 2019), achieving performance gains with it. Monotonic autoregressive models typically achieve a superior performance than their non-monotonic and non-autoregressive counterparts (Zhou et al., 2020). Bérard et al. (2017) propose a model that predicts a sequence of actions, which is closer to our approach, although they impose a left-to-right order. As expected, we do not outperform the results of the monotonic autoregressive model. However, we beat Bérard's action-based model, even though we use a smaller training set due to requiring keystrokes (16,086 samples instead of 23,000). This gain could be due to the pretraining of the BERT encoder used in our model, but also because of a largely different architecture (e.g. we use a Transformer encoder instead of a LSTM).

5.2 Learned orderings

Regarding the orderings learned by our model, they largely resemble the behaviour of the training data. Similar values for Kendall's τ distance indi-

	Kendall's τ	Δ K's τ	%loops	%do-noth
l2r	0.04	+0.04	15.6	10.5
shuff	0.50	+0.02	12.9	11.2
h-ord	0.16	0.00	16.0	9.8

Table 6: Statistics on the actions predicted by the 3 different models, measured on a single run of the development set. Δ K's τ refers to the difference between Kendall's τ distance of the model's output and of the corresponding training data. %loops counts samples that entered a loop, and %do-noth counts samples where the first predicted action was STOP.

cate a similar amount of non-monotonicity in each of the three scenarios, as seen in Table 6. The only exception is the left-to-right model which, unlike the training data, becomes slightly non-monotonic during inference time. This is shown by the increase in Kendall's τ distance and illustrated by Figure 4. This imprecision in the decoding order may be expected since the model does not have an explicit memory of what has already been done.

6 Related Work

Non-monotonic models. Recent work explored alternatives for neural sequence generation that do not impose a left-to-right generation order. On the one hand, this allows for bidirectional attention to both left and right context of the token being generated. On the other hand, it is a more challenging task since it implies learning a generation order from a number of possibilities that grows exponentially. Generation order is usually treated as a latent variable, and our work differs in that we use supervision from human post-editors.

Gu et al. (2019a) propose an insertion-based model which avoids re-encoding by using relative attention, and has two ways of learning order: one using pre-defined orders, the other searching for orders that maximize the sequence likelihood, given the current model parameters. Emelianenko et al. (2019) train using sampled orders instead, to better escape local optima. They also drop the relative attention mechanism together with its better theoretical bound on time complexity – showing that, in practice, inference remains feasible.

Welleck et al. (2019) propose a model that generates text as a binary tree. They learn order from a uniform distribution that slowly shifts to search among the model's own preferences, or alternatively using a deterministic left-to-right oracle.

Lawrence et al. (2019) use placeholders to represent yet-to-insert tokens, allowing for bidirectional attention without exposing future tokens. Decoding is either done left-to-right or by picking the most certain prediction. Alternatively all tokens can be decided in parallel, but with significant loss in performance.

Non-autoregressive models. Another class of models focuses on parallel decoding of multiple tokens, moving away from the traditional autoregressive paradigm. This unlocks faster inference, but brings the difficult challenge of learning dependencies between tokens (Gu et al., 2018). Stern et al. (2019) explore both non-monotonic autoregressive and non-autoregressive decoding with the Insertion Transformer. They use loss functions that promote either left-to-right order, a uniform distribution or a balanced binary tree for maximal parallelization.

The recently proposed Levenshtein Transformer (Gu et al., 2019b) introduces a Delete operation, and can generate or refine text by iterating between parallel insertions and parallel deletions — allowing to tackle the task of MT and also APE. Ruis et al. (2020) add a Delete operation to the Insertion Transformer and evaluate on artificial tasks. Our work differs in that we keep our model autoregressive, tackle the non-monotonicity by providing supervision to the order, analyze learned orders and focus on the APE task.

In general, this class of models is difficult to train and relies on several tricks. Knowledge distillation can bring improvements (Zhou et al., 2020), recently allowing Levenshtein Transformer to close the gap in translation quality between autoregressive monotonic and non-autoregressive models. In our setup, the tools proposed by Zhou et al. (2020) to measure data complexity could be used, for instance, for filtering out samples which are too complex.

Automatic post-editing. APE was initially proposed to combine rule-based translation systems with statistical phrase-based post-editing (Simard et al., 2007). As the quality of MT systems improves, there is less benefit in post-editing its mistakes, in particular if the MT system is trained on in-domain data. Current neural MT systems tend to generate very fluent output, therefore to fix their mistakes it is not enough to look at the mt output, but more deeply seek information from the src to fix adequacy errors. Top-performing systems for post-editing currently rely on tricks such as round-trip translation (Junczys-Dowmunt and Grundkiewicz, 2016) to increase dataset size, leveraging on pre-trained models (Correia and Martins, 2019) and using conservativeness penalties (Lopes et al., 2019) to avoid over-editing. Bérard et al. (2017) post-edit by predicting a sequence of actions with an imposed left-to-right order. Another recent work directly models edits, without including order information but allowing to re-use edits in unseen contexts (Yin et al., 2019).

Human post-editing. Previous work has explored keystrokes to understand the behavior of human editors. O'Brien (2006) investigates the relationship between pauses and cognitive effort, while later research (Lacruz et al., 2012; Lacruz and Shreve, 2014) examines keystroke logs for the same effect. Specia et al. (2017) introduce a dataset of human post-edits, containing information on keytrokes. Recently it was shown that detailed information from post-editing, such as sequences of edit-operations combined with mouseclicks and waiting times, contain structured information (Góis and Martins, 2019). The same work provides evidence that this kind of information allows to identify and profile editors, and may be helpful in downstream tasks.

7 Conclusions

In this work we explored different ways to order the edit operations necessary to fix mistakes in a translated sentence. In particular, we studied which orderings are produced by humans, and whether they can be used to guide the training of a non-monotonic post-editing system.

We found that humans tend to use nearly left-to-right order, although with exceptions, such as preferring to fix punctuation and verbs first. We then proposed a Transformer-based model pre-trained with BERT that learns to automatically post-edit translations in a flexible order. We learned this model in three different ways: by supervising it with orderings performed by humans, by using a left-to-right ordering, or with random orderings. In all three settings, the model outperformed the uncorrected machine translation baseline and a previous system also designed to predict actions (Bérard et al., 2017).

Training the model with human orderings achieved performance equivalent to left-to-right, or even superior. The random order consistently yielded slightly lower results. The model learned to mimic the proposed orders in all three cases.

Acknowledgments

We would like to thank Iacer Calixto, António Lopes, Fábio Kepler, Sean Welleck, Nikita Nangia, and the anonymous reviewers for their insightful comments. This work was partially supported by the EU/FEDER programme under PT2020 (contracts 027767 and 038510) and by the European Research Council (ERC StG DeepSPIN 758969).

References

Bahdanau, Dzmitry, Kyunghyun Cho, and Yoshua Bengio. 2015. Neural machine translation by jointly learning to align and translate. In *3rd International Conference on Learning Representations, ICLR 2015*.

Bérard, Alexandre, Laurent Besacier, and Olivier Pietquin. 2017. LIG-CRIStAL submission for the WMT 2017 automatic post-editing task. In *Proceedings of the Second Conference on Machine Translation*, pages 623–629, Copenhagen, Denmark, September. Association for Computational Linguistics.

Chatterjee, Rajen, José GC de Souza, Matteo Negri, and Marco Turchi. 2016. The fbk participation in the wmt 2016 automatic post-editing shared task. In *Proceedings of the First Conference on Machine Translation: Volume 2, Shared Task Papers*, pages 745–750.

Chatterjee, Rajen, Matteo Negri, Raphael Rubino, and Marco Turchi. 2018. Findings of the wmt 2018 shared task on automatic post-editing. In *Proceedings of the Third Conference on Machine Translation, Volume 2: Shared Task Papers*, pages 723–738, Belgium, Brussels, October. Association for Computational Linguistics.

Correia, Gonçalo M and André FT Martins. 2019. A simple and effective approach to automatic post-editing with transfer learning. In *Proceedings of the 57th Annual Meeting of the Association for Computational Linguistics*, pages 3050–3056.

Devlin, Jacob, Ming-Wei Chang, Kenton Lee, and Kristina Toutanova. 2019. BERT: Pre-training of deep bidirectional transformers for language understanding. In *Proceedings of the 2019 Conference of the North American Chapter of the Association for Computational Linguistics: Human Language Technologies, Volume 1 (Long and Short Papers)*, pages 4171–4186, Minneapolis, Minnesota, June. Association for Computational Linguistics.

Emelianenko, Dmitrii, Elena Voita, and Pavel Serdyukov. 2019. Sequence modeling with unconstrained generation order. In *Advances in Neural Information Processing Systems*, pages 7698–7709.

Góis, António and André FT Martins. 2019. Translator2vec: Understanding and representing human post-editors. In *Proceedings of Machine Translation Summit XVII Volume 1: Research Track*, pages 43–54.

Gu, Jiatao, James Bradbury, Caiming Xiong, Victor O.K. Li, and Richard Socher. 2018. Non-autoregressive neural machine translation. In *International Conference on Learning Representations*.

Gu, Jiatao, Qi Liu, and Kyunghyun Cho. 2019a. Insertion-based decoding with automatically inferred generation order. *Transactions of the Association for Computational Linguistics*, 7:661–676.

Gu, Jiatao, Changhan Wang, and Junbo Zhao. 2019b. Levenshtein transformer. In *Advances in Neural Information Processing Systems*, pages 11179–11189.

Junczys-Dowmunt, Marcin and Roman Grundkiewicz. 2016. Log-linear combinations of monolingual and bilingual neural machine translation models for automatic post-editing. In *Proceedings of the First Conference on Machine Translation: Volume 2, Shared Task Papers*, pages 751–758.

Kendall, Maurice G. 1938. A new measure of rank correlation. *Biometrika*, 30(1/2):81–93.

Kingma, Diederik P. and Jimmy Ba. 2015. Adam: A method for stochastic optimization. In *3rd International Conference on Learning Representations, ICLR 2015, San Diego, CA, USA, May 7-9, 2015, Conference Track Proceedings*.

Klein, Guillaume, Yoon Kim, Yuntian Deng, Jean Senellart, and Alexander Rush. 2017. OpenNMT: Open-source toolkit for neural machine translation. In *Proceedings of ACL 2017, System Demonstrations*, pages 67–72, Vancouver, Canada, July. Association for Computational Linguistics.

Koehn, Philipp, Hieu Hoang, Alexandra Birch, Chris Callison-Burch, Marcello Federico, Nicola Bertoldi, Brooke Cowan, Wade Shen, Christine Moran, Richard Zens, Chris Dyer, Ondřej Bojar, Alexandra Constantin, and Evan Herbst. 2007. Moses: Open source toolkit for statistical machine translation. In *Proceedings of the 45th Annual Meeting of the Association for Computational Linguistics Companion Volume Proceedings of the Demo and Poster Sessions*, pages 177–180, Prague, Czech Republic, June. Association for Computational Linguistics.

Lacruz, Isabel and Gregory M. Shreve. 2014. Pauses and cognitive effort in post-editing. *Post-editing of machine translation: Processes and applications*, page 246.

Lacruz, Isabel, Gregory M Shreve, and Erik Angelone. 2012. Average pause ratio as an indicator of cognitive effort in post-editing: A case study. In *AMTA 2012 Workshop on Post-Editing Technology and Practice (WPTP 2012)*, pages 21–30. AMTA.

Lawrence, Carolin, Bhushan Kotnis, and Mathias Niepert. 2019. Attending to future tokens for bidirectional sequence generation. In *Proceedings of the 2019 Conference on Empirical Methods in Natural Language Processing and the 9th International Joint Conference on Natural Language Processing (EMNLP-IJCNLP)*, pages 1–10, Hong Kong, China, November. Association for Computational Linguistics.

Lopes, António V, M Amin Farajian, Gonçalo M Correia, Jonay Trénous, and André FT Martins. 2019. Unbabel's submission to the wmt2019 ape shared task: Bert-based encoder-decoder for automatic post-editing. In *Proceedings of the Fourth Conference on Machine Translation (Volume 3: Shared Task Papers, Day 2)*, pages 118–123.

O'Brien, Sharon. 2006. Pauses as indicators of cognitive effort in post-editing machine translation output. *Across Languages and Cultures*, 7(1):1–21.

Paszke, Adam, Sam Gross, Francisco Massa, Adam Lerer, James Bradbury, Gregory Chanan, Trevor Killeen, Zeming Lin, Natalia Gimelshein, Luca Antiga, et al. 2019. Pytorch: An imperative style, high-performance deep learning library. In *Advances in Neural Information Processing Systems*, pages 8024–8035. Curran Associates, Inc.

Pereyra, Gabriel, George Tucker, Jan Chorowski, Łukasz Kaiser, and Geoffrey Hinton. 2017. Regularizing neural networks by penalizing confident output distributions. *arXiv preprint arXiv:1701.06548*.

Ruis, Laura, Mitchell Stern, Julia Proskurnia, and William Chan. 2020. Insertion-deletion transformer. *arXiv preprint arXiv:2001.05540*.

Simard, Michel, Nicola Ueffing, Pierre Isabelle, and Roland Kuhn. 2007. Rule-based translation with statistical phrase-based post-editing. In *Proceedings of the Second Workshop on Statistical Machine Translation*, pages 203–206, Prague, Czech Republic, June. Association for Computational Linguistics.

Specia, Lucia, Kim Harris, Aljoscha Burchardt, Marco Turchi, Matteo Negri, and Inguna Skadina. 2017. Translation quality and productivity: A study on rich morphology languages. In *Machine Translation Summit XVI*, pages 55–71.

Srivastava, Nitish, Geoffrey Hinton, Alex Krizhevsky, Ilya Sutskever, and Ruslan Salakhutdinov. 2014. Dropout: A simple way to prevent neural networks from overfitting. *Journal of Machine Learning Research*, 15(56):1929–1958.

Stern, Mitchell, William Chan, Jamie Kiros, and Jakob Uszkoreit. 2019. Insertion transformer: Flexible sequence generation via insertion operations. In *International Conference on Machine Learning*, pages 5976–5985.

Vaswani, Ashish, Noam Shazeer, Niki Parmar, Jakob Uszkoreit, Llion Jones, Aidan N Gomez, Łukasz Kaiser, and Illia Polosukhin. 2017. Attention is all you need. In *Advances in neural information processing systems*, pages 5998–6008.

Welleck, Sean, Kianté Brantley, Hal Daumé III, and Kyunghyun Cho. 2019. Non-monotonic sequential text generation. In *International Conference on Machine Learning*, pages 6716–6726.

Wolf, Thomas, Lysandre Debut, Victor Sanh, Julien Chaumond, Clement Delangue, Anthony Moi, Pierric Cistac, Tim Rault, R'emi Louf, Morgan Funtowicz, and Jamie Brew. 2019. Huggingface's transformers: State-of-the-art natural language processing. *ArXiv*, abs/1910.03771.

Yin, Pengcheng, Graham Neubig, Miltiadis Allamanis, Marc Brockschmidt, and Alexander L. Gaunt. 2019. Learning to represent edits. In *International Conference on Learning Representations*.

Zhou, Chunting, Jiatao Gu, and Graham Neubig. 2020. Understanding knowledge distillation in non-autoregressive machine translation. In *International Conference on Learning Representations*.

What's the Difference Between Professional Human and Machine Translation? A Blind Multi-language Study on Domain-specific MT

Lukas Fischer [1]   **Samuel Läubli** [1,2]

[1] TextShuttle AG

[2] Department of Computational Linguistics, University of Zurich

Abstract

Machine translation (MT) has been shown to produce a number of errors that require human post-editing, but the extent to which professional human translation (HT) contains such errors has not yet been compared to MT. We compile pre-translated documents in which MT and HT are interleaved, and ask professional translators to flag errors and post-edit these documents in a blind evaluation. We find that the post-editing effort for MT segments is only higher in two out of three language pairs, and that the number of segments with wrong terminology, omissions, and typographical problems is similar in HT.

1   Introduction

Machine translation (MT) quality has improved substantially over the past years, allegedly to the degree that it is no longer distinguishable from professional human translation (HT). The first claims of human–machine parity were based on MT systems geared to news translation (Hassan et al., 2018; Popel, 2018), and soon refuted due to weaknesses in the evaluation methodology. Reproductions with professional translators rather than crowd workers and full documents rather than single sentences likewise concluded that HT was superior to MT in terms of both accuracy and fluency (Toral et al., 2018; Läubli et al., 2018).

Human–machine parity claims may not hold with MT systems for broad domains such as news articles, but systems geared to narrower domains have been shown to achieve far better quality (e.g., Levin et al., 2017), and it is unclear how they compare to specialised human professionals. In this paper, we propose an evaluation design that avoids the weaknesses identified in previous human–machine comparisons (Section 2), and relies on metrics that are arguably better quantifiable and interpretable than adequacy and fluency judgments: error counts and edit distance (Section 2.2). Evaluators are asked to flag errors in and post-edit full documents, where half of the sentences are MT and the other half are HT (Section 3). We analyse data collected in a study involving three language pairs and ten professional translators, and find that professional translators post-edit professional HT almost as much as MT, and rate the two similarly in terms of issues with terminology, omission, and typography (Section 4). We also contextualise our results within the ongoing discussion on human–machine parity, suggesting that further assessments will need to focus specifically on what professional translators can do better than MT systems – and vice versa – rather than comparing their "overall quality" (Section 5). Our method should provide a means to assess the viability of MT in specific professional translation contexts, and may possibly help decrease resistance against the technology among professional translators.

2   Background

How to tell whether a translation is good or bad is one of the most important and one of the most difficult questions asked in connection with translation. Best practices for evaluating HT and MT differ, and assessments of human–machine parity have largely ignored the former.

Martins, Moniz, Fumega, Martins, Batista, Coheur, Parra, Trancoso, Turchi, Bisazza, Moorkens, Guerberof, Nurminen, Marg, Forcada (eds.)
Proceedings of the 22nd Annual Conference of the European Association for Machine Translation, p. 215–224
Lisboa, Portugal, November 2020.

2.1 Evaluation of HT

Quality assurance in professional translation workflows typically means manual identification of errors in (a sample of) translations. The error types depend on the quality standard. LISA, the first quality standard that gained widespread adoption in the translation industry, defines 20–123 error types and three severity levels: minor, major, and critical. SAE J2450, originating from the automotive industry, uses fewer error types and only two severity levels: minor and major. In contrast to LISA, SAE J2450 focusses exclusively on linguistic quality (i.e., no style and formatting, etc.). More recently, a joint academia-industry initiative has proposed the Multidimensional Quality Metrics (MQM) framework, which allows the definition of custom quality standards by choosing a subset of (weighted) error types.

The quality score of a given translation is computed as a linear combination of error counts and severity levels (i.e., weights). The error categories are defined in the quality standard; the number of errors per category and the severity of each error are determined by a single qualified rater. A translation is considered fit for purpose if its quality score does not exceed a given threshold.

2.2 Evaluation of MT

While there are various automatic metrics such as BLEU (Papineni et al., 2002) or TER (Snover et al., 2006), human evaluation is considered the only reliable method in MT quality evaluation.[1] Rather than specific error categories, human evaluation of MT quality has been focussed on two rather abstract dimensions: adequacy and fluency. Human raters judge the degree to which a translation adequately expresses meaning of its source text or constitutes a fluent sentence in the target language, respectively, on either an absolute or relative scale. 5-point adjectival scales were used at the first large-scale MT evaluation campaigns, but soon replaced by relative ranking because categories such as "[the translation preserves] most meaning" and "[the translation preserves] much meaning" proved hard to distinguish (Koehn and Monz, 2006). Relative rankings show better inter- and intra-rater agreement (Callison-Burch et al., 2007), but since they only tell if but not by how

Error Type	Definition (MQM)
Terminology	A term (domain-specific word) is translated with a term other than the one expected for the domain or otherwise specified.
Omission	Content is missing from the translation that is present in the source.
Typography	Issues related to the mechanical presentation of text. This category should be used for any typographical errors other than spelling.

Table 1: Error types and definitions.

much two or more translations differ – raters chose between better, same (tie), or worse –, the research community has lately embraced continuous Likert-like scales (referred to as direct assessment, see Graham et al., 2013).

The score of a given system output, typically a few hundred to a few thousand sentences, is computed by aggregating the adequacy and fluency judgements of multiple bi- and monolingual raters, respectively. Raters are typically MT researchers (e.g., Barrault et al., 2019) and/or crowd workers, but rarely qualified translators.

2.3 Assessment of Human–Machine Parity

In summary, the evaluation of HT focusses on quality: raters are qualified translators and give feedback on specific errors (such as the number of severe terminology problems). Because qualified feedback is expensive, few segments are evaluated by a single translator. The evaluation of MT, on the contrary, focusses on quantity: many segments are evaluated by multiple raters, but those raters are not qualified and give feedback on overall quality (such as how adequate a translation is on a 100-point scale).

Given the different evaluation traditions for HT and MT, it could be assumed that a comparison of HT and MT quality would aim at combining the two. However, the first evaluation that claimed MT had reached parity with HT – in one language pair and domain, i.e., Chinese to English news translation – used an MT evaluation design: bilingual crowd workers rated a large number of translated sentences in terms of adequacy (Hassan et al., 2018). Two reproductions of Hassan et al.'s (2018) evaluation showed that their evaluation design disadvantaged HT. Because the translated sentences were shown to raters in random order, they could

---

[1] At WMT 2019, human quality judgements for the strongest MT systems were negatively correlated with BLEU, the most widely used automatic metric (Ma et al., 2019, p. 79).

ID	Source (DE)	Target (EN)	Origin
1	Dieses Arbeitspapier beschränkt sich auf die notwendigen Funktionalitäten für die Bestandsführung.	This **work paper** is limited to the necessary functions for portfolio management.	MT
2	Das Kapitel zur Benutzerverwaltung befindet sich noch in Erstellung.	The user administration chapter is still being prepared.	MT
3	Voraussetzungen	Requirements:	HT
4	Die in der Lohnbuchhaltung erfassten Personen müssen voll arbeitsfähig sein.	The persons entered in payroll accounting must be fully capable of working.	HT
5	Es werden weiters ausschliesslich Personen mit Jahreslohn adressiert und keine Personen, welche auf Stundenlohnbasis arbeiten.	Furthermore, only persons receiving an annual salary are addressed and not persons working on an hourly wage basis.	HT
6	Für die später beschriebenen Mutationen **inkl. Eintritt / Austritt** wird von der Web API eine Korrelations ID zurückgegeben.	A correlation ID is returned by the Web API for the changes described later.	MT

Table 2: Example of a pre-translated document in which HT and MT are interleaved, including a segment with wrong terminology (ID 1), an error in typography (3), and an omission (6). The errors in segments 3 and 6 have been fabricated for the purpose of illustration.

not consider phenomena related to document-level cohesion, such as consistent translation of a product name throughout a news article. When raters compared full articles rather than single sentences, HT was rated significantly better than MT (Läubli et al., 2018). Even with isolated sentences, HT was rated significantly better than MT when professional translators rather than crowd workers carried out the evaluation (Toral et al., 2018).

3 Evaluation Design

We propose an experimental design for combined evaluation of HT and MT that avoids the weaknesses of previous assessments on human–machine parity in translation (Section 2).

3.1 Materials

The evaluation is based on a source text (ST) that is segmented into either sentences or paragraphs. We obtain two translations of the entire source text: one created by a professional translator (HT), the other by the MT system (MT). The result is a segment-aligned text where each source segment (e.g., ST-1) has two translations (HT-1 and MT-1). HT is translated from scratch, i.e., without any MT system. The creator of HT has the same background as the raters (see below), but no further involvement in the experiment.

For each rater, we prepare a translation that combines ST with a mix of HT and MT. To this end, we split ST into sections of equal length. We

then randomly pair each source segment with either its corresponding HT or MT, making sure to include an equal number of translations from both sources. An example is shown in Table 2. Note that the scrambling of HT and MT may introduce disfluencies, as further discussed in Section 5.1.

3.2 Raters

Since our evaluation involves post-editing (see below), and because translation quality is judged differently by professional translators and laypeople (Toral et al., 2018), we engage professional translators as raters. Their area of expertise matches the source text.

3.3 Procedure

The evaluation is organised as a task in which raters are instructed to evaluate the segments in their prepared translation (see above). Raters are told that the entire translation is MT. The primary motivation for this experimental manipulation is that we want raters to focus on evaluating segments rather than guessing if they are MT or HT. The latter would likely occur if they knew that both are present, not least because many professional translators fear "being replaced by a machine" (Cadwell et al., 2018). Translators might also be inclined to evaluate (what they believe is) MT more critically than HT because they have more negative perceptions about the former (Läubli and Orrego-Carmona, 2017).

	HT	MT
Omission	14	12
No Omission	223	226
Total	237	238

Table 3: Contingency table for two binary variables. Raters flagged omissions in 14 segments originating from HT, and in 12 segments originating from MT. Omission does not depend on segment origin (HT vs. MT) according to a two-tailed Fisher's exact test ($p = 0.693$). Data corresponds to Figure 2b.

	DE–EN	DE–FR	DE–IT
Segments			
ID	527,526	1,177,704	905,302
OOD	20,000,000	7,760,035	6,925,296
Ratio	10:1	6:1	7:1
Terms			
Train	10,332	11,551	10,537
Test	3,256	4,915	4,817

Table 4: Training Data

The evaluation of each segment involves three subtasks. First, raters are asked to post-edit the segment. They are instructed to correct spelling and grammatical errors, but not style. Second, raters are asked to flag the presence (but not count the number) of errors in the original target segment. We use a subset of MQM error types that has been shown to be particularly relevant for post-editing of domain-specific MT (Castilho et al., 2018), as listed in Table 1, but note that other subsets or quality standards (Section 2.1) could be used instead. Third, raters have the option to leave a comment for the segment if they wish to give more specific feedback.

Raters complete the experiment within a fixed time frame. While the practical consideration here is limiting experimental cost, time pressure is common in professional translation (Ehrensberger-Dow et al., 2016) and has been shown to increase cognitive function in controlled translation experiments (Campbell, 1999).

3.4 Analysis

We calculate the minimum edit distance (MED) between each original and post-edited segment, as well as corpus-level HTER (Snover et al., 2006) for all HT and MT segments in each target language. While HTER correlates better with human judgements of MT quality, MED is easier to interpret, particularly for individuals outside the MT research community. In reference to industry-focussed studies on post-editing (e.g., Volk et al., 2010), we group post-edited segments into exact matches (MED = 0), non-exact matches (MED >0), and high effort (MED >5).

Besides descriptive statistics, we test if the presence of errors and post-editing effort depends on whether target segments originate from HT or MT. Target segment origin is our binary independent variable, and we test if its proportion varies among the proportion of a single binary dependent variable using a two-tailed Fisher's exact test as implemented in R (Bailey, 1995). An example is shown in Table 3.

4 Experimental Results

We use the evaluation design described in the previous section to compare HT to MT in an experiment with three language pairs and ten professional translators. The study is conducted within the language services department of a multinational insurance company.

4.1 MT System

We train a Transformer (big) model (Vaswani et al., 2017) as implemented in Sockeye (Hieber et al., 2017) with FFN size 2048 for each language pair. The training data is listed in Table 4. We combine publicly available out-of-domain data (OOD) from OPUS (Tiedemann, 2016), from which we discard the lowest-scoring 75% by means of dual conditional cross-entropy filtering (Junczys-Dowmunt, 2018), with in-domain data (ID). We oversample ID to match OOD where possible, with a maximum oversampling factor of 10.

We also integrate domain-specific terminology by means of data augmentation (Dinu et al., 2019). We use two different sets of terms for training and testing (i.e., use in production). For training, we automatically filter the insurance company's full terminology, removing terms with low frequencies in the training data for reasons of time efficiency, and using a stop word list to remove terms that occur frequently in regular text ("normal words"). In addition, we discard terms in 30% of the training segments to increase robustness in constraint-free scenarios. For testing, we use a smaller terminology that was narrowed down by the company's professional terminologists.

	DE–EN		DE–FR		DE–IT	
	HT (N=150)	**MT** (N=150)	**HT** (N=237)	**MT** (N=238)	**HT** (N=244)	**MT** (N=248)
Error Analysis						
Terminology	8 (5.33)	15 (10.00)	27 (11.39)	39 (16.39)	18 (7.38)	19 (7.66)
Omission	1 (0.67)	5 (3.33)	14 (5.91)	12 (5.04)	4 (1.64)	1 (0.40)
Typography	3 (2.00)	4 (2.67)	5 (2.11)	3 (1.26)	8 (3.28)	6 (2.42)
MED						
>0	* 20 (13.33)	* 37 (24.67)	* 67 (28.27)	* 90 (37.82)	65 (26.64)	50 (20.16)
>5	12 (8.00)	19 (12.67)	* 53 (22.36)	* 75 (31.51)	30 (12.30)	27 (10.89)
min	0	0	0	0	0	0
max	85	43	118	150	34	130
avg	1.56	2.89	6.89	7.83	2.39	2.92
med	0	0	0	0	0	0
sd	7.85	7.86	17.41	17.43	6.17	13.07
HTER						
Corpus-level	2.22	4.71	7.42	7.99	3.67	3.81

Table 5: Results. Counts denote the number of segments for which a given variable holds true for HT or MT, respectively; relative numbers are shown in brackets. Pairs of significantly different proportions according to a two-tailed Fisher's exact test (at $p \leq 0.05$) are marked with *. Example: In DE–FR, 5/237 HT segments and 3/238 MT segments contain a typographical error. The difference is not statistically significant. Visualisations and p values are shown in Figures 1–3.

4.2 Texts and Raters

For each language pair, we select a document that contains terminology and language specific to the company's insurance sector: the description of business processes in a customer application (DE–EN) and a text on specialist training in sales (DE–FR, DE–IT).

We have all three documents translated by external translators who are regularly contracted by the company. We also translate the documents using the MT systems described above, and prepare a pre-translated version of each document in which half the target segments stem from the external translators and the other half from the MT system (Section 3.1).

The raters participating in the experiment are in-house translators at the company, and have not previously seen these documents. The number of raters differs between language pairs: four raters each for DE–FR and DE–IT, and two for DE–EN. Each rater is allocated 150 consecutive segments of the document, so the number of experimental items (segments) amounts to 600 for DE–FR and DE–IT, and to 300 for DE–EN.

The raters were given 90 minutes to complete the task. Two raters for DE–FR and one rater for DE–IT did not finish in time, reducing the number of items in our analysis to 475 and 492, respectively.

4.3 Error Analysis

Experimental results are listed in Table 5. We first analyse the proportion of segments that contain at least one terminology, omission, or typography error originating from HT and MT. The number of segments with terminology errors is higher for MT than HT. While almost twice as many segments are affected in DE–EN, the difference is less marked in DE–FR, and very small in DE–IT. Omissions are found in more segments originating from MT in DE–EN, and in more segments originating from HT in DE–FR and DE–IT. The number of segments containing omissions are considerably lower in DE–EN and DE–IT than in DE–FR. In terms of typography, the number of affected segments is low for both HT and MT. HT is slightly better than MT in DE–EN, and slightly worse in DE–FR and DE–IT.

The proportion of erroneous segments is similar for HT and MT overall. A two-tailed Fisher's exact test shows no significant difference between HT and MT in any error category and language pair. p-values are shown in Figures 1–3.

4.4 Post-editing Effort

We compute corpus-level HTER for all HT and MT segments in each language pair (Table 5, last row). We observe very low scores overall, and small differences between HT and MT in DE–FR and DE–IT.

We also compute MED between each pre-translated and post-edited target segment. Descriptive statistics are listed in Table 5. In all language pairs, raters post-edited less characters in HT on average (avg), but again, the differences are small, particularly for DE–IT. The segment that required most post-editing (max) stemmed from HT in DE–EN, and from MT in DE–FR and DE–IT.

We observe a low number of segments that required any post-editing at all. The proportion of these segments is referred to as >0 in Table 5. For example, only 37 out of 150 MT segments in DE–EN were post-edited; raters decided that raw MT was good enough for the remaining segments. However, the proportion of segments that needed any editing was even lower for HT in DE–EN, significantly so according to a two-tailed Fisher's exact test ($p\leq.05$). The difference between the proportion of segments with an MED of more than five characters (>5), on the other hand, is not significant ($p=0.255$) in DE–EN. In DE–FR, both >0 and >5 segments are significantly more frequent in MT (both at $p\leq.05$). In DE–IT, where raters post-edited more HT than MT segments (see >0), the difference is not significant at $p=0.110$ and $p=0.674$, respectively.

5 Discussion

We discuss design decisions in our evaluation and alternative approaches to inference testing, and contextualise our results within the ongoing discussion on human–machine parity in language translation.

5.1 Experimental Validity

Our evaluation is based on pre-translated documents in which target segments from HT and MT are interleaved (Table 2). In contrast to other MT quality evaluation experiments (e.g., Green et al., 2013; Hassan et al., 2018), this enables raters to consider document-level context, but the shuffling of MT and HT may introduce disfluencies that would not occur if all segments stemmed from either MT or – particularly – HT. In DE–FR, for example, the German term *Einzelfirma* (sole

proprietorship), which occurred in seven source segments, was translated as *raison individuelle* and *entreprise individuelle* by HT and MT, respectively. The first three instances were translated by MT, and noting the inconsistency with the fourth instance translated by HT, the rater in charge flagged the segment as erroneous and commented that "[the term translations] should be harmonised". The MT system's translation was consistent with the company's terminology database (TB) in this case, and the flagging of HT as erroneous was correct. However, if MT and HT used different translations for a term not specified in the TB, the translation introduced second would likely be marked as wrong even if it was used consistently within HT and MT. This may increase the number of terminology errors overall, but since the order in which MT and HT appear in documents is randomised in our evaluation design, it would not disadvantage one over the other with sufficient sample size. We also note that combining segments from different sources is common in professional translation workflows: when translations for adjacent source segments are retrieved from a translation memory (TM), these translations may (and typically will) stem from different documents and translators. The documents we prepared for our experiment are what translators would normally see in their computer-aided translation (CAT) tool, with HT corresponding to exact matches, except that segment origin (HT or MT) is not shown in the experiment.

We did not use a CAT tool in our experiment, but presented the pre-translated documents as spreadsheets with dedicated columns for error annotations and comments. A downside of this design decision is that the company's TB was not directly integrated into the translation environment. In the CAT tool that the in-house translators (the raters in this experiment) use in their daily work, terms contained in the TB are highlighted in source segments, and term translations are shown in a dedicated window. While raters had access to the TB during the experiment, it is likely that they missed a few terminology errors because terms were not highlighted in the experiment. On the contrary, we noticed that they marked a variety of other mistakes as terminology errors, such as wrong choice of pronoun (e.g., *que* instead of *soi* in DE–FR) or wrong verb forms (e.g., *data already exists* instead of *data already exist* in DE–EN). Since raters blindly evaluated HT and MT segments the same way, this may affect the true number of terminology errors in our analysis, but not the proportion between errors in HT and MT.

The blind evaluation of pre-translated segments – the fact that we did not tell raters that half of the pre-translations were HT, and that we did not show that pre-translations originated from different sources (HT and MT) – is another design decision that warrants discussion. Whether a pre-translated segment was retrieved from a TM (as an exact or fuzzy match) or an MT system is important information to professional translators and thus prominently shown in CAT tools. However, beliefs about (non-)presence of MT have been shown to impact how willing people are to tolerate translation mistakes (Gao et al., 2014), and surveys have shown that professional translators tend to have negative perceptions about MT (Läubli and Orrego-Carmona, 2017; Cadwell et al., 2018). Our experimental manipulation was aimed at fostering equal rigour in evaluating HT and MT, and preventing raters from guessing if segments are HT or MT rather than focussing on actual evaluation.

5.2 Statistical Analysis

A limitation of using contingency tables (see Table 3 for an example) is that we can only use categorical variables as dependent variables. To that end, we binarised MED with fixed and arguably arbitrary thresholds (>0 and >5; see Section 3.4). Predicting MED in a regression model would seem more appropriate, and offers the advantage of accommodating further predictors such as segment length, but violated the assumption of normally distributed residuals in our data even when extreme values were removed. Futher analysis, including factors other than origin (HT/MT) that may explain the variance in presence of errors and post-editing distance, is left to future work.

We use Fisher's exact test to analyse contingency tables, the null hypothesis being that the likelihood of a segment showing a certain property – such as containing wrong terminology or having been post-edited (MED >0) – is not influenced by its origin (HT or MT). Fisher's exact test has been criticised as rather conservative (see Martín Andrés and Herranz Tejedor, 1995), but is more appropriate than χ^2 or G tests of independence when sample sizes are small (Ruxton and

Neuhäuser, 2010).[2]

It would also be desirable to include more raters in the experiment. The limited number of participants is often criticised in translation experiments, justifiably so because translation performance varies considerably between individuals (e.g., Koehn and Germann, 2014). With sufficient participants, this variance can be accounted for by means of mixed-effects modelling (Green et al., 2013), but quite apart from budgetary constraints, there may just not be enough qualified raters in domain-specific settings. The in-house translation department we work with in this study, for example, employs 2–4 specialised translators per language pair. Non-experts who could be involved to increase the number of raters have been shown to evaluate MT less critically (Toral et al., 2018). In the present study, we prioritised rater qualification over quantity.

5.3 Human–Machine Parity?

Our results illustrate that the question whether MT quality reaches parity with HT is a matter of definition. Hassan et al. (2018), who analysed quality judgements by crowd workers in Chinese to English news translation, concluded that parity was reached because the difference between judgements of HT and MT is not statistically significant. The same holds for our experiment: professional translators flagged errors in segments originating from HT and MT, and the proportion of erroneous HT and MT segments does not differ significantly for any error type and language pair (Section 4.3). This is mainly because error rates are fairly low for both HT and MT, which indicates that both translation methods achieve high quality. However, MT produced more erroneous segments than professional translators (HT) overall, and the fact that statistical tests (Section 5.2) find no significant difference between HT and MT either means that there really is none, which would imply parity, or that the number of analysed segments (the sample size) is too small to infer a significant difference. Consider the proportion of segments with omissions in DE–EN (Table 5): 1/150 in HT vs. 5/150 in MT. Omissions are rare in both, and the difference is attributed to chance (p=0.214,

---

[2]Using a χ^2 or G test of independence has no effect on any finding of (non-)significance reported in this paper. We observe the largest difference when testing for independence of origin and omission in DE–EN with a G test (p=0.085) instead of a two-tailed Fisher's exact test (p=0.214, see Figure 1b).

see also Figure 1b), but in the very document we analysed, omissions were five times more common in MT segments nonetheless. If assessing human–machine parity was the aim of our study, a larger sample size would be imperative to come to understand if such effects are true or random. Nevertheless, the observation that MT produced less erroneous segments than HT in at least one language pair per error type in our experiment – except for terminology, where MT only came close to HT in DE–IT with 19/248 vs. 18/244 erroneous segments, respectively – is noteworthy.

While our error analysis was limited to three specific phenomena – terminology, omission, and typography – the comparison of pre-translated to post-edited segments yields insights about HT and MT quality overall. MT produced significantly more segments that needed post-editing at all (MED >0) in DE–EN and DE–FR. In DE–EN, however, the proportion of segments that needed substantial post-editing (more than five characters, i.e., MED >5) was not significantly higher in MT, and in DE–IT, the number of segments that needed any (MED >0) and substantial (MED >5) post-editing was lower in MT than in HT. This is a remarkable finding, given that HT was produced by an expert translator with experience in the textual domain we investigate. The implication here is that domain-specific MT (Section 4.1) achieves strong results, and it may be insightful to contrast it with generic MT. Moreover, feedback from raters, who had the option to leave a comment for each segment, does not suggest that the experimental manipulation – the mixture of MT with HT – was noticeable. In one particular instance, a rater commented "NMT hat überkorrigiert" ("NMT has overcorrected"), when in fact the segment in question originated from HT.

6 Conclusion

In a blind evaluation, ten specialised translators post-edited and flagged errors in pre-translated documents in which domain-specific MT was interleaved with professional HT. The evaluation comprised three language pairs: DE–EN, DE–FR, and DE–IT. MT required more post-editing than HT on average, but surprisingly, the difference is not significant in DE–IT, where MT produced more segments that needed no post-editing at all, and slightly less segments that needed substantial post-editing. We also analysed if the propor-

tion of segments that contain wrong terminology, omissions, or typographical errors varies among HT and MT, and found no significant dependency in any language pair. MT produced considerably more segments with wrong terminology in two out of three language pairs, but slightly less segments with omissions or typographical errors in at least one language pair each.

Apart from implying that MT can now reach remarkable quality in domain-specific settings, our results show that professional translators may post-edit professional HT almost as much as MT, and tend to rate the two similarly in terms of issues with terminology, omission, and typography. The caveat here and an aspect that warrants further investigation is that we made our participants believe that the HT they were evaluating was MT. From a methodological point of view, it would be interesting to test if this experimental manipulation would also work the other way around, and analyse if translators treat HT and MT differently depending on what they believe it is. From a more practical perspective, it might also be worth exploring whether the proposed evaluation design could help demonstrate the potential benefits of MT to people who are still sceptical about the technology.

References

Bailey, Norman T. J. 1995. *Statistical Methods in Biology*. Cambridge University Press, 3rd edition.

Barrault, Loïc, Ondřej Bojar, Marta R. Costa-jussà, Christian Federmann, Mark Fishel, Yvette Graham, Barry Haddow, Matthias Huck, Philipp Koehn, Shervin Malmasi, Christof Monz, Mathias Müller, Santanu Pal, Matt Post, and Marcos Zampieri. 2019. Findings of the 2019 Conference on Machine Translation (WMT19). In *Proceedings of WMT*. Florence, Italy, pages 1–61.

Cadwell, Patrick, Sharon O'Brien, and Carlos S. C. Teixeira. 2018. Resistance and accommodation: factors for the (non-) adoption of machine translation among professional translators. *Perspectives* 26(3):301–321.

Callison-Burch, Chris, Cameron Fordyce, Philipp Koehn, Christof Monz, and Josh Schroeder. 2007. (Meta-) evaluation of machine translation. In *Proceedings of WMT*. Prague, Czech Republic, pages 136–158.

Campbell, Stuart. 1999. A cognitive approach to source text difficulty in translation. *Target* 11(1).

Castilho, Sheila, Joss Moorkens, Federico Gaspari, Rico Sennrich, Andy Way, and Panayota Georgakopoulou. 2018. Evaluating MT for massive open online courses. *Machine Translation* 22(3):255–278.

Dinu, Georgiana, Prashant Mathur, Marcello Federico, and Yaser Al-Onaizan. 2019. Training neural machine translation to apply terminology constraints. In *Proceedings of ACL*. Florence, Italy, pages 3063–3068.

Ehrensberger-Dow, Maureen, Andrea Hunziker Heeb, Gary Massey, Ursula Meidert, Silke Neumann, and Heidrun Becker. 2016. An international survey of the ergonomics of professional translation. *Revue de l'Institut des langues et cultures d'Europe, Amérique, Afrique, Asie et Australie* (27).

Gao, Ge, Bin Xu, Dan Cosley, and Susan R. Fussell. 2014. How beliefs about the presence of machine translation impact multilingual collaborations. In *Proceedings of CSCW*. Baltimore, Maryland, USA, pages 1549–1560.

Graham, Yvette, Timothy Baldwin, Alistair Moffat, and Justin Zobel. 2013. Continuous Measurement Scales in Human Evaluation of Machine Translation. In *Proceedings of the 7th Linguistic Annotation Workshop & Interoperability with Discourse*. Sofia, Bulgaria, pages 33–41.

Green, Spence, Jeffrey Heer, and Christopher D. Manning. 2013. The efficacy of human post-editing for language translation. In *Proceedings of CHI*. Paris, France.

Hassan, Hany, Anthony Aue, Chang Chen, Vishal Chowdhary, Jonathan Clark, Christian Federmann, Xuedong Huang, Marcin Junczys-Dowmunt, William Lewis, Mu Li, Shujie Liu, Tie-Yan Liu, Renqian Luo, Arul Menezes, Tao Qin, Frank Seide, Xu Tan, Fei Tian, Lijun Wu, Shuangzhi Wu, Yingce Xia, Dongdong Zhang, Zhirui Zhang, and Ming Zhou. 2018. Achieving human parity on automatic chinese to english news translation. *arXiv preprint* 1803.05567.

Hieber, Felix, Tobias Domhan, Michael Denkowski, David Vilar, Artem Sokolov, Ann Clifton, and Matt Post. 2017. Sockeye: A toolkit for neural machine translation. *arXiv preprint* 1712.05690.

Junczys-Dowmunt, Marcin. 2018. Microsoft's submission to the wmt2018 news translation task: How i learned to stop worrying and love the data. In *Proceedings of the Third Conference on Machine Translation*. Belgium, Brussels, pages 429–434.

Koehn, Philipp and Ulrich Germann. 2014. The impact of machine translation quality on human post-editing. In *Proceedings of the EACL 2014 Workshop on Humans and Computer-assisted Translation*. Gothenburg, Sweden, pages 38–46.

Koehn, Philipp and Christof Monz. 2006. Manual and automatic evaluation of machine translation between european languages. In *Proceedings of the Workshop on Statistical Machine Translation (WMT)*. New York, NY, USA, pages 102–121.

Levin, Pavel, Nishikant Dhanuka, and Maxim Khalilov. 2017. Machine translation at booking.com: Journey and lessons learned. *arXiv preprint* 1707.07911.

Läubli, Samuel and David Orrego-Carmona. 2017. When Google Translate is better than some human colleagues, those people are no longer colleagues. In *Proceedings of the 39th Conference on Translating and the Computer*. London, UK.

Läubli, Samuel, Rico Sennrich, and Martin Volk. 2018. Has machine translation achieved human parity? A case for document-level evaluation. In *Proceedings of EMNLP*. Brussels, Belgium, pages 4791–4796.

Ma, Qingsong, Johnny Wei, Ondřej Bojar, and Yvette Graham. 2019. Results of the WMT19 metrics shared task: Segment-level and strong MT systems pose big challenges. In *Proceedings of WMT*. Florence, Italy, pages 62–90.

Martín Andrés, Antonio and Inmaculada Herranz Tejedor. 1995. Is Fisher's exact test very conservative? *Computational Statistics & Data Analysis* 19(5):579–591.

Papineni, Kishore, Salim Roukos, Todd Ward, and Wei-Jing Zhu. 2002. BLEU: A method for automatic evaluation of machine translation. In *Proceedings of ACL*. Philadelphia, PA, USA, pages 311–318.

Popel, Martin. 2018. CUNI Transformer Neural MT System for WMT18. In *Proceedings of WMT*. Brussels, Belgium, pages 486–491.

Ruxton, Graeme D. and Markus Neuhäuser. 2010. Good practice in testing for an association in contingency tables. *Behavioral Ecology and Sociobiology* 64:1505–1513.

Snover, Matthew, Bonnie Dorr, Rich Schwartz, Linnea Micciulla, and John Makhoul. 2006. A study of translation edit rate with targeted human annotation. In *Proceedings of AMTA*. Boston MA, USA.

Tiedemann, Jörg. 2016. OPUS – parallel corpora for everyone. In *Proceedings of EAMT*. Riga, Latvia, page 384.

Toral, Antonio, Sheila Castilho, Ke Hu, and Andy Way. 2018. Attaining the unattainable? Reassessing claims of human parity in neural machine translation. In *Proceedings of WMT*. Brussels, Belgium, pages 113–123.

Vaswani, Ashish, Noam Shazeer, Niki Parmar, Jakob Uszkoreit, Llion Jones, Aidan N. Gomez, Lukasz Kaiser, and Illia Polosukhin. 2017. Attention is all you need. In *Proceedings of NIPS*.

Volk, Martin, Rico Sennrich, Christian Hardmeier, and Frida Tidström. 2010. Machine translation of TV subtitles for large scale production. In *Proceedings of the 2nd joint EM+/CNGL Workshop "Bringing MT to the user: research on integrating MT in the translation industry"*. Denver, Colorado, USA, pages 53–62.

A   Visualisations

Figures 1–3 visualise the main results listed in Table 5. Each plot corresponds to a 2x2 contingency table for two binary variables (Table 3). We compute p-values using Fisher's exact test (see Section 3.4). Error bars show 95% confidence intervals.

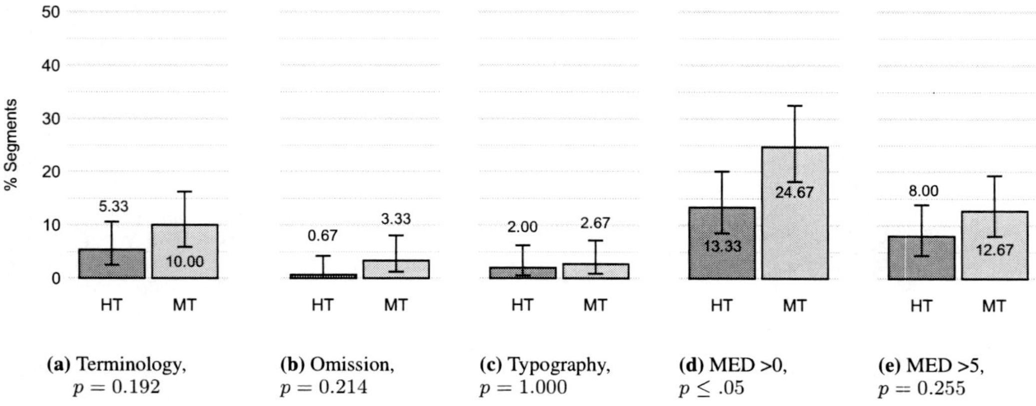

(a) Terminology, $p = 0.192$	**(b)** Omission, $p = 0.214$	**(c)** Typography, $p = 1.000$	**(d)** MED >0, $p \leq .05$	**(e)** MED >5, $p = 0.255$

Figure 1: German–English

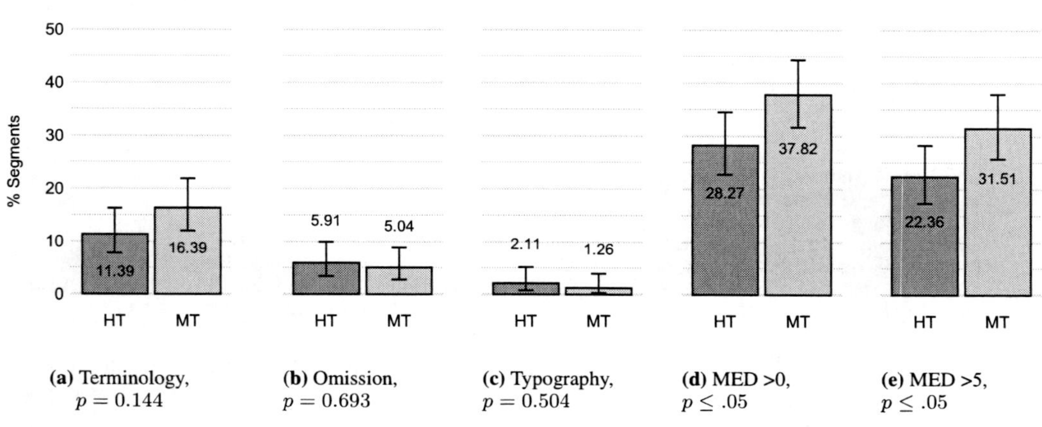

(a) Terminology, $p = 0.144$	**(b)** Omission, $p = 0.693$	**(c)** Typography, $p = 0.504$	**(d)** MED >0, $p \leq .05$	**(e)** MED >5, $p \leq .05$

Figure 2: German–French

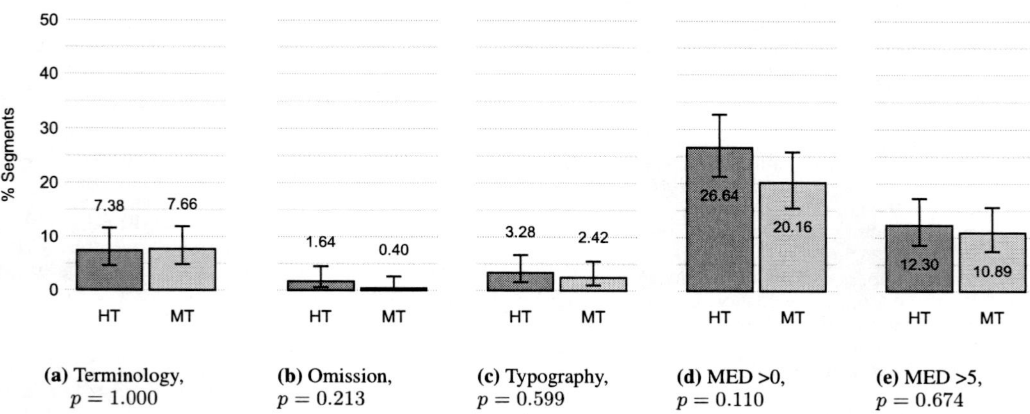

(a) Terminology, $p = 1.000$	**(b)** Omission, $p = 0.213$	**(c)** Typography, $p = 0.599$	**(d)** MED >0, $p = 0.110$	**(e)** MED >5, $p = 0.674$

Figure 3: German–Italian

Document-level Neural MT: A Systematic Comparison

António V. Lopes[1]   **M. Amin Farajian**[1]   **Rachel Bawden**[2]
Michael Zhang[3]   **André F. T. Martins**[1]
[1]Unbabel, Rua Visc. de Santarém 67B, Lisbon, Portugal
[2]University of Edinburgh, Scotland, UK
[3] University of Washington, Seattle, WA, USA
{antonio.lopes, amin, andre.martins}@unbabel.com
rachel.bawden@ed.ac.uk, mjqzhang@cs.washington.edu

Abstract

In this paper we provide a systematic comparison of existing and new document-level neural machine translation solutions. As part of this comparison, we introduce and evaluate a document-level variant of the recently proposed Star Transformer architecture. In addition to using the traditional metric BLEU, we report the accuracy of the models in handling anaphoric pronoun translation as well as coherence and cohesion using contrastive test sets. Finally, we report the results of human evaluation in terms of Multidimensional Quality Metrics (MQM) and analyse the correlation of the results obtained by the automatic metrics with human judgments.

1   Introduction

There has been undeniable progress in Machine Translation (MT) in recent years, so much so that for certain languages and domains, when sentences are evaluated in isolation, it has been suggested that MT is on par with human translation (Hassan et al., 2018). However, it has been shown that human translation clearly outperforms MT at the document level, when the whole translation is taken into account (Läubli et al., 2018; Toral et al., 2018; Laubli et al., 2020). For example, the Conference on Machine Translation (WMT) now considers inter-sentential translations in their shared task (Barrault et al., 2019). This sets a demand for context-aware machine translation: systems that take the context into account when translating, as opposed to translating sentences independently.

Translating sentences in context (i.e. at the document level) is essential for correctly handling discourse phenomena whose scope can go beyond the current sentence and which therefore require document context (Hardmeier, 2012; Bawden, 2018; Wang, 2019). Important examples include anaphora, lexical coherence and cohesion, deixis and ellipsis; crucial aspects in delivering high quality translations which often are poorly evaluated using standard automatic metrics.

Numerous context-aware neural MT (NMT) approaches have been proposed in recent years (Tiedemann and Scherrer, 2017; Zhang et al., 2018; Maruf et al., 2019; Miculicich et al., 2018; Voita et al., 2019b; Tu et al., 2018), integrating source-side and sometimes target-side context. However, they have often been evaluated on different languages, datasets, and model sizes. Certain models have also previously been trained on few sentence pairs rather than in more realistic, high-resource scenarios. A direct comparison and analysis of the methods, particularly concerning their individual strengths and weaknesses on different language pairs is therefore currently lacking.

We fill these gaps by comparing a representative set of context-aware NMT solutions under the same experimental settings, providing:

- A systematic comparison of context-aware NMT methods using large datasets (i.e. pre-trained using large amounts of sentence-level data) for three language directions: English (EN) into French (FR), German (DE) and Brazilian Portgueuse (PT_br). We evaluate on (i) document translation using public data for EN→{FR,DE} and (ii) chat translation using proprietary data for all three directions. We use targeted automatic evaluation and human assessments of quality.

Martins, Moniz, Fumega, Martins, Batista, Coheur, Parra, Trancoso, Turchi, Bisazza, Moorkens, Guerberof, Nurminen, Marg, Forcada (eds.)
Proceedings of the 22nd Annual Conference of the European Association for Machine Translation, p. 225–234
Lisboa, Portugal, November 2020.

- A novel document-level method inspired by the Star transformer approach (Guo et al., 2019), which can leverage full document context from arbitrarily large documents.

- The creation of an additional open-source large-scale contrastive test set for EN→FR anaphoric pronoun translation.[1]

2 Neural Machine Translation

2.1 Sentence-level NMT

NMT systems are based on the encoder-decoder architecture (Bahdanau et al., 2014), where the encoder maps the source sentence into word vectors, and the decoder produces the target sentence given these source representations. These systems, by assuming a conditional independence between sentences, are applied to sentence-level translation, i.e. ignoring source- and target-side context. As such, current state-of-the-art NMT systems optimize the negative log-likelihood of the sentences:

$$p(y^{(k)}|x^{(k)}) = \prod_{t=1}^{n} p(y_t^{(k)}|y_{<t}^{(k)}, x^{(k)}), \quad (1)$$

where $x^{(k)}$ and $y^{(k)}$ are the kth source and target training sentences, and $y_t^{(k)}$ is the tth token in $y^{(k)}$.

In this paper, the underlying architecture is a Transformer (Vaswani et al., 2017). Transformers are usually applied to sentence-level translation, using the sentence independence assumption above. This assumption precludes these systems from learning inter-sentential phenomena. For example, Smith (2017) analyzes certain discourse phenomena that sentence-level MT systems cannot capture, such as obtaining consistency and lexical coherence of named entities, among others.

2.2 Context-aware NMT

Context-aware NMT relaxes the independence assumption of sentence-level NMT; each sentence is translated by conditioning on the current source sentence as well as other sentence pairs (source and target) in the same document. More formally, given a document D containing K sentence pairs $\{(x^{(1)}, y^{(1)}), (x^{(2)}, y^{(2)}), \ldots, (x^{(K)}, y^{(K)})\}$, the probability of translating $x^{(k)}$ into $y^{(k)}$ is:

$$p(y^{(k)} \mid x^{(k)}) = \prod_{t=1}^{n} p(y_t^{(k)} \mid y_{<t}^{(k)}, X, Y^{(<k)}), \quad (2)$$

where $X := \{x^{(1)}, \ldots, x^{(K)}\}$ are the document's source sentences and $Y^{(<k)} := \{y^{(1)}, \ldots, y^{(k-1)}\}$ the previously generated target sentences.

2.3 Chat translation

A particular case of context-aware MT is chat translation, where the document is composed of utterances from two or more speakers, speaking in their respective languages (Maruf et al., 2018; Bawden et al., 2019).

There are two main defining aspects of chat: the content type (shorter, less planned, more informal and ungrammatical and noisier), and the context available (past utterances only, from multiple speakers in different languages). Specifically, chat is an online task where only the past utterances are available and context-aware models (see §3) need to be adapted to cope with multiple speakers. In this work we introduce tokens to distinguish each speaker and modifying the internal flow of the method to incorporate both speakers' context. There is also an additional challenge in how to handle both language directions and how using gold or predicted context affects chat models. In this work we consider a simplification of this problem by assuming the language direction of the first speaker is always from a gold set, leaving for future work the assessment of the impact of using predictions of the other speaker's utterances.

3 Context-aware NMT methods

We compare three previous context-aware approaches (concatenation, multi-source and cache-based) in our experiments. As well as illustrating different methods of integrating context, they vary in terms of which context (source/target, previous/future) and how much context (number of sentences) they can exploit, as shown in Table 1. Although other context-aware methods do exist, we choose these three methods as being representative of the number of context sentences and usage of both source and target side context.

Concatenation: Tiedemann and Scherrer (2017) use the previous sentence as context, i.e. $X^{(k-1)}$ and $Y^{(k-1)}$, concatenated to the current sentence, i.e. $X^{(k)}$ and $Y^{(k)}$, separated by a special token. It is called 2to1 when just the source-side context is used, and 2to2 when the target is used too.

Multi-source context encoder: Zhang et al. (2018) model the previous source sentences,

---

[1]The dataset and scripts are available at https://github.com/rbawden/Large-contrastive-pronoun-testset-EN-FR

$X^{(<k)}$ with an additional encoder. They modify the transformer encoder and decoder blocks to integrate this encoded context; they introduce an additional *context encoder* in the source side that receives the previous two source sentences as context (separated by a special token), encodes them and passes the context encodings to both the encoder and decoder, integrating them using additional multi-head attention mechanisms. Similar to the concatenation-based approach, here the context is limited to the previous few sentences.

Cache-based: Tu et al. (2018) model all previous source and target sentences, $X^{(<k)}$ and $Y^{(<k)}$ with a cache-based approach (Grave et al., 2016), whereby, once a sentence has been decoded, its decoder states and attention vectors are saved in an external key-value memory that can be queried when translating subsequent sentences. This is one of the first approaches that uses the global context.

Other methods have been proposed to use both source and target history with different ranges of context. (Miculicich et al., 2018) attends to words from previous sentences with a 2-stage hierarchical approach, while (Maruf et al., 2019), similarly, attends to words in specific sentences using sparse hierarchical selective attention. (Voita et al., 2019a), which extends the concatenation-based approach to four sentences in a monolingual Automatic Post-Edition (APE) setting; whereas Junczys-Dowmunt (2019) proposes full document concatenation with a BERT model to improve the word embeddings through document context and full document APE. Ng et al. (2019) proposes a noisy channel approach with reranking, where the language model (LM) operates at document-level but the reranking does not. Yu et al. (2019) extends the previous work using conditionally dependent sentence reranking with the document-level LM.

	#Prev	#Fut	Src	Trg
Concat2to1 (1)	1	-	✓	
Concat2to2 (1)	1	-	✓	✓
Multi-source context encoder (2)	2	-	✓	
Cache-based (3)	all	-	✓	✓
Star (4) - (see §4)	all	all (src)	✓	✓
Target APE (5)	3	3		✓
Sparse Hierarchical attn. (6)	all	-	✓	✓

Table 1: A summary of the methods compared (1-4). We also include (5-6) in this summary table for comparative purposes.

4 Doc-Star-Transformer

We propose a scalable approach to document-level NMT inspired by the Star architecture (Guo et al., 2019) for sentence-level NMT. We have an equivalent relay node and build sentence-level representations; we propagate this non-local information at document-level and enrich the word-level embeddings with context information.

To do this, we augment the vanilla sentence-level Transformer model of Vaswani et al. (2017) with two additional multi-headed attention sub-layers. The first sub-layer is used to summarize the global contribution of each sentence into a single embedding. The second layer then uses these sentence embeddings to update word representations throughout the document, thereby incorporating document-wide context.

In §4.1, we describe our model assuming it can attend to context from the entire document without practical memory constraints. Then in §4.2 we show how to extend the model to arbitrarily long contexts by introducing sentence-level recurrence.

4.1 Document-level Context Attention

We begin by describing the encoder of the Doc-Star-Transformer (Figure 1). We refer to the sentence and word representations of the kth sentence at layer i as $\mathbf{s}_i^{(k)}$ and $\mathbf{w}_i^{(k)}$ respectively. Our Doc-Star-Transformer model makes use of the Scaled Dot-Product Attention of Vaswani et al. (2017) to perform alternating updates to sentence and word embeddings across the document to efficiently incorporate document-wide context; our method can efficiently capture local and non-local context (at document-level) and, like the Star Transformer, also eliminates the need to compute pairwise attention scores for each word in the document .

Intermediate word representations, $\mathbf{H}_i^{(k)}$, are updated with sentence-level context. These intermediate representation are then used in a second stage of multi-headed attention to generate an embedding for each sentence in the document.

$$\mathbf{H}_i^{(k)} = \text{Transformer}(\mathbf{w}_{i-1}^{(k)}), \qquad (3)$$
$$\mathbf{s}_i^{(k)} = \text{MultiAtt}(\mathbf{s}_{i-1}^{(k)}, \mathbf{H}_i^{(k)}), \qquad (4)$$

We then concatenate the newly constructed sentence representations and allow each word in sentence k to attend to all preceding sentences' representations.[2] Finally, we apply a feed-forward net-

---

[2] We describe our method in the online setting and to match

work, which uses two linear transformations with a ReLU activation to get the layer's final output.

$$\mathbf{H}_{i'}^{(k)} = \text{MultiAtt}(\mathbf{H}_i^{(k)}, [\mathbf{s}_i^{(k)}; \mathbf{s}_i^{(k-1)}; \ldots; \mathbf{s}_i^{(1)}]), \tag{5}$$

$$\mathbf{w}_i^{(k)} = \text{ReLu}(\mathbf{H}_{i'}^{(k)}), \tag{6}$$

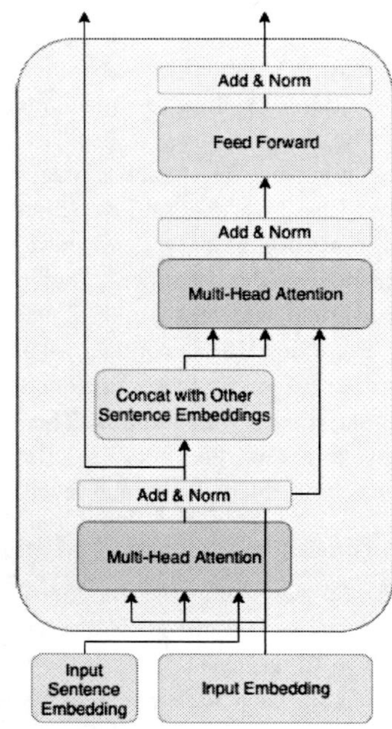

Figure 1: Doc-Star-Transformer encoder.

The Doc-Star-Transformer decoder follows a similar structure to the encoder, except that the decoder does not have access to the sentence representation of the current sentence k, thus, removing sentence $\mathbf{s}_i^{(k)}$ from (5). Source-side context is added through concatenation of the previous sentence embeddings from the final layer of the encoder with the decoder's in (5).

4.2 Sentence-level Recurrence

To overcome practical memory constraints (due to very long documents), we introduce a sentence-level recurrence mechanism with state reuse, similar to that used by Dai et al. (2019). During training, a constant number of sentence embeddings are cached to provide context when translating the next segment. We cut off gradients to these cached sentence embeddings, but allow them to

be used to model long-term dependencies without context fragmentation. More formally, we allow τ to be the number of previous sentence embeddings maintained in the cache and update as follows:

$$\mathbf{H}_i^{(k')} = \text{MultiAtt}(\mathbf{H}_i^{(k)}, [\mathbf{s}_i^{(k)}; \mathbf{s}_{i-1}^{(k)}; \ldots; \mathbf{s}_i^{(B)};$$
$$\text{SG}(\mathbf{s}_i^{(B)}); \ldots; \text{SG}(\mathbf{s}_i^{(B-\tau)})]),$$

where B is the index of the first sentence in the batch and SGs are the sentence representations with stopped gradients. In contrast with previous approaches, such as Hierarchical Attention (Maruf et al., 2019), this gradient caching strategy has the advantage of letting the model attend to full source context regardless of document lengths and therefore to avoid practical memory issues.

5 Evaluating Context-Aware NMT

The evaluation of context-aware MT is notoriously tricky (Hardmeier, 2012); standard automatic metrics such as BLEU (Papineni et al., 2002) are poorly suited to evaluating discourse phenomena (e.g. anaphoric references, lexical cohesion, deixis, ellipsis) that require document context. We therefore evaluate all models using a range of phenomenon-specific contrastive test sets.

Contrastive sets are an automatic way of evaluating the handling of particular phenomena (Sennrich, 2017; Rios Gonzales et al., 2017). The aim is to assess how well models rank correct translations higher than incorrect (contrastive) ones. For context-aware test sets, the correctness of translations depends on context. Several such sets exist for a range of discourse phenomena and for several language directions: EN→FR (Bawden et al., 2018), EN→DE (Müller et al., 2018) and EN→RU (Voita et al., 2019b). In this article, we evaluate using the following test sets for our two language directions of focus, EN→DE and EN→FR:

EN-FR: anaphora, lexical choice (Bawden et al., 2018):[3] two manually crafted sets (200 contrastive pairs each), for which the previous sentence determines the correct translation. The sets are balanced such that each correct translation also appears as an incorrect one (a non-contextual baseline achieves 50% precision). Anaphora examples include singular and plural personal and possessive pronouns. In addition to standard contrastive examples, this set also contains contextually correct examples, where the antecedent is translated

---

the decoder side. In the document-MT setting, (5) concatenates all sentences' representations to include context from future source-side sentences during translation.

---

[3] https://github.com/rbawden/discourse-mt-test-sets

strangely, designed to test the use of past translation decisions. Lexical choice examples include cases of lexical ambiguity (cohesion) and lexical repetition (cohesion).

EN→DE: anaphoric pronouns (ContraPro) (Müller et al., 2018).[4] A large-scale automatically created set from OpenSubtitles2018 (Lison et al., 2018), in which sentences containing the English anaphoric pronoun *it* (and its corresponding German translations *er*, *sie* or *es*) are automatically identified, and contrastive erroneous translations are automatically created. The test set contains 4,000 examples for each target pronoun type, and the disambiguating context can be found in any number of previous sentences.

EN→FR: large-scale pronoun test set We automatically create a large-scale EN→FR test set from OpenSubtitles2018 (Lison et al., 2018) in the style of ContraPro, with some modifications to their protocol due to the limited quality of available tools. The test set is created as follows:

1. Instances of *it* and *they* and their antecedents are detected using NEURALCOREF.[5] Unlike Müller et al. (2018), we only run English coreference due to a lack of an adequate French tool.

2. We align pronouns to their translations (*il, elle, ils, elles*) using FastAlign (Dyer et al., 2013).

3. Examples are filtered to only include subject pronouns (using Spacy[6]) with a nominal antecedent, aligned to a nominal French antecedent matching the pronoun's gender. We also remove examples whose antecedent is more than five sentences away to avoid cases of imprecise coreference resolution.

4. Contrastive translations are created by inverting the pronouns' gender (cf. Figure 2). We modify the gender of words that agree with the pronoun (e.g. adjectives and some past participles) using the Le*fff* lexicon (Sagot, 2010)).

The test set consists of 3,500 examples for each target pronoun type (cf. Table 2 for the distribution of coreference distances).

6 Experimental Setup

As mentioned in §1, we aim to provide a systematic comparison of the approaches over the same

[4]https://github.com/ZurichNLP/ContraPro
[5]https://github.com/huggingface/neuralcoref
[6]https://spacy.io

Context sentence
Some red **roses** for Your Ladyship.
Des **roses**$_{\text{fem.}}$ pour madame.

Current sentence	
	Who could **they** be from?
✓	De qui peuvent-**elles**$_{\text{fem.}}$ bien être ?
✗	De qui peuvent-**ils**$_{\text{masc.}}$ bien être ?

Figure 2: An example from the large-scale EN→FR test set.

Pronoun	# examples at each distance					
	0	1	2	3	4	5
il	1,628	1,094	363	213	127	75
elle	1,658	1,144	356	166	106	70
ils	1,165	1,180	501	302	196	156
elles	1,535	1,148	409	199	128	81

Table 2: The distribution of each pronoun type according to distance (in #sentences) from the antecedent.

datasets, training data sizes and language pairs. We study whether pre-training with larger resources (in a more realistic high-resource scenario) has an impact on the methods on language directions that are challenging for sentence-level MT. We consider translation from English into French (FR), German (DE) and Brazilian Portuguese (PT_br), which all have gendered pronouns corresponding to neuter anaphoric pronouns in English (*it* for all three and *they* for FR and PT_br).

We compare the three previous methods (§3) plus the Doc-Star-Transformer in two scenarios: (i) document MT, testing on TED talks (EN→FR and EN→PT_br), and (ii) chat MT testing on proprietary conversation data for all three directions.

6.1 Data

For both scenarios, we pre-train baseline models on large amounts of publicly available sentence-level parallel data ($\sim$18M, $\sim$22M and $\sim$5M sentence pairs for EN→DE, EN→FR, and EN→PT_br respectively). We then separately fine-tune them to each domain. For the document MT task, we consider EN→DE and EN→FR and fine-tune on IWSLT17 (Cettolo et al., 2012) TED Talks, using the test sets 2011-2014 as dev sets, and 2015 as test sets. For the chat MT task, we fine-tune on (anonymized) proprietary data of 3 different domains and on an additional language pair (EN→PT_br). Dataset sizes are shown in Table 3 (sentence-level pre-training data) and Tables 4–5 (document and chat task data respectively).

	Train	Dev
EN-DE	18M	1K
EN-FR	20M	1K
EN-PT_br	5M	1K

Table 3: Sentence-level corpus sizes (#sentences)

	Train	Dev	Test
EN-DE	206K	5.4K	1.1K
EN-FR	233K	5.8k	1.2K

Table 4: TED talks document-level corpus sizes (#sentences)

		Domain1	Domain2	Domain3
EN-DE	Train	674k	62K	13K
	Dev	37K	3.2K	0.6K
	Test	35K	3.6K	0.7K
EN-FR	Train	395K	108K	110K
	Dev	21K	6.3K	6.1K
	Test	22K	6.2K	6.3K
EN-PT_br	Train	235K	61K	13K
	Dev	13K	3.4K	0.7K
	Test	13K	3.2K	0.7K

Table 5: The corpora sizes of the chat translation task. We consider both speakers for this count.

6.2 Training Configuration

For all experiments we use the *Transformer base* configuration (hidden size of 512, feedforward size of 2048, 6 layers, 8 attention heads) with the learning rate schedule described in (Vaswani et al., 2017). We use label smoothing with an epsilon value of 0.1 (Pereyra et al., 2017) and early stopping of 5 consecutive non-improving validation points of both accuracy and perplexity. Self-attentive models are sensitive to batch size (Popel and Bojar, 2018), and so we use batches of $32k$ tokens for all methods.[7] For all tasks, we use a subword unit vocabulary (Sennrich et al., 2016) with $32k$ operations. We share source and target embeddings, as well as target embeddings with the final vocab projection layer (Press and Wolf, 2017).

For the document translation experiments, we run the same experimental setting with 3 different seeds and average the scores of each model.

For the approaches that fine-tune just the document-level parameters (i.e. cache-based, multi-source encoder, and Doc-Star-Transformer), we reset all optimizer states and train with the same configuration as the baselines (with the base parameters frozen), as described in (Tu et al., 2018; Zhang et al., 2018). For Doc-Star-Transformer we use multi-heads of 2 and 8 heads. All methods are

implemented in Open-NMT (Klein et al., 2017).

6.3 Chat-specific modifications

In the case of the concatenation-based approaches, multi-source context encoder, and the Doc-Star-Transformer, we add the speaker symbol as special token to the beginning of each sentence. For the cache-based systems, we introduce two different caches, one per speaker, and investigate different methods for deep fusing them (Tu et al., 2018): (i) deep fusing the first speaker's cache first and next fusing with the second speaker's cache, (ii) the same method but with the second speaker first, and (iii) jointly integrating the caches. In addition, for the cache-based system we explore the effect of storing full words or subword units in the external memory For the full word approach, we use subword units in the vocab but merge the words when adding to the cache.

6.4 Evaluation setup

We perform both automatic and manual evaluation, in order to gain more insights into the differences between the models.

Automatic evaluation: We first evaluate all methods with case-sensitive detokenized BLEU (Papineni et al., 2002).[8] We then evaluate context-dependent discourse-level phenomena using the previously described contrastive test sets. For EN→DE this corresponds to the large-scale anaphoric pronoun test set of Müller et al. (2018) and for EN→FR our own analogous large-scale anaphoric pronoun test set (described in §5),[9] as well as the manually crafted test sets of Bawden et al. (2018) for anaphora and coherence/cohesion.

Manual evaluation: In the case of the chat translation task (using proprietary data), in addition to BLEU, we also manually assess the performance of the systems with professional human annotators, who mark the errors of the systems with different levels of severity (i.e. minor, major, critical). In the case of extra-sentential errors such as agreements we asked them to mark both the pronoun and its antecedent. We score the systems' performance using Multidimensional Quality Metrics (MQM) (Lommel, 2013):

$$MQM = 100 - \frac{\text{minor} + \text{major} * 5 + \text{critical} * 10}{\text{Word count}}$$

---

[7]The optimizer update is delayed to simulate the $32k$ tokens.

[8]Using Moses' (Koehn et al., 2007) `multi-bleu-detok`.

[9]For both large-scale test sets, we make sure to exclude the documents they include from the training data.

By having access to the full conversation, the annotators can annotate both intra- and extra-sentential errors (e.g. document-level error examples of agreement or lexical consistency).

We prioritize documents with a large number of edits compared to the sentence-level baseline (normalized by document length) due to document-level systems tending to perform few edits with respect to the high performance non-context-aware systems. We request annotations of approximately 200 sentences per language pair and method.

7　Results and analysis

7.1　Document Translation Task

Table 6 shows the results of the average performance of each system on IWSLT data according to BLEU. Although the approaches have previously shown improved performance compared to a baseline, when a stronger baseline is used, we see marginal to no improvements over the baseline for both language directions.

	EN→DE	EN→FR
Baseline	32.08	40.92
Concat2to1	31.84	40.67
Concat2to2	30.89	40.57
Cache SubWords	32.10	40.91
Cache Words	**32.12**	40.88
Zhang et al. 2018	31.03	**40.95**
Star, 2 heads, gold target ctx	31.76	**41.00**
Star, 2 heads, predicted target ctx	31.39	40.72
Star, 8 heads, gold target ctx	31.74	40.74
Star, 8 heads, predicted target ctx	31.29	40.58

Table 6: BLEU score results on the IWSLT15 test set (averaged over 3 different runs for each method).

Table 7 shows the average performance of each system for all contrastive sets. The results differ greatly from BLEU results; methods on par or below the baseline according to BLEU perform better than the baseline when evaluated on the contrastive test sets. This is notably the case of the Concat models, which achieve some of the best results on the both large-scale pronoun sets (EN→DE and EN→FR), as shown by the high percentages on the more difficult feminine pronoun *Sie* for EN→DE and all pronouns for EN→FR.

Most models struggle to achieve high performances for the feminine *sie* and masculine *er*, which is likely due to neuter *es* being the majority class in the training data. For French, although the feminine pronouns are also usually challenging, the high scores seen here are possibly due to

the fact that many examples have an antecedent within the same sentence. The Concat2to2 method however performs well across the board, proving to be an effective way of exploiting context. It also achieves the highest scores on both the anaphora and coherence/cohesion test set, which is only possible when the context is actually being used, as the test set is completely balanced. This appears to confirm the findings of Bawden et al. (2018) that target-side context is most effectively used when channelled through the decoder. Surprisingly, the multi-source encoder approach degrades the baseline with respect to this evaluation, suggesting that the context being used is detrimental to the handling of these phenomena.

We note that using OpenSubtitles as a resource for context-dependent translation or scoring, has additional challenges. Figure 3 illustrates four of these, which could make translation more challenging if they affect the context being exploited.

7.2　Chat Translation Task

Table 8 shows BLEU score results on the proprietary data, with the modifications described in §3 to address the chat task. As expected, document-level information has a larger impact for the lowest resource language pair, EN→PT_br, with marginal improvements on EN→FR and EN→DE.

The performance of these methods depends on the language pair and domain. Although it is not conclusive which method performs best, our proposed method improves over the baseline consistently, whereas the cache-based and Concat2to2 methods also perform well in some scenarios. For our Doc-Star-Transformer approach, using predictions rather than the gold history harms the model at inference, showing that bridging this gap could lead to a better handling of target-side context.

There is little correlation between BLEU scores and the human MQM scores (as shown by the comparison for 3 methods in Table 9). Although the difference between BLEU scores are marginal, MQM indicates that quality differences can be seen by human evaluators: the document-level systems (Cache and Star) both achieve higher results for EN→PT_br (although the Star approach underperforms for EN→FR). This shows that for certain language directions, the document-level approaches do learn to fix some errors and therefore improve translation quality. This also confirms previous suggestions that BLEU is not a good met-

	EN→DE				EN→FR					Anaphora	Coherence/ cohesion(%)
						it		they			
	Total	Es	Sie	Er	Total	elle	il	elles	ils	All	All
Baseline	45.0	91.9	22.9	20.2	79.7	88.1	82.7	76.1	72.2	50.0	50.0
Concat2to1	48.0	91.6	**27.1**	**25.3**	**80.9**	**88.4**	**83.3**	**77.2**	**73.9**	50.0	**52.5**
Concat2to2	70.8	91.8	**61.9**	**58.7**	**83.2**	**89.2**	**86.2**	**80.4**	**77.6**	**82.5**	**55.0**
Cache (Subwords)	45.2	**92.1**	**23.5**	19.9	79.7	88.0	82.7	76.0	72.0	50.0	50.0
Multi-src Enc	42.6	62.3	**33.9**	**31.5**	59.0	62.0	61.3	57.2	57.3	47.0	46.5
Star, 8 heads	45.9	91.3	**27.0**	19.5	79.6	88.0	82.6	76.1	72.0	50.0	50.0

Table 7: Accuracies (in %) for the contrastive sets. Methods outperforming the baseline are in bold.

		Domain1			Domain2			Domain3		
		EN-DE	EN-FR	EN-PT_br	EN-DE	EN-FR	EN-PT_br	EN-DE	EN-FR	EN-PT_br
Baseline		78.53	79.71	81.21	72.11	76	73.94	69.67	74.76	74.95
Concat2to1	S1,S2 + speaker tag	78.04	79.65	80.36	71	75.35	73.02	**69.92**	74.57	74.82
	S1	77.97	79.55	80.26	70.95	75.21	73.33	**69.77**	74.47	74.84
Concat2to2	S1,S2 + speaker tag	**79.84**	79.3	80.33	70.56	74.87	73.52	**69.74**	74.37	74.56
	S1	**78.88**	79.15	79.92	70.13	74.9	73.33	69.59	74.25	74.33
Cache S1 + Cli	JointPolicy Subwords	**78.62**	79.66	80.79	**72.12**	75.03	73.47	69.47	74.77	75.04
	JointPolicy Words	78.52	79.63	80.93	71.66	75.93	73.54	69.55	74.77	74.97
Cache S1 only	Subwods	78.41	79.46	81.17	71.73	75.92	**74.41**	69.68	**74.8**	74.94
	Words	78.28	79.54	81.04	71.9	75.87	**74.33**	69.51	**74.82**	74.94
Multi-src enc	SEP + speaker tag	78.23	79.64	81.04	71.5	75.87	73.78	-	74.66	74.82
Star	S1,S2 2 heads Gold target ctx	**79.7**	**80.08**	**82.64**	71.79	75.62	73.67	**71.36**	**74.87**	**75.03**
	S1,S2 2 heads Predicted target ctx	**78.81**	79.38	79.63	71.72	75.58	73.7	**69.38**	74.77	**75.11**
	S1 2 heads Gold target ctx	**79.35**	79.58	**82.52**	72.16	75.95	**74.1**	**71.33**	**75.01**	**75.48**
	S1 2 heads Predicted target ctx	78.17	79.24	79.83	**72.24**	75.68	73.9	**70.24**	74.65	**75.21**

Table 8: BLEU scores on the chat translation task (proprietary data for 3 different domains and language pairs). S1 and S2 refer to the speakers in the case of chat translation task.

	EN→FR		EN→PT_br	
	BLEU	MQM	BLEU	MQM
Baseline	74.76	87.46	74.95	92.47
Cache	74.82	**89.02**	74,94	**93.20**
Star 2 heads	75.01	86.80	75.48	**95.20**

Table 9: The results of automatic and manual evaluation of the context-aware NMT methods in terms of BLEU and MQM on English→French and English→Portuguese.

ric to distinguish between strong NMT systems.

8 Conclusion

We provided a systematic comparison of several context-aware NMT methods. One of the methods in this comparison was a new adaptation of the recently proposed StarTransformer architecture to document-level MT. In addition to BLEU, we reported results of the contrastive evaluation of context-dependent phenomena (anaphora and coherence/cohesion), creating an additional large-scale contrastive test set for EN→FR anaphoric pronouns, and we carried out human evaluation in terms of Multidimensional Quality Metrics (MQM). Our findings suggest that existing context-aware approaches are less advantageous in scenarios with larger datasets and strong sentence-level baselines. In terms of the targeted context-dependent evaluation, one of the promising approaches is one of the simplest: the Concat2to2, where translated context is channelled through the decoder, although our Doc-Star-Transformer method achieves good results according to the manual evaluation of MT quality.

Acknowledgments

We thank the anonymous reviewers for their valuable feedback. This work is supported by the EU in the context of the PT2020 project (contracts 027767 and 038510) and the H2020 GoURMET project (825299), by the European Research Council (ERC StG DeepSPIN 758969), by the Fundação para a Ciência e Tecnologia through contract UID/EEA/50008/2019 and by the UK Engineering and Physical Sciences Research Council (MTStretch fellowship grant EP/S001271/1).

References

Bahdanau, D., K. Cho, and Y. Bengio. 2014. Neural machine translation by jointly learning to align and translate. *arXiv preprint arXiv:1409.0473*.

Barrault, Loïc, Ondřej Bojar, Marta R. Costa-jussà, Christian Federmann, Mark Fishel, Yvette Graham, Barry Haddow, Matthias Huck, Philipp Koehn, Shervin Malmasi, Christof Monz, Mathias Müller, Santanu Pal, Matt Post, and Marcos Zampieri. 2019.

Difficulty	English	French
Colloquialisms	Well, they just ain't a-treatin' me right	Eh bien, elles me traitent mal 'Well, they're treating me badly'
Paraphrasing	Do not forget your friends, they are always with you heart and soul!	N'oubliez pas vos amis: ils sont toujours près de vous! 'Don't forget your friends: they are always near to you'
Truncation	Neighbor. what have you done?	Voisin ? 'Neighbour?'
Free translation	I don't understand either.	Moi non plus. 'me neither'

Figure 3: Examples of four challenges for MT of OpenSubtitles: (i) colloquialisms, (ii) paraphrasing, (iii) subtitle truncation (can be due to space constraints), and (iv) free translations that fulfill the same discursive role.

Findings of the 2019 Conference on Machine Translation (WMT19). In *Proceedings of the 4th Conference on Machine Translation*.

Bawden, Rachel, Rico Sennrich, Alexandra Birch, and Barry Haddow. 2018. Evaluating Discourse Phenomena in Neural Machine Translation. In *Proceedings of the 2018 Conference of the North American Chapter of the Association for Computational Linguistics; Human Language Technologies*.

Bawden, Rachel, Sophie Rosset, Thomas Lavergne, and Eric Bilinski. 2019. DiaBLa: A Corpus of Bilingual Spontaneous Written Dialogues for Machine Translation.

Bawden, Rachel. 2018. *Going beyond the sentence: Contextual Machine Translation of Dialogue*. Ph.D. thesis, LIMSI, CNRS, Université Paris-Sud, Université Paris-Saclay, Orsay, France.

Cettolo, Mauro, Christian Girardi, and Marcello Federico. 2012. WIT³: Web Inventory of Transcribed and Translated Talks. In *Proceedings of the 16th Conference of the European Association for Machine Translation*.

Dai, Zihang, Zhilin Yang, Yiming Yang, Jaime G. Carbonell, Quoc V. Le, and Ruslan Salakhutdinov. 2019. Transformer-XL: Attentive Language Models Beyond a Fixed-Length Context. In *Proceedings of the 57th annual meeting on association for computational linguistics*.

Dyer, Chris, Victor Chahuneau, and Noah A. Smith. 2013. A simple, fast, and effective reparameterization of IBM model 2. In *Proceedings of the 2013 Conference of the North American Chapter of the Association for Computational Linguistics: Human Language Technologies*.

Grave, Edouard, Armand Joulin, and Nicolas Usunier. 2016. Improving neural language models with a continuous cache. *arXiv preprint arXiv:1612.04426*.

Guo, Qipeng, Xipeng Qiu, Pengfei Liu, Yunfan Shao, Xiangyang Xue, and Zheng Zhang. 2019. Star-transformer. In *Proceedings of the 2019 Conference of the North American Chapter of the Association for Computational Linguistics: Human Language Technologies*.

Hardmeier, Christian. 2012. Discourse in Statistical Machine Translation. a survey and a case study. *Discours*, 11.

Hassan, Hany, Anthony Aue, Chang Chen, Vishal Chowdhary, Jonathan Clark, Christian Federmann, Xuedong Huang, Marcin Junczys-Dowmunt, William Lewis, Mu Li, et al. 2018. Achieving human parity on automatic Chinese to English news translation. *arXiv preprint arXiv:1803.05567*.

Junczys-Dowmunt, Marcin. 2019. Microsoft translator at wmt 2019: Towards large-scale document-level neural machine translation. In *Proceedings of the Fourth Conference on Machine Translation*.

Klein, Guillaume, Yoon Kim, Yuntian Deng, Jean Senellart, and Alexander M. Rush. 2017. OpenNMT: Open-source toolkit for neural machine translation. In *Proceedings of the 55th Annual Meeting of the Association for Computational Linguistics*.

Koehn, Philipp, Hieu Hoang, Alexandra Birch, Chris Callison-Burch, Marcello Federico, Nicola Bertoldi, Brooke Cowan, Wade Shen, Christine Moran, Richard Zens, Chris Dyer, Ondřej Bojar, Alexandra Constantin, and Evan Herbst. 2007. Moses: Open source toolkit for statistical machine translation. In *Proceedings of the 45th Annual Meeting of the Association for Computational Linguistics*.

Läubli, Samuel, Rico Sennrich, and Martin Volk. 2018. Has machine translation achieved human parity? a case for document-level evaluation. In *Proceedings of the 2018 Conference on Empirical Methods in Natural Language Processing*.

Laubli, Samuel, Sheila Castilho, Graham Neubig, Rico Sennrich, Qinlan Shen, and Antonio Toral. 2020. A set of recommendations for assessing human–machine parity in language translation. *Journal of Artificial Intelligence Research (JAIR)*, 67.

Lison, Pierre, Jörg Tiedemann, and Milen Kouylekov. 2018. OpenSubtitles2018: Statistical rescoring of sentence alignments in large, noisy parallel corpora. In *Proceedings of the 11th International Conference on Language Resources and Evaluation*.

Lommel, Arle Richard. 2013. Multidimensional quality metrics: a flexible system for assessing translation quality.

Maruf, Sameen, André F. T. Martins, and Gholamreza Haffari. 2018. Contextual neural model for translating bilingual multi-speaker conversations. In *Proc. of the 3rd Conference on Machine Translation*.

Maruf, Sameen, André F. T. Martins, and Gholamreza Haffari. 2019. Selective Attention for Context-aware Neural Machine Translation. In *Proceedings of the 2019 Conference of the North American Chapter of the Association for Computational Linguistics: Human Language Technologies*.

Miculicich, Lesly, Dhananjay Ram, Nikolaos Pappas, and James Henderson. 2018. Document-Level Neural Machine Translation with Hierarchical Attention Networks. In *Proceedings of the 2018 Conference on Empirical Methods in Natural Language Processing*.

Müller, Mathias, Annette Rios, Elena Voita, and Rico Sennrich. 2018. A large-scale test set for the evaluation of context-aware pronoun translation in neural machine translation. In *Proceedings of the Third Conference on Machine Translation*.

Ng, Nathan, Kyra Yee, Alexei Baevski, Myle Ott, Michael Auli, and Sergey Edunov. 2019. Facebook fair's wmt19 news translation task submission. In *Proceedings of the Fourth Conference on Machine Translation (Volume 2: Shared Task Papers, Day 1)*.

Papineni, Kishore, Salim Roukos, Todd Ward, and Wei-Jing Zhu. 2002. BLEU: a method for Automatic Evaluation of Machine Translation. In *Proceedings of the 40th Annual Meeting on Association for Computational Linguistics*.

Pereyra, Gabriel, George Tucker, Jan Chorowski, Łukasz Kaiser, and Geoffrey Hinton. 2017. Regularizing neural networks by penalizing confident output distributions. In *Proceedings of the 5th International Conference on Learning Representations*.

Popel, Martin and Ondřej Bojar. 2018. Training tips for the transformer model. *The Prague Bulletin of Mathematical Linguistics*, 110(1).

Press, Ofir and Lior Wolf. 2017. Using the output embedding to improve language models. In *Proceedings of the 15th Conference of the European Chapter of the Association for Computational Linguistics*.

Rios Gonzales, Annette, Laura Mascarell, and Rico Sennrich. 2017. Improving word sense disambiguation in neural machine translation with sense embeddings. In *Proceedings of the 2nd Conference on Machine Translation*.

Sagot, Benoît. 2010. The lefff, a freely available and large-coverage morphological and syntactic lexicon for French. In *Proceedings of the 7th International Conference on Language Resources and Evaluation*.

Sennrich, Rico, Barry Haddow, and Alexandra Birch. 2016. Neural machine translation of rare words with subword units. In *Proc. of the 54th Annual Meeting of the Association for Computational Linguistics*.

Sennrich, Rico. 2017. How Grammatical is Character-level Neural Machine Translation? In *Proceedings of the 15th Conference of the European Chapter of the Association for Computational Linguistics*.

Smith, Karin Sim. 2017. On integrating discourse in machine translation. In *Proceedings of the Third Workshop on Discourse in Machine Translation*.

Tiedemann, Jörg and Yves Scherrer. 2017. Neural machine translation with extended context. In *Proceedings of the 3rd Workshop on Discourse in Machine Translation*.

Toral, Antonio, Sheila Castilho, Ke Hu, and Andy Way. 2018. Attaining the Unattainable? Reassessing Claims of Human Parity in Neural Machine Translation. In *Proceedings of the Third Conference on Machine Translation*.

Tu, Zhaopeng, Yang Liu, Shuming Shi, and Tong Zhang. 2018. Learning to remember translation history with a continuous cache. *Transactions of the Association for Computational Linguistics*, 6.

Vaswani, Ashish, Noam Shazeer, Niki Parmar, Jakob Uszkoreit, Llion Jones, Aidan N Gomez, Łukasz Kaiser, and Illia Polosukhin. 2017. Attention is all you need. In *Advances in neural information processing systems*.

Voita, Elena, Rico Sennrich, and Ivan Titov. 2019a. Context-aware monolingual repair for neural machine translation. In *Proceedings of the 2019 Conference on Empirical Methods in Natural Language Processing and the 9th International Joint Conference on Natural Language Processing*.

Voita, Elena, Rico Sennrich, and Ivan Titov. 2019b. When a good translation is wrong in context: Context-aware machine translation improves on deixis, ellipsis, and lexical cohesion. In *Proceedings of the 57th Annual Meeting of the Association for Computational Linguistics*.

Wang, Longyue. 2019. *Discourse-Aware Neural Machine Translation*. Ph.D. thesis, Dublin City University, Dublin, Ireland.

Yu, Lei, Laurent Sartran, Wojciech Stokowiec, Wang Ling, Lingpeng Kong, Phil Blunsom, and Chris Dyer. 2019. Putting machine translation in context with the noisy channel model.

Zhang, Jiacheng, Huanbo Luan, Maosong Sun, Feifei Zhai, Jingfang Xu, Min Zhang, and Yang Liu. 2018. Improving the Transformer Translation Model with Document-Level Context. In *Proceedings of the 2018 Conference on Empirical Methods in Natural Language Processing*.

Automatic Translation for Multiple NLP tasks:
a Multi-task Approach to Machine-oriented NMT Adaptation

Amirhossein Tebbifakhr
FBK, Trento, Italy
University of Trento, Italy
atebbifakhr@fbk.eu

Matteo Negri
FBK, Trento, Italy
negri@fbk.eu

Marco Turchi
FBK, Trento, Italy
turchi@fbk.eu

Abstract

Although machine translation (MT) traditionally pursues "human-oriented" objectives, humans are not the only possible consumers of MT output. For instance, when automatic translations are used to feed downstream Natural Language Processing (NLP) components in cross-lingual settings, the translated texts should ideally pursue "machine-oriented" objectives that maximize the performance of these components. Tebbifakhr et al. (2019) recently proposed a reinforcement learning approach to adapt a generic neural MT (NMT) system by exploiting the reward from a downstream sentiment classifier. But what if the downstream NLP tasks to serve are more than one? How to avoid the costs of adapting and maintaining one dedicated NMT system for each task? We address this problem by proposing a multi-task approach to machine-oriented NMT adaptation, which is capable to serve multiple downstream tasks with a single system. Through experiments with Spanish and Italian data covering three different tasks, we show that our approach can outperform a generic NMT system, and compete with single-task models in most of the settings.

1 Introduction

Neural Machine Translation (NMT) systems are typically developed considering humans as the end-users, and are hence optimized pursuing human-oriented requirements about the output quality. To meet these requirements, supervised NMT models are trained to maximize the probability of the given parallel corpora (Bahdanau et al., 2015; Sutskever et al., 2014), which embed the adequacy and fluency criteria essential for the human comprehension of a translated sentence. In another line of research, these objectives are directly addressed in Reinforcement Learning (Ranzato et al., 2016; Shen et al., 2016) and Bandit Learning (Kreutzer et al., 2017; Nguyen et al., 2017), where model optimization is driven by the human feedback obtained for each translation hypothesis.

However, humans are not the only possible consumers of MT output. In a variety of application scenarios, MT can in fact act as a pre-processor to perform other natural language processing (NLP) tasks. For instance, this is the case of text classification tasks for which, in low-resource conditions, the paucity of training data provides a strong motivation for exploiting translation-based solutions. In tasks like sentiment classification, hate speech detection or document classification (the three application scenarios addressed in this paper) a translation-based approach would allow: *i)* translating the input text data from an under-resourced language into a resource-rich target language for which high-performance NLP components are available, *ii)* run a classifier on the translated text and, finally, *iii)* project the results back to the original language.

This approach represents a straightforward solution in low/medium-resource[1] language settings

---

[1] Jain et al. (2019) consider as "medium-resource" languages those for which, although annotated training corpora do not exist, off-the-shelf (MT) systems like Google Translate are available.

Martins, Moniz, Fumega, Martins, Batista, Coheur, Parra, Trancoso, Turchi, Bisazza, Moorkens, Guerberof, Nurminen, Marg, Forcada (eds.)
Proceedings of the 22nd Annual Conference of the European Association for Machine Translation, p. 235–244
Lisboa, Portugal, November 2020.

where reliable NLP components for specific tasks are not available, and represents a strong baseline in a variety of multilingual and cross-lingual NLP tasks (Conneau et al., 2018). However, the NMT systems normally used are still optimized by pursuing human-oriented adequacy and fluency objectives, which are not necessarily the optimal ones for this pipelined solution. These models can indeed produce translations in which some properties of the input text are altered or even lost. For instance, as shown in (Mohammad et al., 2016), this happens in sentiment classification, where automatic translations can fail to properly project core traits of the input text into the target language. When this happens, the downstream linguistic processor will likely produce results of lower quality.

In light of these considerations, Tebbifakhr et al. (2019) argued that when the role of NMT is to feed a downstream NLP component instead of a human, translating into fluent and adequate sentences is not necessarily the main priority. Rather, if the goal is producing translations that are "easy to process" by the downstream component, other optimization strategies might be more effective, even if they result in low-quality output from the point of view of human comprehension. Back to the sentiment classification example: before meaning and style, a "machine-oriented" translation should prioritize the optimal projection of the sentiment traits of the input text, which are the key clues from the automatic sentiment classification standpoint.

To pursue machine-oriented translation objectives, Tebbifakhr et al. (2019) proposed Machine-Oriented Reinforce (MO-Reinforce), a method based on Reinforce (Williams, 1992; Ranzato et al., 2016). While in Reinforce the objective is to maximize the reward given by humans to NMT systems' output, in MO-Reinforce the human feedback is replaced by the reward coming from a downstream NLP system. Focusing on sentiment classification, where the classifier's output is a probability distribution over the classes for each input text, they define the reward as the probability of predicting the correct class. Evaluation results computed on Twitter data show that a downstream English sentiment classifier performs significantly better when it is fed with machine-oriented translations rather than the human-oriented ones produced by a general-purpose NMT system.

Despite its potential usefulness, MO-Reinforce has a limitation that might reduce its general applicability: it requires one NMT model for each downstream task. This represents a possible bottleneck in real industry scenarios, where training and maintaining multiple task-oriented NMT systems (one for each possible downstream task) would be costly and time-consuming, if not unfeasible. To overcome this limitation, in this paper we explore the possibility to simultaneously address multiple downstream tasks with a single NMT system. In this direction, we propose a multi-task learning approach that has two main potential strengths. One is the higher flexibility for industrial deployment due to its architectural simplicity. The other is the possibility to exploit knowledge transfer across similar tasks (Zhang and Yang, 2017), eventually improving the results achieved by the single-task MO-Reinforce approach.

We test the viability of our multi-task approach on two source languages (Spanish and Italian[2]) for which data covering different tasks (sentiment classification, hate speech detection and document classification) have to be translated into English and then processed by dedicated NLP components. Our results show that translating with the proposed multi-task extension yields significant gains in classification performance with respect to both *i)* a generic NMT system and *ii)* the original single-task MO-Reinforce by Tebbifakhr et al. (2019).

Besides exploring for the first time a multi-task approach to "machine-oriented" NMT, this paper provides two technical contributions that explain the reported performance gains, namely: *i)* a reward normalization strategy to weigh the importance of each sample in the course of training, and *ii)* the application of dropout while sampling the translation candidates, which makes the model more reactive and avoids local optima. On the experimental side, another contribution of this work is the first evaluation on multi-class classification data (i.e., those used for the document classification task), a more challenging scenario compared to the binary task considered by Tebbifakhr et al. (2019).

---

[2]Although one of the motivations for machine-oriented translation is to support NLP in under-resourced settings, the chosen source languages do not fall in this category. The choice is motivated by the fact that they provide us with all the necessary infrastructure (e.g. test data) to perform a sound comparative evaluation. Here, indeed, we focus on testing the general applicability of our approach, while its evaluation in real under-resourced settings (conditioned to the availability of benchmarks for multiple tasks) is left for future work.

2 Background

2.1 Human-oriented NMT

Formally, in MT, the probability of generating the translation $\mathbf{y}$ with length of N given a source sentence $\mathbf{x}$ is computed as follows:

$$P(\mathbf{y}|\mathbf{x}) = \prod_{i=1}^{N} p_\theta(\mathbf{y}_i|\mathbf{y}_{<i}, \mathbf{x}) \qquad (1)$$

where p_θ is a conditional probability defined by sequence-to-sequence NMT models (Bahdanau et al., 2015; Sutskever et al., 2014; Vaswani et al., 2017). In these models, an encoder first encodes the source sentence and then, at each time step, a decoder outputs the probability distribution over the vocabulary conditioned on the encoded source sentence and the translation prefix $\mathbf{y}_{<i}$. In supervised NMT, the parameters of the model θ are trained by maximizing the log-likelihood of the given parallel corpus $\{\mathbf{x}^s, \mathbf{y}^s\}_{s=1}^{S}$:

$$
\begin{aligned}
\mathcal{L} &= \sum_{s=1}^{S} \log P(\mathbf{y}^s|\mathbf{x}^s) \\
&= \sum_{s=1}^{S} \sum_{i=1}^{N^s} \log p_\theta(\mathbf{y}_i^s|\mathbf{y}_{<i}^s, \mathbf{x})
\end{aligned}
\qquad (2)
$$

By maximizing this objective, the model indirectly pursues the human-oriented objectives of adequacy and fluency embedded in the training parallel corpora.

In addition to normal NMT training, these objectives can be directly addressed using reinforcement learning methods such as Reinforce (Ranzato et al., 2016). This method maximizes the expected reward from the end-user:

$$
\begin{aligned}
\mathcal{L} &= \sum_{s=1}^{S} E_{\hat{\mathbf{y}} \sim P(.|\mathbf{x}^s)} \Delta(\hat{\mathbf{y}}) \\
&= \sum_{s=1}^{S} \sum_{\hat{\mathbf{y}} \in \mathbf{Y}} P(\hat{\mathbf{y}}|\mathbf{x}^s) \Delta(\hat{\mathbf{y}})
\end{aligned}
\qquad (3)
$$

where $\Delta(\hat{\mathbf{y}})$ is the reward of the sampled translation candidate $\hat{\mathbf{y}}$, and $\mathbf{Y}$ is the set of all the possible translation candidates. Since the size of this set $\mathbf{Y}$ is exponentially large, Equation 3 is estimated by sampling one translation candidate out of this set using multinomial sampling or beam search:

$$\hat{\mathcal{L}} = \sum_{s=1}^{S} P(\hat{\mathbf{y}}|\mathbf{x}^s) \Delta(\hat{\mathbf{y}}), \hat{\mathbf{y}} \sim P(.|\mathbf{x}^s) \qquad (4)$$

Since collecting human rewards is costly, the process can be simulated by comparing the sampled translation candidates with the corresponding reference translations using automatic evaluation metrics like BLUE (Papineni et al., 2002).

The two learning strategies (supervised and reinforcement) have two main commonalities: *i)* the learning objectives are human-oriented, and *ii)* they both need parallel data, respectively for maximizing the probability of the translation pair in supervised learning and for simulating the human reward in reinforcement learning.

2.2 Machine-oriented NMT

To pursue machine-oriented objectives and to bypass the need for parallel corpora, in the MO-Reinforce algorithm proposed by (Tebbifakhr et al., 2019), the human reward is replaced by the reward from a downstream classifier (in that case, a polarity detector predicting the positive/negative sentiment of a translated sentence). This reward is defined as the probability of labeling the translated text with the correct class and it can be easily computed since the output of the downstream classifier is a probability distribution over the possible classes. Therefore, given a small amount of labeled data in the source language[3] $\{\mathbf{x}^s, \mathbf{l}^s\}_{s=1}^{S}$, in which $\mathbf{l}$ is the label of the corresponding source text $\mathbf{x}$, Equation 4 can be redefined as follows:

$$\hat{\mathcal{L}} = \sum_{s=1}^{S} P(\hat{\mathbf{y}}|\mathbf{x}^s) \Delta(\hat{\mathbf{y}}, \mathbf{l}^s), \hat{\mathbf{y}} \sim P(.|\mathbf{x}^s) \qquad (5)$$

where $\Delta(\hat{\mathbf{y}}, \mathbf{l}^s)$ is the probability that the downstream classifier assigns $\mathbf{l}^s$ to a sampled candidate.

In order to increase the contribution of the reward and to sample "useful" translation candidates, the proposed sampling strategy randomly extracts K candidates and eventually chooses the one with the highest reward to update the model. This strategy results in the selection of candidates that influence the initial model towards translations that maximize the performance of the downstream processor. For instance, in the sentiment classification scenario, these are NMT outputs that preserve, or even emphasize, relevant aspects like the proper handling of sentiment-bearing terms. Although they are poor in terms of the human-oriented notion of quality (as shown by BLEU scores close

---

[3] In (Tebbifakhr et al., 2019), MO-Reinforce is shown to result in better classification performance than the original Reinforce (Ranzato et al., 2016) with few hundred labeled instances ($\sim$ 500).

to zero when compared against human references), their high sentiment polarization considerably simplifies the polarity labelling task.

Despite the significant gains compared to the classification performance achieved by translating with a generic NMT system, a limitation of MO-Reinforce lies in its applicability to one task at a time. Serving multiple tasks would only be possible by training multiple NMT models (one for each possible downstream classifier), which is a sub-optimal solution for the actual deployment of the approach in real industrial settings. To overcome this issue, in the next section we propose an extension aimed at simultaneously serving multiple classifiers with a single NMT system. Later, in the experimental part of the paper (sections 4 and 5), we will evaluate it in a multi-task scenario involving both binary and multi-class tasks.

3 Multi-task Machine-oriented NMT

Our multi-task extensions of MO-Reinforce include: *i)* prepending task-specific tokens to the input for managing multiple domains and computing normalized rewards to avoid under/over-fitting (Section 3.1), and *ii)* adding randomness to the sampling process to push for higher exploration of the probability space (Section 3.2).

3.1 Normalized Reward

To serve multiple downstream classifiers with a single NMT system, the model has to be trained on a mixture of the labeled datasets available for the different tasks. To define the target task, we prepend a task-specific token to each input sample within the corresponding dataset. In this way, the NMT model is informed about the target downstream application for which the input text has to be translated. This idea is drawn from multilingual NMT, in which an effective solution is to prepend to the input sentences a token defining the desired target language (Johnson et al., 2017).

To avoid under/over-fitting when training the NMT model on mixed datasets that can have different sizes, we need to schedule the sampling from these datasets. In multilingual NMT, two fixed sampling schedules have been proposed, namely: *i)* proportionally with respect to the dataset size (Luong et al., 2015), or *ii)* uniformly from each dataset (Dong et al., 2015). However, these fixed scheduling approaches are not optimal solutions. The first one gives higher importance to tasks with larger datasets, so that those with less training material might remain under-fitted. The second one gives equal importance to all the tasks, which implies that larger datasets for some tasks will not be fully exploited, reducing systems' performance on those tasks.

To overcome these limitations, adaptive scheduling strategies can be adopted to update the importance of each task in the course of training. The idea is that, when the performance of the model is low on one task, higher importance is given to that task. This can be done by keeping the schedule fixed and scaling the gradients (Chen et al., 2017), or directly by changing the sampling weights (Jean et al., 2019). In the first approach by Chen et al. (2017), the adaptation is done based on the magnitude of the gradients. However, the computed gradients loosely correlate with the performance of the model and do not directly measure model's performance for the corresponding task. The second one (Jean et al., 2019), requires knowing the performance of the single-task models for each task on the development set before starting the training. Then, after each epoch, the results of the multi-task model on the same development set are compared with those achieved by the single-task models, and the weights get updated accordingly. As a direct indicator, models' performance on the development set represents a more reliable alternative compared to exploiting the indirect information provided by gradients' magnitude. However, it is more computationally intensive and it assumes knowing in advance the performance of the single-task models, which is not always available.

We hence opt for the idea of scaling the gradients while keeping the schedule fixed and uniform across tasks. We make the adaptation based on the reward from the downstream task, which reflects the performance of the model for the corresponding input sample. Equation 6 shows the stochastic gradient of the MO-Reinforce objective function.

$$\nabla \hat{\mathcal{L}} = \sum_{s=1}^{S} \Delta(\hat{\mathbf{y}}, \mathbf{l}^s) \nabla \log P(\hat{\mathbf{y}}|\mathbf{x}^s) \qquad (6)$$

In this formulation, since the magnitude of the reward scales the computed gradient for each sample, those samples with higher rewards will also have higher influence on the model adaptation process. This can have a negative impact when the samples come from challenging tasks or even from challenging classes within a specific task. These samples, in fact, will likely get lower reward leaving the corresponding tasks/classes under-fitted.

To avoid this problem and to boost performance when dealing with challenging samples, we propose a reward normalization step, which extends MO-Reinforce with the possibility to weight the importance of each sample during training. The idea is that the average reward for the K translation candidates sampled by MO-Reinforce in order to chose the most useful one (see Section 2.2) can be considered as an indicator of the level of difficulty of each task. Therefore, to normalize the reward, this average value can be subtracted from the original reward as follows:

$$\hat{\Delta}(\hat{\mathbf{y}}, \mathbf{l}) = \Delta(\hat{\mathbf{y}}, \mathbf{l}) - \frac{\sum_{k=1}^{K} \Delta(\hat{\mathbf{y}}_k, \mathbf{l})}{K} + \alpha \quad (7)$$

where K is the number of sampled translation candidates. We add a constant value α to prevent zero reward for the cases in which all the rewards have the same value. This normalization reduces more the reward of easy samples, whose average is high, and subsequently results in giving more importance to challenging samples with low reward.

3.2 Noisy Sampling

Two sampling strategies are used for sampling the translation candidates in reinforcement learning. The first one is *beam search* (Sutskever et al., 2014). It is a heuristic search, which maintains a pool of highest probability translation prefixes with size B. At each step, the prefixes in the pool are expanded by B highest probability words from the model's distribution output. Then, the resulting $B \times B$ hypotheses are pruned by keeping B-highest probability prefixes. The search continues until all the prefixes in the pool reach the *EOS* token. The second one is *multinomial sampling* (Ranzato et al., 2016) where, at each time step, a word is generated by sampling from the model's distribution output. The generation is terminated when the *EOS* token is generated.

For a given application, the choice between the two sampling strategies depends on the known trade-off between exploration and exploitation in reinforcement learning. Indeed, while beam search exploits more the model's knowledge, multinomial sampling is more oriented to exploring the probability search space. In light of this difference, in MO-Reinforce the sampling is done using multinomial sampling, which achieves better results in NMT (Wu et al., 2018). This is needed, since the parameters of the model are initialized by a generic NMT system, which is trained on parallel data pursuing human-oriented objectives. Pushing for the exploration of the probability space instead of exploiting the original model's knowledge will promote the generation of more diverse candidates and eventually increase the chance to influence system's behaviour towards our machine-oriented objectives.

Although for these reasons multinomial sampling represents a better choice compared to beam search, in MO-Reinforce the exploration of the probability space does not always result in a boost of candidates' diversity. For instance, the higher randomness in generating the translation candidates might not suffice when the model's probability distribution is very peaked (i.e. when, at a given time step, the number of plausible options for the next word is very small). In this case, multinomial sampling will likely generate the same candidate at different iterations on the data. If its reward is the highest one among the K samples, this candidate will be chosen and the model will be updated to increase the candidate's probability. The result will be an even more peaked distribution that, in turn, will increase the chance of making the model stuck in a local optimum by repeatedly generating the same candidate.

To avoid these local optima and make MO-Reinforce more reactive to handle multi-task data, our last extension aims to perturb the model's probability distribution. We do this by enabling *dropout* (Srivastava et al., 2014) while generating the candidates, which is usually disabled while generating the translation outputs. Dropout adds permutation in sampling, which helps the model to generate different translation candidates at different passes over the data even in the case of highly peaked probability distributions.

4 Experiments

Our multi-task extension of MO-Reinforce is evaluated on two source languages: Spanish and Italian. For Spanish, we consider the downstream tasks of document classification and hate speech detection. For Italian, we select document classification and sentiment analysis. The evaluation is done by feeding dedicated English classifiers (one for each downstream task) with translations produced by different NMT models, namely: *i)*

| | Spanish Tasks | | | | | |
| | MLDoc | | | | Hate Speech | |
	CCAT	ECAT	GCAT	MCAT	Non-Hateful	Hateful
Train	100	100	100	100	400	400
Developement	314	201	208	277	500	500
Test	1246	731	794	1229	278	222

| | Italian Tasks | | | | | |
| | MLDoc | | | | Sentiment | |
	CCAT	ECAT	GCAT	MCAT	Negative	Positive
Train	100	100	100	100	2289	1450
Developement	239	248	238	275	254	161
Test	963	1066	976	995	733	316

Table 1: Statistics of datasets used for the Spanish and Italian tasks.

	Europarl	JRC	Wikipedia	ECB	TED	KDE	News11	News	Total
Es-En	2M	0.8M	1.8M	0.1M	0.2M	0.2M	0.3M	0.2M	5.6M
It-En	2M	0.8M	1M	0.2M	0.2M	0.3M	0.04M	0.02M	4.56M

Table 2: Statistics of the parallel corpora used for training the generic NMT systems

a general-purpose NMT system, *ii)* the original single-task MO-Reinforce, and *iii)* different variants of our multi-task extension. The goal is to maximize the classification performance on each downstream task. As another term of comparison for the three translation-based solutions, we consider the results obtained by directly processing the input sentences with task-specific Spanish and Italian classifiers trained on the same small datasets used to adapt the general-purpose NMT system.

In line with (Tebbifakhr et al., 2019), the multi-task approach is expected to outperform the generic (human-oriented) NMT system, as well as the task/language-specific classifiers trained on few data points. Ideally, thanks to the solutions proposed in Section 3, it should also compete with the single-task (machine-oriented) models. This would indicate the viability of a single-model approach to simultaneously address multiple tasks.

In the following, we describe the task-specific data used for model adaptation and evaluation, as well as the parallel corpora used for training the generic NMT system. Their statistics are respectively reported in Tables 1 and 2.

Document Classification. For this multi-class labelling task, we use the MLDoc corpora (Schwenk and Li, 2018), which cover 8 languages, including English, Spanish and Italian. They comprise news stories labeled with 4 different categories: CCAT (Corporate/Industrial), ECAT (Economics), GCAT (Government/Social), and MCAT (Markets). For each language, the training, de-

velopment and test sets respectively contain 10K, 1K, and 4K documents uniformly distributed into the 4 classes. Following (Bell, 1991), for training and evaluation we only consider the first sentence of each document, which usually provides enough information about the general content of the document. We use the whole English training set to build our downstream classifiers. To simulate an under-resourced setting, we randomly sample 100 documents for each class from the Spanish and Italian training sets. We use these samples to adapt the generic NMT system for the downstream task, while for development and test we use the whole sets.

Hate Speech Detection. For this binary task, we use the English and Spanish datasets published for the multilingual hate speech detection shared task at SemEval 2019 (Basile et al., 2019). We train the downstream classifier on the whole English training set, including 3,783 hateful and 5,217 non-hateful Twitter messages. We randomly sample 400 tweets for each class from the Spanish training set in order to simulate the under-resourced setting. Since the test set is not publicly available, we use the development set as final evaluation benchmark, and we sample 500 tweets for each class from the rest of the training set as the development set.

Sentiment Classification. For this binary task, we use a collection of annotated tweets released for the Italian sentiment analysis task at Evalita 2016 (Barbieri et al., 2016). After filtering out the subjective tweets and the ones with mixed polarity,

Models	Spanish-English		Italian-English	
	MLDoc	Hate Speech	MLDoc	Sentiment
Generic	82.58	54.49	75.43	51.89
Source	84.86	75.29	73.24	64.06
Single-task MO-Reinforce	88.36	64.24	76.86	**70.27**
Multi-task MO-Reinforce (proportional sampling)	86.18	62.93	10.83	70.11
Multi-task MO-Reinforce (uniform sampling)	86.45	55.07	68.26	68.01
Multi-task MO-Reinforce (normalization)	86.98	66.52	75.11	66.70
Multi-task MO-Reinforce (dropout)	87.73	**77.56**	80.31	68.98
Multi-task MO-Reinforce (dropout & normalization)	**90.13**	77.08	**80.90**	66.73

Table 3: Classification results (F1) obtained by: *i)* translating with the *Generic* NMT system, *ii)* directly processing the untranslated data *(Source)*, *iii)* translating with separate *Single-task MO-Rinforce* models, *iv)* one *Multi-task MO-Reinforce* model with different sampling strategies, *v)* one *Multi-task MO-Reinforce* model with reward normalization and noisy sampling.

we train the downstream system using a balanced set of 1.6M negative and positive tweets (Go et al., 2009).

Generic NMT systems We train the generic NMT system using the parallel corpora reported in Table 2. After filtering out long and imbalanced pairs, we encode the corpora using 32K byte-pair codes (Sennrich et al., 2016). Our NMT model uses Transformer with parameters set as in the original paper (Vaswani et al., 2017). In all the settings, we start the training by initializing the NMT model with the trained generic NMT systems. Then, we continue the training for 50 epochs and choose the best performing checkpoint based on the average F1 score measured on the development set of each task. We set K (i.e. the number of sampled translation candidates at each time step) to 5, and used the development set to evaluate different values of α (i.e. the constant value added to prevent zero rewards – see Section 3.1). The best-performing value of 0.1 was then used in all the experiments. For developing the classifiers (both the downstream English ones and the language-specific ones used as baseline), we fine-tune the multilingual BERT (Devlin et al., 2019).

5 Results and Discussion

Our experimental results are shown in Table 3, which reports the classification performance (F1) obtained on each downstream task by:

- Feeding the English classifiers with translations from different NMT models (i.e. *Generic, Single-task MO-Reinforce* and different variants of *Multi-task MO-reinforce*);

- Running language-specific classifiers on the original untranslated data *(Source)*.

The F1 scores obtained by the *Generic* NMT systems in document classification (MLDoc) show that the simplest translation-based approach produces competitive results compared to those achieved by language-specific classifiers trained on small in-domain data. The situation is different for tasks whose data differ significantly from those used to train the general-purpose system. On the user-generated content used for hate speech detection and sentiment classification (i.e. Twitter data), the *Generic* results are indeed poor. This shows that NMT models trained by only pursuing human-oriented criteria might not fit to target downstream tasks, for which machine-oriented adaptation becomes necessary.

Machine-oriented adaptation with single-task *MO-Reinforce* yields the expected benefits, with improvements (+3.25 F1 points for document classification, +18.38 for sentiment classification in Italian) that allow to outperform the language-specific *(Source)* classifiers in three tasks out of four. These gains confirm and validate on multiple tasks (including multi-class classification) the findings of Tebbifakhr et al. (2019), showing that *MO-Reinforce* can leverage the feedback from external linguistic processors to adapt the NMT model towards translations that maximize the performance in downstream applications.

The middle part of Table 3 shows the first results obtained by our multi-task adaptation of *MO-Reinforce*. This is done by prepending the task-specific tokens and comparing the two fixed sampling schedules (proportional to datasets' size and uniform). As expected (see Section 3.1), when sampling proportionally, the task with less training data (MLDoc) starves in training and remains under-fitted. This is particularly evident for Italian, where the document classification dataset is ten

Models	Spanish-English		Italian-English	
	MLDoc	Hate Speech	MLDoc	Sentiment
Single-Task MO-Reinforce	88.36	64.24	76.86	70.27
Single-Task MO-Reinforce (dropout)	**89.91**	35.73	**81.87**	65.67
Single-Task MO-Reinforce (dropout & normalization)	88.55	**78.33**	81.22	**70.97**

Table 4: Classification results (F1) obtained by translating with the original single-task MO-Reinforce and two variants of multi-task MO-Reinforce (with noisy sampling – dropout – alone and combined with reward normalization).

times smaller than the sentiment analysis one, and performance is particularly low (10.83). On Spanish, where the hate-speech dataset is only twice as big as the document classification one, the problem exists but it is less evident. Although uniform sampling helps the task with less training data (MLDoc) to achieve better performance, it harms those with more data, which remain under-fitted (lower performance than proportional sampling). Analysing the performance of the multitask and single task variants of *MO-Reinforce*, we notice that, although the former still outperforms the *Generic* NMT system in three tasks out of 4, its results are worse compared to the single-task *MO-Reinforce*. For the task with the most unbalanced data (MLDoc Italian), uniform sampling helps to increase the performance, but it is not sufficient to reach the scores achieved by *Generic* NMT. On hate speech data, the results of the language-specific classifiers (*Source*) are still the highest ones. The results reported so far would not allow a user to replace the single task systems with the multitask one.

The bottom part of Table 3 reports the classification results obtained by *MO-Reinforce* with reward normalization and noisy sampling (both separately and together). As it can be seen, reward normalization is beneficial for both the Spanish tasks, with a larger performance gain on hate speech with respect to both the sampling strategies (+3.59 and +11.45 F1 points). For Italian, reward normalization helps in the MLDoc task (+6.85 over the best sampling strategy), but it results in a performance drop in sentiment classification (-1.31). In general, reward normalization shows to be useful for tasks that tend to remain under-fitted with proportional or uniform sampling. Concerning the sentiment analysis task, our intuition is that, in presence of a large quantity of task-specific data in the target language, both the English classifier and the computed rewards are reliable enough. Scaling the rewards with their average value (see Eq. 7) reduces the learning capability of the NMT sys-

tem, resulting in an under-fitted model. Although adding reward normalization reduces the gap in performance with respect to the single-task *MO-Reinforce* and the Source classifiers, it is not yet sufficient to replace them.

The results are significantly better with the noisy sampling approach discussed in Section 3.2. In both the languages and in all the tasks, the reported F1 scores approach those obtained by the single-task variant of *MO-Reinforce* (which in two cases is even outperformed) and always improve over the language-specific Source classifiers. This confirms that enabling dropout while generating the translation candidates avoids the model to get stuck in local optima, and promotes diversity in producing candidates that eventually receive higher rewards.

Combined, the two contributions of this paper (reward normalization and noisy sampling) yield mixed outcomes. For Spanish, we observe a further improvement compared to noisy sampling in document classification (+2.40), which comes at the cost of a small drop in hate speech detection (-0.48). Also for Italian there is an improvement over noisy sampling alone in document classification (+0.59), but a larger drop in sentiment classification performance (-2.25). However, it's worth remarking that: *i)* the size of the Italian sentiment analysis dataset is almost 10 times larger than the size of the document classification dataset, and *ii)* the data used to train the English classifiers are even more unbalanced. Being able to harmonize the results of the two task hence becomes quite difficult. Nevertheless, combining reward normalization and noisy sampling has a general positive effect, which allows the multi-task *MO-Reinforce* system to approach and, in some tasks, even to outperform the single task models.

In our final analysis, we investigate the effect of introducing dropout and reward normalization when *MO-Reinforce* is used in the single-task scenario. As shown in Table 4, enabling dropout improves the document classification results in both the languages. The reported scores show that the

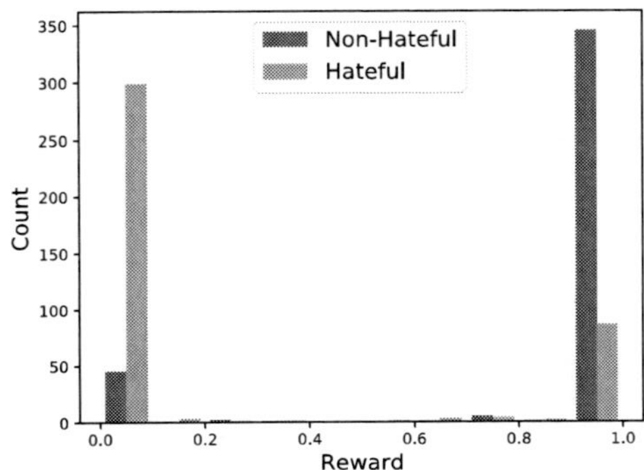

Figure 1: Rewards distribution for the hate speech detection training set translated with the *Generic* NMT system.

added noise introduced by dropout helps the model to explore more the probability space and avoid local optima, even when dealing with a single task. However, for hate speech detection in Spanish and sentiment analysis in Italian, this exploration of the probability space results in lower performance compared to the original *MO-Reinforce*. To understand the reasons of this drop, Figure 1 shows the distribution of the rewards obtained in hate speech detection when translating the training set with the generic NMT system. This distribution shows that the downstream classifier is very biased toward the non-hateful class (right side of Figure 1), with most of the hateful samples obtaining zero reward (left side). While the model is exploring the probability space, this extreme imbalance in the rewards does not allow the hateful samples to get a non-zero reward, and this drastically scales down their gradients preventing the NMT system to actually learn from these samples. Eventually, this results in a "catastrophic forgetting", where the NMT system learns only from one class and totally forgets the other. Whatever it will receive in input, this system will generate a translation with no hate nuances, which will be classified as non-hateful by the downstream classifier. The very low F1 (35.73) is the result of this process.

Adding reward normalization minimizes the "catastrophic forgetting" effect by keeping the magnitude of the rewards balanced across the classes. In terms of performance, hate speech detection and sentiment analysis benefit of it by achieving higher results compared to the original *MO-Reinforce* (respectively, +14.09 and +0.77). On both the languages, the document classifi-

cation results slightly drop compared with *MO-Reinforce* with dropout, but they still outperform those achieved by translating with the original approach by (Tebbifakhr et al., 2019).

Looking at the output of the system, we noticed that the translations are shorter and are not adequate compared to the output of the *Generic* system. For instance, in document classification, the samples belonging to the Corporate class are usually translated to *"The company."*, or the positive samples in sentiment analysis are translated to *"I'm very happy."*, which are easier to be classified by the downstream classifiers.

6 Conclusion

We proposed an extension of the MO-Reinforce algorithm, targeting "machine-oriented" NMT adaptation in a multi-task scenario. In this scenario, different NLP components are fed with translations produced by a single NMT system, which is adapted to generate output that is "easy to process" by the downstream processing tools. To close the performance gap between the single and the multi-task variants of MO-Reinforce, we enhanced the latter with reward normalization and noisy sampling strategies. Our experiments show that, with these two features, the multi-task MO-Reinforce approach achieves significant gains in performance that make it competitive with the single-task solution (though, having one single model to build and maintain, at considerably lower deployment costs). Furthermore, we show that reward normalization and noisy sampling can also help in the single-task setting, where our approach outperforms the original MO-Reinforce in four tasks.

References

Bahdanau, Dzmitry, Kyunghyun Cho, and Yoshua Bengio. 2015. Neural machine translation by jointly learning to align and translate. In Proc. of ICLR 2015, San Diego, CA, USA, May.

Barbieri, F, V Basile, D Croce, M Nissim, N Novielli, and V Patti. 2016. Overview of the evalita 2016 sentiment polarity classification task. In Proc. of EVALITA 2016, Naples, Italy, December.

Basile, Valerio, Cristina Bosco, Elisabetta Fersini, Debora Nozza, et al. 2019. SemEval-2019 task 5: Multilingual detection of hate speech against immigrants and women in twitter. In Proc. of SEMEVAL 2019, pages 54–63, Minneapolis, Minnesota, USA, June.

Bell, A. 1991. The Language of News Media. Language in society. Blackwell.

Chen, Zhao, Vijay Badrinarayanan, Chen-Yu Lee, and Andrew Rabinovich. 2017. Gradnorm: Gradient normalization for adaptive loss balancing in deep multitask networks. arXiv preprint arXiv:1711.02257.

Conneau, Alexis, Ruty Rinott, Guillaume Lample, Adina Williams, Samuel Bowman, et al. 2018. XNLI: Evaluating cross-lingual sentence representations. In Proc. of EMNLP 2018, pages 2475–2485, Brussels, Belgium, November.

Devlin, Jacob, Ming-Wei Chang, Kenton Lee, and Kristina Toutanova. 2019. BERT: Pre-training of deep bidirectional transformers for language understanding. In Proc. of NAACL-HLT 2019, pages 4171–4186, Minneapolis, Minnesota, June.

Dong, Daxiang, Hua Wu, Wei He, Dianhai Yu, and Haifeng Wang. 2015. Multi-task learning for multiple language translation. In Proc. of ACL 2015, pages 1723–1732, Beijing, China, July.

Go, Alec, Richa Bhayani, and Lei Huang. 2009. Twitter sentiment classification using distant supervision. CS224N Project Report, Stanford, 1(12):2009.

Jain, Alankar, Bhargavi Paranjape, and Zachary C. Lipton. 2019. Entity projection via machine translation for cross-lingual NER. In Proc. of EMNLP 2019, pages 1083–1092, Hong Kong, China, November.

Jean, Sébastien, Orhan Firat, and Melvin Johnson. 2019. Adaptive scheduling for multi-task learning. arXiv preprint arXiv:1909.06434.

Johnson, Melvin, Mike Schuster, Quoc V. Le, Maxim Krikun, et al. 2017. Google's multilingual neural machine translation system: Enabling zero-shot translation. Transactions of the Association for Computational Linguistics, 5:339–351.

Kreutzer, Julia, Artem Sokolov, and Stefan Riezler. 2017. Bandit structured prediction for neural sequence-to-sequence learning. In Proc. of ACL 2017, pages 1503–1513, Vancouver, Canada, August.

Luong, Minh-Thang, Quoc V Le, Ilya Sutskever, et al. 2015. Multi-task sequence to sequence learning. arXiv preprint arXiv:1511.06114.

Mohammad, Saif M., Mohammad Salameh, and Svetlana Kiritchenko. 2016. How translation alters sentiment. Journal of Artificial Intelligence Research, 55(1):95–130, January.

Nguyen, Khanh, Hal Daumé III, and Jordan Boyd-Graber. 2017. Reinforcement learning for bandit neural machine translation with simulated human feedback. In Proc. of EMNLP 2017, pages 1464–1474, Copenhagen, Denmark, September.

Papineni, Kishore, Salim Roukos, Todd Ward, and Wei-Jing Zhu. 2002. BLEU: a method for automatic evaluation of machine translation. In Proc. of ACL 2002, pages 311–318, Philadelphia, PA, USA, July.

Ranzato, Marc'Aurelio, Sumit Chopra, Michael Auli, and Wojciech Zaremba. 2016. Sequence level training with recurrent neural networks. In Proc. of ICLR 2016, San Juan, Puerto Rico, May.

Schwenk, Holger and Xian Li. 2018. A Corpus for Multilingual Document Classification in Eight Languages. In Proc. of LREC 2018, Miyazaki, Japan, May.

Sennrich, Rico, Barry Haddow, and Alexandra Birch. 2016. Neural machine translation of rare words with subword units. In Proc. of ACL 2016, pages 1715–1725, Berlin, Germany, August.

Shen, Shiqi, Yong Cheng, Zhongjun He, Wei He, et al. 2016. Minimum risk training for neural machine translation. In Proc. of ACL 2016, pages 1683–1692, Berlin, Germany, August.

Srivastava, Nitish, Geoffrey Hinton, Alex Krizhevsky, Ilya Sutskever, and Ruslan Salakhutdinov. 2014. Dropout: A simple way to prevent neural networks from overfitting. Journal of Machine Learning Research, 15(56):1929–1958.

Sutskever, Ilya, Oriol Vinyals, and Quoc V Le. 2014. Sequence to sequence learning with neural networks. In Advances in Neural Information Processing Systems 27, pages 3104–3112. Curran Associates, Inc.

Tebbifakhr, Amirhossein, Luisa Bentivogli, Matteo Negri, and Marco Turchi. 2019. Machine translation for machines: the sentiment classification use case. In Proc. of EMNLP 2019, pages 1368–1374, Hong Kong, China, November.

Vaswani, Ashish, Noam Shazeer, Niki Parmar, Jakob Uszkoreit, et al. 2017. Attention is all you need. In Advances in Neural Information Processing Systems 30, pages 5998–6008. Curran Associates, Inc.

Williams, Ronald J. 1992. Simple statistical gradient-following algorithms for connectionist reinforcement learning. Machine learning, 8(3-4):229–256.

Wu, Lijun, Fei Tian, Tao Qin, Jianhuang Lai, and Tie-Yan Liu. 2018. A study of reinforcement learning for neural machine translation. In Proc. of EMNLP 2018, pages 3612–3621, Brussels, Belgium, November.

Zhang, Yu and Qiang Yang. 2017. A survey on multi-task learning. arXiv preprint arXiv:1707.08114.

MT syntactic priming effects on L2 English speakers

Natália Resende
ADAPT Centre
Dublin City University
School of Computing
natalia.resende@
adaptcentre.ie

Benjamin Cowan
ADAPT Centre
University College Dublin
School of Information and
Communication Studies
benjamin.cowan@
ucd.ie

Andy Way
ADAPT Centre
Dublin City University
School of Computing
andy.way@
adaptcentre.ie

Abstract

In this paper, we tested 20 Brazilian Portuguese speakers at intermediate and advanced English proficiency levels to investigate the influence of Google Translate's MT system on the mental processing of English as a second language. To this end, we employed a syntactic priming experimental paradigm using a pretest-priming design which allowed us to compare participants' linguistic behaviour before and after a translation task using Google Translate. Results show that, after performing a translation task with Google Translate, participants more frequently described images in English using the syntactic alternative previously seen in the output of Google Translate, compared to the translation task with no prior influence of the MT output. Results also show that this syntactic priming effect is modulated by English proficiency levels.

1 Introduction

Machine Translation systems (MT), especially Google Translate, have become popular in the last decades (Clifford et al., 2013). The popularity of these systems has grown not only due to technical improvements, but also due to the facilitation of users' access through the proliferation of mobile applications containing a number of functions that allow users to translate from texts, from speech or from a text image (Gupta and Dhawan, 2019; Chinnery, 2008). The rapid development of

MT technologies is the result of massive research investment in the field over the past decades focusing on language resources, new methods and techniques with the aim of improving the quality of the MT output. Consequently, the progress made in MT technology has changed the way people are engaging with these systems (Gaspari and Hutchins, 2007).

In the past, MT systems were used mainly for gisting purposes, but nowadays they are also being used as a tool supporting writing skills, grammar skills and language production in a second language (L2) (Niño, 2006; Garcia and Pena, 2011). However, research in the MT field focusing on end-users is limited so that, currently, little we know about what the users' interaction with an MT system could bring to the mental processing of a second language. In this paper, we aim at investigating the role MT systems play, especially, the role that the popular MT system Google Translate plays on the processing of English as a second language. Specifically, we investigate the influence of Google Translate on the processing of English as L2 by testing whether the MT output can influence the way MT users process English syntax. We address the following research questions:

1. Is the use of MT capable of affecting the way a second language is being processed by users when speaking in a second language?

2. Can MT systems facilitate the access and processing of syntactic structures that pose a challenge to L2 English speakers?

To the best of our knowledge, these questions remain unaddressed in the MT literature and deserve further scrutiny.

To accomplish this paper's goal, we carried out a syntactic priming study, an experimental paradigm

Martins, Moniz, Fumega, Martins, Batista, Coheur, Parra, Trancoso, Turchi, Bisazza, Moorkens, Guerberof, Nurminen, Marg, Forcada (eds.)
Proceedings of the 22nd Annual Conference of the European Association for Machine Translation, p. 245–253
Lisboa, Portugal, November 2020.

commonly used by researchers in the field of psycholinguistics, as an way to understand aspects of the representation and processing of language syntax (Braningan et al., 2000). The syntactic priming approach enabled us to understand the influence of the MT in participants' linguistic behaviour after exposition to the MT output. Due to differences in syntactic structures, we focused in particular on Portuguese-English (PT–EN) translation.

Before presenting our methodology in detail, we highlight the progress that has been made in previous research focusing on syntactic processing adopting the syntactic priming methodological paradigm.

2   Related work

The syntactic priming effect, known as *syntactic alignment* or *structural alignment*, occurs when people, in a communicative context, repeat the same syntactic structure previously seen, heard or read (Bock, 1986).

The first priming effect was reported by Levelt and Kelter (1982) who observed a repetition in grammatical structure in a question-and-answer telephone experiment in which merchants were asked either (a) *"At what time does your store close?"* or (b) *"What time does your store close?"*. The researchers observed that the merchants were much more likely to respond to (a) with a sentence also starting with a preposition, such as *"At 6 o'clock"*, and to questions such as (b) with a noun-phrase, such as *"6 o'clock"*. Bock (1986) was the first to implement a laboratory study to investigate this repetition effect and developed an experimental paradigm to understand its characteristics in a controlled and naturalistic manner at the syntactic level. The experiment consisted of reading a sentence and asking participants to repeat out loud the same sentence. Listening and repeating the sentence was considered the "prime phase" of the experiment as the experimenter could control participants' exposure to different syntactic structures. Following the "prime phase", participants were requested to describe an image so that the researcher could observe if participants would use the same structure they had just produced in the prime phase in the subsequent utterance. Bock (1986) noticed that in their subsequent utterance participants tended to use the same syntactic structure previously heard and repeated. After this seminal study, a number of studies have shown syntactic priming evidence between human interlocutors in L1 (Bock, 1986; Bock and Kroch, 1989; Bock et al., 1992; Hartsuiker and Kolk, 1998; Bock and Griffin, 2000) and L2 (McDonough, 2006; Shin and Christianson, 2012) interactions. These studies have also revealed that less frequent syntactic structures prime more than more frequent structures (Ferreira and Bock, 2006). For example, passive structures which are less frequently used by English and Dutch speakers prime more than active structures that are more frequently used (Bock, 1986). Some researchers call this effect as the "inverse preference effect" and they claim that the most uncommon structures drive the priming effect (Heyselaar et al., 2017a; Heyselaar et al., 2017b).

This repetition effect (Heyselaar et al., 2017a) has also been shown between humans and computers (Branigan et al., 2003). Cowan et al. (2015) found syntactic alignment in human-computer speech-based interactions for both dative structures (e.g. *give the waitress an apple* vs. *give the apple to the waitress*) and noun phrase structures (e.g. *a purple circle* vs. *a circle that is purple*) evidencing that a computer system can also influence a speaker's grammatical choices in speech-based interactions.

Virtual reality studies have also demonstrated syntactic alignment between humans and computer avatars. Heyselaar et al. (2017b) observed a priming effect for passives and actives, although the priming effect was stronger for passives than for actives. Suzuki and Katagiri (2007) have also found prosodic alignment between humans and computers. In their experiment, people exhibited alignment of loudness and response latency in their speech in response to computer-generated speech. Oviatt et al. (2004) found that children talking to computer partners spontaneously adapt several basic acoustic and prosodic features of their speech by 10–50%, with the largest adaptations involving utterance pause structure and amplitude. In addition, both naturalistic (Stoyanchev and Stent, 2009) and laboratory research (Branigan et al., 2003) investigating speech-based interactions between humans and computers have also shown that people tend to align syntactically with computers.

From the findings presented above, it is possible to conclude that, in an interactive context, speakers tend to syntactically align with their interlocutors both in first and second languages as well as with computer partners. Importantly, these studies show that syntactic priming plays a central role in successful communication since it can promote mutual understanding through the semantic and structural representations shared by interlocutors (Pickering and Garrod, 2004).

In this paper, we report the preliminary results of a study that investigates whether human participants, specifically L2 speakers of English, syntactically align with MT output after performing a translation task. In other words, we investigate whether users are primed by the MT output when speaking in a second language. We expect that if, after performing a translation task using an MT system, the syntactic structure from the translation task is observed in the speakers' subsequent utterance, then MT output can influence the syntactic processing of English as a second language.

Despite a number of studies demonstrating syntactic priming between humans and computers, to the best of our knowledge, this is the first time syntactic alignment between an MT system and a human partner has been investigated.

The present study also expands previous syntactic priming studies. For the first time syntactic priming is tested from text (comprehension) to speech (production) by means of a cross-linguistic task (translation task) using a computer tool. Based on previous findings, we hypothesize that when translating a text using an MT, the user's syntactic choices when producing speech in a second language will mirror the syntax of the MT output.

To test these hypotheses, we carried out a behavioural syntactic priming study using an experimental paradigm commonly used in syntactic priming studies in the field of psycholinguistics (Pickering and Ferreira, 2008). Based on Shin and Christianson (2012), we adopted a pretest-priming design as it enabled us to study the influence of the MT on participants' performance in a picture description priming task as compared to the pretest baseline. In addition to the two general research questions presented above, by adopting the syntacting priming methodological paradigm we aim at answering the following specific research question:

- Would Portuguese speakers use a more difficult syntactic structure to process in English in their subsequent speech after exposure to this structure through Google Translate's output?

In the following sections, we describe the methodology employed in detail.

3 Method

3.1 Participants

We recruited 20 native speakers of Brazilian Portuguese (14 women) to take part in the study, through posts on social networks and the distribution of advertisements in English schools in Dublin, Ireland. Participants received a € 10 voucher in return for taking part. We excluded one participant from the dataset as the person reported difficulties in completing the tests, leaving 19 participants in the sample. Prior to the experimental sessions, all participants gave written informed consent to participate in the experiments and read the plain language statement.

All participants were living in Dublin, Ireland, at the time of data collection and reported having received formal instruction in English. The average age of the sample was 33.7 years (sd=5.6) with all participants being either at intermediate or advanced English proficiency levels according to the online Cambridge General English test[1] (25 question test; Mean test score= 13.8 (sd=4,5)).

3.2 Dependent Variable- Noun Phrase Syntax

Our research focuses on the participant's production of an English noun phrase with a relation of possession between nouns (e.g. *the cutlery handles are colourful* or *the handles of the cutlery are colourful*). We focused on this structure as this type of noun phrase varies across the participants' native and non-native language.

In Portuguese, only one syntactic alternative exists to represent a relation of possession between nouns. The relation is always encoded in the preposition *do* (de + o) or *da* (de + a) (e.g. *a mesa do escritório está cheia* or *a porta da casa está fechada*). Yet in English this relation can be represented using either a prepositional noun phrase (PNP), which follows the same word order as in Portuguese (e.g. *the table of the office is full*), or a non-prepositional noun phrase (NP) (e.g. *the office table is full*), which differs from Portuguese in word order. This allows us to identify whether syntactic priming by the MT output can lead Portuguese participants to produce NP structures more frequently in English which is an unfamiliar, and

---

[1] https://www.cambridgeenglish.org/test-your-english/general-english/

more complex structure for these L2 speakers to process.

3.3 Experiment Task

Participants were asked to take part in an experimental game involving two stages; a pretest and a priming test phase. In the pretest phase, participants were asked to translate sentences depicting images from Portuguese into English using words provided below each image. In the priming test phase, participants had to describe, after a translation task using Google translate, the images displayed on a computer screen using speech. This is similar to the design used in previous second language syntactic priming studies (Shin and Christianson, 2012).

To construct the stimuli trials used in the pretest and priming test, we used a total of 104 images all of them retrieved from an online image repository[2]. The stimuli were presented on a computer screen using *Psychopy* software[3]. During the pretest and priming test, all verbal responses were recorded on Quick Player voice recorder.

3.4 Google Translate output

Prior to the construction of the experiment materials, we tested how Google would translate the Portuguese sentences created for the priming phase of the experiment. We observed that all sentences in Portuguese were translated from Portuguese into English using a NP structure far more frequently than a PNP structure. All the 40 sentences used in the priming phase were Google translated with a NP structure which is, as already mentioned, a more challenging syntactic alternative to Portuguese speakers. Based on this observation, we hypothesize that participants will produce more NP constructions after being exposed to the MT output than PNP constructions, but they will produce more PNP constructions in the pretest because the pretest does not involve participants' exposure to MT output. Observing the use of NP structure after being exposed to the output would suggest that the MT system would be facilitating the access to a syntactic alternative that is more complex to process for Portuguese speakers.

[2]https://elements.envato.com/
[3]https://www.psychopy.org/

3.4.1 Pretest stage
3.4.2 Materials

The pretest consisted of 26 trials which were presented in a random order. The game was self-paced, i.e., all trials were presented until the participants responded. Participants were allowed to reformulate their answer once in case they noticed a mistake.

From the 26 trials, 20 trials consisted of images depicting a scene that was described in a sentence in Portuguese composed of a noun phrase subject, an auxiliary verb and a complement (e.g. *Os armários da cozinha estão organizados* – "kitchen cabinets are tidy"). The 6 remaining trials were filler trials (30% of the priming trials) consisting of sentences composed of a subject (definite article + noun), an auxiliary verb and complement (e.g. *A porta está trancada* – "the door is locked") as well as images depicting those sentences. These 20 pretest trials provided a baseline because they enabled us to test the frequency at which participants produced the different syntactic alternatives in English when translating without any influence of an MT system.

3.4.3 Procedure - Prestest stage

Participants were instructed to orally translate the sentences on the computer screen from the Portuguese into English. All sentences depicting the images involved a relation of possession so that they all could be translated into English using either a PNP construction or a NP construction. Below each image, we provided the words in Portuguese and their equivalents in English so that the use of participants' preferable syntactic alternative to translate the sentences was not hindered by any lexical retrieval issues. Figure 1, below, shows examples of pretest trials.

3.4.4 Priming stage
3.4.5 Materials

The priming test consisted of 26 trials, comprised of prime-target (prime condition) and filler prime-target (filler condition) pairs. Like the pretest stage, the priming stage was also self-paced. The items were presented in a random order one after another in one go, imediately after completing the pretest.

Each trial included two items preceding a target description item. There were 20 trials where two items acted as primes for the English MT translated structure (prime-target trials)and 6 filler trials

Figure 1: Examples of trials presented in the baseline pretest. Participants translated the sentences depicting images out loud using the words provided below each image.

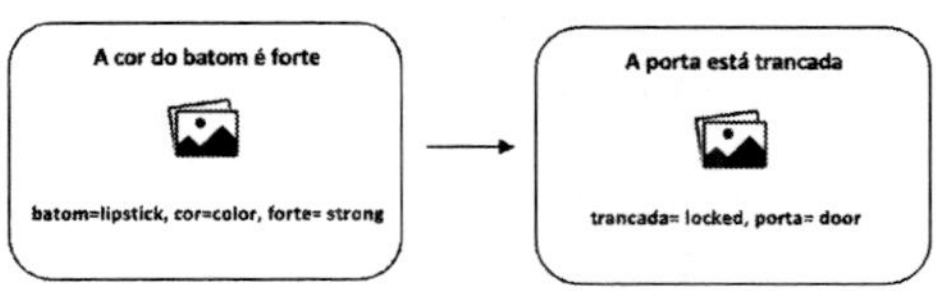

(30% of the 20 prime trials) where the two items primed an unrelated syntactic structure (i.e. intransitive structure). The prime trials were created using 40 sentences in Portuguese with a relation of possession and pictures depicting those sentences (e.g. *A mesa do escritório está cheia*). Targets were constructed using 20 images presented to participants with three words appearing on top of each one (e.g. *room,rug, dirty*). In the filler condition, the prime sentences in Portuguese and pictures depicting those sentences were constructed using 12 intransitive sentences (e.g. *O homem está trabalhando*) and 6 target pictures presented to participants for description using one intransitive verb (e.g. *praying, smiling, studying*) appearing on top of each image. Prime items and target items were different as no words were repeated between them. This procedure allowed us to isolate the syntactic priming effect from syntactic repetition effect boosted by word repetition (Pickering and Branigan, 1998).

3.4.6 Procedure - Priming stage

Participants were instructed to Google translate into English the two prime sentences in Portuguese depicting the image using the Google Translate aplication on their own mobile device and repeat the MT output out loud, thus triggering the syntactic priming effect (Konopka and Bock, 2009). Immediately after this task, in the target images, participants were instructed to construct and speak out loud a sentence in English without the help of Google Translate using the three words (prime condition) or the intransitive verb (filler condition) presented right above the images. They were also instructed to keep the sentence as simple as possible by avoiding adding words that were not on the computer screen or using prepositions of location (such as *in, on, at*) to construct the sentences. This procedure allowed us to test whether participants would describe the image mirroring the NP syntactic alternative of the Google Translate output (which differs from the Portuguese word order) or

whether they would describe the image using the PNP syntactic alternative which is easier to process.

Two prime-target trials in the two conditions that did not appear in the main experiment were introduced for participants' training before the start of the priming test.

Below, Figure 2 shows one example of trial of the priming test.

4 Analysis and coding

Verbal responses were transcribed and manually coded for the syntactic structure used to create the factorial dependent variable *Prime*. We coded a sentence as "1" if participants produced NP constructions mirroring Google Translate syntactic alternative and as "0" if they produced PNP constructions or any other syntactic construction such as *the office's table is full* or *the window in the house is broken* that have not appeared in the output of the MT.

After coding participants' responses (20 pretest and 20 priming test), we obtained a dataset containing 760 data points (19 x 40 = 760). The dataset was modelled using mixed-effects logit model and the glmer function of the lme4 package version 1.1.-4; (Bates et al., 2011) in R (R Core Development Team, 2011).

The mixed-effects logit model is a linear regression model used to handle the repeated measures nature of a dataset whose dependent variable is binomial. As fixed effects, we included the English proficiency test score (continuous) to investigate the influence of this variable on participants' responses and a factorial predictor *Test* with two levels: baseline pretest and priming test.

Following Barr et al. (2013), we used a maximal random-effects structure. We began with a maximal model and then performed a step-wise reduction procedure to find the simplest model that did not differ significantly from the full model in terms of variance explained. The numeric predictor (En-

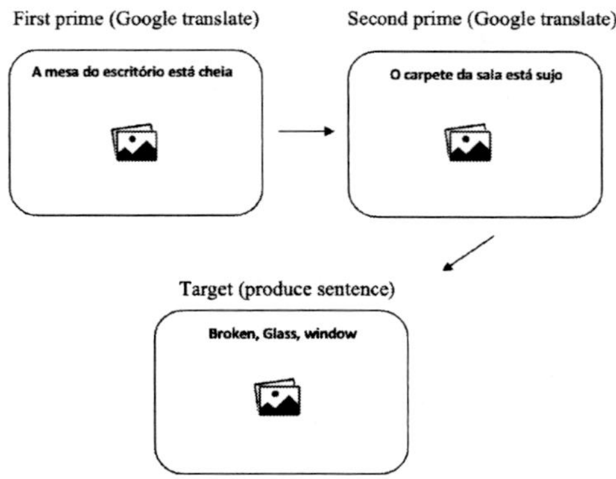

Figure 2: Example of trial presented in the priming test. Participants Google translated the sentences of the first and second primes in the two conditions and, in the target item, were instructed to describe the images out loud using the words provided above each image.

glish test score) was centered and the factorial predictor (Test) was dummy coded (all means compared to a reference group). P-values reported here were obtained by means of ANOVA type 3, test Chisquare. In order to make sure that the inclusion of the random slopes and random intercepts are justified we used Likelihood ratio tests which allowed us to compare the models (Baayen et al., 2008). Based on this process, the final model included by participant random slopes for Test and by-item random intercepts as random effects.

5 Results

Figure 3 below shows the influence of Language Proficiency on priming effect. Participants at higher English proficiency levels tended to produce more NP constructions during the priming test phase than participants at lower English proficiency levels.

Table 1 shows average percentages of structures produced by participants in the pretest and priming test. In the pretest, participants produced on average 38.42% of PNP constructions, 33.42% of NP constructions and 26.16% of other constructions such as *The window in my room is wide* or *The office's table is full*. In the prime test, participants produced on average 10.5% of PNP constructions, 55% of NP constructions and 34% of other constructions. Thus, as predicted, in the pretest (i.e.the test without any prior influence of syntactic constructions), participants produced on average more PNP constructions. However, after being primed by the NP constructions produced by the Google Translate output, the average percentage of PNP constructions decreased 27.92% while the average percentage of NP constructions increased 21.58%.

Table 1: Average percentages of NP, PNP and other response choices

Structure	Pretest	Priming
PNP	38,42%	10,50%
NP	33,42%	55%
Other	28,16%	34%

Table 2 summarizes the fixed and random effects of the model fit for this dataset.

In the priming test condition, more NP constructions were produced compared to the baseline (p < .001). This indicates that, after performing a translation task using Google Translate, participants tended to use significantly more NP constructions, thus mirroring the syntactic structure previously seen in the Google Translate output when speaking in English.

Results also show a significant effect of language proficiency (p< .001), demonstrating a difference between participants' responses at higher and lower levels of English proficiency as well as a significant interaction (p<.05) between factors *Test* (Baseline vs. Priming Test) and EnglScore (participants' English proficiency test score) suggesting that participants at higher levels of English proficiency produced more NP constructions during the priming test than participants at lower levels of English proficiency.

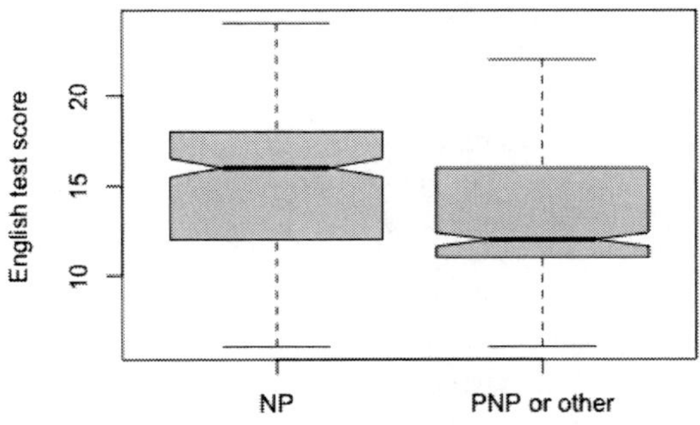

Table 2: Summary of the best mixed effects logit model for participants' strucuture choices. Estimate (Est), Variance (Var), Standard Deviation (SD), Correlation (Corr), Standard Error (SE), Random effects (RE) and Fixed effects (FE). Final model formula: Prime ˜ EnglishTestScore * Test + (1 + Test | $Subject$) + (1 | $items$)

RE				
	Name	**Var**	**SD**	**Corr**
items	intercept	0,02529	0,1590	
subject	intercept	1,49830	1,2240	
	PrimingTest	0,55407	0,7444	-0,57

FE				
	Est	**SE**	**Z-value**	**P-value**
(Intercept)	0,9207	0,3226	2,853	0,00432
PrimingTest	-1,4193	0,3520	-4,032	5.52e-05
EnglScore	-1,2223	0,2582	-4,733	2.21e-06
PrimingTest: EnglScore	0,6045	0,3053	1,980	0,04769

6   General discussion and conclusions

To test the influence of MT output on the syntactic processing of English, we measured the effect of priming when performing a translation task using Google Translate. To this end, we used a common syntactic priming experimental design allowing us to compare the priming magnitude in the participant's speech before and after the task.

In line with our predictions and the literature, our results show that, after interacting with an MT system, participants tend to use the same syntactic alternative previously seen in the output of the MT system more frequently in their subsequent speech. That is, they tended to use more NP constructions after the translation task with Google Translate. Importantly, after being primed by the Google Translate output, participants used noun phrase structures without a preposition, as a direct result of exposure to sentences with these structures in English. This structure represents the syntactic alternative more likely to elicit processing difficulties due to word ordering differences between Portuguese and English. This result suggests that an MT system is capable of facilitating the syntactic processing of a second language by allowing users to access a structure that poses a challenge to the syntactic processing mechanism of Brazilian Portuguese native speakers. In contrast, this processing facilitation triggered by the MT system was more evident at higher English proficiency levels. We hypothesize that the effect of English proficiency observed is related to the participants' focus of attention when processing the second language. A number of studies (e.g. Marinis et al. (2005)) have shown that language learners at lower levels of proficiency are less sensitive to syntax than more proficient bilinguals because they focus their attention more on resolving semantic ambiguities than on resolving parsing problems. However, at higher proficiency levels it is possible to observe more automaticity in second language parsing. Accordingly, our results suggest that MT systems can be useful in English language learning as it can facilitate end-users to access or construct problematic syntactic structures in English due to the structural differences between the languages. Moreover, based on some psycholinguistic studies (e.g. (Heyselaar et al., 2017a; Charny, 1966)) evidencing that people tend to syntactically align more often with people they like, the priming effect observed may suggest that people enjoy interacting with Google Translate.

Although this study provides evidence for the influence of MT on English syntactic processing as a second language, especially NP structures, it also reveals the possiblity that other syntactic structures may show the same effect as well as other language pairs. Therefore, in follow-up studies, we will test whether the same effect can be observed for other challenging syntactic structures for Portuguese speakers such as dative constructions with and without prepositions. In future studies, we also aim at increasing the number of participants, testing whether the popularity of the system plays a role on the magnitude of the effect and, finally, testing whether the participants mimic the Google Translate syntactic structure consciously or unconsciously. Nonetheless, we claim that this first attempt to check syntactic alignment between an MT system and MT users provides an important investigation as the methodology has been tested and produced results comparable to results found in the literature in the field of psycholinguistics, second language learning and human-computer interaction.

Acknowledgments

The ADAPT Centre for Digital Content Technology (www.adaptcentre.ie) at Dublin City University is funded by the Science Foundation Ireland Research Centres Programme (Grant 13/RC/2106) and is co-funded by the European Regional Development Fund. This project was funded by the European Union's Horizon 2020 research and innovation programme under the Marie Sklodowska-Curie grant agreement number 843455.

References

Baayen, R.H., D.J. Davidson, and D.M. Bates. 2008. Mixed-effects modeling with crossed random effects for subjects and items. *Journal of Memory and Language*, 59(4):390 – 412. Special Issue: Emerging Data Analysis.

Barr, Dale J., Roger Levy, Christoph Scheepers, and Harry J. Tily. 2013. Random effects structure for confirmatory hypothesis testing: Keep it maximal. *Journal of Memory and Language*, 68(3):255 – 278.

Bates, Douglas, Martin Mächler, and Bin Dai. 2011. *lme4: Linear Mixed-Effects Models Using S4 Classes*, volume 0.999375-33. 01.

Bock, Kathryn and Zenzi M. Griffin. 2000. The persistence of structural priming: Transient activation or implicit learning?. *Journal of Experimental Psychology: General*, 129(2):177 – 192.

Bock, J. Kathryn and Antony S. Kroch. 1989. The isolability of syntactic processing. In M.K., Carlson G.N.and Tanenhaus, editor, *Linguistic Structure in Language Processing. Studies in Theoretical Psycholinguistics*, volume 7. Springer), Dordrecht.

Bock, Kathryn, Helga Loebell, and Randal Morey. 1992. From conceptual roles to structural relations: Bridging the syntactic cleft. *Psychological Review*, 99(1):150 – 171.

Bock, J.Kathryn. 1986. Syntactic persistence in language production. *Cognitive Psychology*, 18(3):355 – 387.

Branigan, Holly P., Martin J. Pickering, Jamie Pearson, Janet F. McLean, and Clifford I. Nass. 2003. Syntactic alignment between computers and people: the role of belief about mental states. In Alterman, Richard and David Kirsh, editors, *Proceedings of the 25th Annual Conference of the Cognitive Science Society, July 31 - August 2 2003, Boston, Massachusetts*, pages 186–191. Lawrence Erlbaum Associates.

Braningan, Holly P., Martin J. Pickering, Andrew J. Stewart, and Janet F. Mclean. 2000. Syntactic priming in spoken production: Linguistic and temporal interference. *Memory and Cognition*, 28(8):1297–1302.

Charny, Israel W. 1966. Integrated individual and family psychotherapy. *Family Process*, 5(2):179–198.

Chinnery, George. 2008. You've got some gall: Google-assisted language learning. *Language Learning Technology*, 12(1):3–11.

Clifford, Joan, Lisa Merschel, and Joan Munné. 2013. Surveying the landscape: What is the role of machine translation in language learning? *Revista d'innovacio educativa*, (10):108–121.

Cowan, Benjamin R., Holly P. Branigan, Mateo Obregón, Enas Bugis, and Russell Beale. 2015. Voice anthropomorphism, interlocutor modelling and alignment effects on syntactic choices in humancomputer dialogue. *International Journal of Human-Computer Studies*, 83:27 – 42.

Ferreira, Victor S. and Kathryn Bock. 2006. The functions of structural priming. *Language and Cognitive Processes*, 21(7-8):1011–1029. PMID: 17710210.

Garcia, Ignacio and María Isabel Pena. 2011. Machine translation-assisted language learning: writing for beginners. *Computer Assisted Language Learning*, 24(5):471–487.

Gaspari, Federico and John Hutchins. 2007. Online and free ! ten years of online machine translation : Origins , developments , current use and future prospects.

Gupta, Brij M. and S. M. Dhawan. 2019. Machine translation research a scientometric assessment of global publications output during 2007 16. *DESIDOC Journal of Library Information Technology*, 39(1):31–38, 01.

Hartsuiker, Robert J. and Herman H.J. Kolk. 1998. Syntactic facilitation in agrammatic sentence production. *Brain and Language*, 62(2):221 – 254.

Heyselaar, Evelien, Peter Hagoort, and Katrien Segaert. 2017a. How social opinion influences syntactic processing—an investigation using virtual reality. *PLOS ONE*, 12(4):1–21, 04.

Heyselaar, Evelien, Peter Hagoort, and Katrien Segaert. 2017b. In dialogue with an avatar, language behavior is identical to dialogue with a human partner. *Behavior Research Methods*, (49):46–60.

Konopka, Agnieszka E. and Kathryn Bock. 2009. Lexical or syntactic control of sentence formulation? structural generalizations from idiom production. *Cognitive Psychology*, 58(1):68 – 101.

Levelt, Willem J.M and Stephanie Kelter. 1982. Surface form and memory in question answering. *Cognitive Psychology*, 14(1):78 – 106.

Marinis, Theodore, Leah Roberts, Claudia Felser, and Harald Clahsen. 2005. Gaps in second language sentence processing. *Studies in Second Language Acquisition*, 27(1):53–78.

McDonough, Kim. 2006. Interaction and syntactic priming: English l2 speakers' production of dative constructions. *Studies in Second Language Acquisition*, 28(2):179–207.

Niño, Ana. 2006. *Evaluating the suitability of using raw machine translation output as input for foreign language written production*. Ph.D. thesis.

Oviatt, Sharon, Courtney Darves, and Rachel Coulston. 2004. Toward adaptive conversational interfaces: Modeling speech convergence with animated personas. *ACM Trans. Comput.-Hum. Interact.*, 11(3):300–328, September.

Pickering, Martin J. and Holly P. Branigan. 1998. The representation of verbs: Evidence from syntactic priming in language production. *Journal of Memory and Language*, 39(4):633 – 651.

Pickering, Martin J. and Victor S. Ferreira. 2008. Structural priming: A critical review. *Psychological Bulletin*, 134(3):427 – 459.

Pickering, Martin J. and Simon Garrod. 2004. Toward a mechanistic psychology of dialogue. *Behavioral and Brain Sciences*, 27(2):169–190.

R Core Development Team, R. 2011. *R: A language and environment for statistical computing*. Viena, Austria.

Shin, Jeong-Ah and Kiel Christianson. 2012. Structural priming and second language learning. *Language Learning*, 62(3):931–964.

Stoyanchev, Svetlana and Amanda Stent. 2009. Lexical and syntactic priming and their impact in deployed spoken dialog systems. In *Proceedings of Human Language Technologies: The 2009 Annual Conference of the North American Chapter of the Association for Computational Linguistics, Companion Volume: Short Papers*, NAACL-Short '09, page 189–192, USA. Association for Computational Linguistics.

Suzuki, N. and Y. Katagiri. 2007. Prosodic alignment in human-computer interaction. *Connection Science*, 19(2):131 – 141.

User papers

Domain Informed Neural Machine Translation: Developing Translation Services for Healthcare Enterprise

Sahil Manchanda and Galina Grunin
Optum
{sahil_manchanda, galina.grunin}@optum.com

Abstract

Neural Machine Translation (NMT) is a deep learning based approach that has achieved outstanding results lately in the translation community. The performance of NMT systems, however, is dependent on the availability of large amounts of in-domain parallel corpora. The business enterprises in domains such as legal and healthcare require specialized vocabulary but translation systems trained for a general purpose do not cater to these needs. The data in these domains is either hard to acquire or is very small in comparison to public data sets.

This is a detailed report of using an open-source library to implement a machine translation system and successfully customizing it for the needs of a particular client in the healthcare domain. This report details the chronological development of every component of this system, namely, extraction of data from in-domain healthcare documents, a pre-processing pipeline for the data, data alignment and augmentation, training and a fully automated and robust deployment pipeline. This work proposes an efficient way for the continuous deployment of newly trained deep learning models. The deployed translation models are optimized for both inference time and cost.

1 Introduction

The emergence of Neural Machine Translation (NMT) was sparked by the use of Recurrent Neural Networks (RNN) for machine translation. The RNN encoder in this approach is responsible for encoding the source language phrase into a fixed-length vector. This vector is then decoded into the target language (Cho et. al., 2014). Some approaches also use Long Short Term Memory (LSTM) (Hochreiter, 1997) for this task (Sutskever et al., 2014).

Sequence to Sequence models with attention (Bahdanau et al., 2014) started coming to fruition with the advent of the idea that the LSTM layers stacked on top of each other stopped improving at about a depth of 4. The attention-based models were essentially of two types, local and global. The attention models proved to be much more efficient in translating long sentences as compared to non-attention models (Luong et al., 2015). But long sentences still exhibited "exposure bias" which led to the emergence of attention models that attend over the input and generated outputs separately (Paulus, Xiong, Socher, 2017).

Despite these remarkable advances in NMT, one of the major problems still faced by some enterprises is domain-specific translation where the general-purpose translators do not perform well. Leveraging in-domain corpora to skew a general purpose translator successfully has been an area of interest in NMT in recent years. One of the successful techniques to do this has been mixed fine-tuning (Chu, Chenhui and Wang, Rui, 2018) which suggests to train an NMT model on out-of-domain corpora until model convergence and then resume training from step 1 on a mix of in-domain and out-of-domain data.

Martins, Moniz, Fumega, Martins, Batista, Coheur, Parra, Trancoso, Turchi, Bisazza, Moorkens, Guerberof, Nurminen, Marg, Forcada (eds.)
Proceedings of the 22nd Annual Conference of the European Association for Machine Translation, p. 255–261
Lisboa, Portugal, November 2020.

This paper tackles the challenge of translating in-domain correspondence letters for one such health-care enterprise. The documents that these enterprises send out to their clients contain confidential information, legal/medical clauses that need to be translated in an enterprise-specific manner. Some parts of text like entity names, addresses, text in a language different from the language of the document do not need to be translated. In addition, the human-translated data that we leverage is present in sources such as HTML pages, or .doc/.docx forms, so intelligent parsing is required to extract parallel text.

In this paper, we illustrate the construction and deployment of a translation system from English to Spanish. First, we describe the training from the ground up of a general-purpose translator using an open-source library, OpenSeq2Seq (Ginsburg et al., 2018). Then, we describe an iterative process to customize this model for two use cases: medical handwritten text and formal medical correspondence letters. We use various resources from our clients at our disposal. First, we scanned the human-translated documents that were sent to the end-users to extract domain-specific sentences in the source and reference languages, cleaned the data, and built a parallel corpus. We also utilized another resource obtained from the enterprise, a translation memory, which is an XML to XML mapping that human translators used to refer to for the translation of specific sentences and form sections of a letter. We used these domain-specific parallel corpora to fine-tune the general-purpose model while making sure it did not overfit.

This study also proposes continuous deployment architecture for these models that is highly efficient at inference time and seamlessly deploys newly trained models with zero downtime.

The rest of the report is organized as follows:
Section 2 describes all the data sets used in this work, section 3 outlines how the data from different sources was made suitable for training, section 4 describes the architecture and evaluation procedures used. Section 5 explains the experiments and customization of the model towards the target domain, section 6 describes an efficient and inference-optimized architecture for our model and we conclude in section 7.

2 Data sets

Our data sets included two sources from the public domain, one used for training and one for evaluation for the general domain. For the customization part of the training process, various resources internal to the customer were leveraged. The customer sends medical claim correspondence letters which are manually translated in Spanish. We used the translations from these documents as a major part of our in-domain data set. Also, human translators use a translation memory to refer to the correct translation of some phrases or sentences. Translation memory consists of XML mapping files that contained source XML in English and reference XML in Spanish. Table 1 summarizes the size and source of the data sets used in this work. Note that the size of correspondence letters and translation memory is measured before they are extracted and pre-processed (3).

Data Fragment	Source	Sentences
Paracrawl [1]	Public	38M
WMT-News	Public	14K
Correspondence Letters (M&R)	Customer Internal	492K
Translation Memory (M&R)	Customer Internal	15K

Table (1)   Data sets used in this work and corresponding source and number of sentences in each.

3 Data Preparation

While our baseline experiment used the raw version of the public data, we cleaned and aligned all the data sets to ensure the quality of data on which the model is trained. This step was especially critical to the customer documents, as they were word document files (Docx) containing tables and forms and not only plain text. This needed special attention as described in the following sections.

3.1 Public Data

The Paracrawl [1] v5 open corpus data set is used for the public section of this model's training data. This data contains 38,971,347 sentences of English and Spanish. The data was subjected to

[1] http://paracrawl.eu.

256

the following alignment and pre-processing procedures:

1. **Sentence Alignment**
   A mismatch in the corresponding text in the source and reference language can cause the translator to learn wrong short term dependencies. Hence, the sentences in the data set were aligned using "Yet Another Sentence Aligner" (Lamraoui, Langlais, 2013) which has shown to improve the quality of statistical machine translation. The sentences which were not successfully aligned were discarded.

2. **Language Check Elimination**
   Sentences not from the intended language were eliminated.

3. **Redundant Characters Elimination**
   On closer inspection of the data, we found a lot of acronyms, and language idiosyncrasies in the provided files like '...' instead of a '.'. For the purpose of a medical correspondence letter translator, it was assumed that the letter would follow the correct English language syntax. Hence, the idiosyncrasies of the text were neutralized.

4. **Data Augmentation**
   Some documents contain text with incorrect casing and punctuation, for instance, the text in a bullet list, prescriptions, forms, etc. The system has to be robust enough to endure the incorrect casing and punctuation that it can encounter in a text. So, we converted 20% of the data to its lowercase or punctuation-less form. 80% of the data remained as is.

The Paracrawl data set of size 38M sentences was reduced to 24M after the pre-processing steps were done. We have used both raw and pre-processed versions of this data set for our experiments to note the effects of these steps on translation quality. The WMT-News (J. Tiedemann, 2012) data set was kept as is for evaluation purposes.

3.2 Customer Data

We requested manually translated documents from the source to reference language from our customer. Since the customer is a medical entity sending out medical claim acceptance or refusal letters in English and Spanish, we were able to obtain 22,292 pairs of claim refusal letters that they sent to their subscribers. The text was extracted from these documents and the following operations were applied to make it ready for training.

1. **Data Extraction**
   Data was extracted from the correspondence letters of the customer. This included names, addresses, medical terminologies, law terms, etc. All confidential data was deleted and the rest of the text was utilized.

2. **Record of Untranslated Text**
   The text that was the same in both the source and reference documents was recorded for further analysis. This could be due to various reasons: some text could be personal data that should not undergo translation, or it could be medical/legal terms that should stay as they are. They can be leveraged in our systems as lookup tables to aid in translation.

3. **Sentence Alignment**
   As was done with public data, we aligned the extracted text to eliminate any mismatch between source and reference language texts. YASA (Lamraoui, Langlais, 2013) was used to align these sentences.

The final count of the sentences that were extracted from the customer documents was 323,161, reduced from 492K due to pre-processing steps. This data set was divided into two parts for our experiments, part 1, comprising of 182,143 sentences, and part 2, comprising of 141,018 sentences. The division was random and based on the order in which these documents were sent to us. Part 1 was utilized to skew our model to the customer domain while part 2 served as our in-domain test data set.

4 Model Training

4.1 Model Architecture

The OpenSeq2Seq (Ginsburg et al., 2018) toolkit for experimentation with Natural Language Processing has been used in our experiments. This toolkit has access to various sequence to sequence architectures. For experiments in this paper, we have used a transformer-based model architecture with self-attention (Vaswani et al., 2018). This model is based on an encoder-decoder sequence to sequence architecture which has been found to outperform vanilla RNNs and CNNs in terms of machine translation. The Transformer starts by generating initial representations, or vector embeddings, for each word. Then, using self-attention, it aggregates information from all of the other words, generating a new representation per word informed by the entire context.

4.2 Evaluation

We evaluate the models on a general-purpose data set and text from in-domain customer documents. This section specifies the metric and the fractions of the data sets we used for evaluation.

4.2.1 Metric

The experiments presented in this work use the metric of BLEU Score (Papineni, Roukos, Ward and Zhu, 2002) both at training and test time. The BLEU Score matches the presence of the exact tokens in the source and reference document.

4.2.2 Evaluation Data Sets

The following data sets are used for evaluation.

1. **WMT-News**
   This part of the evaluation data set represents how close our system is to a general-purpose translation system. The WMT-News data set is a different domain from the customer data set and hence is a good verification step against overfitting. The entire WMT-News data set of 14K sentences is used here. All the text in this data set is converted to lowercase to test if the system is robust against wrong casing.

2. **Customer Correspondence Letters**
   The customer correspondence letters, part 2, comprising of 141,018 sentences are used here. These are sentences from in-domain letters that the customer often uses.

5 Experiments and Results

The following experiments are done on the Transformer model[2] with fixed training hyperparameters using OpenSeq2Seq (Ginsburg et al., 2018).

1. **Experiment 1: Reference Baseline**
   First, we trained a model from only the raw public data set (without any preprocessing steps) and tested it on the two evaluation sets. This model is considered as our reference baseline.

---

[2]https://nvidia.github.io/OpenSeq2Seq/html/machine-translation/transformer.html

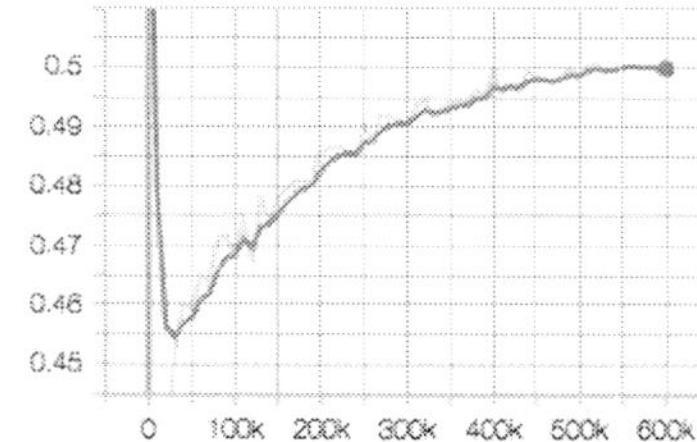

(a) Experiment 1: Reference Baseline

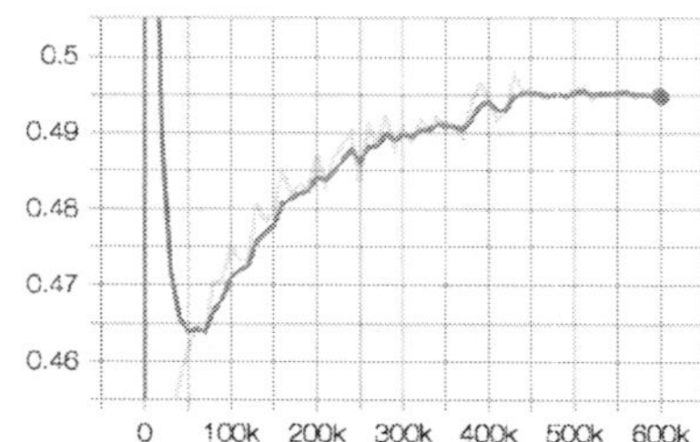

(b) Experiment 2: Clean and Augmented Data

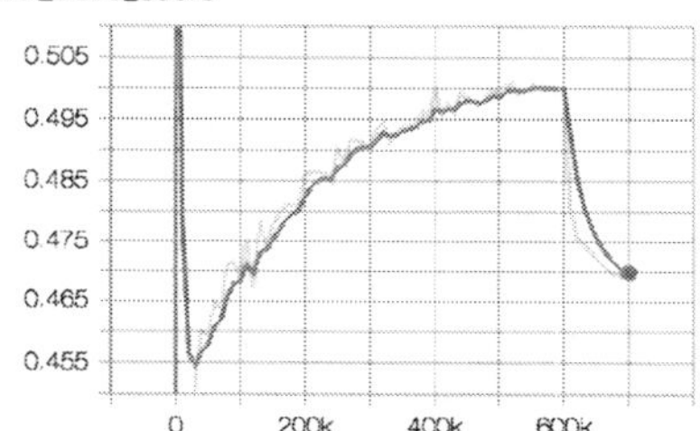

(c) Experiment 3: Fine-tuning on the Customer Data

Figure (1)   BLEU score at each training step

2. **Experiment 2: Clean and Augmented Data**
   We use the alignment tool by YASA (Lamraoui, Langlais, 2013) to align sentences. Then we eliminate address lines, augment the data with random punctuation and casing. This reduces the amount of training data but enhances the quality of it.

3. **Experiment 3: Fine-tuning on the Customer Data**
   The model from experiment 2 performed better on the customer evaluation data set. Hence, it was chosen for fine-tuning on the customer correspondence letters (part 1). The attention dropout parameter is slightly increased to protect against overfitting.

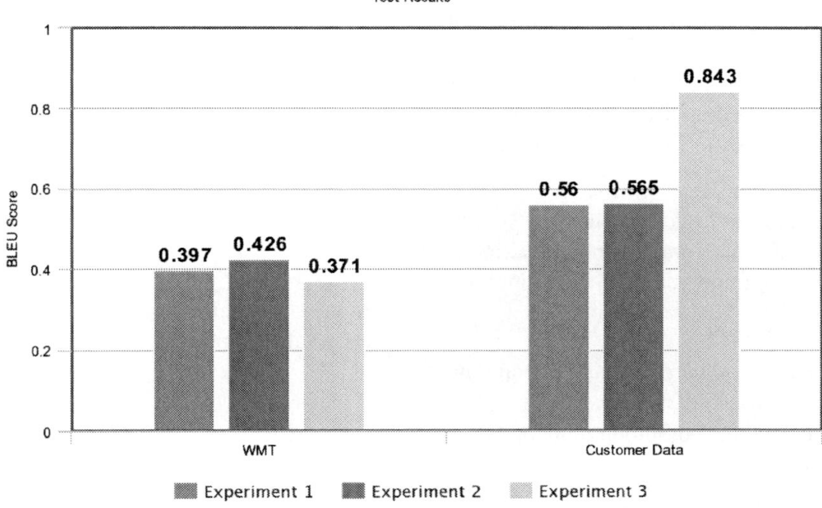

Figure (2)   BLEU scores on evaluation data sets

Figure 1 shows the BLEU score evaluation graphs during training for all the above mentioned experiments. We can see that at train time experiments 1 and 2 perform almost identically and in experiment 3, the BLEU score drops slightly in the fine-tuning phase. This is due to the domain difference between the public and customer data sets. Note that the language model in experiment 3 is the same as experiment 2.

The BLEU scores on the test data for these experiments are shown in figure 2. As we can see with 38M sentences, the baseline reference performs well but falls short in the customer domain with a BLEU score of 0.560 on the customer evaluation data set. Also, this model trained only on raw public data does not perform as well on WMT-News lowercase.

Experiment 2, which involves the aligned, cleaned, and augmented data, starts improving on WMT-News but, it is still mediocre on the customer data set. This further validates the argument that the translator trained on a general data set can not cater to domain-specific needs.

Experiment 3 involves fine-tuning the model from experiment 2 on the customer correspondence letters (part 1). While it shows no improvement at train time, the BLEU score on the in-domain evaluation data set improves greatly and reaches 0.8.

6   NMT Inference Service Deployment

We built a scalable, performance-oriented, and cost-optimized deployment pipeline targeting a cloud-native environment. We separated all text processing from neural model inference. Text processing and clients serving rest APIs were implemented as light-weight microservices that run on CPU. Neural models are served by TensorRT inference Server containers (Nvidia, 2019), which are provisioned with GPU. Models are placed on persistent storage accessible to the TensorRT Inference Servers (Figure 3).

We chose TensorRT inference server because of the following features that it provides:

- Concurrent model execution
  Since TensorRT can access multiple models or multiple instances of the same model at the same time, it can be decided at run time which model will be used for inference.

- Seamless model deployment
  Models are stored in the file system-based model repository. Each model is represented by a directory. This directory contains a model configuration file that describes the framework, scheduling, batching, concurrency, and other model serving parameters. Each model can have one or more versions available in the model repository. Each version is stored in its own, numerically named

subdirectory where the name of the subdirectory corresponds to the version number of the model. The server monitors all changes in the model store and adds or removes models or model versions from serving without any restarts of TensorRT Inference Server.

- Batching support
  It provides multiple batching and scheduling algorithms that combine individual inference requests to improve inference throughput.

- Optimized models
  - Layer and tensor fusion and elimination of unused layers
  - Precision Calibration (support for FP16 and INT8 precision)
  - Kernel Auto-tuning
  - Efficient memory reuse

- Scalable and reliable deployment
  Since the model serving and processing of text are independent of each other and model serving is dynamic, a new version of the model can be deployed without a server restart or any downtime in the service. Since multiple versions are present, rollback to a previous version is easy to implement.

- Extensible Architecture

- Inference and server monitoring API

Utilizing a TensorRT inference server decreases the inference response time by a factor of three, due to the use of optimized models and GPU sharing. Our approach also allows a separate auto-scaling of CPU and GPU resources.

6.1 Model Deployment Pipeline

Due to the independence of the neural model serving and pre/post-processing, the model can be deployed and rolled back without rebuilding the images and restarting TensorRT Inference Server containers – all that is needed to be done is to change environment variables and restart CPU microservices. Here is how it is achieved.

1. A Git repository contains the code of the service and the configuration YAML of the model deployed. It also contains a neural model metadata file. Model metadata file includes parameters like the corresponding language model location, output, input tensor name, and model version.

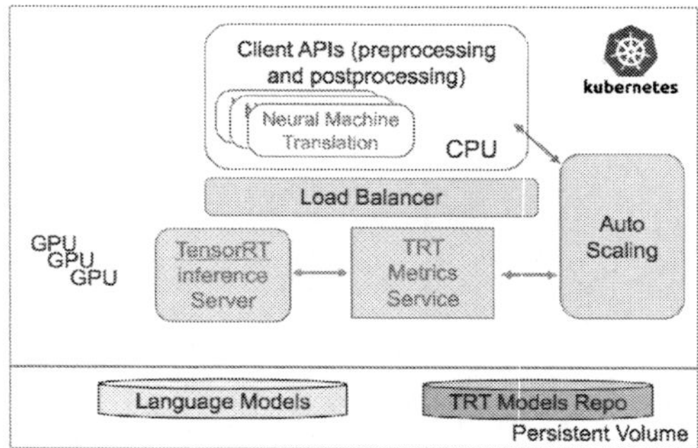

Figure (3) Current architecture of Translation system deployed.

2. Anytime a new neural model is trained, and subsequently the parameters of the metadata are changed and committed, a minimal testing docker container is automatically created. The new language model and inference model are deployed to the persistent volume storage, accessible to the TensorRT Inference Server and text processing containers. TensorRT Inference Server automatically starts serving a new version of the model in addition to the current one. General sentences are passed through the model to check its sanity. The deployment only goes further if the model translates these source language phrases correctly.

3. Depending upon which customer/use case the model will serve, the model is then evaluated on sentences of a specific domain.

4. If the aforementioned steps are successful all that is needed to be done is environment variable changes for text processing (TensorRT client) container. The rolling update with the new environment variables is initiated. After this update, APIs are serving the new model.

6.2 Online Learning

The API lets the customer upload a document and then shows all the parts of the document and corresponding translated parts simultaneously. This allows the enterprise users to edit the translations if they want any modification in the translated document. The customer can download the modified document containing the changes they made.
These corrections are being recorded so that the model could be improved periodically. How to judge the accuracy of customer corrections and

how to use that information for online learning makes a top priority in our future work.

7 Conclusion

Our experiments demonstrate how a general-purpose neural machine translation framework can be customized to a specific use case for a specialized domain enterprise. They also show how different versions of the same model architecture can serve different needs. For instance, experiment 2 yields a model that is suitable for a manually typed general language data but not suitable for medical claim correspondence letters for the customer. Experiment 3, however, yields a model that performs exceedingly well in the given customer scenario and has a BLEU score of 0.8 which would be very hard to manifest for a general-purpose translator.

In this work, we also describe an architecture for the deployment of deep learning models (specifically neural machine translation) optimized for inference using TensorRT. We explain how the models can be automatically deployed and changed at run time following the customer's needs. For instance, the translation model of experiment 2 is served for a human typing interface, whereas the fine-tuned model from experiment 3 is provided for medical correspondence letters.

Acknowledgements: We would like to thank our colleagues Ajay Ajit Maity, Brian Carter and Declan Atkins for their contribution.

References

Cho et al. 2014. *Learning Phrase Representations using RNN Encoder–Decoder for Statistical Machine Translation* Prentice-Hall, Englewood Cliffs, NJ.

Sepp Hochreiter and Jürgen Schmidhuber. Long short-term memory. 1997. *Neural computation.* 9(8):1735–1780, 1997.

Ilya Sutskever, Oriol Vinyals, and Quoc VV Le. Sequence to sequence learning with neural networks. 2014. *Advances in Neural Information Processing Systems*, 3104–3112, 2014. (2)

Dzmitry Bahdanau, Kyunghyun Cho, and Yoshua Bengio. 1981. Neural machine translation by jointly learning to align and translate. *CoRR*, abs/1409.0473, 2014. (1).

Yonghui Wu, Mike Schuster, Zhifeng Chen, Quoc V Le, Mohammad Norouzi, Wolfgang Macherey, Maxim Krikun, Yuan Cao, Qin Gao, Klaus Macherey, et al. 2016. Google's neural machine translation system: Bridging the gap between human and machine translation. *arXiv preprint arXiv:1609.08144*

Minh-Thang Luong, Hieu Pham, and Christopher D Manning. 2015. Effective approaches to attention-based neural machine translation. *arXiv preprint arXiv:1508.04025*

Rafal Jozefowicz, Oriol Vinyals, Mike Schuster, Noam Shazeer, and Yonghui Wu. 2016. Exploring the limits of language modeling. *arXiv preprint arXiv:1602.02410*

Ankur Parikh, Oscar Tackstrom, Dipanjan Das, and Jakob Uszkoreit. 2016. A decomposable attention model. *Empirical Methods in Natural Language Processing*

Romain Paulus, Caiming Xiong, and Richard Socher. 2017. A deep reinforced model for abstractive summarization. *arXiv preprint arXiv:1705.04304*

Zhouhan Lin, Minwei Feng, Cicero Nogueira dos Santos, Mo Yu, Bing Xiang, Bowen Zhou, and Yoshua Bengio 2017. A structured self-attentive sentence embedding. *arXiv preprint arXiv:1703.03130, 2017.*

Fethi Lamraoui, Philippe Langlais, 2013. Yet Another Fast, Robust and Open Source Sentence Aligner. Time to Reconsider Sentence Alignment? *Machine Translation summit, 2013*

Kishore Papineni, Salim Roukos, Todd Ward, and Wei-Jing Zhu 2002. BLEU: a Method for Automatic Evaluation of Machine Translation *Proceedings of the 40th Annual Meeting of the Association for Computational Linguistics (ACL), Philadelphia, July 2002, pp. 311-318. Kishore Papineni, Salim Roukos, Todd Ward, and Wei-Jing Zhu*

Oleksii Kuchaiev and Boris Ginsburg and Igor Gitman and Vitaly Lavrukhin and Jason Li and Huyen Nguyen and Carl Case and Paulius Micikevicius 2018. Mixed-Precision Training for NLP and Speech Recognition with OpenSeq2Seq *arXiv 1805.10387 cs.CL*

Ashish Vaswani, Noam Shazeer, Niki Parmar, Jakob Uszkoreit, Llion Jones, Aidan N. Gomez, Lukasz Kaiser, Illia Polosukhin 2017. Attention Is All You Need *arXiv 1706.03762cs.CL*

Ashish Vaswani, Noam Shazeer, Niki Parmar, Jakob Uszkoreit, Llion Jones, Aidan N. Gomez, Lukasz Kaiser, Illia Polosukhin 2012. Parallel Data, Tools and Interfaces in OPUS *In Proceedings of the 8th International Conference on Language Resources and Evaluation (LREC 2012)*

Chu, Chenhui and Wang, Rui 2018. A Survey of Domain Adaptation for Neural Machine Translation *Proceedings of the 27th International Conference on Computational Linguistics*

Nvidia-TensorRT 2019. https://github.com/NVIDIA/TensorRT

Evaluating the usefulness of neural machine translation for the Polish translators in the European Commission

Karolina Stefaniak
European Commission, Directorate General for Translation
1-7 Boulevard Pierre Frieden, L-1543 Luxembourg
Office: T2 00/B076
karolina.stefaniak@ec.europa.eu

Abstract

The mission of the Directorate General for Translation (DGT) is to provide high-quality translation to help the European Commission communicate with EU citizens. To this end DGT employs almost 2000 translators from all EU official languages. But while the demand for translation has been continuously growing, following a global trend, the number of translators has decreased. To cope with the demand, DGT extensively uses a CAT environment encompassing translation memories, terminology databases and recently also machine translation. This paper examines the benefits and risks of using neural machine translation to augment the productivity of in–house DGT translators for the English–Polish language pair. Based on the analysis of a sample of NMT-translated texts and on the observations of the working practices of Polish translators it is concluded that the possible productivity gain is still modest, while the risks to quality are quite substantial.

1   Introduction

Machine translation arrived at the European Commission in 1976 with the purchase of Systran, a rule-based technology, for the English-French language pair. This initial version was then developed and adapted as EC Systran to respond to the Commission's needs; specialized terminology and dictionaries were imported, and, over time, other language pairs were added. By 2010, some 2 million pages were translated per year with Systran, used both by EU and Member States' officials to provide quick drafts of texts in unfamiliar languages, and by EU translators. However, while the quality was fine for getting the gist of short, repetitive texts with standardized structure and terminology, the system was rather unsuitable for translating legislation, and so its use among translators never really caught up (Petritis, 2001; Eisele, 2017a).

EC Systran was discontinued in December 2010 and since then the Commission has been working on its own machine translation system, developed by the Directorate-General for Translation. MT@EC, based on Moses, an open-source statistical machine translation (SMT) toolkit, and improved by rule-based pre- and post-processing, went operational in June 2013. By 2017 it offered 78 direct language pairs, covering all EU official languages (Eisele 2017b). It proved to be quite helpful for certain language pairs (English–French or English-Portuguese, for example) and quite unusable for other (like English-Hungarian or English-Finnish). Polish, with its free word order, rich inflectional morphology and complex orthography, was also quite challenging for the system, which produced very mixed results, from acceptable translations to unintelligible nonsense. As a result, few Polish translators tried to use it as a resource in the translation process. An internal evaluation performed in the Polish Language Department of DGT in 2017 revealed that SMT was useful only for certain text types and that only half of the SMT output was suitable for post-editing and thus likely to bring some productivity gains. Moreover, the post-editing speed depended strongly on the typing speed of the translator in question: translators with good

Martins, Moniz, Fumega, Martins, Batista, Coheur, Parra, Trancoso, Turchi, Bisazza, Moorkens, Guerberof, Nurminen, Marg, Forcada (eds.)
Proceedings of the 22nd Annual Conference of the European Association for Machine Translation, p. 263–269
Lisboa, Portugal, November 2020.

typing skills benefited much less from using SMT than those with poorer skills[1].

In November 2017 the Directorate-General for Translation launched eTranslation, a neural machine translation system, as part of the Connecting Europe Facility. The aim of eTranslation is not only to deliver raw machine translation to the public administration or to interested SMEs in EU Member States, but also to provide MT as a tool for translators in EU institutions, to be embedded within their CAT workflow. With the introduction of eTranslation the question arose as to whether NMT actually provides better results than SMT as far as productivity and quality of translation is concerned. Based on the literature on the subject (e.g. Bentivogli et al., 2016), one would expect for example less lexical, inflectional morphology and word order errors in the NMT output when compared to SMT, and overall less editing effort, measured by automatic metrics such as BLEU and TER. However, studies on the performance of machine translation involving the Polish language are very limited (e.g. Skadiņš et al., 2014; Wołk and Marasek, 2015), and since the specific types of errors are dependent on the particular language pair involved and are influenced by the morphosyntactic features of the target language, a simple extrapolation of the results obtained with one language pair to another language pair is not possible. Therefore in the Polish Language Department of DGT it was decided to conduct an evaluation on the benefits and risks of using NMT produced by eTranslation as a translation aid, beside translation memory, for the English–Polish language pair, concentrating in particular on the post-editing efficiency and the risks to quality.

The paper is organized as follows. Section 2 provides a description of the data and methods used in the evaluation. Section 3 reports on the results and in section 4 the outcomes are discussed and final observations are offered.

2   Data and methods

DGT's aim is to provide high-quality translations that are fit for publication. To this end translators have at their disposal a number of tools, most notably translation memories (Euramis) and a terminology database (IATE), integrated in a CAT environment. Machine translation is provided during pre-processing and can be included as a resource to complement the translation memory. Hence, machine translation is presented for editing only when no TM match is found. The threshold for TM matches is set at 75%. When opting to use MT, translators can choose whether they want to use it in the Autosuggest mode only (which is a feature that can speed up typing by presenting words and phrases from the MT translation memory after a few characters have been typed in an empty segment) or whether they want to have MT suggestions inserted in the segment every time no TM match is found.

For the purpose of the present evaluation a group of 9 translators was recruited. They worked in their usual way, assisted by translation memory, but were instructed to always choose MT when downloading translation resources and to use it for all 'new' segments, i.e. segments that did not have a TM match, consistently and for all their translation assignments. They were also asked to put down any comments and opinions regarding the quality of the NMT output, including examples of mistakes, for each translation assignment. Each of them translated between 1 and 13 texts. The texts varied in length from 1 page to over 150 pages and reflected well the text types and subject domains usually translated by DGT. The text types covered both legislative texts (Commission regulation, Commission decision, proposal for a Council decision, proposal for a regulation of the European Parliament and the Council, proposal for a directive of the European Parliament and the Council, report from the Commission, communication from the Commission, impact assessment to a proposal for a regulation) and non-legislative texts (public consultation, report of an audit, notification of a concentration, list of phrases for a database, press release, description of a game for children, letter to a citizens, letter to the national authorities, text on the e-Justice portal, text on the Europa portal). The subject domains included: agriculture, climate, human health, maritime affairs, fisheries, internal market, industry, transport, competition, taxation, customs union, justice, trade, regional policy, banking, finance, external relations, internal affairs and migration. The test period lasted three months (July-September 2018).

---

[1] That evaluation followed a similar approach to the one presented here, however, a comparison of the performance of SMT and NMT is beyond the scope of this article.

In total, during the test period the testing group translated 57 texts. 48 texts (22 legislative and 26 non-legislative) were used for further analysis (9 translations were discarded for reasons such as very few or no MT segments, shared project and problems with TER processing). Also, for each raw MT segment (3178 MT segments in total) the TER score was calculated using the final translation as a reference.

Since it was not possible to record the post-editing time automatically during translation, small-scale productivity tests on isolated sentences were conducted. Six translators (out of the 9 participating in the evaluation) were asked to perform the test. A subsample of 12 sentence pairs was randomly selected from the texts translated during the test period with the aim to collect sentences with increasing TER scores to see whether post-editing speed depended on the quality of the NMT sentence as indicated by the TER score. The source sentences contained 29 words on average. Translators were divided into two groups and each translator was asked to translate 6 sentences from scratch and to edit 6 different NMT-produced sentences. In this way each sentence from the subsample was translated or post-edited by three translators. They worked directly in a Word document, but were asked to proceed in their usual way (consult terminology database, translation memory database etc.). The time needed for both activities was measured by the author of this evaluation with a stop watch separately for each sentence and then averaged for each sentence and for each translator.

3 Results

3.1 Quality of the NMT output

The usefulness of machine translation can be assessed by analyzing the type of errors found in the raw MT output, as some errors have more impact on the quality of the final product than other. This data was gathered by means of feedback from translators performing the post-editing. They reported that NMT produced rather fluent sentences, with few linguistic errors, but at the same time lacking consistency, which made ensuring textual coherence more difficult. Moreover, the accuracy mistakes produced by NMT were often difficult to detect and only a careful comparison with the original could reveal the mistake. For example, in the translation below the phrase 'must be respected' is missing entirely

from the NMT translation, which is nevertheless still fluent and grammatically correct:

EN: The capacity ceilings set out in Annex II to Regulation (EU) No 1380/2013 on the CFP must be respected and any granting of aid for purchasing a new vessel must not lead to exceeding these capacity ceilings.

NMT: Pułapy zdolności połowowej określone w załączniku II do rozporządzenia (UE) nr 1380/2013 w sprawie WPRyb oraz przyznawanie pomocy na zakup nowego statku nie mogą prowadzić do przekroczenia tych pułapów zdolności.

[The capacity ceilings set out in Annex II to Regulation (EU) No 1380/2013 on the CFP and any granting of aid for purchasing a new vessel must not lead to exceeding these capacity ceilings.]

Errors in terminology were also reported to be common, ranging from deprecated or obsolete terms chosen in place of the preferred ones, to a wrong equivalent in the given context. For example:

EN: For the purpose of this flexibility exercise, the eligibility of requested stock transfers and the state of exploitation of these stocks have been taken into account.

NMT: Do celów tej elastyczności uwzględniono kwalifikowalność wnioskowanych transferów zapasów oraz stan eksploatacji tych stad.

[For the purpose of this flexibility exercise, the eligibility of requested *stock* transfers and the state of exploitation of these *fishstocks* have been taken into account.]

In this translation, the second occurrence of the term 'stocks' has been wrongly translated as 'fishstocks' (fisheries term) and not as 'inventories' (financial term). Mistakes of that kind were common especially for single-word homonyms and are also an example of errors in consistency; both types of mistakes are related as terms need to be translated consistently. Inconsistencies could occur even in the same sentence, like in the example above, but were most often found across sentences. All testers agreed that using NMT made keeping terminology coherent in the translation more difficult.

These finding are consistent with the literature on the subject (see section 1 above) and so these two types of errors could be considered typical for NMT irrespective of the language pair and the text type. The issues mentioned in the feedback that seem specific for the translation from

English into Polish were wrong word order, calqued from the original sentence, and errors in verbs forms (tense, voice, aspect or mood). Pronouns, too, were often mistranslated due to their ambiguity in the English original, which had to be resolved in the translation into Polish, like in the following example:

> EN: The plastic gives the article its essential character as its [plastic's] presence is predominant in quantity and because of its determinant role in relation to the use of the article.

> NMT: Tworzywo sztuczne nadaje artykułowi jego zasadniczy charakter, ponieważ występuje on w przeważającej ilości oraz z powodu jego decydującej roli w odniesieniu do użytkowania artykułu.

> [The plastic gives the article its essential character as its [article's] presence is predominant in quantity and because of its determinant role in relation to the use of the article.]

Here the masculine pronoun 'on' is used in the NMT output, which refers to 'the article'; to refer to the 'the plastic' the neuter pronoun 'ono' should have been selected. Thus, in spite of being grammatical, the translation is wrong.

Specific in the context of DGT were frequent mistranslations of the titles of legal acts, since they should not have been retranslated and needed to be quoted verbatim the way they had been published in the Official Journal. The same was true for quotations. Also, when confronted with abbreviations, proper names, including given names, Latin names, chemical nomenclature etc., as well as other infrequent words the NMT engine could get very creative, from misplacing letters ('Łukasz Brasszek' instead of 'Łukasz Brzenczek') to producing new 'words' ('femzabójstwa', a non-existing word as an equivalent of 'femicides'), to creating unintended comical effects ('newborns' translated as 'nowe borówki', literally 'new berries'). This may be explained by the fact that eTranslation had been trained on corpus of predominantly legal texts, as they constitute the majority of texts translated by DGT.

3.2 Post-editing effort

The quality of the MT output is reflected, too, in the technical effort of post-editing, i.e. in the number of insertions, deletions and word shifts that the translator has to perform to produce a translation of the required quality. The technical effort can be measured by means of automatic evaluation metrics, such as TER (translation edit rate) (Snover et al., 2006). TER scores range from 0 (best) and 1 (worst). The score can be greater than 1, if the number of edits between the MT and reference segment is greater than the number of words in the reference segment.

TER scores were obtained for all sentences in the sample and then averaged for individual texts and for the sample as a whole. The average TER score for individual texts in the sample varied from 0.14 to 1.1; the average TER score for the whole sample was 0.42. The median TER score varied from 0.10 to 0.67. The median for the whole sample was 0.33. The share of MT segments with TER=0 (i.e. segments that did not require any editing) varied from 0% to 40.9% (12.7% on average). The first quartile was at the level of 0.31 and the 3rd quartile at 0.49.

Significant differences between legislative and non-legislative texts were observed. The average TER score for individual legislative texts varied from 0.14 to 0.61 (average: 0.34, median 0.32). The average TER score for non-legislative texts varied from 0.2 to 1.1 (average: 0.49, median: 0.42). The summary of the results is presented in Table 1.

	All	Legislative	Non-Legislative
Average TER	0.42	0.34	0.49
Median TER	0.33	0.32	0.42
1st Quartile	0.31	0.28	0.38
3rd Quartile	0.49	0.38	0.64
TER=0	12.7%	11.7%	13.5%

Table 1. Comparison of legislative vs. non-legislative texts

These quantitative results clearly show that for the English–Polish language pair NMT performs much better for legislative texts in comparison to non-legislative texts. This may be explained by the fact that in general MT performs better for standard, repetitive texts featuring characteristic terms and phrases (which is typical for legislative texts), while it does not give equally good results for texts containing new terminology or rare words, including idioms, metaphors or proper names (which occur more often in non-legislative texts).

When interpreting the results, one has to remember that metrics like TER largely ignore notions of semantic equivalence and say nothing about the reason of the edits. Neither do TER scores fully capture the cognitive effort of post-editing, as some corrections may be more demanding than other, depending on the type and severity of the errors (see also Koponen et al., 2012). This is particularly problematic in the evaluation of NMT, which produces fluent, grammatical sentences that may nonetheless contain serious accuracy mistakes (see section 3.1 above). Another problem with metrics relying on the post-editing distance is that even minor errors might require substantial changes to the MT output, or the other way round, minor edits may suffice to correct severe mistakes (see also Burchardt and Lommel, 2017). In other words, the technical effort may not necessarily correlate with the temporal effort, i.e. the speed at which the translator processes the MT output. This is discussed in the next section 3.3.

3.3 Productivity gain

Although it seems intuitive to predict that MT-produced segments with low TER scores, i.e. segments that require little or no intervention, require also short editing times, this correlation is by no means straightforward. In particular, 'establishing the exact threshold on HTER scores above which translations should be considered too bad to be post-edited is a complex problem in itself' (Specia and Farzindar, 2010: 38). The research on this subject is inconclusive. For example, Gaspari et al. (2014) reported only a weak correlation between the evaluation metrics (BLEU, TER and METEOR) and the post-editing time. On the other hand, de Gibert Bonet (2018) found out that the higher the TER score, the longer translators needed to correct the MT-produced sentence. The TER threshold she established for productivity gain was 0.33. Also Parra Escartín and Arcedillo (2015) reported a productivity gain for segments with TER≤ 0.3.

To determine such productivity threshold for the purpose of the present evaluation, small-scale productivity tests with 6 translators were conducted. The results per sentence are shown in Table 2.

	TER	Average translation speed	Average post-editing speed
Sentence 1	0.11	0.21	0.16
Sentence 2	0.15	0.23	0.48
Sentence 3	0.21	0.32	0.53
Sentence 4	0.22	0.17	0.21
Sentence 5	0.33	0.18	0.32
Sentence 6	0.34	0.24	0.52
Sentence 7	0.41	0.21	0.25
Sentence 8	0.46	0.16	0.39
Sentence 9	0.50	0.32	0.29
Sentence 10	0.61	0.17	0.20
Sentence 11	0.63	0.18	0.30
Sentence 12	0.71	0.20	0.25

Table 2. Average translation and post-editing speed (in words/second) per sentence.

The post-editing speed varied greatly between sentences with the same TER. No clear correlation between the TER score and the post-editing speed could have been established and no clear productivity threshold. Rather, based on the observations of translators during the productivity tests, the processing speed seemed to depend more on the syntactic complexity of the source sentence, its terminological density and the number of references it contained that needed to be checked. Consider the following sentence:

> Article 14(1)(b) of Commission Regulation (EC) No 2535/2001 provides that licence applications lodged from 1 to 10 June may be used for imports during the period from 1 July to 31 December following.

To make sure the MT output is correct, the translator has to look up the regulation in question, find the appropriate article and compare the source text and the translation as published in the Official Journal to the text under translation and the machine translation output, respectively. Only then can they make the decision on the accuracy of the MT. This may take as much time as translating from scratch, or more, because there is no text to compare when translating from scratch. In this case, indeed, post-editing took more time that translation from scratch (on average 0.16 vs. 0.21 words/second).

These observations are consistent with the conclusions of Tatsumi (2009), who suggests that there may not be a linear relationship between the post-editing speed and the differences measured by automatic metrics, and that other variables like sentence length or error types influence the processing time.

The post-editing speed varied greatly also among the 6 translators. It could be observed, for example, that translators who felt unfamiliar with the subject domain needed more time for post-editing in comparison to their colleagues specializing in that subject. Still, on average, all translators were faster when post-editing the NMT output than when translating from scratch, even though the difference was sometimes minimal. The average translation speed was 0.22 words/second; the average post-editing speed was 0.32 words/second. This is shown in Table 3.

	Average translation speed	Average post-editing speed
Translator A	0.23	0.40
Translator B	0.29	0.37
Translator C	0.20	0.32
Translator D	0.17	0.32
Translator E	0.26	0.27
Translator F	0.18	0.24

Table 3. Average translation and post-editing speed (in words/second) per translator.

Using the average processing speed for translating from scratch of 0.20 words/second and the post-editing speed for NMT of 0.32 words/second the potential productivity gain could be calculated. A productivity gain is the difference between the time necessary to translate a page with the help of translation memory (TM) matches only and the time needed to translating the same page using TM supplemented with MT suggestions:

productivity gain = (time to edit TM matches + time to translate from scratch) – (time to edit TM matches + time to post-edit MT)

Because translation and post-editing speed are expressed in words/second, a standard page of 350 words was assumed. In the sample, the average share of 'empty' segments that did not yield any TM matches and which could thus potentially benefit from using NMT was 44.9%. Also, since the processing speed of TM matches was not measured, it was assumed to equal the post-editing speed. The productivity gain thus calculated was only 4 minutes or 17 % per page on average. Similarly modest results, when post-editing speed is measured in an actual working environment and when TM matches is taken into account, are reported in the literature so far. For example, Castilho et al. (2017), who compared the translation of texts from educational domain from English into German, Greek, Portuguese and Russian, also found no clear improvement with regard to productivity, suggesting that 'NMT for production may not as yet offer more than an incremental improvement in temporal PE effort' (Castilho et al., 2017: 127).

4   Conclusions

The initial driving force behind the development of machine translation back in the 1940s was the firm belief that high-quality fully automated translation is not only possible, but is a matter of a few years. After seven decades of research one needs to face the fact that when it comes to MT there is no one-size-fits-all solution. Machine translation engines have to be customized to accommodate the desired terminology, style, domain and other requirements, including whether the MT translation is meant for publication and dissemination or rather for short-lived internal use. In other words, 'the degree of human involvement required (…) will depend on the purpose, value and shelf-life of the content' (Way 2013).

The requirements placed on DGT translators, especially regarding the quality of the translation of legal acts, are even higher than the usual requirements on the translation market for texts meant for publication. This is because mistakes in legal texts impact not only on DGT's image, they also have legal consequences. Beside accuracy, consistency within the text and with any related texts is of particular importance, e.g. terminological consistency with the acts in the same domain or lexical and terminological consistency with the basic legal act. Hence the usefulness of machine translation must be evaluated in view of these particular requirements.

For the Polish language, neural machine translation usually produces rather well-formed sentences suitable for post-editing. Hence, correcting the NMT output was not perceived to be very cumbersome by translators participating in the evaluation. On the other hand, on average only less than 20 % of NMT segments did not contain any errors; and most of the mistakes in the remaining segments were mistakes in accuracy or terminology, which poses serious challenges to the quality of the final translation. Legal texts seem to benefit more from NMT than non-legal texts, probably because of their repetitive and standard character. In non-legal texts NMT suggestions often need extensive adaptation of style and register and therefore are in general perceived to be less useful.

There seems to be only a weak correlation between the TER score and the post-editing time, although a bigger sample is necessary to corroborate this finding. The calculated productivity gain when NMT is used to complement TM matches is still modest. However, this finding needs to be confirmed with more data obtained under more controlled conditions. Also, observations of the working practices of the Polish translators at DGT point out to the possibility that there might be a stronger relationship between other variables and the post-editing speed, such as the experience of the translator in the subject domain and the number of terms and references or quotations in the sentence. This hypothesis, too, would require further testing.

References

Bentivogli, Luisa, Arianna Bisazza, Mauro Cettolo and Federico Marcello. 2016. Neural versus Phrase-Based Machine Translation Quality: a Case Study. *Proceedings of the 2016 Conference on Empirical Methods in Natural Language Processing*, 257-267.

Burchardt, Aljoscha and Arle Lommel. 2017. Quality Management for Translation. In Jörg Porsiel (ed.). 2017. *Machine Translation. What Language Professionals Need to Know.* Berlin: BDÜ Weiterbildungs- und Fachverlagsgesellschaft GmbH, 128-147.

Castilho, Sheila, Federico Gaspari and Maria Gialama. 2017. A Comparative Quality Evaluation of PBSMT and NMT using Professional Translators. *Proceedings of the 2016 Conference on Empirical Methods in Natural Language Processing (EMNLP 2016)*, 257-267.

Eisele, Andreas. 2017a. Machine Translation at the European Commission. In Jörg Porsiel (ed.). 2017. *Machine Translation. What Language Professionals Need to Know.* Berlin: BDÜ Weiterbildungs- und Fachverlagsgesellschaft GmbH, 209-220.

Eisele, Andreas 2017b. From MT@EC to eTranslation in CEF. Overview for the DGT QT21 Workshop. http://www.qt21.eu/wp-content/uploads/2018/02/02-20170315-DGT-overview-March-2017.pdf (consulted on 24.3.2019).

Gaspari, Federico, Antonio Toral, Sudip Kumar Naskar, Ddecla Groves and Andy Way. 2014. Perception vs Reality: Measuring Machine Translation Post-Editing Productivity. Sharon O'Brien, Michel Simard and Lucia Specia (eds). 2014. *Proceedings of the 11th conference of the Association for Machine Translation in the Americas: workshop on post-editing technology and practice (WPTP3)*, Vancouver, 60-72.

de Gibert Bonet, Ona. 2018. *To post-edit or to translate… That is the question. A case study of a recommender system for Quality Estimation of Machine Translation based on linguistic features.* MA Thesis. University of Basque Country.

Koponen, Maarit, Wilker Aziz, Luciana Ramos and Lucia Specia. 2012. Post-editing time as a measure of cognitive effort. *AMTA 2012 Workshop on Post-Editing Technology and Practice (WPTP 2012)*, 11-20.

Parra Escartín, Carla and Manuel Arcedillo. 2015. A fuzzier approach to machine translation evaluation: A pilot study on post-editing productivity and automated metrics in commercial settings. *Proceedings of the Fourth Workshop on Hybrid Approches to Translation (HyTRA@ACL 2015)*, 40-45.

Petritis, Angeliki. 2001. *EC Systran: The Commission's Machine translation system.* European Commission Translation Service. http://mt-archive.info/Petrits-2001.pdf (consulted on 27.03.2019).

Skadiņš, Raivis, Mārcis Pinnis, Andrejs Vasiļjevs, Inguna Skadiņa and Tomáš Hudík. 2014. Application of Machine Translation in Localization into Low-Resourced Languages. *Proceedings of the Seventeenth Annual Conference of the European Association for Machine Translation (EAMT 2014)*, 209-216.

Specia, Lucia and Atefeh Farzindar. 2010. Estimating Machine Translation Post-Editing Effort with HTER. *Proceedings of the AMTA-2010 Workshop Bringing MT to the User: MT Research and the Translation Industry*, 33-41.

Snover, Matthew, Bonnie Dorr, Richard Schwartz, Linnea Micciulla and John Makhoul. 2006. A Study of Translation Edit Rate with Targeted Human Annotation. *Proceedings of Association for Machine Translation in the Americas*, 223-231.

Tatsumi, Midori. 2009. Correlation Between Automatic Evaluation Metric Scores, Post-editing speed, and Some other Factors. *Proceedings of MT Summit XII*, 332-339.

Way, Andy. 2013. Traditional and emerging use-cases for machine translation. *Proceedings of Translating and the Computer 35*, London.

Wołk, Krzysztof and Krzysztof Marasek. 2015. Neural-based machine translation for medical text domain. Based on European Medicines Agency leaflet texts. *Procedia Computer Science 64*, 2-9.

Terminology-Constrained Neural Machine Translation at SAP

Miriam Exel **Bianka Buschbeck** **Lauritz Brandt** **Simona Doneva**[*]
SAP SE
Dietmar-Hopp-Allee 16, 69190 Walldorf
Germany

University of Mannheim
68131 Mannheim
Germany

`firstname.lastname@sap.com sdoneva@mail.uni-mannheim.de`

Abstract

This paper examines approaches to bias a neural machine translation model to adhere to terminology constraints in an industrial setup. In particular, we investigate variations of the approach by Dinu et al. (2019), which uses inline annotation of the target terms in the source segment plus source factor embeddings during training and inference, and compare them to constrained decoding. We describe the challenges with respect to terminology in our usage scenario at SAP and show how far the investigated methods can help to overcome them. We extend the original study to a new language pair and provide an in-depth evaluation including an error classification and a human evaluation.

1 Introduction

With over one billion words per year, SAP deals with a huge translation volume; covering product localization and translation of documentation, training materials or support instructions for up to 85 languages. With a wide range of product lines in different industries, translation settings are diverse. There are over 100 active translation domains for which we maintain translation resources such as translation memories and terminologies. At SAP we usually train multi-domain neural machine translation (NMT) engines, whose input consists of a multitude of data sources including the contents of the company-internal translation memories from various domains. The result-ing NMT system produces high-quality technical translations, but has difficulties generating appropriate and coherent terminology in specific contexts. Given the great importance of correct and consistent terminology in technical translation, this is a nuisance for the translators that work in a post-editing scenario as well as for users consuming machine translation (MT) in a self-service scenario.

In our translation environment, translators are assigned projects along with the relevant translation domain's terminology. To achieve term consistency, SAP maintains SAPterm[1], a large terminology database which also specifies viable term translations. Translators can easily select target terms from SAPterm in a computer-assisted translation (CAT) environment, but applying terminology constraints in NMT is a challenge. As we do not have reliable term recognition or morphological inflection generation tools for all our productive languages at our disposal, we require an approach that not only enforces the correct terminology but also learns its contextually appropriate inflections.

To that end, we investigate the approach presented in Dinu et al. (2019), which combines inline annotation with source factors (Sennrich and Haddow, 2016), that provide an additional input stream with terminology annotation, to show how domain-specific terminology can be enforced in a multi-domain NMT model. The approach should be capable of handling unseen terminology while retaining NMT's ability to produce fluent output sequences without the need for additional resources such as morphological generators and without drastically reducing decoding speed. We will present results for variations of this approach which were not investigated in Dinu et al. (2019),

---

[*] Employed as a working student at SAP during this project.

[1] http://www.sapterm.com/

Martins, Moniz, Fumega, Martins, Batista, Coheur, Parra, Trancoso, Turchi, Bisazza, Moorkens, Guerberof, Nurminen, Marg, Forcada (eds.)
Proceedings of the 22nd Annual Conference of the European Association for Machine Translation, p. 271–280
Lisboa, Portugal, November 2020.

but could be of interest to users of NMT who plan to implement that approach in a productive system.

While the WMT news translation task that Dinu et al. (2019) evaluate on is a viable test bed for new methods, we aim to validate that the method is also applicable to other scenarios, such as the translation of texts from the business and IT context of SAP, when constraining it with entries from SAPterm. We furthermore extend the original study to a new language pair (English–Russian) and provide an in-depth evaluation including a human assessment. Our study yields very promising results, amongst others improvements of up to 11 BLEU points on terminology data, and paves the way to the customization of NMT at SAP: a selected SAPterm glossary can be applied directly when producing MT proposals for a translation project. This yields better translation quality, helps to reduce post-editing costs and eases translators' frustration with correcting terms.

2 Related Work

Several approaches to make NMT adapt to a domain-specific terminology have been proposed in the literature. Fine-tuning on in-domain training data on-the-fly (Farajian et al., 2018; Huck et al., 2019) is shown to improve translation quality and term accuracy but creates additional technological challenges for model management and increases infrastructure costs. Additionally, terminology constraints cannot be specified on a sentence or document level, but instead need to be distinctly present in the available training data, which often is not the case in a productive scenario. The latter argument also holds for domain-aware MT (Kobus et al., 2017), where a multi-domain model distinguishes the translation domains using a domain tag, which is prepended to the source segment.

Since terminology databases are available in most translation environments, integrating them into NMT at run-time to enable domain-specific translation is an ongoing research topic. Early approaches use placeholder tokens for source and target (for example (Crego et al., 2016)). Placeholder approaches often suffer from disfluency as the NMT model does not have access to the term and therefore has difficulties creating a fluent and morphologically sound translation.

Constrained decoding is one of the most prominent approaches to enforcing terminology in NMT. The decoder is subject to a set of constraints that are strictly enforced during decoding (Hokamp and Liu, 2017; Chatterjee et al., 2017). Some issues with constrained decoding have already been addressed, such as better positioning of target terms by exploiting the correspondence between source and target terms (Hasler et al., 2018), and improving performance for the base approach (Post and Vilar, 2018; Hu et al., 2019). Nevertheless, the increase in decoding time compared to unconstrained decoding is still considerable (cf. Section 5). Also the output surface form is enforced exactly as provided by the constraint and no morphological adaptation is applied by the decoder. This leads to misplaced constraints and broken sentences (Burlot, 2019) as well as special cases where surface form variants of an enforced term are being produced by the decoder but not picked up by the constraint, leading to a duplication as the constraint produces the terminology again (Dinu et al., 2019).

Dinu et al. (2019) offer a different approach to applying terminology constraints in NMT. The target terms are inserted into the source string during training and decoding, and thus the model learns a copying behavior. An indication of which words are source terms, target terms or no terms is provided to the model via an additional input stream. This input is encoded as source factors, in the same way that linguistic features can be encoded (Sennrich and Haddow, 2016). For the English–German WMT 2018 news translation task, moderate improvements in BLEU and term accuracies >90% are reported. The zero-shot nature of this approach enables the application of unseen terminology at test time. Furthermore, Dinu et al. (2019) report cases of generating morphological variants of terminology entries in the output, while decoding times are not increased compared to the base model. As the ability to apply terminology constraints is *trained* into the NMT model *by* either appending the target term to the source term or *by* replacing it, Dinu et al. (2019) refer to their models as *train-by* models, and we will continue doing so.

Many commercial providers of MT offer an option to upload a user dictionary in order to customize the NMT output to enforce a certain terminology.[2] This is a feature that users became ac-

---

[2] Accessed on February 21st, 2020:
Amazon Translate: https://aws.amazon.com/blogs/machine-learning/introducing-amazon-translate-custom-terminology/
Google Translate: https://cloud.google.com/translate/docs/advanced/glossary
Microsoft Translator: https://docs.microsoft.com/en-us/azure/cognitive-services/translator/dynamic-dictionary

customed to in rule-based and statistical MT, and consequently they expect a similar functionality for NMT as well. Naturally, the commercial providers usually leave us in the dark about the technology that is used for the implementation of that feature. Such custom terminology features are described more for marketing purposes rather than from an objective technical viewpoint. Usually, no transparent evaluation results are available. Some product descriptions are nevertheless fair enough to describe the limitations of the feature and best practices.

3 Methodology

We experiment with variants of the *train-by* approach introduced by Dinu et al. (2019), which is a form of inline term annotation. Target terms t_t are inserted into a source sentence by either appending them to the source term t_s (*append*) or by replacing t_s completely (*replace*). An additional signal is provided by a term annotation for each input token, where 1 means part of a source term, 2 means part of a target term and 0 is the default. An example for the input is provided in Table 1.

The term annotations are presented as source factors and have their own embedding vectors, which are combined with the respective (sub-) word embeddings to represent the input of the encoder in an encoder-decoder NMT architecture (Sennrich and Haddow, 2016). The two embedding vectors can be combined by either concatenating (*concat*) or summing (*sum*) them. This makes the dimensionality of the source factor embedding either a variable-sized (*concat*) or a fixed sized (*sum*) vector. While Dinu et al. (2019) only report results for the concatenation strategy with an embedding size of 16, we investigate an embedding size of 8 as well as the vector summarization combination.

We are also interested in the impact of the source factors themselves, and thus investigate whether the additionally provided annotation is actually necessary by using only the inline annotation and no term factor annotation.

The source sentences are annotated as described for all terminology entries (t_s, t_t), when t_s is present in the source and t_t occurs in the reference. To check whether a term occurs in a sentence, we use a matching strategy that also covers morphological variants. This is essential as our terminological database contains base forms only. Note that we insert t_t into the source in its base form, because this will also be the scenario at test time.

During training, the model learns to copy the injected target terms to the output. We expect to see morphological variants of the base terms in the output in accordance with the context of the sentence, as is reported in Dinu et al. (2019).

4 Experimental Setup

We evaluate the application of terminology constraints in the usage scenario of MT at SAP, for two language pairs English–German (en–de) and English-Russian (en–ru). We use target languages that are relatively morphologically rich because we want to investigate whether the approach is able to produce the target terms in an appropriate morphological form.

4.1 Data and Data Preparation

Corpus Our parallel data consists of a large collection of proprietary translation memories from within SAP. It is a multi-domain corpus covering different content types, such as documentation, user interface strings and training material in relation to various SAP products. For all our training/validation/test sets we use 5,000,000/2,000/3,000 parallel segments respectively. We use two test sets, where the first is targeted towards the evaluation of terminology and contains at least one terminology entry pair in each sentence, whereas the other does not have terminology annotated. We will refer to them as *terminology* and *no-terminology* test sets respectively.

Terminology SAPterm is organized into concepts where terms that are translations of each other are linked. A concept can cover different term types, such as a main term entry, its synonyms, acronyms or abbreviations. To generate a high-quality glossary, we only consider source-target term pairs consisting of main term entries and their synonyms. To avoid common words and spurious entries, we filter out high-frequency and low-frequency entries.[3] We therefore only select a subset of all entries in SAPterm, consisting of

SDL: https://www.sdl.com/about/news-media/press/2018/sdls-neural-machine-translation-sets-new-industry-standards-with-state-of-the-art-dictionary-and-image-translation-features.html
Systran: https://blog.systransoft.com/our-neural-network-just-learned-syntax/

[3]We filter out term pairs where the English side occurs more than 5,000 times or less than 100 times in a large corpus (>20 million sentences) of proprietary SAP data.

append	en	This$_0$ indicator$_0$ is$_0$ only$_0$ necessary$_0$ for$_0$ **manual$_1$ depreciation$_1$ manuelle$_2$ Abschreibung$_2$** and$_0$ write-ups$_0$.$_0$
replace	en	This$_0$ indicator$_0$ is$_0$ only$_0$ necessary$_0$ for$_0$ **manuelle$_2$ Abschreibung$_2$** and$_0$ write-ups$_0$.$_0$
Ref.	de	Das Kennzeichen wird nur für manuelle Abschreibungen und Zuschreibungen benötigt .

Table 1: Example input for the two term injection methods *append* and *replace*. Source factors are indicated as indices. The terminology entry is (manual depreciation, manuelle Abschreibung).

	en–de	en–ru
train	784,666	582,281
validation	303	238
terminology test	4,868	3,510
no-terminology test	0	0

Table 2: Number of term annotations

116,188 entries for English–Russian and 153,417 entries for English–German.

We apply a fuzzy matching strategy to find and annotate the terms in our data, as motivated in Section 3. Specifically, we lemmatize[4] on the English side, and allow for differences of two characters on the target side. In case of multiple overlapping matches, we keep only the longest match. Inspired by Dinu et al. (2019), we strictly separate training and testing terminology entries and select our parallel data accordingly to demonstrate the zero-shot learning capabilities of the model. For *train-by* methods we annotate 10% of the training and validation segments with terminology using the training terms. The term annotation statistics can be found in Table 2.

Preprocessing We tokenize all data using *NLTK*[5] and perform a joint source and target BPE encoding (Sennrich et al., 2016) using 89.5k merge operations. We furthermore inject the target terms for annotated terms according to the *append* and *replace* methods and generate source factors on BPE-level accordingly (cf. Table 1).

4.2 NMT Models

We make use of the Sockeye toolkit (Hieber et al., 2018) for this investigation. It supports source factors and constrained decoding out-of-the-box.[6]

For all our experiments, we use a transformer network (Vaswani et al., 2017). We configure two encoding and two decoding layers, unless stated otherwise. We also conduct experiments with a six layer setup (*6 layers*), which corresponds to the base configuration of Vaswani et al. (2017). The early stopping criterion is computed on the validation data (32 validation runs without improvement). All evaluations are performed with beam size 5.

For both the *append* and *replace* method, we train and evaluate models in which the embedding of the term annotation is added or concatenated to the corresponding subword embedding. We experiment with embedding sizes of 8 and 16 for concatenation. To investigate the impact of the term annotation in the form of source factors, we also train and evaluate models without source factors (*nofactors*), while still using the term injection of the *append* and *replace* method.

For comparison, we train a baseline without injected terms and source factors. We further compare against Sockeye's implementation of constrained decoding, which is based on Post and Vilar (2018). For this, we use the baseline model and constrain the output to contain the target terms of the terminology entries that are annotated in the *terminology* test set.

5 Automatic Evaluation

In this section we present the results of our experiments using automatic evaluation.

5.1 Metrics

To automatically assess the translation quality, we report BLEU (Papineni et al., 2002) and CHRF (Popović, 2015) on de-BPEed output, using the implementation in *NLTK*[7]. To evaluate how well the models adhere to the terminology constraints, we report *term rates* (TR), computed as the percentage of times the target term is generated in the MT output out of the total number of term annotations. We also employ the previously used fuzzy matching strategy to match the words in the output against the annotated terms in the reference. Note that we are not interested in generating the exact morpho-

---

[4] http://www.nltk.org/api/nltk.stem.html#module-nltk.stem.wordnet

[5] https://www.nltk.org/api/nltk.tokenize.html

[6] https://awslabs.github.io/sockeye/training.html

[7] https://www.nltk.org/api/nltk.translate.html

logical form of the term that occurs in the reference or in the terminology database, but we want the term in whatever form is required in the sentential context of the MT output. We also report the *variant term rate* (variant TR), in which a target term is also counted as correct if it coincides with one of the other possible translations of the source term according to SAPterm. We are aware that those term rates only approximate the truth, as do all automatic MT evaluation metrics. Hence we quantify some shortcomings in Section 7.2 and add a human evaluation in Section 6.

5.2 Results

Results for en–de and en–ru can be found in Tables 3 and 4 respectively. Our *train-by* systems are labeled according to whether they use the *append* or *replace* method from Dinu et al. (2019) and which kind of source factor embedding strategy they employ. We present results for the test sets *terminology* and *no-terminology* separately. The first allows us to demonstrate how the different approaches fare in terms of translation quality and term accuracy, while the latter serves as a sanity check to make sure that the general translation quality does not suffer for data without terminology.

The first thing to note is that BLEU scores for en–ru on the *terminology* data set are a lot higher than for en–de. This can be explained by the test sets that differ in sentence length and grammatical complexity. With an average of 17.7 words, the en–de data contains a large number of longer sentences with a higher term density. The en–ru data in contrast contains many short simple sentences with an average of 9.04 words per segment with mostly only one term.

Terminology test data It can be easily seen that, for both language pairs, all *train-by* models outperform the baseline in terms of translation quality and term rate by a wide margin. Comparing the term rate with the variant term rate for the individual models reveals that, while the baseline sometimes chooses an alternative translation for a term, this does not hold for the *train-by* models where the two term rates are basically the same. Overall, the results show that the *train-by* approach is effective in improving the translation quality using terminology constraints in the evaluated usage scenario of SAP data annotated with terminology from SAPterm.

Taking all results into account, the *append* method works better than the *replace* method for our experimental setup. Looking only at the *append* method results, concatenation of the two embedding vectors works better than summarization. From the approaches that use source factors, the *append-concat16* setting consistently performs best, both in terms of overall translation quality and term rate. This finding holds for both language pairs.

We rerun the most promising setting as well as the baseline with the six-layer transformer for en–de. As expected, both show an improvement for all metrics over their respective two-layer counterpart. The finding that the *append-concat16* approach outperforms the baseline in terms of translation quality and term rate by a wide margin thus holds for the shallow model as well as for the deeper model.

Somewhat surprisingly, we can observe that the impact of source factors is small for en–de and nonexistent, or even slightly detrimental for en–ru. It seems that the model has learned the code switching that happens in the source sentence and the intended copy behavior of the injected terms to the output, without requiring the additional input signal. We hypothesize that the different scripts of English and Russian, Latin and Cyrillic, are the reason why the model picks up the code switching better than for en-de, which both use the Latin alphabet.

Finally, when comparing the *train-by* methods to constrained decoding, we observe that even though constrained decoding reaches almost perfect term rates (>99%), the overall translation quality that is achieved with the *train-by* models is clearly superior. The decrease in BLEU further confirms observations that have previously been made in the literature (cf. Section 2), namely that constrained decoding can sometimes lead to questionable translation quality. In addition, it is important to note that constrained decoding caused an approximate sixfold increase in translation time in our experiments, while no such impact was observed for the *train-by* models.

Test data without terminology The results of the individual approaches on the *no-terminology* test data show slight differences in translation quality as measured by BLEU and CHRF. We deem those to be within the regular variation that we see amongst different training runs with the same data

	terminology				no-terminology	
	BLEU	CHRF	TR	Variant TR	BLEU	CHRF
Baseline	42.74	72.11	71.20	76.73	48.02	71.87
Constrained decoding	41.81	73.91	**99.51**	**99.65**	– " –	– " –
Append-concat16	**47.08**	**76.06**	96.40	96.52	48.22	72.01
Append-concat8	46.72	75.81	96.30	96.50	47.67	71.59
Append-sum	46.45	75.74	96.24	96.42	47.83	71.62
Replace-concat16	45.41	75.31	96.30	96.34	47.79	71.67
Replace-sum	45.75	75.46	96.44	96.50	48.21	71.99
Append-nofactors	46.19	75.58	95.06	95.43	47.26	71.56
Replace-nofactors	45.50	75.16	95.37	95.52	48.04	72.13
Baseline (6 layers)	43.50	72.66	71.98	77.31	48.66	72.52
Append-concat16 (6 layers)	47.45	76.60	96.87	97.16	48.98	72.79

Table 3: Results for English–German on the *terminology* and *no-terminology* test sets

	terminology				no-terminology	
	BLEU	CHRF	TR	Variant TR	BLEU	CHRF
Baseline	50.24	72.57	64.10	69.09	41.79	63.21
Constrained decoding	42.10	78.08	**99.12**	**99.23**	– " –	– " –
Append-concat16	61.23	81.06	95.72	95.81	41.80	63.02
Append-sum	60.94	80.91	95.30	95.32	41.77	62.99
Replace-concat16	60.30	80.46	94.92	94.92	42.04	63.11
Replace-sum	60.29	80.33	95.10	95.10	41.87	63.15
Append-nofactors	**61.47**	**81.48**	96.07	96.18	41.98	63.14
Replace-nofactors	60.83	80.67	95.33	95.33	41.78	62.99

Table 4: Results for English–Russian on the *terminology* and *no-terminology* test sets

and configuration. We thus conclude that the *train-by* approach in the investigated setting generally does not seem to have a negative impact on data without terminology constraints.

6 Translators' Assessment

As we apply MT in post-editing scenarios, it is of importance that our translators approve of our proposed solution of enforcing SAP-specific terminology. Taking the shortcomings of automatic metrics for MT into account, we therefore also conducted a human evaluation.

6.1 Setup

For the human evaluation, we chose to compare the baseline and the two best-performing *train-by* models *append-concat16* and *append-nofactors* from the automatic evaluation. The latter scored surprisingly well, requires less involved preprocessing and a simpler network architecture, which is appealing in a commercial setup. We selected 100 segments from the *terminology* test set (cf. Section 4.1). As we were primarily interested in the differences between the three systems, we made sure that none of the three translations are identi-

cal to each other or to the reference translation. We made sure that 35 of the test sentences contain more than one term annotation, to also cover this particular case.

For both language pairs, we had three testers who evaluated the same 300 translations in a blind evaluation using our in-house MT evaluation tool. Testers were shown the source with highlighted terminology, the relevant terminology entries and one translation at a time in random order. They were asked to rate the target term accuracy and the overall translation quality, both on a scale from one (poor) to six (excellent). Note that the human target term accuracy does not directly correspond to the automatic term rates (cf. Section 5), as testers were advised to also consider whether target terms appear in the expected syntactic position and fit mophologically into their context.

6.2 Results

To consolidate the results of the human evaluation, the accuracy and quality ratings of all testers were averaged for each evaluated segment. Table 5 shows the respective results. Generally, they confirm the findings of the automatic evaluation in

	Term accuracy		Transl. quality	
	en–de	en–ru	en–de	en–ru
Baseline	4.52	4.99	4.40	4.90
Append-concat16	5.74	5.70	4.54	4.98
Append-nofactors	5.79	5.69	4.50	4.90

Table 5: Results of human evaluation: term accuracy rating and translation quality rating

Rating	baseline		nofactors		concat16	
	ende	enru	ende	enru	ende	enru
excellent	50%	53%	86%	80%	87%	77%
very good	6%	12%	9%	13%	7%	14%
good	5%	15%	2%	2%	0%	4%
medium	13%	8%	0%	0%	1%	2%
poor	14%	8%	1%	3%	2%	3%
very poor	12%	4%	2%	2%	3%	0%

Table 6: Distribution of term accuracy ratings for baseline and *append* systems

Section 5. In addition, Table 6 shows the distribution of the average term accuracy ratings.

The accuracy of the term translations of the baseline model clearly lags behind the *train-by* models for both language pairs. The results however also show that terminology is quite well covered by the baseline model already.

The term accuracies for *append-concat16* and *append-nofactors* approach the maximum score for both language pairs, and are very close to each other. This gives rise to the conclusion that the approach works similarly well for enforcing terminology on both morphologically average (de) as well as rich (ru) target languages.

In terms of overall translation quality, the difference between the baseline and the *append* systems is less pronounced than suggested by the automatic scores. For both language pairs, the quality ratings of the *append* models are comparable. Term enforcement does not seem to have noticeable negative side effects on overall translation quality.

Human evaluation also reveals that there is no quality loss when more than one term is injected into a sentence. In the 35% of test segments with multiple terms, term accuracies of the *append* models are even sightly higher than for sentences with one term. This also has an effect on the overall translation quality. For *append-concat16*, for example, we see a positive difference of 0.13 (en–de) and 0.18 (en–ru) points between the average quality ratings of sentences with one and with multiple terms.

7 Examples & Discussion

In this section, we present examples of correct term translations as well as an in-depth human analysis of the terms that were not produced according to the automatic evaluation. Examples for en–de and en–ru are displayed in Table 7.

7.1 Analysis of Term Translations

With the high term rates of all *train-by* models (cf. Tables 3 and 4) it is expected that the models adhere well to the terminology constraints. When taking a closer look into the output of *append-concat16*, we make the following observations (examples taken from Table 7):

- Terminology integrates smoothly into the context of the target language using correct morphological forms (ex. 2). This is especially important for a highly inflecting language like Russian where case information is properly transferred (ex. 5, 6)

- Single terms can build natural compound words in German (ex. 3).

- When enforcing nominal terminology, English verb-noun ambiguities are often resolved towards nouns, which is reflected in the translation (ex. 5 compared to baseline). Another effect is the verbal translation of English imperatives instead of using its nominalization (ex. 7 compared to baseline).

- Enforcing nominal terminology leads to less compounding and prevents over-compounding in German target (ex. 4).

- Abbreviations in the translation are prevented. In our case, they are caused by large amounts of training data from heavily abbreviated content (ex. 4 reference and ex. 8 baseline).

- The baseline translation often uses synonyms of the expected term (ex. 2, 6). This means that the translation does not adhere to the terminology constraint, but that it is not completely wrong either.

7.2 Missed Term Translations

We also analyzed sentences for which term enforcement did not work as expected, i.e. the remaining 3.6% and 4.3% from *append-concat16* in Tables 3 and 4 respectively. For this, 75 segments with missing term translations according to the automatic evaluation were analyzed manually. The results of this investigation are shown in Table 8.

| (1) | | product substitution | – | Produktsubstitution |
		location substitution	–	Lokationsfindung
Source	**Product Substitution** e.g. no **location substitution** for oversea customer			
Baseline	Produktersetzung, z.B. keine Lokationsersetzung für ÜberseeKunde			
Append-concat16	**Produktsubstitution** z.B. keine **Lokationsfindung** für Überseekunden			
Reference	**Produktsubstitution**; Beispiel: keine **Lokationsfindung** für Überseekunden			

| (2) | | budget hierarchy | – | Haushaltsstruktur |
		budget	–	Haushalt
Source	Defining a **budget hierarchy** is the first step in setting up an overall **budget**.			
Baseline	Die Definition einer Budgethierarchie ist der erste Schritt bei der Einrichtung eines Gesamtbudgets.			
Append-concat16	Die Definition einer **Haushaltsstruktur** ist der erste Arbeitsschritt im Aufbau eines **Haushalts**.			
Reference	Der Aufbau einer **Haushaltsstruktur** ist der erste Schritt beim Einrichten eines **Haushalts**.			

| (3) | | inconsistency | – | Inkonsistenz |
		program error	–	Programmfehler
Source	The table **inconsistency** is probably due to a program error.			
Baseline	Wahrscheinlich liegt ein **Programmfehler** vor.			
Append-concat16	Die Tabelle**inkonsistenz** wird wahrscheinlich durch einen **Programmfehler** verursacht.			
Reference	Die Tabelle**inkonsistenz** ist vermutlich durch einen **Programmfehler** entstanden.			

(4)		processing time	–	Bearbeitungszeit
Source	Field: Goods receipt **processing time**			
Baseline	Feld: Wareneingangs**bearbeitungszeit**			
Append-concat16	Feld: **Bearbeitungszeit** für den Wareneingang			
Reference	Field: WE **Bearbeitungszeit**			

| (5) | | release order | – | отзыв |
		package number	–	номер пакета
Source	Purchase order: **release order package number**			
Baseline	Заказ на поставку: деблокировать **номер пакета** заказов			
Append-concat16	Заказ на поставку: **номер пакета отзыва**			
Reference	Заказ на поставку: **номер пакета отзыва**			

| (6) | | logical port | – | логический порт |
		proxy class	–	прокси-класс
Source	No **logical port** found for the **proxy class** &1			
Baseline	**Логический порт** для класса прокси &1 не найден			
Append-concat16	**Логический порт** для **прокси-класса** &1 не найден			
Reference	**Логический порт** для **прокси-класса** &1 не найден			

| (7) | | markup | – | надбавка |
		replacement category	–	тип замены
Source	To define a relative **markup**, choose the Relative **Markup** value in the **Replacement Category** field.			
Baseline	Для определения относительной наценки выберите значение Относительная наценка в поле **Тип замены**.			
Append-concat16	Чтобы определить относительную **надбавку**, выберите значение Относительная **надбавка** в поле **Тип замены**.			
Reference	Чтобы определить относительную **надбавку**, выберите значение Относительная **надбавка** в поле **Тип замены**.			

(8)		table key	–	ключ таблицы
Source	**Table Key** > 70 Char			
Baseline	Табл. ключ > 70 символов			
Append-concat16	**Ключ таблицы** > 70 символов			
Reference	**Ключ таблицы** > 70 символов			

Table 7: Examples for en–de and en–ru. Terminology constraints are provided above each example. Underlining is used to highlight linguistic aspects described in Section 7.1.

Type of term match	en–de	en–ru
True negative (unmatched)	56%	55%
False negative (matched)	44%	45%

Table 8: Results of analysis of negative term rate samples

It was found that among the analyzed examples there are many false negatives, i.e. the expected term translations were indeed produced. The reason is that our fuzzy term matching strategy on which the term rates are based does not cover them. In the investigated examples, for both languages, around 45% of the terms were not recognized by the term rate for the following reasons:

- The term occurs in an inflected form that escapes the fuzzy match of the term rate (ex. 7).
- The term is part of a compound word that escapes the fuzzy match of the term rate (ex. 3).

When analyzing truly problematic terms, i.e. the true negatives that were not generated in the translation at all, patterns that hint at a reason are harder to detect. Generally, there are three types of behavior: most of the time, the term in question is translated by a synonym, sometimes it is mistranslated, and in rare cases it is dropped. For en–ru, there are a few terms in our test set that were not produced by the NMT model, for example *transaction control* - управление транзакциями. The problem also occurs for en–de but to a lesser extent. All those missed terms are properly annotated in the source text and, as the other terms in the test set, all segments containing these terms were removed from the training data. Without looking at the decoder in detail, we cannot draw any conclusions for now. It is possible that some translations are not enforced since another translation is too "strong", or the target word does not exist in the training data and is therefore difficult to assemble and produce. We also noticed some problems in compounding, for example an incorrect connecting element on non-head words.

From our analysis we conclude that term enforcement using the *train-by* method does not always work perfectly - but we also know that MT in general does not always work perfectly either. Nevertheless, we have shown that the term rate is higher than what we have reported in Tables 3 and 4. This is due to the large number of false negatives of the term rate caused by the automatic evaluation strategy.

7.3 Considerations for a Production Setting

With the high term rates paired with an improved translation quality and no negative impact on translation speed, the *train-by* method, specifically the *append* variant, offers a good trade-off for terminology enforcement in a production setting, particularly compared to current alternatives in the class of constrained decoding. Whether term rates are high enough for a productive scenario obviously depends on the specific requirements on the MT system and cannot be answered universally.

Note that we did not perform a human analysis of segments without terminology and only interpret the automatic scores. It remains to be seen whether the inline annotation, particularly if used without source factors, is reliable enough to not apply the learned copy mechanism in unsuitable occasions.

Clearly, the results of this approach depend to a high extent on the quality of the term dictionary. Grammatical and lexical ambiguity of terms as well as the quality of translation correspondences are to be considered. Performance and precision of the term recognition mechanism are additional key factors for making this approach work.

8 Conclusion

We have investigated a new approach for terminology integration into NMT, originally proposed by Dinu et al. (2019), in an real-world setup. Our experimental setting was IT-related corporate data from SAP with terminology from SAP's terminology database, for two language pairs with rather morphologically rich target languages. Our study yields positive results, namely term rates >95% and improvements in translation quality compared to a baseline model as well as constrained decoding, with neither impacting the translation speed nor the translation quality on data without terminology. The improvements in term accuracy were furthermore confirmed in a human evaluation for both language pairs. In an additional manual investigation, we inspected the problematic cases and found that almost half of them are false negatives, meaning that term rates are in fact even higher. We have furthermore confirmed that with this approach the term translations are used flexibly in the surface form required by the sentential context. Overall, it seems to be a promising approach for applying terminology constraints.

References

Burlot, Franck. 2019. Lingua custodia at WMT'19: Attempts to control terminology. In *Proceedings of the Fourth Conference on Machine Translation*, pages 147–154, Florence, Italy. Association for Computational Linguistics.

Chatterjee, Rajen, Matteo Negri, Marco Turchi, Marcello Federico, Lucia Specia, and Frédéric Blain. 2017. Guiding neural machine translation decoding with external knowledge. In *Proceedings of the Second Conference on Machine Translation*, pages 157–168, Copenhagen, Denmark. Association for Computational Linguistics.

Crego, Josep, Jungi Kim, Guillaume Klein, Anabel Rebollo, Kathy Yang, Jean Senellart, Egor Akhanov, Patrice Brunelle, Aurelien Coquard, Yongchao Deng, Satoshi Enoue, Chiyo Geiss, Joshua Johanson, Ardas Khalsa, Raoum Khiari, Byeongil Ko, Catherine Kobus, Jean Lorieux, Leidiana Martins, Dang-Chuan Nguyen, Alexandra Priori, Thomas Riccardi, Natalia Segal, Christophe Servan, Cyril Tiquet, Bo Wang, Jin Yang, Dakun Zhang, Jing Zhou, and Peter Zoldan. 2016. Systran's pure neural machine translation systems.

Dinu, Georgiana, Prashant Mathur, Marcello Federico, and Yaser Al-Onaizan. 2019. Training neural machine translation to apply terminology constraints. In *Proceedings of the 57th Annual Meeting of the Association for Computational Linguistics*, pages 3063–3068, Florence, Italy. Association for Computational Linguistics.

Farajian, M. Amin, Nicola Bertoldi, Matteo Negri, Marco Turchi, and Marcello Federico. 2018. Evaluation of terminology translation in instance-based neural MT adaptation. In *Proceedings of the 21st Annual Conference of the European Association for Machine Translation*, pages 149–158, Alacant, Spain.

Hasler, Eva, Adrià de Gispert, Gonzalo Iglesias, and Bill Byrne. 2018. Neural machine translation decoding with terminology constraints. In *Proceedings of the 2018 Conference of the North American Chapter of the Association for Computational Linguistics*, pages 506–512, New Orleans, Louisiana. Association for Computational Linguistics.

Hieber, Felix, Tobias Domhan, Michael Denkowski, David Vilar, Artem Sokolov, Ann Clifton, and Matt Post. 2018. The Sockeye Neural Machine Translation toolkit at AMTA 2018. In *Proceedings of the 13th Conference of the Association for Machine Translation in the Americas*, pages 200–207, Boston, MA. Association for Machine Translation in the Americas.

Hokamp, Chris and Qun Liu. 2017. Lexically constrained decoding for sequence generation using grid beam search. In *Proceedings of the 55th Annual Meeting of the Association for Computational Linguistics*, pages 1535–1546, Vancouver, Canada. Association for Computational Linguistics.

Hu, J. Edward, Huda Khayrallah, Ryan Culkin, Patrick Xia, Tongfei Chen, Matt Post, and Benjamin Van Durme. 2019. Improved lexically constrained decoding for translation and monolingual rewriting. In *Proceedings of the 2019 Conference of the North American Chapter of the Association for Computational Linguistics*, pages 839–850, Minneapolis, Minnesota. Association for Computational Linguistics.

Huck, Matthias, Viktor Hangya, and Alexander Fraser. 2019. Better OOV translation with bilingual terminology mining. In *Proceedings of the 57th Annual Meeting of the Association for Computational Linguistics*, pages 5809–5815, Florence, Italy. Association for Computational Linguistics.

Kobus, Catherine, Josep Crego, and Jean Senellart. 2017. Domain control for neural machine translation. In *Proceedings of the International Conference Recent Advances in Natural Language Processing*, pages 372–378, Varna, Bulgaria. INCOMA Ltd.

Papineni, Kishore, Salim Roukos, Todd Ward, and Wei-Jing Zhu. 2002. Bleu: a method for automatic evaluation of machine translation. In *Proceedings of the 40th Annual Meeting of the Association for Computational Linguistics*, pages 311–318, Philadelphia, Pennsylvania, USA. Association for Computational Linguistics.

Popović, Maja. 2015. chrF: character n-gram f-score for automatic MT evaluation. In *Proceedings of the Tenth Workshop on Statistical Machine Translation*, pages 392–395, Lisbon, Portugal. Association for Computational Linguistics.

Post, Matt and David Vilar. 2018. Fast lexically constrained decoding with dynamic beam allocation for neural machine translation. In *Proceedings of the 2018 Conference of the North American Chapter of the Association for Computational Linguistics*, pages 1314–1324, New Orleans, Louisiana. Association for Computational Linguistics.

Sennrich, Rico and Barry Haddow. 2016. Linguistic input features improve neural machine translation. In *Proceedings of the First Conference on Machine Translation*, pages 83–91, Berlin, Germany. Association for Computational Linguistics.

Sennrich, Rico, Barry Haddow, and Alexandra Birch. 2016. Neural machine translation of rare words with subword units. In *Proceedings of the 54th Annual Meeting of the Association for Computational Linguistics*, pages 1715–1725, Berlin, Germany. Association for Computational Linguistics.

Vaswani, Ashish, Noam Shazeer, Niki Parmar, Jakob Uszkoreit, Llion Jones, Aidan N Gomez, Łukasz Kaiser, and Illia Polosukhin. 2017. Attention is all you need. In Guyon, I., U. V. Luxburg, S. Bengio, H. Wallach, R. Fergus, S. Vishwanathan, and R. Garnett, editors, *Advances in Neural Information Processing Systems 30*, pages 5998–6008. Curran Associates, Inc.

Ellipsis Translation for a Medical Speech to Speech Translation System

Jonathan Mutal[1], Johanna Gerlach[1], Pierrette Bouillon[1], and Hervé Spechbach[2]

[1]FTI/TIM, University of Geneva, Switzerland
[2]Hôpitaux Universitaires de Genève (HUG), Switzerland
{Jonathan.Mutal, Johanna.Gerlach, Pierrette.Bouillon}@unige.ch
herve.spechbach@hcuge.ch

Abstract

In diagnostic interviews, elliptical utterances allow doctors to question patients in a more efficient and economical way. However, literal translation of such incomplete utterances is rarely possible without affecting communication. Previous studies have focused on automatic ellipsis detection and resolution, but only few specifically address the problem of automatic translation of ellipsis. In this work, we evaluate four different approaches to translate ellipsis in medical dialogues in the context of the speech to speech translation system BabelDr. We also investigate the impact of training data, using an undersampling method and data with elliptical utterances in context. Results show that the best model is able to translate 88% of elliptical utterances correctly.

1 Introduction

Ellipsis is one of the least studied discursive phenomena in automatic translation. Like anaphora, ellipsis require context to be understood, but contrary to anaphora, there is no indicator that there is a missing part in the sentence[1]. The characterising feature of ellipsis is that "elements of semantic content are obtained in the absence of any corresponding form. The syntax thus appears to be incomplete. More specifically, the implicit semantic context is recovered from elements of linguistic and extralinguistic context" (Ginzburg and Miller, 2018).

In NLP, different studies have focused on automatic ellipsis detection and resolution either with rules (patterns or grammars) (for example, the pioneer work from Hardt, 1992) or classification techniques (for example, Hardt and Rambow, 2001; Bos and Spenader, 2011; Liu et al., 2016; Kenyon-Dean et al., 2016; McShane and Babkin, 2016; Rønning et al., 2018). However, only few studies specifically address this problem in machine translation (MT), despite the recent interest for context modelling in neural machine translation (see for example, Bawden et al., 2018). Very recently, some qualitative studies showed the negative impact of ellipsis on generalist neural systems (DeepL, Google Translate, etc.) from a translation point of view in the English-French pair (for example, Hamza, 2019).

In this paper, we focus on automatic translation of ellipsis in medical dialogues, in the particular context of BabelDr, a speech to speech translation system for the medical domain (Spechbach et al., 2019)[2]. Elliptical utterances are very common in dialogues, since they ensure the principle of economy and provide a way to avoid duplication (Hamza et al., 2019). In the medical dialogues we are interested in, ellipsis allows doctors to question patients in a more efficient way (Where is your pain? In the back? Is the pain severe? Moderate?) (Tanguy et al., 2011). Literal translation of these elliptical utterances is rarely possible without affecting communication, in particular with structurally different languages which do not share the same type of ellipsis. For example in Japanese, adjectival ellipsis are very informal and should be

---

[1]Ellipsis is "a case of anaphora, where the anaphor is a null proform (zero-anaphora)" (Ginzburg and Miller, 2018)

---

[2]https://babeldr.unige.ch/

Martins, Moniz, Fumega, Martins, Batista, Coheur, Parra, Trancoso, Turchi, Bisazza, Moorkens, Guerberof, Nurminen, Marg, Forcada (eds.)
Proceedings of the 22nd Annual Conference of the European Association for Machine Translation, p. 281–290
Lisboa, Portugal, November 2020.

translated by complete sentences (Bouillon et al., 2007). The following examples illustrate elliptical utterances where literal translation is problematic, as it produces agreement errors, wrong prepositions or other syntactical or grammatical issues that can make the elliptical utterance difficult to understand.

```
Source: is the pain intense?
->MT: la douleur est-elle intense
Source: sudden?
-> MT: *soudain

Source: do you have pain in
your stomach?
-> MT: le duele el estómago?
Source: in your head?
-> MT: *en la cabeza?

Source: is the pain severe
-> MT: hageshii itami desu ka?
Source: moderate?
-> MT: *chuuteido?
```

The aim of this paper is to compare different approaches to translate ellipsis in the context of BabelDr. Section 2 describes the BabelDr system. Section 3 outlines the methodology, including the objective and research questions, the test data and the evaluation metrics. Section 4 presents the approaches and models, followed by Section 5 which describes the different sets of training data. Section 6 presents the results and Section 7 concludes.

2 The context: BabelDr

2.1 The BabelDr system

BabelDr is a speech-enabled fixed-phrase translator designed to allow French speaking doctors to carry out diagnostic interviews with patients with whom they don't have any common language in emergency settings where no interpreters are available. It combines speech recognition with manually pre-translated sentences, grouped by diagnostic domains. Doctors can freely speak their questions, the system maps the recognised utterance (hereafter: *variation*) to the closest pre-translated sentence (hereafter: *core sentence*), and, after approval by the doctor, the core sentence is translated for the patient. This ensures the reliability of speech recognition and of translation, essential for safe use in the medical domain.

The scarcity of training data available for this domain, a consequence of data confidentiality issues and of the minority languages involved (e.g., Tigrinya, Farsi, Albanian), has at first led to the development of a grammar-based approach. A Synchronous Context Free Grammar (SCFG, Aho and Ullman, 1969) which describes source language variation patterns and their mapping to core sentences is used to compile a language model used by Nuance for speech recognition. This grammar based speech recognition produces high quality results for in coverage items. To handle sentences that are out of grammar coverage, BabelDr also includes a large vocabulary recogniser. Results from this recogniser must then be mapped to the closest core sentences, a task to which several approaches have been applied, including tf-idf indexing and dynamic programming (DP, Rayner et al., 2017) and, more recently, a NMT approach (Mutal et al., 2019). The latter is one of the approaches evaluated in the present study, where it has been extended to handle elliptical utterances.

2.2 Ellipsis in BabelDr

In the BabelDr context, instead of producing a literal translation of the ellipsis, we aim at mapping elliptical utterances to the closest non-elliptical core sentence, for which translations are available in the system. This presents the advantage of removing all ambiguity related to ellipsis and their translation. To resolve the ellipsis, we use context information, which in a diagnostic interview is the previous translated utterance. The proposed ellipsis processing workflow is illustrated in Figure 1 and will be discussed in further detail in Section 4.

3 Methodology

3.1 Objective and research question

The aim of this study is to evaluate the performance of four different approaches for the ellipsis translation task: indexing, classification, neural machine translation and hybrid.

The research questions guiding our experiments are listed as follows 1) What is the best approach to handle ellipsis in this context? 2) How does the distribution of class instances affect the performance of the proposed models? 3) Does inclusion of ellipsis-specific training data improve performance?

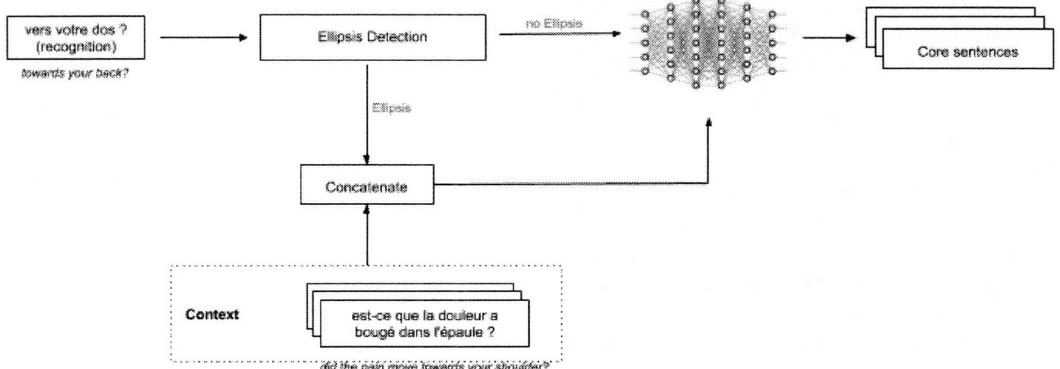

Figure 1: Ellipsis translation task in BabelDr: overview.

3.2 Test data

Since the currently deployed version of babelDr only handles ellipsis in a limited manner, doctors were instructed to use only complete sentences. Consequently, real usage data contains very few elliptical utterances. For this study, we have therefore used a test suite based on the BabelDr coverage and described in (Rayner et al., 2018). This was created by extracting the list of available core sentences for the abdominal domain and transforming complete sentences into elliptical sentences where possible, for example:

```
avez-vous mal au ventre
avez-vous mal dans le bas-ventre
    --> dans le bas-ventre
avez-vous mal dans le haut du
ventre
    --> le haut du ventre
```

Each elliptical utterance was associated with a corresponding complete utterance to serve as context. Five native francophone subjects were then asked to speak the pairs (context and elliptical utterance) in a natural way, freely varying the wording, but with the instruction to respect the distinction between elliptical and plain utterances. Data were collected using a web tool which prompted the subjects and recorded their responses. This produced a total of 1'676 recorded utterances. Each utterance was then transcribed and matched to the most plausible core sentence by two judges and when necessary disagreement between judges resolved. If the second sentence of the pair was not elliptical because subjects did not follow instructions, they were removed from the test suite.

This process finally produced 838 recorded pairs, with the corresponding core sentences. The average utterance length was 8.96 words for the plain utterances and 3.14 words for the elliptical utterances (Rayner et al., 2018).

Since the focus of this study is not on speech recognition performance, but on the subsequent processing, we performed our experiments with the transcriptions as input rather than the speech recogniser output, thereby assuming recognition is perfect.

3.3 Evaluation

We want to compare the different approaches at the task level, namely how many elliptical utterances will result in a correct translation for the patient. Since the system relies on human pre-translation (cf. Section 2), a correct core sentence is equivalent to a correct translation. We therefore measured the sentence error rate (SER), defined as the percentage of utterances for which the resulting core sentence is not identical to the annotated correct core sentence.

Since the target is a finite set of sentences, we also measured system performance on the test data using three standard metrics for classification: recall, precision and F1. As the test data is not perfectly balanced, we computed the performance for each class, and then averaged over the number of classes, i.e. by macro-averaging. The macro-average better reflects the statistics of the smaller classes and therefore is more appropriate when all classes are equally important (Jurafsky and Martin, 2014). We could have applied the standard BLEU score for the evaluation of the MT approaches, but since it is not applicable to the other approaches, it is not appropriate for our comparison.

The metrics were calculated using a module in Sklearn[3].

4 Approaches

As mentioned earlier, our objective is to use the context (previous utterance) to map elliptical utterances to the closest core sentence. Figure 1 provides an overview of the ellipsis translation task as it would be performed in BabelDr. Starting with a source sentence, we perform ellipsis detection using a binary classifier (support-vector machine) trained on handcrafted features. In this context, elliptical sentences can easily be detected by sentence length and syntactic structure. Therefore, the sentence length, the first word of the sentence and its part-of-speech are used as features to train the classifier. This method achieves 98% of accuracy on ellipsis detection. If the utterance is identified as an ellipsis, it is concatenated with the previous utterance from the dialog (Tiedemann and Scherrer, 2017). This concatenated sentence is then processed like other utterances.

In the following sections, we describe the four approaches applied after concatenation. The same training data (described in Section 5) was used for all approaches. The source sentences were preprocessed using the same method for all the models: they have been lower cased and tokenized. Each approach has its own built-in tokenization method to reach optimal results, except for machine translation where we applied BPE.

4.1 Indexing

In this approach, the task is to find the source variations that are the closest matches for a new utterance. To do so, each sentence was represented by a vector and a similarity metric was used to compare them. We employed two approaches to embed each sentence:

tf-idf The first approach uses a customised tf-idf (Salton and Buckley, 1988), where tf-idf was applied to subword occurrences (two to four characters) in variations for a given core sentence. Common pre-processing methods for tf-idf are lemmatizing and removing stop words; however, since accurate preservation of meaning is imperative in a medical dialog context, e.g. in terms of verb

tenses, in our experiments words were left as word forms.

Universal Sentence Encoder The second approach uses the current state-of-the-art for multilingual encoding (Chidambaram et al., 2019). To encode each source sentence, we used an already trained Universal Sentence Encoder[4] (hereafter *uencoder*).

We then used the approximate nearest neighbor search (Andoni and Indyk, 2006) to extract the closest variation sentence with cosine similarity, and return the corresponding core sentence.

4.2 Sequence Classification

In this approach, the task is to classify each variation into a core sentence using a distance based classification method (Xing et al., 2010). We trained two different neural classifiers:

CamemBERT This classifier uses the current state-of-the-art for French based on RoBERTa (Liu et al., 2019), which is used for many NLP tasks. We used the CamemBERT pre-trained model (Martin et al., 2019) and added a classification layer on top of the model to fine-tune it with our data (Sun et al., 2019). To do so, we set-up 10 epochs using the Transformer framework for python (Wolf et al., 2020).

fastText The second approach uses a sequence classification baseline based on bag of tricks (Joulin et al., 2017). We used fastText on bigrams with 100 epochs and a learning rate of 0,2. The other hyper parameters were set by default[5].

4.3 Machine Translation

With these approaches, the task is to translate the source utterance into a core sentence. We have trained two different NMT models:

LSTM We trained a neural machine translation model with an embedding size of 512 in the encoder and decoder. Encoder and decoder were each composed of two LSTM (Hochreiter and Schmidhuber, 1997) with an attention mechanism on the decoder side (Bahdanau et al., 2014; Luong et al., 2015). The model was trained with a dropout rate of 0.3 and a batch size of 64 examples. This system is described in detail in (Mutal et al., 2019).

---

[3]https://scikit-learn.org/stable/modules/generated/
sklearn.metrics.classification_report.html

[4]https://tfhub.dev/google/universal-sentence-encoder-
multilingual/3
[5]https://fasttext.cc/docs/en/supervised-tutorial.html

Corpus	Subset	#sentences	#words	#vocabulary
All data	Train	21M	322M	3121
	Dev	2M	35M	2923
Sampled	Train	143'011	1.5M	3'095
	Dev	15'891	176'816	2'413
Ellipsis	Train	394'767	4.7M	3'218
Corpus	Dev	43'863	528'175	2'593

Table 1: Number of sentences, words and vocabulary on source variations for each training data.

Ellipsis	Core sentence
aux épaules (shoulders)	la douleur se déplace vers les épaules ? (the pain moves towards the shoulders?)
	la douleur au ventre irradie-t-elle vers les épaules ? (does the belly pain radiate to the shoulders?)
	avez-vous aussi mal aux épaules ? (do your shoulders hurt as well?)
du foie (liver)	avez-vous eu un examen du foie ? (have you had a liver exam?)
	avez-vous eu un contrôle médical du foie ? (have you had a liver checkup?)
	avez-vous un cancer du foie ? (do you have liver cancer?)

Table 2: Two examples of ellipsis with corresponding possible core sentence

Transformer The second model relies on a transformer based architecture for machine translation (Vaswani et al., 2017) with default parameters and size[6].

For both architectures, early stopping was used to reduce the number of training steps by monitoring the performance on the development set. We used OpenNMT (Klein et al., 2017) to train the models.

4.4 Hybrid

The hybrid approach combines the best neural machine translation model with the best classification model to build an N-best list of sentences, in this experiment a 2-best list which includes the core sentence generated by machine translation and one sentence from the classification results. To select the best result in this list, we used the log probability of the generated core sentence from the neural machine translation: if it was below a threshold (< -0.25), we kept the core sentence generated by the classifier, else we kept the NMT result. The threshold was set based on the observation that 93% of the sentences above that threshold were mistranslated.

5 Training Data

In this section, we describe the training data sets used for this study. All data were generated from a recent version of the BabelDr SCFG for the abdominal diagnostic domain and consist of variation-core pairs. Table 1 summarises the number of sentences, words and vocabulary for each set.

5.1 All Data

The main data set includes 23M variations, of which 321'698 are ambiguous (i.e. sentences that can be mapped to more than one core sentence). Most of these ambiguous sentences are elliptical. Table 2 shows two examples of such sentences. The variations are mapped to the 4'132 different core sentences available for the abdominal domain. These core sentences are not represented equally in the corpus: 50% of the 4'132 core sentences occur less than 52 times in the data. For example, the core sentence "avez-vous pris des médicaments contre la douleur ?" (have you taken any painkillers?) is mapped to 3'496'503 source variations (14% of the entire dataset) whereas "avez-vous de l'oxygène à la maison ?" (do you have oxygen at home?) is only mapped to 5 source variations.

Since we are interested in evaluating the complete set of core sentences, we have maintained the same distribution when splitting the data into development and training.

---

[6]https://opennmt.net/OpenNMT-tf/model.html

	Source variation	Core sentence
Generated from grammar		
Context	la douleur a bougé dans l'épaule ? (did the pain move to your shoulder?)	la douleur se déplace vers les épaules ? (does the pain move to your shoulders?)
Ellipsis	vers votre dos ? (towards your back?)	la douleur se déplace vers le dos ? (the pain moves towards your back?)
Concatenated for training		
Ellipsis	la douleur a bougé dans l'épaule vers votre dos ? (did the pain move to your shoulders towards your back?)	la douleur se déplace vers le dos ? (the pain moves towards your back?)

Table 3: Example of generated ellipsis training data, composed of variation-core pairs : one complete (context), followed by a corresponding elliptical utterance. For training, elliptical variations are concatenated with the preceding variation (context)

5.2 Sampled Data

As mentioned in the previous section, our main corpus is highly imbalanced. In this context, where all core sentences are relevant for the task, the exclusion or misclassification/translation of minority categories (in our case, core sentences) on the dataset could lead to a heavy cost (Haixiang et al., 2017). Therefore, we used resampling techniques to rebalance the sample space in order to alleviate the effect of the skewed class distribution on the learning process. We applied under-sampling, which is suggested as the best alternative when the training sample size is too large (Mazurowski et al., 2008; Haixiang et al., 2017).

To reduce the number of variations by core sentence while keeping data as representative as possible, we propose a new algorithm for under-sampling based on bigrams consisting in the following steps:

1. For each core sentence, extract all bigrams present in the associated variations.

2. Build a new list of variations by iteratively extracting variations from a list in randomised order until all bigrams are covered.

After under-sampling, the resulting corpus contained 159'902 variations and 87 ambiguous samples. Furthermore, 75% of the core sentences were mapped to less than 32 variations. Even though we managed to reduce most of the categories, minority classes were still under-represented compared to the majority classes. For example, "avez-vous mal au ventre en position de chien de fusil ?" (do you have abdominal pain in a fetal position?) still had 731 variations whereas "combien de kilos avez-vous pris ?" (how much weight did you gain?) had only 1.

5.3 Ellipsis Corpus

To generate training data for ellipsis in context, we exploit grammar rules that contain variables. These variables are placeholders that are replaced by different values at system-compile time, e.g. "avez-vous pris [des anti-douleurs|des medicaments contre l'acidité|...] récemment ?" ("Did you take [painkillers|antacids|...] recently?"). To produce elliptical utterances, we have kept only the value of the variable as source variation, associated with a corresponding complete core sentence. Each of these elliptical variation-core pairs follows a matching complete variation-core pair which serves as context, as shown in Table 3.

To train the models, we transformed the elliptical source variations by concatenating them with the context source variation. The same concatenation was performed on the test data.

6 Results

In this section we first describe the evaluation of the under-sampling method (subsection 6.1). We then give results for different models trained with under-sampled data (subsection 6.2). Finally, including only the best model for each approach in terms of F1, we evaluate the impact of training on Ellipsis data (subsection 6.3).

6.1 Under-sampling

To evaluate the under-sampling method, we ran the experiment with two approaches, machine translation (LSTM, Transformer) and classification (fastText), trained with two different data sets: under-sampled data (hereafter *sampled*) and all data. We then compared performance by calculating SER, precision, recall and F1. Table 4 shows the results on test data.

Model	Data	SER	Precision	Recall	F1
LSTM	all data	0.29	0.56	0.54	0.56
	sampled	0.28	0.60	0.63	0.59
Transformer	all data	0.32	0.55	0.61	0.56
	sampled	0.30	0.58	0.62	0.57
fastText	all data	0.32	0.54	0.55	0.52
	sampled	0.29	0.56	0.57	0.55

Table 4: Models trained with under-sampled (sampled) and all training data (all data).

Approach	Model	SER	Precision	Recall	F1
Indexing	tf-idf	0.53/0.39	0.34/0.51	0.32/0.47	0.32/0.47
	uencoder	0.62/0.49	0.27/0.39	0.23/0.39	0.23/0.37
Classification	fastText	0.52/0.29	0.32/0.56	0.28/0.57	0.28/0.55
	CamemBERT	0.44/0.23	0.41/0.66	0.39/0.71	0.39/0.66
Machine Translation	LSTM	0.53/0.28	0.34/0.60	0.30/0.63	0.30/0.60
Hybrid	LSTM + CamemBERT	0.23/0.17	0.54/0.75	0.50/0.77	0.50/0.74

Table 5: Results on elliptical utterances/all on under-sampled training data for different models on indexing, classification, machine translation and hybrid.

We observe that the proposed under-sampling method (fastText-sampled, LSTM-sampled and Transformer-sampled) produces better results in this particular context indicating that a more balanced data set improves performance in terms of SER, precision, recall and F1.

Regarding the machine translation approaches, while results suggest that both architectures are suitable for the task, we observe that LSTM-sampled and LSTM slightly outperform Transformer and Transformer-sampled on SER, precision, recall and F1. Because of training data size and number of parameters, training time was considerably lower for the LSTM architecture with sampled data. Accordingly, we carried out the subsequent experiments using the LSTM model for the machine translation approach.

6.2 Approaches

In order to select the best approach and model to handle ellipsis in this context, we measured the performance of two different models for each approach (cf. section 4), except for machine translation where we already chose LSTM (cf. subsection 6.1).

Table 5 presents the SER, precision, recall and F1 for elliptical and all sentences.

Classification, with CamemBERT, achieves the best scores across all approaches for both ellip-

tical and all sentences. For elliptical sentences only, tf-idf is the second best approach with 0.53, 0.34, 0.32, 0.32 for SER, precision, recall and F1. However, LSTM outperforms tf-idf for all sentences, showing that LSTM is better suited for non-elliptical sentences.

Based on the observation that sentences that were not well classified by CamemBERT were classified correctly by LSTM, we decided to combine LSTM and camemBERT to build a hybrid system. This hybrid achieved 0.23 and 0.50 on elliptical sentences for SER and F1, outperforming the best model by 0.21 and 0.11 for those metrics respectively. For those sentences that the hybrid classifies/translates adequately, 52% are well translated/classified by both models, 20% by LSTM only and the rest by CamemBERT only.

6.3 Ellipsis Training Data

To determine if the inclusion of ellipsis data in the training data affects performance, we selected the three best models based on the results described in the previous section and trained them with the ellipsis corpus described in section 5.3 in addition to the sampled training data. Table 6 shows final results for each model.

Results show that training models with elliptical sentences improves performance in terms of SER, precision, recall and F1. CamemBERT trained

Approach	Model	SER	Precision	Recall	F1
Classification	CamemBERT	0.15/0.08	0.75 /0.84	0.73/0.85	0.73/0.84
Machine Translation	LSTM	0.23/0.15	0.60/0.71	0.57/0.71	0.57/0.70
Hybrid	CamemBert + LSTM	**0.12**/0.06	0.78/0.86	0.77/0.87	0.76/0.86

Table 6: Results on elliptical utterances/all with ellipsis corpus added to training data.

with the additional ellipsis corpus outperforms the one trained with only the sampled data by 0.29, 0.34, 0.34 and 0.34 for each metric respectively.

With the additional ellipsis training data, Hybrid also outperforms the other approaches (88% of elliptical utterances are translated correctly), yet the difference is not as large as with plain training data only (cf. Table 5). We observed that 85% of the elliptical sentences were well classified by both models. 11% of the sentences were classified correctly by CamemBERT and badly by LSTM, and 4% the other way around.

Closer investigation of the 15% of elliptical sentences which were badly classified revealed several cases. Some of the classification errors were due to ambiguous cases where more than one core sentence would be appropriate for a given elliptical utterance. We also observe many cases where the core sentence was very close to the correct one, but more or less generic.

With these results, we confirmed that in this context, training models with ellipsis improves performance in terms of SER, precision, recall and F1.

7   Conclusion

In this study we have applied different approaches to an ellipsis translation task, in the context of a medical speech translator. We have also experimented with different forms of training data generated from the BabelDr SCFG. Results show that under-sampling the training data improves results for all tested approaches. Of all the tested systems, the hybrid approach, combining neural machine translation and classification models is the most successful both in terms of our task specific metric (SER) and in terms of precision/recall/F1. We also observe that the inclusion of ellipsis training data further improves results.

One limitation of this study is the annotation of the test data. Each source variation has been annotated with a single correct core sentence, but this does not reflect the real use case: the purpose of BabelDr is to allow doctors to collect information from the patient, not to translate their exact utterance. Often, even if the core sentence is not an exact match (e.g. ""in the lower part" vs "in the lower part of the abdomen"), in context it still allows the doctor to obtain the required information. In future work, a more task-oriented annotation approach would be interesting.

A further aspect worth investigating is exploring novel architectures to add the context in different ways: train a context aware decoder to correct translations (Voita et al., 2019, for neural machine translation,) or train a dual-source BERT (Correia and Martins, 2019) adding context on the tuning step for sequence classification.

Finally, future work will also include the replication of these experiments with data from real diagnostic interviews and with data from other diagnostic domains.

Acknowledgements

This project is funded by the "Fondation Privée des Hôpitaux Universitaires de Genève".

References

Aho, A. and Ullman, J. (1969). Syntax directed translations and the pushdown assembler. *Journal of Computer and System Sciences*, 3(1):37–56.

Andoni, A. and Indyk, P. (2006). Near-optimal hashing algorithms for approximate nearest neighbor in high dimensions. In *2006 47th Annual IEEE Symposium on Foundations of Computer Science (FOCS'06)*, page 459–468.

Bahdanau, D., Cho, K., and Bengio, Y. (2014). Neural machine translation by jointly learning to align and translate. *3rd International Conference on Learning Representations, ICLR 2015 - San Diego, United States.* arXiv: 1409.0473.

Bawden, R., Sennrich, R., Birch, A., and Haddow, B. (2018). Evaluating discourse phenomena in neural machine translation. In *Proceedings of the 2018 Conference of the North American Chapter of the Association for Computational Linguistics: Human Language Technologies, Volume 1 (Long Papers)*, page 1304–1313. Association for Computational Linguistics.

Bos, J. and Spenader, J. (2011). An annotated corpus for the analysis of vp ellipsis. *Language Resources and Evaluation*, 45(4):463–494.

Bouillon, P., Rayner, E., Starlander, M., and Santaholma, M. E. (2007). Les ellipses dans un système de traduction automatique de la parole. In *Actes de TALN/RECITAL*, pages 53–62. ID: unige:3452.

Chidambaram, M., Yang, Y., Cer, D., Yuan, S., Sung, Y., Strope, B., and Kurzweil, R. (2019). Learning cross-lingual sentence representations via a multi-task dual-encoder model. In *Proceedings of the 4th Workshop on Representation Learning for NLP (RepL4NLP-2019)*, pages 250–259, Florence, Italy. Association for Computational Linguistics.

Correia, G. M. and Martins, A. F. T. (2019). A simple and effective approach to automatic postediting with transfer learning. In *Proceedings of the 57th Annual Meeting of the Association for Computational Linguistics*, pages 3050–3056, Florence, Italy. Association for Computational Linguistics.

Ginzburg, J. and Miller, P. (2018). Ellipsis in head-driven phrase structure grammar. In van Craenenbroeck, J. and Temmerman, T., editors, *The Oxford Handbook of Ellipsis*, page 74–121. The Oxford Handbook of Ellipsis. Oxford University Press.

Haixiang, G., Yijing, L., Shang, J., Mingyun, G., Yuanyue, H., and Bing, G. (2017). Learning from class-imbalanced data: Review of methods and applications. *Expert Systems with Applications*, 73:220–239.

Hamza, A. (2019). *La détection et la traduction automatiques de l'ellipse : enjeux théoriques et pratiques*. PhD thesis, Université de Strasbourg STRASBOURG.

Hardt, D. (1992). An algorithm for VP ellipsis. In *30th Annual Meeting of the Association for Computational Linguistics*, pages 9–14, Newark, Delaware, USA. Association for Computational Linguistics.

Hardt, D. and Rambow, O. (2001). Generation of vp ellipsis: a corpus-based approach. In *Proceedings of the 39th Annual Meeting on Association for Computational Linguistics - ACL '01*, page 290–297. Association for Computational Linguistics.

Hochreiter, S. and Schmidhuber, J. (1997). Long short-term memory. *Neural Comput.*, 9(8):1735–1780.

Joulin, A., Grave, E., Bojanowski, P., and Mikolov, T. (2017). Bag of tricks for efficient text classification. In *Proceedings of the 15th Conference of the European Chapter of the Association for Computational Linguistics: Volume 2, Short Papers*, page 427–431. Association for Computational Linguistics.

Jurafsky, D. and Martin, J. H. (2014). *Speech and language processing*. Always learning. Pearson Education, 2. ed., pearson new internat. ed edition.

Kenyon-Dean, K., Cheung, J. C. K., and Precup, D. (2016). Verb phrase ellipsis resolution using discriminative and margin-infused algorithms. In *Proceedings of the 2016 Conference on Empirical Methods in Natural Language Processing*, page 1734–1743. Association for Computational Linguistics.

Klein, G., Kim, Y., Deng, Y., Senellart, J., and Rush, A. (2017). Opennmt: Open-source toolkit for neural machine translation. In *Proceedings of ACL 2017, System Demonstrations*, page 67–72. Association for Computational Linguistics.

Liu, Y., Ott, M., Goyal, N., Du, J., Joshi, M., Chen, D., Levy, O., Lewis, M., Zettlemoyer, L., and Stoyanov, V. (2019). Roberta: A robustly optimized bert pretraining approach. *arXiv:1907.11692 [cs]*. arXiv: 1907.11692.

Liu, Z., Gonzàlez Pellicer, E., and Gillick, D. (2016). Exploring the steps of verb phrase ellipsis. In *Proceedings of the Workshop on Coreference Resolution Beyond OntoNotes (CORBON 2016)*, page 32–40. Association for Computational Linguistics.

Luong, T., Pham, H., and Manning, C. D. (2015). Effective approaches to attention-based neural machine translation. In *Proceedings of the 2015 Conference on Empirical Methods in Natural Language Processing*, pages 1412–1421, Lisbon, Portugal. Association for Computational Linguistics.

Martin, L., Muller, B., Suárez, P. J. O., Dupont, Y., Romary, L., de la Clergerie, V., Seddah, D., and Sagot, B. (2019). Camembert: a tasty french language model. *arXiv:1911.03894 [cs]*. arXiv: 1911.03894.

Mazurowski, M. A., Habas, P. A., Zurada, J. M., Lo, J. Y., Baker, J. A., and Tourassi, G. D. (2008). Training neural network classifiers for medical decision making: The effects of imbalanced datasets on classification performance. *Neural Networks*, 21(2–3):427–436.

McShane, M. and Babkin, P. (2016). Detection and resolution of verb phrase ellipsis. *Linguistic Issues in Language Technology – LiLT, Volume 13, Issue 1*, page 36.

Mutal, J. D., Bouillon, P., Gerlach, J., Estrella, P., and Spechbach, H. (2019). Monolingual back-translation in a medical speech translation system for diagnostic interviews - a nmt approach. In for Machine Translation, E. A., editor, *Proceedings of Machine Translation Summit XVII Volume 2: Translator, Project and User Tracks*, pages 169–203. ID: unige:123138.

Rayner, E., Gerlach, J., Bouillon, P., Tsourakis, N., and Spechbach, H. (2018). Handling ellipsis in a spoken medical phraselator. In Dutoit T., Martín-Vide C., P. G., editor, *Statistical Language and Speech Processing. SLSP 2018*, pages 140–152. Springer. ID: unige:110589.

Rayner, E., Tsourakis, N., and Gerlach, J. (2017). Lightweight spoken utterance classification with cfg, tf-idf and dynamic programming. In Camelin, N., Estève, Y., and Martín-Vide, C., editors, *Statistical Language and Speech Processing*, page 143–154. Springer International Publishing.

Rønning, O., Hardt, D., and Søgaard, A. (2018). Sluice resolution without hand-crafted features over brittle syntax trees. In *Proceedings of the 2018 Conference of the North American Chapter of the Association for Computational Linguistics: Human Language Technologies, Volume 2 (Short Papers)*, page 236–241. Association for Computational Linguistics.

Salton, G. and Buckley, C. (1988). Term-weighting approaches in automatic text retrieval. *Inf. Process. Manage.*, 24(5):513–523.

Spechbach, H., Gerlach, J., Mazouri Karker, S., Tsourakis, N., Combescure, C., and Bouillon, P. (2019). A speech-enabled fixed-phrase translator for emergency settings: Crossover study. *JMIR Medical Informatics*, 7(2). ID: unige:117081.

Sun, C., Qiu, X., Xu, Y., and Huang, X. (2019). How to fine-tune bert for text classification? In Sun, M., Huang, X., Ji, H., Liu, Z., and Liu, Y., editors, *Chinese Computational Linguistics*, page 194–206. Springer International Publishing.

Tanguy, L., Fabre, C., Ho-Dac, L.-M., and Rebeyrolle, J. (2011). Caractérisation des échanges entre patients et médecins : approche outillée d'un corpus de consultations médicales. *Corpus, 10 |2011*, pages 137–154.

Tiedemann, J. and Scherrer, Y. (2017). Neural machine translation with extended context. In *Proceedings of the Third Workshop on Discourse in Machine Translation*, pages 82–92, Copenhagen, Denmark. Association for Computational Linguistics.

Vaswani, A., Shazeer, N., Parmar, N., Uszkoreit, J., Jones, L., Gomez, A. N., Kaiser, , and Polosukhin, I. (2017). Attention is all you need. In Guyon, I., Luxburg, U. V., Bengio, S., Wallach, H., Fergus, R., Vishwanathan, S., and Garnett, R., editors, *31st Conference on Neural Information Processing Systems (NIPS 2017), Long Beach, CA, USA*, page 5998–6008. Curran Associates, Inc.

Voita, E., Sennrich, R., and Titov, I. (2019). When a good translation is wrong in context: Context-aware machine translation improves on deixis, ellipsis, and lexical cohesion. In *Proceedings of the 57th Annual Meeting of the Association for Computational Linguistics*, pages 1198–1212, Florence, Italy. Association for Computational Linguistics.

Wolf, T., Debut, L., Sanh, V., Chaumond, J., Delangue, C., Moi, A., Cistac, P., Rault, T., Louf, R., Funtowicz, M., and et al. (2020). Huggingface's transformers: State-of-the-art natural language processing. *arXiv:1910.03771 [cs]*. arXiv: 1910.03771.

Xing, Z., Pei, J., and Keogh, E. (2010). A brief survey on sequence classification. *SIGKDD Explor. Newsl.*, 12(1):40–48.

Bifixer and Bicleaner: two open-source tools to clean your parallel data

Gema Ramírez-Sánchez, Jaume Zaragoza-Bernabeu, Marta Bañón, Sergio Ortiz Rojas
Prompsit Language Engineering, S.L.
Campus UMH, Edifici Quorum III
Av. de la Universitat, s/n. 03202. Elx. Spain
{gramirez, jzaragoza, mbanon, sortiz}@prompsit.com

Abstract

This paper shows the utility of two open-source tools designed for parallel data cleaning: Bifixer and Bicleaner. Already used to clean highly noisy parallel content from crawled multilingual websites, we evaluate their performance in a different scenario: cleaning publicly available corpora commonly used to train machine translation systems. We choose four English–Portuguese corpora which we plan to use internally to compute paraphrases at a later stage. We clean the four corpora using both tools, which are described in detail, and analyse the effect of some of the cleaning steps on them. We then compare machine translation training times and quality before and after cleaning these corpora, showing a positive impact particularly for the noisiest ones.

1 Introduction

Parallel corpora are usually the main source of information used to learn machine translation models. The availability of corpora has encouraged the advance of machine translation in both academy and industry settings. Publicly available parallel corpora (Europarl, News Commentary, United Nations, etc.) have been used for decades now, not only to produce machine translation but also other by-products such as dictionaries, concordances, synonyms, paraphrases, etc. In machine translation, due to the ability of statistical models to hide imperfections without statistical significance, filtering out noise from these corpora was not very

important. Now that neural models have superseded statistical ones, we need to be more careful about noise in the input as it has a higher impact on the output, as discussed in (Khayrallah and Koehn, 2018) and (Rikters, 2018).

Inspired by recent work on filtering parallel corpora to maximize the quality of machine translation from the shared tasks organised at WMT18[1] and WMT19[2], we review how noisy some of the most popular or recent publicly available corpora are and how this impacts the quality of the output of state-of-the-art neural machine translation. Our motivation is twofold: getting high-quality monolingual and bilingual data and getting high-quality machine translation for English–Portuguese. We will further use this resources to compute paraphrases in the framework of a research project.

In order to inspect and filter out noise, we use Bifixer and Bicleaner,[3] a couple of publicly available cleaning tools released as part of the ParaCrawl European project.[4] These tools have been mainly used to filter out noise from the raw version of automatically crawled parallel corpora in more than 30 language combinations. Here we use them in a very different scenario: we take already released publicly available corpora, either widely used in the past or recent. We analyse the main problems of the corpora and review the cleaning steps and their impact on the final size of the corpora.

---

[1] http://www.statmt.org/wmt18/
parallel-corpus-filtering.html
[2] http://www.statmt.org/wmt19/
parallel-corpus-filtering.html
[3] Code available at https://github.com/bitextor/
bifixer and https://github.com/bitextor/
bicleaner
[4] See more info and available corpora on https://
paracrawl.eu

Martins, Moniz, Fumega, Martins, Batista, Coheur, Parra, Trancoso, Turchi, Bisazza, Moorkens, Guerberof, Nurminen, Marg, Forcada (eds.)
Proceedings of the 22nd Annual Conference of the European Association for Machine Translation, p. 291–298
Lisboa, Portugal, November 2020.

To evaluate the effect of cleaning, we train neural machine translation systems before and after filtering them and report both performance results and evaluation through automatic metrics. We do so for English and Portuguese in both translation directions as Portuguese is one of the target languages in our research project related to paraphrasing. Our focus for this paper is, though, the evaluation of the cleaning tools intrinsically and extrinsically through machine translation.

The rest of the paper is organised as follows: in section 2 we discuss the cleaning steps applied to the corpora and analyse the type of noise found in them; section 3 describes the MT experiments and reports on the results; finally, section 4 depicts the conclusions and some ideas for future work.

2 Cleaning parallel corpora

Although parallel corpora cleaning has been explored in previous works, the most recent state-of-the-art can be found as part of the findings of the shared tasks on Parallel Corpora Filtering in WMT18 (Koehn et al., 2018) and WMT19 (Koehn et al., 2019). Participants in these shared tasks applied a bunch of techniques looking for high-quality data inside noisy corpora. Most of these techniques are a mixture of pre-filtering rules for obvious noise, scoring functions of all sorts (language models, neural translation models, etc.) and classification to discriminate between high-quality and low-quality sentence pairs. Diverse techniques have been applied to both high-resource and low-resource languages.

The results encourage filtering, especially for high-resource scenarios involving neural machine translation. On the other hand, no clear trend was devised for low-resource scenarios nor for statistical machine translation.

Some of these techniques have been already implemented and evaluated in Bicleaner (Sánchez-Cartagena et al., 2018). Bifixer adds a different way of exploring corpora cleaning: restorative cleaning. With this step, we aim at fixing content and getting unique parallel sentences before filtering out noise.

2.1 Cleaning by restoring

The first step taken for corpora cleaning in the most recent ParaCrawl pipeline is restorative cleaning. It is performed by Bifixer. Currently, the following sub-steps are applied to the sentences of an input parallel corpus:

- **empty side removal**: lines without content in either source or target are removed

- **character fixing**: sentences with encoding issues (Mojibake), HTML entities issues, wrong alphabet characters and space or punctuation issues are fixed

- **orthography fixing**: words with frequent and straightforward typos are rewritten. It is currently available for Danish, German, English, Spanish, Dutch, Norwegian, Portuguese and Turkish

- **re-splitting**: using NLTK[5] on sentences over 15 tokens by default, and taking into account source and target, re-splitting is applied. Only if the number of splits is equal on both sides, the new splitting is kept, otherwise the original one remains.

- **duplicates identification**: a hash identifier is calculated and added to each pair of sentences in order to identify both duplicate and, optionally, near-duplicate (i.e. ignoring casing, accents, diacritics and digits) parallel sentences. A score is calculated in order to decide the best near-duplicate to be chosen. We will apply both duplicate and near-duplicate marking in our experiments. [6]

The rationale behind the steps performed by Bifixer is to have the best possible content for machine translation: fixing encoding or typos will produce a more consistent content; too long sentences by themselves or because they are two glued sentences, are normally discarded from training sets; finally, duplicates and near duplicates are poor content to be given to learning systems.

2.2 Cleaning by filtering

After restorative cleaning, sentence pairs are sent to Bicleaner, a parallel sentence noise filter and classifier tool. Bicleaner was first released in 2018 as part of the ParaCrawl software, and has been used outside the project in several works such as (Morishita et al., 2019), (Defauw et al., 2019) and (Chaudhary et al., 2019). The tool performs the following sub-steps:

---

⁵`https://www.nltk.org/`
[6]Please note that Bifixer will not actually remove the duplicates, it will just mark them. An additional processing needs to be added for removal.

1. **Pre-filtering** based on rules is the first step in Bicleaner. There is a set of 37 rules currently implemented. Some of the rules are language-dependent and use language identification based on CLD2[7] for filtering. While some of them look into one of the sides of the corpus, some others take into account both sides. In general, they filter obvious noise such as sentences with a very different length in source and target. They were designed to target noise from web crawled content but most of the rules apply to any corpus. We do perform an analysis of the most productive rules for different scenarios in subsection 2.3. When a pair of sentences matches a rule in this step, it is set as "0" score, meaning that it should be discarded.

2. **Language model fluency scoring** allows filtering in a more refined way. It is language-dependent and uses a character-based language model. Using characters instead of n-grams reduces the amount of data needed to train the model, although it limits the usage for some languages with very scarce resources or special alphabets. The fluency filter provides a score for each sentence pair against the language model. Only pairs below a set threshold (0.5) are matched to a 0 score for the rest of the pipeline, meaning that they must be discarded. Recently, the fluency filter was integrated as the last pre-filtering rule in the workflow. This step will be disabled for our experiments in this paper as it is mainly intended for very big-sized corpora.

3. **Classification** based on a random-forest machine learning model is the last step. The classifier takes all sentences not marked with a score of 0 from previous steps and classifies them by providing a score between 0 (bad) and 1 (good). The official ParaCrawl released corpora contain only sentences above a score of 0.7. Other studies have reported better machine translation scores using sentences above 0.5. We will explore both thresholds in our experiments.

2.3 Applying cleaning to popular corpora

To better understand the effect of cleaning, we take four corpora from the bunch of publicly available parallel ones in English and Portuguese. Except for WikiMatrix[8], all of them are taken from OPUS:[9]

- Europarl, version 7, (Koehn, 2005): it is a widespread used corpus in machine translation, last released in 2011, containing parallel sentences from the proceedings of the European Parliament. This version for English–Portuguese contains 2.2 million sentences.

- OpenSubtitles 2018, version 6, (Lison and Tiedemann, 2016): this is also a very popular corpus. It comes mostly from volunteers translating subtitles on the net.[10] The last version from 2018 contains more than 33 million parallel sentences for English–Portuguese.

- JW300 (Agic and Vulic, 2019): it is a very recent corpus with only one version released. It was compiled by crawling the `jw.org` website and contains 2.1 million sentences in English–Portuguese.

- WikiMatrix (Schwenk et al., 2019): also recently released, it is an effort to compile translations found in Wikipedia. The corpus in English–Portuguese contains 4.4 million of parallel sentences.

In our setting, Bifixer was used without modifications applying deduplication also for near duplicates.[11] Bicleaner provides pre-trained classifiers for many languages including English–Portuguese,[12] But, in order to avoid misleading results, we trained new models leaving out the corpora that we intend to analyse.[13] Corpora, training times and sizes are compiled in Table 1. Training corpora are all taken from and cleaned with Bifixer and the pre-filtering rules step in Bicleaner before training. The training of Bicleaner models has been run in an Intel Core i9 using 32 cores and the cleaning of corpora has been run in an Intel Core i7 using 8 cores.

---

[7] `https://github.com/CLD2Owners/cld2`

[8] `https://github.com/facebookresearch/LASER/tree/master/tasks/WikiMatrix`
[9] `http://opus.nlpl.eu/`
[10] `http://www.opensubtitles.org/`
[11] Cloned from Github on 17th February 2020
[12] `https://github.com/bitextor/bicleaner-data/releases/tag/v1.3`
[13] To train our special models for Bicleaner, we follow the guidelines in `https://github.com/bitextor/bicleaner/wiki/How-to-train-your-Bicleaner`

After completing the training step, we apply Bifixer and Bicleaner to the selected corpora. Firstly, after Bifixer, we observe that:

- **we get more data**: by mean, 1,1% new sentences are recovered after re-splitting. The impact on size is almost negligible but it will be noticeable in the quality of the final subset of sentences retained.

- **we keep only unique data**: by mean, 9.8% duplicates or near-duplicates are removed. The biggest impact can be seen in OpenSubtitles (8.1 million sentences representing 24.5% of the whole corpus are removed). It is also noticeable in JW300 where more than 10% is removed at this step.

- **we get a better output**: by mean, 4.6% of the sentences have been fixed (typos, encoding, HTML entities, trailing spaces, etc.) as described in section 2.1.

Secondly, from Bicleaner pre-filtering rules[14] we observe that:

- **most of the content is still retained after pre-filtering rules**: by mean, 85.7% goes to the classifier step. It drops down to 67.7% for OpenSubtitles and is as high as 96.3% for Europarl.

- **none of the corpora matches all the 37 pre-filtering rules**: WikiMatrix matches 35, OpenSubtitles matches 33, Europarl 28 and JW300 only 25.

- **the main source of noise is equivalent across corpora**: it comes from sentences with language identification issues (both source and target are in the same language, the identified languages are not reliable), length issues (unusual length ratio between source and target, sentences have just 1 or 2 tokens in both sides) or quality issues (sentences contain mainly non-alphabetic characters).

It is worth comparing this analysis to the one obtained from ParaCrawl raw files. The raw files contain preliminary and very noisy candidate parallel sentences from crawled websites. For English–Portuguese, version 5 of the raw corpus,[15] a significantly smaller portion is retained after pre-filtering rules compared to our current scenario: only 27.2% of the raw corpus goes to the classifier step. The main reasons why sentences are removed are, though, very similar to the ones applying to the corpora in this paper. From all the 37 rules matched:

- 25.8% is removed by rules matching length issues: very short sentences (only 1 or 2 tokens on both sides) from web crawled content are often badly aligned and of poor quality. On the other side, very long ones (more than 1024 bytes) are often problematic. Too odd length ratios are the cause of the removal of 9,7% of the content.

- 19.5% is removed by rules matching language identification or encoding issues: same language on both sides, languages unreliably identified and characters out of the range of Unicode char sets

- 15.2% is removed by rules matching quality issues: sentences are mainly symbols or URLs, upper and lowercase distribution is odd on either side, match code-like patterns, contain poor language, etc.

- additionally, 9.3% is removed because source and target are identical or just differ in numbers and punctuation

For our four corpora, the last step is scoring with Bicleaner classifier. After classification, we filter sentence pairs below a couple of thresholds: 0.5 and 0.7. For the most aggressive threshold, 0.7, we remove by mean 22.9% of the corpora, being WikiMatrix the most impacted corpus by this step, with a 37.3% of discarded sentences, followed by OpenSubtitles (32.5%). With the threshold set to 0.5, the removal drops to a mean of 10.9%. In this scenario, WikiMatrix loses 21.1% of the corpus, followed by OpenSubtitles (15.5%).

In all (see table 2), for the most aggressive cleaning, the 0.7 classifier score scenario, we observe that the initial sizes of the corpora are reduced by a mean of 37.2% after applying Bifixer and Bicleaner. OpenSubtitles is the corpus with

---

[14]We disable the fluency filter for our experiments, as it is mainly intended for very big-sized corpora.

[15]www.paracrawl.eu/releases

the biggest percentage of removals which represents 64.8% of the total. The classifier step is the most frequent reason for discarding sentences. Europarl is the corpus with the smallest percentage of removals, only 12.5% of the corpus is lost during cleaning.

2.4 Quick evaluation of cleaned data

After cleaning, we sample 100 random sentences from each corpus and manually annotate them with KEOPS,[16] an open-source tool which provides a framework for manual evaluation of parallel sentences. KEOPS was also released as part of the ParaCrawl project. Error annotation is done following the European Language Resource Coordination (ELRC) validation guidelines. [17] We annotate each sentence pair as Valid or as containing one of the following 7 errors: Wrong Language Identification, Wrong Alignment, Wrong Tokenization, Machine Translation, Translation Error or Free translation.

From manual annotation, we get the following insight:

- in Europarl only 2 sentences out of 100 present issues with sentence splitting either in source or in target.

- in JW300 we discover an issue with the original tokenization: hyphens and quotes are separated from the words they belong to (e.g. `lembra - se "` instead of `lembra-se"` in Portuguese). Ignoring those, only 2 sentences are badly split, 2 contain translation errors and 3 are too free translations.

- in OpenSubtitles, 11 sentences out of 100 present issues: 5 are badly tokenized, 2 are clearly bad machine translations and 4 are too free translations.

- in WikiMatrix, 30 sentences out of 100 present issues: 7 are miss-aligned, 4 are badly tokenized, 5 contain bad machine translation, 10 contain translation errors and 4 are too free translations.

These results show room for improvement for the cleaning tools that will be taken into account

as future work. They also give an idea of the characteristics of the corpus, a valuable piece of information to keep in mind when selecting corpora for a number of natural language processing tasks.

3 Evaluation through machine translation

In order to evaluate the impact of cleaning, we train neural machine translation systems before and after cleaning for each of the four corpora inspected. This allows us to see if better and reduced versions of the corpora produce a better machine translation output. We measure the impact of cleaning in the output by using automatic metrics. We also measure training times to see if size reduction and a more consistent content leads to a more efficient training process.

Machine translation systems are trained on each corpus before and after cleaning, for both translation directions and for both 0.7 and 0.5 Bicleaner thresholds. We train Transformer-base models with 32,000 vocabulary using Marian (Junczys-Dowmunt et al., 2018) and SentencePiece. We use development and test sets from TED Talks proposed by (Ye et al., 2018) and report BLEU scores computed with sacreBLEU[18]. Results for BLEU scores for all the 24 systems are reported in table 3 while training times are shown in table 4.

From the results, we can see that cleaning has a positive impact on all the corpora, both in speeding up training times and in slightly improving BLEU scores for almost all corpora and translation directions: only Europarl, English-Portuguese, just stays the same. Thus, no degradation is introduced with corpora size reduction, but rather the opposite: the most aggressive cleaning (0.7) scenario, leading to the smallest corpora sizes, gets consistently better BLEU scores for all the experiments. This scenario leads also to the best training times in most cases. Indeed, the highest improvements in BLEU scores (from +1 to +2.2 absolute BLEU points) are obtained when 22M sentences (two-thirds of the corpus) are filtered out from Open-Subtitles.

4 Conclusions

We have applied Bifixer and Bicleaner, two open-source tools built inside the ParaCrawl project, to

---

[18]Signature:
`BLEU+case.mixed+lang.pt-en+numrefs.1`
`+smooth.exp+tok.13a+version.1.4.2`

clean four publicly available parallel corpora for English–Portuguese. After a review of the tools and the cleaning steps performed to the four corpora, we evaluate the output of neural machine translation before and after cleaning them to see their impact.

Cleaning reduces the size of the corpora. For some of them (Europarl, JW300), the reduction is low but for others, cleaning removes half of the corpus (WikiMatrix) or up to two thirds (OpenSubtitles).

Cleaned corpora, in the most aggressive cleaning scenario (Bicleaner scores above 0.7), lead consistently to equal or slightly better results for BLEU scores in machine translation, not degrading the results in any case and speeding up machine translation training times.

At bigger scale (more languages, bigger sizes for all corpora together) all this could result in remarkable savings of disk space and training times without compromising machine translation quality and producing higher-quality corpora.

Both tools can be currently used without any further effort for more than 30 language combinations and prove to be a cheap and effective step before using parallel corpora for machine translation or other natural language processing tasks. For non-supported languages, Bifixer will only require a list of monolingual safe replacements for typos. Bicleaner, though, will require training resources and time, although much less than other methods.

From a closer look, we observe that, for less noisy corpora as Europarl, some of the Bicleaner pre-filtering rules are too severe and could probably be relaxed. In particular, the removal of too short sentences should be further inspected for already high-quality data.

As further work, although Bifixer and Bicleaner have been used for many other languages inside the ParaCrawl project, it would be interesting to validate the results obtained in this paper for other language combinations and corpora.

Outside machine translation, we believe that cleaning is also good for other tasks such as improving sentence alignment or paraphrase extraction. Both, and specially paraphrase extraction, will be explored as further work as part of a research project that will use the results of this paper as best practices to pre-process corpora.

Acknowledgment

Work supported by project ParaCrawl, actions number 2017-EU-IA-0178 and 2018-EU-IA-0063, funded under the Automated Translation CEF Telecom instrument managed by INEA at the European Commission. Also supported by the Spanish research program *Impulso a las Tecnologías habilitadoras digitales*, action number TS1-100905-2019-4 from the Secretary of State for Digitalisation and Artificial Intelligence currently under the Ministry of Economic Affairs and Digital Transformation. We thank Carmen Iniesta López for her valuable feedback and suggestions.

References

Agic, Zeljko and Ivan Vulic. 2019. Jw300: A wide-coverage parallel corpus for low-resource languages. In Korhonen, Anna, David R. Traum, and Lluís Màrquez, editors, *ACL (1)*, pages 3204–3210. Association for Computational Linguistics.

Chaudhary, Vishrav, Yuqing Tang, Francisco Guzmán, Holger Schwenk, and Philipp Koehn. 2019. Low-resource corpus filtering using multilingual sentence embeddings. In *Proceedings of the Fourth Conference on Machine Translation (Volume 3: Shared Task Papers, Day 2)*, pages 261–266, Florence, Italy, August. Association for Computational Linguistics.

Defauw, Arne, Tom Vanallemeersch, Sara Szoc, Frederic Everaert, Koen Van Winckel, Kim Scholte, Joris Brabers, and Joachim Van den Bogaert. 2019. Collecting domain specific data for mt: an evaluation of the paracrawl pipeline. In *Proceedings of Machine Translation Summit XVII Volume 2: Translator, Project and User Tracks*, pages 186–195.

Junczys-Dowmunt, Marcin, Roman Grundkiewicz, Tomasz Dwojak, Hieu Hoang, Kenneth Heafield, Tom Neckermann, Frank Seide, Ulrich Germann, Alham Fikri Aji, Nikolay Bogoychev, André F. T. Martins, and Alexandra Birch. 2018. Marian: Fast neural machine translation in C++. In *Proceedings of ACL 2018, System Demonstrations*, pages 116–121, Melbourne, Australia, July. Association for Computational Linguistics.

Khayrallah, Huda and Philipp Koehn. 2018. On the impact of various types of noise on neural machine translation. In *Proceedings of the Second Workshop on Neural Machine Translation and Generation*, Melbourne. Association for Computational Linguistics.

Koehn, Philipp, Huda Khayrallah, Kenneth Heafield, and Mikel L. Forcada. 2018. Findings of the WMT 2018 shared task on parallel corpus filtering. In *Proceedings of the Third Conference on Machine Translation: Shared Task Papers*, Belgium, Brussels, October. Association for Computational Linguistics.

Koehn, Philipp, Francisco Guzmán, Vishrav Chaudhary, and Juan Pino. 2019. Findings of the WMT 2019 shared task on parallel corpus filtering for low-resource conditions. In *Proceedings of the Fourth Conference on Machine Translation, WMT 2019, Florence, Italy, August 1-2, 2019 - Volume 3: Shared Task Papers, Day 2*, pages 54–72. Association for Computational Linguistics.

Koehn, Philipp. 2005. Europarl: A Parallel Corpus for Statistical Machine Translation. In *Conference Proceedings: the tenth Machine Translation Summit*, pages 79–86, Phuket, Thailand. AAMT, AAMT.

Lison, Pierre and Jörg Tiedemann. 2016. Opensubtitles2016: Extracting large parallel corpora from movie and tv subtitles. In Calzolari, Nicoletta, Khalid Choukri, Thierry Declerck, Sara Goggi, Marko Grobelnik, Bente Maegaard, Joseph Mariani, Hélène Mazo, Asunción Moreno, Jan Odijk, and Stelios Piperidis, editors, *LREC*. European Language Resources Association (ELRA).

Morishita, Makoto, Jun Suzuki, and Masaaki Nagata. 2019. Jparacrawl: A large scale web-based english-japanese parallel corpus. *arXiv preprint arXiv:1911.10668*.

Rikters, Matīss. 2018. Impact of Corpora Quality on Neural Machine Translation. In *In Proceedings of the 8th Conference Human Language Technologies - The Baltic Perspective (Baltic HLT 2018)*, Tartu, Estonia.

Sánchez-Cartagena, Víctor M., Marta Bañón, Sergio Ortiz-Rojas, and Gema Ramírez-Sánchez. 2018. Prompsit's submission to WMT 2018 Parallel Corpus Filtering shared task. In *Proceedings of the Third Conference on Machine Translation, Volume 2: Shared Task Papers*, Brussels, Belgium, October. Association for Computational Linguistics.

Schwenk, Holger, Vishrav Chaudhary, Shuo Sun, Hongyu Gong, and Francisco Guzmán. 2019. Wikimatrix: Mining 135m parallel sentences in 1620 language pairs from wikipedia. *CoRR*, abs/1907.05791.

Ye, Qi, Sachan Devendra, Felix Matthieu, Padmanabhan Sarguna, and Neubig Graham. 2018. When and why are pre-trained word embeddings useful for neural machine translation. In *HLT-NAACL*.

Bicleaner	Corpora	Subset (#sentences)		Time
Training: probabilistic dictionaries	**DGT**	3.5M	10M	10h
	EuBookshop	3.5M		
	JRC	1M		
	Capes	1M		
	Tilde	1M		
Training: classifier model	**SCielo**	50k	100k	10'
	NewsCommentary	25k		
	Global Voices	25k		
Cleaning: pre-filtering and classifying	**Europarl**	2.2M		20'
	JW300	2.1M		20'
	WikiMatrix	4.4M		46'
	OpenSubtitles	33.2M		112'

Table 1: Corpora, sizes, training and cleaning times for Bicleaner.

<table>
<tr><td rowspan="2"></td><td rowspan="2"></td><td rowspan="2"></td><td colspan="2">Europarl</td><td colspan="2">JW300</td><td colspan="2">WikiMatrix</td><td colspan="2">OpenSubtitles</td></tr>
<tr><td># sent</td><td>%</td><td># sent</td><td>%</td><td># sent</td><td>%</td><td># sent</td><td>%</td></tr>
<tr><td></td><td>Original</td><td></td><td>2,002,943</td><td>100</td><td>2,102,425</td><td>100</td><td>4,458,124</td><td>100</td><td>33,222,606</td><td>100</td></tr>
<tr><td rowspan="7">Bicleaner / Bifixer</td><td>Re-split</td><td></td><td>+17,648</td><td>+0.8</td><td>+55,874</td><td>+2.6</td><td>+39,670</td><td>+0.8</td><td>+9,951</td><td>+0.03</td></tr>
<tr><td>Dedup</td><td></td><td>-65,728</td><td>-3.2</td><td>-228,043</td><td>-10.8</td><td>-32,151</td><td>-0.7</td><td>-8,157,302</td><td>-24.5</td></tr>
<tr><td>Pre-filter</td><td></td><td>-25,755</td><td>-1.2</td><td>-91,659</td><td>-4.3</td><td>-392,648</td><td>-8.8</td><td>-2,594,724</td><td>-7.8</td></tr>
<tr><td rowspan="2">Classify</td><td>0.5</td><td>-40,814</td><td>-2.0</td><td>-105,385</td><td>-5.0</td><td>-941,887</td><td>-21.1</td><td>-5,151,005</td><td>-15.5</td></tr>
<tr><td>0.7</td><td>-177,825</td><td>-8.8</td><td>-275,696</td><td>-13.1</td><td>-1,666,923</td><td>-37.3</td><td>-10,814,463</td><td>-32.5</td></tr>
<tr><td></td></tr>
<tr></tr>
<tr><td rowspan="2">Total</td><td>0.5</td><td>-114,649</td><td>-5.7</td><td>-369,213</td><td>-17.5</td><td>-1,327,016</td><td>-29.7</td><td>-15,893,080</td><td>-47.8</td></tr>
<tr><td>0.7</td><td>-251,660</td><td>-12.5</td><td>-539,524</td><td>-25.6</td><td>-2,052,052</td><td>-46.0</td><td>-21,556,538</td><td>-64.8</td></tr>
<tr><td rowspan="2">Final</td><td>0.5</td><td>1,888,294</td><td>94.2</td><td>1,733,212</td><td>82.4</td><td>3,131,108</td><td>70.2</td><td>17,329,526</td><td>52.16</td></tr>
<tr><td>0.7</td><td>1,751,283</td><td>87.4</td><td>1,562,901</td><td>74.3</td><td>2,406,072,00</td><td>53.9</td><td>11,666,068</td><td>35.1</td></tr>
</table>

Table 2: Number of sentences added (+) or removed (-) after each cleaning step.

<table>
<tr><td rowspan="3"></td><td rowspan="3"></td><td colspan="3">Europarl</td><td colspan="3">JW300</td><td colspan="3">WikiMatrix</td><td colspan="3">OpenSubtitles</td></tr>
<tr><td rowspan="2">size</td><td colspan="2">BLEU score</td><td rowspan="2">size</td><td colspan="2">BLEU score</td><td rowspan="2">size</td><td colspan="2">BLEU score</td><td rowspan="2">size</td><td colspan="2">BLEU score</td></tr>
<tr><td>en–pt</td><td>pt–en</td><td>en–pt</td><td>pt–en</td><td>en–pt</td><td>pt–en</td><td>en–pt</td><td>pt–en</td></tr>
<tr><td colspan="2">Before cleaning</td><td>2.2</td><td>**26.2**</td><td>31.5</td><td>2.1</td><td>29.0</td><td>34.1</td><td>4.4</td><td>35.8</td><td>36.8</td><td>33.2</td><td>31.2</td><td>37.9</td></tr>
<tr><td rowspan="2">After cleaning</td><td>0.5</td><td>1.8</td><td>26.0</td><td>31.5</td><td>1.7</td><td>29.1</td><td>34.2</td><td>3.1</td><td>36.2</td><td>36.8</td><td>17.3</td><td>31.9</td><td>39.5</td></tr>
<tr><td>0.7</td><td>1.7</td><td>**26.2**</td><td>**31.7**</td><td>1.5</td><td>**29.4**</td><td>**34.4**</td><td>2.4</td><td>**36.3**</td><td>**37.0**</td><td>11.6</td><td>**32.2**</td><td>**40.1**</td></tr>
</table>

Table 3: BLEU scores for all NMT systems trained after and before cleaning in both translation directions and for two different Bicleaner classifier thresholds. Sizes of corpora are provided. Best NMT systems are shown in bold.

<table>
<tr><td rowspan="3"></td><td rowspan="3"></td><td colspan="3">Europarl</td><td colspan="3">JW300</td><td colspan="3">WikiMatrix</td><td colspan="3">OpenSubtitles</td></tr>
<tr><td rowspan="2">size</td><td colspan="2">training time</td><td rowspan="2">size</td><td colspan="2">training time</td><td rowspan="2">size</td><td colspan="2">training time</td><td rowspan="2">size</td><td colspan="2">training time</td></tr>
<tr><td>en–pt</td><td>pt–en</td><td>en–pt</td><td>pt–en</td><td>en–pt</td><td>pt–en</td><td>en–pt</td><td>pt–en</td></tr>
<tr><td colspan="2">Before cleaning</td><td>2.2</td><td>21.6</td><td>20.4</td><td>2.1</td><td>18.4</td><td>17.7</td><td>4.4</td><td>28.4</td><td>36.2</td><td>33.2</td><td>54.7</td><td>44.1</td></tr>
<tr><td rowspan="2">After cleaning</td><td>0.5</td><td>1.8</td><td>20.5</td><td>**18.7**</td><td>1.7</td><td>16.2</td><td>**18.4**</td><td>3.1</td><td>29.3</td><td>29.5</td><td>17.3</td><td>25.9</td><td>**33.3**</td></tr>
<tr><td>0.7</td><td>1.7</td><td>**18.8**</td><td>21.6</td><td>1.5</td><td>**13.3**</td><td>**18.4**</td><td>2.4</td><td>**23.9**</td><td>**26.8**</td><td>11.6</td><td>**22.1**</td><td>33.4</td></tr>
</table>

Table 4: Training times in hours for all the NMT systems. Sizes of corpora are provided. Best training times are shown in bold.

An English–Swahili parallel corpus and its use for neural machine translation in the news domain

Felipe Sánchez-Martínez,[‡] Víctor M. Sánchez-Cartagena,[‡] Juan Antonio Pérez-Ortiz,[‡] Mikel L. Forcada,[‡] Miquel Esplà-Gomis,[‡] Andrew Secker,[†] Susie Coleman,[†] Julie Wall[†]

‡Dep. de Llenguatges i Sistemes Informàtics, Universitat d'Alacant
E-03690 Sant Vicent del Raspeig (Spain)
{fsanchez, vmsanchez, japerez, mlf, mespla}@dlsi.ua.es

†The British Broadcasting Corporation
BBC Broadcasting House, Portland Place, London, W1A 1AA. (UK)
{andrew.secker, susie.coleman, julie.wall}@bbc.co.uk

Abstract

This paper describes our approach to create a neural machine translation system to translate between English and Swahili (both directions) in the news domain, as well as the process we followed to crawl the necessary parallel corpora from the Internet. We report the results of a pilot human evaluation performed by the news media organisations participating in the H2020 EU-funded project GoURMET.

1 Introduction

Large news media organisations often work in a multilingual space in which they both publish their material in numerous languages and monitor the world's media across video, audio, printed and on-line sources. As regards *content creation*, one way in which efficient use is made of journalistic endeavour is the republication of news originally authored in one language into another; by using machine translation, and with the appropriate user interfaces, a journalist is able to take a news story or script, in the case of an audio or video report, and quickly obtain a preliminary translation that will be then manually post-edited to ensure it has the quality required to be presented to the audience. Concerning *news gathering*, expert monitors and journalists have to currently perform a lot of manual work to keep up with a growing amount of broadcast and social media streams of data; it is becoming imperative to automate tasks, such as translation, in order to free monitors and journalists to perform more journalistic tasks that cannot be achieved with technology.

In order to cope with these requirements, promoting both the reach of the news published to underserved audiences and the world-wide broadcasting of local information, the H2020 EU-funded project GoURMET (Global Under-Resourced Media Translation),[1] aims at improving neural machine translation (NMT) for under-resourced language pairs with special emphasis in the news domain. The two partner media organisations in the GoURMET project, the BBC in the UK and Deutsche Welle (DW) in Germany, publish news content in 40 and 30 different languages, respectively, and gather news in over 100 languages. In particular, both media partners gather news in and produce content in Swahili.

According to Wikipedia, Swahili has between 2 and 15 million first-language speakers and 90 million second-language speakers. As one of the largest languages in Africa and the recognised *lingua franca* of the East African community, BBC and DW see Swahili as an important language in which to make content available. The NMT systems described and evaluated herein can be deployed to support them in this domain specific context.

The rest of the paper is organised as follows. Next section describes the corpora we used to train our English–Swahili NMT systems in both translation directions. Section 3 then describes the crawling of the additional corpora we used and made publicly available. Section 4 describes the main linguistic contrasts between English and Swahili and the challenges they pose for building MT systems between them. Section 5 describes the resources, other than corpora, that we used to build our own systems and the technical details of the training of the NMT systems. Section 6 discussed the results of

---

[1]https://gourmet-project.eu/

Martins, Moniz, Fumega, Martins, Batista, Coheur, Parra, Trancoso, Turchi, Bisazza, Moorkens, Guerberof, Nurminen, Marg, Forcada (eds.)
Proceedings of the 22nd Annual Conference of the European Association for Machine Translation, p. 299–308
Lisboa, Portugal, November 2020.

Corpus	Sent's	en tokens	sw tokens
GoURMET v1	156 061	3 334 886	2 981 699
SAWA	272 544	1 553 004	1 206 757
Tanzil v1	138 253	2 376 908	1 734 247
GV v2017q3	29 698	534 270	546 107
GV v2015	26 033	467 353	476 478
Ubuntu v14.10	986	2 486	2 655
EUbookshop v2	17	191	228
GNOME v1	40	168	170
total	623 632	8 269 266	6 948 341

Table 1: Parallel English–Swahili corpora used to train the NMT systems described in this work. *GV* stands for the GlobalVoices corpus.

Corpus	Sent's	Tokens
NewsCrawl (en)	18 113 311	359 823 264
NewsCrawl (sw)	174 425	3 603 035
GoURMET (sw)	5 687 000	174 867 482

Table 2: Monolingual Swahili and English corpora used to build synthetic parallel data through back-translation.

automatic evaluation measures, describes a manual evaluation we are conducting and provides preliminary results. The paper ends with some concluding remarks.

2 Monolingual and bilingual corpora

Parallel data is the basic resource required to train NMT. Additionally, it is common practice to use synthetic parallel corpora obtained by back-translating monolingual data (Sennrich et al., 2016b). This section describes the corpora we used to train the NMT systems described in Section 5.

Tables 1 and 2 describe the parallel and monolingual corpora we used, respectively. As regards parallel corpora, with the exception of GoURMET and SAWA, all of them were downloaded from the OPUS website,[2] one of the largest repositories of parallel data on the Internet.[3] We used two additional parallel corpora: the SAWA corpus (De Pauw et al., 2011), that was kindly provided by their editors, and the GoURMET corpus, that was crawled from the web following the method described in Section 3.

As regards monolingual data, only three corpora were used: the NewsCrawl (Bojar et al., 2018) for English (en) and for Swahili (sw),[4] and the GoURMET monolingual corpus for sw. The first two corpora were chosen because they belong to the news domain, the same domain of application of our NMT systems. Given that the size of the sw monolingual corpus is much smaller than the size of the en monolingual corpus, additional monolingual data in sw was obtained as a by-product of the process of crawling parallel data from the web.

3 Crawling of additional corpora

The amount of data for en–sw is clearly low, even if one compares it to the amount of data available for other under-resourced language pairs, such as English–Maltese or English–Icelandic.[5] For this reason, a new corpus was crawled from the Internet (see the GoURMET corpus in Table 1). This corpus has been made publicly available.[6]

The GoURMET corpus was obtained by using Bitextor (Esplà-Gomis and Forcada, 2010; Esplà-Gomis et al., 2019), a free open/source software that allows to identify parallel content on multilingual websites. Bitextor is organised as a pipeline that performs a sequence of steps to obtain parallel data from a list of URLs; for each of these steps, Bitextor supports different approaches that require different resources. In this section, the specific configuration of Bitextor for this work is described, as well as the resulting corpora crawled from the Web.

Crawling. Crawling is the first step of the pipeline implemented in Bitextor and consists of downloading any document containing text from the websites specified by the user. We used wget[7] to crawl documents from 3 751 websites;[8] these websites were obtained by leveraging automatic-language-identification metadata from the CommonCrawl corpus:[9] we consider those websites with at least 5 kB of text in en and in sw.

Every website was crawled during a period of 12 hours and only documents in en or sw were kept; CLD2[10] was used for automatic language identification. Plain text was extracted from HTML/XML and, after this, sentence splitting was applied to every document. From the collection of 3 751 preselected websites, 519 were not available at the time

---

[2] http://opus.nlpl.eu/

[3] Table 1 contains the parallel corpora available at OPUS at the time of training our systems. New corpora have been added recently, such as the large JW300 corpus (Agić and Vulić, 2019), which we did not use.

[4] http://data.statmt.org/news-crawl/sw/

[5] For example, in OPUS one can find about 3M sentence pairs for English–Icelandic and 7.6M sentence pairs for English–Maltese, whereas only 1.2M are available for en–sw.

[6] http://data.statmt.org/gourmet/corpora/ GoURMET-crawled.en-sw.zip

[7] https://www.gnu.org/software/wget/

[8] The list of crawled websites can be found in the hosts.gz file accompanying the corpus.

[9] https://commoncrawl.github.io/ cc-crawl-statistics/plots/languages

[10] https://github.com/CLD2Owners/cld2

of crawling and, from the remaining 3 232, only 908 ended up containing data in both languages.

Document alignment. In this step, documents that are likely to contain parallel data are identified. Bitextor supports two strategies for document alignment: one based on bilingual lexicons and another based on MT. The last option was not feasible in this work as no high-quality MT system between sw and en was available; therefore, the first one was used. This method combines information from bilingual lexicons, the HTML structure of the documents, and the URL to obtain a confidence score for every pair of documents to be aligned (Esplà-Gomis and Forcada, 2010). The bilingual lexicon used was automatically obtained from the word alignments obtained with mgiza++ (Gao and Vogel, 2008) for the following corpora: EUBookshop v2, Ubuntu and Tanzil (see Table 1). A total of 180 520 pairs of documents were obtained by using this method.

Sentence alignment. In this step, aligned documents are segmented and aligned at the sentence level. Two sentence-alignment tools are supported by Bitextor: Hunalign (Varga et al., 2007) and BLEUalign (Sennrich and Volk, 2010). We used Hunalign because BLEUalign requires an MT system to be available. The same bilingual dictionary used for document alignment was provided to Hunalign in order to improve the accuracy of the alignment. After applying Hunalign, 2 051 678 unique segment pairs were obtained.

Cleaning. Bicleaner[11] (Sánchez-Cartagena et al., 2018) was used to clean the raw corpora obtained after sentence alignment. Cleaning implies removing the noisy sentence pairs that are either incorrectly aligned or not in the expected languages.[12] Bicleaner cleaning models require some language-dependent resources:

- Two probabilistic bilingual dictionaries, one for each direction for the language pair, built from the corpora used to build the bilingual lexica for document alignment.

- A parallel (ideally clean) corpus to train the regressor used to score the segment pairs in the raw corpus: the preexisting GlobalVoices v2015 parallel corpus was used, as Bicleaner

requires parallel data used to train the dictionaries and the regressor to be different.

- A collection of pairs of segments that are wrongly aligned to train a language model: following Bicleaner's documentation, this collection was obtained from the raw parallel corpus by applying the "hard rules" implemented in Bicleaner.

Bicleaner was used to score all the sentence pairs in the raw corpus with two different scores: one coming from the regressor, which may be interpreted as the probability that the pair of sentences are parallel, and one coming from the language model, which is the probability that one of the sentences in the pair is malformed. After sampling a small fraction of the corpus, the score thresholds were set to 0.68 and 0.5, respectively. The resulting parallel corpus consisted of 156 061 pairs of segments.

In addition to the parallel corpus obtained after cleaning, a large amount of Swahili monolingual data was obtained as a by-product of crawling and released as a monolingual corpus. Monolingual data cleaning consisted of discarding those sentences not deemed fluent enough to be used for NMT training. Sentences were ranked by perplexity computed by a character-based 7-gram language model and only the 6 million sentences with the lowest perplexity were kept. The language model was trained[13] on the concatenation of the sw side of the parallel corpora listed in Table 1, excluding GoURMET. Moreover, those sentences that were automatically identified not to be in sw,[14] or contained more numeric or punctuation characters than alphabetic characters were also discarded.

4 Contrasts and challenges for MT

Swahili belongs to a very large African language family, the Niger–Congo family, and more specifically to the Bantu group. Swahili is currently written in the Latin script, with no diacritics; the apostrophe is used in the seldom-occurring combination *ng'* which represents the sound of *ng* in *singer* (not *finger*); one common example is *ng'ombe*, ('cow').

Swahili is morphologically and syntactically quite different from English, in spite of the fact that both are subject–verb–object languages. Swahili verb morphology is rich and agglutinative, and a

---

[11]https://github.com/bitextor/bicleaner/
[12]This additional language checking is required as document-level language identification may be too general and small fragments in other languages can be included in the sentence-aligned corpus.

[13]The language model was trained with KenLM (Heafield, 2011) with modified Kneser-Ney smoothing (Ney et al., 1994).
[14]Automatic language identification was carried out by using CLD3: https://github.com/google/cld3

large number of morphologically-marked nominal genders participate in nominal and verbal agreement. Table 3 provides a summary of the main linguistic contrasts between en and sw; some examples are from Perrott (1965) and the table is mostly based on `https://wals.info`.

The challenges to build an MT system for news translation between en and sw are twofold. On the one hand, parallel corpora are rather scarce. On the other hand, a number of challenges stem from the linguistic divergences between the two languages:

- The absence of definite and indefinite articles in sw may make the generation of grammatical en tricky.
- Genders in sw do not mark sex (in fact, all nouns designating people are in the same gender or class); generating the correct en 3rd-person pronouns and possessives may be challenging.
- When translating into sw, the presence of many noun classes and their agreement inside noun phrases and with verbal affixes may be an important obstacle.
- Swahili interrogatives have to be reordered when translating to en.
- Fortunately, most word-order differences seem to occur locally (basically inside the noun phrase). This may only be a problem for longer noun phrases.

5 Neural machine translation model

This section describes the steps followed to build en→sw and sw→en NMT systems from the corpora described in Section 2. We firstly describe corpora preprocessing and give details about the NMT architecture used and the process followed to choose it. Secondly, we present the strategies followed in order to take advantage of monolingual corpora and to integrate linguistic information into the NMT systems.

5.1 Corpus preparation

In order to properly train NMT systems, we need a development corpus to help the training algorithm decide when to finish, and a test corpus that allows us to estimate the quality of the systems.

We obtained both of them from the GlobalVoices parallel corpus. We randomly selected 4 000 parallel sentences from the concatenation of GlobalVoices-v2015 and GlobalVoices-v2017q3, and split them into two halves (with 2 000 sentences

each), which were used respectively as development and test corpora. The half reserved to be used as test corpus was further filtered to remove the sentences that could be found in any of the monolingual corpora.

The remaining sentences from GlobalVoices-v2015 and GlobalVoices-v2017q3, together with the other parallel corpora listed in Table 1 were de-duplicated to obtain the final parallel corpus used to train the NMT systems.

All corpora were tokenised with the Moses tokeniser (Koehn et al., 2007) and truecased. Parallel sentences with more than 100 tokens in either side were removed. Words were split in sub-word units with byte pair encoding (BPE; Sennrich et al. (2016c)). Table 4 reports the size of the corpora after this pre-processing.

5.2 Neural machine translation architecture

We trained the NMT models with the Marian toolkit (Junczys-Dowmunt et al., 2018). Since training hyper-parameters can have a large impact in the quality of the resulting system (Lim et al., 2018), we carried out a grid search in order to find the best hyper-parameters for each translation direction. We explored both the Transformer (Vaswani et al., 2017) and recurrent neural network (RNN) with attention (Bahdanau et al., 2014) architectures. Our starting points were the Transformer hyper-parameters[15] described by Sennrich et al. (2017) and the RNN hyper-parameters[16] described by Sennrich et al. (2016a).

For each translation direction and architecture, we explored the following hyper-parameters:

- Number of BPE operations: 15 000, 30 000, or 85 000.
- Batch size: 8 000 tokens (trained on one GPU) or 16 000 tokens (trained on two GPUs).
- Whether to tie the embeddings for both languages (Press and Wolf, 2017)

We trained a system for each combination of hyper-parameters, using only the parallel data described above. Early stopping was based on perplexity on the development set and patience was set to 5. We selected the checkpoint that obtained the

---

[15]`https://github.com/marian-nmt/marian-examples/tree/master/wmt2017-transformer`
[16]`https://github.com/marian-nmt/marian-examples/tree/master/training-basics`

Feature	Value in English	Value in Swahili	Examples
Coding of plurality in nouns	Plural suffix	Plural prefix	*kichwa* ('head'), *vichwa* ('heads'); *jicho* ('eye'), *macho* ('eyes')
Number of categories encoded in a single-word verb	Few (number, person, tense)	Many ("STROVE", that is, number and person of subject, tense, aspect and mood, optional relatives, number and person of object, verb root, and optional extensions)	*nimekinunua kitabu* 'I have bought the book', where: *ni* 'I', subject; *me*, present perfect; *ki*, 'it', object; *nunua*, 'buy', verb root.
Definite articles	Definite word distinct from demonstrative	Demonstrative (seldom) used as definite article	*kitabu* ('book', 'the book', 'a book').
Noun Phrase Conjunction	*And* different from *with*	*And* identical to *with*	*Lete chai na maziwa* ('Bring tea and milk'); *Yesu alikuja na Baba yake* ('Jesus came with his Father').
Inflectional morphology	Suffixing	Mainly prefixing	*kitabu* ('book'), *vitabu* ('books'); *nilinunua* ('I bought'), *ulinunua* ('You bought'); but *jenga* ('build'), *jengwa* ('be built')
Reduplication	No productive reduplication	Productive full and partial reduplication	*Mimi ninasoma kitabu* 'I am reading the book'; *mimi ninasomasoma kitabu* 'I am reading the book bit by bit'
Number of genders	Three, sex-based, only in 3rd person singular pronouns and possessives	Many, not based on sex (called *classes*)	*kitabu* 'book' (*ki-vi*-class): plural *vitabu* 'books' ; *mtoto* 'child' (*m-wa*-class): plural *watoto* 'children' ; etc. Note that adjectives and verbs have to agree: *kitabu kidogo* 'small book', *vitabu vidogo* 'small books'; *mtoto mdogo* 'small child', etc.
Order of genitive and noun	No dominant order	Noun–genitive	*gari la mama* 'Mom's (*mama*) car (*gari*)'; *paa la nyumba* 'The roof (*paa*) of the house (*nyumba*)'.
Order of adjetive and noun	adjective–noun	noun–adjective	*mtoto mdogo* 'small child', lit. 'child small'
Order of demonstrative and noun	demonstrative–noun	noun–demonstrative	*gari hili* 'this car', lit. 'car this'
Order of numeral and noun	numeral–noun	noun–numeral	*vitabu viwili* ('two books', lit. 'books two')
Expression of Pronominal Subjects	Obligatory pronouns in subject position	Subject affixes on verb	*Nilinunua* ('I bought'), *ulinunua* ('You bought')
Negation	Particle or construction	Negative form of verb	*Ninasoma* ('I am reading'), *Sisomi* ('I am not reading'); *Unasoma* ('You are reading'), *husomi* ('You are not reading');
Position of Interrogative Phrases in Content Questions	Initial interrogative phrase	Not initial interrogative phrase	*Unasoma vitabu* ('You are reading books'); *Unasoma nini?* ('What are you reading', lit. 'you are reading what?')
Polar questions	Change in word order, use of auxiliaries	No change in word order	*Amesoma* ('He has read'); *Amesoma?* ('Has he read?')
Comparative	Comparative form of adjective ('-er') or 'more'	Absolute form of adjective	*Virusi ni ndogo* ('A virus is small') *Virusi ni ndogo kuliko bakteria* ('A virus is smaller than a bacterium', lit. 'A virus is small where there is a bacterium')
Predicative Possession	'have'	conjunctional ('to be with')	*Nina swali* ('I have a question', lit. 'I-am-with question')

Table 3: A summary of linguistic contrasts between English and Swahili.

highest BLEU (Papineni et al., 2002) score on the development set.

We obtained the highest test BLEU scores for en→sw with an RNN architecture, 30 000 BPE operations, tied embeddings and single GPU, while the highest ones for sw→en were obtained with a Transformer architecture, 30 000 BPE operations, tied embeddings and two GPUs.

5.3 Leveraging monolingual data

Once the best hyper-parameters were identified, we tried to improve the systems by making use of the monolingual corpora via back-translation. Back-translation (Sennrich et al., 2016b) is a widespread method for integrating target-language (TL) monolingual corpora into NMT systems. The quality of a system trained on back-translated data is usually

Corpus	Sentences	en tokens	sw tokens
parallel	424 821	7 536 537	6 191 959
NewsCrawl (en)	40 000 000	796 199 072	-
NewsCrawl (sw)	414 598	-	8 377 157
GoURMET mono (sw)	5 687 000	-	174 867 482
development	2 000	41 726	42 037
test (en-sw)	1 863	41 097	41 188
test (sw-en)	1 969	43 149	43 174

Table 4: Size of the corpora used to build the NMT systems after preprocesing. For the en NewsCrawl corpus, only the size of the subset that has been used for training is displayed. Token counts were calculated before BPE splitting.

correlated with the quality of the system that translates the TL monolingual corpus into the source language (SL) (Hoang et al., 2018, Sec. 3). We took advantage of the fact that we are building systems for both the en→sw and sw→en directions and applied an iterative back-translation (Hoang et al., 2018) algorithm that simultaneously leverages monolingual sw and monolingual en data. It can be outlined as follows:

1. With the best identified hyper-parameters for each direction we built a system using only parallel data.

2. en and sw monolingual data were back-translated with the systems built in the previous step.

3. Systems in both directions were trained on the combination of the back-translated data and the parallel data.

4. Steps 2–3 were re-executed 3 more times. Back-translation in step 2 was always carried out with the systems built in the most recent execution of step 3, hence the quality of the system used for back-translation improved with each iteration.

The sw monolingual corpus used in step 2 was the GoURMET monolingual corpus. The en monolingual corpus was a subset of the NewsCrawl corpus, the size of which was duplicated after each iteration. It started at 5 million sentences.

Since the sw NewsCrawl corpus was made available near the end of the development of our MT systems, it could not be used during the iterative back-translation process. Nevertheless, we added it afterwards: the sw NewsCrawl was back-translated with the last available sw→en system obtained after completing all the iterations, concatenated to the

existing data for the en→sw direction and the MT system was re-trained.

5.4 Integrating linguistic information

In addition to the corpora described above, linguistic information encoded in a more explicit representation was also employed to build the MT systems. In particular, we explored the *interleaving* (Nadejde et al., 2017) of linguistic tags in the TL side of the training corpus with the aim of enhancing the grammatical correctness of the translations.

Morphological taggers were used to obtain the interleaved tags added to the training corpus. The sw text was tagged with TreeTagger (Schmid, 2013). We used a model[17] trained on the Helsinki Corpus of Swahili.[18] The en text was tagged with the Stanford tagger (Qi et al., 2018), which was trained on the English Web Treebank (Silveira et al., 2014).

Figure 1 shows examples of en→sw and sw→en training parallel sentences with interleaved tags. While the tags returned by the sw tagger were just part-of-speech tags, en tags contained also morphological inflection information. Interleaved tags are removed from the final translations produced by the system.

6 Evaluation

This section reports the scores obtained on the test corpus using automatic evaluation metrics. It then describes the manual evaluation we are conducting at the time of writing these lines and provides preliminary results.

6.1 Automatic evaluation

Table 5 shows the BLEU and chrF2++ scores, computed on the test set, for the different steps in the development of the MT systems. All systems were trained with the hyper-parameters described in Section 5.2. As a reference, we also show the scores obtained by the translation obtained with Google Translate[19] on 6th March 2020 using the web interface.

It is worth noting the positive effect of adding monolingual data during the iterative back-translation iterations and that interleaved tags also help to improve the systems according to the automatic evaluation metrics.

<hr>

[17] Available at https://www.cis.uni-muenchen.de/~schmid/tools/TreeTagger/
[18] https://korp.csc.fi/download/HCS/a-v2/hcs-a-v2-dl
[19] https://translate.google.com/

en (SL): he 's studying law at No@@ tre D@@ ame .
sw (TL): VFIN A@@ nj@@ ifunza N sheria PRON huko PROPNAME No@@ tre PROPNAME D@@ ame

sw (SL): A@@ nj@@ ifunza sheria huko Notre Dame
en (TL): PRON|Nom|Masc|Sing|3|Prs he AUX|Ind|Sing|3|Pres|Fin 's VERB|Pres|Part studying
NOUN|Sing law ADP at PROPN|Sing No@@ tre PROPN|Sing D@@ ame

Figure 1: Examples of parallel sentences after interleaving linguistic tags. The @@ symbol is placed at the end of each BPE sub-word when it is not the last sub-word of a token. The tag corresponding to the morphological analysis of a token is interleaved before the first sub-word unit of the token.

Strategy	it.	BLEU	chrF++
en→sw			
only parallel	-	22.23	46.34
iter. backt.	1	25.59	50.08
iter. backt.	2	26.22	50.91
iter. backt.	3	26.36	51.09
iter. backt.	4	26.58	51.39
+ NewsCrawl	4	26.77	51.46
+ NewsCrawl + tags	4	27.42	52.11
Google Translate	-	23.24	48.80
sw→en			
only parallel	-	22.66	44.62
iter. backt.	1	29.29	51.19
iter. backt.	2	29.70	51.82
iter. backt.	3	29.99	51.98
iter. backt.	4	30.19	52.10
+ tags	4	30.55	52.72
Google Translate	-	30.36	53.32

Table 5: Automatic evaluation results obtained for the different development steps of the MT systems: *only parallel* stands for the systems trained only on parallel data with the best hyper-parameters; *iter. backt.* represents systems obtained after iteratively back-translating monolingual data (iteration number is shown in column *it.*); *+NewsCrawl* means that the sw NewsCrawl corpus was back-translated and added; and *+ tags* indicates that TL linguistic tags were interleaved.

Finally, our system clearly outperforms Google Translate for the en→sw direction, while their performances are close for the opposite direction. We noticed that the sw→en Google Translate system improved dramatically since we built our systems, which suggests that their systems may be trained on data that was not available at OPUS website at that time.

6.2 Manual evaluation

Manual evaluation requires the use of humans to give subjective feedback on the quality of translation, either directly or indirectly. All manual evaluation undertaken within the GoURMET project uses in-domain data, i.e. test data derived from news sources. Two types of subjective evaluation have been selected and applied in order to generate the most insight for the media partners:

- *Direct assessment* (Graham et al., 2016a; Graham et al., 2016b) (DA) is used to test

en→sw. This corresponds to the content creation use case which will use translation predominantly in this direction, and where the correctness of the translation is key.

- *Gap filling* (Forcada et al., 2018) (GF) is used to test sw→en. This corresponds to the media monitoring use case which will use translation almost exclusively in this direction and where getting the gist of the meaning of a sentence is enough to fulfil the use-case, perfect translation of sentence structure is less important.

Custom interfaces were created to support both evaluations; see figures 2 and 3 for DA and GF, respectively.

Evaluators were recruited from within the media partner organisations to complete the DA and GF tasks. Evaluators were required to have an excellent level of comprehension in the TL (i.e. sw for DA and en for GF) and precedence was given to journalists who write exclusively or predominately in one of the two target languages.

Media partners (BBC, DW) prepared test data using previously published articles. For DA this consisted of 205 sentences drawn at random from six different articles originally published in en by DW. The test data was further augmented with 5 sentences written in the TL by a human and used as *calibration* examples resulting in a total of 210 sentences shown to each evaluator in random order. All evaluators were asked to rate the quality of the translated sentence on a sliding scale from 0 to 100 for two criteria according to the statement *"For the pair of sentences below read the text and state how much you agree that: Q1) The black text adequately expresses the meaning of the grey text and Q2) The black text is a well written phrase or sentence that is grammatically and idiomatically correct"*. The ratings for the first five sentences were discarded as practice evaluations while the results for the five sentences used for calibration were discarded, leaving 200 pairs of results for each evaluator. Four evaluators completed the task.

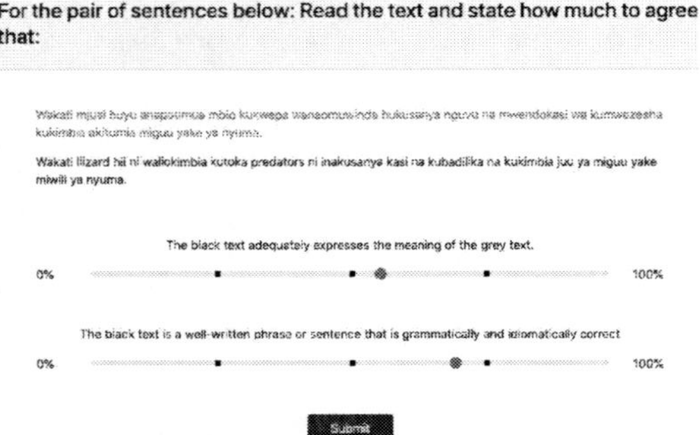

Figure 2: Custom Direct Assessment interface.

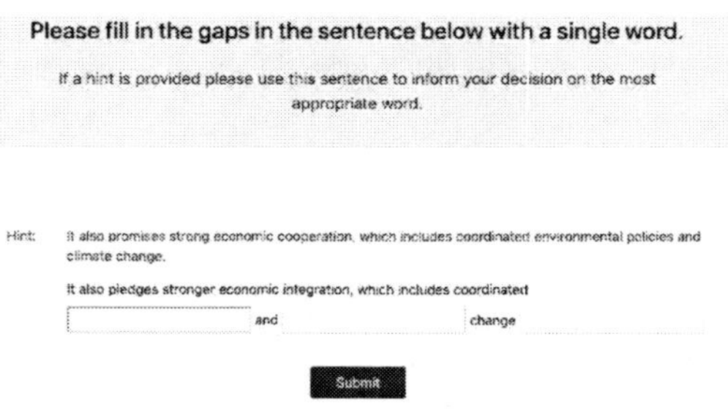

Figure 3: Custom Gap Filling interface.

Hint type	Success rate
No hint	26.45%
Google	60.60%
GoURMET	54.34%

Table 6: Gap-filling success rates for each hint type

For GF 30 sentences were selected from six different articles originally published in sw by DW. Each sentence was translated into en by a professional translator and it was ensured that once translated, each sentence was 15 words or more in length. For each sentence in en, 20% of the content words were removed, making sure there were no two consecutive gaps, typically leaving between 1 and 8 missing words in each sentence, averaging 2.67, for a total of 70 different missing-word problems. Each sentence in sw was translated into en by the GoURMET MT system described here, and Google Translate. The work of seventeen human evaluators was collected and their work on each of the 30 sentences was evaluated in three different ways: one evaluator saw the gapped sentence with no hint; one evaluator saw the gapped sentence with the GoURMET MT output as a hint; finally, one evaluator saw the gapped sentence with the Google Translate output as a hint. A total of 210 different missing-word/hint type configurations were therefore evaluated by an average of 17/3=5.67 evaluators. Sentences were distributed in such a way that no evaluator ever saw the same sentence twice. The GF evaluation requires the evaluator to fill in the missing words using the hint (if present). The accuracy is simply a *success rate*: the fraction of gaps correctly filled.

6.3 Manual evaluation results

Gap-filling (GF) success rates are shown in Table 6. As may be seen, Google Translate seems to be more helpful in this gisting task than the system created in this paper. To get an idea of how significant this difference is, Figure 4 shows a box-and-whisker plot of the distribution of success rates for each hint type by evaluator. As may be seen, the boxes for Google Translate and GoURMET clearly overlap, meaning that the difference in usefulness is not significant. However we also notice a slight overlap between the GoURMET success-rate distribution and that when there is no hint (NONE); this overlap does not occur with Google Translate.

Direct asssesment (DA): evaluators 1 and 2 scored the calibration sentences with values close to the expected ones (0 or 100 depending on the sentence), but evaluators 3 and 4 provided relatively inconsistent scores. Besides that, there is a weak positive correlation among the evaluators' answers (Pearson correlation coefficients between 0.22 and 0.46 for Q1, and between 0.24 and 0.49 for Q2, the highest values corresponding to evaluators 1 and 2 in both cases). Consequently, Table 7 shows the average score per evaluator. Unfortunately, these scores do not allow us to extract reliable conclusions.

7 Concluding remarks

We have described the development and evaluation of an NMT system to translate in the news domain between English and Swahili in both directions. We have also described the crawling of a new parallel corpus from the Internet which we have made publicly available.

We performed an automatic evaluation of both systems. According to it, the en→sw NMT system performs better than *Google Translate*, whereas the sw→en systems performs on par with it. In addition, the sw→en NMT system was manually evaluated to ascertain it usefulness for gisting purposes, and the en→sw NMT system as regards

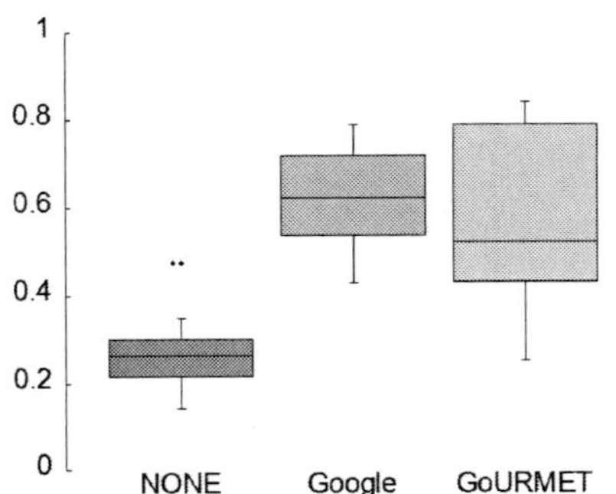

Figure 4: Gap-filling success rate distribution across evaluators for each hint type.

	Q1	Q2
Evaluator 1	77.65 ± 3.97	70.80 ± 4.30
Evaluator 2	47.30 ± 6.20	52.94 ± 5.97
Evaluator 3	48.42 ± 3.28	60.20 ± 3.75
Evaluator 4	54.40 ± 3.92	56.53 ± 4.02

Table 7: Average score and confidence intervals (estimated via standard significance testing) for questions Q1 and Q2 in the direct assessment evaluation.

its fluency and adequacy. The preliminary results of both evaluations show that the sw→en system performs similarly to *Google Translate* (which is consistent with the automatic evaluation), and that the en→sw system needs to be further evaluated because evaluators provided quite different scores.

As future work, and in view of the scarcity of bilingual resources available, we plan to try approaches based on monolingual corpora (Artetxe et al., 2018). We also plan to study if a correct segmentation of verbs, which are very rich and complex (see Table 3), as a pre-processing step helps improve performance.

Acknowledgements: Work funded by the European Union's Horizon 2020 research and innovation programme under grant agreement number 825299, project Global Under-Resourced Media Translation (GoURMET). We thank the editors of the SAWA corpus for letting us use it for training. We also thank Wycliffe Muia (BBC) for help with Swahili examples and DW for helping in the manual evaluation.

References

Agić, Ž. and I. Vulić. 2019. JW300: A wide-coverage parallel corpus for low-resource languages. In *Proceedings of the 57th Annual Meeting of the Association for Computational Linguistics*, pages 3204–3210, Florence, Italy, July.

Artetxe, M., G. Labaka, and E. Agirre. 2018. Unsupervised statistical machine translation. *arXiv preprint arXiv:1809.01272*.

Bahdanau, D., K. Cho, and Y. Bengio. 2014. Neural machine translation by jointly learning to align and translate. *CoRR*, abs/1409.0473.

Bojar, O., C. Federmann, M. Fishel, Y. Graham, B. Haddow, P. Koehn, and C. Monz. 2018. Findings of the 2018 conference on machine translation (WMT18). In *Proceedings of the Third Conference on Machine Translation: Shared Task Papers*, pages 272–303, Belgium, Brussels, October. Association for Computational Linguistics.

De Pauw, G., P.W. Wagacha, and G.-M. De Schryver. 2011. Exploring the SAWA corpus: collection and deployment of a parallel corpus English–Swahili. *Language resources and evaluation*, 45(3):331.

Esplà-Gomis, M., M.L. Forcada, G. Ramírez-Sánchez, and H. Hoang. 2019. ParaCrawl: Web-scale parallel corpora for the languages of the EU. In *Proceedings of Machine Translation Summit XVII Volume 2: Translator, Project and User Tracks*, pages 118–119, Dublin, Ireland, August.

Esplà-Gomis, M and M.L. Forcada. 2010. Combining content-based and url-based heuristics to harvest aligned bitexts from multilingual sites with bitextor. *The Prague Bulletin of Mathematical Linguistics*, 93:77–86.

Forcada, M.L., C. Scarton, L. Specia, B. Haddow, and A. Birch. 2018. Exploring gap filling as a cheaper alternative to reading comprehension questionnaires when evaluating machine translation for gisting. *CoRR*, abs/1809.00315.

Gao, Q. and S. Vogel. 2008. Parallel implementations of word alignment tool. In *Software Engineering, Testing, and Quality Assurance for Natural Language Processing*, pages 49–57, Columbus, Ohio, USA, June.

Graham, Y., T. Baldwin, M. Dowling, M. Eskevich, T. Lynn, and L. Tounsi. 2016a. Is all that glitters in machine translation quality estimation really gold? In *Proceedings of the 26th International Conference on Computational Linguistics: Technical Papers*, pages 3124–3134, Osaka, Japan.

Graham, Y., T. Baldwin, A. Moffat, and J. Zobel. 2016b. Can machine translation systems be evaluated by the crowd alone. *Natural Language Engineering*, 23(1):3–30.

Heafield, K. 2011. KenLM: faster and smaller language model queries. In *Proceedings of the EMNLP 2011 Sixth Workshop on Statistical Machine Translation*, pages 187–197, Edinburgh, Scotland, UK, July.

Hoang, V.C.D., P. Koehn, G. Haffari, and T. Cohn. 2018. Iterative back-translation for neural machine translation. In *Proceedings of the 2nd Workshop on Neural Machine Translation and Generation*, pages 18–24, Melbourne, Australia, July.

Junczys-Dowmunt, M., R. Grundkiewicz, T. Dwojak, H. Hoang, K. Heafield, T. Neckermann, F. Seide, U. Germann, A. Fikri Aji, N. Bogoychev, A.F.T. Martins, and A. Birch. 2018. Marian: Fast neural machine translation in C++. In *Proceedings of ACL 2018, System Demonstrations*, pages 116–121, Melbourne, Australia, July.

Koehn, P., H. Hoang, A. Birch, C. Callison-Burch, M. Federico, N. Bertoldi, B. Cowan, W. Shen, C. Moran, R. Zens, C. Dyer, O. Bojar, A. Constantin, and E. Herbst. 2007. Moses: Open source toolkit for statistical machine translation. In *Proceedings of the 45th Annual Meeting of the Association for Computational Linguistics Companion Volume Proceedings of the Demo and Poster Sessions*, pages 177–180, Prague, Czech Republic, June.

Lim, R.V., K. Heafield, H. Hoang, M. Briers, and A.D. Malony. 2018. Exploring hyper-parameter optimization for neural machine translation on GPU architectures. *CoRR*, abs/1805.02094.

Nadejde, M., S. Reddy, R. Sennrich, T. Dwojak, M. Junczys-Dowmunt, P. Koehn, and A. Birch. 2017. Predicting target language CCG supertags improves neural machine translation. In *Proceedings of the Second Conference on Machine Translation, Volume 1: Research Papers*, pages 68–79, Copenhagen, Denmark, September.

Ney, H., U. Essen, and R. Kneser. 1994. On structuring probabilistic dependences in stochastic language modelling. *Computer Speech & Language*, 8(1):1 – 38.

Papineni, K., S. Roukos, T. Ward, and W.-J. Zhu. 2002. BLEU: a method for automatic evaluation of machine translation. In *Proceedings of the 40th Annual Meeting on Association for Computational Linguistics*, pages 311–318, Philadelphia, PA, USA, July.

Perrott, D.V. 1965. *Teach Yourself Swahili*. English Universities Press.

Press, O. and L. Wolf. 2017. Using the output embedding to improve language models. In *Proceedings of the 15th Conference of the European Chapter of the Association for Computational Linguistics: Volume 2, Short Papers*, pages 157–163, Valencia, Spain, April.

Qi, P., T. Dozat, Y. Zhang, and C.D. Manning. 2018. Universal dependency parsing from scratch. In *Proceedings of the CoNLL 2018 Shared Task: Multilingual Parsing from Raw Text to Universal Dependencies*, pages 160–170, Brussels, Belgium, October.

Sánchez-Cartagena, V.M., M. Bañón, S. Ortiz-Rojas, and G. Ramírez-Sánchez. 2018. Prompsit's submission to wmt 2018 parallel corpus filtering shared task. In *Proceedings of the Third Conference on Machine Translation, Volume 2: Shared Task Papers*, Brussels, Belgium, October.

Schmid, H. 2013. Probabilistic part-of-speech tagging using decision trees. In *New methods in language processing*, page 154.

Sennrich, R. and M. Volk. 2010. MT-based sentence alignment for ocr-generated parallel texts. In *Proceedings of the Ninth Conference of the Association for Machine Translation in the Americas*, Denver, USA, October.

Sennrich, R., B. Haddow, and A. Birch. 2016a. Edinburgh Neural Machine Translation Systems for WMT 16. In *Proceedings of the First Conference on Machine Translation*, pages 371–376, Berlin, Germany, August.

Sennrich, R., B. Haddow, and A. Birch. 2016b. Improving neural machine translation models with monolingual data. In *Proceedings of the 54th Annual Meeting of the Association for Computational Linguistics (Volume 1: Long Papers)*, pages 86–96, Berlin, Germany, August.

Sennrich, R., B. Haddow, and A. Birch. 2016c. Neural machine translation of rare words with subword units. In *Proceedings of the 54th Annual Meeting of the Association for Computational Linguistics (Volume 1: Long Papers)*, volume 1, pages 1715–1725, Berlin, Germany, August.

Sennrich, R., A. Birch, A. Currey, U. Germann, B. Haddow, K. Heafield, A.V. Miceli Barone, and P. Williams. 2017. The University of Edinburgh's Neural MT Systems for WMT17. In *Proceedings of the Second Conference on Machine Translation, Volume 2: Shared Task Papers*, pages 389–399, Copenhagen, Denmark, September.

Silveira, N., T. Dozat, M.-C. de Marneffe, S. Bowman, M. Connor, J. Bauer, and C.D. Manning. 2014. A gold standard dependency corpus for English. In *Proceedings of the Ninth International Conference on Language Resources and Evaluation (LREC-2014)*, pages 2897–2904, Reykjavik, Iceland, May.

Varga, D., P. Halácsy, A. Kornai, V. Nagy, L. Németh, and V. Trón. 2007. Parallel corpora for medium density languages. *Amsterdam Studies In The Theory And History Of Linguistic Science Series 4*, 292:247.

Vaswani, A., N. Shazeer, N. Parmar, J. Uszkoreit, L. Jones, A.N. Gomez, Ł. Kaiser, and I. Polosukhin. 2017. Attention is all you need. In *Advances in Neural Information Processing Systems 30*, pages 5998–6008.

Machine Translation Post-Editing Levels: Breaking Away from the Tradition and Delivering a Tailored Service

Mara Nunziatini
Welocalize Italy S.r.l.
Via Alserio 22, Milan, Italy
mara.nunziatini@welocalize.com

Lena Marg
Welocalize Inc.
Frederick, MD, United States
lena.marg@welocalize.com

Abstract

While definitions of full and light post-editing have been around for a while, and error typologies like DQF and MQM gained in prominence since the beginning of last decade, for a long time customers tended to refuse to be flexible as for their final quality requirements, irrespective of the text type, purpose, target audience etc. We are now finally seeing some change in this space, with a renewed interest in different machine translation (MT) and post-editing (PE) service levels. While existing definitions of light and full post-editing are useful as general guidelines, they typically remain too abstract and inflexible both for translation buyers and linguists. Besides, they are inconsistent and overlap across the literature and different Language Service Providers (LSPs). In this paper, we would like to comment on existing industry standards and share our experience on several challenges, as well as ways to steer customer conversations and provide clear instructions to post-editors.

1 Introduction

As one of the largest multilingual LSPs, we have been offering machine translation post-editing services for many years, and our team supports more than 30 of our largest customers in the Enterprise or Regulated space with MT and post-editing programs in often 30+ language pairs. When implementing machine translation for a new customer, we always provide a post-editing training to the linguists working on the program.

During this training, among other relevant topics, we focus on the basics of post-editing and we explain what the client's requirements are regarding final translation quality.

Based on experience, we found that it can be very complicated to communicate what is expected of linguists in different post-editing levels. While it is easier to explain what is expected of light versus full post-editing, there are some grey areas that don't fall either into the full post-editing or the light post-editing service. Furthermore, our customers will often not be experts of translation quality assurance methodologies, and also not be familiar with the common definitions of the different levels of post-editing. As such, they are themselves often not entirely sure which approach would meet, exceed or fall short of their requirements. It is therefore crucial to guide them and define their requirements from the very outset, also in order to be able to clearly communicate them to the post-editors. This is extremely important since post-editors might feel confused if they do not receive clear instructions, and will probably end up delivering a quality that is either too high – in this case they will not be productive – or too low – and the clients' quality requirements will not be met.

Ultimately, the effort of the post-editor depends strictly on clients' quality requirements, therefore, it is not always advisable to rely exclusively on the current, most commonly used post-editing guidelines. In order to precisely define the quality requirements for each post-editing task, we reference the DQF-MQM error matrix and the TAUS DQF content types to align all parties on what types of errors are acceptable for a translation request given its purpose, target audience etc.

In this paper, we would like to share our experience on existing industry standards,

Martins, Moniz, Fumega, Martins, Batista, Coheur, Parra, Trancoso, Turchi, Bisazza, Moorkens, Guerberof, Nurminen, Marg, Forcada (eds.)
Proceedings of the 22nd Annual Conference of the European Association for Machine Translation, p. 309–318
Lisboa, Portugal, November 2020.

challenges, and ways to steer customer conversations and provide clear instructions to post-editors.

2 Existing Industry Definitions and Standards

As for quality, two error typologies were proposed in the last years: DQF by TAUS, 2011 (O'Brien et al., 2011) and MQM by QT21, 2014 (Lommel et al., 2014). These provide more flexible and dynamic ways to assess quality, and apply the same approach to machine translation and human translation. While they can also be used separately, the two typologies were brought together in 2015 into the MQM-DQF quality framework. These error typologies also aim to move away from the LISA QA model (LISA, 2006), used for a long time in the localization industry to rate translation quality. We like the DQF-MQM error typology because the error hierarchy, made up of well-structured main criteria and sub-criteria, allows for a granular categorisation of the quality issues in the translation.

Regarding post-editing, as mentioned above, it is common knowledge and generally accepted in the translation industry that there are different levels of post-editing, aimed at obtaining a final text that satisfies diverse predefined purposes and quality standards. However, there appears to be no recognised industry-wide standard and the definition and guidelines of each level of post-editing are inconsistent across the literature and different LSPs. Currently, the most commonly used and referenced definitions of light and full post-editing in the localization industry are probably those provided by the International Organization for Standardization, GALA, TAUS and Sharon O'Brien (O'Brien, 2010). While the last two were already analysed by Hu and Cadwell, we would like to summarize what ISO and GALA say on the different levels of post-editing, before we proceed with the comparative analysis.

2.1 ISO Standard No. 18587

The ISO standard defines the requirements for full and light post-editing, as well as post-editors' competences. According to the standard, the final output after full post-editing should be equivalent to human translation. Therefore, if we had to reference the DQF-MQM high-level error types, the post-editor should focus on Accuracy, Fluency, Terminology, Style and Design. Plus, post-editors should edit any inappropriate content (see Appendix B).

The standard is less precise regarding light post-editing, but it still calls out that the post-editor should focus on Accuracy and disregard Style. For both light and full PE there are some less clear instructions regarding inappropriate content, that should be edited, and restructuring of the sentence, which should happen only in case of unclear meaning.

2.2 GALA

GALA references an article from Juan Rowda (Rowda, 2016): *Better, Faster, and More Efficient Post-editing* to explain the differences between light and full post-editing. According to Rowda, full post-edited output should be close to human translation quality. During full post-editing, the linguist should focus on Language (grammar and spelling), Terminology, Style and Accuracy error types.

On the other hand, light post-editing should aim at fixing major/blatant errors only, while minor issues are acceptable. More precisely, during light post-editing, linguists should focus on accuracy. They should not focus on punctuation, style and spelling, and preferential changes should be avoided. While these guidelines are in line with other common definitions of light post-editing, they remain vague for a post-editor to implement. An interesting aspect of these guidelines is that the checklist for light post-editing also mentions that light post-editing should allow for a fast turn-around.

In addition to these, there are older and helpful guidelines found in translation studies publications, which we will leave aside here.

3 Challenges with Existing Definitions of Post-Editing

The main challenge with terms like "light", "medium" and "full" is that they remain very abstract. Hu and Cadwell showcased already in 2016 that the literature seems to offer inconsistent and/or overlapping nomenclature, definitions and guidelines for post-editing.

Having said this, it seems to be broadly accepted that light post-editing should focus on conveying the meaning of the source text in an accurate way. Therefore, if we had to use the DQF-MQM error types as a reference – instead of the categories from the LISA QA Model (Localization Industry Standards Association Quality Assurance Model) and SAE (Society of Automotive Engineers) J2450 translation quality metric, as suggested by Hu and Cadwell – we could say that light post-editing should focus on fixing Accuracy error types, while it should not focus on Style, Design, Locale Convention and Verity error types, as long as the information is delivered accurately. Whether Terminology, Spelling and Grammar errors should be penalized in a light post-editing task seems to remain controversial and unclear – the requirements as for these error types are inconsistent (see Appendix A).

On the other hand, if we consider the findings from Hu and Cadwell as well as the ISO standard No. 18587, it seems to be broadly accepted that full post-editing should focus on readability. However, there appears to be no common agreement as to whether full-post editing should be of equal quality to conventional human translation from scratch. Considering the different guidelines we analysed, we could say that full post-editing should focus on Accuracy, Fluency and Terminology error types. Style is discussed controversially, as there is no agreement on its importance between all the different guidelines (see Appendix B). According to the TAUS guidelines, the style "may not be as good as that achieved by a native-speaker human translator",[1] while stylistic and textuality problems should be ignored according to O'Brien. On the other hand, we read that the ISO standard No. 18587 recommends that client's stylistic guidelines are followed, and highlights that the style should be appropriate for the text type. Lastly, GALA simply points out that the style should be consistent and appropriate.

Some LSPs also provide "medium post-editing" services, but the guidelines for this quality level are even more vague and inconsistent, and this level of post-editing is mentioned only sporadically in the literature. Generally speaking, when performing medium post-editing, we expect the post-editor to put more effort into editing Terminology, Fluency and Style compared to light post-editing, but not to the same extent as they would for full post-editing. There appear to be no medium post-editing definitions in the literature that we could reference here; the easiest way to derive a distinction between full and medium post-editing, for instance, might be via the text type and translation purpose, i.e. texts that

are more stylistically challenging and complex by definition would always require full post-editing, whereas text types with a simpler structure (often technical manuals) could fold into medium post-editing. However, this might ultimately be an unnecessary definition as such, that could also be covered by the full post-editing requirement for "appropriate" style.

As we can see, these guidelines leave some grey areas when it comes to a hands-on post-editing task. For example, if I am performing full post-editing, should I check that bullets are consistent in the same list of items? That the headers are all title case? And what happens if I notice that the target language is using masculine form – for example, "amigo" in Spanish – when the source language might refer both to feminine and masculine gender – for example, "friend" in English? Should I edit all of these, or is it ok to leave those as they are?

There is also a potential problem in that existing definitions appear to assume that only one linguist should ever post-edit the machine translated output – irrespective of full or light. In other words, there appear to be no guidelines specifying how many linguists should be involved in the different post-editing levels, and the ISO standard No. 18587 does not set any requirement in this sense. It just mentions the requirement of a process to make sure that the final product meets the specifications. In the localization industry, however, it is still very common for translation buyers to enshrine a so-called "4-eye process" in the contract, i.e. irrespective of MT, that content needs to undergo post-editing plus a separate review or revision step, and potentially even a quality assurance step, which in some cases might be performed by a third party. In other words, customers still tend to buy a specific process (TEP, translation only, etc.), rather than an agreed service level or translation quality. This becomes even more stringent in the Regulated sectors, i.e. patent, life sciences, finance etc., where these additional steps can be mandatory to comply with other ISO standards and certification requirements.

Another challenge with the terms "light" and "full" post-editing is that often people misunderstand that these describe how much editing needs to be done, or in other words, how much effort the post-editor should put into the task, rather than what the final translation quality should be. More precisely, some people might erroneously

---

think that, if they were to translate the same content in multiple languages, depending on the quality of the raw MT output, some languages will require light post-editing while others will require full post-editing. For example, User-generated Content machine translated into Spanish will require light post-editing as the raw output's quality is good, while Finnish will require full post-editing, because the raw output isn't as good as for Spanish. This is a fairly common misunderstanding and yet another reason why we think it is better to focus on final translation quality requirements, than the vaguer definitions of light and full PE.

4   Challenges with Error Typologies

Since the lack of a clear, common approach highlighted by Hu and Cadwell (2016) is still a very present issue, translation service providers need to define their own methodology, in order to provide a flexible service offering, linked to transparent pricing for the client and fairer rates for the post-editors. What is ultimately needed is a highly flexible and granular approach, since the effort of the post-editor is essentially decided by the exact quality requirements of a given customer.

Rather than working with the somewhat vague definitions of "light", "medium" and "full" post-editing, we find that it is easier for all parties to define quality requirements by aligning on what types of errors are admissible for a translation request given its purpose, target audience etc. Considering the purpose of the text and the document type, and referencing the DQF-MQM error matrix, we help the clients choose what error categories are acceptable for them and what are not. Also, for each error category they decide how many (if any) major and/or minor errors they are admissible. We use the same framework for Quality Assurance (QA) steps to understand if the quality of the MTPE projects meets client's requirements – this way the linguists performing this task are fully aware of what they should focus on and we get full consistency as for quality requirements from the start until the end of the process.

In order to make this possible, first we created different groups of domains, considering the purpose of the document and the text type (based on TAUS DQF content types), and then we created different sets of standard checks for each one of these groups, aimed at getting a translation which is free of certain predefined unacceptable errors.

For example, for User-generated Content, we could propose a set of post-editing checks that focuses purely on the accurate transfer of meaning. User-generated Content would be an example of text type typically accepting a high error threshold – especially in light of the source input itself being known for being characterized by errors (O'Curran, 2014). At the other end of the spectrum we might find text types such as marketing materials with a focus on brand's style and tone of voice. We like to call the above-mentioned sets of standard checks "full", "medium" and "light" post-editing too, as our guidelines show some similarity with the most popular industry MTPE guidelines mentioned above. Then, building on these sets of pre-defined standard checks, we add or remove applicable error categories as per client's preferences, and we raise or lower the threshold of the acceptable number of minor and/or major errors.

As mentioned above, the error categories are also based on the DQF-MQM error typology. The DQF-MQM framework involves the use of a list of error categories, and the content quality is judged based on the amount and severity of the errors found. The errors can have different severity levels: critical, major, minor and neutral. "Neutral" applies when an issue should be flagged to the translator but is not counted as an error and does not influence whether the translation is considered a PASS or a FAIL. During our QA step, a post-edited text (or a sample of it) is evaluated by a linguist who marks the errors; all errors are added up, based on severity, and output a PASS or FAIL score, depending on the defined threshold. The thresholds are flexible and depend on content type, text purpose and perishability of the text. In practice, this strategy is extremely helpful, as we can agree with customers, post-editors and reviewers at a very granular level what issues need to be addressed during post-editing, and which are of purely preferential nature.

However, while error typologies for quality assurance are fairly common among professional translators and reviewers, it can be trickier to agree on error categories and severities with translation buyers. This is primarily due to the fact that the owner of a given machine translation initiative on customer side may not be an expert in translation quality assurance methodologies. On the other hand, on post-editor and reviewer side, the main challenge is changing the mindset, and getting professional translators to accept that for certain content types and translation purposes, it is acceptable to leave certain types of issues in the machine translation output unedited. However, by providing a granular breakdown of what constitutes an error in a given translation request, it is much easier to train and support post-editors, and to monitor their actual productivity for the task at hand.

5 Use Cases Examples and Strategies

As we have seen on a high level, clients often have specific requirements that cannot easily and universally be categorized with the typical definitions of full, medium or light post-editing. In the following section, we will showcase some examples to explain our approach: based on the purpose of the document, the content type and the error types that the client is willing to accept or not, we build custom requirements and instructions for post-editors.

5.1 Use Case 1

A good example for "light post-editing" presented itself with a client who needed to translate Knowledge Base content within a defined budget. For the content and purpose, light post-editing seemed the appropriate approach, as the main goal was to provide final translations that accurately transfer the meaning, while maximising translator throughput within a defined budget. However, for this particular client it was important that product names were handled correctly, in this case kept in English also in the target language. Light post-editing per se does not typically focus on terminology (Hu and Cadwell, 2016); this requirement therefore implied additional editing effort, especially in cases of product names that were unknown to the MT engine at a given point in time, or not handled consistently in the data used to train the MT system. In this case, we therefore added the specific terminology check requirement to the obligatory checks for post-editing, still classifying the task as light post-editing.

Below you can see an example in which the MT engine translated an unknown product name literally from English into Portuguese. Standard light post-editing instructions don't necessarily require post-editors to review such instances, and post-editors could be tempted to leave this unchanged.

Source	**Bugcheck** 7E
Raw MT	**Verificação de bugs** 7E
Final	**Bugcheck** 7E

Table 1: Example of correctly edited DNT ("Do Not Translate") term.

Post-editors working on this account received a list with all product names to be left untranslated, and before project kick-off they were also trained to perform light post-editing while still ensuring product names were in line with the client's requirements.

5.2 Use Case 2

Another client translating Online Help content wanted to have medium post-editing performed on the raw MT output: this was defined as providing usable and accurate translations, without a need for stylistic flourishes or lengthy terminology research. One requirement, however, was that the translations should all use the formal tone of voice, in line with the brand's style. This again goes slightly beyond what we would typically define as "medium" post-editing, so this instruction was added to the mandatory checks for post-editors; see an example below from English into Spanish:

Source	**Change** the size of the logo on the traveler ticket **if desired**.
Raw MT	**Si lo deseas, cambia** el tamaño del logotipo de la entrada del viajero.
Final	**Si lo desea, cambie** el tamaño del logotipo de la entrada del viajero.

Table 2: Example of correctly edited tone of voice.

In this case, raw machine translation output would have been accurate and correct according to the typical medium post-editing guidelines, however it would not have met client's requirements.

5.3 Use Case 3

In this instance, we are using MT and post-editing for UI and UA content. Typically, for this content type we would recommend medium post-editing, as the focus is on accuracy and correct terminology, while style should not usually play a key role. However, this client wanted to also include stylistic requirements to reflect brand and voice. The impact of this was so significant, that this was ultimately classified as full post-editing. In the interest of maximising productivity, we typically train our post-editors to use as much of the raw MT output as possible, in line with the standard task definitions (TAUS MT Post-Editing Guidelines and ISO Standard No. 18587, just to mention two of those). In this case, however, they were instructed to make sure to always follow the client's preferred terminology and style – this implied editing the machine translation suggestions to reflect the client's style guide, preferred terminology, punctuation, spelling (i.e. capitalization), tone and register.

Even when a client's requirements and post-editing guidelines are seemingly clear, we have experienced many challenges. For example, sometimes post-editors – also depending on how experienced they are (de Almeida et al., 2010) – find it difficult to understand what is expected of them and end up editing too much (over-editing) or not enough (under-editing).

5.4 How We Measure Adequate Editing Effort

If the post-editors are over-editing, they are not making an efficient use of the MT output because they are introducing unnecessary preferential changes. Generally speaking, we can recognise over-editing by comparing the raw MT output and the final post-edited files with our proprietary scoring tool and analysing common industry metrics like BLEU, GTM, Nist, Meteor, Precision, Recall, TER, and Levenshtein Edit Distance (Levenshtein, 1966). If we notice that the metrics are not in line with our expectations, and Edit Distance (ED) and/or TER are especially high compared to other target languages of the same project, or compared to what we usually see for a given language and domain, we might suspect that the post-editor is over editing. We would then check what was changed of the raw output, focusing on the segments with the higher edit distance, to find out where the post-editors are putting most of their effort and we investigate if the edits introduced are actually necessary to reach the agreed quality standards. In the example below, for instance, ED was particularly high:

Source	Milford, **MA**, USA
Raw MT	Milford, **MA**, USA
Light PE	Milford, **Massachusetts**, USA

Table 3: Over-editing in light post-editing.

The post-editor was instructed to perform light post-editing. Edits like the one in the example above are typically not in line with light post-editing expectations, as the raw output was perfectly understandable. If unnecessary edits like the one above are frequent in the final target text, it probably means that the post-editors were not clear about what was expected of them and were therefore unproductive.

On the other hand, if the post-editors are under-editing, they will deliver a final translation that does not meet the agreed quality standards and will fail Quality Assurance checks. If the Edit Distance for a given translation is suspiciously low, i.e. it is especially low compared to other target languages of the same project, or compared to what we usually see for a given language and domain, we would check closely the quality of the final translation to make sure the post-editor actually implemented all the necessary edits.

If we come across over-editing or under-editing issues, we follow up with the post-editors and provide feedback as well as extra training, to make sure they understand their task, mind their productivity and align with client's requirements.

6 How We Provide Guidance and Set Expectations

In order to help clients understand what service level best fits their needs and to make it clear to post-editors what is required of them, there are different strategies an LSP can put in place.

6.1 Supporting Post-Editors

To support post-editors and make sure they have a clear understanding of what is expected of them, we find it very useful to have meetings at the start of a new engagement.

On these calls we explain the project, the quality level agreed with the customer, we go through the post-editing guidelines (full, light or medium, depending on project requirements), the agreed quality assurance process and applicable error types, and we offer post-editors any extra guidance needed to reach the quality level, i.e. anything that would not be clear by simply reading the post-editing guidelines, or any exception: for example, the service required is medium post-editing but for the German target audience, the client insists on n-dashes being replaced by m-dashes. We also explain what MT engine we are using, how it was customized, its known strengths and weaknesses, and we discuss any areas the neural MT struggles with in general, and where the machine translated output might fall short of the client's particular requirements. This way, post-editors are aware of what is expected of them and know exactly what to look for in the raw output, we reduce the risk of mis-understandings and we also set expectations on the final quality of the output. These calls are also a good chance to clarify any doubt post-editors might have or answer their questions.

These calls are often followed by a quick questionnaire to make sure post-editors are clear on the topics presented during the call, as well as brief instructions summarizing the key take-aways. Once a program has started, we continue monitoring performance, typically via Levenshtein Edit Distance analysis, and check for unexpected behaviour. As mentioned above, if we notice anything unexpected, i.e. under-editing or over-editing, we get in touch with post-editors to explain what we observed and give them further support or correct any wrong behaviour.

6.2 Supporting Clients

It can be very difficult for clients to understand the distinction between the different definitions of post-editing service levels. The differences between light and full post-editing are easily enough understood where content types very clearly require different approaches, e.g. user-generated content versus patents or branded website content. However, it is harder to explain the different requirements for technical content and stylistically demanding content, especially if the person overseeing the MT effort at client end is not familiar with different quality assurance methodologies. It still remains crucial to clearly define the client's requirements, so that they will know what they are buying, and what contributes to the productivity gains and compensation models. For this purpose, it can be useful to provide samples of the text to be translated with different post-editing approaches, and applicable error categories. This way they will see how the target text changes and choose what service they prefer:

Source	Raw MT	Light PE	Medium PE	Full PE
Dopo la cottura, la "verace pizza napoletana" (vera pizza napoletana) presenta un diametro variabile che non deve superare 35 cm, con il bordo rialzato (cornicione) e con la partecentrale coperta dai condimenti.	After baking the "real Neapolitan pizza" has a variable diameter that must exceed 35cm, the edge (cornion) and the participant covered by the seasonings.	After baking the "real Neapolitan pizza" (original Neapolitan pizza) has a variable diameter that must not exceed 35cm, the raised edge (cornicione) and the central part covered by the seasonings.	After baking, the "verace pizza napoletana" (original Neapolitan pizza) has a variable diameter that must not exceed 35cm, the raised edge (cornicione) and the central part covered by the seasonings.	After baking, the "verace pizza napoletana" (original Neapolitan pizza) has a variable diameter that must not exceed 35 cm, a raised edge (cornicione) and the central part covered with toppings.

Table 4: Different levels of PE.

It is important to guide the client and provide recommendations in order for them to get the appropriate post-editing level for the content type and translation purpose they are looking to address, and to help them achieve the cost and time savings they were hoping to see.

7 Conclusions

There is no gold standard for post-editing guidelines nor universally applicable definitions of different post-editing services. While still being useful for initially steering conversations, we saw that the generic guidelines overlap in key aspects. At this point in time, we find that in order to effectively communicate with different stakeholders in the localization industry, it is necessary to refer both to definitions of light, medium, full post-editing, but to also supplement these with very hands-on, practical definitions of what constitutes an error in a given scenario, and how quality assurance is provided. Instructions, error categories and penalty thresholds need to be defined on a case-by-case basis with customers and need to be communicated very clearly to post-editors. Metrics such as TER or Edit Distance can help analyse and monitor the actual post-editing effort, and can be used to fine-tune and revisit requirements, productivity expectations and fair compensation.

References

De Almeida G. and S. O'Brien 2010. Analysing Post-Editing Performance: Correlations with Years of Translation Experience. Accessed January 2020. Available at http://www.mt-archive.info/EAMT-2010-Almeida.pdf.

Hu, Ke and Patrick Cadwell. 2016. A Comparative Study of Post-editing Guidelines. *Baltic J. Modern Computing*, Vol. 4 (2016), No. 2, 346-353.

International Organization for Standardization. 2017. Translation services — Post-editing of machine translation output — Requirements (ISO Standard No. 18587).

Levenshtein, Vladimir Iosifovich. 1966. Binary Codes Capable of Correcting Deletions, Insertions and Reversals. *Soviet Physics Doklady*.

LISA. 2006. LISA QA Model 3.1: Assisting the localization development, production and quality control processes for global product distribution (press release). Romainmôtier: LISA.

Lommel, Arle and Uszkoreit, Hans and Burchardt, Aljoscha. 2014. Multidimensional quality metrics

(MQM): A framework for declaring and describing translation quality metrics. *Tradumàtica: tecnologies de la traducció*, (12):455–463.

O'Brien, S. 2010. Introduction to Post-Editing: Who, What, How and Where to Next? Accessed January 2020. Available at http://amta2010.amtaweb.org/AMTA/papers/6-01-ObrienPostEdit.pdf

O'Brien, S., Choudhury, R., Van der Meer, J., Aranberri Monasterio, N. 2011. TAUS Dynamic Quality Evaluation Framework: TAUS Labs report, Accessed January 2020. Available at https://www.taus.net/thinktank/reports/evaluate-reports/translation-quality-evaluation-is-catching-up-with-thetimes

O'Curran, Elaine. 2014. Machine Translation and Post-Editing for User Generated Content: An LSP Perspective. Proceedings of AMTA 2014, vol. 2: MT Users Vancouver, BC.

Rowda, Juan. 2016. Better, Faster, and More Efficient Post-editing. Accessed January 2020. Available at https://www.gala-global.org/publications/better-faster-and-more-efficient-post-editing

TAUS. 2010. MT Post-editing Guidelines. Accessed January 2020. Available at https://www.taus.net/academy/best-practices/postedit-best-practices/machine-translation-post-editing-guidelines

Appendix A. Comparative Analysis of Light PE Guidelines based on DQF-MQM framework

Error Type		O'BRIEN 2010	ROWDA 2016	TAUS 2016	ISO 2017
Accuracy	Addition	The message transferred should be accurate	Accuracy is key	Ensure that no information has been accidentally added or omitted	Ensure that no information has been added or omitted
	Omission	The message transferred should be accurate	Accuracy is key	Ensure that no information has been accidentally added or omitted	Ensure that no information has been added or omitted
	Mistranslation	The message transferred should be accurate	Accuracy is key	Aim for semantically correct translation	Restructure sentences in the case of incorrect or unclear meaning
	Over-translation	The message transferred should be accurate	Accuracy is key	Ensure that no information has been accidentally added or omitted	Ensure that no information has been added or omitted
	Under-translation	The message transferred should be accurate	Accuracy is key	Ensure that no information has been accidentally added or omitted	Ensure that no information has been added or omitted
	Untranslated text	The message transferred should be accurate	Accuracy is key		
	Improper exact TM match				
Fluency	Punctuation		Variations in style, punctuation, and spelling are OK		
	Spelling	All basic rules regarding spelling still apply	Variations in style, punctuation, and spelling are OK	Basic rules apply	
	Grammar	Not a big concern, unless grammatical problems interfere with accuracy		May not be perfect	
	Grammatical register				
	Inconsistency				
	Link/cross-reference				
	Character encoding				
Terminology	Inconsistent with termbase	Do not spend time researching terms			
	Inconsistent use of terminology	Do not spend time researching terms			
Style	Awkward	Ignore stylistic problems	Variations in style, punctuation, and spelling are OK	No need to implement corrections that are of a stylistic nature only	Need not be stylistically adequate
	Company style	Ignore stylistic problems	Variations in style, punctuation, and spelling are OK	No need to implement corrections that are of a stylistic nature only	Need not be stylistically adequate
	Inconsistent style	Ignore stylistic problems	Variations in style, punctuation, and spelling are OK	No need to implement corrections that are of a stylistic nature only	Need not be stylistically adequate
	Third-party style	Ignore stylistic problems	Variations in style, punctuation, and spelling are OK	No need to implement corrections that are of a stylistic nature only	Need not be stylistically adequate
	Unidiomatic	Ignore stylistic problems	Variations in style, punctuation, and spelling are OK	No need to implement corrections that are of a stylistic nature only	Need not be stylistically adequate
Design	Length				
	Local formatting				
	Markup				
	Missing text				
	Truncation/text expansion				
Locale convention	Address format				
	Date format				
	Currency format				
	Measurement format				
	Shortcut key				
	Telephone format				
Verity	Culture-specific reference	Edit any offensive, inappropriate or culturally unacceptable information		Edit any offensive, inappropriate or culturally unacceptable content	Edit any inappropriate content
Other			Fix major/blatant errors only. Minor issues are acceptable. Avoid stylistic and preferential changes.		
		Throughput expectations: very high Quality expectations: low	Fast turn-around	Use as much of the raw MT output as possible	Use as much of the raw MT output as possible

Appendix B. Comparative Analysis of Full PE Guidelines based on DQF-MQM framework

Error Type		O'BRIEN 2010	ROWDA 2016	TAUS 2016	ISO 2017
Accuracy	Addition	The message transferred should be accurate		No information has been accidentally added or omitted	No information has been added or omitted
	Omission	The message transferred should be accurate		No information has been accidentally added or omitted	No information has been added or omitted
	Mistranslation	The message transferred should be accurate	All mistranslations fixed	Aim for grammatically, syntactically and semantically correct translation	Restructure sentences in the case of incorrect or unclear meaning
	Over-translation	The message transferred should be accurate	All mistranslations fixed	No information has been accidentally added or omitted	No information has been added or omitted
	Under-translation	The message transferred should be accurate	All mistranslations fixed	No information has been accidentally added or omitted	No information has been added or omitted
	Untranslated text	The message transferred should be accurate		Untranslated terms belong to the client's list of "Do Not Translate"	
	Improper exact TM match				
Fluency	Punctuation	All basic rules regarding spelling, punctuation and hyphenation still apply		Basic rules regarding spelling, punctuation and hyphenation apply	Apply spelling, punctuation and hyphenation rules
	Spelling	All basic rules regarding spelling, punctuation and hyphenation still apply	Detailed corrections, no grammar or spelling errors should be ignored	Basic rules regarding spelling, punctuation and hyphenation apply	Apply spelling, punctuation and hyphenation rules
	Grammar	Grammar should be accurate	Detailed corrections, no grammar or spelling errors should be ignored	Aim for grammatically, syntactically and semantically correct translation	Produce grammatically, syntactically and semantically correct target language content
	Grammatical register			Aim for grammatically, syntactically and semantically correct translation	Ensure that the style appropriate for the text type is used and that stylistic guidelines provided by the client are observed
	Inconsistency				
	Link/cross-reference				
	Character encoding				
Terminology	Inconsistent with termbase	Ensure that key terminology is correctly translated	Accurate terminology	Key terminology is correctly translated	Adhere to client and/or domain terminology
	Inconsistent use of terminology	Ensure that key terminology is correctly translated	Accurate terminology	Correcting inconsistencies in terminology, terminology disambiguation	Adhere to client and/or domain terminology
Style	Awkward	Ignore stylistic and textuality problems	Style should be consistent and appropriate	May not be as good as that achieved by a native-speaking human translator	Ensure that the style appropriate for the text type is used and that stylistic guidelines provided by the client are observed
	Company style	Ignore stylistic and textuality problems	Style should be consistent and appropriate	May not be as good as that achieved by a native-speaking human translator	Ensure that the style appropriate for the text type is used and that stylistic guidelines provided by the client are observed
	Inconsistent style	Ignore stylistic and textuality problems	Style should be consistent and appropriate	May not be as good as that achieved by a native-speaking human translator	Ensure that the style appropriate for the text type is used and that stylistic guidelines provided by the client are observed
	Third-party style	Ignore stylistic and textuality problems	Style should be consistent and appropriate	May not be as good as that achieved by a native-speaking human translator	Ensure that the style appropriate for the text type is used and that stylistic guidelines provided by the client are observed
	Unidiomatic	Ignore stylistic and textuality problems	Style should be consistent and appropriate	May not be as good as that achieved by a native-speaking human translator	Ensure that the style appropriate for the text type is used and that stylistic guidelines provided by the client are observed
Design	Length			Ensure that formatting is correct	Apply formatting rules
	Local formatting			Ensure that formatting is correct	Apply formatting rules
	Markup	For tagged formats, ensure all tags are present and in the correct positions		Ensure that formatting is correct	Apply formatting rules
	Missing text			Ensure that formatting is correct	Apply formatting rules
	Truncation/text expansion			Ensure that formatting is correct	Apply formatting rules
Locale convention	Address format			Handling of measurements and locale-specific punctuation, date formats and alike	
	Date format			Handling of measurements and locale-specific punctuation, date formats and alike	
	Currency format			Handling of measurements and locale-specific punctuation, date formats and alike	
	Measurement format			Handling of measurements and locale-specific punctuation, date formats and alike	
	Shortcut key			Handling of measurements and locale-specific punctuation, date formats and alike	
	Telephone format			Handling of measurements and locale-specific punctuation, date formats and alike	
Verity	Culture-specific reference	Edit any offensive, inappropriate or culturally unacceptable information		Edit any offensive, inappropriate or culturally unacceptable content	Edit any inappropriate content
Other		Retain as much raw translation as possible		Use as much of the raw MT output as possible	Use as much of the MT output as possible
		Throughput expectations: high Quality expectations: medium	Close to human translation quality		Produce an output which is indistinguishable from human translation output

A User Study of the Incremental Learning in NMT

Miguel Domingo[1] and **Mercedes García-Martínez**[2] and **Álvaro Peris**[3] and **Alexandre Helle**[2]
and **Amando Estela**[2] and **Laurent Bié**[2] and **Francisco Casacuberta**[1] and **Manuel Herranz**[2]

[1]PRHLT Research Center - Universitat Politècnica de València
{midobal, fcn}@prhlt.upv.es
[2]Pangeanic / B.I Europa - PangeaMT Technologies Division
{m.garcia, a.helle, a.estela, l.bie, m.herranz}@pangeanic.com
[3]Independent Researcher
lvapeab@gmail.com

Abstract

In the translation industry, human experts usually supervise and post-edit machine translation hypotheses. Adaptive neural machine translation systems, able to incrementally update the underlying models under an online learning regime, have been proven to be useful to improve the efficiency of this workflow. However, this incremental adaptation is somewhat unstable, and it may lead to undesirable side effects. One of them is the sporadic appearance of made-up words, as a byproduct of an erroneous application of subword segmentation techniques. In this work, we extend previous studies on on-the-fly adaptation of neural machine translation systems. We perform a user study involving professional, experienced post-editors, delving deeper on the aforementioned problems. Results show that adaptive systems were able to learn how to generate the correct translation for task-specific terms, resulting in an improvement of the user's productivity. We also observed a close similitude, in terms of morphology, between made-up words and the words that were expected.

1 Introduction

Despite its improvements and obtaining admissible results in many tasks, machine translation (MT) is still very far from obtaining automatic high-quality translations (Dale, 2016; Toral et al., 2018). Thus, a human agent needs to supervise and correct the outputs generated by an MT system. This process is known as *post-editing* and is a common use case of MT in the industrial environment. As MT systems are continuously improving their capabilities, it has acquired major relevance in the translation market (Guerberof, 2008; Pym et al., 2012; Hu and Cadwell, 2016; Turovsky, 2016).

Throughout the post-editing process, new data are continuously generated. These new data have valuable properties—they are domain-specific training samples. Thus, it can be leveraged to continuously adapt the system towards a given domain or the style of the post-editor. A common way of achieving this consists in following an online-learning paradigm (Ortiz-Martínez, 2016; Peris and Casacuberta, 2019). Each time the user validates a post-edit, the system's models are updated incrementally with this new sample. Hence, when the system generates the next translation, it will consider the previous post-edits made by the user and it is expected to produce higher quality translations (or, at least, more suited to the post-editor's preferences).

Domingo et al. (2019b) conducted a preliminary user study for professional post-editors, who had a positive perception of the adaptive systems. However, they noticed that, in some cases, there were occurrences of some made-up words. In this work, we study the impact of this phenomenon. Additionally, we extend their user study by involving three more participants and providing additional measures for the increase in productivity gained with the adaptive system.

2 Related work

Post-editing MT hypotheses is a practice that was adopted in the translation industry a long time ago (e.g., Vasconcellos and León, 1985). Its relevance grew as MT technology advanced and improved. The capabilities of MT post-editing have been demonstrated through many user studies (Aziz et al., 2012; Bentivogli et al., 2016; Castilho et al., 2017; Green et al., 2013a).

Parallel to the rise of the post-editing protocol, using user post-edits to adapt MT systems has also attracted the attention of researches and industry. This was studied in the CasMaCAT (Alabau et al., 2013) and MateCAT (Federico et al., 2014) projects and phrase-based statistical MT systems based on online learning were developed (Ortiz-Martínez, 2016). With the breakthrough in neural MT (NMT) technology (Bahdanau et al., 2015; Wu et al., 2016; Vaswani et al., 2017), research shifted towards constructing adaptive systems via online learning in this post-editing scenario. The use of online learning to adapt an NMT system to a new domain with post-edited samples was proposed by Peris et al. (2017) and Turchi et al. (2017). Other works refined these adaptation techniques and applied them to new use cases (Kothur et al., 2018; Wuebker et al., 2018; Peris and Casacuberta, 2019).

The evaluation of MT post-edits is a hard topic that

Martins, Moniz, Fumega, Martins, Batista, Coheur, Parra, Trancoso, Turchi, Bisazza, Moorkens, Guerberof, Nurminen, Marg, Forcada (eds.)
Proceedings of the 22nd Annual Conference of the European Association for Machine Translation, p. 319–328
Lisboa, Portugal, November 2020.

Corpus	#Sentences	# Tokens		# Types		Average length	
		En	Es	En	Es	En	Es
Training	23.4M	702M	786M	1.8M	1.9M	30.0	33.6
Document 1	150	1.7K	-	618	-	11.3	-
Document 2	150	2.6K	-	752	-	17.3	-

Table 1: Corpora statistics in terms of number of sentences, number of tokens, number of types (vocabulary size) and average sentence length. K denotes thousands and M, millions.

is currently being actively researched (e.g., Toral, 2019; Freitag et al., 2020; Läubli et al., 2020). Several works conducted user studies for MT post-editing systems, either phrase-based (Alabau et al., 2013; Green et al., 2013b; Denkowski et al., 2014; Bentivogli et al., 2016) or NMT (Daems and Macken, 2019; Koponen et al., 2019; Jia et al., 2019). Moreover, two studies showed improvements in terms of productivity time and translation quality with the application of an online learning protocol (Karimova et al., 2018; Domingo et al., 2019b). This latter study is tightly related to ours. We extend it by performing a finer-grained evaluation of the outputs of the adaptive systems.

3 Experimental framework

As we extended the work of Domingo et al. (2019b), we used their same data and systems. The task at hand consisted of a small medico-technical (description of medical equipment) corpus from their production scenario. It contains specific vocabulary from a very closed domain. It was conformed by two documents of 150 sentences, which contained 1.7 and 2.7 thousand words respectively. The translation direction was English to Spanish. The system was trained using the data from WMT'13's translation task (Bojar et al., 2013) and samples selected by the feature decay selection technique (Biçici and Yuret, 2015). The data features are summarized in Table 1. We applied joint byte pair encoding (Sennrich et al., 2016), using $32,000$ merge operations. The system was built with OpenNMT-py (Klein et al., 2017), using a long short-term memory (Gers et al., 2000) recurrent encoder–decoder with attention (Bahdanau et al., 2015). All model dimensions were 512. The system was trained using Adam (Kingma and Ba, 2014) with a fixed learning rate of 0.0002 (Wu et al., 2016) and a batch size of 60. A label smoothing of 0.1 (Szegedy et al., 2015) was applied. At inference time, we used beam search with size 6.

The adaptation process followed the findings from Peris and Casacuberta (2019). We tuned the hyperparameters for the adaptation process on our development set, under simulated conditions. For each new post-edited sample, we applied two plain SGD updates, with a fixed learning rate of 0.05.

As translation environment we used the one designed by Domingo et al. (2019a). It connects our adaptive NMT engine with the SDL Trados Studio interface, which is used by the post-editors in our production

workflow. In addition, it also allowed us to trace the productivity metrics and user behavior.

3.1 Evaluation

We evaluated two main aspects of the adaptation process: productivity of the post-editors and quality of the NMT systems. The former was assessed by computing the average post-editing time per sentence and the number of words generated by the post-editor per hour. For the latter, we employed two well-known MT metrics: (h)BLEU (Papineni et al., 2002) and (h)TER (Snover et al., 2006). In order to ensure consistent BLEU scores, we used sacreBLEU (Post, 2018). Since we computed per-sentence BLEU scores, we used exponential BLEU smoothing (Chen and Cherry, 2014).

We applied approximate randomization tests (Riezler and Maxwell, 2005), with $10,000$ repetitions and a p-value of 0.05, to determine whether two systems presented statistically significant differences.

3.2 Human post-editors

Six professional translators were involved in the experiment. Some profiling details about them can be found in Table 2.

User	Sex	Age	Professional experience
User 1	Male	24	1.5 years
User 2	Female	25	5 years
User 3	Female	30	5 years
User 4	Female	24	1 month
User 5	Female	22	1 year
User 6	Male	48	22 years

Table 2: Information about the human post-editors that took part in the experiment, regarding their sex, age and years of professional experience.

The static experiment consisted in post-editing using the initial NMT system, which remained fixed along the complete process. For the adaptive experiment, all users started with the initial system, which was adapted to each user through the process using their own post-edits. Therefore, at the end of the process, each user obtained a tailored system. In order to avoid the influence of translating the same text multiple times, each participant post-edited a different document set under each scenario (static and adaptive), as shown in Table 3.

User	Document 1	Document 2
User 1	Static	Adaptive
User 2	Adaptive	Static
User 3	Static	Adaptive
User 4	Adaptive	Static
User 5	Static	Adaptive
User 6	Adaptive	Static

Table 3: Distribution of users, document sets and scenarios. All users conducted first the experiment which involved post-editing document 1 and then document 2 (e.g., user 2 first post-edited document 1 on an adaptive scenario and, then, document 2 on a static scenario).

4 User study

In our study, we focus on the differences between static and adaptive systems based on three main aspects: the productivity of post-editors, the quality of post-edits and the generation differences.

4.1 On the productivity of the post-editors

Table 4 shows the average gains obtained in terms of translation quality. These results demonstrate how the adaptive systems benefits from the user post-edits to improve the translation quality, yielding gains of up to 6.7 TER points and 8.0 BLEU points.

Test	System	hTER [↓]	hBLEU [↑]
Document 1	Static	39.5	47.9
	Adaptive	32.8†	55.9†
Document 2	Static	36.2	42.9
	Adaptive	34.3†	50.5†

Table 4: Results of the user experiments, in terms of translation quality. These numbers are averages over the results obtained by the different post-editors. *Static system* stands for conventional post-editing—without adaptation. *Adaptive system* refers to post-editing in an environment with online learning. *hTER* and *hBLEU* refer to the TER and BLEU of the system hypothesis computed against the post-edited sentences. † indicates statistically significant differences between the static and the adaptive systems.

Table 5 presents the productivity improvements yielded by the adaptive system. With two exceptions, the adaptive system significantly reduced the averaged time needed to post-edit a sentence (with gains from 4.0 up to 33.5 seconds per sentence). These two exceptions were for user 2—whose average time was the same for both systems—and user 4—whose average time was bigger when using the adaptive system. This last case can be explained by taking into account that user 4 is one of the least experienced users and that she conducted the experiment involving the adaptive scenario first (see Tables 2 and 3). Therefore, as time goes on, user 4 feels more comfortable with the task and tools and, thus, the post-editing time decreases. This phenomenon was already observed during the CasMaCAT project (Alabau et al., 2013).

When measuring productivity in terms of number

User	System	Time [↓]	Words per hour [↑]
User 1	Static	37.9	1685
	Adaptive	33.0†	1935†
User 2	Static	30.5	2091
	Adaptive	30.4	2097†
User 3	Static	38.0	1678
	Adaptive	27.0†	2364†
User 4	Static	37.5	1701
	Adaptive	47.4†	1346†
User 5	Static	80.2	795
	Adaptive	46.7†	1367†
User 6	Static	53.7	1188
	Adaptive	49.7†	1284†

Table 5: Results of the user experiments, in terms of productivity. *Static system* stands for conventional post-editing, without adaptation. *Adaptive system* refers to post-editing in an environment with online learning. *Time* corresponds to the average post-editing time per sentence, in seconds. *Words per hour* represents the number of words generated by the post-editors per hour. Users 4 to 6 has less experience, in this particular domain, than users 1 to 3. † indicates statistically significant differences between the static and the adaptive systems.

of words generated per hour, the adaptive systems achieved significant gains for all cases except for user 4—which is coherent with the results obtained in terms of time per sentence. These gains range from 6—for user 2, who took the same average time for both scenarios—to 686 words per hour. Therefore, both metrics showcase how adaptive systems are able to significantly improve productivity.

4.1.1 User feedback

Following Domingo et al. (2019b) post-editors filled a questionnaire (see Appendix A) regarding the task they had just performed. We asked them about their level of satisfaction of the translations they had produced; whether they would have preferred translating from scratch instead of post-editing; and their opinion about the automatic translations, in terms of grammar, style and overall quality. Additionally, we also requested them to give, as an open-answer question, their feedback on the task.

While post-editors were generally satisfied with the system and the translations they produced (as also reported by Domingo et al. (2019b)), they spotted some issues regarding the adaptive NMT system: they noticed that domain-specific term were "forgotten" by the system, being wrongly translated. In addition, the users spotted the occurrence of some nonexistent words in the target language (e.g., "absolvido"). We delve deeper into these problems in Section 5.

4.2 On the quality of the post-edits

In order to assess and compare the quality of the human post-edits using the static and adaptive systems, a

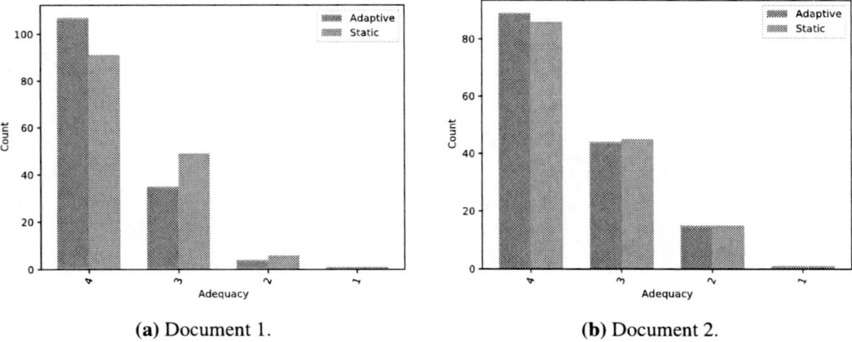

(a) Document 1.　　　　　　(b) Document 2.

Figure 1: Sentence-level adequacy scores. Count values are the average between both evaluators.

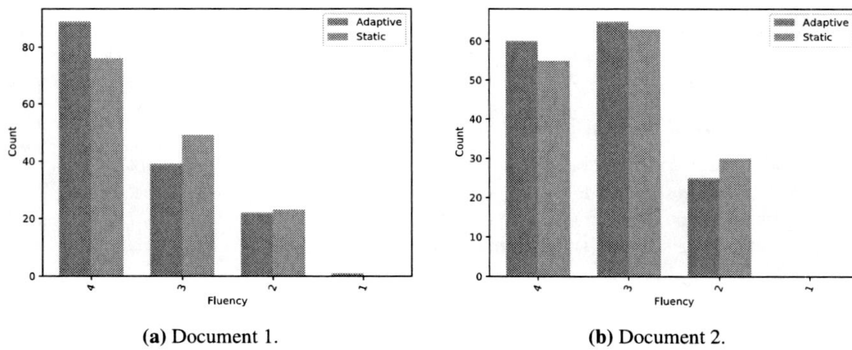

(a) Document 1.　　　　　　(b) Document 2.

Figure 2: Sentence-level fluency scores. Count values are the average between both evaluators.

human evaluation was conducted with the help of two professional translators—who had not taken part in the user study. In this evaluation, the evaluators were given a source sentence and the post-edits produced by each user—three of which had used the static system, and the other three the adaptive system.

Following Castilho et al. (2019) and TAUS adequacy/fluency guidelines[1], they were asked to assess, on a 4-point scale, the adequacy (how much of the meaning is represented in the translation) and the fluency (the extent to which the translation is well-formed grammatically, has correct spellings, adheres to common use of terms, titles and names, is intuitively acceptable and can be sensibly interpreted by a native speaker) of each post-edit.

In total, they evaluated 600 sentences: the post-edits of the first 50 sentences of Document 1 and the post-edits from the first 50 sentences of Document 2 (see Section 3). To avoid biases, evaluators were not given any information regarding the origin of the translations. Figs. 1 and 2 present the results of the evaluation.

In terms of adequacy, results show that, for both systems, most of the post-edits convey the full meaning of

the original sentence or most of it (represented by the scores 4 and 3). Just a few of them convey little or none of the original meaning (represented by the scores of 2 and 1). While both system behave similarly, we observe that a larger amount of the post-edits generated using the adaptive system have the highest adequacy score. This difference is more noteworthy for the post-edits from document 1 than for those from document 2. Similar conclusions can be reached according to fluency: Most post-edits, independently of the system used, are either flawless or good (represented by scores 4 and 3) regarding the extent to which they are constructed. Just a few are considered to be dis-fluent or incomprehensible (represented by a score of 2). Again, both systems are perceived to be similar in document 2, while the adaptive system is perceived as slightly more fluent.

Finally, it is worth noting sine particularities of the task that may have influenced the results of the evaluation: the task consists in the description of medical equipment and, thus, contains several singularities such as specific acronyms (with which the target audience may be more familiar in their original language than with their translation) or description of parts of an equipment (taking into account that the physical equipment may have tags in its original language). Since the evaluators were given no specific instruction about how

---

[1]`https://www.taus.net/academy/`
`best-practices/evaluate-best-practices/`
`adequacy-fluency-guidelines`.

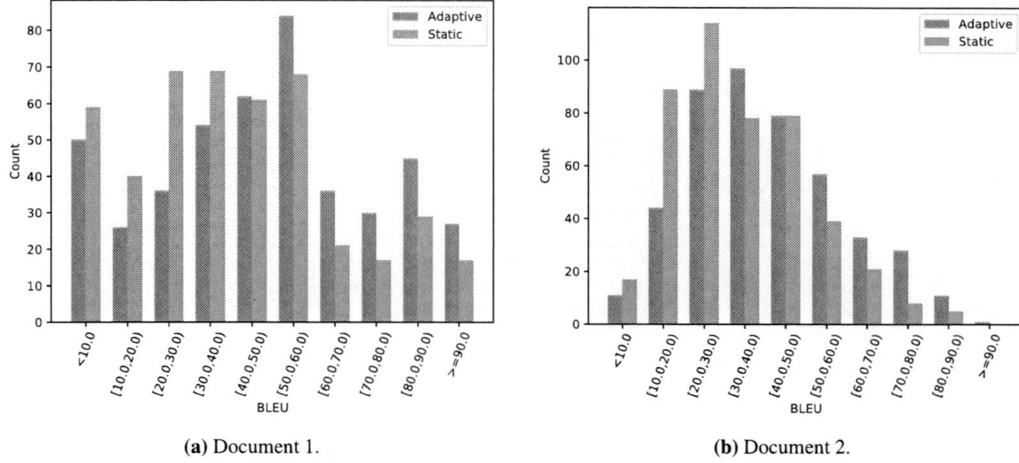

(a) Document 1.   (b) Document 2.

Figure 3: Histogram of sentence-level BLEU scores. The counts are distributed in buckets of range 10.

to solve those particularities, their personal criteria may had an impact in the evaluation results.

4.3 On differences in the generation

Next, we compare both adaptive and static systems in terms of the translations generated. To this end, we employed the discriminative language model method (Akabe et al., 2014) implemented in the `compare-mt` (Neubig et al., 2019) tool, comparing sentence-level BLEU and word n-grams.

In terms of translation quality, we show a histogram of sentence-level BLEU scores in Fig. 3. For both documents, we observe similar trends: the static system generated low-scored sentences more frequently than the adaptive systems. The adaptive systems placed more hypotheses from bucket $[50, 60)$ onward, for both test documents. Moreover, the differences in frequencies between adaptive and static systems were kept at a similar proportion along all high-score buckets. Hence, adaptive systems were able to outperform the static one in these high-score ranges.

The study of the different n-grams helped us to identify common patterns across all users: adaptive systems were able to effectively learn ad-hoc sequences for the task at hand. We discovered several phenomena among the most common n-gram matches of adaptive systems: the correct translation of acronyms, entities relating a particular device and specific task terminology. See Fig. 4 for examples of these phenomena. We found these common constructions to be one of the major causes of the differences in terms of translation quality.

5 Generation of made-up words

On their feedback, the users reported that, in some cases, the system's hypothesis contained words which were not real words (e.g., "absolvido"). This phe-

nomenon, although infrequent, was a bit cumbersome. Most likely, it is caused by an incorrect segmentation of a word via the byte pair encoding process which, according to their frequency, splits words into multiple tokens. In order to assess its impact, we start by quantifying the issue. Table 6 shows the total of made-up words generated per user.

User	System	Words
User 1	Static	3
	Adaptive	6
User 2	Static	8
	Adaptive	5
User 3	Static	3
	Adaptive	17
User 4	Static	8
	Adaptive	5
User 5	Static	3
	Adaptive	14
User 6	Static	8
	Adaptive	4

Table 6: Total made-up words generated per user.

While this phenomenon is not very frequent (it represents from 0.2 up to 0.8% of all the words generated by a given system), it is present in all systems. Depending on the user, this problem was more present using the static or the adaptive system. Since users were using a different document set for each scenario (see Table 3) and there is a significant difference between documents in terms of total words and vocabulary (see Table 1), we need to compute the average per document in order to evaluate how the problem of made-up words generation affects the different scenarios. These results are shown in Table 7.

Although it could be expected for the adaptive sys-

323

Phenomenon	System	Example
Acronyms	Source	QSE Number
	Post-edit	Número **de ESC**
	Adaptive	Número **de ESC**
	Static	Número QSE
Entities	Source	Show the R Series ALS
	Post-edit	Mostrar **la serie R** ALS
	Adaptive	Mostrar **la serie R** ALS
	Static	Mostrar el R Series ALS
Terminology	Source	There are several steps involved with sidestream end tidal CO2 setup.
	Post-edit	La configuración del CO2 **espiratorio final** de flujo lateral se realiza en varios pasos.
	Adaptive	Hay varias etapas de la configuración del CO2 **espiratorio final** del ajuste.
	Static	Hay varias etapas que involucran la configuración del CO2 maremoto del CO2 maremoto

Figure 4: Examples of the n-gram differences between adaptive and static systems. In **boldface** we highlight the differences introduced by adaptive systems.

Document	System	Words
Document 1	Static	5
	Adaptive	4
Document 2	Static	8
	Adaptive	12

Table 7: Average of made-up words generated per document for all users.

tem—which has to deal with a higher number of out-of-vocabularies, introduced by the user—to generate made-up words with a higher frequency, both systems behave similarly: on document 1 case, the static system generated 0.1% more made-up words and, in the other case (document 2), it was the adaptive system which generated 0.1% more made-up words. Furthermore, when comparing both documents, we observe that, despite document 2 having a bigger vocabulary, both static systems generated the same percentage of made-up words. However, Document 2's adaptive systems generated 0.2% of made-up words on average. Most likely, since we did not have an in-domain corpus for training the systems (see Section 3), the bigger the document's vocabulary is, the easier an out-of-vocabulary word may results in an incorrect subword segmentation.

5.1 Error analysis

Fig. 5 shows some example of made-up words generated by the static system.

From the examples, we observe that while the made-up words do not have any sense, they resemble real words (e.g., *pacio* resembles *espacio*; *escaga* resembles *escala*; etc). However, the words they resemble are semantically very different to the correct words (e.g., while *pacio* resembles *espacio*, the correct word would be *estimulación*).

The adaptive systems generates similar made-up words (see Fig. 6 for some examples). However, in this case we observe that some made-up words are almost correct: while *los válvulos* does not exist (*valve* is a

1. La zona verde es para **pacio**.

2. Roll al paciente a su lado, y luego rodar el electrodo hacia la espalda del paciente a la izquierda de su columna y debajo de la **escaga**.

3. Presione la tecla del **softón**.

4. Sin embargo, el metrónomo **absolvido** si las compresiones son inferiores a las directrices.

5. Que el dispositivo puede hacer un choque de prueba de 30 **jojuelas**.

Figure 5: Example of sentences with made-up words (denoted in **bold**) from the static system. The first word should have been *estimulación*, the second one *omóplato*, the third one *RCP*, the fourth one *sonará* and the fifth one *julios*.

1. Al mover el Selector de modo a Pacer se activará la puerta del **pidante** para abrir.

2. Coloque el sensor con el adaptador instalado fuera de todas las fuentes de CO2 (incluidos los **válvulos** de aire de respiración y respiratorio) exhalado.

3. Las **marcapasas** de estimulación deben producirse aproximadamente cada centímetro en la tira.

4. El conector de autoprueba funciona solo cuando el envase del electrodo es **inabierto** y conectado a la serie R Series.

5. Para aplicar los electrodos OneStep, introduzca primero el electrodo trasero para evitar la **herración** del electrodo delantero.

Figure 6: Example of sentences with made-up words (denoted in **bold**) from the adaptive systems. The first word should have been *marcapasos*, the second one *válvulas*, the third one *marcadores*, the fourth one *cerrado* and the fifth one *deformación*.

feminine word in Spanish), it would be correct, from a morphological point of view, if *valve* were masculine. Something similar, but with the opposite gender, happens with *las marcapasas* (which should be *los marca-*

pasos) although, in this case, the correct word would be *marcadores*. While we do not have the means for evaluating the impact in the cognitive effort, we believe this kind of errors are more difficult for the users to deal with due to their similarity with the correct words. However, we need to assess the real impact in a future work.

When comparing both type of systems, there are times in which the adaptive systems are able to generate the correct word when the static system had generated a made-up word; times in which the adaptive systems generate the same made-up word than the static system; and times in which the adaptive systems generate a made-up word when the static system was able to generate the correct word. Note that the behavior of the adaptive systems depend on their user (see Fig. 7 for an example).

Static system: Coloque el sensor con el adaptador instalado fuera de todas las fuentes de CO2 (incluido el del paciente) y *sus válvulas* de escape para el aire libre exhalado y el ventilador del ventilador.

Adaptive system$_{User 1}$**:** Coloque el sensor con el adaptador instalado fuera de todas las fuentes de CO2 (incluido el del paciente y *su respiración* y el respirador exhalado) .

Adaptive system$_{User 3}$**:** Coloque el sensor con el adaptador instalado fuera de todas las fuentes de CO2 (incluidos *los válvulos* de aire de respiración y respiratorio) exhalado.

Adaptive system$_{User 5}$**:** Coloque el sensor con el adaptador alejado de todas las fuentes de CO2 incluido el paciente, y *sus válvulas* de respiración y respiración exhalados).

Figure 7: Example of the different behaviors of the adaptive systems. At a certain point of the translation hypothesis, the static system generates the words *sus válvulas*. In their place, the adaptive system for user 1 generates the words *su respiración*. However, the adaptive system for user 3 generates the words *los válvulos*—making-up the word *válvulos*. Finally, the adaptive system for user 5 coincides with the static system in generating the words *sus válvulas*.

Finally, we tried to compare, using edit distance, the made-up words with the closest words (in morphological terms) from the vocabulary in order to have a better understanding of this phenomenon. However, this study did not show any significant information: in almost all the cases, made-up words had a lot of morphological similitudes with words from the vocabulary but those words had no semantic relation with the correct word.

6 Conclusions and future work

In this work, we extended a previous user study of an adaptive NMT system. We conducted new experiments with the help of professional translators, and observed significant improvements of the translation quality—measured in terms of hTER and hBLEU—and significant improvements of the user's productivity—measured in terms of post-editing time and number of words generated. We also conducted, with the help of two additional professional translators, a human evaluation that verified the quality of the post-edits generated during the user study.

The users were pleased with the system. They noticed that corrections applied on a given segment generally were reflected on the successive ones, making the post-editing process more effective and less tedious. When comparing the translations generated by both kind of systems, we identified that adaptive systems were able to generate the correct translation of acronyms, entities relating a particular device and specific task terminology.

An undesirable side effect mentioned by the users was the sporadic apparition of made-up words. We studied this phenomenon and reached the conclusion that due to the increase in the number of out-of-vocabularies as part of the post-editing process, adaptive systems suffer this problem more than static systems. Furthermore, sometimes these made-up words are very similar, in morphological terms, to the correct words—such as a feminine word converted into its non-existent masculine equivalent—which made them harder to detect. However, the cognitive impact in the post-editors will need to be assesed before reaching categorical conclusions.

In regards to future work, we should try to assess the cognitive impact of the made-up words phenomenon. We would also like to study the degradation of domain-specific terms, and analyze the impact on the amount of work required to post-edit subsequent sentences as the user provides corrected examples. Additionally, we will integrate our adaptive systems together with other translation tools, such as translation memories or terminological dictionaries, with the aim of fostering the productivity of the post-editing process. With this feature-rich system, we would like to conduct additional experiments involving more diverse languages and domains, using domain-specialized NMT systems, testing other models (e.g., Transformer, Vaswani et al., 2017) and involving a larger number of professional post-editors. Finally, we also intend to implement the interactive–predictive machine translation protocol (Lam et al., 2018; Peris and Casacuberta, 2019) in our translation environment, and compare it with the regular post-editing process.

Acknowledgements

The authors wish to thank the anonymous reviewers for their careful reading and in-depth criticisms and suggestions. The research leading to these results has received funding from the Spanish Centre for Technological and Industrial Development (Centro para el Desarrollo Tecnológico Industrial) (CDTI); the European Union through *Programa Operativo de Crecimiento Inteligente* (Project IDI-20170964) and through *Programa Operativo del Fondo Europeo de Desarrollo Regional (FEDER)* from Comunitat Valenciana

(20142020) under project *Sistemas de frabricación inteligentes para la indústria 4.0* (grant agreement ID-IFEDER/2018/025); and Generalitat Valenciana (GVA) under project *Deep learning for adaptive and multimodal interaction in pattern recognition (DeepPattern)* (grant agreement PROMETEO/2019/121). We gratefully acknowledge the support of NVIDIA Corporation with the donation of a GPU used for part of this research; and the translators and project managers from Pangeanic for their help with the user study.

References

Akabe, K., Neubig, G., Sakti, S., Toda, T., and Nakamura, S. (2014). Discriminative language models as a tool for machine translation error analysis. In *Proceedings of COLING 2014, the 25th International Conference on Computational Linguistics: Technical Papers*, pages 1124–1132.

Alabau, V., Bonk, R., Buck, C., Carl, M., Casacuberta, F., García-Martínez, M., González-Rubio, J., Koehn, P., Leiva, L. A., Mesa-Lao, B., Ortiz-Martínez, D., Saint-Amand, H., Sanchis-Trilles, G., and Tsoukala, C. (2013). CASMACAT: An open source workbench for advanced computer aided translation. *The Prague Bulletin of Mathematical Linguistics*, 100:101–112.

Aziz, W., Castilho, S., and Specia, L. (2012). Pet: a tool for post-editing and assessing machine translation. In *In proceedings of The International Conference on Language Resources and Evaluation*, pages 3982–3987.

Bahdanau, D., Cho, K., and Bengio, Y. (2015). Neural machine translation by jointly learning to align and translate. *arXiv:1409.0473*.

Bentivogli, L., Bertoldi, N., Cettolo, M., Federico, M., Negri, M., and Turchi, M. (2016). On the evaluation of adaptive machine translation for human post-editing. *IEEE/ACM Transactions on Audio, Speech and Language Processing*, 24(2):388–399.

Biçici, E. and Yuret, D. (2015). Optimizing instance selection for statistical machine translation with feature decay algorithms. *IEEE/ACM Transactions on Audio, Speech and Language Processing*, 23(2):339–350.

Bojar, O., Buck, C., Callison-Burch, C., Haddow, B., Koehn, P., Monz, C., Post, M., Saint-Amand, H., Soricut, R., and Specia, L., editors (2013). *Proceedings of the Eighth Workshop on Statistical Machine Translation*.

Castilho, S., Moorkens, J., Gaspari, F., Calixto, I., Tinsley, J., and Way, A. (2017). Is neural machine translation the new state of the art? *The Prague Bulletin of Mathematical Linguistics*, 108(1):109–120.

Castilho, S., Resende, N., Gaspari, F., Way, A., ODowd, T., Mazur, M., Herranz, M., Helle, A., Ramírez-Sánchez, G., Sánchez-Cartagena, V., Pinnis, M. a., and Šics, V. (2019). Large-scale machine translation evaluation of the iADAATPA project. In *Proceedings of the Machine Translation Summit*, pages 179–185.

Chen, B. and Cherry, C. (2014). A systematic comparison of smoothing techniques for sentence-level bleu. In *Proceedings of the Ninth Workshop on Statistical Machine Translation*, pages 362–367.

Daems, J. and Macken, L. (2019). Interactive adaptive smt versus interactive adaptive nmt: a user experience evaluation. *Machine Translation*, pages 1–18.

Dale, R. (2016). How to make money in the translation business. *Natural Language Engineering*, 22(2):321–325.

Denkowski, M., Dyer, C., and Lavie, A. (2014). Learning from post-editing: Online model adaptation for statistical machine translation. In *Proceedings of the 14th Conference of the European Chapter of the Association for Computational Linguistics*, pages 395–404.

Domingo, M., García-Martínez, M., Estela Pastor, A., Bié, L., Helle, A., Peris, Á., Casacuberta, F., and Herranz Pérez, M. (2019a). Demonstration of a neural machine translation system with online learning for translators. In *Proceedings of the 57th Annual Meeting of the Association for Computational Linguistics: System Demonstrations*, pages 70–74.

Domingo, M., García-Martínez, M., Peris, Á., Helle, A., Estela, A., Bié, L., Casacuberta, F., and Herranz, M. (2019b). Incremental adaptation of NMT for professional post-editors: A user study. In *Proceedings of the Machine Translation Summit*, pages 219–227.

Federico, M., Bertoldi, N., Cettolo, M., Negri, M., Turchi, M., Trombetti, M., Cattelan, A., Farina, A., Lupinetti, D., Martines, A., Massidda, A., Schwenk, H., Barrault, L., Blain, F., Koehn, P., Buck, C., and Germann, U. (2014). The matecat tool. In *Proceedings of the 25th International Conference on Computational Linguistics: System Demonstrations*, pages 129–132.

Freitag, M., Grangier, D., and Caswell, I. (2020). Bleu might be guilty but references are not innocent. *arXiv:2004.06063*.

Gers, F. A., Schmidhuber, J., and Cummins, F. (2000). Learning to forget: Continual prediction with LSTM. *Neural computation*, 12(10):2451–2471.

Green, S., Heer, J., and Manning, C. D. (2013a). The efficacy of human post-editing for language translation. In *Proceedings of the SIGCHI Conference on Human Factors in Computing Systems*, pages 439–448.

Green, S., Wang, S., Cer, D., and Manning, C. D. (2013b). Fast and adaptive online training of feature-rich translation models. In *Proceedings of the 51st Annual Meeting of the Association for Computational Linguistics*, volume 1, pages 311–321.

Guerberof, A. (2008). Productivity and quality in the post-editing of outputs from translation memories and machine translation. *Localisation Focus*, 7(1):11–21.

Hu, K. and Cadwell, P. (2016). A comparative study of post-editing guidelines. In *Proceedings of the 19th Annual Conference of the European Association for Machine Translation*, pages 34206–353.

Jia, Y., Carl, M., and Wang, X. (2019). Post-editing neural machine translation versus phrase-based machine translation for english–chinese. *Machine Translation*, pages 1–21.

Karimova, S., Simianer, P., and Riezler, S. (2018). A user-study on online adaptation of neural machine translation to human post-edits. *Machine Translation*, 32(4):309–324.

Kingma, D. P. and Ba, J. (2014). Adam: A method for stochastic optimization. *arXiv preprint arXiv:1412.6980*.

Klein, G., Kim, Y., Deng, Y., Senellart, J., and Rush, A. M. (2017). OpenNMT: Open-source toolkit for neural machine translation. In *Proceedings of the Association for the Computational Linguistics*, pages 67–72.

Koponen, M., Salmi, L., and Nikulin, M. (2019). A product and process analysis of post-editor corrections on neural, statistical and rule-based machine translation output. *Machine Translation*, pages 1–30.

Kothur, S. S. R., Knowles, R., and Koehn, P. (2018). Document-level adaptation for neural machine translation. In *Proceedings of the 2nd Workshop on Neural Machine Translation and Generation*, pages 64–73.

Lam, T. K., Kreutzer, J., and Riezler, S. (2018). A reinforcement learning approach to interactive-predictive neural machine translation. In *Proceedings of the European Association for Machine Translation conference*, pages 169–178.

Läubli, S., Castilho, S., Neubig, G., Sennrich, R., Shen, Q., and Toral, A. (2020). A set of recommendations for assessing human–machine parity in language translation. *Journal of Artificial Intelligence Research*, 67:653–672.

Neubig, G., Dou, Z.-Y., Hu, J., Michel, P., Pruthi, D., and Wang, X. (2019). compare-mt: A tool for holistic comparison of language generation systems. In *Proceedings of the 2019 Conference of the North American Chapter of the Association for Computational Linguistics (Demonstrations)*, pages 35–41.

Ortiz-Martínez, D. (2016). Online learning for statistical machine translation. *Computational Linguistics*, 42(1):121–161.

Papineni, K., Roukos, S., Ward, T., and Zhu, W.-J. (2002). BLEU: a method for automatic evaluation of machine translation. In *Proceedings of the Annual Meeting of the Association for Computational Linguistics*, pages 311–318.

Peris, Á. and Casacuberta, F. (2019). Online learning for effort reduction in interactive neural machine translation. *Computer Speech & Language. In Press.*

Peris, Á., Cebrián, L., and Casacuberta, F. (2017). Online learning for neural machine translation post-editing. *arXiv:1706.03196*.

Post, M. (2018). A call for clarity in reporting bleu scores. In *Proceedings of the Third Conference on Machine Translation: Research Papers*, pages 186–191.

Pym, A., Grin, F., Sfreddo, C., and Chan, A. (2012). The status of the translation profession in the european union. Technical report.

Riezler, S. and Maxwell, J. T. (2005). On some pitfalls in automatic evaluation and significance testing for mt. In *Proceedings of the ACL workshop on intrinsic and extrinsic evaluation measures for machine translation and/or summarization*, pages 57–64.

Sennrich, R., Haddow, B., and Birch, A. (2016). Neural machine translation of rare words with subword units. In *Proceedings of the Annual Meeting of the Association for Computational Linguistics*, pages 1715–1725.

Snover, M., Dorr, B., Schwartz, R., Micciulla, L., and Makhoul, J. (2006). A study of translation edit rate with targeted human annotation. In *Proceedings of the Association for Machine Translation in the Americas*, pages 223–231.

Szegedy, C., Liu, W., Jia, Y., Sermanet, P., Reed, S., Anguelov, D., Erhan, D., Vanhoucke, V., and Rabinovich, A. (2015). Going deeper with convolutions. In *Proceedings of the IEEE Conference on Computer Vision and Pattern Recognition*, pages 1–9.

Toral, A. (2019). Post-editese: an exacerbated translationese. In *Proceedings of Machine Translation Summit XVII Volume 1: Research Track*, pages 273–281.

Toral, A., Castilho, S., Hu, K., and Way, A. (2018). Attaining the unattainable? reassessing claims of human parity in neural machine translation. In *Proceedings of the Third Conference on Machine Translation: Research Papers*, pages 113–123, Brussels, Belgium. Association for Computational Linguistics.

Turchi, M., Negri, M., Farajian, M. A., and Federico, M. (2017). Continuous learning from human post-edits for neural machine translation. *The Prague Bulletin of Mathematical Linguistics*, 108(1):233–244.

Turovsky, B. (2016). Ten years of Google Translate.

Vasconcellos, M. and León, M. (1985). SPANAM and ENGSPAN: machine translation at the pan american health organization. *Computational Linguistics*, 11(2-3).

Vaswani, A., Shazeer, N., Parmar, N., Uszkoreit, J., Jones, L., Gomez, A. N., Kaiser, Ł., and Polosukhin, I. (2017). Attention is all you need. In *Advances in Neural Information Processing Systems*, pages 5998–6008.

Wu, Y., Schuster, M., Chen, Z., Le, Q. V., Norouzi, M., Macherey, W., Krikun, M., Cao, Y., Gao, Q., Macherey, K., Klingner, J., Shah, A., Johnson, M., Liu, X., Kaiser, Ł., Gouws, S., Kato, Y., Kudo, T., Kazawa, H., Stevens, K., Kurian, G., Patil, N., Wang, W., Young, C., Smith, J., Riesa, J., Rudnick, A., Vinyals, O., Corrado, G., Hughes, M., and Dean, J. (2016). Google's neural machine translation system: Bridging the gap between human and machine translation. *arXiv:1609.08144*.

Wuebker, J., Simianer, P., and DeNero, J. (2018). Compact personalized models for neural machine translation. In *Proceedings of the 2018 Conference on Empirical Methods in Natural Language Processing*, pages 881–886.

Appendix A   User Questionnaire

How satisfied are you with the translation you have produced?

- Very satisfied.

- Somewhat satisfied.

- Neutral.

- Somewhat dissatisfied.

- Very dissatisfied.

Would you have preferred to work on your translation from scratch instead of post-editing machine translation?

- Yes.

- No.

Do you think that you will want to apply machine translation in your future translation tasks?

- Yes, at some point.

- No, never.

- I'm not sure yet.

Based on the post-editing task you have performed, how much do you rate machine translation outputs on the following attributes?

	Well below average	Below average	Average	Above average	Well above average
Grammatically					
Style					
Overall quality					

Based on the post-editing task you have performed, which of these statements will you go for?

- I had to post-edit ALL the outputs.

- I had to post-edit about 75 % of the outputs.

- I had to post-edit 2550 % outputs.

- I only had to post-edit VERY FEW outputs.

Based on the post-editing task you have performed, how often would you have preferred to translate from scratch rather than post-editing machine translation?

- Always.

- In most of the cases (75 % of the outputs or more).

- In almost half of the cases (approximately 50 %).

- Only in a very few cases (less than 25 %).

Which of the tasks do you think was the one that contained online learning? *(Note: This question was only asked after both tasks had been completed.)*

- Task 1.

- Task 2.

Give your opinion about the task you have performed.

NICE: Neural Integrated Custom Engines

Daniel Marín Buj[1], Daniel Ibáñez García[1], Zuzanna Parcheta[1], Francisco Casacuberta[2]

```
daniel.marin@cdt.europa.eu
{daniel.ibanez,zuzanna.parcheta}@ext.cdt.europa.eu
fcn@prhlt.upv.es
```

[1] Translation Centre for the Bodies of the European Union
[2] PRHLT Research Center, Universitat Politecnica de València

Abstract

In this paper, we present a machine translation system implemented by the Translation Centre for the Bodies of the European Union. The main goal of this project is to create domain-specific machine translation engines to support machine translation services and applications for the Translation Centre's clients. In this article, we explain the entire implementation process of NICE: Neural Integrated Custom Engines. We describe the problems identified and the solutions provided, and present the final results for different language pairs. Finally, we describe the work that will be done on this project in the future.

1 Project description

Set up in 1994, the Translation Centre for the Bodies of the European Union (CdT) delivers an average of 750,000 pages a year to over 60 European Union institutions, agencies and bodies across Europe. It has grown steadily, hand in hand with an increasing number of official European Union (EU) languages. To meet the needs of its clients and to cope with very specialised fields and growing translation volumes, the CdT has decided to enhance its services with state-of-the-art technologies such as neural machine translation (NMT) (Wu, 2016; Castilho, 2017).

The business goal of this project is to provide raw machine translation of source texts that enable translators to produce final translations that are indistinguishable from human translations with less effort than it would take to produce the same translations from scratch (Jia, 2019). Also, we aim to create engines that are fully integrated into CdT's translation management system and fine-tuned for specific needs, such as post-editing particular document types, which cannot be achieved by existing systems. Finally, the purpose is to keep maximum confidentiality in the inference process by assuring an adapted, on-premise infrastructure.

In this work, we focus on two different domains: intellectual property (IP) and public health (PH). Although the scope of the project includes all 24 official EU languages, each domain has its requirements in terms of language coverage. Thus, we targeted specific pairs for the development phase of the engines, with English being the common language for all models.

The practice adopted for the development of machine translation engines included extensive preprocessing of data. After such data preparation, a generic model (GEN) was trained using data from all available domains. Then, the generic model was fine-tuned with in-domain data (IND). After training the IND model, we tested it using fixed test sets, and with five standard metrics. After the automatic evaluation against high-quality references, human translators assessed another set of representative samples by applying predefined metrics at a segment level, such as adequacy and fluency (Koehn, 2006), and by post-editing the raw output to measure potential productivity gains (Levenshtein distance (Marg, 2016)). All steps of NMT engine creation will be explained in the following sections.

Martins, Moniz, Fumega, Martins, Batista, Coheur, Parra, Trancoso, Turchi, Bisazza, Moorkens, Guerberof, Nurminen, Marg, Forcada (eds.)
Proceedings of the 22nd Annual Conference of the European Association for Machine Translation, p. 329–338
Lisboa, Portugal, November 2020.

2 Data available

The available data for all language pairs belong to existing domains: IP, PH, other domains and generic material.

Within each domain, the data was split into an extendable number of sets depending on the quality for the purpose, ordered from the most suitable (1) to the less suitable (5), with each number reflecting the relative and presumed quality of the set, as follows:

1. Validated translations from CdT translation memories.

2. Non-validated translations from CdT translation memories.

3. Verified sentence-based alignments from CdT legacy data.

4. Non-CdT data sources (public).

5. Synthetic data (CdT and non-CdT).

Each sentence pair extracted from the quality sets is linked to metadata labels indicating the date and the quality set number to which the pair belongs. This metadata was used in the preprocessing pipeline. Most of the data was parsed as TMX 1.4b; however, publicly available data was obtained in different formats such as plain text or other TMX versions.

For low-resource pairs with English as source language, we generated synthetic data to enlarge the training corpora. We consider low-resource language pairs when the IND dataset contains less than 150,000 bilingual sentences. The synthetic data consists of back translations of monolingual sets extracted from non-English language pairs, such as Croatian–French, being the Croatian the low-resource language in this case. As described in Koehn et al. (2017), successful applications of this idea used equal amounts of synthetic and true data to train the final system. However, generating this amount of synthetic data is not always possible. Besides, to generate synthetic data, a reverse translation system is required. Since most CdT machine translation engines are unidirectional from English, we used `eTranslation` platform for generating synthetic data via back-translation.[1]

[1] `https://ec.europa.eu/cefdigital/`
`eTranslation`

`eTranslation` (Oravecz, 2019) is the European Commission's machine translation service, supported by the Connecting Europe Facility (CEF) and developed by the Directorate-General for Translation. Available engines can translate documents between all official EU languages and a few non-EU languages, providing quality machine translation in a secure system that protects privacy. As an EU body, the CdT contributes to its development and maintenance and has access to its platform. These engines were used for back-translation because of the high-quality output, as demonstrated in experiments to benchmark both `eTranslation` and our translation system.

To determine whether and to what extent synthetic data improves the quality of the PH engine, different experiments were conducted with the English–Croatian pair, using all available data and comparing the model trained with synthetic data (quality sets 1-5) against a baseline trained without any synthetic data (quality sets 1-4). The detailed amounts of data are shown in Table 1 (EN—HR). From Figure 1 we can appreciate that the GEN model obtains lower sacreBLEU (Post, 2018) with synthetic data. It can be due to the fact that the GEN model is large enough (1.4 millions of bilingual sentences) and the added 460,000 bilingual synthetic sentences are of lower quality than the original data from the generic model. The fact that the validation and test sets belong to IND makes the potential degradation of the GEN scores less relevant, as long as IND scores improve. In the case of the IND model, the sacreBLEU score of the model trained with synthetic data is around 0.5 points higher when using synthetic data in the GEN and IND models. The IND data contains only 83,000 sentences, so the addition of 33,000 bilingual synthetic sentences had a positive effect on the final score. The last experiment with synthetic data was the fine-tuning of the original GEN model (without synthetic data) with an IND dataset including synthetic data. The obtained sacreBLEU score was 52.4, which implies a reduction of 0.6 sacreBLEU points compared to 53 sacreBLEU points from the previous experiment. Therefore, the best approach found was to apply synthetic data to both GEN and IND models.

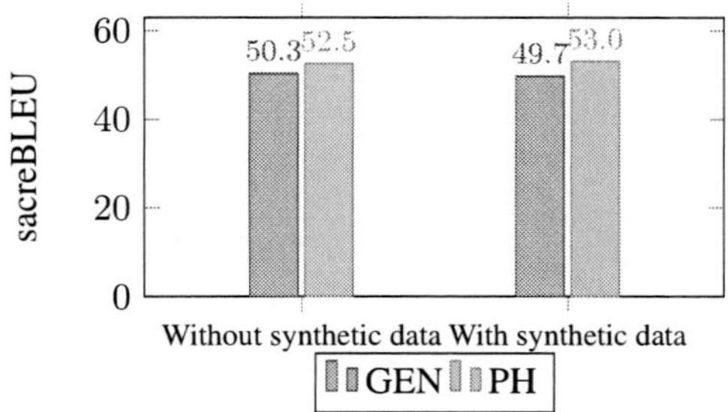

Figure 1: Comparison of the PH model output quality with and without synthetic data for English–Croatian using sacreBLEU.

3 Data preparation

In this section, we describe the entire data preparation process, which is as follows:

1. **Extraction of parallel sentences from TMX files**: we extracted translation units for the relevant languages from the available quality-graded sets.

2. **Cleaning of anomalous data**: we filtered out pairs according to different criteria, such as sentence pairs with identical source and target, sentences without words, or anomalous size ratios between source and target lengths.

3. **Deduplication**: we deduplicated pairs when the same source was translated in different ways more than once keeping the most recent translation with the highest quality. To keep the best pairs in the deduplication step, the quality labels described previously were used.

4. **Removal of oversized sentences**: to accommodate differences among languages, we used a parameter that indicates the percentage of sentences to keep by length. We applied a value of 0.99, which removes 1% of the sentences.

5. **Data normalisation**: we used regular expressions to protect numbers, URLs, emails, codes and certain acronyms, and replaced them with the corresponding token, e.g. numbers with ((NUMBER 0)), as described in Post et al. (2019). Where sentences contained several matches of the same pattern, we numbered each of them, e.g ((NUMBER 0)), ((NUMBER 1)).

6. **Vocabulary model training**: we trained a byte-pair encoding model using the `sentencepiece` sub-word tokeniser (Kudo, 2018), which omits the previously protected tokens.

7. **Training data encoding**: we tokenised training data with the `sentencepiece` model.

8. **Advanced data filtering**: we applied `fast_align` (Dyer, 2013) to train an alignment model on good quality data (i.e. quality sets 1 and 2) for the corresponding language pair. `fast_align` allows an alignment model to be computed that contains negative log-likelihood between source and target words. Once the alignment model was built, we scored the clean data and obtained a $z - score$ for each sentence. The scored bilingual sentences were normalised by the source length of each bilingual pair and the vector was standardised using Equation 1, where μ is the mean of scores and σ is its standard deviation.

$$z = \frac{x - \mu}{\sigma} \qquad (1)$$

In Figure 2, the grey field represents the sentences below a fixed threshold that are filtered out; in this case, -1. Where the dataset was very small, we applied a lower threshold so the filtering would be more tolerant.

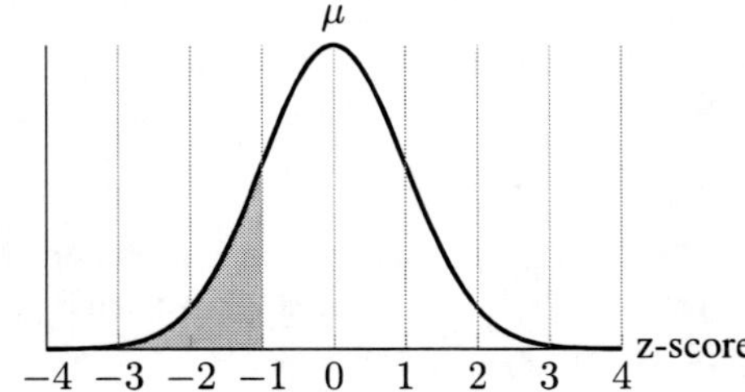

Figure 2: Z-score filtering.

We conducted experiments using `fast_align` data filtering method for English–Polish and English–German. Figure 3 shows the sacreBLEU scores and demonstrates the significant improvement in engine quality using `fast_align` for language pairs with many resources such as

English–German (EN–DE) and low-resource language such as English–Polish (EN–PL) pairs.

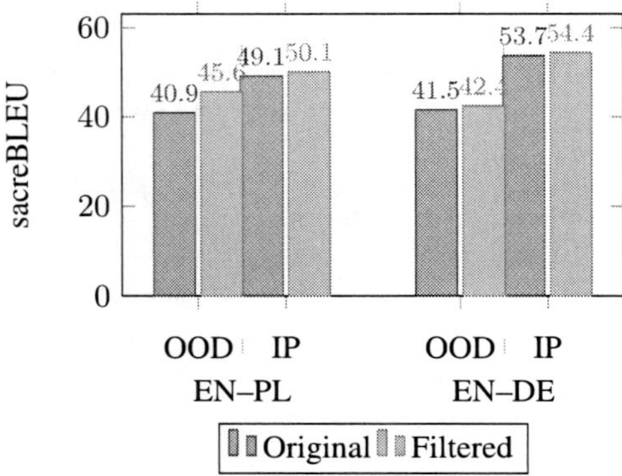

Figure 3: Quality comparison using English–Polish (EN–PL) and English–German (EN–DE) language pairs. 'Original' data means that the data was not cleaned and 'filtered' means that the data was filtered using `fast_align`. The sacreBLEU scores come from the evaluation of the normal test set.

Table 1: Example sizes of parallel corpora for a given language pair before and after data preparation.

Pair	Quality	Domain	Before	After
EN–ES	1	GEN	1.1M	460k
		PH	141k	90k
	2	GEN	649k	257k
		PH	57k	31k
	3	GEN	1M	590k
		PH	226k	144k
	4	GEN	13.5M	6.7M
		PH	1.5M	443k
	5	GEN	0	0
		PH	0	0
	Total	GEN	16.2M	8M
		PH	1.9M	708k
EN–HR	1	GEN	542k	266k
		PH	110k	60k
	2	GEN	268k	121k
		PH	37k	14k
	3	GEN	238k	132k
		PH	12k	8.7k
	4	GEN	1.9M	931k
		PH	0	0
	5	GEN	560k	460k
		PH	42k	33k
	Total	GEN	3.5M	1.9M
		PH	201k	116k

A large amount of data was discarded after the data preparation process. Table 1 shows the number of sentence pairs available for each quality set for a language pair with sufficient resources, such as English–Spanish (EN–ES), compared to a low-resource language pair, such as English–Croatian (EN–HR), before and after data preprocessing.

4   Training

All our engines are built with `OpenNMT-tf` (Klein, 2017), which is an open-source toolkit for NMT and neural sequence learning with a TensorFlow backend.

4.1   Architecture

The architecture used to train our models is TransformerBig, a large transformer network based on Vaswani et al. (2017).

The transformer is based on an encoder-decoder structure (Bahdanau, 2014; Cho, 2014). The encoder maps an input sequence of symbol representations $(x_1, \ldots, x_n)$ to a sequence of continuous representations $(z_1, \ldots, z_n)$. Given z, the decoder then generates an output sequence $(y_1, \ldots, y_m)$ of symbols one element at a time. At each step the model is auto-regressive (Graves, 2014), consuming the previously generated symbols as additional input when generating the next. The transformer follows this overall architecture using stacked self-attention and point-wise, fully connected layers for both the encoder and decoder.

4.2   Hyperparameters

During the training process, we used Adam as optimisation method (Kingma, 2014). A dropout layer of 30% probability was applied and a weight decay value of 10^{-4}. We calculated the number of validation steps based on the size of the training data and considering a buffer of 500,000 shuffled sentences, including at least two validation cycles per epoch. That way, the validation steps depend on the corpora and the batch size, which is usually of 64 examples. We stored the last ten checkpoints and applied early stopping (Prechelt, 1998) with a patience value of five evaluations. Once the training was stopped, we averaged the five best stored models.

4.3   Instance description

The training was done in Amazon Elastic Compute Cloud (Amazon EC2).[2] EC2 is a cloud service enabling developers to instantiate machines, which can be configured on-demand in terms of speed, storage and mathematical calculation.

---

[2]`https://aws.amazon.com/ec2`

We used a 'p3.8xlarge' instance to train translation models. This instance type includes 4 NVIDIA Tesla V100 GPUs with 16 GiB of GPU memory each, which allows an in-domain model to be trained using a TransformerBig architecture in 7-12 hours depending on the language pair.

5 Evaluation

In this section, we describe the validation process and test set generation and which type of sentences each test set contains. We describe the final evaluation of the models by human translators and the benchmarking exercise against two state-of-the-art systems: `eTranslation` and `DeepL Pro`.[3]

5.1 Validation and test

A random test file containing 2,000 sentences was generated from the IND dataset. In addition, several test files were generated to check the quality of specific types of segments, such as very long or very short sentences, sentences with numbers, etc. Those files were produced just once, and were used for all experiments for a given domain and language pair. To generate the test files, we first prepared the training data and, from there, calculated several parameters to use when producing the test sets. These parameters included the threshold indicating when a sentence is considered too long. Each test set can be described as follows:

- Normal: 2,000 pairs; this set is extracted from the IND dataset and is used to check the quality of the trained model.

- Long: 1,000 pairs; it contains long sentences. A sentence is considered long when it is longer than 80% of the sentences in the training set.

- Short: 1,000 pairs; it contains short sentences to translate. The default length of short sentences is two full words but this parameter is configurable.

- Numbers: 1,000 pairs; it contains sentences with numbers, dates and codes, e.g. 578,850 euros, or 40%.

- Uppercase: 1,000 pairs; sentences that contain uppercase letters, e.g. entity names.

To validate the model during the training process, we used a validation set of 2,000 sentence pairs, which was extracted as a normal test set from the IND dataset. It was also generated once and the same validation file was used in all experiments for a given language pair.

5.2 Metrics

We used several standard metrics to evaluate the test files described above. We evaluated each file at document and sentence level based on the following metrics: sacreBLEU (Post, 2018), NIST (Doddington, 2002), TER (Snover, 2006), CHARCUT (Lardilleux, 2017) and METEOR (Denkowski, 2011). Even though sacreBLEU's purpose is to evaluate whole documents, we also used it to evaluate each sentence. The sentence evaluation is only used for our internal records, to collect data for future experiments and to facilitate deeper analysis of the sentences.

5.3 Human evaluation

The final validation of the engines was done by translators. This assessment was carried out with a minimum of one in-house translator (worst-case scenario) and up to three professional linguists, depending on the language pair and the domain. The results for engines in the PH and IP domains are described separately below.

The human assessment focused on the following categories and metrics:

- Fluency: assesses to what extent a translated text is grammatically informed, whether it contains spelling errors, and how it is perceived by a native speaker. It is manually entered by the translator according to a scale of 1 (lowest mark) to 4 (highest mark).

- Adequacy: assesses to what extent the meaning in the source text is expressed in the translation. It is manually entered by the translator according to a scale of 1 (lowest mark) to 4 (highest mark).

- Productivity: computed automatically at a segment level by comparing the raw machine translation against the post-edited version as the normalised edit distance. It considers the minimum number of character edits (i.e.

---

[3] `https://www.deepl.com`

insertions, deletions or substitutions) that are required to transform the original string into the final version of the same string. Scientific research (Marg, 2016) suggests a strong correlation between edit distance and post-editing productivity metrics.

The acceptance threshold for quality criteria (fluency and adequacy) was set at 2.75 by a consensus among the specialists involved in the project. Also, the acceptance criteria for productivity were as follows: a maximum of 25% of text should be classified as 'Re-translation required', and a minimum of 50% of text should be classified as 'Acceptable as is' or 'Little post-editing needed'. The mapping between these categories and the normalised edit distances was decided by a consensus among the specialists of the project. The results for IP and PH domains are reported separately below.

IP domain: models created for the IP domain cover eight language pairs: {DE, ES, FR, IT}–EN and EN–{DE, ES, FR, IT}. Figure 4 shows the quality of IP documents in eight different languages in terms of fluency and adequacy. The post-editing effort of documents from the IP domain is shown in Figure 5.

The results presented reflect the quality of the first builds that yielded acceptable ratings during the human evaluation, resulting in eight out of eight language pairs deemed fit for purpose according to the fluency and adequacy marks of 1,567 segments. All models were considered as fit for assimilation and post-editing.

PH domain: models created for the PH domain cover seven language pairs: EN–{BG, DA, DE, ES, FR, PL, SV}. Human evaluation was done at a subdomain level, each corresponding to a specialised EU agency (EMA,[4] EU-OSHA,[5] ECDC,[6] EMCDDA[7]), by CdT translators evaluating linguistic quality and productivity aspects. The main difference between the subdomains is that EMA document types can be considered technical, i.e. medical prospects, reports or scientific documentation. Other subdomain texts (EU-OSHA, ECDC, EMCDDA)

are of an informative or educational nature, such as web articles, press releases or content for the general public. In total, 1,533 sentences were evaluated by human translators; the number of sentences evaluated from each subdomain is shown in Table 2. Figure 6 shows the quality of EMA documents for seven different language pairs. Figure 7 shows the productivity results for the EMA subdomain.

Table 2: Number of segments evaluated per subdomain.

Subdomain	Segments evaluated
ECDC	161
EMA	854
EMCDDA	168
EU-OSHA	350
Grand Total	1533

The productivity evaluation between different agencies is shown in Figure 8.

Following the acceptance criteria for productivity, six out of seven languages pairs evaluated from the EMA subdomain were considered as fit for assimilation and post-editing. EMCDDA and EU-OSHA results were fit for assimilation and post-editing only for a limited set of language pairs. ECDC subdomain results were not fit for assimilation and post-editing. The language pairs from different subdomains that do not meet the acceptance requirements are shown in Table 3.

Table 3: Subdomains failing at quality and/or productivity.

Subdomain	Pair	Quality	Productivity
EMA	EN–SV	✓	✗
ECDC	EN–FR	✓	✗
	EN–DE	✓	✗
	EN–SV	✓	✗
EU-OSHA	EN–PL	✗	✗
	EN–DE	✓	✗
	EN–DA	✓	✗
	EN–SV	✗	✗
EMCDDA	EN–FR	✓	✗
	EN–DA	✓	✗
	EN–BG	✓	✗
	EN–DE	✗	✗
	EN–ES	✗	✗
	EN–SV	✓	✗

In total, 14 out of 28 cases (language pair plus PH subdomain) did not meet the acceptance requirements in terms of productivity.

In terms of fluency and adequacy, the non-technical documents received much lower scores than technical documents (EMA).

---

[4] https://www.ema.europa.eu
[5] https://osha.europa.eu
[6] https://www.ecdc.europa.eu
[7] http://www.emcdda.europa.eu

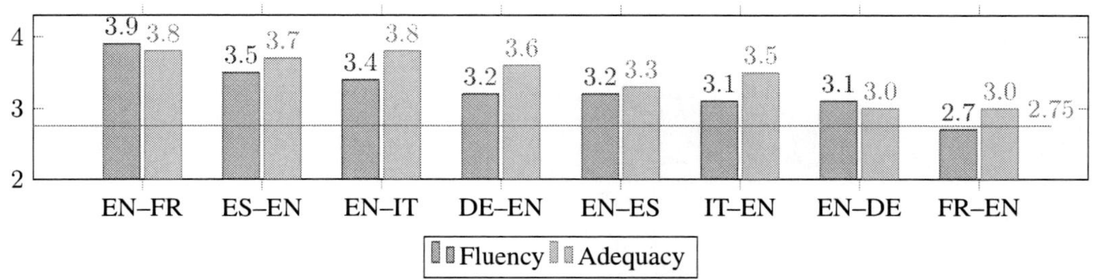

Figure 4: Fluency and adequacy, weighted by segment length in the IP domain.

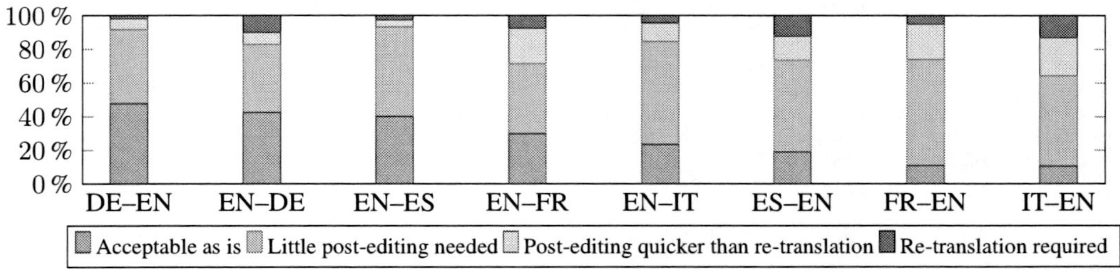

Figure 5: Post-editing effort per segment, weighted by segment length. Based on the calculation of the normalised edit distance at segment level weighted by the segment length in a total of 3,726 segments (85,577 words) post-edited by professional linguists.

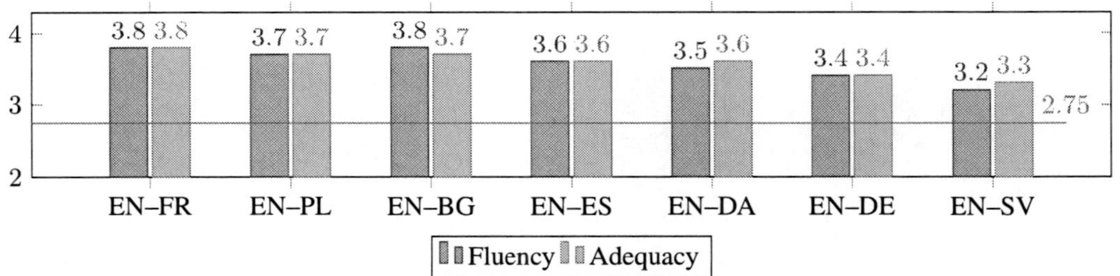

Figure 6: Fluency and adequacy, weighted by segment length from EMA documents.

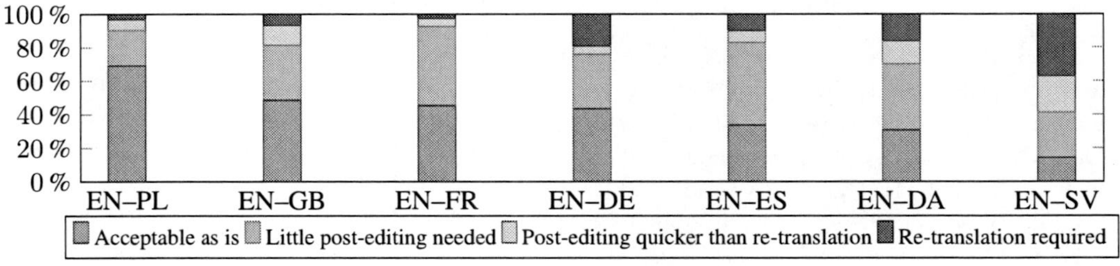

Figure 7: Post-editing effort per segment, weighted by segment length. Based on the calculation of the normalised edit distance at segment level weighted by the segment length in a total of 854 segments from EMA documents post-edited by CdT linguists.

5.4 Benchmarking

The benchmarking was done against `eTranslation` and `DeepL Pro`, which are top-quality machine translation platforms in the industry. However, the system comparison may not be representative enough since the samples used for benchmarking had never been seen before by `NICE`, while this could not be guaranteed in the case of `DeepL Pro` and `eTranslation`. Therefore, results are only indicative and cannot be used to draw any conclusion. The systems for each domain are compared separately below.

IP benchmarking: Figure 9 shows the comparison of quality in terms of fluency and adequacy against `eTranslation` and `DeepL`.

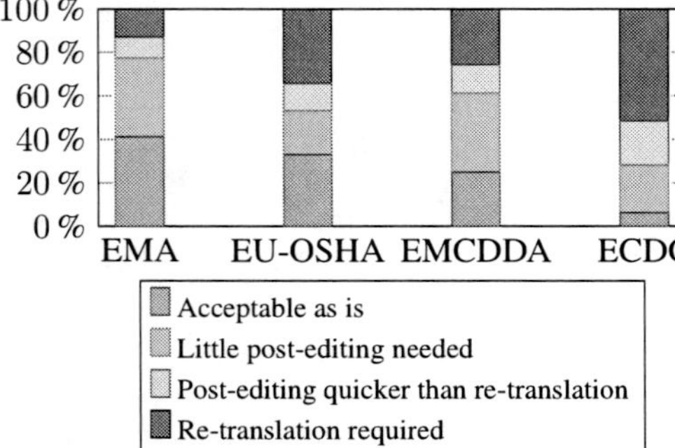

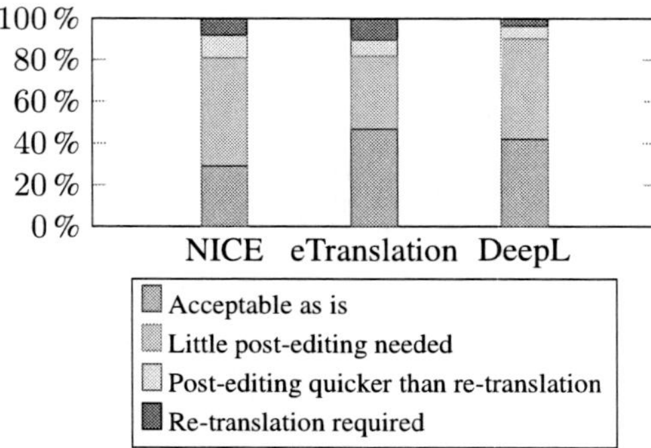

Figure 8: Post-editing effort per segment, weighted by segment length. Based on the calculation of the normalised edit distance at segment level weighted by the segment length in a total of 854 segments from documents of all subdomains from the PH domain post-edited by CdT linguists.

Figure 10: Post-editing effort per segment, weighted by segment length. Based on the calculation of the normalised edit distance at segment level weighted by the segment length in a total of 854 segments from the IP domain post-edited by CdT linguists.

The productivity of benchmarked systems is shown in Figure 10. All three systems show comparable results. Both quality and productivity pass the acceptance threshold.

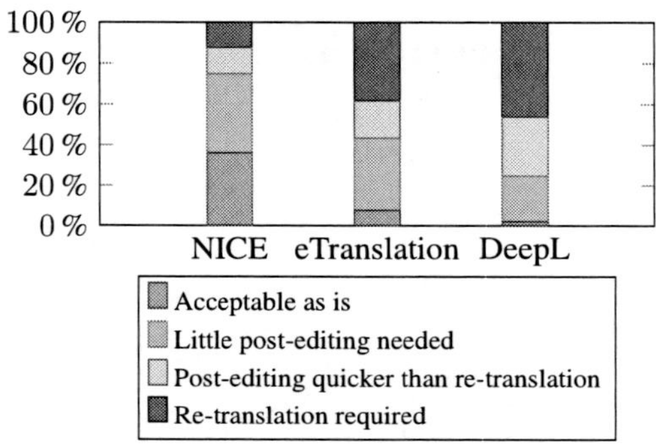

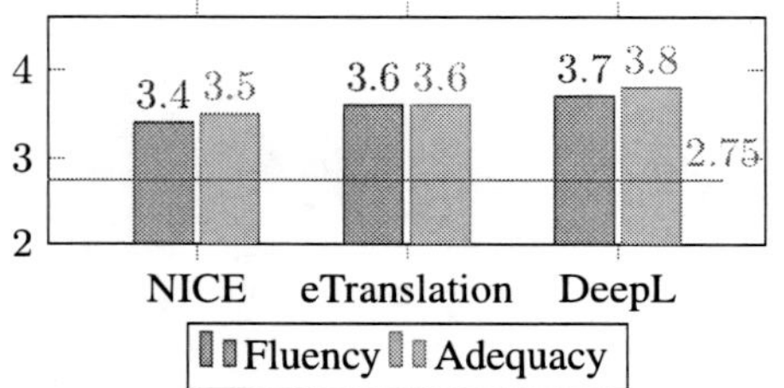

Figure 11: Post-editing effort per segment, weighted by segment length. Based on the calculation of the normalised edit distance at segment level weighted by the segment length in a total of 1 533 segments from documents of all agencies from the PH domain post-edited by CdT linguists.

Figure 9: Fluency and adequacy ratings per segment, weighted by segment length for the IP domain.

PH benchmarking: Figure 12 shows the comparison of quality in terms of fluency and adequacy against eTranslation and DeepL Pro. The productivity of benchmarked systems is shown in Figure 11. The quality of all compared systems is acceptable in terms of quality and fluency. In terms of productivity, only NICE meets the requirements. Although NICE fails to meet the acceptance requirements for some language pairs from different subdomains, it gets the best score compared to other benchmarked systems.

6 Deployment

For deployment, weight pruning (See, 2016; Zhu, 2017) was applied to accelerate prediction. Weight pruning has several advantages: 1) the inference time is much lower; 2) the model size is reduced. The pruning experiments were done with the CTranslate2 tool, which is an optimised inference engine for OpenNMT-py and OpenNMT-tf models supporting both CPU and GPU execution.[8] This library is geared towards an efficient serving of standard translation models, but is also a place for experimentation around model compression and inference acceleration. Table 4 shows the different experiments. The CPU used in the experiment from Figure 4 was i7-7800X CPU 3.5GHz*1.2 and the GPU GeForce GTX 1080 Ti 11GB. Finally, models were pruned using CTranslate2 and the inference executed on CPU. In our view, the loss of quality is not significant and the inference speed is fast enough for the project purposes.

The final goal of this project is to integrate the custom neural engines into the workflows of the

---

[8] https://github.com/OpenNMT/CTranslate2

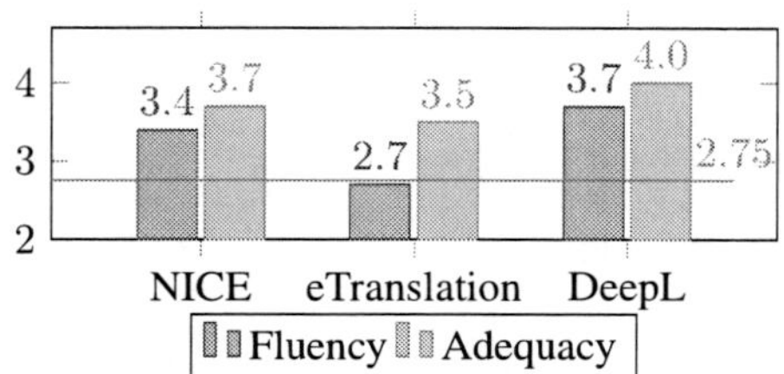

Figure 12: Fluency and adequacy ratings per segment, weighted by segment length for the PH domain.

CdT's advanced translation management system via a web service, allowing for optimised and more efficient translation services.

7 Conclusions and future work

This paper describes the implementation of NICE: Neural Integrated Custom Engines, which was developed by CdT in collaboration with the European Union Intellectual Property Office (EUIPO). The system described in this article includes a sophisticated data preprocessing pipeline. Different techniques for data filtering were applied with satisfactory results. Depending on the language pair, we also applied data augmentation techniques, which improved the output quality.

In this work, we focused on two domains: IP and PH. Nevertheless, the system has been designed to allow the rapid implementation of new EU-related domains, such as legal or finance.

Of the 36 samples evaluated in both domains, 22 were fit for post-editing purposes. NICE produced very satisfactory results for the IP domain and technical documents from the PH domain.

NMT development is an iterative process and it can be assumed that quality will improve over time. The database of high-quality translations produced by CdT contractors and in-house translators is growing day by day. As the CdT collects more data from revised and post-edited translations, incremental learning will be applied (Peris, 2017; Peris, 2019).

Still, there is room for improvement by other means, such as named entity recognition (NER) (Kai, 2019). For example, NER can be applied in the PH domain, where the use of names of medicines and active substances is very frequent, and for which sentencepiece does not manage well, tending to create new words. Another technique under development is the neural quality estimation for translation hypothesis selection (Shah, 2014), which allows the translation quality to be rated without references at run-time.

Finally, another technique is the application of advanced domain adaptation methods to enlarge IND datasets, mainly for languages with fewer resources. We are working to adapt a state-of-the-art classifier from Parcheta et al. (2019) for domain adaptation. The goal is to select more suitable pairs of sentences from the GEN dataset and include them in IND.

Soon, other custom engines will be implemented for other domains, such as the legal domain. We are working on collecting data.

The final step in this project will be to implement a simple web service that seamlessly integrates custom engines into the CdT's advanced translation workflows, allowing translators to work directly with our state-of-the-art, in-domain NMT technology NICE.

Acknowledgements

This work has been carried out under a cooperation programme between the CdT and the EUIPO. The authors would like to thank the valuable contributions and support received from Rafael Sáez Mendoza (EUIPO) and the different departments and persons involved in this programme in both organisations.

Table 4: Comparison of inference time and quality using weight pruning on CPU/GPU.

Hardware	cTranslate2	Model size	sentences/sec	sacreBLEU
CPU	NO	4GB	0.0267	57.9
CPU	YES	1.5GB	3.33	57.1
GPU	NO	4GB	30	57.9
GPU	YES	1.5GB	50	57.1

References

Bahdanau D., Cho K. and Bengio Y. 2015. Neural machine translation by jointly learning to align and translate. *Proc. of 3rd ICLR*

Castilho S., Moorkens J., Gaspari F., Calixto I., Tinsley J. and Way A. 2017. Is neural machine translation the new state of the art? *The Prague Bulletin of Mathematical Linguistics* Vol. 108, N° 1, 109–120.

Cho K., Van Merrienboer B., Gülçehre Ç., F. Bougares, Schwenk H. and Bengio Y. 2014. Learning Phrase Representations using RNN Encoder-Decoder for Statistical Machine Translation. *Proc. of EMNLP* 1724–1734

Denkowski M. and Lavie A. 2011. Meteor 1.3: Automatic metric for reliable optimization and evaluation of machine translation systems. *Proc. of 6th WMT*. Edinburgh, Scotland. 85–91.

Doddington G. 2002. Automatic evaluation of machine translation quality using n-gram co-occurrence statistics. *Proc. of the second Int. Conf. on Human Language Technology Research* San Diego, California, USA. 138–145.

Graves A. 2013. Generating sequences with recurrent neural networks. *arXiv:1308.0850v5*

Hakala K. and Pyysalo S. 2019. Biomedical Named Entity Recognition with Multilingual BERT. *Proc. of BioNLP*. Hong Kong, China. 56–61.

Jia Y., Carl M., and Wang X. 2017. How does the post-editing of neural machine translation compare with from-scratch translation? A product and process study. The Journal of Specialised Translation Vol. 31, 61–86.

Kingma D. P. and Ba J. 2014. Adam: A Method for Stochastic Optimization. *Proc. of 3rd ICLR*

Klein G., Kim Y.,Deng Y., Senellart J. and Rush A. M. 2017. OpenNMT: Open-Source Toolkit for Neural Machine Translation. *arXiv:1701.02810v2*

Koehn P. 2017. Neural Machine Translation. Available at `http://mt-class.org/jhu/assets/nmt-book.pdf`

Koehn P. and Monz C. 2017. Manual and automatic evaluation of machine translation between european languages. *Proceedings on the Workshop on Statistical Machine Translation* 102–121.

Kudo T. and Richardson J. 2018. SentencePiece: A simple and language independent subword tokenizer. *arXiv:1808.06226v1*

Lardilleux A. and Lepage Y. 2017. CHARCUT: Human-Targeted Character-Based MT Evaluation with Loose Differences. *Proc. of IWSLT*. Tokyo, Japan. 146–153.

Lui M. and Baldwin T. 2012. A Simple, Fast, and Effective Reparameterization of IBM Model 2. *Proc. of the NAACL 2013: Human Language Technologies*. Atlanta, USA. 644–648.

Marg L. 2016. The Trials and Tribulations of Predicting Post-Editing Productivity. *Proc. of LREC*. Portorož, Slovenia. 146–153.

McCallum A. and Nigam K. 1998. A comparison of event models for naive Bayes text classification. *AAAI-98 Workshop on learning for text categorization* 41–48.

Oravecz C., Bontcheva K., Lardilleux A., Tihanyi L. and Eisele A. 2019, eTranslation's Submissions to the WMT 2019 News Translation Task. *proc. WMT*. Florence, Italy. 320–326.

Papineni K., Roukos S., Ward T. and Wei-Jing Z. 2002. BLEU: A Method for Automatic Evaluation of Machine Translation. *Proc. of the 40th Annual Meeting on ACL*. Philadelphia, Pennsylvania, USA. 311–318.

Parcheta Z., Sanchis-Trilles G., Casacuberta F. and Redahl R. 2019. Multi-input CNN for Text Classification in Commercial Scenarios. *Proc. of the IWANN*. Gran Canaria, Spain. 596–608.

Peris Á. and Casacuberta F. 2019. Online learning for effort reduction in interactive neural machine translation. 98–126. *Computer Speech & Language*

Peris Á., Cebrián L. and Casacuberta F. 2017. Online learning for neural machine translation post-editing. *arXiv:1706.03196v1*

Post M. 2018. A call for clarity in reporting BLEU scores. 186–191. *Proc. of WMT*.

Post M., Ding S., Martindale M. and Wu W. 2019. An Exploration of Placeholding in Neural Machine Translation, *Proc. of MT Summit XVII. Research Track, Volume 1*, Dublin, Ireland. 182–192.

Prechelt L. 1998. Early stopping – but when? *Neural Networks: Tricks of the trade*. 55–69.

See A. , Luong M.-T. and Manning C. D. 2016. Compression of neural machine translation models via pruning. *CoNLL* 291—301.

Shah K. and Specia L. 2014. Quality Estimation for Translation Selection. *Proc. of EAMT*. Dubrovnik, Croatia. 109–116.

Snover M. , Dorr B., Schwartz R., Micciulla L. and Makhoul J. 2006. A study of translation edit rate with targeted human annotation. *Proc. of AMTA*. Cambridge, Massachusetts, USA. Vol. 200, N° 6, 186–191.

Wu Y., Schuster M., Chen Z., Le Q. V, et al. 2017. Google's neural machine translation system: Bridging the gap between human and machine translation. *arXiv*

Vaswani A., Shazeer N., Parmar N., Uszkoreit J., Jones L., Gomez A. N., Kaiser L. and Polosukhin I. 2017. Attention Is All You Need. *Advances in neural information processing systems* 5998–6008.

Zhu M. and Gupta S. 2018. To prune, or not to prune: exploring the efficacy of pruning for model compression. *Proc. of ICLR*

Estimation vs Metrics: is QE Useful for MT Model Selection?

Anna Zaretskaya   **José Conceição**   **Frederick Bane**
TransPerfect
Passeig de Gràcia, 11, Esc B 5-2
08007 Barcelona, Spain
{azaretskaya, jconceicao, fbane}@translations.com

Abstract

This paper presents a case study of applying machine translation quality estimation (QE) for the purpose of machine translation (MT) engine selection. The goal is to understand how well the QE predictions correlate with several MT evaluation metrics (automatic and human). Our findings show that our industry-level QE system is not reliable enough for MT selection when the MT systems have similar performance. We suggest that QE can be used with more success for other tasks relevant for translation industry such as risk prevention.

1 Introduction

Machine translation quality estimation (QE) is a technique for predicting machine translation (MT) quality (Specia et al., 2009). As MT becomes the dominant tool in the translation industry, accurate estimation of the quality of MT output would be of great benefit to many business concerns such as budget allocation for human post-editing, estimating the usefulness of the MT output for gisting purposes, and selecting the best MT system out of a selection of systems. In addition to that, a reliable QE model would also help linguists make more efficient use of their time.

As opposed to MT evaluation, where MT output is compared to one or several human reference translations, QE attempts to perform the much more challenging task of predicting MT quality in the absence of a reference translation. QE can be performed on a word, sentence or document level,

and the output of a QE system is typically a score that is intended to correlate with a certain automatic or human MT evaluation metric.

In this paper we present a case study where QE models were applied for the purpose of ranking different MT engines for a given document or text corpus. Our approach is based on obtaining segment-level QE scores for all segments in the document/corpus and using the average to select the best MT system. We use two QE systems to score the output of different MT engines and compare the results of the QE model with several automatic MT evaluation metrics, which include the post-editing distance (PED), HTER, BLEU score (Papineni et al., 2002), and weighted and unweighted sentence embedding similarity, as well as with human MT evaluation scores. We conclude the paper by reflecting on the usefulness of QE for MT engine selection, possible improvements to QE, and the limitations of our model and method.

2 Background and Motivation

The main motivation of exploring the QE method for MT model selection is the fact that we are often faced with a scenario where we need to choose the best MT system without a reference translation. The only existing method for this is involving human evaluators, which is, however, quite costly and requires more time. We are looking for a more cost-efficient and fast (almost immediate) way of deciding which MT system to use.

QE is a very well explored topic in Natural Language Processing given that predicting MT quality has clear practical benefits (Specia et al., 2018). Multiple QE frameworks have been developed, some of which are open-source: QuEst++ (Specia et al., 2015), POSTECH (Kim et al., 2017),

Martins, Moniz, Fumega, Martins, Batista, Coheur, Parra, Trancoso, Turchi, Bisazza, Moorkens, Guerberof, Nurminen, Marg, Forcada (eds.)
Proceedings of the 22nd Annual Conference of the European Association for Machine Translation, p. 339–346
Lisboa, Portugal, November 2020.

QEBrain (Wang et al., 2018), OpenKiwi (Kepler et al., 2019), YiSi (Lo, 2019) and others. Details about state-of-the-art QE tools are presented in detail in the corresponding WMT2019 shared task (Fonseca et al., 2019).

Despite the extensive research interest in QE, there is less information on how useful it actually is in specific commercial workflows. For example, Shterionov et al. (2019) compare the performance of various QE models using specific user business metrics, as well as implementation and computation cost. They demonstrate that the system with the highest performance can be also the most computationally expensive and simpler, faster systems can provide satisfactory results. More aspects of applying QE in commercial settings are discussed in (de Souza et al., 2015) and (Astudillo et al., 2018).

We believe that evaluation of the performance of any NLP system must firstly take into account the end use of the system. In our case, the goal is to be able to automatically select the best MT engine out of two or more engines on a segment level in scenarios where a reference translation is not available. It is relevant to mention that our goal is not to fully replace automatic MT evaluation metrics; the findings from Task 3 of the shared task on QE (Fonseca et al., 2019) confirm that this is still a challenge. Rather, the objective of this study is to investigate whether our QE systems are reliable enough to be used to select the best among multiple MT engines.

Segment-level QE is typically evaluated by calculating the correlation of the QE predictions with human judgement or one or several MT evaluation metrics, most commonly with HTER (Snover et al., 2006a), using the Root Mean Square Error (RMSE) and/or Mean Absolute Error (MAE) (Specia et al., 2018). Apart from that, Avramidis et al. (2018) describe a more fine-grained, linguistically-informed evaluation method which enables greater understanding of the behaviour of the QE system.

For this study, in addition to the standard metrics, we utilize the metrics that correspond to our business goals. One of the most important metrics for us is the post-editing distance (PED), a standard MT quality metric used at the company and is the current industry standard. Similarly to HTER, PED represents post-editing effort in terms of the number of editing operations, but it is character-based (while HTER is word-based) and therefore more accurately reflects the effort expended in editing. Another important metric for us is the BLEU score (Papineni et al., 2002), which is used mostly for MT development in order to measure improvement over a baseline.

There are many valid criticisms of automatic MT evaluation metrics such as BLEU (Callison-Burch et al., 2006), one of the most salient of which is the fact that they require one or more reference translations against which MT output is compared. However, a given sentence can have multiple correct translations depending on a certain context and end use, and for this reason reference-based metrics cannot always cover the entire space of valid translations for the sentence. For this reason, we also include human MT evaluation - direct assessment of the MT output by linguists, which is not reference-dependant. In addition, we experiment with text similarity metrics (Chan and Ng, 2008). In particular, we use word embedding similarity in order to reflect how semantically close the MT translation is to the reference translation. We produced sentence embeddings for the MT output and the reference translation, and calculated the cosine distances between these embeddings. Cosine distances between sentence embeddings capture how closely the meanings of two sentences correspond in high-dimensional vector space, and as such are less sensitive to the substitution of similar words in alternative translations. While this latter metric is insufficient on its own as a measure of translation quality (due to its insensitivity to word-order, among other reasons), we hypothesize that it may be a useful auxiliary metric.

3 Methodology

Our primary research goal was to investigate how well the scores from QE systems correlate with commonly-used metrics for evaluating translation quality, and based on these results understand how useful QE is for MT model selection in cases when a reference translation is not available. As a secondary goal, we also studied the impact of content domain on these correlations. Domain is known to be a highly significant factor in the performance of MT engines, and we hypothesized that this would also be true of QE systems. Therefore, for this study we used two QE models: one in a general domain (QE-gen) and the other in the domain of life sciences (QE-domain). Below we present implementation details about these models.

3.1 QE Systems

The QE models used to perform these experiments were implemented using the OpenKiwi framework (Kepler et al., 2019). The framework was chosen as it was the foundation of the winning systems of the word-, sentence-, and document-level tasks of the WMT 2019 shared task on QE, and furthermore because of its adoption as the baseline system for this task (Fonseca et al., 2019).

When it comes to the architecture, we chose to use the Predictor-Estimator (Kim et al., 2017), a two-phase, end-to-end neural QE model which had the most noteworthy benchmarks of all OpenKiwi's available architectures (excluding ensembles and stacks). The Predictor-Estimator architecture attempts to overcome challenges faced by previous architectures, such as a shortage of QE data and dependence on hand-engineered features to capture the complex relationships between feature sets and QE annotations.

This architecture uses word prediction as a pretask to boost performance and reduce the amount of QE data needed to achieve state-of-the-art results. This task takes in source and target sentences, masks a target word at random, and then attempts to predict the masked word. Word prediction uses a bidirectional long short-term memory (LSTM) to encode the source and two unidirectional LSTMs to process the target: LSTM-L2R (left to right) and LSTM-R2L (right to left) (Kepler et al., 2019). These LSTMs are trained using a large parallel corpus. This structure allows the use of both left and right target context to generate predictions of the masked word.

Before diving into detailed descriptions of the models, it is worth noting that the systems used in scientific research are normally ensembles or stacks of different architectures, which typically outperform individual stand-alone systems. However, at this stage we think the difference is not substantial enough to justify the increased costs of training several models for each language pair instead of one, which can skyrocket when taking into consideration the number of language pairs that our company handles. Both QE models (the domain and the generic one) used the same word predictor model, built from a large generic parallel corpus. The primary difference is due to the different text types from which the data were sampled:

QE-domain model was trained exclusively on texts from the Life Sciences domain and QE-gen was trained on a mixed corpus. In both cases, the training data was compiled from previously post-edited projects. Table 1 shoes the training corpora size used for each of the models.

The first step in the pre-processing pipeline was to query our SQLite database, specifying our language and other settings such as the maximum number of tokens per sentence. We then refined the data using the langdetect python package to filter out any rows that weren't flagged with the language pair we had specified. To generate the OK/BAD tags (the tags marking whether a specific word is correct or wrong in the translation), we relied on the industry standard TERCOM tool (Snover et al., 2006b). For each token in each sentence, if the token is present in the target sentence, the token is labeled OK; if it was deleted or modified during PE, the token is labeled BAD. Insertions are ignored. At the end, sentences are updated such that only the ones without any error in identifying the tags are kept. Both models achieved industry-standard F1-mult scores. F1-mult is a word-level prediction score that evaluates the performance of identifying correct and incorrect words in the translation (Table 1).

	QE-gen	QE-domain
F1-mult	55.73	57.85
Test corpus	2893	1998
Training corpus	134438	92341

Table 1: Training and testing corpus size in number of sentence pairs and the F1-mult score of the two QE models.

3.2 Experiments

Equipped with these two models, we conducted two separate experiments, one in the general domain and one in the life sciences domain. In the first, we obtained translations for the generic data set from two freely available MT engines, Google and Bing. The QE-gen model was used to predict the quality of these translations, then these scores were compared with several metrics for evaluating translation quality. The data obtained from these comparisons were considered a baseline by which to judge the performance of the two QE models on domain-specific content in the second experiment.

In the second experiment, we used a dataset of life sciences content to compare the performance of the QE-gen and QE-domain models. In the first experiment we found that the Bing and Google MT engines performed quite similarly in terms of the quality of their output. Thus, for this experiment we also used a specialized proprietary life sciences MT engine, which we expected to perform significantly better than the two more general engines. Translations were obtained from all three engines, and these translations were scored by the QE-domain and QE-gen models. The resulting QE scores were then compared to the same MT evaluation metrics.

In addition to measuring how well our QE models correlate with MT quality metrics, we also calculated the probabilities of the QE models to correctly identify the best MT engine out of several.

3.3 Test Data

We used two sets of data for the evaluation. The first set contained 1756 sentences translated from English into Spanish by professional translators from the corporate communication domain. We selected these texts because they have a general style and do not have any specific or technical terminology. The average source sentence length was 17.91 words.

The second data set contained 2048 sentences from the Life Sciences domain and contained texts with highly specialized terminology and style. The average sentence length in this data set was 14.29 words. Both data sets were cleaned to remove sentences with less than four and more than 200 tokens as well as any sentences where the MT outputs of the engines were identical.

3.4 Evaluation

Each QE system (QE-gen and QE-domain) was evaluated based on

- the correlation of the QE scores and PED (Pearson's r);

- the correlation of the QE scores and BLEU (Pearson's r);

- the correlation of the QE scores and the two sentence similarity metrics (Pearson's r);

- the RMSE (root mean square error) for HTER;

- the MAE (mean absolute error) for HTER;

- the percentage of sentences where the QE model correctly selected the best MT engine based on each of the quality metrics;

- correlation with human assessment of the MT quality.

PED was calculated using the Levenshtein distance algorithm at the character level and normalized based on the length of the strings. HTER scores were calculated as explained in (Snover et al., 2006a). BLEU scores were assigned using NLTK's built-in BLEU score function. The text similarity metrics were calculated as the cosine distances between the weighted and unweighted sentence embeddings of the MT output and the human translation. As such, lower values indicate more similar sentences. Unweighted sentence embeddings were calculated as a simple mean of Word2Vec word embeddings for each word in the sentence, while weighted sentence embeddings were calculated by averaging the word embeddings after weighting them based on the inverse frequency of the word in the Word2Vec[1] training corpus. The Scipy and Numpy python libraries were used to perform data analysis, and the Pearson's correlation coefficient (PCC) was used to assess correlation between the QE scores and our other translation quality metrics.

For the human evaluation we have used 200 sentences from each dataset, which were evaluated by two different annotators on a 1 to 100 scale. During the evaluation, the reference translations of the segments were not provided. The Human judgement scores were then averaged between the two annotators. Then, we followed the procedure described in (Ma et al., 2019) to calculate the Kendall's τ scores that show the correlation between the QE scores and the human judgment. It has to be noted that we removed all the instances of ties in human judgment, i.e. all the segments where the MT engines were assigned the same average human score. After removing all the human judgment ties, we ended up with 134 segments in each of the datasets. As to the ties in the QE scores, these were penalized, meaning that we counted as *Discordant* the segments where the predicted QE scores for different MT systems were equal (and the human scores were not).

---

[1]https://arxiv.org/pdf/1310.4546.pdf

4 Results

We evaluated the two QE models on the corresponding data sets in terms of the model performance. Table 2 shows the Pearson's correlation results with the automatic MT evaluation metrics. In the Generic Use Case, we used QE-gen and the generic data set. Here, we compare the results only for the two generic (not customized) MT systems. In the Domain use case, we used QE-domain and the Life Sciences data set. In the Mixed Use Case, we used QE-gen and the Life Sciences data set. In the latter two cases we also consider the results of the domain specific MT system trained for life sciences content. The Mixed case allows us to compare the performance of a domain-specific QE system with that of a generic QE system. Similar results would suggest no clear benefit from training different systems for each genre of content.

		Google	Bing	LifeSci
Generic Case	PED	0.301	0.278	
	HTER	0.148	0.089	
	BLEU	-0.308	-0.271	
	Sim1	0.296	0.203	
	Sim2	0.198	0.141	
Domain Case	PED	0.284	0.199	0.127
	HTER	0.308	0.273	0.135
	BLEU	-0.324	-0.302	-0.195
	Sim1	0.315	0.308	0.184
	Sim2	0.180	0.166	0.118
Mixed Case	PED	0.261	0.182	0.125
	HTER	0.280	0.276	0.138
	BLEU	-0.269	-0.290	-0.188
	Sim1	0.245	0.269	0.175
	Sim2	0.159	0.172	0.090

Table 2: Pearson's correlation results between the predicted sentence-level QE score and the particular MT metrics. Sim1 refers to unweighted sentence similarity, while Sim2 refers to weighted sentence similarity.

In general, we found only weak correlation with most of the metrics and in some cases almost no correlation at all. While the F1-mult scores indicated that our QE models achieved industry-level performance, the poor correlations with the evaluation metrics were unexpected. Out of all the metrics considered, the highest correlation observed was for the BLEU score. Interestingly, the correlation with HTER was particularly weak (practically no correlation) in the generic case, but stronger for life sciences domain content. When it comes to the word embedding similarity, using unweighted embeddings proved to yield a stronger correlation with QE than weighted embeddings. This may be partially explained by the fact that our weighted embeddings distinguish words in terms of their frequency, while QE systems and unweighted word embeddings treat all words equally.

Table 3 shows the RMSE and the MAE scores for the predicted HTER. Based on RMSE, the predicted HTER scores differ from the actual HTER scores by about 5 percentage points, while based on MAE calculation the difference is about 3 percentage points.

		QE-domain	QE-gen
RMSE↓	Google	5.186	4.949
	Bing	5.190	5.156
	LifeSci	5.450	5.373
MAE↓	Google	3.574	3.437
	Bing	3.606	3.541
	LifeSci	3.656	3.732

Table 3: RMSE and MAE of each of the QE models applied to the output of the three MT engines.

Finally, the correlation with human judgment in terms of Kendall's τ is also weak or non-existing. For the generic dataset, the τ score was equal to 0.119 (slightly better than random) while for the in-domain dataset the τ score was equal to −0.059 (practically random). Note that the τ score can take value from −1 to 1.

The observations indicate how well our QE systems perform and how similar their behavior is to the various metrics. However, we want to understand whether their performance level is sufficient to be able to replace MT evaluation metrics for the purpose of engine selection. Therefore, we also provide a comparison of the average metrics scores for the different MT engines with the average QE scores (Tables 4 and 5).

As can be seen from these results, the performance of the two generic MT systems (Bing and Google) was very similar according to all the metrics and also the average QE scores. While Google and Bing score better according to the automatic metrics, human evaluation ranked Google first, and the QE system is in line with the human score. In general, though, the differences between the two were negligible.

On the other hand, the tendency changes when the Life Sciences MT engine comes into the pic-

	Google	Bing
PED ↓	0.321	0.311
HTER ↓	0.468	0.459
BLEU ↑	0.682	0.699
Sim1 ↓	0.081	0.079
Sim2 ↓	0.010	0.010
Human ↑	83.5	82.6
QE-gen ↓	0.312	0.325

Table 4: Average values for the automatic and human MT evaluation metrics compared to average QE score QE-gen on the Generic data set.

	Google	Bing	LifeSci
PED ↓	0.296	0.282	0.183
HTER ↓	0.413	0.397	0.253
BLEU ↑	0.328	0.350	0.561
Sim1 ↓	0.055	0.052	0.027
Sim2 ↓	0.006	0.005	0.003
Human ↑	83.6	85.3	88.5
QE ↓	0.396	0.392	0.372

Table 5: Average values for the automatic and human MT evaluation metrics compared to average QE score of QE-gen (for Google and Bing MT systems) and QE-domain (for LifeSci MT system) on the Life Sciences data set.

ture (Table 5); its performance is significantly higher according to all the metrics, and therefore the QE system also correctly identifies it as the best engine out of three (although the difference is rather small). This is also illustrated in Figure 1, which shows the distribution of PED scores and QE scores for the three engines on the Life Sciences data set. These results suggest that QE systems are more likely to choose the best model in cases where one MT engine clearly outperforms

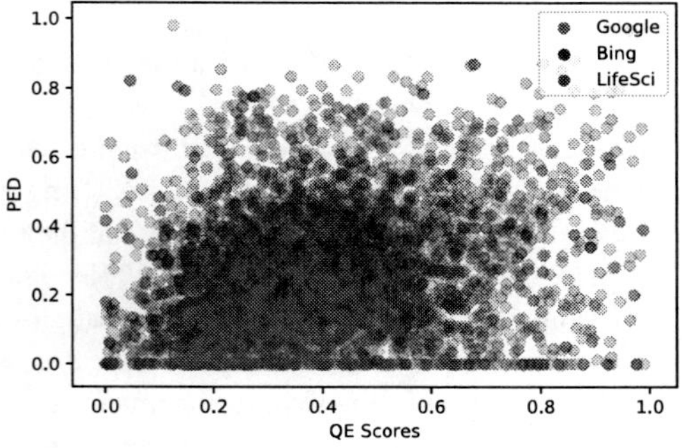

Figure 1: Distributions of QE scores and PED for the three engines on life sciences data. Note the "squashing" of the distribution for the LifeSci engine

the others. This conclusion is also in line with the findings of the WMT19 Metrics Shared Task (Ma et al., 2019), which conclude that the metrics and QE tasks become more challenging when comparing multiple strong systems with similar performance as opposed to scenarios where the performance level of the systems is more varied.

	Generic	Domain	Mixed
PED	53.4%	44.8%	47.8%
HTER	41.0%	44.5%	49.0%
BLEU	51.6%	39.5%	45.1%
Sim1	51.0%	43.5%	46.6%
Sim2	47.7%	43.0%	46.2%

Table 6: Percentage of cases where QE correctly selected the best MT engine based on each of the automatic MT evaluation metrics. Note that for the generic case only 2 MT engines were used, so the results are essentially random.

Finally, we consider the percentage of cases (segments) where the QE systems correctly identified the best engine based on each of the metrics (Table 6). In the Generic case (two generic MT engines used on generic data), the results are practically random. In the Domain and Mixed scenarios, where three MT engines were used, the best engine is correctly identified in about 50% of the cases. These results are noticeably better than a random guess (which would be correct 33% of the time), but are not sufficient to meet the standard of usability in our workflow.

In summary, we observe mediocre results. Based on the weak correlation with the MT evaluation metrics and the human judgment we can conclude that our QE systems do not perform well enough in order to be used on a sentence level. On the other hand, when considering the average QE scores across the entire test set, we do see that a superior MT engine does tend to have lower average QE scores. This suggests that, at the document level, our QE models might do better at identifying the best MT engine in scenarios where the performance of the MT engines is significantly different - this is still to be confirmed by further studies.

We did not observe a significant gap in performance between the QE model trained entirely on life sciences data and the generic model when applied to life sciences content. Indeed, despite the fact that the QE-domain achieved superior a F1-mult score, this model performed worse than the QE-gen model at predicting the best sentence on every metric.

5 Discussion and Future Work

In this paper we explored how well industry-standard QE models correlate with traditional measures of MT quality, both in a specific domain and in a general domain scenario. Our goal was to establish if these models can be used for automatic MT engine ranking. Our models used the OpenKiwi framework and achieved F1-mult scores similar to currently reported scores for similar single models. However, we failed to find strong evidence that these scores translate reliably into predictions of which MT engine's translation has better quality.

While the results we obtained are better than random guessing, we can conclude that QE in its current state can be fruitfully applied for MT model selection only in very specific scenarios, namely when the given MT models are known or expected to differ significantly in performance. Nevertheless, it is encouraging that there is some observable correlation between QE and our various metrics, and that our QE systems did show a tendency to choose the best model when there was a clearly superior choice. Indeed, in real production scenarios, there is no risk of choosing a slightly worse MT system when its performance is comparable to the other candidates, while it is more important to filter out the systems with significantly lower performance. In addition, we suggest that a very useful application of QE to explore is risk prevention: instead of selecting the best MT system out of several, we would be able to predict with a high degree of confidence that the performance of an MT system is significantly lower than average. This is one of the directions we are planning to explore in future studies.

One of the immediate steps in our research will be qualitative analysis of the data, especially the of the segments where a significant discrepancy was observed between the human evaluation scores and the QE scores. We hope to obtain an more profound understanding of the data and the reasons for the weak correlation.

When it comes to the actual performance of our QE system, the question becomes, how can we improve ours so that it may be more useful in the future? The first idea that presents itself is to reduce the class imbalance during the training stage. In the dataset on which we trained our QE models, OK tags outnumbered BAD tags by a factor of nearly 10:1. We hypothesize that the performance of the classifier may improve if we better balance the examples of the OK and BAD classes. One way to accomplish this goal is through the use of synthetic training data. In addition to real examples, we could create additional examples by replacing words randomly with other words from the vocabulary (either sampled uniformly or weighted based on the frequency that the word is associated with a BAD tag), thereby increasing the number of BAD tags the system sees during training.

Another possible way to improve the performance of QE models is through adversarial training. Using an architecture similar to a GAN, we could train a generator to create predictions for each word in a sentence, and simultaneously use the output of this system and human-annotated sentences to train a discriminator to distinguish model-generated output from human-annotated sentences. At this time we are not aware of any study which attempts to implement these methods for QE.

One important observation about the QE system's performance that we can draw from this study is that contrary to our expectations, there was no boost in performance compared with the generic model when an in-domain QE model was used on in-domain content. One reason for this might be that the QE-gen model was exposed to more data (including all the data used to train the QE-domain model), and so it may have developed a more sophisticated and robust language model than its counterpart trained on only a subset of those data. Another possibility is that domain simply does not play as significant a role in QE modeling as it does in more complex generative tasks like translation. In any case, it is a rather positive finding, as it proves that there is no need to train a QE model for each domain and training one generic model on a corpus that contains data from different domains is sufficient.

References

Astudillo, Ramón, João Graça, and André Martins, editors. 2018. *Proceedings of the AMTA 2018 Workshop on Translation Quality Estimation and Automatic Post-Editing*, Boston, MA, March. Association for Machine Translation in the Americas.

Avramidis, Eleftherios, Vivien Macketanz, Arle Lommel, and Hans Uszkoreit. 2018. Fine-grained evaluation of quality estimation for machine translation based on a linguistically motivated test suite. In *Proceedings of the AMTA 2018 Workshop on Transla-*

tion Quality Estimation and Automatic Post-Editing, pages 243–248, Boston, MA, March. Association for Machine Translation in the Americas.

Callison-Burch, Chris, Miles Osborne, and Philipp Koehn. 2006. Re-evaluating the role of Bleu in machine translation research. In *11th Conference of the European Chapter of the Association for Computational Linguistics*, Trento, Italy, April. Association for Computational Linguistics.

Chan, Yee Seng and Hwee Tou Ng. 2008. MAXSIM: A maximum similarity metric for machine translation evaluation. In *Proceedings of ACL-08: HLT*, pages 55–62, Columbus, Ohio, June. Association for Computational Linguistics.

de Souza, Jose G. C., Marcello Federico, and Hassan Sawaf. 2015. Mt quality estimation for e-commerce data. In *Proceedings of MT Summit XV, vol. 2: Users' Track*, pages 20–29, Maiami, Florida.

Fonseca, Erick, Lisa Yankovskaya, AndrÃ© F. T. Martins, Mark Fishel, and Christian Federmann. 2019. Findings of the WMT 2019 shared tasks on quality estimation. In *Proceedings of the Fourth Conference on Machine Translation (Volume 3: Shared Task Papers, Day 2)*, pages 1–12, Florence, Italy, August. Association for Computational Linguistics.

Kepler, Fabio, Jonay Trénous, Marcos Treviso, Miguel Vera, and André F. T. Martins. 2019. OpenKiwi: An open source framework for quality estimation. In *Proceedings of the 57th Annual Meeting of the Association for Computational Linguistics: System Demonstrations*, pages 117–122, Florence, Italy, July. Association for Computational Linguistics.

Kim, Hyun, Jong-Hyeok Lee, and Seung-Hoon Na. 2017. Predictor-estimator using multilevel task learning with stack propagation for neural quality estimation. In *Proceedings of the Second Conference on Machine Translation*, pages 562–568, Copenhagen, Denmark, September. Association for Computational Linguistics.

Lo, Chi-kiu. 2019. YiSi - a unified semantic MT quality evaluation and estimation metric for languages with different levels of available resources. In *Proceedings of the Fourth Conference on Machine Translation (Volume 2: Shared Task Papers, Day 1)*, pages 507–513, Florence, Italy, August. Association for Computational Linguistics.

Ma, Qingsong, Johnny Wei, Ondřej Bojar, and Yvette Graham. 2019. Results of the WMT19 metrics shared task: Segment-level and strong MT systems pose big challenges. In *Proceedings of the Fourth Conference on Machine Translation (Volume 2: Shared Task Papers, Day 1)*, pages 62–90, Florence, Italy, August. Association for Computational Linguistics.

Papineni, Kishore, Salim Roukos, Todd Ward, and Wei-Jing Zhu. 2002. Bleu: A method for automatic evaluation of machine translation. In *Proceedings of the 40th Annual Meeting on Association for Computational Linguistics*, ACL '02, pages 311–318, Stroudsburg, PA, USA. Association for Computational Linguistics.

Shterionov, Dimitar, Félix do Carmo, Joss Moorkens, Eric Paquin, Dag Schmidtke, Declan Groves, and Andy Way. 2019. When less is more in neural quality estimation of machine translation. an industry case study. In Forcada, Mikel L., Andy Way, John Tinsley, Dimitar Shterionov, Celia Rico, and Federico Gaspari, editors, *Proceedings of Machine Translation Summit XVII Volume 2: Translator, Project and User Tracks, MTSummit 2019, Dublin, Ireland, August 19-23, 2019*, pages 228–235. European Association for Machine Translation.

Snover, Matthew, Bonnie Dorr, Richard Schwartz, Linnea Micciulla, and John Makhoul. 2006a. A study of translation edit rate with targeted human annotation. In *Proceedings of Association for Machine Translation in the Americas*.

Snover, Matthew, Bonnie Dorr, Richard Schwartz, Linnea Micciulla, and John Makhoul. 2006b. A study of translation edit rate with targeted human annotation. In *Proceedings of Association for Machine Translation in the Americas, 2006*.

Specia, Lucia, Nicola Cancedda, Marc Dymetman, Marco Turchi, and Nello Cristianini. 2009. Estimating the sentence-level quality of machine translation systems. In *Proceedings of the 13th Annual Conference of the European Association for Machine Translation (EAMT 2009)*, pages 28–35, Barcelona, Spain.

Specia, Lucia, Gustavo Henrique Paetzold, and Carolina Scarton. 2015. Multi-level translation quality prediction with QuEst++. In *Proceedings of ACL-IJCNLP 2015 System Demonstrations*, pages 115–120, Beijing, China.

Specia, L., C. Scarton, and G. H. Paetzold. 2018. *Quality Estimation for Machine Translation*, volume 11(1) of *Synthesis Lectures on Human Language Technologies*. Morgan & Claypool Publishers.

Wang, Jiayi, Kai Fan, Bo Li, Fengming Zhou, Boxing Chen, Yangbin Shi, and Luo Si. 2018. Alibaba submission for WMT18 quality estimation task. In *Proceedings of the Third Conference on Machine Translation: Shared Task Papers*, pages 809–815, Belgium, Brussels, October. Association for Computational Linguistics.

Persistent MT on software technical documentation - a case study

María Concepción Laguardia
Senior Information Developer
Citrix Systems
Cambridge, UK
conchita.laguardia@citrix.com

Abstract

We report on the features and current challenges of our on-going implementation of a Persistent MT workflow for Citrix Product Documentation, to increase localization coverage to 100% content in docs.citrix.com, into our Tier-1[1] languages.

By the end of 2019, we had processed seven million words of English documentation with this model, across the 24 doc sets of the Citrix portfolio (Digital Workspace, Networking, and Analytics), and raised localization coverage from 40% to 100% of the content of our documentation repositories.

The current implementation requires a process of Light Post-editing (LPE) for all languages, in order to fix over-translations, out-of-domain words, inline tags, and markdown errors in the raw output.

1 Background

The Localization team at Citrix Systems introduced Machine Translation in its documentation workflows in 2013, with an in-house implementation of Moses engines from English into German, French, and Spanish. Statistical MT was the basis for a full post-editing workflow performed by in-house linguists and a small pool of trusted contractors. With the advent of Neural Machine Translation in 2017, we switched to Google generic engines, and later on incorporated Amazon Translate and Microsoft Custom Translator. The adoption of cloud Translation Management Platforms with built-in connectors for the main generic Neural MT providers, allowed us to mature the post-editing workflows and expand them to Japanese and Simplified Chinese. This now classic workflow of MT pre-translation followed by full human post-editing has since been our default model for the documentation use-case.

Productivity increased dramatically since introducing NMT as a base for full post-editing. This had a positive impact on time-to-market and reduction of localization costs. However, the actual coverage of our localization infrastructure remained at 40% of all the Citrix Product Documentation volume, mainly into Tier-1 languages, with a few doc sets into Korean and Brazilian Portuguese. The cost of sustained localization of the remaining content using MT plus human full post-editing was prohibitively high. It was evident that just integrating MT in the workflows was not enough to produce global-ready content at the increasing speeds and volumes necessary in today's competitive market.

2 The plan

Encouraged by the better fluency and adequacy of NMT output, at the end of 2018, it was proposed to expand our localization coverage to the remaining 60% wordcount of our documentation by using raw MT (MT without post-editing).

By then we were familiar with Microsoft's successful implementation of raw MT in their technical and end-user support documentation, which Microsoft now considers "proven for all support content types" (Schmidtke and Groves, 2019). We particularly liked some of the front-end features of

[1]Citrix Tier-1 languages: German, French, Spanish, Japanese and Simplified Chinese.

Martins, Moniz, Fumega, Martins, Batista, Coheur, Parra, Trancoso, Turchi, Bisazza, Moorkens, Guerberof, Nurminen, Marg, Forcada (eds.)
Proceedings of the 22nd Annual Conference of the European Association for Machine Translation, p. 347–352
Lisboa, Portugal, November 2020.

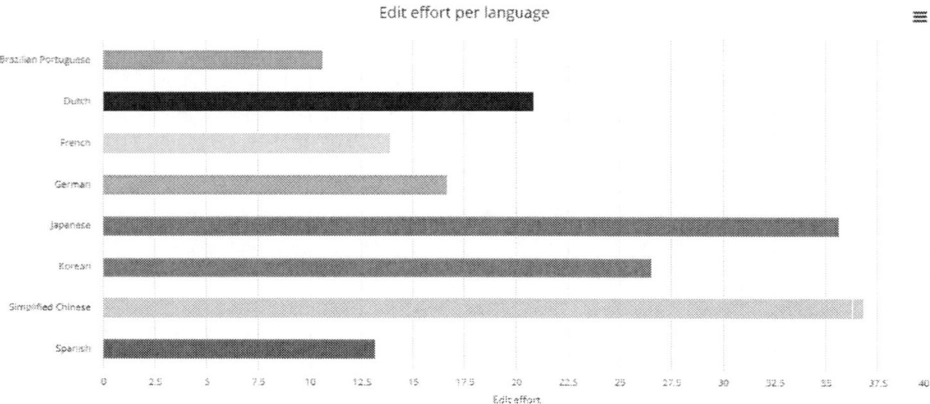

Figure 1: Edit Effort of fully post-edited documentation, measured with Okapi tools. Scale: 0-100

their deployment in docs.microsoft.com, like the switch-to-English toggle and the banner with the MT warning, and we looked at the Microsoft case as a good reference for our implementation.

We have since come across the Adobe[2] case, where similar features have been used to implement raw MT in their documentation web site.

Our focus was on **usability** as the criteria for publication, and the philosophy behind the idea was to offer this MT content as a **service** to the customer. The plan was to use the current technology we already used for full post-editing: a generic MT provider and the TMS system in place. We remained open to exploring bespoke MT engines and other TMS, depending on the results.

This solution would only be applied to technical documentation of products where the user interface is not localized, and therefore their documentation would not have been a candidate for human/fully post-edited translation in the first place.

2.1 MT *on-the-fly* vs Persistent MT

We had initially experimented with an MT *on-the-fly* implementation, which would allow customers to translate un-localized English articles on an on-demand basis, by sending an HTTPS POST request from the front-end to the Google Translate API. The main advantages of this solution were that the machine translated content would always be in sync with the latest English version, and that it would completely bypass TMS processing. The formatting of the output was also mostly correct, as

the MT request was performed on the HTML output, rather than from a conversion from markdown to XLIFF, which brings its own set of problems.

However, site navigation and user experience would significantly suffer from having to send individual API requests for each topic of the English content that they would like to read in another language. Also, we would have no control over the linguistic quality of the dynamic output, and no way of fixing any quality shortcomings, should we consider this step necessary to provide usable content to our customers. There were also cost considerations: we would not be able to easily predict demand and costs of the translation API in the MT *on-the-fly* context.

In the interest of providing optimal user experience, applying a certain level of quality control, and having better visibility on costs, a decision was made to offer a solution of **Persistent MT** instead: all un-localized content in docs.citrix.com would be pre-translated into French, Spanish, German, Japanese, and Simplified Chinese using raw MT, and then published in the specific language sites of docs.citrix.com. The MT content would be permanently available to our global customers and updated regularly, alongside the human post-edited documentation sets.

3 Evaluation phase

The MT engine of choice for the Persistent MT implementation was Amazon Translate, as we had been using it successfully for the full post-edit workflow.

We found that overall quality in terms of fluency and adequacy was similar between the NMT pro-

---

[2]https://docs.adobe.com/content/help/es-ES/target/using/activities/auto-allocate/automated-traffic-allocation.translate.html

vided by Google and Amazon, but the latter offered a Custom Terminology feature which was crucial to solve the issue of over-translation of product names. This issue was severe in doc sets related to products where generic nouns are used as part of the product name (for example: "App Layering", "Workspace", "Endpoint Management").

In order to collect data on the current quality gap between the raw output of generic NMT and our human translations, we started measuring Edit Effort[3] in the full post-edit workflow. The data thus obtained corroborated our human assessment of the quality that could be expected from the Amazon generic MT engine on the Tier-1 languages (see Figure 1). Edit Effort was chosen over BLEU scores, as we understand BLEU tends to underestimate the quality of NMT (Shterionov et al., 2017).

We also ran quality assessment checks on the MT output using a popular QA tool, Xbench[4], in order to scrutinize the raw MT output and identify quality shortcomings, error patterns, their estimated frequency, and their severity.

In addition, we ran a human evaluation test on 55 articles (topics) of Citrix documentation, where in-house linguists, contractors, and native speakers of the target languages were asked to rate the quality of the MT output with a criteria of *usability*, using scores from 1 to 5.

The scores were to be given at topic-level, rather than segment-level. The idea was to assess whether the translated content would be enough for the user to complete the task described in a particular topic. Evaluators were asked to penalise output that would confuse the user to the point of being unable to follow or understand the text. The averaged result across all 55 topics was 4 for the European languages, and 2 for the Asian languages. However, there were some discrepancies in the ratings, consistent with the subjectivity of human evaluation based on *usability* criteria.

4 The implementation

The Persistent MT workflow uses the current TMS already in place for the human/fully post-edited documentation workflow. This simplifies both the MT processing and the leverage of human quality translations from our Translation Memories.

The Persistent MT workflow is very similar to the default full post-edit workflows: source files are taken from Bitbucket repositories in markdown format and uploaded to the TMS, where the Translation Memory is leveraged before processing new content with MT. The target files are then downloaded from the TMS and uploaded to Bitbucket for publication in docs.citrix.com. Unlike the default human post-editing workflow, only in-context and 100% matches are leveraged from the TM. All fuzzy matches (99% and lower) are sent to MT for processing, together with new words.

In order to maximize the usability of the machine-translated content, and to manage customer expectations, the documentation website features the following:

- **Explicit warning and legal disclaimer**, to inform the user that the content is MT output.

- **Switch to English** toggle, to direct the user to the English version.

- **Parallel browsing**: a pop-up window that allows the readers to see the underlying English source of a paragraph when they hover over the text.

- A *verbatim* **customer feedback** form, where we ask the user whether the translated content was useful or not, and allows them to enter comments when the answer is "No". We are aware that in other implementations like Adobe's or Microsoft's, there is no option to enter further feedback about the translation, only a "yes/no" reply. However, we have opted for allowing customers to enter comments, so that we can get some insights on their perception of quality. It may also guide any action on our part to improve the service (for example, a targeted PE/fix process based on specific feedback).

These MT docs usage data is collected via Google Analytics *events*. Since the addition of the customer feedback feature is fairly recent, we are unable to report significant insights at this time.

5 The challenges

5.1 Regular updates

Sustaining the increasing volumes of localized documentation updates is the main challenge we face at the moment, as the default process of manual file handling and TMS job creation is not scalable to the Persistent MT workflow. For this purpose, we are currently developing an automation platform that will smart-trigger localization

---

[3]Edit Effort is a measurement based on edit distance and fuzzy match scores of two samples. `https://okapiframework.org/wiki/index.php/Translation_Comparison_Step`
[4]`https://www.xbench.net/`

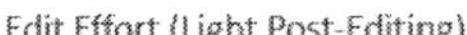

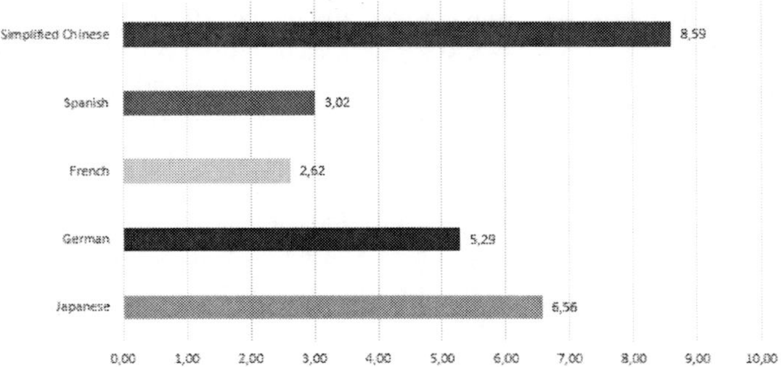

Figure 2: Light Post-Editing effort measured with Okapi tools. Scale: 0-100

jobs from the Bitbucket source repositories, based on the volume of changes in the English content and/or a predefined update schedule.

The platform is meant to be TMS- and MT-engine agnostic. This will facilitate the use of any MT engine available (not only the ones currently available in the TMS). Also, it will allow us to overcome TMS bottlenecks that may happen when increasing volumes of documentation are sent for localization simultaneously.

5.2   Output

We are also facing some challenges with regards to the actual quality obtained from generic MT engines when processed through the TMS and rendered as HTML in docs.citrix.com.

Processing the MT via third-party platforms and having no control over the quality delivered by third-party engines introduces a lot of uncertainty in our process, and it forces us to implement continuous quality estimation on each output. There is a difficulty in finding the root cause of some issues on the output, as it is unclear whether they come from the actual MT engine, or whether they are due to specific TMS-processing choices (markdown to XLIFF parsing, the way the MT API is called, and so on):

1. Inline tags: normally correspond to markdown formatting for highlighted text and URLs (for example, double-asterisk for bold text). These can be misplaced in the MT output, and we currently have no means to automatically fix the target. We have observed a disparity of tag placement behaviour when processing MT via different TMS systems, which seems to point at the root cause

for these issues being on the TMS processing side, rather than the MT engine behaviour.

2. Whitespace added or removed: this can completely break the markdown formatting. For example, when spaces are added after and before the double-asterisk for bold text.

3. Terminology deviations and out of domain words: some non-translatables and brand names are currently successfully handled with the Amazon Custom Terminology setting. We also keep blacklists containing some predictable out-of-domain words that arise when polysemous words appear in the source. However, the uncertainty of the output remains, as we cannot possibly blacklist every out-of-domain word that generic MT can produce. Even when we can detect terminology deviations, we are not capable of automating fixes for them in all cases as this would require a more complex solution than a simple search and replace mechanism.

4. Total or partial over-translation of file paths, command names, and parameter names. We are working on implementing a pre-processing step in order to mask file/command line paths in the source files, where possible.

5. Other issues: spurious characters added in Asian languages, and rarely, wrong target language for a segment (Portuguese instead of Spanish, for example) or non-existent (*made-up*) words in the target.

Most LPE and post-processing efforts (see figure 2) go into fixing issues 1 and 2 above. While the volume of LPE and post-processing work is small, the importance of these manual edits is considered high as they may impact usability (over-translated parameter names, file paths) and the look and feel of the content.

5.3 Quality definition

The very definition of what is *publishable* quality has also been challenging. Without any data from customer feedback to establish a baseline on what is the expected quality for machine-translated documentation, we relied on the in-house Citrix Translation Services team to develop the criteria and associated thresholds that define quality for the Citrix Persistent MT use-case. These criteria were then implemented in the form of specific linguistic checks used for quality estimation (see subsection 5.4)

The adequacy of these quality criteria still needs to be confirmed by actual data from the customer feedback mechanism in place.

5.4 Quality estimation

Quality is estimated based on linguistic features that can be detected using Checkmate, the quality assessment tool available in the Okapi Framework.

We apply language-specific custom checks (non-translatables lists, blacklists for banned or non-preferred terms, alphanumeric mismatches, known error regex patterns, camel-case word mismatches, and so on).

We have expanded the default Checkmate code in order to integrate these checks into the automated delivery platform of Persistent MT under development.

In order to deal with terminology deviations and non-existent words appearing occasionally in the output, we are considering a process which will compare each MT output to a normalized reference vocabulary obtained from the human-translated documentation, and flag any differences between them.

We are also implementing a scoring system, in order to produce a quality report for each documentation update, which will include the error categories found, and the associated quality score, per category and for the whole doc update. The score for a doc set will be based on an overall *translation issue density* value: weighted issues per 1000 words. The higher this value, the lower the quality score.

The idea is to eventually be able to use this report as a quality gate for publication. This would allow us to directly publish the content if the score is optimal, or else re-route to a process of targeted PE if the score is too low.

However, we are aware of the limitations of this method of estimation, as it relies on predefined issues (leaving out potential problems in the output that we cannot foresee). Also, human intervention is necessary to review these reports and discard false positives. It also relies on human-assigned, subjective, scores, which can be difficult to fine-tune.

This naive implementation of linguistic checks in order to estimate output quality is a short-term solution, as we expect to rely on machine learning-based QE in the mid-term.

Our challenges in this area are the lack of QE tools readily available to plug into our workflows. As such, we are researching some available open-source frameworks (Quest++, OpenKiwi).

However, these ML-based tools require some ML and engineering expertise in order to use them reliably. They also require substantial efforts in building the right data pipeline and infrastructure to sustain the necessary workflows for model training/updating that will help us implement ML-based QE with confidence.

Ideally, we would wish to have a sentence and document-level QE tool that can be easily used by our in-house Translation team, to train and evaluate models by uploading our Translation Memories, without requiring substantial training in ML or coding experience.

6 Conclusion

We have achieved localization coverage of 100% of Citrix product documentation using Persistent MT for Spanish, German, French, Japanese, and Simplified Chinese. However, sustaining the update cadence of the English documentation proves challenging without an automation platform, and without a solid quality estimation process in place for each MT output. The same factors make scalability into other languages difficult.

Besides, we are not truly ready to move to a raw MT without review workflow. A process of LPE is still considered necessary, even for the languages where linguistic quality, fluency, and adequacy of the raw MT is very good. This LPE process targets mainly inline tags, over-translations, and blacklisted terms. We are aware that other successful implementations of raw MT in docs, like

Microsoft's, rely on a tighter control and customisation capabilities of their MT engines, and this is a crucial difference between their case and ours. In this respect, we are currently testing the customisation capabilities of Google AutoML and Microsoft Custom Translator, to train English-Japanese and English-Chinese engines.

In addition, due to the constraints of the source format (markdown), we have encountered further limitations in the quality of the raw output. The markdown errors in the output affect formatting and rendering, and some of them cannot be fixed with automated processes. They require human intervention to pass the validators in place, before publication in the docs web site.

Quality estimation remains an important challenge, as we observe a lack of readily available tools that we can integrate into MT workflows in a production environment. As a workaround, we use current QA tools in the market to perform *estimation* tasks, but these tools are best used in traditional localization workflows where the quality checks are aimed at helping human intervention (PE), rather than bypassing it.

A TMS-agnostic, reliable and customisable QE tool that we could plug in our current workflows would significantly reduce the burden on our Translation Project Managers and post-editors, and accelerate the end-to-end workflow by allowing the implementation of an automated quality gate.

Also, we still depend on a third-party TMS to process the MT content. This dependency adds a certain degree of uncertainty to our processes and restricts the MT engines we can test and use for optimal output.

We believe an in-house custom tool to support the entire Persistent MT pipeline would be beneficial and this is part of the automation platform we are currently working on.

References

Amazon Translate. 2019. Amazon Translate Developer Guide. *https://docs.aws.amazon.com/*.

Felice, Mariano. 2012. Linguistic Indicators for Quality Estimation of Machine Translations. *Master's thesis. University of Wolverhampton, UK.*

Google Translation. 2019. Cloud Translation Documentation. *https://cloud.google.com/translate/docs.*

Kepler, Fabio, Jonay Trénous, Marcos Treviso, Miguel Vera, and André Martins. 2019. OpenKiwi: An Open Source Framework for Quality Estimation. *https://arxiv.org/abs/1902.08646*

Microsoft Custom Translator. 2019. Custom Translator documentation *https://docs.microsoft.com/en-us/azure/cognitive-services/translator/custom-translator/overview*

Okapi Framework. 2019. Okapi Documentation Wiki *https://okapiframework.org*

Schmidtke, D. and Declan Groves. 2019. Automatic Translation for Software with Safe Velocity. *Electronic proceedings of MT Summit, Dublin 2019.*

Shterionov, Dimitar, Pat Nagle, Laura Casanellas, Riccardo Superbo and Tony O'Dowd. 2017. Empirical evaluation of NMT and PBSMT quality for large-scale translation production. *Electronic proceedings of EAMT 2017 (User track).*

Specia, Lucia, Gustavo H. Paetzold, and Carollina Scarton. Multi-level Translation Quality Prediction with QUEST++. 2015. *Proceedings of ACL-IJCNLP 2015 System Demonstrations.* Association for Computational Linguistics and The Asian Federation of Natural Language Processing.

Specia, Lucia, Carolina Scarton, and Gustavo H. Paetzold. 2018b. Quality Estimation for Machine Translation. *Synthesis Lectures on Human Language Technologies.* Morgan & Claypool Publishers.

Way, Andy. 2013. Traditional and Emerging Use-Cases for Machine Translation. In: *Proceedings of Translating and the Computer 34, London*

Insights from Gathering MT Productivity Metrics at Scale

Georg Kirchner
Dell Technologies
42 South Street
Hopkinton, MA, 01748, U.S.A.
Georg.Kirchner@dell.com

Abstract

In this paper, we describe Dell EMC's framework to automatically collect MT-related productivity metrics from a large translation supply chain over an extended period of time, the characteristics and volume of the gathered data, and the insights from analyzing the data to guide our MT strategy.

Aligning tools, processes and people required decisions, concessions and contributions from Dell management, technology providers, tool implementors, LSPs and linguists to harvest data at scale over 2+ years while Dell EMC migrated from customized SMT to generic NMT and then customized NMT systems.

For content in two quality tiers, we ranked language pairs by productivity, graphed trendlines, compared the time needed to edit machine translations versus fuzzy matches, studied the time spent on segments with no post-edits, and going by the post-edit density, reviewed segment distribution on a post-edit scale of 1 to 10 and any correlation between the extent of edits and segment length.

1 Gathering Data at Scale

Dell's translation efforts produce significant amounts of linguistic data. Getting to the data, however, is not trivial since it originates with hundreds of linguists who are one or two organizational layers removed in Dell's external supply chain. Each linguist may prefer a different CAT tool, with or w/o the necessary features to track metrics for productivity or quality. Especially if desktop CAT tools require manual configuration from linguists, the constant churn in the resource pool makes it difficult to collect data reliably over time.

For various operational needs, when looking for alternatives six years ago, we qualified translation technology and implemented it as a collaborative environment for linguists to share data in real time. After we had integrated this environment, GlobalLink[1], with the TAUS DQF Dashboard[2], we were ready to harvest metrics on productivity from our Microsoft Translator[3] MT systems automatically between August 2017 and February 2020.

2 The Metrics

We will discuss the following MT metrics: productivity and post-edits. We chose to measure both metrics at the first linguistic step, Translation, although our linguists may have made further changes downstream at the Editing, Proofing, Client Review and Feedback Implementation steps.

The TAUS DQF Dashboard expresses productivity in words post-edited per hour. This number is calculated from the number of words in segments and the milliseconds these segments are active in the CAT tool for editing.

As for post-edits (PED), the TAUS DQF Dashboard distinguishes between post-edit density (PEDe) and post-edit distance (PEDi). Both are calculated with the Levenshtein algorithm (1966).

---

[1] https://www.translations.com/globallink/index.html
[2] https://qd.taus.net/
[3] https://www.microsoft.com/en-us/translator/business/translator-api/

Martins, Moniz, Fumega, Martins, Batista, Coheur, Parra, Trancoso, Turchi, Bisazza, Moorkens, Guerberof, Nurminen, Marg, Forcada (eds.)
Proceedings of the 22nd Annual Conference of the European Association for Machine Translation, p. 353–362
Lisboa, Portugal, November 2020.

PEDe expresses changes across the entire sample in percentages, in the average number of characters changed per 100 characters.

At the segment level, PEDi expresses the changes in absolute numbers, i.e., in characters changed per segment; we will call it aPEDi. Normalized to the length of the segment, the PEDi expresses changes on a scale of 0 to 10; we will call it nPEDi. As an example: 10 characters changed in a 20 character-long segment will result in an aPEDi of 10 and an nPEDi of 5.

3   Caveats

As we analyzed the accumulated data for this paper, we found that post-edits made in a single CAT tool session at the translation step correctly capture the full extent of post edits, even if the linguist revisits a segment multiple times in the same session. If the linguist edited the same segment in separate CAT tool sessions, only the edits made in the last session are captured. Because of this, we are underreporting the post-edit distance for an unknown number of segments.

Another caveat is that we decided not to track productivity for human translations (HT). We originally expected that for a given quality tier, we would either MTPE or HT all jobs. And comparing productivity between MTPE and HT jobs across quality tiers would not result in a fair comparison. Later on, we found that our PMs did apply HT workflows selectively to MTPE quality tiers. Had we adjusted our setup, we would now have data to benchmark MTPE against HT productivity.

4   Ranking by Productivity

The most basic exercise is to rank our major language pairs by productivity. These hourly word numbers below result from dividing cumulative MT words by cumulative post-editing time between August 2017 and December 2019.

Good enough				High quality		
Souce	Target	Words / Hour		Source	Target	Words / Hour
EN-US	pt-BR	2147		EN-US	pt-BR	1486
EN-US	it-IT	1801		EN-US	fr-FR	1445
EN-US	fr-FR	1729		EN-US	zh-CN	1204
EN-US	zh-CN	1409		EN-US	it-IT	1195
EN-US	es-MX	1373		EN-US	es-MX	1120
EN-US	de-DE	1314		EN-US	de-DE	1040
EN-US	ko-KR	1304		EN-US	ko-KR	952
EN-US	ja-JP	991		EN-US	ja-JP	787
EN-US	ru-RU	905		EN-US	ru-RU	743

Table 1: Average number of MT words post-edited per hour and quality tier

The hourly throughput does not account for elapsed time, such as research while segments in the CAT tool are inactive and the time tracker is not running. Therefore these productivity numbers are somewhat theoretical and do not mean that our PT-BR linguists post-edit 2147 x 8 = 17,176 words per day. But they surely suggest that the historic translation output of 2000 words per day is outdated and the actual productivity is significantly higher due to translation technology.

While the language ranking is roughly as expected, there are surprises: ZH-CN ranks relatively high compared to JA-JP and KO-KR; and ES-MX (Latin American Spanish) ranks low compared to FR-FR, IT-IT and PT-BR.

Productivity clearly varies by quality tiers, being higher for Good enough than High quality content. This may be due to varying levels of linguistic complexity and expectations, or the simple fact that Good enough jobs are bigger than High quality jobs, think of product documentation vs. marketing material. And the more volume in a given job, the easier it is for linguists to pick up speed.

EN-US > DE-DE	Good enough	High quality
Total words	1,115,804	2,633,399
# of jobs	484	3,463
Average words / job	2,305	760

Table 2: Average number of new words per job.

Let's see if there is a correlation between BLEU scores generated automatically by Microsoft's MT system customization environment, Custom Translator[4], and our language ranking.

---

[4] https://docs.microsoft.com/en-us/azure/cognitive-services/translator/custom-translator/overview

Source	Target	Training	Dictionary	BLEU - Dell	BLEU - Baseline
EN-US	ES-MX	1,499,349	0	71.19	49.03
EN-US	PT-BR	1,215,351	2,308	67.16	51.79
EN-US	JA-JP	2,825,902	0	63.02	43.27
EN-US	FR-FR	1,379,887	0	62.58	47.45
EN-US	ZH-CN	1,513,565	2,308	59.93	44.48
EN-US	DE-DE	1,363,042	2,307	58.41	41.36
EN-US	IT-IT	623,477	2,364	56.18	37.68
EN-US	KO-KR	1,099,853	2,364	50.18	32.52
EN-US	RU-RU	556,592	2,364	34.48	20.21

Table 3: Automatically generated BLEU scores during NMT system customization

Training means bi-lingual TMX files containing human translations or post-edited machine translations. The training data is counted in Translation Units (TUs); assume 14 words per TU. *Dictionary* means a phrase table of mostly do-not-translate items such as product names. *BLEU – Dell* is the score based on the customization effort; *BLEU – Baseline* is the Microsoft Translator stock NMT system.

Within the overall correlation between BLEU and productivity, the top-ranking BLEU score for ES-MX failed to predict average post-editing productivity; similarly, the better-than-expected BLEU score for JA-JP failed to predict low post-editing productivity. It has been observed before that productivity and BLEU scores do not correlate necessarily (Koponen, 2016).

There is a caveat to our correlation of productivity and BLEU since productivity was calculated using data collected since August 2017, while the BLEU score is for customized NMT systems deployed only since March 2019.

Productivity ranking of MT systems provides helpful context when triaging linguist feedback on MT output quality, especially when combining the ranking with nPEDi distributions for a particular language or across languages for a given job. Please zoom in.

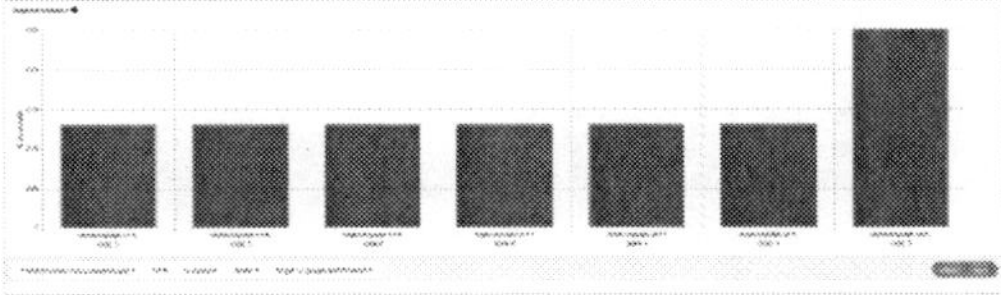

Table 4: Job-level comparison of nPEDi distribution between FR-FR and PT-BR in the TAUS DQF Dashboard.

Also, knowing your numbers allows you to place your MT technology relative to potential alternatives in the market.

5 Productivity and PEDe Trendlines

We wanted to understand if our MT output is getting better, worse or is stable over time.

For this, we compiled productivity and PEDe trends by transcribing monthly averages from the TAUS DQF Dashboard into MSFT Excel and applying linear trendlines. We then noted start and end values of these trendlines along with the number of words machine translated for statistical context.

Target	GE - Words	GE - Prod	GE - PEDe	HQ - Words	HQ - Prod	HQ - PEDe
ZH-CN	1,431,924	20%	-24%	3,232,031	9%	28%
JA-JP	1,607,365	0%	-46%	2,847,134	21%	20%
KO-KR	794,571	-7%	-48%	2,110,117	26%	-15%
DE-DE	1,027,343	33%	-48%	1,862,915	14%	-23%
FR-FR	1,116,151	-5%	-43%	1,814,899	25%	-19%
PT-BR	1,013,459	10%	-29%	1,717,225	14%	-29%
ES-MX	1,147,095	0%	-46%	1,689,249	32%	-28%
IT-IT	549,231	145%	-28%	1,346,025	36%	-22%
RU-RU	530,633	16%	-24%	1,104,929	67%	-6%
NL-NL				520,293	64%	-28%
SV-SE				223,052	-56%	28%
AR-SA				175,560	21%	19%

Table 5: Productivity and PED gains and losses between June 2018 and November 2019.

The higher the productivity, the better; the lower the PED, the better. In the above table a positive percentage for productivity (Prod) means that the hourly edited words increased by x%, while a negative value indicates productivity loss. Conversely, a negative PEDe value means that average number of edits fell over time (good), while a positive value means an increase in edits (bad).

For Good enough content, PEDe fell for our top nine languages. Likewise, productivity increased for these languages for High quality content. Productivity for Good enough content and PEDe for High quality content, however, have outliers.

Ideally, falling PEDe should result in rising productivity. While DE-DE exemplifies hoped-for results, there are obvious exceptions. Korean, for example, at the Good enough quality tier has PEDe falling by 48%, while productivity is dropping by 7%, when it should be rising in correlation.

The table below shows how the numbers above came about.

355

EN > DE	Good enough	High quality
Words	1,027,343	1,862,915
Prod Start	1200	1010
Prod Finish	1600	1150
Increase	33%	14%
PED Start	29	26
PED Finish	15	20
Reduction	48%	23%

Table 6: Productivity and PED gains [and losses] expressed in percentages.

The following two graphs provide bird's-eye views of trendlines for our top nine languages between January 2018 and November 2019. This timeframe spans the three MSFT Translator deployment phases of customized SMT, generic NMT and customized NMT. Please zoom in.

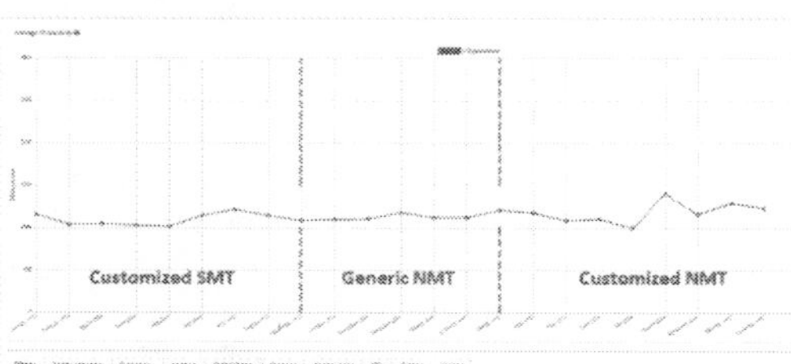

Figure 1: Productivity for 9 languages rising from 1050 words per hour to 1300.

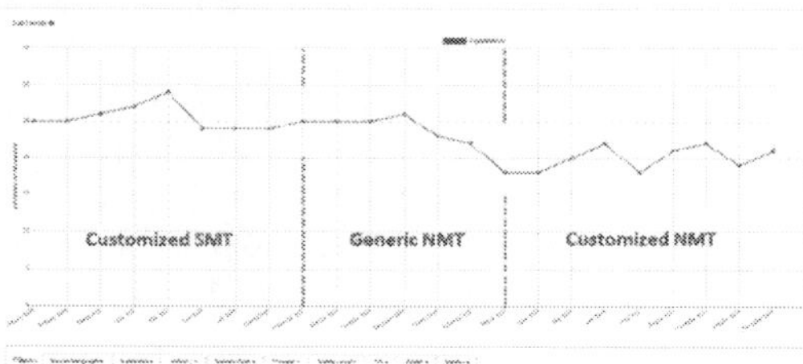

Figure 2: PEDe for 9 languages falling from 25 to 20 characters per 100 characters.

The trendline for PEDe appears to be more robust than for productivity. Also, within the discernable trends over 23 months, we see monthly ups and downs, suggesting that productivity is driven by multiple factors, not only MT quality.

The following graph compares productivity trendline and PEDe for EN-US to Dutch, a language pair for which we never customized NMT systems.

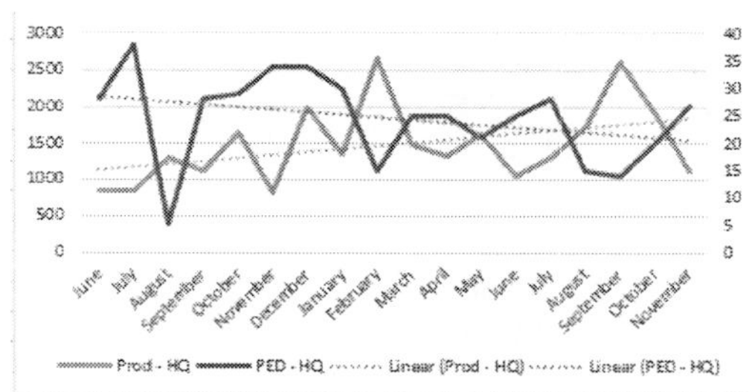

Figure 3: Well correlated trendlines: falling PED and rising productivity, going from generic SMT to generic NMT.

In summary, we can observe the overall benefits of customized NMT systems, especially when rolling up trendlines for all top nine languages. Looking at individual language pairs we can see exceptions. Pronounced discrepancies between PED and productivity we plan to review with our translation and MT technology providers.

6 Cut-off between MT and TM

In the following exercise, we wanted to find out if post-editing machine translations is faster than editing fuzzy matches. Depending on the language pair and NMT system, customized vs. generic, machine translated segments require fewer post-edits than fuzzy matches (Zaretskaya, 2019). Assuming that fewer post-edits mean shorter post-editing times, i.e., higher productivity, we should raise the MT-to-TM cut-off from 75% to x.

We looked at jobs machine translated against our customized NMT system from EN-US to DE-DE between March 2019 and 2020.

Match rate	Segments	Sentences per bracket	Bracket	Milliseconds
0	15,090	15,090	0	43,812
75	314			
76	304			
77	323			
78	319			
79	324	1,584	75-79	25,032
80	324			
81	328			
82	299			
83	305			
84	315	3,155	75-84	24,584
85	385			
86	424			
87	395			
88	379			
89	333			
90	362			
91	347			
92	355			
93	393			
94	404	3,777	85-94	20,968
95	405			
96	382			
97	670			
98	1,500	2,957	95-98	13,199
99	12,096	12,096	99	3,700
100	101,916	101,916	100	58
Grand Total	138,991			

Table 7: Distribution of 138,991 segments on leverage scale of $0 - 100$, grouped by matching bands.

As expected, post-editing times diminish with increasing match rates. But it takes significantly longer to post-edit MT segments than 75%-84% fuzzies: 44 vs. 25 seconds. Increasing the MT-to-TM cut-off to 85% would drastically reduce productivity.

EN-US > DE-DE	Time in segs	Avg. secs	Total segs
0 - 10 nPEDi	Any	44	14,889
75-84 fuzzies	Any	25	3,155
0 - 10 nPEDi	0 - 120 secs	22	13,537
75 - 84 fuzzies	0 - 120 secs	17	3,044
0 - 10 nPEDi	0 - 60 secs	15	12,118
75 - 84 fuzzies	0 - 60 secs	12	2,848

Table 8: EN-US-to-DE-DE MT and fuzzy-match segments grouped by average active time. "Any" contains outliers.

Sorting segments by post-edit time, we noticed outliers that were active much longer than typically necessary for editing. The biggest outlier was active in the CAT tool for 16 minutes. When only considering segments active for 60 seconds – which means 81% of all MT segments - the editing time gap shrinks from 76% to 25%.

EN-US > FR-FR	Time in segs	Avg. secs	Total segs
0 - 10 nPEDi	Any	42	13,515
75-84 fuzzies	Any	26	2,866
0 - 10 nPEDi	0 - 120 secs	20	12,283
75 - 84 fuzzies	0 - 120 secs	15	2,724
0 - 10 nPEDi	0 - 60 secs	12	11,010
75 - 84 fuzzies	0 - 60 secs	11	2,561

Table 9: EN-US-to-FR-FR MT and fuzzy-match segments grouped by average active time. "Any" contains outliers.

For the EN-US-to-FR-FR language pair, the post-editing time gap between fuzzy matches and MT shrinks to 9% when only considering segments active for 60 seconds. This convergence likely applies to other well-performing MT language pairs as well: English to Brazilian Portuguese, Chinese, French, Italian and Spanish.

But as long as editing time for MT segments doesn't fall below editing time for fuzzy matches, raising the MT-to-TM cut-off would be counterproductive.

Let's see if the PED tells a different story.

EN > DE: w/o OL	MT	75-84	85-94	95-98	99
Segments	14,302	2,758	3,363	2,487	11,926
Avg aPEDi	23	23	16	12	3
Avg Words	14	10	14	12	7

Table 10: Average aPEDi for EN-US to DE-DE by match band, without outliers.

For EN-US to DE-DE, the average absolute PED for MT and the adjacent fuzzy match segments is the same, 23 characters. But, it takes 25% longer to edit the MT segments.

EN > FR: w/o OL	MT	75-84	85-94	95-98	99
Segments	13,180	2,675	2,708	1,836	14,769
Avg aPEDi	17	21	15	10	2
Avg Words	17	13	18	14	9

Table 11: Average aPEDi for EN-US to FR-FR by match band, without outliers.

For EN-US to FR-FR, the average PED for MT segments is 17 characters vs. 21 characters for 75%-84% fuzzy matches. While MT segments require 19% fewer post-edits, it takes 9% longer to edit them. It has been noted before, that post-edits and post-editing time, i.e., technical and temporal efforts do not necessarily correlate (Krings, 2001).

While we couldn't demonstrate that our MT segments can be edited faster than our fuzzies, we did gain a couple of useful insights. For one, we need to optionally exclude outliers from our data to produce a richer picture of our MT productivity. About 10% of MT segments inflate both average post-editing time and PED noticeably.

EN > DE: with OL	MT	75-84	85-94	95-98	99
Segments	14,889	3,155	3,777	2,957	12,096
Avg aPEDi	28	75	80	62	6
Avg Words	15	11	15	12	8

Table 12: Average aPEDi for EN-US to DE-DE by match band, with outliers.

EN > FR: with OL	MT	75-84	85-94	95-98	99
Segments	13,515	2,866	2,958	2,180	14,881
Avg aPEDi	20	43	47	48	4
Avg Words	17	14	19	14	9

Table 13: Average aPEDi for EN-US to FR-FR by match band, with outliers.

The tables above contain outliers, segments with inline tags relatively easy to handle by linguists in the CAT tool, but with large character counts to the Levenshtein algorithm. In one sample, a segment with 7 words and 6 tags resulted in an aPEDi of 1015 characters. Going by the standard ratio of 1:5 for words to characters, the calculated aPEDi vastly overstates the human effort of placing a few tags and minor textual changes.

For two, 99% fuzzy matches deserve special consideration in SLAs, assuming they constitute a good portion of overall word count. In our 12-month sample, they account for 9% of total words, and require a fraction of editing time compared to other match bands. They ought to be broken out for dedicated costing.

7   Time spent on 0 nPEDi segments

In this section we discuss the time linguists spent on segments that required no post-editing. Ideally, CAT tools should flag these segments to linguists so that they can skip them.

The following table breaks down segments machine translated from EN-US into DE-DE between March 2019 and March 2020.

EN-US > DE-DE	0 nPEDi	1 nPEDi	0 - 10 nPEDi
HT + MT Segments	113,308	7,520	138,991
MT Segments	1,890	3,210	14,889
Segs with 0 Time in segment	1,389	219	1,778
Segs with Time in segment	501	2,991	13,111
Avg. time in segment *	8	19	50
Avg. segment length *	7	16	15

Table 14: Editing time for segments with 0 post-edits. Excluding segments with no time in segment (*).

Linguists didn't post-edit 1,890 (or 12%) of all MT segments. And the CAT tool didn't record post-editing time for 1389 segments of these unchanged segments, suggesting that the linguist had signed off on them unseen. We realized that the CAT tool allows linguists to sign off on segments w/o activating them. Because linguists can by-pass the time-tracker for unchanged segments, our hourly MT productivity is slightly overstated.

Of the unchanged segments (0 nPEDi), linguists did activate 501 for review. These segments were on average 7 words long and took linguists 8 seconds on average to conclude that no edits were needed.

In the 1 nPEDi bracket, linguists made minor changes, e.g., to correct compounds, punctuation, or word casing. For 219 segments the CAT tool recorded changes, but no time in segment. We found that search and replace operations register as PED, but not editing time. In the 1 nPEDi bracket, for the 2991 segments requiring editing time, the segment length goes up to 16 words, in line with the overall MT segment length of 15 words, yet the average time to edit is only 19 seconds versus 50 seconds for all MT segments.

To increase ROI from MT, we would need to achieve three things: for accurate productivity tracking, the CAT tool needs to optionally force linguists to activate segments for sign-off, even if no post edits are needed. To increase the modest 12% of MT segments that do not require post-editing, we need to improve MT output by retraining our NMT systems against the latest base model and by adjusting our Style Guides to make allowances for immaterial linguistic deviations.

If we manage to increase the percentage of segments that don't require post-editing, we need to find a way to flag these for linguists in the CAT tool via quality estimation models. Similar to how we opt to selectively skip review of repetitions or 100% matches, we may choose to skip review of low-risk MT segments.

8 Segments by nPEDi

To understand how segments are distributed on the nPEDi scale of $1 - 10$, we looked at Good enough and High quality material, machine translated with our customized NMT system between March 2019 and February 2020.

The following diagram shows that most segments for FR-FR and DE-DE fall into the nPEDi range of 0 to 4. In line with the overall ranking of languages by productivity, FR-FR performs better than DE-DE, with more segments in the nPEDi range of 0 to 1.

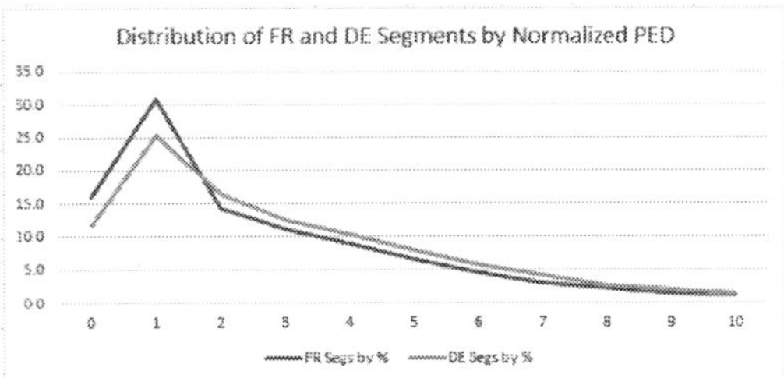

Figure 4: Distribution of segments on nPEDi scale of 0 to 10.

Since we omitted to track productivity for HT workflows, we need to go by the industry assumption that linguists are faster post-editing MT output than translating from scratch (HT) if the nPEDi is below 5. Going by this assumption, our customized NMT system boosts FR-FR productivity for 81% of the segments.

Norm. PED	Segs by #	FR Segs by %	Cummulative %
0	2,301	16.0	16.0
1	4,462	30.9	46.9
2	2,057	14.3	61.1
3	1,590	11.0	72.2
4	1,280	8.9	81.0
5	933	6.5	
6	669	4.6	
7	442	3.1	
8	304	2.1	
9	212	1.5	
10	175	1.2	
	14,425		

Table 15: nPEDi distribution for EN-US to FR-FR segments by percentages.

For DE-DE, our customized NMT system boosts productivity for 76% of the segments.

Norm. PED	Segs by #	DE Segs by %	Cummulative %
0	2,293	11.7	11.7
1	4,959	25.3	37.0
2	3,228	16.5	53.5
3	2,449	12.5	66.0
4	2,009	10.3	76.3
5	1,547	7.9	
6	1,112	5.7	
7	806	4.1	
8	504	2.6	
9	391	2.0	
10	292	1.5	
	19,590		

Table 16: nPEDi distribution for EN-US to DE-DE segments by percentages.

We are planning to analyze segments in the nPEDi range of 1 to 2 to understand if aligning styleguide requirements to MT capabilities or automated post-editing rules will elevate these low nPEDi to 0 nPEDi segments.

9 Correlating nPEDi and segment length

We approached the exercise of correlating nPEDi and segment length with the assumption that MT systems translate segments of a certain length best, segments that are not too short and not too long. Similar to linguists, MT systems may struggle with short segments for lack of context and with long segments because of complexity.

We tried to confirm this assumption with two different methods on segments machine translated with our customized NMT systems between March 2019 and February 2020.

In the first exercise, we simply expanded the nPEDi distribution table, by adding the total source language word count for each nPEDi mark and dividing it by the number of segments.

nPEDi	Segs	Words	FR W / S
0	2,301	22,821	10
1	4,462	69,311	16
2	2,057	30,723	15
3	1,590	23,312	15
4	1,280	18,483	14
5	933	12,673	14
6	669	8,056	12
7	442	4,242	10
8	304	2,730	9
9	212	1,511	7
10	175	950	5
	14,425	194,812	14

Table 17: Average segment length per nPEDi bracket.

nPEDi	Segs	Words	DE W / S
0	2,293	16,461	7
1	4,959	77,968	16
2	3,228	50,936	16
3	2,449	42,690	17
4	2,009	34,667	17
5	1,547	25,172	16
6	1,112	17,139	15
7	806	11,070	14
8	504	5,923	12
9	391	3,512	9
10	292	1,773	6
	19,590	287,311	15

Table 18: Average segment length per nPEDi bracket.

While short segments appear at both ends of the 1 − 10 nPEDi scale, 75% of them are in the 0 nPEDi bracket. This does mean that shorter strings machine translate more successfully.

In the next method, we grouped DE-DE segments by word length and, calculated the average aPEDi and nPEDi for each length.

Length	Segments	Avg. nPEDi	Avg. aPEDi
1	317	2.06	3
2	776	2.77	6
3	945	2.95	8
4	958	3.15	11
5	988	2.69	11
6	939	2.89	13
7	914	2.96	16
8	866	2.94	18
9	812	3.03	20
10	751	2.9	21
11	713	3.03	23
12	678	2.94	25
13	680	2.92	26
14	666	2.89	27
15	636	2.91	28
20	507	2.94	38
25	324	3.04	46
30	226	3.15	60
35	100	3.12	71
40	58	2.7	65
	12,854		

Table 19: Average nPEDi and aPEDi by segment length in words.

With the exception of segments 1, 2, 5 and 40 words long, the nPEDi hovers around 3 for segments of any length, even for the longer ones. We assume that the average nPEDi for longer segments doesn't increase noticeably because linguists may revisit these long and complicated segments in separate CAT sessions and therefore only record a portion of the actual post-edits.

The lighter (orange) line in the graph below illustrates the lower nPEDi for the very short segments and the otherwise relatively stable nPEDi:

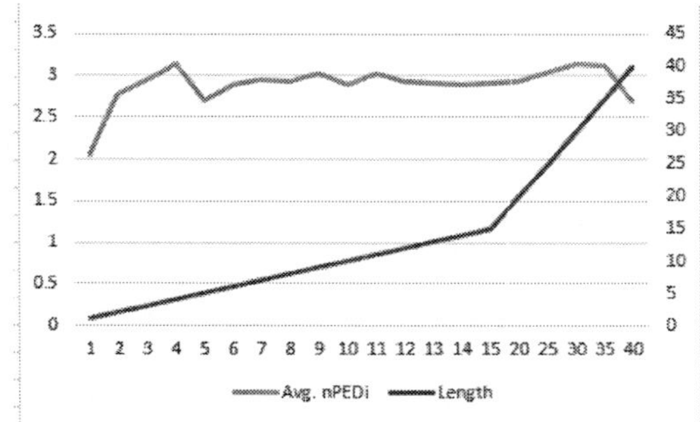

Figure 5: nPEDi in characters by segment length in words.

Naturally, the aPEDi generally increases with segment length. The lines diverge because segment length is counted in words while aPEDi is counted in characters.

360

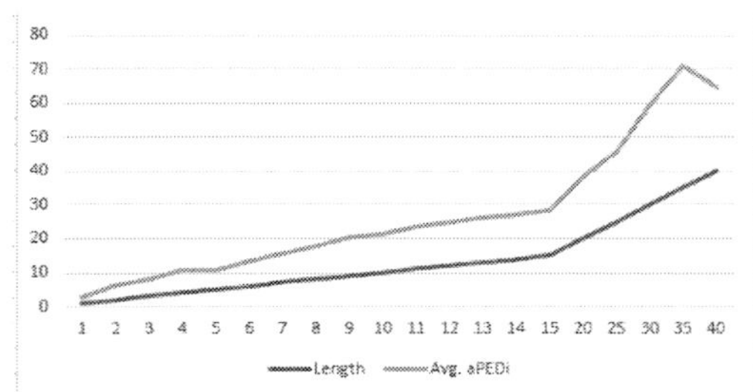

Figure 6: aPEDi in characters by segment length in words.

The first exercise clearly indicates that it is the majority of shorter segments that machine translate better than longer strings. A minority of shorter strings fails to translate well, probably for lack of context. The second exercise is inconclusive, but highlights one of the imperfections in our productivity tracking setup.

10 Future work

Users will benefit from several enhancements to GlobalLink to more accurately record post-editing efforts in this particular translation management system. Above all, the setup needs to capture all edits, whether performed in one or multiple CAT tool sessions. MT segments should only be included in the metrics if linguists signed off on them. To track editing time comprehensively, the CAT tool should optionally require activation also for segments that do not need post-edits. Batch changes that do not trigger the time tracker should be accounted for somehow. Tracking editing effort for HT segments is essential to establish a baseline. The comprehensive audit trail capabilities of GlobalLink allowed us to pinpoint these opportunities for improvement.

We hope that TAUS will use our findings to develop certification test plans for tools integrators to ensure that productivity metrics are consistently calculated across organizations using different CAT tools. Also, the TAUS DQF Dashboard should allow users to exclude outliers for an alternate productivity view.

For full access to our productivity data currently stored in the TAUS DQF Dashboard, Dell needs to integrate its BI tools.

11 Conclusion

Tracking MT productivity at scale needs to become an integral capability in the translation industry to be available regardless of which tools and services providers we partner with.

Even though our productivity metrics are after the fact, they are a statistically robust addition to small-scale human evaluations, BLEU scores and emerging risk calculation models. Together, these MT quality assurance methods help us focus our continuous improvement efforts.

Our numbers show that we are on the right track: productivity is steadily rising and post-edits falling. Our challenge will be to turn the many segments requiring few post-edits to ones that require none and to flag these segments in the CAT tool so that linguists can skip them.

We like to think that the imperfections we discovered in our setup balance each other out as some inflate and some deflate our productivity numbers. We are also reminded that within MTPE jobs, we apply machine translations to new words only, about 10% of total word count. The remaining 90% are leveraged from translation memories. While MT is an important productivity aid, it is not the only one in a linguist's tool chest.

Overall, 70% of our production translation jobs use MT to pre-translate new words. We will expand MT usage by starting to pre-translate software as well. The biggest expansion of MT usage at Dell, however, occurs somewhere else. To operate within a global enterprise, many of our colleagues produce raw MT in self-service mode. And data scientists machine translate vast amounts of data into English for processing by BI engines. This last use case dwarfs all others by volume. Closely monitoring machine translation quality in our human-assisted production workflows will benefit Dell's two use cases of unedited MT output as well.

Acknowledgements

The following individuals and organizations were instrumental in creating an environment to harvest MT metrics automatically for Dell EMC: Nancy Anderson, head of the EMC translation team at the time supported the proposal to take translations "online". She negotiated with our LSPs the necessary process and tools concessions. Keith Brazil and his team at Translations.com optimized GlobalLink as a collaborative platform for a multi-vendor supply chain. Jaap van der Meer proposed an integration with the TAUS DQF Dashboard. TAUS and

Translations.com then worked together to connect systems to calculate and record MT productivity metrics. Last but not least, our MLVs, their numerous SLVs and the many linguists agreed to trade their preferred CAT tools for a common technology platform.

References

Levenshtein, Vladimir Iosifovich. 1966. *Binary Codes Capable of Correcting Deletions, Insertions and Reversals*. Soviet Physics Doklady.

Zaretskaya, Anna. 2019. *Raising the TM Threshold in Neural MT Post-Editing: a Case-Study on Two Datasets*. Proceedings of MT Summit XVII, volume 2. 213-218.

Krings, Hans P. 2001. *Repairing Texts: Empirical Investigations of Machine Translation Post-Editing Processes*. Kent State University Press, Kent, Ohio.

Koponen, Maarit. 2016. *Is Machine Translation Postediting Worth the Effort? A Survey of Research into Post-editing and Effort*. The Journal of Specialised Translation.

Translators' papers

On the differences between human translations

Maja Popović
ADAPT Centre
School of Computing
Dublin City University, Ireland
maja.popovic@adaptcentre.ie

Abstract

Many studies have confirmed that translated texts exhibit different features than texts originally written in the given language. This work explores texts translated by different translators taking into account expertise and native language. A set of computational analyses was conducted on three language pairs, English-Croatian, German-French and English-Finnish, and the results show that each of the factors has certain influence on the features of the translated texts, especially on sentence length and lexical richness. The results also indicate that for translations used for machine translation evaluation, it is important to specify these factors, especially when comparing machine translation quality with human translation quality.

1 Introduction

Many studies have demonstrated that translated texts (human translations, HTs) have different lexical, syntactic and other textual features than texts originally written in the given language (originals). These special traits of HTs are result of a compromise between two often antagonised aspects of the translation process: fidelity to the source text and naturalness of the generated target language text. Although all studies confirm the existence of unique HT features, two categories of these features are distinguished in the literature. One category, "translation universals", represents a general set of features shared by all translations, independent of the characteristics of involved languages

(Baker et al., 1993). Another category, "interference", reflects the impact of the source language, the "trace" which the source language leaves in the translation (Toury, 1979). Some studies investigate and demonstrate the existence of both categories, sometimes called "source universals" and "target universals" (Chesterman, 2004; Koppel and Ordan, 2011).

Our research aims to find out whether differences between translators have any influence on the text features. We investigate impact of the translator's expertise and native language. We present results of a computational analysis of a set of HTs originating from the news domain and involving three distinct language pairs, English-Croatian, German-French and English-Finnish. The analysis is guided by the following research questions:

RQ1 Are there differences between HTs related to translator's expertise?

RQ2 Are there differences between HTs related to translator's native language and translation direction? (from or into translator's native language)

The main contribution of this work is empirical, showing evidence of differences between text features of HTs produced by different translators. We expect our findings to motivate and drive future research in this direction in order to better understand these differences by identifying and analysing underlying linguistic phenomena.

Moreover, differences between HTs may have practical impact on evaluation of machine translation (MT) systems. Several recent studies (Toral et al., 2018; Läubli et al., 2018; Zhang and Toral, 2019; Freitag et al., 2019) have shown that the

Martins, Moniz, Fumega, Martins, Batista, Coheur, Parra, Trancoso, Turchi, Bisazza, Moorkens, Guerberof, Nurminen, Marg, Forcada (eds.)
Proceedings of the 22nd Annual Conference of the European Association for Machine Translation, p. 365–374
Lisboa, Portugal, November 2020.

translation direction has impact on the results of evaluation of MT outputs, so that it is important to specify whether originals or HTs were used as source texts for MT systems. Taking into account these studies and the findings reported in this work, potential effects of translators' backgrounds on MT should be investigated too.

2 Related work

Analysis of translated texts A lot of work has been done exploring differences between HTs and originals. Some studies (Baker et al., 1993) have emphasised the existence of "translation universals", general features of translated texts, "simplification" and "explicitation" being the most well-known. Other studies (Toury, 1979) have pointed out the influence of the source language, "interference", whereas some (Chesterman, 2004) concentrate on both categories, called "S-universals" and "T-universals".

Since many text features can be measured quantitatively, a number of publications demonstrated that HTs can be automatically distinguished from originals (Baroni and Bernardini, 2006; Koppel and Ordan, 2011; Volansky et al., 2015; Rabinovich and Wintner, 2015; Rubino et al., 2016). The features used for the classifiers are partly motivated by the theoretical categories mentioned above, however many features are not directly related to a particular category, and many can belong to more than one category. The most common features are lexical variety (percentage of distinct words in a text), lexical density (sometimes called information density, percentage of content words in a text), sentence length, word length, as well as frequencies of certain POS categories, function words and collocations.

Rabinovich et al. (2016) include analysis of non-native texts, namely texts originally written in the given language but by non-native speakers. They found that these texts generally exhibit different features than native originals and HTs, thus representing yet another text category. On the other hand, their features are closer to those of HTs than to native originals, indicating the influence ("interference") of the native language.

In addition to analysis of HTs, more and more publications report analysis of machine translated texts. Ahrenberg (2017) compares MT outputs with HTs by means of automatically calculated text features as well as by manual analysis of divergences (shifts) from the source text. The main finding is that MT output is much more similar to the source text than HT. Another study of machine translated texts (Vanmassenhove et al., 2019) reports significantly lower lexical richness in MT outputs in comparison to originals and HTs.

Post-editing (PE) of MT outputs has lead to yet another type of translated text which has been analysed extensively in the recent years (Čulo and Nitzke, 2016; Daems et al., 2017; Farrell, 2018; Toral, 2019; Castilho et al., 2019). These studies demonstrated that PEs represent an additional text category with the features lying between those of HTs and of MT outputs.

Relations between machine and human translation As machine translation (MT) technology improves, more and more work has been done on investigating relations between different aspects of MT and HT direction. First publications on this topic (Kurokawa et al., 2009; Lembersky et al., 2013) demonstrated that the direction of HT plays an important role for building a statistical MT system, and recommend training on parallel corpora which were translated in the same direction as the MT system (i.e. using originals as source and HTs as target).

Recently, several publications (Läubli et al., 2018; Toral et al., 2018; Freitag et al., 2019; Zhang and Toral, 2019) demonstrated that the translation direction plays an important role both for human as well as for automatic evaluation of MT systems. Before these findings were published, this aspect has not been taken into account at all in the MT community.[1] Afterwards, as a consequence, using only originals as source test texts and HTs as reference test texts has become a common practice in the WMT shared tasks[2] from 2019. The main reason is to avoid all possible side effects, since Toral et al. (2018) have shown that the use of HTs as source texts facilitates the MT process mainly because of the decreased lexical variety. On the other hand, Freitag et al. (2019) recommend using both, albeit separated, original as well as HT source texts precisely in order to be able to take into account and better understand all effects.

Apart from the impact of translation direction, the impact of divergences from a source text in HT

---

[1] For example, in the WMT shared tasks, even texts written in an "external" original language were used extensively, e.g. English HTs from Czech texts were used as source for English-to-German MT systems.

[2] http://www.statmt.org/wmt19/

used as MT data has been investigated, too. The potential influence of different translation strategies and resulting divergences (shifts) on MT evaluation was discussed in (Popović, 2019), whereas Vyas et al. (2018) explored automatic identification of such divergences and their effects on MT training.

Texts translated by different translators Despite of a large body of work dealing with analysis of different translated texts in different contexts, there is, however, not much work about texts translated by different translators. Rubino et al. (2016) explored effects of translator's expertise to some extent, and reported that texts translated by students could be automatically distinguished from originals with higher accuracy than texts translated by professional translators. This indicates that the features of professional HTs are more similar to the features of originals. To the best of our knowledge, our work is the first attempt to systematically compare texts translated by different translators.

3 Data sets

For our experiments, we used three available parallel data sets involving three different language pairs and five translation directions: English→Croatian ($EnHr$), German↔French ($DeFr$) and English↔Finnish ($EnFi$). All data sets belong to the news domain and originate from the publicly available WMT shared tasks.

Ideally, each data set should have been designed specifically for one particular RQ, and created under the same conditions: each of the translators should have translated the same, sufficiently large source text. In addition, all source language texts should be originally written in that language, not being translated from some other language. Table 1 summarises the properties of our three data sets, and the following limitations can be noted:

* None of the data sets were specifically designed for one RQ: only the $EnHr$ data set is (almost) ideal for translation expertise (RQ1). The $DeFr$ is appropriate for both expertise (RQ1) and native language (RQ2), whereas the $EnFi$ data set is suitable for native language (RQ2).

* The $EnHr$ data set is, as mentioned above, almost ideal for exploring translation expertise, although one HT was generated from a different source text than the other three. The main drawback is that both source language texts were not written originally in English, but are HTs: they

were translated from Czech in the framework of the WMT 2012 and WMT 2013 shared task However, this fact has no influence on the results of our experiment, because all HTs are coming from the same original language.

* The main limitation of the $DeFr$ data set is its small size: while in the other two data sets at least 1000 source sentences were translated by each translator, this data set ranges from 100 to 750 sentences. Another drawback is the lack of a common source text for all translators – therefore, different HTs represent a comparable corpus instead of a parallel corpus. The same limitation represents the main drawback of the $EnFi$ data set.

In addition, several domains/genres should ideally be covered, whereas all our data sets come from the news domain. Nevertheless, an ideal data set is, to the best of our knowledge, currently not available for any of our research questions. Therefore, we carried out our first experiments on the described available texts which, despite of their flaws, represent a good starting point for this research direction. The data sets are made publicly available for further research.[3] No personal information (such as name, gender, age, working place) about the translators are shared. The details and statistics of each of the texts used are presented together with the results in the corresponding sections.

4 Text features

The set of text features used in our experiments is inspired by the features frequently used in the literature (Baroni and Bernardini, 2006; Koppel and Ordan, 2011; Volansky et al., 2015; Toral, 2019). Although they are also motivated by two theoretical categories, simplification (Baker et al., 1993) and interference (Toury, 1979), they do not represent any of these categories exclusively. The choice of features is based on a hypothesis that the selected features might vary depending on the factors addressed in our work, namely translator's experience, native language and translation strategies.

For all features, punctuation marks were separated and counted as words. POS tags for all languages are generated by TreeTagger.[4] The features

---

[3] https://github.com/m-popovic/different-HTs
[4] https://www.cis.uni-muenchen.de/~schmid/

property		$EnHr$	$DeFr$	$EnFi$
RQ1: expertise		+	+	−
RQ2: translation direction and native language		−	+	+
same source language text for each translator		±	−	−
$\geq$1000 sentences per translator		+	−	+
source language is the original language		−	+	+

Table 1: Properties of the three data sets; "−" denotes lack of a specific property.

are defined and calculated in the following way:

Sentence length: Number of words in each sentence of the text.

Some translators might tend to generate longer sentences in the target text than others. Some translators might keep the number of words in the translated sentences closer to the number of source text words than others.

Mean word length: The total number of characters in the text divided by total number of words.

Some translators might prefer longer (potentially more complex) words than others.

Lexical variety: The total number of distinct words in the text divided by the total number of words in the text.

$$lexVar = \frac{N(distinct\ words)}{N(words)} \quad (1)$$

Previous work has shown that vocabulary of HTs is generally less rich than vocabulary of originals. However, some translators might use more distinct words (a richer vocabulary) than others.

Morpho-syntactic variety: The total number of distinct POS tags in the text divided by the total number of words.

$$morphsynVar = \frac{N(distinct\ POS)}{N(words)} \quad (2)$$

Some translators might use more complex and/or more diverse grammatical structures than others. Some might keep the grammatical structure of translated sentences closer to the one of the source text than others.

Lexical density: The ratio between the total number of content words (adverbs, adjectives, nouns and verbs) and the total number of words.

$$lexDens = \frac{N(content\ words)}{N(words)} \quad (3)$$

HTs have been found to have a lower percentage of content words than originals. However, some translators might use more content words than others.

5 Experimental set-up

For each feature, we calculate relative difference between the feature value of the original source text $f(source)$ and the feature value of its translation $f(ht)$.

$$\Delta(f) = \frac{f(source) - f(ht)}{f(source)} \quad (4)$$

The main benefits of reporting relative differences are:

- relative difference reduces impact of distinct source languages (language pairs);

- relative difference minimalises effects of using comparable instead of parallel HTs.

Table 2 shows an example of lexical varieties of two comparable HTs. The values of the two target language lexical varieties $f(ht)$ imply that the second HT is lexically richer. However, the reason for that difference might simply be the initially higher lexical variety of the second source text. Relative difference, though, clearly demonstrates that the second translation is lexically less rich and also closer to the source text.

	$f(ht)$	$f(source)$	$\Delta(f)$
source 1	0.721	0.434	**66.1%**
source 2	**0.832**	0.548 (!)	51.8%

Table 2: Example of analysing lexical varieties of two comparable HTs and advantage of using relative differences.

For each text and each feature, relative difference is calculated as average value over chunks of 100 sentences[5] (approximately 2000 words), similarly to some previous work (Volansky et al.,

---

tools/TreeTagger/

[5]50 sentences (1000 words) for the $DeFr$ corpus due to the small size

2015). The purpose of averaging over small chunks is manifold: to make sure that the length of a text does not interfere with the feature values, to avoid issues related to the small size of some texts, and to further minimise the potential effects of using comparable instead of parallel translations.

For each of the research questions, the obtained values are reported and discussed in the following section. It is worth noting that the numbers differ between the data sets due to distinct properties of the language pairs. For example, relative difference between Finnish and English lexical and POS varieties are much larger than those between German and French.

We did not perform any text classification in this experiment, because the sizes of the currently available texts are not sufficient for training a classifier.

6 Results

6.1 RQ1: Influence of expertise and different cohorts

The $EnHr$ data set and the appropriate part of the $DeFr$ data set were used to examine the potential influence of different translator cohorts on text features. The statistics showing number of sentences and translator cohorts for both data sets is shown in Table 3. All translators were native speakers of the target language.

The $EnHr$ data set was created in the framework of the Abu-MaTran project.[6] A subset of the English test set[7] from WMT 2012 (1011 sentences) was translated into Croatian in two ways: professional translation and crowdsourcing via the CrowdFlower platform.[8] The options on the platform were configured in a way that enables the best possible translation quality: geography was limited to Croatia, and only the contributors on the top performance level were considered. In this way, 30 different crowdsourcing contributors participated in translation. In total, three HTs were created from this English source text: one by a professional translator and two by different crowd contributors. In a later phase of the project, 1000 English sentences[9] from the WMT 2013 were translated by a student, thus representing a third translator cohort, although as a comparable text.

The $DeFr$ data set was created for the WMT 2019 shared task. A subset of 1327 sentences was originally written in German and translated by translators with three different levels of expertise: student (326 sentences), professional translator (756 sentences), and specialist[10] (245 sentences).

6.1.1 Results on the *EnHr* data set

The main tendencies which can be observed in Table 4 are variations in sentence length and lexical variety, and to a lesser extent, in morphosyntactic variety. In addition, the features of the two crowd HTs are very similar, and more distinct than the features of the other two HTs. The sentence length indicates that the crowd produced shorter Croatian translations than the professional translator and the student. Higher lexical and morphosyntactic varieties are probably a consequence of a large number of different contributors which lead to a decrease in consistency. Here, it should be noted that a large lexical and/or grammatical variety as well as a large divergence from the source text are not necessarily positive.

Effects on automatic MT evaluation Since the $EnHr$ data set is the only one containing parallel (instead of comparable) HTs, it represents a perfect data set for testing the behaviour of automatic MT evaluation scores calculated on distinct reference translations. For this purpose, we translated the English source text by two online MT systems,[11] Google Translate[12] and Bing Translator.[13] We then calculated the widely used BLEU score (Post, 2018) and two recently proposed character-based metrics, F-score (Popović, 2015) and edit distance (Wang et al., 2016). All scores are calculated by comparing MT output with each of the HTs.

The resulting scores in Table 5 lead to different conclusions depending on the used reference HT. According to the professional HT, the Google MT output is substantially better than the Bing output in terms of all three evaluation metrics. If the first crowd HT is used as a reference, the differences between the two systems become small according to BLEU and chrF, whereas characTER even says that the Bing MT output is better. A similar tendency can be observed if the student HT is

---

[6]https://www.abumatran.eu/
[7]HT from Czech, as mentioned in Section 3
[8]http://crowdflower.com/
[9]also HT from Czech

[10]not a professional translator by vocation, but experienced
[11]in November 2019
[12]https://translate.google.com/
[13]https://www.bing.com/translator

data set	parallel text	translator	translation expertise	number of sentence pairs
$EnHr$	2012 en→hr	Thr_1	professional	1011
	2012 en→hr	Thr_2	crowd	
	2012 en→hr	Thr_3	crowd	
	2013 en→hr	Thr_4	student	1000
$DeFr$	2019 de→fr	Tfr_1	student	326
	2019 de→fr	Tfr_2	specialist	245
	2019 de→fr	Tfr_3	professional	756

Table 3: Characteristics of the texts used to examine the influence of translation expertise: language pair, translator, translator's expertise and number of sentences.

$EnHr$ en→hr	translator expertise	Thr_1 prof.	Thr_2 crowd	Thr_3 crowd	Thr_4 stud.
$\frac{SRC(en)-HT(hr)}{SRC(en)}$	Δ(sentence length)	8.06	12.8	13.4	11.3
	Δ(word length)	-13.7	-14.3	-15.0	-14.8
	Δ(lexical variety)	-32.6	-40.3	-41.6	-35.6
	Δ(POS variety)	-413	-426	-423	-406
	Δ(lexical density)	51.9	51.6	51.8	53.1

Table 4: Relative differences (%) between features of the original texts and features of the translated texts for English→Croatian texts translated by translators with different expertises: professional, crowd and student.

used, albeit the comparison is not completely appropriate since the source text is different. If the second crowd HT is used, the BLEU score of the Bing output becomes slightly better, the characTER score becomes substantially better, whereas the chrF score is slightly worse than Google.

The fact that automatic scores calculated on different reference translations are different is, of course, nothing new. However, here we point out that translator cohort providing the reference HT can have influence on the scores and perceptions of systems' quality, and therefore represents a factor which should be taken into account in MT evaluation.

6.1.2 Results on the *DeFr* data set

Table 6 shows the text features of the $DeFr$ data set. In spite of differences between this corpus and the $EnHr$ corpus in terms of expertise levels, languages, as well as comparable HTs instead of parallel HTs, the same general tendencies can be observed, namely variations in sentence length, lexical variety and morpho-syntactic variety. The sentences in the professional HT are longest and the lexical variety is highest, which could be intuitively expected – professional translators tend to divert more from the source language and to use richer vocabulary. Morpho-syntactic variety, however, is highest in the specialist HT, although not much higher than in the other two. All the findings indicate that translation expertise has influence on sentence length, lexical and morpho-syntactic va-

riety, however a deeper analysis is needed in the future to identify the nature of these differences.

Lexical density, however, varies only in the $DeFr$ data set, especially for the specialist's translation. This feature should certainly be analysed further in order to determine whether the variations are related to the translator expertise, or maybe to some other factors such as distinct nature of the language pair, translator's individual preferences, etc.

6.2 RQ2: Influence of native language and translation direction

The differences between native and non-native HTs were analysed on appropriate portions of the $DeFr$ and $EnFi$ data sets. The statistics of the texts used are shown in Table 7. As already mentioned in Section 3, both data sets contain comparable HTs.

The $DeFr$ texts, created for the WMT 2019 shared task, enable two ways of investigating influence of (non-)native language. One is to compare two translation directions of one translator: a French native specialist Tfr_2 was translating in both directions: from French into German (from their native language) and from German into French (into their native language). Another way is to compare two translators working on the same translation direction: a French native specialist Tfr_2 and a German native specialist Tde_1 both were translating from French into German.

The $EnFi$ data set enables only the first type

EnHr, en→hr	BLEU ↑		chrF ↑		characTER ↓	
reference	Google	Bing	Google	Bing	Google	Bing
Thr_1 (professional)	41.9	34.9	65.5	60.3	30.3	33.4
Thr_2 (crowd)	32.9	32.6	59.8	59.0	**34.1**	**33.4**
Thr_3 (crowd)	**29.5**	**29.6**	57.6	57.4	**36.2**	**35.0**
Thr_4 (student)	34.7	31.2	58.8	57.5	**35.9**	**35.7**

Table 5: Three automatic evaluation scores (BLEU, chrF and characTER) for English-to-Croatian on-line MT systems calculated on reference translations produced by translators with different expertises: professional, crowd and student.

DeFr **de→fr**	translator expertise	Tfr_1 stud.	Tfr_2 spec.	Tfr_3 prof.
	Δ(sentence length)	-21.3	-23.4	-26.1
	Δ(word length)	10.6	11.4	10.9
$\frac{SRC(de)-HT(fr)}{SRC(de)}$	Δ(lexical variety)	12.8	10.3	14.8
	Δ(POS variety)	39.8	40.9	38.7
	Δ(lexical density)	-10.2	-5.62	-13.2

Table 6: Relative differences (%) between features of the original texts and features of the translated texts for German→French texts translated by translators with different expertises: student, specialist and professional.

of analysis, namely comparison of two translation directions done by one translator. It contains three HTs produced by a Finnish native professional: one English into Finnish (into their native language) translation and two Finnish to English (from their native language) translations.

Table 8 presents text features for all native and non-native HTs. **Texts translated by one translator in two different translation directions** are compared in Table 8(a). The following general tendencies can be observed for both translators and both language pairs: sentence length, word length and lexical variety substantially differ depending on the translation direction. Word length and lexical variety are higher when translating into the native language, indicating that the translators tend to choose longer words more often and to use a richer vocabulary in their native language, as intuitively can be expected. As for sentence length, the differences tend in opposite directions: for $DeFr$, the length of non-native HTs is closer to the source text (which can be intuitively expected), whereas for $EnFi$ is the other way round. The reason might lay in sheer differences between the two language pairs, which should be investigated in future work. Deeper analysis of reasons and underlying phenomena is also needed for POS variety and lexical density, because the tendencies are very different for the two language pairs: in $DeFr$ texts, lexical density varies whereas there are no large differences in POS variety, and in $EnFi$ texts is the other way round.

Table 8(b) shows the features of **texts translated from French into German by two translators with different native languages**. It can be seen that the variations in sentence length, word length and lexical variety observed in Table 8(a) are confirmed. Furthermore, word length and lexical variety are again higher in the native translations. Sentence length of the non-native HT is closer to the source language, same as the other $DeFr$ non-native HT presented in Table 8(a) – this also indicates that the reason for the opposite tendency observed on the $EnFi$ language pair might indeed be the different nature of the language pair itself. In any case, a detailed analysis is definitely necessary, as well as for morpho-syntactic variety and lexical density.

Despite the fact that certain tendencies should be investigated further, it can be noted that native and non-native translated texts generally exhibit different traits, especially regarding sentence length, word length and lexical variety. Therefore, the native language of the translator should also be taken into account for MT evaluation.

7   Conclusions

This work presents results of a set of computational analyses on three data sets containing three language pairs and five translation directions with the aim of finding out whether different human translations exhibit different traits. Despite certain limitations, our findings represent a good base for analysing different human translations.

The main contribution of this work is empirical, showing that each of the investigated factors has certain influence on the features of translated texts. Sentence length and lexical variety are affected by

data set	parallel text	translator	translation direction	number of sentence pairs
DeFr	2019 de→fr	Tfr_2	into native	245
	2019 fr→de	Tfr_2	from native	235
	2019 fr→de	Tde_1	into native	100
EnFi	2017 en→fi	Tfi_1	into native	1502
	2017 fi→en	Tfi_1	from native	1500
	2019 fi→en	Tfi_1	from native	1996

Table 7: Characteristics of the texts used to examine the influence of native language and translation direction: language pair, translator, translation direction, and number of sentences.

(a) one translator, two translation directions

DeFr Tfr$_2$	translation direction	de→fr (into native)	fr→de (from native)
$\frac{SRC-HT}{SRC}$	Δ(sentence length)	-23.4	0.21
	Δ(word length)	11.4	-4.96
	Δ(lexical variety)	10.3	-2.82
	Δ(POS variety)	40.9	-41.3
	Δ(lexical density)	-5.62	19.0

EnFi Tfi$_1$	translation direction	en→fi (into native)	fi→en (from native)	fi→en (from native)
$\frac{SRC-HT}{SRC}$	Δ(sentence length)	21.5	-51.4	-46.8
	Δ(word length)	-55.5	36.2	35.0
	Δ(lexical variety)	-46.7	39.4	36.3
	Δ(POS variety)	-393	79.8	79.3
	Δ(lexical density)	-26.5	24.3	26.2

(b) one translation direction, two translators

DeFr fr→de	translator	Tde_1 (into native)	Tfr_2 (from native)
$\frac{SRC(fr)-HT(de)}{SRC(fr)}$	Δ(sentence length)	5.46	0.21
	Δ(word length)	-9.64	-4.96
	Δ(lexical variety)	-3.42	-2.82
	Δ(POS variety)	-24.4	-41.3
	Δ(lexical density)	22.9	19.0

Table 8: Relative differences (%) between features of native and non-native HTs; one translator working on two translation directions (a) and two translators working on one translation direction (b).

all factors, whereas word length varies depending on native language. As for POS variety and lexical density, a deeper analysis is needed to understand the observed tendencies. While we believe that the trends observed in the reported results are not incidental, more research is needed to find linguistic explanations. Our study is based on rather superficial text features at word and POS level – therefore, for future work, different HTs should be analysed in depth, including over- or under-using particular words, collocations and POS categories, as well as presence or absence of different types of translation shifts and semantic divergences. Furthermore, as described in Section 3, this study is carried out on sub-optimal data sets – providing and investigating larger data sets containing parallel HTs generated from the same source text is necessary. More data will also enable another line of work, namely automatic discrimination between different HTs.

More (ideal) data will also enable better analysis of potential effects on human and automatic MT evaluation. Nevertheless, even the presented preliminary results suggest that it is important to specify which kind of HTs were used for MT evaluation, especially for evaluations which involve comparing human and machine translation quality. As MT quality improves, such comparisons are becoming more and more frequent, and are also becoming a part of WMT shared tasks – at the WMT 2019 shared task ((Barrault et al., 2019), Section 3.8), for the German-English language pair it is reported that "many systems are tied with human performance", as well as that "Facebook-FAIR system achieves super-human translation performance". For this type of evaluation, we highly recommend that researchers/evalutaors specify the details about the HTs used.

8 Acknowledgments

The ADAPT SFI Centre for Digital Media Technology is funded by Science Foundation Ireland through the SFI Research Centres Programme and is co-funded under the European Regional Development Fund (ERDF) through Grant 13/RC/2106.

Special thanks to Maarit Koponen, Antonio Toral, Barry Haddow, Loïc Barrault, Franck Burlot, Tereza Vojtěchová and Mārcis Pinnis for all invaluable information and support.

References

Ahrenberg, Lars. 2017. Comparing machine translation and human translation: A case study. In *Proceedings of the 1st Workshop on Human-Informed Translation and Interpreting Technology (HiT-IT 2017)*, pages 21–28, Varna, Bulgaria, September.

Baker, Mona, Gill Francis, and Elena Tognini-Bonelli. 1993. Corpus linguistics and translation studies: Implications and applications. *Text and Technology: in Honour of John Sinclair*, pages 233–250.

Baroni, Marco and Silvia Bernardini. 2006. A new approach to the study of translationese: Machine-learning the difference between original and translated text. *Literary and Linguistic Computing*, 21(3):259–274, September.

Barrault, Loïc, Ondřej Bojar, Marta R. Costa-jussà, Christian Federmann, Mark Fishel, Yvette Graham, Barry Haddow, Matthias Huck, Philipp Koehn, Shervin Malmasi, Christof Monz, Mathias Müller, Santanu Pal, Matt Post, and Marcos Zampieri. 2019. Findings of the 2019 Conference on Machine Translation (WMT19). In *Proceedings of the Fourth Conference on Machine Translation (WMT 2019)*, pages 1–61, Florence, Italy, August.

Castilho, Sheila, Natalia Resende, and Ruslan Mitkov. 2019. What influences the features of post-editese? a preliminary study. In *Proceedings of the 2nd Workshop on Human-Informed Translation and Interpreting Technology (HiT-IT 2019)*, pages 20–28, Varna, Bulgaria, September.

Chesterman, Andrew. 2004. Beyond the particular. In *Translation universals: Do they exist?*, pages 33–50. John Benjamins.

Čulo, Oliver and Jean Nitzke. 2016. Patterns of terminological variation in post-editing and of cognate use in machine translation in contrast to human translation. In *Proceedings of the 19th Annual Conference of the European Association for Machine Translation (EAMT 2016)*, pages 106–114, Riga, Latvia.

Daems, Joke, Orphée De Clercq, and Lieve Macken. 2017. Translationese and post-editese: how comparable is comparable quality? *Linguistica Antverpiensia New Series – Themes in Translation Studie*, 16:89–103.

Farrell, Michael. 2018. Machine translation markers in post-edited machine translation output. In *Proceedings of the 40th Conference on Translating and the Computer (TC40)*, pages 50–59, London, UK, November.

Freitag, Markus, Isaac Caswell, and Scott Roy. 2019. APE at Scale and Its Implications on MT Evaluation Biases. In *Proceedings of the Fourth Conference on Machine Translation (WMT 2019)*, pages 34–44, Florence, Italy, August.

Koppel, Moshe and Noam Ordan. 2011. Translationese and its dialects. In *Proceedings of the 49th Annual Meeting of the Association for Computational Linguistics: Human Language Technologies (ACL-HLT 2011)*, pages 1318–1326, Portland, Oregon, June.

Kurokawa, David, Cyril Goutte, and Pierre Isabelle. 2009. Automatic detection of translated text and its impact on machine translation. In *In Proceedings of MT Summit XII*, pages 81–88, Ottawa, Canada, August.

Läubli, Samuel, Rico Sennrich, and Martin Volk. 2018. Has machine translation achieved human parity? a case for document-level evaluation. In *Proceedings of the 2018 Conference on Empirical Methods in Natural Language Processing (EMNLP 2018)*, pages 4791–4796, Brussels, Belgium, October-November.

Lembersky, Gennadi, Noam Ordan, and Shuly Wintner. 2013. Improving statistical machine translation by adapting translation models to translationese. *Computational Linguistics*, 39(4):999–1023.

Popović, Maja. 2015. chrF: character n-gram f-score for automatic MT evaluation. In *Proceedings of the Tenth Workshop on Statistical Machine Translation*, pages 392–395, Lisbon, Portugal, September.

Popović, Maja. 2019. On reducing translation shifts in translations intended for MT evaluation. In *Proceedings of Machine Translation Summit XVII*, pages 80–87, Dublin, Ireland, 19–23 August.

Post, Matt. 2018. A call for clarity in reporting BLEU scores. In *Proceedings of the Third Conference on Machine Translation: Research Papers*, pages 186–191, Brussels, Belgium, October.

Rabinovich, Ella and Shuly Wintner. 2015. Unsupervised identification of translationese. *Transactions of the Association for Computational Linguistics*, 3:419–432, December.

Rabinovich, Ella, Sergiu Nisioi, Noam Ordan, and Shuly Wintner. 2016. On the similarities between native, non-native and translated texts. In *Proceedings of the 54th Annual Meeting of the Association for Computational Linguistics (ACL 2016)*, pages 1870–1881, Berlin, Germany, August.

Rubino, Raphael, Ekaterina Lapshinova-Koltunski, and Josef van Genabith. 2016. Information density and quality estimation features as translationese indicators for human translation classification. In *Proceedings of the 2016 Conference of the North American Chapter of the Association for Computational Linguistics: Human Language Technologies (NAACL-HLT 2016)*, pages 960–970, San Diego, California, June.

Toral, Antonio, Sheila Castilho, Ke Hu, and Andy Way. 2018. Attaining the Unattainable? Reassessing Claims of Human Parity in Neural Machine Translation. In *Proceedings of the 3rd Conference on Machine Translation (WMT 2018)*, pages 113–123, Belgium, Brussels, October.

Toral, Antonio. 2019. Post-editese: an exacerbated translationese. In *Proceedings of Machine Translation Summit XVII*, pages 273–281, Dublin, Ireland, 19–23 August.

Toury, Gideon. 1979. Interlanguage and its manifestations in translation. *Meta*, 24(2):223–231.

Vanmassenhove, Eva, Dimitar Shterionov, and Andy Way. 2019. Lost in translation: Loss and decay of linguistic richness in machine translation. In *Proceedings of Machine Translation Summit XVII*, pages 222–232, Dublin, Ireland, 19–23 August.

Volansky, Vered, Noam Ordan, and Shuly Wintner. 2015. On the features of translationese. *Digital Scholarship in the Humanities DSH*, 30(1):98–118, April.

Vyas, Yogarshi, Xing Niu, and Marine Carpuat. 2018. Identifying semantic divergences in parallel text without annotations. In *Proceedings of the 2018 Conference of the North American Chapter of the Association for Computational Linguistics: Human Language Technologies (NAACL-HLT 2018)*, pages 1503–1515, New Orleans, Louisiana, June.

Wang, Weiyue, Jan-Thorsten Peter, Hendrik Rosendahl, and Hermann Ney. 2016. Character: Translation edit rate on character level. In *Proceedings of the First Conference on Machine Translation*, pages 505–510, Berlin, Germany, August.

Zhang, Mike and Antonio Toral. 2019. The effect of translationese in machine translation test sets. In *Proceedings of the 4th Conference on Machine Translation (WMT 2019)*, pages 73–81, Florence, Italy, August. Association for Computational Linguistics.

Re-design of the Machine Translation Training Tool MT^3

Emiliano Cuenca
Paula Estrella
Laura Bruno
Faculty of Languages & FaMaF
University of Córdoba
Argentina
Emiliano.Cuenca@unc.edu.ar
Paula.Estrella@unc.edu.ar
lbruno@unc.edu.ar

Jonathan Mutal
Sabrina Girletti
Lise Volkart
Pierrette Bouillon
FTI/TIM, University of Geneva
Switzerland
Jonathan.Mutal@unige.ch
Sabrina.Girletti@unige.ch
Lise.Volkart@unige.ch
Pierrette.Bouillon@unige.ch

Abstract

We believe that machine translation (MT) must be introduced to translation students as part of their training in preparation for their professional life. In this paper, we present a new version of the tool called MT^3, which builds and extends on a joint effort undertaken by the Faculty of Languages of the University of Córdoba and the Faculty of Translation and Interpreting of the University of Geneva to develop an open-source web platform to teach MT to translation students. We also report on a pilot experiment with the goal of testing the viability of using MT^3 in an MT course. The pilot allows us to identify areas for improvement and collect feedback from students on the tool's usability.

1 Introduction

Machine translation (MT) has made enormous progress over the past few years with the development of neural systems (Koehn and Knowles, 2017), and the translation industry has therefore been increasingly integrating it into daily workflow processes. This may have a direct impact on translators, who need to learn how to work with MT in a step called post-editing (O'Brien and Moorkens, 2014). It is therefore important to help translation students understand the underlying concepts of MT, including how MT systems are trained from bilingual corpora, what distinguishes systems from one another in terms of the algorithms they use, as well as the impact of their internal functioning on translation quality and, hence,

on the post-editing task. Even if the idea behind these systems sounds simple (producing the most likely translation), it can be challenging to explain to non-tech savvy students how these systems produce a final output. Currently, there are many open-source tools available to train statistical and neural MT models (the most widely used are Moses (Koehn et al., 2007) for statistical MT and TensorFlow[1] or OpenNMT (Klein et al., 2017) for neural MT) or commercial tools (such as KantanMT[2] or Microsoft Custom Translator[3]). However, it is difficult to integrate them in the classroom because open-source tools are mostly designed for IT professionals, who do not need a graphical user interface (GUI), as opposed to translation students; as for commercial tools, the costs are far too steep for some institutions.

The Faculty of Languages of the University of Córdoba (FL-UNC) and the Faculty of Translation and Interpreting of the University of Geneva (FTI-UniGe) have been collaborating since 2017 to design and prototype a tool that will support lecturers in the classroom.

In this paper, we present a new version of the tool called MT^3, which builds and extends on a joint effort undertaken by both institutions to develop an open-source web platform to teach MT to non-technical students. We also report on a pilot experiment with the goal of testing the viability of using MT^3 for an MA course on MT. After the lecturer presented the topic to students, they had to carry out an exercise using the tool and then complete a questionnaire. The goal of the pilot was not only to test the tool and identify areas for improvements, but also to get subjective feedback from the

---

[1] https://www.tensorflow.org/
[2] https://kantanmt.com/
[3] https://portal.customtranslator.azure.ai/

Martins, Moniz, Fumega, Martins, Batista, Coheur, Parra, Trancoso, Turchi, Bisazza, Moorkens, Guerberof, Nurminen, Marg, Forcada (eds.)
Proceedings of the 22nd Annual Conference of the European Association for Machine Translation, p. 375–382
Lisboa, Portugal, November 2020.

students on its usability.

2   MT in the classroom

MT is one of the topics that should be introduced to translation students in preparation for their professional life, as lacking the necessary skill-set to take on post-editor roles or other technical roles, such as language engineer or MT engineer, could have a negative impact on their future employability, as many researchers and lecturers have observed (Lara, 2019; Koponen, 2015; Doherty and Kenny, 2014; Kenny and Doherty, 2014; Rico, 2017; Temizöz, 2016; Mellinger, 2017; Guerberof and Moorkens, 2019).

The EMT Expert Group (2017, p. 7) "recognises that the ability to interact with MT in the translation process is now an integral part of professional translation competence". Furthermore, as part of the technological competence (p. 9), they highlight the inclusion of "basic knowledge of MT technologies and the ability to implement MT according to potential needs". This reflects the current need of many translation and localization companies to hire specialists with a background in translation or linguistics who know how to train and assess the quality of MT engines. As Lara (2019), Kenny and Doherty (2014) and Doherty and Kenny (2014) explain, MT does not depend exclusively on informatics, but requires a close collaboration with language experts for the creation of corpora, labelling, quality assessment, terminology management, controlled-language definition and text preprocessing.

The importance of introducing these concepts as part of translator training lies in having a set of specific tools that can serve as a playground on which translation students can gain hands-on experience, while also learning about the concepts related to MT. As Pym (2013, p. 494) points out, "students should not learn just one tool step-by-step. They have to be left to their own devices, as much as possible, so they can experiment and become adept at picking up a new tool very quickly, relying on intuition, peer support, online help groups, online tutorials, instruction manuals, and occasionally a human instructor to hold their hand".

However, a major roadblock when teaching technical content such as MT to non-technical audiences (like translation students) is a lack of suitable platforms that allow users to create MT engines without having to deal with low-level pro-

gramming languages, Unix consoles or command lines. This is the main motivation for prototyping MT^3.

3   Support tools for teaching MT/PE

To our knowledge, there are only few active open-source platforms that can be used for teaching MT: Joey NMT (Kreutzer et al., 2019), MTradumàtica (Doğru et al., 2017) and Interactive Teaching Tool (ITT) (Khayrallah et al., 2019). However, they do not provide all the desired features, e.g. MTradumàtica and ITT do not provide neural MT (NMT) models, nor the possibility to visualize intermediate results, and Joey NMT does not have a GUI to train and test models. A valuable resource for practicing post-editing and evaluating MT systems is PET (Aziz et al., 2012), however, this tool does not offer an integrated MT module. Using several tools in an unintegrated way may present new challenges to students, such as compatibility (e.g. file formats) or confidentiality issues. It would therefore be desirable to work on the same platform with intranet restrictions.

The lack of free tools that meet our desiderata has fuelled the joint development of an open-source web platform called *Machine Translation Training Tool - MT^3*. This platform aims at providing a playground for translation students and non-tech savvy users, helping them get hands-on experience with two main kinds of MT technology: statistical MT (SMT), which is less used in the market, but is helpful for pedagogical and comparative purposes, and neural MT, which is the current state-of-art and is more difficult to teach since it involves more complex algorithms and intermediate processing steps. The main goal of this tool is to make abstraction of the technical details by letting users focus on the important processing steps and helping them understand the internals by visualizing intermediate processing results.

Additionally, we consider MT^3 to be a teaching aid that may be useful for developing and testing a syllabus that focuses on MT topics, including practical activities that can be carried out using this platform; hence, it might be possible to measure the acquisition of competences through self-efficacy measures (Bandura, 1977, 2006; Compeau and Higgins, 1995). At the time of writing there is a similar initiative called *MultiTraiNMT - Machine Translation training for multilingual citi-*

zens.[4]

4 Previous versions of MT^3

The first version of this tool was created almost three years ago (Bouillon et al., 2017). In this initial stage, the tool worked only as a desktop application and consisted of a Python module that executed different scripts and processes in the background through a GUI. This GUI, shown in Figure 1, consisted of a series of tabs associated with the well-defined steps of creating a baseline engine with the Moses toolkit. [5]

Each tab consisted of a set of fields where the user inserted the arguments; a button that activated the task in question, for which the internal engine executed one or more sub-programs; and an area on which the output of these sub-programs was printed. With this version, it was possible to train and evaluate statistical models, as well as post-edit the raw output by using a simple table with source and raw MT.

The obvious drawbacks of this version are that the computer can become blocked due to the memory-intensive processes, and it is also highly dependent on electrical power (possibly for several hours or even days) to ensure that the computations that have been carried out are not lost.

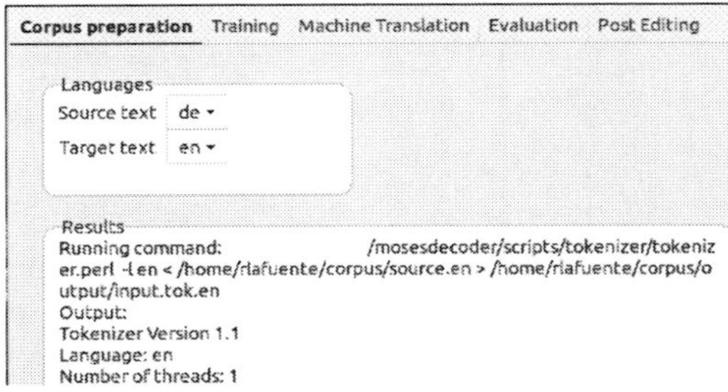

Figure 1: MT^3 version 1: screenshot of the Python-GTK GUI.

An improved version consisted of adapting the previous work to the web, while keeping the original distribution of tabs and a very similar look and feel. Besides overcoming the roadblocks of a desktop version, this version also incorporated the use of Docker (Merkel, 2014) to run all heavy processes on the server inside a Docker container; this

allows for a quicker deployment and maintenance of the tool.

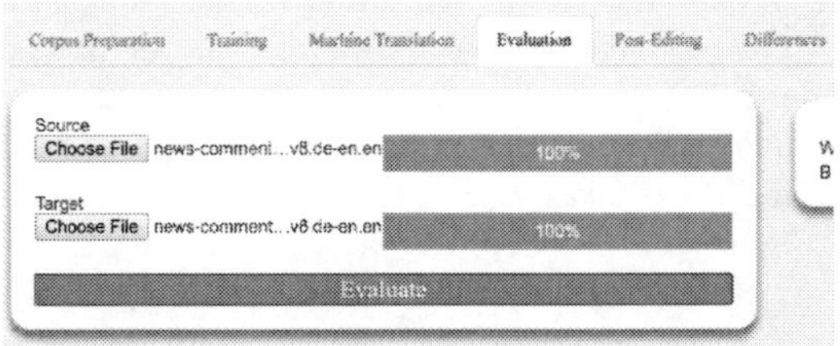

Figure 2: MT^3 version 2: screenshot of the Web GUI.

In addition to the above-mentioned functionalities, a new functionality was included to visualize the modifications made by the post-editor to the raw output, and some basic statistics, like the total amount of time spent on a segment and the number of edit operations, were also added.

Despite the improvements, some structural issues remained, since most of the work was done by students in Computer Science as part of their Masters' graduation projects. This version provided the starting point for the current version, which is presented in the next section.

5 Current version of MT^3

For the new version, the back-end was completely re-designed to provide a more reliable infrastructure that would be suitable for neural models. The GUI was also re-designed to include key functionalities that were missing in previous versions, such as user registration and authentication, or model sharing. Figure 3 shows the new architecture of the server with the major additions: the use of several (as opposed to only one) dedicated persistent Docker containers for special services (web API, database, task manager) and non-persistent containers for smaller tasks.

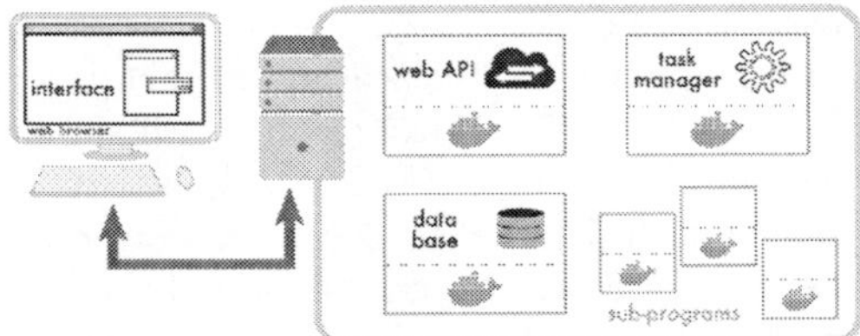

Figure 3: Proposed architecture for version 3 of MT^3.

The following sections provide some details about the server and the client (user GUI).

---

[4] Information available at https://ec.europa.eu/programmes/ erasmus-plus/projects/eplus-project-details/#project/2019-1-ES01-KA203-064245

[5] These steps can be found at http://www.statmt.org/moses/?n=Moses.Baseline

5.1 Server-side architecture

The server uses a REST API, which is accessible through a network connection via the usual HTTP protocol. This type of architecture allows for a distributed computation of the tasks, so that the most demanding work is carried out on the server, while the client takes care of issues related to presentation and interaction with the user. This role assignment is particularly convenient as it allows the user to run the software on a machine with modest resources, without the need for any installation, since all operating systems include a web browser by default.

As for the building blocks of the server, we have based the new version on Docker[6], an open-source Platform-as-a-Service (PaaS) that allows for the isolation of each module and its dependencies from the underlying operating system.

The server creates and destroys containers dynamically to execute tasks related to training statistical MT engines with Moses, neural engines with OpenNMT, and the application of standard evaluation metrics WER, TER (Snover et al., 2006) and BLEU (Papineni et al., 2002).

5.2 GUI functionalities

We have kept the main functionalities of the previous versions and added major ones, namely user management (register and authentication), persistence of user's data (models, translations and evaluations), neural engine training capability (based on OpenNMT's encoder-decoder model), visualization of intermediate results for statistical engines (an online visualization with no need to download) and engine sharing (for more ecological use of resources by avoiding training big engines with the same data multiple times).

Screenshots provided in Figures 4 to 7 show the current state of the tool. After logging, the menu on the left-hand side can be used to access the different modules (Figure 4). Data used in previous training sessions will appear in the right pane, as shown in Figure 5, where three statistical MT models appear: the first one is owned by our test user and the other two are shared by other users. Owned models can be deleted and any model can be explored, tested and used for translation. Figure 6 shows a shared engine being tested: the user is requesting the translation of *the cat is sleeping* and the result shows *le chat dort*. Note that these are

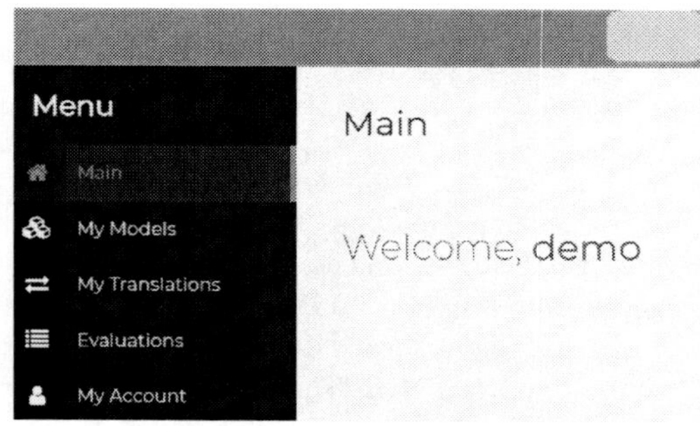

Figure 4: After successful login, the menu on the left shows the modules that can be accessed by the user.

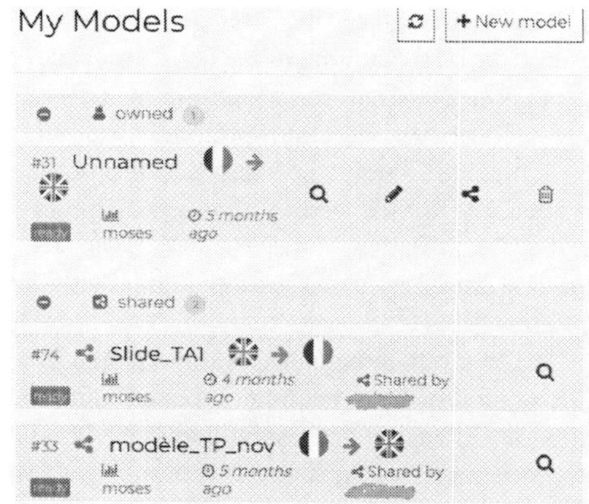

Figure 5: The interface shows the models owned and shared by other users

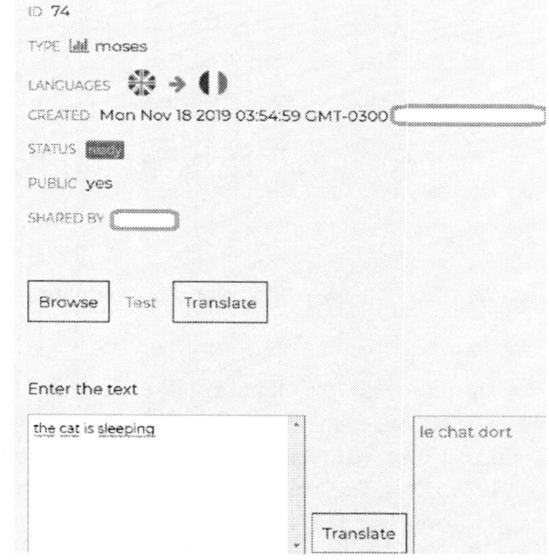

Figure 6: To test a model or run MT on a small number of strings, the "Test" option can be used; it is also possible to "Browse" the training files of the engine and to "Translate" files.

---

[6]https://hub.docker.com/

tiny models built for the purposes of a course on MT where the tool was tested, but the sharing option offers the lecturer the possibility of training a big, robust model, sharing it with students and letting them build smaller engines to compare their quality to the bigger one.

The functionalities to translate and evaluate MT output are very intuitive and follow standard practices; for example, Figure 7 shows the result of one of the evaluations.

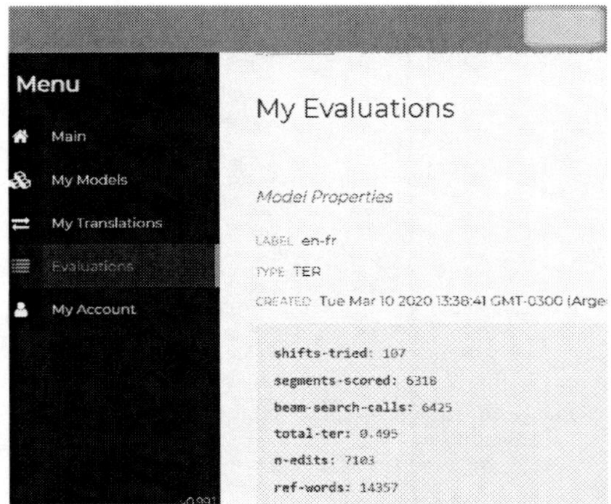

Figure 7: Automatic evaluations can be done using BLEU, TER or WER, and results are stored for future reference.

6 Pilot use in the classroom

In November 2019, a pilot test was carried out in the classroom as part of an MT course (*"Traduction automatique 1"*) at the FTI-UniGe. This experiment was aimed at evaluating the performance and usefulness of the tool for MT classes. Given that the tool is still under development, we decided to start testing parts separately and, at the time of the pilot, we focused on the functionalities related to statistical MT. As part of the development roadmap we will include a second pilot to test the NMT functionalities and add a post-editing tab.

For the first pilot, students were provided with a publicly available statistical model previously trained by the lecturer for the language direction French-to-English. They had to explore the files generated during the training phase and perform quick translations (tests) in order to answer the following questions:

1. What is the target language of the model?

2. Was the model trained with the phrase *Les avocats dorment*?

3. Is the word alignment correct for *aime/like*? Explain your answer.

4. Do the bigrams *avocados.* and *lawyers.* have the same logarithmic probability?

5. Has *J'aime* been properly segmented into two tokens during the tokenization phase?

6. Does the system have the translation of *j'* (in lower case) in the lexical translation model?

7. What is the probability of *hope - espère*?

8. If you write the phrase *J'espère les avocats* in the test interface, you will get the translation *I hope The lawyers*. Why is *The* capitalized?

9. What happens if we try to translate a sentence that contains a word that is not in the training corpus?

10. Is the model a bigram or a trigram one?

At the end of the class, students were invited to complete a survey on their experience with the tool.

The questionnaire addressed different aspects, such as the previous MT experience of each user. Given that the users were translation students, technical concepts related to the software were presented in an accessible way, striving to maintain a balance between simplicity and precision. The survey was distributed via Google Forms, and the most relevant questions were:

1. Did you have any previous knowledge of MT before taking this course?

2. Did you have previous knowledge of post-editing before taking this course?

3. What language pair do you work with?

4. Did you use MT^3 during this course?

5. How much do you agree with the following statement: "I have used MT^3 to practice and it has helped me to better understand the theoretical concepts presented in class"?

6. How much do you agree with the following statement: "The MT^3 interface is friendly and intuitive (i.e. users can perform assigned tasks without having to click here and there to find what they need)"?

7. How much do you agree with the following statement: "Considering that it is in development, MT^3 seems to be reliable enough to perform MT tasks (it is capable of performing the desired function without fail, or, in case there are failures, these are clearly reported to the user)"?

The following are the results of the survey, obtained from the responses received. We are aware that the number of respondents is small (9 valid replies in total) as the survey was not mandatory. Nonetheless, it provides valuable initial feedback and the whole pilot served as an assessment of the development process, helping us to identify a roadmap for future use and development.

Of the total number of respondents, three had prior knowledge of MT and post-editing. All of them worked at least with the French-English language pair, while two of them also worked with the French-German language pair, two others with French-Spanish, one with French-Italian and one with French-Russian.

Replies to question 4 indicate that 4 of the respondents had only seen the teacher using the tool, without using it themselves, while another 4 had used it in class. The final respondent said that he had also used it from home.

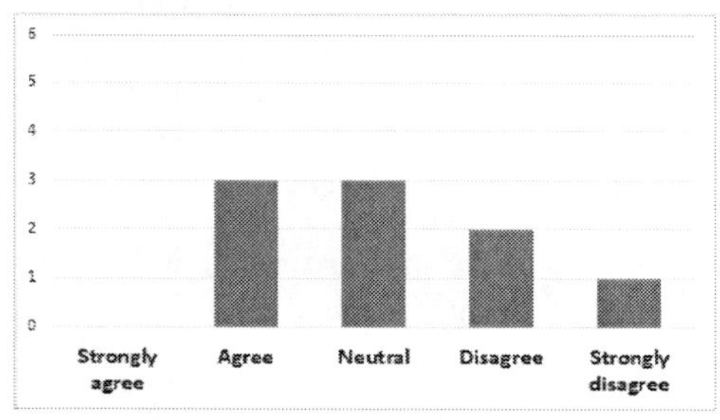

Figure 8: Results obtained for question 5, related to the usefulness of the tool as support for learning theoretical concepts.

As to whether the tool was useful in supporting the theoretical content, 3 agreed, while another 3 were neutral; 2 disagreed and 1 strongly disagreed. These results are shown in Figure 8.

As to whether the interface was friendly and intuitive, 4 respondents agreed, while 3 disagreed, and 2 were neutral. These results are shown in Figure 9. Regarding the reliability of the tool, 3 respondents considered the tool to be sufficiently reliable, as opposed to 1, who thought otherwise, while 5 respondents remained neutral, as shown in

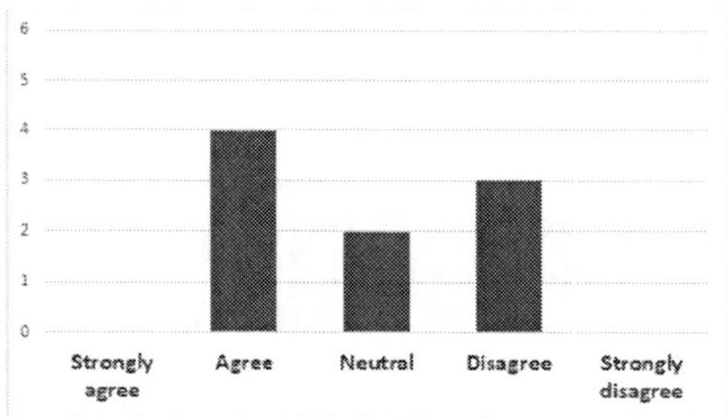

Figure 9: Results obtained for question 6, related to the user-friendliness of the GUI.

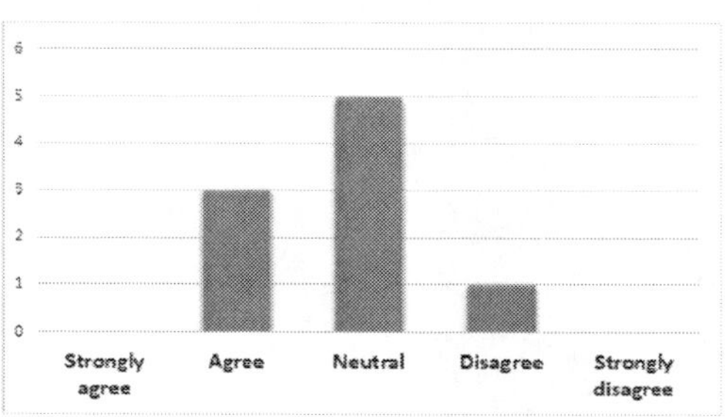

Figure 10: Results obtained for question 7, related to the reliability of the tool.

Figure 10.

Only one respondent reported having problems using the tool, particularly with the expiration of the session forcing him to log in again.

Finally, a student suggested highlighting some relevant files in the model, to avoid searching through all the files, which may generate some confusion.

7 Conclusions and future work

We have presented a new version of MT^3, an open-source web platform intended for teaching MT to translation students and others interested in the topic, who have little or no technical skills. It allows the students to create statistical models using Moses and neural models using OpenNMT, which can be shared among other users. It also includes user management, such as authentication and a basic system of privileges to perform actions on certain resources. User activities, such as translations and evaluations, can be stored. In addition, it aims to show MT models as white boxes, enabling navigation and access to the files generated during the training process.

We have also reported on a pilot experiment based on a real-life MT course for translators, given at the FTI-UniGe. Although the pilot gave us insights on the usefulness of the tool, the clear limitation was the small number of participants. The result of this experience was overall very encouraging, demonstrating that the tool can be installed and used to a certain extent as a support for practical activities in order to apply theoretical concepts.

The work carried out so far was not intended to achieve a final definitive version, but rather an intermediate step towards a more reliable and extensible platform that will serve as a starting point for future developments. These include the visualization of data created during the training of neural engines, the integration of a post-editing tab and a better logging mechanism to provide more specific error messages. As for the utilization of the tool, we are planning another pilot to further test it with students. Finally, we intend to make the platform available in the future to the translation teaching community.

Acknowledgements

This project was financed by SeedMoneyGrant 2019 as part of a joint research project between FL-UNC and FTI-UniGe.

References

Wilker Aziz, Sheila Castilho, and Lucia Specia. Pet: a tool for post-editing and assessing machine translation. In *LREC*, pp. 3982–3987, 2012.

Albert Bandura. Self-efficacy: toward a unifying theory of behavioral change. *Psychological review*, 84(2): 191, 1977.

Albert Bandura. Guide for constructing self-efficacy scales. *Self-efficacy beliefs of adolescents*, 5(1): 307–337, 2006.

Pierrette Bouillon, Sabrina Girletti, Paula Estrella, and Roxana Lafuente. MTTT – Machine Translation Training Tool: A tool to teach MT, evaluation and post-editing. In *The 20th Annual Conference of the European Association for Machine Translation (EAMT)*, p. 18, 2017.

Deborah Compeau and Christopher Higgins. Computer self-efficacy: Development of a measure and initial test. *MIS quarterly*, pp. 189–211, 1995.

Gökhan Doğru, Adrià Martín-Mor, and Sergio Ortiz-Rojas. MTradumàtica: Free statistical machine translation customisation for translators. In *20th Annual Conference of the European Association for Machine Translation*, 2017.

Stephen Doherty and Dorothy Kenny. The design and evaluation of a statistical machine translation syllabus for translation students. *The Interpreter and Translator Trainer*, 8(2): 295–315, 2014.

EMT Expert Group. European Master's in Translation competence framework, 2017.

Réka Eszenyi and Brigitta Dóczi. Rage against the machine–will post-editing assignments outnumber translations in the future? *Fit-For-Market Translator and Interpreter Training in a Digital Age*, pp. 119–133, 2020.

Federico Gaspari, Hala Almaghout, and Stephen Doherty. A survey of machine translation competences: Insights for translation technology educators and practitioners. *Perspectives*, 23(3): 333–358, 2015.

Ana Guerberof Arenas and Joss Moorkens. Machine translation and post-editing training as part of a master's programme. *Jostrans: The Journal of Specialised Translation*, (31): 217–238, 2019.

Dorothy Kenny and Stephen Doherty. Statistical machine translation in the translation curriculum: overcoming obstacles and empowering translators. *The Interpreter and translator trainer*, 8(2): 276–294, 2014.

Huda Khayrallah, Rebecca Knowles, Kevin Duh, and Matt Post. An interactive teaching tool for introducing novices to machine translation. In *Proceedings of the 50th ACM Technical Symposium on Computer Science Education*, SIGCSE '19. ACM, 2019.

Guillaume Klein, Yoon Kim, Yuntian Deng, Jean Senellart, and Alexander M Rush. Opennmt: Opensource toolkit for neural machine translation. *arXiv preprint arXiv:1701.02810*, 2017.

Philipp Koehn, Hieu Hoang, Alexandra Birch, Chris Callison-Burch, Marcello Federico, Nicola Bertoldi, Brooke Cowan, Wade Shen, Christine Moran, Richard Zens, et al. Moses: Open source toolkit for statistical machine translation. In *Proceedings of the 45th annual meeting of the association for computational linguistics companion volume proceedings of the demo and poster sessions*, pp. 177–180, 2007.

Philipp Koehn and Rebecca Knowles. Six challenges for neural machine translation. *arXiv preprint arXiv:1706.03872*, 2017.

Maarit Koponen. How to teach machine translation post-editing? Experiences from a post-editing course. In *4th Workshop on Post-Editing Technology and Practice (WPTP4)*, pp. 2–15, 2015.

Julia Kreutzer, Joost Bastings, and Stefan Riezler. Joey nmt: A minimalist nmt toolkit for novices. *arXiv preprint arXiv:1907.12484*, 2019.

Cristina Plaza Lara. Swot analysis of the inclusion of machine translation and post-editing in the master's degrees offered in the EMT network. *Journal of Specialised Translation*, (31): 260–280, 2019.

Jiwei Li, Xinlei Chen, Eduard Hovy, and Dan Jurafsky. Visualizing and understanding neural models in nlp. *arXiv preprint arXiv:1506.01066*, 2015.

Zachary C Lipton. The mythos of model interpretability. *arXiv preprint arXiv:1606.03490*, 2016.

Christopher D. Mellinger. Translators and machine translation: knowledge and skills gaps in translator pedagogy. *The Interpreter and Translator Trainer*, 11(4): 280–293, 2017.

Dirk Merkel. Docker: lightweight linux containers for consistent development and deployment. *Linux journal*, 2014(239): 2, 2014.

Grégoire Montavon, Wojciech Samek, and Klaus-Robert Müller. Methods for interpreting and understanding deep neural networks. *Digital Signal Processing*, 73: 1–15, 2018.

Sharon O'Brien and Joss Moorkens. Towards intelligent post-editing interfaces. In *Proceedings of FIT XXth World Congress*, Berlin, Germany, 2014.

Kishore Papineni, Salim Roukos, Todd Ward, and Wei-Jing Zhu. BLEU: a method for automatic evaluation of machine translation. In *Proceedings of the 40th annual meeting on association for computational linguistics*, pp. 311–318. Association for Computational Linguistics, 2002.

Celia Rico Pérez. La formación de traductores en Traducción Automàtica. *Tradumàtica: traducció i tecnologies de la informació i la comunicació*, (15): 75–96, 2017.

Matthew Snover, Bonnie Dorr, Richard Schwartz, Linnea Micciulla, and John Makhoul. A study of translation edit rate with targeted human annotation. In *Proceedings of association for machine translation in the Americas*, volume 200, 2006.

Özlem Temizöz. Postediting machine translation output: Subject-matter experts versus professional translators. *Perspectives*, 24(4): 646–665, 2016.

Multidimensional assessment of the eTranslation output for English–Slovene

Mateja Arnejšek
European Commission
Directorate-General for Translation
Slovene Language Department
mateja.arnejsek@ec.europa.eu

Alenka Unk
European Commission
Directorate-General for Translation
Slovene Language Department
alenka.unk@ec.europa.eu

Abstract

The Slovene language department of the European Commission Directorate-General for Translation has always been an early adopter of new developments in the area of machine translation. In 2018, the department started using neural machine translation produced by the eTranslation in-house engines. In 2019, a multidimensional assessment of the eTranslation output for the language combination English–Slovene was carried out. It was based on two user satisfaction surveys, an analysis of reported errors and an ex post analysis of a sample. As part of the assessment effort, a categorisation of errors was devised in order to raise awareness among translators of the potential pitfalls of neural machine translation.

1 Machine translation in DGT

eTranslation[1] is one of the Building Blocks for a Digital Connected Europe in the framework of the Connecting Europe Facility (CEF).[2] It was launched in November 2017 with the progressive addition of engines for different language combinations. eTranslation took over from MT@EC, which had been fully operational since June 2013. MT@EC was a statistical machine translation (SMT) system based on the MOSES open-source translation toolkit.[3] The Directorate-General for Translation (DGT) of the European Commission had developed MT@EC under the Interoperability Solutions for European Public Administrations (ISA) programme with co-funding from EU research and innovation programmes. CEF eTranslation followed the field's move into neural machine translation (NMT).

DGT is organised into language departments (LDs), one for each official language of the EU.[4] Right from the launch of the NMT engines, LDs were provided with practical guidelines that aim to ensure that machine translation is used consistently and effectively within DGT, encouraging translators to at the very least try using machine translation, but still allowing for different approaches to cater to specific needs. Training has also been organised to present the new technology and its known general pitfalls. Based on the guidelines and the training, the LDs adopted different approaches to the uptake of NMT and used it in different ways and to differing extents.

In autumn 2018, after the initial period of introduction, uptake and testing, DGT decided to assess NMT output in the LDs, gathering general opinions on how useful neural engines are for the individual LDs and on the kind of impact these engines can have on the efficiency and quality of translation. The objectives of the exercise were to check which of the two engines, NMT or SMT, was preferred as the default engine in the automated pre-processing of translation requests and what the translators should be aware of when using NMT. It also aimed to promote machine translation among users. Since the quality of machine translation output varies depending on the target language, each LD had to carry out the assessment individually, following broad pre-set guidelines.

---

[1] https://webgate.ec.europa.eu/etranslation.

[2] CEF is a key EU funding instrument to promote growth, jobs and competitiveness through targeted infrastructure investment at European level.

[3] Koehn et al. (2007).

[4] Irish is an exception since it is not yet a fully-fledged department in terms of the number of translators.

Martins, Moniz, Fumega, Martins, Batista, Coheur, Parra, Trancoso, Turchi, Bisazza, Moorkens, Guerberof, Nurminen, Marg, Forcada (eds.)
Proceedings of the 22nd Annual Conference of the European Association for Machine Translation, p. 383–392
Lisboa, Portugal, November 2020.

2 Machine translation in SL LD

The Slovene Language Department (SL LD) of DGT has always been an early adopter of new technologies, including machine translation. In an online survey conducted in November 2012, presented by Leal Fontes (2013), the majority of users of the English–Slovene machine translation of the time (SMT from MT@EC) already responded that they used machine translation for around 50 % of their translation jobs.

By the time eTranslation was launched, MT@EC had been regularly and extensively used. Following the announcement of the launch of the English–Slovene NMT engine on 4 April 2018, interested members of the department started testing NMT output. After the initial DGT training on NMT on 25 April 2018, the SL LD on 29 April 2018 invited all members of the department to test NMT. Three months afterwards, a survey was carried out in the SL LD that showed that the use of NMT was widespread and preferred to the use of SMT. Consequently, the decision was taken to switch to NMT as the default output prepared automatically for every translation request, as of 5 July 2018 for a trial period of three months. After those three months, a new user survey was carried out that confirmed that users were satisfied with NMT and the use of NMT as the default engine was confirmed on a permanent basis.

The method and extent of machine translation use has always been left to the discretion of the translators. They can include machine translation as one of the reference memories in their CAT tool (with a 25 % penalty) in their translation projects. They can use this machine translation as a typing aid (based on an autocomplete functionality), look up the machine translation results in concordance searches, decide to use individual segments and post-edit them, or opt for a combination of these methods. It is also possible to pre-translate the whole document using machine translation and post-edit the result, but such use has not yet been recorded in the department.[5]

The typing aid approach and concordance use are sub-segment-based types of MT use. The translators using NMT in this way use only limited phrases from the machine translation output at a time. The typing aid approach follows the push principle, as the autocomplete suggestions are automatically shown while the translator is typing. The concordance use, on the other hand, applies the pull principle, as the translator needs to select a phrase and launch a search. In neither of these types of use does the translation file contain any record of the machine translation origin of the used phrases.

If, however, the translator uses entire NMT segments and post-edits them, either by recalling them from NMT output individually or in the hypothetical case of pre-translating the document with NMT output, the metadata of the segment in the translation file registers machine translation as the starting point of the translation, regardless of whether the NMT segment has been edited or to what extent.

Since the first user survey, department members were invited to report any examples of very noticeable or repetitive errors. Their contributions were gathered into a list, along with possible causes and explanations that could serve as useful tips to users when working with NMT. To ensure a more objective and comprehensive insight into the usefulness of EN–SL NMT to feed into the DGT-wide assessment of NMT, the department also carried out an ex post analysis to check the quality of NMT in April 2019. The three-step exercise that included gauging user satisfaction (see section 3), an analysis of reported errors (see section 4) and an analysis of a sample (see section 5) allowed for a broad and thorough assessment of the EN–SL eTranslation NMT.

3 User satisfaction

3.1 Summer 2018 survey

The first user satisfaction survey was carried out at the meetings of the two SL LD units (29 June 2018 in SL.1 and 2 July 2018 in SL.2). At that moment, both units combined had 51 active translators (and 2 trainees), 39 of whom attended the two meetings and 35 responded to the survey.

It transpired that the use of NMT was already widespread in the department at that point (only 3 respondents out of 35 did not use NMT and 1 respondent reported that their use of NMT depended on the type of document). Nearly all respondents also preferred NMT to SMT; in fact, all translators who used NMT liked it better than

---

5   Lesznyák (2019) reports that also in the Hungarian LD the translators apply divergent practices to integrate NMT into their workflow.

SMT except for 1 respondent, who answered that they did not notice any difference between SMT and NMT.

I use NMT …		I don't use NMT
and I prefer it to SMT	and I prefer SMT	
SL.1: 14*	SL.1: /	SL.1: 3
SL.2: 18**	SL.2: /	SL.2: /
Total: 32	Total: /	Total: 3

*1 uses NMT depending on the type of document
**1 uses NMT, but doesn't see the difference

Table 1: *Summer 2018 survey in SL LD*

The only purpose of the survey was to determine if it would make sense to switch to NMT as the default machine translation product in the automated pre-processing of translation requests. It merely gauged the uptake of NMT at the time and the first impression of how it compares to SMT. There were no questions about the usefulness or quality of machine translation.

The results of the survey showed that at least 32 members of the SL LD were already using NMT, even though it was not part of the automated workflow (at that time SMT was provided automatically with every translation request). This meant that they were regularly requesting the NMT output manually via the eTranslation portal. Therefore, the decision was made to switch from SMT to NMT in the automated pre-processing for a trial period of three months.

3.2 Autumn 2018 survey

A new user survey was carried out in November 2018, this time online, among all 55 active translators in the department. Its purpose was to check the state of play and whether the department would continue using NMT as the default machine translation product.

Out of the 43 respondents, a majority (29 respondents) used machine translation with every or almost every translation and another 7 respondents used it often. Only 2 respondents rarely used machine translation and just 1 replied that they never used it. All 43 respondents (even those who rarely or never used machine translation) expressed their preference for NMT over SMT in pre-processing. The use of NMT as the default machine translation product was con-

firmed. Again, there were no questions regarding the quality of machine translation as such.[6]

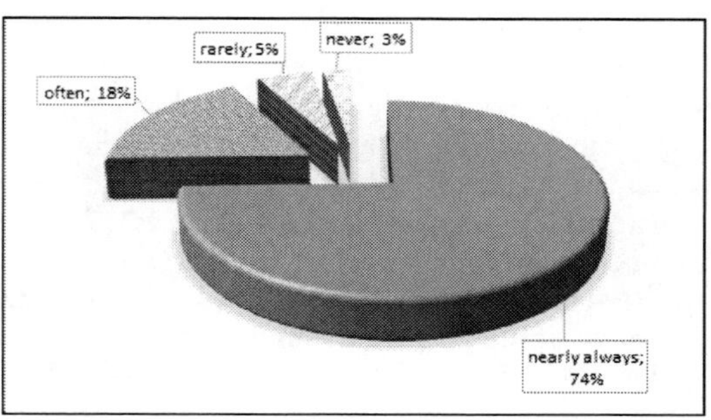

Chart 1: *Autumn 2018 survey in SL LD*

When asked to compare SMT with NMT, translators said that SMT might be more (terminologically) consistent, but had more incorrect inflections and the sentence structure followed the source language more closely rather than adapting to the structure of the target language, which is consistent with the findings of Toral and Sánchez-Cartagena (2017). In some instances, following the structure of the source language too closely resulted in awkward wording, wrong theme–rheme structure and, in the worst cases, mistranslation. This meant that translators had to edit the text heavily. Furthermore, although the mistakes were more obvious and therefore might be easier to spot and correct, the translators might still miss some mistakes simply due to their frequency and introduce new errors in the process of correcting the text. This is consistent with the findings of Lacruz et al. (2014) that transfer errors (which are those that require the MT user to review the source text to understand the meaning) generate a greater cognitive demand than mechanical errors (which are those that can routinely be fixed without reference to the source text), translators noted that NMT errors might require more attention and concentration as they are not easy to spot. The trust placed in NMT is also generally higher than that accorded to SMT. Both of these factors might lead to oversights.

---

[6] Lesznyák (2019) reports a different approach in the Hungarian LD: structured interviews with the majority of the translators were carried out from June 2018 to January 2019 (which is approximately the same period as when the two surveys in the SL LD took place) to gauge the translators' views on NMT in more detail than the SL LD surveys did, and the interviews also served to elicit typical errors and quality issues.

4 Analysis of reported errors

Since the introduction of eTranslation NMT in the department, translators were invited on several occasions to report striking or repetitive errors in the NMT output. We gathered them in a list with each assigned a possible cause or plausible explanation as to its origin. The purpose of the exercise was to provide translators with useful tips for working with NMT. Over time, the list has been split into sections for different categories of NMT issues. These share many similarities with the findings of Van Brussel et al. (2018) for English–Dutch NMT:

• <u>NMT includes polysemic misinterpretations</u> (e.g. "swings" translated as "gugalnice", so in the meaning of playground swings instead of statistical fluctuations, which would translate as "nihanja"). This phenomenon invariably produces terminological errors in NMT output.

• <u>NMT includes complete semantic blunders</u>. Some of these erroneous translations seem to come from mix-ups of similar-looking words. The similarity might exist either in the source language (e.g. "skill", which should have been "spretnost" or "veščina", translated rather as "ubijanje", which means "kill(ing)"; or "Slavery" (capitalised) translated not as "suženjstvo" but as "slovanski", meaning "Slavic"). A similar type of error is presented by Van Brussel et al. (2018), who analysed NMT for English–Dutch, with the example of "grace" ~ "graze". The similarity might also exist in the target language (e.g. "moving away" translated as "odmiranje", which back-translates as "dying off", instead of "odmikanje", meaning "distancing"). Some semantic mistakes at least remain in the same field (e.g. "Cypriot" translated as "evropski", meaning "European"). Some of these errors, however, are utterly perplexing to the human user as their origin remains unclear (e.g. "hosting" in technological context translated as "počitek", which back-translates to "rest").

• <u>NMT output includes "neural neologisms"</u>, a new type of lexical mistake in NMT output, evidenced also by Macken (2019), consisting of words that do not exist in the target language, invented by the NMT engine. It seems that when the engine encounters words not included in the data sets used in its training, the machine starts inventing translations based on statistically probable patterns, creating nonsensical words. "Reformed" Protestant Church, for example, was not translated as "Reformirana", but as "retvorna".

Apparently the elements of the word in the source text were identified ("re" + "formed"), the second element was translated into "tvoren" (which could make sense as a Slovene translation) and the feminine gender was applied ("retvorna"). "Becoming a Maltese citizen", on the other hand, was translated as "popolanje malteškega državljana", where "popolanje" is a non-existent word with no apparent semantic associations with (any meaning of) becoming, but still with the expected gerundial ending. A document with religious vocabulary was especially rife with such neural neologisms (e.g. "Chief Rabbi" as "Chiebi Rabi" instead of "glavni rabin"), probably because such vocabulary is not very common in the material on which NMT engines were trained.

• <u>NMT does not handle proper nouns well</u> as they tend not to be repeated in the data on which NMT is trained. The engine changes them or tries to translate them (e.g. "KRIEGER" becomes "KRIMEGER" and the city of "Christchurch" is translated as "božična cerkev", which back-translates as "Christmas church"). Van Brussel et al. (2018) also note this feature of NMT of translating proper names.

• <u>NMT has trouble translating abbreviations</u> (e.g. "PM" translated not as "predsednica" – feminine form is needed, because it referred to Theresa May – but as "podpredsednica", correctly in feminine form, but meaning "Madame Vice President").

• <u>NMT omits some words</u> (e.g. elements in enumerations), sometimes in such a way as to produce the opposite meaning in the translation (e.g. omitting the negative particle, i.e. "not" or similar). Sometimes it omits also whole parts of sentences, which reflects the finding of Van Brussel et al. (2018) that in omission errors NMT omits more words than SMT.

• <u>NMT sometimes adds words or elements</u> in a sentence – or repeats some of the elements (e.g. "the Portuguese-Spanish border" translated as "portugalsko portugalsko-španska meja").

• <u>NMT has trouble with structures with implicit relationships between words</u>, such as long compound noun phrases. "Short-term travel possibilities", for example, was translated as "kratkoročne možnosti potovanja" – "short-term possibilities for travel" instead of "možnosti za kratkoročno potovanje" – "possibilities for short-term travel". <u>A similar problem occurs with</u>

structures involving explicit relationships between words, misrendering syntactical relations, sometimes even producing the opposite meaning (e.g. "requirements on SMEs" translated not as "zahteve za MSP" but as "zahteve MSP", which back-translates as "requirements of SMEs").

- NMT can have problems with bulleted content. This might be caused by the structure in the bullet points deviating from the structure of normal text. The bulleted items are text fragments and not syntactically complete sentences. Furthermore, the engine might be attempting to translate the bullet symbol (e.g. "State of the Union Address 2016 …" translated as "barbara, govor o stanju v Uniji 2016 …" – translation of "–" ("bar"?) as "Barbara"?).

- NMT has trouble translating misspelt words, which does not come as a surprise (e.g. "Strenghtening" translated with a neural neologism "Strengnetenje", creating a Slovene-sounding gerund with a non-existent stem). What is surprising is that it sometimes manages to translate incorrectly spelt words correctly (e.g. "TheDirective" translated as "Direktiva") – this is something that SMT was not able to do.

- NMT sometimes reproduces spelling mistakes. An error was reported, and we discovered that it originated in a spelling mistake in the data set used to train the NMT engine ("audiovisual" translated as "avdiovizulani" instead of "avdiovizualni"). There was only one spelling mistake in the data, but the error was reproduced several times in the NMT output. This highlights the importance of the quality of data that is used to train NMT engines.

5 Analysis of a sample in April 2019

5.1 Sampling

The sample on which the eTranslation English–Slovene NMT output was to be checked was chosen from among the English-to-Slovene translations of the SL LD. Documents were selected to include legislative, non-legislative and general public documents from different domains.

The documents were chosen from the finalised translation requests received in the department between 1 September 2018 and 31 March 2019. Finalised requests were needed so that a final human translation to which NMT could be compared would be available. The selected period corresponded to the period when NMT was automatically available to translators, in order to facilitate the process of the ex post review (comparing the NMT output to the final translation).

Although the NMT output used for the analysis was actually the one available to the translators at the time of translation, we did not attempt to find out if or how translators had used NMT. Without disproportionate further efforts, it would be difficult to ascertain whether NMT was indeed used in the translation of these documents. Moreover, it would be almost if not completely impossible with the means and tools available to determine in which parts of the text it was used. Checking the segment attributes in xliffs would reveal if machine translation was used, but only if it was used as the starting point of translation. However, machine translation can also be used as a typing aid (based on the autocomplete functionality of the CAT tool) or in concordance searches, and the xliff does not register this.

We only chose documents translated in-house and with a low match rate. The quality of NMT is most relevant in translating documents with a low match rate. If there are no other sources, there is a greater need for machine translation and a greater probability that translators will use it. In addition, this minimises interference from other sources. However, as Lesznyák (2019) points out, NMT for documents with a low match rate might be less useful, as the low match rate indicates that there might have been less material in the databases on which the NMT engines were trained than would be the case of documents with a higher match rate.

Type	Document title
Legislative	Commission Implementing Regulation entering the name 'Havarti'(PGI) in the register of protected designations of origin and protected geographical indications
	Proposal for a Council Decision on the position to be taken on behalf of the European Union in the World Customs Organization in relation to the Harmonised System
	Annex to the Commission Delegated Regulation supplementing ITS Directive 2010/40/EU of the European Parliament and of the Council with regard to the provision of cooperative intelligent transport systems

	Communication from the Commission to the European Parliament, the European Council, the European Central Bank, the European Economic and Social Committee and the Committee of the Regions – Capital Markets Union: progress on building a single market for capital for a strong Economic and Monetary Union (CMU report)
Non-legislative	Report from the Commission to the European Parliament and the Council – EU and the Paris Climate Agreement: Taking stock of progress at Katowice COP (Climate action progress report)
	Replies of the Commission to the Special Report of the European Court of Auditors "The control system for organic products has improved, but some challenges remain"
General public	Citizens' Dialogues and Citizens' Consultations Progress report
	Questions and answers on the EU list of non-cooperative tax jurisdictions
	Health-EU Newsletter 223 - link group
	MEMORY GAME - Match the flags!

Table 2: Sampled documents

We selected two consecutive pages in each of the ten selected documents, which produced a sample of 20 pages.[7]

5.2 Methodology

Each document section in the sample was pre-translated using the automatically provided eTranslation NMT and the result was compared (using the Microsoft Word compare function) to the final, human translation, which is considered the gold standard also to Maučec and Donaj (2020) in all types of evaluations of MT quality. The SL LD quality officer[8] checked the comparison file and inserted comments for the differences that amounted to errors according to the DGT and SL LD standards. The annotated differences were labelled with the error categories found in the error grid used in DGT for the evaluation of freelance translations, so as mistranslations, omissions, or errors relating to terminology, reference documents, clarity, grammar, punctuation or spelling; all of them further classified as minor or major errors.[9, 10] Further observations were added to the labels to make it easier to draw conclusions. Additionally, to gain a better understanding of the gravity of errors in NMT, the categorised errors were fed into the internal quality assessment tool to see where NMT ranks compared to human translations.

As the analysis was based on the differences between NMT and the final translation, potential mistakes in NMT that were present in the final translation as well were not detected (false negatives). Differences between NMT and the final translation where there was no mistake in NMT were disregarded (false positives). As the quality of the final translation itself fell outside the scope of this exercise, any errors in the final translation were also disregarded, whether these were caused by NMT or not.

5.3 The result

More examples for already identified error categories

The analysis confirmed the occurrence of errors that had already been reported by users (see section 4). For certain categories of errors in the eTranslation NMT output, the examples found during the ex post review offered a greater overview:

• NMT output contains terminological errors, with generic words instead of terms. For example, in a document on Protected Geographical Indication, "opponents" were translated as the generic "nasprotniki", which back-translates as "adversaries", "antagonists", instead of the domain specific "vložniki ugovorov", meaning persons who oppose the registration of a designation.

• NMT output contains wrong terms. For example, in an act on the service of judicial and extrajudicial documents, "service" was translated in the economic sense "storitev" instead of as "vročanje" – "delivery".

• NMT can be highly terminologically inconsistent. For example, "operators" within one document translated as different valid terms, but

____

[7]   Pages were counted as standard DGT pages, defined as 1500 characters without spaces.

[8]   For the role of quality officers, see Drugan et al. (2018).

[9]   For more information on the error grid and other elements of evaluation of freelance translations, see Strandvik (2017).

[10]   At the time of this writing, DGT is preparing for new outsourcing contracts with a new error categorisation based on multidimensional quality metrics (MQM).

stemming from other areas of regulation; first as "nosilci dejavnosti", which verbatim back-translates as "activity holders", and in the next sentence as "izvajalci" – "implementers", when they should both have been "gospodarski subjekti" – "economic subjects").

• The problems of NMT with abbreviations are exacerbated by inconsistency. "CA", which in a sampled document stood for "certification authority", was translated in six different ways on the two consecutive pages, including as "pristojni organ" – "competent authority" and "organ za konkurenco" – "competition authority". This was a technical annex, therefore the English abbreviation should have been kept, otherwise it could have been translated as "overitelj potrdil".

• NMT has many problems with structures which (if the context is disregarded) allow for different interpretations (e.g. "awareness on the benefits of earlier hepatitis and HIV testing" translated as "ozaveščenost o koristih prejšnjega hepatitisa in testiranju HIV", which back-translates as "awareness about benefits of earlier hepatitis and (awareness) about testing for HIV").

New error categories

The ex post analysis also produced examples of other types of errors in the eTranslation NMT output that had not been reported before:

• NMT seems to have problems with or around punctuation. Full stops went missing after numbers in numbered paragraphs or points (e.g. "70." translated as "70"). The wrong type of quotation marks was used and spaces around them were added (e.g. „ xyz „ instead of „xyz"). There were redundant spaces around formatted text.

Although easy to correct, these errors are as time consuming to correct as semantic mistakes. Some had originated from the pre-processing of the text before being sent to the engine (formatting converted to tags, subsequently replaced by spaces). Pre-processing has improved and such errors now occur less frequently.

NMT and different document types

The analysis also provided an insight into the usefulness of eTranslation NMT for different document types:

• In legislative documents, in the acts the biggest problem with NMT seems to be terminological errors and inconsistency, but as a tool it is generally useful. In terminology-heavy Annexes, the terminological errors and inconsistency might make NMT useless, especially if there are tables with fragmented text and many abbreviations.

• In non-legislative documents, the NMT output is in general at least somewhat useful. Terminology is still problematic, but as these documents are less terminology-heavy as a rule, machine translation produces fewer errors. However, domain-specific vocabulary still causes errors in the NMT output.

• NMT seems to be least useful for documents for the general public. Although terminology is mostly unproblematic, due to the less standardised vocabulary, complex structures and metaphors, NMT suggestions are mostly useless. In segments with problematic elements in the source, NMT output was poor not only due to handling them badly, but also did worse in the aspects where it is usually superior to SMT (e.g. incorrect inflections or awkward word order).

Legislative documents are still the bulk of the SL LD source texts. Even in the case of low match rate documents, there is more appropriate material in NMT engines' training. Consequently, NMT might produce better results for these than for other types of documents. The nature of these texts makes any errors critical, however. The document sample for the ex post analysis was small (three or four (partial) documents per category) and possibly not representative of the categories. Other documents might demonstrate NMT as more (or less) useful.

Application of the quality assessment tool

DGT uses an internally developed quality assessment calculator to evaluate outsourced translations. Errors are categorised according to the above-mentioned error grid and entered in the calculator, which assigns to them language-specific weights based on the type of document and the length of the sample. The final grade is displayed after deducting points from the initial 100.[11] The tool produced devastating marks for all sample documents of eTranslation NMT output. All received the lowest grade (<21/100 points), in each case reaching negative values. The table below includes the number of points awarded, the number of errors and remarks.

---

[11]   As already stated, at the time of this writing, DGT is preparing for new outsourcing contracts, with a new error categorisation and a new evaluation procedure.

Implementing Regulation regarding 'Havarti' (PGI)							*final mark: −79*
sens[12] = 1	om = 0	term = 1	rd = 1	cl = 5	gr = 1	pt = 3	sp = 0
SENS = 5	OM = 1	TERM = 4	RD = 0	CL = 0	GR = 2	PT = 0	SP = 1
• wrong and inconsistent terminology, also inconsistencies in wording							
• problem with proper nouns (missing capitalisation, misspelling)							
Council Decision regarding HS (WCO)							*final mark: −34*
sens = 0	om = 0	term = 1	rd = 3	cl = 1	gr = 2	pt = 3	sp = 0
SENS = 0	OM = 0	TERM = 5	RD = 1	CL = 4	GR = 1	PT = 0	SP = 0
• incorrect standard phrases and terminology							
Annex to the Delegated Regulation supplementing ITS Directive							*final mark: −690*
sens = 0	om = 1	term = 4	rd = 0	cl = 6	gr = 5	pt = 2	sp = 0
SENS = 37	OM = 4	TERM = 9	RD = 0	CL = 7	GR = 5	PT = 0	SP = 0
• incorrect or nonsense translations due to the table format with text fragments							
• the many repeated abbreviations translated incorrectly and inconsistently							
• wrong and inconsistent terminology							
CMU report							*final mark: −89*
sens = 5	om = 0	term = 1	rd = 0	cl = 6	gr = 2	pt = 2	sp = 0
SENS = 3	OM = 2	TERM = 4	RD = 0	CL = 1	GR = 1	PT = 0	SP = 0
• several mistranslations of the domain specific financial vocabulary							
• some wrong and inconsistent terminology							
Climate action progress report							*final mark: −215*
sens = 6	om = 2	term = 1	rd = 1	cl = 18	gr = 4	pt = 4	sp = 0
SENS = 10	OM = 0	TERM = 0	RD = 0	CL = 3	GR = 2	PT = 1	SP = 0
• many mistranslations of the domain specific vocabulary							
• quite some reader unfriendly translations that needed rewording							
Replies of the Commission to an ECA Special Report							*final mark: −50*
sens = 1	om = 2	term = 4	rd = 0	cl = 12	gr = 6	pt = 2	sp = 0
SENS = 3	OM = 0	TERM = 1	RD = 0	CL = 2	GR = 0	PT = 0	SP = 0
• many minor mistranslations of the domain specific vocabulary							
Citizens' Dialogues and Consultations Progress report							*final mark: −335*
sens = 13	om = 1	term = 1	rd = 0	cl = 44	gr = 6	pt = 5	sp = 1
SENS = 10	OM = 2	TERM = 0	RD = 0	CL = 4	GR = 2	PT = 0	SP = 0
• many mistranslations and difficult to understand translations due to metaphorical language and vocabulary otherwise not frequently used in the translated documents							
Q&A on the EU list of non-cooperative tax jurisdictions							*final mark: −145*
sens = 6	om = 0	term = 3	rd = 0	cl = 12	gr = 3	pt = 1	sp = 0
SENS = 9	OM = 2	TERM = 0	RD = 0	CL = 3	GR = 0	PT = 0	SP = 0
• many mistranslations and difficult to understand translations due to rare vocabulary							
Health-EU Newsletter 223							*final mark: −140*
sens = 2	om = 0	term = 3	rd = 0	cl = 11	gr = 3	pt = 2	sp = 0
SENS = 9	OM = 0	TERM = 0	RD = 0	CL = 7	GR = 0	PT = 0	SP = 0
• mistranslations due to wrong deciphering of complex structures							
• non-translation of titles (considered proper nouns?)							
• difficult to understand translations of text fragments							
Memory game - Match the flags!							*final mark: −620*
sens = 24	om = 1	term = 0	rd = 0	cl = 23	gr = 9	pt = 4	sp = 1
SENS = 34	OM = 1	TERM = 0	RD = 0	CL = 8	GR = 1	PT = 0	SP = 0
• an extraordinary number of mistranslations and neural neologisms due to rare vocabulary and unusual structures							
• problems with proper nouns							

Table 3: Results per document

---

[12] The abbreviations in this table reflect the ones in the error grid and the quality assessment calculator: sens/SENS – mistranslation, om/OM – omission, term/TERM – terminology, rd/RD – reference documents, cl/CL – clarity, gr/GR – grammar, pt/PT – punctuation, sp/SP – spelling. Lowercase is used for minor errors and uppercase for major errors.

These results cannot, however, be taken as the definitive quality marks for the eTranslation NMT, as the methodology for the ex post review did not focus on the revision of the NMT, but on the analysis of the differences between the NMT and the final translation. Therefore, there is a possibility of false negatives (mistakes occurring in the NMT output and in the final translation). Moreover, in some documents with many errors (the document with the fewest comments contained 25 marked errors on the two pages and the document with the most contained a whopping 100 comments), some errors might not have been counted. Therefore, it is highly likely that a revision of NMT would have given even lower marks.

However, it should be born in mind that NMT was assessed against the criteria for human translation and that a specialised set of criteria might have given a different result. Consequently, a low mark earned by the output of NMT does not mean that NMT as a tool is not useful, but that the NMT output cannot be used as a final product. Maučec and Donaj (2020) also indicate a difference between evaluating the quality of MT output as a final product and evaluating its usability to human translators. Numerical results were assigned relatively low importance in the ex post analysis due to the methodological issues with using the quality assessment calculator on NMT and the small size of the sample that cannot produce representative results. The main focus was on consolidating and expanding the error categorisation started with the reported errors, as such indications can direct the translators' attention to the problem areas, and improve and speed up working with NMT.

6 Conclusion and follow-up

eTranslation NMT is widely used in the SL LD and is highly appreciated by the translators. They have assessed it to be a better tool than the SMT previously used. This corresponds to the finding of Burchardt et al. (2017) that turning from a phrase-based to a neural engine produced a striking improvement. Nevertheless, it has been clearly demonstrated that NMT is just a tool and not the final product (against the high standards required for Commission translations).

The reported errors revealed a variety of problems in the NMT output (polysemic misinterpretations, complete semantic blunders, terminological mistakes and inconsistencies, neural neolo-

gisms, omissions and additions; problems with proper nouns and abbreviations, complex structures and text fragments, text containing spelling errors and with (and/or next to) punctuation).

The ex post analysis confirmed that NMT output cannot be used as is. None of the sampled documents when simply pre-translated with the NMT output is a fit-for-purpose translation (fit for publication). A contributing factor for the poor result might also have been the fact that the sampled documents had a low match rate.

How much if any time is saved by machine translation remains unknown.[13] Furthermore, we gathered no definitive data to support the claim that the use of NMT saves time in comparison with the use of SMT.[14] Even though translators prefer working with NMT to working with SMT, we cannot claim that NMT use is necessarily easier and that it accelerates the translation process when compared to SMT. Maučec and Donaj (2020) identify three levels of post-editing effort: temporal, cognitive and technical. The use of NMT involves different types of issues that need to be dealt with and might be considered more mentally taxing than those inherent in the use of SMT (problems at higher levels of grammar and beyond grammar).

Clearly a skilled human is needed to guarantee a high quality of translation. This means NMT as a tool needs to be understood better in order to be used better, which requires educating and training its users, which is in line with Maučec and Donaj (2020), who emphasize the need of research on and teaching of skills specific to post-editing. Therefore, we extended the list of categorised reported errors with additional examples and added to the list new categories of recurring problems discovered during the ex post analysis. The list now paints as comprehensive a picture as possible of all potential English–Slovene NMT pitfalls. A department-level training was held to familiarise translators with the list and with the

---

[13]   At least for the users of the EN–SL eTranslation NMT output. Macken et al. (2020) have worked with the French and Finnish LDs of DGT to assess how much time translators gain (or lose) in real-world conditions when they use machine translation, and observed the average speed gain of 14 % for English–Finnish NMT (and 12 % for English–French phrase-based SMT).

[14]   In their analyses, Bentivogli et al. (2016), and Toral and Sánchez-Cartagena (2017), do arrive to the conclusion that NMT decreases post-editing effort compared to SMT. Klubička et al. (2017) also arrive to the same conclusion, and for a Slavic language close to Slovene.

results of the ex post analysis. The training raised awareness of expected error types among translators and informed our reflection on how to best use NMT. The request for translators to report examples remains open – the reporting is not systematic and the analysed sample was small, so it is possible that some errors elude categorisation due to a low number of occurrences and that some error types have not been detected yet.

Acknowledgement

The authors would like to thank the management of DGT for the opportunity to present our experience. We give our thanks to Jan Bednarich, the Head of the Slovene Language Department, for his continued support and to our colleagues Mojca Šauperl, Maksimiljan Gulič and Sarah Butcher for their indispensable help in improving the text, as well as to Markus Foti, the eTranslation Project Manager, for his insights.

References

Bentivogli, Luisa, Arianna Bisazza, Mauro Cettolo, and Marcello Federico. 2016. Neural versus phrase-based machine translation quality: A case study. In *Proceedings of the 2016 Conference on Empirical Methods in Natural Language Processing*, pages 257–267, Austin.

Burchardt, Aljoscha, Vivien Macketanz, Jon Dehdari, Georg Heigold, Jan-Thorsten Peter, and Philip Williams. 2017. A linguistic evaluation of rule-based, phrase-based, and neural MT engines. *The Prague Bulletin of Mathematical Linguistics*, 108.1: 159–170.

Drugan, Joanna, Ingemar Strandvik, and Erkka Vuorinen. 2018. Translation quality, quality management and agency: Principles and practice in the European Union institutions. In Joss Moorkens, Sheila Castilho, Federico Gaspari, and Stephen Doherty, editors, *Translation Quality Assessment: From Principles to Practice*, Springer, Cham, pages 39–68.

Klubička, Filip, Antonio Toral, and Víctor M. Sánchez-Cartagena. 2017. Fine-grained human evaluation of neural versus phrase-based machine translation. *The Prague Bulletin of Mathematical Linguistics*, 108.1: 121–132.

Koehn, Philip, Hieu Hoang, Alexandra Birch, Chris Callison-Burch, Marcello Federico, Nicola Bertoldi, Brooke Cowan, Wade Shen, Christine Moran, Richard Zens, Chris Dyer, Ondřej Bojar, Alexandra Constantin, and Evan Herbst. 2007. Moses: Open source toolkit for statistical machine translation. In *Proceedings of the 45th Annual Meeting of the Association for Computational Linguistics Companion Volume Proceedings of the Interactive and Demonstration Sessions*, pages 177–180, Prague.

Lacruz, Isabel, Michael Denkowski, and Alon Lavie. 2014. Cognitive demand and cognitive effort in post-editing. In *Proceedings of the Third Workshop on Post-Editing Technology and Practice*. Association for Machine Translation in the Americas, pages 73–84, Vancouver.

Leal Fontes, Hilário. 2013. Evaluating machine translation: Preliminary findings from the first DGT-wide translators' survey. *Languages and Translation*, 6: 10–11.

Lesznyák, Ágnes. 2019. Hungarian translators' perceptions of neural machine translation in the European Commission. In *Proceedings of Machine Translation Summit XVII Volume 2: Translator, Project and User Tracks*, pages 16–22, Dublin.

Macken, Lieve, Laura Van Brussel, and Joke Daems. 2019. NMT's wonderland where people turn into rabbits. A study on the comprehensibility of newly invented words in NMT output. *Computational Linguistics in the Netherlands Journal*, 9: 67–80.

Macken, Lieve, Daniel Prou, and Arda Tezcan. 2020. Quantifying the effect of machine translation in a high-quality human translation production process. *Informatics*, 7(2):12.

Maučec, Mirjam Sepesy, and Gregor Donaj. 2019. Machine translation and the evaluation of its quality. [Online First], IntechOpen, DOI: 10.5772/intechopen.89063. Available from: https://www.intechopen.com/online-first/machine-translation-and-the-evaluation-of-its-quality.

Strandvik, Ingemar. 2017. Evaluation of outsourced translations. State of play in the European Commission's Directorate-General for Translation (DGT). In Tomáš Svoboda, Łucja Biel and Krzysztof Łoboda, editors, *Quality aspects in institutional translation*, 8, pages 123–137, Berlin.

Toral, Antonio, and Víctor M. Sánchez-Cartagena. 2017. A multifaceted evaluation of neural versus phrase-based machine translation for 9 language directions. In *Proceedings of the 15th Conference of the European Chapter of the Association for Computational Linguistics: Volume 1, Long Papers*, pages 1063–1073, Valencia.

Van Brussel, Laura, Arda Tezcan, and Lieve Macken. 2018. A fine-grained error analysis of NMT, PBMT and RBMT output for English-to-Dutch. In *Proceedings of the Eleventh International Conference on Language Resources and Evaluation (LREC 2018)*, pages 3799–3804, Miyazaki.

How do LSPs compute MT discounts? Presenting a company's pipeline and its use

Randy Scansani
Acolad
Rimini, Italy
rscansani@acolad.com

Lamis Mhedhbi
Acolad
Paris, France
lmhedhbi@acolad.com

Abstract

In this paper we present a pipeline developed at Acolad to test a Machine Translation (MT) engine and compute the discount to be applied when its output is used in production. Our pipeline includes three main steps where quality and productivity are measured through automatic metrics, manual evaluation, and by keeping track of editing and temporal effort during a post-editing task. Thanks to this approach, it is possible to evaluate the output quality and compute an engine-specific discount. Our test pipeline tackles the complexity of transforming productivity measurements into discounts by comparing the outcome of each of the above-mentioned steps to an estimate of the average productivity of translation from scratch. The discount is obtained by subtracting the resulting coefficient from the per-word rate. After a description of the pipeline, the paper presents its application on four engines, discussing its results and showing that our method to estimate post-editing effort through manual evaluation seems to capture the actual productivity. The pipeline relies heavily on the work of professional post-editors, with the aim of creating a mutually beneficial cooperation between users and developers.

1 Introduction

Over the last few years, the number of companies starting to integrate machine translation (MT) in their workflow has increased dramatically. In 2018, for the first time, more than half of the companies and individual professionals taking part in the Language Industry Survey stated that they used MT (Elia et al., 2018). The same survey repeated in 2019 showed that MT was one of the highest priorities for companies, with 51% of them willing to increase its use and 62% stating that they were planning investments on MT (Elia et al., 2019).

At the same time, all categories involved in the 2019 Language Industry Survey mentioned price pressure as the main negative trend, with MT and post-editing identified as one of the major causes. In the previous year, one of the main concerns of the language industry components were the "technological advances that are not initiated or controlled by the respondents" (Elia et al., 2018, p. 31).

These surveys point out that individuals and companies are embracing a technology that they themselves see as a threat to the sustainability of the translation industry. This seems to suggest that there might be a strong disagreement regarding the price models to be adopted when MT is included in the workflow. One of the priorities of MT users and developers should therefore be the creation of shared models and/or methods to measure quality and productivity with a view to computing discounts to be applied when MT is used. However, to the best of our knowledge this topic has been underinvestigated so far.

The "Pricing Machine Translation Post-editing Guidelines" published by TAUS have tried to fill the gap in this field.[1] They claim that a model to price post-editing should be predictive (able to es-

---

[1] TAUS is an industry organization in the field of translation and languages. The guidelines can be found here: `https://bit.ly/2PlTCUd`.

Martins, Moniz, Fumega, Martins, Batista, Coheur, Parra, Trancoso, Turchi, Bisazza, Moorkens, Guerberof, Nurminen, Marg, Forcada (eds.)
Proceedings of the 22nd Annual Conference of the European Association for Machine Translation, p. 393–401
Lisboa, Portugal, November 2020.

timate prices in advance), fair (involving all parties and providing them with a reliable estimate), and appropriate for both the language pair and the content characteristics. To achieve this aim, three main indicators should be combined: human evaluation, automatic metrics, and productivity assessments. Despite the usefulness of these guidelines, many questions on how to convert quality scores and/or judgements into rates – especially word-based ones – or discounts remain unanswered. For example, if automatic metrics are used, what would a TER of 0.4 imply in terms of productivity? If a sentence is evaluated as very fluent by a human translator, how could this judgement be converted into a discount? At the same time, if productivity assessments on a machine translated sample reveals that, e.g., 200 words per hour were post-edited, what would be the most reliable and consistent way to turn this productivity rate into a fair per-word rate for post-editing? Indeed, measuring post-editing productivity might be a difficult task *per se*, since post-editing effort is multidimensional and composed of time needed to edit a text (temporal effort), number of edits performed (editing effort) and identification and correction of issues (cognitive effort) (Krings, 2001). Computing discounts adds an additional challenge, i.e. converting productivity measures into post-editing rates.

Building upon TAUS guidelines, in the present work we introduce a pipeline to estimate an engine-specific discount to be applied to per-word rates for post-editing. The pipeline is composed of different steps that involve the use of automatic metrics, post-editing effort measurements and human evaluation processes, carried out as follows:

1. Automatic scores. TER (Snover et al., 2006) is used to evaluate the engine and gain a first insight into its quality (see Section 3.1).

2. Manual evaluation. One linguist is asked to manually evaluate and score, based on the amount of editing required, each sentence of a sample of 3,000 words (see Section 3.2).

3. Real Condition test (RCT). One post-editor is asked to perform full post-editing on a sample of 5,000 words. Both editing and temporal effort are measured (see Section 3.3).

To tackle the aforementioned challenge of converting quality scores and productivity rates into discounts for per-word rates, the outcomes of the second and third steps are contrasted against what would be the average productivity of a linguist translating from scratch. The resulting coefficient is then subtracted from the per-word rate applied to no-match sentences (see Section 3.4). A high coefficient thus results in a low discount and *vice versa*.

Our model complies with the three requirements listed by TAUS. It computes discounts in advance, and being engine-specific it provides a discount that is appropriate for a content type and a language pair. Also, the Acolad pipeline involves all parties, since it strongly relies on the work of post-editors who perform the tasks listed above (and described in Section 3.2 and 3.3) and fill in a feedback module on the output quality at the end of each post-editing task. Besides being desirable according to TAUS guidelines and useful to better understand an engine quality, involving post-editors allows us to collect data coming from the final users of our custom engines and to raise awareness of our MT-related processes, especially those focused on MT quality, which might help translators to feel more comfortable when performing post-editing tasks.

The present work is structured as follows. Section 2 provides a brief overview on articles and lines of research that are relevant for the topic handled here. Each stage of our pipeline is detailed in Section 3 and its subsections, while the pipeline application is presented in Section 4. To conclude, results of the application are discussed in Section 5, and limitations and future work are outlined in Section 6.

2   Related work

Quality estimation (QE) models – i.e. models trained to output a quality indicator of a translation without the need of comparing it to a reference – have been examined by a large amount of papers in the last decade and would serve the need of estimating the output quality, the post-editing time or the amount of editing needed on a whole text or on each of its sentences (Specia et al., 2009; Escartín et al., 2017; Scarton et al., 2019). Despite the relevance of this line of research for the present paper, we are not aware of QE models aimed at predicting discounts or post-editing effort that are ready to be integrated in CAT tools, which would be key for translation companies. One exception is

Memsource MTQE functionality, which computes a match rate for machine translated sentences – similarly to what CAT tools usually do for translation memory (TM) matches. However Memsource MTQE is still in a Beta version, and as of today it is not able to estimate quality for all language pairs and sentences.[2]

Companies operating in the translation field have published articles on their experience in computing discounts for post-editing. Cattelan (2013) describes an experiment carried out in the framework of the MateCat project aimed to understand the maximum discount translators are willing to accept for post-editing tasks.[3] Translators working on different language combinations were asked to choose between translating 1,000 words from scratch or post-editing a lower number of words at the same per-word rate. The number of words paid for post-editing was gradually increased until at least 75% of the translators chose post-editing over translation from scratch. However, the author claimed that this method was not suitable for establishing discount rates, since for some language combinations translators chose post-editing over translation only when the former was paid more than the latter. The article then suggests a combination of editing effort, temporal effort and output quality to understand the usefulness of MT for post-editors.

A rather straightforward approach at computing post-editing discounts is the one presented by Lizuka (2018) in an SDL blog post.[4] The author suggests that a post-editing test is set up where a linguist is asked to post-edit a text sample for one hour. After that, the post-editor hourly rate is divided by the number of translated words to obtain the discount. However, since post-editing rates should be computed based on the content and language pair (see Section 1), this test should be carried out every time a post-editor is working on a new content, or on a text belonging to a different domain or on a target language they have never post-edited. This would not be the most efficient solution.

The different approaches presented here suggest that developing a reliable method to compute post-editing discounts is not an easy task. As a matter of fact, to the best of our knowledge, as of today the translation world lacks a shared model to establish MT discounts upfront. In the next sections we will present the pipeline developed and currently in use at Acolad to compute an engine-specific discount (see Section 3). To gain a better insight into its functioning, four use cases are also presented (see Section 4).

3   Pipeline description

Our pipeline is mainly composed of the three steps that were introduced in Section 1. These will be detailed in the following sections, together with a final step in which the final coefficient is computed.

3.1   Automatic scores

After each (re-)training, our MT engine quality is measured based on TER on a held-out set of 2,500 sentence pairs. This step is carried out for two main reasons. First, it produces a quality indicator whose results are comparable across different versions of the engine. Moreover it provides a first insight into the output quality. If TER results are not satisfactory, tests described in Section 3.2 and 3.3 are not launched. Instead, analyses are carried out on the hypothesis to understand the reason for such poor quality.

3.2   Manual evaluation

As mentioned in Section 1, including a manual evaluation in the creation of a pricing model is a practice suggested by TAUS guidelines. Also, from a more practical point of view, asking more than one linguist to post-edit a whole sample would be too costly. A manual evaluation step allows the collection of observations from a different person than the one involved in the RCT (see Section 3.3) in a relatively short span of time.

Regarding the reliability of such procedure, De Sousa et al. (2011) found a high correlation between subjective scores based on the predicted post-editing effort and the actual post-editing time. On the other hand, works such as the one by Moorkens et al. (2015) have shown that correlations between ratings of predicted post-editing effort and actual temporal effort are only moderate. However, the authors also stated that such re-

---

[2] A description of the Memsource MTQE feature can be found at this link: `https://bit.ly/2u1exEO`, while the supported language pairs are listed here `https://bit.ly/2wCHDuR`.

[3] MateCat is a free online CAT tool developed in the framework of a three-year project funded by the European Union in 2011.

[4] SDL is a company offering translations services and software.

sults were probably influenced by the instructions provided to participants. Also, participants were researchers or academic staff members. Results might be different in our scenario, since linguists dealing with translation and post-editing tasks on a daily basis are involved.

Developing a manual evaluation method and an approach to turn the scores assigned by the evaluator into a discount was arguably the most complex part in the creation of the whole pipeline. Due to confidentiality reasons, we cannot reveal the formula currently in use at Acolad. Nevertheless, in the rest of this section details will be provided regarding the manual evaluation setup and method.

A sample of 3,000 words is randomly extracted from a held-out set of sentence pairs and the source text is machine translated with the engine that is being tested. This sample size was chosen to collect a reasonable number of observations, at the same time without asking the evaluator to score a high number of sentences, which might be perceived as a repetitive task, introducing a fatigue effect.

One evaluator is asked to evaluate the sample by assigning a score to each sentence. As in Specia (2009), scores range from 1 to 4 and describe the amount of editing that would be needed in a full post-editing scenario[5]:

1. No editing required

2. Minor editing required. Edits in these sentences are usually related to word order, wrong word class, wrong use of plural/singular forms, etc.

3. Major editing required. Edits require quite some effort, but post-editing is still more efficient than translating from scratch

4. Re-translation required: post-editing would be less efficient than translating from scratch

The evaluator might be negatively influenced by a preconception against MT, or by low quality in the first sentences of the sample, since human evaluation is inherently subjective. To reduce the number of sentences assigned the worst score despite their acceptable quality, we ask the evaluator to provide a correct version of the sentence when this is labelled with the worst score (4). Also, the evaluator is paid based on the time required to finish

---

[5] Differently from the approach present in this paper, in Specia (2009) the worst score is 1 and the best score is 4.

the task, so as to avoid a situation whereby the outcome of the task is influenced by unfair per-word rates.

At the end of the evaluation, each score is treated as a fuzzy match percentage. For example, sentences with the best score (1) are treated as 100% matches, while sentences with the worst score (4) are treated as 0% matches. Based on these percentages and on the number of words assigned to each score, a formula determines the coefficient in a way similar to the one used to compute weighted word counts in CAT tools.

It is worth noting that a penalty is added to 0% matches, assuming that re-translating an MT output would take longer than translating the same sentence from scratch. The post-editor would need to first read and analyse both the source and the target sentence, and then to delete and re-translate the latter. A 5% margin is then added to the coefficient, in order to take into account the subjectivity of manual scores. Henceforth, the resulting coefficient will be referred to as the *manual evaluation coefficient* (see Section 3.4).

3.3 Real condition test

In the RCT, a sample of 5,000 words is randomly extracted from a held-out set of sentence pairs and machine translated by the engine that is being tested. This sample size was chosen because it should allow the measurement of productivity over a reasonable span of time. The machine translated sample is sent to one post-editor, who is asked to perform full post-editing on the output. The RCT and the manual evaluation (see Section 3.2) are carried out by two different linguists. At this stage, reliable information on the discount to be applied is not available. For this reason, the post-editor taking part in the RCT is paid based on his/her per-word rate for translation from scratch. The post-editor can choose his/her preferred CAT tool to perform this task. This is in line with previous works suggesting that experiments on post-editing productivity should be carried out with the same tools that are normally used in the translation industry (Macken et al., 2020; Läubli et al., 2013).

There are two main outputs of this test. First, the editing effort is obtained computing HTER (Snover et al., 2006) between the raw output and its post-edited version. Time spent on the whole task is tracked by the post-editor, who then provides this datum at delivery. HTER is not used to compute a coefficient, since it might not take into account all edits performed on a text/sentence or the required cognitive effort (Lacruz et al., 2014). Moreover, the number of edits might not correlate with time measurements (Tatsumi, 2009; Macken et al., 2020).

On the other hand, combining HTER with temporal effort provides an overview on productivity and a better understanding of how time was used. The informativeness of a comparison between these two types of post-editing effort will be shown in Section 4.

The time spent on the whole task and the total number of source words are used to compute the result of this test (henceforth, the *RCT coefficient*). First, we retrieve the throughput (source words per hour). Then, we compute the difference between the post-editing throughput and an estimated throughput for translation from scratch, i.e. 357 words per hour (the language industry standard of 2,500 words per day if we consider a seven-hour workday). The ratio between the resulting difference and the estimated throughput for translation from scratch provides the *increased speed*. To conclude, the RCT coefficient is computed using the following formula:

$$RCT\ coeff. = \frac{1}{1 + increased\ speed} \quad (1)$$

Our method is similar to the one used in Plitt and Masselot (2010), and in Guerberof (2014), except for two differences. First, the RCT coefficient measures the throughput improvement, while the formula reported by Plitt and Masselot and by Guerberof (2014) focuses on time savings (i.e. throughput improvement is subtracted from 100). As a result, if the RCT formula outputs a 77% coefficient, the formula by the authors mentioned above would report a 23% of time saved. Also, in Guerberof (2014) and Plitt and Masselot (2010) the actual throughput for translation from scratch is computed, which is not possible for us due to time and budget constraints (this limitation is further discussed in Section 3.4 and 6).

At the end of the task, the post-editor is asked to fill in a feedback form, in which he/she rates the quality of the whole output assigning a score from 1 (worst score) to 5 (best score) to each of the following categories: accuracy, fluency, terminology translation, formatting and punctuation. An optional field for comments is also provided. For cases in which a high number of terminology issues are spotted, post-editors can list examples of wrong target terms found in the output, together with their source and the correct version. This module helps understanding if a low productivity is confirmed by low quality judgements, or if a perceived low quality is contradicted by a high productivity rate. Receiving a general feedback from the final users of our engines can be useful in different ways. As mentioned in Section 1, besides being recommended by TAUS guidelines, this feedback should help post-editors to feel more involved in MT-related processes. On the other hand, our MT team can undoubtedly benefit from linguists' feedback. It is also worth noting that this module is filled in after each post-editing task, so that quality can be consistently monitored thanks to the work of post-editors.

3.4 Computing the final coefficient

If no specific issues were identified during any of the steps described above, the RCT coefficient and the manual evaluation coefficient are averaged to obtain the *final coefficient*. This will be then subtracted from the per-word rate for no-match segments when MT is used.

When averaging the two coefficients, the result is rounded up to the nearest whole number. This is done – together with the margin added to the manual evaluation coefficient and introduced in Section 3.2 – to take into account variability between different post-editors or different texts in terms of productivity. As a matter of fact, rounding up the coefficient reduces the discount. Although the best solution would be to have more than one evaluator and more than one post-editor being involved in the pipeline for each engine test (and a larger sample to be evaluated or post-edited) this is often not feasible due to either budget or time constraints (see Section 6). Only one linguist is usually involved in each task. He/she is chosen from among the linguists who often translate for the customer for which the engine was created. On the other hand, if the outcomes of the test steps are contradictory, too high, or too low, the test is repeated with a different linguist.

From a practical point of view, a further step is required once the coefficient has been computed. Having a large number of engines – with a specific coefficient each – and being a company with a large number of employees, an effort has to

Evaluation step	Outcome	En–De		De–It	
		Fashion	Medical	Medical	Legal
Automatic score	**TER**	61.60	49.86	46.75	48.88
RCT	**HTER**	41.00	29.89	40.77	34.45
	Coefficient	59%	81%	62.00%	72%
Manual evaluation	**Coefficient**	66.00%	80.50%	63.70%	74.20%
Final coefficient		63%	81%	63%	73%

Table 1: Results of each step of our test pipeline for two language combinations (En–De and De–It) on engines developed for customers in the following domains: Fashion, Medical, Legal. For consistency with the coefficients, (H)TER values are presented as a percentage score. TER values (first row) were obtained comparing the MT output to a pre-existing reference translation, while data in the other rows are based on the work by translators involved in the test pipeline. The final coefficient is an average – rounded up – of the other two coefficients and is subtracted from the rate for no match segments. The lower the coefficient, the higher the productivity and the discount.

be made to make sure that project managers can quickly find the best engine for their project (if any) and that they know which discount to apply. For this reason, we developed an automation step that, for each project, suggests the engine that suits the project manager's needs and provides its coefficient. Also, newsletters are sent out to project managers every time a new set of engines is ready to be used.

4 Use cases

4.1 MT engines

After having introduced the different steps of our test pipeline and their outcomes, in this section we present 4 use cases (see Table 1), each of them related to an engine trained for a specific customer. For confidentiality issues, we only reveal the domain the customers operate in. Two engines are trained on English–German data and their domains are fashion and medical. Two engines are trained on German–Italian data and their domains are medical and legal.

The rationale behind the choice of En–De and De–It is that in the first language combination the evaluation steps were carried out on a Germanic language, while in the second language combination, evaluations were carried out on a Romance language. Since different issues might be found in the output, e.g. based on the target language syntax, the post-editing effort (and therefore evaluation results) might be influenced by them. After having chosen the language combinations, medical, legal and fashion were chosen to provide examples for 3 domains with wide differences in terms of sentence structure and terminology.

4.2 Results

Looking at Table 1, we can see that there usually is a large difference between TER in the automatic score step and HTER in the RCT – except for the Medical De–It engine. This is to be expected since the reference test used for TER is a manual translation produced from scratch, while in the case of HTER we are measuring the edit distance between a raw MT output and its post-edited version. At the same time, we are reporting the HTER for the RCT for the sake of completeness and comparison, although – as explained in Section 3.3 – the RCT coefficient is computed based on the productivity increase.

The Fashion En–De engine, which has a TER score of 61.60, seemed to provide rather poor quality. However, once the test pipeline was completed, it was shown to be able to increase productivity by 37%. The exact same result was obtained by the Medical De–It engine. The other Medical engine (En–De) reached a 81% final coefficient – the highest value in the table and thus the worst productivity increment. To conclude, Legal De–It engine reached a 73% final coefficient. According to our coefficients, all engines are thus able to produce an output that increases post-editor productivity by at least 19%.

Comparing the two outcomes of the RCT for all engines, we see many discrepancies. In the fashion En–De engine, for example, 41% of the sample was edited. However, productivity increased by 41% according to the coefficient. In Section 3.3 the low correlation between HTER and productivity measurements was illustrated. This becomes evident when considering RCT results for Medical En–De, Medical De–It and Legal De–It. An HTER increase corresponds to a decrease of the

RCT coefficient, and thus to a productivity increment, confirming that a lower number of edits does not necessarily imply a lower post-editing time and thus a higher productivity.

The RCT coefficient and the manual evaluation coefficient are similar for three engines out of four, with their differences ranging from 0.5 to 2.2%. For fashion En–De, they differ by 7%. Since the manual evaluation coefficient is higher (66%), it is possible that the fashion En–De evaluator was particularly strict when manually scoring sentences, thus causing the coefficient to increase. In the feedback form for the RCT, the post-editor stated that the source text was often translated literally or using an incorrect sentence structure. As shown by Koponen (2012), target sentences involving more reordering tend to be perceived as requiring a high editing effort. It is thus possible that sentences in the manual evaluation sample received a score that reflected a higher post-editing effort than that actually required during RCT.

5 Discussion

We have presented four use cases of our pipeline to test an MT engine and estimate the productivity increase that can be reached when its output is used in post-editing tasks.

Results in Table 1 have shown that when a higher HTER is computed, productivity increases and *vice versa*. Indeed previous works found a low correlation between HTER and temporal effort (see Section 3.3). For example, small edits might require a high cognitive and temporal effort, thus having a large negative impact on productivity.

The small differences between the RCT coefficient and the manual evaluation coefficient seem to suggest that the approach adopted to estimate post-editing effort through manual scoring reflects the actual temporal (and cognitive) effort. This might not always be the case as testified by the fashion En–De engine. Therefore, keeping both coefficients and computing an average of the two seems to be the best solution.

6 Conclusions and future work

The present work aimed at introducing our test pipeline to measure MT quality and engine-specific discounts. Future work might present a higher number of use cases than those described in Section 4.2, in order to provide a better overview of how the pipeline works. Also, adding examples of raw sentences together with the score assigned to them during the manual evaluation and their post-edited versions can better explain differences between the two coefficients or between the two outcomes of the RCT. However, it has to be taken into account that it is often not possible to provide such examples due to confidentiality issues.

The feedback module described in Section 3.3 has been recently added to our pipeline. Before that, post-editors were only asked to provide a general feedback on the output quality and its main issues. However, such general feedback was often too generic and/or difficult to interpret. For this reason, in this paper we are not reporting the feedback received, except for the fashion En–De engine in Section 4.2. Future work could compare HTER and the coefficients with the results of the new feedback module, discussing the accuracy and fluency ratings assigned to the four engines.

Our MT group is constantly working on the improvement of our processes, including improvements of our test pipeline. In the future, language-specific or domain-specific formulas to compute the two coefficients could be developed, since productivity can be highly influenced by the text and/or domain post-editors are working on.

Also, as introduced in Section 3.3, using an average productivity increase to compute discounts to be applied to the work of any post-editor does not take into account differences between professionals. Several studies on post-editing concluded that there is a high degree of variability between post-editors when it comes to productivity (Macken et al., 2020; Guerberof Arenas, 2014; Plitt and Masselot, 2010). However, we fully agree with Guerberof (2014), who argues that using an average productivity increase to compute discounts for all post-editors is not beneficial for less productive post-editors, but further maintains that this is what happens with fuzzy match discounts as well, and finding a solution is not an easy task. To improve the fairness of our discounts, when allowed by deadlines and by the budget, we plan to involve more than one linguist per stage.

To conclude, the authors are aware of the need to develop a pipeline that can be applied to all production tasks involving post-editing. Producing continuous reports on the output quality of an engine – and how this influences productivity – is of the essence for an increasingly efficient and fair use of MT, similarly to what has been introduced by TAUS Dynamic Quality Framework (DQF).[6] However, developing such a complex pipeline will require a long research and pilot phase.

These possible improvements should not hide the fact that, to the best of our knowledge, this is the first work presenting a company's approach to test engines and method of computing its specific discount rates, reporting also on examples of the practical use of this pipeline.

Acknowledgements

The authors would like to thank the whole Acolad MT team for its contribution to the development of the processes described in the present work, and two anonymous reviewers for insightful comments on the first draft of this paper.

References

Cattelan, Alessandro. 2013. A fair rate for post-editing. https://bit.ly/38FO1Pj. Last accessed: 2020-04-20.

de Sousa, Sheila C. M., Wilker Aziz, and Lucia Specia. 2011. Assessing the post-editing effort for automatic and semi-automatic translations of DVD subtitles. In *Proceedings of the International Conference Recent Advances in Natural Language Processing 2011*, pages 97–103, Hissar, Bulgaria, September. Association for Computational Linguistics.

Elia, EMT, EUATC, FIT Europe, GALA, and LIND. 2018. 2018 Language Industry Survey – Expectations and concerns of the European language industry. https://bit.ly/3bogf3X. Last accessed: 2020-04-20.

Elia, EMT, EUATC, FIT Europe, GALA, and LIND. 2019. 2019 Language Industry Survey – Expectations and concerns of the European language industry. https://bit.ly/3btV2pf. Last accessed: 2020-04-20.

Escartín, Carla Parra, Hanna Béchara, and Constantin Orasan. 2017. Questing for quality estimation a user study. *Prague Bull. Math. Linguistics*, 108:343–354.

Guerberof Arenas, Ana. 2014. Correlations between productivity and quality when post-editing in a professional context. *Machine Translation*, 28(3/4):165–186.

Koponen, Maarit. 2012. Comparing human perceptions of post-editing effort with post-editing operations. In *Proceedings of the Seventh Workshop on Statistical Machine Translation*, pages 181–190, Montréal, Canada, June. Association for Computational Linguistics.

Krings, Hans P. 2001. *Repairing Texts: Empirical Investigations of Machine Translation Post-Editing Processes*. Kent State University Press, Kent, Ohio.

Lacruz, Isabel, Michael Denkowski, and Alon Lavie. 2014. Cognitive Demand and Cognitive Effort in Post-Editing. In *Proceedings of the Third Workshop on Post-Editing Technology and Practice*, pages 73–84. Association for Machine Translation in the Americas.

Läubli, Samuel, Mark Fishel, Gary Massey, Maureen Ehrensberger-Dow, and Martin Volk. 2013. Assessing post-editing efficiency in a realistic translation environment. In O'Brien, Sharon, Michel Simard, and Lucia Specia, editors, *Proceedings of MT Summit XIV Workshop on Post-editing Technology and Practice (Nice, September 2, 2013)*, pages 83–91, Allschwil, September. European Association for Machine Translation.

Lizuka, Izabella. 2018. Isn't it time to embrace machine translation post-editing? The localization use case for MT. https://bit.ly/3cJsOCF. Last accessed: 2020-04-20.

Macken, Lieve, Daniel Prou, and Arda Tezcan. 2020. Quantifying the effect of machine translation in a high-quality human translation production process. *Informatics*, 7(2).

Moorkens, Joss, Sharon O'Brien, Igor A. L. da Silva, Norma B. de Lima Fonseca, and Fábio Alves. 2015. Correlations of perceived post-editing effort with measurements of actual effort. *Machine Translation*, 29:267–284.

Plitt, Mirko and François Masselot. 2010. A productivity test of statistical machine translation postediting in a typical localisation context. In *Prague Bulletin of Mathematical Linguistics, 93:7–16, 2010. URL http://ufal.mff.cuni.cz/pbml/93/art-plitt-masselot.pdf*.

Scarton, Carolina, Mikel L. Forcada, Miquel Esplà-Gomis, and Lucia Specia. 2019. Estimating post-editing effort: a study on human judgements, task-based and reference-based metrics of mt quality.

Snover, Matthew, Bonnie Dorr, Richard Schwartz, Linnea Micciulla, and John Makhoul. 2006. A study of translation edit rate with targeted human annotation. In *Proceedings of Association for Machine Translation in the Americas*, pages 223–231, Cambridge, Massachussets.

Specia, Lucia, Nicola Cancedda, Marc Dymetman, Marco Turchi, and Nello Cristianini. 2009. Estimating the sentence-level quality of machine translation systems. In *In EAMT*, pages 28–35.

---

[6]DQF is a framework to evaluate quality and productivity for translation tasks. https://bit.ly/2VVfVUP

Tatsumi, Midori. 2009. Correlation between automatic evaluation metric scores , post-editing speed , and some other factors. In *Proceedings of the AMTA 2012 Workshop on Post-editing Technology and Practice*, pages 69–77. Association for Machine Translation.

PosEdiOn: Post-Editing Assessment in PythOn

Antoni Oliver
Universitat Oberta de Catalunya
aoliverg@uoc.edu

Sergi Alvarez
Universitat Pompeu Fabra
salvarezvid@uoc.edu

Toni Badia
Universitat Pompeu Fabra
toni.badia@upf.edu

Abstract

There is currently an extended use of post-editing of machine translation (PEMT) in the translation industry. This is due to the increase in the demand of translation and to the significant improvements in quality achieved in recent years. PEMT has been included as part of the translation workflow because it increases translators' productivity and it also reduces costs. Although effective post-editing requires sufficiently high quality MT output, usual automatic metrics do not always correlate with post-editing effort. We describe a standalone tool designed both for industry and research that has two main purposes: to collect sentence-level information from the post-editing process (e.g. post-editing time and keystrokes) and to visually present multiple evaluation scores so they can be easily interpreted by a user.

1 Introduction

Post-editing of machine translation (PEMT) is a very common practice in the translation industry. It has been included as part of the translation workflow because it increases productivity when compared with human translation (Aranberri et al., 2014) and reduces costs (Guerberof, 2009) without having a negative impact on quality (Plitt and Masselot, 2010). Post-editors "edit, modify and/or correct pre-translated text that has been processed by an MT system from a source language into (a) target language(s)" (Allen, 2003, p. 296).

In the last few years, both research and industry have become very interested in neural machine translation (NMT) because it has produced very successful results in terms of quality, for example in WMT 2017 (Bojar et al., 2017), WMT 2018 (Bojar et al., 2018) and WMT 2019 (Barrault et al., 2019). Given the overall performance of NMT, it is necessary to study all the potential this approach can offer to post-editing. One of the main problems is that automatic scores give a general idea of the MT output quality but do not always correlate with post-editing effort (Koponen, 2016; Shterionov et al., 2018). Many professional translators state that if the quality of the MT output is not good enough, they delete the remaining segments and translate everything from scratch (Parra Escartín and Arcedillo, 2015).

One of the main goals both of industry and research is to establish a correlation between the quality measurements of the MT output and translators' performance. Research is especially focused on the effort this activity entails, mainly taking into account the temporal, technical, and cognitive effort (Krings, 2001). The use of tools that can log these three dimensions becomes a paramount challenge for research.

Professional translators usually use commercial products to translate and post-edit. In the 2018 Language Industry Survey[1] conducted by EUATC, Elia, FIT Europe, GALA and LINDWeb, SDL Trados[2] was the most used product with more than half of the market quota, followed by MemoQ,[3]

---

[1] http://fit-europe-rc.org/wp-content/uploads/2019/05/2018-Language-Industry-Survey-Report.pdf
[2] https://www.sdl.com/
[3] https://www.memoq.com

Martins, Moniz, Fumega, Martins, Batista, Coheur, Parra, Trancoso, Turchi, Bisazza, Moorkens, Guerberof, Nurminen, Marg, Forcada (eds.)
Proceedings of the 22nd Annual Conference of the European Association for Machine Translation, p. 403–410
Lisboa, Portugal, November 2020.

Memsource,[4] Wordfast,[5] and Across.[6] However, these existing post-editing environments have a restricted availability and flexibility. As proprietary tools, they are difficult to modify and do not usually provide translator activity data that may be used to study post-editing effort. However, other open-source computer-assisted translation (CAT) environments such as OmegaT,[7] have been modified and used for data collection (Moran et al., 2014).

Instead of trying to reproduce the working conditions of translators, which vary greatly among individuals, other tools establish controlled conditions in order to obtain non-biased data. For this purpose, translators use a post-editing tool that records the post-editing information, can be easily accessed from any platform and has an easy-to-use interface.

In this paper we present PosEdiOn, a simple standalone tool that allows post-editing of MT output and records information of the post-editing effort (time and keystrokes) at sentence-level. It also includes multiple evaluation scores that the user can interpret easily to assess the post-editing process (such as edit distance, HBLEU and HTER). As it does not depend on any specific CAT tool, it allows the collection of post-editing data in a controlled way. It can be used by professionals to assess the convenience of post-editing a certain MT output and by researchers to study post-editing effort.

In Section 2 we analyze some of the previous tools developed for this purpose. The tool and its mains characteristics are presented in Section 3. In Section 4 we describe the PosEdiOn analyzer, which is used to perform all the analysis, and Section 5 includes the conclusions and future work.

2 Previous Work

In order to analyze the different components of post-editing effort, it becomes paramount to use tools that are able to log time, keyboarding, and other potential indicators of cognitive effort (e.g. gaze data). Currently there is a proliferation of these tools (Vieira, 2013), mainly because each research project has specific requirements.

Some of the tools developed focus more on pro-

ductivity as part of an industry scenario. For example, the Qualitivity[8] plugin can be added to SDL Trados to measure post-editing effort. Alternatively, TAUS developed DQF,[9] which can be used as a standalone benchmark or as an SDL Trados plugin. There has also been EU-funded research to develop open-source workbenches to help improve quantitative measurements of effort (CASMACAT[10] and Matecat[11]).

Other tools collect gaze data, which can be used to study post-editing effort. Tobii Pro Lab is the commercial Windows-oriented eye-tracking software that accompanies Tobii eye trackers. It can calculate a variety of eye-tracking metrics and create visual representations of the data.

Another similar product is Translog-II (Carl, 2012), which is a Windows-oriented program that records user activity data (UAD), that is, all the keystrokes and gaze movements. It is meant specifically for translation process research (TPR) and it offers the possibility of further processing the data with the scripts included in the TPR database of the Centre for Research and Innovation in Translation and Technology (CRITT TPR-DB). Even though these tools collect extensive information, they have specific and demanding settings which are not suitable for all experiments.

Some products devised for a specific experiment are not made available to the public afterwards (Plitt and Masselot, 2010; Green et al., 2013). Other tools focus on obtaining as much information as possible with an easy-to-use product. For example, TransCenter (Denkowski and Lavie, 2012) is an open-source, web-based tool that allows users to carry out PE tasks and logs time and keyboard/mouse activity at a sentence level.

Another tool useful for quantitative investigations specifically designed for post-editing is PET (Aziz et al., 2012). It can also be accessed from any platform, although it is based in Java, which can sometimes be challenging for end-users who need to open the tool from their desktop computers. In addition to recording time and effort indicators at a segment level, PET also allows users to perform evaluation tasks on different customizable scales and criteria. The data file with all the information is saved in xml. However, it does not offer graphics or any other visual information with

---

[4]https://www.memsource.com
[5]https://www.wordfast.net
[6]https://www.across.net
[7]https://omegat.org

[8]https://appstore.sdl.com/language/app/qualitivity/612/
[9]https://www.taus.net/dqf
[10]https://www.casmacat.eu
[11]https://www.matecat.com

the results nor does it include an analyzer which produces multiple automatic metrics.

3 PosEdiOn

PosEdiOn is a post-editing tool developed mainly to collect information on different implicit and explicit effort indicators. It records time and keystrokes, and it also calculates some of the main indirect effort estimation measures (HTER, HBLEU and edit distance). It produces a file with the raw measurements but it also includes a results file with visually structured information that can be easily understood by any user.

It was developed completely in Python3 and it works in any platform which has Python installed. Translators tend to work from home with a great variety of platforms and devices, and do not always have the computer skills to solve any compatibility errors they may encounter with the tools they are about to use. A Windows executable file is also available, which allows to run PosEdiOn without the need of installing the Python interpreter.

3.1 Files and tasks

PosEdiOn is designed to facilitate the distribution of post-editing tasks in an easy and error-free way. The user receives a zip compressed folder with all the needed elements:

- The PosEdiOn program itself, usually as a Python file. Optionally, a Windows executable can be also used. In this case, sending the zipped file by e-mail can cause problems as some mail providers block attachments with executable files. Alternatively, a link to the zipped file can be used to distribute the post-editing tasks.

- The configuration file (*config.yaml*) that provides all the information necessary for the post-editing task. See section 3.3.

- The post-editing task itself as a tab delimited plain text file. The text file is structured in four fields: source text, machine translated text, post-edited text and segment status.

For translation tasks, only the first field is compulsory. In this case, the translator will be presented only with the source text. For post-editing tasks, the first two fields are compulsory and the post-editor will be presented with the source text and the output text from MT. Each time a segment

is validated, this file and the status of the segment are updated.

Once the compressed file is received, it must be unzipped. After executing the program, the task is directly presented. When the translator begins to work on the new task, a new file (*actions.txt* or any other file name stated in the configuration file) is created. All actions including keystrokes, mouse actions and button clicks are stored in this file along with the time it is performed. An example can be seen in the following figure:

```
START 1 2020-02-22 22:28:04.979308
F 1 2020-02-22 22:28:04.996692 Focus_in
M 1 2020-02-22 22:28:08.840216 Mouse.button1
F 1 2020-02-22 22:28:08.840857 Focus_in
K 1 2020-02-22 22:28:09.742533 Key.letter.u 1.6
M 1 2020-02-22 22:28:13.129137 Mouse.button1
OUT 1 2020-02-22 22:28:23.827548
IN 2 2020-02-22 22:28:23.829034
K 2 2020-02-22 22:28:25.018297 Command.CtrlReturn 1.8
OUT 2 2020-02-22 22:28:25.020480
IN 3 2020-02-22 22:28:25.046122
K 3 2020-02-22 22:28:29.602347 Key.navigation 2.5
....
```

Figure 1: File with the actions recorded

All analysis and measurements can be obtained from this actions file. Each line contains several information fields separated by tabs:

- The first field provides information about the kind of action. The actions are: START (task is started); PAUSE (task is paused); EXIT (user exits the application); RESTART (user restarts the task); IN (user enters into a segment); OUT (user exits a segment); K (keyboard action); M (mouse action); C (command action); B (user clicks a button on the application); F (application loses or gains focus); CLEAR (user clears all the content of the translation); RESTORE (user restores the content of the translation).

- The second field indicates the segment number.

- The third field gives the time and date of the event.

- Some actions have a fourth field which provides more detailed information about the event. For example, the key pressed, the text copied or pasted, and so on.

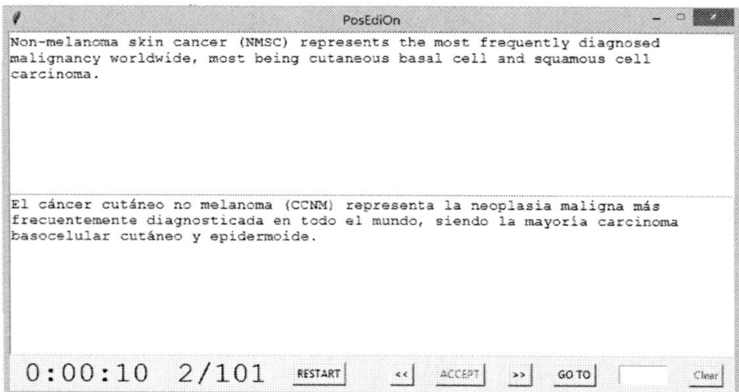

Figure 2: PosEdiOn interface

- Key actions have another field indicating the position in the target text where the key is pressed.

The user can pause and even stop the task and close the PosEdiOn program. Once the task is restarted, the new data will be appended to the existing actions file.

When the task is finished, the folder containing the program should be compressed again and sent back to the person who has to carry out the analysis.

3.2 User Interface

The interface displays the source and target language segments one on top of the other. Figure 2 shows the PosEdiOn interface, where the upper window contains the source segment and the lower window enables the translator to edit the text. Translators can see a wider context using the toolbar buttons located on the lower part, which can be used to move along the whole document.

Each unit is translated/edited one at a time and navigation through the different segments of the document can be achieved in four ways:

- Once the translator has finished post-editing a segment, he needs to validate it using the Ctrl+Enter keys. When this is done, the tool moves automatically to the next segment.

- To validate a segment, the user can also use the ACCEPT button. Once pressed, it also moves to the next segment.

- Using the << or >> buttons in the toolbar located at the lower part of the screen.

- Using the GO TO box, where you can write the number of the segment you want to move to.

Once a segment is accepted, its background turns green. The user can mark a segment as validated (green) using Ctrl+g; or he can change the state to undone (white background) using Ctrl+w. Segments can also be marked as red (Ctrl+r) to indicate a problematic status. Red segments can be reached directly using Ctrl+s.

3.3 Customization

In order to facilitate customization, certain elements can be modified in the *config.yaml* file without having to access the Python script.

As shown in Figure 4, users can customize the following elements:

- The size of the tool's window. Both height and width can be changed.

- Whether the source segment text can be edited or not. The edits introduced in the source segment are not registered by the tool. If the source segments can be edited, users can select and copy fragments of the source text.

- The size and type of font used for the source and target segments.

- Whether or not to show the chronometer.

- The name of the text file containing the task to translate or post-edit.

- The name of the actions file, where all the information containing the user's actions is stored.

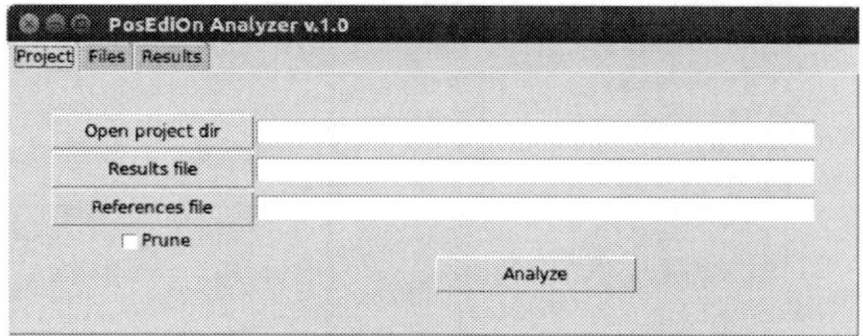

Figure 3: PosEdiOn analyzer interface

- The source and target language codes.

- The set of characters to be considered as symbols or punctuation. It also includes up to three user-defined groups of characters. In the example, a user-defined group called *mathematical* (containing symbols of mathematical operations) is defined.

```
Size:
    height: 10
    width: 80

Behaviour:
    allowEditSL: True

Font:
    font: courier 12

Chronometer:
    status: show
    #possible values: show / hide

Text:
    file: test-Google-1.txt

Actions:
    file: actions.txt

Languages:
    source: eng
    target: spa

Definition:
    symbols: "! @ # $ % ^ & ( ) _ { } [ ]"
    punctuation: ", : ; ."
    nameuserdef1: mathematical
    userdef1: "+ - * / ="
    nameuserdef2: None
    userdef2: None
    nameuserdef3: None
    userdef3: None
```

Figure 4: View of the customizable elements

4 PosEdiOn analyzer

PosEdiOn has a companion program, PosEdiOn analyzer, that performs different analyses on the PosEdiOn project files and offers a wide range of measurements. More specifically, it can calculate:

- Time spent editing each segment.

- HTER (Snover et al., 2006), the TER value comparing the raw MT output with the post-edited segment. A value of HTER is provided for each segment. The value of TER is calculated using tercom.[12]

- HBLEU, a BLEU (Papineni et al., 2002) value obtained comparing the raw MT output with the post-edited segment.

- HEd, an edit distance (Leveshtein distance) value calculated comparing the raw MT output with the post-edited segment.

- Keystrokes for each segment.

If a reference translation file is provided, the following measurements are also calculated:

- TER comparing the raw MT output with the reference translations. A value of TER is calculated for each segment.

- BLEU comparing the raw MT output with the reference translations. A value of BLEU is calculated for each segment.

- Ed, edit distance value calculated comparing the raw MT output with the post-edited segment.

To calculate the normalization of time, HEd (and eventually Ed) and keystrokes values, users can chose three different criteria: segment, token or character. All these values are provided both for each segment and for the whole document. On top of that, the mean and standard deviation are also calculated.

Users can choose to prune results. The pruning is based on a maximum value of normalized time and on a maximum value of normalized

---

[12]https://github.com/jhclark/tercom

segmentID	tokens	time	$time_{norm}$	HTER	HBLEU	HEd	HEd_{norm}	keys	$keys_{norm}$
1	5	38.02	7.6	0.1905	0.6703	18	3.6	18	3.6
2	11	48.81	4.44	0.12	0.6775	6	0.55	238	21.6
3	1	21.31	21.31	0.3333	0	8	8.0	10	10.0
4	29	279.69	9.64	0.2785	0.2318	72	2.48	148	5.1
5	15	72.12	4.81	0.0606	0.7242	2	0.13	50	3.3

Figure 5: Detailed information for each segment

keystrokes. These maximum values are calculated with the mean value and two times the standard deviation. All segments with a normalized time greater than the maximum or with a normalized number of keystrokes greater than the maximum are not taken into account to calculate the pruned values of all scores. The results are provided as numeric values and with a visual presentation of the results following the ideas of the Vis-Eval Metric Viewer (Steele and Specia, 2018).

4.1 Configuration

The configuration of the tool is performed using a Yaml configuration file (*config-analyzer.yaml*) as shown in Figure 6:

```
Filepath:
  path_in: /home/user/directory
  path_out: /home/user/directory
Results_file:
  prefix: results-
  sufix:
  extension: txt
Measures:
  bysegment: True
  normalization: tokens
  #one of segment, token, char
  HTER: True
  HBLEU: True
  HEd: True
  round_time: 2
  round_keys: 2
  round_HTER: 4
  round_HBLEU: 4
  round_HEd: 2
  round_other: 1
  TER: True
  BLEU: True
  ED: True
  round_TER: 4
  round_BLEU: 4
  round_Ed: 2
```

Figure 6: Yaml configuration file

The file paths including the location of the project and the results can be specified. The name of the results file can also be customized by adding a prefix, a suffix and an extension to the name of the project. If no prefix, suffix or extension is required, any of these fields can be left blank. The measurements can also be customized, and users can decide whether or not to show measurements by segment, the normalization criteria, which measurements will be calculated and shown, as well as the number of decimal points. Remember that the values of TER, BLEU and Ed will be calculated and shown only if a reference file is provided, regardless of the values in the configuration file.

4.2 Use of PosEdiOn analyzer

PosEdiOn analyzer can work both in text command and in graphical mode. To start the graphical user interface (shown in Figure 2) the program can be called with no parameters or with the --gui parameter. If no parameters or incomplete parameters are given, the GUI interface starts (see Figure 3). To use it in command line mode, you need to provide a set of parameters that can be checked using the --h option.

Usually we simply set the path for the directory containing the PosEdiOn project to analyze and the name of the output file containing the results:

```
python3 PosEdiOn-analyzer.py -p ./project
-o results.txt
```

If we want the results to be pruned, the option --prune should be used. Eventually we can set the name of a reference file containing the reference translation. The reference file is a text file that includes the reference translation aligned line by line with the text in the project.

PosEdiOn analyzer can also work with a set of files instead of a PosEdiOn project. This can be done using the Files tab, where the user can select the raw MT (option --raw), the post-edited files (--ped) and, optionally, the reference files (--refs) to calculate HTER, HBLEU and HEd values. If the reference files are provided, TER, BLEU and Ed values are also calculated. This allows PosEdiOn analyzer to be used independently from PosEdiOn tool.

4.3 Results

The analyzer can provide the following global results: time normalized, keystrokes normalized,

HTER, HBLEU and HEd. Remember that the normalization factor can be segment, token and character and can be set by the user. For each measurement, the mean and the standard deviation are provided. Pruned values are calculated rejecting the values lower than the mean minus two times the standard deviation or higher than the mean plus two times the standard deviation.

```
------------------------------------------
PRUNING:
------------------------------------------
time norm. mean: 9.19
time norm. std. dev.: 33.97
keys norm. mean: 6.36
keys norm. std. dev.: 28.25
max. norm. time: 77.14
max. norm. keystrokes: 62.86
------------------------------------------
IGNORED SEGMENT 9 norm.
time: 387.3 norm. kestrokes: 192.0
IGNORED SEGMENT 15 norm.
time: 212.24 norm. kestrokes: 301.0
IGNORED SEGMENT 19 norm.
time: 215.58 norm. kestrokes: 219.0
IGNORED SEGMENT 120 norm.
time: 122.75 norm. kestrokes: 3.5
IGNORED SEGMENT 189
norm. time: 67.42 norm. kestrokes: 75.0
------------------------------------------
TIME:
TIME TOTAL 19864.11
TIME NORM. MEAN 90.7
TIME NORM. STD 92.74


------------------------------------------
KEYS:
KEYS TOTAL: 12717
KEYS NORM MEAN 2.9
KEYS NORM STD 4.75
------------------------------------------
HTER:
HTER MEAN 0.1611
HTER STD 0.1172
------------------------------------------
HBLEU:
HBLEU MEAN 0.5303
HBLEU STD 0.2714
------------------------------------------
HEd NORM:
HEd NORM MEAN 1.28
HEd NORM STD 1.19
------------------------------------------
```

Figure 7: View of the results file

If the user has selected the detailed results through the *config-analyzer.yaml* file, the output file includes the following information for each segment (see Figure 5): segment ID, number of tokens or characters, time, time normalized, HTER, HBLEU, HEd, HEd normalized, number of pressed keys, number of pressed keys normalized.

PosEdiOn is able to generate graphics using the data, as the one shown in Figure 8 created from the pruned HTER values. The user can choose which data should be used to generate graphics.

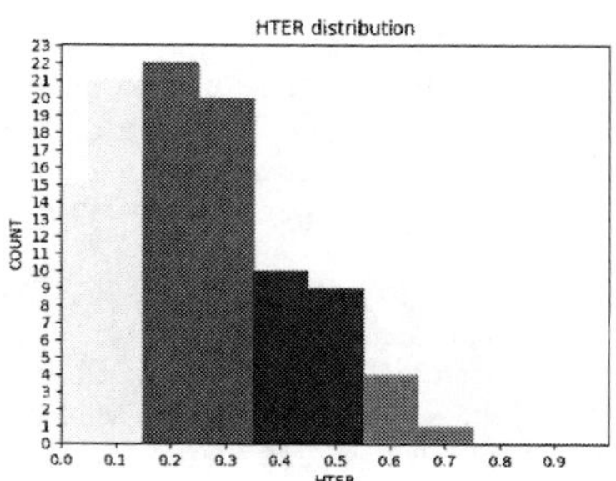

Figure 8: Graphic of the pruned HTER distribution

The results are stored in a tabulated text file, so they can be easily imported into any spreadsheet to perform further calculations.

5 Conclusions and future work

In this paper we have presented PosEdiOn, a tool to perform evaluations of post-editing tasks, and its companion program PosEdiOn analyzer, which allows to user to easily analyze the data obtained with PosEdiOn. Both programs are released under a free license (GNU GPL v3) and can be freely downloaded from the SourceForge page created for the project.[13]

We plan to use this tool in several studies related to post-editing and to implement new features such as the evaluation of fluency and adequacy and an error mark-up tool. Both programs are developed in Python3 and they can be easily adapted and improved. As the data are stored as tabbed text files, they can be easily processed or imported into any spreadsheet program to perform further analysis or data visualization.

Acknowledgements: The training of the neural machine translation systems used to develop and test PosEdiOn has been possible thanks to the NVIDIA GPU grant programme.

References

Allen, Jeffrey H. 2003. Post-editing. In Sommer, Harold, editor, *Computers and Translation: A translator's guide*. John Benjamin, Amsterdam.

[13]https://sourceforge.net/projects/posedion/

Aranberri, Nora, Gorka Labaka, Arantza Ilarraza, and Kepa Sarasola. 2014. Comparison of Post-Editing Productivity between Professional Translators and Lay Users. In *Proceedings of the Third Workshop on Post-Editing Technology and Practice (WPTP - 3)*, Vancouver, Canada.

Aziz, Wilker, Sheila C. M. De Sousa, and Lucia Specia. 2012. PET: a Tool for Post-editing and Assessing Machine Translation. In *Proceedings of the Eight International Conference on Language Resources and Evaluation (LREC'12)*, pages 3982–3987.

Barrault, Loïc, Ondřej Bojar, Marta R. Costa-jussà, Christian Federmann, Mark Fishel, Yvette Graham, Barry Haddow, Matthias Huck, Philipp Koehn, Shervin Malmasi, Christof Monz, Mathias Müller, Santanu Pal, Matt Post, and Marcos Zampieri. 2019. Findings of the 2019 Conference on Machine Translation (WMT19). In *Proceedings of the Fourth Conference on Machine Translation (Volume 2: Shared Task Papers, Day 1)*, pages 1–61, Florence, Italy, August. Association for Computational Linguistics.

Bojar, Ondřej, Rajen Chatterjee, Christian Federmann, Yvette Graham, Barry Haddow, Shujian Huang, Matthias Huck, Lmu Munich, Philipp Koehn, Jhu Edinburgh, Qun Liu, Varvara Logacheva, Mipt Moscow, Christof Monz, Matteo Negri, Matt Post, Johns Hopkins, Raphael Rubino, and Marco Turchi. 2017. Findings of the 2017 Conference on Machine Translation). In *Proceedings of the 2017 Conference on Machine Translation (WMT17))*, volume 2, pages 169–214.

Bojar, Ondřej, Christian Federmann, Mark Fishel, Yvette Graham, Barry Haddow, Matthias Huck, Philipp Koehn, and Christof Monz. 2018. Findings of the 2018 Conference on Machine Translation. In *Proceedings of the 2018 Conference on Machine Translation (WMT18)*, volume 2, pages 272–303.

Carl, Michael. 2012. Translog-II: A Program for Recording User Activity Data for Empirical Reading and Writing Research. In *Proceedings of the Eighth International Conference on Language Resources and Evaluation (LREC'12)*, pages 4108–4112, Istanbul, Turkey, May. European Language Resources Association (ELRA).

Denkowski, M. and A. Lavie. 2012. TransCenter: Web-Based Translation Research Suite. In *AMTA 2012 Workshop on Post-Editing Technology and Practice Demo Session*, May.

Green, Spence, Jeffrey Heer, and Christopher D. Manning. 2013. The Efficacy of Human Post-editing for Language Translation. In *Proceedings of the SIGCHI Conference on Human Factors in Computing Systems - CHI 13*. ACM Press.

Guerberof, Ana. 2009. Productivity and Quality in MT Post-editing. In *Proceedings of Machine Translation Summit XII*.

Koponen, Maarit. 2016. Is Machine Translation Post-editing Worth the Effort? A Survey of Research into Post-editing and Effort. *The Journal of Specialised Translation*, pages 131–148.

Krings, Hans P. 2001. *Repairing texts: Empirical investigations of machine translation post-editing process*. The Kent State University Press, Kent, OH.

Moran, J., D. Lewis, and C. Saam. 2014. Analysis of Post-editing Data: A Productivity Field Test using an Instrumented CAT Tool. In O'Brien, Sharon, Laura Winther Balling, Michael Carl, Michel Simard, and Lucia Specia, editors, *Post-editing of Machine Translation: Processes and Applications*, chapter 6. Cambridge Scholars Publishing, United Kingdom.

Papineni, Kishore, Salim Roukos, Todd Ward, and Wj Zhu. 2002. BLEU: A Method for Automatic Evaluation of Machine Translation. In *ACL '02: Proceedings of the 40th Annual Meeting on Association for Computational Linguistics*, number July, pages 311–318.

Parra Escartín, Carla and Manuel Arcedillo. 2015. A Fuzzier Approach to Machine Translation Evaluation: A Pilot Study on Post-editing Productivity and Automated Metrics in Commercial Settings. In *Proceedings of the ACL 2015 Fourth Workshop on Hybrid Approaches to Translation (HyTra)*, volume 1, pages 40–45.

Plitt, Mirko and François Masselot. 2010. A Productivity Test of Statistical Machine Translation Post-Editing in a Typical Localisation Context. *The Prague Bulletin of Mathematical Linguistics NUMBER*, 93:7–16.

Shterionov, Dimitar, Riccardo Superbo, Pat Nagle, Laura Casanellas, Tony O'Dowd, and Andy Way. 2018. Human versus Automatic Quality Evaluation of NMT and PBSMT. *Machine Translation*, 32(3):217–235, Sep.

Snover, Matthew, Bonnie Dorr, Richard Schwartz, Linnea Micciulla, and John Makhoul. 2006. A Study of Translation Edit Rate with Targeted Human Annotation. In *Proceedings of Association for Machine Translation in the Americas*, pages 223–231, August.

Steele, David and Lucia Specia. 2018. Vis-eval Metric Viewer: A Visualisation Tool for Inspecting and Evaluating Metric Scores of Machine Translation Output. In *Proceedings of the 2018 Conference of the North American Chapter of the Association for Computational Linguistics: Demonstrations*, pages 71–75.

Vieira, Lucas Nunes. 2013. An Evaluation of Tools for Post-editing Research: The Current Picture and Further Needs. In *Proceedings of the MT Summit XIV Workshop on Post-editing Technology and Practice (WPTP-2)*, pages 93–101, Nice.

Quantitative Analysis of Post-Editing Effort Indicators for NMT

Sergi Alvarez
Universitat Pompeu Fabra
salvarezvid@uoc.edu

Antoni Oliver
Universitat Oberta de Catalunya
aoliverg@uoc.edu

Toni Badia
Universitat Pompeu Fabra
toni.badia@upf.edu

Abstract

The recent improvements in machine translation (MT) have boosted the use of post-editing (PE) in the translation industry. A new MT paradigm, neural MT (NMT), is displacing its corpus-based predecessor, statistical machine translation (SMT), in the translation workflows currently implemented because it usually increases the fluency and accuracy of the MT output. However, usual automatic measurements do not always indicate the quality of the MT output and there is still no clear correlation between PE effort and productivity. We present a quantitative analysis of different PE effort indicators for two NMT systems (transformer and seq2seq) for English-Spanish in-domain medical documents. We compare both systems and study the correlation between PE time and other scores. Results show less PE effort for the transformer NMT model and a high correlation between PE time and keystrokes.

1 Introduction

The use of machine translation (MT) systems for the production of drafts that are later post-edited has become a widespread practice in the translation industry. Research has concluded that post-editing of machine translation (PEMT) is usually more efficient than translating from scratch (Plitt and Masselot, 2010; Federico et al., 2012; Green et al., 2013). Thus, it has been included in the translation workflow because it increases productivity

when compared with human translation (Aranberri et al., 2014) and reduces costs (Guerberof, 2009) without having a negative impact on quality (Plitt and Masselot, 2010). Post-editors "edit, modify and/or correct pre-translated text that has been processed by an MT system from a source language into (a) target language(s)" (Allen, 2003, p. 296).

In recent years, neural machine translation (NMT) has produced promising results in terms of quality, for example in WMT 2019 (Barrault et al., 2019). This has increased the interest in this new paradigm for the translation industry, which has begun to substitute its corpus-based predecessor, statistical machine translation (SMT), with new NMT models. It has also boosted the incorporation of PEMT in many translation workflows. In the 2018 Language Industry Survey,[1] 37% of the respondents reported an increase of MT post-editing and an additional 17% indicated that they had started implementing this practice.

Given the improved-quality performance of NMT and its widespread use in industrial scenarios, it is necessary to study the potential this approach can offer to post-editing. One of the main problems is that automatic scores give a general idea of the MT output quality but do not always correlate to post-editing effort (Koponen, 2016; Shterionov et al., 2018). However, many professional translators state that if the quality of the MT output is not good enough, they delete the remaining segments and translate everything from scratch (Parra Escartín and Arcedillo, 2015).

One of the main goals both of industry and research is to establish a correlation between the quality measurements of the MT output and translators' performance. Regarding post-editing ef-

[1] http://fit-europe-rc.org/wp-content/uploads/2019/05/2018-Language-Industry-Survey-Report.pdf?x77803

Martins, Moniz, Fumega, Martins, Batista, Coheur, Parra, Trancoso, Turchi, Bisazza, Moorkens, Guerberof, Nurminen, Marg, Forcada (eds.)
Proceedings of the 22nd Annual Conference of the European Association for Machine Translation, p. 411–420
Lisboa, Portugal, November 2020.

fort, all research uses the three separate but inter-related, dimensions established by Krings (2001): temporal, technical and cognitive. Temporal effort measures the time spent post-editing the MT output. Technical effort makes reference to the insertions and deletions applied by the translator and is usually measured with keystroke analysis, HTER (Snover et al., 2006) or Levenshtein distance (edit distance). Cognitive effort relates to the cognitive processes taking place during post-editing and has been measured by eye-tracking or think-aloud protocols. Krings (2001) claimed that post-editing effort could be determined as a combination of all three dimensions. Even though no current measure includes them all, cognitive effort was found to correlate with technical and temporal PE effort in a study by Moorkens et al. (2015).

In this paper we present a preliminary comparative quantitative analysis of different post-editing effort indicators (technical and temporal) for two NMT systems for English-Spanish in-domain medical documents. First of all, we trained a transformer and seq2seq model and compared them with Google Translate and an SMT engine (check section 4.1 for further detail on the results). As the NMT systems produced better quality results, we used them to translate three English-to-Spanish medical texts. Then, two different translators post-edited each version with PosEdiOn,[2] a post-editing tool developed mainly to collect information on different direct and indirect effort indicators (technical and temporal effort).

In Section 2 we analyse some of the previous work on post-editing effort. We explain the different NMT architectures in Section 3. In Section 4 we detail the MT systems and corpora used. We explain the experimental settings in Section 5 and we present the results in Section 6.

2 Previous Work

NMT is not a new architecture, but it can only be applied once the computational limitations have been solved (Cho et al., 2014; Bahdanau et al., 2015). The promising results obtained in automatic metrics such as BLEU (Papineni et al., 2002) have been paired with excellent scores in human evaluation of NMT (Wu et al., 2016; Junczys-Dowmunt et al., 2016; Isabelle et al., 2017) when compared to SMT, which has been the predominant MT architecture so far.

Once the improvement in quality has been determined, it was necessary to analyse its benefits for post-editing. One of the first complete papers studying the impact of SMT and NMT in post-editing was (Bentivogli et al., 2016). They carried out a small scale study on post-editing NMT and SMT outputs of English to German translated TED talks. They conclude that NMT in general terms decreases the post-editing effort, but degrades faster than SMT with sentence length. One of the main strengths of NMT is reordering of the target sentence.

Toral and Sánchez-Cartagena (2017) increase the initial scope of the study by Bentivogli et al. (2016) by increasing the language combinations and the metrics. One of the main conclusions is an improvement in quality when using NMT, although it is not the same for all the language combinations.

Castilho et al. (2017) report on a comparative analysis of phrase-based SMT (PBSMT) and NMT. They compare four language pairs and different automatic metrics and human evaluation methods. General results show a quality increase for NMT, although it also highlights some of the weaknesses of this new system. It focuses on post-editing and uses the PET interface (Aziz et al., 2012) to compare educational domain outputs from both systems using different metrics. NMT is shown to reduce word order errors and improve fluency. However, even if keystrokes are reduced, temporal PE effort exhibits no significant reduction.

Koponen et al. (2019) present a comparison of PE changes performed on NMT, rule-based MT (RBMT) and SMT output for the English-Finnish language combination. A total of 33 translation students participate in this English-to-Finnish PE experiment. It outlines the strategies participants adopt to post-edit the different outputs, which contributes to the understanding of NMT, RBMT and SMT approaches. It also concludes that PE effort is lower for NMT than for SMT.

In industrial scenarios, Shterionov et al. (2018) show that NMT systems obtain higher rankings by human reviewers than phrased-based SMT in all cases. They highlight that automatic measures such as BLEU, F-measure (Chinchor, 1992) and TER scores do not always correlate with NMT quality. Rather, they usually tend to underestimate it. Even in closely-related languages, which

---

[2] https://sourceforge.net/projects/posedion/

System	BLEU	NIST	WER	DA
Marian S2S	0.3601	7.6142	0.6893	64
Marian Transformer	0.3616	7.3863	0.6334	68
Moses	0.3942	7.8146	0.7386	46
Google Translate	0.3304	7.1197	0.7788	56

Table 1: Automatic and DA evaluation figures

are traditionally post-edited with RBMT systems, NMT systems with worse automatic metrics show better results in human evaluation (Costa-Jussà, 2017; Alvarez et al., 2019).

Regarding PE effort indicators, PE time is one of the most commonly-used elements to study MT quality, although research shows considerable variation among translators (Koponen et al., 2019). HTER is another measure frequently used in the industry due to its theoretical correlation to PE effort (Specia and Farzindar, 2010). However, research has shown it does not always correspond to translators' perception of quality (Koponen, 2012; Graham et al., 2016). In fact, some authors suggest new ways of measuring PE effort taking into account different scores (Scarton et al., 2019) or a multidimensional approach that combines some of the currently existing measures (Aranberri et al., 2014).

Given the undeniable improvements in quality NMT offers for post-editing, we study two different NMT systems and how they affect different indicators of post-editing effort. We also analyse the correlation of PE time with different direct and indirect measures of technical effort (keystrokes, HBLEU, HTER and edit distance). As far as we are aware, there are no studies comparing how two different NMT outputs affect post-editing for English to Spanish in-domain texts.

3 NMT architectures

The basic architecture of NMT models (Cho et al., 2014; Sutskever et al., 2014) consists of an encoder and a decoder. First of all, each word included in the input sentence is introduced as a separate element into the encoder so that it can encode it into an internal fixed-length representation called the context vector. It contains the meaning of the whole sentence. Then, the decoder decodes the context vector and predicts the output sequence.

Instead of encoding the input sequence into a single fixed context vector, attention (Bahdanau et al., 2015) is proposed as a solution to the limitation of the encoder-decoder model encoding the input sequence to one fixed length vector. It develops a context vector that is filtered specifically for each output time step.

Transformer (Vaswani et al., 2017) follows mainly the encoder-decoder model with attention passed from encoder to decoder. It employs a self-attention mechanism that allows the encoder and decoder to account for every word included in the entire input sequence. Transformer proposes to encode each position, apply self-attention in both decoder and encoder, and enhance the idea of self-attention by calculating multi-head attention. This improves performance expanding the model's ability to focus on different positions and gives the attention layer multiple sets of weight matrices. There are no recurrent networks, only a fully connected feed-forward network.

4 MT systems and training corpora

4.1 MT systems

For the experiments, we used Marian[3] (Junczys-Dowmunt et al., 2018) to train two NMT systems. For the first one (1) we used an RNN-based encoder-decoder model with attention mechanism (s2s), layer normalization, tied embeddings, deep encoders of depth 4, residual connectors and LSTM cells. For the second one (2), the transformer, we used the configuration in the example of the Marian documentation,[4] that is, 6 layer encoder and 6 layer decoder, tied embeddings for source, target and output layer, label smoothing, learn rate warm-up and cool down.

To establish a comparison baseline, we trained a Moses model with the same corpus, and also used Google translate. We assessed the resulting engines with standard automatic metrics (see Table 1). The best scores for BLEU were obtained by the Moses engine, even though WER was better for the two NMT systems. This is in line with the

---

[3]https://marian-nmt.github.io
[4]https://github.com/marian-nmt/marian-examples/tree/master/transformer

Corpus	Segments/Entries	Tokens eng	Tokens spa
BMTR	816,544	14,726,693	16,836,428
Medline Abstracts	100,797	1,772,461	1,964,860
UFAL	258,701	3,202,162	3,437,936
Kreshmoi	1,500	28,454	32,158
IBECS	72,168	13,575,418	15,014,299
SciELO	741,407	17,464,256	19,305,165
MedLine	140,479	1,649,869	1,846,374
MSD Manuals	241,336	3,719,933	4,467,906
EMEA	366,769	5,327,963	6,008,543
Portal Clinic	8,797	159,717	169,294
Glossary MeSpEn	125,645	-	-
ICD10-en-es	5,202	-	-
SnowMedCT Denom.	887,492	-	-1
SnowMedCT Def.	4,268	177,861	184,574
Total	**4,430,765**	**66,147,518**	**74,663,550**

Table 2: Size of the corpora and glossaries used to create the corpus to train the MT systems

results of recent research, which has shown certain automatic metrics tend to underestimate NMT systems (Shterionov et al., 2018; Alvarez et al., 2019).

Additionally, we conducted a manual evaluation of a 30-segment sample for the three MT outputs employing monolingual direct assessment (DA) of translation adequacy (Graham and Baldwin, 2014; Graham and Liu, 2016). We used this DA setup because it simplifies the task of translation assessment (usually done as a bilingual task) into a simpler monolingual assessment task. We obtained the results averaging the assessment of two annotators and the NMT systems received higher marks.

As it can be seen in Table 1, DA classified Moses as the worst rated. Therefore, we decided to include only the two NMT systems for the post-editing tasks.

4.2 Corpora

To train the system we have used several publicly available corpora in the English-Spanish pair:

- Biomedical translation repository (BMTR)[5]
- Medline abstracts training data provided by Biomedical Translation Task 2019[6]
- The UFAL Medical Corpus[7] v1.0.
- The Khresmoi development data[8]

- The IBECS[9] (*Spanish Bibliographical Index in Health Sciences*) corpus.
- The SciELO corpus[10]
- The EMEA[11] (*European Medicines Agency*) corpus.

We have also created several corpora from websites with medical content:

- Medline Plus[12]: we have compiled our own corpus from the web and we have combined this with the corpus compiled in MeSpEn.
- MSD Manuals[13] English-Spanish corpus, compiled for this project under permission of the copyright holders.
- Portal Clínic[14] English-Spanish corpus, compiled by us for this project.

We have also used several glossaries and glossary-like databases treating them as corpora. These resources contain a lot of useful terms and expressions in the medical domain. Namely, we have used the English-Spanish glossary from MeSpEn, the 10th revision of the International Statistical Classification of ICD and SnowMedCT. With all the corpora and glossaries we have created an in-domain training corpus of 4,430,765 segments and entries.

[5]https://github.com/biomedical-translation-corpora/corpora
[6]http://www.statmt.org/wmt19/biomedical-translation-task.html
[7]https://ufal.mff.cuni.cz/ufal_medical_corpus
[8]https://lindat.mff.cuni.cz/repository/xmlui/handle/11234/1-2122
[9]http://ibecs.isciii.es
[10]https://sites.google.com/view/felipe-soares/datasets
[11]http://opus.nlpl.eu/EMEA.php
[12]https://medlineplus.gov/
[13]https://www.msdmanuals.com/
[14]https://portal.hospitalclinic.org

	T1 (S2S)		T2 (S2S)		T3 (T)		T4 (T)	
	mean	st. dev.	mean	st. dev.	mean	st. dev.	mean	st. dev.
HTER	0.16	0.12	0.11	0.09	0.17	0.17	0.12	0.17
HBLEU	0.53	0.27	0.65	0.27	0.56	0.29	0.67	0.33
HEd	1.28	1.19	0.84	0.94	1.56	2.04	1.09	2.07
Keys/tok	6.36	28.25	3.38	5.25	7.53	27.62	5.91	25.59
PETpT	9.19	33.97	4.61	8.56	4.57	12.22	3.03	8.69

Table 3: PE-based metrics (mean and standard deviation) for the task

	S2S NMT		Transf. NMT	
	mean	st. dev.	mean	st. dev.
HTER	0.13	0.10	**0.11**	0.09
HBLEU	0.59	0.27	**0.65**	0.27
HEd	1.06	1.06	**0.84**	0.94
Keys/tok	4.87	16.75	**3.38**	5.25
PETpT	6.90	21.26	**4.61**	8.56

Table 4: Total PE-based metrics for each NMT model

In Table 2 the size of all corpora and glossaries used for training the MT systems is shown. Figures are calculated eliminating all the repeated source segment-target segment pairs in the corpora.

5 Experiment

We used the two NMT systems (transformer and s2s) trained with the corpora described above to translate from English into Spanish three texts (1468, 631 and 2247 words respectively) from the medical domain.

Four professional translators with at least one year of post-editing experience carried out the task: two of them post-edited the s2s output (T1 and T2) and the other two, the transformer output (T3 and T4). They were asked to produce publishable quality translations. As we wanted to reduce the external variables as much as possible, they all used PosEdiOn[15], a computer-assisted translation tool specifically designed for assessing post-editing effort, which logs both post-editing time and edits (keystrokes, insertions and deletions, that is, technical effort). The main characteristics of the post-editing tool were also explained to them before starting the task.

In order to avoid any bias, translators never post-edited the same text twice. However, they were told that an NMT system was used to produce the output. They received previous information on

the tool and a three day period to test it before doing the task. They were paid their usual rate and had a two-week deadline. Two of them expressed concerns about the tool, as they preferred to work with their usual tools. However, they did not think it would affect the final quality of their job or their usual working speed. While post-editing, they could search for all the required information in order to produce the final translation. They could also pause the post-editing task whenever they wanted.

6 Results

6.1 PE effort indicators

Once translators finished post-editing, we calculated the following task-specific (PE based) metrics (showed in Table 3):

- **PETpT**, PE time in seconds normalised by the length of the target segment in tokens.
- **HTER**, the TER value comparing the raw MT output with the post-edited segment.
- **HBLEU**, the BLEU score obtained by comparing the raw MT output with the post-edited segment.
- **HEd**, an edit distance value (Levenshtein distance) calculated comparing the raw MT output with the post-edited segment.
- **Keystrokes** normalized by the number of tokens.

[15]https://sourceforge.net/projects/posedion/

Post-editor	Unmodified seg.
T1 (S2S)	22
T2 (S2S)	31
T3 (T)	19
T4 (T)	58

Table 5: Unmodified segments after post-editing

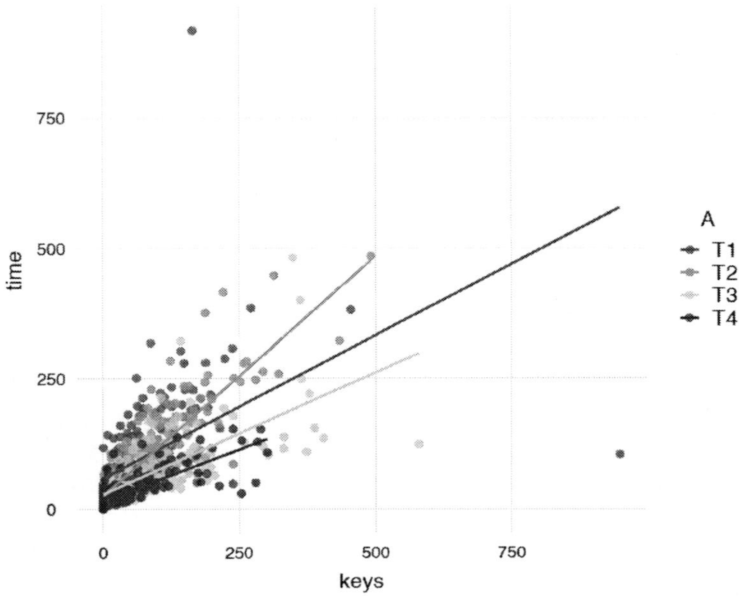

Figure 1: Scatter plot of keystrokes and time for all of the translators

In order to avoid the maximum number of outliers, we did not include those segments in which (normalized) time or (normalized) keystrokes doubled the mean plus the standard deviation of the total time or number of keystrokes. As usually happens in these types of tasks, post-editing effort indicators show a considerable variation among different translators. For the seg2seg model, translators showed a difference of 4.58 PETpT between them. This difference was reduced to 1.54 in the case of the transformer model. However, if we check the total figures for each of the systems (see Table 4), post-editing time is clearly reduced for the transformer model, as well as all the other scores.

We also used the distribution-agnostic Kolmogorov–Smirnov test to compare the distribution of PETpT for the two translators of each NMT model. We found there was no clear distribution (considering $p < 0.05$). This would seem to indicate the need to increase the number of translators for any given post-editing test to obtain a more representative mean.

Another interesting figure to understand PE effort is the number of unmodified segments. Even though that does not mean those segments imply no PE effort, it could give an indication of MT output. Table 5 shows the number of unmodified segments per translators from a total of 224 segments. There is not a clear tendency for any MT system, but rather a preference corresponding to the individual translator, especially T4, who didn't modify a high number of segments, which correlates to the low PE time recorded.

We also checked PETpT related to segment length, as research has shown longer segments tend to imply higher PE effort (Bentivogli et al., 2016). We studied segments with more than 35 tokens to see if PETpT or any other PE effort indicator increased. We could find no statistically sig-

	T1 (S2S)	T2 (S2S)	T3 (T)	T4 (T)	ALL
HTER	0.309*	0.545*	0.418*	0.00705*	0.49*
HBLEU	-0.072	-0.209	-0.148	-0.370*	-0.21*
HEd	0.043*	0.706	0.0770*	0.809*	0.66
Keys	**0.823***	**0.868***	**0.824***	**0.822***	**0.82***

Table 6: Spearman's correlation with time as a gold standard for different effort indicators (*p<0.001)

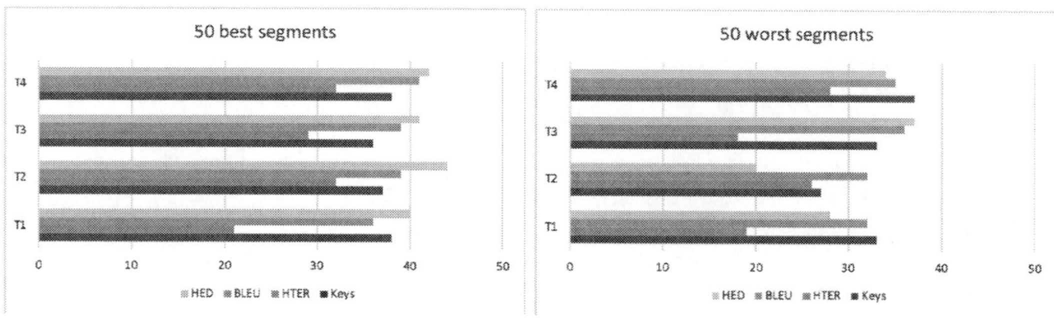

Figure 2: Correlation for best and worst segments

nificant evidence linking segment length to translators' effort in our experiments. This could indicate newer NMT models do not always reduce MT quality in longer segments.

Our results with a limited number of translators confirm previous studies (Castilho et al., 2017; Shterionov et al., 2018; Alvarez et al., 2019) and further, more extensive experimentation is needed in order to obtain meaningful indicators of MT output quality.

6.2 Correlation between scores

Once we established the overall results per each model, we tried to identify which metric produced scores that were closest to the total time spent per segment. We calculated Spearman's correlation coefficient between the total amount of time and all other metrics.

As can be seen in Table 6, the best overall correlation is found with the number of keys (see Figure 1) for all translators as well as for the total, followed by the calculated edit distance. Most of the results obtained show a statistically significant correlation, especially those figures relating to the number of keystrokes (*p<0.001).

These results are in line with the conclusions reported by previous work (Graham et al., 2016; Scarton et al., 2019) that found no clear correlation between temporal effort and the most frequent metrics, even though the number of keystrokes was the metric more closely related.

6.3 Tails distribution

There was a lack of correlation between the distribution of PE time among translators, and between this indicator and the others. We wanted to take a closer look at the best and worse segments to analyse if the correlation improved. We counted the number of common segments between the 50 best and worst time segments and all other metrics calculated.

As can be seen in Figure 2, there is a better correlation for the segments in which less time was spent. Furthermore, the edit distance shows the best correlation in these cases. For the segments with the higher time recorded, correlation is notably reduced in all cases and the edit distance and the number of keystrokes show a higher correlation.

7 Concluding remarks

There is a need for reliable metrics to evaluate MT quality in order to produce outputs which translators can post-edit without too much effort. Our experiments have shown that no single PE indicator can provide all the information necessary to assess the quality of the MT output. PE time provides a useful measure, even though it does not always correspond with other PE metrics and includes a great variation among translators. The only score that seems directly related to temporal effort are keystrokes (technical effort), but not

HTER or HBLEU.

In industrial scenarios, the quality of a certain MT output is usually linked to PE time. The results of our experiments suggest that the analysis of temporal effort can indicate the quality of the MT output, but we believe a multidimensional approach that includes different effort indicators would be a safer path to assess to convenience of post-editing a certain MT output.

Our future work will study further indicators of MT quality for post-editing in depth, mainly the characterization of source text to assess PE effort.

Acknowledgements: This work was supported by Universitat Pompeu Fabra (grant COMPLE-MENTA 2019).

The training of the neural machine translation systems has been possible thanks to the NVIDIA GPU grant programme.

References

Allen, Jeffrey H. 2003. Post-editing. In Sommer, Harold, editor, *Computers and Translation: A translator's guide*, pages 297–317. John Benjamin, Amsterdam.

Alvarez, Sergi, Antoni Oliver, and Toni Badia. 2019. Does NMT Make a Difference when Post-editing Closely Related Languages? The Case of Spanish-Catalan. In *Proceedings of Machine Translation Summit XVII Volume 2: Translator, Project and User Tracks*, pages 49–56, Dublin, Ireland, August. European Association for Machine Translation.

Aranberri, Nora, Gorka Labaka, Arantza Ilarraza, and Kepa Sarasola. 2014. Comparison of Post-Editing Productivity between Professional Translators and Lay Users. In *Proceedings of the Third Workshop on Post-Editing Technology and Practice (WPTP - 3)*, Vancouver, Canada.

Aziz, Wilker, Sheila C. M. De Sousa, and Lucia Specia. 2012. PET: A Tool for Post-editing and Assessing Machine Translation. In *Proceedings of the Eight International Conference on Language Resources and Evaluation (LREC'12)*, pages 3982–3987.

Bahdanau, Dzmitry, Kyunghyun Cho, and Yoshua Bengio. 2015. Neural Machine Translation by Jointly Learning to Align and Translate. In Bengio, Yoshua and Yann LeCun, editors, *3rd International Conference on Learning Representations, ICLR 2015, San Diego, CA, USA, May 7-9, 2015, Conference Track Proceedings*.

Barrault, Loïc, Ondřej Bojar, Marta R. Costa-jussà, Christian Federmann, Mark Fishel, Yvette Graham, Barry Haddow, Matthias Huck, Philipp Koehn, Shervin Malmasi, Christof Monz, Mathias Müller, Santanu Pal, Matt Post, and Marcos Zampieri. 2019. Findings of the 2019 Conference on Machine Translation (WMT19). In *Proceedings of the Fourth Conference on Machine Translation (Volume 2: Shared Task Papers, Day 1)*, pages 1–61, Florence, Italy, August. Association for Computational Linguistics.

Bentivogli, Luisa, Arianna Bisazza, Mauro Cettolo, and Marcello Federico. 2016. Neural versus Phrase-Based Machine Translation Quality: a Case Study. In *Proceedings of the 2016 Conference on Empirical Methods in Natural Language Processing*, pages 257–267. Association for Computational Linguistics.

Castilho, Sheila, Joss Moorkens, Federico Gaspari, Rico Sennrich, Vilelmini Sosoni, Yota Georgakopoulou, Pintu Lohar, Andy Way, Antonio Miceli Barone, and Maria Gialama. 2017. A Comparative Quality Evaluation of PBSMT and NMT using Professional Translators. In *Proceedings of MT Summit XVI, vol.1: Research Track*, pages 116–131, 9.

Chinchor, Nancy. 1992. MUC-4 Evaluation Metrics. In *Proceedings of the Fourth Message Understanding Conference*, pages 22–29.

Cho, Kyunghyun, Bart van Merriënboer, Dzmitry Bahdanau, and Yoshua Bengio. 2014. On the Properties of Neural Machine Translation: Encoder-Decoder Approaches. In *Proceedings of SSST-8, Eighth Workshop on Syntax, Semantics and Structure in Statistical Translation*, Doha, Qatar. Association for Computational Linguistics.

Costa-Jussà, Marta R. 2017. Why Catalan-Spanish Neural Machine Translation? Analysis, Comparison and Combination with Standard Rule and Phrase-based Technologies. *Proceedings of the Fourth Workshop on NLP for Similar Languages, Varieties and Dialects (VarDial)*, pages 55–62.

Federico, M., A. Catttelan, and M. Trombetti. 2012. Measuring User Productivity in Machine Translation Enhanced Computer Assisted Translation. In *Proceedings of the 10th Conference of the AMTA*, pages 44–56. AMTA.

Graham, Yvette and Timothy Baldwin. 2014. Testing for Significance of Increased Correlation with Human Judgment. In *Proceedings of the 2014 Conference on Empirical Methods in Natural Language Processing (EMNLP)*, pages 172–176, Doha, Qatar, October. Association for Computational Linguistics.

Graham, Yvette and Qun Liu. 2016. Achieving Accurate Conclusions in Evaluation of Automatic Machine Translation Metrics. In *Proceedings of the 15th Annual Conference of the North American Chapter of the Association for Computational Linguistics: Human Language Technologies*, San Diego, CA. Association for Computational Linguistics.

Graham, Yvette, Timothy Baldwin, Meghan Dowling, Maria Eskevich, Teresa Lynn, and Lamia Tounsi. 2016. Is all that Glitters in Machine Translation Quality Estimation really Gold? In *Proceedings of COLING 2016, the 26th International Conference on Computational Linguistics: Technical Papers*, pages 3124–3134, Osaka, Japan, December. The COLING 2016 Organizing Committee.

Green, Spence, Jeffrey Heer, and Christopher D. Manning. 2013. The Efficacy of Human Post-editing for Language Translation. In *Proceedings of the SIGCHI Conference on Human Factors in Computing Systems - CHI 13*. ACM Press.

Guerberof, Ana. 2009. Productivity and Quality in MT Post-editing. In *Proceedings of MT Summit XII*, pages 8–14. Association of Machine Translation.

Isabelle, Pierre, Colin Cherry, and George F. Foster. 2017. A Challenge Set Approach to Evaluating Machine Translation. *CoRR*, abs/1704.07431.

Junczys-Dowmunt, Marcin, Tomasz Dwojak, and Hieu Hoang. 2016. Is Neural Machine Translation Ready for Deployment? A Case Study on 30 Translation Directions. *CoRR*, abs/1610.01108.

Junczys-Dowmunt, Marcin, Roman Grundkiewicz, Tomasz Dwojak, Hieu Hoang, Kenneth Heafield, Tom Neckermann, Frank Seide, Ulrich Germann, Alham Fikri Aji, Nikolay Bogoychev, André F. T. Martins, and Alexandra Birch. 2018. Marian: Fast Neural Machine Translation in C++. *Proceedings of ACL 2018, System Demonstrations*, pages 116–121, July.

Koponen, Maarit, Leena Salmi, and Markku Nikulin. 2019. A Product and Process Analysis of Post-editor Corrections on Neural, Statistical and Rule-based Machine Translation Output. *Machine Translation*, (33, pages 61–90).

Koponen, Maarit. 2012. Comparing Human Perceptions of Post-editing Effort with Post-editing Operations. *Proceedings of the Seventh Workshop on Statistical Machine Translation*, pages 181–190.

Koponen, Maarit. 2016. Is Machine Translation Post-editing Worth the Effort? A Survey of Research into Post-editing and Effort. *The Journal of Specialised Translation*, pages 131–148.

Moorkens, Joss, Sharon O 'brien, Igor A L Da Silva, Norma B De, Lima Fonseca, Fabio Alves, and Norma B De Lima Fonseca. 2015. Correlations of perceived post-editing effort with measurements of actual effort. *Machine Translation*, 29:267–284.

Papineni, Kishore, Salim Roukos, Todd Ward, and Wj Zhu. 2002. BLEU: A Method for Automatic Evaluation of Machine Translation. Number July, pages 311–318.

Parra Escartín, Carla and Manuel Arcedillo. 2015. A Fuzzier Approach to Machine Translation Evaluation: A Pilot Study on Post-editing Productivity and Automated Metrics in Commercial Settings. *Proceedings of the ACL 2015 Fourth Workshop on Hybrid Approaches to Translation (HyTra)*, 1(2010):40–45.

Plitt, Mirko and François Masselot. 2010. A Productivity Test of Statistical Machine Translation Post-Editing in a Typical Localisation Context. *The Prague Bulletin of Mathematical Linguistics NUMBER*, 93:7–16.

Scarton, Carolina, Mikel L. Forcada, Miquel Esplà-Gomis, and Lucia Specia. 2019. Estimating Post-editing Effort: A Study on Human Judgements, Task-based and Reference-based Metrics of MT Quality. In *Proceedings of IWSLT 2019*, volume abs/1910.06204, Hong Kong, China.

Shterionov, Dimitar, Riccardo Superbo, Pat Nagle, Laura Casanellas, Tony O'Dowd, and Andy Way. 2018. Human versus Automatic Quality Evaluation of NMT and PBSMT. *Machine Translation*, 32(3):217–235, Septembre.

Snover, Matthew, Bonnie Dorr, Richard Schwartz, Linnea Micciulla, and John Makhoul. 2006. A Study of Translation Edit Rate with Targeted Human Annotation. *Proceedings of Association for Machine Translation in the Americas*, (August):223–231.

Specia, Lucia and Atefeh Farzindar. 2010. Estimating Machine Translation Post-editing Effort with HTER. *AMTA-2010 Workshop Bringing MT to the User: MT Research and the Translation Industry*, page 33–41.

Sutskever, Ilya, Oriol Vinyals, and Quoc V Le. 2014. Sequence to Sequence Learning with Neural Networks. In Ghahramani, Z., M. Welling, C. Cortes, N. D. Lawrence, and K. Q. Weinberger, editors, *Advances in Neural Information Processing Systems 27*, pages 3104–3112. Curran Associates, Inc.

Toral, Antonio and Víctor M. Sánchez-Cartagena. 2017. A Multifaceted Evaluation of Neural versus Phrase-Based Machine Translation for 9 Language Directions. In *Proceedings of the 15th Conference of the European Chapter of the Association for Computational Linguistics*, volume 1, Long Papers, pages 1063–1073, East Stroudsburg. Association for Computational Linguistics (ACL).

Vaswani, Ashish, Noam Shazeer, Niki Parmar, Jakob Uszkoreit, Llion Jones, Aidan N. Gomez, Lukasz Kaiser, and Illia Polosukhin. 2017. Attention is all you need. In *Advances in Neural Information Processing Systems 30 (NIPS)*.

Wu, Yonghui, Mike Schuster, Zhifeng Chen, Quoc V. Le, Mohammad Norouzi, Wolfgang Macherey, Maxim Krikun, Yuan Cao, Qin Gao, Klaus Macherey, Jeff Klingner, Apurva Shah, Melvin Johnson, Xiaobing Liu, Lukasz Kaiser, Stephan Gouws,

Yoshikiyo Kato, Taku Kudo, Hideto Kazawa, Keith Stevens, George Kurian, Nishant Patil, Wei Wang, Cliff Young, Jason Smith, Jason Riesa, Alex Rudnick, Oriol Vinyals, Gregory S. Corrado, Macduff Hughes, and Jeffrey Dean. 2016. Google's Neural Machine Translation System: Bridging the Gap between Human and Machine Translation. *ArXiv*, abs/1609.08144.

Comparing Post-editing based on Four Editing Actions against Translating with an Auto-Complete Feature

Félix do Carmo
Centre for Translation Studies
University of Surrey
f.docarmo@surrey.ac.uk

Abstract

This article describes the results of a workshop in which 50 translators tested two experimental translation interfaces, as part of a project which aimed at studying the details of editing work. In this work, editing is defined as a selection of four actions: deleting, inserting, moving and replacing words. Four texts, machine-translated from English into European Portuguese, were post-edited in four different sessions in which each translator swapped between texts and two work modes. One of the work modes involved a typical auto-complete feature, and the other was based on the four actions. The participants answered surveys before, during and after the workshop. A descriptive analysis of the answers to the surveys and of the logs recorded during the experiments was performed. The four editing actions mode is shown to be more intrusive, but to allow for more planned decisions: although they take more time in this mode, translators hesitate less and make fewer edits. The article shows the usefulness of the approach for research on the editing task.

1 Introduction

1.1 Purpose

This article describes an experiment that is based on a theoretical framework in which editing is defined as being composed of four actions (delete, insert, move and replace). This framework also includes the definition of an editing threshold, which is a rate above which one may consider that the translator is no longer editing but translating the segment. The editing threshold was experimentally set at 25% for the project, as an inversion of the 75% fuzzy match initial band used in the translation industry. (do Carmo 2017)

The motivation for the experiment was to investigate how translators edited machine translation (MT) output, with and without consideration for the four editing actions.

At the beginning of the project, there was the expectation that this could contribute to the development of smart editing tools, which could learn patterns of editing based on these four actions, and then use this learned knowledge to support translators' editing work. If such systems employed features like Online Learning (Ortiz-Martínez et al. 2016) to record and reuse, for example, the word substitutions that are required, each edit could be made more efficiently. Such a system would show the translator good candidates for deletion, suggest words that might be missing from the MT output and indicate possible new positions for words being moved. These features are particularly useful in texts with high internal repetition, and when the output only requires minor editing.

After an analysis of the scope of the project, it was decided to focus on testing forms of interface for supporting editing work. The practical part was outlined as the comparison of an experimental interface based on the four editing actions, against an interface based on an auto-complete feature. This comparison of a novel interface against the main form of support offered by interactive translation tools to help translators while they edit (see below section 1.2) would create the opportunity to study in detail effects of different modes of work.

The specific research objectives for the experiment were two: (i) to collect opinions and effects of this description of editing, in a qualitative and quantitative study with professional translators and (ii) to compare two modes of editing, and measure the effects on editing practices of these two modes. The research questions explored

Martins, Moniz, Fumega, Martins, Batista, Coheur, Parra, Trancoso, Turchi, Bisazza, Moorkens, Guerberof, Nurminen, Marg, Forcada (eds.)
Proceedings of the 22nd Annual Conference of the European Association for Machine Translation, p. 421–430
Lisboa, Portugal, November 2020.

during the workshop are presented in section 3.4, together with the variables that were measured.

1.2 Related research

In the localisation industry, professional translators not only translate texts from one language to another and revise translated texts, but they also regularly post-edit MT content. Several studies have highlighted the differences between the processes of translation, revision and post-editing (PE) (Alves and Vale 2011; Carl, Dragsted, and Jakobsen 2011; Carl et al. 2016).

PE is a demanding process, which requires that the translator pays a lot of attention to details, while using diverse resources and repeating very minute technical actions. Krings (2001) first described the three dimensions for which researchers must collect data to study the effort required by PE: temporal, technical and cognitive. While the most important dimension for the improvement of the processes is the cognitive effort, this is the hardest dimension to collect data from.

Despite a reasonable body of research, and research on the development of tools that integrate MT features to minimise translation effort (Green et al. 2014; Forcada and Sánchez-Martínez 2015), the computer aided-translation (CAT) tools used by professional translators are mostly the same for the three processes, and are oriented towards the use of translation memory (TM) features rather than for MT (Moorkens and O'Brien 2017).

In research on interactive translation, there are two main paradigms to feed MT content into translation tools: by presenting a full MT suggestion, which must then be edited by the translators, or by presenting suggestions to complete the translation, as it is typed. The first model is known as typical PE, and the second as Interactive Machine Translation (IMT) (Green et al. 2014; Sanchis-Trilles et al. 2014; Forcada and Sánchez-Martínez 2015; Ortiz-Martínez 2016).

. Current interactive tools, like CasMaCat (Alabau et al. 2013) and Lilt (Green et al. 2014) offer a type of support which is based on IMT: translators type their translation from beginning to end and there is an auto-complete feature that suggests how to finish the word or sentence the translator is typing. (The distinction between PE and IMT concerns the features that form the interaction and interface with the user, at the segment level. Other adaptive features are not used for this distinction.) It is not clear yet whether this type of IMT feature will be fully adopted by translators, as it has been shown that it implies a big cognitive interference with the translation effort (Alabau et al. 2016).

Translation process research collects data from keylogs at the character-level, producing a detailed output that is hard to interpret. Levels of recursiveness, non-linearity in the writing actions, the fact that several edits may not be linked to specific words, cutting and pasting or moving words, all these factors increase the difficulty (Carl and Jakobsen 2009; Alves and Hurtado Albir 2010).

Extensive research has been done using translation edit rate (TER) (Snover et al. 2006) and other edit distances as identifiers of the editing operations that are required to transform one version of a text into another. Implementations of TER start by aligning words in source and target segments, and then estimate the least number of insertions, deletions and replacements that are necessary for the second version generation. Word movements are calculated afterwards. This means that TER is calculated from finished products, not during the process. As demonstrated in do Carmo (2017), TER is quite accurate at identifying insertions, deletions and replacements when only one word is edited in a segment, but this metric is not so accurate when editing involves more actions. Movements of words are very difficult to estimate accurately, especially at the end of a segment.

2 The experiment setting

This section describes the set-up of a three-hour workshop with 50 translators, which was performed in January 2017. This included a two-hour presentation and discussion on the conceptual framework of this project, followed by a one-hour hands-on experiment. This article summarises the experiment, which is described in detail in do Carmo (2017).

The setup of the experiment was exploratory. Our main purpose was to test a novel interface in as many scenarios as possible in a short time, and to collect translators' impressions on it. In this sense, this could be framed as an extensive pilot test, even though there were no plans for a proper test to the novel interface.

The use of edit distances to estimate operations performed by translators was one of the dimensions being tested during the experiments. As we wanted to collect data on the actual actions (the words that were deleted, inserted and replaced, besides those that were moved, together with a record of all the positions these edits were made on), we would need an interface that recorded those actions while they were being performed, not post-process estimations as edit distances are. It was also clear that this new interface would ask for conscious decisions from translators on using only the four actions.

The tool developed during the study had usability issues, but it allowed us to explicitly ask translators to consider which words to delete, insert, move or replace, before performing any of those actions. This allowed us to gather information which would not be possible from an unconstrained work environment, in which translators could, for example, delete a whole MT suggestion, and write the whole translation, eventually retyping words already in the suggestion.

2.1 Translation tool and interfaces

The translation tool used in the experiment was HandyCAT (Hokamp and Liu 2015), in a specific implementation that Chris Hokamp agreed to create for this workshop.[2] This version included two modes of interaction:

Auto-complete (AC mode): Figure 1 - this is an implementation of the technical principles of predictive writing, used in IMT. Users type their translations and get suggestions on how to complete each word.

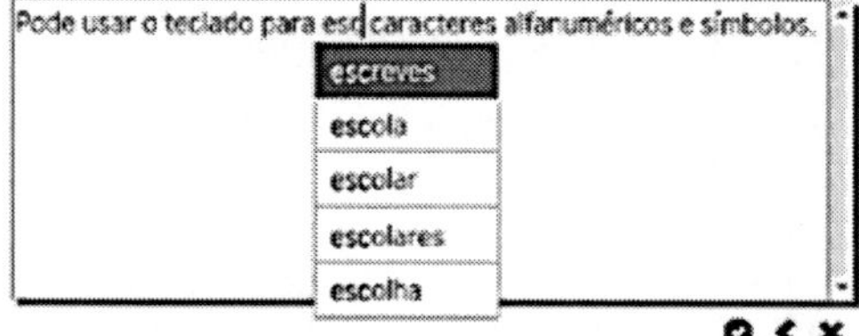

Figure 1 – Auto-complete mode (AC mode).

Post-editor (PE mode): Figure 2 - this mode constrained the users to select a token and then choose from a contextual menu one of the four editing actions to apply to that token.

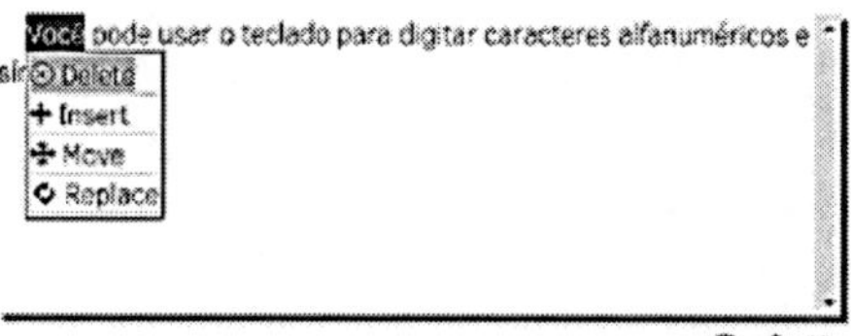

Figure 2 – Post-editor mode (PE mode).

2.2 Workshop and data collection

After a presentation and a discussion on the theoretical foundations of the project, translators received an explanation of the work sessions that they were going to perform and their purpose. In this explanation, it was mentioned that there would be no evaluations of the quality of the translations they produced, because we were only interested in collecting data on *how* they used the two interfaces.

During the hands-on sessions, translators edited four texts, from English into European Portuguese. Each text was extracted from a different technical document, aiming at a diversified experience from the participants. One of the texts was extracted from an electronic device instruction guide (text A), another from a marketing questionnaire (text B), the third text (C) was part of a product catalogue, and the last one (text D) was the initial paralegal text of a technical manual. The texts had been pre-translated using MateCAT (Federico et al. 2014).

Text A was used for familiarisation with both working modes (AC and PE), and there was no data collection from this stage. Then, users edited the MT outputs of the other 3 texts, in a random distribution, in four different sessions. In the first session, each translator edited one of the three available texts (B, C or D) in AC mode for 10 minutes. Next, they edited one of the other texts in PE mode for 15 minutes, so to allow for a richer experience with a method that was new for all users. After these two sessions, they performed two 5-minute sessions with the third text, first in AC mode and then in PE mode. All 50 translators edited each of the 3 texts, but not in the same mode, nor in the same sequence.

The length of each text varied, between 500 and 970 words, but there was no requirement to finish editing any of the texts, since all sessions were time-limited. Thus, we released each translator from concerns about speed.

We analysed data that corresponded to a total of 26 hours of work, during which 8565 segments were edited by the 50 translators.

Before, during, and after the workshop, participants filled in questionnaires, to identify their opinions on the conceptual structure of the project, and on the use of the two modes of interaction in a translation tool (the results of these 150 questionnaires are presented in section 3). Besides,

---

[2] This version of HandyCat is available from https://github.com/chrishokamp/handycat/releases/tag/porto_v0.1.

HandyCAT collected activity logs, which were also used in the data analysis (section 4). To collect edit scores, we used an add-on of SDL Trados Studio called Post-Edit Compare, or PEC (Hartnett and SDL Community 2014).

3 Data analysis

3.1 Characteristics of the participants

The selection of participants in the workshop was non-probabilistic and purposive (Trochim 2006), as the aim was to get specialised feedback. Most participants in the workshop were freelancers (58%) or they worked in translation agencies (36%). There was a fair distribution between experience ranges, of 1 year to 20 or more years. Most users were very comfortable with technology, and a fair majority (68%) preferred to type over the source text than to write the translation in an empty window. 90% of the users worked with suggestions from CAT tools, and most also used predictive writing features and/or support by MT systems. 75% of the users had some or a lot of experience in doing PE. Finally, a big proportion of users (66%) considered that the new technologies will not have a negative impact on the profession.

3.2 Receptivity to the proposal

Although the workshop was a pilot test on concepts that were still in development, most participants (80%) accepted that the concepts discussed in the workshop were useful for clarifying the tasks that they perform, and a large majority (90%) said at the end that the workshop had allowed them to rethink what they do when they post-edit.

3.3 Specialised answers

Data collected from activity logs confirmed most of the intuitive answers these specialised users gave in the questionnaires. For example, the texts that, after a quick reading, were classified as more complex and which showed a lower MT quality were the ones that later required the highest TER scores. Users also identified the mode in which they edited more (AC mode), and the actions they used the most (replace, followed by delete) – see section 4.5.

They classified AC mode as faster, easier to work with and more adjusted to translation work; they classified PE mode as slower, more intrusive, and more adapted to PE work, namely when only small changes were necessary. Another positive outcome was visible after the qualitative answers were codified and analysed. Translators considered, for example, that PE mode forced them to think and plan the changes that were required, and to focus on priority issues. They also said that their view on PE had changed, as an effect of the work they had done at the workshop.

3.4 Data variables in the activity logs

The input variables, the main questions related to them, and the sections in which these are presented are shown below:

- **Texts:** Did text features influence the editing practices? (Section 4.1)
- **Segments:** Did longer or shorter segments affect the results? (Section 4.2)
- **Users:** Is it possible to distinguish users according to numbers of edits and speed? (Section 4.3)
- **Modes:** Did work modes affect how translators edited? (Section 4.4)
- **Actions:** Which differences can be observed in the way users applied the different editing actions? (Section 4.5).

The main dependent variables in the study were:

- **Edit scores:** number of edits per segment and TER scores (number of edits divided by segment length).
- **Speed:** number of seconds per edit.

Section 4.6 focuses on the results obtained by looking for the most influential factors for the results shown by the two dependent variables.

4 Discussion of results

4.1 Text variable

With only 3 texts being used, and for a short time, it would not be possible to extract strong evidences that different texts were associated with different editing practices. However, interesting patterns started emerging at this level. The main two results at the level of texts were the edit scores, and the related editing threshold.

	AC	*PE*	*Total*
B - Questionnaire	17%	18%	**18%**
C - Catalogue	34%	29%	**31%**
D - Manual	29%	24%	**26%**
Total average	**26%**	**24%**	**25%**

Table 1 – Average TER per text and mode.

Text B (a marketing questionnaire) had the lowest TER score, Text C (a catalogue of office supplies) the highest TER score, and Text D (the initial instructions of a manual) presented an intermediate edit score. Across all texts, the average editing score is 25% (at our proposed editing threshold). This result might be read as a global indicator of the high quality of the MT output, since it only required that circa 25% of the words were edited. However, this hid a more complex situation, since text C in AC mode required editing to more than 33% of its words. The features of this text (a list of short descriptions of products) might justify this, but the study was not planned to collect enough contrastive data on text types to make such a claim.

4.2 Segment variable

Segments allowed for a more detailed analysis of the values collected at text level, but this presented its own challenges. The main research question at this level was whether longer or shorter segments had affected the results, but it was not possible to identify a meaningful correlation between segment length and editing scores or speed. This is related to the dependence of segment level to text type. In fact, the text with the longest segments was also the text with the shortest segments (B – Questionnaire). This was also the text in which more segments were edited, almost double than those for text C, the catalogue. Apart from this, the fact that users could spend a long time in a short segment and make only one edit, skewed the influence of those data points in all estimates related to segments.

At segment level, it was interesting to analyse edit scores, especially at the extremes (segments with zero edits and high number of edits in specific segments). Globally, 34% of the segments required editing above the 25% editing threshold, but in text C – Catalogue 53% of the segments were above the threshold. Figure 3 shows the spread of scores in all segments, with the percentage of edited segments per text and mode in the vertical axis, and the distribution in TER ranges in the horizontal axis.

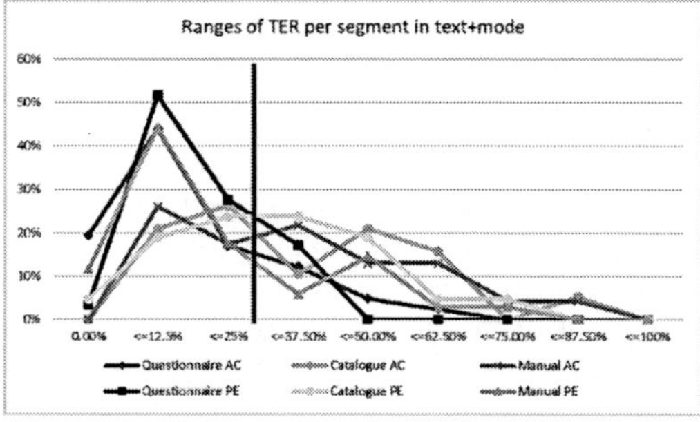

Figure 3 – Segment distribution in TER ranges.

Although most segments, in both modes and all texts, have edit scores below or equal to the 25% threshold (as described by the highest points in all curves at the second and third ranges at the left of the chart), there is a fair number of segments that show higher edit scores, up to 87.5%, as we move to the right of the chart. Catalogue shows the highest number of segments above the threshold, as is visible in the data points of the two curves (one for each mode) that describe this text, especially at and above the 50% editing range.

Next, we looked at extreme editing. We measured numbers of zero edited segments (see the first column of data points in Figure 3), but the results in the opposite extreme were more interesting. In all texts, there were five segments that presented editing scores above 50% on average, among all users. At this level of intense editing, there are not only long segments, as might be expected, if we consider the strong correlation between editing effort and segment length (Popovic et al. 2014). In fact, only two of these five segments have more than six words. This shows that short segments, like the ones one finds in software localisation, in the translation of lists of technical terminology, and in other types of length-restricted projects, may imply an editing effort which is not proportional to their size.

4.3 Users variable

The analysis of the different behaviours of users showed a few outliers, which were essentially users who had had technical problems and only reported a few of the work sessions. Besides this, there were users who had left segments open for a long time, and others who came back and reopened segments. This behaviour had not been anticipated, but it was possible to reclassify the data and get more accurate records of the number of times users opened and closed segments, with or without editing them, or to re-edit them. We could then see that this behaviour was more frequent in AC mode than in PE mode.

Users' editing behaviour tends to be more consistent in PE mode than in AC mode. For example, they tend to edit each segment in PE mode in a time range from 01:15 to 02:15, but in AC mode it ranges from 01:00 to 03:45. This wider variation of values in AC mode was visible in other scores.

Figure 5 shows the distribution of users in each mode according to TER scores, in ranges of 5%. The averages in PE mode are more concentrated in central cases, and they go up to users with an average of 46-50% edit scores. In AC mode, there are users with very small edit score averages and with very high edit scores. The number of users with average editing scores above the 25% threshold is the same for both modes (56%) and is higher than those below the threshold.

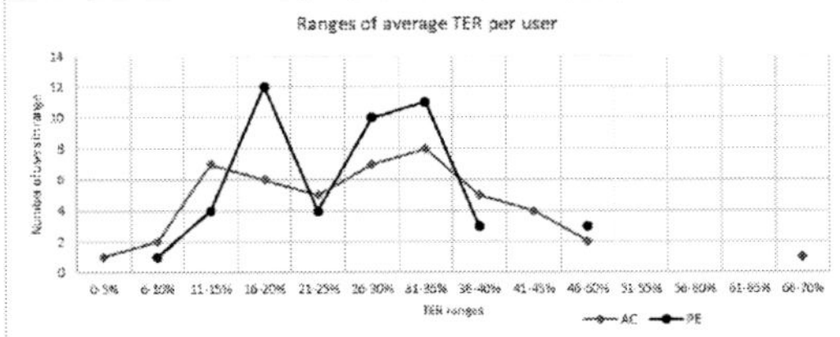

Figure 5 – Distribution of TER in both modes.

Another interesting result of the analyses based on users was a matrix of sorted results in terms of speed and TER, which showed four clear clusters of users, as described in Figure 6.

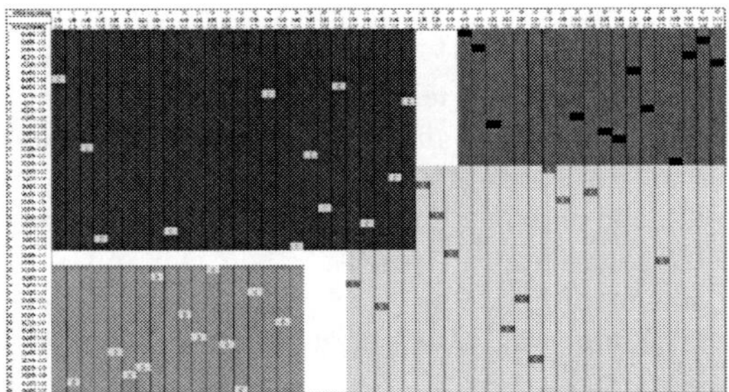

Figure 6 – Groups of users per TER and speed.

This figure was created by placing each user in a matrix which ranked them from the highest TER score to the lowest (vertical axis), and the highest speed to the lowest (horizontal axis). Separating lines around each area were then drawn, at the frontiers that divided each variable by the same number of users: the 12 faster users separated from the 12 slowest, and the 12 users who edited more separated from the 12 who edited less. These groups could be further explored, in terms of their characteristics, but none of the analysis employed showed a strong consistency. We found this clustering of users an interesting outcome of our experiment, but our position is that this should not be used in any form of profiling translators, since many other factors, not measured in our experiment, have to be taken into account when quality is discussed in professional uses.

4.4 Modes variable

The general perception that PE mode created more difficulties for the users is confirmed by the scores obtained. However, PE mode may have helped users achieve higher efficiency. For example, assuming that users are trying to produce a similar edited result in both modes, they tend to reopen and re-edit segments less often when they are in PE mode. They also make less edits (2.85 edits per segment in PE mode, against 3.21 in AC mode).

The total average TER scores are very similar for both modes, but PE mode has a higher score, slightly above the threshold (26% against 24% in AC mode). The fact that these global averages are so close to the suggested threshold does not recommend immediately that the threshold should be revised and repositioned. If more experiments identify a very frequent number of cases around this threshold (i.e. if most segments and texts require that around a quarter of the words are edited), we suggest that the threshold should become an object of study in itself. Arguments for studies focusing on the threshold, besides its statistical relevance, would include quality and effort, since, as Krings (2001) mentions, medium quality segments seem to be the ones that require the highest cognitive effort.

Mode is the variable in which considerations on speed are more relevant, related to users' efficiency. In fact, speed reveals a clearer separation between the two work modes than edit intensity.

In the four work sessions (two in each work mode), each edit took 16 seconds on average in PE mode, but only 10 seconds in AC mode. This difference can be attributed to the intrusiveness of the PE mode, but there are other factors to take into account, like the fact that AC is a method that some users already knew and used regularly, whereas none of the users had ever used PE mode. The two final sessions, in which the same text was edited in the two different modes (first AC and then PE), confirmed that users were still faster applying each edit in AC mode (10 seconds on average, against 12 seconds in PE mode).

The two sessions (second and fourth) with PE mode also show an interesting result: users improved their times when they applied the PE method for the second time. The average speed for each edit in the first session in PE mode was 19 seconds, but this improved to 12 seconds in the second session, when translators edit for the second time the same content they had edited in AC mode. This might simply arise from repetition, but it shows that the constraints of the PE mode can be overcome with that repetition.

We stress again that we make no claims on the usability of the method — this only shows that repetition (of method and text) may lead to a high increase in speed (37%), which may be considered relevant for a feature that had implementation issues. We should also note that questions on the quality and reasonability of the edits made by the translators at any of these sessions cannot be answered in this experimental setup and are not considered in these observations.

4.5 Actions variable

The last variable that was studied involved the four editing actions. For this variable, we chose a more descriptive research question: which differences can be observed in the way users applied the different editing actions?

First, we wanted to know how accurate the estimations of edit distances are, in relation to real actions performed by users. The analysis of this data requires a detailed description of the methods of collection and treatment of data by the tools that we used.

Every time a user selected an action (delete, insert, move or replace) in PE mode from HandyCAT's contextual menu, this event was recorded in a separate row in the log. So, we might have only one row or many rows describing each segment, according to the number of events for that segment: the edits each translator did in that segment. This data was then analysed in terms of TER edits measured by PEC, and a comparison was made between them. This confirmed the initial analysis of a disconnection between the users' actual actions and the description of TER.

Table 2 summarises these results. The first columns represent the events selected in HandyCAT; the four last columns, under 'Edits by PEC', summarise the total numbers of each type of edit that PEC estimated. In each row in the table, we show the number and types of edits PEC estimated for each type of action selected by the participants.

Actions	No. events	Edits by PEC			
		Delete	Insert	Move	Replace
PE.delete	1122	1280	0	0	273
PE.insert	570	22	650	1	174
PE.move	265	107	46	184	107
PE.replace	1470	118	342	1	1197
Total	3427	1527	1038	186	1751

Table 2–Relation between actions/events and TER.

If we look to the first row of table 2, we can see that users chose the 'delete' action (PE.delete) from the contextual menu in HandyCAT, 1122 times in total. When PEC compared the effect of each of these deletions in each segment, it identified 1280 deletions, more than those actually performed. Furthermore, it also identified in the same deletion events 273 substitutions. This illustrates the lack of reliability in descriptions of editing behaviour based on the estimations made by edit distances like TER.

Replace was the action most often well identified by PEC (of the 1470 times replace was selected, 1197 times a replacement was identified by PEC, an accuracy of 81%). Move was the action most often wrongly identified (the accuracy was 69%). In total, TER estimated 31% more actions than those chosen in HandyCAT (a total 4502 against 3427).

Then, we looked at the distribution of the editing actions chosen by the participants. Replace was the action most frequently chosen by participants (43% of the events), followed by delete (33%), then insert (17%), and finally move (only 7%). This is in line with the results obtained by Krings (2001) – in very different technical circumstances – and Snover et al (2006).

Part of the disconnection between the actions chosen in a menu and the estimates by PEC may be due to technical issues, such as the fact that edits to spaces and capitalisation are registered by HandyCAT, but not counted by PEC. There may also be errors in user's selection of actions, which we analysed carefully in our data. However, the differences in these numbers are mainly related to the way PEC estimates the edits, using an estimation optimised for efficiency, which is not necessarily the method used by translators.

We also investigated how edit distances considered contiguous edits: when the user applied the same action (e.g. delete) to two consecutive words, it could be expected that PEC would identify this as just one edit (one deletion of two words). However, edits are estimated per word, which means that the average number of edited words for most estimated actions is one. Movement is an exception to this: TER implementations, as the one PEC applies, maximise efficiency for movement by starting to estimate movements of phrases. This is the reason why there was an exceptional average of 1.68 words being edited in each row where one move action was selected.

The values for speed of each editing action are easy to understand. Delete is the fastest action to apply (an average 8 seconds), then move (11 seconds), while insert and replace take, with a slight rounding, the same time (14 seconds). The delay in both these actions is associated with the time required to type the new words. Choosing move is faster than deleting and inserting a word.

4.6 Factors for editing scores and speed

After all the results were compiled, we did an analysis per user, combining answers from questionnaires and activity logs, by applying different statistical tests and tools in R (R Development Core Team 2008). The objective was to identify the factors that most contributed to the values obtained in each dependent variable (edit scores and speed).

One of the tools that presented the clearest results was a decision tree approach, a tool which, although not having a very strong explanatory power, shows interesting trends in the data. We fed a total of 27 factors to the decision tree, some of which were codified qualitative answers to the questionnaires (like experience with PE, or opinion on the impact of the workshop) and others performance indicators (like the number of segments with zero edits, ranking according to speed, average and total edit scores and speeds, etc.). Then, we estimated which of these factors had a stronger relation with the distribution of results for TER and speed.

For TER scores, this tool showed that the 'text' was the most influential factor, as we can see in Figure 6. The second factor, some way behind it, was 'experience with PE'. However, the influence of text was so determining that if we removed the data for 'text' from the list of factors, the program could not calculate and produce a decision tree.

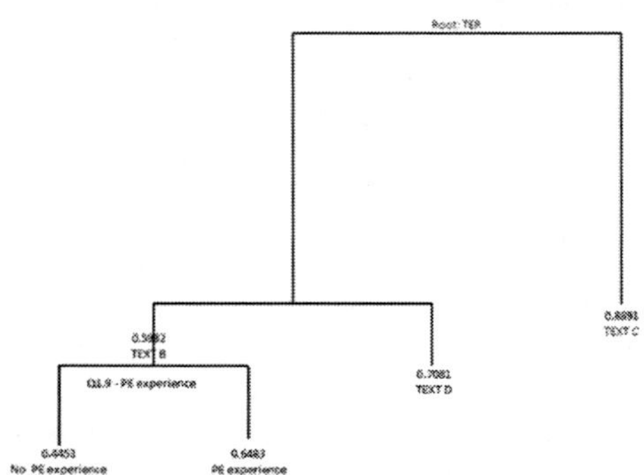

Figure 6 – Decision tree for TER scores.

The results for speed were different. Speed seems to be a measure that depends more on the work method used. That was an impression collected from users, and it was confirmed in the global analysis of the data collected. The second most influential factor was the previous use or not of predictive writing features by translators, and finally their experience with MT or PE. The text, for example, does not appear in the sequence of influencing factors for speed of editing, as shown in Figure 7.

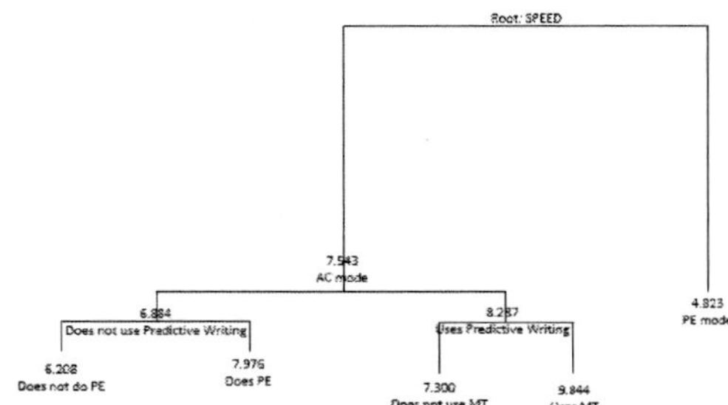

Figure 7 – Decision tree for speed factors.

5 Discussion and conclusions

Following the aim of the project, we could confirm in the workshop that there is a research interest, from different points of view, in the approach of editing as being formed by four actions.

First, it was confirmed by the participants in the surveys conducted during the workshop. Although it was related to a disruption in work habits, translators admitted that this perspective made sense as a description of what they do when they edit MT text, at least from a technical perspective. As commented in the final surveys, the main advantage of this method, which is related to its intrusiveness, is the demand for translators to plan their editing strategy before applying it, thus bringing to light an often-unconscious decision process, forcing them to make more efficient actions. This efficiency, measured only as technical action data, is, naturally, meaningless if we aim at relating it to effectiveness, but it is relevant for the development of better forms of support in translation tools.

As admitted from the outset, the four editing actions interface tested during the workshop was not appropriate for commercial settings, because of its lack of usability development. There are, however, potential research and pedagogical implications in this mode of work. The work mode based on the four editing actions gives visibility to the decision process in time-constrained and efficiency demanding work contexts, as is the case of PE.

This study, namely in its analysis of the lack of correspondence between the estimations of edit distances and the actions employed by translators, also calls the attention to the complexity of editing work. This calls for a cautious use of metrics like TER as descriptors of processes, and to the need to study in closer detail the different levels of complexity in PE. Our suggestion of an editing threshold that sets a boundary between levels in which editing can be easily described and others in which it cannot is a contribution to this type of study.

The methodology applied in this study was adjusted to the objectives and constraints of the experiment. The amount of questions this exploratory approach raised meant that a choice had to be made between extensiveness or depth of statistical analysis. This approach enabled a rich discussion with the participants, on the two work modes and around concepts and practices that were novel, and to collect data for the comparison between the two modes, thus fulfilling the experiment objectives.

The analysis of the results of our experiment exploited the weight of different dimensions of PE. The suggested editing threshold of 25% was the most frequent global average in the different levels of analysis, but relevant differences in editing intensity in different texts, by different users and using different work modes were also observed. We also saw how the number of edits and speed may be associated with different factors, text and work mode, respectively, but also how these two dependent variables helped us group users in four different clusters. This shows how the threshold may act as an important instrument to highlight varied degrees of complex editing in MT content.

The experiment also showed that users were more consistent, and, in a certain sense, more efficient in PE mode, since they made fewer edits and returned fewer times to the same segment. This efficiency is contradicted by the fact that PE mode requires more time per edit, but we also observed improvements in speed of use of this work method. This highlights the usefulness of making the decision process more conscious, something which may be explored in pedagogic contexts.

Finally, this work showed how the four editing actions are useful features to describe and research editing work. The most frequent action employed by translators was replace, followed by delete, then insert and finally move, a result confirmed in similar experiments. Insert and replace take longer to perform because they require typing. A tool that aims at supporting the actions performed by translators needs to act on all of these actions. This presents implementation challenges, not only at the data collection stage, but also regarding the usefulness and usability of the interfaces. For example, actions that require typing (like insert and replace) may be supported by auto-complete features, but delete and move only have an added value if they can appear previously as suggestions to the users, highlighting words which may have to be deleted and positions where words may be moved into. So, a combination of methods, flexibly adjusted to different degrees of editing, seems to be the most reasonable approach.

Although it focused on micro actions, this project allowed us to learn many things about the editing task. It has raised relevant questions related to technical effort, productivity, usability and usefulness of action support features, and on how to support specialised users. We suggest that more research around the editing actions and the editing threshold, besides new applications to support editing actions, should be pursued by translation technology researchers and developers.

Acknowledgements

This Project has received funding from the European Union's Horizon 2020 research and innovation programme under the EDGE COFUND Marie Skłodowska-Curie Grant Agreement no. 713567. This publication has emanated from research supported in part by a research grant from Science Foundation Ireland (SFI) under Grant Number 13/RC/2077.

References

Alabau, Vicent, Ragnar Bonk, Christian Buck, Michael Carl, Francisco Casacuberta, Mercedes García-Martínez, Jesús González, et al. 2013. "CASMACAT: An Open Source Workbench for Advanced Computer Aided Translation." *The Prague Bulletin of Mathematical Linguistics* 100 (100): 101–12. https://doi.org/10.2478/pralin-2013-0016.

Alabau, Vicent, Michael Carl, Francisco Casacuberta, Mercedes García Martínez, Jesús González-Rubio, Bartolomé Mesa-Lao, Daniel Ortiz-Martínez, Moritz Schaeffer, and Germán Sanchis-Trilles. 2016. "Learning Advanced Post-Editing." In *New Directions in Empirical Translation Process Research*, edited by Michael Carl, Srinivas Bangalore, and Moritz Schaeffer, 95–110. Heidelberg: Springer International Publishing Switzerland. https://doi.org/10.1007/978-3-319-20358-4_5.

Alves, Fábio, and Amparo Hurtado Albir. 2010. "Cognitive Approaches." In *Handbook of Translation Studies - Volume I*, edited by Yves Gambier and L. van Doorslaer. Amsterdam/Philadelphia: John Benjamins Publishing Company.

Alves, Fábio, and Daniel Couto Vale. 2011. "On Drafting and Revision in Translation: A Corpus Linguistics Oriented Analysis of Translation Process Data." *Translation: Computation, Corpora, Cognition* 1 (1): 105–22. http://www.mt-archive.info/TC3-2011-Alves.pdf.

Carl, Michael, Barbara Dragsted, and Arnt Lykke Jakobsen. 2011. "On the Systematicity of

Human Translation Processes." In *Tralogy 2011. Translation Careers and Technologies: Convergence Points for the Future*. Paris, France. http://research.cbs.dk/en/publications/on-the-systematicity-of-human-translation-processes(0225f368-7eea-4ed2-8a35-9a7d9efbce6c).html.

Carl, Michael, and Arnt Lykke Jakobsen. 2009. "Towards Statistical Modelling of Translators' Activity Data." *International Journal of Speech Technology* 12 (4): 125–38. https://doi.org/10.1007/s10772-009-9044-6.

Carl, Michael, Isabel Lacruz, Masaru Yamada, and Akiko Aizawa. 2016. "Measuring the Translation Process." In *The 22nd Annual Meeting of the Association for Natural Language Processing, NLP 2016*, 0–3. Japan. http://openarchive.cbs.dk/bitstream/handle/1039 8/9280/Michael Cral_2016_02.pdf.

do Carmo, Félix. 2017. "Post-Editing: A Theoretical and Practical Challenge for Translation Studies and Machine Learning." Universidade do Porto. https://repositorio-aberto.up.pt/handle/10216/107518.

Federico, Marcello, Nicola Bertoldi, Mauro Cettolo, Matteo Negri, Marco Turchi, Marco Trombetti, Alessandro Cattelan, et al. 2014. "The Matecat Tool." *Proceedings of COLING 2014, the 25th International Conference on Computational Linguistics: System Demonstrations* 7 (287688): 129–32. http://aclweb.org/anthology/C14-2028.

Forcada, Mikel L, and Felipe Sánchez-Martínez. 2015. "A General Framework for Minimizing Translation Effort: Towards a Principled Combination of Translation Technologies in Computer-Aided Translation." *Proceedings of the 18th Annual Conference of the European Association for Machine Translation*, 27–34. http://aclweb.org/anthology/W15-4904.

Green, Spence, Jason Chuang, Jeffrey Heer, and Christopher D Manning. 2014. "Predictive Translation Memory: A Mixed-Initiative System for Human Language Translation." In *Proceedings of the 27th Annual ACM Symposium on User Interface Software and Technology (UIST '14)*. New York: ACM. https://doi.org/http://dx.doi.org/10.1145/264291 8.2647408.

Hartnett, Patrick, and SDL Community. 2014. "Post-Edit Compare." 2014. http://posteditcompare.wiki-site.com/index.php/Main_Page.

Hokamp, Chris, and Qun Liu. 2015. "Handycat: The Flexible CAT Tool for Translation Research." In *EAMT 2015*. Istanbul.

Krings, Hans P. 2001. *Repairing Texts: Empirical Investigations of Machine Translation Post-Editing Processes*. Edited by Geoffrey S. Koby. Kent, Ohio & London: The Kent State University Press.

Moorkens, Joss, and Sharon O'Brien. 2017. "Assessing User Interface Needs of Post-Editors of Machine Translation Interfaces for Editing Human Translation and Post-Editing Machine." In *Human Issues in Translation Technology*, edited by Dorothy Kenny and Jenny Williams. London: Routledge.

Ortiz-Martínez, Daniel. 2016. "Online Learning for Statistical Machine Translation." *Computational Linguistics* 42 (1 (March 2016)): 121–61. https://doi.org/http://dx.doi.org/10.1162/COLI_a _00244.

Ortiz-Martínez, Daniel, Jesús González-Rubio, Vicent Alabau, German Sanchis-Trilles, and Francisco Casacuberta. 2016. "Integrating Online and Active Learning in a Computer-Assisted Translation Workbench." In *New Directions in Empirical Translation Process Research*, edited by Michael Carl, Srinivas Bangalore, and Moritz Schaeffer, 57–76. Heidelberg: Springer International Publishing Switzerland. https://doi.org/10.1007/978-3-319-20358-4-3.

Popovic, Maja, Arle Richard Lommel, Aljoscha Burchardt, Eleftherios Avramidis, and Hans Uszkoreit. 2014. "Relations between Different Types of Post-Editing Operations, Cognitive Effort and Temporal Effort." In *The Seventeenth Annual Conference of the European Association for Machine Translation (EAMT 14)*, 191–98.

R Development Core Team. 2008. "R: A Language and Environment for Statistical Computing." Vienna, Austria. http://www.r-project.org.

Sanchis-Trilles, Germán, Vicent Alabau, Christian Buck, Michael Carl, Francisco Casacuberta, Mercedes García-Martínez, Ulrich Germann, et al. 2014. "Interactive Translation Prediction versus Conventional Post-Editing in Practice: A Study with the CasMaCat Workbench." *Machine Translation* 28 (3–4): 217–35. https://doi.org/10.1007/s10590-014-9157-9.

Snover, Matthew, Bonnie Dorr, Richard Schwartz, Linnea Micciulla, and John Makhoul. 2006. "A Study of Translation Edit Rate with Targeted Human Annotation." *Proceedings of AMTA 2006*, no. August: 223–31. https://doi.org/10.1.1.129.4369.

Trochim, Joachim. 2006. "The Research Methods Knowledge Base." 2006. http://www.socialresearchmethods.net/kb/index. php.

A human evaluation of English-Irish statistical and neural machine translation

Meghan Dowling
meghan.dowling@adaptcentre.ie
Joss Moorkens
joss.moorkens@adaptcentre.ie
Andy Way
andy.way@adaptcentre.ie

Sheila Castilho
sheila.castilho@adaptcentre.ie
Teresa Lynn
teresa.lynn@adaptcentre.ie

ADAPT Centre, Dublin City University, Dublin, Ireland

Abstract

With official status in both Ireland and the EU, there is a need for high-quality English-Irish (EN-GA) machine translation (MT) systems which are suitable for use in a professional translation environment. While we have seen recent research on improving both statistical MT and neural MT for the EN-GA pair, the results of such systems have always been reported using automatic evaluation metrics. This paper provides the first human evaluation study of EN-GA MT using professional translators and in-domain (public administration) data for a more accurate depiction of the translation quality available via MT.

1 Introduction

The Irish language enjoys the status of both the first official language of Ireland and an official European Union language. As a result of this status is there is a requirement for official public content to be made available in Irish in both Ireland[1] and the EU.[2] There is currently a derogation on the amount of Irish content published by the EU, due to be lifted at the end of 2021 (Publications Office of the European Union, 2011). At this point, the already high demand for professional Irish translators will increase significantly. With this demand for the production of Irish-language text, usually with English as the source language, it is important that any available EN→GA MT systems are robust and fit-for-purpose.

Despite MT having been established as a useful tool in the workflow of a professional translator, it is not yet the norm for Irish translators, whether freelance or within a translation company.[3] As a lesser-resourced and minority language, Irish faces a barrier to state-of-the-art technology shown to be effective for majority languages (European Language Resource Coordination, 2020).

While there has been research on improving EN→GA MT (Dowling et al., 2015; Arcan et al., 2016; Defauw et al., 2019; Dowling et al., 2019) to date there have been no publications describing a human evaluation (HE) study for EN→GA MT. This study aims to provide the first EN→GA MT HE study, investigating the measurable usefulness of EN→GA in a professional translation capacity. In an attempt to closely match the context in which EN→GA MT is intended to be used, professional translators will undertake post-editing (PE) tasks using MT output.

Another aim of this study is to provide a human-derived comparison of EN→GA statistical machine translation (SMT) and neural machine translation (NMT). In previous work, a preliminary comparison of EN→GA SMT and NMT showed that SMT fared better than NMT in terms of automatic metrics (Dowling et al., 2018). More recent publications (Defauw et al., 2019; Dowling et al., 2019) show a more positive picture for EN→GA NMT, but without a direct comparison to SMT. The SMT/NMT comparison presented in this paper will take into account both the quantitative metadata gathered during the study (time per seg-

---

[1]The Official Languages Act (2003) requires all official public information and services to be available in both Irish and English: http://www.irishstatutebook.ie/eli/2003/act/32/enacted/en/html

[2]Irish has been a full EU language since 2006.

[3]A recent study by Moorkens (2020) reported that "...few participants appear to use MT at present..."

Martins, Moniz, Fumega, Martins, Batista, Coheur, Parra, Trancoso, Turchi, Bisazza, Moorkens, Guerberof, Nurminen, Marg, Forcada (eds.)
Proceedings of the 22nd Annual Conference of the European Association for Machine Translation, p. 431–440
Lisboa, Portugal, November 2020.

ment, number of keystrokes, etc.) as well as the qualitative opinions and recommendations of the participants.

This paper is presented as follows: Section 2 describes related work in the areas of EN→GA MT, HE, etc. In Section 3 we provide details of the data and parameters used in our SMT and NMT systems, while Section 4 describes the methodology used in this HE study. We present our results in Section 5 and provide some conclusions and avenues for future work in Section 6.

2 Related work

As Irish is a poorly-resourced language (Judge et al., 2012), the quality of MT output has struggled to reach the same level of quality as well-supported languages. Several studies (Dowling et al., 2015; Arcan et al., 2016; Dowling et al., 2016) thus focused on improving EN→GA SMT, as discussed in Section 1. In previous work comparing EN-GA SMT and NMT, preliminary results suggest that SMT seems to outperform NMT (Dowling et al., 2018), although we show a number of examples where the score may be misleading and recommend that a HE study may be necessary to fully understand the quality of each system type. More recent studies (Defauw et al., 2019; Dowling et al., 2019) show the effects of adding artificially-created training data to EN-GA NMT.

In terms of Irish translators' attitudes to MT, Moorkens' (2020) extensive survey reports varying attitudes between translators based on terms of employment, with freelance translators appearing to be poorly disposed towards MT.

Koehn and Knowles (2017) include low–resource languages as one of the main challenges still present in MT research. Unable to exploit cutting-edge techniques that require huge resources, MT researchers must look to creative solutions to improve low–resource MT. Such approaches include the creation of artificial parallel data, e.g. through back-translation (Poncelas et al., 2018), exploiting out-of-domain data (c.f. Imankulova et al., (2019)) and using a better-resourced language as a pivot (Wu and Wang, 2007; Liu et al., 2018; Cheng, 2019).

HE is a vital component of MT research (Castilho et al., 2018), with many of the major MT conferences including a translator track to encourage such publications. They are especially valuable in low-resource or minority contexts (e.g.

Spanish-Galician MT (Bayón and Sánchez-Gijón, 2019), Russian-Japanese MT (Imankulova et al., 2019)) where the languages may be overlooked by global MT companies.

There have been comparisons of SMT and NMT since NMT first emerged in the field. The conference on machine translation (WMT) regularly feature both systems, with HE at the forefront (Bojar et al., 2016; Ondřej et al., 2017; Barrault et al., 2019). Castilho et al. (2017) describe an extensive comparison of SMT and NMT using both automatic metrics and HE. Mixed results overall highlight the need for language-specific HE studies.

Recently, Läubli et al., (2020) published a set of recommendations for performing HE of MT. They advocate for (1) the use of professional translators over novices, (2) translations to be evaluated on a document-level, (3) fluency to be evaluated in addition to adequacy, (4) reference translations not to be heavily edited for fluency and (5) the use of original source texts (rather than translated text as input). We take these recommendations into account when designing this HE study.

3 MT systems set-up

To compare SMT and NMT through HE it is first necessary to train a system of each type using the same training data. This section describes the data used in building both MT systems, their specific parameters and the automatic evaluation scores generated for each.

3.1 Data

Both SMT and NMT rely on large amounts of high-quality parallel data. This is especially true of NMT, a type of MT system that is highly data-driven. Although there are legal requirements regarding the creation of public Irish text (see Section 1) we may still describe Irish as a 'less-resourced' language. As mentioned previously, the derogation on the status of Irish has limited the amount of Irish content generated by the EU. Furthermore, the Irish Language Act (2003) does not enforce bilingual production of all public text and, until relatively recently, translation memories were not usually requested by public bodies when outsourcing translation work (Lynn et al., 2019).

Table 1 shows the sources and number of GA words of all datasets used to build the SMT and NMT systems. In line with previous work (Dowl-

Source	# words (GA)
DCHG	1,085,617
EU	439,262
Crawled	254,772
CnaG	21,365
Teagasc	32,908
UT	15,377
IT	57,314
Paracrawl	20,803,088
ELRC	415,648
ELRI	628,669
TOTAL	**23,754,020**

Table 1: Source and number of Irish words of data sources used to build the MT systems described in this paper

ing et al., 2019), in-domain data from the Department of Culture, Heritage and the Gaeltacht (DCHG) is used. This is supplemented with data from EU sources,[4] crawled data,[5] Conradh na Gaeilge[6] (CnaG), Teagasc,[7] University Times (UT) and the Irish Times (IT). The two latter sources contain monolingual Irish text only. As in Defauw et al., (2019), we include the Paracrawl corpus, a large corpus of webcrawled data (Esplà-Gomis et al., 2019). Further to this, we add two new corpora, referred to in Table 1 as ELRC and ELRI. ELRC refers to the European Language Resource Coordination,[8] an initiative led by the European Commission to gather language resources for all EU official languages. ELRI[9] is an initiative which focuses on the building and sharing of language resources within France, Ireland, Portugal and Spain (Etchegoyhen et al., 2018) (European Language Resource Infrastructure).

3.2 SMT parameters

When training the SMT system, we follow parameters identified in previous work. Moses (Koehn et al., 2007), the standard tool for building SMT systems, along with the data described in Section 3.1,

is used to train our SMT model. KenLM (Heafield, 2011) is used to train a 6-gram language model using the GA portion of the parallel data, as well as the monolingual GA data. This wider-context language model (3-gram is the default) along with hierarchical reordering tables are used in an attempt to address the divergent word orders of EN and GA (EN having subject-verb-object and GA having verb-subject object word order.)

3.3 NMT parameters

As in other research on EN-GA NMT (Defauw et al., 2019; Dowling et al., 2018), we use Open-NMT (Klein et al., 2017) as the basis for training our NMT system. We implement a transformer-based approach (Vaswani et al., 2017), which has shown promising results for low-resource NMT with other language pairs (Lakew et al., 2017; Murray et al., 2019). We use parameters recommended by Vaswani et al., (2017).

3.4 Test data

1,500 sentences of gold-standard data,[10] with an average sentence length of 20 words per sentence, were held out from training data in order to perform automatic evaluation. This data contains extracts from DCHG sources such as official correspondence, public announcements, etc.

3.5 Automatic evaluation

Automatic evaluation metrics, while best used to track developmental changes in one particular MT system over time, can also be used to gauge differences in quality between two different MT systems. In this study we generate BLEU (Papineni et al., 2002), TER (Snover et al., 2009), CharacTER (Wang et al., 2016) and ChrF scores (Popović, 2015).

	BLEU↑	TER↓	ChrF↑	CharacTER↓
SMT	45.13	43.51	66.26	0.29
NMT	**46.58**	**40.85**	**67.21**	**0.28**

Table 2: Automatic evaluation scores for the SMT and NMT systems used to generate MT output, rounded to 2 decimal places. The best score in each column is highlighted in bold.

With automatic evaluation, the source side of the test data (EN) is translated using the MT system. BLEU and TER both compute scores by comparing words in the MT output to those in the GA por-

---

[4] Parallel texts from two EU bodies: the Digital Corpus of the European Parliament (DCEP) and Directorate General for Translation, Translation Memories (DGT-TM)

[5] Crawled from various sources including Citizens Information, an Irish government website that provides information on public services

[6] Conradh na Gaeilge is a public organisation tasked with the promotion of the Irish language

[7] The state agency providing research, advisory and education in agriculture, horticulture, food and rural development in Ireland.

[8] http://www.lr-coordination.eu/

[9] http://www.elri-project.eu/

[10] Professionally translated data within the same domain (from the DCHG corpus).

tion of the test data. CharacTER and chrF, however, compute a score based on a character-level comparison, which can be more accurate for inflected languages.

Table 2 shows the BLEU, TER, CharacTER and ChrF scores for the SMT and NMT systems. These scores can then be compared to the results provided through HE. Both BLEU and ChrF are precision based, with higher scores indicating higher precision and, in theory, higher quality. This is indicated with a ↑ in Table 2. TER (translation error rate) and CharacTER (TER on character level) are error-based metrics. Accordingly, a lower score represents a lower error rate, indicated with a ↓ in Table 2.

It can be seen from Table 2 that the NMT system achieves a better score across all four metrics, whether calculated on a word or character level.

4 Study methodology and set-up

MT HE can take many forms, e.g. ranking of MT output, annotation of incorrect parts of speech or post-editing of MT output. A HE study can also be carried out by providing the translators with MT output and asking them to post-edit it. One benefit of this method is that subjectivity can be decreased – data gathered through translator post-editing (e.g. time spent per segment, number of keystrokes, etc.) is used to assess the MT system rather than the participant being required to give a judgement per word/segment. It is also faster than error annotation and requires less training, particularly if the translators already have experience of post-editing MT output. It is also the method which is closest to the situation in which MT is intended to be used, and as a result translator opinions of the post-editing tasks can also be elicited. For these reasons, we see post-editing as the HE method that best suits the needs and intended outputs of this study. This section describes the set-up and methodology of the PE task and related survey.

4.1 PET tool and guidelines

Post-editing tool (PET) (Aziz et al., 2012) was chosen as the software with which to collect data for this study as it is freely available online and specifically designed for use in HE studies of MT. We configure PET with the default parameters and compose guidelines and instructions for the participants. For example, participants were permitted to use dictionaries while editing the output, but were not permitted to use another MT tool. The guidelines were written in Irish, the target language of this study.

4.2 Pilot study

Prior to the main study, we conducted a pilot study to ensure that the tool was set up correctly and to test the robustness of the guidelines. Two Irish linguists each post-edited 10 machine–translated sentences. We then updated the guidelines as per the feedback of both pilot study participants.

4.3 Data

Two subsets were extracted from the test data described in Section 3.1, each containing 100 EN sentences, and then translated with the SMT and NMT systems described in 3.2 and 3.3 respectively. With the merits of document-level translation raised in recent MT research (Toral et al., 2018; Werlen et al., 2018) and the importance of context in work using MT for dissemination, we choose to keep the sequence of sentences, rather than extract each of the 200 sentences individually at random.

Recent studies have shown that MT can have a negative impact on the linguistic richness of MT output (Vanmassenhove et al., 2019) and post-edited translations (Toral et al., 2018). To demonstrate the differences in linguistic richness between SMT and NMT, we calculate standardised type-token ratio (STTR) with the outputs.[11] Table 3 shows that, although a small difference can be seen between jobs for both systems, in average both MT systems have a very similar STTR.

System	Job 1	Job 2	Average
SMT	41.71	42.69	42.20
NMT	43.84	41.33	42.59

Table 3: Comparison of STTR between SMT and NMT outputs normalised per 1000 words

4.4 Participants

With EN-GA MT more likely to be used as a tool to help publish translated content in an official context rather than a gisting tool, it is important that the participants in this study match the profile of the intended user, namely a professional translator. To this end, we recruited participants with an ac-

---

[11]Type-token ratio normalised per 1,000 words.

creditation in EN-GA translation.[12] We recruited four accredited translators, referred to from now on as P1, P2, P3 and P4 respectively.

Each participant was asked to post-edit 210 sentences: 10 practice sentences, 100 sentences translated using SMT and 100 sentences translated using NMT. The same source text was provided to all 4 translators. Figure 1 shows the distribution of MT output across participants. Two participants (P1 and P3) were presented with the SMT output using Job 1 data and the NMT output using Job 2 data (set-up A). The other two participants (P2 and P4) were asked to post-edit set-up B, consisting of Job 1 machine-translated using NMT and Job 2 machine-translated using SMT. Both set-up A and set-up B contain 10 practice sentences from a similar source (Dublin City Council) so that the translators could try out the PET environment and get used to the software without worrying about speed. The output files and associated metadata from the practice segment are not included in the results.

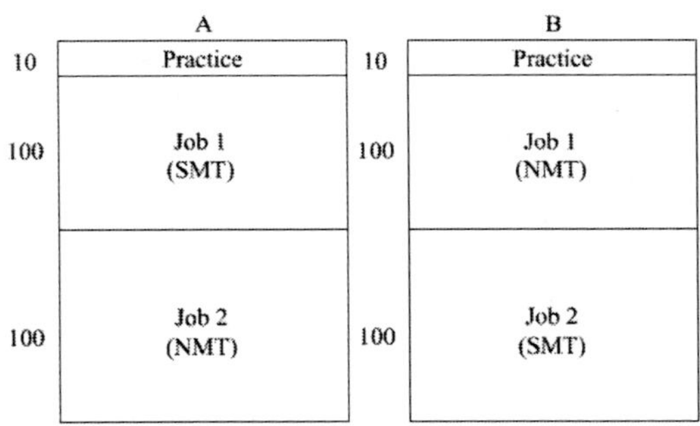

Figure 1: Distribution of MT output (not to scale)

4.5 Survey questions

A post-task survey was implemented to gather information about the participants' experience and their opinions of the two MT outputs. Participants were not informed whether the MT output was produced by an SMT or NMT system. The survey was distributed via Google sheets. The following information was gathered in the survey:

- months/years experience as a professional translator

- months/years experience post-editing MT in a professional capacity

- view of MT as a tool to be used by professional translators

- which system seems most fluent

- which system seems most accurate

- which system the translator would prefer to post-edit

- a text box for additional comments

5 Results and analysis

In this section we present the survey results and the results gathered via the PET output.

5.1 Survey results

The survey results show that all 4 participants are experienced translators. P1 has 25 years of experience, P2 5 years, P3 10 years part-time, and P4 13 years. Two of the participants' (P2 and P4) have experience post-editing (PE) MT in a professional capacity, with 3 years (P2) and 5 years (P4) of PE experience each (see Table 4).

Participant	Translator exp.	PE exp.
P1	25 years	N/A
P2	5 years	3 years
P3	10 years†	N/A
P4	13 years	5 years

Table 4: Table displaying the amount of experience (exp.) each participant has a professional EN-GA translator and, if relelvant, how much experience each has PE EN-GA output. A dagger (†) signifies that the experience is in a part-time capacity.

When asked for their views of MT as a tool to be used by professional translators, answers varied from positive ("It's a very useful tool") to cautious ("I think it depends very much on what the machine has been fed!"; "Improving constantly, but insufficient at present";) to negative ("It's not much use for English to Irish translation. It would take the same length of time to translate from scratch"). The positive but guarded responses came from participants with post-editing (PE) experience, whereas those without PE experience answered negatively. This may be an indication that there is a learning curve with PE before MT can be a valuable and useful addition to translation workflow.

<hr>

Table 5 shows the survey results pertaining to differences between the two systems (SMT and NMT). The question "In general, which output did you perceive to be the most fluent-sounding?" is represented by the heading 'fluency'. 'Accuracy' is the heading used to represent the question "In general, which output did you did you perceive to be the most accurate in terms of semantics? (i.e. conveyed the meaning the best, fluency aside)." The final question dealing with SMT versus NMT, "Which output would you prefer to post-edit?" is represented with the heading 'prefer.' The participants were not aware which output was produced by which system; they were simply presented with two separate translation jobs.

Participant	fluency	accuracy	prefer
P1	NMT	NMT	No diff.
P2	No diff.	NMT	NMT
P3	No diff.	No diff.	No diff.
P4	NMT	NMT	NMT

Table 5: Survey responses relating to differences between SMT and NMT fluency, accuracy and participant preference.

5.2 PET results

Interestingly, none of the four participants gave SMT as an answer to any of these questions. This contradicts previous work comparing EN-GA SMT and NMT using automatic metrics (Dowling et al., 2018). It does, however, line up with the automatic metrics gathered during this study (BLEU, TER, ChrF and CharacTER scores suggested that the NMT output was of greater quality than that of SMT – see section 3 for more details).

The results gathered from PET provided us not only with the post-edited output, but also with the number of keystrokes, annotations, and seconds spent on each segment. We used this data to calculate the average seconds per segment, average keystrokes per segment, and the average unchanged segments per system per participant. These figures, as well as the human-targetered TER (HTER) scores (Snover et al., 2006), are displayed in Table 6. Where MT for dissemination is concerned, temporal effort, or time spent PE, is arguably the most important metric as payment is usually based on words translated. Two of the four participants in this study (P1 and P4) were more productive when working with NMT output. The difference for P4 was sizeable (an average of 48.53 seconds per segment for NMT compared to 193.06

for SMT), although it should be noted that P4 was required to repeat the PE task for the NMT job due to a technical error. It is likely that this led to a faster PE time for this job, and that other values for this job are also skewed. P2 and P3 were more productive using SMT, although for P2 the difference is negligible (an average of 119.86 seconds per segment for SMT PE in comparison to 120.59 for NMT).

HTER is a metric for evaluating MT output based on TER (see Section 3). Using HTER, a human translator post-edits MT output and the score is calculated using the post-edit distance and the length of the reference. A low HTER score should equate to low PE effort, although in practice, post-editors may delete and retype text rather than taking the shortest possible route from raw MT to PE.

In the case of P1, P2 and P4, HTER was lower for NMT than SMT. Results from P3 showed negligible difference between the HTER of both systems (a difference of 0.0004).

In the survey, P1 reported that the NMT output was more fluent-sounding and more accurate. This is reflected in the data. From Table 6 we can see that P1 was quicker, used fewer keystrokes, and left more segments unchanged when PE NMT output. P1 did, however, choose 'no difference' when asked which output they would prefer to PE.

P2 also voiced a preference for NMT output over SMT output, although reported 'no difference' in fluency. Scores generated from PET data indicated little/no difference in time, keystrokes, and unchanged segments, although the HTER score was markedly improved for NMT.

Although P3 answered 'no difference' to all three questions comparing SMT and NMT, this is not reflected in the time and keystrokes, which indicated more favourable results for SMT, nor in the unchanged segments for which NMT had a higher score. It is, however, reflected in the HTER scores which are almost identical for both outputs.

P4 reported NMT to be more fluent sounding, more accurate, and the output they would most prefer to post-edit. This is reflected in all metrics present in Table 6, where the results for the NMT output show a marked improvement over those of the SMT output, apart from the number of unchanged segments. However, as mentioned in Section 5.1, P4 had to repeat the entire PE task for the NMT output. This may have lead to a faster PE time with fewer keystrokes and, relatedly, a lower

participant	system	avg. time/seg.	avg. keys./seg.	avg unchanged segs.	HTER
1	SMT	102.4	91.47	0.12	0.33
1	NMT	89.16	89.16	0.2	0.28
2	SMT	119.86	207.09	0.11	0.52
2	NMT	120.59	205.61	0.12	0.43
3	SMT	173.15	90.44	0.17	0.36
3	NMT	207.21	139.9	0.2	0.36
4	SMT	193.06	100.49	0.1	0.43
4	NMT	48.53	48.73	0.18	0.24

Table 6: Table displaying the average (avg.) number of seconds (time) per segment (seg.), average number of keystrokes (keys.) per segments, average unchanged segments and HTER of each system for each participant.

HTER score. Overall, these results suggest HTER to be a more valuable indication than other metrics gathered.

5.3 PE output

With both the survey responses and figures generated using results from PET varying substantially from translator to translator we chose to take a closer look at the differences in PE output provided by the four participants. To identify potentially interesting sentences, we used compare-mt (Neubig et al., 2019), a tool designed to analyse MT output and provide the user with sentences which differ greatly. Although human-generated translations are not the intended input for compare-mt, it was still useful in identifying cases where the participants gave different translations.

Input:	If you have been allocated as a decision-maker..
SMT:	Má tá tú mar a déantóir cinntí..* *If you are a decision manufacturer..*
P1:	Más cinnteoir thú air.. *If you are a decision-maker for it..*
P3:	Má ainmníodh thú mar chinnteoir.. *If you are named as a decision-maker..*
NMT:	Má roghnaíodh mar chinnteoir thú.. *If you are chosen as a decision-maker..*
P2:	Má shanntar ról mar chinnteoir ort.. *If the role of decision-maker is assigned to you..*
P4:	Má roghnaíodh mar chinnteoir thú.. *If you are chosen as a decision-maker..*

Table 7: A portion of the PE output from P1, P2, P3 and P4. The EN data provided to the translators as input is also provided. The relevant MT output provided to translators is given above the participants' output. A gloss for each sentence is indicated in italics below each GA output. An asterix (*) indicates that the segment is not grammatically correct.

Table 7 shows a shortened portion of a segment of PE output produced by P1, P2, P3 and P4. It can be seen, even to those who do not speak Irish, that all four translators chose to post-edit the MT input in a different way. In fact, there is no word which is repeated (with the same inflections) throughout all four translations. Despite all being correct, it stands to reason that automatic values generated for this output, such as HTER and number of keystrokes, would also differ. This highlights the limitations of such metrics, as well as the need for multiple references when generating automatic evaluation scores.

Similarly, in Table 8, all four participants chose slightly different translations of the source text. In this example, the importance of context can be seen. In the source text, the acronym for Freedom of Information (FOI) is not expanded. Despite this, only P3 chooses to use the equivalent Irish acronym – possibly due to both MT systems producing the expanded acronym (shown in bold). The three other translators (P1, P2 and P4) chose to preserve the expanded acronym in the GA PE sentence. It could be the case that, in Irish, the acronym is not as instantly recognised as its English counterpart. This is quite common, when an acronym is commonly used in one language but not in another. Without training data to reflect this, it is unlikely that an MT system would produce such an output. This inconsistent spelling-out of the acronym in the post-edited texts again indicates the importance of in-domain training data and of seeking the advice of professional translators when training MT systems.

6 Conclusions and Future Work

We have presented the first HE study for EN-GA SMT and NMT. We have shown that, while auto-

Source	to ensure.. in the **FOI** legislation..
SMT:	chun a chinntiú.. sa reachtaíocht um **Shaoráil Faisnéise**.. *to ensure.. in legislation surrounding the Freedom of Information..*
P1:	cinntiú.. sa reachtaíocht um **Shaoráil Faisnéise**. *ensure.. in the legislation surrounding the Freedom of Information..*
P3:	chun a chinntiú.. sa reachtaíocht **SF**. *to ensure.. in the **FOI** legislation..*
NMT:	féachaint.. sa reachtaíocht um **Shaoráil Faisnéise**.. *see.. in the legislation surrounding the Freedom of Information..*
P2:	a fheacháint.. i reachtaíocht um **Shaoráil Faisnéise**.. *to see.. in legislation surrounding the Freedom of Information..*
P4:	féachaint.. sa reachtaíocht um **Shaoráil Faisnéise**.. *see.. in the legislation surrounding the Freedom of Information..*

Table 8: A portion of the PE output from P1, P2, P3 and P4. The EN data provided to the translators as the source text is also provided. The relevant MT output provided to translators is given above the participants output. A gloss for each sentence is indicated in italics below each GA output.

matic metrics can be useful in obtaining a rough idea of MT system quality, it does not always correlate with HE. Although in automatic metrics NMT was identified as the 'better' system and was the system translators deemed most accurate,[13] this did not consistently align with the scores generated using the PET output, nor the translators' perceptions of fluency or the system which they would most prefer to post-edit.[14]

Overall, we can see that, even with just four participants, results can vary from translator to translator with both automatic metrics and those gathered as a direct result of PE. As a result, it is unreasonable to expect any one automatic metric to perfectly mirror HE.

Within this study, we have observed HTER as the metric which most closely matches our participants' survey responses. However, it is important to note that with this study being limited to four

participants we are unable to make definitive conclusions as to the best metric with which to guide EN→GA MT system development. As might be expected, the recommended approach would be to use HE wherever possible, and, in cases where this is not feasible, a combination of automatic metrics will provide the broadest snapshot of MT quality.

In terms of future work, we propose a similar study with more participants. We have seen that translators vary in MT PE approaches, experience and opinion. Accordingly, more participants would provide us with a more accurate picture of EN→GA MT quality and would provide us with a greater amount of data points to extrapolate from. We also suggest a more fine-grained evaluation of EN→GA MT output. In the survey portion of this study we elicit opinions of MT quality over 100-sentence documents in general. In the future it may be beneficial to examine specific differences between EN-GA SMT and NMT at the sentence-level, examining variations in errors in case, semantics, tense, etc.

On a final note, it is worth considering that with the derogation of EN→GA translation within the EU lifting in 2021, there is an urgent requirement for Irish language translation with too few translators available to satisfy the demand as well as a lack of Irish language resources. This means that we have a greater need than ever for EN-GA MT systems designed with the end-user in mind.

Acknowledgements The ADAPT SFI Centre for Digital Media Technology is funded by Science Foundation Ireland through the SFI Research Centres Programme and is co-funded under the European Regional Development Fund through Grant #13/RC/2106. We thank the reviewers for their useful comments, and the four participants for their invaluable contribution to this research; go raibh míle maith agaibh.

References

Arcan, Mihael, Caoilfhionn Lane, Eoin O Droighneáin, and Paul Buitelaar. 2016. IRIS: English-Irish machine translation system. In *The International Conference on Language Resources and Evaluation*, pages 566–572, Portoroz, Slovenia.

Aziz, Wilker, Sheila Castilho, and Lucia Specia. 2012. PET: a tool for post-editing and assessing machine translation. In *The International Conference on Language Resources and Evaluation*, pages 3982–3987, Istanbul, Turkey.

---

[13]Three of the four translators chose the NMT system as the most accurate output in the post-task survey, see Table 5.

[14]Two of the four chose NMT for both 'fluency' and 'prefer' in Table 5.

Barrault, Loïc, Ondřej Bojar, Marta R Costa-jussà, Christian Federmann, Mark Fishel, Yvette Graham, Barry Haddow, Matthias Huck, Philipp Koehn, Shervin Malmasi, et al. 2019. Findings of the 2019 conference on machine translation (wmt19). In *Proceedings of the Fourth Conference on Machine Translation (Volume 2: Shared Task Papers, Day 1)*, pages 1–61, Florence, Italy.

Bayón, María Do Campo and Pilar Sánchez-Gijón. 2019. Evaluating machine translation in a low-resource language combination: Spanish-galician. In *Proceedings of Machine Translation Summit XVII Volume 2: Translator, Project and User Tracks*, pages 30–35, Dublin, Ireland.

Bojar, Ondřej, Rajen Chatterjee, Christian Federmann, Yvette Graham, Barry Haddow, Matthias Huck, Antonio Jimeno Yepes, Philipp Koehn, Varvara Logacheva, Christof Monz, et al. 2016. Findings of the 2016 conference on machine translation. In *Proceedings of the First Conference on Machine Translation: Volume 2, Shared Task Papers*, pages 131–198, Berlin, Germany.

Castilho, Sheila, Joss Moorkens, Federico Gaspari, Rico Sennrich, Vilelmini Sosoni, Panayota Georgakopoulou, Pintu Lohar, Andy Way, Antonio Valerio Miceli Barone, and Maria Gialama. 2017. A comparative quality evaluation of pbsmt and nmt using professional translators. page 116–131.

Castilho, Sheila, Stephen Doherty, Federico Gaspari, and Joss Moorkens. 2018. Approaches to human and machine Translation Quality Assessment. In *Translation Quality Assessment: From Principles to Practice*, volume 1 of *Machine Translation: Technologies and Applications*, pages 9–38. Springer International Publishing, July.

Cheng, Yong. 2019. Joint training for pivot-based neural machine translation. In *Joint Training for Neural Machine Translation*, pages 41–54. Springer.

Defauw, Arne, Sara Szoc, Tom Vanallemeersch, Anna Bardadym, Joris Brabers, Frederic Everaert, Kim Scholte, Koen Van Winckel, and Joachim Van den Bogaert. 2019. Developing a neural machine translation system for Irish. In *Proceedings of the 2nd Workshop on Technologies for MT of Low Resource Languages*, pages 32–38, Dublin, Ireland.

Dowling, Meghan, Lauren Cassidy, Eimear Maguire, Teresa Lynn, Ankit Srivastava, and John Judge. 2015. Tapadóir: Developing a statistical machine translation engine and associated resources for Irish. In *Proceedings of the The Fourth LRL Workshop: "Language Technologies in support of Less-Resourced Languages"*, pages 314–318, Poznan, Poland.

Dowling, Meghan, Teresa Lynn, Yvette Graham, and John Judge. 2016. English to Irish machine translation with automatic post-editing. In *PARIS Inalco du 4 au 8 juillet 2016*, page 42, Paris, France.

Dowling, Meghan, Teresa Lynn, Alberto Poncelas, and Andy Way. 2018. SMT versus NMT: Preliminary comparisons for Irish. In *Association for Machine Translation in the Americas (AMTA)*, pages 12–20, Boston, USA.

Dowling, Meghan, Teresa Lynn, and Andy Way. 2019. Investigating backtranslation for the improvement of English-Irish machine translation. *TEANGA, the Journal of the Irish Association for Applied Linguistics*, 26:1–25.

Esplà-Gomis, Miquel, Mikel L Forcada, Gema Ramírez-Sánchez, and Hieu Hoang. 2019. Paracrawl: Web-scale parallel corpora for the languages of the eu. In *Proceedings of Machine Translation Summit XVII Volume 2: Translator, Project and User Tracks*, pages 118–119, Dublin, Ireland.

Etchegoyhen, Thierry, Borja Anza Porras, Andoni Azpeitia, Eva Martínez Garcia, Paulo Vale, José Luis Fonseca, Teresa Lynn, Jane Dunne, Federico Gaspari, Andy Way, et al. 2018. ELRI. European language resource infrastructure. page 351.

European Language Resource Coordination. 2020. *ELRC WHITE PAPER Sustainable Language Data Sharing to Support Language Equality in Multilingual Europe*. OVD Verlag Saarbrucken, Saarbrucken.

Heafield, Kenneth. 2011. Kenlm: Faster and smaller language model queries. In *Proceedings of the Sixth Workshop on Statistical Machine Translation*, pages 187–197, Edinburgh, Scotland.

Imankulova, Aizhan, Raj Dabre, Atsushi Fujita, and Kenji Imamura. 2019. Exploiting out-of-domain parallel data through multilingual transfer learning for low-resource neural machine translation. In *Proceedings of Machine Translation Summit XVII Volume 1: Research Track*, pages 128–139, Dublin, Ireland.

Judge, John, Ailbhe Ní Chasaide, Rose Ní Dhubhda, Kevin P. Scannell, and Elaine Uí Dhonnchadha. 2012. *An Ghaeilge sa Ré Dhigiteach – The Irish Language in the Digital Age*. META-NET White Paper Series. Georg Rehm and Hans Uszkoreit (Series Editors). Springer. Available online at `http://www.meta-net.eu/whitepapers`.

Klein, Guillaume, Yoon Kim, Yuntian Deng, Jean Senellart, and Alexander M Rush. 2017. Opennmt: Open-source toolkit for neural machine translation. In *Proceedings of ACL 2017, System Demonstrations*, pages 67–72, Vancouver, Canada.

Koehn, Philipp and Rebecca Knowles. 2017. Six challenges for neural machine translation. In *Proceedings of the First Workshop on Neural Machine Translation*, pages 28–39, Vancouver, Canada.

Koehn, Philipp, Hieu Hoang, Alexandra Birch, Chris Callison-Burch, Marcello Federico, Nicola Bertoldi, Brooke Cowan, Wade Shen, Christine Moran,

Richard Zens, et al. 2007. Moses: Open source toolkit for statistical machine translation. In *Proceedings of the 45th annual meeting of the ACL on interactive poster and demonstration sessions*, pages 177–180, Prague, Czech Republic.

Lakew, Surafel M, Mattia A Di Gangi, and Marcello Federico. 2017. Multilingual neural machine translation for low resource languages. In *Fourth Italian Conference on Computational Linguistics*, page 189, Rome, Italy.

Läubli, Samuel, Sheila Castilho, Graham Neubig, Rico Sennrich, Qinlan Shen, and Antonio Toral. 2020. A set of recommendations for assessing human–machine parity in language translation. *Journal of Artificial Intelligence Research*, 67:653–672.

Liu, Chao-Hong, Catarina Cruz Silva, Longyue Wang, and Andy Way. 2018. Pivot machine translation using chinese as pivot language. In *China Workshop on Machine Translation*, pages 74–85, Wuyishan, China.

Lynn, Teresa, Micheál Ó Conaire, and Jane Dunne, 2019. *Country Profile Ireland*, pages 92–97. German Research Center for Artificial Intelligence (DFKI), Saarbrucken, Germany.

Moorkens, Joss. 2020. Comparative satisfaction among freelance and directly-employed Irish-language translators. *The International Journal for Translation & Interpreting Research*, 12(1):55–73.

Murray, Kenton, Jeffery Kinnison, Toan Q Nguyen, Walter Scheirer, and David Chiang. 2019. Autosizing the transformer network: Improving speed, efficiency, and performance for low-resource machine translation. In *Proceedings of the 3rd Workshop on Neural Generation and Translation*, pages 231–240, Hong Kong.

Neubig, Graham, Zi-Yi Dou, Junjie Hu, Paul Michel, Danish Pruthi, and Xinyi Wang. 2019. compare-mt: A tool for holistic comparison of language generation systems. In *Proceedings of the 2019 Conference of the North American Chapter of the Association for Computational Linguistics (Demonstrations)*, pages 35–41, Minneapolis, Minnesota.

Ondřej, Bojar, Rajen Chatterjee, Federmann Christian, Graham Yvette, Haddow Barry, Huck Matthias, Koehn Philipp, Liu Qun, Logacheva Varvara, Monz Christof, et al. 2017. Findings of the 2017 conference on machine translation (wmt17). In *Second Conference onMachine Translation*, pages 169–214, Copenhagen, Denmark.

Papineni, Kishore, Salim Roukos, Todd Ward, and Wei-Jing Zhu. 2002. Bleu: a method for automatic evaluation of machine translation. In *Proceedings of the 40th annual meeting on association for computational linguistics*, pages 311–318, Philadelphia, Pennsylvania.

Poncelas, Alberto, Dimitar Shterionov, Andy Way, Gideon Maillette de Buy Wenniger, and Peyman Passban. 2018. Investigating backtranslation in neural machine translation. In *Proceedings of the 21st Annual Conference of the European Association for Machine Translation*, pages 249–258, Alacant, Spain.

Popović, Maja. 2015. chrf: character n-gram f-score for automatic mt evaluation. In *Proceedings of the Tenth Workshop on Statistical Machine Translation*, pages 392–395, Lisbon, Portugal.

Publications Office of the European Union. 2011. *Interinstitutional style guide*. Available online at `http://publications.europa.eu/resource/cellar/e774ea2a-ef84-4bf6-be92-c9ebebf91c1b.0018.03/DOC_2`.

Snover, Matthew, Bonnie Dorr, Richard Schwartz, Linnea Micciulla, and John Makhoul. 2006. A study of translation edit rate with targeted human annotation. In *Proceedings of the 7th Conference of the. Association for Machine Translation of the Americas*, pages 223–231, Cambridge, Massachusetts, USA.

Snover, Matthew G, Nitin Madnani, Bonnie Dorr, and Richard Schwartz. 2009. Ter-plus: paraphrase, semantic, and alignment enhancements to translation edit rate. *Machine Translation*, 23(2-3):117–127.

Toral, Antonio, Sheila Castilho, Ke Hu, and Andy Way. 2018. Attaining the unattainable? reassessing claims of human parity in neural machine translation. In *Proceedings of the Third Conference on Machine Translation: Research Papers*, pages 113–123, Brussels, Belgium.

Vanmassenhove, Eva, Dimitar Shterionov, and Andy Way. 2019. Lost in translation: Loss and decay of linguistic richness in machine translation. In *Proceedings of Machine Translation Summit XVII Volume 1: Research Track*, pages 222–232.

Vaswani, Ashish, Noam Shazeer, Niki Parmar, Jakob Uszkoreit, Llion Jones, Aidan N Gomez, Łukasz Kaiser, and Illia Polosukhin. 2017. Attention is all you need. In *Advances in neural information processing systems*, pages 5998–6008, California, USA.

Wang, Weiyue, Jan-Thorsten Peter, Hendrik Rosendahl, and Hermann Ney. 2016. Character: Translation edit rate on character level. In *Proceedings of the First Conference on Machine Translation: Volume 2, Shared Task Papers*, pages 505–510, Berlin, Germany.

Werlen, Lesly Miculicich, Dhananjay Ram, Nikolaos Pappas, and James Henderson. 2018. Document-level neural machine translation with hierarchical attention networks. *CoRR*, abs/1809.01576.

Wu, Hua and Haifeng Wang. 2007. Pivot language approach for phrase-based statistical machine translation. *Machine Translation*, 21(3):165–181.

Machine Translation Quality: A comparative evaluation of SMT, NMT and tailored-NMT outputs

Maria Stasimioti
Vilelmini Sosoni
Department of Foreign Languages,
Translation and Interpreting
Ionian University
Corfu, Greece
stasimioti@ionio.gr
sosoni@ionio.gr

Despoina Mouratidis
Katia Kermanidis
Department of Informatics
Ionian University
Corfu, Greece
c12mour@ionio.gr
kerman@ionio.gr

Abstract

The present study aims to compare three systems: a generic statistical machine translation, a generic neural machine translation and a tailored-NMT system focusing on the English to Greek language pair. The comparison is carried out following a mixed-methods approach, i.e. automatic metrics, as well as side-by-side ranking, adequacy and fluency rating, measurement of actual post editing effort and human error analysis performed by 16 postgraduate Translation students. The findings reveal a higher score for both the generic NMT and the tailored-NMT outputs as regards automatic metrics and human evaluation metrics, with the tailored-NMT output faring even better than the generic NMT output.

1 Introduction

Latest technological advances in machine translation (MT) have led to a wider availability of MT systems for various language pairs and neural machine translation (NMT) has been widely hailed as a significant development in the improvement of the quality of MT, given that NMT models have been proven to consistently outperform statistical machine translation (SMT) models in shared tasks, as well as in various project outcomes (Toral and Sánchez-Cartagena, 2017; Castilho et al., 2017a, 2017b, 2018; Klubička et al., 2017, 2018; Popović, 2017, 2018).

MT has been moved "from the peripheries of the translation field closer to the centre" (Koponen, 2016a, p. 131) and has been integrated in the translation workflow, by using machine translated text as a raw translation to be further post-edited by a translator (Lommel and DePalma, 2016; Koponen, 2016b).

The differences between various MT systems, as regards the quality of their output and the types of errors included therein, have been reported by several recent studies. Some (Bahdanau et al., 2015; Jean et al., 2015; Junczys-Dowmunt, 2016; Dowling et al., 2018) relied on automatic evaluation metrics (AEMs) like BLEU (Papineni et al., 2002) and HTER (Snover et al., 2006); others used human evaluations of the MT output quality, employing adequacy and fluency ratings (Bentivogli et al., 2016), manual error analyses (Klubička et al., 2017, 2018; Popović, 2018) or a combination of methods (Burchardt et al., 2017; Castilho et al., 2017a, 2017b, 2018; Toral and Sánchez-Cartagena, 2017; Shterionov et al., 2018; Koponen et al., 2019; Jia et al., 2019; Stasimioti and Sosoni, 2019).

Drawing on these studies, the present study aims to compare three systems: a generic SMT, a generic NMT and a tailored-NMT system, namely a factored or custom-trained NMT system, focusing on the English to Greek language pair. The comparison is performed following a mixed-methods approach, i.e. automatic metrics, as well as side-by-side ranking, adequacy and fluency rating, measurement of actual post-editing (PE) effort and human error analysis. To the best of our knowledge there are no studies to date for the English to Greek language pair which compare generic and custom-trained MT systems, while there are only a few related studies to date comparing SMT and NMT systems (Castilho et al., 2017b; Stasimioti and Sosoni, 2019)

2 Methodology

A mixed-methods approach was adopted in the present study with a view to producing reliable results. AEMs and human evaluation metrics, including eye-tracking and keystroke logging data for measuring the effort expended by translators while carrying out full PE of the MT output

Martins, Moniz, Fumega, Martins, Batista, Coheur, Parra, Trancoso, Turchi, Bisazza, Moorkens, Guerberof, Nurminen, Marg, Forcada (eds.)
Proceedings of the 22nd Annual Conference of the European Association for Machine Translation, p. 441–450
Lisboa, Portugal, November 2020.

generated by three different systems (Google Translate SMT system, Google Translate NMT system, tailored-NMT system), side-by-side ranking of the MT outputs, adequacy and fluency rating and human error classification were used to evaluate the quality of the MT output of these three MT systems and investigate their differences.

A series of experiments were carried out during the 2018-2019 Spring Semester at the Department of Foreign Languages, Translation and Interpreting of the Ionian University. Twenty Greek students enrolled on the MA in the Science of Translation initially participated in this study. However, only sixteen completed all tasks, since the participation in the tasks was optional. All participants signed a consent form, while all stored data were fully anonymised in accordance with Greek Law 2472/97 (as amended by Laws 3783/2009, 3917/2011 and 4070/2012).

2.1 Participants and training

As can be seen in Table 1, all participants were female, the majority belonged to the 18-24 and 25-34 age groups, they all had an undergraduate degree either in Translation or in a related field, while only five of the participants had professional experience in translation. In addition, none of the participants had experience in PE.

Gender	Female	16
	18-24	10
Age distribution	25-34	5
	45-54	1
	Undergraduate degree holder	13
Education level	Postgraduate degree holder	2
	PhD holder	1
Degree type	Translation	9
	Other	7
Experience in Translation	Yes	4
	No	12
Experience in PE	Yes	0
	No	16

Table 1. Participants' gender, age distribution, education level, degree type and experience in translation and PE

PE training was a prerequisite for participating in this study. For that reason, specific training was offered in the context of the compulsory module "Translation Tools" and aimed to introduce students to MT and PE as well as to the recent developments in the respective fields. Upon completion of the training, students were expected, among others, to be able to (i) use MT during the pre-translation process, (ii) evaluate MT output using both automatic and human evaluation metrics and (iii) post-edit MT output according to the expected level of quality (full/light PE).

To that end, the topics covered included, among others, the theory and history of MT and PE, the basic principles of MT technology, analysis of the dominant systems in the market, the importance of controlled language and pre-editing for MT, quality metrics and evaluation of MT output, PE levels of quality, PE effort and productivity (temporal, technical and cognitive effort), MT output error identification, MT engine implementation in the translation workflow and post-editor profile and associated skills (O'Brien, 2002; Depraetere, 2010; Doherty et al., 2012; Doherty and Kenny, 2014; Kenny and Doherty, 2014; Koponen, 2015; Guerberof and Moorkens, 2019).

2.2 Source Texts

The source texts (STs) used in this study were 4 short (~140 words) semi-specialised texts about the 2019 EU elections selected from the British daily newspaper *The Guardian*. They all had comparable Lexile® scores (between 1200L and 1300L), i.e. they were suitable for 11th/12th graders (see Table 2). The Lexile Analyzer[1] was used as it relies on an algorithm to evaluate the reading demand – or text complexity – of books, articles and other materials.

	Text 1	Text 2	Text 3	Text 4
Lexile® Measure	1200L–1300L	1200L–1300L	1200L–1300L	1200L–1300L
Number of sentences	7	6	8	8
Mean sentence length	20.86	23.50	20.00	19.71
Word count	146	141	140	138

Table 2. Lexile® scores for the STs used in the study

---

[1] https://la-tools.lexile.com/free-analyze/

2.3 MT systems

As already mentioned, for the present study we used three different MT systems: the SMT system developed by Google (Google Translate SMT system - GSMT), the NMT system developed by Google (Google Translate NMT system - GNMT) and a tailored-NMT system. The first two are generic MT systems, i.e. general purpose systems, trained with huge amounts of data from various subject areas and thus suitable to translate texts in all subject areas or domains. Google Translate, in particular, is the best known MT service, which can be used either free of charge as a standalone tool (translate.google.com) or for a small fee via an API for translating large amounts of text or for using it within a CAT tool. The third system is a custom-trained system developed by Kanavos and Nadalis (2019) with the Open NMT toolkit (Klein et al., 2017) and trained with publicly available parallel corpora, including a parallel corpus compiled from the RAPID multilingual parallel corpus compiled from all press releases of the Press Release Database of European Commission released between 1975 and end of 2016[2] as well as a parallel corpus of English and South-East European Languages which is based on the content published on the SETimes.com[3] news portal. Although generic MT systems provide "reasonable quality" (Vasiljevs et al., 2016: 134) for many language pairs (Aiken, 2019), they do not perform particularly well for domain and user-specific texts and are much less effective than custom-trained MT systems, which in most cases produce better results (Ping, 2009).

2.4 Evaluation

In order to evaluate the MT output generated by each MT system we used both AEMs and human evaluation metrics.

2.4.1 Automatic Evaluation Metrics (AEMs)

The AEMs used in this study were BLEU, METEOR, WER and TER. BLEU measures the similarity between the MT output and a reference translation, METEOR (Lavie and Agarwal, 2007) is based on the weighted harmonic mean of unigram precision and recall, while WER (Zechner and Waibel, 2000) and TER are based on Levenshtein distance and calculate the number of edits required to make an MT output match the reference translation. It should be noted that we used two (2) reference translations by professional translators, since the use of a single human-translated reference tends to introduce bias (Popovic et al., 2016).

2.4.2 Human Evaluation

As pointed out, human evaluation included eye-tracking and keystroke logging data for measuring the effort expended by translators while carrying out full PE of each MT output, side-by-side ranking of the MT outputs, adequacy and fluency rating and error classification. As regards the PE, the participants were asked to perform full PE of the MT output (either the output from the generic SMT system, the generic NMT system or the tailored-NMT system) of four semi-specialised texts, which were presented to them in a random order. All participants were asked to rank and rate for adequacy and fluency all the segments from each MT output for all four texts (87 segments in total) and perform a classification of all the errors found therein. Each participant performed the tasks in one go, starting from the PE and moving on to the ranking, rating and error analysis tasks. The questionnaires were filled right after the completion of the PE tasks.

2.4.2.1 Measurement of PE effort (temporal, technical and cognitive)

According to Krings (2001), there are three categories of PE effort: (i) temporal effort, (ii) technical effort and (ii) cognitive effort (Krings, 2001, p.179). Cognitive effort is directly related to temporal effort and technical effort.

For the aims of this study, the participants were asked to carry out PE tasks while the temporal effort (total task time), the technical effort (keystrokes: insertions and deletions) and the cognitive effort (number of fixations, mean fixation duration and total gaze time) expended were registered using a Tobii X2-60 remote eye-tracker and the Translog-II software (Carl, 2012). The effectiveness of using eye-tracking as an MT evaluation technique has been proven by previous studies (Doherty et al., 2010). Although using eye-tracking involves humans, much of the subjectivity involved in human evaluation of MT quality is removed as the processes that eye-tracking measures are largely unconscious (Doherty et al., 2010).

Prior to the execution of the tasks, a group meeting was organised during which the participants were informed about the nature of the experiments, the task requirements and the general as well as task-specific guidelines they

---

[2] http://europa.eu/rapid/

[3] http://www.setimes.com

had to follow. In particular, the participants were asked to carry out full PE of the MT output generated by the aforementioned three MT systems, according to the task-specific guidelines, i.e retain as much raw MT translation/output as possible, transfer the message accurately, fix any omissions and/or additions (at the level of sentence, phrase or word), correct mistranslations, correct morphological errors, correct misspellings and typos, fix incorrect punctuation if it interferes with the intended message, correct erroneous terminology, fix inconsistent use of terms and do not introduce stylistic changes. The task began with a warm-up PE task which aimed to familiarise each participant with the procedure; the data from the warm-up task were not included in the ensuing analysis and discussion. The actual experimental task involved the full PE of the MT output of four semi-specialised texts by each one of the participants. The texts for full PE were presented to the participants in a random order. During the experiment, the ST was displayed in the Translog-II software at the top half of the screen and the MT output at the bottom half. The participants were asked to carry out the tasks at the speed at which they would normally work in their everyday work as translators; therefore, no time constraint was imposed. In addition, they worked directly on the MT output.

2.4.2.2   Side-by-side ranking

After the eye-tracking experiments the participants were given a side-by-side task for each text (Text 1, Text 2, Text 3 and Text 4) and were asked to read the Greek translations of each English source segment carefully and rank them in order from best to worst. The SMT, NMT and tailored-NMT outputs were presented to participants using Google Forms in a random order.

2.4.2.3   Adequacy and fluency

Following the ranking task, the participants were asked to rate each segment from each MT output for all four texts (87 segments in total) for adequacy and fluency (defined as the extent to which a target segment is correct in the target language and reflects the meaning of the source segment) on a five-point Likert scale for each segment.

In particular, the translators were asked to rate adequacy in response to the question "Is the MEANING of the English sentence kept in the translation?". A five-point Likert scale was used, where 1 is "Not at all", 2 is "Barely", 3 is "Partly",

4 is "Mostly" and 5 is "Fully". Similarly, the translators were asked to rate fluency in response to the question "Considering only GRAMMAR and SPELLING, the translated sentence is:". Like in the case of adequacy, a five-point Likert scale was used where 1 is "Very poor", 2 is "Poor", 3 is "Fair", 4 is "Good" and 5 is "Excellent".

2.4.2.4   Error classification

The last task for the participants was an error classification task. The error typology used in this study was suggested by Stasimioti and Sosoni (2019) and was a combination of the subset of the Dynamic Quality Framework (DQF) and Multidimensional Quality Metrics (MQM) harmonized error typology suitable for MT analysis as suggested by Lommel and Melby (2018) and the MQM error typology which was widely used in previous studies mainly due to the flexibility of the error types and their granularity (Klubička et al., 2017; 2018; Carl and Báez, 2019).

In particular the participants were asked to classify the errors of each segment in two main error categories and their subcategories; adequacy errors: addition, omission, mistranslation, untranslated text, terminology error and fluency errors: error in grammar, error in punctuation, error in style, spelling error and typo.

3   Findings and discussion

3.1   Automatic Evaluation Metrics (AEMs)

Table 3 shows the scores of the AEMs we used per system.

	SMT	NMT	tailored-NMT
BLEU	0.34	0.39	**0.46**
METEOR	0.48	0.52	**0.56**
WER	0.50	0.49	**0.43**
TER	0.52	0.51	**0.39**

Table 3. Average of AEMs per system

The tailored-NMT system outperformed both the SMT and the NMT systems. In further detail, it is observed that the tailored-NMT output shared more common words with the reference translations (higher BLEU score) than did the SMT and NMT outputs. In addition, the higher METEOR score observed at both segment and system levels in the tailored-NMT output showed that there are significant matches between words and phrases in the tailored-NMT output and the reference translations. As regards TER and WER, the majority of edits observed were substitutions and deletions. The tailored-NMT system achieved the lowest score between the systems. Given that TER and WER are edit-distance metrics, a lower score indicates better performance. As far as the SMT and NMT systems are concerned, the latter performed better in all cases achieving higher BLEU and METEOR scores and lower TER and WER scores.

3.2 Human evaluation

3.2.1 Measurement of PE effort (temporal, technical and cognitive)

Temporal effort

As far as the temporal effort is concerned, we measured the average time (in minutes) the participants needed to post-edit each MT output. As it emerges from Figure 1, the MT output generated by the tailored-NMT system required less time for full PE ($M = 8.73$, $SD = 3.16$) compared to the MT outputs generated by the NMT system ($M = 9.85$, $SD = 3.55$) and the SMT system ($M = 12.76$, $SD = 5.11$). A one-way ANOVA was conducted to compare the effect of the MT output on temporal effort (task duration) when post-editing the SMT output, the NMT output and the tailored-NMT output. There was a significant effect of the MT output on temporal effort for these three conditions $F(2,45) = 4.28$, $p = 0.019$. Post hoc comparisons indicated that mean task duration when post-editing the SMT output was significantly different, i.e. higher, than mean task duration when post-editing the tailored-NMT output. However, mean task duration when post-editing the NMT output did not significantly differ from mean task duration when post-editing the SMT output and the tailored-NMT output.

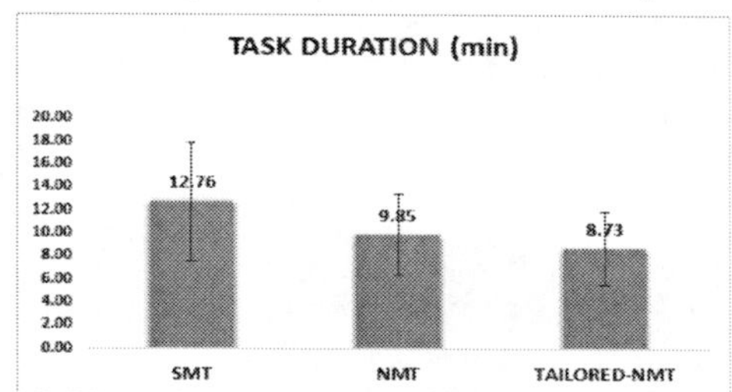

Figure 1. Temporal effort: Mean and standard deviation of task duration per system

Technical effort

Technical effort is generally measured by the number of keystrokes, which can be distinguished into insertions and deletions. As it emerges from Figure 2 and similarly to temporal effort, the participants performed fewer keystrokes when post-editing the tailored-NMT output ($M = 228$, $SD = 114$) compared to the keystrokes performed when post-editing the NMT output ($M = 362$, $SD = 116$) and the SMT output ($M = 520$, $SD = 208$). A one-way ANOVA yielded a statistically significant difference $F(2,45) = 14.72$, $p < 0.05$ for the average number of keystrokes (insertions and deletions), as well as for the insertions $F(2,45) = 14.18$, $p < 0.05$ and deletions $F(2,45) = 14.12$, $p < 005$ separately. Post hoc comparisons indicated that the average number of keystrokes performed when post-editing the SMT output was significantly different, i.e. higher, than the average number of keystrokes performed when post-editing the NMT output and the tailored-NMT output. In addition, the average number of keystrokes performed when post-editing the tailored-NMT output was significantly different, i.e lower, than the average number of keystrokes performed when post-editing the NMT output. The same applies for the insertions and deletions separately.

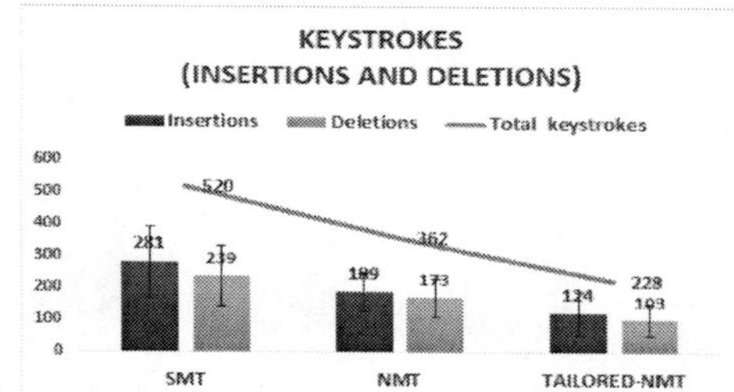

Figure 2. Technical effort: Mean and standard deviation of keystrokes per system

Cognitive effort

Pause duration and pause density (Lacruz and Shreve, 2014; Daems et al., 2017; Koponen et al., 2019; Jia et al., 2019), fixation count, fixation duration and gaze time (Mesa-Lao, 2014; Moorkens et al., 2015) have been used in previous studies as indicators of cognitive effort. In our study we measured the average fixation count, the mean fixation duration (in milliseconds) as well as the average total gaze time (in minutes), i.e. the sum of all fixation durations, on both areas of the screen (ST at the top half of the screen and MT output at the bottom half of the screen) in order to compare the cognitive effort expended by the translators when post-editing each MT output. As far as the average fixation count is concerned (see Figure 3), this was higher when post-editing the SMT output ($M = 1460$, $SD = 547$) than the NMT output ($M = 1154$, $SD = 421$) and the tailored-NMT output ($M = 1089$, $SD = 375$). Apart from the higher average fixation count, the SMT output also triggered longer gaze time ($M = 7.97$, $SD = 2.90$) than the NMT ($M = 6.32$, $SD = 2.31$) and the tailored-NMT output ($M = 5.59$, $SD = 1.86$) (see Figure 4). The mean fixation duration was exactly the same when post-editing the SMT and the NMT output ($M = 329$, $SD = 34$ and $M = 329$, $SD = 28$ respectively) and slightly lower when post-editing the tailored-NMT output ($M = 311$, $SD = 33$) (see Figure 5). A one-way ANOVA yielded a statistically significant difference $F(2,45) = 4.11$, $p = 0.023$ for the total gaze time, but not for the number of fixations $F(2,45) = 3.05$, $p = 0.057$ or the mean fixation duration $F(2,45) = 1.63$, $p = 0.206$. Post hoc comparisons indicated that total gaze time when post-editing the SMT output was significantly different, i.e. longer, than total gaze time only when post-editing the tailored-NMT output. In addition, the average fixation count when post-editing the SMT output was significantly different, i.e. higher, than the average fixation count only when post-editing the tailored-NMT output.

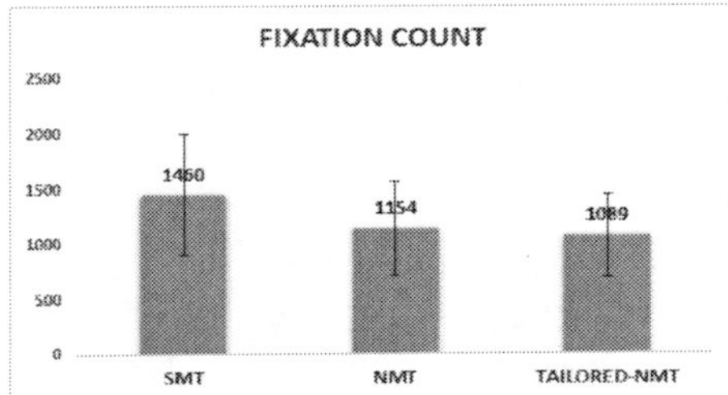

Figure 3. Cognitive effort: Mean and standard deviation of fixation count per system

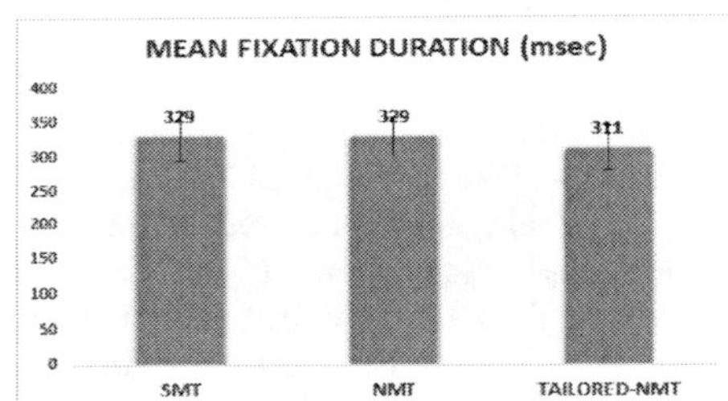

Figure 4. Cognitive effort: Mean and standard deviation of mean fixation duration per system

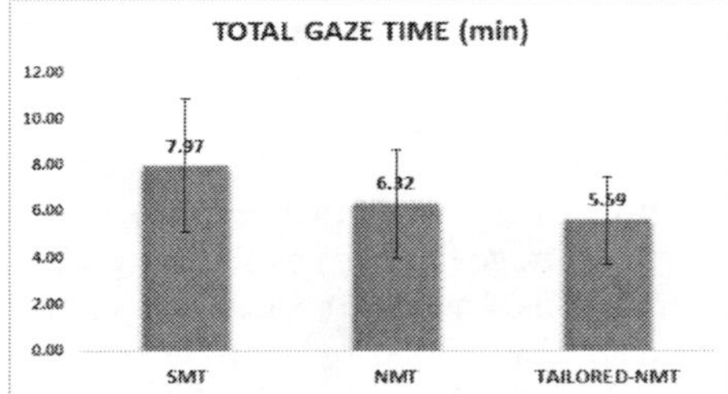

Figure 5. Cognitive effort: Mean and standard deviation of total gaze time per system

3.2.2 Side-by-side ranking

As it emerges from Figure 6, the tailored-NMT output was ranked as the best by 37% of the participants, compared to 34% for the SMT output and 29% for the NMT output. The SMT output was ranked as the worst by almost half (45%) of the participants, while the NMT output was ranked second by 53% of the participants. It is observed that quite a high percentage, namely 38% of the participants, ranked tailored-NMT output as the worst. This may be explained by the higher number of omissions and punctuation errors found in the output as can be seen in the error classification in 3.2.4. To assess the agreement between the annotators we computed Fleiss' kappa coefficient (Fleiss, 1971). Inter-annotator agreement shows fair agreement among the annotators ($\kappa = 0.40$).

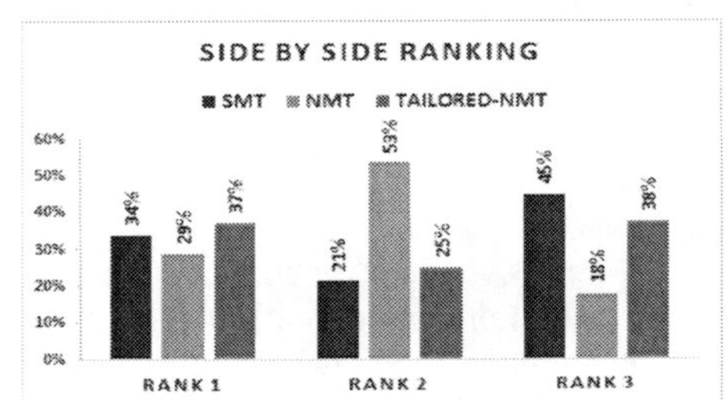

Figure 6. Average percentage of ranking per system

3.2.3 Adequacy and fluency

As it emerges from Figure 7, the tailored-NMT output was rated higher for both adequacy and fluency followed by the NMT output. In particular, both the tailored-NMT and the NMT outputs were deemed to be good by the translators/annotators, both as regards the grammaticality and the conveyance of meaning, while the SMT output was deemed to be fair in both respects. Inter-annotator agreement shows fair agreement among the annotators for fluency ($\kappa = 0.29$) and slight agreement for adequacy ($\kappa = 0.10$).

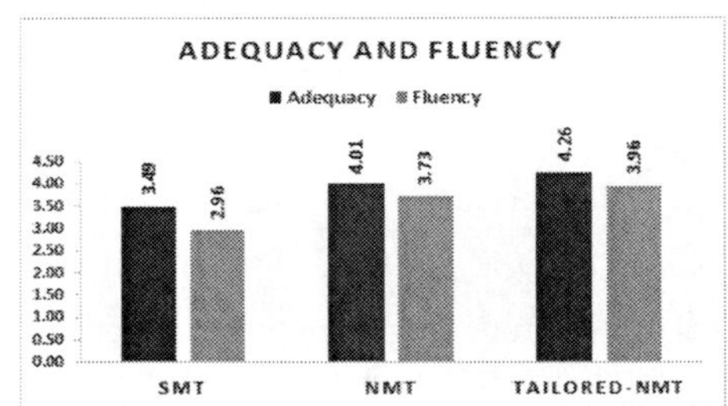

Figure 7. Weighted average of adequacy and fluency rating per system

3.2.4 Error classification

As far as the number of errors is concerned (see Figure 8), the tailored-NMT output contains the lowest number of errors overall, while the SMT output contains the highest number of errors overall.

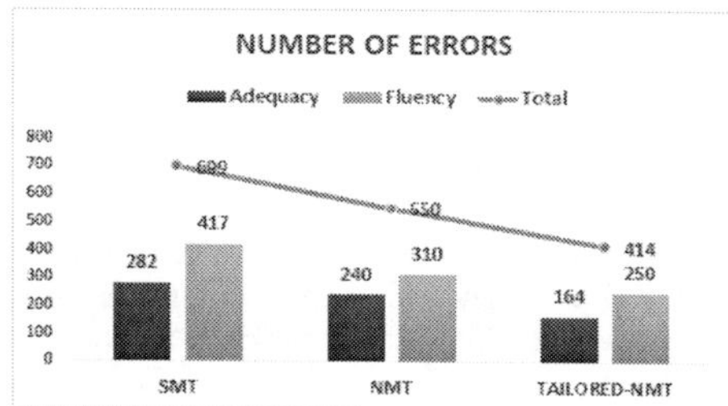

Figure 8. Total number of errors per system

As far as the types of errors are concerned (see Figures 8 and 9), we observed that all MT outputs contain more errors at the level of fluency than at the level of adequacy.

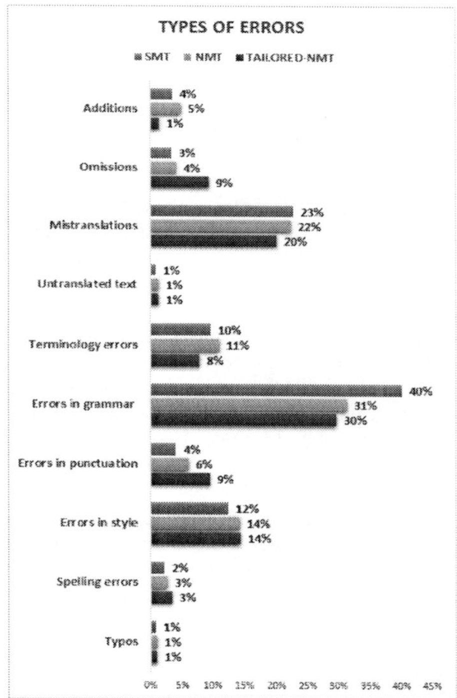

Figure 9. Average percentage of error types per system

As regards the category of fluency, the SMT output contains significantly more grammatical errors than the NMT and tailored-NMT outputs. Another interesting finding as regards fluency involves the category of punctuation. The tailored-NMT output contains almost 60% more punctuation errors than the SMT output and almost 30% more than the NMT output. This difference is due to the fact that the em dashes found in the STs are omitted in the tailored-NMT output in all cases. As far as the category of adequacy is concerned, the tailored-NMT output contains slightly fewer mistranslations, terminological errors and additions but more omissions than the NMT and SMT outputs. Inter-annotator agreement shows fair agreement among the annotators ($\kappa = 0.22$).

4 Discussion and conclusion

This paper reports on a comparative evaluation of generic SMT, generic NMT and tailored-NMT outputs for the English to Greek language pair using AEMs and human evaluation metrics, including eye-tracking and keystroke logging data, side-by-side ranking of the MT outputs, adequacy and fluency rating and error classification. As regards the differences between the SMT and NMT outputs, this study shows that the NMT systems produce translations of higher quality and thus corroborates the findings of previous studies on various language pairs (Toral and Sánchez-Cartagena, 2017; Klubička et al., 2017, 2018; Jia et al., 2019; Koponen et al., 2019), including the English-Greek language pair (Castilho et al., 2017a, 2017b; Stasimioti and Sosoni, 2019). In particular, the analysis reveals a higher score for both the generic NMT and the tailored-NMT outputs as regards automatic metrics and human evaluation metrics, with the tailored-NMT output faring even better than the generic NMT output. In addition, the tailored-NMT output was ranked as the best and was rated higher for both adequacy and fluency, a fact which explains the reduced temporal, technical and cognitive effort expended during its PE.

The decrease in PE effort can also be explained by the lowest number of errors found in the tailored-NMT output. Another interesting finding is that all the MT outputs contain more errors at the level of fluency than at the level of adequacy with the most typical fluency errors being grammatical errors. Both NMT outputs contain fewer grammatical errors than the SMT output, confirming thus the findings of previous studies for improved quality of the NMT systems at the level of fluency - not only for the English-Greek language pair (Castilho et al., 2017a, 2017b; Stasimioti and Sosoni, 2019) but also for other language-pairs, such as English-Czech, English-German, English- Finnish, English-Romanian,

English-Russian, English-Croatian and English-Chinese (Toral and Sánchez-Cartagena, 2017; Klubička et al., 2017, 2018; Jia et al., 2019). However, no difference between the generic NMT and the tailored-NMT outputs was reported. Another interesting finding involves the category of punctuation where the tailored-NMT output fares worse than both the generic NMT and the generic SMT output. Finally, in terms of adequacy, the tailored-NMT output fares better with slightly fewer mistranslations, terminological errors and additions than the generic NMT and the generic SMT outputs, although it includes more omissions than the former.

The findings point to the fact that there are limits to generic MT models, as they are not tuned to provide translations that are unique to a specific genre and thus business or industry. Although the development of a tailored-NMT system can be particularly compute intensive, and therefore too expensive and time-consuming – especially in cases where there are not enough parallel data to train a new good quality and appropriately adapted system – the higher quality and the reduced cognitive, technical and temporal effort suggest that it is worth exploring further.

Acknowledgement We would like to thank the HUBIC Lab (Raptis and Giagkou, 2016) for providing the Tobii X2-60 remote eye-tracker for the purposes of this study.

References

Aiken, Milam. 2019. An Updated Evaluation of Google Translate Accuracy. *Studies in Linguistics and Literature*. 3:253.

Bahdanau, Dzmitry, Kyunghyun Cho, and Yoshua Bengio. 2015. Neural Machine Translation by Jointly Learning to Align and Translate. In *Proceedings of the 3rd International Conference on Learning Representations*. San Diego, CA, USA.

Bentivogli, Luisa, Arianna Bisazza, Mauro Cettolo, and Marcello Federico. 2016. Neural versus phrase-based machine translation quality: a case study. In EMNLP 2016 *Proceedings of the 2016 conference on empirical methods in natural language processing*. Austin, Texas, 1-5 November 2016. Association for Computational Linguistics, 257–267.

Burchardt, Aljoscha, Vivien Macketanz, Jon Degdari, Georg Heigold, Jan-Thorsten Peter, and Philip Williams. 2017. A linguistic evaluation of rule-based, phrase-based, and neural MT engines. *Prague Bulletin of Mathematical Linguistics*, 108: 159–170.

Carl, Michael. 2012. Translog – II: A program for recording user activity data for empirical reading and writing research. In *Proceedings of the 8th international conference on language resources and evaluation*. Istanbul, Turkey, 21-27 May 2012. European Language Resources Association (ELRA), 4108–4112.

Carl, Michael, and María Cristina Toledo Báez. 2019. Machine Translation Errors and the Translation Process: A Study across Different Languages. *Journal of Specialised Translation*, 31:107-132.

Castilho, Sheila, Joss Moorkens, Federico Gaspari, Iacer Calixto, John Tinsley, and Andy Way. 2017a. Is neural machine translation the new state of the art? *Prague Bulletin of Mathematical Linguistics*, 108:109–120.

Castilho, Sheila, Joss Moorkens, Federico Gaspari, Rico Sennrich, Vilelmini Sosoni, Yota Georgakopoulou, Pintu Lohar, Andy Way, Antonio Miceli Barone, and Maria Gialama. 2017b. A Comparative quality evaluation of PBSMT and NMT using professional translators. In *Proceedings of Machine Translation Summit XVI*, vol.1: Research Track. Nagoya, Japan, 18-22 September 2017. 16th Machine Translation Summit, 116–131.

Castilho, Sheila, Joss Moorkens, Federico Gaspari, Rico Sennrich, Yota Georgakopoulou, Andy Way, Antonio Miceli Barone, and Maria Gialama. 2018. Evaluating MT for massive open online courses: A multifaceted comparison between PBSMT and NMT systems. *Machine Translation*, 32(3):255–278.

Daems, Joke, Sonia Vandepitte, Robert J. Hartsuiker, and Macken, Lieve. 2017. Identifying the Machine Translation Error Types with the Greatest Impact on Post-editing Effort. *Frontiers in Psychology*. 8: 1282.

Depraetere, Ilse. 2010. What counts as useful advice in a university post-editing training context? Report on a case study. In François Yvon and Viggo Hansen (eds). 2010. *EAMT 2010: Proceedings of the 14th annual conference of the European association for machine translation*, 27-28 May 2010 Saint-Raphaël Congrès, Saint-Raphaël, France, European Association for Machine Translation.

Doherty, Stephen, Sharon O' Brien, and Michael Carl. 2010. Eye tracking as an Automatic MT Evaluation Technique. *Machine Translation*. 24:1-13.

Doherty, Stephen, Dorothy Kenny, and Andy Way. 2012. Taking statistical machine translation to the student translator. In AMTA-2012 *The Tenth Biennial Conference of the Association for Machine Translation in the Americas*. San Diego, USA, 28 October-1 November 2012. AMTA, n.p.

Doherty, Stephen, and Dorothy Kenny. 2014. The design and evaluation of a statistical machine translation syllabus for translation students. *The Interpreter and Translator Trainer*, 8(2):295–315.

Dowling, Meghan, Teresa Lynn, Alberto Poncelas and Andy Way. 2018. SMT versus NMT: preliminary comparisons for Irish. In *AMTA 2018 Workshop: LoResMT 2018*, 17-21 Mar 2018, Boston, MA. USA.

Guerberof, Anna and Joss Moorkens. 2019. Machine translation and post-editing training as part of a master's programme. *Jostrans: The Journal of Specialised Translation*, 31:217–238.

Fleiss, Joseph. L. 1971. Measuring nominal scale agreement among many raters. *Psychological Bulletin* 76(5):378-382.

Jia, Yanfang, Michael Carl, and Xiangling Wang. 2019. Post-editing neural machine translation versus phrase-based machine translation for English–Chinese. *Machine Translation* (2019).

Jean, Sébastien, Orhan Firat, Kyunghyun Cho, Roland Memisevic, and Yoshua Bengio. 2015. Montreal Neural Machine Translation Systems for WMT'15. In *Proceedings of the Tenth Workshop on Statistical Machine Translation*. Lisbon, Portugal, 134–140.

Junczys-Dowmunt, Marcin, Dwojak Tomasz and Hoang Hieu. 2016. Is Neural Machine Translation Ready for Deployment? A Case Study on 30 Translation Directions. In *Proceedings of the International Workshop on Spoken Language Translation 2016*. 1 edn, vol. 1, 4, Japan.

Kanavos, Panos, and Costas Nadalis. 2019. MT Systems and MT Training. Presentation at the *Crash Course in Machine Translation* organized by Dimetra Academy. 26-28 June 2019, Athens, Greece.

Kenny, Dorothy, and Stephen Doherty. 2014. Statistical machine translation in the translation curriculum: Overcoming obstacles and empowering translators. *The Interpreter and Translator Trainer*, 8(2), 276–294.

Klein, Guillaume, Yoon Kim, Yuntian Deng, Jean Senellart and Alexander M. Rush. 2017. OpenNMT: Open-Source Toolkit for Neural Machine Translation. In *Proceedings of the 55th Annual Meeting of the Association for Computational Linguistics*. Association for Computational Linguistics, Vancouver, Canada, 67-72.

Klubička, Filip, Antonio Toral, and Victor M. Sánchez-Cartagena. 2017. Fine-grained human evaluation of neural versus phrase-based machine translation. *Prague Bulletin of Mathematical Linguistics*, 108:121–132.

Klubička, Filip, Antonio Toral, and Victor M. Sánchez-Cartagena. 2018. Quantitative fine-grained human evaluation of machine translation systems: a case study on English to Croatian. *Machine Translation*, 32(3): 195–215.

Koponen, Maarit. 2015. How to teach machine translation post-editing? Experiences from a post-editing course. In *Proceedings of 4th Workshop on Post-Editing Technology and Practice* (WPTP4). Miami, United States, 30 October-3 November 2015. AMTA, 2–15.

Koponen, Maarit. 2016a. Is machine translation post-editing worth the effort? A survey of research into post-editing and effort. *Jostrans: The Journal of Specialised Translation*, 25:131–148.

Koponen, Maarit. 2016b. *Machine translation post-editing and effort: Empirical Studies on the post-editing effort*. PhD. Helsinki: University of Helsinki.

Koponen, Maarit, Leena Salmi, and Markku Nikulin. 2019. A product and process analysis of post-editor corrections on neural, statistical and rule-based machine translation output. *Machine Translation* (2019).

Krings, Hans. (2001). *Repairing texts: Empirical investigations of machine translation post-editing processes*. Kent: Kent State University Press.

Lacruz, Isabel, and Gregory M. Shreve. 2014. Pauses and cognitive effort in post-editing. In Sharon O'Brien, Laura Winther Balling, Michael Carl, Michel Simard, and Lucia Specia. (eds.) *Post-editing of machine translation*. Newcastle: Cambridge Scholars Publishing.

Lavie, Alon, and Abhaya Agarwal. 2007. METEOR: An Automatic Metric for MT Evaluation with High Levels of Correlation with Human Judgments. In *Proceedings of the Second ACL Workshop on Statistical Machine Translation*. Association for Computational Linguistics, 228-231

Lommel, Arle, and Donald A. DePalma. 2016. *Europe's leading role in Machine Translation: How Europe is driving the shift to MT. Technical report.* Boston: Common Sense Advisory.

Lommel, A. and Melby, A.K. (2018). MQM-DQF: A good marriage (Translation quality for the 21st century). Tutorial at the *13th Conference of The Association for Machine Translation in the Americas.* Boston, USA, 17 March 2018. AMTA. https://www.aclweb.org/anthology/W18-1925

Mesa-Lao, Bartolome. 2014. Gaze behaviour on source texts: An exploratory study comparing translation and post-editing. In Sharon O'Brien, Laura Winther Balling, Michael Carl, Michel Simard, and Lucia Specia, (eds.) *Post-editing of machine translation.* Newcastle: Cambridge Scholars Publishing.

Moorkens, Joss, Sharon O'Brien., Igor A.L. Silva, Norma Fonseca, and Fabio Alves. 2015. Correlations of perceived post-editing effort with measurements of actual effort. *Machine Translation* 29(3): 267–284.

O'Brien, Sharon. 2002. Teaching post-editing: A proposal for course content. In EAMT 2002 *Proceedings of the 6th annual conference of the European association for machine translation.* Manchester, UK, 14-15 May 2002. European Association for Machine Translation, 99–106.

Papineni, Kishore, Roukos Salim, Ward Todd, and Zhu Wei-Jing. 2002. BLEU: a method for automatic evaluation of machine translation. In *Proceedings of the 40th annual meeting on association for computational linguistics*, Association for Computational Linguistics, Philadelphia, 311-318.

Ping, Ke. 2009. Machine translation. In Mona Baker, and Gabriela Saldanha (Eds.), *Routledge encyclopedia of translation studies* 2: 162 168. London: Routledge.

Popovic, Maja, Mihael Arčan and Arle Lommel. 2016. Potential and Limits of Using Post-edits as Reference Translations for MT Evaluation. *Baltic J. Modern Computing*, 4(2):218-229.

Popović, Maja. 2017. Comparing language related issues for NMT and PBMT between German and English. *Prague Bulletin of Mathematical Linguistics,* 108(1):209–220.

Popović, Maja. 2018. Language-related issues for NMT and PBMT for English–German and English–Serbian. *Machine Translation*, 32(3):273–252.

Raptis, Spyros, and Maria Giagkou. 2016. From capturing to generating human behavior: closing the interaction loop at the HUBIC Lab. In *Proceedings of the 20th Pan-Hellenic Conference on Informatics (PCI) with International Participation*, Patras, Greece, 10-12 November 2016. ACM Digital Library, International Conference Proceedings Series.

Shterionov, Dimitar, Riccardo Superbo, Pat Nagle, Laura Casanellas, and Tony O'Dowd. 2018.. Human versus automatic quality evaluation of NMT and PBSMT. *Machine Translation* 32:217–235.

Snover, Matthew, Bonnie Dorr, Schwartz Richard, Linnea Micciulla, and John Makhoul. 2006. A study of translation edit rate with targeted human annotation. In *Proceedings of the 7th Conference of the Association for Machine Translation in the Americas,* The Association for Machine Translation in the Americas, Cambridge, 223-231.

Stasimioti, Maria, and Vilelmini Sosoni. 2019. MT output and post-editing effort: Insights from a comparative analysis of SMT and NMT output for the English to Greek language pair and implications for the training of post-editors. In C. Szabó & R. Besznyák (eds) *Teaching Specialised Translation and Interpreting in a Digital Age - Fit-For-Market Technologies, Schemes and Initiatives.* Wilmington: Vernon Press.

Stymne, Sara. 2011. BLAST: A Tool for Error Analysis of Machine Translation Output. In *Proceedings of the 49th Annual Meeting of the Association for Computational Linguistics: Human Language Technologies*, 19-24 June, Portland, Oregon, USA - System Demonstrations, 56-61.

Toral, Antonio, and Victor M. Sánchez-Cartagena 2017. A multifaceted evaluation of neural versus phrase-based machine translation for 9 language directions. In *Proceedings of the 15th conference of the European Chapter of the Association for Computational Linguistics*: Volume 1, Long Papers. Valencia, Spain, 3-7 April 2017. ACL, 1063–1073.

Vasiļjevs, Andrejs, Jan Hajic, Jochen Hummel, Josef van Genabith, and Rihards Kalniņš. 2016. European Platform for the Multilingual Digital Single Market: Conceptual Proposal. In Inguna Skadiņa and Roberts Rozis (eds.) *Human Language Technologies – The Baltic Perspective.* Amsterdam: IOS Press BV.

Zechner, Klaus and Alex Waibel. 2000. Minimizing word error rate in textual summaries of spoken language. *1st Meeting of the North American Chapter of the Association for Computational Linguistics.*

Project/product descriptions

QE Viewer: an Open-Source Tool for Visualization of Machine Translation Quality Estimation Results

Felipe Soares
University of Sheffield
Broomhall
Sheffield S10 2TG
United Kingdom
fs@felipesoares.net

Anna Zaretskaya
TransPerfect
Passeig de Gràcia, 11
Esc B 5-2
08007 Barcelona, Spain
azaretskaya@translations.com

Diego Bartolomé
TransPerfect
Passeig de Gràcia, 11
Esc B 5-2
08007 Barcelona, Spain
dbartolome@translations.com

Abstract

QE Viewer is a web-based tool for visualizing results of a machine translation quality estimation (QE) system. It allows users to see information on the predicted post-editing distance (PED) for a given file or sentence, and highlighted words that were predicted to contain MT errors. The tool can be used in a variety of academic, educational and commercial scenarios.

1 Introduction

This paper presents a web-based tool for visualization of machine translation quality estimation (QE) (Specia et al, 2018) results. The tool allows users to submit one or several bilingual files with machine translation (MT) output and see information about its estimated quality, namely the predicted post-editing distance (PED), the distribution of segments with different PED scores in the file, and general information about the file in terms of number of segments and word count. Most importantly, the tools also allows to see all segments in the file and highlights words that potentially contain MT errors.

The source code is available at: `https://github.com/soares-f/qe-viewer`.

2 Functionality of the Tool

2.1 Features

QE Viewer is an easy-to-use web interface that allows users to upload a bilingual file in TMXL[1] format (or multiple TMXL files in a .zip archive) that contains source segments and MT segments. The user also has the option to introduce a unique identifier for that submission, allowing possible integration with other MT workflows.

Once the file is submitted it is processed with the QE system and the user sees the results page that contains a sensitivity bar allowing the user to adjust the system's prediction; file-level information on total number of segments, total number of words, predicted average PED; a histogram representing the distribution of segments in the file with different level of predicted PED (Figure 1); segment-level information showing the predicted PED for each segment in the file, while also highlighting the words that, according to the QE system's prediction, contain MT errors (Figure 2).

2.2 Integration with Different QE Frameworks

The tool is system-agnostic which means that it can be integrated with any QE framework, given that a pre-defined API request can be met. For this purpose, we implemented a wrapper for the OpenKiwi framework (Kepler et al., 2019) that handles the requests.

3 Technical Implementation

QE Viewer is implemented in Flask,[2] which is a Python micro-framework for web development that allows quick development and at the same time it can scale up to complex applications. In addition to the Flask framework, we used SQLAlchemy[3] as the object relational mapper, since it can abstract the database operations handling and allows easy database migration and scaling.

[1] TXML format is an XML-based format of bilingual files used at TransPerfect.

[2] `https://github.com/pallets/flask`
[3] `https://www.sqlalchemy.org/`

Martins, Moniz, Fumega, Martins, Batista, Coheur, Parra, Trancoso, Turchi, Bisazza, Moorkens, Guerberof, Nurminen, Marg, Forcada (eds.)
Proceedings of the 22nd Annual Conference of the European Association for Machine Translation, p. 453–454
Lisboa, Portugal, November 2020.

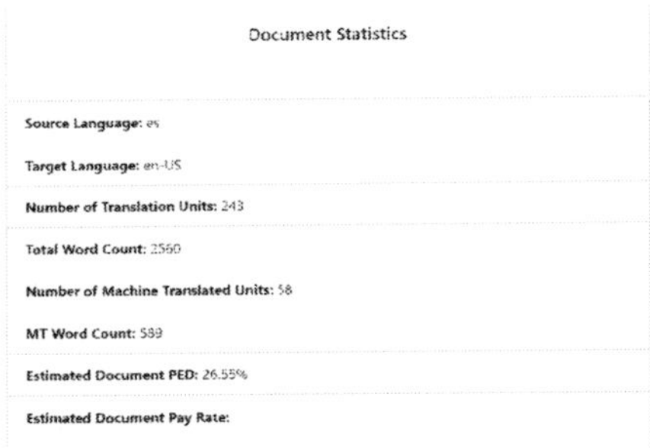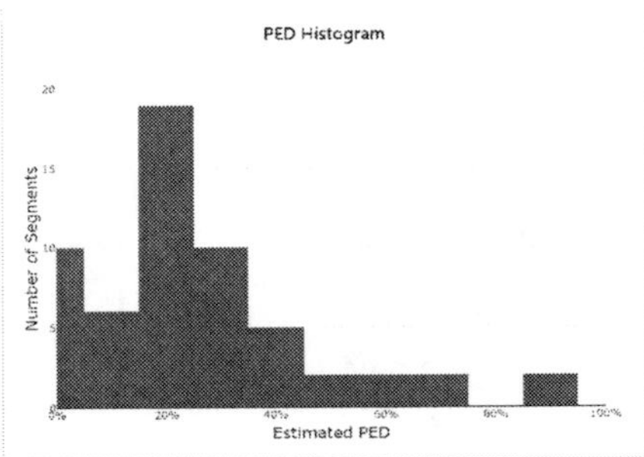

Figure 1: Histogram showing the distribution of segments with different PED.

ID	Source	Machine Translated	PE Dist.
1	ARE YOU COMPLYING	¿ESTA CUMPLIENDO	93.75%
2	WITH THE LIFE SAVING RULES ?	CON LAS REGLAS PARA SALVAR VIDAS ?	17.65%

Figure 2: Segment-level information.

When a file is submitted, the system checks if it is a ZIP file or a single TMXL file. Then the files are validated and a record is created both in the submission table and in the file information table. Once this step is done, the system will iterate over all available files for that submission and their segments, submitting calls to the QE system. The results are then stored in a table, such that the QE API will not need to be queried again when visualizing the same submission.

When visualizing, the system will look for the information stored in the corresponding tables and render the final page.

Regarding style and template, we employed Bootstrap[4] (v4.3) with the native Jinja2 templating system. Bootstrap is a responsive front-end component that can be easily modified to reflect the users' needs.

4 Conclusions

In this paper, we presented an open-source tool for visualization of QE results called QE Viewer. Its aim is to enable users to obtain and understand QE results in practical scenarios, such as translation industry or translation training. The tool is system-agnostic and can be integrated with any QE framework. QE Viewer has proven to be useful in a variety of commercial scenarios, including estimating the budget for post-editing, predicting MT errors and selecting the best MT system. In addition, it can be successfully used for educational purposes in translation and post-editing training.

References

Specia, L., Scarton, C. and Paetzold G. H. 2018. *Synthesis Lectures on Human Language Technologies*, volume 11(1). Morgan & Claypool Publishers.

Kepler, Fabio, Trénous, Jonay, Treviso, Marcos, Vera, Miguel and Martins, André F. T.. 2019 OpenKiwi: An Open Source Framework for Quality Estimation. *Proceedings of the 57th Annual Meeting of the Association for Computational Linguistics: System Demonstrations*, Florence, Italy. 117–122.

---

[4] https://github.com/twbs/bootstrap

Document-Level Machine Translation Evaluation Project: Methodology, Effort and Inter-Annotator Agreement

Sheila Castilho
ADAPT Centre
School of Computing
Dublin City University
sheila.castilho@adaptcentre.ie

Abstract

Recently, document-level (doc-level) human evaluation of machine translation (MT) has raised interest in the community after a few attempts have disproved claims of "human parity" (Toral et al., 2018; Läubli et al., 2018). However, little is still known about best practices regarding doc-level human evaluation. This project aims to identify methodologies to better cope with i) the current state-of-the-art (SOTA) human metrics, ii) a possible complexity when assigning a single score to a text consisted of 'good' and 'bad' sentences, iii) a possible tiredness bias in doc-level set-ups, and iv) the difference in inter-annotator agreement (IAA) between sentence and doc-level set-ups.

1 Introduction

Although currently an active community is working on developing document-level (doc-level) MT systems, their evaluation has primarily been performed at the sentence level. In 2019, for the first time, WMT19 attempted a doc-level human evaluation for the news domain, after considering criticisms by Toral et al. (2018) and Läubli et al. (2018) regarding the current best practices in MT evaluation. Both papers independently reassessed the claims of MT "achieving human parity" and found that the lack of extra-sentential context has a great effect on quality assessment.

In a recent survey with native speakers, Castilho et al. (2020) tested the context span for the translation of three different domains (reviews, subtitles,

and literature). Results show that over 33% of the sentences tested (300 in total) required more content than the sentence itself to be translated, and from those, 23% required more than two previous sentences to be properly translated. Some of the issues which the participants found to most hinder the translation include word ambiguity, terminology, and gender agreement. Moreover, the authors found that there are differences in issues and context span between domains. This shows that doc-level evaluation enables to assess suprasentential context, textual cohesion and coherence types of errors.

In one of the few studies on doc-level evaluation, Läubli et al. (2018) use pairwise rankings of fluency and adequacy in which raters give one single score to the full document. For WMT19, the direct assessment task asked crowdworkers to give a single score (0–100) to full documents for accuracy, where only one MT output is shown each time (no comparison with other MT system).

With that in mind, this project aims at identifying methodologies to better cope with the SOTA human metrics, namely ratings of fluency and adequacy, error mark up and ranking evaluations (Castilho et al., 2018). We will gauge the complexity when assigning a single score to full texts, since they can consist of 'good' and 'bad' sentences, which could mean that instead of a single score, translators would prefer to give scores to different chunks of the texts while seeing the whole text. We will investigate the difference in IAA between sentence and document level set-ups. Furthermore, a possible tiredness bias in doc-level set ups will also be investigated, for example, the extend to which translators judge a long text on the quality of its first sentences. For that end, we will run a series of experiments with the WMT newstest2019, with

Martins, Moniz, Fumega, Martins, Batista, Coheur, Parra, Trancoso, Turchi, Bisazza, Moorkens, Guerberof, Nurminen, Marg, Forcada (eds.)
Proceedings of the 22nd Annual Conference of the European Association for Machine Translation, p. 455–456
Lisboa, Portugal, November 2020.

professional translators.

2 Methodology

The evaluation setup is made up of two sequential stages: (1) Fluency/adequacy and error markup, and (2) Pairwise ranking. Four professional translators will carry out the tasks in two scenarios: (A) evaluation at the sentence level, showing randomised sentences, one at a time, and (B) evaluation at a document level. While Scenario A will be the baseline as it follows common practice in MT evaluation, Scenario B will show how translators will make the decisions and what influences them when they have to give one score for full texts. After each task, translators will answer a post-task questionnaire about the tasks. The documents and scenarios are randomised to avoid participants evaluating the same source twice. Table 1 shows how documents and sentences are randomised by participant.

Documents (groups)	P1	P2	P3	P4
A (1–500 sentences)	S_1	S_2	D_1	D_2
B (501–1000 sentences)	D_2	D_1	S_2	S_1

Table 1: Distribution of tasks where S is sentence level and D is document level, and 1 and 2 are the order of the tasks.

The corpus used is the WMT *newstest2019* English corpora, which has an average document length of 17 sentences (minimum 4 sentences, maximum 30 sentences). Full documents that amount to 1000 sentences are selected, totalling 64 documents. The English documents are translated into Brazilian Portuguese with Google Translate for stage 1, and with both Google Translate and DeepL for stage 2.

The choice of language is because as it is the principal researcher's mother tongue, this will make it possible to analyse it more carefully and see possible patterns in the process. Moreover, being Portuguese a Romance language, it is possible that the results of this pilot can be extended to the language family.

The tasks are set in two tools. For fluency, adequacy, and error mark up, PET tool (Aziz et al., 2012) is used as it allows time tracking. For the ranking tasks, an online spreadsheet is used and extension to track time is also implemented. Translators are also requested to keep track of their time while performing the evaluation.

After stages 1 and 2 are complete, a second round of evaluation will designed. This time, doc-level evaluation will be performed with translators giving one score per chunks/sentence in the text while having access to the full document. That way we will be able to compare effort and IAA between the two methodologies for doc-level.

3 Final Remarks

This project aims at shedding light at methodology, effort and IAA and systematically improve human evaluation of MT at the doc-level. Preliminary results will be available by June 2020, and data sets will be fully available at the end of the project.

Acknowledgements This project is funded by the EAMT under its programme "2019 Sponsorship of Activities". The ADAPT Centre for Digital Content Technology at Dublin City University is funded by the Science Foundation Ireland Research Centres Programme (Grant 13/RC/2106) and is co-funded by the European Regional Development Fund.

Thank you all the translators for providing us with annotations and feedback.

References

Aziz, Wilker, Sheila Castilho, and Lucia Specia. 2012. PET: a Tool for Post-editing and Assessing Machine Translation. In *Proceedings of the Eight International Conference on Language Resources and Evaluation (LREC'12)*, pages 3982–3987, Istanbul, Turkey, may.

Castilho, Sheila, Stephen Doherty, Federico Gaspari, and Joss Moorkens. 2018. Approaches to human and machine Translation Quality Assessment. In *Translation Quality Assessment: From Principles to Practice*, volume 1 of *Machine Translation: Technologies and Applications*, pages 9–38. Springer International Publishing, July.

Castilho, Sheila, Maja Popović, and Andy Way. 2020. On Context Span Needed for Machine Translation Evaluation. In *Proceedings of the Twelfth International Conference on Language Resources and Evaluation (LREC'20)*, Marseille, France, may.

Läubli, Samuel, Rico Sennrich, and Martin Volk. 2018. Has Machine Translation Achieved Human Parity? A Case for Document-level Evaluation. In *Proceedings of EMNLP*, pages 4791–4796, Brussels, Belgium.

Toral, Antonio, Sheila Castilho, Ke Hu, and Andy Way. 2018. Attaining the Unattainable? Reassessing Claims of Human Parity in Neural Machine Translation. In *Proceedings of WMT*, pages 113–123, Brussels, Belgium.

SOCKEYE 2:
A Toolkit for Neural Machine Translation

Felix Hieber and **Tobias Domhan** and **Michael Denkowski** and **David Vilar**
Amazon
`{fhieber,domhant,mdenkows,dvilar}@amazon.com`

Abstract

We present SOCKEYE 2, a modernized and streamlined version of the SOCKEYE neural machine translation (NMT) toolkit. New features include a simplified code base through the use of MXNet's Gluon API, a focus on state-of-the-art model architectures, and distributed mixed precision training. These improvements result in faster training and inference, higher automatic metric scores, and a shorter path from research to production.

1 Introduction

SOCKEYE (Hieber et al., 2017) is a versatile toolkit for research in the fast-moving field of NMT. Since the initial release, it has been used in at least 25 scientific publications, including winning submissions to WMT evaluations (Schamper et al., 2018). Based on the deep learning library MXNet (Chen et al., 2015), SOCKEYE also powers Amazon Translate, showing industrial-strength performance in addition to the flexibility needed in academic environments. Moreover, we are excited to see hardware manufacturers contributing optimizations to MXNet and SOCKEYE. Intel has demonstrated large performance gains for SOCKEYE inference on Intel Skylake processors.[1] NVIDIA is working on significant performance improvements for SOCKEYE's transformer (Vaswani et al., 2017) implementation through fused operators and optimized beam search. This

paper discusses SOCKEYE 2's streamlined Gluon implementation (§2), support for state of the art architectures (§3), and improved model training (§4).

2 Gluon Implementation

SOCKEYE 2 adopts Gluon, the latest and preferred application programming interface (API) of the MXNet deep learning library. Gluon simplifies the code while improving overall performance. Developers can define building blocks of neural network architectures as Python classes and seamlessly switch between eager execution for step-by-step debugging and cached computation graphs for maximum performance. Migration to Gluon simplifies training and inference code in SOCKEYE 2, reducing the overall number of lines of Python code by 25%. The hybridized Gluon transformer implementation in SOCKEYE 2 improves training speed by 14%, compared to SOCKEYE.

3 Focus on State-of-the-Art Models

Due to the success of self-attentional models we concentrated development of SOCKEYE 2 on the transformer (Vaswani et al., 2017), removing support for recurrent and convolutional models. Using the pre-norm configuration by default allows for learning rate warm-up-free training.

We found deep encoders and shallow decoders for transformers to be competitive in BLEU while significantly increasing decoding speed due to computational workload being shifted to the encoder side. On WMT19 (EN–FI, FI–EN, EN–DE, DE–EN), a 20-encoder and 2-decoder layer configuration improves on average by 0.2 BLEU over the baseline, while reducing decoding time by 50%.

We also improved support for source factors by allowing to tie source factor and word embeddings,

---

[1]`https://www.intel.ai/amazing-inference-performance-with-intel-xeon-scalable-processors/#gs.wrgsji`

Martins, Moniz, Fumega, Martins, Batista, Coheur, Parra, Trancoso, Turchi, Bisazza, Moorkens, Guerberof, Nurminen, Marg, Forcada (eds.)
Proceedings of the 22nd Annual Conference of the European Association for Machine Translation, p. 457–458
Lisboa, Portugal, November 2020.

	DE–EN		EN–FI	
	BLEU	Time	BLEU	Time
Ott et al. (2018)	34.7	30h	20.1	14h
Plateau Reduce	**34.9**	**28h**	**20.7**	**12h**

Table 1: SacreBLEU (Post, 2018) scores (newstest2019) and training times (8 NVIDIA V100 GPUs) for a 20-encoder 2-decoder layer transformer using the training setup described by Ott et al. (2018) and Plateau Reduce, both implemented in SOCKEYE 2.

as well as specifying different types of embedding combinations (concatenation or summation).

4 Training Improvements

SOCKEYE 2 significantly accelerates training with Horovod[2] integration (Sergeev and Balso, 2018) and MXNet's automatic mixed precision (AMP). Horovod extends synchronous training to any number of GPUs (including across nodes) while AMP automatically detects and converts parts of the model that can run in reduced-precision mode (FP16) without loss of quality.

SOCKEYE also provides a data-driven alternative to the popular "inverse square root" learning schedule used by Vaswani et al. (2017) and Ott et al. (2018): "Plateau Reduce" keeps the same learning rate until validation perplexity does not increase for several checkpoints, at which time it reduces the learning rate and rewinds all model and optimizer parameters to the best previous point. Training concludes when validation perplexity reaches an extended plateau. In a WMT19 benchmark (Barrault et al., 2019), Plateau Reduce training produces stronger models in slightly less time than the setup described by Ott et al. (2018). Results are presented in Table 1 where all values are averages over 3 independent training runs with different random initializations. Full hyperparameters for SOCKEYE 2's large batch training can be found in the toolkit's documentation.

5 Licensing and availability

SOCKEYE 2 is available[3] under the Apache 2.0 license. It includes a Docker build to easily run training or inference on any supported platform.

6 Conclusion

SOCKEYE 2 provides out-of-the-box support for quickly training strong transformer models for re-search or production. Extensive configuration options and the simplified code base enable rapid development and experimentation. We invite the community to contribute their ideas to SOCKEYE 2 and hope that the new programming model and performance improvements enable others to conduct effective and successful research.

References

Barrault, Loïc, Ondřej Bojar, Marta R. Costa-jussà, Christian Federmann, Mark Fishel, Yvette Graham, Barry Haddow, Matthias Huck, Philipp Koehn, Shervin Malmasi, Christof Monz, Mathias Müller, Santanu Pal, Matt Post, and Marcos Zampieri. 2019. Findings of the 2019 conference on machine translation (WMT19). In *Procs. of the Fourth Conference on Machine Translation (Vol. 2: Shared Task Papers)*, pages 1–61, Florence, Italy, August.

Chen, Tianqi, Mu Li, Yutian Li, Min Lin, Naiyan Wang, Minjie Wang, Tianjun Xiao, Bing Xu, Chiyuan Zhang, and Zheng Zhang. 2015. Mxnet: A flexible and efficient machine learning library for heterogeneous distributed systems. *arXiv preprint arXiv:1512.01274*.

Hieber, Felix, Tobias Domhan, Michael Denkowski, David Vilar, Artem Sokolov, Ann Clifton, and Matt Post. 2017. Sockeye: A toolkit for neural machine translation. *ArXiv e-prints*, abs/1712.05690.

Ott, Myle, Sergey Edunov, David Grangier, and Michael Auli. 2018. Scaling neural machine translation. In *Procs. of the Third Conference on Machine Translation, Vol. 1: Research Papers*, pages 1–9, Belgium, Brussels, October.

Post, Matt. 2018. A call for clarity in reporting bleu scores. In *Procs. of the Third Conference on Machine Translation, Vol. 1: Research Papers*, pages 186–191, Belgium, Brussels, October.

Schamper, Julian, Jan Rosendahl, Parnia Bahar, Yunsu Kim, Arne Nix, and Hermann Ney. 2018. The RWTH Aachen University supervised machine translation systems for WMT 2018. In *Procs. of the Third Conference on Machine Translation, Vol. 2: Shared Task Papers*, pages 500–507, Belgium, Brussels, October.

Sergeev, Alexander and Mike Del Balso. 2018. Horovod: fast and easy distributed deep learning in tensorflow. *CoRR*, abs/1802.05799.

Vaswani, Ashish, Noam Shazeer, Niki Parmar, Jakob Uszkoreit, Llion Jones, Aidan N Gomez, Łukasz Kaiser, and Illia Polosukhin. 2017. Attention is all you need. In *Advances in neural information processing systems*, pages 5998–6008.

[2]https://github.com/horovod/horovod
[3]https://github.com/awslabs/sockeye

CEF Data Marketplace:
Powering a Long-term Supply of Language Data

Amir Kamran[†], **Dace Dzeguze**[†], **Jaap van der Meer**[†], **Milica Panic**[†],
Alessandro Cattelan[‡], **Daniele Patrioli**[‡],
Luisa Bentivogli[⋆], **and Marco Turchi**[⋆]

[†] TAUS - Language Data Network, Netherlands {amir,dace,jaap,milica}@taus.net
[‡] Translated, Italy {alessandro,daniele.patrioli}@translated.com
[⋆] FBK, Italy {bentivo,turchi}@fbk.eu

Abstract

We describe the CEF Data Marketplace project, which focuses on the development of a trading platform of translation data for language professionals: translators, machine translation (MT) developers, language service providers (LSPs), translation buyers and government bodies. The CEF Data Marketplace platform will be designed and built to manage and trade data for all languages and domains. This project will open a continuous and long-term supply of language data for MT and other machine learning applications.

1 Introduction

The CEF Data Marketplace project is an initiative co-funded by the European Union under the Connecting Europe Facility programme, under Grant Agreement INEA/CEF/ICT/A2018/1816453. The project has a duration of 24 months and started in November 2019.

With over 350^1 million new Internet users in 2019 and the annual digital growth of 9%, there is insufficient content available in the local languages. The automated translation platforms support merely about a hundred of the 4,000 languages with an established writing system. The CEF Data Marketplace will be the first platform that facilitates the buying and selling of language data to help businesses and communities reach scale with their language technologies while offering a way for the language data creators to monetize their work.

2 Platform Description

The platform focuses on the integration and maintenance of the already available technologies for managing and trading translation data. Specifically, the following features will be added to an existing underlying translation data repository:

- An easy-to-use mechanism to upload and annotate data-sets for data sellers, as well as options to upload updates to the data-sets;

- an easy-to-explore mechanism to find the right data for specific languages and domains for data buyers;

- an easy-to-trade transaction system for data sellers to earn monetary rewards by trading their data with data buyers;

- an easy-to-trust reputation system to improve the confidence of data buyers towards the marketplace and to ensure quality of data.

3 State-of-the-art Processing Tools

Advanced data processing services will be integrated to enable and facilitate data exchange through the marketplace and to encourage data sellers and buyers to join the platform. These services consist of software for cleaning, anonymizing and clustering the data to ensure that the data-sets available in the Marketplace are of high quality. These services will be provided through APIs and will be available free of charge to data providers or against a fee for users not publishing their data through marketplace. The software will

[1] https://wearesocial.com/blog/2019/01/digital-2019-global-internet-use-accelerates

Martins, Moniz, Fumega, Martins, Batista, Coheur, Parra, Trancoso, Turchi, Bisazza, Moorkens, Guerberof, Nurminen, Marg, Forcada (eds.)
Proceedings of the 22nd Annual Conference of the European Association for Machine Translation, p. 459–460
Lisboa, Portugal, November 2020.

also be released open source for the industrial and research communities.

4 Data Acquisition Strategy

To acquire as much data as possible with added value for the CEF Automated Translation (CEF-AT) Core Platform our strategy is to create a vibrant, broader market serving the needs of translation providers and translation buyers across various desired language combinations and domains. The legal framework of TAUS Data is updated to build trust[2] of the data owners to participate in the Marketplace. Clear guidelines are provided about data ownership to safeguard the copyrights and to support the royalty-based model.

5 Acknowledgement

The sole responsibility of this publication lies with the author. The European Union is not responsible for any use that may be made of the information contained therein.

---

[2]http://hdl.handle.net/11346/TAUS-PZNM

QRev: Machine Translation of User Reviews: What Influences the Translation Quality?

Maja Popović
ADAPT Centre
School of Computing
Dublin City University, Ireland
maja.popovic@adaptcentre.ie

Abstract

This project aims to identify the important aspects of translation quality of user reviews which will represent a starting point for developing better automatic MT metrics and challenge test sets, and will be also helpful for developing MT systems for this genre. We work on two types of reviews: Amazon products and IMDb movies, written in English and translated into two closely related target languages, Croatian and Serbian.

1 Description

Data sets used for MT research include mainly "formal written text" (such as news) and "formal speech" (such as TED talks). Recently, there has been an increase of interest in the translation of "informal written text" which focuses on very noisy texts originating from sources like WhatsApp, Twitter and Reddit. On the other hand, other types of "informal written text" such as user reviews have not been investigated thoroughly, although they are important both from commercial and from a user perspective – user reviews of products have become an important feature that many customers expect to find.

This project focusses on user reviews in order to investigate which new challenges this "mid-way" kind of text poses for current MT systems. The main goal is to identify important quality aspects for MT of user reviews which will enable:

- development of appropriate automatic evaluation metrics;
- design of test suites specialised for important factors;
- definition of directions for improving MT systems.

Although the focus of the project are user reviews translated into Serbian and Croatian (as a case involving mid-size less-resourced morphologically rich European languages), the proposed evaluation strategy is completely genre/domain/language independent, so it can be applied to any genre, domain and language pair.

2 Data sets

We are working with two types of publicly available user reviews:

- IMDb movie reviews[1]
- Amazon product reviews[2]

3 MT systems

The main goal of the project is to find the common aspects important for the translation quality, and not to evaluate or compare particular MT systems. We are currently analysing MT outputs[3] of three on-line systems: Google Translate[4], Bing[5] and Amazon translate[6]. We are also developing our own system using publicly available data, which will be analysed in the later stages of the project.

---

[1] https://ai.stanford.edu/~amaas/data/sentiment/
[2] http://jmcauley.ucsd.edu/data/amazon/
[3] generated at the end of January 2020
[4] https://translate.google.com/
[5] https://www.bing.com/translator
[6] https://aws.amazon.com/translate/

Martins, Moniz, Fumega, Martins, Batista, Coheur, Parra, Trancoso, Turchi, Bisazza, Moorkens, Guerberof, Nurminen, Marg, Forcada (eds.)
Proceedings of the 22nd Annual Conference of the European Association for Machine Translation, p. 461–462
Lisboa, Portugal, November 2020.

4 Evaluation procedure

Our evaluation procedure is based on comprehensibility and fidelity (adequacy) (Roturier and Bensadoun, 2011), and it is being carried out on the review level (not on the sentence level). It should be noted that comprehensibility is not fluency – a fluent text can be incomprehensible, and vice versa. The novelty of our procedure is asking the annotators to concentrate on problematic parts of the text and to mark them, without assigning any scores or classifying errors. The procedure can also be guided by other evaluation criteria, not only comprehensibility and adequacy. The annotators were computational linguistics students and researchers fluent in the source language and native speakers of the target language. The annotation consisted of two independent subsequent tasks with the following guidelines:

Comprehensibility   A monolingual task without access to the original source language text. Which parts of the translated review are not understandable? Distinguish two levels: "completely incomprehensible" and "not fully clear due to grammatic or stylistic errors".

Fidelity (Adequacy)   A bilingual task with access to the original source language text. Which parts of the translated review do not correspond to the meaning of the original? Distinguish two levels: "the meaning of the original text is changed" and "not an optimal translation choice". If there are any problems in the source language, mark it, too (spelling or other errors, incomprehensible, unfinished, etc.).

The annotation started on 2 February 2020 and finished in April 2020. The annotated texts will be further analysed in order to identify common mistakes and linguistic phenomena which have the largest influence on comprehensibility and adequacy. The main aim of the analysis is to find the most important patterns and aspects which then can serve as a basis for automatic metrics, test suites, as well as for system improvements. In addition, the analysis will show in which way and to which extent particular phenomena contribute to comprehensibility and adequacy.

In total, 28 IMDb and 122 Amazon reviews (16807 untokenised English source words) are covered in this evaluation. However, not all generated MT hypotheses (6 for each review) are included. Each of the 270 included hypotheses is annotated by two annotators. The annotated data sets will be publicly released under the Creative Commons CC-BY licence.

5 First results: inter-annotator agreement and percentage of issues

Inter-annotator agreement (IAA) is shown in Table 1 in the form of F-score and normalised edit distance (WER).

IAA (%)	C	F (A)
F-score ↑	85.5	86.6
WER ↓	27.2	23.9

Table 1: Inter-annotator agreement (IAA): F-score and normalised edit distance WER.

Percentage of words with issues for the two target languages is shown in Table 2.

% of issues		C	F (A)
hr	major	9.0	8.0
	minor	12.3	12.5
sr	major	13.1	12.1
	minor	19.4	14.4

Table 2: Percentages of words problematic for comprehensibility (C) and fidelity/adequacy (F (A)).

Acknowledgments

This research is being conducted with the financial support of the European Association for Machine Translation under its programme "2019 Sponsorship of Activities" at the ADAPT Research Centre at Dublin City University. The ADAPT SFI Centre for Digital Media Technology is funded by Science Foundation Ireland through the SFI Research Centres Programme and is co-funded under the European Regional Development Fund (ERDF) through Grant 13/RC/2106.

We would like to thank all the evaluators for providing us with annotations and feedback.

References

Lohar, Pintu, Maja Popović, and Andy Way. 2019. Building English-to-Serbian Machine Translation System for IMDb Movie Reviews. In *Proceedings of the 7th Workshop on Balto-Slavic Natural Language Processing (BSNLP 2019)*, Florence, Italy, August.

Roturier, Johann and Anthony Bensadoun. 2011. Evaluation of MT Systems to Translate User Generated Content. In *Proceedings of the MT Summit XIII*, Xiamen, China, September.

ELITR: European Live Translator

Ondřej Bojar[1]   Dominik Macháček[1]   Sangeet Sagar[1]   Otakar Smrž[1]
Jonáš Kratochvíl[1]   Peter Polák[1]   Ebrahim Ansari[1]
Dario Franceschini[2]   Chiara Canton[2]   Ivan Simonini[2]
Thai-Son Nguyen[3]   Felix Schneider[3]   Sebastian Stüker[3]   Alex Waibel[3]
Barry Haddow[4]   Rico Sennrich[4]   Philip Williams[4]
[1]Charles University, [2]PerVoice, [3]Karlsruhe Institute of Technology, [4]University of Edinburgh
Coordinator email: `bojar@ufal.mff.cuni.cz`

Abstract

ELITR (European Live Translator) project aims to create a speech translation system for simultaneous subtitling of conferences and online meetings targetting up to 43 languages. The technology is tested by the Supreme Audit Office of the Czech Republic and by alfaview®, a German online conferencing system. Other project goals are to advance document-level and multilingual machine translation, automatic speech recognition, and meeting summarization.

1 Description

ELITR (European Live Translator, `elitr.eu`) is a three-year EU H2020 Research and Innovation Programme running from 2019 to 2021. The consortium consists of Charles University, University of Edinburgh, Karlsruhe Institute of Technology (research partners), PerVoice (integrator) and alfatraining (user partner).

2 Objectives

ELITR objectives are research and innovations in the field of spoken language and text translation and automatic summarization of meetings.

2.1 Simultaneous Subtitling

In ELITR, we aim to develop a system for simultaneous subtitling of conferences and online meetings. Our affiliated user partner is the Supreme Audit Office of the Czech Republic. It is hosting a congress of EUROSAI (European Organization of Supreme Audit Institutions). The congress participants are natives of 43 languages, and many of them have difficulties in understanding any of the six congress official languages, into which it is interpreted by humans, or to understand some non-native accents. For this and other similar cases, we develop a simultaneous speech translation system from 7 spoken languages (English, German, Russian, Italian, French, Spanish, and experimentally Czech) subtitling into 43 languages, including those for which a human interpreter would not be available for capacity reasons. The 43 languages are 24 EU official languages and 19 others, spoken between Morocco and Kazachstan.

With our other user partner, alfatraining, we connect our system with an online meeting platform, alfaview®.

2.2 Other Research Topics

The most visible application goal of live subtling is supported by our advancements in the related areas. We research into document-level machine translation to enable conference participants to translate documents between all the 43 languages in high-quality, taking inter-sentential phenomena into account (Voita et al., 2019a; Voita et al., 2019b; Vojtěchová et al., 2019; Popel et al., 2019; Rysová et al., 2019).

We research into multilingual machine translation to reduce the cost of targeting many languages at once, and to leverage multiple language variants of the source for higher quality (Zhang et al., 2019; Zhang and Sennrich, 2019).

To face challenges of simultaneous translation, such as robustness to noise, out-of-vocabulary words, domain adaptation, and non-standard accents (Macháček et al., 2019), latency and quality trade-off, we aim to improve automatic speech

Martins, Moniz, Fumega, Martins, Batista, Coheur, Parra, Trancoso, Turchi, Bisazza, Moorkens, Guerberof, Nurminen, Marg, Forcada (eds.)
Proceedings of the 22nd Annual Conference of the European Association for Machine Translation, p. 463–464
Lisboa, Portugal, November 2020.

recognition. We also explore cascaded and fully end-to-end neural spoken language translation (Pham et al., 2019; Nguyen et al., 2019; Nguyen et al., 2020) and co-organize shared tasks at WMT and IWSLT.

2.3 Automatic Minuting

The last objective of our project is an automatic system for structured summaries of meetings. It is a challenging and high-risk goal, but potentially very profitable. We aim to lay the necessary foundations for research in this area by collecting and releasing relevant datasets (Nedoluzhko and Bojar, 2019; Çano and Bojar, 2019a; Çano and Bojar, 2019b) and plan to run shared tasks.

3 ELITR SLT System

ELITR's integration of components of spoken language translation builds on a proprietary software solution by the project integrator PerVoice. The central point is a server called the "mediator". "Workers" for SLT subtasks, such as automatic speech recognition, machine translation, and intermediate punctuating component for specific languages, potentially in event-specific or experimental versions, are provided by research labs in the consortium, ran on their hardware and connected to the mediator. A client requests a specific task, for example, German audio into Czech translation, and the mediator connects a cascade of workers to deliver the requested output. The last worker finally publishes subtitles on a webpage. Meeting participants follow subtitles and slides on personal devices.

The system provides simultaneous low latency translation. We follow the re-translation approach of Niehues et. al (2018). The translation is first displayed around 1 second after the speaker, and then it is occasionally corrected and finalized after approximately 7 seconds.

Acknowledgement

This project has received funding from the European Union's Horizon 2020 Research and Innovation Programme under Grant Agreement No. 825460.

References

Çano, Erion and Ondřej Bojar. 2019a. Efficiency Metrics for Data-Driven Models: A Text Summarization Case Study. *arXiv e-prints*, page arXiv:1909.06618.

Çano, Erion and Ondřej Bojar. 2019b. Keyphrase generation: A text summarization struggle. In *NAACL/HLT*, June.

Macháček, Dominik, Jonáš Kratochvíl, Tereza Vojtěchová, and Ondřej Bojar. 2019. A Speech Test Set of Practice Business Presentations with Additional Relevant Texts. In *SLSP*.

Nedoluzhko, Anna and Ondřej Bojar. 2019. Towards Automatic Minuting of Meetings. In *ITAT: Slovenskočeský NLP workshop (SloNLP 2019)*.

Nguyen, Thai-Son, Sebastian Stueker, Jan Niehues, and Alex Waibel. 2019. Improving sequence-to-sequence speech recognition training with on-the-fly data augmentation. *arXiv preprint arXiv:1910.13296*.

Nguyen, Thai-Son, Sebastian Stüker, and Alex Waibel. 2020. Toward Cross-Domain Speech Recognition with End-to-End Models. *arXiv preprint arXiv:2003.04194*.

Niehues, Jan, Ngoc-Quan Pham, Thanh-Le Ha, Matthias Sperber, and Alex Waibel. 2018. Low-latency neural speech translation. *arXiv preprint arXiv:1808.00491*.

Pham, Ngoc-Quan, Thai-Son Nguyen, Jan Niehues, Markus Müller, and Alex Waibel. 2019. Very Deep Self-Attention Networks for End-to-End Speech Recognition. *Proc. Interspeech, Graz, Austria*.

Popel, Martin, Dominik Macháček, Michal Auersperger, Ondřej Bojar, and Pavel Pecina. 2019. English-Czech Systems in WMT19: Document-Level Transformer. In *WMT Shared Task Papers*.

Rysová, Kateřina, Magdaléna Rysová, Tomáš Musil, Lucie Poláková, and Ondřej Bojar. 2019. A Test Suite and Manual Evaluation of Document-Level NMT at WMT19. In *WMT Shared Task Papers*.

Voita, Elena, Rico Sennrich, and Ivan Titov. 2019a. Context-Aware Monolingual Repair for Neural Machine Translation. In *EMNLP/IJCNLP*.

Voita, Elena, Rico Sennrich, and Ivan Titov. 2019b. When a Good Translation is Wrong in Context: Context-Aware Machine Translation Improves on Deixis, Ellipsis, and Lexical Cohesion. In *ACL*.

Vojtěchová, Tereza, Michal Novák, Miloš Klouček, and Ondřej Bojar. 2019. SAO WMT19 Test Suite: Machine Translation of Audit Reports. In *WMT Shared Task Papers*.

Zhang, Biao and Rico Sennrich. 2019. Root Mean Square Layer Normalization. In *NIPS*, Vancouver, Canada.

Zhang, Biao, Ivan Titov, and Rico Sennrich. 2019. Improving Deep Transformer with Depth-Scaled Initialization and Merged Attention. In *EMNLP/IJCNLP*.

Progress of the PRINCIPLE Project:
Promoting MT for Croatian, Icelandic, Irish and Norwegian

**Petra Bago,[1] Jane Dunne,[2] Federico Gaspari,[2] Andre Kåsen,[3] Gauti Kristmannsson,[4]
Helen McHugh,[2] Jon Arild Olsen,[3] Dana D. Sheridan,[5] Páraic Sheridan,[5]
John Tinsley,[5] Andy Way[2]**

[1] Faculty of Humanities and Social Sciences, University of Zagreb, 10000 Zagreb, Croatia
[2] ADAPT Centre, School of Computing, Dublin City University, Dublin 9, Ireland
[3] National Library of Norway, Henrik Ibsens gate 110, 0203 Oslo, Norway
[4] University of Iceland, Saemundargata 2, 101 Reykjavik, Iceland
[5] Iconic Translation Machines, Invent Building, Dublin City University, Dublin 9, Ireland

```
pbago@ffzg.hr, {jane.dunne,federico.gaspari,helen.mchugh,
andy.way}@adaptcentre.ie, {andre.kasen,jon.olsen}@nb.no,
gautikri@hi.is, {dana,paraic,john}@iconictranslation.com
```


Abstract

This paper updates the progress made on the PRINCIPLE project, a 2-year action funded by the European Commission under the Connecting Europe Facility (CEF) programme. PRINCIPLE focuses on collecting high-quality language resources for Croatian, Icelandic, Irish and Norwegian, which have been identified as low-resource languages, especially for building effective machine translation (MT) systems. We report initial achievements of the project and ongoing activities aimed at promoting the uptake of neural MT for the low-resource languages of the project.

1 Background

PRINCIPLE is a 2-year initiative that started in September 2019, funded by the European Commission under the Connecting Europe Facility (CEF) programme. The project is coordinated by the ADAPT Centre at Dublin City University (DCU, Ireland), and the consortium includes the Faculty of Humanities and Social Sciences of the University of Zagreb (Croatia), the National Library of Norway in Oslo, the University of Iceland in Rejkyavik, and Iconic Translation Machines (Ireland). PRINCIPLE focuses on the identification, collection and processing of high-quality language resources (LRs) for Croatian, Icelandic, Irish, and Norwegian (covering both varieties of Bokmål and Nynorsk), which are severely under-resourced. The uptake of machine translation (MT) for these languages has been hampered so far by the lack of extensive high-quality LRs that are required to build effective systems, especially parallel corpora. PRINCIPLE aims to improve LR collection efforts in the respective languages, prioritising the two strategic Digital Service Infrastructures (DSIs)[1] of eJustice and eProcurement. The LRs assembled and curated in PRINCIPLE will be validated to demonstrate improved MT quality, and will be uploaded via ELRC-SHARE to enhance MT systems provided by eTranslation, that are available to public administrations in Europe, thus promoting language equality for low-resource languages.

Way and Gaspari (2019) introduced the PRINCIPLE project at its start, giving a high-level overview of its main objectives, along with the planned activities and the overall approach to data collection and validation. They also explained its position within the wider eco-system of related, recently finished CEF projects such as iADAATPA (Castilho et al., 2019) and ELRI.[2] This paper provides an update on the progress of PRINCIPLE, focusing on its initial achievements and describing ongoing activities, especially in terms of engaging with stakeholders and MT users, and concludes with future plans to promote the continued collection of LRs with a view to improving and extending MT use.

---

[1] https://ec.europa.eu/digital-single-market/en/news/connecting-europe-facility-cef-digital-service-infrastructures
[2] www.elri-project.eu

Martins, Moniz, Fumega, Martins, Batista, Coheur, Parra, Trancoso, Turchi, Bisazza, Moorkens, Guerberof, Nurminen, Marg, Forcada (eds.)
Proceedings of the 22nd Annual Conference of the European Association for Machine Translation, p. 465–466
Lisboa, Portugal, November 2020.

2 Achievements and Ongoing Activities

Most of PRINCIPLE's key activities are already well underway and will continue into the second year of the action. Such activities include coordination; use-case analysis, data requirements and data preparation; development, evaluation and deployment of MT systems; identification, collection and consolidation of LRs; and, finally, dissemination. In contrast, most of the work on exploitation and sustainability will take place from July 2020, when more mature results will be available to share with the community.

The progress of the project is constantly monitored via milestones that help to verify that the work is on track to achieve the goals of the action. At the time of writing, in its first eight months, PRINCIPLE has already achieved three of these milestones, namely (i) the adoption of the jointly written project implementation plan that defines key aspects of how the action operates, (ii) the preparation of a detailed report on the use-cases, data requirements and data preparation agreed with various stakeholders in each participating country, and more recently (iii) the design of the software architecture of the MT systems to be built by Iconic for the early adopters (EAs) as part of the project, with a view to releasing the first batch by October 2020.

The EAs are data contributors who have also agreed to work with the PRINCIPLE consortium to introduce custom-built MT engines developed by Iconic into their translation workflow on the basis of their defined use-cases and requirements. These domain-adapted MT systems will be evaluated by DCU with flexible protocols including state-of-the-art automatic metrics and human/manual techniques matching the use-cases and scenarios that have been previously defined. This is a crucial step to validate the quality of the LRs in real user settings, thereby confirming their value to the actual improvement of MT system development, before uploading the data sets collected in the project to ELRC-SHARE.

As part of this ongoing effort, the consortium has already established, and continues to seek, partnerships with public and government bodies as well as private entities in Croatia, Iceland, Ireland and Norway who can provide valuable LRs to the project. By way of example, at the time of writing three data providers in Croatia have confirmed that they will be contributing LRs, thereby offering access to over 1,250 documents of varying length, and containing data from various DSIs. The Croatian PRINCIPLE partner is currently inspecting these documents to check their relevance to eJustice and eProcurement as well as their quality, before selecting those that are deemed suitable for further processing.

3 Future Plans

Preliminary indications suggest that the project is on track to achieve its ambitious objectives for LR collection, and the consortium partners will continue to collaborate with existing and new data contributors in Croatia, Iceland, Ireland and Norway to focus on the eJustice and eProcurement DSIs that are prioritised by the action.

Work to be done in the remainder of the project includes exploring the feasibility of creating new National Relay Stations[3] for the coordinated collection of LRs in Croatia, Iceland and Norway, after their successful introduction by the ELRI project. Finally, future plans also involve expanding and consolidating the LRs collected by the project, and intensifying dissemination activities, with a series of workshops scheduled in the four countries represented in PRINCIPLE by July 2021.

Acknowledgements

PRINCIPLE is generously co-financed by the European Union Connecting Europe Facility under Action 2018-EU-IA-0050 with grant agreement INEA/CEF/ICT/A2018/1761837.

References

Castilho, Sheila, Natalia Resende, Federico Gaspari, Andy Way, Tony O'Dowd, Marek Mazur, Manuel Herranz, Alex Helle, Gema Ramírez-Sánchez, Victor Sánchez-Cartagena, Mārcis Pinnis, and Valters Sics. 2019. Large-scale Machine Translation Evaluation of the iADAATPA Project. *Proceedings of Machine Translation Summit XVII, Volume 2*, Dublin, Ireland 179-185.

Way, Andy, and Federico Gaspari. 2019. PRINCIPLE: Providing Resources in Irish, Norwegian, Croatian and Icelandic for the Purposes of Language Engineering. *Proceedings of Machine Translation Summit XVII, Volume 2*, Dublin, Ireland 112-113.

---

[3] www.elri-project.eu/resources/D1.3_ELRI_Public_Final_Report.pdf

MTUOC: easy and free integration of NMT systems in professional translation environments

Antoni Oliver
Universitat Oberta de Catalunya
aoliverg@uoc.edu

Abstract

In this paper the MTUOC project, aiming to provide an easy integration of neural and statistical machine translation systems, is presented. Almost all the required software to train and use neural and statistical MT systems is released under free licences. However, their use is not always easy and intuitive and medium-high specialized skills are required. MTUOC project provides simplified scripts for preprocessing and training MT systems, and a server and client for easy use of the trained systems. The server is compatible with popular CAT tools for a seamless integration. The project also distributes some free engines.

1 Introduction

MTUOC is a project from the Arts and Humanities department at the Universitat Oberta de Catalunya (UOC) to facilitate the use and integration of neural and statistical machine translation systems.

Most of the software needed for training and using such systems is distributed under free permissive licences. So this technology is, in principle, freely available for any professional, company or organization. The use of MT toolkits presents some problems:

- *Technological skills*: medium-high technological skills are required. Knowledge of some programming (as Python, for example) and scripting (as Bash, for example) languages are necessary. On the other hand, the documentation of these toolkits is not always detailed enough and some time in trial and error is spent.

- Integration: the resulting systems are not easily integrable in existing workflows. Most of the toolkits provide access through some kind of API, usually using a server-client configuration. Some CAT tools offer plugins to access some existing systems. But not all CAT Tool - MT system combinations are available.

- *Hardware*: relatively high hardware requirements are present, especially for training the systems. For training SMT systems lots of RAM memory is required. For training NMT systems one or more powerful GPU units are compulsory.

MTUOC tries to offer solutions for the first two problems. Regarding the *technological skills problem*, it provides a series of easy-to-use and easy-to-understand Python and Bash scripts for corpus pre-processing and training. All these scripts are well documented and can be adapted and extended in an easy way. Regarding the *integration problem*, a fully configurable server and client are provided. The server can mimic the behaviour of several kinds of servers, so it can be used with a large range of CAT tools. For example, the server can use a Marian engine but behave as a Moses server so it can be directly integrated with OmegaT. The client can deal with several widely used file formats (as XLIFF, for example) and generate TMX translation memories that can be used in any CAT tool. Regarding the *hardware problem*, several facts should be borne in mind. Firstly, hardware requirements for training are much harder than for translating. Once an engine is trained, it can be

Martins, Moniz, Fumega, Martins, Batista, Coheur, Parra, Trancoso, Turchi, Bisazza, Moorkens, Guerberof, Nurminen, Marg, Forcada (eds.)
Proceedings of the 22nd Annual Conference of the European Association for Machine Translation, p. 467–468
Lisboa, Portugal, November 2020.

used in any consumer computer. So many potential users can benefit from the freely available engines. Several providers can offer the service of training tailored machine translation systems. UOC can sign technology-transfer agreements with companies and organizations to train tailored systems at very competitive rates. This service is free for NGOs. Secondly, the price of hardware is getting lower over time and powerful GPU units are now available at affordable prices.

2 Components

The MTUOC project offers six main components:

- *Python modules*: providing several functionalities as tokenization, truecasing, etc.

- *Scripts* written in Python and Bash and several configuration files:

    - Corpus pre-processing scripts: to process the training corpora for training the systems
    - Training scripts and configuration files: for several SMT and NMT toolkits
    - Evaluation scripts: providing some widely used MT evaluation metrics (as BLEU, NIST, WER, TER, edit distance)

- *MTUOC Server*: the component that receives a segment to translate from the client or CAT tool, process it (tokenization, truecasing and so on) and sends it to the translation server. After receiving the translation this component post-processes it (detruecasing, detokenization and so on) and sends it back to the client or CAT tool.

- *MTUOC Client*: this component can handle several translation formats, send segments to the server, receive the translations and create the translated file.

- *MTUOC Virtual Machine*: as most toolkits work under Linux, this virtual machine is useful for Windows users to run all the required components.

- *Pre-trained translation engines* that can be freely used with MTUOC

3 MT Toolkits

MTUOC-server can be used with the following MT toolkits.

- Moses[1] (Koehn et al., 2007)

- Marian[2] (Junczys-Dowmunt et al., 2018)

- OpenNMT[3] (Klein et al., 2017)

- ModernMT[4] (Bertoldi et al., 2018)

4 Obtaining MTUOC

All the components of MTUOC can be downloaded from its SourceForge page.[5] The documentation of the systems is available in the Wiki space of the project page. All the MTUOC components are released under a free licence, namely GNU GPL version 3.

Acknowledgements: The training of the neural MT systems distributed by MTUOC has been possible thanks to the NVIDIA GPU grant programme.

References

Bertoldi, Nicola, Davide Caroselli, and Marcello Federico. 2018. The ModernMT project.

Junczys-Dowmunt, Marcin, Roman Grundkiewicz, Tomasz Dwojak, Hieu Hoang, Kenneth Heafield, Tom Neckermann, Frank Seide, Ulrich Germann, Alham Fikri Aji, Nikolay Bogoychev, André F. T. Martins, and Alexandra Birch. 2018. Marian: Fast neural machine translation in C++. In *Proceedings of ACL 2018, System Demonstrations*, pages 116–121, Melbourne, Australia, July. Association for Computational Linguistics.

Klein, Guillaume, Yoon Kim, Yuntian Deng, Jean Senellart, and Alexander M. Rush. 2017. OpenNMT: Open-source toolkit for neural machine translation. In *Proc. ACL*.

Koehn, Philipp, Hieu Hoang, Alexandra Birch, Chris Callison-Burch, Marcello Federico, Nicola Bertoldi, Brooke Cowan, Wade Shen, Christine Moran, Richard Zens, et al. 2007. Moses: Open source toolkit for statistical machine translation. In *Proceedings of the 45th annual meeting of the association for computational linguistics companion volume proceedings of the demo and poster sessions*, pages 177–180.

---

[1]http://www.statmt.org/moses/
[2]https://marian-nmt.github.io/
[3]https://opennmt.net/
[4]https://github.com/modernmt/modernmt
[5]https://sourceforge.net/projects/mtuoc/

INMIGRA3: building a case for NGOs and NMT

Celia Rico[*]
Universidad Europea de Madrid

María del Mar Sánchez Ramos[**]
Universidad de Alcalá

Antoni Oliver[***]
Universitat Oberta de Catalunya

*celia.rico@universidadeuropea.es
**mar.sanchezr@uah.es
***aoliverg@uoc.edu

Abstract

INMIGRA3 is a three-year project that builds on the work of two previous initiatives: INMIGRA2-CM[1] and CRISIS-MT[2]. Together, they address the specific needs of NGOs in multilingual settings with a particular interest in migratory contexts.

Work on INMIGRA3 concentrates in the analysis of how to use NMT for the purposes of translating NGOs documentation.

1 Translation needs of non-governmental organisations

The third sector is experiencing an increasing relevance as the number of people in vulnerable circumstances grows. Natural catastrophes, wars, political and religious persecutions, or economic crisis are some of the conditions that leave people unprotected. These are situations that pose a challenge as complex linguistic situations arise (Federici and O'Brien, 2020). And migration flows are not an exception.

Previous research has revealed a series of gaps still to be filled if we are to understand the true nature of multilingual needs in not-for-profit settings. For instance, which are their working conditions as related to multilingual needs? How technology can be best put to use? (see, for instance, the work of INTERACT project[3], *Language on the Move*[4] or *Translators without Borders*[5]).

In the case of NGOs working in the migratory context, one the main issues is that usually the budget allocated to translation resources is scarce or non-existent. This might explain why catering for the multilingual needs of migrant population is not considered among their core activities —at least in the minds of official donors (Footitt, Crack and Tesseur, 2018). Consequently, translation is mostly conducted as volunteer work and using *ad hoc* materials and tools. In the case of MT, volunteers mostly use free online engines (Rico, 2020). This involves a high risk when dealing with confidential and personal data such as donors' information, reports to official bodies regarding field actions or personal documentation from most vulnerable people.

2 Building a case for the use of neural machine translation

INMIGRA3 aims at building a case for the use of NMT for the specific translation needs of NGOs. This involves an experimental setting along the following lines:

- The participation of two NGOs working with migrant people and refugees in Spain: Cáritas Española[6] and the Spanish Committee for Refugee Help (CEAR)[7].

---

[1] The work of INMIGRA2-CM was presented at EAMT 2017: https://ufal.mff.cuni.cz/eamt2017/user-project-product-papers/Conference_Booklet_EAMT2017.pdf
[2] CRISIS-MT is a project funded by Universidad de Alcalá (CCG2018/HUM-043). Among other objectives, it aims at designing an MT system that can be easily put to use in multilingual crisis communication.

[3] INTERACT website:
https://sites.google.com/view/crisistranslation/home?authuser=0
[4] Language on the move website:
https://www.languageonthemove.com/
[5] TWB website: https://translatorswithoutborders.org/
[6] Cáritas Española is the Spanish chapter of *Caritas Internationalis*, a not-for-profit organization associated to the Roman Catholic Church.
[7] CEAR's website: https://www.cear.es/

Martins, Moniz, Fumega, Martins, Batista, Coheur, Parra, Trancoso, Turchi, Bisazza, Moorkens, Guerberof, Nurminen, Marg, Forcada (eds.)
Proceedings of the 22nd Annual Conference of the European Association for Machine Translation, p. 469–470
Lisboa, Portugal, November 2020.

- Definition of a use-case scenario according to the specific needs of the two NGOs participating in the project. This involves different text typologies and topics: donors' funding information, economic reports to official bodies, documentation for asylum petition, administrative forms and instructions for housing benefits, workshop materials in food safety and health issues, tax waiver forms, and informative texts on access to education. The source language of all texts is Spanish and target languages are English, French, Russian, Arabic and Chinese[8].

- A compact NMT engine developed at the Universitat Oberta de Catalunya that can be used offline in a regular consumer computer. As demonstrated in Oliver et al (2019) it is possible to develop neural MT systems that can be integrated in a very compact set of applications that work in computers with limited hardware resources and without Internet connection. In our implementation, we are using the Marian toolkit with an s2s architecture. The subword-nmt algorithm (Sennrich, 2016) has been applied to both sides of the corpus to minimize the effect of out-of-vocabulary words. As a training corpus, we use MultiUN corpus.

- The evaluation of the MT output in terms of text usability (Suojanen et al, 2015).

- The publication of a best practice report with specific recommendations for NGOs on how to implement NMT. This will include specifications on how these systems can be adapted to the needs of a given situation (language pairs, subjects, etc.), and how to implement them in a regular consumer computer to provide a useful solution to communication needs in migratory contexts.

References

Federici, F.M. and O'Brien, S. 2020, *Translation in Cascading Crisis*. London: Routledge.

Footitt, HA, Crack, A & Tesseur, W. 2018, *Respecting Communities in International Development: Languages and Cultural Understanding.* https://www.intrac.org/resources/respecting-communities-international-development-languages-cultural-understanding/

Oliver, A., M. Sánchez Ramos and C. Rico. Building offline, compact, ready to use MT systems for crisis translation. *Workshop on Crisis Machine Translation ("Crisis MT") at MT Summit 2019* https://sites.google.com/view/crisistranslation/crisis-mt-workshop

Rico, C. 2020. Mapping translation technology and the multilingual needs of NGOs along the aid chain. In Federici, F.M. and O'Brien, S. 2020, *Translation in Cascading Crisis*. London: Routledge.

Sennrich, R. Barry Haddow and Alexandra Birch (2016): Neural Machine Translation of Rare Words with Subword Units *Proceedings of the 54th Annual Meeting of the Association for Computational Linguistics* (ACL 2016). Berlin, Germany.

Suojanen, T., Koskinen, K. and Tuominen, T. 2015. User-Centered Translation. London and New York: Routledge.

Acknowledgements

INMIGRA3 is a project jointly funded by the Autonomous Community of Madrid (Spain) and the European Social Fund under grant H2019/HUM-5772 (start date: 1 Jan 2020; end date: 31 Dec 2023).

---

[8] We are aware that these languages do not cover the full spectrum of languages spoken by migrant people in Spain. Less resourced languages are not the specific subject of this project as the participating NGOs issue their content in the language combinations mentioned.

The Multilingual Anonymisation Toolkit for Public Administrations (MAPA) Project

Ē. Ajausks†, V. Arranz‡, L. Bié*, A. Cerdà-i-Cucó*, K. Choukri‡, M. Cuadros§,
H. Degroote*, A. Estela*, T. Etchegoyhen§, M. García-Martínez*,
A. García-Pablos§, M. Herranz*, A. Kohan*, M. Melero**, M. Rosner¶,
R. Rozis†, P. Paroubek◇, A. Vasiļevskis†, P. Zweigenbaum◇ *

†Tilde {eriks.ajausks,roberts.rozis,arturs.vasilevskis}@tilde.lv

‡ELDA/ELRA {arranz,choukri}@elda.org

*Pangeanic - PangeaMT {l.bie,a.cerda,h.degroote,a.estela,m.garcia,m.herranz,a.kohan}@pangeanic.com

**Barcelona Supercomputing Center maite.melero@bsc.es ◇ Université Paris-Saclay, CNRS, LIMSI {pap,pz}@limsi.fr

¶University of Malta mike.rosner@um.edu.mt §Vicomtech {agarciap,mcuadros,tetchegoyhen}@vicomtech.com

Abstract

We describe the MAPA project, funded under the Connecting Europe Facility programme, whose goal is the development of an open-source de-identification toolkit for all official European Union languages. It will be developed since January 2020 until December 2021.

1 Introduction

De-identification may provide the means to share language data while also protecting private or sensitive data by spotting then deleting, obfuscating, pseudoymising or encrypting personally identifiable information. De-identification is typically performed for the purpose of protecting an individual's private activities while maintaining the usefulness of the gathered data for research and development purposes.

The Multilingual Anonymisation toolkit for Public Administrations (MAPA) project aims to leverage natural language processing tools to develop an open-source toolkit for effective and reliable text de-identification, focusing on the medical and legal domains. The project is funded by the Connecting Europe Facility (CEF) programme, under grant N° A2019/1927065, and will run from January 2020 until December 2021.

The toolkit developed by the MAPA partners (Pangeanic[1], Tilde[2], CNRS[3], ELDA[4], University of Malta[5], Vicomtech[6] and SEAD[7]) will address all official EU languages, including underresourced ones such as Latvian, Lithuanian, Estonian, Slovenian and Croatian, and severely underresourced ones such as Irish and Maltese.

As a part of the project, a connection to eTranslation,[8] an online machine translation service provided by the European Commission, will be established to foster the provision of multilingual datasets by public administrations that may in turn improve the coverage and quality of machine translation systems.

2 Approach

At its core, the MAPA anonymisation toolkit will rely on Named Entity Recognition and Classification (NERC) techniques using neural networks and deep learning techniques. The latest deep learning architectures and the availability of pre-trained multilingual language models, such as BERT (Devlin et al., 2019) have pushed the state of the art in NERC to new levels of performance.

In addition, thanks to the transfer learning capabilities shown by this type of deep learning models, new systems can be trained using smaller datasets of manually labelled data, and the knowledge acquired for a given domain or language can be reused in a cross-domain or cross-language setting (García-Pablos et al., 2020). MAPA will leverage the most innovative technology to provide robust models for the 24 official European languages, trained to detect named entities that involve sensitive information, depending on the application do-

---

All authors have contributed equally to this work.

[1] https://pangeamt.com/
[2] https://www.tilde.com/
[3] http://www.cnrs.fr/
[4] http://www.elra.info/en/

[5] https://www.um.edu.mt/
[6] https://www.vicomtech.org/en/
[7] https://avancedigital.gob.es/
[8] https://ec.europa.eu/info/resources-partners/machine-translation-public-administrations-etranslation_en

Martins, Moniz, Fumega, Martins, Batista, Coheur, Parra, Trancoso, Turchi, Bisazza, Moorkens, Guerberof, Nurminen, Marg, Forcada (eds.)

Proceedings of the 22nd Annual Conference of the European Association for Machine Translation, p. 471–472

Lisboa, Portugal, November 2020.

main (e.g., medical, legal).

MAPA will contain a general NERC model, that will be further fine-tuned to detect domain-specific entities. The system will then be tailored to fulfil the specific needs of each use case. Since some severely under-resourced languages such as Maltese, one of the official EU languages, are not included in the pre-trained multilingual BERT model, a separate solution will be developed in this case.

The deep learning NERC approach will be complemented with other configurable mechanisms, such as pattern detection based on regular expressions, to deal with pattern-based entities: email addresses, ID numbers, telephone numbers, bank accounts, etc. It will also be capable of using user-defined dictionaries to detect specific uses of entity names known in advance.

All these subsystems will be seamlessly combined into an integrated system that will provide a powerful and customisable de-identification engine. For each EU language, a separate docker image will be published, which will take text as input and return it in de-identified form.

3 Use cases

The project includes two specific deployment cases for public institutions in an EU country: one for the health domain and one for the legal domain. Both domains were selected given their strong de-identification requirements prior to any sharing of the data. In each deployment case, the system will be tailored to the specific needs of the relevant institution.

L-Università ta' Malta (University of Malta) will take care of the deployment case for the MAPA toolkit in Malta. In Spain, the deployment case will be executed under the umbrella of the Language Technology Plan[9], which is already running actions in the Health sector in close collaboration with the Ministry and regional institutions, and is willing to expand its activities to the Legal public sector.

4 Data Collection

MAPA will count on a data collection activity to provide the necessary training and testing data for the toolkit development. Data is currently being identified and collected for the 24 relevant European languages. One million sentence corpora are targeted per language, prioritising both medical and legal data, but also containing some general-language data for training. Testing will make use of sample data sets which will be manually annotated with named entities addressing the de-identification needs of the covered domains in the 24 languages. Specific annotation guidelines are currently being defined for that purpose.

The performance of the produced system will be evaluated for each language on held-out sample data sets for each of the two prioritized domains. This evaluation will inform use case designers and users about the expected performance of the base system so that they can assess their need for further adaptation.

5 Conclusion

The MAPA project will develop an open-source anonymisation toolkit for all official EU languages, which will support public administrations in sharing their data while complying with the GDPR requirements. The toolkit will be publicly available and particularly targeted to public administrations in the health and legal domains, as a result of the specific use cases addressed during the development of the project.

References

Devlin, Jacob, Ming-Wei Chang, Kenton Lee, and Kristina Toutanova. 2019. BERT: Pre-training of Deep Bidirectional Transformers for Language Understanding. In *Proceedings of the 2019 Conference of the North American Chapter of the Association for Computational Linguistics: Human Language Technologies, Volume 1 (Long and Short Papers)*, pages 4171–4186.

García-Pablos, Aitor, Naiara Perez, and Montse Cuadros. 2020. Sensitive Data Detection and Classification in Spanish Clinical Text: Experiments with BERT. In *Proceedings of the 12th International Conference on Language Resources and Evaluation (LREC'20)*.

---

[9]https://www.plantl.gob.es/tecnologias-lenguaje/PTL/Paginas/plan-impulso-tecnologias-lenguaje.aspx

APE-QUEST: a Quality Gate for Routing MT

Joachim Van den Bogaert, Heidi Depraetere, Sara Szoc, Tom Vanallemeersch
CrossLang, Kerkstraat 106, 9050 Gentbrugge, Belgium
`{first.lastname}@crosslang.com`

Lucia Specia, Julia Ive
University of Sheffield
`{initial.lastname}@sheffield.ac.uk`

Maxim Khalilov
Unbabel, Rua Visconde de Santarém, 67B, 1000-286 Lisboa, Portugal
`maxim@unbabel.com`

Abstract

The APE-QUEST project (2018–2020) provides a quality gate connected to the eTranslation system of EC's Connecting Europe Facility (CEF). The quality gate supports translation in specific domains and involves quality estimation (QE), automatic post-edition (APE) of machine translation (MT) output, human post-editing (PE) and secure data transfer. Public PE datasets are provided. Evaluations involving three language pairs are ongoing.

1 Overview

The APE-QUEST project (Automated Post-editing and Quality Estimation) is funded by the EC's CEF Telecom programme (project 2017-EU-IA-0151) which started in October 2018 and runs until September 2020. The project offers a quality gate connected to the eTranslation MT system, developed by the Directorate-General for Translation and provided by the CEF Automated Translation building block of the Directorate-General for Communications Networks, Content and Technology (DG CNECT) as a service to Digital Service Infrastructures (DSIs) of the EC and to public administrations of Member States. The project consortium consists of two companies, CrossLang (coordinator) and Unbabel, and the University of Sheffield.

APE-QUEST consists of a quality gate which injects QE and APE into the translation workflow. The main goals of this injection are (1) to reach the desired translation quality in an efficient and reliable way using MT and PE and (2) to create data aggregation opportunities by making translations and post-edits "locally owned", as data is generated and curated at the end user's site, in accordance with the similar main principle of the EC's ELRC action.[1]

The APE-QUEST project focuses on mature technologies by integrating systems for MT, QE and APE. Tests involve three language pairs (English to Portuguese, French and Dutch) and three domains (legal-domain text, procurement and online dispute resolution).

2 Architecture

The workflow consists of three tiers: (1) MT output with acceptable quality flows directly to the end user or connected system, (2) moderate-quality MT is enhanced through APE, and (3) low-quality MT is sent to a workflow for human PE. The input consists of text snippets (messages) or full text documents from the project's stakeholders, such as DSIs, public services in Member States, and organisations involved in CEF Telecom projects adopting eTranslation. The input is provided through an API or user interface and is segmented into sentences to allow for routing sentences to different tiers based on the detected quality.

---

[1]   http://lr-coordination.eu (European Language Resources Coordination)

Martins, Moniz, Fumega, Martins, Batista, Coheur, Parra, Trancoso, Turchi, Bisazza, Moorkens, Guerberof, Nurminen, Marg, Forcada (eds.)
Proceedings of the 22nd Annual Conference of the European Association for Machine Translation, p. 473–474
Lisboa, Portugal, November 2020.

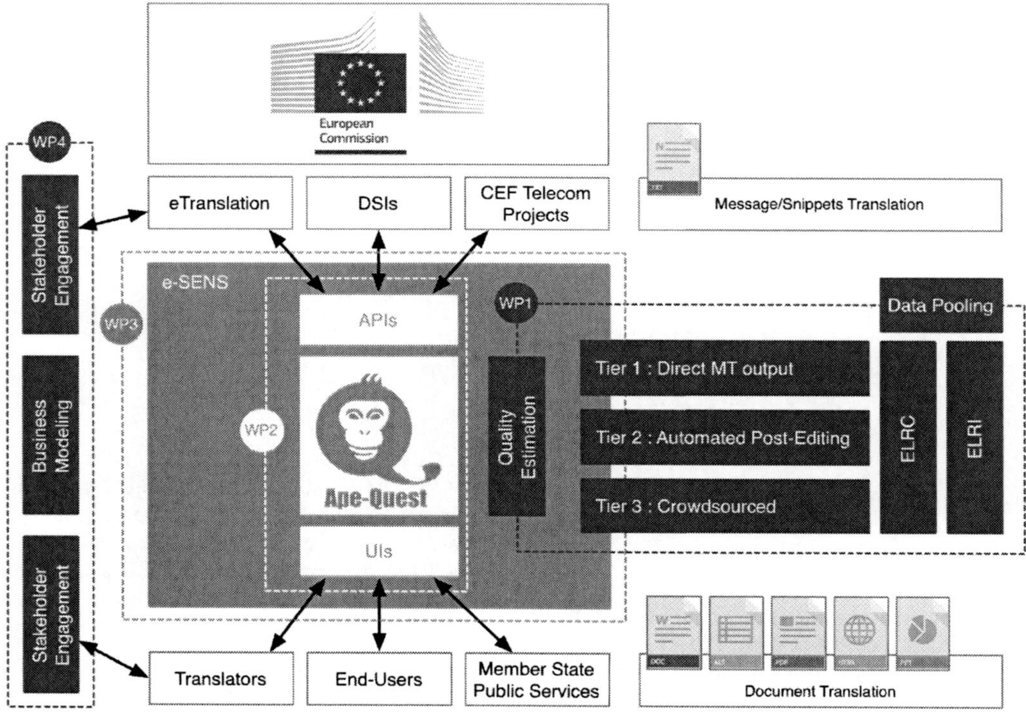

Figure 1 Architecture of APE-QUEST

The PE workflow allows for collecting user data for system improvement, i.e. data for adapting the MT system and re-training QE and APE systems.

The components of the workflow have been successfully integrated and it is fully operational. It is interoperable with the eTranslation system, it is conformant with the EC's eDelivery building block in order to ensure secure and reliable data transfer, and it contains a portal-style front end (an adaptation of MateCat).[2]

3 Outcome

The human PE data created in the framework of the project is available in the ELRC-SHARE repository,[3] which collects, prepares and shares language resources. This data consists of around 30K tuples including a source sentence, a corresponding neural MT output, a post-edited version created by a professional translator, and the original reference translation crawled from parallel language websites in the legal domain. All data were anonymized.

Tests with the quality gate are ongoing in order to determine QE thresholds. The APE component for these tests is based on neural *copycat* networks, while the open-source framework *OpenKiwi* is used for QE. Both are described in Ive et al. (2020). The thresholds aim at establishing a trade-off between automatic processing (MT and APE) and human PE, in terms of translation speed, quality and cost. The tests involve two use cases, i.e. dissemination and assimilation of translated texts.

Acknowledgement

APE-QUEST is funded by the EC's CEF Telecom programme (project 2017-EU-IA-0151).

References

Ive, Julia, Lucia Specia, Sara Szoc, Tom Vanallemeersch, Joachim Van den Bogaert, Eduardo Farah, Christine Maroti, Artur Ventura, and Maxim Khalilov. 2020. A Post-Editing Dataset in the Legal Domain: Do we Underestimate Neural Machine Translation Quality? To appear in Proceedings of LREC 2020.

---

[2] http://www.matecat.com

[3] Name of the resource: "Post-editing corpus English to Dutch/French/Portuguese, legal domain"

MICE: Adapting MT through Middleware

Joachim Van den Bogaert, Heidi Depraetere, Tom Vanallemeersch
CrossLang
Kerkstraat 106
9050 Gentbrugge
Belgium
{first.lastname}@crosslang.com

Abstract

The MICE project (2018–2020) will deliver a middleware layer for improving the output quality of the eTranslation system of EC's Connecting Europe Facility through additional services, such as domain adaptation and named-entity recognition. It will also deliver a user portal, allowing for human post-editing.

1 Objectives

The MICE project (Middleware for Customer eTranslation), which is funded by the CEF Telecom programme (Connecting Europe Facility) and runs from October 2018 to September 2020, delivers a middleware layer for the improvement of the eTranslation machine translation (MT) system. The latter is developed by DG Translation, supports all 24 official EU languages, and is provided by the CEF Automated Translation building block of DG CNECT as a service to Digital Service Infrastructures (DSIs) of the EC and to public administrations of Member States. The project consortium of MICE consists of two companies, CrossLang (coordinator) and Tilde, and two public organisations, NBN (Bureau for Standardisation, Belgium) and RIK (Centre of Registers and Information Systems, Estonia).

The middleware layer consists of the following services:

- domain adaptation;
- terminology resolution;
- named-entity recognition;
- document filtering;
- normalisation.

MICE also provides a human and automated post-editing (PE) environment for CEF eTranslation output, based on MateCat.[1] This will help users to dynamically enhance the MT output and aggregate data for further system improvement.

The tests in the project involve several languages (English, Dutch, French, Estonian), domains (standards and e-Business/e-Land register information) and countries (Belgium, Estonia). Domain-specific neural MT systems will be made available by the project consortium.

2 Architecture

MICE will expose its middleware layer for customisation through APIs and a user portal, in order to increase its impact and usability. Tasks will be performed in real-time or offline, depending on user preference. The input consists of text snippets (messages in plain text of maximally 5,000 characters) or full text documents (Microsoft Office, open document formats, etc.). The MICE architecture, which is shown in Figure 1, is compliant with the eDelivery building block.

The MICE project will create a reference implementation for the automated translation of standards and e-Business/e-Land register information in Belgium and Estonia. It will be extensible in order to allow for future add-ons of MT-related services, such as automated domain detection or combination of MT systems.

3 Test results

In both use cases (NBN, RIK), similar tests for domain adaptation were performed. We will illustrate them based on the NBN use case.

---

[1] http://www.matecat.com

Martins, Moniz, Fumega, Martins, Batista, Coheur, Parra, Trancoso, Turchi, Bisazza, Moorkens, Guerberof, Nurminen, Marg, Forcada (eds.)
Proceedings of the 22nd Annual Conference of the European Association for Machine Translation, p. 475–476
Lisboa, Portugal, November 2020.

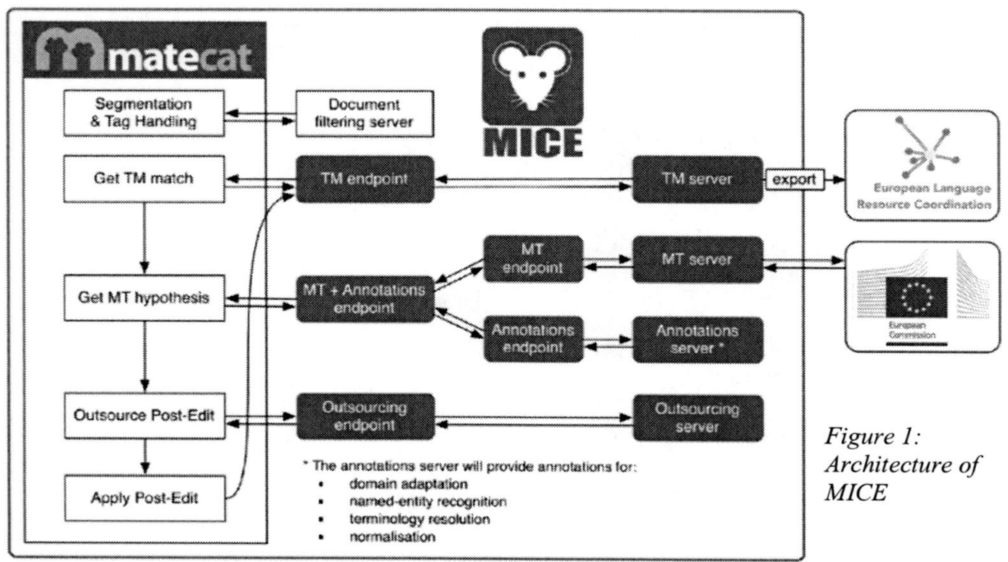

Figure 1: Architecture of MICE

In-domain English–French and English–Dutch MT systems were built by extracting and aligning sentences from PDF files of NBN. In addition, parallel synthetic data were created by backtranslating text from in-domain monolingual target language data, and other parallel text was obtained by scraping the NBN website and aligning web pages and sentence pairs in them. Overfitting on the domain was avoided by enriching the training data with text from other domains.

Further domain adaptation involved a preprocessing step before training the MT systems. This step consisted of named-entity recognition and detection of numbers, URLs, email addresses and technical entities. Sentences were normalized by replacing the detected parts with placeholders. When applying the MT system to new sentences, the placeholders in the output were replaced by a copy of the source text (e.g. person names) or a localized version (in case of numbers). Another type of domain adaptation consisted of enriching MT training data with bilingual term lists automatically extracted using TermCalc (Vanallemeersch and Kockaert 2010).

Domain-adapted MT systems were trained with OpenNMT (Klein et al. 2017) and evaluated using a manually cleaned in-domain test set, as well as using out-of-domain test sets (legal domain) in order to prevent a risk of overfitting. The BLEU scores shown in Table 1 and 2 indicate that MT systems with in-domain training data perform better than systems without, and that the use of bilingual terms further improves

the results. The scores for the legal domain, on the other hand, are more or less constant.

Test Train	In-domain	Legal 1	Legal 2
Various domains	23.2	37.9	46.2
+ In-domain	35.7	35.8	44.6
+ Bilingual terms	35.9	37.1	45.1

Table 1 BLEU scores English–Dutch

Test Train	In-domain	Legal 1	Legal 2
Various domains	29.1	34.8	40.1
+ In-domain	49.5	34.9	39.5
+ Bilingual terms	51.3	35.3	40.6

Table 2 BLEU scores English–French

Acknowledgement

MICE is funded by the EC's CEF Telecom programme (project 2017-EU-IA-0169).

References

Klein, Guillaume, Yoon Kim, Yuntian Deng, Jean Senellart, and Alexander Rush. 2017. OpenNMT: Open-Source Toolkit for Neural Machine Translation. *ACL 2017, System Demonstrations*, Vancouver, Canada 67–72.

Vanallemeersch, Tom and Hendrik Kockaert. 2010. Automated Detection of Inconsistent Phraseology Translation. *Southern African Linguistics and Applied Language Studies*, 28(3):283–290.

Neural Translation for the European Union (NTEU) Project

**L. Bié*, A. Cerdà-i-Cucó*, H. Degroote*, A. Estela*,
M. García-Martínez*, M. Herranz*, A. Kohan*, M. Melero‡,
T. O'Dowd§, S. O'Gorman§, M. Pinnis†, R. Rozis†,
R. Superbo§, A. Vasiļevskis†***

‡Barcelona Supercomputing Center `maite.melero@bsc.es`
§KantanMT{`sineadog,tonyod,riccardos`}`@kantanmt.com`
*Pangeanic-PangeaMT{`l.bie,a.cerda,h.degroote,a.estela,m.garcia,m.herranz,a.kohan`}`@pangeanic.com`
†Tilde{`roberts.rozis,marcis.pinnis,arturs.vasilevskis`}`@tilde.lv`

Abstract

The Neural Translation for the European Union (NTEU) project aims to build a neural engine farm with all European official language combinations for eTranslation,[1] without the necessity to use a high-resourced language as a pivot. NTEU started in September 2019 and will run until August 2021.

1 Introduction

Normally, data for translation are available in English from or to another language. With a few exceptions, all eTranslation MT engines include English as either source or target. Thus, to translate between two non-English languages, English must be used as a pivot.

The NTEU partners, Pangeanic,[2] Tilde,[3] KantanMT[4] and SEAD[5], have been awarded EU funds to build direct machine translation (MT) engines between any of the 24 EU official languages (e.g. Spanish to German, Croatian to Italian, Greek to Polish, etc.) without pivoting through English (around 550 translation engines in total).

2 Approach

NTEU will provide a capacity service to eTranslation by building a near-human-professional-quality neural engine farm which includes all EU language combinations. State-of-the-art technologies such as the transformer (Vaswani et al., 2017) architecture will be implemented. Moreover, lower-resourced languages (for example, Irish or Maltese) will be a challenge, and more effort will be required to obtain well-performing engines for them. In order to obtain the best results, we will experiment with techniques to supplement the original data, such as generating synthetic data by doing back-translation (Sennrich et al., 2016), checking of sentence alignments, transfer learning (Zoph et al., 2016) and unsupervised learning on a monolingual corpus (Artetxe et al., 2019).

In addition to providing the trained engines, the NTEU consortium will gather and clean data from all language combinations so that the engines can be retrained with other technologies in the future. As part of the national digital data gathering efforts, NTEU will also act as a bridge between previous efforts, putting to work the results of the ELRC[6] repository and other European data gathering efforts such as the NEC TM[7] and ParaCrawl[8] projects. Therefore, the project will promote the free flow of data between public administrations themselves and EU bodies.

3 Evaluation methodology

The results of the MT will be manually evaluated in an open-source platform created by the consortium. Following industry and WMT[9] practices for human evaluation, the evaluation dataset has been carefully chosen so as to represent real-world, whole, human-translated documents, purposely excluded from the training data. Human

---

[1] https://ec.europa.eu/info/resources-partners/machine-translation-public-administrations-etranslation_en
[2] https://pangeamt.com/
[3] https://www.tilde.com/
[4] https://kantanmt.com/
[5] Spanish Agency for Digital Advancement, dependant on the Ministry of Economy
[6] https://elrc-share.eu/
[7] https://www.nec-tm.eu/
[8] https://paracrawl.eu/
[9] http://www.statmt.org/wmt19/

Martins, Moniz, Fumega, Martins, Batista, Coheur, Parra, Trancoso, Turchi, Bisazza, Moorkens, Guerberof, Nurminen, Marg, Forcada (eds.)
Proceedings of the 22nd Annual Conference of the European Association for Machine Translation, p. 477–478
Lisboa, Portugal, November 2020.

evaluators will score the MT for fluency, adequacy and fit-for-purpose, in a range between 0 and 100. The human evaluator —who will be a native speaker of the target language, but not necessarily knowledgeable of the source language— will be presented with the reference translation in context, plus two automatic translations (one from our engines and one from a third party state-of-the-art system), both unidentified. Each translation will be evaluated by two different human evaluators. The aim of the evaluation platform is to make human evaluation of MT faster, more efficient and more consistent. Automatic evaluation using a larger dataset, also excluded from training, is foreseen as well. The objective is to extensively reduce the time required to build and approve production-ready MT engines with continuous evaluator feedback that reinforces data selection and training procedures.

4 Conclusion

In conclusion, the NTEU project will yield a state-of-the-art neural MT engine farm, which will include all EU language combinations without pivoting through English for eTranslation. Special emphasis will be put on the low-resourced language combinations. The collected data will be provided so it can be used in future technologies. Moreover, an open-source platform will be developed to facilitate human evaluation of the MT engines. Finally, the project will be promoted between public administrations and will put to work previous European data-gathering initiatives.

Acknowledgements

The work reported in this paper was conducted during the NTEU project, which was funded by Innovation and Network Executive Agency (INEA) through grant Nº INEA/CEF/ICT/A2018/1816500 as part of the EU's CEF Telecommunications Program.

References

Artetxe, Mikel, Gorka Labaka, and Eneko Agirre. 2019. Unsupervised neural machine translation, a new paradigm solely based on monolingual text. *Procesamiento del Lenguaje Natural*, 63:151–154.

Sennrich, Rico, Barry Haddow, and Alexandra Birch. 2016. Improving neural machine translation models with monolingual data. In *Proceedings of the 54th Annual Meeting of the Association for Computational Linguistics (Volume 1: Long Papers)*, pages 86–96, Berlin, Germany, August. Association for Computational Linguistics.

Vaswani, Ashish, Noam Shazeer, Niki Parmar, Jakob Uszkoreit, Llion Jones, Aidan N Gomez, Łukasz Kaiser, and Illia Polosukhin. 2017. Attention is all you need. In *Advances in Neural Information Processing Systems*, pages 5998–6008.

Zoph, Barret, Deniz Yuret, Jonathan May, and Kevin Knight. 2016. Transfer learning for low-resource neural machine translation. In *Proceedings of the 2016 Conference on Empirical Methods in Natural Language Processing*, pages 1568–1575, Austin, Texas, November. Association for Computational Linguistics.

OPUS-MT – Building open translation services for the World

Jörg Tiedemann
Department of Digital Humanities
HELDIG
University of Helsinki

Santhosh Thottingal
Wikimedia Foundation

1 Introduction

Equality among people requires, among other things, the ability to access information in the same way as others independent of the linguistic background of the individual user. Achieving this goal becomes an even more important challenge in a globalized world with digital channels and information flows being the most decisive factor in our integration in modern societies. Language barriers can lead to severe disadvantages and discrimination not to mention conflicts caused by simple misunderstandings based on broken communication. Linguistic discrimination leads to frustration, isolation and racism and the lack of technological language support may also cause what is known as the *digital language death* (Kornai, 2013).

Machine translation (MT) has developed into a useful tool that diminishes and partially removes such language barriers. Modern MT engines enable people to communicate, to access information in foreign languages and to build efficient resources for new communities. The mission of OPUS-MT[1] is to provide open translation services and tools that are free from commercial interests and restrictions. The idea is to make automatic translation accessible for anyone in a transparent and secure way without exploitation plans and hidden agendas compromising privacy and placing marketing strategies. We also want to focus on the support of minority and low-resource languages with the aim to introduce a community effort for the benefit of all.

OPUS-MT has successfully launched its first pilot system and currently collaborates with the Wikimedia foundation in the setup of translation services for the production of Wikipedia content in new languages based on more elaborated resources available in, e.g. English. Currently, the project provides over 1,000 pre-trained translation models that are free to download and use. OPUS-MT also contains open-source software for launching translation services as web applications. The on-going effort focuses on the improvement of translation quality, language coverage and emphasizes specific test cases to study the applicability of the approach. More details about the implementation and current status of the project are given below.

2 OPUS-MT models

The models that we train are based on state-of-the-art transformer-based neural machine translation (NMT). We apply Marian-NMT[2] in our framework, a stable production-ready NMT toolbox with efficient training and decoding capabilities (Junczys-Dowmunt et al., 2018). Our models are trained on freely available parallel corpora collected in the large bitext repository OPUS[3] (Tiedemann, 2012). The architecture is based on a standard transformer setup with 6 self-attentive layers in both, the encoder and decoder network with 8 attention heads in each layer. The hyper-parameters follow the general recommendations given in the documentation of the software. All the details can be seen in the training procedures that we also release as open source in our GitHub repository.[4]

OPUS-MT supports both, bilingual as well as multilingual models. For the latter, we apply the language label approach proposed by (Johnson et al., 2017). Our package implements generic

[1] `https://github.com/Helsinki-NLP/Opus-MT`

[2] `https://marian-nmt.github.io`
[3] `http://opus.nlpl.eu`
[4] `https://github.com/Helsinki-NLP/Opus-MT-train`

Martins, Moniz, Fumega, Martins, Batista, Coheur, Parra, Trancoso, Turchi, Bisazza, Moorkens, Guerberof, Nurminen, Marg, Forcada (eds.)
Proceedings of the 22nd Annual Conference of the European Association for Machine Translation, p. 479–480
Lisboa, Portugal, November 2020.

model	BLEU	chrF$_2$
English–Finnish	22.9	0.548
+ back-translation	23.7	0.562
+ fine-tuning	25.7	0.578

Table 1: Test results for the English–Finnish OPUS-MT model based on the news translation task from WMT 2019. Fine-tuning was done using the English–Finnish news translation test sets from earlier years.

procedures that make it easy to train a large number of translation models from the existing data in the OPUS collection. The procedures take care of proper pre-processing and training setups to enable batch-processes without the immediate need for further adjustments. We try to reduce the burden of time-consuming optimization and focus on rather generic models for the time being in order to quickly achieve a good language coverage without significantly compromising translation quality that can be achieved.

We use common benchmarks and test sets that are extracted on the fly from held-out data to monitor the quality of the NMT models. Test sets and results are released together with the models, pre- and post-processing scripts and basic information about their usage. The table of currently supported language pairs can be accessed on-line.[5]

We also develop generic fine-tuning and data augmentation procedures that can be used to further improve the translation models. We implemented a pipeline for backtranslation of Wikimedia content (coming from Wikipedia, Wikibooks, Wikisource, etc.) to augment existing training data. Backtranslation is known to significantly boost performance and to enable simple domain adaptation based on in-domain target language data. Furthermore, we also provide procedures for fine-tuning that can adjust model parameters according to some small in-domain data set, another successful strategy for domain adaptation. The impact of fine-tuning and backtranslation can be seen on the example of the English–Finnish OPUS-MT model listed in Table 1.

3 OPUS-MT servers

Finally, we also provide simple web applications that can be used to launch translation services based on the pre-trained models. The most straightforward setup is implemented as a dockerized Tornado-besed web application that can be set up with a few simple commands. The configuration can be adjusted and extended to serve any bilingual trans-

lation model that we provide. Each service can accommodate several language pairs and may connect multiple servers. The current implementation is based on CPU-based decoding as a cost-efficient setup for every-day users but it should be adjustable to a GPU-based setup without major changes. A running service demonstrating the app is hosted by the Wikimedia foundation at `https://opusmt.wmflabs.org`.

Another websocket based application is also provided, which enables the support of multilingual models, a simple translation cache and the retrieval of token alignment information, which is supported by most models that we train with the guided alignment feature of Marian-NMT. Further improvements of the web applications are planned once we have finished our tests of the current implementation in a production environment for selected test cases.

4 Conclusions

This paper presents OPUS-MT, a project that focuses on the development of free resources and tools for machine translation. The current status is a repository of over 1,000 pre-trained neural MT models that are ready to be launched in on-line translation services. For this we also provide open-source implementations of web applications that can run efficiently on average desktop hardware with a straightforward setup and installation.

The work is supported by the European Union's Horizon 2020 projects FoTran and MeMAD as well as by the Finnish IT Center for Science, CSC.

References

Johnson, M., Schuster, M., Le, Q. V., Krikun, M., Wu, Y., Chen, Z., Thorat, N., Viégas, F., Wattenberg, M., Corrado, G., et al. (2017). Google's multilingual neural machine translation system: Enabling zero-shot translation. *Transactions of the Association of Computational Linguistics*, 5(1):339–351.

Junczys-Dowmunt, M., Grundkiewicz, R., Dwojak, T., Hoang, H., Heafield, K., Neckermann, T., Seide, F., Germann, U., Aji, A. F., Bogoychev, N., Martins, A. F. T., and Birch, A. (2018). Marian: Fast neural machine translation in C++. In *Proceedings of ACL 2018, System Demonstrations*, pages 116–121.

Kornai, A. (2013). Digital language death. *PloS one*, 8(10). :e77056.

Tiedemann, J. (2012). Parallel data, tools and interfaces in OPUS. In *Proceedings of LREC*, Istanbul, Turkey.

---

[5] `http://opus.nlpl.eu/Opus-MT/`

OCR, Classification & Machine Translation (OCCAM)

**Joachim Van den Bogaert, Arne Defauw,
Frederic Everaert, Koen Van Winckel,
Alina Kramchaninova, Anna Bardadym,
Tom Vanallemeersch**
CrossLang
Kerkstraat 106
9050 Gentbrugge
Belgium
{first.lastname}@croslang.com

Pavel Smrž, Michal Hradiš
Brno University of Technology
Božetěchova 2
612 00 Brno
Czech Republic
smrz@fit.vut.cz,
ihradis@fit.vutbr.cz

Abstract

The OCCAM project (Optical Character recognition, ClassificAtion & Machine translation), which runs from 2019 to 2021, and is carried out by CrossLang and Brno University of Technology, aims at integrating the CEF (Connecting Europe Facility) Automated Translation service with image classification, translation memories, optical character recognition, and machine translation. It will support the automated translation of scanned business documents (a document format that, currently, cannot be processed by the CEF eTranslation service) and will also lead to a tool useful for the digital humanities domain.

1 Introduction

The European Commission's Business Registers Interconnection System (BRIS) facilitates the access to information on EU companies and ensures that all EU business registers can communicate to each other electronically, in relation to cross-border mergers and foreign branches.[1] Its main task is to synchronize the information that is present within Members States' business registers.

The CEF has planned an integration of BRIS with the CEF eTranslation[2] Digital Service Infrastructure (DSI), to make draft translations of company information available via the European e-Justice Portal,[3] but a large volume of scanned documents would remain untranslated, because it consists of raw images that are not machine-readable.

A similar problem occurs in the digital humanities domain: while there are plenty of optical character recognition (OCR) frameworks available (both open source and proprietary), the need for OCR and translation within the digital humanities domain remains pressing. The European Newspaper Survey Report,[4] as conducted during the Europeana Newspapers project, revealed that access to twentieth-century content remains problematic, and only few libraries use OCR when scanning documents. At the same time, there is a growing interest in gaining multilingual access to cultural heritage resources.

2 Proposed solution for BRIS

Existing content within the member state databases will be leveraged to recognise, classify and translate legacy and new content. The presence of database links to scanned documents, and the template-like nature of administrative documents will be exploited to optimize OCR and translation. Since a *pipelined* (cascaded) implementation (i.e. an OCR step followed by a machine translation (MT) step) has the inherent risk of error accumulation, OCCAM proposes a more informed classification-based approach, as outlined in Figure 1, to:

---

[1] https://ec.europa.eu/cefdigital/wiki/pages/viewpage.action?pageId=46992657

[2] https://ec.europa.eu/cefdigital/wiki/display/CEFDIGITAL/eTranslation

[3] https://e-justice.europa.eu/

[4] http://www.europeana-newspapers.eu/wp-content/uploads/2012/04/D4.1-Europeana-newspapers-survey-report.pdf

Martins, Moniz, Fumega, Martins, Batista, Coheur, Parra, Trancoso, Turchi, Bisazza, Moorkens, Guerberof, Nurminen, Marg, Forcada (eds.)
Proceedings of the 22nd Annual Conference of the European Association for Machine Translation, p. 481–482
Lisboa, Portugal, November 2020.

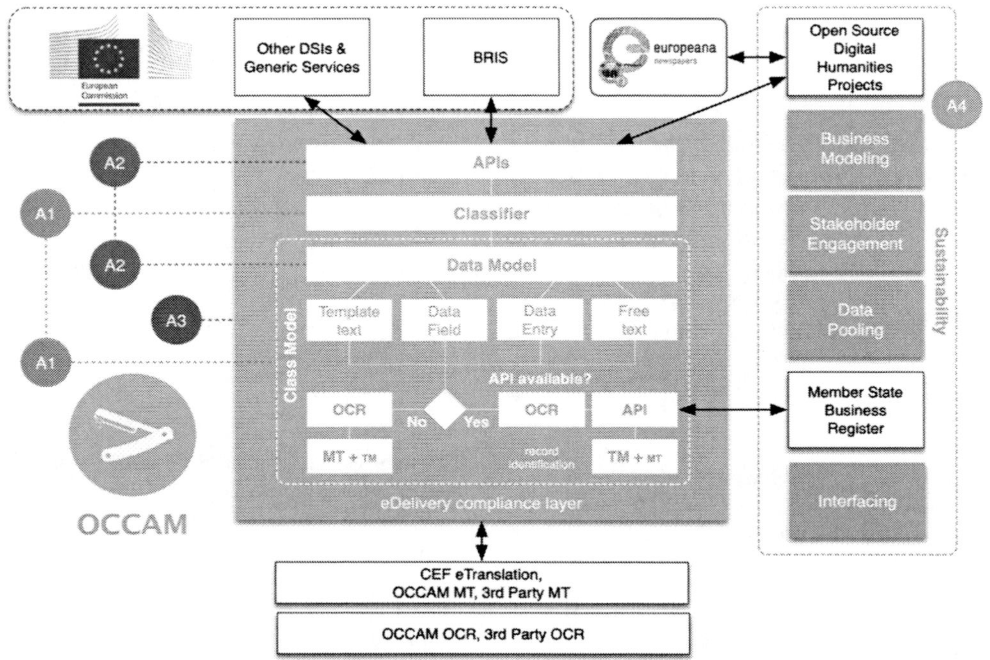

Figure 1: OCCAM system architecture

- recognise document types and link them to a corresponding data model (consisting of template text, data fields, data entries and free text);
- identify entities within documents and link them to corresponding entries in member state databases (e.g. by using OCR to recognise VAT numbers and retrieve the corresponding data from a national business register);
- retrieve translations from translation memoriess associated with the data model;
- use class-adapted OCR and MT for the remaining free text.

Brno University of Technology will provide the image classification and OCR tools, using the open source packages OpenCV,[5] Tesseract,[6] and TensorFlow,[7] and an in-house neural OCR system currently developed for the analysis of challenging historical documents in a project called PERO,[8] aimed at improving accessibility of cultural heritage. These tools are distributed under commercially-friendly (non-viral) licenses (3-clause BSD and Apache 2.0).

CrossLang will build MT engines using CEF eTranslation's MT system and its own Moses-based SMT (distributed under LGPL license) and OpenNMT-based (distributed under MIT license) systems. The developed MT systems will incorporate maned-entity recognition and terminology technology, and target the following language pairs: Dutch, French, German, and Czech into English.

The resulting OCCAM solution will be built as a reference implementation and made publicly available at the end of the project. The licenses of the used components will ensure that the implementation can be distributed freely, and adapted for use by business registers across Europe, after the project has ended.

For the digital humanities domain, a technology roadshow will be organised and tutorials will be published, to make researchers acquainted with the technology, so they can easily develop and adapt their own models.

Acknowledgement

OCCAM is funded by the EC's CEF Telecom programme (project 2018-EU-IA-0052).

---

[5] https://opencv.org/

[6] https://github.com/tesseract-ocr/tesseract

[7] https://www.tensorflow.org/

[8] http://www.fit.vutbr.cz/units/UPGM/grants/index.php.en?id=1165

CEFAT4Cities, a Natural Language Layer for the ISA^2 Core Public Service Vocabulary

Joachim Van den Bogaert, Arne Defauw, Sara Szoc, Frederic Everaert, Koen Van Winckel, Alina Kramchaninova, Anna Bardadym, Tom Vanallemeersch

CrossLang
Kerkstraat 106
9050 Gentbrugge
Belgium
`{first.lastname}@croslang.com`

Abstract

The CEFAT4Cities project (2020–2022) will create a "smart cities natural language context" (a software layer that facilitates the conversion of natural-language administrative procedures, into machine-readable data sets) on top of the existing ISA^2 interoperability layer for public services. Integration with the FIWARE/ORION "Smart City" Context Broker, will make existing, paper-based, public services discoverable through "Smart City" frameworks, thus allowing for the development of more sophisticated and more user-friendly public services applications. An automated translation component will be included, to provide a solution that can be used by all EU Member States. As a result, the project will allow EU citizens and businesses to interact with public services on the city, national, regional and EU level, in their own language.

1 Introduction

eGovernment tools and data sets provided by public sector organisations, are typically too fragmented across institutional levels and entities. This is known as the silo effect. To alleviate this effect, the ISA and ISA^2 (Interoperability Solutions for European Public Administrations) programmes[1] have been supporting the development of interoperability solutions for cross-border and cross-sector public services, for more than a decade. While ISA^2 Actions, such as the Core Vocabularies and the Core Public Service Vocabulary Application Profile (CPSV-AP) provide public administrations with templates and tools for describing their public services in a uniform way, one important aspect is still missing, i.e. user-centredness: existing infrastructures are primarily designed to facilitate computer-to-computer interaction, using a common, machine-readable vocabulary. But EU citizens do not speak in standardized data fields. Instead, they use 24 official EU languages to talk to their government: for instance, for an Austrian national living in Belgium, and starting up a new business, it is more important to find an eGovernment procedure in his or her mother tongue, than to know that all data is represented in ISA^2-compliant fields.

2 Proposed solution

To speed up the development and adoption of multilingual, cross-border eGovernment services, the CEFAT4Cities project, which runs from April 2020 to March 2022, will build:

- a quality-assured workflow that assists in transforming natural-language eGovernment administrative procedures into multilingual interoperable solutions. CEF eTranslation will be integrated as a tool for developing multilingual resources.
- an open linked data repository containing the results of applying this workflow, i.e. multilingual vocabularies.
- a FIWARE/ORION[2] extension that allows the context broker to be integrated with the envisaged workflow and resources.

---

[1] `https://ec.europa.eu/isa2/isa2_en`, ISA and ISA^2 support the development of digital solutions that enable public administrations, businesses and citizens in Europe to benefit from interoperable cross-border and cross-sector public services.

[2] `https://fiware-orion.readthedocs.io/en/master/`

Martins, Moniz, Fumega, Martins, Batista, Coheur, Parra, Trancoso, Turchi, Bisazza, Moorkens, Guerberof, Nurminen, Marg, Forcada (eds.)
Proceedings of the 22nd Annual Conference of the European Association for Machine Translation, p. 483–484
Lisboa, Portugal, November 2020.

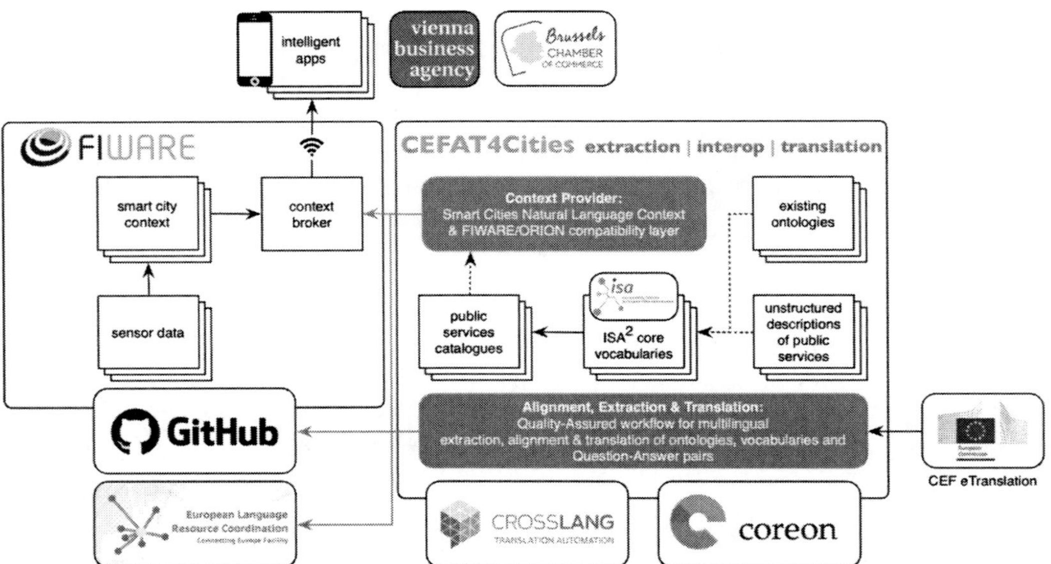

Figure 1: CEFAT4Cities system architecture

To promote the use of the CEFAT4Cities infrastructure within the smart cities community, a dissemination and communication plan, along with a roadmap for future funding, will be developed.

3 Use cases

The effectiveness of the solution will be demonstrated by three use cases:

- CEFAT4Cities will be integrated into the Context Broker Digital Service Infrastructure and the CPSV-AP and OSLO² templates, as a general Natural Language Processing (NLP) layer;
- the Vienna Business Agency will make its public services discoverable in multiple languages;
- the Brussels Chamber of Commerce will create a multilingual wizard for starting a new business in Brussels and showcase how CEFAT4Cities contributes to bringing local public services to a European scale.

The following tangible results will be produced:

- parts of CEFAT4Cities will be distributed as open source software components, enabling the Context Broker to deal with multilingual public service catalogues, through a connection with the CEF eTranslation service.
- the Vienna Business Agency will be able to connect its Content Management System to a multilingual resource, semantically linked across languages.

- the Brussels Chamber of Commerce will have a multilingual app for non-Belgian company founders.
- resources for the following languages will be developed and committed to the ELRC repository: Dutch, English, French, German, Italian, Slovenian, Croatian and Norwegian.

4 Consortium

CEFAT4Cities will be implemented by a consortium of five partners, representing three different countries (Austria, Belgium and Germany), demonstrating a diversified expertise, with access to various stakeholder communities. CrossLang (Belgium) and Coreon (Germany) have a strong track record in NLP, Machine Translation, and Knowledge Management. The FIWARE Foundation (Germany) has plenty of experience in productizing research code and working with the open source community. Vienna Business Agency (Austria) and Brussels Chamber of Commerce (Belgium) have both immediate access to other regions and cities. The targeted users, represented by the cities of Maribor (Slovenia) and Trento (Italy), will involve their networks of problem owners to test the project results and to promote the outcomes.

Acknowledgement

CEFAT4Cities is funded by the EC's CEF Telecom programme (project 2019-EU-IA-0015).

Assessing the Comprehensibility of Automatic Translations (ArisToCAT)

Lieve Macken, Margot Fonteyne, Arda Tezcan and Joke Daems
LT[3], Language and Translation Technology Team
Ghent University
Belgium
`Lieve.Macken@ugent.be`

Abstract

The ArisToCAT project aims to assess the comprehensibility of 'raw' (unedited) MT output for readers who can only rely on the MT output. In this project description, we summarize the main results of the project and present future work.

1 Introduction

Machine translation (MT) systems cannot guarantee that the text they produce will be fluent and coherent in both syntax and semantics. Errors occur frequently in machine-translated text, leaving the reader to guess parts of the intended message. With the arrival of neural machine translation (NMT), however, the quality of machine translation has increased significantly. As such, machine translation is becoming an attractive solution to deal with the increased need for translated content. This could mean that, in the near future, readers will be more often confronted with 'raw' (unedited) MT output.

2 Quality of MT output

To assess the quality improvements in MT, we compared the quality of three different MT systems for English–Dutch: a commercial neural system, a phrase-based system and a predominantly rule-based system. We used Web-Anno[1] as annotation tool and adopted a two-step approach to annotate all errors in the MT output. In a first step, only the target text was visible and we marked all fluency errors; in a second step all accuracy errors

were labelled in both source and target text and were linked. Van Brussel et al. (2018) found that the neural system, in general, outperformed the phrase-based and rule-based systems when considering fluency. The output of the neural system contained fewer grammatical errors and hardly any spelling mistakes. For accuracy, the improvements of NMT are less apparent. The target sentence does not always contain traces of the errors or clues of omissions, which might have an impact on the comprehension.

3 Reading comprehension tests

In a pilot study, Macken and Ghyselen (2018) selected three texts of the English MT Evaluation version of the Corpus of Reading Comprehension Exercises (Scarton and Specia, 2016) and set up a reading comprehension test for both human translated and raw MT texts. Ninety-nine participants were asked to read the translation very carefully after which they had to answer comprehension questions without having access to the translated text. Human translations received the best overall clarity scores, but the reading comprehension tests provided much less unequivocal results.

4 Comprehensibility of newly invented words in NMT output

NMT systems occasionally generate non-existing words, i.e words that are not part of the vocabulary of the target language and were thus invented by the NMT system. In cases in which readers only have access to the MT output without the source text, such non-existing words can affect comprehension. There are several reasons why an NMT system creates new non-existing words. One reason is that, although NMT systems have

[1]https://webanno.github.io/webanno/

Martins, Moniz, Fumega, Martins, Batista, Coheur, Parra, Trancoso, Turchi, Bisazza, Moorkens, Guerberof, Nurminen, Marg, Forcada (eds.)
Proceedings of the 22nd Annual Conference of the European Association for Machine Translation, p. 485–486
Lisboa, Portugal, November 2020.

made huge progress, they sometimes still generate a too literal translation for different types of multi-word expressions such as compounds, another reason, specific for NMT systems, is that they operate at sub-word level to reduce vocabulary size. Macken et al. (2019) set up an experiment in which eighty-six participants were given 15 non-existing words (5 single words and 10 noun compounds) and were either asked to describe the meaning of these words or to select the correct meaning from a predefined list. The words were presented either in isolation or in sentence context. Non-existing words indeed impaired comprehension as on average in 60% of the cases the participants gave a wrong answer. Sentence context, however, made it easier for the participants to determine the meaning of the non-existing word as the percentage of wrong answers is much higher (77%) when the words were presented in isolation.

5 NMT for literary translation

To assess whether, with the improved quality, NMT systems are able to produce high-quality translations for more creative text types such as literature, we translated Agatha Christie's novel *The Mysterious Affair at Styles* with Google's NMT system into Dutch and applied the two-step error annotation. Fonteyne et al. (2020) found that 44% of the MT sentences did not contain any errors. The accuracy subcategory *mistranslation* was the most frequent error type encountered in the novel, followed by the fluency subcategories *coherence* and *style & register*. Tezcan et al. (2019) further investigated how the MT version differs from the published professionally human-translated (HT) Dutch version of the book. Measures of lexical richness (type-token ratio and mean segmental type-token ratio) gave inconclusive results. They also looked at word translation entropy (Carl et al., 2016), which indicates the degree of uncertainty to choose a particular translation from a set of target words based on the number and distribution of different translations that are available for a given word in a given context and found that the average word translation entropy scores were higher in HT than in MT, meaning that there was more variety in the translations in HT. At the syntactic level, the MT generally follows more closely the structure of the source sentence compared to the HT version.

6 Future work

In future work, we will set up eye-tracking experiments and expand the Ghent Eye-Tracking Corpus (Cop et al., 2017) with eye-tracking data for the NMT version of the novel. This will allow us to analyse to what extent MT impacts the reading process, and which errors impact this reading process the most.

Acknowledgements: The ArisToCAT project is a four-year research project (2017–2021) funded by the Research Foundation – Flanders (FWO) – grant number G.0064.17N assigned to prof. dr. Lieve Macken. All research is carried out at the University of Ghent (Belgium).

References

Carl, M., M. Schaeffer and S. Bangalore 2016. The CRITT Translation Process Research Database. In *New Directions in Empirical Translation Process Research: Exploring the CRITT TPR-DB.*, Cham, Heidelberg, New York, Dordrecht, London: Springer, 13–54.

Cop, U., N. Dirix, D. Drieghe and W. Duyck 2017. Presenting GECO: An eyetracking corpus of monolingual and bilingual sentence reading. *Behavior Research Methods*, 49:602–615.

Fonteyne, M., A. Tezcan, and L. Macken. Accepted. Literary MT under the Magnifying Glass: Assessing the Quality of an NMT-Translated Agatha Christie Novel. *Proceedings of LREC 2020*

Macken, L. and I. Ghyselen. 2018. Measuring comprehension and acceptability of neural machine translated texts: a pilot study. *Proceedings of the 40th Conference Translating and the Computer*, London, UK, pp. 120–126.

Macken, L., L. Van Brussel and J. Daems 2019. NMT's wonderland where people turn into rabbits. A study on the comprehensibility of newly invented words in NMT output. *Computational Linguistics in the Netherlands Journal*, 9:67–80.

Scarton, C. and L. Specia. 2016. A reading comprehension corpus for machine translation evaluation. *Proceedings of LREC 2016*, Portorož (Slovenia).

Tezcan, A., J. Daems, and L. Macken. 2019. When a 'sport' is a person and other issues for NMT of novels. *Proceedings of the Qualities of Literary Machine Translation*, Dublin, Ireland: European Association for Machine Translation, pp. 40–49

Van Brussel, L., A. Tezcan and L. Macken. 2018. A fine-grained error analysis of NMT, SMT and RBMT output for English-to-Dutch. *Proceedings of LREC 2018*, Miyazaki, Japan.

Use MT to simplify and speed up your alignment for TM creation

Judith Klein
STAR Group
Wiesholz 35, 8262 Ramsen
Switzerland
`judith.klein@star-group.net`

Giorgio Bernardinello
STAR Group
Wiesholz 35, 8262 Ramsen
Switzerland
`giorgio.bernardinello
@star-group.net`

Abstract

Large quantities of multilingual legal documents are waiting to be regularly aligned and used for future translations. Due to time restraints and the effort and cost required, manual alignment is not an option. Automatically aligned segments are suitable for concordance search but are unreliable for fuzzy search and pre-translation. MT-based alignment could be the key to improving the results.

1 Why align if there is MT?

Today, in the translation sector, many texts and documents in different sectors and areas and in many different language combinations are translated using MT or with MT support. Why go to the effort of using alignment to create a Translation Memory (TM) for a CAT tool from existing translations? This is because precisely the existing verified translations are required. MT can probably provide precisely these translations by chance, but not reliably.

2 What data and for what purpose?

The Systematic Collection of Legislation (SR)[1] of the Swiss Federal Administration (Bund) is currently automatically aligned and provided as a TM[2] four times a year. It consists of over 5000 MS Word documents in German, French and Italian, each with over two million segments or almost 20 million words[3]. The final version of the legal text is synchronised or translated into all three languages in the original document.

Since the legal texts have been automatically aligned and not translated in the CAT tool, there is no TM with reliable segment alignment. The TM can therefore be used via concordance search[4] but is not suitable for fuzzy search or pretranslation.

3 STAR's translation technology

From 2020, the Bund will use STAR's translation technology as its general translation solution with the translation memory tool Transit as the core system. An alignment tool is integrated into Transit as standard. The MT interface makes it easy to use machine translations from different MT systems.

4 Interactive alignment in Transit

In alignment projects, the document pairs are imported in the respective languages and segmented independently of each other. The segment alignment then does not match, for example, if two sentences in one document correspond to just one sentence in the other document, if a sentence has no equivalent in the other text, or if the sentence order is different.

As usual with alignment tools, formal (e.g. sentence length, numbers, formatting) and lexical parameters (e.g. dictionary entries or unchanged words, such as company names) are used to calculate the segment alignment.

---

[1] https://www.admin.ch/gov/de/start/bundesrecht/systematische-sammlung.html

[2] Previously in MultiTrans.

[3] Version: March 2020

---

[4] In Transit, the user can open the aligned document pair in the Transit editor directly from the concordance result and copy the corresponding section of text. The same applies for fuzzy hits, but this would not be an efficient way of using the fuzzy search.

Martins, Moniz, Fumega, Martins, Batista, Coheur, Parra, Trancoso, Turchi, Bisazza, Moorkens, Guerberof, Nurminen, Marg, Forcada (eds.)
Proceedings of the 22nd Annual Conference of the European Association for Machine Translation, p. 487–489
Lisboa, Portugal, November 2020.

4.1 TM for the segment alignment

In addition to formal and lexical parameters, the TM can also be used to calculate the segment alignment. The Transit fuzzy algorithm[5] calculates the similarity between the target-language segment in the TM and the target-language segment in the aligned document. This value has the strongest weighting.

However, a TM that contains 100% hits is only available for an alignment project in exceptional cases, because, if there were a 100% hit for lots of segments, it would not be necessary to create another TM.

4.2 Alignment mode

The alignment tool uses the criteria to dynamically calculate the segment alignment. Change proposals are displayed graphically and in colour in the alignment editor. Manual checking and correction guarantees reliable segment alignment, meaning that the material can be used for the fuzzy search and pretranslation.

However, no matter how well the interactive alignment supports the user, interactive alignment alone is not an effective solution for such vast quantities of text as the SR.

5 Machine alignment in Transit

5.1 MT for the segment alignment

Sennrich and Volk (2010) have already reported on the successful use of MT for alignment, provided that the MT system produces good translations. This is not a question of the quality of the translation as such, but about its similarity to the existing translation, which is determined using "BleuAlign". BleuAlign is a part of BiTextor, which is used within the Paracrawl project to create a vast quantity of bilingual corpora.[6]

5.2 Machine alignment function

In the same way that the alignment tool uses the Transit fuzzy value from the TM translation for the segment alignment, it also uses the similarity value from the MT translation.

The selected MT system is specified in the alignment project. The following steps are automatically carried out when the "machine alignment" function is used:

- Machine translation of the source-language documents

- Evaluation of the MT similarity for the segment alignment

- Automatic modification of the segment alignment based on the results of the calculation

The changes are based on the segmentation of the source language and consist of (a) joining source- or target-language segments[7] in the case of 1:N or N:1 relationships, (b) inserting empty segments where there is missing target-language text[8], (c) deleting source- and target-language segments if multiple segments cannot be aligned, and (d) moving target-language segments.

5.3 Machine alignment of the SR

The machine alignment of the SR will be carried out automatically every three months via the "STAR CLM" workflow system[9]. In the subsequent runs, only changed or new texts are sent to the MT system (in this case, DeepL Pro[10]), since the other MT translations are already available. Whether and when the entire SR will be machine-translated again depends on whether innovations in the MT system could further improve the segment alignment.

6 Conclusion

The perfect interaction between the alignment tool and the MT interface in Transit means that machine translation can be directly integrated into the calculation of the segment alignment. This additional information can be used to improve the alignment, making both the

---

[5] Proven algorithm for the similarity calculation of source-language segments for pretranslation and fuzzy search.

[6] https://www.slideshare.net/TAUS/bitextor-harvest-your-own-parallel-corpora-from-the-web-miquel-esplgomis-universitat-dalacant, https://paracrawl.eu/

[7] To find out how "virtual join" works for the source language, see: https://www.star-group.net/en/downloads/transit-termstar.html

[8] Transit ignores a segment if the target is empty.

[9] The first cycle is planned for June 2020.

[10] https://www.bk.admin.ch/bk/de/home/dokumentation/medienmitteilungen.msg-id-77610.html

interactive and the automatic alignment easier and quicker.

We are still investigating whether machine alignment can be used to achieve reliable segment alignment in such a way that the material can be used not only for concordance search, but also for fuzzy search and pretranslation.

References

Sánchez-Gijón, Pilar, Joss Moorkens and Andy Way. 2019. Post-editing neural machine translation versus translation memory segments. *Machine Translation* 33(1-2):31-59

Sennrich, Rico and Martin Volk. 2010. MT-based sentence alignment for OCR-generated parallel text. *AMTA 2010. 9th Conference of the Association for Machine Translation in the Americas.* Denver, Colorado

An Overview of the SEBAMAT Project

Reinhard Rapp
[1]ILSP / Athena R.C.,
[2]Magdeburg-Stendal University of
Applied Sciences, [3]University of Mainz
reinhardrapp@gmx.de

George Tambouratzis
ILSP / Athena R.C.,
6 Artemidos & Epidavrou, Maroussi,
15125, Greece
giorg_t@ilsp.gr

Abstract

SEBAMAT (semantics-based MT) is a Marie Curie project intended to contribute to the state of the art in machine translation (MT). Current MT systems typically take the semantics of a text only in so far into account as they are implicit in the underlying text corpora or dictionaries. Occasionally it has been argued that it may be difficult to advance MT quality to the next level as long as the systems do not make more explicit use of semantic knowledge. SEBAMAT aims to evaluate three approaches incorporating such knowledge into MT.

1 The current state of the art in MT

SEBAMAT aims to show ways on how to improve the translations produced by current MT systems. For several decades the *rule-based approach* was dominant (Arnold et al., 1994) which focused on grammatical well-formedness. In the *statistical approach* (SMT, Brown et al. 1990), linguistic rules were replaced by statistical patterns as automatically extracted from large monolingual and parallel text corpora. Recently, the dominance of SMT has been contested by *neural MT* (NMT), which almost consistently generates better results. Although NMT represents the current state of the art, technical issues and problems have been raised, including NMT's inferior performance to SMT for limited training data, reduced portability across domains, and sensitivity to semantic divergence in the training data (Koehn & Knowles (2017), Carpuat et al. (2017). Sennrich & Zang (2019) improve NMT for small corpora, but marked improvements are gained using larger corpora.

However, despite considerable advances, the quality of current MT systems is still limited, and the likely reason is that the algorithms used are of a mechanical nature, employing statistical rules or deep learning architectures, without a human-like understanding of the texts to be translated. Amongst others, Kevin Knight pointed out that MT systems do not sufficiently take into account semantic considerations such as *who did what to whom, when where and why*. This is also true for NMT, where the translations are typically fluent but often semantically inadequate. SEBAMAT will suggest steps to raise MT quality by taking into account semantics more explicitly than has usually been done so far. Three main directions will be investigated.

2 Explicit semantic disambiguation

Up to now, almost all MT work involving parallel and monolingual corpora has been based on raw texts. However, recently there have been significant advances in word sense induction and disambiguation using corpus-based automatic methods. Inspired by Vintar & Fiser (2016), we suggest to pre-process parallel corpora using word sense disambiguation software, and then apply classical SMT word alignment procedures on the disambiguated rather than the original corpora. That is, word senses rather than words are aligned, and bilingual dictionaries of word senses rather than dictionaries of words are extracted. If the disambiguation can be done with sufficiently high accuracy, this may lead to an improvement in translation quality. The reason is that the average translation ambiguity of a word sense can be expected to be considerably lower than that of a word, which should make the task of finding the correct translation easier.

Of course, other MT systems also (though implicitly) try to select the target words which translate the correct senses of the given source words. However, e.g. in the case of NMT, initially only a single embedding is assigned to each

Martins, Moniz, Fumega, Martins, Batista, Coheur, Parra, Trancoso, Turchi, Bisazza, Moorkens, Guerberof, Nurminen, Marg, Forcada (eds.)
Proceedings of the 22nd Annual Conference of the European Association for Machine Translation, p. 491–492
Lisboa, Portugal, November 2020.

word or sub-word unit, regardless of sense, and only when building sentence representations senses come into play. This has at least the disadvantage that it is almost impossible to understand what happens internally (black box behavior), so system improvements are typically achieved by trial and error. Also, only the suggested approach delivers a new type of resource, namely a dictionary of sense translations.

3 Semantically annotated corpora

We will also research the promising approach for semantics-based translation proposed by Jones et al. (2013) which uses synchronous hyperedge replacement grammars. For training, this requires semantically annotated corpora, whereby we will focus on language-neutral annotations which can be considered as an interlingua. Our annotation scheme will probably adapt abstract meaning representations (AMR) along the lines of the AMR bank (https://amr.isi.edu/). By default these annotations are done by human experts using Ulf Hermjakob's AMR editor, but as we require large amounts of data we will also investigate how far it is possible to automate this via algorithms for semantic role labeling (Gormley et al., 2014). The next step is to train MT systems on large parallel corpora which are annotated in this way. Synchronous hyperedge replacement grammars can then be used to translate into and from such graph-shaped intermediate meaning representations. Hereby it is possible to extract synchronous grammar rules, and to also combine this with syntactic annotations. For languages with Frame-Net[1] style resources, we investigate whether these are suitable for semantics-based translation.

4 Association-based MT

The novel paradigm of association-based machine translation is cognitively motivated and based on the concept of multi-stimulus association. The underlying hypothesis is that the meaning of a short sentence or phrase can be characterized by its associations. That is, the content words in this sentence/phrase are used as multi-word stimuli, and a *meaning vector* is computed. The relation between two sentences can be computed by comparing their corresponding meaning vectors using a vector similarity metric.

To translate a source language phrase, we first compute its meaning vector. Presupposing the existence of a basic dictionary, in analogy to Rapp (1999) we can translate this meaning vector into the target language. Assuming that we already know the meaning vectors of a very large number of target language phrases, we select the target language meaning vector which is most similar to the source language meaning vector. The corresponding target language phrase is considered the translation of the source phrase. This is an unsupervised vector space approach requiring meaning vectors for huge numbers of phrases, but no parallel corpora nor training.

5 Project details

SEBAMAT is a 2-year Marie Curie individual fellowship funded by the European Commission's Horizon 2020 program. It supports the first author to conduct research at Athena R.C. For details see the upcoming project website and https://cordis. europa.eu/project/id/844951.

References

Arnold, D., Balkan, L., Lee Humphreys, R., Meijer, S., Sadler, L. (1994). *Machine Translation. An Introductory Guide.* Manchester: Blackwell.

Brown, P., Cocke, J., Della Pietra, S., Della Pietra, V., Jelinek, F., Lafferty, J., Mercer, R, Rossin, P. (1990). A statistical approach to machine translation. *Computational Linguistics*, 16 (2), 79–85.

Carpuat, M., Vyas, Y., Niu, X., (2017) Detecting cross-lingual semantic divergence for neural machine translation, *Proceedings of the First Workshop on NMT*, Vancouver, Canada, 69–79.

Gormley, M.R., Mitchell, M., Van Dumme, B., Dredze, M. (2014). Low-resource semantic role labeling. Proc. 52nd ACL, Baltimore, MD, 1177–1187.

Jones, B., Andreas, J., Bauer, D., Hermann, K.M., Knight, K. (2013): Semantics-based machine translation with hyperedge replacement grammars. *Proceedings of COLING 2012*, Mumbai, 1359–1376.

Koehn, P., Knowles, R. (2017), Six challenges for neural machine translation, *Proc. of the 1st Workshop on NMT*, Vancouver, Canada, 28–39.

Rapp, R. (1999). Automatic identification of word translations from unrelated English and German corpora. *Proceedings of 37th ACL*, 1999, 519–526.

Sennrich, R., Zhang, B. (2019) Revisiting low-resource neural machine translation: a case study. *Proc. of 57th ACL 2019*, Florence, Italy, 211–221.

Vintar, S., Fiser, D. (2016). Using WordNet-based word senses to improve MT performance. In: Costa-jussa, M. et al. (eds.): *Hybrid Approaches to Machine Translation*. Springer, 191–205.

---

[1] https://framenet.icsi.berkeley.edu/fndrupal/

DeepSPIN: Deep Structured Prediction for Natural Language Processing

André F. T. Martins, Vlad Niculae, Erick Fonseca, Ben Peters,
Gonçalo Correia, Tsvetomila Mihaylova, Marcos Treviso, Pedro Martins

Instituto de Telecomunicações and Unbabel,
Lisbon, Portugal

`andre.t.martins@tecnico.ulisboa.pt`

Abstract

DeepSPIN[1] is a research project funded by the European Research Council (ERC) whose goal is to develop new neural structured prediction methods, models, and algorithms for improving the quality, interpretability, and data-efficiency of natural language processing (NLP) systems, with special emphasis on machine translation and quality estimation applications.

1 Description

Neural network models became the standard in NLP applications, with impressive results in machine translation (Bahdanau et al., 2015; Vaswani et al., 2017). New language interfaces (digital assistants, customer service bots) are emerging as the next technologies for seamless, multilingual communication among humans and machines. From a machine learning perspective, many problems in NLP can be characterized as *structured prediction*: they involve predicting structurally rich and interdependent outputs. In spite of this, current neural NLP systems ignore the structural complexity of human language, relying on simplistic and error-prone greedy search procedures. This leads to critical mistakes in MT, such as words being dropped or named entities mistranslated.

The DeepSPIN project attacks these fundamental problems by bringing together deep learning and structured prediction. This is done in three fronts: better generation strategies, beyond left-to-right search; induction of sparse latent structure to make networks more interpretable; and incorporation of weak supervision to reduce the need for labeled data. We focus here on the applications to machine translation, including some results that have already been obtained in the project.

Alternate Generation Strategies. In Peters et al. (2019), we introduced *sparse sequence-to-sequence models*, with encouraging results in MT. These sparse losses endow MT systems with a small set of choices for the next word to be generated. When the model is fully confident, it auto-completes longer phrases (Figure 1). This property is appealing for building interactive MT systems. A current problem with left-to-right decoders is exposure bias (MT systems not exposed to their own predictions at training time). To mitigate this problem, we proposed a new scheduled sampling technique to avoid teacher forcing in transformers Mihaylova and Martins (2019). Future work will look at alternate generation strategies for MT, inspired by preliminary work in sequence tagging (Martins and Kreutzer, 2017).

Sparse Attention and Interpretability. One big goal of the DeepSPIN project is to make neural networks amenable to interpretation by humans. This is particularly useful in a scenario mixing MT and human post-editing. Our recent work on *sparse and structured attention* (Martins and Astudillo, 2016; Niculae et al., 2018) presents a promising avenue for enhancing interpretability (see Figure 1 for sparse word alignments), and we built on this idea in two directions: to reduce repetitions in neural MT by using constrained sparse attention to capture fertility (Malaviya et al., 2018); and using hierarchical sparse attention for document-level MT (Maruf et al., 2019). This idea has also been applied successfully in both RNN

[1]Project website: `https://deep-spin.github.io`.

Martins, Moniz, Fumega, Martins, Batista, Coheur, Parra, Trancoso, Turchi, Bisazza, Moorkens, Guerberof, Nurminen, Marg, Forcada (eds.)
Proceedings of the 22nd Annual Conference of the European Association for Machine Translation, p. 493–494
Lisboa, Portugal, November 2020.

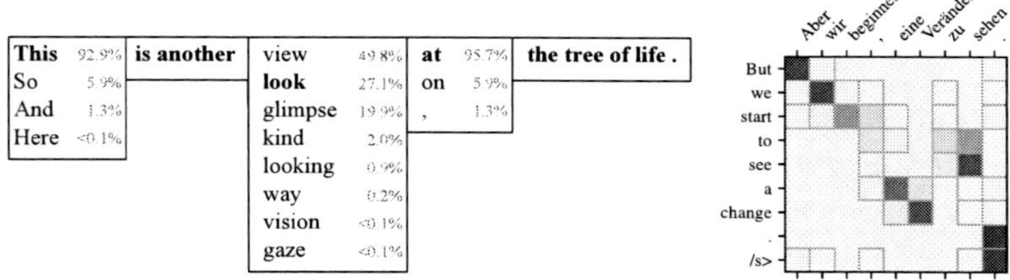

Figure 1: Left: Forced decoding using 1.5-entmax for the German source sentence "Dies ist ein weiterer Blick auf den Baum des Lebens." Only predictions with nonzero probability are shown at each time step. When consecutive predictions consist of a single word, we combine their borders to showcase *auto-completion* potential. The selected gold targets are in boldface. Right: Attention weights produced by a De-En 1.5-entmax model. Nonzero weights are outlined (Peters et al., 2019).

and transformer architectures (Peters et al., 2019; Correia et al., 2019). Future research will push this direction to improve efficiency and compactness of models as well as making MT systems more amenable to interpretation.

Weak Supervision. To avoid the data hunger of neural MT models, DeepSPIN will pursue techniques for weak supervision, such as transfer learning and leveraging of human post-editor activity data. This idea has been explored by Correia and Martins (2019) for automatic post-editing, by fine-tuning a pre-trained BERT model (Devlin et al., 2019). In collaboration with Unbabel, we extracted keystroke information from human post-editors in a crowd-sourced MT platform, and created a new dataset with keystroke sequences (Góis and Martins, 2019). This data[2] has proved extremely informative to understand the behavior of post-editors and predict translation quality.

Released Code and Datasets. To promote research reproducibility, the DeepSPIN project has released software code and datasets that may be useful to other researchers. This includes: OpenKiwi,[3] an open-source toolkit for quality estimation (Kepler et al., 2019); the `entmax` package[4] for sparse attention and losses; a new dataset with post-editor activity data (Góis and Martins, 2019);[2] and a new dataset for document-level quality estimation, used at WMT 2018 and 2019 shared tasks (Fonseca et al., 2019). New datasets are being prepared for shared tasks in WMT 2020.

Acknowledgments. This work was supported by ERC StG DeepSPIN 758969 with AM as PI.

References

Bahdanau, Dzmitry, Kyunghyun Cho, and Yoshua Bengio. 2015. Neural machine translation by jointly learning to align and translate. In *ICLR*.

Correia, Gonçalo M and André F. T. Martins. 2019. A simple and effective approach to automatic post-editing with transfer learning. In *ACL*.

Correia, Gonçalo, Vlad Niculae, and André F. T. Martins. 2019. Adaptively sparse Transformers. In *EMNLP*.

Devlin, Jacob, Ming-Wei Chang, Kenton Lee, and Kristina Toutanova. 2019. Bert: Pre-training of deep bidirectional transformers for language understanding. In *NAACL*.

Fonseca, Erick, Lisa Yankovskaya, André FT Martins, Mark Fishel, and Christian Federmann. 2019. Findings of the wmt 2019 shared tasks on quality estimation. In *WMT*.

Góis, António and André FT Martins. 2019. Translator2vec: Understanding and representing human post-editors. In *MT Summit*.

Kepler, Fabio, Jonay Trénous, Marcos Treviso, Miguel Vera, and André F. T. Martins. 2019. Openkiwi: An open source framework for quality estimation. In *ACL System Demonstrations*.

Malaviya, Chaitanya, Pedro Ferreira, and André FT Martins. 2018. Sparse and constrained attention for neural machine translation. In *ACL*.

Martins, Andre and Ramon Astudillo. 2016. From softmax to sparsemax: A sparse model of attention and multi-label classification. In *ICML*.

Martins, André F. T. and Julia Kreutzer. 2017. Learning what's easy: Fully differentiable neural easy-first taggers. In *EMNLP*.

Maruf, Sameen, André FT Martins, and Gholamreza Haffari. 2019. Selective attention for context-aware neural machine translation. In *NAACL*.

Mihaylova, Tsvetomila and André F. T. Martins. 2019. Scheduled sampling for transformers. In *ACL Student Research Workshop*.

Niculae, Vlad, Andre Martins, Mathieu Blondel, and Claire Cardie. 2018. Sparsemap: Differentiable sparse structured inference. In *ICML*.

Peters, Ben, Vlad Niculae, and André F. T. Martins. 2019. Sparse sequence-to-sequence models. In *ACL*.

Vaswani, Ashish, Noam Shazeer, Niki Parmar, Jakob Uszkoreit, Llion Jones, Aidan N Gomez, Łukasz Kaiser, and Illia Polosukhin. 2017. Attention is all you need. In *NeurIPS*.

---

[2]Available at `https://github.com/Unbabel/translator2vec/releases/download/v1.0/keystrokes_dataset.zip`
[3]`http://github.com/Unbabel/OpenKiwi`
[4]`https://github.com/deep-spin/entmax`

Project MAIA: Multilingual AI Agent Assistant

João Graça[1], Paulo Dimas[1], Helena Moniz[2], André F. T. Martins[1,3], Graham Neubig[4]

[1]Unbabel / Lisbon, Portugal
[2]INESC-ID / Lisboa, Portugal
[3]Instituto de Telecomunicações / Portugal
[4]CMU / Pittsburgh, USA

{joao,pdimas,andre.martins}@unbabel.com,
helena.moniz@inesc-id.pt, gneubig@cs.cmu.edu

Abstract

This paper presents the Multilingual Artificial Intelligence Agent Assistant (MAIA), a project led by Unbabel with the collaboration of CMU, INESC-ID and IT Lisbon. MAIA will employ cutting-edge machine learning and natural language processing technologies to build multilingual AI agent assistants, eliminating language barriers. MAIA's translation layer will empower human agents to provide customer support in real-time, in any language, with human quality.

1 Introduction

Online conversational support – chat – is the fastest growing customer service channel, being the preferred way for millennials to obtain customer service. Today, supporting international customers in this channel is mostly done by using human agents that speak different languages – a scarce and costly resource. The tremendous progress of language technologies (machine translation and dialogue systems) in the last years makes them an appealing tool for multilingual customer service. However, current systems are still too brittle and impractical: first, they require too much data and computing power, failing for domains or languages where labeled data is scarce; second, they do not capture contextual information (e.g. current MT systems work on a sentence-by-sentence basis, ignoring the conversation context); third, fully automatic systems lack human empathy and fail on unexpected scenarios, leading to low customer satisfaction. In MAIA, we will develop a multilingual conversational platform where human agents are assisted by AI agents. This approach will overcome the above limitations by targeting the following scientific and technological goals:

- New memory-efficient neural models for context-aware machine translation, suitable for online and real-time translation. These models will retain key aspects of a conversation (e.g., the gender of the customer), bringing them up whenever needed to translate a message.

- New answer generation techniques where the human agent (e.g., a tourism officer) will receive suggestions that reduce effort and increase the customer's (e.g. a tourist) satisfaction.

- New techniques for conversational quality estimation and sentiment analysis to assess how well the conversation is addressing the customer's needs, while simultaneously increasing "human empathy".

- Integration of the scientific advances above into a full end-to-end product. To this end, two demonstrators will be built to cover concrete use cases in the Travel and Tourism industries.

2 Overview of MAIA

Figure 1 displays a mock-up of the user interface to assist the human agent. Illustrated is the conversation history (on the agent's language), a list of answer suggestions, a message box supporting auto-completion where the agent can type the response, and an indicator of the sentiment of the customer throughout the conversation. The overarching goal of MAIA is to build context-aware, multilingual, empathetic agent assistants. These assistants will help human agents to provide real-time customer

Martins, Moniz, Fumega, Martins, Batista, Coheur, Parra, Trancoso, Turchi, Bisazza, Moorkens, Guerberof, Nurminen, Marg, Forcada (eds.)
Proceedings of the 22nd Annual Conference of the European Association for Machine Translation, p. 495–496
Lisboa, Portugal, November 2020.

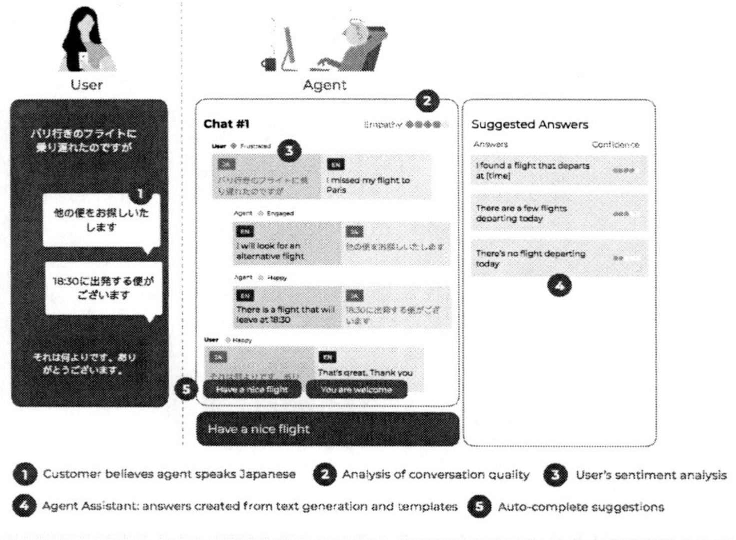

Figure 1: Mock-up of the user interface to assist the human agent.

service in multiple languages. This will be accomplished by pursuing the following objectives:

- **Translation layer for multilingual customer service.** Enabling multilingual customer service by using domain-adapted machine translation for translating messages sent from customers to agents and vice-versa. This will be ensured by developing new neural machine translation models that can be efficiently adapted to new domains and clients, the implementation of automatic retraining of machine translation engines, and an active learning strategy to use the Unbabel community of human post-editors to translate conversations offline, in a recurrent manner, to build an ever-increasing parallel datasets.

- **Conversational context-awareness.** Development of methods for neural machine translation and automatic response generation that take into account the context of the conversation. This requires the development of new machine learning methods that are able to compress the conversation history into a compact memory representation, and to pick the relevant elements whenever needed.

- **Modeling customer satisfaction via sentiment analysis and conversational quality estimation.** Development of a module for conversational quality estimation that is able to detect when the agent is effectively answering to the customer's needs, and react otherwise. This will trigger specific actions for either the machine translation or the answer generation modules. In addition, a sentiment analysis component will estimate the sentiment and emotions of the customer throughout the conversation, informing the agent.

- **Integration of the multilingual conversational platform and acquisition of reference customers.** Implementation of the MAIA platform and execution of Customer Discovery Programs for testing, validating, and improving product prototypes, testing for feasibility, usability, and viability. Execution of a plan for commercial exploitation and use of the plat- forms, systems, and technologies developed in MAIA.

References

André F. T. Martins and Marcin Junczys-Dowmunt and Fabio Kepler and Ramon Astudillo and Chris Hokamp and Roman Grundkiewicz. 2017. Pushing the Limits of Translation Quality Estimation, *Transactions of the Association for Computational Linguistics].*

Jonathan Herzig, Guy Feigenblat, Michal Schmueli-Scheuer, Anat Rafaeli, Daniel Altman, and David Spivak. 2016. Classifying emotions in customer support dialogues in social media. *Proceedings of the 2016 SIGDIAL Conference*, pp. 64.73.

MTrill project: Machine Translation impact on language learning

Natália Resende
ADAPT Centre
School of Computing
Dublin City University
natalia.resende@adaptcentre.ie

Andy Way
ADAPT Centre
School of Computing
Dublin City University
andy.way@adaptcentre.ie

1 Background

Over the last decades, massive research investments have been made in the development of machine translation (MT) systems (Gupta and Dhawan, 2019). This has brought about a paradigm shift in the performance of these language tools, leading to an widespread use of popular MT systems (Gaspari and Hutchins, 2007). Although the first MT engines were used for gisting purposes, in recent years, there has been an increasing interest in using MT tools, specially the freely available online MT tools, for language teaching and learning (Clifford et al., 2013). The literature on MT and Computer Assisted Language Learning (CALL) shows that, over the years, MT systems have been facilitating language teaching and also language learning (Niño, 2006). Research also shows the positive role of MT systems in the development of writing skills in English as well as in improving communication skills in English (Garcia and Pena, 2011). However, to date, the cognitive impact of MT on language acquisition and on the syntactic aspects of language processing has not yet been investigated and deserves further scrutiny.

The MTrill project aims at filling this gap in the literature by examining whether MT is contributing to a central aspect of language acquisition: the so-called language binding, i.e., the ability to combine single words properly in a grammatical sentence (Heyselaar et al., 2017; Ferreira and Bock, 2006). The project focus on the initial stages (pre-intermediate and intermediate) of the acquisition of English syntax by Brazilian Portuguese native speakers using MT systems as a support for language learning.

guage learning.

Below, we present the methodological approach of the project as well as its objectives.

2 Methodological approach and objectives

In order to examine the impact of MT systems on the acquisition and processing of English syntactic structures, this research will implement a syntactic priming laboratory study to investigate how memory systems encode the syntactic information triggered by MT output. Syntactic priming is an experimental paradigm commonly used by researchers in the field of psycholinguistics as an way to understand aspects of the representation and processing of language syntax (Braningan et al., 2000). The Syntactic priming or structural priming can be defined as the tendency speakers have to use a syntactic structure that has been previously encountered (Bock, 1986).

A common syntactic priming experimental paradigm (Bock, 1986) consists of reading a sentence and asking participants to repeat out loud the same sentence. Listening and repeating the sentence is considered the "prime phase" of the experiment as the experimenter could control participants' exposure to different syntactic structures. Following the "prime phase", participants are requested to describe an image so that the researcher could observe if participants would use in the subsequent utterance the same structure they had just produced in the prime phase. In our experiments, we will check whether after being exposed to the output of an MT through a translation task using Google Translate, participants will use the syntactic alternative of the MT output or whether they will choose a different syntactic alternative in their subsequent speech. The language pair investigated

Martins, Moniz, Fumega, Martins, Batista, Coheur, Parra, Trancoso, Turchi, Bisazza, Moorkens, Guerberof, Nurminen, Marg, Forcada (eds.)
Proceedings of the 22nd Annual Conference of the European Association for Machine Translation, p. 497–498
Lisboa, Portugal, November 2020.

is Portuguese–English due to the differences in syntactic structures between them.

The specific objectives of the project are:

- Investigate whether MT systems are capable of eliciting syntactic priming effects.

- Investigate whether any priming effect elicited is of explicit or implicit learning nature.

- Investigate whether the size of the priming effect varies as a function of the gender of the subjects.

- Investigate whether the size of the effect varies as a function of the level of reliability of system or English proficiency levels.

3   First study

In the first study of the MTrill project, 20 Brazilian Portuguese speakers at intermediate and advanced English proficiency levels took part in syntactic priming experiment that investigated the influence of the popular Google Translate MT system on the mental processing of English as a second language.

We adopted a pretest-priming design (Shin and Christianson, 2012). In the pretest phase, participants were instructed to freely translate from Portuguese into English sentences depicting images appearing in a computer screen. Imediately after this pretest, in the priming phase, participants were instructed to translate other sentences depicting images appearing in a computer screen using Google Translate and repeat out loud the output. After this task, they were requested to describe out loud an image using three words provided. This design allowed to test if participants would describe the image mirroring the syntactic structure previously seen in the output of Google Translate and compare participants' language behaviour before and after Google Translate.

The results of this preliminary study show that, after performing a translation task with Google translate, participants described images in English using more frequently the syntactic alternative previously seen in the output of Google Translate when compared to the translation task with no prior influence of the MT output. Results also show that this priming effect is modulated by language proficiency levels.

Acknowledgements

The ADAPT Centre for Digital Content Technology (www.adaptcentre.ie) at Dublin City University is funded by the Science Foundation Ireland Research Centres Programme (Grant 13/RC/2106) and is co-funded by the European Regional Development Fund. This project was funded by the European Union's Horizon 2020 research and innovation programme under the Marie Sklodowska-Curie grant agreement number 843455. Start date 25/04/2019 - End date 24/04/2021.

References

Bock, J.Kathryn. 1986. Syntactic persistence in language production. *Cognitive Psychology*, 18(3):355 – 387.

Braningan, Holly P., Martin J. Pickering, Andrew J. Stewart, and Janet F. Mclean. 2000. Syntactic priming in spoken production: Linguistic and temporal interference. *Memory and Cognition*, 28(8):1297–1302.

Clifford, Joan, Lisa Merschel, and Joan Munné. 2013. Surveying the landscape: What is the role of machine translation in language learning? *Revista d'innovacio educativa*, (10):108–121.

Ferreira, Victor S. and Kathryn Bock. 2006. The functions of structural priming. *Language and Cognitive Processes*, 21(7-8):1011–1029. PMID: 17710210.

Garcia, Ignacio and María Isabel Pena. 2011. Machine translation-assisted language learning: writing for beginners. *Computer Assisted Language Learning*, 24(5):471–487.

Gaspari, Federico and John Hutchins. 2007. Online and free ! ten years of online machine translation : Origins , developments , current use and future prospects.

Gupta, Brij M. and S. M. Dhawan. 2019. Machine translation research a scientometric assessment of global publications output during 2007 16. *DESIDOC Journal of Library Information Technology*, 39(1):31–38, 01.

Heyselaar, Evelien, Peter Hagoort, and Katrien Segaert. 2017. In dialogue with an avatar, language behavior is identical to dialogue with a human partner. *Behavior Research Methods*, (49):46–60.

Niño, Ana. 2006. *Evaluating the suitability of using raw machine translation output as input for foreign language written production*. Ph.D. thesis.

Shin, Jeong-Ah and Kiel Christianson. 2012. Structural priming and second language learning. *Language Learning*, 62(3):931–964.

Sponsors

Gold sponsor

Official Carrier

Media sponsor

Institutional partners